The Compendium of Seminary Texts

THE VERIFICATION AND RENEWAL CURRICULUM SERIES

This publication was made possible through the support of Grant 62642 from the John Templeton Foundation. The opinions expressed in this publication are those of the author(s) and do not necessarily reflect the views of the John Templeton Foundation.

JOHN
TEMPLETON
FOUNDATION

From the Series Editor

بسم الله الرحمن الرحيم

ALL PRAISE IS due to Allah, and may peace and blessings be upon the Prophet Muhammad. The volume which you have before you has been several years in the making. It began with a conversation between Shaykh Khalil Abdur-Rashid and me in the summer of 2017 in Harvard Square from which emerged the Mirani Program, an online reading of Shaykh Muhammad Emin Er's *Jāmiʿ al-mutūn al-dirāsiyya*. Over the course of two years, Shaykh Khalil taught a group of dedicated students from around the country, covering all the treatises in the volume save for those on rhetoric (*balāgha*).

During the first year of the course, I worked with some of my university students to produce draft translations of the first section of the treatise titled *The Tranquil Sea: On the Science of Grammar*, as well as the *ʿAwāmil* of Birgevī and *Bināʾ al-afʿāl*, the former serving as one of two source texts for *The Tranquil Sea* and the latter being the source text for the treatise titled *Turning a Glance: On the Science of Morphology*. These, however, remained only in draft form. After finishing the Mirani Program, some participants discussed a project to translate each of the treatises; however, only a few summary or incomplete drafts emerged. Yet the dream of making this unique text available to a wider Anglophone audience remained, and Shaykh Khalil and I continued to imagine avenues to its completion.

In 2020, Dr. Macksood Aftab, Muhammad Hozien, and I founded the American Society of Islamic Philosophy and Theology with the support of a seed grant from the Templeton Foundation. As our community of students, professors, and scholars grew, it became clear that many of us were working on similar projects connected to curriculum development for Islamic learning institutions. From this realization was born the Verification and Renewal Curriculum, a project funded by a larger grant from the Templeton Foundation to produce Islamic curricular materials for Anglophone learning communities, with an emphasis on producing students and scholars who are uniquely equipped to address contemporary questions of religion, science, and philosophy in a unified manner rooted in the traditional Islamic sciences.

Towards the goal of producing whole, balanced, and learned Muslims who are equally at home in the laboratory, university, market, and mosque, the Verification and Renewal Curriculum consists of an increasing number of texts, syllabi, and resources for students and scholars at varying stages of their educational journey. It is rooted in the study and application of the instrumental sciences, which might be called the "Islamic liberal arts." These pedagogical resources are sometimes produced in-house by a small research team with whom I have the honor of collaborating, but we also lend our time, knowledge, and efforts to partners working in curriculum development around the world—from California to Cairo, Istanbul to India—collaborating with them in the production of unique works ranging from homeschool curricula to graduate school syllabi.

The Compendium of Seminary Texts plays an essential role in the Verification and Renewal Curriculum in that it provides the advanced beginner a single "minimum effective dose" of all of the core foundational and instrumental sciences that support one's further studies in the advanced Islamic sciences. Of the numerous curricular projects under development, *The Compendium of Seminary Texts* is crucial as it treats the instrumental sciences of morphology, grammar (syntax), logic, linguistic theory, rhetoric and its branches, dialectics, and the foundational sciences of jurisprudence, theology, and spiritual purification. All of these sciences are fundamental for any meaningful Islamic engagement with the questions and challenges facing humanity today.

Its author intended to provide the student who had completed the study of this concise yet rigorous volume a sufficient grounding in these sciences so that such a student could then pursue further studies in the sacred sciences, such as law, Quranic exegesis, hadith, and Sufism, among others. Recognizing the urgency of producing well-grounded scholars who can serve their communities in a variety of capacities, this single-volume compendium summarizes, combines, and reframes a number of common core texts of the Ottoman madrasa curriculum and places them between two covers.

Serving this text became an integral part of our Verification and Renewal Curriculum. In 2022, I was able to hire two brilliant and highly skilled young scholars, Mawlana Justin Poe and Marwan Tayyan, both graduates of Zaytuna College's master's program in Islamic texts. Their expert knowledge of the sciences covered in the *Compendium* along with their masterful attention to detail in translation, composition, and editing have been indispensable in bringing this volume to light.

Rather than producing a literal, word-for-word translation, we instead aimed to translate the text in a form that would both deliver the meanings of the original Arabic and frame the subject matter in an accessible prose familiar to the contemporary English speaker.

The goal of this work, then, is to make the content of Shaykh Emin's work available to students whose primary language of instruction is English, not through mere translation but rather a presentation of the content in accessible and readable English. Like any text from the classical madrasa curriculum, one ideally will read this text with a trained scholar or advanced student, preparing the text by referencing commentaries and comparative texts, then reading directly with one's teacher, followed by a careful review, preferably with fellow students. This method of deep preliminary reading (*muṭālaʿa*), followed by a close guided reading with a trained scholar (*dars*), followed by a careful review of the material with fellow students (*mudhākara*) is the nearly lost yet absolutely essential key to unlocking a work like *The Compendium of Seminary Texts*. The reader is urged to find and nurture communities of learners who desire to study in this time-honored and proven method of mastering the instrumental and sacred sciences. We pray that this text will serve and inspire such communities, and we ask all who read and benefit from this book that they pray for its author, translators, teachers, and all who helped bring it light.

All praise is due to Allah; the mistakes are our own.

—Aaron Spevack

MUHAMMAD EMIN ER

The Compendium of Seminary Texts

Twelve parallel English–Arabic teaching texts edited and translated by

MARWAN M. TAYYAN & JUSTIN POE

The American Society of Islamic Philosophy and Theology

The American Society of Islamic Philosophy and Theology
Boston, Massachusetts

asipt.org/contact

Director: Aaron Spevack
Translators: Marwan M. Tayyan and Justin Poe
Editor of the Arabic text: Marwan M. Tayyan

Suggested citation:
Er, Muhammad Emin. *The Compendium of Seminary Texts*. Edited and translated by Marwan M. Tayyan and Justin Poe. Boston: ASIPT, 2024.

ISBN 979-8-9915593-0-0 (color)
ISBN 979-8-9915593-1-7 (noncolor)

Typeset in Brill 11/12.5 and Uthman Taha Naskh 12.5/22.5.

To our teachers

CONTENTS

From the Series Editor iii
Foreword xiii
Translators' Preface xix

Introduction 1
Notes to the Introduction 19

I TURNING A GLANCE
On the science of morphology 21

Introduction 25
Chapter 1. Morphological Classes 27
Chapter 2. Derivatives 39
[Variform Derivatives] 39
Uniform Derivatives 45
Chapter 3. Irregular Roots 52
I. The Doubled Root 52
II. The Resemblant Root 57
III. The Hollow Root 62
IV. The Defective Root 79
V. The Disjointly Weak Root 84
VI. The Conjointly Weak Root 85
VII. The Hamzated Root 88
[Second Method] 91
Notes to Treatise I 114

II THE TRANQUIL SEA
On the science of grammar 121

Chapter 1. The Governor 124
The Abstract Governor 124
The Expressed Governor 125
Chapter 2. The Governed 133
The Primarily Governed 133
The Secondarily Governed 136
Chapter 3. Inflection 138
Chapter 4. The Noun 144
I. Generic Nouns 145
II. Proper Names 145
III. Declinable Nouns 145
IV. Appositives of Declinable Nouns 147
V. Nominative Nouns 148
VI. Accusative Nouns 150
VII. Genitive Nouns 154
VIII. Indeclinable Nouns 156
IX. Dual Nouns 160
X. Plural Nouns 161
XI–XII. Definite and Indefinite Nouns 162
XIII–XIV. Masculine and Feminine Nouns 163
XV. Diminutive Nouns 165
XVI. Relational Nouns 165
XVII. Numeral Nouns 166
XVIII. Nouns Related to Verbs 168
Chapter 5. The Verb 171
I. Perfect Tense Verbs 172
II. Imperfect Tense Verbs 172
III. Imperative and Prohibitive Verbs 177
IV. Transitive and Intransitive Verbs 177
V. Active and Passive Verbs 178
VI. Verbs of Mental Consideration 178
VII. Auxiliary Verbs 179
VIII. Verbs of Proximity 181
IX. Verbs of Praise or Blame 182
X. Verbs of Wonderment 183
Chapter 6. The Particle 184
I. Prepositions 185
II. Verb-Like Particles 189
III. Conjunctions 192
IV. Negative Particles 195
V. Particles of Alerting 196
VI. Vocative Particles 197
VII. Particles of Affirmation 198
VIII. Exceptive Particles 199

IX. Particles of Address 200
X. Particles of Connection 200
XI. Particles of Explanation 201
XII. Infinitive Particles 202
XIII. Particles of Reproach and Exhortation 203
XIV. The Particle of Proximity 203
XV. Particles of Futurity 203
XVI. Interrogative Particles 204
XVII. Conditional Particles 205
XVIII. Particles Expressing the Reason 207
XIX. The Particle of Rebuke 208
XX. *Lām* Particles 208
XXI. The Vowelless *Tā'* of Femininity 209
XXII. The Emphatic *Nūn* ***209***
XXIII. The *Hā'* of Pause 210
XXIV. Nunation 211
Notes to Treatise II 213

III THE ANCIENT ABUNDANCE
On the science of logic 221

Introduction 224
Chapter 1. The Five Universals 234
Essential Universals 235
Accidental Universals 238
[Ontological Divisions of the Universal] 240
The Relations between Universals 240
Chapter 2. Definitions 243
Chapter 3. Propositions 247
Definition and Classification into Categorical and Hypothetical 247
The Quantifiers of Propositions 251
Contradiction, Conversion, and Contraposition 253
Chapter 4. Syllogisms 256
Syllogisms Classified by Form 256
Syllogisms Classified by Categoricity, Conditionality, and Disjunction 264
Syllogisms Classified by Matter 265
Notes to Treatise III 274

IV THE GUSHING WELLSPRING
On the science of linguistic theory 279

Introduction 282
Chapter 1. Individual Assignment 283
Chapter 2. Collective Assignment 288
A Fuller Exposition of Collective Assignment 291
Instructive Notes 295
Notes to Treatise IV 297

V THE RADIANT BLOOM
On the science of metaphor 299

[Introduction] 302
Chapter 1. Simile 304
Chapter 2. Nonliteral Language 311
[Preliminary Classification] 311
[I. Simple Metonymy] 316
[II. Composite Metonymy] 319
[III. Simple Metaphor] 320
[IV. Composite Metaphor] 332
Chapter 3. Implication 334
Notes to Treatise V 338

VI THE QUINTESSENCE
On the science of dialectics 341

Introduction 344
Chapter 1. Assent, or the Claim 345
Challenge 345
Counteraction 351
Confutation 354
Chapter 2. Definition 359
Chapter 3. Division 364
Conclusion 370
Notes to Treatise VI 372

VII THE LORDLY PROFUSION
On the science of rhetorical semantics 375

Introduction 378
Chapter 1. Modes of Declarative Predication 385
Chapter 2. Modes of the Subject 393
Chapter 3. Modes of the Predicate 412
Chapter 4. Modes of Verbal Objects 415
Chapter 5. Restriction 417

Chapter 6. Non-Declarative Speech 420
Chapter 7. Breaking and Joining 424
Chapter 8. Proportionality, Brevity, and Prolixity 428
Notes to Treatise VII 433

VIII THE ELUCIDATION
On the science of figurative language 437

Introduction 440
Chapter 1. Simile 441
Chapter 2. Tropes 444
[Metaphor] 446
Chapter 3. Implication 456
Notes to Treatise VIII 460

IX THE VERNAL DOWNPOUR
On the science of embellishment 461

Notes to Treatise IX 471

X UNDERSTANDING LAW
On jurisprudential theory 473

Sixteen Preliminary Discussions 478
Chapter 1. The Quran 484
Chapter 2. The Sunna 498
Chapter 3. Consensus 508
Chapter 4. Analogy 510
The Components of Analogy 512
The Means for Determining a Legal Cause 518
Disqualifying Factors 521
Conclusion 522
Chapter 5. Adopted Indicants 524
Chapter 6. The Weighing of Indicants 528
Chapter 7. Ijtihad 535
Notes to Treatise X 541

XI THE STURDY ROPE
On creedal theology 547

[The Principles of Creedal Theology] 549
From *al-Fiqh al-Akbar* and Its Commentaries 554
Matters of Which Ignorance Is Harmless and Knowledge Beneficial 559
Notes to Treatise XI 562

XII THE PLENITUDE OF THE GRACIOUS ONE
On the science of spiritual principles 565

Notes to Treatise XII 573

Notes to the Arabic Text 575
Glossary 585
Arabic–English Glossary Key 629
Bibliography 641

FOREWORD

By Khalil Abdur-Rashid

I WAS INTRODUCED to the *ʿulūm al-āla* in Tarim, Hadramawt of Yemen in the summer of 2002. It was my second time there studying traditional Islamic sciences at the Dar al-Mustafa Seminary. I was granted special permission to complete a specialized program of study in Islamic family law, an intensive program that entailed the full study of nine works in Shāfiʿī jurisprudence. While completing the fifth of the nine required legal manuals, I was required to read and complete a special legal commentary known as *Ḥāshiyat al-Bājūrī*. While I read this text line by line with a senior tutor in the seminary, the tutor explained that many of the texts of the legal genre composed by Muslim jurists of the era, such as the text we were studying, were written in a way that required knowledge of the Arabic linguistic and hermeneutical sciences called the *ʿulūm al-āla* ("the instrumental sciences"). The senior tutor explained that the author of *Ḥāshiyat al-Bājūrī* was a master in these sciences, and that, therefore, to truly comprehend the depths of text, I needed to study the *ʿulūm al-āla* in full. He explained that while these sciences are taught at the seminary, the true living masters of *ʿulūm al- āla* are the Kurdish scholars of southeastern Türkiye, notably in the region of Diyarbakır. He said that if I ever had the chance, I should seek them out because they are the best in the field of the *ʿulūm al-āla*, representing the full corpus of Arabic language study necessary for scholarly Islamic legal study and Quranic interpretation.

Two years later, by the will of Allah, I met such a scholar, who taught me these disciplines and authorized me in them. He was arguably not only one of the greatest of our time but the last living scholar of the Ottoman era who preserved the full curriculum of the *ʿulūm al-āla*. His name was Shaykh Muhammad Emin Er, and he authored a unique work that collected all the *ʿulūm al-āla* disciplines into one text, published in Arabic under the title *Jāmiʿ al-mutūn al-dirāsiyya* ("The Compendium of Study Texts"). This work is translated here into English for the first time.

Shaykh Muhammad Emin Er was a remarkable scholar and practitioner of the prophetic path. He was born around the outbreak of World War I, possibly in 1914 or perhaps as early as 1909.[1] The official records of the time are not always accurate, and the exact date of his birth is uncertain. He was born in the late Ottoman era in the village of Külüyan near the town of Çermik, Diyarbakır, in what is today southeastern Türkiye. When Muhammad Emin was a child of three or four, his mother passed away; at the age of ten, his father died, leaving him an orphan. At the time, the Ottoman state extended from North Africa to Yemen and from the Balkans to the frontiers of Persia. But the coordinated attacks that it faced on multiple fronts led to the depletion of its dwindling financial resources. The economic situation became ruinous, resulting in severe material hardship throughout the country, not least in the impoverished regions of eastern Anatolia where the young Muhammad Emin grew up. He spent his early life in straitened circumstances, first under the care of his stepmother and later under the care of his elder brother. High up in the mountains surrounding his village, he shepherded goats to help support his family. Throughout these difficulties, his singular desire was to learn to read and write. Enjoying neither paper nor pen, he used stones to etch words and sentences on flat rocks while tend-

[1] This biographical information is taken from his work entitled *The Soul of Islam: Essential Doctrines and Beliefs*.

ing goats on the mountainsides. He would shed bitter tears imploring Allah to help him learn to read the Quran. He missed no opportunity to seek out those who he thought could teach him. Muhammad Emin would journey on foot for days at a time to visit knowledgeable people in the vicinity of his village, however briefly. Eventually, he learned to write letters and read books in the Ottoman script. But there was no one at the time to introduce him to the Arabic language and the traditional Islamic disciplines, and he sought what knowledge he could from books.

When World War I came to a close, the nascent Turkish Republic abolished the traditional Ottoman script and outlawed all Quranic and Islamic education with harsh, and sometimes mortal, punishment. Families feared teaching the Quran to their children even in the privacy of their own homes. Though the first awakenings of his spiritual quest came to him at a very young age, Shaykh Muhammad Emin recalled that few opportunities to learn were available:

> *From my early childhood, I was anxious with respect to death and the life to come, so I would visit certain teachers and inquire of them about all this. I asked them how to prepare myself for the next life. From early childhood, I was curious about such things. I kept asking older people why we are so interested in this life and the things of this world when we are going to die, absolutely, every one of us. So it became my main goal to seek out a teacher and gain a religious education. But at that time everything was forbidden in Türkiye. Even to read and learn the Quran was forbidden in those days. It was not easy like it is today.*

Shaykh Muhammad Emin resolved to seek his religious learning in Syria, but he was denied entry. When he returned at the age of twenty-five from his first hajj, he undertook extensive travels in eastern Anatolia and later in Syria to seek out Islamic scholars. In the years that followed, Shaykh Muhammad Emin studied Arabic and the rational and Islamic sciences (*ʿulūm al-āla*) with a number of scholars. He studied morphology (*ṣarf*), grammar (*naḥw*), logic (*manṭiq*), linguistic theory (*ʿilm al-waḍʿ*), metaphor (*istiʿāra*), literary style (*adab*), rhetorical semantics (*maʿānī*), figurative language (*bayān*), embellishment (*badīʿ*), the fundamentals of religious belief (*uṣūl al-dīn*), rational theology (*kalām*), Quranic exegesis (*tafsīr*), the rules of Quranic recitation (*tajwīd*), jurisprudential theory (*uṣūl al-fiqh*), the sciences of the prophetic traditions (*uṣūl al-ḥadīth*), jurisprudence (*fiqh*) and the laws of inheritance (*farāʾiḍ*).

He spent considerable time with Molla Rasūl, a classmate of Shaykh Bediüzzaman Said Nursî. In 1951, Shaykh Muhammad Emin completed the last of his studies with Shaykh Muḥammad Maʿshūq, who granted him an *ijāza*, the traditional diploma and authorization to teach, in all of the rational sciences and traditional Islamic disciplines. Concurrent with his studies in the Islamic sciences, Shaykh Muhammad Emin devotedly pursued the study and practice of *taṣawwuf*, *tazkiyat al-nafs*, or *iḥsān*—the normative discipline of spiritual purification, which is the essence of Islam. He had a number of spiritual teachers, all from the Naqshbandī order. Following the death of Shaykh Aḥmad Ghaznawī, whom he met in Syria, he became a student of Shaykh Muḥammad Saʿīd Saydā al-Jazarī and remained under his tutelage until he was granted an *ijāza* to guide students of his own. Shaykh Muhammad Emin was profoundly affected by Shaykh Saʿīd's character (*akhlāq*): his immense kindness and love for all, selfless service towards others, boundless patience, genuine humility, unaffected sincerity, innocent self-effacement, and continuous forbearance and forgiveness. Shaykh Muhammad Emin related that he never heard Shaykh Saʿīd utter a harsh or disparaging word against another and that he would never defend himself. When he heard of others slandering him, he would only respond, "I have more faults than they know." Once, when he was quite elderly, Shaykh Saʿīd learned that fellow villagers were building a house but did not have enough stone to complete the construction. He went to a ruined house, asked his students to place two stones from it on his back, and carried them to the house being constructed. Shaykh Saʿīd rode on donkeys, never horses, due to a constant concern to preserve his humility and ward off ostentation. *Ṣuḥba* with Shaykh Saʿīd was instrumental in shaping Shaykh Muhammad Emin's scholarship, spirituality, character, and pedagogy. Shaykh Muhammad Emin would later say that every spiritual path has its own methods of remembrance (*dhikr*) and practice, but among all of them, the practice of *ṣuḥba* (companionship) is indispensable and uniquely effective.

Until the last breath of his life—and he lived to be over 100 years old—Shaykh Muhammad Emin lived the character (*akhlāq*) that he inherited from his teacher: he was perpetually in a state of divine remembrance (*dhikr*); he lived a life of rigorous worship; he fasted whenever possible; he regularly observed the night vigil prayers (*tahajjud*); he ate, spoke, and slept little; he gave counsel to all those who sought his advice; he magnanimously hosted a steady stream of guests in his modest Ankara apartment; he traveled far and wide to join family and fraternal ties; he tirelessly taught students, sensitive to each student's needs and aptitude; and he continued to write on a variety of subjects. Those who had the divinely gifted grace to spend time with him attest that he did everything, and lived every moment, with an unmatched poetic, innocent, spiritual elegance.[1]

I was first introduced to Shaykh Muhammad Emin Er in 2004 upon my first visit to Istanbul. It was then that I had the distinct honor of studying legal, theological and spiritual sciences with him daily. I was also at that time that I had the privilege of being introduced to the detailed study of the *ʿulūm al-āla*. During that incredibly intensive summer, my understanding of the Islamic studies and the Arabic language transformed profoundly. Though I initially went there for only one summer of study, I ended up leaving the United States the following year and settling in Istanbul, where I was able to devote myself fully to the study of the *ʿulūm al-āla* and other Islamic disciplines under the guidance of Shaykh Muhammad Emin Er and his top students, such as Shaykh Mahsuk Yamac, as well as numerous other Kurdish and Turkish scholars.

In 2010, I was granted full authorization by Shaykh Muhammad Emin Er to transmit all his work and received full *ijāza* from him. Among his final words to me when I was preparing to depart Türkiye were "Teach the *dīn* in its entirety."

The *ʿulūm al-āla* represent the linguistic requirements of learning and teaching the *dīn* of Islam, for knowledge and comprehension of the Quran and its sciences requires knowledge of Arabic language and linguistics.

Upon returning to the United States and completing my graduate and doctoral work, I came to understand the profound importance of teaching the curriculum of the *ʿulūm al-āla* more fully. It is a profoundly effective curriculum for methodically training students to realize their fullest potential in cultivating a deep relationship with the Quran, as encapsulated by the Quranic injunctions *iqraʾ*[2] (to read and cultivating fundamental literacy) and *tadabbar*[3] (to engage in rational contemplation, spiritual reflection, and critical analysis with the heart).

In the beginning, one learns to read; later, one reads to learn. Both levels constitute the beginning and end of the command *iqraʾ*. After continuous reading of the Quran, one learns to think and then

[1] *The Soul of Islam*, 13–40.

[2] The reference for *iqraʾ* in the Quran is "Read! In the name of your Lord..." (Q 96:1).

[3] The reference for *tadabbur* in the Quran is "Do they not contemplate the Quran? Or are their hearts locked?" (Q 47:24).

engages Quranically with other forms of thought and critically analyzes such thought through Quranic lenses. Put differently, one learns to think and then thinks in order to critique. This is the beginning and end of the instruction of *tadabbur*. This, in a nutshell, is Islamic literacy:

*iqra*ʾ (read): learn to read; read to learn
tadabbar (think): learn to think; think to critique

The *ʿulūm al-āla*, as reformulated in the Ottoman era and presented here in English for the first time, are designed to produce Islamic literacy through the study of twelve disciplines:

1. *ṣarf* (morphology) – learn to read
2. *naḥw* (grammar) – read to learn
3. *manṭiq* (logic) – learn to think
4. *waḍʿ* (language theory) – learn to think
5. *majāz* (metaphor) – learn to think
6. *munāẓara* (dialectics) – think to critique
7. *maʿānī* (rhetorical semantics) – think to critique
8. *bayān* (figurative language) – think to critique
9. *badīʿ* (embellishment) – think to critique
10. *uṣūl al-fiqh* (jurisprudential theory) – think to critique
11. *uṣūl al-dīn* (creedal theology) – think to critique
12. *uṣūl al-taṣawwuf* (principles of spiritual devotion) – think to critique

Ṣarf and *naḥw* are co-disciplines that teach the student how words and basic meanings are constructed. *Ṣarf* (morphology) teaches how changes in the beginning and middle of Arabic words produce literal variances in meaning, while *naḥw* (grammar) reveals how changes at the end of the Arabic word influence meaning. Both disciplines teach how structural changes in words have conceptual significance in the mind, which is the arena of *manṭiq*.

Manṭiq (logic), the third discipline, explores the nature of conceptualization and its role in the formation of propositions, which are expressions intended to bear truth-claims about the world. Truth-claims and the tools to understand and assess them are vital, especially in a time when empirical knowledge can be directly called into question due to the new tools of our digital age, in which generative AI, ChatGPT, deepfakes, fake news, virtual reality, and the overall secular age which glorifies the absence of certainty about reality—let alone certainty about a transcendental realm—render it significantly more challenging to cling to claims of truth and reality. *Manṭiq* explores how reasoning distinguishes between valid and invalid truth-claims.

The fourth discipline is *ʿilm al-waḍʿ* (linguistic theory). *Waḍʿ* starts with the understanding that the Arabic language is rooted in a divine system whose structure is engineered to convey a broad range of meanings, one reason for the Quran's being revealed in Arabic. *ʿIlm al-waḍʿ* posits that word families and patterns have given boundaries of built-in meanings, which provides definitive limits for Arabic hermeneutics. These limits, while clearly delineated, have some flexibility, which brings us to the fifth discipline: *ʿilm al-majāz*.

ʿIlm al-majāz (the science of metaphor) explores the range of flexibility within which words may be creatively used to convey poetic or figurative meaning. This is significant for the teaching of the limits of interpretation and for exploring the linguistically permissible range in which speech or a text may be understood. *Majāz* is also useful in understanding how familiar concepts might be recast in new forms and expressed in creative ways to suit contexts where standard forms of expression might make it difficult to articulate those meanings.

The sixth discipline is *munāẓara* (dialectics). The purpose of *munāẓara* is to expound upon the proper rules of engagement of debate for reaching and establishing truth among competing truth-claims. *Munāẓara* is the linguistic arena in which the battle between ideas is joined. Logic, language and intellectual creativity become instruments of discovery and defense when faced with arguments that stand counter to one's own reasoning about a particular position. One learns to combat opinions and ideas through effective argumentation and intellectual interrogation and engages in an exploratory, rational back-and-forth process in order to distinguish truth from falsehood.

The seventh, eighth, and ninth disciplines are a collection of topics that constitute the subject called *ʿilm al-balāgha* (rhetoric). These three disciplines are *ʿilm al-maʿānī* (rhetorical semantics), *ʿilm al-bayān* (figurative language) and *ʿilm al-badīʿ* (embellishment). *Balāgha* explores how speech can be adapted to context to move the listener emotionally and intellectually. It is the true art of linguistic expression and beautiful speech, and it helps the student better appreciate the depths of Quranic eloquence.

The tenth discipline is *uṣūl al-fiqh* (jurisprudential theory). It is said that all of the disciplines above are established for the sole purpose of serving this one. Without all of the previous disciplines, one cannot truly embark on the study of this science, which itself is a prerequisite for the deep study of Islamic jurisprudence, for developing the skill of delivering fatwas, and for the rigorous work of *ijtihād* in general. *Uṣūl al-fiqh* is the grand discipline, comprising the required topics for understanding how to interpret the divine address to humanity through the four primary sources of Islamic jurisprudence: the Quran, the hadith, *ijmāʿ* (consensus), and *qiyās* (analogical reasoning). In addition, *uṣūl al-fiqh* outlines the requirements for utilizing the secondary sources of Islamic jurisprudence such as *maṣlaḥa* (public interests), *istiḥsān* (juristic preference), *ʿurf* (social norms), *qawāʿid fiqhiyya* (legal maxims), *maqāṣid al-sharīʿa* (the objectives of the law), and the requirements for *ijtihād* (expert legal interpretation and reasoning) and limits of *taqlīd* (common adherence to an established legal opinion).

The eleventh discipline is *uṣūl al-dīn* (creedal theology). *Uṣūl al-dīn* comprises the major elements of proper faith and belief in the religion of Islam. A true practitioner of Islamic hermeneutics and scriptural interpretation must be grounded in the most fundamental aspects of Islamic tenets of faith, and this discipline outlines them.

The final discipline is *uṣūl al-taṣawwuf* or *mabādiʾ al-taṣawwuf* (the principles of spiritual devotion). Rational inquiry and the cultivation of the intellect alone is not enough for the believer, for this process may expose the practitioner to dangerous vices of the self like arrogance, pride, anger, and other internal sins. Spiritual cultivation is needed to discipline the self along the journey and to temper the appetites of the self. Comprising the principles of self-purification, this discipline maps the spiritual landscape of the requirements for wayfaring on the spiritual path and the conditions necessary for continued progress, leading to ultimate success in this life and in the next.

These twelve disciplines collectively make up the contents of this manual authored by the late Shaykh Muhammad Emin and translated here into English with the accompanying Arabic text. This work is the culmination of many years of effort, birthed initially from a desire to render this work accessible to English speakers and students of sacred knowledge in the West. Dr. Aaron (Harun) Spevack came to me many years ago and first expressed interest in studying this text with me along with a small cohort of serious students. We began online with the first discipline and slowly progressed, working our way through each of the twelve disciplines. Dr. Harun eventually commissioned two senior specialists with graduate degrees from Zaytuna College, Marwan Tayyan and Justin Poe, to produce a complete translation of the text. Prof. Carl Sharif El-Tobgui was generous enough to offer his scholarly support and valuable time to read a significant portion of the work while it was in development, and he also read the work with Dr. Harun and me. After much labor and determination, the work was completed in the summer of 2024.

I can personally attest to the fact that these four individuals are competent in these disciplines, and I have personally given them *ijāza* in the *ʿulūm al-āla* with my chain (*sanad*) from Shaykh Muhammad Emin.

I am deeply grateful to Shaykh Muhammad Emin for devoting his precious time and energy to this meek servant of Allah who was not worthy of this great honor by such an esteemed master of the Islamic sciences and the prophetic path. I also express my profound gratitude to each and every one of my teachers, especially Shaykh Mahsuk Yamac, for teaching me the *ʿulūm al-āla* and other Islamic sciences. My time with these luminaries was the best part of my life, and it is truly a blessing from Allah Most High to see this work come to fruition. May Allah make it a blessing for others and make it a worthy contribution to the development of this *dīn* in the English-speaking world, and may He grant all of those who helped make it happen a portion of the reward in this life and the next. *Āmīn.*

Dr. Khalil Abdur-Rashid

Muslim Chaplain at Harvard University

Chair of the Board of Religious, Spiritual, and Ethical Life at Harvard University

Islam and Public Policy Lecturer at Harvard Kennedy School of Public Policy

June 2024 / Dhū al-Ḥijja 2, 1445

TRANSLATORS' PREFACE

بسم الله الرحمن الرحيم

THIS EDITION came about in methodical steps under the direction of Dr. Aaron Spevack. The first step was a preliminary one: we assembled a set of comparative glossaries surveying existing translations of Arabic technical terms in the domains of grammar and morphology, logic, dialectics, language theory, and rhetoric.[1] By studying the various approaches that translators over the past 150 years of Anglophone scholarship have brought to the formidable task of translating these technical sciences, we began to form an early idea of the translation methodology we wanted for this project. Above all, we wanted to serve those engaging these texts from within the tradition of learning and teaching for which they were intended. To this end, we viewed translation not as a mere crutch for students with poor Arabic but rather as a tool that, used precisely, can extend an invaluable apparatus of scholarship and knowledge into the vital linguistic space of the English language.

The comparative glossaries were used to produce initial, preparatory draft translations of each treatise in the *Compendium*, with the endeavor to begin by clinging as closely to the literal Arabic as possible, even at the cost of unidiomatic phrasing, so that we could focus our attention first on the technical terms. Marwan produced preparatory drafts of Treatises I, III, IV, VI, XI, XII; Justin produced preparatory drafts of the introduction and Treatises II, V, VII, VIII, IX, and X. These drafts were used as springboards for in-house collaborative review and discussion of methodology, a process in which we were joined by Dr. Spevack.

This was followed by a lengthy process over which Marwan carried out a thorough overhaul of the preparatory draft and produced the final translation alongside the edited Arabic text, while the team convened frequently to read this new draft and to continue discussing and refining the translation. These readings profited immeasurably from the gracious presence of Carl Sharif El-Tobgui, whose expertise saved the translation from many an embarrassing mistake. The introduction and Treatises I, II, III, IV, XI, and XII were read jointly in this manner, line by line, with the occasional company of university students in Boston.[2] The remaining treatises were kindly reviewed by the following experts:

Suheil Laher reviewed the translation of Treatises V, VII, VIII, and IX, which are the treatises on the disciplines of rhetoric, and provided an extensive list of notes and recommendations, for which we are sincerely grateful.

Talal Ahdab met with us to read the greater portion of Treatise X, on jurisprudential theory, along with the translation. His mastery of the science was indispensable in grappling with the complexities of the Arabic text.

Mehmet Fatih Arslan read the translation of Treatise VI, on dialectics, and provided a number of helpful suggestions and remarks.

[1] These glossaries may be accessed at https://asipt.org/glossary. Special credit must be given to Alison Jacques, who had already done some prior work to source the logic glossary.

[2] Nasra Noor deserves special acknowledgment for her dedication to the sessions on morphology and grammar.

We also thank Mahsuk Yamac for his readiness to answer our questions about the text. We are forever indebted to him and the rest of our teachers, especially those at Zaytuna College, for the knowledge and training that made this work possible.

On the Edition and Conventions

The Arabic text of this edition is based on the second edition of Shaykh Muhammad Emin's collected treatises published under the title *Jāmiʿ al-mutūn al-dirāsiyya* by Dār al-Andalus in 2011. Although the second edition corrected many of the errors made in the transcription of the first print edition, which was based on a manuscript in the author's handwriting, we saw it necessary in preparing this edition to correct numerous mistakes that remained in the second edition. These have been marked in the Arabic text with endnotes explaining the changes. Substantive additions or changes as well as minor adjustments to the text for the sake of accuracy, completeness, clarity, or the orderly and helpful presentation of sections are enclosed in square brackets in both the Arabic and the English. It should be noted that the bracketed material is sometimes integral to the phrasing of the English translation; the translation is *not* intended to be coherent with omission of this material.

For most treatises, the Dār al-Andalus edition includes explanatory footnotes at least some of which are clearly in the voice of the author. Unless otherwise indicated in the notes to the Arabic text, the footnotes are retained as footnotes in the parallel bilingual format of this edition. In many cases, we deemed that a statement or passage needed further clarification. These points of clarification, along with the identification of proper names of scholars and books mentioned in the text, we have relegated to endnotes that follow each treatise respectively. To assist the reader in distinguishing footnotes from endnotes, we have enclosed the footnote references in square brackets and set their numbering to restart on every page. Because the total scope of the sciences treated in this volume is so wide, we have done our best to exercise a disciplined approach in providing explanations and commentary in the endnotes, fearing to undertake what would otherwise have quickly become an unmanageable responsibility. Thus, the notes are far from fulfilling the role of a traditional commentary, and substantial assumptions will be made about the reader's knowledge and familiarity with technical jargon throughout the main text. This is an unavoidable consequence of the fact that Shaykh Emin's treatises were intended to be taught and explained by teachers in a seminary setting.

Transliteration follows the guidelines of the *International Journal of Middle East Studies*. Ottoman names (like Birgevī and Gelenbevī) are rendered according to the Ottoman transliteration system. For translations of Quranic verses, we have primarily consulted *The Study Quran*, with frequent and, in many cases, significant modifications, especially in consideration of what is directly relevant to a given passage of discussion.

Several other conventions are noteworthy. Translations in blue-gray are provided after transliterated words, phrases, or sentences in cases where the point of the passage is to discuss the words themselves or illustrate features inherent in the Arabic. The purpose of this coloring is to set these courtesy translations apart from the flow of the larger sentence to allow the reader to follow the main idea uninterrupted. Certain letters, words, and phrases are underlined in the English text of the grammar and rhetoric treatises to indicate the pertinent parts of various examples provided for discussions in the text. Finally, technical terms are italicized when not clearly introduced by a heading or when it otherwise might slip the attention of the reader that a given term is to be read as a technical term.

On the Translation of Terms

Inasmuch as we can make any claim to consistency in the translation of more than seven hundred technical terms, our main principle has been to regard the translation as a means of assisting students in understanding the subject matter. As all translators know, every choice is a matter of balance and judgment. Some choices were easy, others quite difficult. The following is a list of some ways in which we have thought about the task of translating terms and striven to apply the principle above:

1. With a handful of exceptions, we have provided a translation for every technical term, on the premise that many English-speaking students who are learning Arabic will find Arabic with English more useful than either alone, and in view of the fact that translation cannot subtract much since the Arabic will always be there for reference, sitting just parallel to the translated text. The choice to translate all terms in the English text (rather than retaining a significant number of Arabic terms in transliterated form) is not to suggest that we could collectively do without the Arabic but rather to illustrate to the English-speaking student how the concepts may be expressed and utilized successfully in his language. One need not struggle to "think in Arabic" (on pain of futility) in order to grasp and internalize the principles of logic, jurisprudential theory, or even the Arabic sciences. Only in rare instances (e.g., the term *muḍāf ilayhi* and terms present in the Merriam-Webster dictionary like *mujtahid*) did we judge that no available English translation was both precise and clear enough to be more helpful than distracting.

2. We have avoided literal translation when this would have left the intelligibility of the term totally dependent on translating it back into Arabic. In our evaluation, using a technically imprecise literal translation (like using "borrowing" for *istiʿāra* instead of "metaphor") is hardly different from just using the Arabic term. The interested reader is encouraged to flip to the glossary, where we have provided the lexical meanings of Arabic terms when they differed notably from the chosen technical translation. Of course, the reader is also encouraged to avail himself of a good Arabic–English classical dictionary like *Lane's Lexicon*, good classical Arabic dictionaries, and even a good English dictionary!

3. We have avoided translations that rely on the etymology and strict lexical denotation of an English term when this would conflict with usage and cause confusion. Hence, we translate *waḍʿ* as "assignment," not "imposition," though the latter has historically seen some use for this technical meaning. In general, we have tried to avoid words with multiple usages when confusion was likely. For example, we never translate *lafẓī* as "formal," even when this would be accurate as the opposite of *maʿnawī* where "formal" means "in the mere outward aspect or appearance."

4. We have generally avoided contravening well-established precedent, since doing so could confuse a reader who has already learned a particular translation. We have made a few exceptions, however, for the sake of technical accuracy. *Kināya* may well be "metonymy" in Arabic–English dictionaries and various contemporary studies, but "metonymy" is technically to refer to a thing by the name of something associated with it, which is not the technical meaning of *kināya* (in fact, it almost exactly suits the technical meaning of *majāz mursal*, which we do translate thus). It is worth mentioning that there is rarely any consensus in matters of translation beyond the most basic terms.

5. We have not been hindered by fear of "cultural imperialism" in selectively using terms from other traditions, especially terms drawn from western scholastic grammar, logic, or rhetoric (e.g., "preposition," "differentia," and "simile"). Embracing parallels across traditions is not just an exercise in comparative studies; when done responsibly, it trains the student to look past the terms to the meanings. One defeats the higher purpose of seeking real knowledge—a purpose that is arguably the very heart of the traditional sciences—when one insists on relativizing the overwhelming majority of concepts to particular historical traditions, especially when studying sciences that expressly define themselves as universal tools of knowledge. That being said, we have avoided importing neat preexisting terms and categories when we judged that they

would obscure or cause injury to the proper meaning of a term. Hence, for example, *taṣdīq* is "assent," not "judgment" (since the judgment, or *ḥukm*, is often regarded as a conceptual part of propositions, not a mode of knowledge), and *iltifāt* is "shift in person," not "apostrophe" (which is more specific).

6. Though the sciences by their nature often demand the use of complex or unfamiliar terms for abstract concepts (like "predicate-privative" for *maʿdūlat al-maḥmūl* and "*a fortiori* implication" for *faḥwā al-khiṭāb*), we have tried to avoid overly arcane terms when there were clearer, more approachable alternatives. Hence, for instance, the *mubtadaʾ* is the "subject," not the "inchoative"; *jumlat al-sharṭ* is the "condition clause," not the "protasis"; and *mashhūrāt* are "commonplace premises," not "endoxa." Note that in some situations, we bypassed familiar words in order to free up their ordinary, nontechnical significations for use elsewhere. Thus, we use "augmentation" instead of the plainer "addition" to refer to that kind of *ziyāda* that is internal to the morphological classes (*abwāb al-ṣarf*), leaving the word "addition" for use elsewhere in the treatise on morphology, such as in the chapter on modification (*iʿlāl*).

7. We have introduced new translations when we could not find satisfactory precedent according to the standards above—or, in some cases, any precedent at all. In these instances, we prioritized capturing the gist of the technical meaning in a word or short phrase.

How to Use This Book

In consideration of the fact that each of the treatises in this volume is written as a *matn*, or terse seminary primer, it is not expected of a reader lacking prior training in or exposure to the sciences in this *Compendium* to be able to gain the kind of conceptual familiarity and fluency that would traditionally be provided by a good teacher, nor should it be expected of this edition to lend the support that would be provided by a good commentary. A *matn* is meant to be *taught*, its contents unpacked line by line, word by word. Although the reader is of course free to use this edition in any way he finds helpful, we expect that it will serve best in one of three ways:

First, the treatises might be used as texts of classroom instruction in a seminary or seminary-like context where classical Arabic texts are taught primarily in English. Teachers and students alike may also find the text useful as an adjacent supplement to the teaching and study of commonly taught seminary texts, which will be especially feasible because, more often than not, the author closely followed the model and wording of commonly taught texts in writing these treatises. The bilingual format of this text will render it particularly helpful outside the classroom in preparing for instruction or consolidating the material afterward.

Second, students of these sciences and experts alike may find the best use of this edition as a reference work for the translation of technical terms in English. Its wide scope, the effort that has been made to bring a systematic approach to the task of translation, and the extensive glossary of terms will, we hope, allow this edition to serve this role particularly well.

Finally, Anglophone researchers interested in the textual tradition of the late Ottoman madrasa will benefit from the translation not only because these treatises arguably belong to that tradition but also because of the many parallels with its primary texts, and will find the references to commentary texts in the endnotes useful in pointing the way to further research.

❁ ❁ ❁

Advice to the Student and Closing Prayer

Reader of this volume and seeker of sacred knowledge, know that your path towards sacred knowledge begins with learning your individual obligations. Before you dig for the treasures of revelation and the secrets of reality, you must light the torch of faith, warm yourself with its radiation, and construct around it and yourself a barrier to protect you from the winds and bolts of unbelief and ingratitude. You first learn what Allah requires you to know and what actions you must perform, and only then can you pursue what awaits you beyond these foundations. After you know what is required of you and you practice what is expected of you, you may begin the sacred sciences. Our author, Shaykh Muhammad Emin Er (may Allah have mercy on him), gives us these foundations within the first pages of this *Compendium*.

Thereafter, the seeker of sacred knowledge turns and directs his or her attention first towards the instrumental sciences of language: morphology and grammar. These form the foundation of all subsequent sciences the student pursues, opening doors to understanding sacred texts, elevating the student's comprehension, and planting before him or her paradigms and rules to apply and compare to examples encountered in every text and speech. This volume begins with these sciences.

After studying the foundational lexical sciences, the seeker continues on with the remaining instrumental sciences of logic, language theory, dialectics, and rhetoric. Competency in these sciences opens the path before the seeker to move on to sciences at the intermediate level, including jurisprudential theory, creedal theology, and the principles of spirituality. These three sciences assume a strong foundation in the instrumental sciences, especially the lexical sciences.

Seeker, we pray that these treatises assist you in your study of the sacred sciences, whether they form the basis of your studies or serve as supplemental texts. We advise you to gather your attention and direct it towards knowledge that will benefit you in this life and the hereafter. Direct your efforts towards these sciences and then progress to closely studying and reflecting on the divine address and the path of the Messenger ﷺ with the resolve to follow the light poured forth for you.

May Allah, the Bestower and Knowing, grant you the resolve by which to unlock these pages and the humility by which to absorb their meanings. Continue on your path to knowledge with courage. There is no might or power except that which Allah gives. Remember your obligations for they protect you from obscenity, your supplications for they enlighten your path, and the author and your teachers for they have taken your hand towards felicity.

INTRODUCTION

المقدمة

In the Name of Allah,
All-Merciful, Most Compassionate

بسم الله الرحمن الرحيم

ALL PRAISE IS due to Allah, who graciously bestowed upon us belief and submission and by His favor made us part of the community of the best of all creation; may the blessings of Allah ﷻ and His peace be upon him forever and upon his family, his Companions, and his Followers, who have attained paradise, the abode of peace.

To Proceed Says the destitute servant, needful of the mercy of his self-sufficient Lord, may Allah ﷻ by His manifest and subtle kindness grant him and his parents forgiveness, Muḥammad Emīn Er al-Mīrānī al-Kuluyānī al-Jirmikī al-Āmidī and, later, al-Anqarawī, b. Dhulkifl b. ʿAlī b. Aḥmad al-Baghdādī (patrilineally), named Qarw, al-Jarkazī al-Qāfqāsī (matrilineally), al-Shantawī (by residence):

The Motive for Writing Since the Arabic sciences are among the most important sciences, especially the sciences of lexicology, morphology, syntax, logic, language theory, metaphor, dialectics, rhetoric, creedal theology, jurisprudential theory, and the science of spiritual principles—how could they not be so, when they are the means to understanding the book of Allah ﷻ and the Sunna of His messenger ﷺ?—I wanted, by His permission ﷻ, to write

الحمد لله الذي منّ علينا بالإيمان والإسلام وجعلنا بفضله من أمّة خير الأنام صلوات الله تعالى وسلامه عليه على الدوام وعلى آله وصحبه وأتباعه الفائزين بالجنّة دار السلام.

أما بعد فيقول العبد الفقير المفتقر إلى رحمة ربّه الغني، سامحه الله تعالى ووالديه بلطفه الجليّ والخفيّ، **محمد أمين** أر الميراني الكلياني الجرمكي الآمدي ثم الأنقروي بن ذي الكفل بن علي بن أحمد البغدادي أبًا الملقّب بقرو الجركزي القافقاسي أمًّا الشنتوي استيطانًا:

الباعث على التأليف لما كانت العلوم العربية من أجلّ العلوم لا سيما علم اللغة والاشتقاق والإعراب والميزان والوضع والاستعارة والآداب والبلاغة والأصولَين وعلم مبادئ التصوّف[1] — كيف لا وهي وسيلة إلى فهم كتاب الله تعالى وسنّة رسوله ﷺ — أردت

a treatise on each of these sciences that covers its principal questions in a way that facilitates its comprehension for every student, whether bright and clever or otherwise.

The first of these twelve treatises is the treatise entitled *Turning a Glance: On the Science of Morphology*, and the last of them is the treatise entitled *The Plenitude of the Gracious One: On the Science of Spiritual Principles*, bringing [the reader] at last to spiritual excellence and the wholehearted devotion of one's acts to Him ﷻ.

بإذنه تعالى أن أكتب في كل علم منها رسالة تشتمل على عيون مسائله على وجه يسهّل فهمها على كل طالب فطين ذكيّ وغيره.

أوّل تلك الرسائل الاثنتي عشرة الرسالة المسمّاة لفتة الطرف في علم الصرف وآخرها الرسالة المسمّاة فيض الرؤوف في علم مبادئ التصوّف المفضي إلى الإحسان وإخلاص العمل له تعالى.

The Duties of One Who Takes Up a Science

I found it necessary before delving into these treatises to point out what is incumbent on anyone who intends to engage in teaching or learning any science. This is as follows:

1. that one set beforehand the intention to act, to teach, and to remove ignorance both from oneself and from others.
2. that one begin first with what is individually obligatory, in order of importance, then with what is communally obligatory, in the same way, avoiding what crosses into the range of specialized [knowledge], without falling short in any obligation or emphasized sunna, and without plunging into ambiguous matters, into the intricacies of the science of rational theology, or into vain and useless sciences that fetch harm without benefit.

الواجب على من باشر علما

رأيت من الواجب أن أشير قبل الخوض في تلك الرسائل إلى ما يجب على من أراد المباشرة بشيء من العلوم تعليمًا أو تعلّمًا، وهو هذا:

١- أن يقدّم نيّة العمل والتعليم وإزالة الجهل عن نفسه وعن الغير جميعًا.

٢- أن يبدأ أوّلًا بفرض العين الأهمّ فالأهمّ، ثم بفرض الكفاية كذلك غير المتجاوز إلى حدّ الندرة ولا مخلّ بفرض أو سنّة مؤكدة وغير خائض في المتشابهات ودقائق علم الكلام ولا فيما يضرّ ولا ينفع من العلوم الزخرفية العاطلة.

3. that one strengthen his belief by accompanying the righteous, reflecting on the proofs of the clear Quran, and acting rightly, taking what is most precautious in matters of practice and what is conclusively established in matters of creed.
4. that one make his creed sound in accordance with the views of the scholars of the Sunna and the Majority ﵃ rather than what he might have understood from the texts of revelation in a way opposed to the views of the scholars of the Sunna and the Majority, which is the habit of those who follow whimsical inclinations and deviant innovations. Such is pure misguidance; may Allah ﷻ by his grace and generosity protect us from it all.

٣- وأن يقوّي إيمانه بصحبة الصالحين والنظر في أدلّة القرآن المبين وبالأعمال الصالحة آخذًا بالأحوط في الفروع والقواطع في أصول الدين.

٤- أن يصحّح عقيدته وفق آراء علماء أهل السنّة والجماعة رضي الله عنهم لا وفق ما يفهم من النصوص على خلاف آراء أهل السنّة والجماعة كما هو دأب أهل الأهواء والبدع، فذلك ضلالة محضة حفظنا الله تعالى عن ذلك كلّه بمنّه وكرمه.

❋ ❋ ❋

The views of the scholars of the Sunna and the Majority are, in summary, as follows:

1. There is nothing rightly worshipped, nothing that creates anything, and nothing that possesses any [absolute] perfection except Allah.
2. He possesses every perfection and transcends every deficiency. He can do anything that is possible. Whatever He wills is; whatever He wills not is not.
3. He is the First: nothing precedes Him. He is the Last: nothing succeeds Him. He is the Self-Sufficient: He needs no locus or specifier.[1]

وهي أي آراء أهل السنّة والجماعة ملخّصةً:

١- أنه لا معبود بحقّ ولا خالق لشيء ولا متّصف بكمال غير الله.

٢- وأنه متّصف بكل كمال ومنزّه عن كل نقص، وجائز له كل ممكن. ما شاء الله كان وما لم يشأ لم يكن.

٣- وأنه هو الأوّل ليس قبله شيء والآخر ليس بعده شيء والقيّوم ليس يحتاج إلى محلّ أو مخصّص.

4. He is dissimilar to His creation: He does not resemble anything nor does anything resemble Him. “There is nothing like Him” (Q 42:11). He is one, unique, independent; “He neither begets nor was begotten, nor has He any equal” (Q 112:3–4).
5. He is living, knowing, willing, and powerful, equally capable of doing anything He wills without or through causal means. Others besides Him lack the power to do anything, even given the means, unless He ﷻ wills it. He is hearing and seeing. He gives existence to the heavens and the earth, everything in between, and everything within.
6. Muḥammad ﷺ is the messenger of Allah. Truthful, trustworthy, and intelligent, he conveyed all that he was entrusted to convey.
7. He is the seal of the prophets and messengers. He was sent to the entire population of both weighty realms.[2] He is the best of all the creation of Allah.
8. His revealed law abrogated every prior revealed law; it suffices the needs of humanity and suffices for their prosperity in every time and place, and it will remain until just before the final hour.
9. *Religion* is defined as that which Allah ﷻ has revealed to His servants on the tongues of His messengers. According to the verifying position, [the observance of] religion falls into three categories:
   (a) religion insofar as Allah ﷻ reveals it to His servants on the tongues of His messengers but those servants do not believe in it. Such a mode of religion cannot be described either as deficient or as perfect: it saves them neither from everlasting residence [in hell] nor from punishment.

٤- وأنه مخالف لخلقه لا يشبه شيئًا ولا يشبهه شيء ليس كمثله شيء؛ واحد أحد صمد لم يلد ولم يولد ولم يكن له كفوًا أحد.

٥- حيّ، عليم، مريد، قادر يقدر على كل شيء أراده بلا أسباب كما يقدر عليه بأسباب. وغيره لا يقدر على شيء ولو بأسباب بدون إرادته تعالى، سميع، بصير، مكوّن للسماوات والأرض وما بينهما وما فيهما.

٦- أنّ محمدًا ﷺ رسول الله وأنه صادق أمين فطين بلّغ جميع ما أمر بتبليغه.

٧- وأنه خاتم الأنبياء والمرسلين وأنه مبعوث إلى كافّة الثقلين وأنه خير خلق الله أجمعين.

٨- وأنّ شريعته نسخت كل شريعة قبلها وأنها كافية لاحتياج البشر وسعادتهم في كل زمان ومكان وأنها باقية إلى قبيل قيام الساعة.

٩- وأنّ الدين ما بيّنه الله تعالى لعباده على لسان رسله. وأنه على التحقيق على ثلاثة أقسام:

(أ) دين بيّنه الله تعالى لعباده على لسان رسله ولم يؤمنوا به. وهذا دين لا يوصف بأنه ناقص أو كامل، ولا ينجيهم من الخلود ولا من العذاب.

(b) religion insofar as Allah ﷻ reveals it to His servants on the tongues of His messengers and those servants believe in it yet do not act accordingly. Such a mode of religion is deficient: it grants salvation not from punishment but merely from everlasting residence [in hell]—unless Allah pardons such a person by His grace.

(c) religion insofar as Allah ﷻ reveals it to His servants on the tongues of His messengers and those servants believe in it and act accordingly. This mode of religion is complete with respect to some servants, while for others it is all the more perfect because they uphold rigor, take the best course, and [maintain] continual invocation, introspective awareness, and immersion in the meaning of the divine essence (this entailing no likeness or [knowable] modality); it is pleasing to Allah and leads to "groves with rivers running below, therein to abide, and spouses made pure, and supreme good pleasure from Allah" (Q 3:15).

The scholars of theology have defined this complete religion as a divine dispensation and revealed order that leads people of sound intellect, by a praiseworthy exercise of their choice, to righteousness in the present and felicity in the future, that is, righteousness in this worldly life and felicity in the hereafter. Thus, religion includes both creed and worship; it does not refer merely to creed.

Allah ﷻ has elucidated for us in the most concise yet comprehensive phrase what religion is, saying, "Truly, religion in the sight of Allah is submission" (Q 3:19), meaning that [the observance of] religion as pleases Allah and grants salvation from punishment is submission, i.e., that the servant submit himself to his Lord by conforming to what He

(ب) دين بيّنه الله تعالى لعباده على لسان رسله، آمنوا به ولم يعملوا بمقتضاه. وهذا دين ناقص غير منجٍ عن العذاب بل منجٍ من الخلود إلا أن يعفو الله عن صاحبه بفضله.

(ج) دين بيّنه الله تعالى لعباده على لسان رسله، آمنوا به وعملوا بمقتضاه. وهذا دين منجٍ من الخلود والعذاب؛ وهو في بعضهم كامل وفي بعضهم أكمل لأخذهم بالعزائم والأولى ودوام الذكر والمراقبة والاستغراق في معنى الذات بلا مثال ولا كيف؛ ومرضيّ عند الله وموصل إلى جنّات تجري من تحتها الأنهار خالدين فيها وأزواج مطهّرة ورضوان من الله.

وعرّف هذا الدين الكامل علماء علم الأصول بأنه وضع إلهي ونظم سماوي سائق لذوي العقول السليمة باختيارهم المحمود إلى الصلاح في الحال والفلاح في المآل، أي الصلاح في الدنيا والفلاح في العقبى. فقد اشتمل الدين على العقيدة والعبادة جميعًا فليس الدين عبارة عن العقيدة فقط.

وقد بيّن الله تعالى لنا الدين بأوجز عبارة وأشمل لفظ فقال ﴿إِنَّ ٱلدِّينَ عِندَ ٱللَّهِ ٱلۡإِسۡلَٰمُ﴾ [٣/ ١٩] أي إنّ الدين المرضيّ عند الله والمنجي من العذاب هو الإسلام، أي تسليم العبد نفسه لربّه بامتثال ما

commands and avoiding what He forbids. For He ﷻ has bought from His servants their souls in exchange for paradise; thus, they are to submit their souls to their Lord by conforming to what He commands and avoiding what He forbids.

Religion, then, is more comprehensive [than mere belief], including belief, practice, and spiritual excellence. As for belief, it means to believe with conviction in Allah ﷻ, His angels, His books, His messengers, the final day, and destiny—in sum, to believe with conviction in everything that is conclusively established in terms of both authenticity and indication and known of necessity to be part and parcel of the religion. As for practice, it means to do what you are commanded seeking the countenance of Allah ﷻ. And as for spiritual excellence, it means to worship Allah as if you see Him, for though you do not see Him, He surely sees you.

Spiritual excellence has principles. Among them is that you purify yourself from the two kinds of impurity and from filth with water; that you purify yourself from the four excesses by shaving, plucking, cutting, and trimming; that you purify yourself from the sins of the seven bodily parts, from diseases of the heart, and from states of inward heedlessness with the water of repentance.

Repentance means that you repent of all of your sins with remorse over your past actions and determination not to ever revert to anything similar, fulfilling any obligation due to Allah ﷻ by making it up and fulfilling any due that you owe to His servants by returning the due if it be money, presenting yourself to the inheritor if it be a life, or doing much good to the person and making supplication for him and humbling yourself much before Him ﷻ so that He may make the person satisfied with you on the day of recompense if it be honor.

[Also among the principles of spiritual excellence] is that you habituate your soul first with little food, little sleep, little speech, and little mingling with people, then that you rein it in with the

أمر به واجتناب ما نهاه عنه، لأنه تعالى اشترى من عباده أنفسهم بالجنّة فعليهم أن يسلّموا أنفسهم لربّهم بامتثال ما يأمر به والاجتناب عمّا ينهى عنه.

فهو أشمل يشتمل على الإيمان والعمل والإحسان. أمّا الإيمان فهو أن تؤمن جزمًا بالله تعالى وملائكته وكتبه ورسله واليوم الآخر والقدر؛ وإجمالًا أن تؤمن جزمًا بكل ما ثبت بدليل قطعيّ الثبوت والدلالة وعلم من الدين بالضرورة. أمّا العمل فهو أن تفعل ما أمرت به ابتغاء وجه الله تعالى. أمّا الإحسان فهو أن تعبد الله كأنك تراه فإن لم تكن تراه فإنه يراك.

وله مبادئ؛ منها أن تطهّر نفسك عن الحدثين والخبث بالماء، وعن الفضولات الأربعة الشرعية بالحلق والنتف والقصّ والتقليم، وعن ذنوب الأعضاء السبعة والأمراض القلبية والغفلات السرّية بماء التوبة.

وهي أن تتوب من ذنوبك كلها نادمًا على ما مضى، عازمًا على ألّا تعود إلى مثله أبدًا، مؤدّيًا ما عليك من حقّ الله تعالى من الواجبات بالقضاء ومن حقّ عباده بالردّ إن كان مالًا وبتسليم نفسك للوارث إن كان نفسًا وبالخير الكثير والدعاء له وإكثار التضرّع إليه تعالى ليرضيه عنك يوم الجزاء إن كان عرضًا.

وأن تعوّد نفسك أوّلًا بقلّة الطعام وقلّة المنام وقلّة الكلام وقلّة الاختلاط بالأنام، ثم تلجمها بلجام

reins of God-consciousness, bar it from immorality, excess, and inclination, rousing it with fear of His anger ﷻ and a raging hellfire and with hope for His pleasure ﷻ and groves with rivers running below in which [the pious] abide forever. Fear and hope to you are like two wings are to a bird.

[Spiritual excellence also entails] that you charge your soul with complete adherence to the Sunna, rigorous practice, and the best course. Part of what it means to adhere completely to the Sunna is

1. to eat of what is lawful.
2. to purify your intention in all acts.
3. to conform to the best of speech.
4. to preoccupy yourself with what is best in the present time.
5. to maintain constant remembrance in all states, remaining aware that Allah ﷻ sees you; ascending such that it is as though you see Him; bearing with humility; turning away from all else—the lower world, creatures, insinuations, inclinations, and all worries and fleeting thoughts—trusting Allah in your affairs; consigning important matters to Him ﷻ; keeping steadfast in acts of devotion, in moments of tribulation, and in the avoidance of disobedience; remaining content and grateful about the divine decree and destiny; and engaging in invocation in your times of seclusion, forgetting all else and immersing yourself in the meaning of the One remembered who has no like.

Success is through Allah alone.

التقوى وتنهاها عن الفجور والفضول والهوى مهيّجًا بخوف غضبه تعالى ونار تلظّى ورجا مرضاته تعالى وجنّات تجري من تحتها الأنهار خالدين فيها أبدًا، وهما لك كالجناحين للطير.

وتأمرها بكمال الالتزام بالسنّة والعزيمة والأولى.
ومن جملة كمال الالتزام بالسنّة:

١- الأكل من الحلال.

٢- وإخلاص النيّة في جميع الأعمال.

٣- واتّباع الأحسن من الأقوال.

٤- والاشتغال بالأولى في وقت الحال.

٥- ودوام الذكر في جميع الأحوال مستشعرًا[٢] بأنّ الله سبحانه وتعالى يراك، مترقيًّا إلى أن تكون بحيث كأنّك تراه، خاشعًا معرضًا عن السوى من الدنيا والخلق والوسواس والهوى والهموم والخواطر جميعًا، على الله في أمورك متوكّلًا وإليه تعالى في المخطرات مفوّضًا وعلى الطاعات والبلايا وترك المعاصي صابرًا وبالقضاء والقدر راضيًا شاكرًا وفي خلواتك ذاكرًا ناسيًا السوى وفي معنى المذكور اللامثل مستغرقًا.

وبالله وحده التوفيق.

[Obligatory Knowledge]

It is also necessary for such a person[3] to have knowledge of the ritual ablutions, the ritual bath, the ritual prayer, and fasting. It is necessary for one who possesses the alms threshold to have knowledge of zakat, for one on whom the hajj pilgrimage is obligatory to have knowledge of the hajj pilgrimage, and for merchants to have knowledge of transactions so that they avoid dubious and reprehensible matters in all their dealings. The same goes for people of the various trades. Everyone who engages in something is obligated to know the thing and its legal ruling so that he avoids what is forbidden therein.[4]

As stated in *Tabyīn al-maḥārim*:[5] There is no doubt that it is obligatory to know the five obligations; to know sincerity because the soundness of one's actions depends on it; to know what is lawful and what is unlawful; to know ostentation because it deprives a worshipper the reward of his actions; to know envy and self-conceit because they consume one's actions as fire consumes wood; to know selling and buying and marriage and divorce for those who intend to engage in these affairs; and to know what utterances are unlawful or vitiate belief—upon my life, this is one of the most important matters in this age because you will hear many of the common people ignorantly saying things that render a person a disbeliever! The precautious course is that the ignorant person renew his belief every day and renew his marriage to his wife before two witnesses once or twice a month, since a mistake not made by a man is often made by a woman.[6]

It also states: As for the communally obligatory, this is every science that is indispensable for conducting religious or worldly affairs, including medi-

[العلم الواجب]

وعلى من ذكر أيضًا أن يعلم علم الوضوء والغسل والصلاة والصوم وعلم الزكاة لمن له نصاب والحجّ لمن وجب عليه والبيوع على التجّار ليحترزوا عن الشبهات والمكروهات في سائر المعاملات، وكذا أهل الحرف وكل من اشتغل بشيء يفرض عليه علمه وحكمه ليمتنع عن الحرام فيه.

وفي تبيين المحارم: لا شكّ في فرضية علم الفرائض الخمس، وعلم الإخلاص لأنّ صحّة العمل موقوفة عليه، وعلم الحلال والحرام، وعلم الرياء لأن العابد محروم من ثواب عمله بالرياء، وعلم الحسد والعجب إذ هما يأكلان العمل كما تأكل النار الحطب، وعلم البيع والشراء والنكاح والطلاق لمن أراد الدخول في هذه الأشياء، وعلم الألفاظ المحرّمة أو المكفّرة. ولعمري هذا من أهمّ المهمّات في هذا الزمان لأنك تسمع كثيرًا من العوامّ يتكلّمون بما يكفر وهم عنه غافلون؛ والاحتياط أن يجدّد الجاهل إيمانه كل يوم ويجدّد نكاح امرأته عند شاهدين في كل شهر مرّة أو مرّتين إذ الخطأ وإن لم يصدر من الرجل فهو من النساء كثير.

وفيه أيضًا: أمّا فرض الكفاية فهو كل علم لا يستغنى عنه في قوام أمور الدين والدنيا كالطبّ،

cine; arithmetic; grammar; lexicology; rational theology; the Quranic recitations; the transmissional chains of hadith; the distribution of bequests and inheritance; writing; rhetorical semantics, embellishment, and figurative language; jurisprudential theory; and knowledge of what abrogates and what is abrogated, of what is general and what is specific, and of what is unequivocal and what is apparent. Each of these [areas of knowledge] serves as a means to the sciences of Quranic exegesis and hadith. The same holds for the science of narrations and reports; the knowledge of narrators, of their names, and of the names and qualities of the Companions; the knowledge of probity in narrators, the knowledge of their statuses so that the weak can be distinguished from the strong, and the knowledge of the spans of their life; the basic professions like agriculture and weaving; politics; and cupping.

والحساب، والنحو، واللغة، والكلام، والقراءات، وأسانيد الحديث، وقسمة الوصايا والمواريث، والكتابة، والمعاني والبديع والبيان، والأصول، ومعرفة الناسخ والمنسوخ والعامّ والخاصّ والنصّ والظاهر؛ وكل هذه آلة لعلم التفسير والحديث. وكذا علم الآثار والأخبار، والعلم بالرجال وأساميهم وأسامي الصحابة وصفاتهم، والعلم بالعدالة في الرواة والعلم بأحوالهم لتمييز الضعيف من القويّ والعلم بأعمارهم، وأصول الصناعات كالفلاحة والحياكة[٣]، والسياسة، والحجامة.

This is what it is individually and communally obligatory to know, the first of the praiseworthy categories of knowledge.

هذا هو العلم الفرض العيني والكفائي، وأوّل الأقسام الحسنة العلميّة.

Recommended Knowledge

The second of the praiseworthy categories of knowledge is that which it is recommended to know, namely, that one delve deep into jurisprudence and the science of the heart, i.e., ethics, which is a science by which one knows the kinds of virtues and how to acquire them and the kinds of vices and how to avoid them. To delve deep into these sciences is recommended, but it is individually obligatory to study them to the extent that one needs them.

العلم المندوب

ثانيها العلم المندوب وهو التبحّر في الفقه و علم القلب أي علم الأخلاق، وهو علم يعرف به أنواع الفضائل وكيفيّة اكتسابها وأنواع الرذائل وكيفيّة اجتنابها. فالتبحّر في هذين العلمين مندوب، وأمّا قدر ما يحتاج إليه منهما ففرض عين.

Unlawful Knowledge

The third of the categories of knowledge is that which is unlawful, and it is of various kinds.

العلم الحرام

ثالثها العلم الحرام وهو أنواع:

Heretical Philosophy *Falsafa* (philosophy) is a Greek word that in Arabic has come to express "adulterated wisdoms," that is, outwardly embellished and inwardly corrupt, as in the view that the universe is eternal and other views that entail disbelief or are unlawful.

Trickery Trickery is any sleight of hand that resembles sorcery, making something appear to be what it in truth is not.[7] The erudite scholar Ibn Ḥajar[8] issued the fatwa that members of cliques in the alleyways who perform strange feats like cutting off human heads and then restoring them, making things like silver coins out of dirt, and so forth are effectively the same as sorcerers if not actually sorcerers: what they do is impermissible and it is impermissible for a person to stop by [and observe] them. Moreover, it is related from *al-Mudawwana*, a Mālikī work,[9] that a person who cuts off the hand of a man or inserts a blade into his body is to be executed if what he performs is sorcery; otherwise, he is to be punished.[10]

Sorcery Sorcery is a science by the study of which one acquires a trained capacity of the soul to perform strange acts through obscure means. Bīrī's gloss of *al-Īḍāḥ*[11] states: It is unlawful to learn it or to teach it. This applies without qualification even if one learns it to protect the Muslims from harm.

In the hadith, there is a prohibition of magic charms (*tawala*, which is of the morphological pattern of *ʿataba*), namely, what is done to make a husband love his wife. In fact, there is an explicit statement in *al-Khāniyya*[12] that they are unlawful, and Ibn Wahbān[13] cites as the legal cause [for this ruling] that they are a kind of sorcery.

The Disagreement on Whether Sorcery Is Disbelief It is narrated in *Tabyīn al-maḥārim* from Imam Abū Manṣūr[14]: The view that sorcery is unconditionally disbelief is mistaken. It is necessary

الفلسفة الملحدة هو لفظ يوناني وتعريبه «الحكم المموهة» أي مزيّنة الظاهر فاسدة الباطن كالقول بقدم العالم وغيره من المكفّرات والمحرّمات.

الشعوذة وهي خفّة في اليد كالسحر تُري الشيء بغير ما عليه أصله. وأفتى العلّامة ابن حجر في أهل الحِلق في الطرقات الذين لهم أشياء غريبة كقطع رأس إنسان وإعادته وجعل نحو دراهم من التراب وغير ذلك بأنهم في معنى السحرة إن لم يكونوا منهم، فلا يجوز لهم ذلك ولا لأحد أن يقف عليهم. ثم نقل عن المدوّنة من كتب المالكيّة أنّ الذي يقطع يد الرجل أو يدخل السكّين في جوفه إن كان سحرًا قتل وإلا عوقب.

السحر السحر هو علم يستفاد منه حصول ملكة نفسانية يقتدر بها على أفعال غريبة لأسباب خفيّة. وفي حاشية الإيضاح لبيري: تعلّمه وتعليمه حرام. ومقتضى الإطلاق ولو تعلّم لدفع الضرر عن المسلمين.

وفي الحديث النهي عن التِوَلَة بوزن عَتَبَة؛ وهي ما يفعل ليحبّب المرأة إلى زوجها، بل نصّ على حرمتها في الخانيّة، وعلّل ابن وهبان بأنه ضرب من السحر.

الخلاف في كون السحر كفرًا في تبيين المحارم عن الإمام أبي منصور: إنّ القول بأنّ السحر كفر على

to investigate the essence of the act: if it entails any rejection of a necessary condition for belief, then it is disbelief, but otherwise it is not.

Imam al-Qarāfī al-Mālikī[15] has discussed the difference between the kind of sorcery that vitiates belief and other kinds of sorcery. He went on at length, but, in summary, sorcery is of three kinds:

1. *sīmyāʾ*, which is prepared using specific earthly [materials] (e.g., a specific oil or specific words) that cause some or all of the five senses to perceive tastes, smells, or other things that either really exist or are merely imagined.
2. *hīmyāʾ*, which causes the same to occur in addition to occurrences that are not earthly but rather celestial.
3. [a kind of sorcery that makes use of] peculiar properties of things, e.g., to take seven stones and throw them at a type of dog, and then, if it bites the stones, to cast them into water such that, consequently, special effects manifest on any person who drinks that water.

These, then, are the three kinds of sorcery. They may occur by words, actions, or beliefs that entail disbelief, and they may occur otherwise, e.g., placing stones. Thus, not everything that is termed sorcery is disbelief, and this agrees with the statement of Imam Abū Manṣūr al-Māturīdī.

Now, it does not follow from the fact that [one practicing sorcery] has not necessarily committed disbelief that he is not to be executed. This is because the reason for his execution is that he has endeavored to work corruption. Thus, if it is established that he has done harm through his sorcery, even if not by means of anything that entails disbelief, then he is to be executed in order to repel his harm, just like cutthroats and highway bandits.[16]

الإطلاق خطأ ويجب[٥] البحث عن حقيقته، فإن كان في ذلك ردّ ما لزم في شرط الإيمان فهو كفر وإلا فلا.

وقد ذكر الإمام القرافي المالكي الفرق بين ما هو سحر يكفر به وبين غيره وأطال في ذلك، وحاصله أنّ السحر أنواع ثلاثة:

١- السيمياء[٦]، وهي ما يركّب من خواصّ أرضية كدهن خاصّ أو كلمات خاصّة توجب إدراك الحواسّ الخمس أو بعضها بما له وجود حقيقي أو بما هو تخيّل صرف من مأكول أو مشموم أو غيرهما.

٢- الهيمياء، وهي ما يوجب ذلك مضافًا إلى آثار سماوية لا أرضية.

٣- بعض خواصّ الحقائق، كما يؤخذ سبع أحجار يرمى بها نوع من الكلاب فإذا عضّها الكلب وطرحت في ماء فمن شربه ظهرت عليه آثار خاصّة.

فهذه أنواع السحر الثلاثة قد تقع بما هو كفر من لفظ أو فعل أو اعتقاد، وقد يقع بغيره كوضع الأحجار، فليس كل ما يسمّى سحرًا كفر. وهذا موافق لكلام الإمام أبي منصور الماتريدي.

ثم إنه لا يلزم من عدم كفره مطلقًا عدم قتله، لأنّ قتله بسبب سعيه بالفساد. فإذا ثبت إضراره بسحره ولو بغير مكفر يقتل دفعًا لشرّه كالخنّاق وقطّاع الطريق.

Soothsaying Soothsaying is the practice of telling the future of things and claiming to know mysteries. Among soothsayers are those who claim that they have a subordinate who gives them information about things, and among them are those who claim to know things by means of portents—either the words, state, or actions of the one who comes to ask—from which they draw conclusions, and this latter kind of soothsayer is specifically called a psychic. The hadith "Whoever comes to a soothsayer…"[17] includes the psychic and the astrologer; the Arabs call anyone who preoccupies himself with arcane knowledge a "soothsayer."

Logic That Is Not Islamic The logic that is intended here is that which is cited in the books of the philosophers in proving their false doctrines. As for the logic of those in accordance with Islam, which takes for its axioms Islamic principles, there is no respect in which it may be declared unlawful. In fact, al-Ghazālī named it "the standard of the sciences,"[18] and the scholars of Islam have written works on it, including the verifying scholar Ibn al-Humām,[19] who explicated the majority of its questions in the introduction to his book *al-Taḥrīr al-uṣūlī*.[20]

Reprehensible Knowledge

The fourth of the categories of knowledge is that which is reprehensible, namely, the poetry of the postclassical Arabic-speaking generations who succeeded the Arab poets. That of their poetry which is reprehensible is the kind that one takes as a career. This is how the hadith agreed upon [by al-Bukhārī and Muslim] is to be interpreted: "Truly, it would be better that the insides of any among you be full of pus than full of poetry."[21] There is nothing wrong with a moderate amount of it when intended to demonstrate instances of artful skill, even when it

الكهانة الكهانة هي تعاطي الخبر عن الكائنات في المستقبل وادّعاء معرفة الأسرار. ومن الكهانة من كان يزعم أنّ له تابعًا يلقي إليه الأخبار عن الكائنات، ومنهم من كان يزعم أنه يعرف الأمور بمقدّمات يستدلّ بها من كلام من يسأله أو حاله أو فعله؛ يخصّون هذا باسم العرّاف. وحديث «من أتى كاهنًا» يشمل العرّاف والمنجّم، والعرب تسمّي كل من يتعاطى علمًا دقيقًا كاهنًا.

المنطق الغير الإسلامي المراد بالمنطق ههنا هو المذكور في كتب الفلاسفة للاستدلال على مذاهبهم الباطنة؛ أمّا منطق الإسلاميين الذي مقدّماته قواعد إسلاميّة فلا وجه للقول بحرمته، بل سمّاه الغزالي معيار العلوم. وقد ألّف فيه علماء الإسلام ومنهم المحقّق ابن الهمام فإنه أتى منه ببيان معظم مطالبه في مقدّمة كتابه التحرير الأصولي.

العلم المكروه

رابعها العلم المكروه وهو أشعار المولّدين الذين حدثوا بعد شعراء العرب. المكروه من أشعارهم ما جعله صناعة له؛ وبه فسّر الحديث المتّفق عليه: «لأن يمتلئ جوف أحدكم قيحًا خير من أن يمتلئ شعرًا»، فاليسير من ذلك لا بأس به إذا أراد إظهار نحو النكات

consists in the description of cheeks and physiques; indeed, the scholars of embellishment quote such poetry.[22]

وإن كان في وصف الخدود والقدود، فإنّ علماء البديع قد استشهدوا من ذلك.

Permissible Knowledge

The fifth of the categories of knowledge is that which is permissible, namely, that of their poetry that does not involve the demeaning of any Muslim by mentioning his flaws or damaging his honor.[23]

العلم المباح

خامسها العلم المباح وهو أشعارهم التي ليس فيها استخفاف بأحد من المسلمين كذكر عوراته والأخذ في عرضه.

General Exhortations

الوصايا لكل عبد

The First Exhortation The servant must be conscious of Allah wherever he is, dealing with people with good character and remedying every bad act with a good act such that it effaces it. One who keeps conscious of Allah has exercised the utmost prudence in safeguarding his religion and his honor.

الوصية الأولى على العبد أن يتّقي الله حيث كان فيعاشر الناس بخلق حسن ويتبع السيّئة الحسنة تمحها، فمن اتّقى الله استبرأ لدينه وعرضه.

The Second Exhortation He must strengthen his belief by accompanying the righteous, reflecting on the proofs of the noble Quran, affirming what is well founded, acting on what is furthest from doubt, and maintaining remembrance to rouse himself from being heedless of Allah ﷻ, either inwardly or both inwardly and outwardly by [invoking] the name of majesty or the statement of divine oneness.

الوصية الثانية أن يقوّي إيمانه بصحبة الصالحين والتفكّر في أدلّة القرآن الكريم والتصديق بما ثبت والعمل بما هو أبعد عن الشبهة وبدوام ما يوقظه عن الغفلة عن الله تعالى من الذكر قلبًا أو قلبًا وقالبًا بلفظة الجلال أو كلمة التوحيد.

The Third Exhortation He must attend to his spiritual and practical character traits to be among those of immense fortune and among the successful and the steadfast.

الوصية الثالثة أن يعتني بالأخلاق الروحية والعملية حتى يكون من ذوي الحظّ العظيم والصابرين الفائزين.

The spiritual character traits include maintaining relationships with those who spurn you, giving to those who deprive you, forgiving those who wrong you, and showing goodness to those who hurt you. He says ﷻ, "The good deed and the evil deed are not equal. Repel by that which is better, then behold: he between whom and you there was enmity will be as though he were a loyal, protecting friend" (Q 41:34).

The practical character traits include

1. preserving one's good health.
2. cleanliness in accordance with revealed law.
3. putting one's household implements and appliances in order.
4. designating a specific kind of activity for every time.
5. turning one's heart to Allah ﷻ in the ritual prayer and at other times.
6. striving for noble things instead of trivial things. [Worthy of one's striving] are [the virtues of] resoluteness, steadfastness, patience, temperance, command over the lower soul, courage, keeping secrets, contentment, and generosity.
7. safeguarding one's soul in private settings as one safeguards it in public settings. One who accustoms himself to evil deeds in private will be overcome by them in public.
8. the cleanliness of one's body, clothing, and bearing; affability; and good etiquette with one's elders and those advanced in years.
9. visiting one's relatives and the righteous while observing good etiquette with them as appropriate to their status.

من الروحية أن تصل من قطعك وتعطي من حرمك وتعفو عمن ظلمك وتحسن إلى من أذاك. قال تعالى: ﴿وَلَا تَسْتَوِى ٱلْحَسَنَةُ وَلَا ٱلسَّيِّئَةُ ٱدْفَعْ بِٱلَّتِى هِىَ أَحْسَنُ فَإِذَا ٱلَّذِى بَيْنَكَ وَبَيْنَهُۥ عَدَٰوَةٌ كَأَنَّهُۥ وَلِىٌّ حَمِيمٌ﴾ [٤١/ ٣٤].

ومن العمليّة:

١- المحافظة على الصحّة.

٢- النظافة الشرعيّة.

٣- ترتيب أدوات المنزل.

٤- التعيين لكل وقت عملًا خاصًّا.

٥- توجّه القلب إلى الله تعالى في الصلاة وغيرها.

٦- السعي في معالي الأمور بدلًا عن سفسافها؛ منها العزم والثبات والصبر والعفّة وضبط النفس والشجاعة وكتم السرّ والقناعة والكرم.

٧- صون النفس في الخلوات كصونها في الجلوات. من اعتاد السيّئات في خلوته غلبت عليه في علانيته.

٨- نظافة الجسم والثوب والهيئة، وحسن اللقاء، ومراعاة الأدب مع الأكابر وذوي الشيب.

٩- زيارة ذوي الأرحام والصالحين مع مراعاة الأدب معهم حسب منزلتهم.

10. observing the etiquette of travel. This involves redressing wrongs and returning trusts; choosing a pious and intelligent companion who fulfills his promises; bidding farewell to one's family, brethren, and friends; and praying two units of the *istikhāra* prayer at one's home before departing.

11. observing the etiquette of the road. This involves averting one's gaze from what is forbidden; refraining from causing harm; assisting those in need; gently enjoining what is right and forbidding what is wrong; and enduring grievances with patience.

12. observing the etiquette of conversation. This involves that one show one's interlocutor a greater eagerness to learn from him than to teach him; that one's speech be meant to either repel some harm or bring some benefit; and that one's speech come at a time when it is necessary. Every bit of speech has its time, so take care neither to hurry nor to hesitate unduly. [The etiquette of conversation entails] that one's speech and also the elevation of one's voice be to the extent necessary; that one enunciate one's words; and that one refrain from immediately answering when another person is asked a question.

13. observing the etiquette of eating and drinking. This involves eating what is lawful; washing one's hands before the meal; placing the food on a table; intending to invigorate one's body; sitting on one's knees; invoking the name of Allah at the beginning of the meal, reflecting during it, and praising Allah after it; and drinking in sips while seated, having invoked the name of Allah at the beginning and praising Allah at the end.

١٠- مـراعاة آداب السـفر؛ منهـا ردّ المظالـم والودائـع، واختيـار رفيق تقيّ زكيّ منجز الوعـد، وتوديع الأهل والإخوان والأصدقاء، وصلاة ركعتي الاسـتخارة في منزله قبـل أن يخرج.

١١- مـراعاة آداب الطريـق؛ منهـا غـضّ البـصر عـن المحرّمـات، كفّ الأذى، إعانـة ذوي الحاجة، الأمر بالمعـروف والنـهي عـن المنكـر بلـين، والصبر على الأذى.

١٢- مـراعاة آداب المحادثـة؛ منهـا أن تـري محادثـك حرصـك على الاسـتفادة منـه أكثر مـن الحرص على إفادتـك له، كـون الـكلام إمـا أن يكـون لدفـع مضرّة أو جلـب منفعة، كون الـكلام وقت الحاجة فلـكل كلام زمن فاحـذر العجلة أو التـواني، كون الـكلام على قدر الحاجـة وكذا رفع الصـوت، ترتيل الكلمـات، ترك المبـادرة بالجـواب إذا سـئل غيرك.

١٣- مـراعاة آداب الأكل والـشرب؛ منهـا أكل الحـلال، غسـل اليـد قبـل الطعـام، وضـع الطعـام على السـفرة أو المائـدة، نيّـة تقوية البـدن، الجلوس على الركبتـين، البسـملة أوّل الطعـام والفكـر وسـطه والحمدلة آخـره، الشرب مصًّا جالسًـا مع البسـملة أوّلًا والحمدلـة آخـرًا.

14. observing moderation in food, drink, and clothing and in all things.

١٤- مراعاة التوسّط في المأكل والمشرب والملبس وفي كل شيء.

❁ ❁ ❁

Here concludes the introduction by the assistance of Allah ﷻ. By His permission ﷻ, the twelve treatises follow—the first of which is the treatise entitled *Turning a Glance: On the Science of Morphology*, because, as it is said, morphology is the mother of the sciences. We beseech and implore Allah ﷻ the Munificent, the Generous, to accept this and to render it of benefit to us on “the day when neither wealth nor children avail, save for him who comes to Allah with a sound heart” (Q 26:88–89). “Glory to your Lord, Lord of Might, transcending what they describe! Peace be upon the messengers. And praise to Allah, Lord of the worlds” (Q 37:180–82). May Allah send blessings upon our messenger Muḥammad and upon all of his family and Companions.

إلى هنا تمّت المقدّمة بعون الله تعالى. وتليها بإذنه تعالى الرسائل الاثنتا عشرة أوّلها الرسالة المسمّاة لفتة الطرف في علم الصرف لأنه كما قيل أمّ العلوم. نسأل الله تعالى المنّان الكريم ونتضرّع إليه أن يقبلها[٧] ويجعلها نافعة لنا ﴿يَوْمَ لَا يَنفَعُ مَالٌ وَلَا بَنُونَ ۝٨٨ إِلَّا مَنْ أَتَى ٱللَّهَ بِقَلْبٍ سَلِيمٍ﴾ [٢٦/ ٨٨-٨٩]. ﴿سُبْحَٰنَ رَبِّكَ رَبِّ ٱلْعِزَّةِ عَمَّا يَصِفُونَ ۝١٨٠ وَسَلَٰمٌ عَلَى ٱلْمُرْسَلِينَ ۝١٨١ وَٱلْحَمْدُ لِلَّهِ رَبِّ ٱلْعَٰلَمِينَ﴾ [٣٧/ ١٨٠-١٨٢]. وصلّى الله على رسولنا محمد وعلى آله وصحبه أجمعين.

NOTES TO THE INTRODUCTION

1 In metaphysical terms, a locus (*maḥall*) is an entity that another thing subsists in, and a specifier (*mukhaṣṣiṣ*) is an entity that determines which of various existential possibilities will be realized for another thing. Needing a locus or a specifier entails that a given thing is ontologically dependent rather than self-sufficient.

2 *Al-thaqalān* (the two weighty ones) is a word in Sūrat al-Raḥmān (Q 55:31) that is understood as a reference to humanity and the jinn, the two realms of beings who bear the weight of moral responsibility.

3 That is, anyone who intends to engage in teaching or learning a science. This can be counted as the fifth thing necessary for such a person after the four listed at the beginning of the text.

4 Ibn ʿĀbidīn, *Radd al-muḥtār*, 1:42. Citations of *Radd al-muḥtār* in the footnotes of the Arabic text of the introduction have been omitted and are replaced by citations in the English endnotes.

5 A book authored by the Ḥanafī jurist Yūsuf Sinān al-Dīn al-Amāsī (d. 986/1578).

6 Ibn ʿĀbidīn, *Radd al-muḥtār*, 1:42.

7 Al-Ḥamawī, *Ghamr ʿuyūn al-baṣāʾir*, 4:125, [cited by Ibn ʿĀbidīn].

8 This is the Shāfiʿī jurist Ibn Ḥajar al-Haytamī (d. 974/1567).

9 Authored by the Mālikī jurist Saḥnūn b. Saʿīd (d. 240/854).

10 Ibn ʿĀbidīn, *Radd al-muḥtār*, 1:43.

11 This attribution is possibly mistaken, though the same citation appears to be present in the available manuscripts of *Radd al-muḥtār*, the source of this larger passage. According to the editor in Ibn ʿĀbidīn, *Ḥāshiyat Ibn ʿĀbidīn*, 1:146n2, the intended work could be *Ḥāshiyat al-Ashbāh* (the full title of which is *ʿUmdat dhawī al-baṣāʾir li-ḥall muhimmāt al-Ashbāh wa-l-naẓāʾir*) by Ibrāhīm b. Ḥusayn, who is also known as Ibn Bīrī or Pīrī-Zādah (d. 1099/1688).

12 That is, *al-Fatāwā al-khāniyya* by the Ḥanafī jurist al-Ḥasan b. Manṣūr al-Farghānī, known as Qāḍīkhān (d. 592/1196).

13 The Ḥanafī jurist ʿAbd al-Wahhāb b. Aḥmad (d. 768/1367).

14 Abū Manṣūr al-Māturīdī (d. 333/944), the eponym of the Māturīdī school of theology.

15 The Mālikī jurist Shihāb al-Dīn al-Qarāfī (d. 684/1285).

16 Ibn ʿĀbidīn, *Radd al-muḥtār*, 1:44–45, with omissions.

17 The hadith continues, "...and believes what he says has disassociated himself from what was revealed to Muḥammad." Al-Ḥākim, *al-Mustadrak*, 1:46–47; Abū Dāwūd, *al-Sunan*, 4:338 (no. 3899).

18 Abū Ḥāmid Muḥammad al-Ghazālī (d. 505/1111) wrote a book on logic with this title.

19 The Ḥanafī jurist al-Kamāl b. al-Humām (d. 861/1457).

20 Ibn ʿĀbidīn, *Radd al-muḥtār*, 1:45.

21 Al-Bukhārī, *al-Jāmiʿ al-ṣaḥīḥ*, 8:36–37 (no. 6154); Muslim, *Ṣaḥīḥ*, 955 (no. 2258).

22 Ibn ʿĀbidīn, *Radd al-muḥtār*, 1:46.

23 Ibn ʿĀbidīn, *Radd al-muḥtār*, 1:42–46, summarized.

I

TURNING A GLANCE

On the science of morphology

لفتة الطرف في علم الصرف

In the Name of Allah,
All-Merciful, Most Compassionate

بسم الله الرحمن الرحيم

"Morphology is the mother of the sciences, and grammar the father."

"Learn Arabic and teach it to the people."[1]

«الصرف أمّ العلوم والنحو أبوها».

«تعلّموا العربيّة وعلّموها الناس».

ALL PRAISE IS due to Allah, Lord of the worlds. May blessings and peace be upon the seal of the prophets and messengers, Muḥammad, the unlettered prophet, and upon all of his family, Companions, and Followers.

الحمد لله رب العالمين والصلاة والسلام على خاتم الأنبياء والمرسلين محمد النبيّ الأمّي وعلى آله وصحبه وأتباعه أجمعين.

To Proceed Says the destitute servant, needful of the mercy of his self-sufficient Lord, Muḥammad Emīn Er b. Dhulkifl b. ʿAlī b. Aḥmad b. Qarū al-Mīrānī al-Kuluyānī[1] and, later, al-Anqarawī, may Allah ﷻ by His manifest and subtle kindness grant him and his family forgiveness: This is a treatise on the science of morphology. I have entitled it *Turning a Glance: On the Science of Morphology* and arranged it into three chapters.

أما بعد فيقول العبد المسكين المفتقر إلى رحمة ربّه الغنيّ محمد أمين أر بن ذي الكفل بن علي بن أحمد بن قرو الميراني الكُلُيَانِي[١] ثم الأنقروي، غفر الله تعالى له ولوالديه بلطفه الجلي والخفي: إن هذه رسالة في علم الصرف سمّيتها لفتة الطرف في علم الصرف؛ رتّبتها على ثلاثة أبواب.

Chapter 1 concerns *morphological classes*: How many are they? Into how many categories are they sorted? What is the pattern of each class, and what are its typifications? What is its characteristic sign? Does it impart transitivity or not?

الباب الأول في أبواب الصرف: كم هي؟ وإلى كم نوع تتنوع؟ وما وزن كل باب وما موزونه؟ وما علامته؟ أهو للتعدية أم لا؟

---

[1] [Külüyan] is a village in Çermik, Diyarbakır. Diyarbakır was historically called Amed.

[١] قرية في چرميك دياربكر؛ باسمه القديم آمد.

Chapter 2 concerns *derivatives*: What are derivatives? Of how many types are they? How many forms does each type comprise in total? What are the technical names of these forms?

Chapter 3 concerns *irregular roots*: What are irregular roots? Of how many types are they? What is the definition of each type? How is it modified when it is in the perfect or the imperfect and so on until the last of the nine derivatives?

Success and rectitude are from Allah ﷻ alone.

الباب الثاني في الأمثلـة: ما الأمثلة؟ كم قسـمًا هي؟ وإلى كـم صيغة يرتقي كل قسـم؟ وما عنـوان هذه الصيغ؟

الباب الثالـث في المعتـلّ: مـا المعتلّ؟ كم قسـمًا هو؟ ومـا تعريف كل قسم؟ ومـا إعلاله حـال كونـه ماضيًا أو مضارعًا إلى آخر المشـتقّات التسـعة؟

من الله تعالى وحده التوفيق والسداد.

INTRODUCTION

What is the difference between word-formation (*ṣarf*) and the science of morphology (*ʿilm al-ṣarf*)? What is the aim of the science? What is its subject matter?

As technical terms, *ṣarf* and *taṣrīf* (word-formation) have the same meaning, namely, transforming a single original word (namely, the infinitive noun) into various derivative words to express intended meanings that do not otherwise obtain—e.g., transforming *naṣr* (to help), which is an infinitive noun, into *naṣara* (he helped), *yanṣuru* (he helps), *nāṣirun* (one that helps), and other of the *variform derivatives* and into *naṣara*, *naṣarā* (they two [m.] helped), *naṣarū* (they [m.] helped), and other of the *uniform derivatives*.

The science of morphology is a science concerning principles by which one has knowledge of the states of word forms in terms of derivation and modification. Derivation is of two types: (1) theoretical, that is, knowing, for example, that *naṣara* is derived from *naṣr*, and (2) practical, that is, changing a thing into something else, e.g., changing *naṣr* into *naṣara* or other derivative forms by formal alteration and the like. The aim of [the science] is awareness of the correct way to understand a word's meaning. Its subject matter is the word in terms of derivation and the like.

What is meant by a *word* here is a noun or verb. Each may be either (1) *sound*, which means that none of its radicals—those letters that correspond

تقديم

ما الفرق بين الصرف وبين علم الصرف؟

وما غايته؟ وما موضوعه؟

الصرف والتصريف في الاصطلاح بمعنًى واحد وهو تحويل الأصل الواحد أي المصدر إلى أمثلة مختلفة لمعانٍ مقصودة لا تحصل إلا بها، كتحويل «النصر» الذي هو المصدر إلى «نَصَرَ، يَنْصُرُ، نَاصِرٌ» وغيرها من الأمثلة المختلفة وإلى «نَصَرَ، نَصَرَا، نَصَرُوا» وغيرها من الأمثلة المطّردة.

علم الصرف علم بأصول تُعرف بها أحوال أبنية الكلم من حيث الاشتقاق والإعلال. الاشتقاق على قسمين: (١) علمي، وهو أن تعلم مثلًا أن «نَصَرَ» مأخوذ من «النصر»؛ (٢) وعملي، وهو نقل شيء إلى شيء بتغيير كنقل «النصر» إلى «نَصَرَ» وغيره من الأمثلة بتغيير الهيئة ونحوه. غايته الاطّلاع على فهم المعنى على وجه الحقّ. موضوعه الكلمة من حيث الاشتقاق وغيره.

المراد من الكلمة هنا الاسم والفعل. وكل منهما إما (١) سالم، وهو ما سلمت حروفه الأصليّة التي

to *f-ʿ-l* or *f-ʿ-l-l*—are doubled, are weak, or are a *hamza*, e.g., *naṣrun* (help) and *daḥraja* (he rolled s.th.),[2] or (2) *unsound*, which means that its radicals include such a letter, e.g., *madda* (he extended), *waʿada* (he promised), *qāla* (he said), *ghazā* (he purposed), *waqā* (he guarded), *shawā* (he roasted), and *akhadha* (he took), all seven of which are unsound.

The first radical is designated *fāʾ al-fiʿl*,[3] the second *ʿayn al-fiʿl*, and the third *lām al-fiʿl*, given that the word is triliteral like *naṣara*. If it is quadriliteral like *daḥraja*, the third radical is designated *lām al-fiʿl al-ūlā* and the fourth *lām al-fiʿl al-thāniya*. Any letter that has been added to the radicals is designated by its own name, even when converted from another letter: one thus says that *iṣṭalaḥa* (he agreed on s.th.)[4] is of the pattern *iftaʿala*, not the pattern *ifṭaʿala*.[5] An exception is when a [radical] is repeated, whether for conformity[6] or otherwise; [in such cases, the added letter is designated] by the name of the preceding [radical]: one thus says that *jalbaba* (he dressed s.o. in a *jilbāb* [a long, flowing outer garment]) is of the pattern *faʿlala*, not the pattern *faʿlaba*, and that *farraḥa* (he gladdened s.o.) is of the pattern *faʿʿala*, not the pattern *faʿrala*.

تقابَل بـ«فَعَـلَ» أو «فَعْلَلَ» عن حـرف التضعيف والعلّة والهمـزة، نحـو «نَصْرٌ» و«دَحْـرَجَ»؛ وإمـا (٢) غير سـالم، وهـو ما لم يسـلم من تلك الحـروف، نحو «مَدَّ، وَعَـدَ، قَالَ، غَـزَا، وَقَى، شَـوَى، أَخَذَ» فهذه السـبعة كلّها غير السـالم.

ويعبّر عـن الحـرف الأول بـ«فاء الفعـل» وعن الثاني بـ«عين الفعـل» وعـن الثالـث بـ«لام الفعـل» إن كان الفعـل على ثلاثـة أحـرف كـ«نَصَرَ». وإن كان على أربعة أحـرف كـ«دَحْـرَجَ» يـعبّر عـن الحـرف الثالـث بـ«لام الفعـل الأولى» وعن الرابع بـ«لام الفعل الثانيـة». ويعبّر عـن الحـروف الزائـدة على الحـروف الأصليّـة بلفظها وإن كانـت منقلبة عن حـروف أخـرى، فيقـال «اصْطَلَحَ وزن افْتَعَـلَ» لا «...وزن افطعـل»؛ إلا المكـرّرة للإلحاق أو غيره فبلفـظ ما تقدّمهـا، فيقـال «جَلْبَـبَ وزن فَعْلَلَ» لا «...وزن فَعْلَبَ» و«فَـرَّحَ وزن فَعَّلَ» لا «...وزن فَعْرَلَ».

Chapter 1

MORPHOLOGICAL CLASSES

How many are they? Into how many categories are they sorted? What is the name of each category? How many classes belong to each category? What is the pattern of each class, and what are its typifications? What is its characteristic sign? Is it transitive or intransitive?

There are thirty-five morphological classes, and upon them innumerable words are patterned. They can be sorted into ten categories.

1. Simple Triliterals

The first category is that of simple triliterals, and it comprises six classes:

1. The pattern of the first class is *faʿala / yafʿulu*, typified by *naṣara / yanṣuru* (to help). Its characteristic sign is that the second radical possesses *fatḥ*[7] in the perfect tense and *ḍamm* in the imperfect tense.
2. The pattern of the second class is *faʿala / yafʿilu*, typified by *ḍaraba / yaḍribu* (to hit). Its characteristic sign is that the second radical possesses *fatḥ* in the perfect tense and *kasr* in the imperfect tense.
3. The pattern of the third class is *faʿala / yafʿalu*, typified by *fataḥa / yaftaḥu* (to open). Its characteristic sign is that the second radical possesses *fatḥ* in the perfect tense and the imperfect tense. Either the second or the third radical must be a guttural letter,[8] and these are six: *ḥāʾ*, *khāʾ*, *ʿayn*, *ghayn*, *hamza*, and *hāʾ*.

الباب الأول

في أبواب الصرف

كم هي؟ و إلى كم نوع تتنوّع؟ وما عنوان كل نوع؟
كم أبواب كل نوع؟ وما وزن كل باب وما موزونه؟ وما
علامته؟ أهو متعدٍّ أم لازم؟

أبواب الصرف خمسة وثلاثون بابًا توزن بها كلمات لا تُحصى. وتتنوّع إلى عشرة أنواع.

١. الثلاثي المجرد

النوع الأول الثلاثي المجرّد، وهو ستّة أبواب.

١- الباب الأول وزنه فَعَلَ/ يَفْعُلُ؛ موزونه نَصَرَ/ يَنْصُرُ؛ علامته كون عين فعله مفتوحًا في الماضي ومضمومًا في المضارع.

٢- الباب الثاني وزنه فَعَلَ/ يَفْعِلُ؛ موزونه ضَرَبَ/ يَضْرِبُ؛ علامته كون عين فعله مفتوحًا في الماضي ومكسورًا في المضارع.

٣- الباب الثالث وزنه فَعَلَ/ يَفْعَلُ؛ موزونه فَتَحَ/ يَفْتَحُ؛ علامته كون عين فعله مفتوحًا في الماضي والمضارع بشرط أن يكون عين فعله أو لامه حرفًا من حروف الحلق، وهي ستّة: الحاء والخاء والعين والغين والهمزة والهاء.

4. The pattern of the fourth class is *faʿila / yafʿalu*, typified by *ʿalima / yaʿlamu* (to know). Its characteristic sign is that the second radical possesses *kasr* in the perfect tense and *fatḥ* in the imperfect tense.

5. The pattern of the fifth class is *faʿula / yafʿulu*, typified by *ḥasuna / yaḥsunu* (to be good). Its characteristic sign is that the second radical possesses *ḍamm* in the perfect tense and the imperfect tense. Of the variform derivatives, the only ones that occur in this class are the perfect and imperfect tense verbs,[1] the infinitive noun as determined by use [for a given root],[9] the participial, the diminutive noun, and the relational noun.

6. The pattern of the sixth class is *faʿila / yafʿilu*, typified by *ḥasiba / yaḥsibu* (to deem). Its characteristic sign is that the second radical possesses *kasr* in both [tenses].

Each of these six classes is predominantly transitive[2] except for Class *Ḥasuna*, which is always intransitive[3] since it is only for [words that signify] natures and dispositions.

An intransitive verb may become transitive in three ways: (a) by transformation into the class of *ifʿāl*, (b) [by transformation] into the class of *tafʿīl*, or (c) by means of a prepositional particle, e.g., *dhahabtu bihi* in the sense of *adhhabtuhu* (I removed it).

---

[1] This includes [forms of the imperfect tense] that are preceded by *lam*, *lammā*, the negative *mā*, the negative *lā*, *lan*, the imperative *lām*, or the prohibitive *lā*. The second person imperative is also included by the imperfect tense.

[2] Transitivity means that the action of the agent passes to an object.

[3] Intransitivity means that the action of the agent does not pass to an object and instead occurs in the agent.[10]

٤- الباب الرابع وزنه فَعِلَ/ يَفْعَلُ؛ موزونه عَلِمَ/ يَعْلَمُ؛ علامته كون عين فعله مكسورًا في الماضي ومفتوحًا في المضارع.

٥- الباب الخامس وزنه فَعُلَ/ يَفْعُلُ؛ موزونه حَسُنَ/ يَحْسُنُ؛ علامته كون عين فعله مضمومًا في الماضي والمضارع. لا تجيء منه من الأمثلة المختلفة إلا فِعلَا[١] الماضي والمضارع[١] ومصدره المستعمل والصفة المشبّهة واسم التصغير والمنسوب.

٦- الباب السادس وزنه فَعِلَ/ يَفْعِلُ؛ موزونه حَسِبَ/ يَحْسِبُ؛ علامته كون عين فعله مكسورًا فيهما.

وجميع هذه الأبواب الستّة للتعدية[٢] غالبًا إلا باب حَسُنَ فلازم[٣] دائمًا فإنه للطبائع لا غير.

يصير اللازم متعديًا بثلاثة أمور: (١) بالنقل إلى باب الإفعال (٢) وإلى باب التفعيل (٣) وبحرف الجرّ، نحو «ذهبتُ به» بمعنى «أذهبته».

---

[١] ولو دخل عليه «لم» و«لمّا» و«ما» و«لا» النفي و«لن» ولام الأمر و«لا» النهي. وفعل الأمر للمخاطب أيضًا داخل في معنى المضارع.

[٢] ومعنى التعدية تجاوز فعل الفاعل إلى المفعول به.

[٣] ومعنى اللازم عدم تجاوز فعل الفاعل إلى المفعول به بل وقوعه في نفسه.

2. Singly Augmented Triliterals

The second category is that of singly augmented triliterals, and it comprises three classes:

1. The pattern of the first class is *afʿala* / *yufʿilu* / *ifʿālan*, typified by *akrama* / *yukrimu* / *ikrāman* (to honor s.o.). Included in this class is *ammasa*, which is originally *anmasa* (to cause discord [between two people]). When the first radical is a *nūn*, it is converted to be the same as the second radical if the second radical is a letter in the set *y-r-m-l-w-n*.[11] The characteristic sign of this class is the addition of a *hamza* at the beginning.[1]
2. The pattern of the second class is *faʿʿala* / *yufaʿʿilu* / *tafʿīlan*, typified by *farraḥa* / *yufarriḥu* / *tafrīḥan* (to gladden s.o.). The original form of [*tafrīḥan*] is *tafrirḥan*, but the second *rāʾ* is converted to a *yāʾ* for the sake of phonetic alleviation, as it is converted in the verb *farayna* (they [f.] fled), originally *fararna*, in the third-person feminine plural. The characteristic sign of this class is the doubling of the second radical.
3. The pattern of the third class is *fāʿala* / *yufāʿilu* / *mufāʿalatan*,[2] typified by *qātala* / *yuqātilu* / *muqātalatan* (to battle s.o.). Its characteristic sign is the addition of an *alif* between the first and second radicals.

The forms[13] of these three classes are predominantly transitive.[3]

[1] The addition of a *sīn* or *hāʾ* between the *hamza* and the first radical to indicate intensification is valid in contravention of the standard rule, e.g., *asṭāʿa* / *yusṭīʿu* / *isṭāʿan* (to obey [completely]) and *ahrāqa* / *yuhrīqu* / *ihrāqan* (to spill [forcefully]).[12]

[2] Two other infinitive noun forms for this class are sometimes mentioned: *fiʿālan* and *fīʿālan*.

[3] The third class additionally signifies reciprocity, as in *qātala Zaydun ʿAmran* (Zayd fought ʿAmr).

٢. الثلاثي المزيد فيه بحرف

النوع الثاني الثلاثي المزيد فيه بحرف، وهو ثلاثة أبواب.

١- البـاب الأول وزنه أَفْعَـلَ/ يُفْعِـلُ/ إِفْعَـالًا؛ موزونه أَكْـرَمَ/ يُكْـرِمُ/ إِكْرَامًـا. ومنـه أَمَّـسَ وأصلـه أَنْمَـسَ، يقلـب فـاء فعلـه إذا كان نونـًا بجنـس عينـه إذا كان عينـه حرفًا من حـروف «يرملون»؛ علامتـه زيـادة الهمـزة في أوله.[١]

٢- الباب الثـاني وزنه فَعَّـلَ/ يُفَعِّـلُ/ تَفْعِيـلًا؛ موزونه فَـرَّحَ/ يُفَـرِّحُ/ تَفْرِيحًـا، أصلـه تَفْرِرْحًا قلـب الراء الثـاني يـاءً للتخفيـف كمـا قلـب في فَرَيْـنَ أصله فَـرَرْنَ جمـع المؤنـث الغائـب؛ علامتـه تضعيـف عينه .

٣- الباب الثالـث وزنـه فَاعَـلَ/ يُفَاعِـلُ/ مُفَاعَلَـةً؛[٢] موزونـه قَاتَـلَ/ يُقَاتِـلُ/ مُقَاتَلَـةً؛ علامتـه زيـادة الألـف بـين الفـاء والعين.

وبناء هذه الثلاث للتعدية غالبًا.[٣]

[١] يجـوز زيادة السـين أو الهاء بين الهمـزة والفـاء للمبالغة على خلاف القيـاس، نحـو «أَسْـطَاعَ/ يُسْـطِيعُ/ إِسْـطَاعًا» و«أَهْـرَاقَ/ يُهْرِيـقُ/ إِهْرَاقًا».

[٢] ويذكر مصدران آخران لهذا الباب وهما «فِعَالًا» و«فِيعَالًا».

[٣] والباب الثالث للمشاركة أيضًا، نحو «قاتَلَ زيدٌ عمرًا».

3. Doubly Augmented Triliterals

The third category is that of doubly augmented triliterals, and it comprises five classes:

1. The pattern of the first class is *infaʿala / yanfaʿilu / infiʿālan*, typified by *inqaṭaʿa / yanqaṭiʿu / inqiṭāʿan* (to be severed). Included in this class is also *irramala*, originally *inramala*. When the first radical is a letter in the set *y-r-m-l-w-n*, the *nūn* of *infaʿala* is converted to be the same as it and then assimilated. The characteristic sign of this class is the addition of an *alif* and a *nūn* at the beginning. Its form imparts quasi-passivity.[1]
2. The pattern of the second class is *iftaʿala / yaftaʿilu / iftiʿālan*, typified by *ijtamaʿa / yajtamiʿu / ijtimāʿan* (to come together). Included in this class are *khaṣṣama* (he quarreled), originally *ikhtaṣama*, and *iẓẓalama* (he was wronged), originally *iẓtalama*. When the first or the second radical is a letter in the set *a-t-th-d-dh-z-s-sh-ṣ-ḍ-ṭ-ẓ-w-y*, the *tāʾ* in *iftaʿala* is converted to be of its kind and then it is assimilated.[15] The characteristic sign of this class is the addition of an *alif* at the beginning and a *tāʾ* between the first and second radicals. Its form imparts quasi-passivity or transitivity.[16]
3. The pattern of the third class is *ifʿalla / yafʿallu / ifʿilālan*, typified by *iḥmarra / yaḥmarru / iḥmirāran* (to redden). Its characteristic sign is the addition of an *alif* at the beginning and the repetition of the third radical. The form of this class is intransitive.

[1] Quasi-passivity means that the effect of something obtains by means of a transitive action, as in *kasartu al-zujāja fa-inkasara dhālika al-zujāju* (I broke the glass and the glass consequently broke). That the glass broke is an effect that obtained by means of breaking, which is a transitive action.[14]

٣. الثلاثي المزيد فيه بحرفين

النوع الثالث الثلاثي المزيد فيه بحرفين، وهو خمسة أبواب.

١- الباب الأول وزنه اِنْفَعَلَ/ يَنْفَعِلُ/ اِنْفِعَالًا؛ موزونه اِنْقَطَعَ/ يَنْقَطِعُ/ اِنْقِطَاعًا، ومنه اِرَّمَلَ وأصله اِنْرَمَلَ، يقلب نون انفعل بجنس فائه إذا كان فاؤه حرفًا من حروف «يرملون» ثم تدغم؛ وعلامته زيادة الألف والنون في أوله؛ وبناؤه للمطاوعة.[١]

٢- الباب الثاني وزنه اِفْتَعَلَ/ يَفْتَعِلُ/ اِفْتِعَالًا؛ موزونه اجْتَمَعَ/ يَجْتَمِعُ/ اجْتِمَاعًا، ومنه خَصَّمَ أصله اخْتَصَمَ واظَّلَمَ أصله اظْتَلَمَ، يقلب تاء افتعل بجنس عينه وكذا بجنس فائه إذا كان فاؤه أو عينه حرفًا من حروف «اتشذ زسشص ضط ظوي» ثم تدغم؛ وعلامته زيادة الألف في أوله والتاء بين الفاء والعين؛ وبناؤه للمطاوعة والتعدية.

٣- الباب الثالث وزنه اِفْعَلَّ/ يَفْعَلُّ/ اِفْعِلَالًا؛ موزونه اِحْمَرَّ/ يَحْمَرُّ/ اِحْمِرَارًا؛ وعلامته زيادة الألف في أوله وتكرار لام فعله؛ وبناؤه للازم.

[١] معنى المطاوعة حصول أثر الشيء عن تعلّق الفعل المتعدّي، نحو «كسرت الزجاج فانكسر ذلك الزجاج» فإن انكسار الزجاج أثر حصل عن تعلّق الكسر الذي هو فعلٌ متعدٍّ.

4. The pattern of the fourth class is *tafāʿala* / *yatafāʿalu* / *tafāʿulan*, typified by *tabāʿada* / *yatabāʿadu* / *tabāʿudan* (to move away). Included in this class is *iththāqala* (he found s.th. burdensome), originally *tathāqala*. When the first radical is a letter in the set *a-t-th-d-dh-z-s-sh-ṣ-ḍ-ṭ-ẓ-w-y*, the *tāʾ* in *tafāʿala* is converted to be of its kind and then it is assimilated.[17] Its characteristic sign is the addition of a *tāʾ* at the beginning and an *alif* between the first and second radicals. The form of this class signifies reciprocity between two or more.[18]

5. The pattern of the fifth class is *tafaʿʿala* / *yatafaʿʿalu* / *tafaʿʿulan*, typified by *takallama* / *yatakallamu* / *takalluman* (to speak). Included in this class is *iṭṭahhara* (he purified himself), originally *taṭahhara*. When the first radical is a letter in the set *a-t-th-d-dh-z-s-sh-ṣ-ḍ-ṭ-ẓ-w-y*, the *tāʾ* in *tafaʿʿala* is converted to be of its kind and then it is assimilated. Its characteristic sign is the addition of a *tāʾ* at the beginning and the doubling of the second radical. The form of this class implies effort.[1]

4. Triply Augmented Triliterals

The fourth category is that of triply augmented triliterals, and it comprises four classes:

1. The pattern of the first class is *istafʿala* / *yastafʿilu* / *istifʿālan*, typified by *istakhraja* / *yastakhriju* / *istikhrājan* (to extract). Its char-

٤- الباب الرابع وزنه تَفَاعَلَ/ يَتَفَاعَلُ/ تَفَاعُلًا؛ موزونه تَبَاعَدَ/ يَتَبَاعَدُ/ تَبَاعُدًا، ومنه اثَّاقَلَ أصله تَثَاقَلَ، يقلب تاء تَفَاعَلَ بجنس فائه إذا كانت فاؤه حرفًا من حروف «اتشدذ زسشص ضط ظوي» ثم تدغم؛ وعلامته زيادة التاء في أوله والألف بين الفاء والعين؛ وبناؤه للمشاركة بين الاثنين فصاعدًا.

٥- الباب الخامس وزنه تَفَعَّلَ/ يَتَفَعَّلُ/ تَفَعُّلًا؛ موزونه تَكَلَّمَ/ يَتَكَلَّمُ/ تَكَلُّمًا، ومنه اطَّهَّرَ أصله تَطَهَّرَ، يقلب تاء تَفَعَّلَ بجنس فائه إذا كانت فاؤه حرفًا من حروف «اتشدذ زسشص ضط ظوي» ثم تدغم؛ وعلامته زيادة التاء في أوله وتضعيف عينه؛ وبناؤه للتكلّف.[١]

٤. الثلاثي المزيد فيه بثلاثة أحرف

النوع الرابع الثلاثي المزيد فيه بثلاثة أحرف، وهو أربعة أبواب.

١- الباب الأول وزنه اِسْتَفْعَلَ/ يَسْتَفْعِلُ/ اِسْتِفْعَالًا؛ موزونه اسْتَخْرَجَ/ يَسْتَخْرِجُ/ اسْتِخْرَاجًا؛

[1] Effort (*takalluf*) means the realization of an objective gradually, as in "I learned (*taʿallamtu*) the material one topic at a time and graduated from college."

[١] معنى التكلّف تحصيل المطلوب شيئًا بعد شيء، نحو «تعلّمتُ العلم مسألةً بعد مسألة وتخرّجتُ في الكليّة».

acteristic sign is the addition of a *hamza*, a *sīn*, and a *tāʾ* at the beginning. The form of this class is predominantly transitive.[1]

2. The pattern of the second class is *ifʿawʿala / yafʿawʿilu / ifʿīʿālan*, typified by *iʿshawshaba / yaʿshawshibu / iʿshīshāban* (to be abundant in vegetation). The original form of [*iʿshīshāban*] is *iʿshiwshāban*, but the *wāw* is converted to a *yāʾ* because it is vowelless and the preceding letter possesses *kasr*. The characteristic sign of this class is the addition of a *hamza* at the beginning, the addition of a *wāw* after the second radical, and the doubling of the second radical. Its form serves to intensify an intransitive action.

3. The pattern of the third class is *ifʿawwala / yafʿawwilu / ifʿiwwālan*, typified by *ijlawwadha / yajlawwidhu / ijliwwādhan* (to move along quickly). Its characteristic sign is the addition of a *hamza* at the beginning and a doubled *wāw* between the second and third radicals. The form of this class serves to intensify an intransitive action.

4. The pattern of the fourth class is *ifʿālla / yafʿāllu / ifʿīlālan*, typified by *iḥmārra / yaḥmārru / iḥmīrāran* (to redden intensely). The original form of [*iḥmīrāran*] is *iḥmārāran*, but the *alif* following the *mīm* is converted to a *yāʾ* for the sake of phonetic alleviation, and the *mīm* is vowelized with *kasr* [to accord with] the *yāʾ*. Its characteristic sign is the addition of a *hamza* at the beginning, the addition of an *alif* between the second and third radicals, and the repetition of the third radical. The form of this class serves to intensify an intransitive action.

علامته زيادة الهمزة والسين والتاء في أوله؛ وبناؤه للتعدية غالبًا.[١]

٢- الباب الثاني وزنه اِفْعَوْعَلَ/ يَفْعَوْعِلُ/ اِفْعِيعَالًا؛ موزونه اِعْشَوْشَبَ/ يَعْشَوْشِبُ/ اِعْشِيشَابًا؛ أصله اِعْشِوْشَابًا، قلب واوه ياء لسكونه وكسر ما قبله؛ وعلامته زيادة الهمزة في أوله والواو بعد عين فعله وتكرار عين الفعل؛ وبناؤه لمبالغة اللازم.

٣- الباب الثالث وزنه اِفْعَوَّلَ/ يَفْعَوِّلُ/ اِفْعِوَّالًا؛ موزونه اِجْلَوَّذَ/ يَجْلَوِّذُ/ اِجْلِوَّاذًا؛ علامته زيادة الهمزة في أوله والواو المشدّدة بين العين واللام؛ وبناؤه لمبالغة اللازم.

٤- الباب الرابع وزنه اِفْعَالَّ/ يَفْعَالُّ/ اِفْعِيلَالًا؛ موزونه اِحْمَارَّ/ يَحْمَارُّ/ اِحْمِيرَارًا؛ أصله اِحْمَارَارًا، قلب الألف الذي بعد الميم ياء للتخفيف وكُسر الميم للياء؛ وعلامته زيادة الهمزة في أوله والألف بين العين واللام وتكرار اللام؛ وبناؤه لمبالغة اللازم.

[1] It may signify the requesting of an action, as when He ﷻ says, "So they went on until they came upon the people of a town and sought food (*istaṭʿamā*) from them. But they refused to show them any hospitality..." (Q 18:77).

[١] وقد يفيد طلب الفعل، كما في قوله تعالى ﴿فَٱنطَلَقَا حَتَّىٰٓ إِذَآ أَتَيَآ أَهْلَ قَرْيَةٍ ٱسْتَطْعَمَآ أَهْلَهَا فَأَبَوْاْ أَن يُضَيِّفُوهُمَا﴾ [١٨/ ٧٧].

5. Simple Quadriliterals

The fifth category is that of simple quadriliterals, and it comprises one class, whose pattern is *faʿlala* / *yufaʿlilu* / *faʿlalatan, fiʿlālan*, typified by *daḥraja* / *yudaḥriju* / *daḥrajatan, diḥrājan* (to roll s.th.). The characteristic sign of this class is the possession of four radicals. Its form is predominantly transitive.

٥. الرباعي المجرد

النوع الخامس الرباعي المجرّد، وهو باب واحد. وزنه فَعْلَلَ/ يُفَعْلِلُ/ فَعْلَلَةً وفِعْلَالًا؛ موزونه دَحْرَجَ/ يُدَحْرِجُ/ دَحْرَجَةً ودِحْرَاجًا؛ علامته كون أصوله على أربعة؛ وبناؤه للتعدية غالبًا.

6. Singly Augmented Quadriliterals

The sixth category is that of singly augmented quadriliterals, and it comprises one class, whose pattern is *tafaʿlala* / *yatafaʿlalu* / *tafaʿlulan*, typified by *tadaḥraja* / *yatadaḥraju* / *tadaḥrujan* (to roll [intr.]). The characteristic sign of this class is the possession of four radicals and the addition of a *tāʾ* at the beginning. Its form imparts quasi-passivity.

٦. الرباعي المزيد فيه بحرف

النوع السادس الرباعي المزيد فيه بحرف، وهو أيضا باب واحد. وزنه تَفَعْلَلَ/ يَتَفَعْلَلُ/ تَفَعْلُلًا؛ موزونه تَدَحْرَجَ/ يَتَدَحْرَجُ/ تَدَحْرُجًا؛ علامته كون أصوله على أربعة وزيادة التاء في أوله؛ وبناؤه للمطاوعة.

7. Doubly Augmented Quadriliterals

The seventh category is that of doubly augmented quadriliterals, and it comprises two classes:

1. The pattern of the first class is *ifʿalalla* / *yafʿalillu* / *ifʿillālan*, typified by *iqshaʿarra* / *yaqshaʿirru* / *iqshiʿrāran* (to shudder). Its characteristic sign is the possession of four radicals, the addition of a *hamza* at the beginning, and the repetition of the fourth radical. The form of this class serves to intensify an intransitive action.
2. The pattern of the second class is *ifʿanlala* / *yafʿanlilu* / *ifʿinlālan*, typified by *iḥranjama* / *yaḥranjimu* / *iḥrinjāman* (to crowd together). Its characteristic sign is the possession of four radicals, the addition of a *hamza* at the beginning, and the addition of a *nūn* between the second and third radicals. The form of this class imparts quasi-passivity.

٧. الرباعي المزيد فيه بحرفين

النوع السابع الرباعي المزيد فيه بحرفين، وهو بابان.

١- الباب الأول وزنه اِفْعَلَلَّ/ يَفْعَلِلُّ/ اِفْعِلَّالًا؛ موزونه اِقْشَعَرَّ/ يَقْشَعِرُّ/ اِقْشِعْرَارًا؛ علامته كون أصوله على أربعة وزيادة الهمزة في أوله وتكرار اللام؛ وبناؤه لمبالغة اللازم.

٢- الباب الثاني وزنه اِفْعَنْلَلَ/ يَفْعَنْلِلُ/ اِفْعِنْلَالًا؛ موزونه اِحْرَنْجَمَ/ يَحْرَنْجِمُ/ اِحْرِنْجَامًا؛ علامته كون أصوله على أربعة وزيادة الهمزة في أوله والنون بين العين واللام؛ وبناؤه للمطاوعة.

8. Singly Augmented Triliterals That Conform to Class *Daḥraja*

The eighth category is that of singly augmented triliterals that conform to Class *Daḥraja*,[19] the sign of their conformity being that their infinitive nouns have the same form. This category comprises six classes:

1. The pattern of the first class is *fawʿala* / *yufawʿilu* / *fawʿalatan, fīʿālan*, typified by *ḥawqala* / *yuḥawqilu* / *ḥawqalatan, ḥīqālan* (to become decrepit). Its characteristic sign is the possession of three radicals and the addition of a *wāw* between the first and second radicals. The form of this class is intransitive since its meaning does not depend on an object; e.g., *ḥawqala Zaydun* (Zayd became decrepit).
2. The pattern of the second class is *faʿwala* / *yufaʿwilu* / *faʿwalatan, fiʿwālan*, typified by *jahwara* / *yujahwiru* / *jahwaratan, jihwāran* (to pronounce s.th. aloud). Its characteristic sign is the possession of three radicals and the addition of a *wāw* between the second and third radicals. The form of this class is transitive.
3. The pattern of the third class is *fayʿala* / *yufayʿilu* / *fayʿalatan, fīʿālan*, typified by *bayṭara* / *yubayṭiru* / *bayṭaratan, bīṭāran* (to split s.th.). Its characteristic sign is the possession of three radicals and the addition of a *yāʾ* between the first and second radicals. The form of this class is transitive.
4. The pattern of the fourth class is *faʿyala* / *yufaʿyilu* / *faʿyalatan, fiʿyālan*, typified by *ʿathyara* / *yuʿathyiru* / *ʿathyaratan, ʿithyāran* (to trip). Its characteristic sign is the possession of three radicals and the addition of a *yāʾ* between the second and third radicals. The form of this class is intransitive.

٨. الثلاثي المزيد فيه بحرف الملحق بدحرج

النوع الثامن الثلاثي المزيد فيه بحرف الملحق بدَحْرَجَ؛ علامة الإلحاق اتّفاق المصدرين. وهو ستّة أبواب.

١- الباب الأول وزنه فَوْعَلَ/ يُفَوْعِلُ/ فَوْعَلَةً وفِيعَالًا؛ موزونه حَوْقَلَ/ يُحَوْقِلُ/ حَوْقَلَةً وحِيقَالًا؛ علامته كون أصوله ثلاثة وزيادة الواو بين الفاء والعين؛ وبناؤه للّازم لعدم توقّف معناه على المفعول، نحو «حوقلَ زيدٌ»[٢].

٢- الباب الثاني وزنه فَعْوَلَ/ يُفَعْوِلُ/ فَعْوَلَةً وفِعْوَالًا؛ موزونه جَهْوَرَ/ يُجَهْوِرُ/ جَهْوَرَةً وجِهْوَارًا؛ علامته كون أصوله ثلاثة وزيادة الواو بين العين واللام؛ وبناؤه للتعدية.

٣- الباب الثالث وزنه فَيْعَلَ/ يُفَيْعِلُ/ فَيْعَلَةً وفِيعَالًا؛ موزونه بَيْطَرَ/ يُبَيْطِرُ/ بَيْطَرَةً وبِيطَارًا؛ علامته كون أصوله ثلاثة وزيادة الياء بين الفاء والعين؛ وبناؤه للتعدية.

٤- الباب الرابع وزنه فَعْيَلَ/ يُفَعْيِلُ/ فَعْيَلَةً وفِعْيَالًا؛ موزونه عَثْيَرَ/ يُعَثْيِرُ/ عَثْيَرَةً وعِثْيَارًا؛ علامته كون أصوله ثلاثة وزيادة الياء بين العين واللام؛ وبناؤه للّازم[٣].

5. The pattern of the fifth class is *faʿlala* / *yufaʿlilu* / *faʿlalatan, fiʿlālan*, typified by *jalbaba* / *yujalbibu* / *jalbabatan, jilbāban* (to dress s.o. in a *jilbāb*). Its characteristic sign is the possession of three radicals and the repetition of the third radical. The form of this class is transitive.

6. The pattern of the sixth class is *faʿlā* / *yufaʿlī* / *faʿlayatan, fiʿlāʾan*, typified by *salqā* / *yusalqī* / *salqayatan, silqāʾan* (to thrust s.o. down onto his back). Its characteristic sign is the possession of three radicals and the addition of a *yāʾ* at the end. The form of this class is transitive.

9. Doubly Augmented Triliterals That Conform to Class *Tadaḥraja*

The ninth category is that of doubly augmented triliterals that conform to Class *Tadaḥraja*, and it comprises five classes:

1. The pattern of the first class is *tafawʿala* / *yatafawʿalu* / *tafawʿulan*, typified by *tajawraba* / *yatajawrabu* / *tajawruban* (to put on socks). Its characteristic sign is the possession of three radicals, the addition of a *tāʾ* at the beginning, and the addition of a *wāw* between the first and second radicals. The form of this class imparts quasi-passivity.

2. The pattern of the second class is *tafaʿwala* / *yatafaʿwalu* / *tafaʿwulan*, typified by *tarahwaka* / *yatarahwaku* / *tarahwukan* (to walk with a swagger). Its characteristic sign is the possession of three radicals, the addition of a *tāʾ* at the beginning, and the addition of a *wāw* between the second and third radicals. The form of this class is intransitive.

3. The pattern of the third class is *tafayʿala* / *yatafayʿalu* / *tafayʿulan*, typified by *tashayṭana* / *yatashayṭanu* / *tashayṭunan* (to behave like a devil). Its characteristic sign is the pos-

٥- الباب الخامس وزنه فَعْلَلَ/ يُفَعْلِلُ/ فَعْلَلَةً وفِعْلَالًا؛ موزونه جَلْبَبَ/ يُجَلْبِبُ/ جَلْبَبَةً وجِلْبَابًا؛ علامته كون أصوله ثلاثة وتكرار لام الفعل؛ وبناؤه للتعدية.

٦- الباب السادس وزنه فَعْلَى/ يُفَعْلِي/ فَعْلَيَةً وفِعْلَاءً؛ موزونه سَلْقَى/ يُسَلْقِي/ سَلْقَيَةً وسِلْقَاءً؛ علامته كون أصوله ثلاثة وزيادة الياء في آخره؛ وبناؤه للتعدية[٤].

٩. الثلاثي المزيد فيه بحرفين الملحق بتدحرج

النوع التاسع الثلاثي المزيد فيه بحرفين الملحق بتَدَحْرَجَ، وهو خمسة أبواب.

١- الباب الأول وزنه تَفَوْعَلَ/ يَتَفَوْعَلُ/ تَفَوْعُلًا؛ موزونه تَجَوْرَبَ/ يَتَجَوْرَبُ/ تَجَوْرُبًا؛ علامته كون أصوله ثلاثة وزيادة التاء في أوله والواو بين الفاء والعين؛ وبناؤه للمطاوعة.

٢- الباب الثاني وزنه تَفَعْوَلَ/ يَتَفَعْوَلُ/ تَفَعْوُلًا؛ موزونه تَرَهْوَكَ/ يَتَرَهْوَكُ/ تَرَهْوُكًا؛ علامته كون أصوله ثلاثة وزيادة التاء في أوله والواو بين العين واللام؛ وبناؤه للازم.

٣- الباب الثالث وزنه تَفَيْعَلَ/ يَتَفَيْعَلُ/ تَفَيْعُلًا؛ موزونه تَشَيْطَنَ/ يَتَشَيْطَنُ/ تَشَيْطُنًا؛ علامته كون

session of three radicals, the addition of a *tāʾ* at the beginning, and the addition of a *yāʾ* between the first and second radicals. The form of this class is intransitive.

4. The pattern of the fourth class is *tafaʿlala / yatafaʿlalu / tafaʿlulan,* typified by *tajalbaba / yatajalbabu / tajalbuban* (to put on a *jilbāb*). Its characteristic sign is the possession of three radicals, the addition of a *tāʾ* at the beginning, and the repetition of the third radical. The form of this class imparts quasi-passivity.

5. The pattern of the fifth class is *tafaʿlā / yatafaʿlā / tafaʿliyan,* typified by *tasalqā / yatasalqā / tasalqiyan* (to lie on one's back). Its characteristic sign is the possession of three radicals, the addition of a *tāʾ* at the beginning, and the addition of a *yāʾ* at the end. The form of this class is intransitive.

أصـوله ثلاثـة وزيـادة التاء في أوله والياء بين الفاء والـعين؛ وبناؤه لـللازم.

٤- البـاب الرابـع وزنـه تَفَعْلَـلَ/ يَتَفَعْلَـلُ/ تَفَعْلُـلًا؛ موزونـه تَجَلْبَـبَ/ يَتَجَلْبَـبُ/ تَجَلْبُبًـا؛ علامته كون أصـوله ثلاثـة وزيـادة التـاء في أوله وتكـرار لام الفعـل؛ وبنـاؤه للمطاوعـة.

٥- البـاب الخامـس وزنـه تَفَعْلَى/ يَتَفَعْـلَى/ تَفَعْلِيًـا؛ موزونـه تَسَـلْقَى/ يَتَسَـلْقَى/ تَسَـلْقِيًا؛ علامته كون أصـوله ثلاثة وزيادة التـاء في أوله واليـاء في الآخر؛ وبنـاؤه للـلازم.

10. Triply Augmented Triliterals That Conform to Class *Iḥranjama*

The tenth category is that of triply augmented triliterals that conform to Class *Iḥranjama,* and it comprises two classes:

1. The pattern of the first class is *ifʿanlala / yafʿanlilu / ifʿinlālan,* typified by *iqʿansasa / yaqʿansisu / iqʿinsāsan* (to arch one's back). Its characteristic sign is the possession of three radicals, the addition of a *hamza* at the beginning, the addition of a *nūn* between the second and third radicals, and the repetition of the third radical. The form of this class serves to intensify an intransitive action.

2. The pattern of the second class is *ifʿanlā / yafʿanlī / ifʿinlāʾan,* typified by *islanqā / yaslanqī / islinqāʾan* (to lie on one's back). Its characteristic sign is the possession of three

١٠. الثلاثي المزيد فيه بثلاثة أحرف الملحق باحرنجم

النـوع العـاشر الثلاثي المزيـد فيـه بثلاثة أحـرف الملحق باحْرَنْجَـمَ، وهـو بابان.

١- البـاب الأول وزنـه اِفْعَنْلَـلَ/ يَفْعَنْلِـلُ/ اِفْعِنْـلَالًا؛ موزونه اِقْعَنْسَـسَ/ يَقْعَنْسِـسُ/ اِقْعِنْسَاسًا؛ علامته كـون أصـوله ثلاثـة وزيـادة الهمـزة في أوله والنون بـين العـين والـلام وتكـرار لام الفعـل؛ وبنـاؤه لمبالغـة اللازم.

٢- البـاب الثـاني وزنـه اِفْعَنْلَى/ يَفْعَنْـلِي/ اِفْعِنْـلَاءً؛ موزونه اِسْـلَنْقَى/ يَسْـلَنْقِي/ اِسْـلِنْقَاءً؛ علامته كون

radicals, the addition of a *hamza* at the beginning, the addition of a *nūn* between the second and third radicals, and the addition of a *yā'* at the end. The form of this class is intransitive.

أصـوله ثلاثـة وزيـادة الهمـزة في أوله والنـون بين الـعين واللام والياء في الآخـر؛ وبنـاؤه لـللازم.

❁ ❁ ❁

Altogether, the number of morphological classes we have listed under these ten categories totals thirty-five. To enumerate them in brief:

Category 1 includes six classes: *Naṣara, Ḍaraba, Fataḥa, ʿAlima, Ḥasuna, Ḥasiba*

Category 2 includes three classes: *Akrama (Ammasa), Farraḥa, Qātala*

Category 3 includes five classes: *Inqaṭaʿa (Irramala), Ijtamaʿa (Iẓẓalama, Khaṣṣama), Iḥmarra, Takallama (Iṭṭahhara), Tabāʿada (Iththāqala)*

Category 4 includes four classes: *Istakhraja, Iʿshawshaba, Ijlawwadha, Iḥmārra*

Category 5 includes a single class: *Daḥraja*

Category 6 includes a single class: *Tadaḥraja*

Category 7 includes two classes: *Iqshaʿarra, Iḥranjama*

Category 8 includes six classes: *Ḥawqala, Jahwara, Bayṭara, ʿAthyara, Jalbaba, Salqā*

فصار مجموع ما ذكرناه من أبواب الصرف في ضمن هذه الأنواع العشرة خمسة وثلاثين بابًا. ضبطها مختصرًا:

النوع الأول ستّة أبواب: نصر، ضرب، فتح، علم، حسن، حسب.

النوع الثاني ثلاثة أبواب: أكرم (أمَّسَ)، فرّح، قاتل.

النوع الثالث خمسة أبواب: انقطع (ارّمل)، اجتمع (اظّلم/ خصّم)، احمرّ، تكلّم (اطّهر)، تباعد (اثّاقل).

النوع الرابع أربعة أبواب: استخرج، اعشوشب، اجلوذّ، احمارّ.

النوع الخامس باب واحد: دحرج.

النوع السادس باب واحد: تدحرج.

النوع السابع بابان: اقشعر، احرنجم.

النوع الثامن ستة أبواب: حوقل، جهور، بيطر، عثير، جلبب، سلقى.

النوع التاسع خمسة أبواب: تجورب، ترهوك، تشيطن، تجلبب، تسلقى.

Category 9 includes five classes: *Tajawraba, Tarahwaka, Tashayṭana, Tajalbaba, Tasalqā*

النوع العاشر بابان: اقعنسس، اسلنقى.

Category 10 includes two classes: *Iqʿansasa, Islanqā*

Chapter 2

الباب الثاني

DERIVATIVES

في الأمثلة

What are derivatives? How many categories do they have? What is the definition of each category? How many forms arise in each category? What are the technical names for these forms?

ما الأمثلة؟ كم قسمًا هي؟ وما تعريف كل قسم؟ وإلى كم صيغة يرتقي كل قسم؟ وما عنوان تلك الصيغ؟[٦]

Derivatives are [words] derived from the infinitive noun in the way that *naṣara* (he helped), *yanṣuru* (he helps), and *nāṣirun* (one that helps) as well as *yanṣuru*, *yanṣurāni* (they two [m.] help), and *yanṣurūna* (they help) are derived from *naṣr* (to help), which is the infinitive noun. Derivatives are of two categories.

الأمثلة ما تتولّد من المصدر كتولّد «نصر، ينصر، ناصر» و«ينصر، ينصران، ينصرون» من «النصر» الذي هو المصدر. هي قسمان.

[Variform Derivatives]

[الأمثلة المختلفة]

The first of the two categories is called the *variform derivatives*: words that share a common lexical root but have different internal forms and grammatical affixes, like *naṣara*, *yanṣuru*, *nāṣirun*, and *manṣūrun* (one that is helped).

الأول من القسمين يقال لها الأمثلة المختلفة هي صيغ متّحدة مادةً مختلفة هيئةً وعلامةً، نحو «نصر، ينصر، ناصر، منصور».

[Variform Derivatives in Simple Triliteral Classes]

[الأمثلة المختلفة من الثلاثي المجرد]

Under this first of the two categories of derivatives, there arise twenty-five words from [each infinitive noun of] a simple triliteral class other than Class *Ḥasuna*. These derivatives, with their technical names, are as follows:

وهو أي الأول من القسمين يرتقي من الثلاثي المجرّد سوى باب حسن إلى خمس وعشرين صيغة. ها هي ذي مع عنوانها:

1. *naṣara* (he helped). *Perfect tense verb* in the active voice[20] built on *fatḥ*.[21] Thus for all perfect tense verbs unless suffixed with the pronominal *wāw*, whereupon they are built on a *ḍamma*, and unless suffixed with a vowelized pronoun, whereupon they are built on the lack of a vowel.

2. *yanṣuru* (he helps). *Imperfect tense verb* in the active voice[22] with a *ḍamma* for the indicative.[23] Thus for all imperfect tense verbs except the second-person feminine singular, the dual, and the plural,[1] which are suffixed with the inflectional *nūn*.

3. *nāṣirun* (one that helps). *Active participle*. It does not occur in [classes signifying] natures and dispositions,[2] though the participial does.

4. *manṣūrun* (one that is helped). *Passive participle*. It does not occur in intransitive [classes] except with a prepositional particle.[24]

5. *lam yanṣur* (he did not help). [Imperfect tense verb];[25] unconditioned negation of past action.

6. *lammā yanṣur* (he has not helped). [Imperfect tense verb]; negation of all past action [until and including the present].[26]

7. *mā yanṣuru* (he is not helping). Imperfect tense verb; negation of present action.

8. *lā yanṣuru* (he does not help; he will not help). Imperfect tense verb; negation of future action.[27]

9. *lan yanṣura* (he will not help).[28] [Imperfect tense verb]; emphatic negation of future action.

10. *li-yanṣur* (let him help). *Third-person imperative*.[29]

١- نَصَرَ: فعل ماضٍ معلوم مبني على الفتح، وكذا كل فعل ماضٍ إلا إذا اتّصل به واو الضمير فعلى الضمّة أو الضمير المتحرّك فعلى السكون.

٢- يَنْصُرُ: فعل مضارع معلوم مرفوع بالضمّة، وكذا كل مضارع إلا في الواحدة المخاطبة والتثنية والجمع[١] فبنون الإعراب.

٣- نَاصِرٌ: اسم الفاعل؛ ولا يجيء من الطبائع[٢] ويجيء منه الصفة المشبّهة.

٤- مَنْصُورٌ: اسم المفعول؛ ولا يجيء من اللوازم إلا بحرف الجر.[٧]

٥- لَمْ يَنْصُرْ: الجحد المطلق لنفي الماضي.

٦- لَمَّا يَنْصُرْ: الجحد المستغرق لنفي الماضي.

٧- مَا يَنْصُرُ: فعل مضارع نفي الحال.

٨- لَا يَنْصُرُ: فعل مضارع نفي الاستقبال.

٩- لَنْ يَنْصُرَ: تأكيد نفي الاستقبال.

١٠- لِيَنْصُرْ: أمر الغائب.

[1] That is, the masculine plural, e.g., *yanṣurūna* (they [m.] help) and *tanṣurūna* (you all [m.] help).

[2] In Class 5, e.g., *ḥasuna / yaḥsunu* (to be good).

[١] أي جمع المذكّر مثل «ينصرون» و«تنصرون».

[٢] من الباب الخامس مثل «حسُن/ يحسُن».

11. *lā yanṣur* (let him not help). *Third-person prohibitive.*

12. *unṣur* (help). *Second-person imperative.*

13. *lā tanṣur* (do not help). *Second-person prohibitive.*

14. *manṣarun* (help, a place/time of help). *Mimated infinitive;*[30] *noun of time*; *noun of place*. In simple triliterals it takes the form *maf*ʿ*alun*—except when [the imperfect tense verb in its class] has the pattern *yaf*ʿ*ilu* or the first radical is weak, whereupon it takes the form *maf*ʿ*ilun*. In non-triliteral classes it is patterned after the passive participle, lacking a special form of its own.

15. *minṣarun* (an instrument of help). *Noun of instrument.* It does not occur in intransitive or non-triliteral classes, even with an intermediary [preposition].

16. *naṣratun* (an instance of help). *Instantial infinitive noun.* In non-triliteral classes it takes its respective infinitive noun form with an [added] *tā*ʾ, as in *af*ʿ*ala* / *if*ʿ*ālatan*. This treatment extends analogously to other [classes]; e.g., *fa*ʿʿ*ala* / *taf*ʿ*īlatan*, as in *farraḥa* / *tafrīḥatan* (he gladdened / an instance of gladdening).

17. *naṣriyyatun* (a notion of help). *Synthetic infinitive noun.* When one wishes to form an infinitive noun out of a given word, one adds the relational *yā*ʾ and the transmutative *tā*ʾ, e.g., *al-rāmiyyatu* (to be one that throws), *al-marmiyyatu* (to be something that is thrown), and other forms like *if*ʿ*āliyyatun*, a synthetic infinitive form for Class *Akrama*.

18. *niṣratun* (a kind of help). *Infinitive noun of kind.* It does not occur in non-triliteral classes except with an intermediary element.[31]

١١- لَا يَنْصُرْ: نهي الغائب.

١٢- انْصُرْ: أمر الحاضر.

١٣- لَا تَنْصُرْ: نهي الحاضر.

١٤- مَنْصَرٌ: المصدر الميمي، اسم الزمان، واسم المكان؛ هي من الثلاثي المجرّد على مَفْعَل إلا ما كان من يَفْعِلُ أو كان معتلّ الفاء فعلى مَفْعِل، ومن غير الثلاثي على وزن اسم المفعول ليس لهنّ صيغة مستقلّة.

١٥- مِنْصَرٌ: اسم الآلة؛ ولا يجيء من اللوازم ولا من غير الثلاثي ولو بالواسطة.

١٦- نَصْرَةً: مصدر بناء المرّة؛ ويجيء من غير الثلاثي بالمصدر المستعمل مع التاء، نحو أَفْعَلَ/ إِفْعَالَةً ويقاس عليه غيره نحو فَعَّلَ/ تَفْعِيلَةً، كفَرَّحَ/ تَفْرِيحَةً.

١٧- نَصْرِيَّةً: المصدر الصنعي. إذا أريد صنع مصدر من كلمة يزاد عليها ياء النسبة وتاء النقل كـ«الراميّة» و«المرميّة» وغير ذلك مثل «إفعاليّة» مصدر صنعي من باب أَكْرَمَ.

١٨- نِصْرَةً: مصدر بناء النوع؛ لا يجيء من غير الثلاثي إلا بالواسطة.

19. *naṣriyyun* (one related to help). *Relational noun* in the triliteral. In non-triliteral classes it takes the pattern *afʿaliyyun*.

20. *nuṣayrun* (a little one that helps). *Diminutive noun* in the triliteral. In other classes it takes the pattern *ufayʿilun*.

21. *naṣṣārun*[1] (one that helps much). *Active participle intensive*. It does not occur in non-triliteral classes.

22. The *participial* does not occur in transitive or non-triliteral classes. It occurs only in the intransitive simple triliteral, as in *ʿaṭshānu* (one that is thirsty).[32]

23. *anṣaru* (more/most helpful). *Comparative/superlative.*[33] It does not occur in words signifying color or flaws or in non-triliteral classes except with an intermediary element, e.g., *aktharu ikrāman* (greater in honoring). So it is with verbs of wonderment expressed with the particle *mā* or the letter *bāʾ*.

24. *mā anṣarahu* (How helpful he is!). *Verb of wonderment* expressed with the particle *mā*.

25. *anṣir bihi* (How helpful he is!). Verb of wonderment expressed with the letter *bāʾ*. These two forms, like the comparative/superlative, do not occur in words signifying color or flaws or in non-triliteral classes except with an intermediary element, e.g., *mā ashadda ikrāmahu* and *ashdid bi-ikrāmihi* (How great his honoring is!).

١٩- نَصْرِيٌّ: الاسم المنسوب من الثلاثي. ومن غير الثلاثي: أَفْعَلِيٌّ.

٢٠- نُصَيْرٌ: اسم التصغير من الثلاثي. ومن غير الثلاثي: أُفَيْعِلٌ.

٢١- نَصَّارٌ:[١] مبالغة اسم الفاعل؛ ولا يجيء مبالغة اسم الفاعل من غير الثلاثي.

٢٢- لا تجيء الصفة المشبّهة من المتعدّي ولا من غير الثلاثي بل يجيء من الثلاثي المجرّد اللازم، نحو «عطشان».

٢٣- أَنْصَرُ: اسم التفضيل؛ ولا يجيء من الألوان والعيوب ولا من غير الثلاثي إلا بالواسطة، نحو «أَكْثَرُ إِكْرَامًا». وكذا فعلا التعجّب المائي والبائي.

٢٤- مَا أَنْصَرَهُ: فعل التعجّب المائي.

٢٥- أَنْصِرْ بِهِ: فعل التعجّب البائي. وهما كاسم التفضيل لا يجيئان من الألوان والعيوب ولا من غير الثلاثي إلا بالواسطة، نحو «مَا أَشَدَّ إِكْرَامَهُ» و«أَشْدِدْ بِإِكْرَامِهِ».

[1] There are other patterns for the active participle intensive: *faʿūlun* as in *jahūlun* (one that is very ignorant), *fiʿʿīlun* as in *ṣiddīqun* (one that is ever truthful), *fuʿulun* as in *ghufulun* (one that is utterly heedless), *faʿulun* as in *yaquẓun* (one that is completely attentive), *mifʿālun* as in *midrārun* (thing that pours forth very abundantly), *mifʿīlun* as in *mikthīrun* (thing that is very copious), and *fuʿalatun* as in *luʿanatun* (one that incessantly curses others).

[١] هناك أوزان أخرى لمبالغة اسم الفاعل: فَعُولٌ «جَهُولٌ»، فِعِّيلٌ «صِدِّيقٌ»، فُعُلٌ «غُفُلٌ»، فَعُلٌ «يَقُظٌ»، مِفْعَالٌ «مِدْرَارٌ»، مِفْعِيلٌ «مِكْثِيرٌ»، فُعَلَةٌ «لُعَنَةٌ».

Each of these derivative forms occurs in every sound simple triliteral class, with the following exceptions: the noun of instrument, the active and passive participles, the comparative/superlative, and the two verbs of wonderment do not occur in the fifth class, namely, Class *Ḥasuna*, while the participial does.

[Variform Derivatives in Classes That Are Not Simple Triliterals]

Twenty-one words arise from [each infinitive noun of] a class other than Class *Iḥmarra* that is not a simple triliteral.[34] These derivatives, with their technical names, are as follows:

1. *akrama* (he honored). *Perfect tense verb* built on *fatḥ*. Thus for all perfect tense verbs unless suffixed with the pronominal *wāw*, whereupon they are built on a *ḍamma*, and unless suffixed with a vowelized pronoun, whereupon they are built on the lack of a vowel.
2. *yukrimu* (he honors). *Imperfect tense verb* with a *ḍamma* for the indicative. Thus for all imperfect tense verbs except the second-person feminine singular, the dual, and the [masculine] plural, which are suffixed with the inflectional *nūn* for [the indicative].
3. *mukrimun* (one that honors). *Active participle.*
4. *mukramun* (one that is honored). *Passive participle*; *noun of time*; *noun of place*; and *mimated infinitive*. These are distinguished by context.
5. *lam yukrim* (he did not honor). Imperfect tense verb that the jussive particle *lam* renders jussive, eliding the [end] vowel. Thus for all imperfect tense verbs except for the second-person feminine singular, the dual, and the [masculine] plural, which have their inflectional *nūn* elided.
6. *lammā yukrim* (he has not honored). Imperfect tense verb rendered jussive by the jussive particle *lammā*.

وهـذه الأمثلة كلّهـا تجيء من كل بـاب مـن الثلاثي المجرّد السـالم إلا أن اسم الآلـة واسـم الفاعـل والمفعول واسـم التفضيـل وفِعلَي التعجّـب لا يجئن مـن الباب الخامس أي باب حَسُـنَ وتجيء منـه الصفة المشـبّهة.

[الأمثلة المختلفة من غير الثلاثي]

ومـن غير الثلاثي المجرّد سـوى بـاب احمـرّ[٨] تـرتقي إلى إحـدى وعشريـن صيغـة. وهي مـع عنوانهـا:

١- أَكْـرَمَ: فعل مـاضٍ مبني على الفتح، وكـذا كل ماضٍ إلا إذا اتّصـل بـه واو الضمير فعـلى الضمّة أو ضمير متحرّك فعلى السـكون.

٢- يُكْـرِمُ: فعـل مضـارع مرفـوع بالضمّـة، وكذا كل مضـارع إلا في الواحـدة المخاطبة والتثنيـة والجمع فبنـون الإعراب.

٣- مُكْرِمٌ: اسم الفاعل.

٤- مُكْـرَمٌ: اسـم المفعـول والزمـان والمـكان، والمصدر الميـمي؛ والعلامـة القرينة.

٥- لَـمْ يُكْـرِمْ: مضـارع مجـزوم بـ«لَـم» الجـازم بحـذف الحركـة، وكـذا كل مضـارع إلا في الواحـدة المخاطبـة والتثنيـة والجمـع فبحـذف نـون الإعـراب.

٦- لَمّا يُكْرِمْ: مضارع مجزوم بـ«لَمّا» الجازم.

7. *mā yukrimu* (he does not honor). Imperfect tense verb rendered negative by the particle *mā*, negating present action.

8. *lā yukrimu* (he does not honor; he will not honor). Imperfect tense verb rendered negative by the particle *lā*, negating future action.[35]

9. *lan yukrima* (he will not honor). Imperfect tense verb that the subjunctive particle *lan* renders subjunctive, for which it is vowelized with *fatḥ*, and for which the inflectional *nūn* is elided from the second-person feminine singular, the dual, and the [masculine] plural.

10. *li-yukrim* (let him honor). *Third-person imperative* rendered jussive by the imperative *lām*.

11. *lā yukrim* (let him not honor). *Third-person prohibitive* rendered jussive by the prohibitive *lā*.

12. *akrim* (honor). *Second-person imperative*, also called an *imperative* [*proper*].[36] According to the Basrans, this form is derived from the form *li-tuʾakrim*, from which the *lām* and *tāʾ* were elided by frequent use.

13. *lā tukrim* (do not honor). *Second-person prohibitive* rendered jussive by the prohibitive *lā*.

14. *ikrāmatan* (an instance of honoring). *Instantial infinitive noun* formed by adding a *tāʾ* at the end of the respective infinitive form.

15. *ikrāmatan ʿaẓīmatan* (a great kind of honoring). *Infinitive noun of kind* with an adjective as an intermediary element.

16. *ikrāmiyyatan* (a notion of honoring). *Synthetic infinitive noun* formed by adding the relational *yāʾ* and the transmutative *tāʾ* at the end.

17. *ukayrimun* (a little one that honors). *Diminutive noun* formed by adding a *yāʾ* after the first radical.

18. *ikramiyyun* (one related to honoring). *Relational noun* formed by adding the relational *yāʾ* to the end after eliding the *alif* of the infinitive noun form.

٧- مَا يُكْرِمُ: مضارع منفي بـ«مَا» لنفي الحال.

٨- لَا يُكْرِمُ: مضارع منفي بـ«لَا» لنفي الاستقبال.

٩- لَنْ يُكْرِمَ: مضارع منصوب بـ«لَن» الناصبة، ونصبه بالفتحة وفي الواحدة المخاطبة والتثنية والجمع بحذف نون الإعراب.

١٠- لِيُكْرِمْ: أمر الغائب مجزوم بلام الأمر.

١١- لَا يُكْرِمْ: نهي الغائب مجزوم بـ«لا» النهي.

١٢- أَكْرِمْ: أمر الحاضر يقال له أمر [بالصيغة] صيغة مشتقّة من لِتُؤَكْرِمْ عند البصريّين حذفت اللام مع التاء لكثرة الاستعمال.

١٣- لَا تُكْرِمْ: نهي الحاضر مجزوم بـ«لا» النهي.

١٤- إِكْرَامَةً: مصدر بناء المرّة بإلحاق التاء بمصدره المستعمل.

١٥- إِكْرَامَةً عَظِيمَةً: مصدر بناء النوع بواسطة صفة.

١٦- إِكْرَامِيَّةً: المصدر الصنعي بإلحاق ياء النسبة وتاء النقل.

١٧- أُكَيْرِمٌ: اسم التصغير بزيادة الياء بعد الفاء.

١٨- إِكْرَمِيٌّ: الاسم المنسوب بإلحاق ياء النسبة بعد حذف ألف المصدر.

19. *aktharu ikrāman* (greater in honoring). *Comparative/superlative* formed by means of an intermediary element.
20. *mā ashadda ikrāmahū* (How great his honoring is!). *Verb of wonderment* expressed with the particle *mā*.
21. *ashdid bi-ikrāmihī* (How great his honoring is!). Verb of wonderment expressed with the letter *bāʾ*.

Thus, accounting for the augmented triliteral classes, the simple quadriliteral classes, and the augmented quadriliteral classes, there remain only a few classes like Class *Iḥmarra*, and in the latter neither the active and passive participles, the two verbs of wonderment, nor similar forms occur.[1]

Uniform Derivatives

The second of the two types of derivatives is that of uniform derivatives. What are they? How many types of them are there? How many forms arise in each type? What are the technical names of these forms?

Uniform derivatives are words that share a common lexical root and internal form but have different grammatical affixes,[37] e.g., *naṣara* (he helped), *naṣarā* (they two [m.] helped), and *naṣarū* (they [m.] helped). They are of three types: verbal, like *naṣara*; adjectival, like *nāṣir* (one that helps); and nominal, like *manṣar* (place/time of help).

[1. Verbal Derivatives]

The first of the three types is that of verbal derivatives. Whether for a perfect tense verb in the ac-

[1] The participial occurs instead, because this class, like Class *Ḥasuna*, signifies natures and dispositions.

١٩- أَكْثَرُ إِكْرَامًا: اسم التفضيل بالواسطة.

٢٠- مَا أَشَدَّ إِكْرَامَهُ: فعل التعجّب المائي.

٢١- أَشْدِدْ بِإِكْرَامِهِ: فعل التعجّب البائي.

هكـذا مـا بقي مـن الأبـواب الثلاثي المزيـد فيـه والربـاعي المجـرّد والمزيـد فيـه إلا بعـض أبـواب منهـا كبـاب احمـرّ، فإنـه لا يجيء منـه اسـما الفاعـل والمفعول وفِـعلَا التعجّـب ونحوهـا.[١]

[الأمثلة المطردة]

الثاني من قسمي الأمثلة الأمثلة المطّردة. ما هي؟ كم قسمًا هي؟ إلى كم صيغة يرتقي كل قسم؟ ما عنوان هذه الصيغ؟

هي صيـغ متّحدة مـادةً وهيئةً ومختلفة علامـةً، نحو «نصر، نصرا، نصروا». وهي ثلاثـة أقسـام: فِعليّة كـنَصَرَ، وصْفيّة كنَاصِر، اسـميّة كمَنْصَر.

[١. الفعلية]

الأول مـن الأقسـام الثلاثـة الفعليّـة وهي سـواء كانـت ماضيًـا معلومًـا أو مجهـولًا أو مضـارعًا معلومًـا أو مجهولًا

[١] بل تأتي الصفة المشبّهة لأن هذا الباب للطبائع كباب حَسُنَ.

tive or passive voice or an imperfect tense verb in the active or passive voice, and whether for a simple triliteral or otherwise, there are fourteen verbal derivatives:[38] three for the third-person masculine, three for the third-person feminine, three for the second-person masculine, three for the second-person feminine, one for the first-person singular, and one for the first-person dual and plural, as follows:

ثلاثيًّا مجرّدًا أو غيره أربع عشرة صيغة: ثلاث منها لمذكّر غائب، ثلاث منها لمؤنّثة غائبة، ثلاث منها لمذكّر مخاطب، ثلاث منها لمؤنّثة مخاطبة، وواحدة منها لمتكلّم وحده، وأخرى لمتكلّم مع الغير؛ نحو:

Perfect Tense in the Active Voice **الماضي المعلوم**

	PL.	DUAL	SING.
3RD PERS. MASC.	نَصَرُوا	نَصَرَا	نَصَرَ
3RD PERS. FEM.	نَصَرْنَ	نَصَرَتَا	نَصَرَتْ
2ND PERS. MASC.	نَصَرْتُمْ	نَصَرْتُمَا	نَصَرْتَ
2ND PERS. FEM.	نَصَرْتُنَّ	نَصَرْتُمَا	نَصَرْتِ
1ST PERS. (SING.)			نَصَرْتُ
1ST PERS. (D. & PL.)	نَصَرْنَا		

Thus in total there are fourteen forms.

فالمجموع أربع عشر صيغة.

Perfect Tense in the Passive Voice The passive perfect is that in which the second last radical possesses *kasr* and the previous vowelized letters possess *ḍamm*, e.g., *nuṣira* (he was helped) and *ustukhrija* (it was extracted).

الماضي المجهول وهو ما يكسر ما قبل آخره ويضمّ حروفه المتحركة التي قبله، نحو «نُصِرَ» و«اسْتُخْرِجَ».

	PL.	DUAL	SING.
3RD PERS. MASC.	نُصِرُوا	نُصِرَا	نُصِرَ
3RD PERS. FEM.	نُصِرْنَ	نُصِرَتَا	نُصِرَتْ
2ND PERS. MASC.	نُصِرْتُمْ	نُصِرْتُمَا	نُصِرْتَ
2ND PERS. FEM.	نُصِرْتُنَّ	نُصِرْتُمَا	نُصِرْتِ
1ST PERS. (SING.)			نُصِرْتُ
1ST PERS. (D. & PL.)	نُصِرْنَا		

Imperfect Tense in the Active Voice

المضارع المعلوم

	PL.	DUAL	SING.
3RD PERS. MASC.	يَنْصُرُونَ	يَنْصُرَانِ	يَنْصُرُ
3RD PERS. FEM.	يَنْصُرْنَ	تَنْصُرَانِ	تَنْصُرُ
2ND PERS. MASC.	تَنْصُرُونَ	تَنْصُرَانِ	تَنْصُرُ
2ND PERS. FEM.	تَنْصُرْنَ	تَنْصُرَانِ	تَنْصُرِينَ
1ST PERS. (SING.)			أَنْصُرُ
1ST PERS. (D. & PL.)	نَنْصُرُ		

Imperfect Tense in the Passive Voice The passive imperfect is that in which the imperfect tense prefix possesses *ḍamm*, the second last radical possesses *fatḥ*, and the remaining letters retain their original vowels, e.g., *yuḍrabu* (he is hit) and *yustakhraju* (it is extracted).

المضارع المجهول وهو ما يضمّ حرف المضارعة ويفتح ما قبل آخره ويبقى الباقي على حاله، نحو «يُضْرَبُ» و«يُسْتَخْرَجُ».

	PL.	DUAL	SING.
3RD PERS. MASC.	يُنْصَرُونَ	يُنْصَرَانِ	يُنْصَرُ
3RD PERS. FEM.	يُنْصَرْنَ	تُنْصَرَانِ	تُنْصَرُ
2ND PERS. MASC.	تُنْصَرُونَ	تُنْصَرَانِ	تُنْصَرُ
2ND PERS. FEM.	تُنْصَرْنَ	تُنْصَرَانِ	تُنْصَرِينَ
1ST PERS. (SING.)			أُنْصَرُ
1ST PERS. (D. & PL.)	نُنْصَرُ		

[2. Adjectival Derivatives]

[٢. الوصفية]

The second of the types of uniform derivatives is that of adjectival derivatives. Whether for the active participle, the passive participle, the diminutive noun, the relational noun, the active participle intensive, the participial, or the comparative/superlative, there are six adjectival derivatives, discounting the broken plural.[39]

الثاني من أقسام الأمثلة المطّردة الوصفيّة وهي سواء كانت اسم الفاعل أو اسم المفعول أو اسم التصغير أو اسم المنسوب أو مبالغة اسم الفاعل أو الصفة المشبّهة أو اسم التفضيل ستّ صيغ سوى الجمع المكسّر.

Active Participle — اسم الفاعل

	BROKEN PL.	SOUND PL.	DUAL	SING.
MASC.	نُصَّارٌ، نُصَّرٌ، نَصَرَةٌ	نَاصِرُونَ	نَاصِرَانِ	نَاصِرٌ
FEM.	نَوَاصِرُ	نَاصِرَاتٌ	نَاصِرَتَانِ	نَاصِرَةٌ

Passive Participle — اسم المفعول

	BROKEN PL.	SOUND PL.	DUAL	SING.
MASC.	مَنَاصِرُ	مَنْصُورُونَ	مَنْصُورَانِ	مَنْصُورٌ
FEM.		مَنْصُورَاتٌ	مَنْصُورَتَانِ	مَنْصُورَةٌ

Diminutive Noun — اسم التصغير[٩]

	PL.	DUAL	SING.
MASC.	نُصَيْرُونَ	نُصَيْرَانِ	نُصَيْرٌ
FEM.	نُصَيْرَاتٌ	نُصَيْرَتَانِ	نُصَيْرَةٌ

Relational Noun — اسم المنسوب[١٠]

	PL.	DUAL	SING.
MASC.	نَصْرِيُّونَ	نَصْرِيَّانِ	نَصْرِيٌّ
FEM.	نَصْرِيَّاتٌ	نَصْرِيَّتَانِ	نَصْرِيَّةٌ

Active Participle Intensive — مبالغة اسم الفاعل

	PL.	DUAL	SING.
MASC.	نَصَّارُونَ	نَصَّارَانِ	نَصَّارٌ
FEM.	نَصَّارَاتٌ	نَصَّارَتَانِ	نَصَّارَةٌ

Participial الصفة المشبّهة

	PL.	DUAL	SING.
MASC.	عِطَاشٌ	عَطْشَانَانِ	عَطْشَانُ
FEM.	عِطَاشٌ	عَطْشَيَانِ	عَطْشَى

Comparative/Superlative اسم التفضيل

	BROKEN PL.	SOUND PL.	DUAL	SING.
MASC.	أَنَاصِرُ	أَنْصَرُونَ	أَنْصَرَانِ	أَنْصَرُ
FEM.	نُصَرُ	نُصْرَيَاتٌ	نُصْرَيَانِ	نُصْرَى

[3. Nominal Derivatives] [٣. الاسمية]

The third of the types of uniform derivatives is that of nominal derivatives. Whether for the mimated infinitive, the non-mimated infinitive, the noun of time or place, the noun of instrument, the instantial infinitive, or the infinitive of kind, there are three nominal derivatives.[40]

الثالث من أقسام الأمثلة المطّردة الاسميّة، ترتقي إلى ثلاث صيغ سواء كانت المصدر الميمي أو المصدر غير الميمي أو اسم الزمان أو المكان أو اسم الآلة أو مصدر بناء المرّة أو مصدر بناء النوع.

Non-Mimated Infinitive المصدر الغير الميمي

PL.	DUAL	SING.
نَصْرَاتٌ	نَصْرَانِ	نَصْرٌ

Mimated Infinitive; Noun of Time; Noun of Place المصدر الميمي واسم الزمان والمكان

PL.	DUAL	SING.
مَنَاصِرُ	مَنْصَرَانِ	مَنْصَرٌ

Noun of Instrument — اسم الآلة

PL.	DUAL	SING.
مَنَاصِرُ	مِنْصَرَانِ	مِنْصَرٌ

Instantial Infinitive — مصدر بناء المرّة

PL.	DUAL	SING.
نَصْرَاتٌ	نَصْرَتَانِ	نَصْرَةٌ

Infinitive of Kind — مصدر بناء النوع

PL.	DUAL	SING.
نِصْرَاتٌ	نِصْرَتَانِ	نِصْرَةٌ

Instructive Note

The technical names we have provided are for simple [verb tenses]. As for the names of compound [verbal constructions],[41] they are numerous. We list twenty of them below:[42]

1. *kāna faʿala* (he had done) – past perfect.
2. *in faʿala* (if he does/did) – conditional.
3. *in kāna faʿala* (if he did; if he had done) – past conditional.
4. *idh ḥīna faʿala* (when he did) – expressive of the time.
5. *ḥaythu faʿala* (where he did) – expressive of the place.
6. *mā dāma yafʿalu* (as long as he does) – temporally extensive.
7. *mā zāla yafʿalu* (he continues doing; he still does) – expressive of persistence.

تنبيه

ما ذكرناه من العناوين هي عناوين المفردات، أما عناوين المركّبات فكثيرة؛ نذكر منها عشرين عنوانًا:

١- كَانَ فَعَلَ: حكائيّة.

٢- إِنْ فَعَلَ: شرطيّة.

٣- إِنْ كَانَ فَعَلَ: شرطيّة حكائيّة.

٤- إِذْ حِينَ فَعَلَ: توقيتيّة.

٥- حَيْثُ فَعَلَ: محلّيّة.

٦- مَا دَامَ يَفْعَلُ: توقيتيّة امتداديّة.

٧- مَا زَالَ يَفْعَلُ: دائميّة.

8. *mundhu faʿala* (since he did) – expressive of the time of commencement.
9. *ḥattā faʿala* (until he did; to the point that he did) – expressive of the point of termination.
10. *wa-in faʿala/wa-law faʿala* (even if he does/did/had done)[1] – anti-exceptive.
11. *a-faʿala, hal faʿala* (did he do?) – interrogative.
12. *a-kāna faʿala, hal kāna faʿala* (had he done?) – past perfect interrogative.
13. *hallā faʿala* (why did he not do?)[43] – expressive of reproach.
14. *hallā yafʿalu* (why does he not do?) – expressive of exhortation.
15. *laʿallahu faʿala* (perhaps he will do) – expressive of hope.
16. *laytahu faʿala* (would that he had done) – expressive of wish.
17. *law faʿala* (if he had done) – counterfactual hypothetical.[2]
18. *lā budda an yafʿala* (he must do) – expressive of obligation or necessity.
19. *yanbaghī an yafʿala* (he should do) – expressive of what is proper or appropriate.
20. *yaqdiru an yafʿala* (he can do) – expressive of ability.

[1] As in the phrase, "even if (*wa-law*) We brought the like thereof to replenish it," in His saying ﷻ, "Say, 'If the sea were ink for the words of my Lord, the sea would be exhausted before the words of my Lord were exhausted'—even if We brought the like thereof to replenish it" (Q 18:109).

[2] This form signifies the non-reality of one thing due to the non-reality of another, as when He ﷻ says, "Were there (*law kāna*) gods other than Allah in [the heavens and the earth], they would surely have been corrupted. So glory to Allah, Lord of the Throne, transcending what they describe!" (Q 21:22).

٨- مُنْذُ فَعَلَ: ابتدائيّة.

٩- حَتَّى فَعَلَ: انتهائيّة.

١٠- وَإِنْ، وَلَوْ فَعَلَ:[١] وصليّة.

١١- أَفَعَلَ، هَلْ فَعَلَ: استفهاميّة.

١٢- أَكَانَ فَعَلَ، هَلْ كَانَ فَعَلَ: استفهاميّة حكائيّة.

١٣- هَلَّا فَعَلَ: تنديبيّة.

١٤- هَلَّا يَفْعَلُ: تحضيضيّة.

١٥- لَعَلَّهُ فَعَلَ: رجائيّة.

١٦- لَيْتَهُ فَعَلَ: تمنّيّة.

١٧- لَوْ فَعَلَ: امتناعيّة.[٢]

١٨- لَا بُدَّ أَنْ يَفْعَلَ: وجوبيّة.

١٩- يَنْبَغِي أَنْ يَفْعَلَ: لياقتيّة.

٢٠- يَقْدِرُ أَنْ يَفْعَلَ: قدرتيّة.

[١] مثل «ولو جئنا بمثله مددًا» في قوله تعالى ﴿قُل لَّوْ كَانَ ٱلْبَحْرُ مِدَادًا لِّكَلِمَـٰتِ رَبِّى لَنَفِدَ ٱلْبَحْرُ قَبْلَ أَن تَنفَدَ كَلِمَـٰتُ رَبِّى وَلَوْ جِئْنَا بِمِثْلِهِۦ مَدَدًا﴾ [١٨/ ١٠٩].

[٢] هذه الصيغة لامتناع شيء لامتناع غيره، نحو قوله تعالى ﴿لَوْ كَانَ فِيهِمَآ ءَالِهَةٌ إِلَّا ٱللَّهُ لَفَسَدَتَا فَسُبْحَـٰنَ ٱللَّهِ رَبِّ ٱلْعَرْشِ عَمَّا يَصِفُونَ﴾ [٢١/ ٢٢].

Chapter 3

الباب الثالث

IRREGULAR ROOTS

المعتــــل

On unsound roots, which are termed irregular roots. What are irregular roots? How many types of them are there? What is the first type of irregular root and then the next, and so forth?

غير السالم ويقال له المعتلّ: ما المعتلّ؟ وكم قسمًا هو؟ وما أول أقسام المعتلّ ثم فثم؟

The irregular root[44] is that one of whose radicals is a doubled letter, a *wāw*, a *yā'*, or a *hamza*, e.g., *madda* (he extended), *wa'ada* (he promised), *qāla* (he said), *ghazā* (he purposed), *waqā* (he guarded), *shawā* (he roasted), and *akhadha* (he took). It has seven types: doubled, resemblant, hollow, defective, disjointly weak, conjointly weak, and hamzated.

المعتلّ هو ما كان أحد حروفه الأصليّة حرف تضعيف أو واوًا أو ياءً أو همزةً، نحو «مَدَّ، وَعَدَ، قَالَ، غَزَا، وَقَى، شَوَى، أَخَذَ». وأقسامه سبعة أوّلها المضاعف ثم المثال ثم الأجوف ثم الناقص ثم اللفيف المفروق ثم اللفيف المقرون ثم المهموز.

I. The Doubled Root

(١) المضاعف

The first of the types of irregular roots is the doubled root. What is the doubled root? In how many classes does it occur? What is the modification[45] of the doubled root in the perfect, the imperfect, and so on until the last of the nine derivatives, which are the perfect, the imperfect, the imperative, the prohibitive, the active participle, the passive participle, the nouns of time and place, and the mimated infinitive?

الأول من أقسام المعتلّ المضاعف: ما المضاعف؟ ومن كم باب يجيء؟ وما إعلال أبواب المضاعف ماضيًا، مضارعًا، ثم فثم إلى آخر المشتقّات التسعة التي هي الماضي، المضارع، الأمر، النهي، اسم الفاعل، اسم المفعول، اسما الزمان والمكان، والمصدر الميمي؟

The doubled root in simple and augmented triliteral classes is that whose second and third radicals are the same, e.g., *madda* (he extended s.th.) and *amadda* (he provided). In simple and augmented quadriliteral classes it is that whose first and third

المضاعف هو من الثلاثي المجرّد والمزيد فيه ما كان عين فعله ولامه من جنس واحد، نحو «مَدَّ» و«أَمَدَّ»؛ ومن الرباعي المجرّد والمزيد فيه ما كان فاء فعله ولامه الأولى

radicals are the same and whose second and fourth radicals are the same, e.g., *zalzala* (to shake s.th.) and *tazalzala* (to shake [intr.]).

مـن جنس واحد وكذلـك عين فعله ولام فعلـه الثانية من جنس واحد، نحو «زَلْـزَلَ» و«تَزَلْزَلَ».

If the letter before the identical letters in a doubled root is vowelized, then elision and assimilation are necessary, e.g., *madda* (he extended s.th.). If it lacks a vowel, then transfer and assimilation are necessary, e.g., *yamuddu* (he extends s.th.). Of the two identical letters, if the one that is the third radical is originally vowelless, then assimilation cannot occur, e.g., *madadna* (they [f.] extended s.th.). If its vowelless state is not original, then assimilation can occur, e.g., *lam yamuddi* (he did not extend s.th.).[1] Memorize these rules.

وإن كان مـا قبـل المتجانـسين فيـه متحـرّكًا فالحذف والإدغام واجـب، نحو «مَـدَّ». وإن سـاكنًا فالنقل والإدغام واجـب، نحـو «يَمُـدُّ». وإن كان لام المتجانـسين سـاكنًا بسـكون أصلي فـالإدغام ممتنـع، نحـو «مَـدَدْنَ». وإن كان بسـكون عـرضي فـالإدغام جائـز، نحـو «لَـمْ يَمُـدِّ».[1] فاحفـظ هـذه القواعد.

The doubled root occurs in nine classes:

1. Class *Naṣara*: *madda* (to extend s.th.).
2. *Ḍaraba*: *farra* (to flee).
3. *ʿAlima*: *ʿaḍḍa* (to bite).
4. *Akrama*: *amadda* (to provide).
5. *Qātala*: *mādda* (to delay).
6. *Inqaṭaʿa*: *inmadda* (to be extended).
7. *Ijtamaʿa*: *imtadda* (to be extended).
8. *Tabāʿada*: *tamādda* (to stretch s.th. together with s.o.).
9. *Istakhraja*: *istamadda* (to draw from).

يجيء من تسعة أبواب:

١- باب نَصَرَ: مَدَّ.
٢- ضَرَبَ: فَرَّ.
٣- عَلِمَ: عَضَّ.
٤- أَكْرَمَ: أَمَدَّ.
٥- قَاتَلَ: مَادَّ.
٦- اِنْقَطَعَ: اِنْمَدَّ.
٧- اِجْتَمَعَ: اِمْتَدَّ.
٨- تَبَاعَدَ: تَمَادَّ.
٩- اِسْتَخْرَجَ: اِسْتَمَدَّ.

Classes with doubled roots are modified as follows:

إعلال أبواب المضاعف:

[1] [It is valid to read this] with any of the three ways of vowelizing the *dāl*: with a *fatḥa* (*lam yamudda*) since it is phonetically the lightest vowel, with a *kasra* (*lam yamuddi*) since a vowelless letter when vowelized is normally vowelized with *kasr*, and with a *ḍamma* (*lam yamuddu*) in imitation of the second radical. Another [valid reading] is to dissolve the assimilation: *lam yamdud*.

[١] بحـركات الدال الثلاث: بالفتحـة «لـم يَمُـدَّ» لأنه أخـفّ الحركات، وبالـكسرة «لـم يَمُـدِّ» لأن السـاكن إذا حـرّك حـرّك بالـكسر، وبالضمـة «لـم يَمُـدُّ» اتبـاعًا للـعين؛ وبفـكّ الإدغام «لَـمْ يَمْـدُدْ».

[The Doubled Perfect]

In the perfect tense, classes with doubled roots are modified (1) through elision and assimilation or (2) through transfer and assimilation:

1. The first is [for] *madda* (he extended s.th.), whose original form is *madada* of the pattern *faʿala* as in *naṣara* (he helped). Through elision, because the letter preceding the two identical letters is vowelized, and then through assimilation, this becomes *madda*. Examples like *madda*: *farra* (he fled), *ʿaḍḍa* (he bit), *mādda* (he delayed), *inmadda* (it was extended), *imtadda* (it was extended), *tamādda* (he stretched s.th. together with s.o.).
2. The second is [for] *amadda* (he provided), originally *amdada* of the pattern *afʿala* as in *akrama* (he honored). Through transfer, because the letter preceding the doubled letter lacks a vowel, and then through assimilation, this becomes *amadda*. Example like *amadda*: *istamadda* (he drew from s.th.).

As for words like *madadna* (they [f.] extended s.th.), they cannot be modified because the vowelless state of the third radical is original. However, modification through elision of the third radical is possible in some cases for the sake of phonetic alleviation, e.g., *ẓalna* (they [f.] remained), originally *ẓalilna* of the pattern *faʿilna* as in *ʿalimna* (they [f.] knew). Moreover, the third radical is sometimes converted to a *yāʾ*, e.g., *dassā* (he inserted), originally *dassasa*[1] of the pattern *faʿʿala* as in *farraḥa* (he gladdened s.o.).

[The Doubled Imperfect]

In the imperfect tense, classes with doubled roots are modified (1) through transfer and assimilation or (2) through elision and assimilation:

[1] Like *taẓannā* with respect to *taẓannana* (he surmised).

[الماضي من المضاعف]

إعلال أبواب المضاعف ماضيًا (١) بالحذف والإدغام، (٢) وبالنقل والإدغام:

١- الأول مَدَّ؛ أصله مَدَدَ على وزن فعل كنَصَرَ؛ فبالحذف لكون ما قبل المتجانسين متحركًا والإدغام صار مدّ. كـ«مدّ»: فَرَّ، عَضَّ، مَادَّ، انْمَدَّ، امْتَدَّ، تَمَادَّ.

٢- الثاني أَمَدَّ؛ أصله أَمْدَدَ على وزن أَفْعَلَ كأكرم؛ فبالنقل لكون ما قبل حرف التضعيف ساكنًا والإدغام صار أمدّ. كـ«أمدّ»: اسْتَمَدَّ.

أما الإعلال في نحو مَدَدْنَ فممتنع لكون سكون اللام فيه أصليًا. ولكن الإعلال قد يجوز في بعض الصور للتخفيف بحذف اللام، نحو ظَلْنَ أصله ظَلِلْنَ وزن فَعِلْنَ كعَلِمْنَ، وبقلبها ياءً، نحو دَسَّى[١١] أصله دَسَّسَ[١] وزن فَعَّلَ كفرّح.

[المضارع من المضاعف]

إعلال أبواب المضاعف مضارعًا (١) بالنقل والإدغام، (٢) وبالحذف والإدغام:

[١] كما يقال «تَظَنَّى»[١٢] في «تَظَنَّنَ».

1. The first is [for] *yamuddu* (he extends s.th.), originally *yamdudu* of the pattern *yafʿulu* as in *yanṣuru* (he helps). Through transfer, because the letter before the doubled letter lacks a vowel, and then through assimilation, this becomes *yamuddu.* Examples like *yamuddu*: *yafirru* (he flees), *yaʿaḍḍu* (he bites), *yumiddu* (he provides), *yamtaddu* (it is extended), *yastamiddu* (he draws from).
2. The second is [for] *yumāddu* (he stretches s.th.), originally *yumādidu* of the pattern *yufāʿilu* as in *yuqātilu* (he fights). Through elision, since the letter before the doubled letter is vowelized, and then through assimilation, this becomes *yumāddu.* Example like *yumāddu*:46 *yatamāddu* (he stretches s.th. together with s.o.), for the vowelless *alif* is as someone dead; it is not taken into account.

[The Doubled Imperative]

In the imperative proper, classes with doubled roots are modified (1) through transfer and elision and then vowelizing and assimilation or (2) through elision, vowelizing, and assimilation:

1. The first is [for] *muddi* (extend s.th.), originally *umdud* of the pattern *ufʿul* as in *unṣur* (help). Its modification occurs first through transfer and elision and then through vowelizing and assimilation. Examples like *muddi*: *firri* (flee), *ʿaḍḍi* (bite), *amiddi* (provide), *istamiddi* (draw from).[1]
2. The second is [for] *māddi* (delay), originally *mādid* of the pattern *fāʿil* as in *qātil* (fight). Its modification occurs first through elision, since the letter before the doubled letter is vowelized, then through vowelizing and assimilation. Thus, this becomes *māddi.* Examples like *māddi*: *imtaddi* (be extended), *tamāddi* (stretch s.th. together with s.o.).

[1] Also valid are the forms *ifrir, iʿḍaḍ, amdid,* and *istamdid,* with the assimilation dissolved.

١- الأول يَمُدُّ؛ أصله يَمْدُدُ على وزن يَفْعُلُ كينصر؛ وبالنقل لكون ما قبل حرف التضعيف ساكنًا والإدغام صار يمدّ. كـ«يمدّ»: يَفِرُّ، ويَعَضُّ، ويُمِدُّ، ويَمْتَدُّ، ويَسْتَمِدُّ.

٢- الثاني يُمَادُّ؛ أصله يُمَادِدُ على وزن يُفَاعِلُ كيقاتل؛ وبالحذف لكون ما قبل حرف التضعيف متحرّكًا والإدغام صار يمادّ. كـ«يمادّ»: يَتَمَادُّ١٣؛ إذ الألف الساكنة كالميت لا اعتداد بها.

[الأمر من المضاعف]

إعلال أبواب المضاعف أمرًا بالصيغة (١) بالنقل والحذف ثم التحرّك والإدغام، (٢) وبالحذف والتحرّك والإدغام:

١- الأول مُدِّ؛ أصله امْدُدْ على وزن افْعُلْ كانصر؛ إعلاله أولًا بالنقل والحذف ثم التحرك والإدغام. كـ«مدّ»: فِرِّ، وعَضِّ، وأمِدِّ، واسْتَمِدِّ.[١]

٢- الثاني مَادِّ١٤؛ أصله مَادِدْ على وزن فَاعِلْ كقاتل؛ إعلاله أولًا بالحذف لكون ما قبل حرف التضعيف متحركًا ثم التحرك والإدغام فصار مادّ. كـ«مادّ»: امْتَدّ، وتَمَادّ.

[١] ويجوز «افْرِرْ، اعْضَضْ، أَمْدِدْ، اسْتَمْدِدْ» بفكّ الإدغام.

[The Doubled Prohibitive]

In the prohibitive, classes with doubled roots are modified (1) through transfer, vowelizing, and assimilation or (2) through elision and assimilation:

1. The first is [for] *lā tamuddi* (do not extend s.th.), originally *lā tamdud* of the pattern *lā tafʿul* as in *lā tanṣur* (do not help). Through transfer, vowelizing, and assimilation, this becomes *lā tamuddi*. Examples like *lā tamuddi*: *lā tafirri* (do not flee), *lā taʿaḍḍi* (do not bite), *lā tumiddi* (do not provide).
2. The second is [for] *lā tumāddi* (do not delay), originally *lā tumādid* of the pattern *lā tufāʿil* as in *lā tuqātil* (do not fight). Through elision and assimilation, this becomes *lā tumāddi*. Examples like *lā tumāddi*: *lā tanmaddi* (do not be extended), *lā tamtaddi* (do not be extended), *lā tatamāddi* (do not stretch s.th. together with s.o.).

[النهي من المضاعف]

إعلال أبـواب المضاعـف نهيًـا (١) بالنقـل والتحريـك والإدغام، (٢) وبالحـذف والإدغام:

١- الأول لا تَمُـدِّ؛ أصلـه لا تَمْـدُدْ على وزن لا تَفْعُـلْ كلا تنـصر؛ وبالنقـل والتحـرك والإدغام صـار لا تمـدّ. كـ«لا تمـدّ»: لا تَفِـرِّ، ولا تَعَـضِّ، ولا تُمِدِّ.

٢- الثـاني لا تُمَـادِّ؛ أصلـه لا تُمَـادِدْ على وزن لا تُفَاعِـلْ كلا تقاتـل؛ فبالحـذف والإدغام صـار لا تمـادّ. كـ«لا تمـادّ»: لا تَنْمَـدِّ، ولا تَمْتَـدِّ، ولا تَتَمَـادِّ.

[The Doubled Active Participle]

In the active participle, simple triliteral classes with doubled roots are modified through elision and assimilation as in *māddun* (one that extends s.th.), *fārrun* (one that flees), and *ʿāḍḍun* (one that bites), originally *mādidun*, *fārirun*, and *ʿāḍiḍun*, of the pattern *fāʿilun* as in *nāṣirun* (one that helps), *ḍāribun* (one that hits), and *ʿālimun* (one that knows).

Classes that are not simple triliterals adopt the modification of the active imperfect with the exception that you replace the imperfect tense prefix with a *mīm* possessing *ḍamm*, e.g., *mumiddun* (one that provides) and *yumiddu* (he provides), which are of the same pattern.

[اسم الفاعل من المضاعف]

إعلال أبـواب المضاعـف حـال كونها اسـم الفاعـل فمن الثلاثي المجرّد يكـون إعلاله بالحـذف والإدغام نحو: مَادٌّ وفَـارٌّ وعَاضٌّ؛ أصلها مَـادِدٌ وفَارِرٌ وعَاضِـضٌ على وزن فَاعِلٌ كناصر ضـارب عالم.

ومـن غير الثلاثي المجـرّد يكـون إعلاله إعلال الفعـل المضـارع المعلـوم إلا أنـك تبـدّل حـرف المضارعـة بالميم المضمومـة، نحـو: مُمِـدٌّ، يُمِـدُّ، متفقـان وزنًا.

[The Doubled Passive Participle]

Simple triliteral classes are not modified, e.g., *mamdūdun* (thing that is extended).

[اسم المفعول من المضاعف]

إعلال أبـواب المضاعـف حـال كونها اسـم المفعـول فمن الثلاثي المجـرّد لا يعـلّ، نحو: مَمْـدُودٌ.

Classes that are not simple triliterals are patterned after the passive imperfect with the exception that you replace the imperfect tense prefix with a *mīm* possessing *ḍamm*, e.g., *mumaddun* (one that is provided), which shares the pattern of *yumaddu* (he is provided), and *mumdadun* (one that is provided), which shares the pattern of *yumdadu* (he is provided).

ومِـن غير الثلاثي المجـرّد يكـون على وزن الفعـل المضـارع المجهـول إلا أنـك تبـدّل حـرف المضارعـة بالميـم المضمومـة، نحـو: مُمَـدٌّ على وزن يُمَـدُّ، ومُمْـدَدٌ على وزن يُمْـدَدُ.

[The Doubled Noun of Time; Noun of Place; Mimated Infinitive]

[اسم الزمان، اسم المكان، المصدر الميمي من المضاعف]

Simple triliteral classes are modified through transfer and assimilation as in *mamaddun* (place/time of extension, extension), originally *mamdadun* of the pattern *maf'alun* as in *manṣarun* (place/time of help, help) and *maḍrabun* (place/time of hitting, hitting).

إعلال أبـواب المضاعف حال كونها اسـم الزمـان والمكان والمصدر الميمي إعلالها مـن الثلاثي المجرّد بالنقل والإدغام نحو: مَمَدٌّ، أصلـه مَمْدَدٌ على وزن مَفْعَـلٌ كمنصر ومضرب.

Classes that are not simple triliterals are patterned after the passive participle and are distinguished [from it] by context.

ومـن غير الثلاثي المجـرّد يكـون على وزن اسـم المفعول، والفـارق القرينة.

II. The Resemblant Root

(٢) المثال

The second of the seven types of irregular roots is that whose first radical is weak, and it is termed the resemblant root. The definition of the resemblant root, its classes, and the modification of every class individually in the perfect and so on until the last of the nine derivatives are as follows.

الثاني من الأقسام السبعة المعتلّة معتلّ الفاء ويقال له المثال: تعريفه، أبوابه، إعلال كل باب على حدة ماضيًا ثم فثم إلى آخر المشتقات التسعة

The resemblant root is that whose first radical is a weak letter, whether a *wāw* or a *yā'*.

هو ما كان فاؤه حرف علّة واوًا أو ياءً.

As for *wāw*, it is elided in the pattern *yaf'ilu* because the second radical possesses *kasr*. This rule exists on account of the difficulty of pronouncing the *wāw* when it is between a *yā'* and a *kasra*, and it is extended to words of the pattern *taf'ilu* on account of the formal resemblance. It is also elided in its infinitive form, which is of the pattern *fi'latun*, with the first rad-

أمـا الـواو فتحـذف مـن يَفْعِـلُ بكسر الـعين لثقـل الـواو بين الياء والـكسرة، وحُمـل نحـو تَفْعِـلُ على يَفْعِـلُ للمشـاكلة؛ ومـن مصـدره الذي على فِعْلَـةً بكسر الفـاء، نحـو «عِـدَةً/ وِعْـدَةً». وحذفـت مـن

ical possessing *kasr*, e.g., *ʿidatun* (promise), originally *wiʿdatun*. It is elided in *yaḍaʿu* (he places) because it is originally of the pattern *yafʿilu*,[1] [the *ḍād* being] vowelized with *fatḥ* for the sake of phonetic alleviation. It is not elided in *yūsiru* (he lives in easy circumstances) so as not to do injury to the word by eliding two letters.

As for *yāʾ*, it remains in all cases, with the exception that both it and *wāw* are converted to a *tāʾ* and assimilated when they occur as the first radical in the pattern *iftaʿala*, e.g., *ittaʿada* (he reached an agreement), originally *iwtaʿada*; and *ittasara* (he divided [the slaughtered camel]), originally *iytasara*.

The resemblant root occurs in eleven classes:

1. Class *Ḍaraba*: *waʿada* (to promise).
2. *Fataḥa*: *waḍaʿa* (to place).
3. *ʿAlima*: *wajila* (to be afraid).
4. *Ḥasuna*: *wajuha* (to be notable).
5. *Ḥasiba*: *wamiqa* (to love).
6. *Akrama*: *awʿada* (to promise).
7. *Inqaṭaʿa*: *nātara*.
8. *Ijtamaʿa*: *ittaʿada* (to reach an agreement).
9. *Iḥmarra*: *ījazza*.
10. *Iḥmārra*: *ījāzza*.
11. *Istakhraja*: *istawlada* (to render pregnant).

The modification of each class individually is as follows:

[1] Thus *yawḍiʿu*.

يَضَعُ لكونه على وزن يَفْعِلُ في الأصل[1] وفُتح للخفّة. ولم تحذف من يُوسِرُ لئلا يلزم إجحاف في الكلمة بحذف الحرفين.

وأما الياء فتثبت في الكل إلا أنها هي والواو إذا وقع كل منهما فاء اِفْتَعَلَ تقلب تاءً وتدغم، نحو «اتَّعَدَ/ اِوْتَعَدَ»، «اتَّسَرَ/ اِيْتَسَرَ».

يجيء من أحد عشر بابًا:

١- باب ضرب: وَعَدَ.
٢- فتح: وَضَعَ.
٣- علم: وَجِلَ.
٤- حسن: وَجُهَ.
٥- حسب: وَمِقَ.
٦- أكرم: أَوْعَدَ.
٧- انقطع: نَاتَرَ.
٨- اجتمع: اِتَّعَدَ.
٩- احمرّ: اِيجَزَّ.
١٠- احمارّ: اِيجَازَّ.
١١- استخرج: اِسْتَوْلَدَ.

إعلال كل باب على حدة:

[١] أي يَوْضِعُ.

[1. The Resemblant Class *Ḍaraba*]

Class *Ḍaraba* is [modified to be] like *waʿada* / *yaʿidu* (he promises), whose original form is *yawʿidu* of the pattern *yafʿilu* as in *yaḍribu* (he hits). The *wāw* is elided due to the difficulty of pronouncing it between a *yāʾ* and a *kasra*. This rule is extended to cases like *taʿidu* (she promises / you [m.] promise) on account of the formal resemblance.

For its infinitive noun, one says *ʿidatun* (promising), originally *wiʿdatun*, of the pattern *fiʿlatun*. Its *kasra* is transferred to the second radical, and the *wāw* is elided in conformity with its elision in the verb; thus the word becomes *ʿidatun*, of the pattern *ʿilatun*.

For the second-person imperative, one says *ʿid* (promise), originally *iwʿid* of the pattern *ifʿil* as in *iḍrib* (hit). This is modified through conversion and then double elision, becoming *ʿid* like *ʿil*.

For the second-person prohibitive, one says *lā taʿid* (do not promise), originally *lā tawʿid* of the pattern *lā tafʿil* as in *lā taḍrib* (do not hit). This is modified through elision, in accordance with the modification of *lā yaʿid*.

For the active participle, one says *wāʿidun* (one that promises), and for the passive participle *mawʿūdun* (one that is promised).

For the nouns of time and place: *mawʿidun* (place/time of promising), of the pattern *mafʿilun*.

For the noun of instrument: *mīʿadun* (instrument of promising), originally *miwʿadun*, of the pattern *mifʿalun*. The *wāw* is converted to a *yāʾ* because whenever the *wāw* is vowelless and the preceding letter possesses *kasr*, the *wāw* is converted to a *yāʾ*.

[١. باب ضرب من المثال]

باب ضرب نحو: وَعَدَ/ يَعِدُ؛ أصله يَوْعِدُ على وزن يَفْعِلُ كيضرب؛ حذفت الواو لثقلها بين الياء والكسر. وحُمل عليه نحو تَعِدُ للمشاكلة.

تقول في مصدره: عِدَةً؛ أصلها وِعْدَةً على وزن فِعْلَةً؛ نقل كسرها إلى العين وحذفت لحذفها من فعلها فصار عدة على وزن عِلَةً.

وتقول في أمر الحاضر: عِدْ؛ أصله اِوْعِدْ على وزن اِفْعِلْ كاضرب؛ إعلاله بالقلب والحذفين فصار عِدْ كعِلْ.

وفي نهي الحاضر: لا تَعِدْ؛ أصله لا تَوْعِدْ على وزن لا تَفْعِلْ كلا تضرب؛ إعلاله بالحذف حملًا على لا يعد.

وتقول في اسم الفاعل: وَاعِدٌ، واسم المفعول: مَوْعُودٌ.

وفي اسم الزمان والمكان: مَوْعِدٌ على وزن مَفْعِلٌ.

وفي اسم الآلة: مِيعَدٌ؛ أصله مِوْعَدٌ على وزن مِفْعَلٌ؛ قلبت الواو ياءً لأن الواو إذا كانت ساكنة وما قبلها مكسورًا قلبت ياءً.

[2. The Resemblant Class *Fataḥa*]

Class *Fataḥa* is [modified to be] like *waḍaʿa* / *yaḍaʿu* (he places). The *wāw* is elided in *yaḍaʿu*, for it is originally *yawḍiʿu*, but it is vowelized with *fatḥ* on account of the phonetic heaviness of the guttural letter.

[٢. باب فتح من المثال]

باب فتح نحو: وَضَعَ/ يَضَعُ؛ حذفت الواو من يضع لأنها كانت في الأصل يَوْضَعُ فتحت لثقل حرف الحلق.

Its imperative form is *ḍaʿ* (place); its prohibitive *lā taḍaʿ* (do not place); its active participle *wāḍiʿun* (one that places); its passive participle *mawḍūʿun* (thing that is placed); and its noun of time, noun of place, and mimated infinitive *mawḍiʿun* (place/time of placing, placing).

Its noun of instrument is *mīḍaʿun* (instrument of placing), originally *miwḍaʿun* of the pattern *mifʿalun*. The *wāw* is converted to a *yāʾ* because it is vowelless and the preceding letter possesses *kasr*.

وصيغة الأمر منه: ضَعْ؛ والنهي: لا تَضَعْ؛ واسم الفاعل: وَاضِعٌ؛ واسم المفعول: مَوضُوعٌ؛ واسم الزمان والمكان والمصدر الميمي: مَوْضِعٌ.

واسم الآلة: مِيضَعٌ؛ أصله مِوْضَعٌ على وزن مِفْعَلٌ؛ قلبت الواو ياءً لسكونها وانكسار ما قبلها.

[3. The Resemblant Class *ʿAlima*]

Class *ʿAlima* is [modified to be] like *wajila* / *yawjalu* (he is afraid).

Its imperative is *ījal* (be afraid), originally *iwjal* of the pattern *ifʿal* as in *iʿlam*. The *wāw* is converted to a *yāʾ* because it is vowelless and the preceding letter possesses *kasr*.

Its prohibitive is *lā tawjal* (do not be afraid); its active participle *wājilun* (one that is afraid); its passive participle *mawjūlun* (thing that is feared); and its noun of time, noun of place, and mimated infinitive *mawjilun* (place/time of being afraid, being afraid).

[٣. باب علم من المثال]

باب علم نحو: وَجِلَ/ يَوْجَلُ.

والأمر منه: اِيجَلْ؛ أصله اِوْجَلْ على وزن اِفْعَلْ كاعلم؛ قلبت الواو ياء لسكونها وانكسار ما قبلها.

والنهي: لا تَوْجَلْ؛ واسم الفاعل: وَاجِلٌ؛ واسم المفعول: مَوْجُولٌ؛ واسم الزمان والمكان والمصدر الميمي: مَوْجِلٌ.

[4. The Resemblant Class *Ḥasuna*]

Class *Ḥasuna* is [modified to be] like *wajuha* / *yawjuhu* (he is notable). For its participial, one says *wajīhun* (one that is notable). No other forms besides these three occur in this class,[47] since it signifies natures and dispositions.

[٤. باب حسن من المثال]

باب حسُن نحو: وَجُهَ/ يَوْجُهُ؛ تقول في الصفة المشبّهة: وَجِيهٌ. ولا يجيء من هذا الباب غير هذه ثلاثة لكونه من الطبائع.

[5. The Resemblant Class *Ḥasiba*]

Class *Ḥasiba* is [modified to be] like *wamiqa* / *yamiqu* / *miqatan* (to love), in analogy with *waʿada* / *yaʿidu* / *ʿidatan* (to promise).

[٥. باب حسب من المثال]

باب حسِب نحو: وَمِقَ/ يَمِقُ/ مِقَةً؛ كوَعَدَ/ يَعِدُ/ عِدَةً.

[٦. باب أكرم من المثال]

بـاب أكرم نحـو: أَوْعَـدَ/ يُوعِدُ. لـم تحذف الـواو لئلا يلزم الإجحـاف في كلمـة واحدة.

والأمـر منـه: أَوْعِـدْ؛ والنهي: لا تُوعِـدْ؛ واسـم الفاعـل: مُوعِـدٌ؛ وأسـماء المفعـول والزمـان والمكان والمصـدر المـيمي: مُوعَـدٌ.

[6. The Resemblant Class *Akrama*]

Class *Akrama* is [modified to be] like *awʿada / yūʿidu* (he promises). The *wāw* is not elided so as not to cause a double elision in one word.

Its imperative is *awʿid* (promise); its prohibitive *lā tūʿid* (do not promise); its active participle *mūʿidun* (one that promises); and its passive participle, noun of time, noun of place, and mimated infinitive *mūʿadun* (one that is promised, place/time of promising, promising).

[٧. باب انقطع من المثال]

بـاب انقطع نحـو: نَاتَـرَ/ يَنَاتِـرُ. أصل ناتـر اِنْوَتَـرَ على وزن اِنْفَعَـلَ كانقطع؛ نقلـت حركة الواو إلى النـون وقلبت الواو ألفًـا وحذفت همـزة الوصل للاسـتغناء عنها. وأصـل يناتر يَنْوَتِـرُ على وزن يَنْفَعِـلُ كينقطـع؛ نقلـت حركـة الـواو إلى النـون وقلبت الـواو ألفًا.

لا يجيء من هذا الباب غير الماضي والمضارع.

[7. The Resemblant Class *Inqaṭaʿa*]

Class *Inqaṭaʿa* is [modified to be] like *nātara / yanātiru. Nātara* is originally *inwatara* of the pattern *infaʿala* as in *inqaṭaʿa* (it was severed), but the vowel of the *wāw* is transferred to the *nūn*, the *wāw* is converted to an *alif*, and the connective *hamza* is elided because it is not necessary. *Yanātiru* is originally *yanwatiru* of the pattern *yanfaʿilu* as in *yanqaṭiʿu* (it is severed), but the vowel of the *wāw* is transferred to the *nūn* and the *wāw* is converted to an *alif*.

No other form besides the perfect and the imperfect occurs in this class.

[٨. باب اجتمع من المثال]

باب اجتمـع نحو: اِتَّعَدَ/ يَتَّعِـدُ؛ أصلهما اِوْتَعَـدَ/ يَوْتَعِدُ على وزن اِفْتَعَـلَ/ يَفْتَعِـلُ؛ قلبـت الـواو فيهما تـاءً وأدغمت في الثانيـة لأنه إذا كانت فـاء الافتعال واوًا أو يـاءً انقلبت تاءً وأُدغمـت في الثانية.

[8. The Resemblant Class *Ijtamaʿa*]

Class *Ijtamaʿa* is [modified to be] like *ittaʿada / yattaʿidu* (he reached/reaches an agreement), originally *iwtaʿada / yawtaʿidu* of the pattern *iftaʿala / yaftaʿilu*. The *wāw* in both instances is converted to a *tāʾ* and assimilated to the second *tāʾ*. This is because when the first radical in the class of *iftaʿala* is a *wāw* or a *yāʾ*, it is converted to a *tāʾ* and assimilated to the second *tāʾ*.

[9. The Resemblant Class *Iḥmarra*]

Class *Iḥmarra* is [modified to be] like *ījazza* / *yawjazzu*. *Ījazza* is originally *iwjazza* of the pattern *ifʿalla* as in *iḥmarra*. The *wāw* is converted to a *yāʾ* because it is vowelless and the preceding letter possesses *kasr*.

[٩. باب احمرّ من المثال]

بـاب احمـرّ نحـو: اِيجَـزَّ/ يَوْجَـزُّ؛ أصـل ايجـز اِوْجَـزَّ على وزن اِفْعَـلَّ كاحمـرّ؛ قلبـت الـواو يـاءً لسـكونها وانكسـار مـا قبلهـا.

[10. The Resemblant Class *Iḥmārra*]

Class *Iḥmārra* is [modified to be] like *ījāzza* / *yawjāzzu*. Its modification is exactly like those of the previous cases.

[١٠. باب احمارّ من المثال]

بـاب احمارّ نحـو: اِيجَازَّ/ يَوْجَـازُّ. والإعلال هنـا كإعلال ما قبله بلا فـرق بينهما.

No other forms besides the perfect and the imperfect occur in these last two classes, because they signify natures and dispositions.

لا يجيء منهمـا غير الماضي والمضـارع لكونهمـا مـن الطبائـع.

[11. The Resemblant Class *Istakhraja*]

Class *Istakhraja* is [modified to be] like *istawlada* / *yastawlidu* / *istīlādan* (rendering pregnant), originally *istiwlādan*. The *wāw* is converted to a *yāʾ* because it is vowelless and the preceding letter possesses *kasr*.

[١١. باب استخرج من المثال]

بـاب اسـتخرج نحـو: اِسْـتَوْلَدَ/ يَسْـتَوْلِدُ/ اِسْتِـيلَادًا؛ أصله اِسْـتِوْلَادًا؛ قلبت الواو ياءً لسـكونها وانكسـار مـا قبلها.

III. The Hollow Root

The third of the seven types of irregular roots is that whose second radical is weak, and it is termed the hollow root. The definition of the hollow root, its classes, and its modification in the perfect and so on until the last of the nine derivatives are as follows.

(٣) الأجوف

الثالث من الأقسام السبعة المعتلّة معتلّ العين ويقال له الأجوف: تعريفه، أبوابه، إعلالها ماضيًا ثم فثم إلى آخر المشتقّات التسعة

The hollow root is that whose second radical is a *wāw* or a *yāʾ*.

When the *wāw* or *yāʾ* is vowelized and the preceding letter possesses *fatḥ*, the *wāw* or *yāʾ* is converted to an *alif*, e.g., *qāla* (he said), originally *qawala*, and

هو ما كان عين فعله واوًا أو ياءً.

والـواو والياء تقلبـان ألفًـا إذا تحرّكتـا وانفتـح مـا قبلهمـا، نحـو «قَـالَ/ قَـوَلَ» و«بَـاعَ/ بَيَـعَ». وفي «قُلْـنَ»

bāʿa (he sold), originally *bayaʿa*. In the uniform derivatives *qulna* (they [f.] said), *biʿna* (they [f.] sold), *khifna* (they [f.] were afraid), and so on, the *wāw* or *yāʾ* is converted to an *alif*, then the *alif* is elided due to the impermissible convergence of two vowelless letters,[48] and then the first radical is vowelized with *ḍamm* if the second radical was originally a *wāw*—except in *khāfa* (he was afraid)[49]—and vowelized with *kasr* if the second radical was originally a *yāʾ*, to indicate [the original letter], e.g., *qulna* and *biʿna*. In *khāfa*, the first radical is vowelized with *kasr*, as *khifna*, to indicate that the second radical [originally] possessed *kasr*.

When the *wāw* or *yāʾ* is preceded by a vowelless sound letter, its vowel is transferred to that letter, e.g., *yaqūlu* (he says), *yabīʿu* (he sells), and *yakhāfu* (he is afraid).[1]

When either is succeeded by a vowelless letter, it is elided, e.g., *lam yaqul* (he did not say), *lam yabiʿ* (he did not sell), and *lam yakhaf* (he was not afraid). It is retained when that letter becomes vowelized, e.g., *lam yaqūlā* (they two [m.] did not say), *lam yabīʿā* (they two [m.] did not sell), *lam yakhāfā* (they two [m.] were not afraid), and *la-taqūlanna* (you [m.] will certainly say) with the emphatic *nūn*.

In the active participle, the *wāw* or *yāʾ* is converted to a *hamza* because it is preceded by an added *alif*, e.g., *qāʾilun* (one that says), *bāʾiʿun* (one that sells), and *khāʾifun* (one that is afraid), originally *qāwilun*, *bāyiʿun*, and *khāwifun*, but the *wāw* or the *yāʾ* was converted to a *hamza* because it was preceded by an added *alif*.

The hollow root occurs in nine classes:

1. Class *Naṣara*: [*qāla*] (*qawala*) (to say).
2. *Ḍaraba*: [*bāʿa*] (*bayaʿa*) (to sell).
3. *ʿAlima*: [*khāfa*] (*khawifa*) (to be afraid).
4. *Akrama*: [*ajāba*] (*ajwaba*) (to answer).

[1] Note that the *wāw* in *yakhāfu* is converted to an *alif* as will be explained below by Allah's will.

و«بِعْـنَ» و«خِفْـنَ» إلى آخـره تقـلبن ألفًـا ثـم تحـذف الألـف لالتقـاء السـاكنين على غير حـدِّه، ثـم تضـمّ الفـاء في الـواوي سـوى «خَـافَ» وتكسر في اليائي دلالـةً عليهمـا، نحـو «قُلْـنَ» و«بِعْـنَ». وفي «خَـافَ» تكسر نحـو «خِفْـنَ» ليـدلّ على كسر عين الفعـل.

وإذا كان قبلهمـا حـرف صحيـح سـاكن نقلـت حركتهمـا إليـه، نحـو «يَقُـولُ» و«يَبِيـعُ» و«يَخَـافُ».[١]

وتسـقطان إذا سكـن مـا بعدهمـا، نحـو «لـم يَقُـلْ»، و«لـم يَبِـعْ»، «لـم يَخَـفْ». وتثبتـان إذا تحـرّك، نحـو «لـم يَقُـولَا» و«لـم يَبِيعَـا» و«لـم يَخَافَـا» و«لَتَقُولَـنَّ» بنـون التأكيـد.

وفي اسـم الفاعـل تقلبـان همـزةً لوقوعهمـا بعـد الألـف الزائـدة، نحـو «قَائِـلٌ، بَائِـعٌ، خَائِـفٌ»؛ أصلهـا «قَـاوِلٌ، بَايِـعٌ، خَـاوِفٌ»؛ قلبتـا همـزةً لوقوعهمـا بعـد الألـف الزائـدة.

يأتي من تسعة أبواب:

١- باب نصر: [قَالَ] (قَوَلَ).

٢- ضرب: [بَاعَ] (بَيَعَ).

٣- علم: [خَافَ] (خَوِفَ).

٤- أكرم: [أَجَابَ] (أَجْوَبَ).

[١] غير أن الـواو الذي في «يَخَـافُ» تقلـب ألفًـا كمـا سـيأتي بيانـه إن شـاء الله.

5. *Inqaṭaʿa*: [*innāla*] (*innawala*).
6. *Ijtamaʿa*: [*ikhtāra*] (*ikhtayara*) (to choose).
7. *Istakhraja*: [*istaqāma*] (*istaqwama*) (to straighten up).
8. *Daḥraja*: [*marāḥa*] (*marwaḥa*).
9. *Iqshaʿarra*: [*bādarra*] (*ibwadarra*).

Their modification, i.e., the modification of classes with hollow roots, is as follows:

[*First Arrangement of the Modification of the Hollow Root*]

[The Hollow Perfect]

In the perfect tense, they are modified (1) through conversion or (2) through conversion, elision, and then conversion, as in

1. *qāla* (he said), a perfect tense verb that is originally *qawala* of the pattern *faʿala* as in *naṣara* (he helped). This is modified through conversion because the *wāw* is vowelized and the preceding letter possesses *fatḥ*.
2. in the feminine plural and the forms that follow:[50] *qulna* (they [f.] said) and *qulta* (you [m.] said), originally *qawalna* and *qawalta*, respectively. They are modified through conversion, elision, and then the vowelizing of the first radical with *ḍamm* to indicate the elision of the *wāw*.

Examples like *qāla*: *bāʿa* (he sold), *khāfa* (he was afraid), *innāla*, *ikhtāra* (he chose).

As for *ajāba* (he answered), *istaqāma* (he straightened up), and *marāḥa*, they are modified through transfer and conversion because the *wāw* is vowelized and the preceding letter lacks a vowel, as in *ajwaba*, *istaqwama*, and *marwaḥa*.

٥- انقطع: [انَّالَ] (اِنَّوَلَ)[١٥].
٦- اجتمع: [اخْتَارَ] (اِخْتَيَرَ).
٧- استخرج: [استَقَامَ] (اِسْتَقْوَمَ).
٨- دحرج: [مَرَاحَ] (مَرْوَحَ).
٩- اقشعرّ: [بَادَرَّ] (اِبْوَدَرَّ).

إعلالها، أي إعلال أبواب الأجوف:

[الوجه الأول في إعلال الأجوف]

[الماضي من الأجوف]

إعلالها ماضيًا (١) بالقلب، (٢) وبالقلب والحذف والقلب نحو:

١- قَالَ؛ فعل ماض أصله قَوَلَ على وزن فَعَلَ كنصر؛ إعلاله بالقلب لتحرك الواو وانفتاح ما قبلها.
٢- وفي الجمع المؤنث وما بعده: قُلْنَ/ قُلْتَ/... أصلها قَوَلْنَ/ قَوَلْتَ/... إعلالها بالقلب والحذف ثم ضم فاء الفعل ليدل على حذف الواو.

كـ«قال»: بَاعَ، خَافَ، اِنَّالَ، اِخْتَارَ.

أما أَجَابَ واسْتَقَامَ ومَرَاحَ فإعلالها بالنقل والقلب لتحرك الواو وسكون ما قبلها، نحو أَجْوَبَ واسْتَقْوَمَ ومَرْوَحَ.

However, the modification of *bādarra* is through transfer and conversion and then elision. For it is originally *ibwadarra* of the pattern *ifʿalalla* as in *iqshaʿarra* (he shuddered), but the vowel of the *wāw* is transferred to the preceding letter since it lacks a vowel, then the *wāw* is converted to an *alif*, and then the connective *hamza* is elided because it is not necessary.

[The Hollow Imperfect]

In the imperfect tense, they are modified (1) through transfer, (2) through assimilation and conversion, or (3) through transfer and elision, as in

1. *yaqūlu* (he says), an imperfect tense verb that is originally *yaqwulu* of the pattern *yafʿulu* as in *yanṣuru* (he helps). This is modified through transfer because the *wāw* is preceded by a vowelless letter; thus it becomes *yaqūlu*. Examples like *yaqūlu*: *yabīʿu* (he sells), *yakhāfu* (he is afraid), *yujību* (he answers), *yastaqīmu* (he straightens up), *yumarīḥu*, *yabādirru*.
2. *yannālu*, originally *yannawilu* of the pattern *yanfaʿilu* as in *yanqaṭiʿu* (it is severed). Through assimilation and conversion, because the second radical is vowelized and the preceding letter possesses *fatḥ*, this becomes *yannālu*. Example like *yannālu*: *yakhtāru* (he chooses)—only, the conversion in the former occurs after assimilation, unlike in the latter.
3. As for the modification of the feminine plural and the forms that follow, this occurs through transfer because of the vowelized pronominal suffix and then elision due to the convergence of two vowelless letters, e.g., *yaqulna* (they [f.] say), *yabiʿna* (they [f.] sell), *yakhafna* (they [f.] are afraid), [*yujibna* (they [f.] answer)], *yastaqimna* (they [f.] straighten up), and *yumariḥna*, originally *yaqwulna*, *yabyiʿna*, *yakhwafna*, *yujwibna*, *yastaqwimna*, and *yumarwiḥna*.

غير أن إعلال بَـادَرَّ بالنقـل والقلـب ثـم الحـذف إذ أصلـه اِبْوَدَرَّ على وزن اِفْعَلَلَّ كاقشعرّ؛ فنقلـت حركة الواو إلى مـا قبلها لسـكونه ثـم قلبت الـواو ألفًـا فحذفت همزة الوصل للاستغناء عنها.

[المضارع من الأجوف]

إعلالها مضارعًا (١) بالنقل، (٢) وبالإدغام والقلب، (٣) وبالنقل والحذف[١٦] نحو:

١- يَقُـولُ؛ فعل مضـارع أصلـه يَقْـوُلُ على وزن يَفْعُلُ كينصر؛ إعـلاله بالنقـل لسـكون مـا قبـل الـواو فبالإعلال صـار يقول. كـ«يقـول»: يَبِيـعُ، يَخَافُ، يُجِيـبُ، يَسْتَقِيمُ، يُمَرِيـحُ، يَبَادِرُّ.

٢- ويَنَّـالُ؛ أصلـه يَنْنَـوِلُ على وزن يَنْفَعِـلُ كينقطـع؛ وبـالإدغام والقلب لتحـرك العين وانفتـاح ما قبله صـار ينّـال. كـ«ينّـال»: يَخْتَـارُ؛ إلا أن القلـب في الأول بعـد الإدغام دون الثـاني.

٣- وأمـا الإعـلال في الجمع المؤنـث وما بعـده فبالنقل لاتصـال الضمير المرفـوع المتحـرك بهمـا والحذف لالتقـاء السـاكنين، نحـو: يَقُلْـنَ، يَبِعْـنَ، يَخَفْـنَ، [يُجِبْنَ]، يَسْتَقِمْنَ، يُمَرِحْنَ؛ أصلها يَقْوُلْـنَ، يَبْيِعْنَ، يَخْوَفْـنَ، يُجْوِبْـنَ، يَسْـتَقْوِمْنَ، يُمَرْوِحْنَ.

Two exceptions are *yannalna* and *yakhtarna* (they [f.] choose), which are modified through conversion and elision because the second radical is preceded by a letter possessing *fatḥ* and because of the consecutive occurrence of two vowelless letters, as in *yannālna* and *yakhtārna*.

إلا يَنَّلْـنَ ويَخْتَرْنَ؛ فإعلالهما بالقلب والحذف لانفتـاح مـا قبـل الـعين والتقـاء السـاكنين، نحـو يَنَّالْـنَ ويَخْتَارْنَ.

Another exception is *yabādirirna*, which is modified through transfer and conversion because the second radical is preceded by a vowelless letter, as in *yabwadrirna*.

وإلا[١٧] يَبَـادِرِنَ؛ فإعـلاله بالنقـل والقلـب لسـكون مـا قبـل العـين، نحـو يَبْـوَدْرِرْنَ.

[The Hollow Imperative]

In the imperative, they are modified through elision and addition and then transfer and double elision according to the Kufans, becoming like *qul* (say), a second-person imperative (also termed an *imperative proper*) that is originally *uqwul* of the pattern *ufʿul* as in *unṣur* (help), [derived from] *taqūlu* (you [m.] say). The latter is modified through the elision of the imperfect tense prefix and the addition of the connective *hamza* to accommodate the vowelless beginning. It thus becomes *uqwul*, of the pattern *ufʿul* as in *unṣur*. It is then modified through transfer and double elision and becomes *qul*, of the pattern *ful*. Examples like *qul*: *biʿ* (sell), *khaf* (be afraid), *ajib* (answer), *innal*, *ikhtar* (choose), *istaqim* (straighten up), *mariḥ*, *bādirri*.

[الأمر من الأجوف]

إعلالها أمـرًا بالحـذف والزيـادة ثـم بالنقـل والحـذفين عنـد الكوفـيين نحـو: قُـلْ؛ أمـر الحاضر ويقـال له الأمـر بالصيغـة أصلـه اقْـوُلْ على وزن افْعُـلْ كانصر مـن تَقُـولُ؛ إعلاله بحـذف حـرف المضارعـة وزيـادة الهمـزة للوصـول إلى الابتـداء بالسـاكن فصـار اقْـوُلْ على وزن افْعُـلْ كانصر، ثـم اعتـلّ بالنقـل والحـذفين فصـار قُـلْ على وزن فُـلْ. كـ«قـل»: بِـعْ، خَـفْ، أَجِـبْ، انَّـلْ، اخْتَرْ، اسْـتَقِمْ، مَـرِحْ، بَـادِرِّ.

[The Hollow Prohibitive]

In the prohibitive, they are modified through transfer and elision as in *lā taqul* (do not say), a second-person prohibitive that is originally *lā taqwul* of the pattern *lā tafʿul* as in *lā tanṣur*. This is modified through transfer because the *wāw* is preceded by a vowelless letter and then through elision due to the convergence of vowelless letters. Examples like *lā taqul*: *lā tabiʿ* (do not sell), *lā takhaf* (do not be afraid), *lā tujib* (do not answer), *lā tastaqim* (do not straighten up), *lā tumariḥ*.

[النهي من الأجوف]

إعلالها نهيًـا بالنقـل والحـذف نحـو: لا تَقُـلْ؛ نهي الحاضر أصلـه لا تَقْـوُلْ على وزن لا تَفْعُـلْ كلا تـنصر؛ إعلاله بالنقـل لكـون مـا قبـل الـواو سـاكنًا والحـذف لالتقـاء السـاكنين. كـ«لا تقـل»: لا تَبِـعْ، لا تَخَـفْ، لا تُجِبْ، لا تَسْـتَقِمْ، لا تُمَـرِحْ.

[The Hollow Active Participle]

In the active participle, they are modified through conversion as in *qā'ilun* (one that says), *bā'i'un* (one that sells), and *khā'ifun* (one that is afraid), instances of the active participle that are originally *qāwilun*, *bāyiʿun*, and *khāwifun*, of the pattern *fāʿilun* as in *nāṣirun* (one that helps), *ḍāribun* (one that hits), and *ʿālimun* (one that knows).

Simple triliteral classes are modified through conversion, that is, converting the *wāw* or *yā'* to a *hamza* because they are preceded by an added *alif*. Classes that are not simple triliterals are patterned after the active imperfect with the exception that you replace the imperfect tense prefix with a *mīm* possessing *ḍamm*, e.g., *mujībun* (one that answers), *munnawilun* (one that gives), and *mustaqīmun* (one that straightens up) in relation to *yujību* (he answers), *yannawilu* (he gives), and *yastaqīmu* (he straightens up), respectively.

[اسم الفاعل من الأجوف]

إعلالها اسم الفاعل بالقلب نحو: قَائِلٌ، بَائِعٌ، خَائِفٌ؛ اسم الفاعل أصلها قَاوِلٌ، بَايِعٌ، خَاوِفٌ على وزن فَاعِلٌ كناصر، ضارب، عالم.

إعلالها ثلاثيًا مجرّدًا بالقلب أي بقلب الواو والياء همزة لوقوعها بعد ألف زائدة. ومن غير الثلاثي المجرّد يكون على وزن الفعل المضارع المعلوم غير أنك تبدّل حرف المضارعة بالميم المضمومة، نحو: مُجِيبٌ، مُنَّوِلٌ، مُسْتَقِيمٌ كيُجِيبُ، يَنَّوِلُ، يَسْتَقِيمُ.

[The Hollow Passive Participle]

In the passive participle, they are modified (1) through transfer and elision or (2) through transfer, elision, and double conversion, as in

1. *maqūlun* (thing that is said), *makhūfun* (thing that is feared), and *mabīʿun* (thing that is sold), instances of the passive participle that are originally *maqwūlun*, *makhwūfun*, and *mabyūʿun*, of the pattern *mafʿūlun* as in *manṣūrun* (one that is helped), *maʿlūmun* (thing that is known), and *maḍrūbun* (one that is hit), respectively. These are modified through transfer because the *wāw* or *yā'* is vowelized and the preceding letter lacks a vowel and then through elision due to the convergence of vowelless letters. They become *maqūlan*, *makhūfan*, and *mabūʿan*.

[اسم المفعول من الأجوف]

إعلالها اسم المفعول (١) بالنقل والحذف، (٢) وبهما والقلبين نحو:

١- مَقُولٌ، مَخُوفٌ، مَبِيعٌ؛ اسم المفعول أصلها مَقْوُولٌ، مَخْوُوفٌ، مَبْيُوعٌ على وزن مَفْعُولٌ كمنصور، معلوم، مضروب؛ إعلالها بالنقل لتحرّك الواو والياء وسكون ما قبلهما والحذف لالتقاء الساكنين فصارت مقولًا، مخوفًا، مَبُوعًا.

2. …then,[51] in *mabūʿun*, the *ḍamma* of the letter preceding the *wāw* is converted into a *kasra* to indicate the elision of the *yāʾ*, and then the *wāw* is converted into a *yāʾ* because it is vowelless and the preceding letter possesses *kasr*. It thus becomes *mabīʿun*, of the pattern *mafīlun*.

٢- …ثـم قلبـت ضمّـة مـا قبـل الـواو في مَبُـوعٌ كـسرةً لتـدلّ على حـذف اليـاء ثـم انقلبـت الـواو يـاءً لسـكونها وانكسـار مـا قبلهـا فصـار مَبِيعٌ على وزن مَفِيـلٌ[١٨].

[*Second Arrangement of the Modification of the Hollow Root*]

[الوجه الثاني في إعلال الأجوف]

The following is the modification of the hollow root presented differently, that is, by modifying classes individually rather than collectively.

إعلال أبـواب الأجـوف على وجـه آخـر أي إعلال كل باب منهـا على حـدة لا مجتمعة:

[1. The Hollow Class *Naṣara*]

[١. باب نصر من الأجوف]

[Perfect] In the perfect tense, Class *Naṣara* with hollow roots is modified (1) through conversion or (2) through conversion, elision, and conversion, as in

1. *qāla* (he said), a perfect tense verb whose original form is *qawala* of the pattern *faʿala* as in *naṣara* (he helped). This is modified through conversion, that is, converting the *wāw* to an *alif* because it is vowelized and the preceding letter possesses *fatḥ*.
2. *qulna* (they [f.] said), a third-person feminine plural that is originally *qawalna* of the pattern *faʿalna* as in *naṣarna* (they [f.] helped). This is modified through conversion, elision, and then conversion of the *fatḥa* of the first radical to a *ḍamma* to indicate the elision of the *wāw*. That is, the *wāw* is converted to an *alif* because it is vowelized and the preceding letter possesses *fatḥ*, the *alif* is elided due to the convergence of two vowelless letters, and the first radical is vowelized with *ḍamm* to indicate the elision of the *wāw*.

The same applies to *qulta* (you [m.] said) and *qultumā* (you two said) and so on until *qultu* (I said) and *qulnā* (we said).

[الماضي] إعلال بـاب نصر أجـوف ماضيًـا (١) بالقلب، (٢) وبالقلـب والحـذف ثـم القلب نحو:

١- قَالَ؛ فعـل ماض أصلـه قَـوَلَ على وزن فَعَلَ كنصر؛ إعـلاله بالقلـب أي بقلـب الـواو ألفًـا لتحرّكهـا وانفتـاح مـا قبلها.

٢- وقُلْـنَ؛ جمـع المؤنثـة الغائبة أصلـه قَوَلْـنَ على وزن فَعَلْـنَ كنـصرن؛ إعـلاله بالقلب والحـذف وقلب فتحة الفاء ضمـةً لتدلّ على حذف الـواو أي بقلب الـواو ألفًـا لتحركهـا وانفتـاح مـا قبلهـا وحـذف الألـف لالتقـاء السـاكنين وضـمّ الفـاء ليـدلّ على حـذف الواو.

وكذا حكـم قُلْتَ/ قُلْتُمَا… إلى قُلْتُ/ قُلْنَا.

[Imperfect] In the imperfect tense, it is modified (1) through transfer or (2) through transfer and elision as in

1. *yaqūlu* (he says), an imperfect tense verb that is originally *yaqwulu* of the pattern *yafʿulu* as in *yanṣuru* (he helps). This is modified through transfer alone.
2. *yaqulna* (they [f.] say), a third-person feminine plural imperfect that is originally *yaqwulna* of the pattern *yafʿulna* as in *yanṣurna* (they [f.] help). This is modified through transfer and elision. That is, the vowel of the *wāw* is transferred to the preceding letter and the *wāw* is elided due to the convergence of two vowelless letters. *Taqulna* (you all [f.] say) is like *yaqulna*.

[Imperative] In the second-person imperative, it is modified through transfer and double elision as in *qul* (say), a second-person imperative (also termed an *imperative proper*) whose original form according to the Kufans is *uqwul* of the pattern *ufʿul* as in *unṣur* (help); this is modified through transfer and double elision. According to the Basrans, it is originally *li-taqwul*, and it is modified through elision and the addition of the connective *hamza*; that is, the imperative *lām* and the imperfect tense prefix were elided due to frequent use, and the connective *hamza* was added because a word cannot begin with a vowelless letter. Then it was modified through transfer and double elision and consequently became *qul*, of the pattern *ful*.

[Prohibitive] In the second-person prohibitive, it is modified through transfer and elision as in *lā taqul* (do not say), a second-person prohibitive that is originally *lā taqwul* of the pattern *lā tafʿul* as in *lā tanṣur* (do not help). Through transfer and elision—that is, transferring the vowel of the *wāw* to the preceding letter because the former is vowelized and the latter lacks a vowel and then eliding

[المضارع] إعلاله مضارعا (١) بالنقل، (٢) وبالنقل والحذف نحو:

١- يَقُولُ؛ فعل مضارع أصله يَقْوُلُ على وزن يَفْعُلُ كينصر؛ إعلاله بالنقل فقط.

٢- ويَقُلْنَ؛ فعل مضارع جمع المؤنثة الغائبة أصله يَقْوُلْنَ على وزن يَفْعُلْنَ كينصرن؛ إعلاله بالنقل والحذف أي نقل حركة الواو إلى ما قبلها وحذف الواو لالتقاء الساكنين. كـ«يَقُلْنَ» تَقُلْنَ.

[الأمر] إعلاله أمر الحاضر بالنقل والحذفين نحو: قُلْ؛ أمر الحاضر ويقال له الأمر بالصيغة أصله عند الكوفيين اقْوُلْ على وزن افْعُلْ كانصر؛ إعلاله بالنقل والحذفين. وعند البصريين لِتَقْوُلْ؛ فإعلاله بالحذف وزيادة الهمزة أي حذف لام الأمر مع حرف المضارعة لكثرة الاستعمال وزيادة همزة الوصل لاستحالة الابتداء بالساكن. ثم اعتلّ بالنقل والحذفين فصار بعد النقل والحذفين قُلْ على وزن فُلْ.

[النهي] إعلاله نهي الحاضر بالنقل والحذف نحو: لا تَقُلْ؛ نهي الحاضر أصله لا تَقْوُلْ على وزن لا تَفْعُلْ كلا تنصر؛ فبالنقل والحذف أي نقل حركة الواو إلى ما

the *wāw* due to the convergence of two vowelless letters—this becomes *lā taqul.*

قبلهـا لتحرّكها وسـكون مـا قبلها وحـذف الـواو لالتقاء السـاكنين صـار لا تقل.

[Active Participle] In the active participle, it is modified through conversion as in *qāʾilun* (one that says), an active participle that is originally *qāwilun* of the pattern *fāʿilun* as in *nāṣirun* (one that helps). Through conversion—that is, converting the *wāw* to a *hamza* because it is preceded by an added *alif*—this becomes *qāʾilun.*

[اسـم الفاعـل] إعلاله اسـم الفاعـل بالقلـب نحـو: قَائِلٌ؛ اسـم الفاعـل أصلـه قَـاوِلٌ على وزن فَاعِـلٌ كنـاصر؛ فالقلـب أي قلـب الـواو همـزةً لوقوعهـا بعـد الألـف الزائـدة صـار قائـل.

[Passive Participle] In the passive participle, it is modified through transfer and elision as in *maqūlun* (thing that is said), a passive participle that is originally *maqwūlun* of the pattern *mafʿūlun* as in *manṣūrun* (one that is helped). Through transfer and elision this becomes *maqūlun,* of the pattern *mafūlun.*

[اسـم المفعـول] إعلاله اسـم المفعـول بالنقـل والحـذف نحو: مَقُولٌ؛ اسـم المفعـول أصلـه مَقْـوُولٌ على وزن مَفْعُولٌ كمنصـور؛ فبالنقـل والحذف صـار مقـول على وزن مَفُولٌ.

[Noun of Time; Noun of Place; Mimated Infinitive] In the nouns of time and place and the mimated infinitive, it is modified though transfer and conversion as in *maqālun* (place/time of saying, saying), a noun of time and of place and a mimated infinitive, originally *maqwalun* of the pattern *mafʿalun* as in *manṣarun* (place/time of helping, helping). Through transfer and conversion this becomes *maqālun,* of the pattern *mafaʿlun.*

[اسم الزمان، اسم المكان، المصدر الميمي] إعلاله اسمي الزمان والمكان والمصدر الميمي بالنقل والقلب نحو: مَقَالٌ؛ اسمي الزمان والمكان والمصدر الميمي أصله مَقْوَلٌ على وزن مَفْعَلٌ كمنصر؛ فبالنقل والقلب صار مقال على وزن مَفَعْلٌ.

[2. The Hollow Class *Ḍaraba*]

[٢. باب ضرب من الأجوف]

[Perfect] In the perfect tense, Class *Ḍaraba* with hollow roots is modified through conversion as in *bāʿa* (he sold), a perfect tense verb that is originally *bayaʿa* of the pattern *faʿala* as in *ḍaraba* (he hit). Through conversion this becomes *bāʿa,* of the pattern *faʿla.*

[المـاضي] إعـلال باب ضرب أجـوف ماضيًـا بالقلب[١٩] نحـو: بَـاعَ؛ فعل مـاض أصله بَيَـعَ على وزن فَعَـلَ كضرب؛ فبالقلب[٢٠] صـار بـاع على وزن فَعْلَ.

[Imperfect] In the imperfect tense, it is modified as in *yabīʿu* (he sells), an imperfect tense verb that is originally *yabyiʿu* of the pattern *yafʿilu* as in *yaḍribu* (he hits). This is modified through transfer because the *yāʾ* is vowelized and the preceding letter possesses *kasr.*

[المضـارع] إعلاله مضـارعًا نحـو: يَبِيعُ؛ فعـل مضـارع أصلـه يَبْيِـعُ على وزن يَفْعِـلُ كـيضرب؛ إعلاله بالنقـل لتحـرّك الياء وانكسـار مـا قبلهـا.

[Imperative] In the imperative, it is modified as in *biʿ*, a second-person imperative that is originally *ibyiʿ* (sell) of the pattern *ifʿil* as in *iḍrib* (hit). This is modified through transfer and double elision and becomes *biʿ*, of the pattern *fil*.

[الأمـر] إعلاله أمـر الحاضر نحو: بِعْ؛ أمـر الحاضر أصله ابْيِعْ على وزن افْعِلْ كاضرب؛ إعلاله بالنقـل والحـذفين فصـار بِـعْ على وزن فِلْ.

[Prohibitive] In the prohibitive, it is modified as in *lā tabiʿ* (do not sell), a second-person prohibitive that is originally *lā tabyiʿ*. This is modified through transfer and elision and becomes *lā tabiʿ*, of the pattern *lā tafil*.

[النهي] إعلاله نهي الحاضر نحـو: لا تَبِـعْ؛ نهي الحاضر أصلـه لا تَبْيِـعْ؛ إعلاله بالنقـل والحذف فصـار لا تبع على وزن لا تَفِـلْ.

[Active Participle] In the active participle, it is modified as in *bāʾiʿun* (one that sells), an active participle that is originally *bāyiʿun*. This is modified through conversion to a *hamza* and becomes *bāʾiʿun*, of the pattern *fāʿilun*.

[اسـم الفاعـل] إعلاله اسـم الفاعـل نحـو: بَائِـعٌ؛ اسـم الفاعل أصلـه بَايِـعٌ؛ إعلاله بالقلب همزةً فصـار بائع على وزن فَاعِلٌ.

[Passive Participle] In the passive participle, it is modified as in *mabīʿun* (thing that is sold), a passive participle that is originally *mabyūʿun*, of the pattern *mafʿūlun*. This is modified through transfer, elision, and vowelizing the *bāʾ* with *kasr* to indicate the elision of the *yāʾ*; then the *wāw* is converted to a *yāʾ* because the preceding letter possesses *kasr*.

[اسـم المفعـول] إعلاله اسـم المفعـول نحـو: مَبِيعٌ؛ اسـم المفعـول أصلـه مَبْيُـوعٌ على وزن مَفْعُـولٌ؛ وإعلاله بالنقـل والحـذف وكسر الباء ليـدلّ على حـذف الياء ثـم انقلبـت الواو يـاءً لانكسـار مـا قبلها.

[Noun of Time; Noun of Place; Mimated Infinitive] In the nouns of time and place [and the mimated infinitive], it is modified as in *mabāʿun* (place/time of selling, selling), a noun of time and place and a mimated infinitive that is originally *mabyaʿun*. This is modified through transfer and conversion and becomes *mabāʿun*, of the pattern *mafaʿlun*.

[اسـم الزمـان، اسـم المكان، المصـدر المـيمي] إعلاله اسمي الزمـان والمكان [والمصـدر المـيمي] نحو: مَبَاعٌ؛ اسـما الزمـان والمكان والمصدر الميمي أصله مَبْيَعٌ؛ إعلاله بالنقل والقلـب فصـار مبـاع على وزن مَفْعَلٌ.

[3. The Hollow Class *ʿAlima*]

[٣. باب علم من الأجوف]

[Perfect] In the perfect tense, Class *ʿAlima* with hollow roots is modified (1) through conversion or (2) through conversion, elision, and then conversion, as in

[المـاضي] إعـلال معتـل العين من بـاب علـم[1] ماضيًا (١) بالقلـب، (٢) بالقلـب والحـذف ثـم القلب نحو:

1. *khāfa* (he was afraid), a perfect tense verb that is originally *khawifa*. This is modified through conversion.
2. For the uniform derivatives from the [third-person] feminine plural to the first-person [plural], one says *khifna* (they [f.] were afraid)...*khifnā* (we were afraid), originally *khawifna*...*khawifnā*, respectively. These are modified through conversion and elision and then the conversion of the *fatḥa* of the first radical to a *kasra* to indicate the [original] *kasra* of the second radical.

[Imperfect] In the imperfect tense, it is modified (1) through transfer and conversion or (2) through transfer, conversion, and elision, as in

1. *yakhāfu* (he is afraid), an imperfect tense verb that is originally *yakhwafu*. This is modified through transfer and conversion.
2. For the feminine plural, one says *yakhafna* / *takhafna* (they [f.] are afraid / you all [f.] are afraid), originally *yakhwafna* / *takhwafna*. These are modified through transfer, conversion, and elision.

[Imperative] In the imperative proper, it is modified through elision, the addition of the connective *hamza*, transfer, and double elision as in *khaf* (be afraid), an imperative that is originally *ikhwaf* of the pattern *ifʿal* as in *iʿlam* (know). According to the Basrans, *ikhwaf* is derived from the original *li-takhwaf*, whose imperative *lām* and imperfect tense prefix were elided due to frequent use, and the connective *hamza* was added, such that it became *ikhwaf*. Then through transfer, conversion, and double elision this became *khaf*, of the pattern *fal*.

١- خَافَ؛ فعل ماضٍ أصله خَوِفَ؛ إعلاله بالقلب.

٢- تقول في جمع المؤنث إلى المتكلم: خِفْنَ... خِفْنَا؛ أصلهما خَوِفْنَ... خَوِفْنَا؛ إعلالهما بالقلب والحذف[٢٢] ثم قلب فتحة الفاء كسرةً لتدلّ على كسرة العين.

[المضارع] إعلاله مضارعًا (١) بالنقل والقلب، (٢) بالنقل والقلب والحذف نحو:

١- يَخَافُ؛ فعل مضارع أصله يَخْوَفُ؛ وإعلاله بالنقل والقلب.

٢- تقول في جمعي المؤنّث: يَخَفْنَ وتَخَفْنَ؛ أصلهما يَخْوَفْنَ وتَخْوَفْنَ؛ إعلالهما بالنقل والقلب والحذف.

[الأمر] إعلاله أمرًا بالصيغة بالحذف وزيادة همزة الوصل ثم النقل والحذفين نحو: خَفْ؛ فعل أمر أصله اخْوَفْ على وزن افْعَلْ كاعلم. وأصل اخْوَفْ عند البصريّين من لِتَخْوَفْ، عند البصريّين حذفت لام الأمر مع حرف المضارعة لكثرة الاستعمال وجيء بهمزة الوصل فصار اخوف. فبالنقل والقلب والحذفين صار خف على وزن فَلْ.

[Prohibitive] In the second-person prohibitive, it is modified through transfer, conversion, and elision as in *lā takhaf* (do not be afraid), a second-person prohibitive that is originally *lā takhwaf*. This is modified through transfer, conversion, and elision.

[النهي] إعلاله نهي الحاضر بالنقل والقلب والحذف نحو: لا تَخَفْ؛ نهي الحاضر أصله لا تَخْوَفْ؛ إعلاله بالنقل والقلب والحذف.

[Active Participle] In the active participle, it is modified through conversion as in *khāʾifun* (one that is afraid), an active participle that is originally *khāwifun*. This is modified through conversion, that is, converting the *wāw* to a *hamza* because it is preceded by an added *alif*.

[اسم الفاعل] إعلاله اسم الفاعل بالقلب نحو: خائِفٌ؛ اسم الفاعل أصله خاوِفٌ؛ إعلاله بالقلب أي بقلب الواو همزةً لوقوعها بعد الألف الزائدة.

[Passive Participle] In the passive participle, it is modified through transfer and elision as in *makhūfun* (thing that is feared), a passive participle that is originally *makhwūfun* of the pattern *mafʿūlun* as in *maʿlūmun* (thing that is known). Through transfer and elision this becomes *makhūfun*, of the pattern *mafūlun*.

[اسم المفعول] إعلاله اسم المفعول بالنقل والحذف نحو: مَخُوفٌ؛ اسم المفعول أصله مَخْوُوفٌ على وزن مَفْعُولٌ كمعلوم؛ فبالنقل والحذف صار مخوف على وزن مَفُولٌ.

[Noun of Time; Noun of Place; Mimated Infinitive] In the nouns of time and place and the mimated infinitive, it is modified through transfer and conversion as in *makhāfun* (place/time of being afraid, being afraid), a noun of time, a noun of place, and a mimated infinitive, originally *makhwafun* of the pattern *mafʿalun* as in *maʿlamun* (place/time of knowing, knowing). Through transfer and conversion this becomes *makhāfun*, of the pattern *mafaʿlun*.

·**[اسم الزمان، اسم المكان، المصدر الميمي]** إعلاله اسمي الزمان والمكان والمصدر الميمي بالنقل والقلب نحو: مَخَافٌ؛ اسما الزمان والمكان والمصدر الميمي أصله مَخْوَفٌ على وزن مَفْعَل كمعلم[٢٣]؛ فبالنقل والقلب صار مخاف على وزن مَفَعْلٌ.

[4. The Hollow Class *Akrama*]

[٤. باب أكرم من الأجوف]

[Perfect] In the perfect tense, Class *Akrama* is modified to become *ajāba* (he answered), a perfect tense verb that is originally *ajwaba* of the pattern *afʿala* as in *akrama* (he honored). Through transfer and conversion this becomes *ajāba*, of the pattern *afaʿla*.

·**[الماضي]** إعلال باب أكرم حال كونه أجوف ماضيًا[٢٤]: أَجَابَ؛ فعل ماض أصله أَجْوَبَ على وزن أَفْعَلَ كأكرم؛ فبالنقل والقلب صار أجاب على وزن أَفَعْلَ.

For the [third-person] feminine plural, one says *ajabna* (they [f.] answered), originally *ajwabna*. This is modified through transfer and conversion and then elision. The rest of [the uniform derivatives] until *ajabnā* undergo the same modification.

[Imperfect] In the imperfect tense, it is modified to become *yujību* (he answers), an imperfect tense verb that is originally *yujwibu* of the pattern *yufʿilu* as in *yukrimu* (he honors). This is modified through transfer and conversion and becomes *yujību*, of the pattern *yufiʿlu*.

For the feminine plural, one says *yujibna* / *tujibna* (they [f.] answer / you all [f.] answer), originally *yujwibna* / *tujwibna*, of the pattern [*yufʿilna* / *tufʿilna*]. These are modified through transfer, conversion, and elision and [adopt] the pattern *yufilna* / *tufilna*.

[Imperative] In the imperative, it is modified to become *ajib* (answer), a second-person imperative that is originally *ajwib* of the pattern *afʿil* as in *akrim* (honor). According to the Basrans, *ajwib* is originally *li-tujwib*, from which the imperative *lām* and the imperfect tense prefix are elided, and the [augment] *hamza* that is suppressed in the imperfect tense reappears such that it becomes *ajwib*. Then it is modified through transfer and elision.

[Prohibitive] In the prohibitive, it is modified to become *lā tujib* (do not answer), a second-person prohibitive that is originally *lā tujwib*. This is modified through transfer and elision and adopts the pattern *lā tufil*.

[Active Participle] In the active participle, it is modified as in *mujībun* (one that answers), an active participle that is originally *mujwibun*, of the pattern *mufʿilun*. This is modified through transfer and conversion.

تقول في جمع المؤنّث: أَجَبْنَ؛ أصله أَجْوَبْنَ؛ إعلاله بالنقل والقلب ثم الحذف. وهكذا إعلال ما بعده إلى أَجَبْنَا.

[المضارع] إعلاله مضارعًا: يُجِيبُ؛ فعل مضارع أصله يُجْوِبُ على وزن يُفْعِلُ كيكرم؛ إعلاله بالنقل والقلب صار يجيب على وزن يُفِعْلُ.

وتقول في جمعي المؤنّث: يُجِبْنَ/ تُجِبْنَ؛ أصلهما يُجْوِبْنَ/ تُجْوِبْنَ على وزن [يُفْعِلْنَ/ تُفْعِلْنَ]؛ إعلالهما بالنقل والقلب والحذف على وزني يُفِلْنَ/ تُفِلْنَ.

[الأمر] إعلاله أمر الحاضر: أَجِبْ؛ أمر الحاضر أصله أَجْوِبْ على وزن أَفْعِلْ كأكرم. أصل أجوب عند البصريين لِتُجْوِبْ، حذفت لام الأمر مع حرف المضارعة وعادت الهمزة المتروكة في المضارع فصار أجوب؛ إعلاله بالنقل والحذف.

[النهي] إعلاله نهي الحاضر: لا تُجِبْ؛ نهي الحاضر أصله لا تُجْوِبْ؛ إعلاله بالنقل والحذف على وزن لا تُفِلْ.

[اسم الفاعل] إعلاله اسم الفاعل نحو: مُجِيبٌ؛ اسم الفاعل أصله مُجْوِبٌ على وزن مُفْعِلٌ[٢٥]؛ إعلاله بالنقل والقلب.

[Passive Participle; Noun of Time; Noun of Place; Mimated Infinitive] In the passive participle and its sister forms, it is modified as in *mujābun* (one that is answered, place/time of answering, answering), a passive participle, a noun of time, a noun of place, and a mimated infinitive, originally *mujwabun*, of the pattern *mufʿalun*, derived from the passive imperfect by the addition of a *mīm* possessing *ḍamm* in place of the imperfect tense prefix. This is modified through transfer and conversion.

[اسم المفعول، اسم الزمان، اسم المكان، المصدر الميمي] إعلاله اسم المفعول وأخواته نحو: مُجَابٌ؛ أسماء المفعول والزمان والمكان والمصدر الميمي أصله مُجْوَبٌ على وزن مُفْعَلٌ، مشتقّ من الفعل المضارع المجهول بزيادة الميم المضموم موضع حرف المضارعة؛ إعلاله بالنقل والقلب.

For the non-mimated infinitive noun, one says *ijābatan* (answering), originally *ijwāban*, of the same pattern as *ikrāman* (honoring). The vowel of the *wāw* is transferred to the *jīm*, the *wāw* is converted to an *alif* and elided due to the convergence of two vowelless letters, and then a *tāʾ* is added to the end of the word in compensation for the elided letter. It becomes *ijābatan*, of the pattern *ifālatan*.

تقول في المصدر الغير الميمي: إِجَابَةً؛ أصله إِجْوَابًا على وزن إكرامًا؛ نقلت حركة الواو إلى الجيم وقلبت ألفًا ثم حذفت لالتقاء الساكنين وزيدت التاء في آخره عوضًا عن المحذوف فصارت إجابة على وزن إِفَالَةً.

[5. The Hollow Class *Inqaṭaʿa*]

[٥. باب انقطع من الأجوف]

In Class *Inqaṭaʿa* with hollow roots, the only forms that occur are the perfect tense and the imperfect tense.

إعلال باب انقطع أجوف لا يجيء منه غير الماضي والمضارع.

[Perfect] In the perfect tense, it is modified as in *innāla*, a perfect tense verb that is originally *innawala* of the pattern *infaʿala* as in *inqaṭaʿa* (it was severed). This is modified through assimilation and conversion.

[الماضي] إعلاله ماضيًا نحو: انَّالَ؛ فعل ماضٍ أصله انْنَوَلَ على وزن انْفَعَلَ كانقطع؛ إعلاله بالإدغام والقلب.

[Imperfect] In the imperfect tense, it is modified as in *yannālu*, an imperfect tense verb that is originally *yannawilu* of the pattern *yanfaʿilu* as in *yanqaṭiʿu* (it is severed). This is modified through assimilation and conversion.

[المضارع] إعلاله مضارعًا نحو: يَنَّالُ؛ فعل مضارع أصله يَنْنَوِلُ على وزن يَنْفَعِلُ كينقطع؛ إعلاله بالإدغام والقلب.

[6. The Hollow Class *Ijtamaʿa*]

[٦. باب اجتمع من الأجوف]

[Perfect] Class *Ijtamaʿa* with hollow roots is modified as in *ikhtāra* (he chose), originally *ikhtayara*. This is modified through conversion.

[الماضي] إعلال باب اجتمع حال كونه أجوف نحو: اخْتَارَ؛ أصله اخْتَيَرَ؛ إعلاله بالقلب.

[Imperfect] The imperfect tense is *yakhtāru* (he chooses), originally *yakhtayiru*. This is also modified through conversion.

[المضارع] والمضارع: يَخْتَارُ؛ أصله يَخْتَيِرُ؛ وإعلاله أيضا بالقلب.

[Imperative; Prohibitive] The imperative is *ikhtar* (choose) and the prohibitive *lā takhtar* (do not choose), originally *ikhtayir* and *lā takhtayir*, respectively. These are modified through conversion and elision.

[الأمر، النهي] والأمر: اخْتَرْ. والنهي: لا تَخْتَرْ. أصلهما اخْتَيِرْ، لا تَخْتَيِرْ؛ إعلالهما بالقلب والحذف.

[Active Participle; Passive Participle; Noun of Time; Noun of Place; Mimated Infinitive] The active participle, the passive participle, the nouns of time and place, and the mimated infinitive are *mukhtārun* (one that chooses, one that is chosen, place/time of choice, choice), originally *mukhtayirun* / *mukhtayarun*, with the *yāʾ* possessing *kasr* in the active participle and *fatḥ* in the rest of the forms. This is modified through conversion of the *yāʾ* to an *alif*.

[اسم الفاعل، اسم المفعول، اسم الزمان، اسم المكان، المصدر الميمي] واسم الفاعل والمفعول والزمان والمكان والمصدر الميمي: مُخْتَارٌ؛ أصله مُخْتَيِرٌ بكسر الياء في اسم الفاعل وفتحها في البواقي؛ إعلاله بقلب الياء ألفًا.

[7. The Hollow Class *Istakhraja*]

[٧. باب استخرج من الأجوف]

[Perfect] Class *Istakhraja* with hollow roots is modified in the perfect tense to become *istaqāma* (he straightened up), originally *istaqwama*. This is modified through transfer and conversion.

[الماضي] إعلال باب استخرج أجوفَ الفعلَ الماضي: اسْتَقَامَ؛ أصله اسْتَقْوَمَ؛ إعلاله بالنقل والقلب.

[Imperfect] The imperfect tense verb is *yastaqīmu* (he straightens up), originally *yastaqwimu*. This is modified through transfer and conversion.

[المضارع] والفعل المضارع: يَسْتَقِيمُ؛ أصله يَسْتَقْوِمُ؛ إعلاله بالنقل والقلب.

For the infinitive noun, one says *istiqāmatan* (straightening up), originally *istiqwāman*. This is modified through transfer and conversion, then elision of the converted letter, and then the compensatory addition of a *tāʾ*. It becomes *istiqāmatan*, of the pattern *istifālatan*.

وتقول في المصدر: اسْتِقَامَةً؛ أصله اسْتِقْوَامًا؛ إعلاله بالنقل والقلب ثم حذف المنقلبة وزيادة التاء عوضًا فصار استقامة على وزن اسْتِفَالَةً.

[**Imperative**] The imperative verb is *istaqim* (straighten up).

[**الأمر**] فعل الأمر: اسْتَقِمْ.

[**Prohibitive**] The prohibitive verb is *lā tastaqim* (do not straighten up).

[**النهي**] والنهي: لا تَسْتَقِمْ.

[**Active Participle**] The active participle is *mustaqīmun* (one that straightens up), derived from the active imperfect tense verb.

[**اسم الفاعل**] واسم الفاعل: مُسْتَقِيمٌ؛ مشتق من الفعل المضارع المعلوم.

[**Passive Participle; Noun of Time; Noun of Place; Mimated Infinitive**] The passive participle, the nouns of time and place, and the mimated infinitive are *mustaqāmun* (one that is straightened up, place/time of straightening up, straightening up), derived from the passive imperfect tense verb through the addition of a *mīm* possessing *ḍamm* in place of the imperfect tense prefix.

[**اسم المفعول، اسم الزمان، اسم المكان، المصدر الميمي**] واسم المفعول والزمان والمكان والمصدر الميمي: مُسْتَقَامٌ؛ مشتقّ من الفعل المضارع المجهول بزيادة الميم المضمومة موضع حرف المضارعة.

[8. The Hollow Class *Daḥraja*]

[**٨. باب دحرج من الأجوف**]

[**Perfect**] Class *Daḥraja* with hollow roots is modified in the perfect tense to become *marāḥa*, originally *marwaḥa*. This is modified through transfer and conversion.

[**الماضي**] إعلال باب دحرج أجوفَ الفعلَ الماضي: مَرَاحَ؛ أصله مَرْوَحَ؛ إعلاله بالنقل والقلب.

[**Imperfect**] The imperfect tense is *yumarīḥu*, originally *yumarwiḥu*. This is modified through transfer and conversion.

[**المضارع**] والفعل المضارع: يُمَرِيحُ؛ أصله يُمَرْوِحُ؛ إعلاله بالنقل والقلب.

[**Imperative**] The imperative verb is *mariḥ*, originally *marwiḥ*. This is modified through transfer, conversion, and elision.

[**الأمر**] وفعل الأمر: مَرِحْ؛ والأصل مَرْوِحْ؛ إعلاله بالنقل والقلب والحذف.

[**Prohibitive**] The prohibitive verb is *lā tumariḥ*, originally *lā tumarwiḥ*. This is modified through transfer, conversion, and elision.

[**النهي**] والنهي: لا تُمَرِحْ؛ أصله لا تُمَرْوِحْ؛ إعلاله بالنقل والقلب والحذف.

[Active Participle] The active participle is *mumarīḥun*, originally *mumarwiḥun*. This is modified through transfer and conversion.

[اسم الفاعل] واسم الفاعل: مُمَرِيحٌ؛ أصله مُمَرْوِحٌ؛ إعلاله بالنقل والقلب.

[Passive Participle; Noun of Time; Noun of Place; Mimated Infinitive] The passive participle, the nouns of time and place, and the mimated infinitive are *mumarāḥun*, originally *mumarwaḥun*. This is modified through transfer and conversion.

[اسم المفعول، اسم الزمان، اسم المكان، المصدر الميمي] واسم المفعول والزمان والمكان والمصدر الميمي: مُمَرَاحٌ؛ أصله مُمَرْوَحٌ؛ إعلاله بالنقل والقلب.

[9. The Hollow Class *Iqshaʿarra*]

[٩. باب اقشعرّ من الأجوف]

[Perfect] Class *Iqshaʿarra* with hollow roots is modified in the perfect tense to become *bādarra*, originally *ibwadarra* of the pattern *ifʿalalla* as in *iqshaʿarra* (he shuddered). This is modified through transfer and conversion and then elision of the *hamza*.

[الماضي] إعلال باب اقشعرّ أجوفَ الفعلَ الماضي: بَادَرَّ؛ أصله ابْوَدَرَّ على وزن افْعَلَلَّ كاقشعرّ؛ إعلاله بالنقل والقلب ثم حذف الهمزة.

[Imperfect] The imperfect tense is *yabādirru*, originally *yabwadirru* of the pattern *yafʿalillu* as in *yaqshaʿirru* (he shudders). This is modified through transfer and conversion.

[المضارع] والمضارع: يَبَادِرُّ؛ أصله يَبْوَدِرُّ على وزن يَفْعَلِلُّ كيقشعرّ؛ إعلاله بالنقل والقلب.

[Imperative] The imperative is *bādirri*, originally *ibwadirri* of the pattern *ifʿalilli* as in *iqshaʿirri* (shudder). This is modified through transfer, conversion, and elision.

[الأمر] والأمر: بَادِرّ؛ أصله ابْوَدِرّ على وزن افْعَلِلّ كاقشعرّ؛ إعلاله بالنقل والقلب والحذف.

[Prohibitive] The prohibitive is *lā tabādirri*, originally *lā tabwadirri* of the pattern *lā tafʿalilli* as in *lā taqshaʿirri* (do not shudder). This is modified through transfer and conversion.

[النهي] والنهي: لا تَبَادِرّ؛ أصله لا تَبْوَدِرّ على وزن لا تَفْعَلِلّ كلا تقشعرّ؛ إعلاله بالنقل والقلب.

[Active Participle] The active participle is *mubādirrun*, with the same form as the active imperfect tense verb.

[اسم الفاعل] واسم الفاعل: مُبَادِرٌّ؛ على هيئة فعل المضارع المعلوم.

[Passive Participle; Noun of Time; Noun of Place; Mimated Infinitive] The passive participle is *mubādarrun*, with the same form as the passive imperfect tense verb; the nouns of time and place and the mimated infinitive are the same.

[اسم المفعول، اسم الزمان، اسم المكان، المصدر الميمي]
واسم المفعول: مُبَادَرٌّ؛ على هيئة الفعل المضارع المجهول. وكذا اسما الزمان والمكان والمصدر الميمي.

IV. The Defective Root

(٤) الناقص

The fourth of the seven types of irregular roots is that whose third radical is weak, and it is termed the defective root. The definition of the defective root, its classes, and the modification of its classes are as follows.

الرابع من الأقسام السبعة المعتلّة معتلّ اللام يقال له

الناقص: تعريفه، أبوابه، إعلال أبوابه

The defective root is that whose third radical is a weak letter.

هو ما كان لام فعله حرف علّة.

When the *wāw* or *yā'* is vowelized and the preceding letter possesses *fatḥ*, the *wāw* or *yā'* is converted to an *alif*. An *alif* that has been converted from a *yā'* is written [in the figure of] a *yā'*, as in *ramā* (he threw), *a'ṭā* (he gave), and *ishtarā* (he purchased); however, an *alif* that has been converted from a *wāw* in a simple triliteral is written as an *alif*, as in *ghazā* (he purposed).

تقلب الواو والياء ألفًا إذا تحرّكتا وانفتح ما قبلهما، وتكتب الألف المنقلبة من الياء ياءً، نحو: رَمَى وأَعْطَى واشْتَرَى. ولكن المنقلبة عن الواو في الثلاثي المجرّد تكتب بالألف، نحو: غَزَا.

The third radical in the defective root is always elided in cases like *fa'alū*, and it is elided in cases like *fa'alat* and *fa'alatā*, when the second radical possesses *fatḥ*, e.g., *ghazaw* (they [m.] purposed), *ghazat* / *ghazatā* (she / they two [f.] purposed). In other cases it is retained, e.g., *sarū* (they [m.] were noble and generous), *saruwat* / *saruwatā* (she was / they two [f.] were noble and generous), *raḍū* (they [m.] were content), and *raḍiyat* (she was content).

وتحذف اللام من الناقص في نحو فَعَلُوا مطلقًا، وفي نحو فَعَلَتْ وفَعَلَتَا إذا انفتح العين، نحو: غَزَوْا/ غَزَتْ/ غَزَتَا. وتثبت في غيرها، نحو: سَرُوا، سَرُوَتْ/ سَرُوَتَا، ورَضُوا/ رَضِيَتْ.

The defective root occurs in six classes:

1. Class *Naṣara*: *ghazā* (to purpose).
2. *Ḍaraba*: *ramā* (to throw).
3. *'Alima*: *raḍiya* (to be content).

وهو يأتي من ستّة أبواب:

١- باب نصر: غَزَا.
٢- ضرب: رَمَى.
٣- علم: رَضِيَ.

٧٩

4. *Akrama*: *aʿṭā* (to give).
5. *Ijtamaʿa*: *ishtarā* (to purchase).
6. *Ḥasuna*: *saruwa* (to be noble and generous).

The modification of its classes, i.e., the modification of classes with defective roots, from the perfect tense to the mimated infinitive, is as follows.

[The Defective Perfect]

In the perfect tense, classes with defective roots are modified through conversion as in *ghazā* (he purposed), originally *ghazaw*a of the pattern *faʿala* as in *naṣara* (he helped). This is modified through conversion, that is, converting the third radical, here the *wāw*, to an *alif* because it is vowelized and the preceding letter possesses *fatḥ*.

The third radical converted from a *wāw* is written as an *alif*, e.g., *ghazā*, and that converted from the letter *yāʾ* is written [in the figure of] a *yāʾ*, e.g., *ramā* (he threw).

Examples like *ghazā*: *ramā*, *aʿṭā* (he gave), *ishtarā* (he purchased), *taṣābā* (he behaved like a child), *istadʿā* (he called for), and so on.

Note: The third radical is not converted to an *alif* in Classes *ʿAlima* and *Ḥasuna* because the preceding letter does not possess *fatḥ*, e.g., *raḍiya* (he was content) and *saruwa* (he was noble and generous).

[The Defective Imperfect]

In the imperfect tense, they are modified through elision as in *yaghzū* (he purposes), originally *yaghzuwu* of the pattern *yafʿulu* as in *yanṣuru* (he helps). This is modified through elision, that is, eliding the vowel of the third radical on account of its phonetic heaviness in conjunction with the letters *wāw* and *yāʾ*. Examples like *yaghzū*: *yarmī* (he throws), *yuʿṭī* (he gives), *yanjalī* (it is cleared away), *yataṣābā* (he behaves like a child), *yastadʿī* (he calls for), and so on.

٤- أكرم: أَعْطَى.
٥- اجتمع: اشْتَرَى.
٦- حسن: سَرُوَ.

إعلال أبوابه، أي إعلال أبواب الناقص ماضيًا إلى المصدر الميمي:

[الماضي من الناقص]

إعلالها ماضيًا بالقلب نحو: غَزَا؛ أصله غَزَوَ على وزن فَعَلَ كنصر؛ إعلاله بالقلب أي قلب لام الفعل الذي هو الواو هنا ألفًا لتحركها وانفتاح ما قبلها.

واللام المقلوبة من الواو تكتب ألفًا نحو غَزَا؛ والمقلوبة من الياء تكتب ياءً نحو رَمَى.

كـ«غزا»: رَمَى، أَعْطَى، اشْتَرَى، تَصَابَى، اسْتَدْعَى، ونحوها.

غير أن اللام لا تقلب ألفًا في باب علم وحسن لعدم انفتاح ما قبلها، نحو رَضِيَ وسَرُوَ.

[المضارع من الناقص]

إعلالها مضارعًا بالحذف نحو: يَغْزُو؛ أصله يَغْزُوُ على وزن يَفْعُلُ كينصر؛ إعلاله بالحذف أي حذف حركة اللام لثقلها على الواو والياء. كـ«يغزو»: يَرْمِي، يُعْطِي، يَنْجَلِي، يَتَصَابَى، يَسْتَدْعِي[٢٦]، ونحوها.

Note: The third radical in the classes of *yaʿlamu*, *yaftaḥu*, *yatakallamu*, and *yatabāʿadu* is converted to an *alif* because the preceding letter possesses *fatḥ*, e.g., *yarḍā* (he is content), *yarʿā* (he cares for), *yatarajjā* (he hopes for), and *yataṣābā*.

[The Defective Active Participle]

In the active participle, they are modified (1) through conversion and double elision or (2) through double elision, as in

1. *ghāzin* (one that purposes), originally *ghāziwun* of the pattern *fāʿilun* as in *nāṣirun* (one that helps). This is modified through conversion and double elision, that is, converting the *wāw* to a *yāʾ* because it occurs as the fourth letter and also because of its outermost position, eliding the *ḍamma* on account of its phonetic heaviness in conjunction with the *yāʾ*, and then eliding the *yāʾ* due to the convergence of vowelless letters.[1] Examples like *ghāzin*: *rāʿin* (one that desists).[52]
2. *rāmin* (one that throws), originally *rāmiyun* of the pattern *fāʿilun* as in *ḍāribun* (one that hits). Through double elision this becomes *rāmin*. Example like *rāmin*: *rāʿin* (one that cares for), [*rāḍin* (one that is content), *sārin* (one that journeys by night)].[53]

Classes that are not simple triliterals adopt the form of the active imperfect tense verb; for example, *muʿṭin* (one that gives) is like *yuʿṭī* (he gives). It is originally *muʿṭiwun* of the pattern *mufʿilun*. Its modification is the same as the modification of *rāḍiwun*: it is through conversion and double elision because the *wāw* occurs as the fourth letter and because of its outermost position.

[1] That is, [the convergence of] the converted *yāʾ* and the *nūn* of nunation.

إلا أن اللام في باب يعلم ويفتح ويتكلّم ويتباعد تقلب ألفًا لانفتاح ما قبلها، نحو: يَرْضَى، ويَرْعَى، ويَتَرَجَّى، ويَتَصَابَى.

[اسم الفاعل من الناقص]

وإعلالها اسم الفاعل (١) بالقلب والحذفين، (٢) وبالحذفين نحو:

١- غَازٍ؛ أصله غَازِوٌ على وزن فَاعِلٌ كناصر؛ إعلاله بالقلب والحذفين أي قلب الواو ياءً لوقوعها رابعة وتطرّفها أيضًا، وحذف الضمّة لثقلها على الياء ثم حذف الياء لالتقاء الساكنين.[١] كـ«غازٍ»: رَاعٍ.[٥٢]

٢- رَامٍ؛ أصله رَامِيٌ على وزن فَاعِلٌ كضارب؛ فبالحذفين صار رامٍ. كـ«رامٍ»: رَاعٍ، [رَاضٍ، سَارٍ].

ومن غير الثلاثي المجرّد يكون على هيئة فعل المضارع المعلوم، نحو: مُعْطٍ كيُعْطِي؛ أصله مُعْطِوٌ على وزن مُفْعِلٌ؛ إعلاله كإعلال رَاضِوٌ بالقلب والحذفين لوقوع الواو رابعة ولتطرفها.

[١] أي الياء المقلوبة ونون التنوين.

[The Defective Passive Participle and Sister Forms]

In the passive participle, they are modified (1) through assimilation or (2) through conversion, transfer, and assimilation, as in

1. *maghzuwwun* (thing that is purposed), originally *maghzūwun* of the pattern *mafʿūlun* as in *manṣūrun* (one that is helped). This is modified through assimilation, that is, assimilating the *wāw* in the pattern *mafʿūlun* to the third radical. This is how [defective roots] of Classes *Naṣara* and *Ḥasuna* are modified, as in *masruwwun* (thing that is removed from s.o.).
2. As for Classes *Ḍaraba*, *Fataḥa*, and *ʿAlima*, as in *marmūyun*, their modification is through conversion, transfer, and assimilation. That is, [first] the *wāw* in [the pattern] *mafʿūlun* is converted to a *yāʾ*, because when the letters *wāw* and *yāʾ* coincide within a word and either is preceded by a vowelless letter, the *wāw* is converted to a *yāʾ*. Then the *ḍamma* of the letter preceding the converted *yāʾ* is converted to a *kasra*. Then the one *yāʾ* is assimilated to the other, and the word becomes *marmiyyun* (thing that is thrown), originally *marmūyun* of the pattern *mafʿūlun*. This is how the passive participle is modified when it occurs in a simple triliteral.

When the passive participle occurs in a class that is not a simple triliteral, it joins the nouns of time and place and the mimated infinitive in adopting the pattern of the passive imperfect tense verb, though the imperfect tense prefix is replaced with a *mīm* possessing *ḍamm*; for example, *muʿṭan* (one that is given) is like *yuʿṭā* (he is given), whose remote origin is *yuʿṭawu*. But [in the latter] the *wāw* is converted to a *yāʾ* because it occurs as the fourth letter and because of its outermost position; then the *yāʾ* is converted to an *alif* because it is vowelized and the preceding letter possesses *fatḥ*; and then the imperfect tense prefix is replaced with a *mīm* possessing *ḍamm*. Thus, it becomes *muʿṭan* of the pattern *mufʿal* as in *mukram* (one that is honored).

[اسم المفعول وأخواته من الناقص]

إعلالها اسم المفعول (١) بالإدغام، (٢) وبالقلب والنقل والإدغام نحو:

١- مَغْزُوٌّ؛ أصله مَغْزُووٌ على وزن مَفْعُولٌ كمنصور؛ إعلاله بالإدغام أي إدغام واو المفعول في لام الفعل. وهذا إعلال ما كان من باب نصر أو من باب حسن، نحو مَسْرُوٌّ.

٢- وأما ما كان من باب ضرب أو باب فتح أو باب علم نحو مَرْمُويٌ فالإعلال فيها بالقلب والنقل والإدغام، أي قلب واو المفعول ياءً لأنه إذا اجتمعت الواو والياء في كلمة واحدة وسُبقت إحداهما بسكون قلبت الواو ياءً، ثم قلبت ضمّة ما قبل الياء المقلوبة كسرةً، ثم أدغمت الياء في الياء فصار مَرْمِيٌّ أصله مَرْمُويٌ[٢٨] على وزن مَفْعُولٌ. هذا إعلال اسم المفعول إذا كان من الثلاثي المجرّد.

وأما إذا كان من غير الثلاثي المجرّد فيكون هو واسم الزمان والمكان والمصدر الميمي على وزن الفعل المضارع المجهول غير أنك تبدّل حرف المضارعة بالميم المضمومة، نحو: مُعْطًى كيُعْطَى؛ أصله البعيد يُعْطَوُ؛ قلبت الواو ياءً لوقوعها رابعة ولتطرفها ثم قلبت الياء ألفًا لتحرّكها وانفتاح ما قبلها ثم بدّل ياء المضارعة ميمًا مضمومة فصار معطى على وزن مُفْعَل كمكرم.

[The Defective Imperative]

In the imperative proper, they are modified through double elision and addition of the connective *hamza* as in *ughzu* (purpose), originally *ughzū* of the pattern *ufʿul* as in *unṣur* (help). This, in turn, was originally *li-taghzū* or *taghzū*, in accordance with the dispute between the Basrans and Kufans. The third radical was elided due to the jussive-making imperative *lām*, the imperative *lām* and the imperfect tense prefix were elided by frequent use, and the connective *hamza* was added to resolve the vowelless beginning. It thus became *ughzu*,[1] of the pattern *ufʿu*. Examples like *ughzu*: *irmi* (throw), *ishtari* (purchase), and so on.

Note: After the imperfect tense prefix is elided in the class of *yukrimu*, the suppressed [augment] *hamza* reappears. Thus, the imperative in the class of *yukrimu* is *afʿil* rather than *ifʿil*.

Every verb with a vowelized letter following the imperfect tense prefix does not require the addition of a connective *hamza* in the imperative, e.g., *farriḥ* (gladden), *qātil* (fight), and so on. Otherwise, it does require this, e.g., *unṣur* (help).

[The Defective Prohibitive]

In the prohibitive, they are modified through elision as in *lā taghzu* (do not purpose), originally *lā taghzū* of the pattern *lā tafʿul* as in *lā tanṣur* (do not help). This is modified through elision of only the third radical due to the operation of the jussive-making prohibitive *lā*. Examples like *lā taghzu*: *lā tarmi* (do not throw), *lā tuʿṭi* (do not give), *lā tashtari* (do not purchase), and so on.

[الأمر من الناقص]

إعلالها حال كونها الأمر بالصيغة بالحذفين وزيادة همزة الوصل نحو: اغْزُ؛ أصله اغْزُوْ على وزن افْعُلْ كانصر من لِتَغْزُوْ أو من تَغْزُوْ للخلاف بين البصريّين والكوفين؛ حذفت اللام بلام الأمر الجازم، ثم حذفت لام الأمر مع حرف المضارعة لكثرة الاستعمال، وزيدت الهمزة لدفع الابتداء بالساكن، فصار اغز[١] على وزن افْعُ. كـ«اغز»: ارْمِ، اشْتَرِ، ونحوها.

غير أن باب يكرم بعد حذف حرف المضارعة منه أعيدت الهمزة المتروكة، فالأمر من باب يُكرم أَفْعِلْ لا افْعِلْ.

وكل فعل يكون ما بعد حرف مضارعته متحرّكًا لا يحتاج في صياغة فعل الأمر منه إلى زيادة همزة الوصل كفَرِّحْ وقَاتِلْ ونحوهما؛ وإلا فيحتاج نحو انْصُرْ.

[النهي من الناقص]

إعلالها نهيًا بالحذف نحو: لا تَغْزُ؛ أصله لا تَغْزُوْ على وزن لا تَفْعُلْ كلا تنصر؛ إعلاله بحذف اللام فقط لدخول «لا» الناهية الجازمة عليه. كـ«لا تغز»: لا تَرْمِ، لا تُعْطِ، لا تَشْتَرِ، ونحوها.

[1] The third radical is elided as a sign of the jussive.

[١] حذفت اللام علامةً للجزم.

V. The Disjointly Weak Root

The fifth of the seven types of irregular roots is that whose first and third radicals are weak, and it is termed the disjointly weak root.

The disjointly weak root is that whose first and third radicals are weak, as in *waqā* / *yaqī* (to guard).

This root occurs in eight classes:[54]

1. Class *Ḍaraba*: *waqā* (to guard).
2. *ʿAlima*: *wajiya* (to have one's foot become chafed).
3. *Ḥasiba*: *waliya* (to be close to).
4. *Akrama*: *awṣā* (to bequeath).
5. *Farraḥa*: *wallā* (to turn).
6. *Qātala*: *wārā* (to conceal).
7. *Ijtamaʿa*: *ittaqā* (to guard o.s. against).
8. *Istakhraja*: *istawfā* (to exact in full).
9. *Daḥraja*: *watāla*, originally *watwala*.
10. *Tadaḥraja*: *tātāla*, originally *tawatwala*.
11. *Iḥranjama*: *īsanāsa*, originally *iwsanwasa*.

The modification of the first radical in the disjointly weak root is like the modification of the first radical in the resemblant root, and the modification of the third radical is like the modification of the third radical in the defective root, e.g., *waqā* (he guarded) / *yaqī* (he guards) / *qih* (guard) / *lā taqi* (do not guard) / *wāqin* (one that guards) / *mawqiyyun* (thing that is guarded) / *mawqā* (place/time of guarding), the latter form serving as the noun of time, the noun of place, and the mimated infinitive.

(٥) اللفيف المفروق

الخامس من الأقسام السبعة المعتلّة معتلّ الفاء واللام
ويقال له اللفيف المفروق

هو ما كان فاء فعله ولامه حرف علّة، نحو: وَقَى، يَقِي.

وهو يجيء من ثمانية أبواب:

١- باب ضرب: وَقَى.
٢- علم: وَجِيَ.
٣- حسب: وَلِيَ.
٤- أكرم: أَوْصَى.
٥- فرّح: وَلَّى.
٦- قاتل: وَارَى.
٧- اجتمع: اتَّقَى.
٨- استخرج: اسْتَوْفَى.
٩- دحرج: وَتَالَ (وَتْوَلَ).
١٠- تدحرج: تَاتَالَ (تَوَتْوَلَ).
١١- احرنجم: ايسَنَاسَ (اوْسَنْوَسَ).

وإعلال فائه كإعلال فاء المثال وإعلال لامه كإعلال لام الناقص، نحو: وَقَى/ يَقِي/ قِهْ/ لا تَقِ/ وَاقٍ/ مَوْقِيٌّ[٢٩]/ مَوْقًى[٣٠] اسما الزمان والمكان والمصدر الميمي.

VI. The Conjointly Weak Root

(٦) اللفيف المقرون

The sixth of the seven types of irregular roots is that whose second and third radicals are weak, and it is termed the conjointly weak root.

السادس من الأقسام السبعة المعتلّة معتلّ العين واللام ويقال له اللفيف المقرون

The conjointly weak root is that whose second and third radicals are weak letters, as in *shawā / yashwī* (to roast).

وهــو مــا كان عين فعلــه ولامــه حــرف علّــة، نحــو: شَــوَى، يَشْــوِي.

This root occurs in eight classes:

1. Class *Ḍaraba*: *shawā* (to roast).
2. *ʿAlima*: *qawiya* (to be strong).
3. *Akrama*: *arwā* (to quench s.o.'s thirst).
4. [*Farraḥa*:[55] *rawwā* (to quench s.o.'s thirst).]
5. *Qātala*: *ḥāwā*.[56]
6. *Inqaṭaʿa*: *intawā* (to intend).
7. *Ijtamaʿa*: *iltawā* (to be twisted).
8. *Istakhraja*: *istaḥyā* (to feel shy).

وهو يجيء من ثمانية أبواب:

١- باب ضرب: شَوَى.
٢- علم: قَوِيَ.
٣- أكرم: أَرْوَى.
٤- [فرّح: رَوَّى.]
٥- قاتل: حَاوَى.
٦- انقطع: انْتَوَى[٣١].
٧- اجتمع: الْتَوَى.
٨- استخرج: اسْتَحْيَى.

[The Conjointly Weak Perfect]

In the perfect tense, they are modified through conversion. That is, classes with conjointly weak roots are modified by conversion of the third radical into an *alif* when it is preceded by a letter possessing *fatḥ* and into a *yāʾ* when it is preceded by a letter possessing *kasr*, e.g., *shawā* (he roasted), originally *shawaya* of the pattern *faʿala* as in *ḍaraba* (he hit). This is modified through conversion, that is, converting the third radical into an *alif*—verbally but not in writing—because it is vowelized and the preceding letter possesses *fatḥ*. Examples like *shawā*: *arwā* (he quenched s.o.'s thirst), *ḥāwā*, *intawā* (he intended), *iltawā* (it was twisted), *istaḥyā* (he felt shy).

[الماضي من اللفيف المقرون]

إعلالها ماضيًا بالقلب[٣٢] أي إعلال أبواب اللفيف المقرون بقلب اللام ألفًا إن كانت ما قبلها مفتوحة وياءً إن كانت ما قبلها مكسورة، نحو: شَوَى؛ أصله شَوَيَ على وزن فَعَلَ كضرب؛ إعلاله بالقلب أي بقلب لام الفعل ألفًا تلفظًا لا كتابةً لتحركها وانفتاح ما قبلها. كـ«شوى»: أَرْوَى، حَاوَى، انْتَوَى[٣٣]، الْتَوَى[٣٤]، اسْتَحْيَى.

As for *qawiya* (he was strong), it is originally *qawiwa*[57] of the pattern *faʿila* as in *ʿalima* (he knew). The *wāw* is converted to a *yāʾ* because it lies at an outermost position while the preceding letter possesses *kasr*.

أما قَوِيَ فإنّ أصله قَوِوَ على وزن فَعِلَ كعلم؛ قلبت الواو ياءً لتطرفها وانكسار ما قبلها.

[The Conjointly Weak Imperfect]

In the imperfect tense, they are modified through elision as in *yashwī* (he roasts), originally *yashwiyu* of the pattern *yafʿilu* as in *yaḍribu* (he hits). This is modified through elision, that is, eliding the vowel of the *yāʾ* on account of the phonetic heaviness of the vowel with the *yāʾ*. Examples like *yashwī*: *yurwī* (he quenches s.o.'s thirst), *yuḥāwī*, *yantawī* (he intends), *yaltawī* (it is twisted), *yastaḥyī* (he feels shy).

An exception is [the class of] *yarḍā*;[58] the *yāʾ* in its imperfect tense is converted to an *alif* as in *yaqwā* (he is strong), originally *yaqwayu*. The *yāʾ* is converted to an *alif* because the preceding letter possesses *fatḥ*.

[المضارع من اللفيف المقرون]

·إعلالها مضارعًا بالحذف نحو: يَشْوِي؛ أصله يَشْوِيُ على وزن يَفْعِلُ كيضرب؛ إعلاله بالحذف أي حذف حركة الياء لثقلها عليها. كـ«يشوي»: يُرْوِي، يُحَاوِي، يَنْتَوِي[٣٥]، يَلْتَوِي، يَسْتَحْيِي.

·إلا يَرْضَى[٣٦] فإن الياء في مضارعه تقلب ألفًا نحو: يَقْوَى؛ أصله يَقْوَيُ؛ قلبت الياء ألفًا لانفتاح ما قبلها.

[The Conjointly Weak Imperative]

In the imperative proper, they are modified through double elision and the addition of the connective *hamza* as in *ishwi* (roast), originally *ishwī* of the pattern *ifʿil* as in *iḍrib* (hit). This, in turn, is originally either *tashwī*, as the Kufans hold, or *li-tashwī*, as the Basrans hold. This is modified through double elision and the addition of the connective *hamza* to resolve the vowelless beginning.[59] Examples like *ishwi*: *iqwa* (become strong), *arwi* (quench s.o.'s thirst), *ḥāwi*, *iltawi* (be twisted), *istaḥi* (feel shy).

[الأمر من اللفيف المقرون]

·إعلالها أمرًا بالصيغة بالحذفين وزيادة همزة الوصل نحو: اشْوِ؛ أصله اشْوِيْ على وزن افْعِلْ كاضرب من تَشْوِيْ عند الكوفيين أو من لِتَشْوِيْ عند البصريّين؛ إعلاله بالحذفين وزيادة همزة الوصل لدفع الابتداء بالساكن. كـ«اشو»: اقْوَ[٣٧]، أَرْوِ، حَاوِ، الْتَوِ[٣٨]، اسْتَحِ.

[The Conjointly Weak Prohibitive]

In the prohibitive, classes with conjointly weak roots are modified through elision as in *lā tashwi* (do not roast), originally *lā tashwī* of the pattern *lā tafʿil* as in *lā taḍrib* (do not hit). This is modified through elision, that is, eliding the last letter by

[النهي من اللفيف المقرون]

إعلال أبواب المعتل العين واللام نهيًا بالحذف نحو: لا تَشْوِ؛ أصله لا تَشْوِيْ على

means of the prohibitive *lā*. Examples like *lā tashwi*: *lā taqwa* (do not become strong), *lā turwi* (do not quench s.o.'s thirst), *lā tuḥāwi*, *lā taltawi* (do not be twisted), *lā tastaḥi* (do not feel shy).

[The Conjointly Weak Active Participle]

In the active participle, classes with conjointly weak roots are modified through double elision as in *shāwin* (one that roasts), originally *shāwiyun* of the pattern *fāʿilun* as in *ḍāribun* (one that hits). This is modified through double elision: the *ḍamma* is elided on account of its phonetic heaviness in conjunction with the letter *yāʾ*, and the final letter is elided due to the convergence of two vowelless letters. Examples like *shāwin*: *rāwin* (one that quenches his thirst),[60] *murwin* (one that quenches s.o.'s thirst), *muḥāwin*, *multawin* (thing that is twisted), *mustaḥin* (one that feels shy).

[The Conjointly Weak Passive Participle and Sister Forms]

In the passive participle, classes with conjointly weak roots are modified through double conversion and assimilation as in *mashwiyyun* (thing that is roasted), originally *mashwūyun* of the pattern *mafʿūlun* as in *maḍrūbun* (one that is hit). This is modified through conversion and assimilation. That is, the *wāw* is converted to a *yāʾ* because the two coincide within a word while one of them is preceded by a vowelless letter—here it is the *wāw* that lacks a vowel, so it is converted to a *yāʾ*. It is assimilated to the second *yāʾ*, then the *ḍamma* is converted to a *kasra* to protect the *yāʾ* from conversion. Thus, the word becomes *mashwiyyun* like *marmiyyun* (thing that is thrown).

The modification of *maqwiyyun* (one that is made strong)[61] is the same as the modification of *mashwiyyun*, except that it does not involve the conversion of a *ḍamma* to a *kasra*.

وزن لا تَفْعِلْ كلا تضرب؛ إعلاله بالحذف أي بحذف الآخر بـ«لا» الناهية. كـ«لا تشو»: لا تَقْوَ[٣٩]، لا تُرْوِ، لا تُحَاوِ، لا تَلْتَوِ، لا تَسْتَحِ.

[اسم الفاعل من اللفيف المقرون]

إعلال أبواب المعتل العين واللام اسمَ الفاعل بالحذفين نحو: شَاوٍ؛ أصله شَاوِيٌ على وزن فَاعِلٌ كضارب؛ إعلاله بالحذفين حذف الضمة لثقلها على الياء وحذف الآخر لالتقاء الساكنين. كـ«شاوٍ»: رَاوٍ[٤٠]، مُرْوٍ، مُحَاوٍ، مُلْتَوٍ، مُسْتَحٍ.

[اسم المفعول وأخواته من اللفيف المقرون]

إعلال أبواب المعتل العين واللام حال كونه اسم المفعول بالقلبين والإدغام نحو: مَشْوِيٌّ؛ أصله مَشْوُويٌ على وزن مَفْعُولٌ كمضروب؛ إعلاله بالقلب والإدغام أي قلب الواو ياءً لاجتماعهما في كلمة وسبق إحداهما بسكون، وهي الواو هنا بالسكون فقلبت ياءً وأدغمت في الثانية ثم قلبت الضمّة كسرة لحفظ الياء عن القلب فصار مشويٌّ كمَرْمِيٌّ.

وإعلال مَقْوِيٌّ كإعلال مَشْوِيٌّ إلا أنه ليس فيه قلب الضمّة كسرةً.

The above applies when the passive participle occurs in a simple triliteral. As for when it occurs in a class that is not a simple triliteral, it joins the nouns of time and place and the mimated infinitive in adopting the pattern of the passive imperfect tense verb, the only difference being that you replace the imperfect tense prefix with a *mīm* possessing *ḍamm*; for example, *murwan* (one whose thirst is quenched) is like *yurwā* (his thirst is quenched).

هذا إذا كان اسم المفعول من الثلاثي المجرّد. أما إذا كان من غير الثلاثي المجرّد فيكون هو واسمي الزمان والمكان والمصدر الميمي على وزن الفعل المضارع المجهول غير أنك تبدّل حرف المضارعة بالميم المضمومة فقط، نحو مُرْوًى كيُرْوَى.

VII. The Hamzated Root

The seventh of the seven types of irregular roots is the hamzated root. The definition of the hamzated root, its classes, and the modification of its classes are as follows.

The hamzated root is that one of whose radicals is a *hamza*. If that radical is the first, the root is called *fāʾ*-hamzated, as in *akhadha* (he took); if the second, *ʿayn*-hamzated, as in *saʾala* (he asked); and if the third, *lām*-hamzated, as in *qaraʾa* (he read).

In terms of its conjugations, it is treated like its analogues. When doubled, it is treated like the doubled root, as in *anna* (he moaned); when resemblant, it is treated like the resemblant root, as in *waʾada* (he buried alive); when hollow, it is treated like the hollow root, as in *āna* (he was at ease); when defective, it is treated like the defective root, as in *asā* (he effected a reconciliation); when conjointly weak, it is treated like the conjointly weak root, as in *awā* (he resorted for shelter); and when disjointly weak, it is treated like the disjointly weak root, as in *waʾā* (he promised).

The *hamza* behaves like a sound letter in the various conjugations; nevertheless, it is sometimes phonetically lightened through conversion, as in *āmana / yūminu / īmānun* (to believe); through

(٧) المهموز

السابع من الأقسام السبعة المعتلّة: تعريفه، أبوابه، وإعلال أبوابه

هو ما كان أحد أصوله همزة؛ فإن فاءً فمهموز الفاء كأَخَذَ، وإن عينًا فمهموز العين كسَأَلَ، وإن لامًا فمهموز اللام كقَرَأَ.

وحكمه في تصاريف فعله حكم مماثله؛ فإن مضاعفًا فمضاعف نحو أَنَّ، وإن مثالًا فمثال نحو وَأَدَ، وإن أجوف فأجوف نحو آنَ، وإن ناقصًا فناقص نحو أَسَا، وإن لفيفًا مقرونًا فلفيف مقرون نحو أَوَى، وإن مفروقًا فمفروق نحو وَأَى.

والهمزة كالصحيح في التصاريف ولكنها قد تخفف بالقلب نحو آمَنَ/ يُومِنُ/ إِيمَان؛ والحذف نحو

elision, as in *asalu* instead of *as'alu* (I ask) and *khabun* instead of *khab'un* (concealing); or through its being pronounced halfway, as in *sa'ala* (he asked), *su'ila* (he was asked), and *la'uma* (he was base).[62]

When the *hamza* assumes the position of the third radical, it is written in the figure of [the long vowel] corresponding to the preceding letter's short vowel, as in *qara'a* (he read), *ṣadi'a* (it was rusty), and *hayu'a* (he was well-formed). When the preceding letter is vowelless, the *hamza* is written on its own, as in *shay'un* (thing), *juz'un* (part), and *khab'un* (s.th. concealed).

When it is vowelized and assumes the position of the second radical, it is written in the figure of [the long vowel] corresponding to its own short vowel (the same figure it adopts in the cases when it is pronounced halfway), as in *sa'ala, su'ila,* and *la'uma.* As for a vowelless *hamza* that assumes the position of the second radical, it is written in the figure of [the long vowel] corresponding to the preceding letter's short vowel, as in *ra'sun* (head), *bi'sa* (he is bad), and *bu'sun* (distress).

The hamzated root occurs in twelve classes, six of which are modified. These classes are modified as follows.

[1. The Hamzated Class *Naṣara*]

Class *Naṣara* is modified as in *amala* (he hoped), and the imperfect tense is *ya'mulu* (he hopes).

The imperative is *ūmul* (hope), originally *u'mul.* The second *hamza* is converted to a *wāw* because it is vowelless and the preceding letter possesses *ḍamm.*[63]

The prohibitive is *lā ta'mul* (do not hope); the active participle *āmilun* (one that hopes); and the passive participle and its sister forms *ma'mūlun* (thing that is hoped for, place/time of hoping, hoping).

أَسَلُ = أَسْأَلُ، خَبٌ = خَبْءٌ؛ وبجعلها بين بين نحو سَأَلَ، سُئِلَ، لَؤُمَ.

وتُكتب الهمزة الواقعة لامًا بجنس حركة ما قبلها، نحو: قَرَأَ، وصَدِئَ، وهَيُؤَ. والساكنة ما قبلها تُكتب بلا شيء، نحو: شَيْءٌ، جُزْءٌ، وخَبْءٌ.

والمتحركة الواقعة عينًا فتكتب بجنس حركة نفسها كما في صورة جعلها بين بين، نحو: سَأَلَ، سُئِلَ، لَؤُمَ. أما الساكنة الواقعة عينًا تكتب بجنس حركة ما قبلها، نحو: رَأْسٌ، بِئْسَ، بُؤْسٌ.

هو أي المهموز يأتي من اثني عشر بابًا، ويعلّ منها ستّة أبواب. إعلال أبواب المهموز:

[١. باب نصر من المهموز]

إعلال باب نصر نحو: أَمَلَ؛ المضارع: يَأْمُلُ.

· الأمر: أُومُلْ[٤١]؛ أصله أُؤْمُلْ[٤٢]؛ قلبت الثانية واوًا لسكونها وانضمام ما قبلها.

· والنهي: لا تَأْمُل[٤٣]؛ اسم الفاعل: آمِلٌ؛ اسم المفعول وأخواته: مَأْمُولٌ.

[2. The Hamzated Class *Ḍaraba*]

Class *Ḍaraba* is modified as in *azara* (he assisted), and the imperfect tense is *yaʾziru* (he assists).

The imperative is *īzar* (assist), originally *iʾzir* of the pattern *ifʿil* as in *iḍrib* (hit). The first radical is converted to a *yāʾ* because it is vowelless and the preceding letter possesses *kasr*. Then the *kasra* of the second radical is converted to a *fatḥa* to avoid the succession of four *kasra*s—since the letter *yāʾ* represents two *kasra*s—and it becomes *īzar*.

[٢. باب ضرب من المهموز]

إعلال باب ضرب نحو: أَزَرَ؛ المضارع: يَأْزِرُ.

الأمر: اِيزَرْ؛ أصله اِئْزِرْ على وزن اِفْعِلْ كاضرب؛ قلبت فاء الفعل ياءً لسكونها وانكسار ما قبلها ثم قلبت كسرة العين فتحةً هربًا من توالي أربع كسرات لأن الياء عبارة عن الكسرتين، فصار ايزر.

[3. The Hamzated Class *Fataḥa*]

Class *Fataḥa* is modified as in *ahaba* (he took in preparation) and *saʾala* (he asked),[64] and the imperfect tense is *yaʾhabu* (he takes in preparation).

The imperative is *īhab* (take in preparation), originally *iʾhab* of the pattern *ifʿal* as in *iftaḥ* (open). This is modified through conversion because it is vowelless and the preceding letter possesses *kasr*.

[٣. باب فتح من المهموز]

إعلال باب فتح نحو: أَهَبَ، سَأَلَ؛ المضارع: يَأْهَبُ.

والأمر: اِيهَبْ؛ أصله اِئْهَبْ على وزن اِفْعَلْ كافتح؛ إعلاله بالقلب لسكونها وانكسار ما قبلها.

[4. The Hamzated Class *ʿAlima*]

Class *ʿAlima* is modified as in *arija* (it was fragrant), and the imperfect tense is *yaʾraju* (it is fragrant).

The imperative is *īraj* (be fragrant), originally *iʾraj* of the pattern *ifʿal* as in *iʿlam* (know). This is modified by converting the first radical to a *yāʾ* because it is vowelless and the preceding letter possesses *kasr*, such that it becomes *īraj*.

[٤. باب علم من المهموز]

إعلال باب علم نحو: أَرِجَ؛ والمضارع: يَأْرَجُ.

والأمر: اِيرَجْ؛ أصله اِئْرَجْ على وزن اِفْعَلْ كاعلم؛ وإعلاله بقلب فاء الفعل ياءً لسكونها وانكسار ما قبلها فصار ايرج.

[5. The Hamzated Class *Akrama*]

Class *Akrama* is modified as in *āmana* (he believed), originally *aʾmana* of the pattern *afʿala* as in *akrama* (he honored). This is modified by converting the first radical to an *alif* because it is vowelless and the preceding letter possesses *fatḥ*, such that it becomes *āmana*.

[٥. باب أكرم من المهموز]

إعلال باب أكرم نحو: آمَنَ؛ أصله أَأْمَنَ على وزن أَفْعَلَ كأكرم؛ وإعلاله بقلب فاء الفعل ألفًا لسكونها وانفتاح ما قبلها فصار آمَنَ.

[6. The Hamzated Class *Ijtamaʿa*]

Class *Ijtamaʿa* is modified as in *ittakhadha* (he took for himself), originally *iʾtakhadha* of the pattern *iftaʿala* as in *ijtamaʿa* (it came together). This is modified by converting the first radical to a *yāʾ* because it is vowelless and the preceding letter possesses *kasr* and then to a *tāʾ* because of the rule with which the student is familiar.[65] Then it is assimilated to the second *tāʾ*, and the word becomes *ittakhadha*.

[٦. باب اجتمع من المهموز]

إعلال باب اجتمع نحو: اتَّخَذَ؛ أصله اِئْتَخَذَ على وزن اِفْتَعَلَ كاجتمع؛ إعلاله بقلب فاء الفعل ياءً لسكونها وانكسار ما قبلها، ثم تاءً لما عُلم من القاعدة، ثم إدغامها في التاء الثانية، فصار اتّخذ.

❁ ❁ ❁

[Second Method]

[الوجه الثاني]

The modification of the classes of the seven irregular types is presented in a briefer and easier manner as follows:

إعلال أبواب الأقسام السبعة المعتلّة على وجه أقصر وأسهل:

I. The Doubled Root

First in the modification of the seven irregular types is the modification of classes with doubled roots.

١. المضاعف

الأول من إعلال الأقسام السبعة المعتلّة إعلال أبواب المضاعف.

[The Doubled Perfect] In the perfect tense, [classes with doubled roots] are modified

1. through elision and assimilation, of necessity, when the letter preceding the doubled letter is vowelized as in *madda* (he extended s.th.), whose original form is *madada* of the pattern *faʿala* as in *naṣara* (he helped). Through elision and assimilation this becomes *madda*. Examples like *madda*: *farra* (he fled), *ʿaḍḍa* (he bit), *mādda* (he delayed), *inmadda* (it was extended), *imtadda* (it was extended), *tamādda* (he stretched s.th. together with s.o.).

[الماضي من المضاعف] إعلالها ماضيًا:

١- بالحذف والإدغام وجوبًا لكون ما قبل حرف التضعيف متحركة نحو: مَدَّ؛ أصله مَدَدَ على وزن فَعَلَ كنصر؛ فبالحذف والإدغام صار مدّ. كـ«مدّ»: فَرَّ، عَضَّ، مَادَّ، انْمَدَّ، امْتَدَّ، تَمَادَّ.

2. through transfer and assimilation when the letter preceding the doubled letter lacks a vowel as in *amadda* (he provided), originally *amdada* of the pattern *afʿala* as in *akrama* (he honored). Through transfer and assimilation this becomes *amadda*. An example like *amadda*: *istamadda* (he drew [from s.th.]).

[The Doubled Imperfect] In the imperfect tense, they are modified

1. through transfer and assimilation when the letter preceding the doubled letter lacks a vowel as in *yamuddu* (he extends s.th.), originally *yamdudu* of the pattern *yafʿulu* as in *yanṣuru* (he helps). Through transfer and assimilation this becomes *yamuddu*. Examples like *yamuddu*: *yafirru* (he flees), *yaʿaḍḍu* (he bites), *yumiddu* (he provides), *yastamiddu* (he draws [from s.th.]).
2. through elision and assimilation when the letter preceding the doubled letter is vowelized as in *yumāddu* (he delays), originally *yumādidu* of the pattern *yufāʿilu* as in *yuqātilu* (he fights). Through elision and assimilation this becomes *yumāddu*. Examples like *yumāddu*: *yanmaddu* (it is extended), *yamtaddu* (it is extended), *yatamāddu* (he stretches s.th. together with s.o.).

[The Doubled Imperative] In the imperative, they are modified

1. through transfer, vowelizing, assimilation, and then elision when the letter preceding the doubled letter lacks a vowel as in *muddi* (extend s.th.), originally *umdud* of the pattern *ufʿul* as in *unṣur* (help). Through transfer, vowelizing, assimilation, and then elision of the connective *hamza*, this becomes *muddi*. Examples like *muddi*: *firri* (flee), *ʿaḍḍi* (bite), *amiddi* (provide), *istamiddi* (draw [from s.th.]).

٢- وبالنقل والإدغام لكون ما قبل حرف التضعيف ساكنة نحو: أَمَدَّ؛ أصله أَمْدَدَ على وزن أَفْعَلَ كأكرم؛ وبالنقل والإدغام صار أمدّ. كـ«أمدّ»: اسْتَمَدَّ.

[المضارع من المضاعف] إعلالها مضارعًا:

١- بالنقل والإدغام لكون ما قبل حرف التضعيف ساكنة نحو: يَمُدُّ؛ أصله يَمْدُدُ على وزن يَفْعُلُ كينصر؛ وبالنقل والإدغام صار يمدّ. كـ«يمدّ»: يَفِرُّ، يَعَضُّ، يُمِدُّ، يَسْتَمِدُّ.

٢- وبالحذف والإدغام لكون ما قبل حرف التضعيف متحركة نحو: يُمَادُّ؛ أصله يُمَادِدُ على وزن يُفَاعِلُ كيقاتل؛ وبالحذف والإدغام صار يمادّ. كـ«يمادّ»: يَنْمَدُّ، يَمْتَدُّ، يَتَمَادُّ.

[الأمر من المضاعف] إعلالها أمرًا:

١- بالنقل والتحرّك والإدغام ثم الحذف لكون ما قبل حرف التضعيف ساكنة نحو: مُدِّ؛ أصله أُمْدُدْ على وزن أُفْعُلْ كانصر؛ فبالنقل والتحرك والإدغام ثم حذف همزة الوصل صار مدّ. كـ«مدّ»: فِرِّ، عَضِّ، أَمِدِّ، اسْتَمِدِّ.

Note: The *hamza* in *amiddi* is not elided since it is not the connective *hamza*.

2. through elision, vowelizing the third radical, and assimilation when the letter preceding the doubled letter is vowelized as in *māddi* (delay), originally *mādid* of the pattern *fāʿil* as in *qātil* (fight). Through the modification this becomes *māddi*. Examples like *māddi*: *inmaddi* (be extended), *imtaddi* (be extended), *tamāddi* (stretch s.th. together with s.o.).

[The Doubled Prohibitive] In the prohibitive, they are modified

1. through transfer, vowelizing, and assimilation when the letter preceding the doubled letter lacks a vowel as in *lā tamuddi* (do not extend s.th.), originally *lā tamdud* of the pattern *lā tafʿul* as in *lā tanṣur* (do not help). Through transfer, vowelizing, and assimilation this becomes *lā tamuddi*. Examples like *lā tamuddi*: *lā tafirri* (do not flee), *lā taʿaḍḍi* (do not bite), *lā tumiddi* (do not provide), *lā tastamiddi* (do not draw [from s.th.]).
2. through elision, vowelizing, and assimilation when the letter preceding the doubled letter is vowelized as in *lā tumāddi* (do not delay), originally *lā tumādid* of the pattern *lā tufāʿil* as in *lā tuqātil* (do not fight). Through elision, vowelizing, and assimilation this becomes *lā tumāddi*. Examples like *lā tumāddi*: *lā tanmaddi* (do not be extended), *lā tamtaddi* (do not be extended), *lā tatamāddi* (do not stretch s.th. together with s.o.).

[The Doubled Active Participle] In the active participle, they are modified in simple triliteral classes through elision and assimilation as in *māddun* (one that extends s.th.), originally *mādidun* of the pattern *fāʿilun* as in *nāṣirun* (one that helps). Through elision and assimilation this becomes *māddun*. Examples like *māddun*: *fārrun* (one that flees), *ʿāḍḍun* (one that bites).

غير أن همـزة أَمِـدِّ لا يحـذف لأنهـا ليسـت همـزة الوصـل.

٢- وبالحـذف وتحـرك الـلام والإدغام لكـون مـا قبـل حـرف التضعيـف متحركة نحو: مَـادِّ؛ أصلـه مَادِدْ على وزن فَاعِـلْ كقاتـل؛ فبالإعـلال صـار مـادّ[٤٤]. كـ«مـادّ»: انْمَـدِّ، امْتَـدِّ، تَمَادِّ.

[النهي من المضاعف] إعلالها نهيًا:

١- بالنقـل والتحـرك والإدغام لكـون مـا قبـل حـرف التضعيـف سـاكنة نحـو: لا تَمُـدِّ؛ أصلـه لا تَمْـدُدْ على وزن لا تَفْعُـلْ كلا تنـصر؛ فبالنقـل والتحـرك والإدغام صـار لا تمـدّ. كـ«لا تمـدّ»: لا تَفِـرِّ، لا تَعَـضِّ، لا تُمِـدِّ[٤٥]، لا تَسْـتَمِدِّ.

٢- وبالحـذف والتحـرك والإدغام لكون مـا قبل حرف التضعيـف متحركة نحو: لا تُمَـادِّ؛ أصلـه لا تُمَادِدْ على وزن لا تُفَاعِـلْ كلا تقاتـل؛ فبالحذف والتحرك والإدغام صـار لا تمادّ. كـ«لا تمـادّ»: لا تَنْمَدِّ، لا تَمْتَـدِّ، لا تَتَمَادِّ.

[اسـم الفاعل من المضاعـف] إعلالها حال كونها اسـم الفاعل فمـن الثلاثي المجـرّد بالحـذف والإدغام[٤٦] نحو: مَادٌّ؛ أصلـه مَـادِدٌ على وزن فَاعِـلٌ كنـاصر؛ فبالحـذف والإدغام صار مـادّ. كـ«مادّ»: فَـارٌّ، عَاضٌّ.

In classes that are not simple triliterals, they are patterned after the active imperfect tense verb, with the exception that the imperfect tense prefix is converted to a *mīm* possessing *ḍamm*, e.g., *mukrimun* / *yukrimu* (one that honors / he honors).

[The Doubled Noun of Time; Noun of Place; Mimated Infinitive] In the nouns of time and place and the mimated infinitive, simple triliteral classes [with doubled roots] are modified through transfer and assimilation as in *mamaddun* (place/time of extension, extension), originally *mamdadun* of the pattern *mafʿalun* as in *manṣarun* (place/time of helping, helping). Through transfer and assimilation this becomes *mamaddun*. Examples like *mamaddun*: *mafarrun* (place/time of fleeing, fleeing), *maʿaḍḍun* (place/time of biting, biting).

Classes [with doubled roots] that are not simple triliterals are patterned after the passive participle and are distinguished [from it] by context.[66]

II. The Resemblant Root

[The Resemblant Perfect] In the perfect tense, [classes with resemblant roots] are modified

1. through transfer, conversion, and elision as in *nātara*, originally *inwatara* of the pattern *infaʿala* as in *inqaṭaʿa* (it was severed). Through transfer, conversion, and elision this becomes *nātara*.
2. through conversion and assimilation as in *ittaʿada* (he reached an agreement), originally *iwtaʿada* of the pattern *iftaʿala* as in *ijtamaʿa* (it came together). Through conversion and assimilation this becomes *ittaʿada*.

ومن غير الثلاثي المجرّد تكون على وزن الفعل المضارع المعلوم غير أنّ حرف المضارعة تقلب ميمًا مضمومة، نحو مُكْرِم ويُكْرِم.

[اسم الزمان، اسم المكان، المصدر الميمي من المضاعف] إعلالها حال كونها اسمي الزمان والمكان والمصدر الميمي[٤٧] من الثلاثي المجرّد بالنقل والإدغام نحو: مَمَدٌّ؛ أصله مَمْدَدٌ على وزن مَفْعَلٌ كمنصر؛ فبالنقل والإدغام صار ممدّ. كـ«ممدّ»: مَفَرٌّ، مَعَضٌّ.

ومن غير الثلاثي المجرّد تكون[٤٨] على وزن اسم المفعول؛ والفارق القرينة.

٢. المثال

[الماضي من المثال] إعلالها ماضيًا:

١- بالنقل والقلب والحذف نحو: نَاتَرَ؛ أصله انْوَتَرَ على وزن انْفَعَلَ كانقطع؛ فبالنقل والقلب والحذف صار ناتر.

٢- وبالقلب والإدغام نحو: اتَّعَدَ؛ أصله اوْتَعَدَ على وزن افْتَعَلَ كاجتمع؛ فبالقلب والإدغام صار اتّعد.

3. through conversion—that is, converting the *wāw* to a *yā'* when it is vowelless and the preceding letter possesses *kasr*—as in *ījazza*, originally *iwjazza* of the pattern *ifʿalla* as in *iḥmarra* (he reddened). Through conversion this becomes *ījazza*. An example like *ījazza*: *ījāzza*.

[The Resemblant Imperfect] In the imperfect tense, they are modified

1. through elision of the *wāw* in the position of the first radical if the resemblant root occurs in Classes *Ḍaraba*, *Fataḥa*, *Ḥasiba*, *Iḥmarra*, or *Iḥmārra* as in *yaʿidu* (he promises), originally *yawʿidu* of the pattern *yafʿilu* as in *yaḍribu* (he hits). The *wāw* is elided because it lies between a *yā'* and a *kasra*. This rule is extended to cases like *taʿidu*. Through the modification [*yawʿidu*] becomes *yaʿidu*. Examples like *yaʿidu*: *yaḍaʿu* (he places) (for it originally belongs to Class *Ḍaraba*), *yamiqu* (he loves), *yajazzu*, *yajāzzu*.
2. through transfer and conversion if the resemblant root occurs in Class *Inqaṭaʿa* as in *yanātiru*, originally *yanwatiru* of the pattern *yanfaʿilu* as in *yanqaṭiʿu* (it is severed). Through transfer and conversion this becomes *yanātiru*.
3. through conversion and assimilation if the letter *wāw* occurs as the first radical in Class *Ijtamaʿa* as in *yattaʿidu* (he reaches an agreement), originally *yawtaʿidu* of the pattern *yaftaʿilu* as in *yajtamiʿu* (it comes together). Through conversion and assimilation this becomes *yattaʿidu*.

٣- وبالقلب أي قلب الواو ياءً لسكونها وانكسار ما قبلها نحو: اِيجَزَّ؛ أصله اوْجَزَّ على وزن افْعَلَّ كاحمرّ؛ وبالقلب صار ايجزّ. كـ«ايجزّ»: اِيجَازَّ.

[المضارع من المثال] إعلالها مضارعًا:

١- بحذف الفاء الواوي إن كان المثال من باب ضرب أو فتح أو حسب أو احمرّ واحمارّ نحو: يَعِدُ؛ أصله يَوْعِدُ على وزن يَفْعِلُ كيضرب؛ حذفت الواو لوقوعها بين الياء والكسرة. وحمل عليه نحو تَعِدُ؛ وبالإعلال صار يعد. مثل «يعد»: يَضَعُ لكونه أصلًا من ضرب، ويَمِقُ، ويَجَزُّ، ويَجَازُّ.

٢- وبالنقل والقلب إن كان المثال من باب انقطع نحو: يَنَاتِرُ؛ أصله يَنْوَتِرُ على وزن يَنْفَعِلُ كينقطع؛ وبالنقل والقلب صار يناتر.

٣- وبالقلب والإدغام إن كان الواو فاء الفعل من باب اجتمع نحو: يَتَّعِدُ؛ أصله يَوْتَعِدُ على وزن يَفْتَعِلُ كيجتمع؛ فبالقلب والإدغام صار يتّعد.

[The Resemblant Imperative] In the imperative, they are modified

1. through double elision—that is, eliding the *wāw* in the position of the first radical when it lies between two *kasras* and then eliding the connective *hamza* because it is not necessary—as in *ʿid* (promise), originally *iwʿid* of the pattern *ifʿil* as in *iḍrib* (hit). Through double elision this becomes *ʿid*. Examples like *ʿid*: *ḍaʿ* (place), *miq* (love).

   As for Classes *Ḥasuna*, *Iḥmarra*, and *Iḥmārra*, no other forms occur in them besides the perfect tense, the imperfect tense, and the participial.[67]

2. through conversion and assimilation if the letter *wāw* assumes the position of the first radical in Class *Ijtamaʿa* as in *ittaʿid* (reach an agreement), originally *iwtaʿid*. Through conversion and assimilation this becomes *ittaʿid*.

[The Resemblant Prohibitive] In the prohibitive, they are modified through elision if the letter *wāw* assumes the position of the first radical in Classes *Ḍaraba*, *Fataḥa*, or *Ḥasiba* as in *lā taʿid* (do not promise), originally *lā tawʿid* of the pattern *lā tafʿil* as in *lā taḍrib* (do not hit). Through elision of the *wāw* because it lies between two *kasras* (though merely by extension),[68] this becomes *lā taʿid*. Examples like *lā taʿid*: *lā taḍaʿ* (do not place), *lā tamiq* (do not love).

[The Resemblant Active Participle] In the active participle, simple triliteral classes [with resemblant roots] are not modified, e.g., *wāʿidun* (one that promises). Classes [with resemblant roots] that are not simple triliterals are patterned after the active imperfect tense verb, as already discussed a number of times.

[الأمر من المثال] إعلالها أمرًا:

١- بالحذفين حذف الفاء الواوي لوقوعها بين الكسرات وحذف همزة الوصل للاستغناء عنها نحو: عِدْ؛ أصله اوْعِدْ على وزن افْعِلْ كاضرب؛ فبالحذفين صار عد. كـ«عد»: ضَعْ ومِقْ.

أما باب حسن واحمرّ واحمارّ فلا يجيء منها غير الماضي والمضارع والصفة المشبّهة[٤٩].

٢- وبالقلب والإدغام إن كانت الواو فاء الفعل من باب اجتمع نحو: اتَّعِدْ؛ أصله اوْتَعِدْ؛ بالقلب والإدغام صار اتّعد.

[النهي من المثال] إعلالها نهيًا بالحذف إن كانت الواو فاء الفعل من باب ضرب أو فتح أو حسب نحو: لا تَعِدْ؛ أصله لا تَوْعِدْ على وزن لا تَفْعِلْ كلا تضرب؛ فبحذف الواو لوقوعها بين الكسرات ولو حملا صار لا تعد. كـ«لا تعد»: لا تَضَعْ، ولا تَمِقْ.

اسم الفاعل من المثال لا يعتلّ من الثلاثي المجرّد، نحو وَاعِدٌ. ومن غير الثلاثي المجرّد يكون على وزن الفعل المضارع المعلوم كما مرّ مرارًا.

[The Resemblant Passive Participle and Sister Forms] In the passive participle and its sister forms, simple triliteral classes [with resemblant roots] are not modified, e.g., *mawʿūdun* (one that is promised) and *mawʿidun* (place/time of promising, promising). Classes [with resemblant roots] that are not simple triliterals are patterned after the passive imperfect tense verb, e.g., *mūʿadun* / *yūʿadu* (one that is promised, place or time of promising, promising / he is promised).

III. The Hollow Root

The third of the seven irregular types—the modification of classes with hollow roots:

[The Hollow Perfect] In the perfect tense, [classes with hollow roots] are modified

1. through conversion when the letter preceding the weak letter possesses *fatḥ* as in *qāla* (he said), originally *qawala* of the pattern *faʿala* as in *naṣara* (he helped). The *wāw* is converted to an *alif* because it is vowelized and the preceding letter possesses *fatḥ*, and this becomes *qāla*. Examples like *qāla*: *bāʿa* (he sold), *khāfa* (he was afraid), *innāla*, *ikhtāra* (he chose).
2. through conversion, elision, and then conversion as in *qulna* (they [f.] said), originally *qawalna* of the pattern *faʿalna* as in *naṣarna* (they [f.] helped). The *wāw* is converted to an *alif* and then elided due to the convergence of two vowelless letters. Then [the vowel of] the first radical is converted to a *ḍamma* to indicate the elision of the *wāw*. The word thus becomes *qulna*. Examples like *qulna*: *biʿna* (they [f.] sold), *khifna* (they [f.] were afraid), *innalna*, *ikhtarna* (they [f.] chose).

[اسم المفعول وأخواته من المثال] لا يعتلّ اسم المفعول وأخواته من الثلاثي المجرّد، نحو مَوْعُودٌ ومَوْعِدٌ. ومن غير الثلاثي المجرّد يكون على وزن الفعل المضارع المجهول، نحو مُوعَدٌ/ يُوعَدُ.

٣. الأجوف

الثالث من الأقسام السبعة المعتلة إعلال أبواب الأجوف.

[الماضي من الأجوف] إعلالها ماضيًا:

١- بالقلب لكون ما قبل حرف العلة مفتوحة نحو: قَالَ؛ أصله قَوَلَ على وزن فَعَلَ كنصر؛ قلبت الواو ألفا لتحركها وانفتاح ما قبلها فصار قال. كـ«قال»: بَاعَ، خَافَ، انَّالَ، اخْتَارَ.

٢- وبالقلب والحذف ثم القلب نحو: قُلْنَ؛ أصله قَوَلْنَ على وزن فَعَلْنَ كنصرن؛ قلبت الواو ألفًا ثم حذفت لالتقاء الساكنين ثم قلبت [حركة] الفاء ضمةً لتدلّ على حذف الواو فصار قلن. كـ«قلن»: بِعْنَ، خِفْنَ، انَّلْنَ، اخْتَرْنَ.

Note: In *biʿna*, the *fatḥa* of the first radical is converted to a *kasra* to indicate the elision of the letter *yāʾ*, and in *khifna* to indicate the [original] *kasra* of the second radical.

3. through transfer and conversion when the letter preceding the weak letter lacks a vowel as in *ajāba* (he answered), originally *ajwaba* of the pattern *afʿala* as in *akrama* (he honored). The *fatḥa* of the *wāw* is transferred to the preceding letter, and then since the preceding letter possesses *fatḥ*, the *wāw* is converted to an *alif* such that the word becomes *ajāba*. Examples like *ajāba*: *istaqāma* (he straightened up), *marāḥa*.

   An exception occurs when a vowelized nominative pronoun is suffixed [to the verb]. In such cases it is modified through transfer and elision rather than conversion, as in *ajabna* (they [f.] answered), originally *ajwabna* of the pattern *afʿalna* as in *akramna* (they [f.] honored). The vowel of the second radical is transferred to the first radical because it is vowelless, and the second radical is elided due to the convergence of two vowelless letters, such that the word becomes *ajabna*. Examples like *ajabna*: *istaqamna* (they [f.] straightened up), *maraḥna*.

[The Hollow Imperfect] In the imperfect tense, they are modified

1. through transfer when the letter preceding the weak letter lacks a vowel as in *yaqūlu* (he says), originally *yaqwulu* of the pattern *yafʿulu* as in *yanṣuru* (he helps). The *ḍamma* of the *wāw* is transferred to the preceding letter, and this becomes *yaqūlu*. Examples like *yaqūlu*: *yabīʿu* (he sells), *yakhāfu* (he is afraid).

   Note: Following the transfer in the case of *yakhāfu*, the *wāw* is converted to an *alif* because the preceding letter possesses *fatḥ*.[69]

إلا أنّ فتحة فاء الفعل تقلب[٥٢] كسرةً في بِعْنَ لتدلّ على حذف الياء وفي خِفْنَ تدلّ على كسر عين الفعل.

٣- وبالنقل والقلب، لكون ما قبل حرف العلة ساكنًا نحو: أَجَابَ؛ أصله أَجْوَبَ على وزن أَفْعَلَ كأكرم؛ نقلت فتحة الواو إلى ما قبلها وقلبت الواو ألفًا لانفتاح ما قبلها فصار أجاب. كـ«أجاب»: اسْتَقَامَ، مَرَاحَ.

إلا إذا اتّصل بآخره الضمير المرفوع المتحرك فإعلالها إذن بالنقل والحذف لا بالقلب، كأَجَبْنَ؛ أصله أَجْوَبْنَ على وزن أَفْعَلْنَ كأكرمن؛ نقلت حركة العين إلى الفاء لسكونها وحذفت العين لالتقاء الساكنين فصار أجبن. كـ«أجبن»: اسْتَقَمْنَ، مَرَحْنَ.

[المضارع من الأجوف] إعلالها مضارعًا:

١- بالنقل لكون ما قبل حرف العلة ساكنة نحو: يَقُولُ؛ أصله يَقْوُلُ على وزن يَفْعُلُ كينصر؛ نقلت ضمة الواو إلى ما قبلها فصار يقول. كـ«يقول»: يَبِيعُ، يَخَافُ.

غير أنّ يخاف بعد النقل تقلب واوه ألفًا لانفتاح ما قبلها.

2. through transfer and elision as in *yaqulna* (they [f.] say), originally *yaqwulna* of the pattern *yafʿulna* as in *yanṣurna* (they [f.] help). Through transfer and elision this becomes *yaqulna*. Examples like *yaqulna*: *yabiʿna* (they [f.] sell), *yakhafna* (they [f.] are afraid).
3. through transfer and conversion when the letter preceding the weak letter lacks a vowel and the vowel of [the weak letter] is of a different category as in *yakhāfu* (he is afraid), originally *yakhwafu* of the pattern *yafʿalu* as in *yaʿlamu* (he knows). Through transfer and conversion this becomes *yakhāfu*. Examples like *yakhāfu*: *yastaqīmu* (he straightens up), *yumarīḥu*, *yabādirru*.

[The Hollow Imperative] In the imperative, they are modified

1. through transfer and double elision as in *qul* (say), originally *uqwul* of the pattern *ufʿul* as in *unṣur* (help). Through transfer and double elision this becomes *qul*. Examples like *qul*: *biʿ* (sell), *khaf* (be afraid).
2. through transfer and elision when the letter preceding the weak letter lacks a vowel and there is a convergence of two vowelless letters as in *ajib* (answer), originally *ajwib* of the pattern *afʿil*. Through transfer and elision this becomes *ajib*.
3. through conversion and elision when the letter preceding the weak letter is vowelized as in *ikhtar* (choose), originally *ikhtayir* of the pattern *iftaʿil*. Through conversion and elision this becomes *ikhtar*.
4. through transfer and elision when the letter preceding the weak letter lacks a vowel as in *istaqim* (straighten up), originally *istaqwim* of the pattern *istafʿil* as in *istakhrij* (extract). Through transfer and elision this becomes *istaqim*. Examples like *istaqim*: *mariḥ*, *bādirri*.

٢- وبالنقل والحذف نحو: يَقُلْنَ؛ أصله يَقْوُلْنَ على وزن يَفْعُلْنَ كينصرن؛ وبالنقل والحذف صار يقلن. كـ«يقلن»: يَبِعْنَ، يَخَفْنَ.

٣- وبالنقل والقلب لكون ما قبل حرف العلة ساكنة وكانت حركتها من غير جنسها نحو: يَخَافُ؛ أصله يَخْوَفُ على وزن يَفْعَلُ كيعلم؛ وبالنقل والقلب صار يخاف. كـ«يخاف»: يَسْتَقِيمُ، يُمَرِيحُ، يَبَادِرُّ.

[الأمر من الأجوف] إعلالها أمرًا:

١- بالنقل والحذفين نحو: قُلْ؛ أصله اقْوُلْ على وزن افْعُلْ كانصر؛ وبالنقل والحذفين صار قل. كـ«قل»: بِعْ، وخَفْ.

٢- وبالنقل والحذف لكون ما قبل حرف العلة ساكنة والتقاء الساكنتين نحو: أَجِبْ؛ أصله أَجْوِبْ على وزن أَفْعِلْ؛ وبالنقل والحذف صار أجب.

٣- وبالقلب والحذف لكون ما قبل حرف العلة متحركة نحو: اخْتَرْ؛ أصله اخْتَيِرْ على وزن افْتَعِلْ[٥٣]؛ وبالقلب والحذف صار اختر.

٤- وبالنقل والحذف لكون ما قبل حرف العلة ساكنة نحو: اسْتَقِمْ؛ أصله اسْتَقْوِمْ على وزن اسْتَفْعِلْ كاستخرج؛ وبالنقل والحذف صار استقم. كـ«استقم»: مَرِحْ، وبَادِرِّ.

Note: Following the transfer and elision in the case of *bādirri*, the connective *hamza* is elided because it is not necessary.

إلا أن بـادرّ بعد النقـل والحـذف حذفت منه همـزة الوصل للاسـتغناء عنها.

[The Hollow Prohibitive] In the prohibitive, they are modified

1. through transfer and elision when the letter preceding the weak letter lacks a vowel as in *lā taqul* (do not say), originally *lā taqwul* of the pattern *lā tafʿul* as in *lā tanṣur* (do not help). Through transfer and elision this becomes *lā taqul*. Examples like *lā taqul*: *lā tabiʿ* (do not sell), *lā takhaf* (do not be afraid), *lā tujib* (do not answer), *lā tastaqim* (do not straighten up), *lā tumariḥ*, *lā tabādirri*.

   Note: The modification of *tabādirri* occurs through transfer and conversion rather than transfer and elision because the letter following the weak letter is vowelized.

2. through conversion and elision when the letter preceding the weak letter is vowelized as in *lā takhtar* (do not choose), originally *lā takhtayir* of the pattern *lā taftaʿil*. Through conversion and elision this becomes *lā takhtar*.

[النهي من الأجوف] إعلالها نهيًا:

١- بالنقـل والحـذف لكـون مـا قبـل حـرف العلـة سـاكنة نحـو: لا تَقُـلْ؛ أصلـه لا تَقْـوُلْ على وزن لا تَفْعُـلْ كلا تنـصر؛ وبالنقل والحذف صـار لا تقل. كـ«لا تقل»: لا تَبِعْ، لا تَخَفْ، لا تُجِبْ، لا تَسْـتَقِمْ، لا تُمَـرِحْ، لا تَبَادِرِّ.

إلا أنّ إعلال تبـادرّ بالنقـل والقلب لا بالنقل والحـذف لكون ما بعـد حرف العلـة متحركة.

٢- وبالقلـب والحـذف لكـون مـا قبـل حـرف العلـة متحركة نحـو: لا تَخْـتَرْ؛ أصله لا تَخْتَـيِرْ على وزن لا تَفْتَعِـلْ؛ وبالقلـب والحـذف صـار لا تختر.

[The Hollow Active Participle] In the active participle, simple triliteral classes [with hollow roots] are modified by converting the second radical (whether it is a *wāw* or a *yāʾ*) to a *hamza* because it follows an added *alif* as in *qāʾilun* (one that says), originally *qāwilun* of the pattern *fāʿilun* as in *nāṣirun* (one that helps). By converting the weak letter to a *hamza* this becomes *qāʾilun*. Examples like *qāʾilun*: *bāʾiʿun* (one that sells), *khāʾifun* (one that is afraid).

[اسم الفاعـل مـن الأجـوف] إعلالها اسـم الفاعل من الثـلاثي المجرّد بقلـب العين همزةً واويًـا كان العين أو يائيًا لوقوعهمـا بعـد الألـف الزائدة[٥] نحـو: قَائِـلٌ؛ أصلـه قَاوِلٌ على وزن فَاعِـلٌ كنـاصر؛ وبقلب حـرف العلة همـزةً صار قائـل. كـ«قائل»: بَائِـعٌ، وخَائِفٌ.

Classes [with hollow roots] that are not simple triliterals are patterned after the active imperfect tense verb.

ومــن غير الثلاثي المجـرّد يكــون على وزن الفعــل المضــارع المعلــوم.

[The Hollow Passive Participle] In the passive participle, [classes with hollow roots] are modified

1. through transfer and elision when the second radical is a *wāw* as in *maqūlun* (thing that is said), originally *maqwūlun* of the pattern *mafʿūlun* as in *manṣūrun* (one that is helped). Through transfer and elision this becomes *maqūlun*. An example like *maqūlun*: *makhūfun* (thing that is feared).
2. through transfer, elision, and then double conversion when the second radical is a *yāʾ* as in *mabīʿun* (thing that is sold), originally *mabyūʿun* of the pattern *mafʿūlun* as in *manṣūrun* (one that is helped). Through transfer, elision, and double conversion—that is, converting the *ḍamma* of the first radical to a *kasra* and converting the *wāw* to a *yāʾ*—this becomes *mabīʿun*.

[اسم المفعول من الأجوف] إعلالها اسم المفعول:

١- بالنقل والحذف عند كون عين الفعل واوًا نحو: مَقُولٌ؛ أصله مَقْوُولٌ على وزن مَفْعُولٌ كمنصور؛ فبالنقل والحذف صار مقول. كـ«مقول»: مَخُوفٌ.

٢- وبالنقل والحذف ثم القلبين عند كون عين الفعل ياءً نحو: مَبِيعٌ؛ أصله مَبْيُوعٌ على وزن مَفْعُولٌ كمنصور؛ فبالنقل والحذف والقلبين أي قلب ضمة الفاء كسرةً وقلب الواو ياءً صار مبيع.

[The Hollow Noun of Time; Noun of Place; Mimated Infinitive] In the nouns of time and place and the mimated infinitive, simple triliteral classes [with hollow roots] are modified through transfer and conversion as in *maqālun* (place/time of saying, saying), originally *maqwalun* of the pattern *mafʿalun* as in *manṣarun* (place/time of helping, helping). Through transfer and conversion this becomes *maqālun*. Examples like *maqālun*: *mabāʿun* (place/time of selling, selling), *makhāfun* (place/time of being afraid, being afraid).

[اسم الزمان، اسم المكان، المصدر الميمي من الأجوف] إعلالها حال كونها اسمي الزمان والمكان والمصدر الميمي من الثلاثي المجرّد بالنقل والقلب نحو: مَقَالٌ؛ أصله مَقْوَلٌ على وزن مَفْعَلٌ كمنصر؛ وبالنقل والقلب صار مقال. كـ«مقال»: مَبَاعٌ، مَخَافٌ.

Classes [with hollow roots] that are not simple triliterals are patterned after the passive participle, e.g., *mujābun* (thing that is answered, place/time of answering, answering), and are distinguished [from it] by context.

ومن غير الثلاثي المجرّد يكن على وزن اسم المفعول، كمُجَابٌ؛ والفارق القرينة.

IV. The Defective Root

Fourth in the modification of the classes of the seven irregular types is the modification of classes with defective roots.

[The Defective Perfect] In the perfect tense, [classes with defective roots] are modified through conversion when the weak letter is vowelized and the preceding letter possesses *fatḥ* as in *ghazā* (he purposed), originally *ghazawa* of the pattern *faʿala* as in *naṣara* (he helped). Through conversion this becomes *ghazā*.

This is in contrast to cases like *raḍiya* (he was content) and *saruwa* (he was noble and generous), in which the letter preceding [the weak letter] does not possess *fatḥ*. It is also in contrast to cases like *ghazawā* (they two purposed), in which the letter *alif* mandates that the preceding letter possess *fatḥ*. It is in contrast, moreover, to cases like *ghazaw*, *ghazat*, and *ghazatā* (they [m.] / she / they two [f.] purposed), in which the two [original consecutive] vowelless letters mandate the elision of the converted *alif*.

Examples like *ghazā*: *ramā* (he threw), *aʿṭā* (he gave), *ishtarā* (he purchased), *istadʿā* (he called for).

[The Defective Imperfect] In the imperfect tense, they are modified through elision—that is, eliding the *ḍamma* of the weak letter on account of the phonetic heaviness of the *ḍamma* with it—as in *yaghzū* (he purposes) (the *wāw* vowelless), originally *yaghzuwu* (the *wāw* possessing *ḍamm*) of the pattern *yafʿulu* as in *yanṣuru* (he helps). Through elision this becomes *yaghzū*. Examples like *yaghzū* include [imperfect tense verbs from] the other defective classes, e.g., *yuʿṭī* (he gives), *yashtarī* (he purchases), and *yastadʿī* (he calls for).

٤. الناقص

الرابع من إعلال أبواب الأقسام السبعة المعتلّة إعلال أبواب الناقص.

[الماضي من الناقص] إعلالها ماضيًا بالقلب لتحرّك حرف العلّة وانفتاح ما قبلها نحو: غَزَا؛ أصله غَزَوَ على وزن فَعَلَ كنصر؛ فبالقلب صار غزا.

بخلاف نحو رَضِيَ وسَرُوَ لعدم انفتاح ما قبلهما، وبخلاف نحو غَزَوَا لاقتضاء الألف فتح ما قبلها، وبخلاف نحو غَزَوْا وغَزَتْ وغَزَتَا لاقتضاء الساكنين حذف الألف المقلوبة.

كغزا: رَمَى، أَعْطَى، اشْتَرَى، اسْتَدْعَى.

[المضارع من الناقص] إعلالها مضارعًا بالحذف أي حذف ضمّة حرف العلّة لثقلها عليها نحو: يَغْزُو، بسكون الواو؛ أصله يَغْزُوُ بضم الواو على وزن يَفْعُلُ كينصر؛ فبالحذف صار يغزو. كـ«يغزو» ما بقي من أبواب الناقصة نحو: يُعْطِي، ويَشْتَرِي، ويَسْتَدْعِي.

[The Defective Imperative] In the imperative, they are modified

1. through elision as in *nāji* (converse secretly with), originally *li-tunājī* according to the Basrans; through elision of the third radical and the imperfect tense prefix *tā'* due to frequent use, this became *nāji*.[70] An example like *nāji*: *taṣāba* (behave like a child).
2. through elision and the addition of the connective *hamza* if the letter following the imperfect tense prefix lacks a vowel as in *ughzu* (purpose), originally *li-taghzū* according to the Basrans; through elision and the addition of the connective *hamza* this becomes *ughzu*. An example like *ughzu*: *istad'i* (call for).

[الأمر من الناقص] إعلالها أمرًا:

١- بالحذف نحو: نَاجِ؛ من لِتُنَاجِ عند البصريين؛ فبحذف اللام مع التاء المضارعة لكثرة الاستعمال صار ناجِ. كـ«ناج»: تَصَابَ.

٢- وبالحذف وزيادة همزة الوصل إن كانت ما بعد حرف المضارعة ساكنة نحو: اغْزُ؛ من لِتَغْزُ عند البصريين؛ فبالحذف وزيادة الهمزة صار اغز. كـ«اغز»: اسْتَدْعِ.

[The Defective Prohibitive] In the prohibitive, they are modified through elision of the third radical in the singular as in *lā taghzu* (do not purpose) and elision of the inflective *nūn* in the dual as in *lā taghzuwā*, the plural as in *lā taghzū*, and the second-person feminine singular as in *lā taghzī*. Examples like *lā taghzu*: *lā tarmi* / *lā tarmiyā* / *lā tarmū* / *lā tarmī* (do not throw), *lā tashtari* / *lā tashtariyā* / *lā tashtarū* / *lā tashtarī* (do not purchase).

[النهي من الناقص] إعلالها نهيًا بحذف لام الفعل مفردًا نحو: لا تَغْزُ؛ ونون الإعراب تثنيةً نحو: لا تَغْزُوَا؛ أو جمعًا نحو: لا تَغْزُوا؛ أو واحدةً مخاطبة نحو: لا تَغْزِي[٥٥]. كـ«لا تغز»: لا تَرْمِ/ لا تَرْمِيَا/ لا تَرْمُوا/ لا تَرْمِي، لا تَشْتَرِ/ لا تَشْتَرِيَا/ لا تَشْتَرُوا/ لا تَشْتَرِي.

[The Defective Active Participle] In the active participle, they are modified

1. through conversion and double elision when the third radical is a *wāw* as in *ghāzin* (one that purposes), originally *ghāziwun* of the pattern *fā'ilun* as in *nāṣirun* (one that helps). The *wāw* is converted to a *yā'* because it is the fourth letter, the *ḍamma* is elided on account of its phonetic heaviness with a weak letter, and then the *yā'* [is elided] due to the convergence of two vowelless letters. The word thus becomes *ghāzin*, of the pattern *fā'in*. An example like *ghāzin*: *qāḍin* (one that judges).

[اسم الفاعل من الناقص] إعلالها اسم الفاعل:

١- بالقلب والحذفين عند كون اللام واوًا نحو: غَازٍ؛ أصله غَازِوٌ على وزن فَاعِلٌ كناصر؛ قلب الواو ياءً لوقوعها رابعة وحذف الضمة لثقلها على حرف العلة ثم الياء لالتقاء الساكنين فصار غازٍ على وزن فَاعٍ. كـ«غازٍ»: قَاضٍ.

2. through double elision when the third radical is a *yāʾ* [as in *rāmin* (one that throws), originally *rāmiyun* of the pattern *fāʿilun* as in *ḍāribun* (one that hits). Through double elision, that is, eliding the *ḍamma* on account of its phonetic heaviness with a weak letter and eliding the *yāʾ* due to the convergence of two vowelless letters, this becomes *rāmin*, of the pattern *fāʿin*.] An example like *rāmin*: *rāʿin* (one that cares for).

[The Defective Passive Participle and Sister Forms] In the passive participle, they are modified

1. through assimilation only when the third radical is a *wāw* as in *maghzuwwun* (thing that is purposed), originally *maghzūwun*; through assimilation this becomes *maghzuwwun*.
2. through double conversion and assimilation when the third radical is a *yāʾ*—that is, converting the *wāw* in the pattern *mafʿūl* to a *yāʾ* and the *ḍamma* of the second radical to a *kasra* and then assimilating the first [*yāʾ*] to the second—as in *marmiyyun* (thing that is thrown), originally *marmūyun*; through double elision and assimilation this becomes *marmiyyun*.

The sister forms of the passive participle are modified through conversion—that is, converting the third radical to an *alif*—as in *maghzā* (place/time of purposing, purposing) and *marmā* (place/time of throwing, throwing), originally *maghzawun* and *marmayun*, respectively; through conversion they become *maghzā* and *marmā*.

V. The Disjointly Weak Root

Fifth in the modification of the classes of the seven irregular types is the modification of classes with disjointly weak roots.

٢- وبالحذفين عند كون اللام ياءً [نحو: رَامٍ؛ أصله رَامِيٌ على وزن فَاعِلٌ كضارب؛ وبالحذفين حذف الضمة لثقلها على حرف العلة وحذف الياء لالتقاء الساكنين صار رامٍ على وزن فَاعٍ.][٥٦] كـ«رامٍ»: رَاعٍ.

[اسم المفعول وأخواته من الناقص] إعلالها حال كونها اسم المفعول:

١- بالإدغام فقط عند كون اللام واوًا نحو: مَغْزُوٌّ؛ أصله مَغْزُووٌ؛ فبالإدغام صار مغزوّ.

٢- وبالقلبين والإدغام عند كون اللام ياءً، أي قلب واو المفعول ياءً وضمة العين كسرةً ودغم الأولى في الثانية نحو: مَرْمِيٌّ؛ أصله مَرْمُويٌ؛ فبالقلبين والإدغام صار مرميّ.

وإعلال أخواته بالقلب أي قلب اللام ألفًا نحو: مَغْزَى، مَرْمَى؛ أصلهما مَغْزَوٌ، ومَرْمَيٌ؛ فبالقلب صارا مغزى، مرمى.

٥. اللفيف المفروق

الخامس من إعلال أبواب الأقسام السبعة المعتلّة إعلال أبواب اللفيف المفروق.

[The Disjointly Weak Perfect] In the perfect tense, [classes with disjointly weak roots] are modified

1. through double conversion and assimilation when the disjointly weak root occurs in Class *Ijtamaʿa* as in *ittaqā* (he guarded himself against), originally *iwtaqaya* of the pattern *iftaʿala* as in *ijtamaʿa* (it came together). The third radical is converted to an *alif*, and the *wāw* is converted to a *tāʾ* and then assimilated to the second *tāʾ*. The word thus becomes *ittaqā*.
2. through transfer and conversion when the disjointly weak root occurs in Class *Daḥraja* as in *watāla*, originally *watwala* of the pattern *faʿlala* as in *daḥraja* (he rolled s.th.); through transfer and conversion this becomes *watāla*.
3. through conversion and then transfer and conversion when [the root] occurs in Class *Tadaḥraja* as in *tātāla*, originally *tawatwala* of the pattern *tafaʿlala* as in *tadaḥraja* (he rolled [intr.]); through conversion and then transfer and conversion this becomes *tātāla*.

   They are also modified through conversion and then transfer and conversion when [the root] occurs in Class *Iḥranjama* as in *īsanāsa*, originally *iwsanwasa* of the pattern *ifʿanlala* as in *iḥranjama* (it crowded together); through conversion and then transfer and conversion this becomes *īsanāsa*.

[The Disjointly Weak Imperfect] In the imperfect tense, they are modified

1. through double elision when the disjointly weak root occurs in Class *Ḍaraba* as in *yaqī* (he guards), originally *yawqiyu* of the pattern *yafʿilu* as in *yaḍribu* (he hits); through elision of the *wāw* and the vowel of the third radical, this becomes *yaqī*. An example like *yaqī*: *yalī* (he is close to).

[الماضي من اللفيف المفروق] إعلالها ماضيًا:

١- بالقلبين والإدغام عند كون اللفيف المفروق من باب اجتمع نحو: اتَّقَى؛ أصله اوْتَقَى على وزن افْتَعَلَ كاجتمع؛ فقلبت لام الفعل[٥٧] ألفًا والواو تاءً ثم أدغمت في التاء الثانية فصار[٥٨] اتّقى.

٢- وبالنقل والقلب عند كون اللفيف المفروق من باب دحرج نحو: وَتَالَ؛ أصله وَتْوَلَ على وزن فَعْلَلَ كدحرج؛ فبالنقل والقلب صار وتال.

٣- وبالقلب ثم النقل والقلب عند كونه من باب تدحرج نحو: تَاتَالَ؛ أصله تَوَتْوَلَ على وزن تَفَعْلَلَ كتدحرج؛ فبالقلب ثم النقل والقلب صار تاتال.

وبالقلب ثم النقل والقلب إن كان من باب احرنجم نحو: اِيسَنَاسَ؛ أصله اوْسَنْوَسَ على وزن افْعَنْلَلَ كاحرنجم؛ فبالقلب ثم النقل والقلب صار ايسناس.

[المضارع من اللفيف المفروق] إعلالها مضارعًا:

١- بالحذفين عند كون اللفيف المفروق من باب ضرب نحو: يَقِي؛ أصله يَوْقِيُ على وزن يَفْعِلُ كيضرب؛ فبحذف الواو وحركة اللام صار يقي. كـ«يقي»: يَلِي.

2. through elision—that is, eliding the vowel of the third radical on account of the phonetic heaviness of the *ḍamma* with the *yāʾ*—as in *yūṣī* (he bequeaths), originally *yuwṣiyu* of the pattern *yufʿilu* as in *yukrimu* (he honors); through elision of the vowel of the third radical this becomes *yūṣī*. Examples like *yūṣī*: *yuwallī* (he turns), *yuwārī* (he conceals).
3. through conversion and assimilation when the disjointly weak root occurs in Class *Ijtamaʿa* as in *yattaqī* (he guards himself against), originally *yawtaqiyu* of the pattern *yaftaʿilu* as in *yajtamiʿu* (it comes together); through conversion, assimilation, and elision of the vowel of the third radical, this becomes *yattaqī*.
4. through transfer and conversion when the disjointly weak root occurs in Class *Daḥraja* as in *yuwatīlu*, originally *yuwatwilu* of the pattern *yufaʿlilu* as in *yudaḥriju* (he rolls s.th.); through transfer and conversion this becomes *yuwatīlu*. An example like *yuwatīlu*: *yūsanīsu*.
5. through conversion and then transfer and conversion when [the root] occurs in Class *Tadaḥraja* as in *yatātālu*, originally *yatawatwalu* of the pattern *yatafaʿlalu* as in *yatadaḥraju* (he rolls [intr.]); through conversion and then transfer and conversion, this becomes *yatātālu*.

[The Disjointly Weak Imperative] In the imperative, they are modified

1. through conversion, elision, and then double elision when the disjointly weak root occurs in Class *Ḍaraba* as in *qi* (guard), originally *iwqī* of the pattern *ifʿil* as in *iḍrib* (hit). Through conversion of the *wāw* to a *yāʾ*, elision of the latter, and elision of the *hamza* and the *lām*, this becomes *qi*, of the pattern *ʿi*. A *hāʾ* is added to the end in pause, as in *qih*. An example like *qi*: *li* (be close to), of Class *Ḥasiba*.

٢- وبالحذف أي بحذف حركة اللام لثقل الضمة على الياء نحو: يُوصِي؛ أصله يُوْصِيُ على وزن يُفْعِلُ كيكرم؛ فبحذف حركة اللام صار يوصي. كـ«يوصي»: يُوَلِّي، يُوَارِي.

٣- وبالقلب والإدغام عند كون اللفيف المفروق من باب اجتمع نحو: يَتَّقِي؛ أصله يَوْتَقِيُ على وزن يَفْتَعِلُ[٥٩] كيجتمع؛ فبالقلب والإدغام وحذف حركة اللام صار يتّقي.

٤- وبالنقل والقلب عند كون اللفيف المفروق من باب دحرج نحو: يُوَتِيلُ؛ أصله يُوَتْوِلُ على وزن يُفَعْلِلُ كيدحرج؛ فبالنقل والقلب صار يوتيل. كـ«يوتيل»: يُوسَنِيسُ.

٥- وبالقلب ثم بالنقل والقلب عند كونه من باب تدحرج نحو: يَتَاتَالُ؛ أصله يَتَوَتْوَلُ على وزن يَتَفَعْلَلُ كيتدحرج؛ فبالقلب ثم بالنقل والقلب صار يتاتال.

[الأمر من اللفيف المفروق] إعلالها أمرًا:

١- بالقلب والحذف ثم الحذفين عند كون اللفيف المفروق من باب ضرب نحو: قِ؛ أصله اوْقِيْ على وزن افْعِلْ كاضرب؛ فبقلب الواو ياءً وحذفها وحذف الهمزة واللام صار ق على وزن عِ، تلحق به الهاء حالة الوقف نحو قِهْ. كـ«ق»: لِ، من باب حسب.

2. through conversion of the first radical and elision of the third when the disjointly weak root occurs in Class *ʿAlima* as in *īja* (have your foot become chafed), originally *iwjay* of the pattern *ifʿal* as in *iʿlam* (know); through conversion and elision this becomes *īja*, of the pattern *ifʿa*.
3. through elision only of the third radical as in *awṣi* (bequeath), originally *awṣī* of the pattern *afʿil* as in *akrim* (honor); through elision of the third radical this becomes *awṣi*. Examples like *awṣi*: *walli* (turn), *wāri* (conceal), of Classes *Farraḥa* and *Qātala*, respectively.

[The Disjointly Weak Prohibitive] In the prohibitive, they are modified through double elision as in *lā taqi* (do not guard), originally *lā tawqī* of the pattern *lā tafʿil* as in *lā taḍrib* (do not hit); through double elision this becomes *lā taqi*. An example like *lā taqi*: *lā tali* (do not be close to), of Class *Ḥasiba*.

VI. The Conjointly Weak Root

Sixth in the modification of the seven irregular types is the modification of classes with conjointly weak roots.

[The Conjointly Weak Perfect] In the perfect tense, [classes with conjointly weak roots] are modified

1. through conversion of the third radical to an *alif* because it is vowelized and the preceding letter possesses *fatḥ* as in *shawā* (he roasted), originally *shawaya* of the pattern *faʿala* as in *ḍaraba* (he hit); through conversion this becomes *shawā*. Examples like *shawā*: *arwā* (he quenched s.o.'s thirst), *rawwā* (he quenched s.o.'s thirst), *ḥāwā*, *intawā* (he intended), *iltawā* (it was twisted), *istaḥyā* (he felt shy).

٢- وبقلب الفاء وحذف اللام عند كون اللفيف المفروق من باب علم نحو: اِيجَ؛ أصله اوْجَيْ على وزن افْعَلْ كاعلم؛ فبالقلب والحذف صار ايج على وزن افْعَ.

٣- وبحذف اللام فقط نحو: أَوْصِ؛ أصله أَوْصِي على وزن أَفْعِلْ كأكرم؛ فبحذف اللام صار أوص. كـ«أوص»: وَلِّ، وَارِ، من باب فرّح وقاتل.

[النهي من اللفيف المفروق] إعلالها نهيًا بالحذفين نحو: لا تَقِ؛ أصله لا تَوْقِي على وزن لا تَفْعِلْ كلا تضرب؛ فبالحذفين صار لا تق. كـ«لا تق»: لا تَلِ، من باب حسب.

٦. اللفيف المقرون

السادس من إعلال الأقسام السبعة المعتلّة إعلال أبواب اللفيف المقرون.

[الماضي من اللفيف المقرون] إعلالها ماضيًا:

١- بقلب لام الفعل ألفًا لتحركها وانفتاح ما قبلها نحو: شَوَى؛ أصله شَوَيَ على وزن فَعَلَ كضرب؛ فبالقلب صار شوى. كـ«شوى»: أَرْوَى، رَوَّى[60]، حَاوَى، انْتَوَى، الْتَوَى، اسْتَحْيَى.

2. through conversion of the *wāw* in the position of the third radical to a *yāʾ* because it lies at an outermost position while the preceding letter possesses *kasr* as in *qawiya* (he was strong), originally *qawiwa* of the pattern *faʿila* as in *ʿalima* (he knew); through the modification this becomes *qawiya*.

[The Conjointly Weak Imperfect] In the imperfect tense, they are modified

1. through elision of the vowel of the third radical on account of the phonetic heaviness of the *ḍamma* with the *yāʾ* as in *yashwī* (he roasts), originally *yashwiyu* of the pattern *yafʿilu* as in *yaḍribu* (he hits); through elision of the vowel this becomes *yashwī*, the third radical vowelless. Examples like *yashwī*: *yurwī* (he quenches s.o.'s thirst), *yurawwī* (he quenches s.o.'s thirst), *yuḥāwī*, *yantawī* (he intends), *yaltawī* (it is twisted), *yastaḥyī* (he feels shy).
2. through conversion of the third radical to an *alif* because the preceding letter possesses *fatḥ* as in *yaqwā* (he becomes strong), originally *yaqwayu* of the pattern *yafʿalu* as in *yaʿlamu* (he knows); through conversion this becomes *yaqwā*.

[The Conjointly Weak Imperative] In the imperative, they are modified

1. through elision and addition of the connective *hamza* when the letter following the imperfect tense prefix lacks a vowel as in *ishwi* (roast), derived from *tashwī* according to the Kufans and from *li-tashwi* according to the Basrans.[71] Its original form, that is, the original form of *ishwi*, is *ishwī* of the pattern *ifʿil* as in *iḍrib* (hit). Through the elision of the third radical and the addition of a *hamza*, this becomes *ishwi*, of the pattern *ifʿi*. Examples like *ishwi*: *iqwa* (be strong), *irwa* (drink your fill), *intawi* (intend), *iltawi* (be twisted), *istaḥi* (feel shy).[72]

٢- وبقلب اللام الواوية ياءً لتطرفها وانكسار ما قبلها نحو: قَوِيَ؛ أصله قَوِوَ على وزن فَعِلَ كعلم؛ فبالإعلال صار قوي.

[المضارع من اللفيف المقرون] إعلالها مضارعًا:

١- بحذف حركة اللام لثقل الضمّة على الياء نحو: يَشْوِي؛ أصله يَشْوِيُ على يوزن يَفْعِلُ كيضرب؛ فبحذف الحركة صار يشوي بسكون اللام. كـ«يشوي»: يُرْوِي، يُرَوِّي، يُحَاوِي، يَنْتَوِي، يَلْتَوِي، يَسْتَحْيِي.

٢- وبقلب لام الفعل ألفًا لانفتاح ما قبلها نحو: يَقْوَى؛ أصله يَقْوَيُ[٦١] على وزن يَفْعَلُ كيعلم؛ فبالقلب صار يقوى[٦٢].

[الأمر من اللفيف المقرون] إعلالها أمرًا:

١- بالحذف وزيادة همزة الوصل لكون ما بعد حرف المضارعة ساكنة نحو: اشْوِ؛ من تَشْوِي عند الكوفيين ومن لِتَشْوِ عند البصريّين؛ أصله أي أصل اشو اشْوِي على وزن افْعِلْ كاضرب؛ وبحذف اللام وزيادة الهمزة صار اشو على وزن افْعِ. كـ«اشو»: اقْوَ، ارْوَ، انْتَوِ، الْتَوِ[٦٣]، اسْتَحِ.

2. through only elision when the letter following the imperfect tense prefix is vowelized as in *arwi* (quench s.o.'s thirst), [remotely] derived from *tuʾarwī*. Its [direct] origin is *arwī* of the pattern *afʿil* as in *akrim* (honor); through elision of the third radical this becomes *arwi*, of the pattern *afʿi*. Examples like *arwi*: *rawwi* (quench s.o.'s thirst) and *ḥāwi*.

[The Conjointly Weak Prohibitive] In the prohibitive, they are modified through elision of the third radical in virtue of the addition of the prohibitive [*lā*] as in *lā tashwi* (do not roast), originally *tashwī* of the pattern *tafʿil* as in *taḍrib* (you [m.] hit); through the abovementioned addition and elision, this becomes *lā tashwi*, of the pattern *lā tafʿi*. Examples like *lā tashwi*: *lā taqwa* (do not become strong), *lā turawwi* (do not quench s.o.'s thirst), *lā tuḥāwi*, *lā tastaḥi* (do not feel shy).

[The Conjointly Weak Active Participle, Passive Participle, and Sister Forms] In the active participle, they are modified through conversion and double elision as in *shāʾin* (one that roasts), originally *shāwiyun*. The *wāw* is converted to a *hamza* because it follows an added *alif*, the *ḍamma* of the *yāʾ* is elided due to the phonetic heaviness of the *ḍamma* with the *yāʾ*, and then the *yāʾ* is elided due to the convergence of two vowelless letters. The word thus becomes *shāʾin* of the pattern *fāʿin* as in *rāmin* (one that throws).

In the passive participle, they are modified through double conversion and assimilation as in *mashwiyyun* (thing that is roasted), originally *mashwūyun* of the pattern *mafʿūlun* as in *maḍrūbun* (one that is hit). The second *wāw* is converted to a *yāʾ* due to the rule that when the letters *wāw* and *yāʾ* coincide within a word while either is preceded by a vowelless letter, the *wāw* is converted to a *yāʾ*. Then the *ḍamma* of the second radical is converted to a *kasra* to preserve the *yāʾ*, and it is assimilated. The word thus becomes *mashwiyyun*, like *marmiyyun* (thing that is thrown).

٢- وبالحذف فقط لكون ما بعد حرف المضارعة متحركة نحو: أَرْوِ من تُؤَرْوِي؛ أصله أَرْوِي على وزن أَفْعِل كأكرم؛ فبحذف اللام صار أرو على وزن أَفْعِ. كـ«أرو»: رَوِّ[٦٤]، حَاوِ.

[النهي من اللفيف المقرون] إعلالها نهيًا بحذف لام الفعل بدخول [«لا»] الناهية نحو: لا تَشْوِ؛ أصله تَشْوِي على وزن تَفْعِلْ كتضرب؛ فبالدخول والحذف صار لا تشو على وزن لا تَفْعِ. كـ«لا تشو»: لا تَقْوَ، لا تُرَوِّ، لا تُحَاوِ، لا تَسْتَحِ.

[اسم الفاعل والمفعول وأخواته من اللفيف المقرون] إعلالها اسم الفاعل بالقلب والحذفين نحو: شَاءٍ؛ أصله شَاوِيٌ؛ قلبت الواو همزةً لوقوعها بعد الألف الزائدة وحذفت ضمّة الياء لثقلها عليها ثم حذفت الياء لالتقاء الساكنين فصار شاءٍ على وزن فَاعٍ كرَامٍ.

إعلالها اسم[٦٥] المفعول بالقلبين والإدغام نحو: مَشْوِيٌّ؛ أصله مَشْوُويٌ على وزن مَفْعُولٌ كمضروب[٦٦]؛ قلبت الواو الثانية ياءً لقاعدة إذا اجتمع الواو والياء في كلمة سبقت إحداهما سكون قلبت الواو ياءً، ثم قلبت ضمّة العين كسرةً محافظةً على الياء ثم أدغمت، فصار مشويّ كمَرْمِيٍّ.

In the nouns of time and place and the mimated infinitive, they are modified through conversion as in *mashwā* (place/time of roasting, roasting), which is analogous to *marmā* (place/time of throwing, throwing), and is originally *mashwayun*; the *yāʾ* is converted to an *alif* because it is vowelized and the preceding letter possesses *fatḥ*. The word thus becomes *mashwā*.

واسـما الزمـان والمكان والمصـدر المـيمي بالقلـب نحـو: مَشْـوًى كمَـرْمًى؛ أصله مَشْـوَيٌ؛ قلبت الياء ألفًـا لتحركها وانفتـاح مـا قبلهـا فصار مشـوى.

VII. The Hamzated Root

٧. المهموز

Seventh in the modification of the classes of the seven irregular types is the modification of classes with hamzated roots.

السـابع مـن إعلال أبواب الأقسـام السـبعة المعتلّة إعلال أبـواب المهموز.

[The Hamzated Perfect] In the perfect tense, [classes with hamzated roots] are modified

[الماضي من المهموز] إعلالها ماضيًا:

1. through conversion—that is, converting the *hamza* to an *alif* when it is vowelless and the preceding letter possesses *fatḥ*—as in *āmana* (he believed), originally *aʾmana* of the pattern *afʿala* as in *akrama* (he honored); through conversion this becomes *āmana*.
2. through converting the *hamza* to a *wāw* when it is vowelless and the preceding letter possesses *ḍamm* as in *ūmina* (he was rendered secure), a passive perfect tense verb that is originally *uʾmina* of the pattern *ufʿila* as in *ukrima* (he was honored); through conversion this becomes *ūmina*.
3. through converting the *hamza* to a *yāʾ* when it is vowelless and the preceding letter possesses *kasr*, then [converting the *yāʾ*] to a *tāʾ*, and then assimilating it as in *ittakhadha* (he took for himself), originally *iʾtakhadha* of the pattern *iftaʿala* as in *ijtamaʿa* (it came together); through converting the *hamza* to a *yāʾ* and then to a *tāʾ* and then assimilating it to the [second] *tāʾ*, this becomes *ittakhadha*.

١- بالقلـب أي قلـب الهمـزة ألفًـا لسـكونها وانفتاح مـا قبلهـا نحـو: آمَـنَ؛ أصلـه أأْمَـنَ على وزن أَفْعَلَ كأكـرم؛ فبالقلـب صـار آمن.

٢- وقلبهـا واوًا لسـكونها وانضمـام مـا قبلهـا نحـو: أُومِـنَ؛ ماضٍ مجهول أصلـه أُؤْمِـنَ[٦٧] على وزن أُفْعِلَ كأُكـرِم؛ فبالقلـب صـار أومن.

٣- وقلبهـا ياءً لسـكونها وانكسـار مـا قبلها ثـم تاءً ثـم الإدغام نحـو: اتَّخَـذَ؛ أصلـه اِئْتَخَـذَ[٦٨] على وزن افْتَعَـلَ كاجتمـع؛ وبقلبها يـاءً ثم تاءً ثـم إدغامها في التاء صـار اتّخذ.

[The Hamzated Imperfect] In the imperfect tense, they are modified

1. through conversion—that is, converting the *hamza* to a *wāw* when it is vowelless and the preceding letter possesses *ḍamm*—as in *yūminu* (he believes), originally *yu'minu* of the pattern *yufʿilu* as in *yukrimu* (he honors); through the modification this becomes *yūminu*.
2. through converting the *hamza* to a *yāʾ* when it is vowelless and the preceding letter possesses *fatḥ*, then [converting the *yāʾ*] to a *tāʾ*, and then assimilating it [as in *yattakhidhu* (he takes for himself), originally *ya'takhidhu* of the pattern *yaftaʿilu* as in *yajtamiʿu* (it comes together); through converting the *hamza* to a *yāʾ*, then converting the *yāʾ* to a *tāʾ*, and then assimilating it to the second *tāʾ*, this becomes *yattakhidhu*.]

[The Hamzated Imperative] In the imperative, they are modified

1. through conversion—that is, converting the *hamza* to a *wāw* when it is vowelless and the preceding letter possesses *ḍamm*—as in *ūmul* (hope) and *ūdub* (be well-mannered), originally *u'mul* and *u'dub*, of the pattern *ufʿul* as in *unṣur* (help). Through the modification these become *ūmul* and *ūdub*.
2. through converting the *hamza* to a *yāʾ* when it is vowelless and the preceding letter possesses *kasr* as in *īzar* (assist)[73] and *īhab* (take in preparation), originally *i'zir* and *i'hab*, of the patterns *ifʿil* and *ifʿal*. Through the modification these become *īzar* and *īhab*. The *kasra* of the *zāy*[74] is converted to a *fatḥa* to avoid the [case of four consecutive] *kasras*, since the letter *yāʾ* counts as two.

[المضارع من المهموز] إعلالها مضارعًا:

١- بالقلب أي قلب الهمزة واوًا لسكونها وانضمام ما قبلها نحو: يُومِنُ؛ أصله يُؤْمِنُ على وزن يُفْعِلُ كيكرم؛ فبالإعلال صار يومن.

٢- وبقلبها ياءً لسكونها وانفتاح ما قبلها ثم تاءً ثم الإدغام [نحو: يَتَّخِذُ؛ أصله يَأْتَخِذُ على وزن يَفْتَعِلُ كيجتمع؛ فبقلب الهمزة ياءً ثم تاءً ثم إدغامها في التاء الثانية صار يتّخذ.][٦٩]

[الأمر من المهموز] إعلالها أمرًا:

١- بالقلب أي قلب الهمزة واوًا لسكونها وانضمام ما قبلها نحو: أُومُلْ، وأُودُبْ؛ أصلهما أُؤْمُلْ، أُؤْدُبْ[٧٠] على وزن افْعُلْ كانصر؛ فبالإعلال صارا أُومُلْ، أُودُبْ.

٢- قلبها ياءً لسكونها وانكسار ما قبلها نحو: إِيزَرْ[٧١]، وإِيهَبْ؛ أصلهما إِئْزِرْ، وإِئْهَبْ على وزن افْعِلْ وافْعَلْ؛ فبالإعلال صارا ايزر وايهب، قلبت كسرة الزاي[٧٢] فتحةً هربًا من الكسرات إذ الياء تعدّ كسرتين.

[The Hamzated Prohibitive] In the prohibitive, they are modified by making the first radical vowelless, since the imperfect tense prefix mandates this in simple triliterals,[75] as in *lā taʾmul* (do not hope), *lā taʾzir* (do not assist), and *lā taʾhab* (do not take in preparation), which are like *lā tanṣur* (do not help), *lā taḍrib* (do not hit), and *lā taftaḥ* (do not open), respectively.

[النهي من المهموز] إعلالها نهيًا بإسكان فاء الفعل لاقتضاء حرف المضارعة ذلك في الثلاثي المجرّد نحو: لا تَأْمُلْ، لا تَأْزِرْ[٧٣]، لا تَأْهَبْ؛ كلا تنصر، لا تضرب، لا تفتح.

[The Hamzated Active Participle] In the active participle, they are modified through conversion—that is, converting the added *alif* to be of the same kind as the vowel of the preceding letter[76]—as in *āmilun* (one that hopes), *āzirun* (one that assists), and *āhibun* (one that takes in preparation), originally *ʾāmilun*, *ʾāzirun*, and *ʾāhibun*. Through the modification these become *āmilun*, *āzirun*, and *āhibun*.

[اسم الفاعل من المهموز] إعلالها حال كونها اسم الفاعل بالقلب أي قلب الألف الزائدة بجنس حركة ما قبلها نحو: آمِلٌ، آزِرٌ[٧٤]، آهِبٌ؛ أصلها أَامِلٌ، أَازِرٌ[٧٥]، أَاهِبٌ؛ فبالإعلال صارت آمل، آزر[٧٦]، آهب.

This applies if the active participle occurs in a simple triliteral class. If, on the other hand, it occurs in a class that is not a simple triliteral, then it is patterned after the active imperfect tense verb, with the substitution of a *mīm* possessing *ḍamm* in place of the imperfect tense prefix.

هذا إذا كان اسم الفاعل من الثلاثي المجرّد. أما من غير الثلاثي المجرّد فعلى وزن الفعل المضارع المعلوم بإبدال حرف المضارعة ميمًا مضمومة.

[The Hamzated Passive Participle and Sister Forms] In the passive participle, the nouns of time and place, and the mimated infinitive, simple triliteral classes [with hamzated roots] are modified by making the *hamza* vowelless, as mandated by the prefixion of the *mīm*, as in *maʾmūlun* (thing that is hoped for), *maʾzūrun* (one that is assisted), *maʾhūbun* (thing that is taken in preparation) for the passive participle and *maʾmalun* (place/time of hoping, hoping), *maʾzarun* (place/time of assistance, assistance), and *maʾhabun* (place/time of taking in preparation, taking in preparation) for its sister forms.

[اسم المفعول وما يذكر معه من المهموز] إعلالها حال كونها اسم المفعول واسم الزمان والمكان والمصدر الميمي من الثلاثي المجرّد يكون بإسكان الهمزة لاقتضاء اتّصال الميم ذلك، نحو: مَأْمُولٌ، مَأْزُورٌ[٧٧]، مَأْهُوبٌ في اسم المفعول؛ ومَأْمَلٌ، مَأْزَرٌ[٧٨]، مَأْهَبٌ في أخواته.

Classes [with hamzated roots] that are not simple triliterals are patterned after the passive imperfect tense verb, with the substitution of a *mīm* possessing *ḍamm* in place of the imperfect tense prefix.

ومن غير الثلاثي المجرّد يكون[٧٩] على وزن الفعل المضارع المجهول بإبدال حرف المضارعة بالميم المضمومة[٨٠].

By the assistance of Allah ﷻ, the treatise entitled *Turning a Glance: On the Science of Morphology* is complete. May Allah ﷻ by His grace and generosity render it of benefit to us and all believers. Allah! "Take us not to task if we forget or err!" (Q 2:286). "Glory to your Lord, Lord of Might, transcending what they describe! Peace be upon the messengers. And praise to Allah, Lord of the worlds" (Q 37:180–82). By His permission ﷻ, the second treatise follows, entitled *The Tranquil Sea: On the Science of Grammar*.

تمّت بعون الله تعالى الرسالة المسمّاة بلفتة الطرف في علم الصرف جعلها الله تعالى بمنّه وكرمه نافعة لنا ولسائر المؤمنين. اللّهم لا تؤاخذنا إن نسينا أو أخطأنا. ﴿سُبۡحَٰنَ رَبِّكَ رَبِّ ٱلۡعِزَّةِ عَمَّا يَصِفُونَ ١٨٠ وَسَلَٰمٌ عَلَى ٱلۡمُرۡسَلِينَ ١٨١ وَٱلۡحَمۡدُ لِلَّهِ رَبِّ ٱلۡعَٰلَمِينَ﴾ [٣٧/ ١٨٠-١٨٢]. وتليها بإذنه تعالى الرسالة الثانية المسمّاة البحر الصحو في علم النحو.

NOTES TO TREATISE I

1 A tradition in similar form appears to be attributed to ʿUmar b. al-Khaṭṭāb ﷺ.

2 In the interest of preserving the flow of the translation, dictionary-style abbreviations are utilized in the translation of examples: s.th. = something, s.o. = someone, m. = masculine, f. = feminine, intr. = intransitive.

3 By convention, the first radical, that is, the first root letter, the letter in the first basic position of the Arabic word, is designated by the letter *fāʾ* on the model of the verb *faʿala* (he did). Thus, in *naṣara* (he helped), the first radical, *nūn*, is named "the *fāʾ*"—that is, the *fāʾ* of the verb *naṣara*. The other radicals are named in the same way. In this translation, these Arabic technical names are simply rendered *first radical*, *second radical*, *third radical*, and, in some cases, *fourth radical*.

4 Even though it is in the grammatical singular, the verb *iṣṭalaḥa* in actual usage is more likely to express the action of a plural entity, e.g., *iṣṭalaḥa al-qawm…* (The people agreed on…), but, for the sake of simplicity, the translations of example words in this text attempt to reflect the grammatical features of the Arabic when possible.

5 Certain word patterns consist of augment letters in addition to the three or four radicals, and in some cases these augment letters are modified for phonetic considerations. *Iṣṭalaḥa* originally consists of the root *ṣ-l-ḥ* with the augment letters *alif* and *tāʾ*, but the *tāʾ* is converted to a *ṭāʾ* because it is easier to pronounce a *ṭāʾ* directly after the letter *ṣād*. Now, because the example in the text appears to contradict the rule that it is supposed to illustrate, it is unclear whether the author's intention is that the changed augment letter should be represented by the letter that it was initially (as in *iftaʿala*) or the letter that it became after the modification (as in *ifṭaʿala*). In fact, it is disputed which of these two conventions would be correct; see al-Astarābādī, *Sharḥ*, 1:18–19.

6 As will be seen in Chapter 1, some classes of word forms (like the class that *jalbaba* belongs to) have augment letters that give them the same pattern as another class (like that of *daḥraja*). Despite their common pattern (in this example, *faʿlala*), the distinction between the two classes in such cases is maintained because the augment letters in the conforming class are not considered to have the same significance as they have in the principal class. See Birgevī, *Risāla*, 639; al-Astarābādī, *Sharḥ*, 1:52.

7 The phrase "possesses *fatḥ*" renders the Arabic term *maftūḥ*, meaning that a given consonant has the vowel of *fatḥ*, which represents the *a* sound and is signified by the vowel marker *fatḥa*. In Arabic, the short vowels of *ḍamm*, *fatḥ*, and *kasr* are not treated as independent letters but as phonetic properties of consonants, representing the different ways of vocalizing a letter by various basic movements of the mouth: "contracting" (*ḍamm*) for the sound *u*, "opening" (*fatḥ*) for the sound *a*, and "breaking" (*kasr*) for the sound *i*.

8 That is, with some exceptions, it is the standard rule that the second or third radical is a guttural letter in words with the pattern *faʿala* / *yafʿalu* since *fatḥ* is phonetically light and these letters and phonetically heavy. Al-Buḥayrī, *al-Inbāʾ*, 45–46.

9 The form of the infinitive noun is not counted as a derivative form in the strict technical sense, since derivative forms are derived *from* the infinitive noun. The qualification "determined by use" (*mustaʿmal*) refers to the fact that the infinitive nouns of simple triliteral classes do not follow a universal rule with respect to their forms (i.e., they are not *qiyāsī*), these forms being rather accepted as transmitted from authoritative early users of the Arabic language (i.e., they are *samāʿī*). See Ibn Aḥmad, *al-Maṭlūb*, 114.

10 The author uses the active participle *lāzim*, which translates as "intransitive," but the definition he provides makes it clear that he is referring to the general meaning of intransitivity, or *luzūm*.

11 That is, when the second radical is any one of the letters *yāʾ*, *rāʾ*, *mīm*, *lām*, *wāw*, and *nūn*.

12 That this addition contravenes the standard rule (*khilāf al-qiyās*) means that it is applied only as it is received from the early, authoritative speakers of the language and is not generally valid. The addition of a *sīn* or *hāʾ* for intensification only applies to certain words, like the examples just cited.

13 The Arabic term is *bināʾ*. The forms of morphological classes, that is, their characteristic signs, are not to be confused with the forms of the *variform derivatives* (*amthila mukhtalifa*), which incorporate the characteristic signs of their respective classes into a predetermined system of structures including the various verb forms and the various derived noun forms, like those of the active and passive participles. Ultimately, the individual word's *form*—which may be termed its *bināʾ*, *hayʾa*, *ṣūra*, *ṣīgha*, or *wazn*, often interchangeably—is a function of both (a) the category that it belongs to among the variform derivatives and (b) its morphological class. Thus, for example, *yufāʿilu* is the form of (1a) the imperfect tense verb (1b) in Class *Qātala*; *fāʿala* is the form of (2a) the perfect tense verb (2b) in Class *Qātala*; and *mustafʿilun* is the form of (3a) the active participle (3b) in Class *Istakhraja*.

14 The quasi-passive import of a class's form should not be confused with the passive voice.

15 This is a simplification. To be more precise, when the first radical is a *ṣād*, *ḍād*, *ẓāʾ*, or *ṭāʾ* the *tāʾ* is converted to a *ṭāʾ*, and in the latter case they are necessarily assimilated; when the first radical is a *zāy*, *dhāl*, or *dāl*, the *tāʾ* is converted to a *dāl*, and in the latter case they are necessarily assimilated; when the first radical is a *hamza*, *wāw*, *yāʾ*, or *thāʾ*, the first radical is converted to a *tāʾ* (alternatively, when the first radical is a *thāʾ*, the *tāʾ* can be converted to a *thāʾ*) and they are assimilated; and when the first radical is a *tāʾ*, it is simply assimilated with the *tāʾ*. Some of these rules will be illustrated in Chapter 3; for the rest, see Ibn Aḥmad, *al-Maṭlūb*, 278–86. We were unable to ascertain the role of the *sīn* or *shīn* in the author's list.

16 This is a simplification; this and many of the forms that follow have more possible functions than are listed here. For fuller treatment of these functions and indications, see Ibn al-Ḥājib, *al-Shāfiya*, 18–22; al-Buḥayrī, *al-Inbāʾ*, 39–103; Wright, *Arabic Grammar*, 1:29–49. Especially comprehensive is al-ʿAyshī, *Rūḥ al-shurūḥ*, 61–106.

17 Again, this is a simplification. The rules governing conversion and assimilation in this and the next class are analogous to those discussed in note 15 above.

18 An important function of this class is that it can serve as the quasi-passive (*muṭāwiʿ*) form for Class *Qātala*.

19 See note 6 above on the meaning of conformity.

20 The active voice (*al-maʿlūm*) is the opposite of the passive voice (*al-majhūl*). The grammatical subject, or agent (*fāʿil*), of an active verb signifies the doer of the action, while the grammatical agent of a passive verb signifies the object of the action. The form of a verb in the passive voice is different than in the active voice; in the passive voice, for example, *naṣara* becomes *nuṣira* (he was helped). The passive voice is discussed in the section below on uniform derivatives and also in Treatise II, p. 178.

21 Being "built on *fatḥ*" (*mabnī ʿalā al-fatḥ*) means that the word ends in *fatḥ* and does not take varying inflections. Unlike the imperfect tense, the perfect tense is not inflectable.

22 In the passive voice, *yanṣuru* becomes *yunṣaru* (he is helped).

23 The indicative (*rafʿ*) is one of the three inflections of the imperfect tense; the other two are the subjunctive (*naṣb*) and the jussive (*jazm*). These are discussed in detail in the treatise on grammar.

24 For example, one cannot use the passive participle form *mamrūrun* for the intransitive verb *marra* (he passed) alone, but one can add a preposition: *mamrūrun bihi* (one that is passed by).

25 This remains an imperfect tense form, but by means of the particle *lam* it undergoes a change (*qalb*) from the function of signifying present action to that of signifying past action.

26 Another signification of this form is that of expectation (*tawaqquʿ*) that the action will occur in the future, as in "he has not *yet* helped."

27 The *lā* used with the imperfect tense often includes the present time as well and carries the general idea of continuing into the future; in these cases, it is natural to translate the verb into the English present tense. See Wright, *Arabic Grammar*, 2:20, 2:300. Consider, for instance, *inna Allāha lā yuḥibbu al-fariḥīna* (Allah does not love the exultant) (Q 28:77). Many similar examples can be found in the Quran, including the verse that immediately follows.

28 In some circumstances, the emphasis in the particle *lan* might be expressed in translation by adding a word like "certainly."

29 Unlike the second-person imperative, which has a special form of its own, the third-person imperative uses the imperfect tense form.

30 The mimated infinitive (*maṣdar mīmī*) is a derived noun form with the signification of the infinitive noun. See Surūrī, *Sharḥ al-Amthila*, 617.

31 In classes other than the simple triliteral, one could add an adjective to specify the kind, as in *istifādatan ḥasanatan* (a good way of benefitting). For further discussion, see Surūrī, *Sharḥ al-Amthila*, 620–21.

32 There are many forms of the participial, and these are often determined for a given root simply by received use. Other common forms include *faʿīlun* as in *ʿaẓīmun* (one that is great), *faʿilun* as in *zaminun* (one that is chronically ill), *afʿalu* as in *aḥmaru* (one [m.] that is red), *faʿlāʾu* as in *ḥamrāʾu* (one [f.] that is red), and *faʿlā* as in *ʿaṭshā* (one [f.] that is thirsty). For a more comprehensive list of participial forms, see Ibn Aḥmad, *al-Maṭlūb*, 176–78.

33 Literally the "noun of deeming superior" (*ism al-tafḍīl*), a form that may impart either the function of the comparative or that of the superlative, depending on context.

34 The examples below are from Class *Akrama* and thus do not exactly represent all classes that are not simple triliterals. It is helpful to remember that the characteristic signs of the classes are preserved in their derivative forms. For example, the active participle in Class *Faraḥa* is not *mufriḥun* as identical in pattern to the example *mukrimun* below; it is *mufarriḥun* (one that gladdens) because the characteristic

sign of Class *Farraḥa* is that the second radical is doubled. For discussion of the variform derivatives in these classes, see Ibn Aḥmad, *al-Maṭlūb*, 130–264.

35 See note 27.

36 The second-person imperative is called the *imperative proper* (*al-amr bi-l-ṣīgha*, literally, "the imperative by its form") because it has a special form of its own. The third-person imperative, by contrast, is sometimes called "the imperative by the *lām*" (*al-amr bi-l-lām*) because it is formed by the addition of the *lām* to the imperfect tense form. Al-Taftāzānī, *Sharḥ Taṣrīf al-ʿIzzī*, 129.

37 Grammatical affixes (*ʿalāmāt*) here are prefixes and suffixes that indicate the person, gender, and number. They should not be confused with *state inflections* (also *ʿalāmāt*), which indicate a noun's case or a verb's mood.

38 Verbal derivatives consider number, gender, and person, producing the most possible combinations.

39 Adjectival derivatives consider only number and gender and so produce less combinations than verbal derivatives. The broken plural is discounted here because the number of broken plural forms available for a given word is unpredictable.

40 Because nominal derivatives consider only number, they consist of only three forms.

41 Some of the following can be construed as compound tenses; others can be construed as general constructions formed by adding modal verbs or particles to the simple perfect or imperfect tense verbs to modify the verbal meaning in various ways.

42 The author lists these constructions alongside Turkish equivalents, omitted in this edition.

43 Although this and the next are expressed in the form of questions, their meaning is not to request information but to reproach or exhort, respectively.

44 The text does not use the term *root* (*jadhr*), yet doing so in English translation is more useful and clear than translating a term like *al-muʿtall* literally as "the irregular," which is a standalone adjective. Perhaps the author would have used *word* (*kalima*) instead of *root*, i.e., "the irregular word," where *word* refers to a noun or verb, as outlined in the introduction. Nevertheless, the term *root* is preferable in translation because it draws attention to the particular aspect of the word to which irregularity pertains.

45 *Modification* (*iʿlāl*) refers to changes in a word's form on account of the irregularity of its root, usually for the sake of pronunciation. Depending on the word and the kind of irregularity, the change may be any one or more of the following: *assimilation* (*idghām*): to merge or blend the sounds of two letters; *elision* (*ḥadhf*): to omit a vowel or letter; *transfer* (*naql*): to move a vowel from one letter to another; *conversion* (*qalb*): to replace one vowel or letter with another; and *addition* (*ziyāda*): to add a vowel or letter.

46 The text adds *yastamiddu*, which is already mentioned in category 1. Since the original form of *yastamiddu* is *yastamdidu*, with a vowelless *mīm*, it would appear that this example does not belong to category 2.

47 No other forms, that is, among the forms being considered in this chapter.

48 The impermissible convergence of two vowelless letters (*ijtimāʿ al-sākinayn ʿalā ghayr ḥaddihi*) is distinguished from the permissible convergence of two vowelless letters (*ijtimāʿ al-sākinayn ʿalā ḥaddihi*), which occurs when the first letter is a long vowel and the second is assimilated to another letter, as in the *alif* and *bāʾ* in *dābba* (beast).

49 That is, except in hollow roots belonging to Class *ʿAlima*, like *kh-w-f*.

50 That is, the subsequent forms in the standard listing of verbal conjugations: *qulta*, *qultumā*,

qultum, qulti, qultunna, qultu, and *qulnā*. In common to all of these is that their second radical is elided.

51 The modification here resumes after the steps just above, by which *mabyūʿun* has already become *mabūʿun*; with the following two steps, it becomes *mabīʿun*.

52 Since it is included in category 1, the word *rāʿin* (one that desists) here is of the root *r-ʿ-w*, while the homonymous *rāʿin* (one that cares for) in category 2 is of the root *r-ʿ-y*.

53 We have moved these last two examples from category 1 to category 2 since their third radical appears to be a *yāʾ*. In the case of *sārin*, the text mentions *saruwa* above, but *saruwa* in its usual sense of "was noble and generous" only takes the participial form *sariyyun*.

54 They total eight if the quadriliteral classes listed below with their original forms are not counted.

55 Although Class *Farraḥa* is not listed here in the text, *rawwā* from Class *Farraḥa* is discussed later as a conjointly weak root. We have included it in the list so that the classes add up to eight.

56 It is possible that the intended example is *ḥāyā* (he revived [the fire]), an obscure word in its own right. See al-Taftāzānī, *Sharḥ Taṣrīf al-ʿIzzī*, 299.

57 On the modification of *qawiya* from *qawiwa*, see Ibn Aḥmad, *al-Maṭlūb*, 126, 340; al-Taftāzānī, *Sharḥ Taṣrīf al-ʿIzzī*, 293.

58 That is, Class *ʿAlima*. Note that *yarḍā* itself is defective rather than conjointly weak.

59 There are actually three elisions: elision of the imperative *lām*, elision of the imperfect tense prefix, and elision of the weak third radical.

60 For the imperative and prohibitive forms directly above as well as here, we have replaced the examples representing Class *ʿAlima* (*irḍa, lā tarḍa,* and *rāḍin*, respectively) because they were based on the defective root *r-ḍ-y*, an apparent oversight. In this case, *q-w-y*, which is the root that was supplied to represent the class at the beginning of the section of the conjointly weak root, is unavailable. (Instead of the active participle *qāwin*, one would use the participial form *qawiyyun*.) We have introduced *rāwin* as a substitute based on the root *r-w-y*, the same root in the examples representing Class *Akrama*.

61 Since *qawiya* (he was/became strong) is intransitive, the passive participle *maqwiyyun* can only be used with an accompanying preposition. See note 24 above.

62 "Halfway pronunciation" of the *hamza* in these words means blending the guttural stop with the sound of the short vowel. Ibn Masʿūd, *Marāḥ al-arwāḥ*, 552; al-ʿAyshī, *Rūḥ al-shurūḥ*, 399.

63 Some common *fāʾ*-hamzated words in this class undergo elision in the imperative, as in *khudh* (take) and *kul* (eat).

64 The imperfect and imperative are provided for *ahaba* but not for *saʾala*. For the latter they are *yasʾalu* (he asks) and *isʾal* (ask).

65 See note 15.

66 Note that the modification of the doubled root in the passive participle form (e.g., *mumaddun*) is not mentioned here.

67 See note 47.

68 See the modification of the imperfect tense above.

69 This is because the *wāw* possesses *fatḥ* before the transfer. See category 3 below.

70 The imperative *lām* is also elided.

71 In a number of previous comparable passages, the form given was *li-tashwī*, prior to the elision of the third radical.

72 Note that the forms *istaḥyi* (with only the third radical elided) and *istaḥi* (with both weak radicals elided) are both valid. In fact, these two

readings extend to the perfect and imperfect tenses as well. See al-Taftāzānī, *Sharḥ Taṣrīf al-ʿIzzī*, 300–301.

73 The text uses the root *a-dh-r* instead of *īzar* and its related forms in this section. Since we could not find the root *a-dh-r* in an Arabic lexicon, we have substituted *a-z-r*—the root used for Class *Ḍaraba* in the earlier section on the hamzated root—in these examples. *A-z-r* is also used in al-Taftāzānī, *Sharḥ Taṣrīf al-ʿIzzī*, 320, where it is explained that the meaning of *azara* is *ʿāwana* (he assisted). The example could also be *īdhan* (from *iʾdhan*), as in Ibn Aḥmad, *al-Maṭlūb*, 398.

74 See the previous note. The text has *dhāl*.

75 It should be noted that this is not a modification in the sense of a change made on account of the *hamza*. The same can be said about the passive participle and its sister forms below.

76 This appears to be mistaken, but the following examples are correct. There is no phonetic modification; orthographically, however, the *hamza* is combined with the added *alif*. See Ibn Aḥmad, *al-Maṭlūb*, 405–6.

II

THE TRANQUIL SEA

On the science of grammar

البحر الصحو في علم النحو

In the Name of Allah,
All-Merciful, Most Compassionate

بسم الله الرحمن الرحيم

ALL PRAISE IS due to Allah, Lord of the worlds. May blessings and peace be upon our messenger Muḥammad and upon all of his family, his Companions, and those who follow them.

الحمد لله رب العالمين والصلاة والسلام على رسولنا محمد وعلى آله وصحبه والتابعين لهم أجمعين.

To Proceed This is a treatise on the science of grammar that I have entitled *The Tranquil Sea: On the Science of Grammar*. The treatise comprises two methods: (1) that which conceives of the science of grammar through the categories of the governor, the governed, and inflection, as is the method of Imām Birgevī and those who follow him and (2) that which conceives of it through the categories of the noun, the verb, and the particle, as is the method of Imām al-Zamakhsharī and those who follow him.[1]

أما بعد فهذه رسالة في علم النحو سمّيتها البحر الصحو في علم النحو مشتملة على طريقين: طريق حصر بيان علم النحو في العامل والمعمول والإعراب كما هو طريق الإمام البركوي ومن تبعه وطريق حصر بيانه في الاسم والفعل والحرف كما هو طريق الإمام الزمخشري ومن تبعه.

With His permission ﷻ, we will allot three chapters to each method.

نذكر بإذنه تعالى كل طريق في ثلاثة أبواب.

[Chapter 1], the first chapter of the first method

الباب الأول من الطريق الأول

THE GOVERNOR

العـامـــل

A governor is that which inherently has the effect of making a specific kind of inflection necessary at the end of a word, as *ḍaraba* (hit) makes the nominative inflection necessary [for the subject] in *ḍaraba Zaydun* (Zayd hit). Governors are of two types: the first is *abstract* and the second *expressed.*

العامـل هـو مـا أوجـب آخـر الكلمـة على وجـه مخصـوص من الإعـراب حسـب اقتضائـه، كاقتضـاء «ضَرَبَ» الرفع في «ضَرَبَ زيـدٌ». وهـو أي العامـل على قسـمين أحدهمـا معنـوي والثاني لفظـي.

The Abstract Governor

العامل المعنوي

The first is the abstract governor, namely, that which is not expressed verbally, like [the very state of] being free from expressed governors. It is of two types:

1. The first is what makes the subject and predicate nominative, e.g., *Muḥammadun rasūlu Allāhi* (Muḥammad is the messenger of Allah).[2]
2. The second is what makes the imperfect tense verb indicative, e.g., *yarḥamu Allāhu taʿālā al-tāʾiba* (Allah ﷻ shows mercy to the repentant one).[3]

الأول العامـل المعنـوي وهـو مـا ليـس للّسـان فيـه حظّ، كالتجـرّد عـن العوامـل اللفظيّـة. وهـو على قسـمين:

١- الأول رافـع المبتـدأ والخبر، نحـو «محمـدٌ رسـولُ الله».

٢- الثـاني رافـع الفعـل المضـارع، نحـو «يرحـمُ الله تعـالى التائـب».

The Expressed Governor

The second is the expressed governor, namely, that which is expressed verbally, like *jā'a* (came) in *jā'a Zaydun* (Zayd came), *ḍarab* (hit) in *ḍarabtu Zaydan* (I hit Zayd), and the *bā'* in *marartu bi-Zaydin* (I passed by Zayd). It is of two types: *regular* and *received*.

The Regular Expressed Governor

The first is the regular expressed governor, namely, that concerning whose governance one can give a universal rule, e.g., to say, "Every verb makes [its agent] nominative and every *muḍāf* makes [the *muḍāf ilayhi*] genitive." There are nine regular expressed governors.

1. The Verb As Such First is the verb as such,[4] namely, what signifies a meaning in itself that is bound to one of the three times,[5] as in *ḍaraba* (he hit), *yaḍribu* (he hits), and *sa-yaḍribu* (he will hit). Every verb [makes its agent] nominative, e.g., *khalaqa Allāhu kulla shay'in* (Allah created everything) and *nazala al-Qur'ānu nuzūlan* (The Quran descended [a descending]).

For every verb, there is necessarily a nominative [agent]. If a complete sentence can be made [of the verb] with that [agent], the verb is termed a *complete verb*, e.g., *'alima Allāhu ta'ālā* (Allah ﷻ knows). But if a complete sentence cannot be made [of the verb] with that [agent] but rather requires an accusative predicate, the verb is termed an *auxiliary verb*, e.g., *kāna Allāhu ta'ālā 'alīman ḥakīman* (Allah ﷻ is all-knowing and all-wise), *ṣāra al-'āṣī mustaḥiqqan li-l-'adhābi* (The disobedient one became deserving of punishment), *mā zāla al-mudhnibu ba'īdan min Allāhi ta'ālā* (The sinner remains distant from Allah ﷻ), *tuqbalu al-tawbatu mā dāma al-rūḥu dākhilan fī al-badani* (Repentance is accepted as long as the soul remains within the body), and *laysa Allāhu ta'ālā jisman* (Allah ﷻ is not a corporeal object).

العامل اللفظي

الثاني العامل اللفظيّ وهو ما للّسان فيه حظّ، كـ«جاء» في «جاء زيد» و«ضرب» في «ضربت زيدًا» والباء في «مررت بزيد». وهو على قسمين: قياسي وسماعي.

العامل اللفظي القياسي

الأول العامل اللفظي القياسي وهو ما يمكن أن يُذكر في عمله قاعدة كلّيّة كأن تقول «كل فعل يرفع» و«كل مضاف يجرّ»[1]. وهو أي العامل اللفظي القياسي تسعة عوامل.

١. الفعل مطلقًا الأول الفعل مطلقًا وهو ما دلّ على معنًى في نفسه مقترن بأحد الأزمنة الثلاثة، نحو «ضرب، يضرب، سيضرب». فكل فعل يرفع، نحو «خلق اللهُ كل شيء» و«نزل القرآنُ نزولًا».

ولا بدّ لكل فعل من مرفوع. فإن تمّ به كلامًا يسمّى فعلًا تامًّا، نحو «علم اللهُ تعالى». وإن لم يتمّ به بل احتاج إلى خبر منصوب يسمّى فعلًا ناقصًا، نحو «كان اللهُ تعالى عليمًا حكيمًا» و«صار العاصي مستحقًّا للعذاب» و«ما زال المذنبُ بعيدًا من الله تعالى» و«تقبل التوبة ما دام الروحُ داخلًا في البدن» و«ليس اللهُ تعالى جسمًا».

2. The Active Participle Second is the active participle, namely, what is derived from a verb [to signify] the one who does the *action*, meaning the occurrence.[6] The active participle shares the governance of its active verb,[7] e.g., *kullu ḥasūdin muḥriqun ḥasaduhu ʿamalahu* (Every envier's envy burns away his deeds).

٢. اسم الفاعل الثاني اسم الفاعل وهو ما اشتقّ من فعل لمن قام به الفعل بمعنى الحدوث. وهو يعمل عمل فعله المعلوم، نحو «كل حسود محرق حسدُه عملَه».

3. The Passive Participle Third is the passive participle, namely, what is derived from a verb [to signify] the one to whom the action is done. It shares the governance of its passive verb, e.g., *kullu tāʾibin maqbūlun tawbatuhu* (Every repenter's repentance is accepted).

٣. اسم المفعول الثالث اسم المفعول وهو ما اشتقّ من فعل لمن وقع عليه الفعل. وهو يعمل عمل فعله المجهول، نحو «كل تائب مقبول توبتُه».

4. The Participial Fourth is the participial, namely, what is derived from an intransitive verb [to signify] the one in whom the action subsists, in the sense of a permanent [attribution]. The participial shares the governance of its verb as well, e.g., *al-ʿibādatu ḥasanun thawābuhā wa-l-maʿṣiyatu qabīḥun ʿadhābuhā* (Worship, good is its reward; disobedience, vile is its punishment).

٤. الصفة المشبّهة الرابع الصفة المشبّهة وهي ما اشتقّت من فعل لازم لمن قام به الفعل على معنى الثبوت. وهي أيضا تعمل عمل فعلها، نحو «العبادة حسن ثوابُها والمعصية قبيح عذابُها».

5. The Comparative/Superlative Noun Fifth is the comparative/superlative noun, namely, a noun derived from a verb [to signify] something that possesses [a verbal action or quality] to a greater degree than other things. It shares the governance of its verb as well, e.g., *mā min rajulin aḥsana fīhi al-ḥilmu minhu fī al-ʿālimi* (There is no man in whom discernment is more excellent than it is in the scholar).[8]

٥. اسم التفضيل الخامس اسم التفضيل وهو ما اشتقّ من فعل لموصوف بزيادة على غيره. وهو أيضا يعمل عمل فعله، نحو «ما من رجل أحسن فيه الحلمُ منه في العالم».

6. The Infinitive Noun Sixth is the infinitive noun, namely, the noun of the action that corresponds to the verb, e.g., *ḍarabtu/ḍarban* (I hit / hitting). It shares the governance of its verb, e.g., *yuḥibbu Allāhu taʿālā iʿṭāʾa ʿabdihi lahu faqīran dirhaman* (Allah ﷻ loves His slave's giving a needy person a dirham for His sake).

٦. المصدر السادس المصدر وهو اسم الحدث الجاري على الفعل، نحو «ضربت/ ضربًا». وهو أيضا يعمل عمل فعله، نحو «يحبّ الله تعالى إعطاء عبده له فقيرًا درهمًا».

7. The *Muḍāf* Noun Seventh is the *muḍāf* noun,[9] and it makes [its governed noun] genitive, e.g., *ʿibādatu Allāhi taʿālā khayrun* (Worship of Allah ﷻ is good).

٧. الاسم المضاف السابع الاسم المضاف٩ وهو يعمل الجرّ، نحو «عبادةُ اللهِ تعالى خير».

8. The Disambiguated Noun Eighth is the disambiguated noun, namely, any ambiguous noun [whose meaning] becomes complete through one of four things: nunation, the *nūn* of the dual, the *nūn* of the quasi-plural, or *iḍāfa*. An example of [disambiguation] through (1) nunation is *ʿindī rāqūdun khallan* (I have a large jug of vinegar); an example with (2) the *nūn* of the dual is *ʿindī manawāni samnan* (I have two *manns* of clarified butter);[10] an example with (3) the *nūn* of the quasi-plural is *ʿindī ʿishrūna dirhaman* (I have twenty dirhams); an example with (4) *iḍāfa* is *ʿindī milʾuhu ʿasalan* (I have its fill of honey).

٨. الاسم المبهم التامّ الثامن الاسم المبهم التامّ وهو كل اسم مبهم تمّ بأحد أربعة أشياء: بتنوين أو نون التثنية أو نون شبه الجمع أو الإضافة. أما (١) بالتنوين، فنحو «عندي راقودٌ خلًّا»؛ أما (٢) بنون التثنية، فنحو «عندي منوانِ سمنًا»؛ أما (٣) بنون شبه الجمع، فنحو «عندي عشرونَ درهمًا»؛ أما (٤) بالإضافة، فنحو «عندي ملؤه عسلًا».

A noun that is disambiguated through one of these four things makes the specifying noun accusative, as you know.

فهو أي الاسم المبهم التامّ بواحد من هذه الأربعة يعمل نصبًا على التمييز كما علمت.

9. The Expression with Verbal Import Ninth is the expression with verbal import, namely, any expression from which the meaning of a verb is understood, e.g., *hayhāta al-mudhnibu min Allāhi taʿālā* (Far is the sinner from Allah ﷻ), i.e., *baʿuda minhu taʿālā*, and *tarāki dhanban* (Abandon sin).[11] [This also includes] cases like *mā fī al-dunyā rāḥatun* (There is no comfort in the world)[12] and cases like *yanbaghī li-l-ʿālimi an yakūna muḥammadiyyan khuluquhu* (The scholar should be Muḥammadan in his character).[13]

٩. معنى الفعل التاسع معنى الفعل وهو كل لفظ يفهم منه معنى فعل، نحو «هيهات المذنب من الله تعالى» أي بعد منه تعالى، و«تراكِ ذنبًا»، ونحو «ما في الدنيا راحة»، ونحو «ينبغي للعالم أن يكون محمّديًّا خلقه».

The Received Expressed Governor

The second is the received expressed governor, namely, that concerning whose governance one cannot give a universal rule but must instead resort to what is received [from the early users of the language]. It is of five types.

العامل اللفظي السماعي

الثاني العامل اللفظي السماعي وهو ما لا يمكن أن يُذكر في عمله قاعدة كلية بل يُقتصر فيه على السماع. وهو على خمسة أنواع.

1. Prepositions First are prepositions, namely, [particles] whose linguistically assigned function[14] is to transfer the meanings of verbs to nouns. They are particles that put only a single noun into the genitive case, and they are termed *ḥuruf al-jarr* or *ḥurūf al-iḍāfa* (prepositions). There are twenty of them:[15]

1. the *bāʾ* (by, in, with), as in *āmantu bi-Allāhi wa-bihi la-ubʿathanna* (I believe in Allah and by Him I will be resurrected).
2. *min* (from, of), as in *tubtu min kulli dhanbin* (I repent from every sin).
3. *ilā* (to, until), as in *tubtu ilā Allāhi* (I repent to Allah).
4. *ʿan* (from), as in *kufiftu ʿan al-ḥarāmi* (I was held back from the prohibited).
5. *ʿalā* (on), as in *tajibu al-tawbatu ʿalā kulli mudhnibin* (Repentance is obligatory on every sinner).
6. the *lām* (for, to, of), as in *ana ʿubaydun li-Allāhi taʿālā* (I am a small slave of Allah's ﷻ).
7. *fī* (in), as in *al-muṭīʿu fī al-jannati* (The obedient one is in paradise).
8. the *kāf* (like), as in His statement ﷻ *laysa ka-mithlihi shayʾun* (There is nothing like Him) (Q 42:11).
9. *ḥattā* (until), as in *aʿbudu Allāha taʿālā ḥattā al-mawti* (I will worship Allah until death).
10. *rubba* (many a…), as in *rubba tālin yalʿanuhu al-Qurʾānu* (Many a reciter is cursed by the Quran).
11. the *wāw* of oath, as in *wa-Allāhi lā afʿalu al-kabāʾira* (By Allah, I will not commit any major sins).
12. the *tāʾ* of oath, as in *ta-Allāhi la-afʿalanna al-farāʾiḍa* (By Allah, I will perform the obligatory acts).

١. حروف الجرّ الأول حروف الجرّ وهي ما وُضعت لإفضاء معنى الأفعال إلى الأسماء وهي حروف تجرّ اسمًا واحدًا فقط، تسمّى حروف الجرّ وحروف الإضافة. وهي عشرون.

١- الباء، نحو «آمنت باللهِ وبه لأبعثنّ».

٢- مِنْ، نحو «تبت من كلِّ ذنب».

٣- إلَى، نحو «تبت إلى اللهِ».

٤- عَنْ، نحو «كففت عن الحرامِ».

٥- عَلَى، نحو «تجب التوبة على كلِّ مذنب».

٦- اللام، نحو «أنا عبيد للهِ تعالى».

٧- فِي، نحو «المطيع في الجنّةِ».

٨- الكاف، نحو قوله تعالى ﴿لَيْسَ كَمِثْلِهِۦ شَىْءٌ﴾ [٤٢/ ١١].

٩- حَتَّى، نحو «أعبد الله تعالى حتى الموتِ».

١٠- رُبَّ، نحو «رب تالٍ يلعنه القرآن».

١١- واو القسم، نحو «واللهِ لا أفعل الكبائر».

١٢- تاء القسم، نحو «تاللهِ لأفعلنّ الفرائض».

13. *ḥāshā* (except), as in *halaka al-nāsu ḥāshā al-ʿālimi* (The people will perish except the scholar).
14. *mudh* (since, beginning from), as in *tubtu min kulli dhanbin faʿaltuhu mudh yawmi al-bulūghi* (I repent from every sin I have committed since the day I reached the age of maturity).
15. *mundhu* (since, beginning from), as in *tajibu al-ṣalātu mundhu yawmi al-bulūghi* (The ritual prayer is obligatory beginning from the day one reaches the age of maturity).
16. *khalā* (except), as in *halaka al-ʿālimūna khalā al-ʿāmili bi-ʿilmihi* (The scholars will perish except those who act in accordance with their knowledge).
17. *ʿadā* (except), as in *halaka al-ʿāmilūna ʿadā al-mukhliṣi* (Those who act will perish except the sincere).
18. *lawlā* (were it not), as in *lawlāka yā raḥmata Allāhi la-halaka al-nāsu* (Were it not for you—O mercy of Allah!—then the people would have perished).
19. *kaymah* (why), as in *kaymah ʿaṣayta* (Why did you disobey?).[16]
20. *laʿalla* (perhaps) in the dialect of ʿUqayl, as in *laʿalla Allāhi taʿālā yaghfiru dhanbī* (Perhaps Allah ﷻ will forgive my sins).

2. Verb-Like Particles Second are the verb-like particles, which are particles that make the subject accusative and the predicate nominative. They are termed "verb-like particles" by way of comparison with auxiliary verbs: both take a subject-noun and a predicate. There are six verb-like particles:

1. *inna* (truly),[17] as in *inna Allāha taʿālā ʿālimu kulli shayʾin* (Allah ﷻ truly knows everything).
2. *anna* (that), as in *iʿtaqadtu anna Allāha taʿālā qādirun ʿalā kulli shayʾin* (I believe that Allah ﷻ has power over everything).

١٣- حَاشَا، نحو «هلك الناس حاشا العالِمِ».

١٤- مُذْ، نحو «تبت من كل ذنب فعلته مذ يومِ البلوغ».

١٥- مُنْذُ، نحو «تجب الصلاة منذ يومِ البلوغ».

١٦- خَلَا، نحو «هلك العالمون خلا العاملِ بعلمه».

١٧- عَدَا، نحو «هلك العاملون عدا المخلصِ».

١٨- لَوْلَا، نحو «لولاك يا رحمة الله لهلك الناس».

١٩- كَيْمَهْ، نحو «كيمه عصيت؟».

٢٠- لَعَلَّ في لغة عقيل، نحو «لعلّ اللهِ تعالى يغفر ذنبي».

٢. الحروف المشبّهة بالفعل الثاني الحروف المشبّهة بالفعل وهي حروف تنصب الاسم وترفع الخبر، وتسمّى الحروف المشبّهة بالفعل لتشبيهها بالأفعال الناقصة في دخولهما على المبتدأ والخبر. وهي ستّة أحرف:

١- إنَّ، نحو «إنّ اللهَ تعالى عالمُ كلِّ شيء».

٢- أَنَّ، نحو «اعتقدت أنّ اللهَ تعالى قادرٌ على كل شيء».

3. *ka'anna* (as if, as though), as in *ka'anna al-ḥarāma nārun* (It is as though the prohibited were fire).
4. *lākinna* (but, however), as in *mā fāza al-jāhilu lākinna al-ʿālima fā'izun* (He who is ignorant does not succeed, but he who is knowledgeable is successful).
5. *layta* (would that, if only), as in *layta al-ʿilma marzūqun li-kulli aḥadin* (If only knowledge were granted to everyone).
6. *laʿalla* (perhaps), as in *laʿalla Allāha taʿālā ghāfiru dhanbī* (Perhaps Allah ﷻ will forgive my sins).

This category of particles that make the subject accusative and the predicate nominative also includes the following two particles:[18]

1. *illā* (but not) in a disconnected exception, e.g., *al-maʿṣiyatu mubaʿʿidatun ʿan al-jannati illā al-ṭāʿata muqarribatun minhā* (Disobedience distances one from paradise, but not obedience, which draws one near to it).
2. the *lā* (no) of categoric negation, e.g., *lā fāʿila sharrin fā'izun* (No doer of evil is successful).

3. The *Mā* and *Lā* That Resemble *Laysa* Third are the *mā* and *lā* that resemble *laysa*, which are particles that make the subject nominative and the predicate accusative, and they are called "the *mā* and *lā* that resemble *laysa*":

1. *mā* (not), e.g., *mā Allāhu taʿālā mutamakkinan bi-makānin*... (Allah ﷻ does not reside in a place...).
2. *lā* (not), e.g., ...*wa-lā shay'un mushābihan li-Llāhi taʿālā* (...and nothing resembles Allah ﷻ).

٣- كَأَنَّ، نحو «كأنّ الحرامَ نارٌ».

٤- لَكِنَّ، نحو «ما فاز الجاهل لكنّ العالمَ فائزٌ».

٥- لَيْتَ، نحو «ليت العلمَ مرزوقٌ لكل أحد».

٦- لَعَلَّ، نحو «لعلّ اللهَ تعالى غافرٌ ذنبي».

ومن هذا النوع أي من نوع الحروف التي تنصب الاسم وترفع الخبر حرفان:

١- إِلَّا في الاستثناء المنقطع، نحو «المعصية مبعدة عن الجنّة إلا الطاعةَ[٣] مقرّبةٌ منها».

٢- لَا لنفي الجنس، نحو «لا فاعلَ شرٍّ فائزٌ».

٣. «ما» و«لا» المشبّهتان بـ«ليس» الثالث «ما» و«لا» المشبّهتان بـ«ليس» وهما حرفان يرفعان الاسم وينصبان الخبر، يسمّيان «ما ولا المشبّهتان بليس»:

١- مَا، نحو «ما اللهُ تعالى متمكنًا بمكان».

٢- لَا، نحو «ولا شيءٌ مشابهًا لله تعالى».

4. Subjunctive Particles of the Imperfect Tense Verb Fourth are the subjunctive particles of the imperfect tense verb, which are particles that make the imperfect tense verb subjunctive. They are termed “the subjunctive particles of the imperfect tense verb,” and there are four of them:

1. *an* (to), as in *uḥibbu an uṭīʿa Allāha taʿālā* (I love to obey Allah ﷻ).
2. *lan* (will not), as in *lan yaghfira Allāhu taʿālā li-l-kāfirīna* (Allah ﷻ will not forgive the disbelievers).
3. *kay* (so that, in order to), as in *uḥibbu ṭūla al-ʿumri kay uḥaṣṣila al-ʿilma* (I would like long life in order to acquire knowledge).
4. *idhan* (therefore, then), as in saying, *idhan tadkhula al-jannata* (Then you will enter paradise), to one who says, *uṭīʿu Allāha taʿālā* (I will obey Allah ﷻ).

٤. الحروف الناصبة للفعل المضارع الرابع الحروف الناصبة للفعل المضارع وهي حروف تنصب الفعل المضارع، تسمّى الحروف الناصبة للفعل المضارع. وهي أربعة.

١- أَنْ، نحو «أحب أن أطيعَ الله تعالى».

٢- لَنْ، نحو «لن يغفرَ الله تعالى للكافرين».

٣- كَيْ، نحو «أحب طول العمر كي أحصّلَ العلم».

٤- إِذَنْ، نحو قولك «إذن تدخلَ الجنّة» لمن قال أطيع الله تعالى.

5. Jussive Operators Fifth are the jussive operators, which are words that make the imperfect tense verb jussive.

Some jussive operators make one verb jussive and are called *jussive particles*. There are four of these:

1. *lam* (did not), as in His statement ﷻ *lam yalid wa-lam yūlad* (He neither begets nor was begotten) (Q 112:3).
2. *lammā* (has not), as in *lamma yanfaʿ ʿumrī* (My life has not been beneficial).
3. the imperative *lām*, as in *li-yaʿmal ʿamalan ṣāliḥan* (Let him do good deeds).
4. *lā* (do not) for prohibition, as in *lā tudhnib* (Do not sin).

٥. الكلمات الجازمة الخامس الكلمات الجازمة وهي كلمات تجزم الفعل المضارع.

بعضها يجزم فعلًا واحدًا، يسمّى حروفًا جازمة؛ وهي أربعة.

١- لَمْ، نحو قوله تعالى ﴿لَمْ يَلِدْ وَلَمْ يُولَدْ﴾ [١١٢/ ٣].

٢- لَمَّا، نحو «لمّا ينفعْ عمري».

٣- لام الأمر، نحو «لِيعملْ عملًا صالحًا».

٤- لَا في النهي، نحو «لا تذنبْ».

Some make two verbs jussive, the two verbs being termed the *condition verb* and the *result verb*. There are eleven of these operators:

1. *in* (if), as in *in tatub tughfar dhunūbuka* (If you repent, your sins will be forgiven).
2. *mahmā* (whatever, however much), as in *mahmā tafʿal tusʾal ʿanhu* (Whatever you do you will be asked about).
3. *mā* (whatever), as in *mā tafʿal min khayrin tajidhu ʿinda Allāhi taʿālā* (Whatever good you do you will find with Allah ﷻ).
4. *man* (whoever), as in *man yaʿmal ʿamalan ṣāliḥan yakun nājiyan* (Whoever performs good deeds will be saved).
5. *ayna* (wherever), as in *ayna takun yudrikka al-mawtu* (Wherever you are, death will overtake you).
6. *matā* (whenever), as in *matā taḥsud tahlik* (Whenever you envy, you are ruined).
7. *annā* (whenever, however), as in *annā tudhnib yaʿlamka Allāhu taʿālā* (Whenever you sin, Allah ﷻ is aware of you).
8. *ayyu* (whichever, any), as in *ayyu ʿālimin yatakabbar yubghiḍhu Allāhu taʿālā* (Any scholar who waxes arrogant Allah ﷻ detests).
9. *ḥaythumā* (wherever), as in *ḥaythumā tafʿal yuktab fiʿluka* (Wherever you act, your action is recorded).
10. *idhmā* (whenever), as in *idhmā tatub tuqbal tawbatuka* (Whenever you repent, your repentance is accepted).
11. *idhāmā* (whenever), as in *idhāmā taʿmal bi-ʿilmika takun khayra al-nāsi* (Whenever you act in accordance with your knowledge, you are the best of people).

وبعضها يجزم فعلين مسمّين شرطًا وجزاءً؛ وهي إحدى عشرة كلمة.

١- إِنْ، نحو «إن تتبْ تغفرْ ذنوبك».

٢- مَهْمَا، نحو «مهما تفعلْ تسألْ عنه».

٣- مَا، نحو «ما تفعلْ من خير تجدْه عند الله تعالى».

٤- مَنْ، نحو «من يعملْ عملًا صالحًا يكنْ ناجيًا».

٥- أَيْنَ، نحو «أين تكنْ يدركْك الموت».

٦- مَتَى، نحو «متى تحسدْ تهلكْ».

٧- أَنَّى، نحو «أنّى تذنبْ يعلمْك الله تعالى».

٨- أَيُّ، نحو «أيّ عالم يتكبرْ يبغضْه الله تعالى».

٩- حَيْثُمَا، نحو «حيثما تفعلْ يكتبْ فعلك».

١٠- إِذْمَا، نحو «إذما تتبْ تقبلْ توبتك».

١١- إِذَا مَا، نحو «إذا ما تعملْ بعلمك تكنْ خير الناس».

[Chapter 2], the second chapter of the first method

الباب الثاني من الطريق الأول

THE GOVERNED

المـعـمـــول

What is the governed? Of how many types is it, and what are they?

ما المعمول؟ وكم قسمًا هو وما هي؟

The governed is that on which a governor has an effect, whether the effect be explicit, e.g., *jā'a Zaydun* (Zayd came); implicit, e.g., *jā'a al-qāḍī* (The judge came); or positional, e.g., *jā'a hā'ulā'i* (These came). [Governed elements] are of two categories: the *primarily governed*, e.g., *jā'a Zaydun* (Zayd came), and the *secondarily governed*, that is, [an expression] inflected in the same way as one that it follows, e.g., *jā'a Zaydun al-'ālimu* (Zayd, the scholar, came).

المعمول هـو ما أثّر فيـه العامـل لفظًا نحو «جـاء زيد»، أو تقديـرًا نحو «جـاء القـاضي»، أو محلًّا نحو «جـاء هؤلاء». وهو قسـمان: (١) معمـول بالأصالة، نحو «جـاء زيدٌ»؛ (٢) معمـول بالتبعيّـة أي يكـون إعرابه مثل إعـراب متبوعه نحو «جاء زيـدٌ العالمُ».

The Primarily Governed

المعمول بالأصالة

The primarily governed [expression] is of four types.

المعمول بالأصالة أربعة أنواع.

Nominative/Indicative Expressions

المعمول المرفوع

The first type is the nominative/indicative governed expression, or that which bears the sign of agency,[19] namely, a *ḍamma*, *alif*, or *wāw*. There are nine nominatives:

1. the *agent*, e.g., *raḥima Allāhu ta'ālā al-tā'iba* (Allah ﷻ had mercy on the repentant one).[20]
2. the *substitute agent*, e.g., *ruḥima al-tā'ibu* (The repentant one was shown mercy).

النـوع الأول المعمـول المرفـوع وهـو مـا اشـتمل على علم الفاعليّـة وهـو الضمّـة والألـف والـواو. وهـو تسـعة مرفـوعات.

١- الفاعل، نحو «رحم اللهُ تعالى التائب».

٢- نائب الفاعل، نحو «رُحم التائبُ».

3. the *subject*, e.g., *Zaydun qāʾimun* (Zayd is standing).
4. the *predicate*, e.g., *Muḥammadun khātamu al-anbiyāʾi ʿalayhim al-ṣalātu wa-l-salāmu* (Muḥammad is the seal of the prophets ﷺ).
5. the subject-noun of *kāna* or its sisters, e.g., *kāna Allāhu taʿālā ʿalīman ḥakīman* (Allah ﷻ is all-knowing and all-wise).
6. the predicate of *inna*,[21] e.g., *inna al-baʿtha ḥaqqun* (The resurrection is indeed real).
7. the predicate of the *lā* of categoric negation, e.g., *lā ʿamala murāʾin maqbūlun* (No deed of an ostentatious hypocrite is accepted).
8. the subject-noun of the *mā* and *lā* that resemble *laysa*, e.g., *mā al-takabburu lāʾiqan li-l-ʿālimi* (Arrogance does not suit the scholar) and *lā ḥasadun ḥalālan* (Envy is not lawful).
9. the imperfect tense verb that is free from subjunctive and jussive [governors], e.g., *yuḥibbu Allāhu taʿālā al-tawāḍuʿa* (Allah ﷻ loves humility).

Accusative/Subjunctive Expressions

The second type of primarily governed expression is the accusative/subjunctive governed expression, or that which bears the sign of objectivity, namely, accusative/subjunctive inflection.[22] There are thirteen accusatives/subjunctives:

1. the *action-notion*, e.g., *tubtu tawbatan naṣūḥan* (I repented [a sincere repenting]).
2. the *object*, e.g., *uʿbud Allāha taʿālā* (Worship Allah ﷻ).
3. the *action-place/time*, e.g., *ṣum shahra Ramaḍāna* (Fast in the month of Ramadan).
4. the *action-reason*, e.g., *iʿmal ṭalaban li-marḍāti Allāhi taʿālā* (Work in pursuit of the pleasure of Allah ﷻ).

٣- المبتدأ، نحو «زيدٌ قائم».

٤- الخبر، نحو «محمد خاتمُ الأنبياء عليهم الصلاة والسلام».

٥- اسم «كَانَ» وأخواتها، نحو «كان اللهُ تعالى عليمًا حكيمًا».

٦- خبر «إِنَّ»، نحو «إنّ البعث حقٌّ».

٧- خبر «لَا» لنفي الجنس، نحو «لا عمل مراءٍ مقبولٌ».

٨- اسم «مَا» و«لَا» المشبّهتين بـ«لَيْسَ»، نحو «ما التكبّرُ لائقًا للعالم» و«لا حسدٌ حلالًا».

٩- الفعل المضارع الخالي عن النواصب والجوازم، نحو «يحبُّ الله تعالى التواضع».

المعمول المنصوب

الثاني من المعمول بالأصالة المعمول المنصوب وهو ما اشتمل على علم المفعوليّة وهو النصب. وهو أي المعمول المنصوب ثلاثة عشر منصوبًا.

١- المفعول المطلق، نحو «تبت توبةً نصوحًا».

٢- المفعول به، نحو «عبد اللهَ تعالى».

٣- المفعول فيه، نحو «صم شهرَ رمضان».

٤- المفعول له، نحو «اعمل طلبًا لمرضاة الله تعالى».

5. the *action-accompaniment*, e.g., *yafnā al-mālu wa-tabqā wa-ʿamalaka* (Wealth will perish, and you will remain with your deeds).
6. the *circumstance*, e.g., *uʿbud Allāha taʿālā khāʾifan rājiyan* (Worship Allah ﷻ in a state of fear and hope).
7. the *specification*, e.g., *ṭāba al-ʿālimu ʿibādatan* (The scholar's worship was good).
8. the *exception*,[23] e.g., *yadkhulu al-jannata al-nāsu illā al-kāfira* (All people will enter paradise except the disbeliever).
9. the predicate of *kāna* or its sisters, e.g., *kāna al-malāʾikatu ʿibāda Allāhi taʿālā* (The angels were [and are] servants of Allah ﷻ).
10. the subject-noun of a particle in the class of *inna*, e.g., *inna al-suʾāla ḥaqqun* (The questioning is indeed real).
11. the subject-noun of the *lā* of categoric negation, e.g., *lā ṭāʿata mughtābin maqbūlatun* (No devotional act of a backbiter is accepted).
12. the predicate of the *mā* and *lā* that resemble *laysa*, e.g., *mā al-ghībatu ḥalālan* (Backbiting is not permissible) and *lā namīmatun jāʾizatan* (Talebearing is not permissible).
13. the imperfect tense verb modified by a subjunctive [governor], e.g., *uḥibbu an yughfara dhunūbī* (I would love that my sins be forgiven).

Genitive Expressions

The third type of primarily governed expression is the genitive governed expression, or that which has the sign of the *muḍāf ilayhi*, namely, genitive inflection.[24] Genitive expressions are of two types:

1. those that are genitive due to a preposition, e.g., *iʿmal bi-ikhlāṣin* (Act with sincerity).
2. those that are genitive due to an *iḍāfa* construction, e.g., *dhanbu al-ʿabdi yusawwidu qalbahu* (The sin of a servant blackens his heart).

٥- المفعول معه، نحو «يفنى المال وتبقى وعملَك».

٦- الحال، نحو «اعبد الله تعالى خائفًا راجيًا».

٧- التمييز، نحو «طاب العالم عبادةً».

٨- المستثنى، نحو «يدخل الجنة الناس إلا الكافرَ».

٩- خبر باب «كانَ»، نحو «كان الملائكة عبادَ الله تعالى».

١٠- اسم باب «إنَّ»، نحو «إنّ السؤالَ حقّ».

١١- اسم «لَا» لنفي الجنس، نحو «لا طاعةَ مغتاب مقبولة».

١٢- خبر «مَا» و«لَا» المشبّهتين بـ«لَيْسَ»، نحو «ما الغيبة حلالًا» و«لا نميمة جائزةً».

١٣- الفعل المضارع الذي دخلته إحدى النواصب، نحو «أحبّ أن يغفرَ ذنوبي».

المعمول المجرور

الثالث من المعمول بالأصالة المعمول المجرور وهو ما اشتمل على علم المضاف إليه وهو الجرّ. وهو أي المجرور على قسمين.

١- المجرور بحرف الجرّ، نحو «اعمل بإخلاصٍ».

٢- المجرور بالإضافة، نحو «ذنب العبدِ يسوّد قلبه».

Jussive Expressions

The fourth type of primarily governed expression is the jussive governed expression, or an imperfect tense verb modified by a jussive [governor], e.g., *in tukhliṣ yuqbal ʿamaluka* (If you are sincere, your deeds will be accepted).

المعمول المجزوم

الرابع من المعمول بالأصالة المعمول المجزوم وهو الفعل المضارع الذي دخلته إحدى الجوازم، نحو «إن تخلص يقبلْ عملك».

The Secondarily Governed

المعمول بالتبع

The second [category] is the secondarily governed [expression], namely, that on which the governor has an effect through an intermediary and which conforms to the *principal noun* in inflection and the like. It is of five types.

الثاني المعمول بالتبع وهو ما يكون العامل مؤثّرًا فيه بواسطة موافقًا لمتبوعه في الإعراب ونحوه. وهو خمسة توابع.

Adjectives

The first type is the adjective, e.g., *uʿbud Allāha al-ʿaẓīma* (Worship Allah the Magnificent).

الصفة

الأول الصفة، نحو «اعبد اللهَ العظيمَ».

Conjuncts

The second is conjunction[25] through one of ten particles:

1. the *wāw* (and), e.g., *uṭīʿu Allāha wa-l-rasūla* (I will obey Allah and the Messenger).
2. the *fāʾ* (and then), e.g., *tajibu takbīratu al-iftitāḥi fa-l-qiyāmu* (The opening *takbīra* is obligatory, then standing).
3. *thumma* (and then), e.g., *yajibu al-ʿilmu thumma al-ʿamalu* (It is obligatory to know and then to act).
4. *ḥattā* (even), e.g., *māta al-nāsu ḥattā al-anbiyāʾu ʿalayhim al-ṣalātu wa-l-salāmu* (People have died, even prophets ﷺ).

العطف

الثاني العطف بأحد الحروف العشرة:

١- الواو، نحو «أطيع اللهَ والرسولَ».

٢- الفاء، نحو «تجب تكبيرةُ الافتتاح فالقيامُ».

٣- ثُمَّ، نحو «يجب العلمُ ثم العملُ».

٤- حَتَّى، نحو «مات الناسُ حتى الأنبياءُ عليهم الصلاة والسلام».

5. *aw* (or), e.g., *ṣalli al-ḍuḥā arbaʿan aw thamāniyan* (Pray the midmorning prayer in four or eight [units]).
6. *immā* (either/or), e.g., *iʿmal immā wājiban wa-immā mustaḥabban* (Perform either an obligatory or a recommended act).
7. *am* (or…?), e.g., *a-riḍā Allāhi taṭlubu am sakhaṭahu* (Is it Allah's pleasure you seek or His displeasure?).
8. *lā* (not), e.g., *iʿmal ṣāliḥan lā sayyiʾan* (Do a good deed, not a bad one).
9. *bal* (rather), e.g., *uṭlub ḥalālan bal ṭayyiban* (Seek what is permissible—rather, what is wholesome).
10. *lākin*,[26] e.g., *lā yaḥillu riyāʾun lākin ikhlāṣun* (Ostentation is not permissible; however, sincerity is).

Emphases

The third is the emphasis, whether like *uṭlub al-ikhlāṣa al-ikhlāṣa* (Seek sincerity, sincerity!) or like *utruk al-dhunūba kullahā* (Abandon sins, all of them!).

Substitutes

The fourth is the substitute, whether like *uʿbud rabbaka ilāha al-ʿālamīna* (Worship your Lord, God of the worlds), like *abghiḍ al-nāsa man ʿaṣā Allāha taʿālā minhum* (Detest those people who disobey Allah ﷻ), or like *iḥfaẓ Allāha taʿālā ḥaqqahu* (Be mindful of what is due to Allah ﷻ).[27]

Clarifying Appositives

The fifth is the clarifying appositive, e.g., *āmantu bi-nabiyyinā Muḥammadin ʿalayhi al-ṣalātu wa-l-salāmu* (I believe in our prophet Muḥammad ﷺ).

٥- أَوْ، نحو «صلّ الضحى أربعًا أو ثمانيًا».

٦- إِمَّا، نحو «اعمل إما واجبًا وإما مستحبًّا».

٧- أَمْ، نحو «أرضا الله تطلب أم سخطَه».

٨- لَا، نحو «اعمل صالحًا لا سيّئًا».

٩- بَلْ، نحو «اطلب حلالًا بل طيّبًا».

١٠- لَكِنْ، نحو «لا يحلّ رياءٌ لكن إخلاصٌ».

التأكيد

الثالث التأكيد، نحو «اطلب الإخلاصَ الإخلاصَ»، ونحو «اترك الذنوبَ كلَّها».

البدل

الرابع البدل، نحو «اعبد ربَّك إلهَ العالمين»، ونحو «ابغض الناسَ من عصى الله تعالى منهم»، ونحو «احفظ اللهَ تعالى حقَّه».

عطف البيان

الخامس عطف البيان، نحو «آمنّا بنبيِّنا محمدٍ عليه الصلاة والسلام».

[Chapter 3], the third chapter of the first method

الباب الثالث من الطريق الأول

INFLECTION

الإعراب

What is inflection? How many types of inflection are there, and what are they?

ما الإعراب؟ وكم قسمًا وما هي؟

Inflection is that in which the ending of an inflectable expression varies according to the various governors that modify the expression, e.g., *jāʾa Zaydun* (Zayd came), *raʾaytu Zaydan* (I saw Zayd), and *marartu bi-Zaydin* (I passed by Zayd).

الإعراب هو ما يختلف به آخر المعرب باختلاف العوامل الداخلة عليه، نحو «جاء زيدٌ» و«رأيت زيدًا» و«مررت بزيدٍ».

The Types of Inflection

أقسام الإعراب

Inflection is of three types: short vowels, letters, and elision.

وهو أي الإعراب ثلاثة أقسام: حركة، حرف، حذف.

Short Vowels The first type is short vowels. They are three: (1) the *ḍamma*, e.g., *jāʾa Zaydun* (Zayd came); (2) the *fatḥa*, e.g., *raʾaytu Zaydan* (I saw Zayd); and (3) the *kasra*, e.g., *marartu bi-Zaydin* (I passed by Zayd).

الحركة الأول الحركة وهي ثلاثة: الأولى الضمّة، نحو «جاء زيدٌ»؛ الثانية الفتحة، نحو «رأيت زيدًا»؛ الثالثة الكسرة، نحو «مررت بزيدٍ».

Letters The second type is letters. They are four: (1) the *wāw*, e.g., *jāʾa abūhu* (His father came); (2) the *alif*, e.g., *raʾaytu abāhu* (I saw his father); (3) the *yāʾ*, e.g., *marartu bi-abīhi* (I passed by his father); and (4) the *nūn*, e.g., *yaḍribāni* (They [d.] hit) and *yaḍribūna* (They hit).

الحرف الثاني الحرف وهو أربعة: الأولى الواو، نحو «جاء أبوه»؛ الثانية الألف، نحو «رأيت أباه»؛ الثالثة الياء، نحو «مررت بأبيه»؛ الرابعة النون، نحو «يضربان»، «يضربون».

Elision The third type is elision. This is of three types and is specific to verbs: (1) elision of a short vowel, e.g., *lam yaḍrib* (He did not hit); (2) elision of the final [letter], e.g., *lam yaghzu* (He did not go on a military expedition), *lam yarmi* (He did not throw), and *lam yakhsha* (He did not fear); and (3)

الحذف الثالث الحذف وهو ثلاثة؛ مختصّ بالفعل: الأول حذف الحركة، نحو «لم يضربْ»؛ الثاني حذف

elision of the [inflectional] *nūn*, e.g., *lam yaḍribā* (They [d.] did not hit) and *lam yaḍribū* (They did not hit).

Altogether, the inflections total ten.

The Types of Inflectable Expressions

Inflectable expressions are of nine types with regard to their taking on these ten inflections. These nine types of inflectable expressions fall into six categories: (1) that which is complete in that it takes any short vowel,[28] (2) that which is incomplete in that it takes only some short vowels, (3) that which is complete in that it takes any [inflectional] letter, (4) that which is incomplete in that it takes only some [inflectional] letters, (5) that which is complete in that it takes any of two short vowels and elision, and (6) that which is incomplete in that it takes only one short vowel and elision.

1. Complete in Taking Any Short Vowel The first is that which is complete in that it takes any short vowel: this category is inflected with a *ḍamma* in the nominative, e.g., *jā'a Zaydun* (Zayd came); with a *fatḥa* in the accusative, e.g., *ra'aytu Zaydan* (I saw Zayd); and with a *kasra* in the genitive, e.g., *marartu bi-Zaydin* (I passed by Zayd).

This includes fully declinable singular nouns and fully declinable broken plurals, e.g., *jā'a rajulun* (A man came) and ...*rijālun* (Men [came]), *ra'aytu rajulan* (I saw a man) and ...*rijālan* (...men), and *marartu bi-rajulin* (I passed by a man) and ...*rijālin* (...men).

2. Incomplete in Taking Only Some Short Vowels The second is that which is incomplete in that it takes only some short vowels, and this category has two types.

الآخر، نحو «لم يغزُ»، «لم يرمِ»، «لم يخشَ»؛ الثالث حذف النون، نحو «لم يضربا»، «لم يضربوا».

فصار مجموع الإعراب عشرة.

أقسام المعرب

والمعرب باعتبار ورود هذه الإعراب العشرة عليه تسعة. وهو ستّة أقسام: (١) تامّ الحركة، (٢) ناقص الحركة، (٣) تامّ الحروف، (٤) ناقص الحروف، (٥) تامّ الإعراب بالحركتين والحذف، (٦) ناقص الإعراب بالحرف والحذف.

١. تامّ الحركة الأول تامّ الحركة أي يكون رفعه بالضمّة نحو «جاء زيدٌ»، ونصبه بالفتحة نحو «رأيت زيدًا»، وجرّه بالكسرة نحو «مررت بزيدٍ».

وذلك المفرد المنصرف و الجمع المكسّر المنصرف، نحو «جاء رجلٌ» و«رجالٌ»، «رأيت رجلًا» و«رجالًا»، «مررت برجلٍ» و«رجالٍ».

٢. ناقص الحركة الثاني ناقص الحركة وهو قسمان.

The first is inflected with a *ḍamma* in the nominative and with a *fatḥa* in the accusative and the genitive. This is the partially declinable noun, e.g., *jāʾa Aḥmadu* (Aḥmad came), *raʾaytu Aḥmada* (I saw Aḥmad), and *marartu bi-Aḥmada* (I passed by Aḥmad).

The second is inflected with a *ḍamma* in the nominative and with a *kasra* in the accusative and the genitive. This is the sound feminine plural, e.g., *jāʾanā muʿjizātun* (Miracles came to us), *ṣaddaqnā muʿjizātin* (We affirmed miracles), and *āmannā bi-muʿjizātin* (We believed in miracles), as well as *jāʾa muslimātun* (Female Muslims came), *raʾaytu muslimātin* (I saw female Muslims), and *marartu bi-muslimātin* (I passed by female Muslims).

3. Complete in Taking Any [Inflectional] Letter The third is that which is complete in that it takes any [inflectional] letter: this category is inflected with a *wāw* in the nominative, e.g., *jāʾa abūhu* (His father came); with an *alif* in the accusative, e.g., *raʾaytu abāhu* (I saw his father); and with a *yāʾ* in the genitive, e.g., *marartu bi-abīhi* (I passed by his father).

This includes the six weak nouns when they are singular and non-diminutive and are made the *muḍāf* of something other than a first-person [pronoun]. These are (1) *abūhu* (his father), (2) *akhūhu* (his brother), (3) *ḥamūhu* (his male in-law),[29] (4) *hanūhu* (his thing), (5) *fūhu* (his mouth), and (6) *dhū mālin* (possessor of wealth), e.g., *jāʾanā Abū al-Qāsimi ʿalayhi al-salāmu* (Abū al-Qāsim ﷺ came to us) and *ṣaddaqnā Abā al-Qāsimi ʿalayhi al-salāmu* (We believe Abū al-Qāsim ﷺ) and also *hādhā abūhu* (This is his father), *...akhūhu* (...his brother), *...ḥamūhu* (...his male in-law), *...hanūhu* (...his thing), *...fūhu* (...his mouth), and *...dhū mālihi* (...the possessor of his wealth).

4. Incomplete in Taking Only Some [Inflectional] Letters The fourth is that which is incomplete in that it takes only some [inflectional] letters, and this category has two types.

الأول رفعه بالضمّة ونصبه وجرّه بالفتحة، وذلك غير المنصرف، نحو «جاء أحمدُ»، «رأيت أحمدَ»، «مررت بأحمدَ».

الثاني رفعه بالضمّة ونصبه وجرّه بالكسرة، وذلك جمع المؤنّث السالم، نحو «جاءنا معجزاتٌ» و«صدّقنا معجزاتٍ» و«آمنّا بمعجزاتٍ»، ونحو «جاء مسلماتٌ» و«رأيت مسلماتٍ» و«مررت بمسلماتٍ».

٣. تامّ الحروف الثالث تامّ الحروف أي يكون رفعه بالواو نحو «جاء أبوه»، ونصبه بالألف نحو «رأيت أباه»، وجرّه بالياء نحوْ «مررت بأبيه».

وذلك الأسماء الستّة المعتلّة المضافة إلى غير ياء المتكلّم مفردة مكبّرة. وهي: (١) أبوه، (٢) أخوه، (٣) حموه، (٤) هنوه، (٥) فوه، (٦) ذو مال؛ نحو «جاءنا أبو القاسم عليه السلام»، و«صدّقنا أبا القاسم عليه السلام»، و«آمنا بأبي القاسم عليه السلام»، ونحو «هذا أبوه و... أخوه و... حموه و...هنوه و...فوه و...ذو ماله».

٤. ناقص الحروف الرابع ناقص الحروف وهو قسمان.

The first is inflected with a *wāw* in the nominative, e.g., *jāʾa Zaydūna* (Zayds came), and with a *yāʾ* in the accusative and the genitive, e.g., *raʾaytu Zaydīna* (I saw Zayds) and *marartu bi-Zaydīna* (I passed by Zayds).

This includes (1) the sound masculine plural, (2) *ulū* (possessors of), and (3) *ʿishrūna* (twenty) and its sisters, e.g., *jāʾanā al-mursalūna ʿalayhim al-salāmu* (The messengers ﵇ came to us), *ṣaddaqnā al-mursalīna ʿalayhim al-salāmu* (We deemed the messengers ﵇ truthful), and *āmannā bi-l-mursalīna ʿalayhim al-salāmu* (We believed in the messengers ﵇). Another example is *jāʾanā al-muslimūna* (The Muslims came to us), ...*ulū mālin* (The possessors of wealth [came to us]), and ...*ʿishrūna* (Twenty [came to us]); *raʾaynā al-muslimīna* (We saw the Muslims), ...*ulī mālin* (...the possessors of wealth), and ...*ʿishrīna* (...twenty); and *mararnā bi-l-muslimīna* (We passed by the Muslims), ...*ulī mālin* (...the possessors of wealth), and ...*ʿishrīna* (...twenty).

The second [type] is inflected with an *alif* in the nominative, e.g., *jāʾa Zaydāni* (Two Zayds came), and with a *yāʾ* in the accusative and the genitive, e.g., *rayʾatu Zaydayni* (I saw two Zayds) and *marartu bi-Zaydayni* (I passed by two Zayds).

This includes (1) the dual, (2) *ithnāni* (two), and (3) *kilā* (both) when it is made the *muḍāf* of a personal pronoun, e.g., *jāʾanā al-ithnāni kilāhumā* (The two both came to us)—meaning the Quran and the Sunna—*ittabaʿnā al-ithnayni kilayhimā* (We followed the two both), and *ʿamilnā bi-l-ithnatayni kilayhimā* (We put the two both into practice). Another example is *jāʾanā muslimāni* (Two Muslims came to us), ...*ithnatāni* (Two [came to us]), and ...*kilāhumā* (Both of them [came to us]); *raʾaynā muslimayni* (We saw two Muslims), ...*ithnatayni* (...two), and ...*kilayhimā* (...both of them); and *mararnā bi-muslimayni* (We passed by two Muslims), ...*ithnatayni* (...two), and ...*kilayhimā* (...both of them).

الأول رفعه بالواو نحو «جاء زيدون»، ونصبه وجرّه بالياء نحو «رأيت زيدين»، «مررت بزيدين».

وذلك جمع المذكّر السالم و«أولو» و«عشرون» وأخواتها، نحو «جاءنا المرسلون عليهم السلام» و«صدّقنا المرسلين عليهم السلام» و«آمنا بالمرسلين عليهم السلام»، ونحو «جاءنا المسلمون و...أولو مال و...عشرون»، و«رأينا المسلمين و...أولي مال و...عشرين»، و«مررنا بالمسلمين و...أولي مال و...عشرين».

الثاني رفعه بالألف نحو «جاء زيدان»، ونصبه وجرّه بالياء نحو «رأيت زيدين»، «مررت بزيدين».

وذلك التثنية و«اثنان» و«كلا» مضافًا إلى مضمر، نحو «جاءنا الاثنان كلاهما» أي الكتاب والسنّة و«اتّبعنا الاثنين كليهما» و«عملنا بالاثنين كليهما»، ونحو «جاءنا مسلمان و...اثنان و...كلاهما»، و«رأينا مسلمين و...اثنين و...كليهما»، و«مررنا بمسلمين و...اثنين» و...كليهما».

5. Complete in Taking Any of Two Short Vowels and Elision The fifth is that which is complete in that it takes any of two short vowels and elision, and this category has two types.

The first is inflected with a *ḍamma* in the indicative, e.g., *yaḍribu* (He hits); with a *fatḥa* in the subjunctive, e.g., *lan yaḍriba* (He will not hit); and with elision of the short vowel in the jussive, e.g., *lam yaḍrib* (He did not hit). This includes the imperfect tense verb that has a sound final letter and has no personal pronoun attached to it, e.g., *nuḥibbu an nushaffaʿa wa-lam nuḥram* (We would love that we be given intercession, not having been deprived).

The second is inflected with a *ḍamma* in the indicative, e.g., *naghzū* (We go on a military expedition); with a *fatḥa* in the subjunctive, e.g., *lan naghzuwa* (We will not go on a military expedition); and with elision of the ending in the jussive, e.g., *lam naghzu* (We did not go on a military expedition). This includes the defective imperfect tense verb that has no personal pronoun attached to its end, e.g., *nadʿū Allāha taʿālā an yaʿfuwa ʿannā wa-lam yarminā fī al-nāri* (We pray to Allah ﷻ that He pardon us, not having thrown us into hell).

٥. تامّ الإعراب بالحركتين والحذف الخامس تامّ الإعراب بالحركتين والحذف وهو اثنان.

الأول رفعه بالضمّة نحو «يضربُ»، ونصبه بالفتحة نحو «لن يضربَ»، وجزمه بحذف الحركة نحو «لم يضربْ». وهو الفعل المضارع الصحيح الآخر ولم يتّصل به ضمير، نحو «نحبُّ أن نُشفَّعَ ولم نُحرَمْ»[٦].

الثاني رفعه بالضمّة نحو «يغزو»، ونصبه بالفتحة نحو «لن يغزوَ»، وجزمه بحذف الآخر نحو «لم يغزُ». وذلك الفعل المضارع الناقص الذي لم يتّصل بآخره ضمير، نحو «ندعو الله تعالى أن يعفوَ عنّا ولم يرمِنا في النار»[٧].

6. Incomplete in Taking Only One Short Vowel and Elision The sixth is that which is incomplete in that it takes only one short vowel and elision: this category is inflected with a *nūn* in the indicative, e.g., *yaḍribāni* (They [d.] hit), and with elision of the *nūn* in the subjunctive and the jussive, e.g., *lan yaḍribā* (They [d.] will not hit) and *lam yaḍribā* (They [d.] did not hit).

This includes the imperfect tense verb that has a personal pronoun other than the *nūn* (i.e., other than the *nūn* of the feminine plural) attached to its end, e.g., *al-awliyāʾu wa-l-ʿulamāʾu yashfiʿāni yawma al-qiyāmati fa-narjū an yashfiʿā lanā wa-lam yuʿriḍā ʿannā* (The saints and the scholars will intercede on the day of resurrection; we hope that they will intercede on our behalf, not having turned away from us). Another example is *Zaydun wa-ʿAmrun yaḍribāni* (Zayd and ʿAmr hit), *...lan yaḍribā* (...will not hit), and *...lam yaḍribā* (...did not hit).[30]

٦. ناقص الإعراب بالحرف والحذف السادس ناقص الإعراب بالحرف والحذف أي يكون رفعه بالنون نحو «يضربان»، ونصبه وجزمه[٨] بحذفه نحو «لن يضربا» و«لم يضربا».

وهو الفعل المضارع الذي اتّصل بآخره ضمير غير النون أي غير نون جمع المؤنّث، نحو «الأولياء والعلماء يشفعان يوم القيامة فنرجو أن يشفعا لنا ولم يعرضا عنا»، ونحو «زيد وعمرو يضربان و...لن يضربا و...لم يضربا».

Thus, the types of inflectable expressions total nine: those that are complete in taking any short vowel (one type), those that are incomplete in taking only some short vowels (two types), those that are complete in taking any [inflectional] letter (one type), those that are incomplete in taking only some [inflectional] letters (two types), those that are complete in taking any of two short vowels and elision (two types), and those that are incomplete in taking only one short vowel and elision (one type).

فصار مجموع المعرب تسعة: تامّ الحركة (١)، ناقص الحركة (٢)، تامّ الحروف (١)، ناقص الحروف (٢)، تامّ الإعراب بالحركة والحذف (٢)، ناقص الإعراب بالحرف والحذف (١).

[Another Classification of Inflection]

Inflection is either explicit, implicit, or positional.

1. If the inflection appears in the expression,[31] it is termed *explicit*, e.g., *jāʾa Zaydun* (Zayd came).
2. If it does not appear in the expression but is implicit in the ending,[32] it is termed *implicit*, e.g., *ana al-ʿāṣī* (I am the sinful one).
3. If it does not appear in the expression and is not implicit in the ending, it is termed *positional*,[33] e.g., *jāʾa hāʾulāʾi* (These came).

[تقسيم آخر للإعراب]

ثمّ الإعراب إما لفظي أو تقديري أو محلّي.

١- إن ظهر في اللفظ يسمّى لفظيًّا، نحو «جاء زيدٌ».

٢- وإن لم يظهر في اللفظ بل قدّر في آخره يسمّى تقديريًّا، نحو «أنا العاصي».

٣- وإن لم يظهر في اللفظ ولم يقدّر في آخره يسمّى محلّيًّا، نحو «جاء هؤلاء».

❋ ❋ ❋

The first method is complete by the aid of Allah ﷻ. With His permission ﷻ, we begin with the second method.

تمّ[٩] بعون الله تعالى الطريق الأول ونشرع بإذنه تعالى في الطريق الثاني.

[Chapter 4], the first chapter of the second method

الباب الأول من الطريق الثاني

THE NOUN

الاســـــم

What is the noun? How many are its categories, and what are they?

ما الاسم؟ وكم صنفًا وما هي؟

The noun is [a word] that signifies a meaning in itself that is not bound to one of the three times, as in *Zayd* and *rajul* (man). Some special characteristics of the noun are that it takes nunation, prepositions, and the definite *lām* and that it can be a subject, an agent, or a *muḍāf.* Some nouns can be governors, e.g., the active participle, and some cannot be governors, e.g., *ana* (I) and *anta* (you).

الاسم هو ما دلّ على معنًى في نفسه غير مقترن بأحد الأزمنة الثلاثة، نحو «زيد» و«رجل». ومن خواصّه دخول التنوين وحرف الجرّ ولام التعريف، وكونه مبتدأً وفاعلًا ومضافًا. وبعضه عامل كاسم الفاعل وبعضه غير عامل كـ«أنا» و«أنت».

There are eighteen categories of nouns:

I. Generic nouns

II. Proper names

III. Declinable nouns

IV. Appositives of declinable nouns

V. Nominative nouns

VI. Accusative nouns

VII. Genitive nouns

VIII. Indeclinable nouns

IX. Dual nouns

X. Plural nouns

XI–XII. Definite and indefinite nouns

XIII–XIV. Masculine and feminine nouns

وأصنافه ثمانية عشر صنفًا:

(١) اسم الجنس

(٢) العلم

(٣) المعرب

(٤) توابع المعرب

(٥) المرفوع

(٦) المنصوب

(٧) المجرور

(٨) المبني

(٩) المثنّى

(١٠) المجموع

(١١-١٢) المعرفة والنكرة

(١٣-١٤) المذكّر والمؤنّث

XV. Diminutive nouns
(١٥) المصغّر

XVI. Relational nouns
(١٦) اسم المنسوب

XVII. Numeral nouns
(١٧) أسماء العدد

XVIII. Nouns related to verbs
(١٨) الأسماء المتّصلة بالأفعال

I. Generic Nouns

(١) اسم الجنس

A generic noun is that which is lexically assigned to a thing and to everything that is like it in essence. Generic nouns are of two types: *concrete nouns*, e.g., *rajul* (man), and *abstract nouns*, e.g., *ʿilm* (knowledge).

وهو ما وضع لشيء ولكل ما أشبهه في الحقيقة. وهو على قسمين: اسم عين كـ«رجل»، واسم معنًى كـ«علم».

II. Proper Names

(٢) العلم

A proper name is that which is assigned to a thing individually. Proper names are of three types: *names simpliciter*, e.g., *Zayd*; *surnames*, e.g., *Abū ʿAbdallāh* (Father of ʿAbdallāh) and *Umm Kulthūm* (Mother of Kulthūm); and *titles*, e.g., *Shams al-Dīn* (sun of the religion) and *al-Aʿraj* (the lame).

وهو ما وضع لشيء بعينه وهو على ثلاثة أقسام: اسم كـ«زيد»، وكنية كـ«أبي عبد الله» و«أم كلثوم»، ولقب كـ«شمس الدين» و«الأعرج».

III. Declinable Nouns

(٣) المعرب

A declinable noun is that whose end varies according to the various governors that modify it, e.g., *jāʾa Zaydun* (Zayd came), *raʾaytu Zaydan* (I saw Zayd), and *marartu bi-Zaydin* (I passed by Zayd). Declinable nouns are of two types:

1. *fully declinable nouns*, which can take the genitive inflection and nunation, e.g., *marartu bi-Zaydin* (I passed by Zayd).

وهو ما اختلف آخره باختلاف العوامل الواردة عليه، نحو «جاء زيدٌ»، «رأيت زيدًا»، و«مررت بزيدٍ». وهو على قسمين.

١- منصرف، وهو ما دخله الجرّ والتنوين، نحو «مررت بزيدٍ».

2. *partially declinable nouns*, which cannot take the genitive inflection or nunation and are [instead] vowelized with *fatḥ* in the genitive case, e.g., *marartu bi-Aḥmada̱* (I passed by Aḥmad). This applies unless they are made *muḍāf* or made definite with the *lām*; in such cases they take the genitive inflection, e.g., *marartu bi-Aḥmadiḵum* (I passed by your Aḥmad) and *...bi-l-aḥmari̱* (...by the red one).

Causes of Partial Declinability There are nine factors that play a role in partial declinability:

1. being a proper name, e.g., *Zaynabu*.
2. femininity,[34] e.g., *Ṭalḥatu*.
3. signifying a quality, e.g., *aḥmaru* (red).
4. the pattern of a verb, e.g., *Aḥmadu*.
5. morphological change, which is when a noun changes from its original form to another form, e.g., *ʿUmaru*, which was changed from *ʿĀmirun*.
6. plurality, i.e., a plural form that cannot be pluralized further as a broken plural, e.g., *masājidu* (masjids) and *maṣābīḥu* (lanterns).
7. being a compound noun, e.g., *Maʿdī-karibu*.
8. being [originally] non-Arabic, e.g., *Ibrāhīmu*.
9. the *alif* and *nūn* that resemble the *alif*s of femininity, e.g., *ʿImrānu* and *ʿUthmānu*.

A noun is partially declinable when it is subject to any two of these factors.[35] Additionally, a noun is partially declinable when it is subject to one factor that stands in the place of two, namely, (1) a plural form like *masājid* and *maṣābīḥ*, (2) an *alif maqṣūra* like *ḥublā* (pregnant) and *bushrā* (glad tidings), or (3) an *alif mamdūda* like *ḥamrāʾ* (red [f.]) and *ṣafrāʾ* (yellow [f.]).

٢- وغير منصرف، وهو ما منع عنه الجرّ والتنوين ويفتح في موضع الجرّ، نحو «مررت بأحمدَ»، إلا إذا أضيف أو عرّف باللام فيدخله الجرّ حينئذ، نحو «مررت بأحمدِكم» و«بالأحمرِ».

أسباب منع الصرف أسباب منع الصرف تسعة:

١- العلمية، كـ«زينب».

٢- التأنيث[١٠]، نحو «طلحة».

٣- الوصف، كـ«أحمر».

٤- وزن الفعل، كـ«أحمد».

٥- العدل، وهو خروج الاسم عن صيغته الأصلية إلى صيغة أخرى، كـ«عمر» فإنّه معدول عن «عامر».

٦- الجمع أي جمع يمتنع جمعه مرّة أخرى جمع التكسير، كـ«مساجد» و«مصابيح».

٧- التركيب كـ«معدي كرب».

٨- العجمة، كـ«إبراهيم».

٩- الألف والنون المشبّهتان لألفي التأنيث، كـ«عمران» و«عثمان».

ومتى اجتمع في الاسم سببان لم ينصرف؛ وكذا لو كان في الاسم سبب يقوم مقام السببين، وهو (١) الجمع نحو «مساجد» و«مصابيح»، (٢) والألف المقصورة نحو «حبلى» و«بشرى»، (٣) والألف الممدودة نحو «حمراء» و«صفراء».

IV. Appositives of Declinable Nouns

Appositives of declinable nouns are any [expression] that comes after [a declinable noun] and adopts its declension in the same manner. They are of five types.

Emphases

An emphasis is any appositive that (1) gives confirmation to the principal noun with respect to the predication, e.g., *jāʾanī Zaydun Zaydun* (Zayd, Zayd came to me) and *jāʾanī Zaydun nafsuhu* (Zayd himself came to me), or (2) gives confirmation to the principal noun with respect to its inclusiveness, e.g., *jāʾanī al-rajulāni kilāhumā* (The two men, both of them, came to me) and *jāʾanī al-qawmu kulluhum* (The people, all of them, came to me).

Adjectives

An adjective is an appositive that signifies any meaning in the principal noun, e.g., *jāʾanī rajulun ḍāribun* (A hitting man came to me), …*maḍrūbun* (A beaten [man came to me]), and …*karīmun* (A generous [man came to me]). The adjective conforms to the described noun in its declension; in whether it is singular, dual, or plural; in whether it is definite or indefinite; and in whether it is masculine or feminine. A thing can be described by reference to its [own] action, as in the abovementioned examples, or by reference to the action of a related noun, as in *marartu bi-rajulin manīʿin jāruhu* (I passed by a man whose neighbor is unapproachable).

Substitutes

A substitute is any appositive to which what is predicated of the principal noun is meant to apply instead. It is of four types:

1. substitution of a whole for the whole, e.g., *raʾaytu Zaydan akhāka* (I saw [Zayd] your brother).[36]

(٤) توابع المعرب

وهي كل ثانٍ معرب بإعراب سابقه من جهة واحدة. وهي خمسة.

التأكيد

الأول التأكيد وهو كل تابع يقرّر أمر المتبوع في النسبة، نحو «جاءني زيدٌ زيدٌ» و«جاءني زيدٌ نفسُه»، أو يقرّر أمر المتبوع في الشمول، نحو «جاءني الرجلان كلاهما» و«جاءني القومُ كلُّهم».

الصفة

الثاني الصفة وهو تابع يدلّ على معنًى في متبوعه مطلقًا، نحو «جاءني رجلٌ ضاربٌ» أو «مضروبٌ» أو «كريمٌ». الصفة توافق الموصوف في إعرابه، وإفراده وتثنيته وجمعه، وتعريفه وتنكيره، وتذكيره وتأنيثه. ويوصف الشيء بفعله كما ذكرناه آنفًا وبفعل متعلّقه نحو «مررت برجلٍ منيعٍ جارُه».

البدل

الثالث البدل وهو تابع مقصود بما نسب إلى المتبوع دونه. وهو على أربعة أقسام.

١- بدل الكل من الكل، نحو «رأيت زيدًا أخاك».

2. substitution of a part for the whole, e.g., *ḍarabtu Zaydan ra'sahu* (I hit [Zayd] Zayd's head).
3. associative substitution, e.g., *suliba Zaydun thawbuhu* ([Zayd] Zayd's garment was stolen).
4. substitution of error, e.g., *marartu bi-rajulin bi-ḥimārin* (I passed [by a man] by a donkey).

٢- بدل البعض من الكل، نحو «ضربت زيدًا رأسَه».

٣- بدل الاشتمال، نحو «سلب زيدٌ ثوبُه».

٤- بدل الغلط، نحو «مررت برجلٍ بحمارٍ».

Clarifying Appositives

Clarifying apposition[37] is to mention [a noun] and then use a more familiar name for it,[38] e.g., *jā'anī akhūka Zaydun* (Your brother, Zayd, came to me).

عطف البيان

الرابع عطف البيان وهو أن تُتبع المذكور بأشهر اسميه، نحو «جاءني أخوك زيدٌ».

Conjuncts

A conjunct is an appositive [for which] along with the principal noun the predication is intended. A conjunction comes between the conjunct and the principal noun, e.g., *jā'anī Zaydun wa-ʿAmrun* (Zayd and ʿAmr came to me), ...*fa-ʿAmrun* ([Zayd] and then ʿAmr [came to me]), and ...*thumma ʿAmrun* ([Zayd] and then ʿAmr [came to me]). Both of them, that is, *Zaydun* and *ʿAmrun*, are intended in the predication, which in this case is that they are coming. There are ten conjunctions: the *wāw*, the *fā'*, *thumma*, *ḥattā*, *aw*, *immā*, *am*, *lā*, *bal*, and *lākin*. They will be explained in detail, if Allah ﷻ wills, in the chapter on particles.

العطف بالحروف

الخامس العطف بالحروف وهو تابع مقصود بالنسبة مع متبوعه. ويتوسّط بينه وبين المتبوع واحد من حروف العطف، نحو «جاءني زيدٌ وعمرٌو» أو «فعمرٌو» أو «ثم عمرٌو». وكل منهما أي من زيد وعمرو مقصود بالنسبة التي هي هنا المجيء. وحروف العطف عشرة: الواو والفاء وثُمَّ وحَتَّى وأَوْ وإِمَّا وأَمْ ولَا وبَلْ ولَكِنْ. وسيجيء تفصيلها إن شاء الله تعالى في باب الحرف.

V. Nominative Nouns

(٥) المرفوعات

Marfūʿāt (nominative nouns) is the plural of *marfūʿ*. A nominative noun is that which bears the sign of agency, which is the nominative inflection, e.g., *ḍaraba Zaydun* (Zayd hit) and *ḍuriba Zaydun* (Zayd was hit). Nominative nouns are of two types.

المرفوعات جمع «مرفوع» وهو ما اشتمل على علم الفاعلية وهو الرفع، نحو «ضَرَبَ زيدٌ» أو «ضُرِبَ زيدٌ». وهو على قسمين.

[The Agent]

One type is the basis, namely, the agent, which is that of which a verb or its like[39] is predicated. The latter in either case precedes the agent because it inheres in it,[40] that is, in the agent, e.g., *qāma Zaydun* (Zayd stood) and *Zaydun qāʾimun abūhu* (Zayd's father is standing).

[Appended Nominatives]

The other type is appended to the agent[41] and includes five subtypes:

[1. The Subject and Its Predicate] The first is the subject and its predicate. The *subject* is a noun that is free from any expressed governors and receives predication, and the *predicate* is free from any governors and is that through which predication is made, as in *Zaydun qāʾimun* (Zayd is standing). The subject should be definite, e.g., *Zaydun qāʾimun* (Zayd is standing), but it is sometimes indefinite, e.g., *salāmun ʿalaykum* (Peace be upon you). The predicate should be indefinite, e.g., *Zaydun karīmun* (Zayd is generous), but sometimes both are definite, e.g., *Allāhu rabbunā wa-Muḥammadun nabiyyunā* (Allah is our Lord and Muḥammad is our prophet). The predicate is of two types: an individual word, e.g., *Zaydun qāʾimun* (Zayd is standing), or a clause, e.g., *Zaydun dhahaba abūhu* (Zayd's father went). There must be a personal pronoun in the clause that refers to the subject [of the main sentence], unless the reference would be understood, e.g., *al-burru al-kurru bi-sittīna dirhaman* (Wheat: a *kurr* costs sixty dirhams),[42] which means *al-kurru minhu bi-sittīna* (a *kurr* of it costs sixty).

[2. The Subject-Noun of *Kāna*] The second of the appended nominatives is the subject-noun for the class of *kāna*, e.g., *kāna Zaydun munṭaliqan* (Zayd was departing).

[الفاعل]

أحدهما أصل، وهو الفاعل وهو ما أسند إليه الفعل أو شبهه وقدّم كل منهما عليه على جهة قيام كل منهما به أي بالفاعل، نحو «قام زيدٌ» و«زيد قائمٌ أبوه».

[ملحقات الفاعل]

وثانيهما ملحق به، وهو خمسة أقسام.

[١. المبتدأ والخبر] الأول المبتدأ وخبره. المبتدأ هو الاسم المجرّد عن العوامل اللفظية مسند إليه، والخبر هو المجرّد عن العوامل مسندًا به، نحو «زيدٌ قائمٌ». وحقّ المبتدأ أن يكون معرفة نحو «زيدٌ قائمٌ»، وقد يجيء نكرةً نحو «سلامٌ عليكم». وحقّ الخبر أن يكون نكرة نحو «زيدٌ كريمٌ»؛ وقد يجيئان معرفتين نحو «اللهُ ربُّنا ومحمدٌ نبيُّنا». والخبر على قسمين: مفرد نحو «زيدٌ قائمٌ»، وجملة نحو «زيدٌ ذهبَ أبوه»؛ ولا بدّ في الجملة من ضمير يرجع إلى المبتدأ إلا إذا كان الراجع معلومًا، نحو «البرُّ الكرُّ بستين درهمًا» أي الكرّ منه بستين.

[٢. اسم كان] الثاني من ملحقات الفاعل الاسم في باب كانَ، نحو «كان زيدٌ منطلقًا».

[3. The Predicate of *Inna*] The third is the predicate for the class of *inna*, e.g., *inna Zaydan munṭaliqun* (Indeed Zayd is departing).

[٣. خبر إنّ] الثالث الخبر في باب إنَّ، نحو «إنّ زيدًا منطلقٌ».

[4. The Predicate of the *Lā* of Categoric Negation] The fourth is the predicate of the *lā* of categoric negation, e.g., *lā rajula afḍalu minka* (No man is better than you).

[٤. خبر لا لنفي الجنس] الرابع خبر لَا لنفي الجنس، نحو «لا رجلَ أفضلُ منك».

[5. The Subject-Noun of the *Mā* and *Lā* That Mean *Laysa*] The fifth is the subject-noun of the *mā* and *lā* that mean *laysa*, e.g., *mā Zaydun munṭaliqan* (Zayd is not departing) and *lā rajulun afḍala minka* (A man is not better than you).

[٥. اسم ما ولا بمعنى ليس] الخامس اسم مَا ولَا بمعنى لَيْسَ، نحو «ما زيدٌ منطلقًا» و«لا رجلٌ أفضلَ منك».

VI. Accusative Nouns

(٦) المنصوبات

Manṣūbāt (accusative nouns) is the plural of *manṣūb*. An accusative noun is that which bears the sign of objectivity, which is the accusative inflection, e.g., *Zaydun ḍaraba ʿAmran* (Zayd hit ʿAmr). Accusative nouns are of two types.

المنصوبات جمع «منصوب» وهو ما اشتمل على علم المفعولية وهو النصب، نحو «زيدٌ ضرب عمرًا». المنصوبات على قسمين.

[Actional Accusatives]

[المفعول]

One type is the basis, namely, the actional accusative, and it includes five subtypes:

أحدهما أصل، وهو المفعول. وهو على خمسة أقسام.

[1. The Action-Notion] The action-notion expresses either (1) emphasis, e.g., *ḍarabtu ḍarban* (I hit [quite a] hitting); (2) kind, e.g., *ḍarabtu ḍirbatan* (I hit [a kind of] hitting); or (3) number, e.g., *ḍarabtu ḍarbatan* (I hit [one] hitting). Sometimes the action-notion occurs with a word other than [the noun that specifically corresponds to] the verb, e.g., *qaʿadtu julūsan* (I sat [a sitting]).

[١. المفعول المطلق] الأول المفعول المطلق وهو إما للتأكيد نحو «ضربت ضربًا»، أو للنوع نحو «ضربت ضِربةً»، أو للعدد نحو «ضربت ضَربةً». وقد يكون بغير لفظ الفعل، نحو «قعدت جلوسًا».

[2. The Object] The object expresses that to which the action of the agent occurs, e.g., *ḍarabtu Zaydan* (I hit Zayd). It may be made accusative by a hidden verb, as in saying to a pilgrim, *Makkata*

[٢. المفعول به] الثاني المفعول به وهو ما وقع عليه فعل الفاعل، نحو «ضربت زيدًا». وينصب

(...Makka?), meaning *taqṣidu Makkata* (You are bound for Makka?).

One type of object is the *vocative object,* [a noun signifying the person] whose response is sought through the use of a particle that stands for *adʿū* (I call) either (1) explicitly, e.g., *yā Zaydu* (O Zayd!), or (2) implicitly, e.g., His saying ﷻ, *Yūsufu aʿriḍ ʿan hādhā* ("Yūsuf! Turn away from this") (Q 12:29), meaning *yā Yūsufu aʿriḍ ʿan hādhā*. The vocative object is accusative when it is (1) *muḍāf,* e.g., *yā ʿAbda Allāhi* (O ʿAbdallāh!); (2) similar to the *muḍāf,*[43] e.g., *yā khayran min Zaydin* (O [person who is] better than Zayd!); or (3) indefinite, e.g., *yā rākiban* (O rider!).[44] As for a singular definite vocative object, it has a *ḍamma*, e.g., *yā Zaydu* (O Zayd!).

[3. The Action-Place/Time] The action-place/time expresses that in which a given action occurs. It is of two types.

The first is the *adverb of time,* e.g., *qumtu yawma al-jumuʿati* (I stayed on the day of Friday). The adverb of time is made accusative by the implicit presence of *fī* (in), whether the adverb be specific, e.g., *jiʾtu yawma al-jumuʿati* (I came on the day of Friday), or unspecific, e.g., *ataytuhu yawman* (I came to him one day).

The second is the *adverb of place*, e.g., *sirtu amāmaka* (I traveled in front of you). It is made accusative by the implicit presence of *fī* (in) if it is unspecific, namely, [when expressing any of] the six directions, e.g., *qumtu amāmaka* (I stood in front of you). The adverb of place is not made accusative if it is specific, e.g., *ṣallaytu fī al-masjidi* (I prayed in the masjid).[45]

[4. The Action-Accompaniment] The action-accompaniment is that which comes after a *wāw* that means *maʿa* (with), e.g., *mā ṣanaʿta wa-abāka* (What did you do together with your father?), i.e., *maʿa abīka*, and *mā shaʾnuka wa-Zaydan* (What is your business with Zayd?), i.e., *maʿa Zaydin*. The

بفعل مضمر، كقولك للحجاج «مكّةَ» أي «تقصدُ مكّةَ».

ومن المفعول به المنادى وهو الذي يُطلب إقباله بحرف نائب مناب «أدعو» لفظًا نحو «يا زيد»، أو تقديرًا نحو قوله تعالى ﴿يُوسُفُ أَعْرِضْ عَنْ هَٰذَا﴾ [١٢/ ٢٩] أي «يا يوسف أعرض عن هذا». وينصب المنادى (١) المضاف نحو «يا عبدَ الله»، (٢) والمشابه له نحو «يا خيرًا من زيد»، (٣) والنكرة نحو «يا راكبًا»؛ وأما المنادى المفرد المعرفة فمضموم، نحو «يا زيدُ».

[٣. المفعول فيه] الثالث المفعول فيه وهو ما عمل فيه فعل مذكور. وهو على قسمين.

أحدهما ظرف زمان، نحو «قمت يومَ الجمعة»؛ وهو أي ظرف الزمان ينصب بتقدير «فِي» سواءً كان معيّنًا نحو «جئت يومَ الجمعة» أو مبهمًا نحو «أتيته يومًا».

ثانيهما ظرف مكان، نحو «سرت أمامك»؛ وهو ينصب بتقدير «فِي» إن كان مبهمًا وهو الجهات الستّ نحو «قمت أمامَك»، ولا ينصب إن كان معيّنًا نحو «صليت في المسجد».

[٤. المفعول معه] الرابع المفعول معه وهو المذكور بعد الواو بمعنى «مَعَ»، نحو «ما صنعت وأباك» أي «مع أبيك»، و«ما شأنك وزيدًا» أي «مع زيد». ولا بدّ له

action-accompaniment must be governed either by a verb, as in the first example, or by the meaning of a verb, as in the second example.[46]

من فعل يكون عاملًا فيه كالمثال الأول أو معنى الفعل كالمثال الثاني.

[5. The Action-Reason] The action-reason is anything that is a reason for the action, e.g., *ḍarabtuhu ta'dīban* (I hit him to discipline [him]), i.e., *ḍarabtuhu li-l-ta'dībi.*

[٥. المفعول له] الخامس المفعول له وهو كل ما كان علّة للفعل، نحو «ضربته تأديبًا» أي «ضربته للتأديب».

[Appended Accusatives]

[ملحقات المفعول]

The other type is appended to it; that is, the second type of the accusative nouns is appended to the basis, namely, to the actional accusative. These appended accusatives total seven.

وثانيهما الملحق به أي ثاني قسمي المنصوبات الملحق بالأصل أي بالمفعول. وهو أي الملحق بالمفعول سبعة أشياء.

[1. The Circumstance] The circumstance is an explanation of the state of the agent or the object, e.g., *ḍarabtu Zaydan qā'iman* (I hit Zayd standing). It should be indefinite and that to which the circumstance applies should be definite. If the circumstance precedes that to which it applies, it is valid to make the latter indefinite, e.g., *jā'anī rākiban rajulun* (Riding, a man came to me).

[١. الحال] الأول الحال وهي بيان هيئة الفاعل أو المفعول به، نحو «ضربت زيدًا قائمًا». وحقّها التنكير وحقّ ذي الحال التعريف؛ فإن قدم عليه الحال جاز تنكيره نحو «جاءني راكبًا رجلٌ».

[2. The Specification] The specification is that which removes ambiguity (1) from an individual word, e.g., *ʿindī rāqūdun khallan* (I have a large jug of vinegar), *…manawāni samnan* (…two *manns* of clarified butter), *…ʿishrūna dirhaman* (…twenty dirhams), *…mil'uhu ʿasalan* (…its fill of honey), or (2) from the predication in the sentence, e.g., *ṭāba Zaydun nafsan* (Zayd was in good spirits) and *ṭāra ʿAmrun faraḥan* (ʿAmr flew in happiness).

[٢. التمييز] الثاني التمييز وهو ما يرفع الإبهام عن المفرد نحو «عندي راقود خلًّا» و«منوان سمنًا» و«عشرون درهمًا» و«ملؤه عسلًا»، أو عن النسبة في الجملة نحو «طاب زيد نفسًا» و«طار عمرو فرحًا».

[3. The Exception] The exception is that which comes after *illā* (except) or its sisters. It is of two types:

1. *connected*, i.e., excluded from a group through *illā* or its sisters, e.g., *jā'anī al-qawmu illā Zaydan* (The people came to me except Zayd) and *jā'a al-qawmu ghayra Zaydin* (The people came except Zayd).

[٣. المستثنى] الثالث المستثنى وهو المذكور بعد إِلّا وأخواتها. وهو على قسمين.

١- متّصل وهو مخرج عن المتعدد بإِلّا وأخواتها، نحو «جاءني القوم إلا زيدًا» و«جاء القوم غير زيد».

2. *disconnected*, i.e., what comes after *illā* or its sisters yet is not excluded from a group, e.g., *jā'anī al-qawmu illā ḥimāran* (The people came to me but not a donkey) and *jā'anī al-qawmu ghayra ḥimārin* (The people came to me but not a donkey).

٢- ومنقطع وهو المذكور بعد إِلَّا وأخواتها غير مخرج من المتعدد، نحو «جاءني القوم إلا حمارًا» و«جاءني القوم غير حمار».

The exception as such, connected or disconnected, must be in the accusative case in the following cases:

1. when it comes after an *illā* that does not have the meaning of an adjective, in an affirmative sentence, e.g., *jā'anī al-qawmu illā Zaydan* (The people came to me except Zayd).
2. when it comes before the group from which the exception is made, e.g., *jā'anī illā Zaydan al-qawmu* (Except for Zayd, the people came to me) and *mā jā'anī illā Zaydan aḥadun* (Except for Zayd, no one came to me).
3. when it is disconnected, e.g., *mā jā'anī al-qawmu illā ḥimāran* (The people did not come to me except a donkey).
4. when it comes after *'adā* or *khalā*, according to the majority position, e.g., *jā'anī al-qawmu 'adā Zaydan* (The people came to me except Zayd) and *...khalā Zaydan.*
5. when it comes after *mā 'adā, mā khalā, laysa,* or *lā yakūnu*, e.g., *jā'anī al-qawmu mā 'adā Zaydan* (The people came to me except Zayd), *...mā khalā Zaydan, ...laysa Zaydan,* and *...lā yakūnu Zaydan,* which are equivalent to *jā'anī al-qawmu mā 'adā/mā khalā/laysa/lā yakūnu ba'ḍuhum Zaydan* (The people came to me, none of them being Zayd).

وهو أي المستثنى مطلقًا متصلًا كان أو منقطعًا منصوب وجوبًا:

١- إذا كان بعد إِلَّا التي لا تكون بمعنى الصفة وفي كلام موجب، نحو «جاءني القوم إلا زيدًا».

٢- وإذا كان مقدّمًا على المستثنى منه، نحو «جاءني إلا زيدًا القوم» و«ما جاءني إلا زيدًا أحد».

٣- إذا كان منقطعًا، نحو «ما جاءني القوم إلا حمارًا».

٤- بعد «عَدَا» و«خَلَا» عند الأكثرين، نحو «جاءني القوم عدا زيدًا» و«خلا زيدًا».

٥- بعد «مَا عَدَا» و«مَا خَلَا» و«لَيْسَ» و«لَا يَكُونُ»، نحو «جاءني القوم ما عدا زيدًا / ما خلا زيدًا / ليس زيدًا / لا يكون زيدًا» أي «جاءني القوم ما عدا / ما خلا / ليس / لا يكون بعضهم زيدًا».

In sentences that are not affirmative in which the group from which the exception is made is expressly mentioned, the accusative is valid for the word after *illā* but substitution is preferable, e.g., His statement ﷻ *mā fa'alūhu illā qalīlun minhum* (They would not have done so, save few) (Q 4:66) and *illā qalīlan*. In sentences that are not affirmative in

يجوز النصب ويختار البدل في ما بعد «إِلَّا» في كلام غير موجب وذكر المستثنى منه، نحو قوله تعالى ﴿مَّا فَعَلُوهُ إِلَّا قَلِيلٌ مِّنْهُمْ﴾ [٤/ ٦٦] و«إلا قليلًا». ويعرب

which the group from which the exception is made is *not* expressly mentioned, the exception is declined according to its governors, and this is termed a *vacated exception*, e.g., *mā jā'anī illā Zaydun* (None came to me but Zayd), *mā ra'aytu illā Zaydan* (I saw none but Zayd), and *mā marartu illā bi-Zaydin* (I passed by none but Zayd).

المستثنى على حسب العوامل إذا كان المستثنى منه غير مذكور في كلام غير موجب، ويسمّى هذا مستثنًى مفرّغًا، نحو «ما جاءني إلا زيدٌ» و«ما رأيت إلا زيدًا» و«ما مررت إلا بزيدٍ».

Ghayr (except, other than) takes the same grammatical state as nouns that come after *illā*, e.g., *mā jā'anī al-qawmu ghayru Zaydin* (The people did not come to me except Zayd), *mā ra'aytu ghayra Zaydin* (I saw none but Zayd), and *mā marartu bi-ghayri Zaydin* (I passed by none but Zayd).

وحكم «غَيْرَ» كحكم الاسم الواقع بعد «إلَّا»، نحو «ما جاءني القوم غيرُ زيد» و«ما رأيت غيرَ زيد» و«ما مررت بغيرِ زيد».

[**4. The Predicate of *Kāna***] The fourth [of the appended accusatives] is the predicate for the class of *kāna*, e.g., *kāna Zaydun munṭaliqan* (Zayd was departing).

[**٤. خبر كان**] الرابع الخبر في باب كانَ، نحو «كان زيد منطلقًا».

[**5. The Subject-Noun of *Inna***] The fifth is the subject-noun for the class of *inna*, e.g., *inna Zaydan qā'imun* (Indeed Zayd is standing).

[**٥. اسم إنّ**] الخامس الاسم في باب إنَّ، نحو «إنّ زيدًا قائم».

[**6. The Subject-Noun of the *Lā* of Categoric Negation**] The sixth is the subject-noun of the *lā* of categoric negation when it is *muḍāf*, e.g., *lā ghulāma rajulin ʿindanā* (There is no servant of a man with us), or similar to the *muḍāf*,[47] e.g., *lā khayran minka ʿindanā* (There is nobody better than you with us). As for when the subject-noun is an individual word, it has a *fatḥa* but is not an accusative noun,[48] e.g., *lā ghulāma laka* (You have no servant).

[**٦. لا لنفي الجنس**] السادس اسم لَا لنفي الجنس إذا كان مضافًا نحو «لا غلامَ رجل عندنا»، أو مشابهًا له نحو «لا خيرًا منك عندنا». وأما المفرد فمفتوح ليس من المنصوبات، نحو «لا غلامَ لك».

VII. Genitive Nouns

(٧) المجرورات

Majrūrāt (genitive nouns) is the plural of *majrūr*. A genitive noun is that which bears the sign of the *muḍāf ilayhi*, namely, the genitive inflection, e.g., *ghulāmu Zaydin* (the boy of Zayd). Genitive nouns

وهي جمع «المجرور» وهو ما اشتمل على علم المضاف إليه وهو الجرّ، نحو «غلام زيدٍ». والمجرورات على

are of two types: nouns made genitive through *iḍāfa*, e.g., *ghulāmu Zaydin* (the boy of Zayd), and nouns made genitive through prepositions, e.g., *bihi dā'un* (He has an illness).

Iḍāfa is of two types: *attributive* and *nonattributive.*

Attributive *iḍāfa* is that the *muḍāf* not be a derivative noun,[49] e.g., *ghulāmu Zaydin* (the boy of Zayd), or that it be a derivative noun but not govern the *muḍāf ilayhi*,[50] e.g., *muṣāriʿu Miṣra* (the wrestler of Egypt). It signifies

1. the meaning of the *lām* when the *muḍāf ilayhi* is neither the generic kind of the *muḍāf* nor its place/time, e.g., *ghulāmu Zaydin* (the boy of Zayd).
2. the meaning of *min* when the *muḍāf ilayhi* is the generic kind of the *muḍāf*, e.g., *khātamu al-fiḍḍati* (ring of silver).
3. the meaning of *fī* when the *muḍāf ilayhi* is the place/time of the *muḍāf*, e.g., *ḍarbu al-yawmi* (the hitting of today).

Nonattributive *iḍāfa* is the *iḍāfa* of a derivative noun to an expression it governs, e.g., *Zaydun ḍāribu ʿAmrin* (Zayd is hitting ʿAmr), ...*ḥasanu al-wajhi* (...has a handsome face), and ...*mu'addabu al-khādimi* (...has a well-mannered servant).

Attributive *iḍāfa* makes the *muḍāf* definite when the *muḍāf ilayhi* is a definite noun, e.g., *ghulāmu Zaydin* (the boy of Zayd), and it specifies the *muḍāf* when the *muḍāf ilayhi* is an indefinite noun, e.g., *ghulāmu rajulin* (the boy of a man). Nonattributive *iḍāfa* serves only to abbreviate [the expression] through elision of the nunation in singular nouns, e.g., *ḍāribu Zaydin* (hitting Zayd), or elision of the *nūn* in dual and plural nouns, e.g., *ḍāribā Zaydin* (hitting [d.] Zayd) and *ḍāribū Zaydin* (hitting [pl.] Zayd).

قسمين: مجرور بالإضافة نحو «غلام زيدٍ»، ومجرور بحرف الجرّ نحو «به داء».

والإضافة على قسمين: معنوية ولفظية.

فالمعنوية هي أن يكون المضاف غير مشتقّ، نحو «غلام زيدٍ»، أو مشتقًّا غير مضاف إلى معمول، نحو «مصارع مصرَ». وهي إما:

١- بمعنى اللام إن لم يكن المضاف إليه جنس المضاف ولا ظرفه، نحو «غلام زيدٍ».

٢- أو بمعنى «مِنْ» إن كان المضاف إليه جنس المضاف، نحو «خاتم الفضّةِ».

٣- أو بمعنى «في» إن كان المضاف إليه ظرف المضاف، نحو «ضرب اليومِ».

واللفظية هي إضافة المشتقّ إلى معموله، نحو «زيد ضاربُ عمرٍو» و«حسنُ الوجهِ» و«مؤدَّبُ الخادمِ».

والإضافة المعنوية تفيد تعريف المضاف إذا أضيف إلى المعرفة نحو «غلام زيد»، وتخصيصه إذا أضيف إلى نكرة نحو «غلام رجل». والإضافة اللفظية لا تفيد إلا تخفيفًا بحذف التنوين في المفرد نحو «ضاربُ زيد»، وحذف النون في التثنية والجمع نحو «ضاربَا زيد» و«ضاربُو زيد».

VIII. Indeclinable Nouns

Indeclinable nouns are nouns whose ending does not vary in accordance with the various governors that modify them, e.g., *jāʾa hāʾulāʾi* (These came), *raʾaytu hāʾulāʾi* (I saw these), and *marartu bi-hāʾulāʾi* (I passed by these).

The lack of a short vowel at the end of an indeclinable word is termed a *stop*, e.g., in *kam* (how many). A short vowel at the end of an indeclinable word is termed either *fatḥ*, e.g., in *ayna* (where); *kasr*, e.g., in *hāʾulāʾi* (these); or *ḍamm*, e.g., in *ḥaythu* (where). The cause of the indeclinability of nouns that are *accidentally indeclinable* is their resemblance to expressions that lack [the nominal nature], which are termed *indeclinable by default*.

[Expressions That Are Indeclinable by Default]

These are four categories of indeclinable expressions:

1. perfect tense verbs, e.g., *ḍaraba* (he hit).
2. imperatives proper, e.g., *iḍrib* (hit).
3. particles, e.g., *qad*.
4. clauses, i.e., considered as clauses and not considered with respect to their interpretation as infinitive phrases, e.g., *balaghanī anna Zaydan kātibun* (I have been informed that Zayd is a writer).[51]

[Accidentally Indeclinable Expressions]

Besides the four categories that are indeclinable by default, anything that resembles one of them is indeclinable and is termed *accidentally indeclinable*. This category of indeclinable expressions has many subcategories.

(٨) المبني

وهو ما لا يختلف آخره باختلاف العوامل الواردة عليه، نحو «جاء هؤلاءِ»، «رأيت هؤلاءِ»، «مررت بهؤلاءِ».

سكون آخر المبنيّ يسمّى وقفًا كما في «كَمْ»، وحركة آخره تسمّى فتحًا كما في «أَيْنَ» وكسرًا كما في «هَؤُلَاءِ» وضمًّا كما في «حَيْثُ». وسبب بناء المبني العارضي مناسبته لغير المتمكّن الذي يسمّى مبنيّ الأصل.

[مبني الأصل]

وهو أربع مبنيّات.

١- الفعل الماضي، كـ«ضَرَبَ».

٢- الأمر بالصيغة، كـ«اضْرِبْ».

٣- الحرف، كـ«قَدْ».

٤- الجملة أي بالنظر إلى أنّها جملة من دون النظر إلى تأويلها بالمصدر، نحو «بلغني أنّ زيدًا كاتب».

[المبني العارضي]

وما عدا المبنيّات الأربعة الأصلية كل ما شابه واحدًا منها يكون مبنيًّا ويسمّى مبنيًّا عارضيًّا. وهذا القسم من المبنى كثير.

[Personal Pronouns] It includes personal pronouns, which are of two types.

Attached pronouns. This includes three subtypes—nominative,[52] accusative, and genitive—as follows:[53]

[المضمرات] منه المضمرات؛ وهي على قسمين.

متّصل؛ وهو على ثلاثة أنواع: متّصل مرفوع، متّصل منصوب، متّصل مجرور، نحو:

	3RD PERS.			
	NOM.	ACC.	GEN.	
SING. MASC.	–	ضَرَبَهُ	غُلَامُهُ	بِهِ
DUAL MASC.	ضَرَبَا	ضَرَبَهُمَا	غُلَامُهُمَا	بِهِمَا
PL. MASC.	ضَرَبُوا	ضَرَبَهُمْ	غُلَامُهُمْ	بِهِمْ
SING. FEM.	–	ضَرَبَهَا	غُلَامُهَا	بِهَا
DUAL FEM.	ضَرَبَتَا	ضَرَبَهُمَا	غُلَامُهُمَا	بِهِمَا
PL. FEM.	ضَرَبْنَ	ضَرَبَهُنَّ	غُلَامُهُنَّ	بِهِنَّ

	2ND PERS.			
	NOM.	ACC.	GEN.	
SING. MASC.	ضَرَبْتَ	ضَرَبَكَ	غُلَامُكَ	بِكَ
DUAL MASC.	ضَرَبْتُمَا	ضَرَبَكُمَا	غُلَامُكُمَا	بِكُمَا
PL. MASC.	ضَرَبْتُمْ	ضَرَبَكُمْ	غُلَامُكُمْ	بِكُمْ
SING. FEM.	ضَرَبْتِ	ضَرَبَكِ	غُلَامُكِ	بِكِ
DUAL FEM.	ضَرَبْتُمَا	ضَرَبَكُمَا	غُلَامُكُمَا	بِكُمَا
PL. FEM.	ضَرَبْتُنَّ	ضَرَبَكُنَّ	غُلَامُكُنَّ	بِكُنَّ

	1ST PERS.			
	NOM.	ACC.	GEN.	
SING.	ضَرَبْتُ	ضَرَبَنِي	غُلَامِي	بِي
DUAL & PL.	ضَرَبْنَا	ضَرَبَنَا	غُلَامُنَا	بِنَا

Genitive personal pronouns do not attach to verbs; they attach only to nouns and prepositions.

ولا يتّصل المجرور بالفعل بل يتّصل بالاسم وحرف الجرّ فقط.

Detached pronouns. This includes two subtypes—nominative and accusative—as follows:

منفصل؛ وهو على نوعين: (١) منفصل مرفوع؛ منفصل منصوب، نحو:

	3RD PERS.		2ND PERS.	
	NOM.	ACC.	NOM.	ACC.
SING. MASC.	هُوَ	إِيَّاهُ	أَنْتَ	إِيَّاكَ
DUAL MASC.	هُمَا	إِيَّاهُمَا	أَنْتُمَا	إِيَّاكُمَا
PL. MASC.	هُمْ	إِيَّاهُمْ	أَنْتُمْ	إِيَّاكُمْ
SING. FEM.	هِيَ	إِيَّاهَا	أَنْتِ	إِيَّاكِ
DUAL FEM.	هُمَا	إِيَّاهُمَا	أَنْتُمَا	إِيَّاكُمَا
PL. FEM.	هُنَّ	إِيَّاهُنَّ	أَنْتُنَّ	إِيَّاكُنَّ

	1ST PERS.	
	NOM.	ACC.
SING.	أَنَا	إِيَّايَ
DUAL & PL.	نَحْنُ	إِيَّانَا

[Demonstrative Pronouns] Another subcategory of accidentally indeclinable expressions is the demonstrative pronouns, which are words assigned[54] to signify objects that are physically indicated. There are five of them:

1. *dhā* (this/that) for the [singular] masculine.
2. *tā*, *tī*, *tih*, *tihī*, *dhī*, *dhih*, and *dhihī* (this/that) for the [singular] feminine.
3. *dhāni* (these/those two) for the dual masculine.

[أسماء الإشارة] ومنه أسماء الإشارة وهي ما وضع لمشار إليه حسّي. وهي خمسة:

١- «ذَا» للمذكّر.

٢- «تَا»، «تِي»، «تِهْ»، «تِهِي»، «ذِي»، «ذِهْ»، «ذِهِي» للمؤنّث.

٣- «ذَانِ» للمذكّرين.

4. *tāni* (these/those two) for the dual feminine.
5. *ulāʾi* (these/those), which is plural and common to both [genders].

The particle of attention can be attached to the beginnings of these, e.g., *hādhā* (this), and the *kāf* of address can be attached to their ends, e.g., *dhāka* (that).

[Relative Pronouns] Another subcategory is the relative pronouns, which are words assigned to signify objects that are mentally indicated. For the masculine, they are *alladhī* [sg.], *alladhāni* [d.], and *alladhīna* [pl]. For the feminine, they are *allatī* [sg.], *allatāni* [d.], and six forms for the plural: *allātī, allawātī, allāʾī, allāyi, allāʾi*. Other relative pronouns include *mā*, *ayyu*, *ayyatu*, and the *alif* and *lām* that mean *alladhī* and *allatī*.[55]

Relative pronouns must have a declarative clause that serves as a relative clause for the pronoun, and they must have a personal pronoun [in it] that refers to them, e.g., *jāʾanī alladhī abūhu munṭaliqun* (The one whose father is departing came to me) and *jāʾanī alladhī dhahaba abūhu* (The one whose father left came to me).

The relative clause of the *alif* and *lām* is either an active participle, e.g., *jāʾanī al-ḍāribu* (The one who hit came to me), i.e., *jāʾanī alladhī ḍaraba*, or a passive participle, e.g., *jāʾanī al-maḍrūbu* (The one who was hit came to me), i.e., *jāʾanī alladhī ḍuriba*.

[Quasi-Verbal Nouns] Another subcategory is the quasi-verbal nouns, which are nouns with either

1. the meaning of an imperative verb, e.g., *ṣah*, which means *uskut* (Be quiet); *mah*, which means *ukfuf* (Stop); *dūnaka*, which means *khudhhu* (Take it); *ʿalayka Zaydan*, which means *ilzamhu* (Stay with [Zayd]); *ruwaydan*, which means *amhil* (Give respite); *halumma*, which means *aḥḍir* (Bring);[56] and *ḥayyahal*, which means *asriʿ* (Be quick).

٤- «تَانِ» للمؤنّثين.

٥- «أُولَاءِ» هذا جمع مشترك بينهما.

ويلحق بأوائلها حرف التنبيه نحو «هَـذَا» وبأواخرها كاف الخطاب نحو «ذَاكَ».

[الموصولات] منه الموصولات وهي ما وضع لمشار إليه ذهني. للمذكّر: الَّذِي، اللَّذَانِ، الَّذَيْنِ. وللمؤنّث: الَّتِي، اللَّتَانِ؛ ولجمعها ستّ صيغ: اللَّاتِي، واللَّوَاتِي، واللَّائِي، واللَّايِ، واللَّاءِ. ومن الموصولات: مَا، مَنْ، أَيُّ، أَيَّةُ، الألف واللام بمعنى الَّذِي والَّتِي.

والموصول لا بدّ له من جملة خبرية تقع له صلة ومن ضمير يعود إليه، نحو «جاءني الذي أبوه منطلق» و«جاءني الذي ذهب أبوه».

صلة الألف واللام اسم الفاعل نحو «جاءني الضارب» أي «جاءني الذي ضرب»، أو اسم المفعول نحو «جاءني المضروب» أي «جاءني الذي ضُرب».

[أسماء الأفعال] منه أسماء الأفعال وهي ما كان:

١- بمعنى الأمر، نحو: «صَهْ» أي اسكت، «مَهْ» أي اكفف، «دُونَكَ» أي خذه، «عَلَيْكَ زيدًا» أي الزمه، «رُوَيْدًا» أي أمهل، «هَلُمَّ» أي أحضِر[١١]، «حَيَّهَلْ» أي أسرِع.

2. the meaning of a perfect tense verb, e.g., *hayhāta* (How far-fetched!), which means *baʿuda* (was far), and *shattāna* (What a difference [there is between them]!), which means *iftaraqa* (was separate).

٢- أو بمعنى الماضي، نحو: «هَيْهَاتَ» أي بعُد، و«شَتَّانَ» أي افترق.

[Nouns of Sound] Another subcategory is the nouns of sound, i.e., any expression by which a sound is mimicked, e.g., *ghāqa* (caw), or by which a sound is made to animals, e.g., *nakhkh* (Sit) [to a camel].

[الأصوات] ومنه الأصوات وهي كل لفظ حكي به صوت كـ«غَاق» أو صوّت به للبهام كـ«نَخّ».

[Certain Place/Time Adverbs] Another subcategory includes certain place/time adverbs, including *idh* (when), *idhā* (when), *matā* (when), *ayyāna* (when), *ayna* (where), *annā* (how), *kayfa* (how), *qablu* (before), and *baʿdu* (after).

[بعض الظروف] ومنه بعض الظروف، نحو: إذْ، إذَا، مَتَى، أَيَّانَ، أَيْنَ، أَنَّى، كَيْفَ، قَبْلُ، بَعْدُ.

[Compound Nouns] Another subcategory is compound nouns, i.e., any noun composed of two words between which there is no predicative relation, e.g., *khamsata ʿashara* (fifteen).

[المركبات] ومنه المركّبات وهي كل اسم مركّب من كلمتين ليس بينهما نسبة، نحو «خمسة عشر».

[Vague Pronouns] Another subcategory is the vague pronouns, which are nonspecific expressions used for specific referents, e.g., *kadhā* (such) and *kam* (how many).[57] *Kam* is of two types: the first is interrogative and its specifying noun is singular and accusative, e.g., *kam rajulan ʿindaka* (How many men are with you?); the second is declarative and its specifying noun is genitive and either singular, e.g., *kam rajulin ʿindī* (Many a man is with me), or plural, e.g., *kam rijālin ʿindī* (Many men are with me), i.e., *kathīrun min al-rijāli ʿindī* (Many men are with me).

[الكنايات] ومنه الكنايات وهي ذكر مجملٍ وإرادة مفصّلٍ، نحو «كَذَا» و«كَمْ». وهو على قسمين: الأول استفهامية ومميّزها منصوب مفرد، نحو «كم رجلًا عندك»؛ والثاني خبرية ومميّزها مجرور إما مفرد نحو «كم رجلٍ عندي» أو مجموع نحو «كم رجالٍ عندي» أي «كثير من الرجال عندي».

IX. Dual Nouns

(٩) المثنى

Another category of nouns is the dual noun, which is that to whose end an *alif* is added in the nominative and a *yāʾ* preceded by a *fatḥa* in the accusative and the genitive, as well as a *nūn* vowelized with *kasr* to substitute for a short vowel and nunation

أي من أصناف الاسم المثنّى وهو ما لحقت آخره ألف في حالة الرفع وياء مفتوح ما قبلها في حالة النصب والجرّ، ونون مكسورة عوضًا عن الحركة والتنوين في المفرد،

in the singular, e.g., *jāʾanī muslimāni* (Two Muslims came to me), *raʾaytu muslimayni* (I saw two Muslims), and *marartu bi-muslimayni* (I passed by two Muslims). The *nūn* is elided in *iḍāfa*, e.g., *ghulāmā Zaydin* (the two boys of Zayd). The *alif* of duality is [phonetically] elided when the following letter is vowelless, e.g., *ghulāma ʾl-Ḥasani* (the two boys of al-Ḥasan).

If a *maqṣūr* noun (i.e., that whose ending is an *alif*) is triliteral, then the *alif* reverts to the root letter before the noun is dualized, e.g., *ʿaṣawāni* (two staffs) as the dual form of *ʿaṣā* (staff) and *raḥayāni* (two mills) as the dual form of *raḥā* (mill). If the noun is non-triliteral, the *alif* converts to a *yāʾ*, e.g., *muṣṭafayāni* (two chosen ones) as the dual form of *muṣṭafā* (chosen one). As for a *mamdūd* noun (i.e., that whose ending is a *hamza* after an *alif*), if its *alif* is originally the *alif* of femininity as in *ḥamrāʾ* (red [f.]), then its dual form is *ḥamrawāni* (two red things [f.]). But if the *alif* is part of the lexical root as in *kisāʾ* (cloth), then its dual form is *kisāʾāni* (two cloths).

نحو «جاءني مسلمانِ»، «رأيت مسلمَيْنِ»، «مررت بمسلمَيْنِ». وتسقط النون عند الإضافة، نحو «غلامَا زيدٍ». وتسقط ألف التثنية إذا لاقاها ساكن، نحو «غلامَا الحسن».

والمقصور وهو ما في آخره ألف إن كان ثلاثيًّا ردّ إلى أصله ثم يثنّى، نحو «عصوان» في تثنية «عصا» و«رحيان» في تثنية «رحى»؛ وإن كان غير ثلاثي ردّ إلى الياء، نحو «مصطفيان» في تثنية «مصطفى». والممدود وهو ما في آخره همزة بعد الألف إن كان ألفها ألف التأنيث في الأصل كـ«حمراء» تقول في تثنيتها «حمراوان»؛ وإن كان أصليًّا كما في «كساء» فتقول في تثنيتها «كساءان».

X. Plural Nouns

Another category is the plural noun. Plural nouns are of two types. The first is *sound*, in which the structure of the singular noun remains intact, and this is used for intelligent beings, e.g., *muslimūna* (Muslims [m.]) and *muslimātun* (Muslims [f.]). The second is *broken*, in which the structure of the singular is broken apart, e.g., *rijālun* (men) and *afrāsun* (horses).

Four of the forms of the broken plural—namely, (1) *afʿulun*, e.g., *aklubun* (dogs); (2) *afʿālun*, e.g., *athwābun* (garments); (3) *afʿilatun*, e.g., *aqfizatun* (dry measures); and (4) *fiʿlatun*, e.g., *ghilmatun* (boys)—are [forms of] the *plural of paucity*. All other forms, that is, besides those of the plural of

(١٠) المجموع

أي من أصناف الاسم المجموع. وهو على قسمين: أحدهما مصحّح وهو ما سلم فيه بناء الواحد ويكون لذوي العلم نحو «مسلمون» و«مسلمات»، وثانيهما مكسّر وهو ما تكسر فيه بناء الواحد نحو «رجال» و«أفراس»[١٢].

وأربعة أوزان من الجمع المكسّر وهي (١) أفْعُل كـ«أكْلُب»، (٢) أفْعال كـ«أثواب»، (٣) أفعِلَة كـ«أقفزة»، (٤) فِعْلة كـ«غلمة» جمع قلّة؛ وما عداها

paucity, are [forms of] the *plural of abundance*. The plural of paucity is used to signify ten or less in the absence of a contextual indicant; it can be used for a greater number with a contextual indicant. The plural of abundance is used in the opposite way: it can be used to signify ten or less with a contextual indicant, but in the absence of a contextual indicant it is used for a greater number.

أي ما عدا جمع القلّة جمع كثرة. جمع القلّة يطلق على عشرة وما دونها بلا قرينة وعلى ما فوقها بقرينة، وجمع الكثرة على عكس ذلك أي يطلق على عشرة وما دونها بقرينة وعلى ما فوقها بلا قرينة.

Fawāʿilu is a plural form for *fāʿilun* both in non-derivative nouns, e.g., *kawāhilu* (napes), which is the plural of *kāhilun* (nape), and in derivative nouns that have the [feminine] meaning of *fāʿilatun*, e.g., *ḥawāʾiḍu* (ones who are menstruating), which is the plural of *ḥāʾiḍun* (one who is menstruating). *Fawāʿilu* is also a plural form for *fāʿilatun* both in non-derivative nouns, e.g., *kawāthibu* (withers of a horse), which is the plural of *kāthibatun* (wither), and in derivative nouns, e.g., *ḍawāribu* (ones [f.] that hit), which is the plural of *ḍāribatun* (one [f.] that hits).

وفَواعِل جمع يجمع عليه فاعِل اسمًا أي غير مشتقّ نحو «كواهل» جمع «كاهل»، وصفةً أي مشتقًّا إذا كان بمعنى فاعلة نحو «حوائض» جمع «حائض». ويجمع عليه فاعِلة اسمًا نحو «كواثب» جمع «كاثبة»، وصفةً نحو «ضوارب» جمع «ضاربة».

XI–XII. Definite and Indefinite Nouns

(١١-١٢) المعرفة والنكرة

The categories of nouns include the definite and the indefinite. *Definite nouns* are those that signify things with specificity, e.g., *Zaydun*. They are of five types:

1. proper names, e.g., *Zaydun*.
2. personal pronouns, e.g., *huwa* (he).
3. non-personal pronouns, which includes two things: demonstrative pronouns, e.g., *dhā* (this, that), and relative pronouns, e.g., *al-ladhī* (which, who, that).
4. nouns made definite with the *lām*, e.g., *al-rajulu* (the man).

أي من أصناف الاسم المعرفة والنكرة. المعرفة ما دلّ على شيء بعينه، نحو «زيد». وهي على خمسة أقسام:

١- الأول العلَم، نحو «زيد».

٢- الثاني المضمر، نحو «هو».

٣- الثالث المبهم وهو شيئان: اسم الإشارة نحو «ذا»، والموصولات نحو «الذي».

٤- الرابع المعرَّف باللام، نحو «الرجل».

5. nouns made *muḍāf* to any of the above in an attributive *iḍāfa*, e.g., *ghulāmu Zaydin* (Zayd's boy), *ghulāmuhu* (his boy), *ghulāmu hādhā* (this one's boy), *ghulāmu alladhī abūhu ʿālimun* (the boy of him whose father is a scholar), *ghulāmu al-rajuli* (the man's boy).

٥- الخامس المضاف إلى أحدها إضافة معنوية، نحو «غلام زيد»، «غلامه»، «غلام هذا»، «غلام الذي أبوه عالم»، «غلام الرجل».

Indefinite nouns are those that signify things without specificity, e.g., *jāʾanī rajulun* (A man came to me) and *rakibtu farasan* (I rode a horse).

والنكرة ما دلّ على شيء لا بعينه، نحو «جاءني رجل» و«ركبت فرسًا».

XIII–XIV. Masculine and Feminine Nouns

(١٣-١٤) المذكر والمؤنث

The categories of nouns include the masculine and the feminine. *Masculine nouns* are those that lack the *tāʾ* of femininity and the *alif*s of femininity, and *feminine nouns* are those that possess any of these, e.g., *ghurfatun* (room), *ḥublā* (pregnant), and *ḥamrāʾu* (red).

أي من أصناف الاسم المذكّر والمؤنّث. فالمذكّر ما ليس فيه تاء التأنيث ولا ألفاه، والمؤنّث ما فيه إحداهما كـ«غرفة» و«حبلى» و«حمراء».

Femininity is of two types: *real* and *verbal*. Real femininity is that which corresponds to (i.e., has a counterpart in) a male animal, e.g., the femininity of *marʾa* (woman) and *nāqa* (she-camel). Verbal femininity is that of which this is not the case, whether there be a corresponding masculine non-animal, as with the femininity of *ẓulma* (darkness), which corresponds to a masculine non-animal, namely, *nūr* (light), or there be no corresponding masculine non-animal, as with the femininity of *bushrā* (glad tidings).

والتأنيث على ضربين: حقيقي ولفظي. فالحقيقي ما بإزائه أي حذائه ذكر من الحيوان كتأنيث المرأة والناقة؛ واللفظي بخلافه سواء كان بإزائه ذكر من غير الحيوان كتأنيث «الظلمة» فإن بإزائها ذكرًا من غير الحيوان وهو النور، أو لم يكن بإزائه ذكر كتأنيث «البشرى».

Real femininity is stronger than verbal femininity. Thus, *jāʾa Hindun* (Hind came) is invalid, while *ṭalaʿa al-shamsu* (The sun rose) and *yaṭluʿu al-yawma al-shamsu* (The sun rises today) are valid. If [the verb and the agent] are separated, then the like of *jāʾa al-yawma Hindun* (Hind came today) is valid and *ṭalaʿa al-yawma al-shamsu* (The sun rose today) is [even] preferable. This applies when the verb is predicated

والحقيقي أقوى من اللفظي ولذلك امتنع «جاء هند» وجاز «تطلع الشمس» و«يطلع الشمس». فإن فصل جاز نحو «جاء اليوم هند» وحسن «طلع اليوم الشمس». هذا إذا أسند الفعل إلى

of an explicit feminine noun; as for when the verb is predicated of a personal pronoun that refers to the noun, it is necessary to add the sign of femininity, e.g., *Hindun jāʾat* (Hind came) and *al-shamsu ṭalaʿat* (The sun rose).[58]

In some nouns, the *tāʾ* is implied, e.g., *arḍun* (earth) and *naʿlun* (sandal). The proof of this is [that their diminutive forms are] *urayḍatun* (small earth) and *nuʿaylatun* (small sandal).

Cases in which the masculine and feminine are equally proper include *faʿūlun* regardless of whether it has the meaning of *fāʿilun*, e.g., *baghiyyun* (one who fornicates),[59] or the meaning of *mafʿūlun*, e.g., *ḥalūbun* (one that is milked), and include *faʿīlun* when it has the meaning of *mafʿūlun*, e.g., *qatīlun* (one who is killed) and *jarīḥun* (one who is wounded).

The femininity of plurals is not real femininity. Thus, *faʿala al-rijālu* (The men acted), *jāʾa al-muslimātu* (The Muslim women came), and *maḍā al-ayyāmu* (The days passed) are valid. An exception is the sound plural of intelligent males, which is masculine, so one says, *jāʾa al-Zaydūna* (The Zayds came), and does not say, *jāʾat al-Zaydūna*. As for personal pronouns that refer to the unsound plural of intelligent males, one may either say, *faʿalū* (They did), or say, *faʿalat* (They did). As for the sound [masculine plural] with the *wāw*, and only in this case, one may say, *al-Zaydūna ḍarabū* (The Zayds hit). If [the sound plural] is not masculine, one may use either the *nūn* or the *tāʾ*, e.g., *al-muslimātu jiʾna* and …*jāʾat* (The Muslim women came) and *al-ayyāmu maḍayna* and …*maḍat* (The days passed). As for cases like *al-nakhlu* (palm trees) and *al-tamru* (dates), because they are generic mass nouns, they may be considered masculine with respect to their grammatical expression and feminine with respect to their meaning, e.g., His saying ﷻ, *kaʾannahum aʿjāzu nakhlin khāwiyatin* (as if they were hollowed palm trunks) (Q 69:7), and His saying, *kaʾannahum aʿjāzu nakhlin munqaʿirin* (as if they were uprooted palm trunks) (Q 54:20).

ظاهر الاسم المؤنث؛ أما إذا أسند الفعل إلى ضمير الاسم فإلحاق علامة التأنيث لازم نحو «هند جاءت» و«الشمس طلعت».

والتاء تقدّر في بعض الأسماء نحو «أرض» و«نعل» بدليل «أُرَيْضَة» و«نُعَيْلَة».

ومما يستوي فيه المذكّر والمؤنّث «فَعُول» مطلقًا أي سواء كان بمعنى فاعل نحو «بَغِيّ» أو كان بمعنى مفعول نحو «حلوب»، و«فعيل» بمعنى مفعول نحو «قتيل» و«جريح».

وتأنيث الجموع غير حقيقي ولذلك جاز «فعل الرجال» و«جاء المسلمات» و«مضى الأيام»؛ إلا جمع المذكر العاقل السالم فإنه مذكّر فتقول «جاء الزيدون» ولا تقول «جاءت الزيدون». وتقول في ضمير جمع المذكر العاقل غير السالم «الرجال فعلوا» و«فعلت». وأما السالم بالواو لا غير، نحو «الزيدون ضربوا». وإن كان غير المذكر فتقول بالنون والتاء، نحو «المسلمات جئن» و«جاءت» و«الأيام مضين» و«مضت». ونحو النخل والتمر لكونه اسم الجنس الجمعي يذكّر حملًا على اللفظ ويؤنّث حملًا على المعنى، نحو قوله تعالى ﴿كَأَنَّهُمْ أَعْجَازُ نَخْلٍ خَاوِيَةٍ﴾ [٦٩/ ٧] وقوله ﴿كَأَنَّهُمْ أَعْجَازُ نَخْلٍ مُّنقَعِرٍ﴾ [٥٤/ ٢٠].

XV. Diminutive Nouns

Another category is the diminutive nouns, which are nouns whose first letter is vowelized with *ḍamm*, whose second letter is vowelized with *fatḥ*, and to which a vowelless *yāʾ* is added as the third letter to signify smallness, e.g., *rujaylun* (small man). The letter after the *yāʾ* is vowelized with *kasr* if the noun consists of four letters or more, e.g., *durayhimun* (small dirham) and *dunaynīrun* (small dinars), except in cases like *ujaymālun* (small beautiful one), *ḥumayrāʾu* (little red one [f.]), *sukayrānu* (little intoxicated one), and *ḥubaylā* (little pregnant one), which, to preserve the *alif*s, are not vowelized with *kasr*.

When a noun is made diminutive, it reverts to its original letters. A *tāʾ* of femininity that is implicit in a triliteral noun is added again in the diminutive form, e.g., *udhaynatun* (small ear), which is the diminutive of *udhunun* (ear). However, a *tāʾ* of femininity that is implicit in a quadriliteral noun is not added again, e.g., *ʿuqayribun* (small scorpion), which is the diminutive of *ʿaqrabun* (scorpion).

The diminutive forms of demonstrative pronouns and relative pronouns are different from the diminutive forms of declinable nouns: they are made diminutive by the addition of a *yāʾ* before the end letter and an *alif* after the end letter, e.g., *dhayyā* as the diminutive of *dhā* (this, that) and *alladhayyā* as the diminutive of *alladhī* (which, who, that).

(١٥) المصغر

أي مـن أصناف الاسـم المصغّر وهو الاسـم الذي ضـمّ أوّله وفتـح ثانيـه ولحقه يـاء سـاكنة ثالثـة ليـدلّ على التقليل، نحـو «رُجَيْـل». ويكسر مـا بعـد الياء إن كان الاسـم على أربعة أحـرف فصاعدًا نحـو «دُرَيْهِـم» و«دُنَيْـنِير»، إلا في نحـو «أُجَيْمَـال» و«حُمَيْرَاء» و«سُـكَيْرَان» و«حُبَـيْلَى» لا يكسر للمحافظـة على الألفـات.

والاسـم عند التصغير يرجـع إلى أصله؛ وتـاء التأنيث المقـدّرة في الثلاثي تثبـت في التصـغير نحـو «أذينـة» في تصـغير «أذن»، والمقـدّرة في الربـاعي لا تثبـت نحـو «عـقيرب» في تصـغير «عقـرب».

وتصغير أسـماء الإشـارة والموصولات مخالف لتصغير الأسـماء المعربة وتصغيرهما هو أن يلحق قبـل آخرهما ياء وبعد آخرهما ألف، نحـو «ذيّا» في تصـغير «ذا» و«اللذيّا» في تصغير «الذي».

XVI. Relational Nouns

Relational nouns are nouns to the end of which a doubled *yāʾ* is added to signify a relation to [the thing that is signified by the word] without the *yāʾ*, e.g., *hāshimiyyun* for a relation to Hāshim.

In relational nouns one should elide (1) the *tāʾ* of femininity, e.g., *baṣriyyun* for a relation to Baṣra; (2) the sign of duality, e.g., *hindiyyun* for a relation to

(١٦) الاسم المنسوب

وهـو الاسـم الملحق بآخـره يـاء مشـدّدة[١٣] للنسـبة إلى المجـرّد عـن الياء، نحـو «هاشـميّ» في النسـبة إلى هاشـم.

وحقّـه أن يحـذف منـه تـاء التأنيـث نحـو «بصريّ» في النسـبة إلى البصرة، وعلامـة التثنيـة نحـو «هنـديّ»

Hindāni, the proper name of a place; and (3) the sign of plurality, e.g., *zaydiyyun* for a relation to Zaydūn, a proper name, and *qinnasriyyun* for a relation to Qinnasrīn, the proper name of a place. This holds true according to the view that inflection is inserted before the *nūn*; one thus says, [*jāʾanī hindiyyun* (One that is related to Hindān came to me), ...*zaydiyyun* (One that is related to Zaydūn [came to me]), *raʾaytu hindiyyan* (I saw one that is related to Hindān), ...*zaydiyyan* (...one that is related to Zaydūn), *marartu bi-hindiyyin* (I passed by one that is related to Hindān), and ...*zaydiyyin* (...one that is related to Zaydūn). As for the view that inflection is inserted after the *nūn*—as in *sakrāniyyun* for a relation to Sakrān and *ʿilliyyūniyyun* for a relation to ʿIlliyyūn—one says, *jāʾanī hindāniyyun* (One that is related to Hindān came to me) and ...*zaydūniyyun* (One that is related to Zaydūn [came to me])].

In the relational forms of triliterals whose second radical is vowelized with *kasr*, one should replace the *kasra* with a *fatḥa*, e.g., *namariyyun* for a relation to *namir* (tiger) and *duʾaliyyun* in relation to *duʾil* (jackal). In every [noun of the pattern] *faʿīlatun*, one should elide the *yāʾ* and *tāʾ* and convert the *kasra* to a *fatḥa*, e.g., *ḥanafiyyun* for a relation to Ḥanīfa. In every defective noun [of the pattern] *faʿīlun*, one should elide the first *yāʾ*, convert the second *yāʾ* to a *wāw*, and convert the *kasra* of the second radical to a *fatḥa*, e.g., *ghanawiyyun* for a relation to *ghanī* (rich). Plural forms should revert to the singular form, and the *kasra* of the second radical should be converted to a *fatḥa*, e.g., *faraḍiyyun* for a relation to *farāʾiḍ* (obligatory acts), whose singular form is *farīḍa*, like *Ḥanīfa*.

في النسبة إلى هندان علَما لموضِع، وعلامة الجمع نحو «زيديّ» في النسبة إلى زيدون علَما و«قنّسريّ» في النسبة إلى قنّسرين علَم لبقعة. هذا فيمن يجعل الإعراب قبل النون فيقول [«جاءني هنديٌّ» و«...زيديٌّ» و«رأيت هنديًّا» و«...زيديًّا» و«مررت بهنديٍّ» و«...زيديٍّ»؛ وأما من يجعل الإعراب على النون كما في «سكرانيّ» في النسبة إلى «سكران» و«علّيّونيّ» في النسبة إلى «علّيّون» فهو يقول «جاءني هندانيّ» و«...زيدونيّ»][١٤].

وحقّه في الثلاثي المكسور العين إبدال الكسرة فتحة نحو «نَمَريّ» في النسبة إلى نَمِر و«دُئَليّ» في النسبة إلى دُئِل؛ وفي كل فَعِيلة حذف الياء والتاء وإبدال الكسرة فتحة نحو «حنَفيّ» في النسبة إلى حنيفة؛ وفي كل فَعِيل من الناقص حذف الياء الأولى وقلب الثانية واوًا وإبدال كسرة العين فتحة نحو «غَنَويّ» في النسبة إلى غنيّ. وحقّه في الجمع ردّه إلى واحده وإبدال كسرة العين فتحة كـ«فَرَضيّ» في النسبة إلى فرائض واحده «فرِيضة» كـ«حنيفة».

XVII. Numeral Nouns

(١٧) أسماء العدد

Another category is the numeral nouns, which are those that are assigned to signify discrete quantities. These are based on twelve nouns: *wāḥidun* (one)

أي من أصناف الاسم أسماء العدد وهي ما وضع لكمّية آحاد الأشياء. وأصولها اثنا عشرة كلمة وهي من

through *ʿasharatun* (ten), *miʾatun* (a hundred), and *alfun* (a thousand). Infinitely many numeral nouns may be produced from these.

For the masculine, one says *wāḥidun* (one), *ithnāni* (two), as is the standard rule [concerning gender agreement], and one says *thalāthatun* (three) through *ʿasharatun* (ten) because these numbers refer to a plurality.[60] Every plural that is pluralized without the *wāw* and *nūn* or the *yāʾ* and *nūn* is feminine, as established in grammar. In accordance with this rule, [for the masculine] one says *aḥada ʿashara* (eleven), *ithnā ʿashara* (twelve), *thalāthata ʿashara* (thirteen) through *tisʿata ʿashara* (nineteen); one says *ʿishrūna* (twenty), *wāḥidun wa-ʿishrūna* (twenty-one), *ithnāni wa-ʿishrūna* (twenty-two), *thalāthatun wa-ʿishrūna* (twenty-three) through *tisʿatun wa-tisʿūna* (ninety-nine); and one says *miʾatun* (one hundred) and *alfun* (one thousand).

One treats the feminine as the reverse of the masculine[61] except for *ʿishrūna* (twenty) and its sisters,[62] *miʾatun* (one hundred), and *alfun* (one thousand), which are the same for the masculine and the feminine.

The specifying noun after these numerals[63] is of two types. The first type is genitive and plural, e.g., *thalāthatu rijālin* (three men) through *ʿasharatu rijālin* (ten men), except for the specifying noun after *miʾa* and *alf*, which is genitive and singular, e.g., *miʾatu rajulin* (one hundred men) and *alfu rajulin* (one thousand men). The second type is accusative and singular, e.g., *aḥada ʿashara rajulan* (eleven men) through *tisʿatun wa-tisʿīna rajulan* (ninety-nine men).

The specifying noun after *ʿashara* (ten) or less should be a plural of paucity, e.g., *thalāthatu athwābin* (three garments) and *ʿasharatu aflusin* (ten coins), except when there is no such form, in which case [the specifying noun should be] a plural of abundance, e.g., *thalāthatu shusūʿin* (three sandal straps), which is the plural of abundance for the singular form *shisʿun*, which lacks a plural of paucity like *ashsāʿun* or any such form of the plural of paucity.

«الواحد» إلى «العشرة» و«المائة» و«الألْف». ويتولّد منها أعداد غير متناهية.

تقول في المذكّر «واحد، اثنان» كما هو قياس و«ثلاثة» إلى «عشرة» لكون معدودها جمعًا، وكل جمع غير ما جمع بالواو والنون أو الياء والنون مؤنّث كما هو مقرّر في علم النحو. وعلى هذا القياس تقول «أحد عشر، اثنا عشر، ثلاثة عشر» إلى «تسعة عشر» و«عشرون، واحد وعشرون، اثنان وعشرون، ثلاثة وعشرون» إلى «تسعة وتسعين» و«مائة» و«ألف».

وتقول في المؤنّث بعكس المذكّر، إلا في «عشرين» وأخواتها و«مائة» و«ألف» فهما فيها سواء.

ومميّز هذه الأعداد على قسمين: الأول مجرور مجموع نحو «ثلاثة رجالٍ» إلى «عشرة رجالٍ»، إلا مميّز مائة والألف فمجرور ومفرد نحو «مائة رجلٍ» و«ألف رجلٍ»؛ والثاني منصوب مفرد نحو «أحد عشر رجلًا» إلى «تسعة وتسعين رجلًا».

وحقّ مميّز العشرة فما دونها أن يكون جمع قلّة نحو «ثلاثة أثواب» و«عشرة أفلس»، إلا إذا فُقد فجمع الكثرة نحو «ثلاثة شسوع» وهو جمع الكثرة واحده «شسع» وليس له جمع قلّة كأشساع أو نحوه من جمع القلّة.

XVIII. Nouns Related to Verbs

(١٨) الأسماء المتصلة بالأفعال

To be “related” to verbs means that these nouns are inseparable from verbal import. They are of five types.

ومعنى اتّصالها بها أنها لا تنفكّ عن معنى الأفعال. وهي خمسة أسماء.

Infinitive Nouns

First are infinitive nouns, namely, those from which verbs are morphologically derived, and they share the governance of the corresponding verb, e.g., *ʿajibtu min ḍarbi Zaydin ʿAmran* (I was surprised at Zayd’s hitting ʿAmr).

المصدر

الأول المصدر، وهو الاسم الذي يشتقّ منه الفعل ويعمل عمل فعله، نحو «عجبت من ضربِ زيدٍ عمرًا».

Active Participles

Second is the active participle, namely, what is derived from *yafʿalu* to signify the one who does an action, [which is understood] as a temporary occurrence.[64] It shares the governance of its verb on condition that (1) it have the meaning of the present or the future, e.g., *Zaydun ḍāribun ghulāmuhu ʿAmran al-yawma* (Zayd’s boy is hitting ʿAmr today) or …*ghadan* ([Zayd’s boy will hit ʿAmr] tomorrow). If you were to say …*amsi* (… yesterday), this would be invalid; *iḍāfa* would be necessary instead, e.g., *Zaydun ghulāmuhu ḍaribu ʿAmrin amsi* (Zayd’s boy hit ʿAmr yesterday), and because this has the meaning of the past, the *iḍāfa* would be an attributive *iḍāfa*. Another condition is that (2) the active participle syntactically depend on something like a subject[65] as in *Zaydun qāʾimun abūhu* (Zayd’s father is standing) and *jāʾanī rajulun qāʾimun ghulāmuhu* (A man whose boy is standing came to me).

اسم الفاعل

الثاني اسم الفاعل، وهو ما اشتقّ من «يفعل» لمن قام به فعل بمعنى الحدوث ويعمل عمل فعله بشرط (١) أن يكون بمعنى الحال أو الاستقبال، نحو «زيدٌ ضاربٌ غلامِه عمرًا اليوم» أو «غدًا». ولو قلت «أمس» لم يجز بل يجب الإضافة نحو «زيدٌ غلامُه ضاربُ عمرٍو أمس»؛ ولكونه بمعنى الماضي كانت الإضافة معنوية. وبشرط (٢) أن يعتمد على نحو مبتدأ، نحو «زيدٌ قائمٌ أبوه» و«جاءني رجلٌ قائمٌ غلامه».

Passive Participles

Third is the passive participle, namely, what is derived from *yufʿalu* to signify the one to whom an action occurs. It shares the governance of its verb, e.g., *Zaydun maḍrūbun ghulāmuhu* (Zayd’s boy is being

اسم المفعول

الثالث اسم المفعول، وهو ما اشتق من «يُفعل» لمن وقع عليه الفعل ويعمل عمل فعله، نحو «زيدٌ مضروبٌ

hit), in the same way as in the statement *Zaydun yuḍrabu ghulāmuhu* (Zayd's boy is being hit). The same conditions apply to its governance as apply in the case of the active participle.

Participials

Fourth is the participial, namely, what is derived from an intransitive verb to signify the one who does the "action," [which is understood] as a permanent [attribution], e.g., *Zaydun karīmun ḥasabuhu* (Zayd is of noble descent). It shares the governance of its verb on the condition that it syntactically depend on its antecedent,[66] e.g., *Zaydun ḥasanun wajhuhu* (Zayd's face is handsome).

Comparative/Superlative Nouns

Fifth is the comparative/superlative noun, namely, that which is derived from a verb to signify something that possesses [a verbal action or quality] to a greater degree than other things. It must be indefinite when it occurs with *min*, e.g., *Zaydun afḍalu min ʿAmrin* (Zayd is better than ʿAmr). When it does not occur with *min*, it must be made definite through the *lām* or through *iḍāfa*, e.g., *Zaydun al-afḍalu* (Zayd is the best) and *Zaydun afḍalu al-rijāli* (Zayd is the best of men).

As long as the comparative/superlative noun is used with *min*, the masculine and feminine share the same form, whether singular, e.g., *Zaydun* (or *Hindun*) *afḍalu min ʿAmrin* (Zayd [or Hind] is better than ʿAmr); dual, e.g., *Zaydāni* (or *Hindāni*) *afḍalu min ʿAmrin* (Two Zayds [or two Hinds] are better than ʿAmr); or plural, e.g., *Zaydūna* (or *Hindātun*) *afḍalu min ʿAmrin* (Zayds [or Hinds] are better than ʿAmr). This is because when *min* is used with the comparative/superlative, it becomes like a part of the noun, such that one cannot attach something else to the noun.

غلامُـه» كمـا تقـول «زيـدٌ يُضرَب غلامُه». ويـشترط في عمله مـا يـشترط في عمـل اسـم الفاعل.

الصفة المشبهة

الرابـع الصفـة المشبّهة، وهي مـا اشـتقّ من فعـل لازم لمن قـام به فعـل بمـعنى الثبـوت، نحـو «زيـدٌ كريمٌ حسـبُه». وعملهـا كعمـل فعلهـا بشرط أن تعتمـد على صاحبها، نحو «زيـدٌ حسـنٌ وجهُه».

أفعل التفضيل

الخامـس أفعـل التفضيـل، وهـو مـا اشـتقّ مـن فعـل لموصـوف بزيـادة على غيره ويلزمـه التنـكير مـع «مِنْ»، نحـو «زيـدٌ أفضـلُ مـن عمـرٍو». وإذا فارقـت «مـن» فالتعريـف بـاللام أو الإضافـة لازم، نحـو «زيـد الأفضـل» و«زيـد أفضـل الرجـال».

ومـا دام أفعـل التفضيـل مسـتعملًا بـ«مـن» فيستوي فيـه المذكّـر والمؤنّـث مفـردًا كانـا نحـو «زيـد» أو «هنـد أفضـل مـن عمـرٍو»، أو مـثنًى نحـو «زيـدان» أو «هنـدان أفضـل مـن عمـرٍو»، أو جمعًـا نحـو «زيـدون» أو «هنـدات أفضـل مـن عمـرٍو»، لـصيرورة «مـن» عنـد الاسـتعمال معـه كجـزء فلا يمكـن حينئـذ إلحاق شيء بـه.

When made definite with the *lām*, the noun can be made feminine and can be made dual or plural: one says, *Zaydun al-afḍalu* (Zayd is the best), *al-Zaydāni al-afḍalāni* (The two Zayds are the best), *al-Zaydūna al-afḍalūna* (The Zayds are the best), *Hindun al-fuḍlā* (Hind is the best), *al-Hindāni al-fuḍlayāni* (The two Hinds are the best), and either *al-Hindātu al-fuḍlayātu* (The Hinds are the best) or …*al-fuḍalu*, which is the plural of abundance.

As for when the comparative/superlative noun is made *muḍāf*, both of the following are valid: equivalence [between the forms of the masculine and the feminine], e.g., *al-Zaydūna afḍalu al-rijāli wa-l-Hindātu afḍalu al-nisāʾi* (The Zayds are the best of men, and the Hinds are the best of women); and non-equivalence, e.g., *al-Zaydūna afḍalū al-rijāli wa-l-Hindātu fuḍlayātu al-nisāʾi*. Non-equivalence is necessary in an *iḍāfa* between the comparative/superlative and the noun that it describes when the comparative/superlative is intended to signify a comparatively great degree that is not compared to the *muḍāf ilayhi*; that is, it becomes necessary that the comparative/superlative correspond [to the gender of the noun being described]. In such a case, one says, *al-Zaydūna afḍalū al-rijāli wa-l-Hindātu fuḍlayātu al-nisāʾi*; one does not say, *al-Zaydūna afḍalu al-rijāli wa-l-Hindātu afḍalu al-nisāʾi*.

·فإذا عرّف باللام أنّث وثنّي وجمع، فتقول «زيد الأفضل»، «الزيدان الأفضلان»، «الزيدون الأفضلون»، و«هند الفضلى»، «الهندان الفضليان»، «الهندات الفضليات» أو «الفُضَل»[١٥] جمع الكثرة.

وأما إذا أضيف فجاز فيه الأمران الاستواء نحو «الزيدون أفضل الرجال والهندات أفضل النساء»، وعدم الاستواء نحو «الزيدون أفضلو الرجال والهندات فضليات النساء». ويجب عدم الاستواء أي تجب المطابقة عند الإضافة بين أفعل وبين موصوفه إذا أريد بأفعل زيادة مطلقة لا على من يضاف إليه، فتقول «الزيدون أفضلو الرجال والهندات فضليات النساء» ولا تقول «الزيدون أفضل الرجال والهندات أفضل النساء».

[Chapter 5], the second chapter of the second method

THE VERB

What is the verb? How many are its categories, and what are they?

A verb is [a word] that signifies a meaning in itself that is bound to one of the three times. Some special characteristics of verbs are that they may be preceded by *qad*, e.g., *qad ḍaraba* (he has hit); by the two particles of futurity, e.g., *sa-yaḍribu* and *sawfa yaḍribu* (he will hit); and by jussive governors, e.g., *lam yaḍrib* (he did not hit); and that explicit [nominative] pronouns may be attached to them, e.g., *ḍarabtu* (I hit); as may the vowelless *tāʾ* of femininity, e.g., *ḍarabat* (she hit).

There are ten categories of verbs:

I. Perfect tense verbs

II. Imperfect tense verbs

III. Imperative and prohibitive verbs

IV. Transitive and intransitive verbs

V. Active and passive verbs

VI. Verbs of mental consideration

VII. Auxiliary verbs

VIII. Verbs of proximity

IX. Verbs of praise or blame

X. Verbs of wonderment

الباب الثاني من الطريق الثاني

الفعل

ما الفعل؟ وكم صنفًا وما هي؟

·الفعل هو ما دلّ على معنًى في نفسه مقترن بأحد الأزمنة الثلاثة. ومن خواصّه أنه يصحّ أن يدخله «قد» نحو «قد ضرب»، وحرفا الاستقبال نحو «سيضرب» و«سوف يضرب»، والجازم نحو «لم يضرب»، ويتّصل به الضمير البارز نحو «ضربتُ»[١٦]، وتاء التأنيث الساكنة نحو «ضربتْ».

وأصنافه عشرة:

(١) الماضي

(٢) المضارع

(٣) الأمر والنهي

(٤) المتعدّي وغير المتعدّي

(٥) المبنيّ للفاعل والمفعول

(٦) أفعال القلوب

(٧) الأفعال الناقصة

(٨) أفعال المقاربة

(٩) فعلا المدح والذمّ

(١٠) فعلا التعجّب

I. Perfect Tense Verbs

Perfect tense verbs are those that signify an occurrence in a time before one's present time, e.g., *ḍaraba* (he hit). They are built on *fatḥ*[67] except when influenced by a factor that necessitates a *ḍamma*, e.g., *ḍarabū* (they hit), or the lack of a short vowel, e.g., *ḍarabna* (they [f.] hit) and *ḍarabtu* (I hit).

(١) الماضي

وهو الذي يدلّ على حدث في زمان قبل زمانك، نحو «ضَرَبَ». وهو مبنيّ على الفتح إلا إذا اعترض عليه ما يوجب ضمّه نحو «ضَرَبُوا» أو سكونه نحو «ضَرَبْنَ»، «ضَرَبْتُ».

II. Imperfect Tense Verbs

Imperfect tense verbs are those whose first letter is always one of the letters of the set *a-t-y-n*,[68] e.g., *yaḍribu* (he hits), *taḍribu* (you/she hits), *aḍribu* (I hit), and *naḍribu* (we hit). It may signify just as well the present or the future, e.g., *yaḍribu* (he hits / he will hit), except when preceded by the *lām* of emphasis, e.g., His statement ﷻ *wa-inna rabbaka la-yaʿlamu mā tukinnu ṣudūruhum* (And surely your Lord knows that which their breasts conceal) (Q 27:74), which is specific to the present, or by either *sawfa*, e.g., *sawfa yaḍribu* (he will hit), or the *sīn*, e.g., *sa-yaḍribu* (he will hit), which are specific to the future.

Imperfect tense verbs are inflected like *yaḍribu* (he hits) in the indicative, *lan yaḍriba* (he will not hit) in the subjunctive, and *lam yaḍrib* (he did not hit) in the jussive. They may also be built on the lack of a vowel, as in *yaḍribna* (they [f.] hit), or on *fatḥ*, as in *la-yaḍribanna* (He will certainly hit).

On the indicative mood and so forth:

[The Indicative Mood]

The indicative mood of the imperfect tense verb is the effect of an abstract governor, namely, [the state of] the absence of expressed governors, e.g., *yaḍribu*

(٢) المضارع

وهو ما اعتقب في صدره واحد من حروف «أتين»، نحو: يَضْرِبُ، تَضْرِبُ، أَضْرِبُ، نَضْرِبُ. ويشترك فيه الحال والمستقبل نحو «يضرب»؛ إلا إذا دخله لام التأكيد كقوله تعالى ﴿وَإِنَّ رَبَّكَ لَيَعْلَمُ مَا تُكِنُّ صُدُورُهُمْ﴾ [٢٧/ ٧٤] فيختصّ بالحال، أو «سوف» نحو «سوف يضرب»، أو السين نحو «سيضرب» فيختصّ بالمستقبل.

ويعرب بالرفع نحو «يضربُ»، والنصب نحو «لن يضربَ»، والجزم نحو «لم يضربْ». ويبنى على السكون نحو «يضربْنَ» وعلى الفتح نحو «لَيضربَنَّ».

رفعه وما يليه:

[رفع المضارع]

رفعه بعامل معنويّ وهو تجرّده عن العوامل اللفظية نحو «يضربُ زيد»، وقيل وقوعه موضع الاسم كوقوع «زيد

Zaydun (Zayd hits).[69] It has also been said that the abstract governor is the verb's occupying the place of a noun, e.g., *Zaydun yaḍribu* (Zayd hits) in place of *Zaydun ḍāribun* (Zayd hits), since the default condition of predicates, adjectives, and circumstances is as simple nouns.

[The Subjunctive Mood]

The subjunctive mood is of two types.

[1. The Subjunctive by Means of Particles] The first type occurs by means of one of four verbally expressed particles, which are the following:

1. *an* (that), e.g., *urīdu an akhruja* (I want to go out).
2. *lan* (will not), e.g., *lan yaḍriba* (He will not hit).
3. *kay* (so that), e.g., *kay tukrimanī* (so that you honor me).
4. *idhan* (then), e.g., to tell someone who says, *ana ātīka* (I will come to you), *idhan yadhhaba al-ḥazanu wa-l-ghammu* (Then grief and distress will depart).

[2. The Subjunctive by Means of an Implicit *An*] The second type occurs by means of an implicit *an* (that) after five particles, which are the following:

1. *ḥattā* (so that, until), e.g., *aslamtu ḥattā adkhula al-jannata* (I submitted so that I enter paradise), i.e., *ḥattā an adkhula al-jannata.*
2. the *lām*, that is, the *lām* expressing the reason, e.g., *jiʾtuka li-tukrimanī* (I came to you so that you would honor me), i.e., *li-an tukrimanī.*
3. *aw* in the sense of *ilā* (until), e.g., *la-alzamannaka aw tuʿṭiyanī ḥaqqī* (I will certainly cling to you until you grant me my right), i.e., *ilā an tuʿṭiyanī ḥaqqī.*

يضربُ» موضع «زيد ضاربٌ» إذ الأصل في الخبر والصفة والحال الاسم والإفراد.

[نصب المضارع]

ونصبه على قسمين.

[١. النصب بالحروف] أحدهما بالحروف الأربعة الملفوظة. وهي:

١- أَنْ، نحو «أريد أن أخرجَ».

٢- لَنْ، نحو «لن يضربَ».

٣- كَيْ، نحو «جئتك كي تكرمَني».

٤- إذَنْ، كقولك لمن قال «أنا آتيك» «إذن يذهبَ الحزن والغمّ».

[٢. النصب بأن المقدّرة] وثانيهما بـ«أَنْ» المقدّرة بعد خمسة أحرف. وهي:

١- حَتَّى، نحو «أسلمت حتى أدخلَ الجنة» أي «حتى أن أدخلَ الجنة».

٢- اللام أي لام التعليل، نحو «جئتك لتكرمَني» أي «لأن تكرمَني».

٣- أَوْ بمعنى «إلى»، نحو «لَألزمنّك أو تعطيَني حقّي» أي «إلى أن تعطيَني حقّي».

4. the *wāw* of combination, e.g., *lā taʾkul al-samakata wa-tashraba al-labana* (Do not eat fish and drink milk [at the same time]), i.e., *wa-an tashraba,* meaning, "Do not combine the two."
5. the *fāʾ*, that is, the causal *fāʾ*, which occurs in the result clause in six situations. These are the following:
   (a) the imperative, e.g., *ītinī fa-ukrimaka* (Come to me so that I might honor you), i.e., *fa-an ukrimaka.*
   (b) the prohibitive, e.g., His saying ﷻ, *wa-lā taṭghaw fīhi fa-yaḥilla ʿalaykum ghaḍabī* (Exceed not the limits therein—that is, "in what We have provided you"—lest My wrath be unleashed upon you) (Q 20:81), i.e., *fa-an yaḥilla ʿalaykum ghaḍabī.*
   (c) negations, e.g., *mā taʾtīnā fa-tuḥaddithanā* (You do not come to us such that you might speak with us), i.e., *fa-an tuḥaddithanā.*
   (d) questions, e.g., *hal asʾaluka fa-tujībanī* (Shall I ask you that you might answer me?),[70] i.e., *fa-an tujībanī.*
   (e) expressions of wishful desire, e.g., *laytanī kuntu ʿindaka fa-afūza* (I wish I were with you such that I might succeed), i.e., *fa-an afūza.* (Success means salvation.)
   (f) suggestions, e.g., *a-lā tanzilu binā fa-tuṣība khayran* (Will you not stay with us such that you might attain benefit?), i.e., *fa-an tuṣība khayran.*

[The Jussive Mood]

The jussive mood is of three types.

٤- واو الجمع، نحو «لا تأكل السمكة وتشربَ اللبن» أي «وأن تشربَ» أي «لا تجمع بينهما».

٥- الفاء أي الفاء السببية التي تقع في جواب الأشياء الستّة، وهي:

(أ) أحدها الأمر، نحو «ائتني فأكرمَك» أي «فأن أكرمَك».

(ب) وثانيها النهي، نحو قوله تعالى ﴿وَلَا تَطْغَوْا فِيهِ﴾ أي «فيما رزقناكم» ﴿فَيَحِلَّ عَلَيْكُمْ غَضَبِي﴾ [٢٠/ ٨١] أي «فأن يحلَّ عليكم غضبي».

(ج) ثالثها النفي، نحو «ما تأتينا فتحدّثَنا» أي «فأن تحدّثَنا».

(د) رابعها الاستفهام، نحو «هل أسألك فتجيبَني» أي «فأن تجيبَني».

(ه) خامسها التمنّي، نحو «ليتني كنت عندك فأفوزَ» أي «فأن أفوزَ»؛ الفوز النجاة.

(و) سادسها العرض، نحو «ألا تنزل بنا فتصيبَ خيرًا» أي «فأن تصيبَ خيرًا».

[جزم المضارع]

وجزمه على ثلاثة أقسام.

١٧٤

[1. The Jussive by Means of Particles] The first type occurs by means of one of five particles:

1. *lam* (did not), e.g., *lam yakhruj* (He did not leave).
2. *lammā* (has not), e.g., *lammā yaḥḍur* (He has not attended).
3. the imperative *lām*, e.g., *li-yaḍrib* (Let him hit).
4. the *lā* of prohibition, e.g., *lā tafʿal* (Do not do [it]).
5. the conditional *in*, e.g., *in tukrimnī ukrimka* (If you honor me, I will honor you).

[2. The Jussive by Means of Nouns That Contain the Meaning of the Conditional *In*] The second type occurs by means of one of nine nouns that contain the meaning of the conditional *in*. These are the following:

1. *man* (whoever), e.g., *man yukrimnī ukrimhu* (Whoever honors me, I will honor him).
2. *mā* (whatever), e.g., His statement ﷻ *wa-mā tuqaddimū li-anfusikum min khayrin tajidūhu ʿinda Allāhi* (Whatever good you send forth for your souls, you will find it with Allah) (Q 2:110).
3. *ayyu* (whichever), e.g., *ayyuhum yaʾtinī ukrimhu* (Whichever of them comes to me, I will honor him).
4. *ayna* (wherever), e.g., *ayna takun akun* (Wherever you are, I will be).
5. *matā* (whenever), e.g., *matā takhruj akhruj* (Whenever you leave, I will leave).
6. *ḥaythumā* (wherever), e.g., *ḥaythumā taqʿud aqʿud* (Wherever you sit, I will sit).
7. *idhmā* (whenever), e.g., *idhmā tadkhul adkhul* (Whenever you enter, I will enter).
8. *annā* (wherever), e.g., *annā tadkhul adkhul* (Wherever you enter, I will enter).
9. *mahmā* (whatever), e.g., *mahmā taṣnaʿ aṣnaʿ* (Whatever you do, I will do).

[١. الجزم بالحروف] الأول بخمسة أحرف:

١- لَمْ، نحو «لم يخرجْ».

٢- لَمَّا، نحو «لمّا يحضرْ».

٣- لام الأمر، نحو «لِيضربْ».

٤- لَا النهي، نحو «لا تفعلْ».

٥- وإِنْ الشرطية، نحو «إن تكرمْني أكرمك».

[٢. الجزم بأسماء متضمنة لمعنى إن الشرطية] الثاني بتسعة أسماء متضمّنة لمعنى «إِنْ» الشرطية. وهي:

١- مَنْ، نحو «من يكرمْني أكرمه».

٢- مَا، نحو قوله تعالى ﴿وَمَا تُقَدِّمُواْ لِأَنفُسِكُم مِّنْ خَيْرٍ تَجِدُوهُ عِندَ ٱللَّهِ﴾ [٢/ ١١٠].

٣- أَيُّ، نحو «أيّهم يأتِني أكرمه».

٤- أَيْنَ، نحو «أين تكنْ أكن».

٥- مَتَى، نحو «متى تخرجْ أخرج».

٦- حَيْثُمَا، نحو «حيثما تقعدْ أقعد».

٧- إِذْمَا، نحو «إذما تدخلْ أدخل».

٨- أَنَّى، نحو «أنّى تدخلْ أدخل».

٩- مَهْمَا، نحو «مهما تصنعْ أصنع».

[3. The Jussive by Means of an Implicit *In* in the Result Clause] The third type occurs by means of an implicit *in* (if) in the result clauses of the six situations that prompt the [causal] *fā*ʾ, except for negation. Thus there are five:

1. the imperative, e.g., *ītinī ukrimka* (Come to me and I will honor you).
2. the prohibitive, e.g., *lā takfur tadkhul al-jannata* (Do not disbelieve and you will enter paradise).
3. questions, e.g., *hal as*ʾ*aluka tujibnī* (Shall I ask you? You will answer me).
4. expressions of wishful desire, e.g., *laytanī* ʿ*indaka afuz* (If only I were with you, I would succeed).
5. suggestions, e.g., *a-lā tanzilu binā tuṣib khayran* (Will you not stay with us? You would attain benefit), i.e., *in tanzil binā tuṣib khayran* (If you stay with us, you will attain benefit).

[٣. الجزم بإن مضمرة في الجواب] الثالث بـ«إنْ» مضمرة في جواب الأشياء الستة التي تجاب بالفاء إلا النفي فهو خمسة:

١- الأمر، نحو «ايتني أكرمْك».

٢- النهي، نحو «لا تكفر تدخلْ الجنة».

٣- الاستفهام، نحو «هل أسألك تجبْني».

٤- التمنّي، نحو «ليتني عندك أفزْ».

٥- العرض، نحو «ألا تنزل بنا تصبْ خيرًا» أي «إن تنزل بنا تصبْ خيرًا».

The Imperfect Tense Verb Devoid of Personal Pronouns

In an imperfect tense verb devoid of personal pronouns, if the third radical is a sound letter, e.g., *yaḍrib* (he hits), then the verb is explicitly inflected with a *ḍamma* in the indicative and a *fatḥa* in the subjunctive, and it is inflected with the lack of a short vowel in the jussive. If [the third radical] is a *wāw* or a *yā*ʾ such that the verb is weak, e.g., *yaghzū* (he goes on a military expedition) and *yarmī* (he throws), then the verb is implicitly inflected with a *ḍamma* in the indicative, it is explicitly inflected with a *fatḥa* in the subjunctive, and it is inflected by elision in the jussive. If [the third radical] is an *alif* such that the verb is weak, e.g., *yakhshā* (he fears), then it is implicitly inflected with a *ḍamma* in the indicative and a *fatḥa* in the subjunctive, and it is inflected by elision in the jussive.

المضارع المجرد عن الضمائر

المضارع المجرّد عن الضمائر إن كان صحيح اللام كـ«يضرب» فرفعه بالضمّة ونصبه بالفتحة لفظًا وجزمه بالسكون. وإن كان معتلًّا بالواو أو الياء نحو «يغزو» و«يرمي» فرفعه بالضمّة تقديرًا ونصبه بالفتحة لفظًا وجزمه بالحذف. وإن كان معتلًّا بالألف نحو «يخشى» فرفعه بالضمّة ونصبه بالفتحة تقديرًا وجزمه بالحذف.

III. Imperative and Prohibitive Verbs

Amr (command) means the request to do an action.[71] A second-person agent is commanded through the [form] *ifʿal* (Do), which is termed the *imperative proper*.[72] [A third-person agent is commanded] through the [imperative] *lām*, e.g., *li-yaḍrib Zaydun* (Let Zayd hit); *li-aḍrib ana* (Let me hit); and *li-taḍrib anta* ([Go ahead and] hit). *Nahy* (prohibition) means the request not to do an action,[73] as in *lā taḍrib* (Do not hit).

(٣) الأمر والنهي

الأمر عبارة عن طلب الفعل. ويؤمر الفاعل المخاطب بمثل «افعلْ» ويقال له الأمر بالصيغة، وغيره باللام نحو «لِيضربْ زيدٌ» ونحو «لِأضربْ أنا» ونحو «لِتضربْ أنت». والنهي عبارة عن طلب ترك الفعل نحو «لا تضربْ».

IV. Transitive and Intransitive Verbs

Transitive verbs are those that take an object. They may take a single object, e.g., *ḍarabtu Zaydan* (I hit Zayd); two objects, the second [referring to] something different from the first, e.g., *aʿṭaytu Zaydan dirhaman* (I gave Zayd a dirham); two objects, the second [referring to] the same thing as the first, e.g., *ʿalimtu Zaydan fāḍilan* (I knew Zayd is virtuous); or three objects, e.g., *aʿlamtu ʿAmran Bakran fāḍilan* (I informed ʿAmr that Bakr is virtuous).

Intransitive verbs are those that are restricted to the agent, e.g., *dhahaba Zaydun* (Zayd went). There are three means by which intransitive verbs are made transitive:

1. the *hamza*, e.g., *adhhabtu Zaydan* (I made Zayd go away).[74]
2. doubling the second radical, e.g., *farraḥtu Zaydan* (I gladdened Zayd).[75]
3. prepositions, e.g., *kharajtu bihi* (I took it out). The latter is a general [rule] for making any verb transitive, whether the verb be triliteral or quadriliteral, and whether it be simple or augmented.

(٤) المتعدي وغير المتعدي

المتعدّي هو ما كان له مفعول به. ويتعدّى إلى مفعول واحد نحو «ضربت زيدًا»، وإلى مفعولين وثانيهما غير الأوّل نحو «أعطيت زيدًا درهمًا»، و إلى مفعولين ثانيهما عين الأوّل نحو «علمت زيدًا فاضلًا»، وإلى ثلاثة مفاعيل نحو «أعلمت عمرًا بكرًا فاضلًا».

غير المتعدّي وهو ما يختصّ بالفاعل كـ«ذهب زيد». ولتعديته ثلاثة أسباب:

١- الهمزة، نحو «أذهبت زيدًا».

٢- تشديد عين الفعل، نحو «فرّحت زيدًا».

٣- حرف الجر، نحو «خرجت به». وهذا عام في تعدية كل فعل ثلاثيًا كان أو رباعيًا كل منهما مجرّدًا كان أو مزيدًا فيه.

V. Active and Passive Verbs

Active verbs are those whose agent is mentioned, e.g., *ḍaraba Zaydun ʿAmran* (Zayd hit ʿAmr). Passive verbs are verbs whose agent is not mentioned, as when the agent is unknown, e.g., *ḍuriba Zaydun* (Zayd was hit).

Passive verbs may be grammatically predicated of

1. the object, e.g., *ḍuriba ʿAmrun* (ʿAmr was hit).
2. the action-notion, e.g., *sīra sayrun shadīdun* (Intense travel was undertaken) as in *sāra Zaydun sayran shadīdan* (Zayd undertook intense travel).
3. the adverb of time, e.g., *ṣira yawmu kadhā* (Such and such day was traveled on) as in *sāra Zaydun yawma kadhā* (Zayd traveled on such and such day).
4. the adverb of place, e.g., *sīra farsakhāni* (Two *farsakh*s were traveled)[76] as in *sāra Zaydun farsakhayni* (Zayd traveled two *farsakh*s).

(٥) الفعل المبني للفاعل والمفعول

الفعـل المـبنيّ للفاعل هو ما ذكـر فاعله، نحـو «ضَرَبَ زيدٌ عمـرًا». والفعل المـبنيّ للمفعـول هو الفعـل الذي لم يذكر فاعلـه لنحو الجهـل بالفاعل، نحـو «ضُرِبَ زيدٌ».

ويُسند:

١- إلى المفعول به كـ«ضُرب عمرٌو».

٢- وإلى المفعـول المطلـق نحو «سِيرَ سـيرٌ شـديدٌ» أي «سـار زيدٌ سـيرًا شـديدًا».

٣- وإلى ظـرف الزمان نحو «سِـيرَ يومُ كذا» أي «سـار زيدٌ يـومَ كذا».

٤- وإلى ظـرف المكان نحو «سِيرَ فرسـخان» أي «سـار زيدٌ فرسخَين».

VI. Verbs of Mental Consideration

Another category of verbs is the verbs of mental consideration. There are seven of these: (1) *ẓanantu* (I thought), (2) *ḥasibtu* (I supposed), (3) *khiltu* (I imagined), (4) *ʿalimtu* (I knew), (5) *zaʿamtu* (I believed), (6) *raʾaytu* (I deemed), and (7) *wajadtu* (I found).[77] They are used with a subject and predicate and make both accusative as objects, e.g., *ḥasibtu* (or *khiltu*) *Zaydan qāʾiman* (I supposed that Zayd was standing).

The other verbs—that is, other than *ḥasibtu* and *khiltu*—[also] have other meanings that entail only one object, e.g., *ẓanantuhu*, meaning *ittahamtuhu*

(٦) أفعال القلوب

أي مـن أصنـاف الفعـل أفعـال القلـوب. وهي سـبعة: (١) ظَنَنْـت، (٢) حَسِبْـت، (٣) خِلْـت، (٤) عَلِمْـت، (٥) زَعَمْـت، (٦) رَأَيْـت، (٧) وَجَـدْت. تدخـل على المبتـدأ والخبر فتنصبهمـا على المفعولية، نحو «حسـبت» أو «خلت زيـدًا قائمًا».

ولغيرهمـا أي لغير «حسـبت» و«خلت» مـعنًى آخر لا يقـتضي إلا مفعولًا واحدًا، نحـو «ظننته» أي «اتّهمته»،

«علمتــه» أي «عرفتــه»، «زعمتــه» أي «قلتــه»، «رأيتــه» أي «أبصرتــه»، «وجدتــه» أي «صادفتــه». الفـرق بين العلـم والمعرفـة أن العلـم يسـتعمل في إدراك الكليّـات أي مـع الجزئيـات والمعرفـة في إدراك الجزئيـات، ولذلـك يقــال له تعــالى عالــم ولا يقــال عارف.

(I suspected him); ʿalimtuhu, meaning ʿaraftuhu (I recognized him); zaʿamtuhu, meaning qultuhu (I claimed it); raʾaytuhu, meaning abṣartuhu (I saw him); and wajadtuhu, meaning ṣādaftuhu (I found it). The difference between ʿilm and maʿrifa (knowledge) is that ʿilm is used for the apprehension of the universal, that is, along with the particular, and maʿrifa for the apprehension of [merely] the particular. Accordingly, He ﷻ is said to be ʿālim and is not said to be ʿārif.

ومــن شــأن أفعــال القلــوب جــواز الإلغــاء بالتوسّــط نحــو «زيــدٌ ظننــت قائــمٌ»، والتأخّــر نحــو «زيــدٌ مقيــمٌ ظننــت».

One property of the verbs of mental consideration is that the nullification of their governance is permissible when (1) the verb intervenes between [its two objects], e.g., *Zaydun ẓanantu qāʾimun* (Zayd I thought was standing), or (2) comes afterward, e.g., *Zaydun muqīmun ẓanantu* (Zayd is residing, I thought).

ومــن شــأنها التعليــق أي وجــوب إبطــال العمــل لفظًــا لا مــعنًى قبــل لام الابتــداء نحــو «علمــت لَزيــدٌ منطلــقٌ»، والاســتفهام نحــو «علمــت أَزيــدٌ عنــدك أم عمــرٌو»، وقبــل النفي نحــو «علمــت مــا زيــدٌ قائــمٌ».

Another of their properties is that of *suspension*, i.e., the necessary nullification of their governance with regard to the verbal expression (though not the meaning) when the verb occurs (1) before the *lām* of beginning, e.g., *ʿalimtu la-Zaydun munṭaliqun* (I knew Zayd was certainly departing), (2) before a question, e.g., *ʿalimtu a-Zaydun ʿindaka am ʿAmrun* (I knew whether Zayd was with you or ʿAmr), or (3) before a negation, e.g., *ʿalimtu mā Zaydun qāʾimun* (I knew Zayd was not standing).

(٧) الأفعال الناقصة

أي مــن أصنــاف الفعــل الأفعــال الناقصــة. وهي: كَانَ، صَــارَ، أَصْبَــحَ، أَمْسَى، أَضْحَى، ظَــلَّ، بَــاتَ، آضَ، عَادَ، غَــدَا، رَاحَ، مَــا زَالَ، مَــا انْفَــكَّ، مَــا فَتِــئَ.

VII. Auxiliary Verbs

Another category of verbs is the auxiliary verbs. The auxiliary verbs are *kāna* (was), *ṣāra* (became), *aṣbaḥa* (became [in the morning]), *amsā* (became [in the evening]), *aḍḥā* (became [at midmorning]), *ẓalla* (became [at midday]), *bāta* (became [at night]), *āḍa* (became), *ʿāda* (became [again]), *ghadā* (became [in the morning]), *rāḥa* (became [in the evening]), *mā zāla* (remained), *mā infakka* (remained), and *mā fatiʾa* (remained).

Auxiliary verbs are verbs assigned to signify the affirmation of an attribute for the agent (that is, an attribute other than the attribute signified by their respective infinitive noun). They are used with a subject and predicate, and they make the predicate accusative, e.g., *kāna Zaydun qāʾiman* (Zayd was standing).

Kāna is of five types:

1. an auxiliary verb, e.g., *kāna Zaydun munṭaliqan* (Zayd was departing).
2. a complete verb that means "was the case" or "occurred," e.g., *kāna al-amru* (The matter was so), i.e., "It was the case" or "It occurred."
3. additional, e.g., His saying ﷻ, *kayfa nukallimu man kāna fī al-mahdi ṣabiyyan* ("How shall we speak to one who is yet a child in the cradle?") (Q 19:29), i.e., *man fī al-mahdi ṣabiyyan*.
4. a pronominal word that contains a dummy pronoun; when this is the case, a clause follows that explains that pronoun, e.g., *kāna Zaydun munṭaliqun* (It was [the case] that Zayd was departing), i.e., *kāna al-shaʾnu* (the case was that).
5. [an auxiliary verb] with the meaning of *ṣāra* (became), e.g., His saying ﷻ, *fa-kānat habāʾan munbaththan* (such that they become scattered dust) (Q 56:6), i.e., *ṣārat habāʾan munbaththan*.

Ṣāra signifies change, e.g., *ṣāra Zaydun ʿāliman* (Zayd became a scholar) and *ṣāra al-ṭīnu khazafan* (The clay became pottery). *Aṣbaḥa*, *amsā*, and *aḍḥā* are the same as *ṣāra*, e.g., *aṣbaḥa* (or *amsā*, or *aḍḥā*) *Zaydun faqīran* (Zayd became poor), i.e., *ṣāra faqīran*.

وهي ما وضع لتقرير الفاعل على صفة أي على صفة غير صفة مصدرها. وتدخل على المبتدأ والخبر وتنصب الخبر، نحو «كان زيدٌ قائمًا».

و«كان» على خمسة أنواع:

١- أحدها أن تكون ناقصة، نحو «كان زيد منطلقًا».

٢- ثانيها أن تكون تامّة بمعنى «ثبت ووقع»، نحو «كان الأمر» أي «ثبت ووقع».

٣- وثالثها أن تكون زائدة، نحو قوله تعالى ﴿قَالُواْ كَيْفَ نُكَلِّمُ مَن كَانَ فِي ٱلْمَهْدِ صَبِيًّا﴾ [١٩/ ٢٩] أي «من في المهد صبيًّا».

٤- رابعها أن تكون مضمرًا فيها ضمير الشأن وحينئذ يقع بعدها جملة تفسّر ذلك المضمر، نحو «كان زيدٌ منطلقٌ» أي «كان الشأنُ».

٥- خامسها أن تكون بمعنى «صار»، نحو قوله تعالى ﴿فَكَانَتْ هَبَآءً مُّنبَثًّا﴾ [٥٦/ ٦] أي «صارت هباء منبثا».

و«صار» للانتقال، نحو «صار زيدٌ عالمًا» و«صار الطين خزفًا». ومثل صَارَ: أَصْبَحَ، أَمْسَى، أَضْحَى، نحو «أصبح... وأمسى... وأضحى زيدٌ فقيرًا» أي «صار فقيرًا».

Mā zāla signifies continuity, e.g., *mā zāla Zaydun faqīran* (Zayd remains poor). *Mā bariḥa, mā fatiʾa,* and *mā infakka* are the same as *mā zāla,* e.g., *mā bariḥa* (or *mā fatiʾa,* or *mā infakka*) *Zaydun karīman* (Zayd remains poor).

Āḍa, ʿāda, ghadā, and *rāḥa* are appended to [the category of] the auxiliary verbs.

Thus, three verbs serve as the basis for [the category of] the auxiliary verbs: *kāna, ṣāra,* and *mā zāla.* The reason that they are termed *afʿāl nāqiṣa* (auxiliary verbs)[78] is that their meanings remain incomplete with merely their subject-noun.

و«ما زال» للاستمرار، نحو «ما زال زيدٌ فقيرًا». ومَا بَرِحَ ومَا فَتِئَ ومَا انْفَكَّ مثل مَا زَالَ، نحو «ما برح... وما فتئ... وما انفكّ زيدٌ كريمًا».

و«آض» و«عاد» و«غدا» و«راح» ملحقة بالأفعال الناقصة.

فمرجع أفعال الناقصة إلى ثلاثة أفعال: «كان»، «صار»، «ما زال». وسبب تسميتها ناقصة لعدم تمام معناها باسمها فقط.

VIII. Verbs of Proximity

(٨) أفعال المقاربة

Another category of verbs is the verbs of proximity.

Verbs of proximity are verbs assigned to signify the proximity of the predicate with regard to (1) [what the speaker] hopes is the case, as in *ʿasā Zaydun an yakhruja* (Perhaps Zayd will leave). *An* may be elided due to the resemblance [of *ʿasā* (perhaps)] with *kāda* (almost, about to), e.g., *ʿasā Zaydun yakhruju.* Sometimes *an* occurs together with the imperfect tense verb as an agent for *ʿasā* and suffices with that agent, e.g., *ʿasā an yakhruja Zaydun* (Perhaps Zayd will leave), i.e., *ʿasā khurūju Zaydin.*

The governance of the verbs of proximity is the same as the governance of *kāna* because they are sisters of *kāna.* The reason that they are discussed separately from the auxiliary verbs is that there are properties unique to them.

أي من أصناف الفعل أفعال المقاربة.

وهي ما وضع لدنوّ الخبر (١) رجاءً كما في «عَسَى زيدٌ أن يخرجَ». وقد يحذف «أن» تشبيهًا بـ«كَادَ»، نحو «عسى زيدٌ يخرجُ». وقد يقع «أن» مع الفعل المضارع فاعلًا لـ«عَسَى» ويقتصر على ذلك الفاعل، نحو «عسى أن يخرج زيد» أي «عسى خروجُ زيد».

وعمل أفعال المقاربة كعمل «كَانَ» لأنّها من أخوات كَانَ؛ وإفرادها عن الناقصة لأحكام تخصّها.

[They may also signify proximity] with regard to (2) what is actually the case, as in *kāda* and *awshaka* (almost, about to), e.g., *kādat al-shamsu* (or *awshakat al-shamsu*) *taghrubu* (The sun is about to set), because the predicate of these two verbs must be an imperfect tense verb.

[Finally, they may signify proximity] with regard to (3) the commencing of an action, as in *karaba*, *akhadha*, *jaʿala*, and *ṭafiqa* (began, took to), e.g., *karaba Zaydun yaqraʾu* (Zayd began reading); *akhadha Bakrun yaqūlu* (Bakr took to saying); *jaʿala ʿAmrun yaḍribu* (ʿAmr took to hitting); and *ṭafiqa Khālidun yanṣuru* (Khālid began helping).

أو (٢) حصولًا كما في «كَادَ» و«أَوْشَكَ»، نحو «كادت الشمسُ... أو أوشكت الشمسُ تغرب» لاختصاص خبرها بالمضارع.

أو (٣) شروعًا فيه كما في «كَرَبَ» و«أَخَذَ» و«جَعَلَ» و«طَفِقَ»، نحو «كرب زيدٌ يقرأ» و«أخذ بكرٌ يقول» و«جعل عمرٌو يضرب» و«طفق خالدٌ ينصر».

IX. Verbs of Praise or Blame

Another category of verbs is the verbs of praise or blame, which are verbs that are assigned to express praise or blame, namely, *niʿma* (how good) and *biʾsa* (how bad). They are used with pairs of nominative nouns; the first is termed the *agent*, and the second is termed either *that which is qualified with praise*, e.g., *niʿma al-rajulu Zaydun* (How good a man Zayd is!), or *that which is qualified with blame*, e.g., *biʾsa al-rajulu Bakrun* (How bad a man Bakr is!).

One of three foundations should be present in the first noun, i.e., the agent: either (1) being definite by means of the generic *lām*, e.g., *niʿma al-rajulu Zaydun* (How good a man Zayd is!) and *biʾsa al-rajulu Bakrun* (How bad a man Bakr is!); (2) being *muḍāf* to a noun that is made definite by means of the generic *lām*, e.g., *niʿma ghulāmu al-rajuli Zaydun* (How good a man's boy Zayd is!); or (3) being a hidden noun that is understood through an accusative indefinite noun, e.g., *niʿma rajulan Zaydun* (How good a man Zayd is!), i.e., *niʿma* <u>*al-rajulu*</u>

(٩) فعلا المدح والذم

أي من اصناف الفعل فعلا المدح والذمّ، وهما ما وضع لإنشاء مدح أو ذمّ وهما «نِعْمَ» و«بِئْسَ». يدخلان على اسمين مرفوعين أوّلهما يسمّى الفاعل وثانيهما يسمّى المخصوص بالمدح نحو «نعم الرجلُ زيدٌ» والمخصوص بالذمّ نحو «بئس الرجلُ بكرٌ».

وحقّ الأول أي الفاعل أن يكون فيه أحد الأصول الثلاثة إما (١) تعريفه بلام الجنس نحو «نعم الرجلُ زيد» و«بئس الرجلُ بكر»، أو (٢) إضافته إلى الاسم المعرّف بلام الجنس نحو «نعم غلامُ الرجلِ زيد»، أو (٣) إضماره ويفسّر بنكرة منصوبة نحو «نعم رجلًا زيد» أي «نعم الرجلُ رجلًا زيد». وقد يحذف المخصوص إذا

rajulan Zaydun. The qualified noun may be elided when it is known through contextual indication, e.g., His statement ﷻ *wa-l-arḍa farashnāhā fa-niʿma al-māhidūna* (And the earth We laid out—what excellent outspreaders!) (Q 51:48), i.e., *fa-niʿma al-māhidūna <u>naḥnu</u>* (what excellent outspreaders We are).

Ḥabbadhā (how good) functions the same as *niʿma*, e.g., *ḥabbadhā rajulan Zaydun* (How good a man Zayd is!), which is just like *niʿma rajulan Zaydun*. *Sāʾa* (how bad) functions the same as *biʾsa*, e.g., *sāʾa al-rajulu Bakrun* (How bad the man Bakr is!), which is just like *biʾsa al-rajulu Bakra*.

علم بالقرينة، نحو قوله تعالى ﴿وَٱلْأَرْضَ فَرَشْنَٰهَا فَنِعْمَ ٱلْمَٰهِدُونَ﴾ [٥١/ ٤٨] أي «فنعم الماهدون نحن».

و«حَبَّذَا» يجري مجرى «نعم»، نحو «حبّذا رجلًا زيد» كما يقال «نعم رجلًا زيد». و«سَاءَ» يجري مجرى «بئس»، نحو «ساء الرجلُ بكر» كما يقال «بئس الرجلُ بكر».

X. Verbs of Wonderment

Another category of verbs is the verbs of wonderment. [The form of] wonderment is that which is assigned to express wonderment. These are two verbal forms. The first is *mā afʿala Zaydan*, e.g., *mā aḥsana Zaydan* (How excellent Zayd is!); the second is *afʿil bi-Zaydin*, e.g., *aḥsin bi-Zaydin* (How excellent Zayd is!). Verbs of wonderment are constructed only from simple triliterals that signify neither colors nor visible defects. [The expression of] wonderment can also be achieved otherwise through *ashadda*, *ablagha*, and analogous words according to one's purpose, e.g., *mā ashadda daḥrajatahu* and *ashdid bi-daḥrajatihi* (How intensely he rolls!).

(١٠) فعلا التعجب

أي من أصناف الفعل فعلا التعجّب، وهو أي التعجب ما وضع لإنشاء التعجّب. وهما فعلان أوّلهما «ما أَفْعَلَ زيدًا» نحو «ما أحسن زيدًا»، وثانيهما «أَفْعِلْ بزيدٍ» نحو «أحسن بزيد». ولا يبنى فعلا التعجب إلا من ثلاثيّ مجرّد ليس بلون ولا عيب ظاهر. ويتوصّل إلى التعجّب مما وراء ذلك بـ«أشدّ» و«أبلغ» ونحو ذلك على حسب غرضك، نحو «ما أشدّ دحرجته» و«أشدِدْ بدحرجته».

[Chapter 6], the third chapter of the second method

الباب الثالث من الطريق الثاني

THE PARTICLE

الحــــرف

What is the particle? How many are its categories, and what are they?

ما الحرف؟ وكم صنفًا وما هي؟

The particle is [a word] that signifies a meaning in [a word] other than itself. There are twenty-four categories of particles:

الحـرف هـو مـا دلّ على مـعنًى في غيره. وأصنافـه أربعـة وعشرون صنفًـا.

I. Prepositions

II. Verb-like particles

III. Conjunctions

IV. Negative particles

V. Particles of alerting

VI. Vocative particles

VII. Particles of affirmation

VIII. Exceptive particles

IX. Particles of address

X. Particles of connection

XI. Particles of explanation

XII. Infinitive particles

XIII. Particles of reproach and exhortation

XIV. The particle of proximity

XV. Particles of futurity

XVI. Interrogative particles

XVII. Conditional particles

(١) الحروف الجارّة

(٢) الحروف المشبّهة بالفعل

(٣) حروف العطف

(٤) حروف النفي

(٥) حروف التنبيه

(٦) حروف النداء

(٧) حروف التصديق

(٨) حروف الاستثناء

(٩) حرفا الخطاب

(١٠) حروف الصلة

(١١) حرفا التفسير

(١٢) الحروف المصدريّة

(١٣) حروف التخصيص

(١٤) حرف التقريب

(١٥) حروف الاستقبال

(١٦) حرفا الاستفهام

(١٧) حروف الشرط

XVIII. Particles expressing the reason	(١٨) حرفا التعليل
XIX. The particle of rebuke	(١٩) حرفا الردع
XX. *Lām* particles	(٢٠) اللامات
XXI. The vowelless *tāʾ* of femininity	(٢١) تاء التأنيث الساكنة
XXII. The emphatic *nūn*	(٢٢) النون المؤكّدة
XXIII. The *hāʾ* of pause	(٢٣) هاء السكت
XXIV. Nunation	(٢٤) التنوين

I. Prepositions

One of the categories of particles is the prepositions, which total nineteen:[79]

1. *Min* *Min* (from, of) is used to signify the point of origin, e.g., *sirtu min al-Baṣrati ilā al-Kūfati* (I traveled from Basra to Kufa).

Min is also used for clarification, and this usage is recognizable by the validity of replacing the *min* with *alladhī*, e.g., *fa-ijtanibū al-rijsa min al-awthāni* (So shun the filth of idols) (Q 22:30), i.e., *alladhī huwa al-wathanu* (namely, idols).

It is also used to signify a part of something, and this usage is recognizable by the validity of replacing the *min* with *baʿḍ* (some), e.g., *akhadha min al-darāhimi* (He took some of the dirhams), i.e., *baʿḍahā* (some of them).

Sometimes it is used as an additional [particle], and this usage can be recognized by its being the case that if the *min* were to be omitted, the meaning would not become deficient, e.g., *mā jāʾanī min aḥadin* (No one came to me), i.e., *mā jāʾanī aḥadun*.

(١) الحروف الجارة

أي من أصناف الحرف الحروف الجارّة. وهي تسعة عشر حرفًا.

١. مِنْ وهي للابتداء، نحو «سرت من البصرة إلى الكوفة».

وللتبيين[١٧]، وتعرف بصحة وضع «الذي» مكانه، نحو ﴿فَٱجْتَنِبُواْ ٱلرِّجْسَ مِنَ ٱلْأَوْثَـٰنِ﴾ [٢٢/ ٣٠] أي «الذي هو الوثن».

وللتبعيض، ويعرف بصحّة وضع «البعض» مكانه، نحو «أخذ من الدراهم» أي «بعضها».

وقد تكون زائدة، وتعرف بأنها لو أسقطت لم يختلّ[١٨] المعنى، نحو «ما جاءني من أحد» أي «ما جاءني[١٩] أحد».

2. *Ilā* *Ilā* (to) signifies the end point, e.g., *sirtu min al-Baṣrati ilā al-Kūfati* (I traveled from Basra to Kufa).

It is sometimes used in the sense of *maʿa* (with), e.g., *akaltu al-samakata ilā raʾsihā* (I ate the fish up to [and including] its head), i.e., *maʿa raʾsihā* (with its head).

3. *Ḥattā* *Ḥattā* (up to, with) means *maʿa*, e.g., *akaltu al-samakata ḥattā raʾsihā* (I ate the fish, even its head), i.e., *maʿa raʾsihā* (with its head). This usage is common with *ḥattā* but rare with *ilā*.

4. *Fī* *Fī* (in) signifies in-ness, which is for one thing to inhere in another either in a literal sense, e.g., *al-mālu fī al-kīsi* (The wealth is in the pouch), or in a nonliteral sense, e.g., *al-najātu fī al-ṣidqi* (Salvation is in truthfulness).

In rare cases it is used in the sense of *ʿalā* (on), e.g., His saying ﷻ, *wa-la-uṣallibannakum fī judhūʿi al-nakhli* ("And I shall surely crucify you on the trunks of palm trees") (Q 20:71), i.e., *ʿalā judhūʿi al-nakhli*.

5. The *Bāʾ* The *bāʾ* may signify various meanings:

1. attachment [by way of attribution], e.g., *bihi dāʾun* (He has an illness).
2. availing oneself of means, e.g., *katabtu bi-l-qalami* (I wrote with the pen).
3. accompaniment, e.g., *ishtaraytu al-farasa bi-lijāmihi* (I bought the horse with its bridle).
4. exchange, e.g., *biʿtu hādhā bi-hādhā* (I sold this for this).
5. transitivity, e.g., *dhahabtu bi-Zaydin* (I took Zayd).
6. being in a place/time, e.g., *jalastu bi-l-masjidi* (I sat in the masjid).

It has other usages as well.

٢. إلَى وهي للانتهاء، نحو «سرت من البصرة إلى الكوفة».

وقد تكون بمعنى «مع»، نحو «أكلت السمكة إلى رأسها» أي «مع رأسها».

٣. حَتَّى وهي بمعنى «مع»، نحو «أكلت السمكة حتّى رأسها» أي «مع رأسها». وهذا المعنى في «حتّى» كثير وفي «إلى» قليل.

٤. في وهي للظرفيّة وهي حلول الشيء في الشيء حقيقةً نحو «المال في الكيس»، ومجازًا نحو «النجاة في الصدق».

وقد يكون بمعنى «على» قليلًا، نحو قوله تعالى ﴿وَلَأُصَلِّبَنَّكُمْ فِي جُذُوعِ ٱلنَّخْلِ﴾ [٢٠/ ٧١]، أي «على جذوع النخل».

٥. الباء وهي لمعان:

١- للإلصاق، نحو «به داء».

٢- وللاستعانة، نحو «كتبت بالقلم».

٣- وللمصاحبة، نحو «اشتريت الفرس بلجامه».

٤- وللمقابلة، نحو «بعت هذا بهذا».

٥- وللتعدية، نحو «ذهبت بزيد».

٦- وللظرفيّة، نحو «جلست بالمسجد».

ولغير ذلك.

6. The *Lām* The *lām* also may signify various meanings:

1. specification, e.g., *al-jullu li-l-farasi* (The covering is for the horse).
2. ownership, e.g., *al-mālu li-Zaydin* (The wealth belongs to Zayd).
3. the reason [for an action], e.g., *ḍarabtu Zaydan li-l-ta'dībi* (I hit Zayd to discipline [him]).

٦. اللام وهي أيضا لمعان:

١- للاختصاص، نحو: «الجلّ للفرس».

٢- وللتمليك، نحو «المال لزيد».

٣- وللتعليل، نحو «ضربت زيدًا للتأديب».

7. Rubba *Rubba* (few, perhaps) signifies fewness,[80] and it stands at the beginning of the sentence. It is specific to indefinite nouns qualified by adjectives, e.g., *rubba rajulin karīmin laqītuhu* (I have met a few noble men). The preventing *mā* can attach to *rubba* and nullify its governance, in which case it is used with a sentence, e.g., *rubbamā Zaydun fī al-dāri* (Perhaps Zayd is in the house) and *rubbamā qāma Zaydun* (Perhaps Zayd has stood).

٧. رُبَّ وهي للتقليل. ولها صدر الكلام؛ ويختص بالنكرات الموصوفة، نحو «ربّ رجلٍ كريم لقيته». ويلحقها «ما» الكافّة فتكفّها عن العمل فتدخل حينئذ على الجملة، نحو «ربّما زيد في الدار» و«ربّما قام زيد».

8. The *Wāw* The *wāw* that means *rubba* is the *wāw* that begins a sentence, e.g.,

> *wa-baldatin laysa bihā anīsu*
> (I have seen) a few towns with none
> for company

i.e., *rubba baldatin amurru bihā laysa bihā insun* (I occasionally pass by towns that contain no one).

٨. الواو بمعنى «رُبَّ» هي التي يبتدأ بها أول الكلام، نحو:

> وَبَلْدَةٍ لَيْسَ بِهَا أَنِيسُ

أي «ربّ بلدة أمرّ بها ليس بها إنس».

9–11. The *Wāw*, *Bā'*, and *Tā'* of Oath The *wāw*, *bā'*, and *tā'* of oath [are used] as in *wa-Llāhi* (*bi-Llāhi, ta-Llāhi*) *la-af'alanna kadhā* (By Allah, I will do such and such). The *bā'* of oath can be used in more situations than the *wāw* and *tā'* because the *bā'* can be used whether the verb [of oath] is mentioned or omitted, whether [the context is one of] request or otherwise, and whether with an explicit noun or an implicit pronoun. This is in contrast to the *wāw* and the *tā'*.

٩-١١. واو القسم وباؤه وتاؤه نحو «والله... وبالله... وتالله لأفعلنّ كذا». باء القسم أعمّ استعمالًا من واو القسم وتائه لأن الباء يستعمل مع الفعل وحذفه ومع السؤال وغيره ومع المظهر والمضمر بخلاف الواو والتاء.

These eleven particles just mentioned can only be particles that mandate the genitive case.

وهذه الحروف الأحد عشر المذكورة لا تكون إلا حرفًا لازمة الجر.

12. *ʿAlā* *ʿAlā* (on) signifies being above, e.g., *jalastu ʿalā al-ḥāʾiṭi* (I sat on the wall).

ʿAlā is sometimes a noun with *min* used before it, in which case it means *fawq* (above), e.g., the poet's saying,

> *ghadat min ʿalayhi*
> It departed from atop it[81]

i.e., *min fawqihi.*

13. *ʿAn* *ʿAn* (from) signifies traversal, e.g., *ramaytu al-sahma ʿan al-qawsi* (I shot the arrow from the bow).

ʿAn is sometimes a noun with *min* used before it, in which case it means *jānib* (side), e.g., *min ʿan yamīnihi* (from his right side), i.e., *min jānibi yamīnihi.*

14. The *Kāf* The *kāf* is for simile, e.g., *Zaydun ka-l-asadi* (Zayd is like a lion).

Sometimes it is used as an additional [particle], e.g., *laysa ka-mithlihi shayʾun* (There is nothing like Him) (Q 42:11),[82] i.e., *laysa mithlahu shayʾun.*

15–16. *Mudh* and *Mundhu* *Mudh* and *mundhu* (since, for) have two meanings. The first is the beginning of a duration, e.g., *mā raʾaytuhu mudh yawmi al-jumuʿati* (I have not seen him since Friday). The second is the entirety of a duration, e.g., *mā raʾaytuhu mundhu yawmayni* (I have not seen him for two days).

These five particles from *ʿalā* to *mundhu* are sometimes particles and sometimes nouns, as you have learned.[83]

١٢. عَلَى وهي للاستعلاء، نحو «جلست على الحائط».

وقد تكون اسمًا بدخول «مِنْ» عليها وتكون حينئذ بمعنى الفوق، نحو قول الشاعر:

غَدَتْ مِنْ عَلَيْهِ

أي «من فوقه».

١٣. عَنْ وهي للمجاوزة، نحو «رميت السهم عن القوس».

وقد تكون اسمًا بدخول «مِنْ» عليها فتكون بمعنى الجانب[٢٠]، نحو «من عن يمينه» أي «من جانب يمينه».

١٤. الكاف وهي للتشبيه، نحو «زيد كالأسد».

وقد تكون زائدة، نحو ﴿لَيْسَ كَمِثْلِهِۦ شَيْءٌ﴾ [٤٢/ ١١] أي «ليس مثله شيء».

١٥-١٦. مذ ومُنْذُ ولهما معنيان. أحدهما أول المدّة، نحو «ما رأيته مذ يوم الجمعة». وثانيهما جميع المدّة، نحو «ما رأيته منذ يومين».

فهذه الحروف الخمسة من «على» إلى «منذ» تارة تكون حرفًا وتارة تكون اسمًا كما علمت.

17. *Ḥāshā* *Ḥāshā* (except) [is used] as in *jāʾanī al-qawmu ḥāshā Zaydin* (The people came to me except Zayd). *Hāshā* is most often used as a preposition.

According to al-Mubarrad,[84] *ḥāshā* is a perfect tense verb that means *jānaba* (avoided, was besides), e.g., *hajama al-qawmu ḥāshā Zaydan* (The people attacked, avoiding Zayd).

١٧. حاشَـا نحـو «جـاءني القـوم حاشـا زيـد». وكـون «حاشـا» حـرف جـرّ أكثر.

وعنـد المبرَّد فعل مـاضٍ بمعنى «جَانَـبَ»، نحو «هجم القوم حاشـا زيدًا».

18–19. *Khalā* and *ʿAdā* *Khalā* and *ʿadā* (except) [are used] as in *jāʾanī al-qawmu khalā Zaydin* (or *ʿadā Zaydin*) (The people came to me except Zayd). This is according to some; according to the majority, however, these are verbs that mean *jāwaza* (bypassed); their agent is a concealed pronoun and their object is the exception that follows.

١٨-١٩. خلَا وعَدَا نحو «جاءني القوم خلا زيد أو...عدا زيد». هذا عند البعض؛ وعند الأكثرين أنّهما فعلان بمعنى «جَاوَزَ» فاعلهما مضمر والمستثنى بعدهما مفعول به.

In articulate usage, *ḥāshā* is used as a preposition and *khalā* and *ʿadā* are used as verbs. For, as you now know, these three particles, namely, *ḥāshā*, *khalā*, and *ʿadā*, may be prepositions and they may be verbs.

الفصيـح في اسـتعمال «حاشـا» أن تكـون حـرف جرّ وفي اسـتعمال «خلا» و«عـدا» أن تكونـا فعـلين. فقـد علم أن هـذه الحروف الثلاثة أعني «حاشـا» و«خلا» و«عدا» قد تكـون حرف جـرّ وقد تكـون فعلًا.

II. Verb-Like Particles

(٢) الحروف المشبهة بالفعل

There are six verb-like particles: *inna* (indeed), *anna* (that), *lākinna* (however), *kaʾanna* (as if), *layta* (would that), and *laʿalla* (perhaps).

وهي ستّة: إِنَّ، أَنَّ، لَكِنَّ، كَأَنَّ، لَيْتَ، لَعَلَّ.

1. *Inna* *Inna* is for emphasis, and it constitutes a sentence together with what comes after it. It does not alter the meaning; it reinforces it. Thus, when one says, *inna Zaydan qāʾimun* (Indeed Zayd is standing), this means *Zaydun qāʾimun* (Zayd is standing) along with added emphasis and intensification, as if one had said, *Zaydun qāʾimun al-battata* (Zayd is certainly standing).

١. إنَّ وهي للتأكيـد مـع مـا بعدهـا جملـة لا تـغيّر معناهـا بـل تؤكّـده، فـإذا قلـت «إنّ زيـدًا قائـم» معنـاه «زيـد قائـم» مع زيـادة التأكيـد والمبالغـة كأنّـك قلـت «زيـد قائـم البتـة».

Inna can be phonetically lightened [as *in*]. In such a case, the nullification of its governance is permissible, and it can be used with verbal sentences. The verb must be one of those verbs that take a subject-noun and predicate, e.g., *in kāna Zaydun la-karīmun* (Zayd truly was generous), and the *lām* must always be used to differentiate this from the negative *in*.

2. *Anna* *Anna* is for confirming actuality, and it constitutes a simple expression together with what comes after it. It alters the meaning of the sentence such that the clause after it takes the status of a simple expression.[1]

Anna can be phonetically lightened [as *an*]. In such a case, it necessarily governs an implicit dummy pronoun, e.g., His statement ﷻ *wa-ākhiru daʿwāhum an al-ḥamdu li-Llāhi rabbi al-ʿālamīna* (And the conclusion of their supplication is that praise is due to Allah, Lord of the worlds) (Q 10:10). It can be used with clauses that are nominal, e.g., *balaghanī an Zaydun akhūka* (I have heard that

وتخفّف فيجوز إلغاؤها وتدخل حينئذ على الجملة الفعليّة ويجب أن يكون ذلك الفعل من الأفعال التي تدخل على المبتدأ والخبر، نحو «إنْ كان زيد لَكريم». واللام لازمة لها للفرق بينها وبين «إنْ» النافية.

٢. أنَّ وهي للتحقيق ومع ما بعدها مفرد تغيّر معنى الجملة فيكون معنى الجملة التي بعدها في حكم المفرد.[١]

وتخفّف فتعمل وجوبًا في ضمير شأن مقدّر، نحو قوله تعالى ﴿وَءَاخِرُ دَعْوَىٰهُمْ أَنِ ٱلْحَمْدُ لِلَّهِ رَبِّ ٱلْعَٰلَمِينَ﴾ [١٠/١٠]. وتدخل على الجمل اسمية كانت نحو «بلغني أنْ

[1] One uses [*inna* with] *kasr* where a clause should be, and one uses [*anna* with] *fatḥ* where a simple expression should be. Thus, one uses *kasr* at the beginning of a sentence, e.g., *inna Zaydan munṭaliqun* (Indeed, Zayd is departing); after [the word] *qawl* (saying) [or its derivatives], e.g., *qultu inna Zaydan qāʾimun* (I said that Zayd is standing); after a relative pronoun, e.g., *jāʾanī alladhī inna abāhu qāʾimun* (The one whose father is indeed standing came to me); and after an oath, e.g., *wa-Llāhi innī la-ṣāʾimun* (By Allah, I am fasting). One uses [*anna* with] *fatḥ* in the place of an agent, e.g., *aʿjabanī anna Zaydan qāʾimun* ([The fact] that Zayd was standing pleased me); in the place of an object, e.g., *samiʿtu anna Zaydan kātibun* (I heard that Zayd is a writer); in the place of a subject, e.g., *ʿindī annaka qāʾimun* (That you are standing [is the case], in my estimation); in the place of a predicate, e.g., *ʿalimtu Zaydan annahu yaqūmu laylan* (I knew [of] Zayd that he stands at night); and in the place of a *muḍāf ilayhi*, e.g., *balaghanī [khabaru] anna Zaydan dhāhibun* (News of Zayd's departure reached me).

[١] فاكسر في مظانّ الجمل وافتح في مظانّ المفردات. فاكسر في ابتداء الكلام نحو «إنّ زيدًا منطلق»، وبعد القول نحو «قلت إنّ زيدًا قائم»، وبعد الموصول نحو «جاءني الذي إنّ أباه قائم»، وبعد القسم نحو «والله إنّي لصائم». وافتح في موضع الفاعل نحو «أعجبني أنّ زيدًا قائم»، وموضع المفعول نحو «سمعت أنّ زيدًا كاتب»، وموضع المبتدأ نحو «عندي أنّك قائم»، وموضع الخبر نحو «علمت زيدًا أنّه يقوم ليلًا»، وموضع المضاف إليه نحو «بلغني [خبر] أنّ زيدًا ذاهب».

Zayd is your brother), or verbal, e.g., *balaghanī an lā yaḍribu Zaydun* (I have heard that Zayd does not hit). With a lightened *an* that is used with a verb, there must always be one of the four particles (1) *qad*, (2) *sawfa*, (3) the *sīn*, or (4) a negative particle to differentiate the lightened *an* from the *an* that makes the imperfect tense verb subjunctive, e.g., *ʿalimtu an qad kharaja Zaydun* (I learned that Zayd had left), *...an sa-yaḍribu* (...that he will hit), *...an sawfa yaḍribu* (...that he will hit), and *...an lam yakhruj* (...that he did not leave).

3. ***Lākinna*** *Lākinna* is for rectification, i.e., to obviate an incorrect expectation [that might] arise from a previous statement, e.g., *jāʾanī Zaydun lākinna ʿAmran lam yajiʾ* (Zayd came to me, but ʿAmr did not come).[85]

Lākinna can be phonetically lightened, in which case its governance is nullified and it can be used in a nominal or a verbal clause, e.g., *abūhu qāʿidun lākin akhūhu qāʾimun* (His father is sitting, but his brother is standing) and *dakhala Zaydun lākin kharaja ʿAmrun* (Zayd entered, but ʿAmr left).

A *wāw* can be used with the lightened *lākin*, e.g., His saying ﷻ, *wa-lākin kānū anfusahum yaẓlimūna* (but themselves did they wrong) (Q 2:57), just as a *wāw* can be used with the doubled *lākinna*.

4. ***Kaʾanna*** *Kaʾanna* is for simile, e.g., *kaʾanna Zaydan asadun* (It is as if Zayd were a lion).

Kaʾanna can be phonetically lightened, in which case its governance is nullified according to the most correct usage, e.g., the poet's saying,

> *ka-an thadyāhu ḥuqqāni*
> As if its breasts were vessels

5. ***Layta*** *Layta* is for wishful desire, e.g., *layta al-shabāba yaʿūdu yawman fa-ukhbirahu bimā faʿala al-mashību* (Would that youth would return for a day, that I might tell it what old age has done).

زيد أخوك» أو فعليةً نحو «بلغني أنْ لا يضرب زيد». ولا بدّ لها أي لأنْ المخفّفة الداخلة على الفعل من أن يكون معها أحد الحروف الأربعة، وهي (١) قَدْ، (٢) سَوْفَ، (٣) والسين، (٤) وحرف النفي، للفرق بين أَنْ المخفّفة وبين «أَنْ» الناصبة للفعل المضارع، نحو «علمت أن قد خرج زيد ...وأن سيضرب ...وأن سوف يضرب ...وأن لم يخرج».

٣. **لَكِنَّ** وهي للاستدراك أي لدفع وهم تولّد من كلام سابق، نحو «جاءني زيد لكنّ عمرًا لم يجئ».

وتخفّف فتلغى وتدخل على الجملة الاسمية والفعلية، نحو «أبوه قاعد لكنْ أخوه قائم» ونحو «دخل زيد لكنْ خرج عمرو».

ويجوز ذكر الواو مع «لكن» المخفّفة نحو قوله تعالى ﴿وَلَٰكِن كَانُوٓا۟ أَنفُسَهُمْ يَظْلِمُونَ﴾ [٢/ ٥٧] كما يجوز مع المشدّدة.

٤. **كَأَنَّ** وهي للتشبيه كـ«كأنّ زيدًا أسد»[١].

وتخفّف فتلغى على الأفصح، كقول الشاعر:

> كَأَنْ ثَدْيَاهُ حُقَّانِ

٥. **ليتَ** وهي للتمنّي، نحو «ليت الشبابَ يعود يومًا فأخبره بما فعل المشيب».

6. *Laʿalla* *Laʿalla* is for hopeful desire, e.g., *laʿalla Zaydan yajīʾu* (Perhaps Zayd will come).

٦. لعَلَّ وهي للترجّي، نحو «لعلّ زيدًا يجيء».

❋ ❋ ❋

According to the most correct usage, the preventing *mā* nullifies the governance of verb-like particles, e.g., His statement ﷻ *innamā Allāhu ilāhun wāḥidun* (Allah is only one God) (Q 4:171). When this is so, these particles are used in verbal sentences, e.g., *innamā dhahaba Zaydun* (Only Zayd went), as well as in nominal sentences, e.g., *innamā Zaydun qāʾimun* (Zayd is only standing). The purpose of adding the preventing *mā* to them is to convey restriction along with emphasis and intensification. Thus, the meaning of *innamā dhahaba Zaydun* is *mā dhahaba illā Zaydun* (No one went except Zayd), and the meaning of *innamā Zaydun qāʾimun* is *mā Zaydun illā qāʾimun* (Zayd is not [doing anything] but standing).

ويبطل عمل الحروف المشبّهة بالفعل «مَا» الكافّة على الأفصح، نحو قوله تعالى ﴿إِنَّمَا ٱللَّهُ إِلَٰهٌ وَٰحِدٌ﴾ [٤/ ١٧١]. فحينئذ تدخل الحروف المشبّهة بالفعل على الجملة الفعليّة نحو «إنما ذهب زيد» كما كانت تدخل على الجملة الاسميّة نحو «إنما زيد قائم». والغرض من إدخال «ما» الكافّة عليها الحصر مع التأكيد والمبالغة. فمعنى «إنما ذهب زيد» «ما ذهب إلا زيد»، ومعنى «إنما زيد قائم» «ما زيد إلا قائم».

III. Conjunctions

(٣) حروف العطف

There are ten conjunctions: the *wāw*, the *fāʾ*, *thumma*, *ḥattā*, *aw*, *immā*, *am*, *bal*, *lā*, and *lākin*.

وهي عشرة: الواو، الفاء، ثُمَّ، حَتَّى، أَوْ، إِمَّا، أَمْ، بَلْ، لَا، لَكِنْ.

[1–4. The *Wāw*, the *Fāʾ*, *Thumma*, and *Ḥattā*] The first four, namely, the *wāw*, the *fāʾ*, *thumma*, and *ḥattā*, are for bringing the conjunct and that to which it is conjoined into the same grammatical status.

The *wāw* is for conjoining without [a particular] order, e.g., *jāʾanī Zaydun wa-ʿAmrun* (Zayd and ʿAmr came to me).

[١-٤. الواو والفاء وثُمَّ وحَتَّى] الأربعة الأولى أي الواو والفاء و«ثُمَّ» و«حَتَّى» للجمع بين المعطوف والمعطوف عليه في الحكم.

فالواو للجمع بلا ترتيب، نحو «جاءني زيدٌ وعمرٌو».

The *fā'* and *thumma* are for conjoining as well, but in [a particular] order. *Thumma* contains a sense of delay, but the *fā'* does not, e.g., His saying ﷻ in quoting Ibrāhīm ﵇, *wa-alladhī yumītunī thumma yuḥyīni* ("and who causes me to die and then gives me life") (Q 26:81), and His statement *fa-khalaqnā al-ʿalaqata muḍghatan fa-khalaqnā al-muḍghata ʿiẓāman* (then of the blood clot We created a lump of flesh, then of the lump of flesh We created bones) (Q 23:14).

والفاء و«ثُمَّ» للجمع المذكور مع الترتيب، وفي «ثمّ» تراخٍ دون الفاء، نحو قوله تعالى عن إبراهيم عليه السلام ﴿وَٱلَّذِي يُمِيتُنِي ثُمَّ يُحْيِينِ﴾ [٢٦/ ٨١] وقوله ﴿فَخَلَقْنَا ٱلْعَلَقَةَ مُضْغَةً فَخَلَقْنَا ٱلْمُضْغَةَ عِظَـٰمًا﴾ [٢٣/ ١٤].

Ḥattā contains the meaning of an end point and termination, i.e., that what is [expressed] before *ḥattā* proceeds incrementally until it reaches the element [conjoined] after *ḥattā*. Thus it is necessary that the conjunct by means of *ḥattā* be a part of that to which it is conjoined: either its best part, e.g., *māta al-nāsu ḥattā al-anbiyā'u* (People have died, even the prophets), or its lowest ranking part, e.g., *qadima al-ḥujjāju ḥattā al-mushātu* (The pilgrims arrived, even those walking).

وفي «حَتَّى» معنى الغاية والانتهاء وهو أنّ ما قبل «حتّى» ينقضي شيئًا فشيئًا إلى أن يبلغ ما بعد «حتى». فلذلك يجب أن يكون المعطوف بـ«حتّى» جزءًا من المعطوف عليه إما جزأه الأفضل نحو «مات الناس حتّى الأنبياء» أو جزأه الأدون نحو «قدم الحجاج حتّى المشاة».

5–6. *Aw* and *Immā* *Aw* and *immā* are for referring to one of two things or to one of several things nonspecifically. They can occur in predicates, e.g., *jā'anī Zaydun aw ʿAmrun* (Zayd or ʿAmr came to me) and *jā'anī immā Zaydun wa-immā ʿAmrun* (Either Zayd or ʿAmr came to me), and they can occur in non-declarative sentences, that is, in imperative and interrogative sentences.

٥-٦. أَوْ وإمَّا وهما لأحد الشيئين أو أحد الأشياء مبهمًا. وتقعان في الخبر نحو «جاءني زيد أو عمرو» و«جاءني إما زيد وإما عمرو» وفي الإنشاء أي في الأمر والاستفهام.

An example in an imperative sentence is to say, *iḍrib ra'sahu aw ẓahrahu* (Hit his head or his back) and *iḍrib immā ra'sahu wa-immā ẓahrahu* (Hit either his head or his back).

أما في الأمر فنحو قولك «اضرب رأسه أو ظهره» و«اضرب إما رأسه وإما ظهره».

An example in an interrogative sentence is to say, *a-laqīta ʿAbdallāhi aw akhāhu* (Did you meet ʿAbdallāh or his brother?) and *a-laqīta immā ʿAbdallāhi wa-immā akhāhu* (Did you meet either ʿAbdallāh or his brother?).

وأما في الاستفهام فنحو قولك «ألقيت عبد الله أو أخاه؟» و«ألقيت إما عبد الله وإما أخاه؟»

7. *Am* *Am* is also for referring to one of two things or to one of several things nonspecifically. *Am*, however, is of two types:

٧. أَمْ هي أيضا لأحد الشيئين أو أحد الأشياء مبهمًا، إلا أن «أَمْ» على قسمين:

The first type is *connected* and occurs only in interrogatives with the [interrogative] *hamza*. After *am* comes one of two equally possible alternatives; the other [alternative comes after] the *hamza*, e.g., *a-Zaydun ʿindaka am ʿAmrun* (Is Zayd with you, or [is] ʿAmr?). In this case, the two equally possible alternatives are Zayd and ʿAmr; *ʿAmr* comes after *am*, and *Zayd* comes after the *hamza*.

The second type is *disconnected*, i.e., discontinuous, and means *bal* (rather) together with the *hamza*. The meaning of *bal* is to disregard something after bringing it up. The disconnected *am* may occur in (1) interrogative sentences, e.g., *a-Zaydun ʿindaka am ʿindaka ʿAmrun* (Is Zayd with you, or, rather, is ʿUmar with you?), i.e. *bal a-ʿindaka ʿAmrun*. One asks first whether Zayd is with the person addressed, then one disregards that question in favor of the question whether ʿAmr is with the person addressed. The disconnected *am* may also occur in (2) declarative sentences, e.g., *innahā la-iblun am shāʾun* (Surely it is a camel—or, rather, is it a sheep?), i.e., *bal a-hiya shāʾun*, as if one had seen a body, spontaneously assumed that it was a camel, said, "This is a camel," and then thought that it was in fact a sheep, so he disregarded that statement in favor of a question, asking, *am shāʾun* (Rather, is it a sheep?), i.e., *bal a-hiya shāʾun*.

8. ***Bal*** *Bal* is for disregarding one thing in favor of another, be [the sentence] affirmative, e.g., *jāʾanī Zaydun bal ʿAmrun* (Zayd came to me; rather, ʿAmr [did]), or negative, e.g., *mā jāʾanī Zaydun bal Khālidun* (Zayd did not come to me; rather, Khālid [did]).

9. ***Lā*** *Lā* is for negating, with respect to the conjunct, what had been affirmed for the first element, e.g., *jāʾanī Zaydun lā ʿAmrun* (Zayd came to me, not ʿAmr). It is used only after affirmations; if you were to say, *mā jāʾanī Zaydun lā ʿAmrun* (Zayd did not come to me, not ʿAmr), this would be invalid.

أحدهما متّصلة لا يقع إلا في الاستفهام مع الهمزة؛ يليها أحد الأمرين المستويين والآخر الهمزة، نحو «أزيد عندك أم عمرو؟» والمراد من الأمرين المستويين هنا زيد وعمرو فـ«عمرو» وليها أي وَلِيَ «أم» و«زيد» وَلِيَ الهمزة.

ثانيها منفصلة أي منقطعة وهي بمعنى «بَلْ» والهمزة. معنى «بل» الإعراض عن الشيء بعد الإقبال عليه. وتقع في (١) الاستفهام، نحو «أزيد عندك أم عندك عمرو» بمعنى «بل أعندك عمرو» فسألت أولًا عن حصول زيد عند المخاطب ثم أعرضت عن ذلك السؤال إلى السؤال عن حصول عمرو عنده. وَفي (٢) الخبر، نحو «إنها لإبل أم شاة؟» بمعنى «بل أهي شاة؟» كأنّك رأيت جثّة سبق وهمك إلى أنها إبل فقلت «إنها لابل» ثم ظننت أنها شاء فأعرضت عن ذلك الخبر إلى السؤال فقلت «أم شاء» أي «بل أهي شاء؟».

٨. بَلْ وهي للإعراض عن الأول إلى الثاني موجبًا كان نحو «جاءني زيد بل عمرو» أو منفيًّا نحو «ما جاءني زيد بل خالد».

٩. لَا وهي لنفي ما ثبت للمعطوف عليه عن المعطوف، نحو «جاءني زيد لا عمرو». فلا تجيء إلا بعد الإثبات، فلو قلت «ما جاءني زيد لا عمرو» لم يجز.

10. *Lākin* *Lākin* is for rectification, i.e., to obviate an incorrect expectation [that might] arise from a previous statement. Thus, it intervenes between statements that differ in meaning. When conjoining statements, *lākin* is like *bal*; that is, it comes after either negation or affirmation, e.g., *mā jāʾanī Zaydun lākin ʿAmrun qad jāʾa* (Zayd did not come to me, but ʿAmr did come) and *jāʾanī Zaydun lākin ʿAmrun lam yajiʾ* (Zayd came to me, but ʿAmr did not come). When conjoining individual words, it is the opposite of *lā*; that is, in contrast to *lā*, it comes only after negation, e.g., *mā raʾaytu Zaydan lākin ʿAmran* (I saw not Zayd but ʿAmr), i.e., *lākin ʿAmran raʾaytuhu*.

١٠. لكِـنْ للاستدراك أي لرفع وهم تـولّد مـن كلام سـابق؛ ولذا يتوسّـط بين كلامين متغايريـن مـعنًى. وهي في عطف الجمـل نظيرة «بل» أي تجيء بعـد النفي والإيجاب، نحـو «مـا جـاءني زيد لكـن عمـرو قـد جـاء» و«جاءني زيـد لكـن عمـرو لم يجئ»؛ وفي عطف المفـردات نقيض «لا» أي تجيء بعـد النفي خاصّـة بعكـس «لا»، نحو «ما رأيـت زيـدًا لكن عمـرًا» أي «لكـن عمـرًا رأيته».

IV. Negative Particles

(٤) حروف النفي

Another category of particles is the negative particles. There are six: *mā*, *lā*, *in*, *lam*, *lammā*, and *lan*.

أي مـن أصناف الحـرف حروف النفي وهي سـتّة: مَـا، لَا، إِنْ، لَـمْ، لَمَّـا، لَنْ .

1. *Mā* *Mā* is for negating the present, e.g., *mā yafʿalu al-āna* (He is not doing [it] now). It is also used for negating the recent past, e.g., *mā faʿala* (He did not do [it]).

١. مَـا وهي لنفي الحال، نحـو «مـا يفعـل الآن»؛ ولنفي الماضي القريـب مـن الحال، نحـو «مـا فعـل».

2. *Lā* *Lā* is for negating the future,[86] e.g., *lā yafʿalu ghadan* (He will not do [it] tomorrow).

It is also used for negating the past on condition of its being repeated, e.g., His statement ﷻ *fa-lā ṣaddaqa wa-lā ṣallā* (For he neither confirmed nor prayed) (Q 75:31). In some cases, it is not repeated, e.g., the poet's saying,

> *wa-kāna fī jārātihi lā ʿahda lah*
> And he was among his female neighbors unscrupulous;
>
> [*fa-ayya amrin sayyiʾin lā faʿalah*[87]
> What evil, then, did he not commit?]

Lā is also used for prohibition, e.g., *lā tafʿal* (Do not do [it]).

٢. لَا وهي لنفي المستقبل، نحو «لا يفعل غدًا».

ولنفي الماضي بشرط التكريـر، نحـو قـوله تعـالى ﴿فَلَا صَـدَّقَ وَلَا صَلَّىٰ﴾ [٧٥/٣١]. وقد لا يُكـرّر كقول الشـاعر:

> وَكَانَ فِـــي جَارَاتِـــهِ لَا عَـهْـــدَ لَـــهْ
>
> [فَـــأَيَّ فِـعْـــلٍ سَـــيِّءٍ لَا فَـعَـلَـــهْ]

والنهي، نحو «لا تفعل».

It is used for supplication, e.g., *lā raʿāhu Allāhu* (May Allah not watch over him).

وللدعاء، نحو «لا رعاه الله».

It is used for categoric negation, e.g., *lā rajula fī al-dāri* (There is no man in the house).

ولنفي العام، نحو «لا رجلَ في الدار».

It is also used for non-categoric negation, i.e., that which means *laysa*, e.g., *lā rajulun fī al-dāri wa-lā imraʾatun* (There is not a man in the house nor a woman).

ولغير العام وهي التي بمعنى «ليس»، نحو «لا رجلٌ في الدار ولا امرأة».

3. *In* *In* is like *mā* in negating the present, e.g., *in yafʿalu al-āna* (He is not doing [it] now).

٣. إنْ وهي نظيرة «ما» في نفي الحال، نحو «إن يفعل الآن».

It can be used before both [types of] sentences: nominal, e.g., His statement ﷻ *in al-ḥukmu illā li-Allāhi* (Judgment belongs to none but Allah) (Q 6:57), and verbal, e.g., His statement *in yattabiʿūna illā al-ẓanna* (They follow naught but conjecture) (Q 6:116).

وتدخل على الجملتين الاسميّة كقوله تعالى ﴿إِنِ ٱلْحُكْمُ إِلَّا لِلَّهِ﴾ [٦/ ٥٧] والفعليّة كقوله ﴿إِن يَتَّبِعُونَ إِلَّا ٱلظَّنَّ﴾ [٦/ ١١٦].

4. *Lam* *Lam* is for negating imperfect tense verbs and changing their signification to the past, e.g., *lam yaḍrib* (He did not hit).

٤. لَمْ وهي لنفي المضارع وقلب معناه إلى الماضي، نحو «لم يضرب».

5. *Lammā* *Lammā* is also for negating imperfect tense verbs and changing their signification to the past, but with continuous negation up until the present. It also contains the meaning of expectation and anticipation. One says, *nadima Zaydun wa-lammā yanfaʿ al-nadamu* (Zayd bore regret and the regret has not benefitted [him]), [that is,] as yet, though [his eventual benefit] is expected.

٥. لمَّا وهي أيضا لنفي المضارع وقلب معناه إلى الماضي ولكن مع استمرار النفي إلى الحال، وفيه معنى التوقّع والانتظار. يقال «ندم زيد ولما ينفع الندم» إلى هذا الوقت لكنه متوقع.

6. *Lan* *Lan* is like *lā* in negating the future, but with emphasis. One says, *lan yafʿala* (He will not [ever] do [it]), to emphasize the statement *lā yafʿalu* (He will not do [it]).

٦. لَنْ وهي نظير «لا» في نفي المستقبل ولكن على التأكيد. تقول «لن يفعل» مؤكّدًا لقولك «لا يفعل».

V. Particles of Alerting

(٥) حروف التنبيه

There are three particles of alerting: *hā*, *amā*, and *alā*.

وهي ثلاثة: هَا، أَمَا، أَلَا.

1. *Hā* *Hā* [is used] as in *hā inna Zaydan bi-l-bābi* ([Hey], Zayd is at the door!). Its most common usage is before demonstrative pronouns, e.g., *hādhā* (this [m.]) and *hātā* (this [f.]), and personal pronouns, e.g., *hā anta* (Hey you!) and His saying ﷻ, *hā-antum hāʾulāʾi* (Behold! You are the very same who…) (Q 3:66). It is sometimes used before sentences, e.g., the poet's saying,

> *hā inna tā ʿidhratun in lam takun qubilat*
> Hark! This is an excuse; if it is not accepted,
>
> *fa-inna ṣāḥibahā qad tāha fī al-baladi*
> Then its possessor is lost in the land

that is, "he [is left to] wander at loss in the land."

١. ها نحو «ها إنّ زيدًا بالباب». وأكثر دخولها على أسماء الإشارة نحو «هذا» و«هتا» وعلى الضمائر نحو «ها أنت» وكقوله تعالى ﴿هَـٰٓأَنتُمْ هَـٰٓؤُلَآءِ﴾ [٣/ ٦٦]. وقد تدخل على الجملة، نحو قول الشاعر:

> هَا إِنَّ تَا عِذْرَةٌ إِنْ لَمْ تَكُنْ قُبِلَتْ
> فَإِنَّ صَاحِبَهَا قَدْ تَاهَ فِي البَلَدِ

أي «تحيّر في البلد».

2–3. *Amā* and *Alā* *Amā* and *alā* are used only with sentences, e.g., *amā innaka khārijun* ([Wait, but] you are leaving) and *alā inna Zaydan qāʾimun* ([Behold!] Zayd is standing).

٢-٣. أَمَا وأَلَا وهما لا تدخلان إلا على الجملة، نحو «أما إنّك خارج» و«ألا إنّ زيدًا قائم».

VI. Vocative Particles

(٦) حروف النداء

There are five vocative particles: *yā*, *ayā*, *hayā*, *ay*, and the *hamza*.

وهي خمسة: يَا، أَيَا، هَيَا، أَيْ، الهمزة.

1–3. *Yā*, *Ayā*, and *Hayā* *Yā*, *ayā*, and *hayā* are for [calling] someone who is distant or of some equivalent status, like someone asleep or unaware. When these particles are used to call anyone who does not belong to any of these categories, then this is due to the caller's desire that the one being called turn his attention to him (i.e., towards the one calling) and his desire that the one called be aware of that for which he is calling him. As for a supplicant's saying *yā rabbi* (O my Lord) or *yā Allāhu* (O Allah), this is due to his finding fault in his self and endeavoring to break it, deeming [his supplication] unworthy to be accepted or heard, and expressing his desire that he be answered.

١-٣. يا وأيا وهيا للبعيد أو لمن هو بمنزلته من نائم أو ساهٍ. وإذا نودي بها مَن عداهم فلحرص المنادي على إقبال المدعوّ عليه أي على المنادي ولحرصه على مفاطنة المدعوّ لما يدعوه له. وأما قول الداعي «يا رب» و«يا الله» فاستقصار منه لنفسه وهضم لها واستبعاد عن مظانّ القبول ومظانّ الاستماع وإظهار للرغبة في الإجابة.

4–5. *Ay* and the *Hamza* *Ay* and the *hamza* are for [calling] someone who is near, but the *hamza* implies more nearness, e.g., *ay Zaydu* (O Zayd) and *a-Zaydu* (O Zayd), as in the poet's saying,

> *a-Zaydu akhā warqāʾa in kunta thāʾiran*
> O Zayd, brother of Warqāʾ! If you seek revenge,
>
> *fa-qad ʿaraḍat aḥnāʾu ḥaqqin fa-khāṣimi*
> The bounds of a right have manifested, so dispute!

٤-٥. أي والهمزة وهما للقريب لكن الهمزة للأقرب، نحو «أي زيد» و«أزيد»، كما قال الشاعر:

> أَزَيْدُ أَخَا وَرْقَاءَ إِنْ كُنْتَ ثَائِرًا
>
> فَقَدْ عَرَضَتْ أَحْنَاءُ حَقٍّ فَخَاصِمِ

VII. Particles of Affirmation

(٧) حروف التصديق والإيجاب

There are six particles of affirmation: *naʿam*, *balā*, *ajal*, *jayri*, *inna*, and *ay*.

وهي ستّة: نَعَمْ، بَلَى، أَجَلْ، جَيْرِ، إِنَّ، أَيْ.

1. *Naʿam* *Naʿam* is for confirming what was affirmed or negated, be it (a) a declarative sentence, e.g., saying *naʿam* (Yes) to someone who says, *qāma Zaydun* (Zayd stood), or says, *lam yaqum Zaydun* (Zayd did not stand), or (b) an interrogative sentence, e.g., saying *naʿam* (Yes) to someone who asks, *a-qāma Zaydun* (Did Zayd stand?), or asks, *a-lam yaqum Zaydun* (Did Zayd not stand?).

١. نعم وهي لتصديق الكلام المثبت والمنفيّ سواء كانا في الخبر كقولك «نعم» لمن قال «قام زيد» أو قال «لم يقم زيد» أو كانا في الاستفهام كقولك «نعم» لمن قال «أقام زيد؟» أو قال «ألم يقم زيد؟».

2. *Balā* *Balā* is specifically for affirming what was negated, be it (a) a declarative sentence, e.g., saying *balā* (Rather, [he did]) to someone who says, *lam yaqum Zaydun* (Zayd did not stand), meaning "He did stand," or (b) an interrogative sentence, e.g., saying *balā* (Indeed [he did]) to someone who asks, *a-lam yaqum Zaydun* (Did Zayd not stand?). He ﷺ says, *a-yaḥsabu al-insānu an-lan najmaʿa ʿiẓāmahu balā qādirīna ʿalā an nusawwiya banānahu* (Does man suppose that We shall not gather his bones? Indeed We shall, while able to fashion his very fingertips) (Q 75:3-4).

٢. بلى وهي تختصّ بإيجاب المنفيّ خبرًا كان كقولك «بلى» لمن قال «لم يقم زيد» أي «قد قام» أو استفهامًا كقولك «بلى» لمن قال «ألم يقم زيد؟» أي «قد قام». قال تعالى ﴿أَيَحْسَبُ ٱلْإِنسَـٰنُ أَلَّن نَّجْمَعَ عِظَامَهُۥ ۝٣ بَلَىٰ قَـٰدِرِينَ عَلَىٰٓ أَن نُّسَوِّىَ بَنَانَهُۥ﴾ [٧٥/ ٣-٤].

3–5. *Ajal, Jayri,* and *Inna* *Ajal, jayri,* and *inna* are specifically for expressing assent to someone with respect to his declarative statement, whether it be negative or affirmative. They are not used in response to interrogative sentences. One thus says *ajal, jayri,* or *inna* (That is correct) to someone who says, *qad jāʾaka Zaydun* (Zayd has come to you), or says, *mā jāʾaka Zaydun* (Zayd has not come to you).

6. *Ay* *Ay* conveys affirmation after an interrogative sentence, and it must be accompanied by an oath, e.g., His saying ﷻ, *īy wa-rabbī* ("Yea, by my Lord") (Q 10:53).

VIII. Exceptive Particles

There are four exceptive particles: *illā, khalā, ʿadā,* and *ḥāshā.*

1. *Illā* *Illā* is considered a particle without dispute. The *exception* after it may be accusative, e.g., *jāʾanī al-qawmu illā Zaydan* (The people came to me except Zayd), and it may be nominative, e.g., *mā jāʾanī illā Zaydun* (No one came to me except Zayd). We discussed the details in the chapter on nouns.

2–3. *Khalā* and *ʿAdā* The majority view considers *khalā* and *ʿadā* to be verbs with the meaning of *jāwaza* (bypassed). The exception after them is accusative, e.g., *jāʾanī al-qawmu khalā Zaydan* (or *ʿadā Zaydan*) (The people came to me except Zayd). According to some, they are prepositions and the noun after them is genitive, e.g., *jāʾanī al-qawmu khalā Zaydin* (or *ʿadā Zaydin*).

4. *Ḥāshā* The majority view considers *ḥāshā* to be a preposition. According to one view, it is a verb with the meaning of *jāwaza*, e.g., *jāʾanī al-qawmu ḥāshā Zaydan* (The people came to me except Zayd).

٣-٥. أجل، جير، إن وهذه الثلاثة تختصّ بتصديق المخبر في إخباره نفيًا كان ذلك الإخبار أو إثباتًا ولا تستعمل في جواب الاستفهام، فتقول «أجل» أو «جير» أو «إن» لمن قال لك «قد جاءك زيد» أو «ما جاءك زيد».

٦. أي هي إثبات بعد الاستفهام ويلزمها القسم، نحو قوله تعالى ﴿إِي وَرَبِّي﴾ [١٠/ ٥٣].

(٨) حروف الاستثناء

وهي أربعة: إِلَّا، خَلَا، عَدَا، حَاشَا.

١. إلا هي حرف بلا خلاف وقد يُنصب المستثنى بعده نحو «جاءني القوم إلا زيدًا» وقد يُرفع نحو «ما جاءني إلا زيدٌ». وقد مرّ التفصيل في باب الاسم.

٢-٣. خلا وعدا فالأكثر على أنهما فعلان بمعنى «جاوزَ» ويُنصب المستثنى بعدهما، نحو «جاءني القوم خلا زيدًا ...وعدا زيدًا». وقيل هما حرفا جرّ ويُجرّ الاسم بعدهما، نحو «جاءني القوم خلا زيدٍ ...وعدا زيدٍ».

٤. حاشا فالأكثر على أنها حرف جرّ؛ وبعضهم قال هي فعل بمعنى «جاوزَ»، نحو «جاءني القوم حاشا زيدًا».

IX. Particles of Address

The particles of address are the *kāf* as in *dhālika* (that) and the *tāʾ* as in *anta* (you). The dual, plural, masculine and feminine [endings] attach to them; one says *dhālika, dhālikumā, dhālikum, dhāliki, dhālikumā*, and *dhālikunna*, and one says *anta, antumā, antum, anti, antumā*, and *antunna*.[88]

(٩) حرفا الخطاب

وهما الكاف كما في «ذلك» والتاء كما في «أنت». ويلحقهما التثنية والجمع والتذكير والتأنيث، كما تقول: ذَلِكَ، ذَلِكُمَا، ذَلِكُمْ، ذَلِكِ، ذَلِكُمَا، ذَلِكُنَّ، وتقول: أَنْتَ، أَنْتُمَا، أَنْتُمْ، أَنْتِ، أَنْتُمَا، أَنْتُنَّ.

X. Particles of Connection

The particles of connection, or the *additional particles*, are particles that at times are added in some places for emphasis. There are seven of these particles: *in, an, mā, lā, min*, the *bāʾ*, and the *lām*.

1. *In* *In* is vowelless and has a *kasra* on the *alif*. It is added after the negative *mā* to emphasize the negation, e.g., *mā in raʾaytu Zaydan* (I certainly did not see Zayd), i.e., *mā raʾaytu Zaydan*.

2. *An* *An* is vowelless and has a *fatḥa* on the *alif*. It is added after *lammā*, e.g., His saying ﷻ, *fa-lammā an jāʾa al-bashīru* (And when the bearer of glad tidings came) (Q 12:96), i.e., *fa-lammā jāʾa al-bashīru*.

3. *Mā* *Mā* is for emphasis and is added (1) to the conditional *mā* after the latter's *alif* is converted to a *hāʾ*, e.g., His saying ﷻ, *mahmā taʾtinā bihi min āyatin* ("Whatever sign you may bring us…") (Q 7:132), i.e., *mā taʾtinā bihi min āyatin*; (2) after *ayna* (where), e.g., His statement ﷻ *aynamā takūnū yudrikkum al-mawtu* (Wheresoever you may be, death will overtake you) (Q 4:78), i.e., *ayna takūnū*; (3) after the *bāʾ*, e.g., His statement ﷻ *fa-bimā raḥmatin min Allāhi linta lahum* (Then [it was] by a mercy from Allah that you were gentle with them) (Q 3:159), i.e., *fa-bi-raḥmati Allāhi linta lahum*.

(١٠) حروف الصلة

أي حروف الزيادة هي حروف تزاد أحيانًا في بعض المواضع للتأكيد. وهي سبعة أحرف: إِنْ، أَنْ، مَا، لَا، مِنْ، الباء، اللام.

١. إن وهي بكسر الألف ساكنة تزاد بعد «ما» النافية لتأكيد النفي، نحو «ما إن رأيت زيدًا» أي «ما رأيت زيدًا».

٢. أن وهي بفتح الألف ساكنة تزاد بعد «لمّا»[٢٢]، نحو قوله تعالى ﴿فَلَمَّآ أَن جَآءَ ٱلْبَشِيرُ﴾ [١٢/ ٩٦] أي «فلمّا جاء البشير».

٣. ما وهي للتأكيد زيدت (١) بعد «ما» الشرطيّة بعد قلب ألفها هاءً، نحو قوله تعالى ﴿مَهْمَا تَأْتِنَا بِهِۦ مِنْ ءَايَةٍ﴾ [٧/ ١٣٢] أي «ما تأتنا به من آية»؛ (٢) وبعد «أين»، نحو قوله تعالى ﴿أَيْنَمَا تَكُونُواْ يُدْرِككُّمُ ٱلْمَوْتُ﴾ [٤/ ٧٨] أي «أين تكونوا»؛ (٣) وبعد الباء، نحو قوله تعالى ﴿فَبِمَا رَحْمَةٍ مِّنَ ٱللَّهِ لِنتَ لَهُمْ﴾ [٣/ ١٥٩] أي «فبرحمة الله لنت لهم».

4. *Lā* *Lā* is added (1) after the subjunctive *an*, e.g., His saying ﷻ, *li-an-lā yaʿlama ahlu al-kitābi* (Such that the people of the Book may know) (Q 57:29), i.e., *li-an yaʿlama*, and (2) before the verb of oath, e.g., His saying ﷻ, *lā uqsimu* (I swear) (Q 75:1), i.e., *uqsimu*.

٤. لا وهي[٢٣] تزاد (١) بعد «أَنْ» الناصبة، نحو قوله تعالى ﴿لِّئَلَّا يَعْلَمَ أَهْلُ ٱلْكِتَٰبِ﴾ [٥٧/ ٢٩] أي «لأن يعلم»؛ (٢) وقبل فعل القسم، نحو قوله تعالى ﴿لَآ أُقْسِمُ﴾ [٧٥/ ١] أي «أقسم».

5. *Min* *Min*, namely, the preposition, is added after negation, e.g., *mā jāʾanī min aḥadin* (No one [at all] came to me), i.e., *aḥadun*.

٥. من وهي «مِنْ» جارّة تزاد بعد النفي، نحو «ما جاءني من أحد» أي «أحد».

6. *Bāʾ* The *bāʾ*, namely, the preposition, is added to the predicate of the *mā* that means *laysa*, e.g., *mā Zaydun bi-qāʾimin* (Zayd is not [at all] standing), i.e., *mā Zaydun qāʾiman*.

٦. الباء وهي باء جارّة تزاد في خبر «ما» بمعنى «ليس»، نحو «ما زيد بقائم» أي «ما زيد قائما».

7. The *Lām* The *lām*, namely, the emphatic *lām*,[89] is added in cases like His saying ﷻ, *radifa lakum* (just behind you) (Q 27:72), i.e., *radifakum*.

٧. اللام وهي لام التأكيد تزاد في نحو قوله تعالى ﴿رَدِفَ لَكُم﴾ [٢٧/ ٧٢] أي «ردفكم».

XI. Particles of Explanation

(١١) حرفا التفسير

The particles of explanation are *ay* and *an*.

وهما: أَيْ، وأَنْ.

1. *Ay* *Ay* [is used] as in *raqiya ay ṣaʿida* (Raqiya, that is, "he ascended"). The poet says,

> *tarmīnanī bi-l-ṭarfi ay anta mudhnibun*
> You hurl at me a glance, meaning "You've done wrong";
>
> *wa-taqlīnanī lākinna iyyāki lā aqlī*
> You hate me, but I will not hate you

١. أي نحو «رقى أي صعد». قال الشاعر:

> تَرْمِينَنِي بِالطَّرْفِ أَيْ أَنْتَ مُذْنِبٌ
> وَتَقْلِينَنِي لَكِنَّ إِيَّاكِ لَا أَقْلِي

2. *An* *An* is used as a particle of explanation only after a verb with the meaning of "saying," e.g., His statement ﷻ *wa-nādaynāhu an yā-Ibrāhīm* (We called to him, [meaning We said], "O Ibrāhīm!") (Q 37:104). Thus, *ay* can be used in more situations

٢. أن هي لا تجيء مفسّرة إلا بعد فعل بمعنى القول، نحو قوله تعالى ﴿وَنَٰدَيْنَٰهُ أَن يَٰٓإِبْرَٰهِيمُ﴾ [٣٧/ ١٠٤]. فـ«أي» أعمّ استعمالًا من «أن» لأنها لا تجيء مفسّرة

than *an* because *an* cannot be used as an explanatory particle after the explicit expression *qawl* nor after a verb that lacks the meaning of "saying," in contrast to *ay*. One may not say, *qultu lahu an qum* (I said to him, [meaning I said], "Stand"), nor may one say, *ḍarabtuhu an qum* (I hit him, [meaning I said], "Stand").

XII. Infinitive Particles

There are three infinitive particles: *an*, *mā*, and *anna*.

1–2. *An* and *Mā* *An* and *mā* are specific to verbal clauses because they precede a verbal clause and give it the status of an individual word that is an infinitive noun. Each requires two examples.

An example of *an* with a perfect tense verb is the statement *aʿjabanī an kharaja Zaydun* (It pleased me that Zayd left), i.e., *aʿjabanī khurūjuhu* (His leaving pleased me). An example with an imperfect tense verb is the statement *urīdu an yakhruja Zaydun* (I want Zayd to leave), i.e., *urīdu khurūjahu* (I want his leaving).

An example of *mā* with a perfect tense verb is His saying ﷻ, *ḥattā idhā ḍāqat ʿalayhim al-arḍu bimā raḥubat* (until the earth, though it is wide, closed in upon them) (Q 9:118), i.e., *bi-raḥbihā* (despite its being wide). An example with an imperfect tense verb is the statement *uḥibbu Zaydan mā yuṣallī* (I love that Zayd prays), i.e., *uḥibbu ṣalātahu* (I love his praying).

3. *Anna* *Anna* is one of the verb-like particles and an infinitive particle. It is used with a subject and predicate and gives them the status of an infinitive noun, e.g., *raʾaytu anna Zaydan qāʾimun* (I saw that Zayd was standing), i.e., *raʾaytu qiyāmahu* (I saw his standing). It is specific to nominal clauses, while its two counterparts, namely, *an* and *mā*, are specific to verbal clauses.[90]

بعد «القول» الصريح ولا بعد فعل لا يكون بمعنى القول بخلاف «أي»؛ فلا يقال «قلت له أن قمْ» ولا يقال أيضا «ضربته أن قمْ».

(١٢) الحروف المصدرية

هي ثلاثة: أَنْ، مَا، أَنَّ.

١-٢. أن وما وهما مختصّان بالجملة الفعليّة لأنّهما يدخلان على الجملة الفعليّة ويجعلانها في حكم المفرد الذي هو المصدر. لكل منهما مثالان.

مثال «أن» من الفعل الماضي قولك «أعجبني أن خرج زيد» أي «أعجبني خروجه»، ومن الفعل المضارع قولك «أريد أن يخرج زيد» أي «أريد خروجه».

ومثال «ما» من الفعل الماضي قوله تعالى ﴿حَتَّىٰٓ إِذَا ضَاقَتْ عَلَيْهِمُ ٱلْأَرْضُ بِمَا رَحُبَتْ﴾ [٩/ ١١٨] أي «برحبها»، ومثالها من الفعل المضارع قولك «أحبّ زيدًا ما يصلي» أي «أحبّ صلاته».

٣. أنّ هذه حرف من الحروف المشبّهة بالفعل مصدريّة تدخل على المبتدأ والخبر تجعلهما في حكم المصدر، نحو «رأيت أنّ زيدًا قائم» أي «رأيت قيامه». فهي مختصّة بالجملة الاسميّة كما أن أختيها أعني «أنْ» و«ما» مختصّتان بالجملة الفعليّة.

XIII. Particles of Reproach and Exhortation

The particles of reproach and exhortation are four: *lawlā, lawmā, hallā,* and *alā*. They stand at the beginning of the sentence and are used in reference to the past to express reproach for not doing an action, e.g., *lawlā faʿalta* and *lawmā faʿalta* (Would that you had done [it]), and they are used in reference to the future to express a request, e.g., *lawlā tafʿalu* and *lawmā tafʿalu* (Why don't you do [it]), i.e., *ifʿal* (Do [it]).

Lawlā and *lawmā* may also indicate that something is non-actual due to the actuality of something else, and in such a case they are specific to nouns, e.g., *lawlā ʿAliyyun la-halaka ʿUmaru* (Were it not for ʿAlī, ʿUmar would have been ruined).

(١٣) حروف التحضيض

وهي أربعة: لَوْلَا، لَوْمَا، هَلَّا، أَلَا. ولها صدر الكلام. وتدخل على الماضي للّوم على ترك الفعل نحو «لولا فعلت» و«لوما فعلت». وتدخل على المستقبل للأمر، نحو «لولا تفعل» و«لوما تفعل» أي «افعل».

«لولا» و«لوما»[٩٠] تكونان أيضا لامتناع الشيء لوجود غيره فتختصّان بالاسم، نحو «لولا عليّ لهلك عمر».

XIV. The Particle of Proximity

The particle of proximity is *qad*, and its function when used with a perfect tense verb is to indicate the recency of a past [occurrence]. One says, *qad qāmat al-ṣalātu* (The prayer has begun). *Qad* may also imply [that there was] a sense of expectation and waiting [in the listener].[91]

When used with an imperfect tense verb, it may express either fewness, e.g., *inna al-kadhūba qad yaṣduqu* (The liar may [sometimes] tell the truth), or actuality, e.g., His statement ﷻ *qad yaʿlamu Allāhu al-muʿawwiqīna* (Allah does know those among you who obstruct) (Q 33:18).

(١٤) حرف التقريب

وهو «قَدْ» ومعناه أنه يقرِّب الماضي من الحال إذا دخل على الماضي. تقول «قد قامت الصلاة». وفيه معنى التوقّع والانتظار.

وأنه تارة يقلّل إذا دخل على المضارع نحو «إنّ الكذوب قد يصدق» وتارة يحقق نحو قوله تعالى ﴿قَدْ يَعْلَمُ ٱللَّهُ ٱلْمُعَوِّقِينَ﴾ [٣٣/ ١٨].

XV. Particles of Futurity

There are four particles of futurity: the *sīn, sawfa, lā,* and *lan*. Those who count *in* as a particle of futurity are mistaken; its function is to negate the present, as mentioned in the discussion of the negative particles in the fourth category.

(١٥) حروف الاستقبال

وهي أربعة: سين، سوف، لَا، لَنْ. ومن عدّ «إن» من حروف الاستقبال فقد سها فإنّها لنفي الحال كما مرّ في بحث حروف النفي في الصنف الرابع.

1–2. The *Sīn* and *Sawfa* The *sīn* and *sawfa* are used [as in] *sa-yaʿlamu* and *sawfa yaʿlamu* (He will know). *Sawfa* implies additional delay.

١-٢. سين وسوف نحو «سيعلم» و«سوف يعلم». وفي «سوف» دلالة على زيادة التأخير.

3–4. *Lā* and *Lan* *Lā* and *lan* negate the future, e.g., *lā yadhhabu Zaydun ghadan* (Zayd is not going tomorrow) and *lan yaqraʾa* (He will not recite).[92] *Lan* implies additional prolongation.

٣-٤. لا ولن وهما نافيتان في المستقبل، نحو «لا يذهب زيد غدًا» و«لن يقرأ». وفي «لن» دلالة على زيادة التأخير.

XVI. Interrogative Particles

(١٦) حرفا الاستفهام

The interrogative particles are the *hamza* and *hal*. They stand at the beginning of the sentence, and they may be used with either type of sentence: nominal, e.g., *a-Zaydun qāʾimun* and *hal Zaydun qāʾimun* (Is Zayd standing?), or verbal, e.g., *a-qāma Zaydun* and *hal qama Zaydun* (Did Zayd stand?).

The usage of the *hamza* is more inclusive than that of *hal*, meaning that the *hamza* can be used in places that *hal* cannot be not used:

1. One says, *a-Zaydun qāma* (Did Zayd stand?), but does not say, *hal Zaydun qāma*, because when the predicate is a verb in a nominal sentence, it is valid to use the *hamza* and invalid to use *hal*. This applies in the same way that it is invalid to use *qad*, for *hal* originally means *qad*.
2. One says, *a-Zaydun ʿindaka am ʿAmrun* (Is Zayd with you or ʿAmr?), but not *hal…*, because *hal* is for asking about attributes, not entities, and the question in this case is about specifying an entity.
3. One says, *a-thumma idhā mā waqaʿa* (Is it then, when it comes to pass…) (Q 10:51), as in Sūrat Yūnus; *a-fa-man kāna ʿalā bayyinatin* (What then of the one who stands upon a clear proof) (Q 11:17), as in [Sūrat] Hūd; and *a-wa-man kāna maytan fa-aḥyaynāhu* (Is then he who was dead and to whom We

وهما الهمزة و«هَلْ». ولهما صدر الكلام. وتدخلان على الجملتين الاسميّة نحو «أزيد قائم» و«هل زيد قائم؟»، الفعلية نحو «أقام زيد» و«هل قام زيد؟».

والهمزة أعمّ تصرّفًا من «هل» أي تستعمل الهمزة في مواضع لا يستعمل «هل» فيها:

١- تقول «أزيد قام» ولا تقول «هل زيد قام»، لأن الخبر إذا كان في الجملة الاسميّة فعلًا جاز استعمال الهمزة ولم يجز استعمال «هل» كما لم يجز استعمال «قد» لأنها في الأصل بمعنى «قد».

٢- تقول «أزيد عندك أم عمرو؟» دون «هل...»، لأنّها للسؤال عن الصفة لا الذات وهنا السؤال عن تعيين الذات.

٣- تقول ﴿أَثُمَّ إِذَا مَا وَقَعَ﴾ [١٠/ ٥١] كما في سورة يونس، ﴿أَفَمَن كَانَ عَلَىٰ بَيِّنَةٍ﴾ [١١/ ١٧] كما في هود، ﴿أَوَمَن كَانَ مَيْتًا فَأَحْيَيْنَاهُ﴾ [٦/ ١٢٢] كما

gave life...) (Q 6:122), as in [Sūrat] al-Anʿām, but one may not say *hal*... [in such situations]. This is because the *hamza* can be used with conjunctions and implies the element to which the conjunction is made after the *hamza*, which is not the case with *hal* because it is weak as an interrogative particle. In fact, the position of Sībawayh[93] is that the *hamza* is the sole interrogative particle and that *hal* means *qad*.

في الأنعام دون «هل...»، لأن الهمزة تدخل على حروف العطف وتقدّر المعطوف عليه بعد الهمزة بخلاف «هل» فإنها ضعيفة في باب الاستفهام. حتى إن مذهب سيبويه إن حرف الاستفهام هو الهمزة فقط وإن «هل» بمعنى «قد».

4. One says, *a-taḍribu Zaydan wa-huwa akhūka* (Do you hit Zayd while he is your brother?) but not *hal*... because *hal* is specific to imperfect tense verbs expressing the future, and here the present is intended.

٤- وتقول «أتضرب زيدًا وهو أخوك؟» دون «هل...»، لأن «هل» مخصّصة للفعل المضارع بالاستقبال وهنا المراد به الحال.

The *hamza* may be elided when there is some indication of its elision, e.g., to ask, *Zaydun ʿindaka am ʿAmrun* (Zayd is with you or ʿAmr?). The poet says,

> *la-ʿamruka mā adrī wa-in kuntu dāriyan*
> By your life, I do not know, though [there is much] I know,
>
> *bi-sabʿin ramayna al-jamra am bi-thamāni*
> Whether they pelted the pillar with seven [pebbles] or eight

وقد تحذف الهمزة عند الدلالة على حذفها، كقولك «زيد عندك أم عمرو؟». وقال الشاعر:

> لَعَمْـرُكَ مَـا أَدْرِي وَإِنْ كُنْـتُ دَارِيًـا
>
> بِسَبْـعٍ رَمَيْـنَ الـجَمْـرَ أَمْ بِثَـمَانِ

XVII. Conditional Particles

(١٧) حروف الشرط

There are three conditional particles: *in*, *law*, and *ammā*. They stand at the beginning of the sentence.

وهي ثلاثة: إِنْ، لَوْ، أَمَّا. ولها صدر الكلام.

1. *In* *In* is for the future even when used with a perfect tense verb, e.g., *in tukrimnī ukrimka* and *in akramtanī akramtuka* (If you honor me, I will honor you). The meaning of these examples is the same, i.e., "If your honoring of me occurs in the future, then my honoring of you will also occur in the future."

١. إن وهي للزمان المستقبل ولو دخل على الفعل الماضي، نحو «إن تكرمني أكرمك» و«إن أكرمتني أكرمتك». ومعنى كلا المثالين واحد أي «إن وقع منك إكرامي في الاستقبال وقع مني أيضا إكرامك فيه».

2. *Law* *Law* is for the past even when used with an imperfect tense verb, e.g., *law ḍarabta ḍarabtu* and *law taḍribu aḍribu* (Had you hit, I would have hit). The meaning of these examples is the same, i.e., "Had your hitting of me occurred in the past, then my hitting of you would have also occurred in the past." *Law* may also be used, like *in*, for the future, e.g., His statement ﷻ *wa-la-amatun mu'minatun khayrun min mushrikatin wa-law aʿjabatkum* (Truly a believing slave woman is better than an idolatress, even if she would please you) (Q 2:221).

٢. لـو وهي للزمـان الماضي وإن دخـل على الفعـل المضـارع، نحو «لو ضربت ضربـت» و«لو تضرب أضرب». كلاهمـا بمـعنى واحـد أي «لو وقـع منـك ضربٌ في الماضي فقـد وقع منّي ضربـك أيضا فيـه». وقد تسـتعمل كـ«إنْ» في المسـتقبل، نحـو قـوله تعـالى ﴿وَلَأَمَـةٌ مُّؤْمِنَـةٌ خَيْرٌ مِّن مُّشْرِكَـةٍ وَلَـوْ أَعْجَبَتْكُـمْ﴾ [٢/ ٢٢١].

The *condition clause* must be verbal. As for the *result clause*, it should be verbal by default; sometimes, however, it is nominal, in which case the *fā'* must be used, e.g., *in jā'a Zaydun fa-lahu al-faḍlu* (If Zayd comes, then that is gracious of him). When both clauses are verbal, imperfect tense verbs are necessarily jussive, e.g., *in tukrimnī ukrimka* (If you honor me, I will honor you). However, if the conditional verb is a perfect tense verb, e.g., *in akramtanī ukrim(u)ka* (If you honor me, I will honor you), then [an imperfect tense verb in the result clause] may be either jussive or indicative, though the jussive is more common.

جملـة الشرط يجـب أن تـكـون فعليّـة؛ وأمـا جملـة الجـواب فالأصـل فيها أن تـكـون فعليّة إلا أنهـا قد تجيء اسـميّة فيلزمهـا الفاء، نحـو «إن جـاء زيد فلـه الفضل». وإذا كانـت الجملتـان فعلـيتين فالجزم في المضـارع واجب نحـو «إن تـكـرمني أكرمـك»، إلا إذا كان فعـل الشرط ماضيًـا نحـو «إن أكرمـتني أكرمـك» فالجـزم والرفـع فيه جائـزان إلا أن الجـزم أكثر.

A *fā'* must introduce the result clause in six circumstances:

1. when the result clause is a nominal clause, e.g., *in ji'tanī fa-anta mukramun* (If you come to me, then you will be honored).
2. when the result clause is a perfect tense verb and *qad* precedes it either (a) verbally, e.g., *in akramtanī fa-qad akramtuka* (If you honor me, then I have honored you), or (b) implicitly, e.g., His saying ﷻ, *in kāna qamīṣuhu qudda min qubulin fa-ṣadaqat* ("If his shirt is torn from the front, then she has spoken the truth") (Q 12:26), i.e., *fa-qad ṣadaqat*.
3. when the result clause is imperative, e.g., *in akramaka Zaydun fa-akrimhu* (If Zayd honors you, then honor him).

يجب دخول الفاء في الجواب في ستّة مواضع:

١- إذا كان الجـزاء جملـة اسـميّة، نحـو «إن جئتـني فأنـت مكـرم».

٢- أو كان الجـزاء ماضيًـا ودخلـه «قـدْ» لفظًـا نحـو «إن أكرمتـني فقـد أكرمتـك» أو تقديـرًا نحـو قـوله تعـالى ﴿إِن كَانَ قَمِيصُـهُۥ قُـدَّ مِـن قُبُـلٍ فَصَدَقَـتْ﴾ [١٢/ ٢٦] أي «فقـدْ صدقـت».

٣- أو كان الجـزاء أمـرًا، نحـو «إن أكرمـك زيـد فأكرمْـه».

4. when it is prohibitive, e.g., *in akramaka fa-lā tuhinhu* (If he honors you, then do not disgrace him).
5. when it is an indeclinable verb, e.g., *in akramta Zaydan fa-ʿasā an yukrimaka* (If you honor Zayd, then perhaps he will honor you).
6. when it is negative by means other than *lā*, e.g., *in akramta Zaydan fa-lan yuhīnaka* (or *fa-mā yuhīnuka*) (If you honor Zayd, he will not [*or* he does not] disgrace you).

The rule is that if the conditional particle has an effect [on the result clause], as in the elision of a short vowel, e.g., *in tukrimnī ukrimka* (If you honor me, I will honor you), or the changing of the meaning to the future, e.g., *in akramtanī akramtuka* (If you honor me, I will honor you), then the use of the *fāʾ* is invalid; otherwise, it is necessary, e.g., *in tajiʾnī fa-l-ikrāmu lāzimun* (If you come to me, then honoring [you] is obligatory).

3. *Ammā* *Ammā* contains the meaning of a condition, e.g., *ammā Zaydun fa-munṭaliqun* (As for Zayd, he is departing), the original form of which is *mahmā yakun min shayʾin fa-Zaydun munṭaliqun* (Whatever the case may be, Zayd is departing). For *mahmā* is originally *māmā*; the *alif* of the first *mā* is converted to a *hāʾ*, and it becomes *mahmā*. The original form of *māmā* is a *mā* to which another *mā* is added for emphasis such that it becomes *māmā*.

٤- أو كان نهيًا، نحو «إن أكرمك فلا تهنْه».

٥- أو كان فعلًا غير متصرّف، نحو «إن أكرمت زيدًا فعسى أن يكرمك».

٦- أو كان منفيًّا بغير «لا»، نحو «إن أكرمت زيدًا فلن... أو ...فما يهينك».

الضابط إن كان لحرف الشرط تأثير بنحو حذف الحركة نحو «إن تكرمْني أكرمْك» أو قلب المعنى إلى الاستقبال نحو «إن أكرمتني أكرمتك» فلا يجوز الفاء وإلا فواجب نحو «إن تجئني فالإكرام لازم».

٣. أما فيه معنى الشرط، نحو «أمّا زيد فمنطلق». أصله «مهما يكن من شيء فزيد منطلق». فـ«مهما» أصله «ماما» فقلبت ألف «ما» الأولى هاءً فصار «مهما». وكان أصل «ماما» «ما» زيدت عليها «ما» أخرى للتأكيد فصارت «ماما».

XVIII. Particles Expressing the Reason

The particles expressing the reason are *kay* and the *lām*, e.g., *jiʾtuka kay tuʿṭiyanī mālan* (I came to you so that you would give me wealth) and *zurtuka li-tukrimanī* (I visited you so that you would honor me).

(١٨) حرفا التعليل

وهما «كي» واللام، نحو «جئتك كي تعطيني مالًا» و«زرتك لتكرمني».

XIX. The Particle of Rebuke

The particle of rebuke, or the *particle of reprimand*, namely, *kallā*, [is used] as in your telling someone who says something you deny, like "So-and-so hates you," *kallā* (Absolutely not!), i.e., "Keep back and restrain yourself from saying such a thing."

(١٩) حرف الردع

أي حرف الزجر وهو «كَلَّا»، كقولك لمن قال شيئًا تنكره كأن قال «فلان يبغضك» «كلّا» أي «ارتدعْ وانزجرْ عن هذا القول».

XX. *Lām* Particles

There are eight kinds of *lām* particles: (1) the definite *lām*, (2) the *lām* of oath, (3) the *lām* that anticipates an oath, (4) the *lām* in response to *law* and *lawlā*, (5) the imperative *lām*, (6) the beginning *lām*, (7) the *lām* that differentiates the lightened *in* from the negative *in*, and (8) the prepositional *lām*.

1. The Definite *Lām* The definite *lām* is the vowelless *lām* that is attached to indefinite nouns and makes them grammatically definite to signify either a category [or a specific referent. An example of the former is the statement *ahlaka al-nāsa al-dīnāru wa-l-dirhamu* (Dinars and dirhams have destroyed people), and an example of the latter is] the statement *faʿala al-rajulu kadhā wa-kadhā* (The man did this and that), which one would say in reference to a man who is known to both oneself and the addressee.[94]

2. The *Lām* of Oath The *lām* of oath is [used] as in *wa-Allāhi la-afʿalanna kadhā* (By Allah, I will certainly do such and such!).

3. The *Lām* That Anticipates an Oath The *lām* that anticipates an oath is [used] as in *la-in akramtanī la-ukrimannaka* ([By Allah], if you honor me, I will honor you).

(٢٠) اللامات

وهي ثمانية أنواع: (١) لام التعريف، (٢) لام القسم، (٣) اللام الموطئة للقسم، (٤) لام جواب لو ولولا، (٥) لام الأمر، (٦) لام الابتداء، (٧) اللام الفارقة بين «إن» المخفّفة وبين «إن» النافية، (٨) لام الجر.

١. لام التعريف وهي اللام الساكنة التي تدخل على الاسم النكرة فتعرّفه إما تعريف جنس [أو تعريف عهد. الأول نحو قولك «أهلك الناسَ الدينارُ والدرهمُ»، والثاني] نحو قولك «فعل الرجل كذا وكذا» تقول ذلك لرجل معهود بينك وبين مخاطبك.

٢. لام القسم نحو «والله لأفعلنَّ كذا».

٣. اللام الموطّئة للقسم نحو «لإن أكرمتني لأكرمنَّك[٢٥]».

4. The *Lām* in the Result Clause of *Law* and *Lawlā* The *lām* in the result clause of *law* and *lawlā* is [used] as in His statement ﷻ *law nashāʾu la-jaʿalnāhu ḥuṭāman* (Had We willed, we would have turned it to chaff) (Q 56:65) and as in *lawlā ʿAliyyun la-halaka ʿUmaru* (Were it not for ʿAlī, ʿUmar would have been ruined).

٤. لام جواب لو ولولا نحو قوله تعالى ﴿لَوْ نَشَآءُ لَجَعَلْنَٰهُ حُطَٰمًا﴾ [٥٦/ ٦٥] ونحو «لولا علي لهلك عمر».

5. The Imperative *Lām* The imperative *lām* is [used] as in *li-yaḍrib Zaydun* (Let Zayd hit).

٥. لام الأمر نحو «ليضرب زيد».

6. The Beginning *Lām* The beginning *lām* is [used] as in *la-Zaydun qāʾimun* (Truly, Zayd is standing).

٦. لام الابتداء نحو «لزيد قائم».

7. The *Lām* That Differentiates the Lightened *In* from the Negative *In* The *lām* that differentiates the lightened *in* with *kasr* from the negative *in* is [used] as in *in Zaydun la-qāʾimun* (Indeed Zayd is standing).

٧. اللام الفارقة بين «إن» المكسورة المخفّفة وبين «إن» النافية نحو «إن زيد لقائم».

8. The Prepositional *Lām* The prepositional *lām* is [used] as in *al-mālu li-Zaydin* (The wealth is Zayd's) and *jiʾtuka li-tukrimanī* (I came to you so that you would honor me).[95]

٨. لام الجر نحو «المال لزيد» و«جئتك لتكرمني».

XXI. The Vowelless *Tāʾ* of Femininity

(٢١) تاء التأنيث الساكنة

The vowelless *tāʾ* of femininity is the *tāʾ* that attaches to the end of a perfect tense verb, e.g., *qad qāmat al-ṣalātu* (The prayer has begun) and *ḍarabat Hindun* (Hind hit). Its function is to signal from the outset that the subject is feminine.

وهي التاء اللاحقة بالفعل الماضي نحو «قد قامتْ الصلاة» و«ضربتْ هند». ودخولها للإيذان من أول الأمر بأن المسند إليه مؤنّث.

XXII. The Emphatic *Nūn*

(٢٢) النون المؤكّدة

The emphatic *nūn* is of two types: (1) heavy and vowelized with *fatḥ*, e.g., the statement *wa-Llāhi la-aḍribannaka* (By Allah, I will hit you!), and (2)

وهي على ضربين ثقيلة مفتوحة كقولك «والله لأضربَنَّك» وخفيفة ساكنة كقولك «والله لأضربَنْك». والثقيلة

light and vowelless, e.g., the statement *wa-Llāhi la-aḍribanka*. The heavy type is more emphatic and can be used in more situations because it can be used with dual and plural verbs, e.g., *wa-Llāhi la-taʾkulānni* (By Allah, you [d.] will eat!) or *wa-Llāhi la-taʾkulunna* (By Allah, you [pl.] will eat!); the lightened type cannot, to avoid the impermissible convergence of two vowelless letters.[96]

Only future verbs that contain the meaning of a request[97] can be emphasized with the emphatic *nūn*. This includes (1) imperatives, e.g., *iḍribanna* (Do hit); (2) prohibitives, e.g., *lā takhrujanna* (Do not leave); (3) interrogatives, e.g., *hal taḍribanna* (Will you hit?); (4) suggestions and invitations, e.g., *a-lā tanzilanna binā* (Will you not stay with us?); (5) expressions of wishful desire, e.g., *laytaka taqʿudanna* (If only you would sit!); and (6) oaths, e.g., *bi-Llāhi la-afʿalanna* (By Allah, I will do [it]!).

When it converges with a vowelless letter after itself, the lightened vowelless *nūn* is elided, e.g., *lā taḍriba ʾbnaka* (Do not hit your son). This is in contrast to nunation, which is vowelized with *kasr* and not elided when it converges with a vowelless letter, e.g., *Zaydun-i ʾl-ʿālimu ʿindanā* (Zayd, the scholar, is with us).

أبلغ في التأكيد وأكثر موقعًا فإنّها تقع في فعل الاثنين والجماعة نحو «والله لتأكلانّ» أو «والله لتأكلُنَّ» دون الخفيفة لئلّا يلزم التقاء الساكنين على غير حدّه.

ولا يؤكّد بنون التأكيد إلا فعل مستقبل فيه معنى الطلب كالأمر نحو «اضربنّ» والنهي نحو «لا تخرجنّ» والاستفهام نحو «هل تضربنّ؟» والعرض نحو «ألا تنزلنّ بنا» والتمنّي نحو «ليتك تقعدنّ» والقسم نحو «بالله لأفعلنّ».

النون المؤكّدة الخفيفة إذا لقيت ساكنًا بعده حذفت الخفيفة نحو «لا تضربَ ابنك» بخلاف التنوين فإنه إذا لقي ساكنًا تحرّك بالكسر ولا يحذف نحو «زيدٌ العالم عندنا».

XXIII. The *Hāʾ* of Pause

The *hāʾ* of pause is the *hāʾ* that can be added to any word that [ends with] a non-inflectional short vowel. It is added specifically when one pauses [after pronouncing the word], e.g., *thammah* (there), *ḥayyahalah* (Hasten!), *māliyah* (my wealth), and *sulṭāniyah* (my power).[98] It is always vowelless; vowelizing it is an error.

(٢٣) هاء السكت

وهي الهاء التي تزاد في كل متحرّك حركته غير إعرابيّة تزاد للوقف خاصّة، نحو «ثمّه» و«حيّهله» و«ماليه» و«سلطانيه». ولا تكون إلا ساكنة وتحريكها لحن.

XXIV. Nunation

Nunation is a vowelless *nūn* that follows the short vowel of the end letter without the function of emphasizing verbs. It is of six types.

[1. Nunation of Establishment] The first type is the nunation of establishment, which indicates that the noun is well established in its nominal nature. This applies to every nunation attached to a fully declinable noun, e.g., the nunation in *Zaydun̲* and *rajulun̲* (man).

[2. Indefinite Nunation] The second type is the indefinite nunation, or any nunation that indicates that the [indeclinable] noun to which it is added is indefinite, e.g., when one says, *ṣahin̲* (Silence!), i.e., "Be silent in some manner for some time." When made vowelless [as *ṣah*], the meaning becomes "Be silent now!"

[3. Nunation of Compensation] The third type is the nunation that compensates for the *muḍāf ilayhi*, that is, any nunation that attaches to a *muḍāf* when the *muḍāf ilayhi* is omitted, e.g., when one says *yawma'idhin* (on that day), i.e., *yawma idh kāna kadhā* (on the day when such and such was so).[99]

[4. Counterpart Nunation] The fourth type is counterpart nunation, or any nunation that attaches to the sound feminine plural form as a counterpart to the *nūn* that occurs in the sound masculine plural form, e.g., the nunation in *muslimātin̲* (Muslims [f.]).

[5. Nunation of Nasalization] The fifth type is the nunation of nasalization,[100] or any nunation that takes the place of a long vowel in an unbound metrical rhyme, that is, one in which the last consonant is vowelized, e.g., the poet's saying,

> *aqillī al-lawma ʿādhila wa-l-ʿitāban̲*
> Reduce your censure, O critic, and reproof,

(٢٤) التنوين

وهو نون ساكنة تتبع حركة الآخر لا لتأكيد الفعل. وهو على ستّة أقسام.

[١. تنوين التمكّن] أحدها تنوين التمكّن أي الدالّ على مكانيّة الاسم في الاسميّة، وهو كل تنوين لحق الاسم المعرب المنصرف، كالتنوين في «زيدٌ» و«رجلٌ».

[٢. تنوين التنكير] الثاني تنوين التنكير، وهو كل تنوين يدلّ على أن الاسم الذي دخل عليه نكرة، كقولك «صهٍ» أي «اسكت سكوتًا ما في وقت ما». وإذا أسكنت فالمعنى «افعل السكوت الآن».

[٣. تنوين العوض] الثالث تنوين العوض من المضاف إليه، وهو كل تنوين لحق مضافًا عند حذف المضاف إليه، كقولك «يومئذٍ» أي «يوم إذ كان كذا».

[٤. تنوين المقابلة] الرابع تنوين المقابلة، وهو كل تنوين لحق جمع المؤنّث السالم في مقابلة النون الواقعة في الجمع المذكّر السالم، كالتنوين في «مسلماتٍ».

[٥. تنوين الترنّم] الخامس تنوين الترنّم، وهو كل تنوين جعل مكان حرف المدّ واللين في القوافي المطلقة أي التي حرف الآخر فيها متحرّك، كما في قول الشاعر:

> أَقِلِّي اللَّوْمَ عَاذِلَ وَالعِتَابَنْ

wa-qūlī in aṣabtu la-qad aṣāban̲
And if I am right, say, "He is indeed right"

The last consonant here is the *bāʾ*.

وَقُـــوِلِي إِنْ أَصَبْـتُ لَقَــدْ أَصَـابَـــنْ

حرف الآخر هنا الباء.

[**6. Nunation of Prolongation**] The sixth is the nunation of prolongation, or any nunation attached for the sake of a quavering prolongation of the voice in a fettered metrical rhyme, that is, one in which the last consonant is vowelless, e.g., another poet's saying,

wa-qātimi al-aʿmāqi khāwī al-mukhtaraqn̲
How many an abyss of dark depths,
empty passes,

mushtabihi al-aʿlāmi lammāʿi al-khafaqn̲
Obscure traces, flashes of the
shifting mirage

[**٦. التنويـن الغـالي**] السـادس التنويـن الغـالي، وهو كل تنوين لحـق قافية مقيّـدة للترنّم أي التي حـرف الآخر فيها سـاكن، كما في قـول الآخر:

وَقَاتِـــمِ الأَعْمَـــاقِ خَـــاوِي المُـــخْتَرَقْنْ

مُشْتَبِـــهِ الأَعْلَامِ لَـمَّـــاعِ الخَـــفَقْنْ

❁ ❁ ❁

By the assistance of Allah ﷻ, the treatise entitled *The Tranquil Sea: On the Science of Grammar* is complete. May Allah ﷻ by His grace and generosity render it of benefit to us and all believers. Allah! "Take us not to task if we forget or err!" (Q 2:286). "Glory to your Lord, Lord of Might, transcending what they describe! Peace be upon the messengers. And praise to Allah, Lord of the worlds" (Q 37:180–82). By His permission ﷻ, the third treatise follows, entitled *The Ancient Abundance: On the Science of Logic*.

Sunday, 13 Rabīʿ al-Awwal 1428 AH

تمّت بعون الله تعالى الرسالة المسمّاة بالبحر الصحو في علم النحو جعلها الله تعالى بمنّه وكرمه نافعة لنا ولسائر المؤمنين. اللّهم لا تؤاخذنا إن نسينا أو أخطأنا. ﴿سُبْحَٰنَ رَبِّكَ رَبِّ ٱلْعِزَّةِ عَمَّا يَصِفُونَ ۝١٨٠ وَسَلَٰمٌ عَلَى ٱلْمُرْسَلِينَ ۝١٨١ وَٱلْحَمْدُ لِلَّهِ رَبِّ ٱلْعَٰلَمِينَ﴾ [٣٧/ ١٨٠-١٨٢]. وتليها بإذنه تعالى الرسالة الثالثة المسمّاة الفيض العتيق في علم المنطق.

١٣ ربيع الأول سنة ١٤٢٨هـ يوم الأحد[٢٦]

NOTES TO TREATISE II

1 The method of Muḥammad al-Birkawī (or Meḥmed Birgevī) (d. 981/1573) is outlined in his *al-ʿAwāmil* and his *Iẓhār al-asrār*, and the method of Maḥmūd b. ʿUmar al-Zamakhsharī (d. 538/1144) is outlined in his *al-Mufaṣṣal fī ṣanʿat al-iʿrāb*.

2 The abstract governor in this case is the fact that the subject and predicate are allowed to stand in a relationship of predication (*isnād*) in the absence of any expressed governors (*ʿawāmil lafẓiyya*) that would exercise their governing influence over the pair. Birgevī, *Iẓhār al-asrār*, 84.

3 The abstract governor in this case is the fact that, in the absence of any expressed governors that would make it subjunctive (*manṣūb*) or jussive (*majzūm*), the imperfect tense verb has a status or place like that of a noun: in this example sentence, *yarḥamu* is comparable to the active participle *rāhimun*. See Birgevī, *Iẓhār al-asrār*, 84.

4 The qualification "as such" (*muṭlaqan*) is meant to include both the perfect tense and the imperfect tense.

5 The three times are the past, the present, and the future. These are different from the two *tenses*, the perfect (*māḍī*) and the imperfect (*muḍāriʿ*), which are *forms* of the verb. The perfect tense is a form that usually signifies the past, and the imperfect tense is a form that usually signifies either the present or the future.

6 This qualifying phrase clarifies that the Arabic word *fiʿl* here is not meant in the sense of the grammatical category "verb" but rather in the sense of the real occurrence, the real "doing" or "action" that is signified.

7 "Its" active verb is the active verb that shares the active participle's lexical root and thus corresponds in meaning. In the example that follows, the corresponding active verb is *yuḥriqu* (it burns).

8 *Ḥilm* could also be understood as forbearance or deliberation.

9 The *muḍāf* is the first of two elements in an *iḍāfa* construction. There are two kinds of *iḍāfa*: the attributive (*maʿnawiyya*) and the nonattributive (*lafẓiyya*). In attributive *iḍāfa*, the first element is attributed to the second element—that is, the second element determines the first element—in a specific relationship, particularly, a relationship that could be conveyed by the *lām*, *min*, or *fī*, which are prepositions. In the construction *ʿibādatu Allāhi* (worship of Allah), for instance, the worship is attributed to Allah, and thereby it is determined what kind of worship is being talked about; this could also have been conveyed by the *lām* (i.e., *ʿibādatun li-l-Llāhi*). In nonattributive *iḍāfa*, a participle or participial exercises its verbal government over another word in the abbreviated form of an *iḍāfa*. Both types of *iḍāfa* are discussed in more detail in the second part of this treatise.

10 A *mann*, also called a *manā*, is a measure of weight that is equal to approximately two pounds.

11 These are examples of quasi-verbal nouns (*asmāʾ al-afʿāl*), whose import, or signification, is entirely that of verbs. *Hayhāta* has the import of the perfect tense verb *baʿuda* (is distant), as indicated in the text, and *tarāki* has the import of the imperative verb *utruk* (abandon).

12 In this case, *rāḥatun* (comfort) is the agent of the phrase *fī al-dunyā* (in the world), which

contains the import of the implicit verb *ḥaṣala* (exists). Gelibolī, *Tuḥfat al-ikhwān*, 250.

13 In this case, *khuluquhu* (his character) is the agent of the relational noun *muḥammadiyyan*, which contains the import of the implicit verb *yattaṣif* (adorns itself). Gelibolī, *Tuḥfat al-ikhwān*, 251.

14 The purpose of this relatively long gloss of the word *wuḍiʿat* on its first occurrence in the text is to call the reader's attention to the fact that this is a technical term. The concept of *waḍʿ*, or the "assignment" of a meaning or function to a linguistic expression or form, permeates this treatise. For more detail, see Treatise IV, which is entirely devoted to the theory of *waḍʿ*.

15 The reader will find one or more meanings for prepositions and other particles provided below, but the text does not aim to be exhaustive. Many prepositions take on quite a number of different meanings with context. See Gelibolī, *Tuḥfat al-ikhwān*, 101–49. For a fairly comprehensive English-language exposition of the Arabic prepositions, see Wright, *Arabic Grammar*, 2:129–93.

16 *Kaymah* is composed of the two words *kay* and *mā*, the latter becoming *mah* in this compound. The preposition is the first word, *kay*.

17 *Inna* is a very common particle that, in most cases, gives sentences a level of emphasis too subtle to be conveyed in an English word. We translate it as "truly" here for the sake of clarity.

18 The following two particles are set apart because they are not considered verb-like particles in the full sense. For more detail, see Gelibolī, *Tuḥfat al-ikhwān*, 165.

19 The agent is considered the fundamental nominative. See Gelibolī, *Tuḥfat al-ikhwān*, 266.

20 Although we have translated this as a declarative (*khabarī*) sentence, it would be typical for a sentence like this one to be meant in the non-declarative (*inshāʾī*) sense of a prayer, as in "May Allah ﷻ have mercy on the repentant one."

21 Or of any of the other verb-like particles.

22 That is, a *fatḥa*, *kasra*, *alif*, or *yāʾ*, as discussed in Chapter 3. See al-Jāmī, *al-Fawāʾid*, 181.

23 The corresponding particle, e.g., *illā*, is called the *exceptive particle*.

24 That is, a *fatḥa*, *kasra*, or *yāʾ*, as discussed in the Chapter 3. See al-Jāmī, *al-Fawāʾid*, 301.

25 Strictly speaking, the appositive is the *conjunct* (*maʿṭūf*) that is conjoined to the primarily governed expression through one of these ten particles. Gelibolī, *Tuḥfat al-ikhwān*, 315.

26 When *lākin* conjoins words or simple expressions, as in the example sentence, it affirms for the second element something that was negated of the first element. When it conjoins complete clauses, one clause is affirmative and the other negative, e.g., *jāʾanī Zaydun lākin ʿAmrun lam yajiʾ* (Zayd came to me, but ʿAmr did not come). Gelibolī, *Tuḥfat al-ikhwān*, 326–27.

27 For the difference between these three types of substitution, see the section on appositives in Chapter 4 (the first chapter of the second method in this treatise), pp. 147–48.

28 Being completely inflectable entails having a distinct inflection for each of the three grammatical states. Hence, triptotes are "complete," while diptotes are "incomplete": in a diptote, two of the three states must share an inflection.

29 Birgevī's *al-ʿAwāmil* lists *ḥamūhā*, with a feminine pronoun, instead; Gelibolī comments that the word refers only to the in-laws of the woman. Gelibolī, *Tuḥfat al-ikhwān*, 362.

30 The text provides examples only for the third-person masculine dual (*yafʿalāni*). The reader can construct examples for the dual in the second-person masculine and feminine and the third-person feminine (*tafʿalāni*) as

well as for the plural in the third-person masculine (*yafʿalūna*) and the second-person masculine (*tafʿalūna*) and for the singular in the second-person feminine (*tafʿalīna*).

31 This applies to all of the nine types of inflectable expressions listed just above.

32 The inflection is implicit when the expression is inherently inflectable but something inhibits the inflection's verbalization. This includes the following: (1) words that end with an *alif*, e.g., *al-ʿaṣā* (the stick) and *yakhshā* (he fears); (2) nouns made *muḍāf* to the first-person *yāʾ*, e.g., *baytī* (my house); (3) words that are quoted in the way that they were initially expressed, e.g., if one were told, *ḍarabta Zaydan* (You hit Zayd), one might respond, *mā Zaydan* (What is "Zaydan"?), leaving the word *Zaydan* in the accusative; (4) words that end in a *yāʾ* preceded by a *kasra*, e.g., *al-qāḍī* (the judge), even if the *yāʾ* has been elided, e.g., *qāḍin* (a judge); (5) verbs that end in a *wāw* preceded by a *ḍamma* with no attached pronoun, e.g., *yadʿū* (he calls); (6) words that end in a long vowel before a word that begins with a connective *hamza*, e.g., *ghulāmā ibnika* (your son's two boys); and (7) words whose ending is left vowelless in pause at the end of one's speaking, e.g., *jāʾa Zayd* (Zayd came). Birgevī, *Iẓhār al-asrār*, 128–31; Gelibolī, *Tuḥfat al-ikhwān*, 385–89. Compare al-Mīlānī, *Sharḥ al-Mughnī*, 160–61.

33 The inflection is positional in two cases. The first case is when the expression is inherently uninflectable; in other words, the expression occupies a role in the sentence that *would* give it a certain inflection if it were another kind of expression. This includes indeclinable nouns, e.g., *jāʾa <u>hāʾulāʾi</u>* (These came), where the pronoun *hāʾulāʾi* (these) has the position of a nominative agent, and it includes clauses, e.g., *Zaydun <u>abūhu ʿālimun</u>* (Zayd's father is a scholar), where the clause *abūhu ʿālimun* (his father is a scholar) has the position of a nominative predicate. The second case is when the expression *is* inherently inflectable, but it cannot display the inflection because its ending is "preoccupied" with another inflection. In the sentence *marartu bi-Zaydin* (I passed by Zayd), the word *Zayd* has the position of an accusative in relation to the verb, but it cannot display the accusative inflection because it is "preoccupied" with the genitive inflection on account of the preposition. Birgevī, *Iẓhār al-asrār*, 132; Gelibolī, *Tuḥfat al-ikhwān*, 389–91.

34 We have omitted the text's qualification "with the *tāʾ*," which was too restrictive and likely incomplete. Verbal femininity (*taʾnīth lafẓī*), the kind marked by a *tāʾ* or an *alif*, is not the only type of femininity that causes partial declinability. Nonverbal femininity (*taʾnīth maʿnawī*) also counts; in fact, what makes *Zaynab* (the example just above) partially declinable is that it is a feminine proper name. See al-Mīlānī, *Sharḥ al-Mughnī*, 162–63. One exception is the case of a three-letter feminine name whose second letter is vowelless, e.g., *Hind*; such names may be treated either as fully declinable (*Hindun*) or as partially declinable (*Hindu*). Birgevī, *Iẓhār al-asrār*, 126.

35 To demonstrate how this applies to the examples above, *Zaynab* and *Ṭalḥa* are proper names and feminine, *aḥmar* signifies a quality and has the pattern of a verb, *Aḥmad* is a proper name and has the pattern of a verb, *ʿUmar* is a proper name and underwent morphological change, *Maʿdī-karib* is a proper name and a compound noun, *Ibrāhīm* is a proper name and originally non-Arabic, and *ʿImrān* and *ʿUthmān* are proper names with the *alif* and *nūn*.

36 The principal noun is enclosed in brackets in these examples to highlight the fact that the main idea of the sentence involves the substitute in place of the principal noun. English does not utilize substitution in this way. It should be noted that the case of the English

sentence "I saw Zayd, your brother" would be analogous to clarifying apposition (*ʿatf bayān*) in Arabic, not substitution.

37 We can term the appositive itself a *clarifying appositive*.

38 The appositive need not always be clearer, but the combination of the two nouns at least must produce a measure of clarity. See Ibn Aḥmad, *Fatḥ al-asrār*, 2:235.

39 See the list of nouns with the governance of verbs in the section on the regular expressed governor in Chapter 1, p. 126.

40 That is, the action or quality signified by the verb or noun inheres, or resides, in the real agent signified by the grammatical agent.

41 This is a way of saying that the following nominatives are secondary to the agent, in the sense that the agent is the basis for the nominative role, but that they are analogous to the agent with respect to that role.

42 A *kurr* is a traditional large unit of measurement.

43 That is, it must be a word that is followed by a grammatically connected element that modifies and determines it as the second element in an *iḍāfa* construction determines the *muḍāf*. Al-Mīlānī, *Sharḥ al-Mughnī*, 186 (see also the editor's footnote).

44 The indefinite vocative is used without any specific reference, i.e., for anyone who matches the description. In this example, it is used for a hypothetical generic "rider" rather than for a particular individual.

45 Instead, the phrase *fī al-masjidi* is considered to be positionally (*maḥallan*) accusative. See note 33.

46 In the second example, *mā shaʾnuka* is understood to mean *mā ṣanaʿta* (What have you done…?) or *mā taṣnaʿu* (What are you doing…?). Al-Mīlānī, *Sharḥ al-Mughnī*, 198; al-Jāmī, *al-Fawāʾid*, 246.

47 See note 43.

48 In other words, it is indeclinable (*mabnī*).

49 That is, an active participle, passive participle, or participial.

50 When the *muḍāf* is a derivative noun, it can exercise governance over the *muḍāf ilayhi* via its verbal action, but this makes the *iḍāfa* nonattributive, as will be seen in the examples of nonattributive *iḍāfa* further below.

51 The clause *Zaydun kātibun* (Zayd is a writer) is indeclinable when considered as a clause. But considered as the agent along with *anna* in the larger sentence, the clause is positionally nominative.

52 In cases when they do not have an explicit agent noun (e.g., *ḍaraba Zaydun*), third-person singular verbs have a hidden, detached nominative pronoun (equivalent to *huwa* for the masculine and *hiya* for the feminine), not an attached pronoun.

53 Though the original text provides examples only in the third person, we have provided examples of attached pronouns in all three persons in the tables below. Verbal constructions are illustrated in the perfect tense. For examples with imperfect tense verbs, see Birgevī, *Iẓhār al-asrār*, 96–97, 114; al-Mīlānī, *Sharḥ al-Mughnī*, 237–41. Note that Arabic nominative pronouns correspond to the subjective case in English: "I," "you," "he," "she," "it," "we," and "they." Arabic accusative pronouns and those Arabic genitive pronouns that are governed by prepositions (*ḥurūf al-jarr*) correspond to the English objective case pronouns "me," "you," "him," "her," "it," "us," and "them." Arabic genitive pronouns that are governed by a *muḍāf* correspond to the English possessive case: "my," "your," "his," "her," "its," "our," and "their."

54 See note 14.

55 The relative pronouns, depending on context, can be translated as "that," "which," "that which," "who," "whom," "whose," "the one(s) who," "the one(s) whom," "the one(s) whose," "those which," "they who," and so on.

56 *Halumma* may be used in the transitive sense of *aḥḍir* (bring) or in the intransitive sense of *taʿāla* or *aqbil* (come). Al-Mīlānī, *Sharḥ al-Mughnī*, 250.

57 The pronoun *kaʾayyin* (how many a...) can be counted as a vague pronoun. These pronouns are also called *kināyāt al-ʿadad* (*kināya*s of number); they are expressions that leave the number and kind of their referents vague. In this context, the term *kināya* means "referring to a thing by a name other than its own for some rhetorical purpose." See Ibn ʿAqīl, *Sharḥ*, 4:68–69 (especially the gloss of ʿAbd al-Ḥamīd).

58 Third-person singular verbs avail themselves of a concealed (*mustatir*) pronoun agent in sentences like these where the verb is positioned after the subject. A masculine verb like *jāʾa* (he came) or *yaṭluʿu* (it [m.] rises) would imply a concealed masculine pronoun with the meaning of *huwa*, which would be incompatible with a feminine subject like *Hind* or *al-shams*. See al-Mīlānī, *Sharḥ al-Mughnī*, 239–40; Birgevī, *Iẓhār al-asrār*, 95–98.

59 A clearer example is *ṣabūrun* (one who is very patient). Ibn ʿAqīl, *Sharḥ*, 4:78. *Baghiyyun* is given as an example of the pattern *faʿūlun* because its original form is *baghūyun*, and it is used for the feminine in Sūrat Maryam: "'O sister of Hārūn! Your father was not an evil man, nor was your mother unchaste (*baghiyyan*)'" (Q 19:28). Al-Mīlānī, *Sharḥ al-Mughnī*, 283.

60 That is, when the noun being counted (*al-maʿdūd*) is masculine, the numbers one and two are given the masculine form as would be expected, but the numbers three through ten are given the feminine form because the plural (defined in grammar as what refers to three or more) is grammatically feminine.

61 For a feminine noun, one says *iḥdā ʿashrata* (eleven), *ithnatā ʿashrata* (twelve), and *thalātha ʿashrata* (thirteen) through *tisʿa ʿashrata* (nineteen). Note that in the numbers thirteen through nineteen for the feminine, the first word is made masculine so that it is the reverse of what it is for the masculine, in which the first word is made feminine.

62 That is, *thalāthūna* (thirty), *arbaʿūna* (forty), and so on until *tisʿūna* (ninety).

63 The specifying noun (*mumayyiz*) is the noun that signifies what is being counted by the numeral.

64 See note 6.

65 Other than a subject (*mubtadaʾ*), this may be a noun qualified by an adjective (*ism mawṣūf*), a relative pronoun (*ism mawṣūl*), or a noun qualified by a circumstance (*dhū al-ḥāl*). Alternatively, it suffices that there be an interrogative *hamza* or a negation (*nafī*). Al-Mīlānī, *Sharḥ al-Mughnī*, 305–6.

66 See the previous note.

67 See Treatise I, note 21.

68 That is, a *hamza*, *tāʾ*, *yāʾ*, or *nūn*.

69 See note 3.

70 For further precision, this could be rendered "Shall I ask you *as a result of which* (or *whereupon*) you might answer me?"

71 In the same way that the Arabic term *fiʿl* can be used to mean either "verb" or "action," the Arabic term *amr* can be used as "command," in reference to the requesting of an action, and it can be used as "imperative," in reference to verbal forms or constructions that *signify* commands. Imperative verbs include verbs with forms like *ifʿal* and verbs with the imperative *lām* prefix.

72 See Treatise I, note 36.

73 As with the Arabic term *amr*, the Arabic term *nahy* can be used as "prohibition," in reference to the request not to do an action, and it can be used as "prohibitive," in reference to verbal constructions that *signify* prohibition by use of the particle *lā*.

74 Here, the word *dhahaba* (he went), which belongs to the morphological class of *fataḥa*, is replaced with the word *adhhaba* (he made go), which has the same root but belongs to the morphological class of *akrama*. See Treatise I, Chapter 1, on the morphological classes.

75 See the previous note. In this case, the word that was replaced is *fariḥa* (was glad) of Class *ʿAlima*.

76 The *farsakh* is a measure of distance equivalent to approximately four miles.

77 To provide examples: (1) *bal naẓunnukum kādhibīna* ("Nay, we think that you are liars") (Q 11:27), (2) *yaḥsabuhum al-jāhilu aghniyāʾa* (The ignorant one supposes them to be wealthy) (Q 2:273), (3) *khiltu al-ghūla mukhīfan* (I imagined the ghoul to be terrifying), (4) *fa-in ʿalimtumūhunna muʾminātin* (Then, if you know them to be believers...) (Q 60:10), (5) *zaʿamta Zaydan ṣadīqaka* (You believed Zayd to be your friend), (6) *innahum yarawnahu baʿīdan* (Truly they deem it far off) (Q 70:6), and (7) *wa-wajadū mā ʿamilū ḥāḍiran* (And they find present [in their book] whatsoever they did) (Q 18:49).

78 Lexically, *nāqiṣ* means "incomplete" or "deficient."

79 Not all important meanings and usages of these prepositions are listed below. See note 15.

80 Though its signification of fewness is considered original, *rubba* usually signifies abundance, in which case it may be translated as "many a...," as in "Many a noble man have I met" for *rubba rajulin karīmin laqītuhu*. Al-Jāmī, *al-Fawāʾid*, 545. See also Wright, *Arabic Grammar*, 214–18.

81 This refers to a bird departing from its chick.

82 According to most exegetes, the *kāf* in this verse is an additional particle that conveys emphasis.

83 That is, as has been mentioned above in the case of *ʿalā* and *ʿan*. For more discussion, see al-Mīlānī, *Sharḥ al-Mughnī*, 367–69.

84 The grammarian Abū al-ʿAbbās Muḥammad b. Yazīd, known as al-Mubarrad (d. 285/898).

85 One might say, for simplicity, that *lākinna* indicates contrast.

86 See Treatise I, note 27.

87 The point of the example is the use of *lā* in the second hemistich, which has thus been added.

88 Thus, these particles signal the number and gender of the addressee or addressees.

89 That is, like the *lām* used with *inna* in *inna Zaydan la-karīmun* (Zayd is indeed generous).

90 The infinitive *an* should not be confused with the phonetically lightened *anna*, which is also *an*.

91 Thus, one would use *qad* before a perfect tense verb when confirming an occurrence to someone who is specifically awaiting that news.

92 These two particles were discussed earlier in this chapter as members of the fourth category, the negative particles (pp. 195–96).

93 The great classical grammarian Abū Bishr ʿAmr b. ʿUthmān, known as Sībawayh (d. ca. 180/796).

94 In addition to its possible roles as a generic *lām* (*lām al-jins*) or a specific *lām* (*lām al-ʿahd*), the definite *lām* can serve as a universal *lām* (*lām al-istighrāq*), which refers to all individuals of a category. The signification of the universal *lām* is discussed in Treatise IV, p. 293.

95 This second example is the previously mentioned "*lām* that expresses the reason" (*lām al-taʿlīl*). It is prepositional here in the sense that it serves as a preposition for the infinitive phrase constructed with the implicit *an*. In this exam-

ple, that would be *li-an tukrimanī*, i.e., *li-ikrāmika iyyāya* (for the sake of your honoring of me).

96 See Treatise I, note 48.

97 Most items in the following list express a request; oaths, however, can be listed separately. Note that in the case of affirmative oaths the emphatic *nūn* is in fact necessary. One omission from the list is the case of a condition clause beginning with *immā*, as in *fa-immā tathqafannahum fī al-ḥarbi…* (So if you overcome them in war…) (Q 8:57). See Ibn al-Ḥājib, *al-Kāfiya*, 204; al-Siyālkūtī, *Ḥāshiyat ʿAbd al-Ḥakīm*, 2:578; Ibn ʿAqīl, *Sharḥ*, 3:265–66.

98 The last two examples are from Sūrat al-Ḥāqqa (69:28–29).

99 This category also includes nunation that compensates for an omitted letter, as in *ghawāshin* (coverings), originally *ghawāshī*. Ibn ʿAqīl, *Sharḥ*, 1:26.

100 This and the next type of nunation are dialectical. The nunation of nasalization (*tarannum*, or "quavering and trilling") is so called because the nunation that replaces a long vowel in sung verse can be modulated with a melodious nasalized quavering and prolongation. Al-Jāmī, *al-Fawāʾid*, 593–94; al-Fākihī, *Sharḥ Kitāb al-ḥudūd*, 284.

III

THE ANCIENT ABUNDANCE

On the science of logic

الفيض العتيق في علم المنطق

In the Name of Allah,
All-Merciful, Most Compassionate

بسم الله الرحمن الرحيم

ALL PRAISE IS due to Allah, who guided us to this clear religion. May blessings and peace be upon the seal of the prophets Muḥammad and upon all of his family, Companions, and Helpers.

الحمد لله الذي هدانا لهذا الدين المبين، والصلاة والسلام على خاتم النبيّين محمد وعلى آله وصحبه وأنصاره أجمعين.

To Proceed This is a treatise on the science of logic. I have entitled it *The Ancient Abundance: On the Science of Logic* and arranged it into an introduction and four chapters.

أما بعد فهذه رسالة في علم المنطق سمّيتها الفيض العتيق في علم المنطق. رتّبتها على مقدّمة وأربعة أبواب.

INTRODUCTION

Concerning the definition, subject matter, and aim of logic, as well as the definition of knowledge, the definition of signification, and the definition of the verbal expression.

The Definition of Logic

Logic is a science in which one investigates how knowns that can be conceived or assented to lead to the knowledge of conceptual or assentive unknowns. Also, the science of logic is a science that protects the mind from errors in *reflective thought*, which (i.e., reflective thought) is to arrange things that one knows such that one is led to the knowledge of something unknown.

Thus, the subject matter of logic is inquiry into conceptual and assentive knowns so that one is brought to conceptual and assentive unknowns, and its aim is to know conceptual and assentive unknowns.

Our discussion in this introduction will first concern the definition of knowledge, its classification into conception and assent, and the classification of each into immediate and reflective. It will, second, concern the definition of signification and its classification into that which is assigned and that which is otherwise and into that which is corresponsive and that which is otherwise. And it will, third, concern an explication of verbal expressions and their classification into simple and composite; the simple into particular and universal; the universal into essential and accidental; the essential into genus, species, and differentia; and the accidental into special accident and general accident.

مقدمة

في تعريف المنطق وموضوعه وغايته وتعريف العلم

وتعريف الدلالة وتعريف اللفظ

تعريف المنطق

المنطق علم يبحث فيه عن المعلومات التصوّريّة والتصديقيّة للإيصال إلى مجهولاتهما. وأيضا علم المنطق علم يعصم العقل عن الخطأ في الفكر، وهو أي الفكر ترتيب أمور معلومة للتأدّي إلى معرفة المجهول.

فموضوعه البحث عن المعلومات التصوّريّة والتصديقيّة للإيصال إلى مجهولاتهما، وغايته معرفة المجهولات التصوّريّة والتصديقيّة.

كلامنا فيها فأوّلًا في تعريف العلم وانقسامه إلى التصوّر والتصديق وانقسام كل منهما إلى الضروري والنظري؛ وثانيًا في تعريف الدلالة وانقسامها إلى الوضعيّة وغيرها والمطابقيّة وغيرها؛ وثالثًا في بيان اللفظ وانقسامه إلى مفرد ومركّب، والمفرد إلى جزئي وكلّي، والكلّي إلى ذاتي وعرضي، والذاتي إلى جنس ونوع وفصل، والعرضي إلي خاصّة وعرض عامّ.

Knowledge: Definition and Classifications

Knowledge is the obtaining of a thing's form[1] in the mind. Knowledge is either (1) *conception* alone, which is also termed *pure conception*,1 i.e., conception unaccompanied by any judgment, e.g., the conception of 'human' without any affirmative or negative judgment about humans, or else it is (2) conception with a judgment, e.g., when we conceive 'human' and judge that a human is something that can or cannot write. The combination of these[2] is termed *assent* according to the imam3 and the late-period logicians, though according to the philosophers, assent is the judgment alone. *Judgment* is the attribution of one thing to another by way of affirmation or negation.

Conceptions and assents are not all self-evident, or else we would have no need for reflective reasoning and acquisition to attain any [knowledge]. Nor are they all reflective, or else either circularity or infinite regress would ensue. Rather, some of each kind is self-evident and termed *immediate*, meaning that which, in order to obtain, does not depend on reflective reasoning and acquisition, e.g., the conceptions of heat and coolness[3] and the assents to [the judgments] that negation and affirmation never coincide

[1] Knowledge is a form inscribed in the soul in the same way an image is replicated in a mirror, except that the mirror replicates the semblances of sensible things, whereas the soul is a mirror that replicates the semblances of intelligible things. The [mentally] inscribed form, which is devoid of matter, is an [instance of] knowledge, while the [corresponding] form in extramental existence is an object of knowledge. Thus, knowledge and the thing known are the same thing in essence, though considered from different perspectives.

[2] That is, the combination of the three conceptions: the conception of the subject of the judgment, the conception of the predicate of the judgment, and the conception of the relation.2

[3] Illustrating self-evident conception.

تعريف العلم وانقسامه

العلم هو حصول صورة الشيء[١] في العقل. وهو إما (١) تصوّر فقط، ويقال له التصوّر الساذج أي تصوّر لا حكم معه كتصوّرنا الإنسان من غير حكم عليه بنفي أو إثبات؛ وإما (٢) تصوّر معه حكم كما إذا تصوّرنا الإنسان وحكمنا عليه بأنه كاتب أو ليس بكاتب. ويقال للمجموع[٢] التصديق عند الإمام والمتأخّرين، وأما عند الحكماء فالتصديق هو الحكم فقط. والحكم هو إسناد أمر إلى آخر إيجابًا أو سلبًا.

وليس كل من التصوّر والتصديق بديهيًّا؛ وإلا لما احتجنا في تحصيل شيء إلى نظر وكسب، ولا نظريًّا وإلا لدار أو تسلسل. بل البعض من كل منهما بديهي، ويقال له الضروري وهو الذي لم يتوقف حصوله على نظر وكسب، كتصوّر الحرارة والبرودة،[٣] وكالتصديق بأن النفي والإثبات لا يجتمعان وأن الواحد نصف

[١] والهيئة المنقوشة في النفس كما تنطبع الصورة في المرآة، إلا أن المرآة لا ينطبع فيها إلا مثل المحسوسات، والنفس مرآة تنطبع فيها مثل المعقولات. والصورة المنقوشة العارية عن المادّة علم، والصورة الخارجيّة معلوم. فالعلم والمعلوم متّحدان بالذات، مختلفان بالاعتبار.

[٢] أي مجموع التصوّرات الثلاثة: تصوّر المحكوم عليه وتصوّر المحكوم به وتصوّر النسبة.

[٣] مثال للتصوّر البديهي.

and that one is half of two.[1] All other [conceptions and assents] are *reflective* (also termed *unknown*)[2] and these are the opposite, e.g., the conceptions of angels and jinn and the assent to [the judgment] that the universe originated in time. The reflective is acquired from the self-evident. While conceptual unknowns are acquired from conceptual knowns by means of *definition*, assentive unknowns are acquired from assentive knowns by means of the *syllogism*.

Reflective thought is to arrange things one knows so that one arrives at something one does not know. This process is susceptible to error; thus one needs the rules of logic.

Signification: Definition and Division

Signification[3] is for a thing to be such that [one of the following is true]:

1. knowing the thing entails knowing another thing,[4] e.g., the entailment that runs from knowing that there is smoke to knowing that there is fire.
2. [knowing the thing entails] presuming another thing, e.g., the entailment that runs from knowing that there are clouds to presuming that there is rain.
3. presuming the thing [entails] presuming another thing, e.g., the entailment that runs from presuming that there are clouds (upon observing dense fog in the sky) to presuming that there is rain.

As for entailment that runs from presumption to knowledge, such does not exist.

[1] Illustrating self-evident assent.

[2] They are also termed *acquired*.

[3] The five universals are divisions of the essential and the accidental, which are divisions of the universal, which is a division of the simple expression, which is a division of the verbal expression, which depends on signification. This is why signification is discussed first.

الاثنين.[١] والبعض الآخر نظري، ويقال له المجهول[٢] وهو بخلافه، كتصوّر الملك والجنّ، وكالتصديق بأن العالم حادث. والنظري يكتسب من البديهي لكن المجهول التصوري يكتسب من المعلوم التصوّري بالتعريف، والمجهول التصديقي من المعلوم التصديقي بالقياس.

والفكر هو ترتيب أمور معلومة للتوصل إلى مجهول. وقد يقع فيه الخطأ فاحتيج إلى قواعد المنطق.

تعريف الدلالة وانقسامها

الدلالة[٣] هي كون الشيء بحالة:

١- يلزم من العلم به العلم بشيء آخر، كلزوم العلم بوجود النار من العلم بوجود الدخان.

٢- أو الظنّ بشيء آخر، كلزوم الظنّ بوجود المطر من العلم بوجود السحاب.

٣- أو من الظنّ به الظنّ بشيء آخر، كلزوم الظنّ بوجود المطر من الظنّ بوجود السحاب عند رؤية الدخان في جوّ السماء.

وأما لزوم العلم من الظنّ فلم يوجد.

[١] مثال للتصديق البديهي.

[٢] ويقال له أيضا الكسبي.

[٣] الكلّيات الخمس أقسام للذاتي والعرضي، وهما قسمان للكلّي وهو قسم للفظ المفرد، وهو قسم للفظ، وهو يتوقّف على الدلالة فلذلك قدّم ذكر الدلالة.

والشيء الأول يسمّى دالًّا ودليلًا،[١] والثاني مدلولًا. والدليل إن كان مفيدًا لليقين يسمّى دليلًا برهانيًّا وبرهانًا، وإن كان مفيدًا للظنّ يسمّى دليلًا إقناعيًّا وأمارة.

وهي أي الدلالة قسمان: لفظيّة إن كان الدالّ لفظًا وإلا فغير لفظيّة. واللفظيّة إن كان بجعل الجاعل فوضعيّة، كدلالة «الإنسان» على الحيوان الناطق؛ أو باقتضاء الطبع فطبيعيّة، كدلالة «أخ» على الوجع؛ أو بغيرهما فعقليّة، كدلالة «ديز» المسموع من وراء الجدار على وجود اللافظ. وكذا غير اللفظيّة كدلالة الدوالّ الأربعة وهي الخطوط والعقود والإشارات والنصب على ما يراد بها، وحمرة الخجل وصفرة الوجل عليهما، والأثر على المؤثّر.

والمقصود للمنطقي الدلالة اللفظيّة الوضعيّة، وهي مطابقة وتضمّن والتزام:

١- لأن دلالة اللفظ على تمام ما وضع له من حيث إنه تمامه مطابقة، كدلالة «الإنسان» على الحيوان الناطق.

٢- وعلى جزئه إن كان له جزء من حيث إنه جزؤه تضمّن، كدلالة «الإنسان» على الحيوان فقط أو على الناطق فقط.

[١] والفرق بين الدالّ والدليل أن الدالّ يطلق على التصوّرات والتصديقات، والدليل لا يطلق إلا على التصديقات فالدالّ أعمّ من الدليل.

The first thing is termed a *signifier* or an *indicant*[1] and the second the thing signified[5] or indicated. When an indicant imparts knowledge, it is termed a *demonstrative proof* or *demonstration*, and when it imparts presumption, it is termed a *persuasive proof* or *suggestive indicant*.

Signification is of two types: it is *verbal* when the signifier is a verbal expression, and it is *nonverbal* otherwise. Now, when verbal signification is [established] by someone's determining act, it is *assigned*, e.g., "human" signifying 'rational animal'. When it is [established] as a consequence of [human] nature, it is *natural*, e.g., "Akh!" signifying pain. When it is otherwise, it is *rational*, e.g., [the meaningless utterance] "dayz" as heard behind a wall signifying the presence of the utterer. [These three categories] also apply to nonverbal signification, e.g., the four nonverbal signifiers (which are written expressions, numerical finger gestures, body gestures, and signposts) signifying their meanings; the redness of embarrassment and the paleness of fear [signifying embarrassment and fear], respectively; and an effect [signifying] an effective cause.

[The category] of concern to the logician is that of assigned verbal signification, which is [classified into] correspondence, containment, and concomitance:

1. An expression's signification of its complete assigned meaning inasmuch as it is complete is *correspondence*, as "human" signifies 'rational animal'.
2. An expression's signification of parts of its assigned meaning (if the meaning has parts) inasmuch as they are parts is *containment*, as "human" signifies 'animal' alone or 'rational thing'[6] alone.

[1] The difference between *dāll* (signifier) and *dalīl* (indicant) is that *dāll* is used for conceptions and assents, whereas *dalīl* is used only for assents. Thus, *dāll* is broader than *dalīl*.

3. An expression's signification of things that are mentally concomitant with its assigned meaning inasmuch as they are concomitant is *concomitance*, as "human" signifies 'thing capable of knowledge and of the craft of writing'.

[The latter two relations][1] entail correspondence, but the reverse is not true.[2]

Verbal Expressions: Definition and Types

Lexically, *lafẓ* (verbal expression) means "to throw," and in technical usage it refers to that which the human being articulates. Verbal expressions are either simple or composite.

Simple Expressions A simple expression is that whose parts are not intended to signify parts of the expression's meaning. Simple expressions, with respect to their parts and their signification, are of six types. For the case may be that

1. both the expression and its meaning lack parts, e.g., [the expression] *qi* if it were assigned to refer to instances of 'the endpoint of a line'.[3]
2. or the meaning has parts but the expression does not, e.g., *qi* if it were assigned as a proper name for a person.
3. or the expression has parts but the meaning does not, e.g., the names of the letters of the alphabet in relation to their referents.[4]
4. or both have [parts], but the parts lack signification, e.g., *insān* (human).

[1] That is, containment and concomitance.

[2] That is, containment and concomitance are not entailed by correspondence; correspondence may obtain without either of them.7

[3] A line being the end of a geometric plane.

[4] *Alif* is a name for [the letter-sound] *a*, *bā*ʾ is a name for *ba*, *jīm* is a name for *ja*, and so on.

٣- وعلى ما يلازمه في الذهن من حيث إنه لازمه التزام، كدلالة «الإنسان» على قابل العلم وصنعة الكتابة.

وتلزمهما[١] المطابقة ولا عكس.[٢]

تعريف اللفظ وأقسامه

اللفظ لغةً الرمي، واصطلاحًا ما ينطق به الإنسان. وهو إما مفرد وإما مركّب.

المفرد وهو ما لا يراد بجزء منه الدلالة على جزء معناه، وهو من حيث الجزء والدلالة ستّة أقسام، لأنه:

١- إما أن لا يكون للّفظ جزء ولا لمعناه، كـ«قِ» إذا وضع لما صدق عليه نهاية الخطّ.[٣]

٢- أو للمعنى جزء لا للّفظ، كـ«ق» علمًا لشخص.

٣- أو للفظ جزء لا لمعناه، كأسماء حروف الهجاء لمسمّياتها.[٤]

٤- أو لكليهما لكن لا يدلّ، كـ«الإنسان».

[١] أي التضمّن والالتزام.

[٢] أي التضمّن والالتزام لا يلزمان المطابقة فتوجد المطابقة من دونهما.

[٣] أي نهاية السطح.

[٤] فإن «الألف» اسم لـ«أ» و«الباء» اسم لـ«ب» و«الجيم» اسم لـ«ج»، وغيرها.

5. or they bear signification, but not to parts of the intended meaning, e.g., *ʿAbdallāh* (slave of Allah) as a proper name.
6. or they signify the parts of the intended meaning although this[1] is not intended, e.g., *al-Ḥayawān al-Nāṭiq* (Rational Animal) as a proper name for a human being.

What is meant by *parts* is parts that have an order[2] when one hears them; hence, verbs,[3] whose lexical matter signifies an action and whose morphological structure signifies a time, do not render the definition of the simple expression insufficiently inclusive nor do they render the definition of the composite expression insufficiently exclusive.8

Simple expressions can be classified into various categories:

1. *particles, verbs, and nouns*. If a simple expression is not independent, it is a *particle* (*adāh*).[4] Otherwise, if through its morphological structure it bears signification by assignment to one of the three times, it is a *verb* (*kalima*).[5] If not, it is a *noun*.
2. *real particulars, univocal universals, and modulative universals*. When a simple expression possesses a single meaning, then, (a) if it has individual reference[6] by assignment, it is a *proper name* according to the grammarians and a *real particular* according to the logicians. Otherwise, it is (b) a *univocal univer-*

[1] That is, this significatory relation.

[2] Where one of two parts comes first and the other second.

[3] That is, when a verb's personal pronoun is not implicit—otherwise, it is a composite expression.

[4] Termed a *ḥarf* by the grammarians.

[5] Termed a *fiʿl* by the grammarians.

[6] I.e., it cannot validly apply to multiple things.

٥- أو يدلّ لكن لا على جزء المعنى المقصود، كـ«عبد الله» علمًا.

٦- أو يدلّ عليه لكن لا تكون[١] مرادة، كـ«الحيوان الناطق» علمًا لإنسان.

والمراد بالجزء الجزء المرتّب[٢] في السمع، فلا ينتقض تعريف المفرد جمعًا والمركّب منعًا بالفعل[٣] الدالّ بمادّته على الحدث وبهيئته على الزمان.

اللفظ المفرد ينقسم إلى أمور شتّى:

١- انقسامه إلى أداة وكلمة واسم: فهو إن لم يستقلّ فأداة[٤] وإلا فإن دلّ بهيئته وضعًا على أحد الأزمنة الثلاثة فكلمة[٥] وإلا فاسم.

٢- انقسامه إلى جزئي حقيقي وكلّي متواطئ ومشكّك: فهو (١) إن كان معناه واحدًا فمع تشخّصه[٦] وضعًا فعلم عند النحاة وجزئي حقيقي عند المناطقة؛ (٢) وبدونه كلّي

[١] أي تلك الدلالة.

[٢] بأن يكون أحد الجزئين أوّلًا والآخر ثانيًا.

[٣] أي إذا لم يكن الضمير مستترا فيه وإلا فهو مركب.

[٤] وعند النحاة حرف.

[٥] وعند النحاة فعل.

[٦] أي لا يصلح لأن يصدق على كثيرين.

sal[1] if its mental or[2] extramental instances are equivalent with respect to it, e.g., "human" and "sun."[3] And it is (c) a *modulative universal* if its[4] obtaining in some instances has primacy, priority, or greater intensity in relation to others, e.g., "existence" in relation to the Necessary and the contingent, respectively; "whiteness" in relation to snow and ivory, respectively; and "blackness" in relation to crows and Abyssinians, respectively.

3. *equivocal, general, indefinite, and numeral.* When a simple expression possesses multiple meanings, then (a) if it is assigned to each by distinct assignations,[5] it is *equivocal*, e.g., *al-ʿayn* (the eye, the wellspring, the spy...). If (b) it comprehends all of its possible referents without restriction, it is *general*, e.g., *ḥayawān* (animal). Otherwise, it is either (c) *indefinite*, e.g., *rajulun* (a man),[10] or (d) a *numeral noun*, e.g., *ʿasharatun* (ten).[11]

4. *transferred, literal, and nonliteral.* If a simple expression is assigned to a meaning and then used for another, then (a) if it is no longer used for the first meaning in the absence of contextual indicants, it is either *transferred by revelational usage*, e.g., *ṣalāh* (ritual prayer) and *ṣawm* (devotional fasting); *transferred by a specific convention*,[12] e.g., *fiʿl* (verb); or *transferred by general convention*, e.g., *dābba* (riding

متواطئ[١] إن استوت فيه أفراده الذهنيّة أو[٢] الخارجيّة كـ«الإنسان» و«الشمس».[٣] (٣) ومشكّك إن كان حصوله[٤] في البعض أولى وأقدم وأشدّ من الآخر كـ«الوجود» بالنسبة إلى الواجب والممكن وكـ«البياض» بالنسبة إلى الثلج والعاج وكـ«السواد» بالنسبة إلى الغراب والحبشي.

٣- انقسامه إلى مشترك وعامّ ونكرة واسم عدد: وهو (١) إن كان معناه كثيرًا فإن وضع لكل وضعًا متعدّدًا[٥] فمشترك لفظي كـ«العين»؛ (٢) وإن استغرق جميع ما يصلح له من غير حصر فعامّ كـ«حيوان»؛ وإلا (٣) فنكرة كـ«رجل» أو (٤) اسم عدد كـ«عشرة».

٤- انقسامه إلى منقول وحقيقة ومجاز: فإن وضع لمعنًى ثم استعمل في آخر (١) فإن ترك استعماله في المعنى الأول بلا قرينة فمنقول شرعي كـ«الصلاة» و«الصوم»، أو عرفي خاصّ

---

[1] *Mutawāṭiʾ* (univocal) derives from *tawāṭuʾ*, which means conformity.

[2] The conjunction "or" here is to preclude mutual exclusion.

[3] [The sun signifying] 'star that shines' and the moon 'star that wanes'.[9]

[4] That is, the meaning of the universal.

[5] By means of this qualification, personal pronouns, non-personal pronouns, and the like are excluded. Even though they signify many things and are assigned to each, it is not by means of distinct assignations that this is so—rather, it is by means of a single assignation.

[١] من التواطؤ وهو التوافق.

[٢] «أو» لمنع الخلوّ.

[٣] كوكب درّي والقمر كوكب ذو محق.

[٤] أي معنى الكلّي.

[٥] خرج بهذا القيد المضمرات والمبهمات ونحوها فإنها وإن كثرت معانيها ووضع لكل لكن لا بوضع متعدّد بل بوضع واحد.

animal).[1] Otherwise,[2] it is (b) *literal* with respect to the first meaning and (c) *nonliteral* with respect to the second, e.g., *asad* (lion) used for the predatory animal or a courageous man.

5. *mutual distinction, synonymy, and coextension* with respect to the simple expression's relation to another [expression]. Two expressions are *mutually distinct* if (a) they differ in intension and extension,[13] e.g., "human" and "rock." If (b) they are the same with respect to both, they are *synonymous*, like *layth* (lion) and *asad* (lion). If (c) [they are the same] in extension, they are *coextensive*,[3] e.g., "rational thing" and "writing thing."[4]

6. *particular and universal*. The *particular* is of two types: (a) *real*, i.e., that the conception of whose meaning precludes that it could be shared, e.g., "Zayd"; and (b) *relative*, i.e., that which is more specific than something, e.g., "human."[5] The *universal* is that the conception of whose meaning does *not* preclude that it could be shared. It is also of two types:

كـ«الفعل»، أو عرفي عامّ كـ«الدابّة»؛[١] وإلا[٢] (٢) فحقيقة في الأول (٣) ومجاز في الثاني كـ«الأسد» للحيوان المفترس والرجل الشجاع.

٥- من حيث نسبته إلى آخر ينقسم إلى التباين والترادف والتساوي: اللفظان (١) إن اختلفا في المفهوم والماصدق فمتباينان كـ«الإنسان» و«الحجر»؛ (٢) وإن اتّحدا فيهما فمترادفان كـ«الليث» و«الأسد»؛ أو (٣) في الماصدق فمتساويان[٣] كـ«الناطق» و«الكاتب».[٤]

٦- انقسامه إلى جزئي وكلّي: الجزئي قسمان: (١) حقيقي وهو ما يمنع نفس تصوّر مفهومه عن وقوع الشركة فيه كـ«زيد»؛ (٢) إضافي وهو الأخصّ من شيء كـ«الإنسان»[٥].١ والكلّي هو ما لا يمنع نفس تصوّر مفهومه عن وقوع الشركة فيه، وهو أيضا قسمان:

---

[1] The original lexical usage of *dābba* was for anything that creeps or walks upon land, and then general convention transferred it to creatures with four legs like horses, mules, and donkeys.

[2] That is, if its usage for the first meaning was never abandoned.

[3] 'Coextension' is broader than 'synonymy'; whenever synonymy obtains, coextension obtains, but the reverse does not hold.

[4] The intension of the first is 'entity for which rationality obtains', and the intension of the second is 'entity for which the capacity to write obtains', and their respective extensions are identical.

[5] "Human" is a particular with respect to "animal," "animal" is a particular with respect to "growing body," and "growing body" is a particular with respect to "physical body."

[١] فإنها في أصل اللغة لكل ما يدبّ على الأرض أي يمشي ثم نقله العرف العامّ إلى ذات القوائم الأربع من الخيل والبغال والحمير.

[٢] أي وإن لم يترك استعماله في المعنى الأول.

[٣] وبين التساوي والترادف عموم وخصوص مطلق لأنه كلّما تحقّق الترادف تحقّق التساوي بدون العكس.

[٤] لأن مفهوم الأول ذات ثبت له النطق ومفهوم الثاني ذات ثبت له الكتابة، وماصدقاتهما متّحدة.

[٥] فإنه جزئي بالنسبة إلى الحيوان، والحيوان جزئي بالنسبة إلى الجسم النامي، والجسم النامي جزئي بالنسبة إلى الجسم [المطلق]٢.

(a) *real,* i.e., that under which other things can fall in the supposition of the mind, irrespective of whether they fall under it in extramental existence or not, e.g., "phoenix" and "non-thing," since their universality is by virtue of their respective meanings; and (b) *relative,* i.e., that under which other things fall in actual reality, e.g., "human" and "animal."

The difference between a universal and a whole is predicability and non-predicability: a universal is predicable of each of its particulars, e.g., "Zayd is a human," whereas a whole is not predicable of each of its parts, for one cannot say, "The wall is a house."

Composite Expressions: Definition and Classification Our discussion here concerns the definition of the composite expression; its division into complete and incomplete; the division of the complete into the declarative and the non-declarative; and the division of the non-declarative into questions, commands, requests, supplications, and so forth. A *composite expression* is that whose parts signify parts of the expression's meaning, e.g., *rāmī al-ḥijārati* (one that casts stones) and *Zaydun qā'imun* (Zayd is standing). If upon [uttering] an expression one can appropriately stop speaking, it is *complete*; otherwise it is *incomplete*.

When a complete expression can take on truth or falsity,[1] it is a *declarative expression* and a *proposition*; otherwise, it is a *non-declarative expression*. Non-declarative expressions are of various types. If the expression is assigned [the function of] asking, then (1) to ask someone to tell something is a *question*; (2) to ask someone, while in a superordinate

[1] That is, [if the expression can take on truth or falsity] by its mere conceptual form, irrespective of what is actually the case. This includes "The sky is above us" and "The sky is beneath us" as well.

(١) حقيقي وهو ما يصلح أن يندرج تحته شيء آخر بحسب فرض العقل سواء اندرج في الخارج أو لا كـ«العنقاء» و«اللاشيء» فإن كلّيتهما بالنظر إلى مفهومهما؛ (٢) إضافي وهو ما اندرج تحته شيء آخر في الواقع كـ«الإنسان» و«الحيوان».

الفرق بين الكلّي والكلّ الحمل وعدم الحمل؛ أعني أن الكلّي يحمل على كل واحد من جزئيّاته نحو «زيد إنسان»، والكل لا يحمل على كل واحد من أجزائه فلا يقال «الجدار بيت».

المركّب أي اللفظ المركّب تعريفه وانقسامه كلامنا هنا في تعريف المركّب وانقسامه إلى تامّ وغير تامّ، والتامّ إلى خبر وإنشاء، والإنشاء إلى استفهام وأمر والتماس ودعاء وغير ذلك. المركّب هو ما يدلّ جزء لفظه على جزء معناه، نحو «رامي الحجارة» و«زيد قائم»؛ وهو إن صحّ السكوت عليه فتامّ وإلا فغير تامّ.

والتامّ إن احتمل الصدق والكذب[١] فخبر وقضيّة وإلا فإنشاء. وهو على أقسام: إن وضع للطلب (١) فطلب ذكر الماهيّة استفهام، (٢) وتحصيلها أو تحصيل الكفّ

[١] أي بمجرّد مفهومه مع قطع النظر عن الخارج فيشمل «السماء فوقنا» و«السماء تحتنا».

position, to bring about something or to bring about an abstinence from something is *command* or *prohibition*;[1] (3) [to ask such] while in a coordinate position is *request*; and (4) [to ask such] with deference in the command or prohibition is *entreaty* or *supplication*. Otherwise,[2] it is *notification*, and this includes wishing, hoping, expressing wonderment, swearing an oath, and calling.

عنها مع الاستعلاء أمر ونهي[١] (٣) ومع التساوي التماس (٤) ومع الخضوع في الأمر والنهي سؤال ودعاء؛ وإلا[٢] فتنبيه. ويدخل فيه التمنّي والترجّي والتعجّب والقسَم والنداء.

An incomplete expression is either *restrictive*, e.g., *al-ḥayawānu al-nāṭiqu* (the rational animal), or it is *non-restrictive*, e.g., [expressions] composed of a noun and a particle.[14]

وغير التامّ إما تقييدي كـ«الحيوان الناطق» أو غير تقييدي كالمركّب من اسم وحرف.

❁ ❁ ❁

Here concludes the introduction by the assistance of Allah ﷻ. By His permission ﷻ, the four chapters follow.

إلى هنا تمّت المقدّمة بعون الله تعالى. تليها بإذنه تعالى الأبواب الأربعة.

---

[1] If you were to say: An expression like *yā Zaydu* (O Zayd) does convey asking for the [act] of approaching to be brought about, but it is not a command; therefore, the definition of "command" fails to be sufficiently exclusive. We would say: Implicit definitions such as those resulting from a division are not to be objected to and disputed in this manner. That is not to mention, moreover, that the grammatical *vocative* is assigned [the function of] drawing the attention of the interlocutor, which entails asking that one approach. As for their saying that "one who is called" (*munādā*) is "one who is asked to approach," this is a loose formulation on their part, [defining a thing merely] by citing what it entails.

[2] That is, if the expression is not assigned to signify asking.

[١] فإن قلت إن نحو «يا زيد»[٣] يفيد طلب تحصيل ماهيّة الإقبال وليس بأمر فاختلّ حدّ الأمر منعًا، قلنا: إن الحدود الضمنيّة كالمستفادة من التقسيم لا يتوجّه عليها المؤاخذة والمناقشة بمثل ذلك، على أن النداء وضع لتنبيه المخاطب ويلزم منه طلب الإقبال. وأما قولهم المنادى[٤] هو المطلوب إقباله فتسامح منهم بذكر اللازم.

[٢] أي وإن لم يوضع للطلب.

Chapter 1

THE FIVE UNIVERSALS

Definition and classification

Our discussion in this chapter concerns universals; the division of universals into essential and accidental; the division of the essential into genus, species, and differentia; the division of the accidental into special accident and general accident; and an explication of the kinds of relations between two universals. Success and rectitude are through Allah ﷻ.

Kulliyyāt (universals) is the plural of *kullī*. A *universal* is that whose mere conception[15] does not preclude that it could be shared.[16] Universals are of two types: (1) *essential*, i.e., that which is not external to the essence of its particulars, whether it be identical to their essence, e.g., 'human',[1] or contained within their essence, e.g., 'animal'[2] and 'rational thing',[3] and (2) *accidental*, which is the opposite,[4] e.g., 'laughing thing'[5] and 'breathing thing'.

---

[1] 'Human' is identical to the essence of Zayd, ʿAmr, and other instances of 'human'.

[2] 'Animal' is a universal contained within the essence of its particulars, namely, humans, donkeys, horses, and other instances of animals.

[3] 'Rational thing' is a universal contained within the essence of its particulars, namely, Zayd, ʿAmr, Bakr, and other instances of rational things.

[4] That is, a universal that is external to the essence of its particulars.

[5] 'Laughing thing' is external to the essence of its instances, which are Zayd, ʿAmr, and other instances of laughing things.[17]

الباب الأول

الكليات الخمسة

تعريفه وانقسامه

كلامنا في هذا الباب في الكلّيات وانقسام الكلّي إلى ذاتي وعرضي، والذاتي إلى جنس ونوع وفصل، والعرضي إلى خاصّة وعرض عامّ، وفي بيان النسب بين الكلّيتين. وبالله تعالى التوفيق والسداد.

«الكلّيات» جمع «كلّي»، والكلّي ما لا يمنع نفس تصوّر مفهومه عن وقوع الشركة فيه. وهو قسمان: (١) ذاتي وهو ما لا يخرج عن حقيقة جزئيّاته سواء كان عينها كالإنسان،[١] أو داخلًا فيها كالحيوان[٢] والناطق؛[٣] (٢) عرضي وهو بخلافه[٤] كالضاحك[٥] والمتنفّس.

---

[١] فإنه عين حقيقة زيد وعمرو وغيرهما من أفراد الإنسان.

[٢] فإنه داخل في حقيقة جزئيّاته التي هي الإنسان والحمار والفرس وغيرهما من أفراد الحيوان منه.

[٣] فإنه داخل في حقيقة جزئيّاته التي هي زيد وعمرو وبكر وغيرها من أفراد الناطق منه.

[٤] أي ما يخرج عن حقيقة جزئيّاته منه.

[٥] فإنه خارج عن حقيقة أفراده التي هي زيد وعمرو وغيرهما من أفراده.

Essential Universals

The essential universal is of three types: genus, species, and differentia.

Genus

A genus is said in response to "What is it?"[1] in consideration of what is shared, unconditionally. It is defined as [that which is] predicated of multiple things that have different essences in response to "What is it?" A genus is (1) *direct* if it can correctly be given in response to [a question about] a quiddity and all [other quiddities] with which that quiddity shares the genus. Take 'animal', for example: it can correctly be given in response to [a question about] 'human', 'horse', and everything that shares 'animal' with them. A genus is (2) *remote* if it cannot be correctly given in response to [a question about] a quiddity and all with which it shares the genus, but can [correctly be given in response to a question] about the quiddity and some [other quiddities with which it shares the genus], e.g., 'growing body' in relation to 'human', for it can correctly be given in response [to a question] about [humans] and plants but not [to one] about [humans] and horses.

A remote genus is either [removed] by one rank, e.g., 'growing body'; by two ranks, e.g., 'physical body';[2] or by three ranks, e.g., 'substance'.[3] Now, these can be ordered into an ascending hierarchy: the furthest of them all is termed a *highest genus* or a *genus of genera*, the nearest a *lowest genus*, and any [genus] between the two an *intermediate genus*.

[1] [This question] represents [all forms of] asking about the essence, whether by the expression "What is it?" or "What are the two of them?" or "What are they?" Thus one cannot object that "What is it?" asks about a single thing while the author's phrase "in consideration of what is shared" indicates multiplicity and that there is therefore a contradiction between these two [parts of the definition].

[2] I.e., that which has the three dimensions, which are height, width, and depth.

[3] I.e., that which subsists in itself.

الذاتي

ينقسم إلى ثلاثة: جنس ونوع وفصل.

الجنس

وهو مقول في جواب «ما هو»[١] بحسب الشركة المحضة، ويعرف بأنه مقول على كثيرين مختلفين بالحقائق في جواب «ما هو». وهو (١) قريب إن صلح جوابًا عن الماهيّة وعن جميع مشاركاتها فيه كالحيوان فإنه يصلح جوابًا للإنسان والفرس وجميع ما يشاركهما فيه؛ (٢) وبعيد إن لم يصلح جوابًا عنها وعن جميع المشاركات بل عنها وعن بعضها كالجسم النامي بالنسبة إلى الإنسان فإنه يصلح جوابًا له وللنباتات لا له وللفرس.

والبعيد إما بمرتبة كالجسم النامي أو بمرتبتين كالجسم المطلق[٢] أو ثلاث مراتب كالجوهر.[٣] فهي قد تترتّب متصاعدة ويقال للأبعد من الكل الجنس العالي وجنس الأجناس، وللقريب الجنس السافل، ولما بينهما الجنس المتوسّط.

[١] كناية عن السؤال عن الحقيقة سواء كان بلفظ «ما هو» أو «ما هما» أو «ما هم» فلا يرد أن «ما هو» سؤال عن الواحد وقوله «بحسب الشركة» إشارة إلى التعدّد فبينهما تناف.

[٢] وهو ما له الأبعاد الثلاثة التي هي الطول والعرض والعمق.

[٣] وهو ما يقوم بنفسه.

Species

Species is of two types. A species may be (1) said in response to "What is it?" in consideration of both[1] what is shared and what is unique. This is *real species*, defined as [that which is] said of multiple things with identical essences in response to "What is it?" Or else it may be (2) a universal of which together with other universals a genus is predicated in response to "What is it?"[2] by way of primary predication.[3] This is *relative species*, e.g., 'animal' and 'growing body'.

Species can be ordered into a descending hierarchy: the broadest of them all is termed a *highest species*, the narrowest a *lowest species* or a *species of species*, and any [species] between the two an *intermediate species*.

Differentia

A differentia is not said in response to "What is it?"; rather, it is said in response to "What kind of thing is it essentially?" It is defined as [that which is] predicated of a thing in response to "What kind of thing is it essentially?" A differentia is (1) *direct* if it distinguishes a thing from that with which it shares the direct genus, e.g., 'rational thing', which distin-

النوع

وهو على قسمين: (١) إما مقول في جواب «ما هو» بحسب الشركة والخصوصيّة معًا[١] وهو النوع الحقيقي، ويعرّف بأنه° مقول على كثيرين متّفقين بالحقيقة في جواب «ما هو»؛ (٢) وإما كلّي[٢] يقال عليه وعلى غيره الجنس في جواب «ما هو» قولًا أوّليًّا[٣] وهو النوع الإضافي كالحيوان والجسم النامي.

والأنواع قد تترتّب متنازلة فيسمّى الأعمّ من الكل النوع العالي، والأخصّ منه النوع السافل ونوع الأنواع، وما بينهما النوع المتوسّط.

الفصل

وهو غير مقول في جواب «ما هو» بل مقول في جواب «أيّ شيء هو في حدّ ذاته»، ويعرّف بأنه مقول على الشيء في جواب «أيّ شيء هو في حدّ ذاته». وهو (١) قريب إن ميّز الشيء عما يشاركه في الجنس القريب

[1] That is, *jamīʿan* (in totality).

[2] That is, a universal that has a genus above it. Granted that this would have been more concise to say, I refrained from doing so for the sake of following the precedent of previous authors and training the minds of beginners.

[3] That is, without any intermediary [predication]. This qualification excludes *sorts*, e.g., 'Turk', for it is a universal of which together with another [universal] (e.g., 'donkey') the genus (i.e., 'animal') is predicated in response to "What is it?" though not by way of primary predication but rather by the intermediary predication of 'human'.[18]

[١] أي جميعًا.

[٢] أي كلّي فوقه جنس وإنما لم أقل ذلك مع أنه أخصر تبعًا للمصنّفين وتشحيذًا لذهن المبتدئين.

[٣] أي بلا واسطة. هذا القيد احتراز عن الصنف كالتركي، فإنه كلّي يقال عليه وعلى غيره (وهو الحمار) الجنس (وهو الحيوان) في جواب «ما هو» لكن لا قولًا أوّليًّا بل بواسطة حمل الإنسان عليه.

guishes 'human' from that with which it shares 'animal'. A differentia is (2) *remote* if it distinguishes a thing from that with which it shares a remote genus, e.g., 'sensitive thing', which distinguishes ['human'] from that with which it shares 'growing body'.

Furthermore, when a differentia is considered with respect to (1) what distinguishes [the thing], it is *constitutive*,[1] that is, inherent in the thing's quiddity, e.g., 'rational thing', which is inherent in 'rational animal'. And [when considered with respect] to (2) what is distinguished from [the thing], a differentia is *divisive*,[2] that is, divisive of the genus into its divisions, e.g., 'rational thing' and 'neighing thing' with respect to 'animal' and 'growing thing' with respect to 'physical body'.

Now, anything constitutive of the superordinate—e.g., 'thing extensible in the three dimensions', which is a constitutive differentia for 'physical body' and hence constitutive of 'human' as well—is constitutive of the subordinate universally, without the reverse being true.[3] The case is the opposite for anything divisive—e.g., 'rational thing', which divides 'animal', also divides 'substance'.[4]

[1] That is, inherent within its constitution, i.e., its essence.

[2] That is, entailing divisions.

[3] That is, it is not the case that everything constitutive of the subordinate is constitutive of the superordinate; rather, only some are, that is, those that are [in the first place] constitutive of the superordinate, which is [in turn] constitutive of the subordinate.

[4] That is, everything divisive of a subordinate is divisive of the superordinate universally, without the reverse being true; i.e., it is not the case that everything divisive of the superordinate is divisive of the subordinate. Take, for example, 'sensitive thing': it divides 'substance', which is superordinate, but does not divide 'animal'—instead, it constitutes it. Some, rather, of what is divisive of the superordinate is divisive of the subordinate, e.g., 'rational thing', which divides what is superordinate and divides what is subordinate, namely 'animal'.

كالناطق المميّز للإنسان عما يشاركه في الحيوان؛ (٢) وبعيد إن ميّزه عما يشاركه في الجنس البعيد كالحسّاس المميّز له عما يشاركه في الجسم النامي.

ثم الفصل إذا نسب إلى (١) ما يميّزه فمقوّم[١] أي داخل في ماهيّته، كناطق داخل في الحيوان الناطق؛ وإلى (٢) ما يميَّز عنه فمقسّم[٢] أي مقسّم الجنس إلى أقسامه، كالناطق والصاهل بالنسبة إلى الحيوان والنامي بالنسبة إلى الجسم.

وكل مقوّم للعالي كالقابل للأبعاد الثلاثة وهو فصل مقوّم للجسم المطلق فهو مقوّم للإنسان أيضا مقوّم للسافل ولا عكس كليًّا،[٣] والمقسّم كالناطق فإنه مقسّم للحيوان فهو مقسّم للجوهر أيضا بالعكس.٦[٤]

[١] أي داخل في قوامه أي حقيقته.

[٢] أي فمحصّل قسم منه.

[٣] أي ليس كل مقوّم للسافل مقوّمًا للعالي بل بعضه وهو ما كان مقوّمًا للعالي الذي هو مقوّم للسافل.

[٤] أي كل مقسّم للسافل مقسّم للعالي ولا عكس كليًّا أي ليس كل مقسّم للعالي مقسّمًا للسافل، كالحسّاس مثلًا فإنه مقسّم للجوهر وهو العالي وليس بمقسّم للحيوان بل مقوّم له؛ بل بعض مقسّم العالي مقسّم للسافل، كالناطق فإنه مقسّم للعالي ومقسّم للسافل الذي هو الحيوان.

Accidental Universals

Accidents are of two types: special accidents and general accidents. If an accident (1) is specific to a single essence, it is a *special accident* (e.g., 'laughing'), defined as [that which is] predicated of what falls under only a single essence by way of accidental predication. If it (2) includes more than a single essence, it is a *general accident* (e.g., 'breathing thing'), defined as [that which is] predicated of what falls under different essences by way of accidental predication.

Either of the two is an *inseparable accident* when its separation from a thing is impossible. Inseparable accidents are of three types: (1) *extramentally inseparable* if the accident is inseparable from the thing in extramental existence, e.g., blackness with respect to the Abyssinian; (2) *mentally inseparable* if the accident is inseparable from the thing in the mind, e.g., sight and blindness;[1] or (3) *essentially inseparable* if the accident is inseparable from the thing in both [extramental existence and the mind], e.g., evenness and four.

Each type of inseparable accident, furthermore, is of three types. An inseparable accident may be (1) *strictly evident*: whenever one conceives the implicant, one consequently conceives the inseparable accident. In this case, knowledge of the implicant necessitates knowledge of the implicate, e.g., 'two' being 'double one'.[2] This is the criterion for signification by concomitance according to the verifying scholars.[19] [Second], an inseparable accident may be (2)

[1] The conceptual meaning of 'blindness' is the privation of sight in the kind of thing that can possess sight. One cannot object: 'Blindness' signifies 'sight' by containment since 'sight' is part of its meaning. For we would respond: The meaning of 'blindness' is relational nonexistence, and the relatum, namely, 'sight', is external to the meaning.

[2] Whoever conceives 'two' apprehends that it is 'double one'. Al-Rāzī, *Sharḥ*, 1:279.

العرضي

والعرضي ينقسم إلى اثنين: خاصّة وعرض عامّ. إن (١) اختصّ بحقيقة واحدة فخاصّة كضاحك، وتعرّف بأنها مقولة على ما تحت حقيقة واحدة فقط قولًا عرضيًّا؛ وإن (٢) عمّ حقائق فوق واحدة فعرض عامّ كمتنفّس، ويعرّف بأنه مقول على ما تحت حقائق مختلفة قولًا عرضيًّا.

وكل منهما إن امتنع انفكاكه عن الشيء فلازم، وهو ثلاثة: (١) لازم وجودي إن لزم الشيء في الخارج، كالسواد للحبشي؛ (٢) ولازم ذهني إن لزمه في الذهن، كالبصر للعمى؛[١] (٣) ولازم الماهيّة إن لزمه فيهما، كالزوجيّة للأربعة.

وكل من اللازم أيضا ثلاثة: (١) إما بيّن بالمعنى الأخصّ وهو ما يلزم من تصوّر الملزوم تصوّره أي يكون العلم بالملزوم موجبًا للعلم باللازم، ككون الاثنين ضعف الواحد،[٢] وهذا هو المعتبر في الدلالة الالتزاميّة عند المحقّقين؛ (٢) وإما بيّن بالمعنى الأعمّ

[١] فإن مفهومه عدم البصر عما من شأنه أن يكون بصيرًا. لا يقال دلالة العمى على البصر تضمنيّة لأن البصر جزء من مفهومه، لأنا[٧] نقول أن مفهوم العمى العدم المضاف والمضاف إليه وهو البصر خارج من مفهومه.

[٢] فإن من تصوّر الاثنين أدرك أنه ضعف الواحد (شرح الشمسيّة).

broadly evident: whenever one conceives both,[1] one is consequently certain, without need for proof, that one entails the other,[2] e.g., 'even number' [as entailed by] 'four'. There is disagreement over whether this is a sufficient criterion for signification by concomitance, and the sounder position is that it is insufficient. [Third], an inseparable accident may be (3) *inevident*, i.e., an accident regarding which certainty of the [relationship][3] requires proof, e.g., the universe's entailment of contingency.[4]

But if an accident's separation from a thing is not impossible, then it is *separable*—either (1) *possibly separable*, e.g., the motion of the celestial spheres, continual poverty for one whose material sufficiency is possible, and disbelief for one whose belief is possible, or (2) *actually separating*, whether quickly or gradually, e.g., standing upright and youth.[5]

[1] That is, the implicant and the implicate.

[2] The reason this [relationship] is broader than the first is that whenever it is the case that the conception of the implicant alone entails the conception of the implicate, it is then the case that the conception of both entails the conception of the implicate, and the reverse does not hold.

[3] That is, of one's entailing the other.

[4] This requires that we state that it undergoes change and so on.

[5] If one were to say: This division—the division of the universal into genus, species, differentia, special accident, and general accident—is invalid, since various of its divisions may apply to one and the same thing. Take 'colored thing', for example: it is a genus for 'black thing', 'red thing', and 'yellow thing'; a species for 'qualified thing', as in 'thing that has smell', 'thing that has taste', and 'thing that has color'; a differentia for 'dense thing', which includes 'air'; a special accident for 'physical body', since 'physical body' is 'thing extensible in the three dimensions' and 'colored thing' is external to its essence; and a general accident for 'animal'. I would respond: This division is perspectival, such that a difference with respect to intension suffices for it. And: The qualification of perspective pertains in definitions, whether [the qualification] is mentioned or not.

وهو ما يلزم من تصوّرهما[١] جزم الذهن باللزوم بينهما بلا افتقار إلى دليل،[٢] كالزوجيّة للأربعة، وفي كفايته في الدلالة الالتزاميّة خلاف والأصحّ أنه غير كاف؛ (٣) وإما غير بيّن وهو الذي يحتاج الجزم به[٣] إلى دليل، كلزوم الحدوث للعالم.[٤]

وإن لم يمتنع انفكاكه عن الشيء فمفارق (١) بالإمكان كحركة الأفلاك وكالفقر الدائم لمن يمكن غناؤه وككفر من يمكن إيمانه أو (٢) بالفعل سريعًا أو بطيئًا كالقيام والشباب.[٥]

[١] أي الملزوم واللازم.

[٢] وإنما كان هذا أعمّ من الأول لأنه كلّما تحقّق استلزام تصوّر الملزوم فقط تصوّرَ اللازم تحقّق استلزام تصوّرهما تصوّرَ اللازم من غير عكس.

[٣] أي باللزوم بينهما.

[٤] فإنه يحتاج إلى قولنا «لأنه متغيّر...» إلخ.

[٥] فإن قيل: هذا التقسيم تقسيم الكلّي إلى الجنس والنوع والفصل والخاصّة والعرض العامّ باطل لتصادق أقسامه على شيء واحد، كالملوّن فإنه جنس للأسود والأحمر والأصفر، ونوع للمكيّف كالمشموم والمطعوم والملوّن، وفصل للكثيف كالهواء، وخاصّة للجسم فالجسم^ قابل للأبعاد الثلاثة والملوّن خارج عن حقيقته، وعرض عامّ للحيوان. أجيب بأن هذا التقسيم اعتباري يكفي فيه تغاير الأقسام بحسب المفهوم، وبأن قيد الحيثيّة معتبر في التعاريف ذكرت أو لم تذكر.

[Ontological Divisions of the Universal]

Furthermore, a universal is such that either (1) its extramental existence is impossible, e.g., 'partner of the Creator'; (2) its extramental existence is possible, but it does not exist, e.g., 'phoenix' and 'mountain of rubies'; (3) one[1] exists while others are impossible, e.g., 'the necessarily existent',[2] or (4) while others are possible, e.g., 'sun'; (5) a finite number exists, e.g., the planets; or (6) an infinite number exists, e.g., the things that Allah ﷻ knows.

The concept 'universal'[3] is termed the *logical concept of the universal*, and that which it characterizes[4] is termed a *natural universal*,[5] e.g., 'human', 'horse', 'word', and 'rational thing'. The two in combination are a *conceptualized universal*. The same is the case for 'genus'[6] and its sisters.[7]

The Relations between Universals

The kinds of relations between two universals are confined to four: mutual distinction, coextension, subsumption, and partial overlap:

---

[1] Of the universal's instances.

[2] This is termed the *universal confined to a single instance*.

[3] I.e., that the mere conception of which does not preclude that it could be shared.

[4] I.e., that which universality characterizes.

[5] Since it is a certain nature, that is, a certain essence.

[6] The intension of 'genus', i.e., 'thing predicable of multiple things…', is the *logical concept of the genus*; what it characterizes, e.g., 'animal', 'word', and 'growing body', is a *natural genus*; and the two in combination are a *conceptualized genus*. Extrapolate from this to 'species', 'differentia', 'special accident', and 'general accident'.

[7] Namely, 'species', 'differentia', 'special accident', and 'general accident'.

[أقسام الكلي من حيث الوجود]

ثم الكلّي (١) إما ممتنع الوجود في الخارج، كشريك الباري؛ (٢) أو ممكن ولم يوجد، كالعنقاء وجبل من ياقوت؛ (٣) أو وجد واحد[١] مع امتناع غيره، كواجب الوجود؛[٢] (٤) أو مع إمكانه، كالشمس؛ (٥) أو كثير متناهٍ، كالكواكب السيّارة؛ (٦) أو غير متناهٍ، كمعلومات الله تعالى.

ومفهوم الكلّي[٣] يسمّى كليًّا منطقيًّا، ومعروضه[٤] كليًّا طبيعيًّا[٥] كالإنسان والفرس والكلمة والناطق، والمجموع كليًّا عقليًّا؛ وكذا الجنس[٦] وأخواته.[٧]

بيان النسب بين الكليين

النسب بين الكلّيين منحصرة في أربع: التباين، والتساوي، والعموم والخصوص المطلق، ومن وجه:

---

[١] من أفراد الكلّي.

[٢] ويسمّى الكلّي المنحصر في فرد.

[٣] وهو ما لا يمنع نفس تصوّر مفهومه عن وقوع الشركة فيه.

[٤] أي ما يعرض له الكلّية.

[٥] لأنه طبيعة [من]٩ الطبائع أي حقيقة من الحقائق.

[٦] فمفهومه وهو القول على كثيرين الخ جنس منطقي ومعروضه كالحيوان والكلمة والجسم النامي جنس طبيعي والمجموع جنس عقلي؛ وقس عليه النوع والفصل والخاصّة والعرض العامّ.

[٧] من النوع والفصل والخاصّة والعرض العامّ.

1. If the two universals do not overlap in their extension at all, then there is *mutual distinction* between them, e.g., 'human' and 'rock'. This kind of relation resolves into two universal negative propositions, e.g., 'Every human is not a rock' and 'Every rock is not a human'.
2. If they entirely overlap in their extension [from both perspectives], then there is *coextension*, e.g., 'human' and 'rational thing'. This kind of relation resolves into two universal affirmative propositions, e.g., 'Every human is rational' and 'Every rational thing is a human'. The same applies to their contradictory opposites.[1]
3. If they [entirely] overlap in their extension from one perspective,[20] then there is *subsumption*. This kind of relation resolves into a universal affirmative proposition[2] and a particular negative proposition.[3] The opposite applies to the contradictory opposites of two such universals.[4]
4. And if each diverges from the other in its extension,[21] then there is *partial overlap*, [e.g., 'white thing' and 'human']. This kind of relation resolves into a particular affirmative proposition and two particular negative propositions, e.g., 'Some white things are humans', 'Some humans are not white', and 'Some white things are not humans'.

١- فالكلّيان إن لم يتصادقا أصلًا فبينهما تباين كلّي، كالإنسان والحجر، ومرجعه إلى سالبتين كلّيتين، نحو «لا شيء من الإنسان بحجر» و«لا شيء من الحجر بإنسان».

٢- وإن تصادقا كليًّا فتساوٍ، كالإنسان والناطق، ومرجعه إلى موجبتين كلّيتين، نحو «كل إنسان ناطق» و«كل ناطق إنسان»؛ ونقيضهما[١] كذلك.

٣- وإن تصادقا من جانب واحد فعموم وخصوص مطلق، ومرجعه إلى موجبة كلّية[٢] وسالبة جزئيّة؛[٣] ونقيضاهما بالعكس.[٤]

٤- وإن افترق كل فمن وجه [كالأبيض والإنسان][١]، ومرجعه إلى موجبة جزئيّة وسالبتين جزئيّتين، نحو «بعض الأبيض إنسان» و«بعض الإنسان ليس بأبيض» و«بعض الأبيض ليس بإنسان».

[1] That is, the contradictory opposites of two coextensive universals are coextensive.

[2] From the perspective of the narrower [universal], with the narrower as subject and the broader as predicate.

[3] From the perspective of the broader [universal], with the broader as subject and the narrower as predicate.

[4] That is, the contradictory opposite of the narrow [universal] is broad, and the contradictory opposite of the broad [universal] is narrow.

[١] أي نقيضا المتساويين متساويان.

[٢] من طرف الأخصّ بأن يكون الأخصّ موضوعًا والأعمّ محمولًا.

[٣] من طرف الأعمّ بأن يكون الأعمّ موضوعًا والأخصّ محمولًا.

[٤] أي نقيض الخاصّ عامّ ونقيض العامّ خاصّ.

The contradictory opposites of two partially overlapping universals are either entirely distinct[1] or partially overlapping. Take 'white thing' and 'animal', for example: they partially overlap, and their contradictory opposites also partially overlap. Partially overlapping universals entail partial distinction; they, and also the contradictory opposites of mutually distinct universals, are partially distinct.[2]

The relation between a particular and a universal (e.g., 'Zayd' and 'human') is of subsumption if the former is a particular of the latter. Otherwise, they can only be mutually distinct (e.g., 'Zayd' and 'horse').

Now, these relations sometimes hold on account of predication and instantiation in regard to particulars, e.g., 'Zayd is a human'. And they sometimes hold on account of actualization and existence, as is the case with parts and wholes. Take, for example, 'wall' and 'house': whenever a house actually exists, walls actually exist, though not vice versa. Take also 'four' and 'five': whenever five actually exists, four actually exists, though not vice versa.

وبين نقيضيهما إما تباين كلّي[١] أو عموم وخصوص من وجه، كالأبيض والحيوان فإن بينهما عمومًا وخصوصًا من وجه وبين نقيضيهما أيضا عموم وخصوص من وجه. والتباين الجزئى لازم لهما فبينهما تباين جزئى وكذا بين نقيضي المتباينين.[٢]

والنسبة بين الجزئى والكلّي كزيد والإنسان بالعموم والخصوص المطلق إن كان جزئيًّا له، وإلا فالتباين بينهما لازم فقط كزيد والفرس.

ثم هذه النسب تكون تارة بحسب الحمل والصدق في الجزئى كزيد إنسان، وتارة بحسب التحقّق والوجود كما في الجزء والكل كالجدار والبيت فإنه كلّما تحقّق البيت تحقّق الجدار بدون العكس وكالأربعة والخمسة فإنه كلّما تحقّق الخمسة تحقّق الأربعة دون العكس.

---

[1] Thus, between 'non-human' and 'animal' there is partial overlap, and between their contradictory opposites, namely 'non-animal' and 'human', there is entire distinction.

[2] In some cases the contradictory opposites of mutually distinct universals are entirely distinct. Take, for example, 'existent' and 'nonexistent': they are entirely distinct, and their contradictory opposites, namely 'non-existent' and 'non-nonexistent', are also entirely distinct. But in other cases they partially overlap. Take, for example, 'human' and 'horse': they are entirely distinct, but their contradictory opposites, namely 'non-human' and 'non-horse', partially overlap. Yet both kinds of cases entail partial distinctness; the contradictory opposites of mutually distinct universals are [always] partially distinct.

[١] فإنه بين اللاإنسان والحيوان عموم وخصوص من وجه وبين نقيضيهما اللذين هما لاحيوان وإنسان تباين كلّي.

[٢] فإن بين نقيضيهما تارة تباينًا كليًّا، كالموجود والمعدوم فإن بينهما تباينًا كليًّا وبين نقيضيهما اللذين هما اللاموجود واللامعدوم أيضا تباين كلّي؛ وتارة بينهما عموم وخصوص من وجه، كالإنسان والفرس فإن بينهما تباينًا كليًّا وبين نقيضيهما اللذين هما اللاإنسان واللافرس عموم وخصوص من وجه. والتباين الجزئى لازم لهما فبين نقيضي المتباينين تباين جزئى.

Chapter 2

DEFINITIONS

Also termed *taʿrīf* (definition)
or the *muʿarrif* (definiens)

Our discussion in this chapter, after we explain what definition is, concerns four matters: complete essential definition, incomplete essential definition, complete descriptive definition, and incomplete descriptive definition. Success and rectitude are through Allah ﷻ.

Definition is that whose conception causes one to acquire conception of a thing in its essence[1] or in some nonessential aspect that distinguishes it from all else.[2] It is of four types:

1. *complete essential definition*, if the definition is composed of the thing's direct genus and direct differentia, e.g., 'rational animal'.22
2. *incomplete essential definition*, if the definition is composed of a remote genus of the thing and its direct differentia, e.g., 'rational body'.

The differentia alone—e.g., to say, "Rational," in response to one who asks, "What is the human being?"—could bear the meaning of either [type of essential definition] if either [the direct genus or the remote genus] is implied: complete essential def-

[1] In reference to essential definition.

[2] In reference to descriptive definition.

الباب الثاني

القول الشارح

ويقال له التعريف والمعرِّف

كلامنا في هذا الباب بعد بيان التعريف في أربعة أشياء: حدّ تامّ، حدّ ناقص، رسم تامّ، رسم ناقص. وبالله تعالى التوفيق والسداد.

التعريف هو ما يكون تصوّره سببًا لاكتساب تصوّر الشيء بكنهه[١] أو بوجه غير الكنه يميّزه عما عداه.[٢] وأقسامه أربعة:

١- الأول حدّ تامّ إن تركّب من جنس الشيء وفصله القريبين، كالحيوان الناطق.

٢- والثاني حدّ ناقص إن تركّب من جنسه البعيد وفصله القريب، كالجسم الناطق.

والفصل وحده — كأن تقول «ناطق» في جواب من قال «إن الإنسان ما هو؟» — في معنى أحدهما إن قدّر أحد

[١] إشارة إلى الحدّ.

[٢] إشارة إلى الرسم.

inition if the direct genus is implied and incomplete essential definition if the remote genus is implied.

3. *complete descriptive definition*, if the definition is composed of the direct genus and an inseparable special accident of the thing, e.g., 'laughing animal'.

4. *incomplete descriptive definition*, if the definition is composed (a) of a remote genus and an inseparable special accident of the thing, e.g., 'laughing body'; (b) of a general accident and the differentia, e.g., 'walking rational thing'; (c) of a general accident and a special accident, e.g., 'walking laughing thing'; (d) of the direct differentia and a special accident, e.g., 'rational laughing thing'; (e) of a remote genus, the differentia, and a special accident, e.g., 'rational laughing body'; or (f) of accidents that when taken together are specific to a single essence, e.g., to say in defining 'human' that it is "something that walks on its two feet, has wide nails, bare skin, and an upright bodily form, and by its nature can laugh."

[This division of the types of definition] is accounted for in the following way. A definition is given either through essential universals alone or not. If it is given through essential universals alone, either it incorporates all of them, and this is complete essential definition, or some of them, and this is incomplete essential definition. If it is not given through essential universals alone, either it incorporates the direct genus and an inseparable special accident, e.g., 'laughing animal', and this is complete descriptive definition, or it does not, and this is incomplete descriptive definition.

المذكورين، فحدّ تامّ إن قدّر الجنس القريب وناقص إن قدّر الجنس البعيد.

٣- والثالث رسم تامّ إن تركّب من جنس الشيء القريب وخاصّته اللازمة، كالحيوان الضاحك.

٤- والرابع رسم ناقص إن تركّب (١) من جنسه البعيد وخاصّته اللازمة، كالجسم الضاحك؛ أو (٢) من العرض العامّ والفصل، كالماشي الناطق؛ أو (٣) من العرض العامّ والخاصّة، كالماشي الضاحك؛ أو (٤) من الفصل القريب والخاصّة، كالناطق الضاحك؛ أو (٥) من الجنس البعيد والفصل والخاصّة، كالجسم الناطق الضاحك؛ أو (٦) من عرضيّات تختصّ جملتها بحقيقة واحدة، كقولنا في تعريف الإنسان «إنه ماشٍ على قدميه، عريض الأظفار، بادي البشرة، مستقيم القامة، ضحّاك بالطبع».

وطريق الضبط أن التعريف إما بمجرّد الذاتيّات أو لا؛ فإن كان بمجرّد الذاتيّات فإما أن يكون بجميعها وهو الحدّ التامّ أو ببعضها وهو الحدّ الناقص، وإن لم يكن بمجرّد الذاتيّات فإما أن يكون بالجنس القريب والخاصّة اللازمة كالحيوان الضاحك وهو الرسم التامّ أو لا وهو الرسم الناقص.

It is necessary to avoid defining a thing through what is equally familiar or obscure, e.g., defining 'motion' as 'what is not stillness',[1] and 'even thing' as 'thing that is not odd'.[2] [It is also necessary to avoid] defining a thing through what can be defined only through it,[3] so that circularity is not entailed. This is irrespective of whether the circularity occurs in one step[4]—as when one says, "Quality is that by which similarity obtains," and then says, "Similarity is to possess the same quality"—or whether it occurs in multiple steps—as when one says, "Two (*al-ithnān*) is the first even number," then says, "An even number is what is divisible into two equal numbers," then says, "Two equal numbers are two things neither of which is greater than the other," and then says, "Two things (*shayʾān*) are two (*ithnān*)." It is also [necessary to avoid defining a thing through] terms whose signification is not apparent, through equivocal terms, and, unless the intended meaning is clear, through nonliteral expressions.

Now, definitions of extramentally existing quiddities are termed *real* and those of mentally considered ones *nominal*.23

In both, it is a condition that the definition be sufficiently inclusive and exclusive,[5] restrictive and comprehensive. The early-period scholars, however, deemed it acceptable for an incomplete definition,

[1] 'Motion' ought rather to be defined as 'two states of being in two places at two times, [respectively]', and 'stillness' as 'two states of being in one place at two times, [respectively]'.

[2] 'Even thing' ought rather to be defined as 'thing that is divisible into two equal things'.

[3] That is, the thing [being defined].

[4] This is termed *explicit circularity*.

[5] Defining a thing through what is broader or narrower is invalid since in the former case the definition would not be exclusive, and in the latter it would not be inclusive.

ويجب الاحتراز عن تعريف الشيء بما يساويه في المعرفة والجهالة، كتعريف الحركة بما ليس بسكون[١] والزوج بما ليس بفرد؛[٢] وعن تعريفه بما لا يعرف إلا به[٣] حتى لا يلزم الدور، سواء كان بمرتبة[٤] كما يقال «الكيفيّة ما بها تقع المشابهة» ثم يقال «المشابهة اتّفاق في الكيفيّة»، أو بمراتب كما يقال «الاثنان هو الزوج الأول» ثم يقال «الزوج هو المنقسم بمتساويين» ثم يقال «المتساويان هما الشيئان اللذان لا يفضل أحدهما على الآخر» ثم يقال «الشيئان هما الاثنان»؛ وكذا عن غير ظاهر الدلالة والمشترك والمجاز إلا عند ظهور المراد.

ثم التعريف للماهيّة الموجودة في الخارج يسمّى حقيقيًّا وللاعتباريّة اسميًّا.

وشرط التعريف فيهما أن يكون جامعًا ومانعًا[٥] مطّردًا ومنعكسًا، لكن القدماء جوّزوا في الناقص حدًّا كان أو

[١] بل يقال في تعريفها «الحركة كونان في آنين في مكانين» وفي تعريف السكون «كونان في آنين في مكان».

[٢] بل يقال هو المنقسم بمتساويين.

[٣] أي الشيء.

[٤] ويسمّى دورًا مصرّحًا.

[٥] فلا يجوز التعريف بالأعمّ ولا بالأخصّ إذ حينئذ لا يكون مانعًا في الأول وجامعًا في الثاني.

whether an essential or descriptive definition, to be broader [than the definiendum], and the shaykh Abū ʿAlī b. Sīnā[24] and many of the verifying scholars approved of this.

رسمًا أن يكون أعمّ واستحسنه الشيخ أبو علي بن سينا وكثير من المحقّقين.

To elucidate an expression by means of a clearer expression is termed *lexical definition*, e.g., elucidating *ghaḍanfar* (lion) by means of *asad* (lion). This is the procedure of the lexicologists.

وتفسير لفظ بلفظ أوضح منه يسمّى تعريفًا لفظيًّا، كتفسير «الغضنفر» بـ«الأسد»؛ وهو طريق أهل اللغة.

Chapter 3

PROPOSITIONS

الباب الثالث

القضـايـا

Our discussion in this chapter concerns the definition of the proposition; the division of propositions into categorical and hypothetical, of hypothetical propositions into conditional and disjunctive, of conditional propositions into inherent and coincidental, and of disjunctive propositions into three types; and an explication of the quantifiers of propositions. Success and rectitude are through Allah ﷻ.

كلامنـا في هـذا الباب في تعريـف القضيّـة وانقسـامها إلى حمليّـة وشرطيّـة، والشرطيّـة إلى متّصلـة ومنفصلـة، والمتّصلـة إلى لزوميّـة واتّفاقيّـة، والمنفصلـة إلى ثلاثـة أقسـام؛ وفي بيـان الأسـوار للقضايـا. وبـالله تعـالى التوفيـق والسـداد.

Definition and Classification into Categorical and Hypothetical

تعريف القضية وانقسامها إلى حملية وشرطية

A proposition is a composite expression[25] with the kind of conceptual form that makes it meaningful to say that he who expresses it has spoken truly or falsely.[26]

القضيّـة قـول يصحّ أن يقـال لقائلـه بمجـرّد النظـر إلى مفهومـه أنـه صـادق فيـه أو كاذب فيـه.

[Categorical Propositions]

[القضية الحملية]

A proposition is *categorical* if its two extremes are simple either actually, e.g., *Zaydun qā'imun* (Zayd is standing), or potentially,[27] e.g., *Zaydun qā'imun abūhu* (Zayd is such that his father is standing).

وهي إمـا حمليّـة إن كان طرفاها مفرديـن بالفعل نحو «زيد قائـم» أو بالقوّة نحو «زيـد قائم أبوه». والمحكـوم عليه في

That about which the judgment is made in a categorical proposition is termed the *subject*, that by which the judgment is made the *predicate*, and that which signifies the relation[1] the *copula*.[28]

With respect to the copula, categorical propositions are of two types: (1) *three-part* if the copula is mentioned, e.g., *Zaydun huwa ʿālimun* (Zayd is [*huwa*] a scholar), and (2) *two-part* if the copula is omitted, e.g., *Zaydun ʿālimun* (Zayd is a scholar).

A categorical proposition is

1. *subject-privative* if a negative particle is part of the subject, e.g., "The non-living-thing is inanimate."
2. *predicate-privative* if it is part of the predicate, e.g., "The inanimate thing is non-knowing."
3. *doubly privative* if it is part of both, e.g., "The non-living-thing is non-knowing."
4. or else *non-privative*, also termed *existential*, and this is what is not any of the above.

[Hypothetical Propositions]

A proposition is *hypothetical* if its two extremes are not simple expressions, e.g., the statement "If the sun has risen then it is daytime." The first part of a hypothetical proposition is termed the *antecedent* and the second the *consequent*. Hypothetical propositions can be divided into conditional and disjunctive.

[Conditional Propositions] A conditional proposition is

[1] As in the expression *huwa*, for example.

الحمليّة يسمّى موضوعًا والمحكوم به محمولًا والدالّ على النسبة[١] رابطة.

وهي باعتبار الرابطة اثنتان:[١٢] (١) ثلاثيّة إن ذكرت فيها الرابطة، نحو «زيد هو عالم»؛ (٢) وثنائيّة إن حذفت منها، نحو «زيد عالم».

والحمليّة إما:

١- معدولة الموضوع إن كان حرف السلب جزءًا منه، نحو «اللاحي جماد».

٢- أو معدولة المحمول إن كان جزءًا منه، نحو «الجماد لاعالم».

٣- أو معدولة الطرفين إن كان جزءًا منهما، نحو «اللاحي لاعالم».

٤- أو محصّلة وتسمّى وجوديّة أيضا وهي ما عداها.

[القضية الشرطية]

وإما شرطيّة إن لم يكن طرفاها مفردين، كقولنا «إن كانت الشمس طالعة فالنهار موجود». الجزء الأول من الشرطيّة يسمّى مقدّمًا والثاني تاليًا. وهي تنقسم إلى متّصلة ومنفصلة.

[الشرطية المتّصلة] فالمتّصلة إما:

[١] وهو لفظ «هو» مثلًا.

1. *inherently conditional* when its judgment is that the conditional relation between the two propositions is due to a connection such that
   (a) the antecedent is a cause of the consequent, e.g., "If the sun has risen then it is daytime."
   (b) the antecedent is an effect of the consequent, e.g., "If it is daytime then the sun has risen."
   (c) the two are effects of a single cause, e.g., "If it is daytime then the earth is illuminated."
   (d) there is a *conceptual correlation* between the two, e.g., "If Zayd is the father of ʿAmr then ʿAmr is his child."
2. *coincidentally conditional*[1] when [its judgment is that the conditional relation] is not due to a connection but rather obtains by mere concurrence in truth, e.g., the statement "If the human being is rational then donkeys bray." The truth of the consequent may be considered sufficient for the coincidentally conditional proposition, e.g., "If the human being is inanimate then donkeys bray."29 This [interpretation] is broad, and the former is narrow.[2]

[Disjunctive Propositions] The disjunctive proposition, which is of three types, is either

1. *strict*, i.e., that in which it is judged that two propositions are neither both true nor both false,31 e.g., the statement "This number is either even or odd."

١- لزوميّة إن كان الحكم فيها بالاتّصال بين القضيّتين لعلاقة:

(أ) بأن يكون المقدّم علّة للتالي، نحو «إن كانت الشمس طالعة فالنهار موجود».

(ب) أو معلولًا له، نحو «إن كان النهار موجودًا فالشمس طالعة».

(ج) أو يكونا معلولى علّة واحدة، نحو «إن كان النهار موجودًا فالأرض مضيئة».

(د) أو يكون بينهما تضايف، نحو «إن كان زيد أبا عمرو فعمرو ابنه».

٢- أو اتّفاقيّة[١] إن كان ذلك لا لعلاقة بل بمجرّد توافقهما على الصدق، كقولنا «إن كان الإنسان ناطقًا فالحمار ناهق». وقد يكتفى فيها بصدق التالي، نحو «إن كان الإنسان جمادًا فالحمار ناهق»؛ وهذه عامّة والأولى خاصّة.[٢]

[الشرطية المنفصلة] والمنفصلة وهي ثلاثة أقسام:

١- إما حقيقيّة وهي التي يحكم فيها بالتنافي بين القضيّتين في الصدق والكذب، كقولنا «إما أن يكون هذا العدد زوجًا أو فردًا».

[1] Grammatically conjoined to "inherently conditional."

[2] Because whenever both extremes are true, the consequent is true, but not vice versa.30

[١] عطف على «لزوميّة».

[٢] لأنه كلّما كان الطرفان صادقين كان التالي صادقًا بدون العكس.

2. *anti-inclusive*, i.e., that in which it is judged only that two propositions are not both true, e.g., the statement "This thing is either a tree or a rock."
3. *anti-exclusive*, i.e., that in which it is judged only that two propositions are not both false, e.g., the statement "Zayd is either in a large liquid body[1] or he is not about to drown."

Each of these three types is either

1. *inherently disjunctive*, i.e., that in which the disagreement is due to the respective essences of the disjuncts,[32] as in the examples introduced above.
2. *coincidentally disjunctive*, i.e., that in which the disagreement obtains by mere coincidence, e.g., to say of something that is black and does not write (a) in a strict disjunctive proposition, "This is either black or writes"; (b) in an anti-inclusive disjunctive proposition, "This is either not black or writes"; or (c) in an anti-exclusive disjunctive proposition, "This is either black or does not write."

Disjunctive propositions may take the formal appearance of having more than two disjuncts, e.g., to say in a strict disjunctive proposition, "A number is either abundant (e.g., twelve), deficient (e.g., four), or perfect (e.g., six)";[33] to say in an anti-inclusive disjunctive proposition, "This thing is either a tree, a rock, or an animal"; or to say in an anti-exclusive disjunctive proposition, "This thing is either not a tree, not a rock, or not an animal." Underlying the first example are [the two propositions] "A number is either abundant or not abundant" and "A number that is not abundant is either deficient or perfect." Underlying the second are "This thing is either a

[1] *Baḥr* (sea) here refers to anything liquid.

٢- وإما مانعة الجمع وهي التي يحكم فيها بالتنافي بينهما في الصدق فقط، كقولنا «إما أن يكون هذا الشيء شجرًا[١٣] أو حجرًا».

٣- وإما مانعة الخلوّ وهي التي يحكم فيها بالتنافي بينهما في الكذب فقط، كقولنا «زيد إما أن يكون في البحر[١] أو لا يغرق».

وكل من الثلاث:

١- إما عناديّة وهي التي يكون التنافي فيها لذات الجزئين، كما في الأمثلة المذكورة.

٢- أو اتّفاقيّة وهي التي يكون التنافي فيها بمجرّد الاتّفاق، كقولنا للأسود اللاكاتب (١) في الحقيقيّة «إما أن يكون هذا أسود أو كاتبًا»؛ (٢) وفي مانعة الجمع «إما أن يكون لاأسود أو كاتبًا»؛ (٣) وفي مانعة الخلوّ «إما أن يكون أسود أو لاكاتبًا».

وقد تكون المنفصلات ذوات أجزاء بحسب الظاهر، كقولنا في الحقيقيّة «العدد إما زائد كاثني عشر أو ناقص كأربعة أو مساو كستة»؛ وفي مانعة الجمع «هذا الشيء إما شجر أو حجر أو حيوان»؛ وفي مانعة الخلوّ «هذا الشيء إما لاشجر أو لاحجر أو لاحيوان». فأصل الأولى «العدد إما زائد أو غير زائد، وغير الزائد إما ناقص وإما

[١] والمراد بالبحر المائع.

rock or not a rock" and "What is not a rock is either a tree or an animal." And underlying the third are "This thing is either not a rock or not a non-rock" and "What is not a non-rock is either not a tree or not an animal."

[Negative Hypothetical Propositions] The *negative* of any kind of affirmative [hypothetical] proposition[1] is that which negates [the relation] that its respective affirmative proposition affirms, whether [the relation] is one of inherent conditionality, inherent disjunction, or coincidental conditionality/disjunction. A proposition that negates inherent conditionality is termed the *negative of inherent conditionality*, one that negates inherent disjunction the *negative of inherent disjunction*, and one that negates coincidental conditionality/disjunction the *negative of coincidental conditionality/disjunction*.

The Quantifiers of Propositions

Aswār is the plural of *sūr* (quantifier), namely, an expression that indicates whether a proposition is particular or universal.

1. The quantifiers[2] for [universal affirmative] categorical propositions are *kull*, *jamīʿ*, *qāṭiba*, *kāffa*, the universal *lām*, and similar expressions.34 Those for universal affirmative conditionals are *kullamā*, *matā*, *mahmā*, and expressions of the same meaning,35 and for universal affirmative disjunctions *dāʾiman*.36

[1] That is, each of the eight kinds of propositions, namely, the two conditionals (inherent and coincidental) and the six disjunctions (three inherent and three coincidental), all of which are affirmative. The negative kinds are also eight.

[2] That is, expressions that signify universality or particularity or an equivalent status.

مساوٍ»؛ وأصل الثانية «هذا الشيء إما حجر أو غير حجر، وغير الحجر إما شجر أو حيوان»؛ وأصل الثالثة «هذا الشيء إما لاحجر أو غير لاحجر، وغير اللاحجر إما لاشجر أو لاحيوان».

[الشرطية السالبة] وسالبة كل موجبة[١] هي ما ترفع ما حكم في موجبتها من اللزوم والعناد والاتّفاق. فالتي ترفع اللزوم تسمّى سالبة لزوميّة، والعناد تسمّى سالبة عناديّة، والاتّفاق تسمّى سالبة اتّفاقيّة.

بيان الأسوار للقضايا

«الأسوار» جمع «سور» وهو لفظ دالّ على جزئيّة القضيّة وكلّيتها.

١- السور[٢] للحمليّة: «كل» و«جميع» و«قاطبة» و«كافّة» ولام الاستغراق ونحوها. وللمتّصلة الموجبة الكلّية: «كلّما» و«متى» و«مهما» وما بمعناها. وللمنفصلة الموجبة الكلّية: «دائمًا».

[١] أي كل واحدة من القضايا الثمان وهي هذه متّصلتان لزوميّة واتّفاقيّة وستّ منفصلات ثلاث منها عناديّات وثلاث منها اتّفاقيّات وكلّها موجبات والسوالب أيضا ثمان.

[٢] وهو اللفظ الدالّ على الكلّية أو الجزئيّة أو ما في حكمهما.

2. The quantifiers for particular affirmative categorical propositions are *baʿḍ* and *wāḥid*,[37] and for conditionals and disjunctions *qad*.[38]
3. The quantifiers for universal negative categorical propositions are *lā shayʾ*, *lā wāḥid*, and the indefinite preceded by negation, e.g., in the statement *mā insānun bi-ḥajarin* (No human being is a rock),[39] and for universal negative conditionals and disjunctions *laysa al-battata*.[1]
4. The quantifiers for particular negative categorical propositions are *laysa kull*, *laysa baʿḍ*, and *baʿḍ...laysa*,[41] and for particular negative conditionals and disjunctions, respectively, *qad lā yakūn*, *laysa mahmā*, *laysa matā*, and expressions of the same meaning,[42] and *laysa dāʾiman*.[43]

Laysa baʿḍ (not some)[44] may be used for universal negation by one's treating *baʿḍ* (some) as an indefinite noun in the context of negation.[2] *Baʿḍ... laysa* (some...is not) may be used for affirmation by one's rendering *laysa* (not) a part of the predicate, such that the proposition is an affirmative predicate-privative proposition, e.g., the statement "Some animal is non-human."

An *unquantified proposition* is formulated by omitting the quantifier in categorical propositions or by employing the expressions *law*, *in*, or *idh* in conditionals[45] and *immā* or *aw* in disjunctions.[46]

٢- السور للحمليّة الموجبة الجزئيّة: «بعض» و«واحد». وللمتّصلة والمنفصلة: «قد».

٣- السور للحمليّة السالبة الكلّية: «لا شيء» و«لا واحد» والنكرة بعد النفي كقولنا «ما إنسانٌ بحجر». وللمتّصلة والمنفصلة السالبتين الكلّيتين: «ليس البتة».[١]

٤- السور للحمليّة السالبة الجزئيّة: «ليس كل» و«ليس بعض» و«بعض ليس». وللمتّصلة والمنفصلة السالبتين الجزئيّتين: «قد لا يكون» و«ليس مهما» و«ليس متى» وما بمعناها، و«ليس دائمًا».

و«ليس بعض» قد يُذكر للسلب الكلّي بجعل «بعض» كالنكرة في سياق النفي.[٢] و«بعض ليس» قد يذكر للإيجاب بجعل «ليس» جزءًا من المحمول فتكون القضيّة موجبة معدولة المحمول، كقولنا «بعض الحيوان ليس إنسانًا».

والمهملة تكون بترك أداة السور في الحمليّة وبإطلاق لفظة «لو» و«إن» و«إذا» في المتّصلة و«إما» و«أو» في المنفصلة.

---

[1] And *laysa...aṣlan* and *laysa...qaṭʿan*.[40]

[2] In that its signified meaning is not clarified. In same way that the indefinite in the context of negation imparts generality, so too in this case since the expression may be equally validly read as a negation with respect to any of the given [particulars], and this is universal negation.

[١] و«ليس أصلًا» و«ليس قطعًا».

[٢] في عدم تبيّن مدلوله فكما أن النكرة في سياق النفي يفيد العموم كذلك ههنا أيضا لأنه احتمل أن يفهم منه السلب في أيّ بعض كان وهو السلب الكلّي.

Contradiction, Conversion, and Contraposition

Contradiction

Contradiction is the difference between two propositions[1] in affirmation and negation in a way that inherently mandates that one be true and one false. This occurs only given that the two propositions concur with respect to their *judgmental relation*. Such concurrence presupposes that they concur with respect to the *eight unities* of subject, predicate, time, place, relation, potentiality and actuality, part and whole, condition, and similar [aspects of unity] including cause, instrument, and so forth.

Two quantified propositions must furthermore differ in universality and particularity since two universal propositions can be simultaneously false, e.g., "Every animal is a human being" and "No animal is a human being," and since two particular propositions can be simultaneously true, e.g., "Some animal is a human being" and "Some animal is not a human being," that is, whenever their matter[47] is such that the subject or antecedent is broader.[2] Thus, the universal affirmative and the particular negative are each the contradictory of the other, and the universal negative and the particular affirmative are each the contradictory of the other. The contradictory, then, of the statement "Every human being is an animal" is the statement "Some human being is not an animal," and the contradictory of the statement "No human being is a rock" is the statement "Some human being is a rock."

[1] This excludes the difference between two simple expressions and between a simple expression and a proposition.

[2] Than the predicate or consequent.

بيان التناقض والعكس المستوي وعكس النقيض

التناقض

وهــو اخــتلاف قضــيّتين[١] في الإيجــاب والســلب بحيــث يقــتضي لذاتــه أن تكــون إحداهمــا صادقــة والأخــرى كاذبــة. ولا يتحقّــق إلا بعــد اتّفاقهمــا في النســبة الحكميّــة، واتّفاقهمــا فيهــا يســتلزم اتّفاقهمــا في الوحــدات الثمــاني مــن الموضــوع، والمحمــول، والزمــان، والمكان، والإضافــة، والقــوّة والفعــل، والجــزء والكل، والشرط ونحوهــا مــن العلّــة والآلــة وغيرهــا.

ولا بــدّ في المحصــورتين مــع ذلــك مــن اختلافهمــا بالكلّيــة والجزئيّة لأن الكلّــيتين تكذبان نحــو «كل حيوان إنســان» و«لا شيء مــن الحيــوان إنســان» والجزئيّــتين تصدقــان نحــو «بعض الحيــوان إنســان» و«بعــض الحيوان ليــس بإنســان» في كل مــادّة يكــون الموضــوع أو المقــدّم فيهــا أعــمّ.[٢] فكل مــن الموجبــة الكلّيــة والســالبة الجزئيّــة نقيض الأخــرى وكل من الســالبة الكلّيــة والموجبــة الجزئيّة نقيض الأخــرى، فنقيض قولنا «كل إنســان حيــوان» قولنا «بعض الإنســان ليــس بحيــوان» ونقيض قــولنا «لا شيء من الإنســان بحجــر» «بعض الإنســان حجر».

[١] خرج اختلاف مفردين ومفرد وقضيّة.

[٢] من المحمول أو التالي.

Conversion

Conversion is to mutually transpose the extremes of a proposition while preserving its truth and quality.[1] Affirmative propositions, whether universal or particular, convert to particular affirmative propositions. Thus, the statements "Every human being [is an animal]" and "Some human being is an animal" [both] convert to "Some animal is a human being." They[2] do not convert to universal propositions, because it is possible that the predicate or antecedent be broader, which would make the converse untrue.

One might object: "Some human being is Zayd," though a particular affirmative proposition, does not convert, since one cannot say, "Some Zayd is a human being." I would respond: The meaning [of the former] is "Some human being is named 'Zayd'," so the proposition converts to "Something named 'Zayd' is a human being."

Universal negative propositions convert to universal negative propositions. Thus, the converse of the statement "No human being is a rock" is the statement "No rock is a human being."

Particular negative propositions always lack a converse because it is possible that (1) the subject be broader, as in the statement "Some animal is not a human being," or that (2) the antecedent be broader, as in the statement "Not in every case is it that when this is an animal it is a human being," which would make the converse untrue.

There is no value in the conversion of coincidental [conditionals] or of disjunctions, so the logicians have not given this consideration and there is no need to discuss it. There is also no value in contraposition, since it is not utilized in the sciences and in the production [of conclusions].

[1] That is, affirmation or negation.

[2] That is, universal affirmative propositions.

العكس المستوي

وهو تبديل طرَفَي القضيّة مع بقاء الصدق والكيف.[١] والموجبة كلّية كانت أو جزئيّة تنعكس موجبة جزئيّة، فينعكس قولنا «كل إنسان... أو بعض الإنسان حيوان» إلى قولنا «بعض الحيوان إنسان»، ولا تنعكس[٢] كلّية لجواز عموم المحمول أو التالي فلا يصدق العكس.

إن قيل: «بعض الإنسان زيد» لا تنعكس وهي موجبة جزئيّة إذ لا يقال «بعض زيد إنسان»، أجيب بأن المعنى «بعض الإنسان مسمّى بزيد» فتنعكس إلى قولنا «بعض المسمّى بزيد إنسان».

والسالبة الكلّية تنعكس سالبة كلّية، فعكس قولنا «لا شيء من الإنسان بحجر» قولنا «لا شيء من الحجر بإنسان».

والسالبة الجزئيّة لا عكس لها لزومًا لجواز عموم (١) الموضوع، كقولنا «بعض الحيوان ليس بإنسان»، أو (٢) المقدّم، كقولنا «قد لا يكون إذا كان هذا حيوانًا كان إنسانًا»؛ فلا يصدق العكس.

ولا فائدة في عكس الاتّفاقيّة والمنفصلات فلم يعتبره القوم فلا حاجة لذكره. وكذا لا فائدة في عكس النقيض لعدم استعماله في العلوم والإنتاج.

[١] أي الإيجاب والسلب.

[٢] أي الموجبة الكلّية.

Contraposition

According to the early-period logicians, contraposition is to mutually transpose the contradictory opposites of a proposition's extremes while preserving its truth and quality. Thus, when we say, "Every human being is an animal," the contrapositive would be "Everything that is not an animal is not a human being."

According to the late-period logicians, contraposition is to place the contradictory opposite of the second element of the original proposition first and to place the first element in its original form second while preserving the proposition's truth and changing its quality. Thus, the contrapositive of "Every human being is an animal" would be "[Nothing that] is not an animal is a human being."

عكس النقيض

وهـو عنـد المتقـدّمين تبديـل نقـيضي طـرفى القضيّـة مع بقاء الصدق والكيـف، فإذا قلنا «كل إنسـان حيوان» كان عكســه «كل ما ليس بحيـوان ليس بإنسـان».

وعنـد المتأخّريـن هـو جعـل نقيـض الجـزء الثاني من الأصـل أولًا وعين الأول ثانيًـا مـع بقاء الصـدق والمخالفة في الكيـف، فعكـس «كل إنسـان حيـوان» «[لا شيء مما] ليـس بحيوان إنسـان».

Chapter 4

SYLLOGISMS

الباب الرابع

القـيـاس

On the syllogism its types

القياس وأقسامه

A syllogism is a composite[48] of propositions that, when accepted, inherently entails another [proposition], e.g., to say, "This is an animal: it is a human, and every human is an animal; therefore, this is an animal."[49] With regard to form, there are two types of syllogisms; with regard to categoricity, conditionality, and disjunction, there are six; and with regard to matter, there are five.

القيـاس هو قـول مؤلّف من قضايا متى سـلّمت لـزم عنها لذاتهـا قول آخـر، كقولنا «هـذا حيـوان لأنه إنسـان، وكل إنسـان حيـوان، فهـذا حيـوان». أقسـامه هي مـن حيـث الصورة قسـمان، ومـن حيث الحمل والاتّصـال والانفصال سـتّة أقسـام، ومن حيث المادّة خمسـة أقسـام.

Syllogisms Classified by Form

أقسام القياس من حيث الصورة

There are two types of syllogisms with regard to form: combinative and replicative.

أقسامه من حيث الصورة اثنان: اقتراني واستثنائي.

Combinative Syllogisms

القياس الاقتراني

The combinative syllogism is that which explicitly incorporates neither the conclusion nor its contradictory,[1] e.g., to say, "The universe originated in time: it undergoes change, and everything that

هـو مـا لـم يكـن عين النتيجـة أو نقيضهـا مذكـورة فيه بالفعـل،[١] كقولنا «العالم حـادث لأنه متـغيّر، وكل متغيّر

[1] E.g., to say, "If this is a human then it is an animal, and this is a human; therefore, this is an animal": the conclusion is explicitly incorporated in the syllogism, i.e., in its same form. Or, [alternatively], "This is not an animal; therefore, this is not a human": the contradictory of the conclusion, which was "This is a human being," is mentioned in it explicitly.

[١] كقـولنا «إن كان هـذا إنسـانًا فهو حيـوان، لكنـه إنسـان، ينتج أنه حيـوان» فالنتيجة مذكورة فيـه بالفعل أي بصورتهـا؛ أو «...لكنه ليـس بحيـوان، ينتـج أنـه ليـس بإنسـان» فنقيـض النتيجـة وهـو «هـذا إنسـان» مذكـور فيـه بالفعل.

undergoes change originated in time; therefore, the universe originated in time."

There are four syllogistic figures. For if the middle term is the predicate in the minor premise and the subject in the major premise, that is the first figure. If it is the predicate in both premises, that is the second figure. If it is the subject in both premises, that is the third figure. And if [it is situated] in reverse of the first figure, that is the fourth figure.

[The First Figure] The conditions [for the productivity] of the first figure are that the minor premise be affirmative and the major premise universal; otherwise, there will invariably be a discrepancy that entails unproductivity (as goes for the conditions of the other figures as well).[50] The first figure has four productive moods.

The first comprises two universal affirmative premises and yields a universal affirmative conclusion, e.g., to say, "Every body is composite, and every composite thing was originated in time; therefore, every body was originated in time."

["Every body was originated in time"] is called the *conclusion*. Its subject is called the *minor term*, and the proposition that contains the minor term is called the *minor premise* or the *antecedent*. Its predicate is called the *major term*, and the proposition that contains the major term is called the *major premise* or the *consequent*. The term repeated in the minor and major premises—in this case, "thing that was originated in time"—is called the *middle term*. The coupling of the minor premise with the major premise[51] is called the *combination* or the *mood*, and the form of the composition of the minor and major premises is termed the *figure*.

حادث، فالعالم حادث».

والأشكال أربعة لأن الحدّ الأوسط إن كان محمولًا في الصغرى موضوعًا في الكبرى فهو الشكل الأول؛ أو محمولًا فيهما فهو الشكل الثاني؛ أو موضوعًا فيهما فهو الشكل الثالث؛ أو بعكس الأول فهو الشكل الرابع.

[الشكل الأول] وشرط الشكل الأول إيجاب الصغرى وكلّية الكبرى وإلا لزم الاختلاف الموجب للعقم؛ وكذا الكلام في شرائط سائر الأشكال. وضروبه المنتجة أربعة.

الأول من موجبتين كلّيتين ينتج موجبة كلّية، كقولنا «كل جسم مؤلّف، وكل مؤلّف محدَث، فكل جسم محدَث».

فـ[«كل جسم محدَث»][١٤] يسمّى نتيجة ومطلوبًا، وموضوعه يسمّى حدًّا أصغر، والقضيّة التي هو فيها تسمّى صغرى ومقدّمة، ومحموله يسمّى حدًّا أكبر، والقضيّة التي هو فيها تسمّى كبرى وتالية، والمكرّر بين الأصغر والأكبر وهو هنا «محدَث» يسمّى حدًّا أوسط، واقتران الصغرى والكبرى يسمّى قرينة وضربًا، وهيئة التأليف من الصغرى والكبرى تسمّى شكلًا.

The second [mood] comprises two universal premises, with the major premise negative,[1] and yields a universal negative conclusion, e.g., to say, "Every body is composite, and nothing composite is eternal; therefore, no body is eternal."

The third comprises two affirmative premises, with the major premise universal,[2] and yields a particular affirmative conclusion, e.g., to say, "Some body is composite, and everything composite was originated in time; therefore, some body was originated in time."

The fourth comprises a particular affirmative minor premise and a universal negative major premise and yields a particular negative conclusion, e.g., to say, "Some body is composite, and nothing composite is eternal; therefore, some body is not eternal."

An instructive note: The conclusion takes after the lesser of the two premises.[3] Thus, if the syllogism is composed of an affirmative and a negative premise, it yields a negative conclusion. And if it is composed of a particular and a universal premise, it yields a particular conclusion.

[The Second Figure] The conditions of the second figure are that its premises differ in affirmation and negation[4] and that the major premise be universal. It also has four productive moods.

[1] And with the minor premise affirmative, that is.

[2] And with the minor premise particular, that is.

[3] Regardless which figure.

[4] [This condition applies] whether [the syllogism is] of a familiar or an unfamiliar form, and the same is true for the other figures. What was mentioned above having been deemed sufficient, this generalization was not mentioned in the text here nor below. According to some, the condition here applies only to familiar syllogisms, and unfamiliar syllogisms of the second figure are productive with two affirmative premises as well.52

الثاني من كلّيتين والكبرى سالبة[١] ينتج سالبة كلّية، كقولنا «كل جسم مؤلّف، ولا شيء من المؤلّف بقديم، فلا شيء من الجسم بقديم».

والثالث من موجبتين والكبرى كلّية[٢] ينتج موجبة جزئيّة، كقولنا «بعض الجسم مؤلّف، وكل مؤلّف محدث، فبعض الجسم محدث».

والرابع من موجبة جزئيّة صغرى وسالبة كلّية كبرى ينتج سالبة جزئيّة، كقولنا «بعض الجسم مؤلّف، ولا شيء من المؤلّف بقديم، فبعض الجسم ليس بقديم».

تنبيه: النتيجة تتبع أخسّ المقدّمتين[٣] فإن كان القياس مركّبًا من موجبة وسالبة ينتج سالبة وإن كان مركّبًا من جزئيّة وكلّية ينتج جزئيّة.

[الشكل الثاني] وشرط الشكل الثاني اختلاف مقدّمتيه بالإيجاب والسلب[٤] وكلّية الكبرى. وضروبه المنتجة أيضا أربعة.

[١] أي والصغرى موجبة.

[٢] أي والصغرى جزئيّة.

[٣] في أي شكل كان.

[٤] متعارفًا كان أو غير متعارف وكذا في باقي الأشكال. ولم يذكر هذا التعميم هنا ولا فيما بعده اكتفاءً بما تقدّم. وقيل هنا شرط للمتعارف فقط. وأما غير المتعارف من الشكل الثاني فينتج من موجبتين أيضا.

The first comprises two universal premises, with the minor premise affirmative, and yields a universal negative conclusion, e.g., to say, "All salt is *ribawī*,[53] and no straw is *ribawī*; therefore, no salt is straw."

الأول من كلّيتين والصغرى موجبة ينتج سالبة كلّية، كقولنا «كل ملح ربوي، ولا شيء من التبن بربوي، فلا شيء من الملح بتبن».

The second comprises two universal premises, with the major premise affirmative, and yields a universal negative conclusion, e.g., to say, "No human being is inanimate, and every rock is inanimate; therefore, no human being is a rock."

والثاني من كلّيتين والكبرى موجبة ينتج سالبة كلّية، كقولنا «لا شيء من الإنسان بجماد، وكل حجر جماد، فلا شيء من الإنسان بحجر».

The third comprises a particular affirmative minor premise and a universal negative major premise and yields a particular negative conclusion, e.g., to say, "Some person is a believer, and no polytheist is a believer; therefore, some person is not a polytheist."

والثالث من موجبة جزئيّة صغرى وسالبة كلّية كبرى ينتج سالبة جزئيّة، كقولنا «بعض الناس مؤمن، ولا شيء من المشرك بمؤمن، فبعض الناس ليس بمشرك».

The fourth comprises a particular negative minor premise and a universal affirmative major premise and yields a particular negative conclusion, e.g., to say, "Some word is not in the nominative case, and every agent is in the nominative case; therefore, some word is not an agent."

والرابع من سالبة جزئيّة صغرى وموجبة كلّية كبرى ينتج سالبة جزئيّة، كقولنا «بعض الكلمة ليس بمرفوع، وكل فاعل مرفوع، فبعض الكلمة ليس بفاعل».

[The Third Figure] The conditions of the third figure are that the minor premise be affirmative and that either premise be universal. It[1] yields only particular conclusions because it is possible that the minor term be broader than the major term, and it is impossible to affirm or negate the narrower of every instance of the broader. The third figure has six productive moods.

[الشكل الثالث] وشرط الشكل الثالث إيجاب الصغرى وكلّية إحدى المقدّمتين. ولا ينتج[١] إلا الجزئيّة لجواز أن يكون الأصغر أعمّ من الأكبر وامتناع إيجاب الأخصّ لكل أفراد الأعمّ أو سلبه عنها. وضروبه المنتجة ستّة.

The first comprises two universal affirmative premises, e.g., to say, "Every human being is an animal, and every human being is rational; therefore, some animal is rational."

الأول من موجبتين كلّيتين، كقولنا «كل إنسان حيوان، وكل إنسان ناطق، فبعض الحيوان ناطق».

[1] That is, this third figure.

[١] أي هذا الشكل الثالث.

The second comprises two universal premises, with the major premise negative,[1] e.g., to say, "All wheat is nutritional, and no wheat is something whose sale for an unequal amount of an item of the same kind is permissible; therefore, some nutritional thing is not something whose sale for an unequal amount of an item of the same kind is permissible."

The third comprises two affirmative premises, with the major premise universal,[2] e.g., to say, "Some agent is in the nominative case, and every agent is syntactically integral; therefore, something in the nominative case is syntactically integral."

The fourth comprises a particular affirmative minor premise and a universal negative major premise,[3] e.g., to say, "Some grammatical object is in the accusative case, and no grammatical object is in the genitive case; therefore, something in the accusative case is not in the genitive case."

The fifth comprises two affirmative premises, with the minor premise universal,[4] e.g., to say, "Every human being is an animal, and some human being writes; therefore, some animal writes."

The sixth comprises a universal affirmative minor premise and a particular negative major premise, e.g., to say, "Every fish is an animal, and some fish is not a donkey; therefore, some animal is not a donkey."

[The Fourth Figure] The condition of the fourth figure is that one of two alternative conditions be met: either that both premises be affirmative with the minor premise universal or that the two premises differ in quality with a single premise universal. In accordance with this condition, the fourth figure has eight productive moods.

[1] And yields a negative particular conclusion.

[2] And yields a particular affirmative conclusion.

[3] And yields a negative particular conclusion.

[4] And yields a particular affirmative conclusion.

الثاني من كلّيتين والكبرى سالبة،[١] كقولنا «كل برّ مقتات، ولا شيء من البرّ بجائز بيعه بجنسه متفاضلًا، فبعض المقتات ليس بجائز بيعه بجنسه متفاضلًا».

والثالث من موجبتين والكبرى كلّية،[٢] كقولنا «بعض الفاعل مرفوع، وكل فاعل عمدة، فبعض المرفوع عمدة».

والرابع من موجبة جزئيّة صغرى وسالبة كلّية كبرى،[٣] كقولنا «بعض المفعول منصوب، ولا شيء من المفعول بمجرور، فبعض المنصوب ليس بمجرور».

والخامس من موجبتين والصغرى كلّية،[٤] كقولنا «كل إنسان حيوان، وبعض الإنسان كاتب، فبعض الحيوان كاتب».

والسادس من موجبة كلّية صغرى وسالبة جزئيّة كبرى، كقولنا «كل سمك حيوان، وبعض السمك ليس بحمار، فبعض الحيوان ليس بحمار».

[الشكل الرابع] وشرط الشكل الرابع أحد الأمرين: إيجاب المقدّمتين مع كلّية الصغرى أو اختلافهما في الكيف مع كلّية إحداهما. وضروبه المنتجة بحسب هذا الاشتراط ثمانية.

[١] ينتج سالبة جزئيّة.

[٢] ينتج موجبة جزئيّة.

[٣] ينتج سالبة جزئيّة.

[٤] ينتج موجبة جزئيّة.

The first comprises two universal affirmative premises and for the reason given above[1] yields only particular conclusions, e.g., to say, "Every human being is an animal, and every rational thing is a human being; therefore, some animal is rational."

The second comprises two affirmative premises, with the major premise particular, and yields only particular conclusions, e.g., to say, "Every horse neighs, and some animal is a horse; therefore, something that neighs is an animal."

The third comprises two universal premises, with the minor premise negative, and yields a universal negative conclusion, e.g., to say, "No donkey is a horse, and everything that brays is a donkey; therefore, no horse brays."

The fourth comprises two universal premises, with the minor premise affirmative, and for the abovementioned reason, this mood yields only particular conclusions, e.g., to say, "Every human being is an animal, and no horse is a human being; therefore, some animal is not a horse."

The fifth comprises a particular affirmative minor premise and a universal negative major premise and yields a particular negative conclusion, e.g., to say, "Some fish is an animal, and no donkey is a fish; therefore, some animal is not a fish."

The sixth comprises a particular negative minor premise and a universal affirmative major premise and yields a particular negative conclusion, e.g., "Some animal is not a horse, and every human being is an animal; therefore, some horse is not a human being."

---

[1] In discussing the third figure, when we explained: "...because it is possible that the minor term be broader than the major term, and it is impossible to affirm or negate the narrower of every instance of the broader."

الأول من موجبتين كلّيتين ولا ينتج إلا الجزئيّة لما تقدّم،[1] كقولنا «كل إنسان حيوان، وكل ناطق إنسان، فبعض الحيوان ناطق».

والثاني من موجبتين والكبرى جزئيّة ولا ينتج إلا جزئيّة، كقولنا «كل فرس صاهل، وبعض الحيوان فرس، فبعض الصاهل حيوان».

والثالث من كلّيتين والصغرى سالبة ينتج سالبة كلّية، كقولنا «لا شيء من الحمار فرس، وكل ناهق حمار، فلا شيء من الفرس بناهق».

والرابع من كلّيتين والصغرى موجبة ولا ينتج هذا الضرب إلا الجزئيّة لما تقدّم، كقولنا «كل إنسان حيوان، ولا شيء من الفرس بإنسان، فبعض الحيوان ليس بفرس».

والخامس من موجبة جزئيّة صغرى وسالبة كلّية كبرى ينتج سالبة جزئيّة، كقولنا «بعض السمك حيوان، ولا شيء من الحمار بسمك، فبعض الحيوان ليس بسمك».

والسادس من سالبة جزئيّة صغرى وموجبة كلّية كبرى وينتج سالبة جزئيّة، نحو «بعض الحيوان ليس بفرس، وكل إنسان حيوان، فبعض الفرس ليس بإنسان».

---

[1] في الشكل الثالث من التعليل بقولنا: ...لجواز أن يكون الأصغر أعمّ من الأكبر وامتناع إيجاب الأخصّ لكل أفراد الأعمّ أو سلبه عنها.

The seventh comprises a universal affirmative minor premise and a particular negative major premise and yields a particular negative conclusion, e.g., to say, "Every human being is an animal, and some horse is not a human being; therefore, some animal is not a horse."

The eighth comprises a universal negative minor premise and a particular affirmative major premise and yields a particular negative conclusion, e.g., "No human being is a rock, and some animal is a human being; therefore, some rock is not an animal."

Replicative Syllogisms

The second of the two types of syllogisms is the replicative syllogism, namely, that which explicitly incorporates either the conclusion or the conclusion's contradictory. It is composed of two premises one of which is hypothetical and the other categorical. If the hypothetical proposition within it is conditional, then affirming the antecedent yields the consequent, e.g., to say, "If this is a human being then it is an animal, and this is a human being; therefore, this is an animal," since the existence of an implicant entails the existence of the implicate. Affirming the contradictory of the consequent yields the contradictory of the antecedent,[1] e.g., to say, "If this is a human being then it is an animal, but this is not an animal; therefore, this is not a human being," since the nonexistence of an implicate entails the nonexistence of the implicant.

[1] Thus two conclusions are possible.

والسابع من موجبة كلّية صغرى وسالبة جزئيّة كبرى وينتج سالبة جزئيّة، كقولنا «كل إنسان حيوان، وبعض الفرس ليس بإنسان، فبعض الحيوان ليس بفرس».

والثامن من سالبة كلّية صغرى وموجبة جزئيّة كبرى وينتج سالبة جزئيّة، نحو «لا شيء من الإنسان بحجر، وبعض الحيوان إنسان، فبعض الحجر ليس بحيوان».

القياس الاستثنائي

الثاني من قسمي القياس القياس الاستثنائي وهو ما كان عين النتيجة أو نقيضها مذكورة فيه بالفعل؛ وهو مركّب من مقدّمتين إحداهما شرطيّة والأخرى حمليّة. الشرطيّة الموضوعة فيه إن كانت متّصلة فاستثناء عين المقدّم ينتج عين التالي، كقولنا «إن كان هذا إنسانًا فهو حيوان، لكنه إنسان، ينتج أنه حيوان»، لأن وجود الملزوم يستلزم وجود اللازم. واستثناء نقيض التالي ينتج نقيض المقدّم،[١] كقولنا «إن كان هذا إنسانًا فهو حيوان، لكنه ليس بحيوان، ينتج أنه ليس بإنسان»، لأن عدم اللازم يستلزم عدم الملزوم.

[١] فالمنتج اثنان.

The reverse does not hold[1] in either case when the implicate is broader,[2] e.g., to say, "Whenever this is a human being then it is an animal, and this is a human being; therefore, this is an animal," or alternatively, "...but this is not an animal; therefore, this is not a human being." However, when the implicate is coextensive, e.g., 'rational thing' and 'laughing thing' with respect to 'human', then affirming either the antecedent or the consequent yields the other in its original form, e.g., to say, "Whenever this thing is rational then it laughs, and this thing is rational; therefore, this thing laughs," or alternatively, "...and this thing laughs; therefore, this thing is rational." And, [in the same way], affirming the contradictory of either yields the contradictory of the other.

If the hypothetical proposition within a replicative syllogism is a strict disjunctive proposition, e.g., the statement "The number is either even or odd," then affirming either disjunct in its original form yields the contradictory of the other since mutual inclusion is precluded, and affirming the contradictory of either disjunct yields the other disjunct in its original form since mutual exclusion is precluded. If the hypothetical proposition is anti-inclusive, then affirming either the antecedent or the consequent yields the contradictory of the other, e.g., to say, "This thing is either a rock or a tree, and it is a rock; therefore, this thing is not a tree." If the hypothetical proposition is anti-exclusive, then affirming the contradictory of either of the two disjuncts yields the other in its original form, e.g., to say, "This thing is either not a rock or not a tree, and it is a rock; therefore, this thing is not a tree."

[1] That is, affirming the consequent or the contradictory of the antecedent does not yield anything when what would be entailed is broader. However, if what would be entailed is coextensive, then affirming the consequent also entails the antecedent, and affirming the contradictory of the antecedent also entails the contradictory of the consequent.

[2] Than the implicant.

ولا عكس[١] في شيء منهما إذا كان اللازم أعمّ،[٢] كقولنا «كلّما كان هذا إنسانًا فهو حيوان، لكنه إنسان، ينتج أنه حيوان» أو «...لكنه ليس بحيوان، ينتج أنه ليس بإنسان». وأما إذا كان اللازم مساويًا كالناطق والضاحك للإنسان فاستثناء عين كل من المقدّم والتالي ينتج عين الآخر، كقولنا «كلّما كان هذا ناطقًا فهو ضاحك، لكنه ناطق، ينتج أنه ضاحك» أو «...لكنه ضاحك، ينتج أنه ناطق». واستثناء نقيض كل ينتج نقيض الآخر.

وإن كانت الشرطيّة الموضوعة فيه منفصلة حقيقيّة كقولنا «العدد إما زوج أو فرد» فاستثناء عين أيّ جزء كان ينتج نقيض الآخر لامتناع الجمع، واستثناء نقيض أيّ جزء كان ينتج عين الآخر لامتناع الخلوّ. وإن كانت مانعة الجمع فاستثناء عين كل واحد من المقدّم والتالي ينتج نقيض الآخر، كقولنا «هذا الشيء إما حجر أو شجر، لكنه حجر، ينتج أنه ليس بشجر». وإن كانت مانعة الخلوّ فاستثناء نقيض كل واحد من الجزئين ينتج عين الآخر، كقولنا «هذا الشيء إما لاحجر أو لاشجر، لكنه حجر، ينتج أنه ليس بشجر».

[١] أي لا ينتج استثناء عين التالي ولا نقيض المقدّم شيئًا إذا كان اللازم أعمّ، وأما إذا كان اللازم مساويًا فينتج استثناء عين التالي أيضا عين المقدّم ونقيض المقدّم نقيض التالي.

[٢] من الملزوم.

Syllogisms Classified by Categoricity, Conditionality, and Disjunction

There are six types of syllogisms with regard to categoricity, conditionality, and disjunction.[54]

The first of the six types is composed of two categorical propositions, e.g., "The universe undergoes change, and everything that undergoes change was originated in time."

The second is composed of two conditional propositions, e.g., "If the sun has risen then it is daytime, and whenever it is daytime the earth is illuminated; therefore, if the sun has risen then the earth is illuminated."

The third is composed of two disjunctive propositions, e.g., to say, "Every number is either even or odd, and every even number is either evenly even (like four) or oddly even (like two);[55] therefore, every number is either odd or evenly even or oddly even."

The fourth is composed of a conditional proposition and a categorical proposition, e.g., to say, "Whenever this thing is a human being then it is an animal, and every animal is a body; therefore, whenever this thing is a human being then it is a body."

The fifth is composed of a disjunctive proposition and a categorical proposition, e.g., to say, "The number is either even or odd, and every odd number is not divisible into two equal numbers; therefore, the number is either even or it is not divisible into two equal numbers."

أقسام القياس من حيث الحمل والاتصال والانفصال

أقسام القياس هي من حيث الحمل والاتّصال والانفصال ستّة:

الأول من الأقسام الستّة مركّب من حمليّتين، نحو «العالم متغير، كل متغير حادث».

والثاني من متّصلتين، نحو «إن كانت الشمس طالعة فالنهار موجود، وكلّما كان النهار موجودًا فالأرض مضيئة، ينتج إن كانت الشمس طالعة فالأرض مضيئة».

والثالث من منفصلتين، كقولنا «كل عدد فهو إما زوج وإما فرد، وكل زوج فهو إما زوج الزوج كالأربعة أو زوج الفرد كالاثنين، ينتج كل عدد إما فرد أو زوج الزوج أو زوج الفرد».

والرابع من متّصلة وحمليّة، كقولنا «كلّما كان هذا الشيء إنسانًا فهو حيوان، وكل حيوان جسم، ينتج كلّما كان هذا الشيء إنسانًا فهو جسم».

والخامس من منفصلة وحمليّة، كقولنا «إما أن يكون العدد زوجًا أو فردًا، وكل فرد غير منقسم بمتساويين، ينتج إما أن يكون العدد زوجًا أو غير منقسم بمتساويين».

The sixth is composed of a conditional proposition and an affirmative disjunctive proposition,[1] e.g., to say, "Whenever this is a human being then it is an animal, and every animal is always either moving or still; therefore, whenever this is a human being then it is either moving or still."

Syllogisms Classified by Matter

There are five types of syllogisms with regard to matter.

[Demonstrative Argument]

The first of the five types is demonstrative argument, which is a syllogism composed of two *certain premises*, whether they be immediate or acquired, [its purpose being] to yield certainty. The certain premises are of six types:

1. *self-evident premises*, which are propositions that the intellect affirms by the mere conception of their extremes and consideration of the relation between them, e.g., the statements "One is half of two"[2] and "The whole is greater than the part."
2. *observational premises*, also termed *sensate premises*, which are propositions that are affirmed by means of mere external or internal sensation, e.g., the statements "The sun is shining," "The fire is burning," and "We experience fear and anger."56

[1] Whether it be strict, anti-inclusive, or anti-exclusive.

[2] This serves as a major premise, and the minor premise is implicit, i.e., "This is one, and one is half of two."

والسادس من متّصلة ومنفصلة موجبة،[١] كقولنا «كلّما كان هذا إنسانًا فهو حيوان، ودائمًا إما أن يكون الحيوان متحرّكًا أو ساكنًا، ينتج كلّما كان هذا إنسانًا فهو متحرّك أو ساكن».

أقسام القياس من حيث المادة

أقسامه من حيث المادّة خمسة.

[البرهان]

الأول من الأقسام الخمسة البرهان وهو قياس مؤلّف من مقدّمات يقينيّة ضروريّة كانت أو مكتسبة لإنتاج اليقين. واليقينيّات ستّة أقسام:

١- أوّليّات وهي قضايا يحكم العقل فيها بمجرّد تصوّر طرفيها وملاحظة النسبة بينها، كقولنا «الواحد نصف الاثنين»[٢] و«الكل أعظم من الجزء».

٢- ومشاهدات وتسمّى محسوسات أيضا وهي قضايا يحكم فيها بمجرّد الحسّ الظاهر أو الباطن، كقولنا «الشمس مشرقة» و«النار محرقة» و«إن لنا خوفًا وغضبًا».

[١] سواء كانت حقيقيّة أو مانعة الجمع أو مانعة الخلوّ.

[٢] هذه كبرى والصغرى مطويّة، أي «هذا واحد، والواحد نصف الاثنين».

3. *experiential premises*, which are propositions that are affirmed through the intermediate process of repeated observation, e.g., the statement "Drinking scammony purges yellow bile."
4. *intuitively inferred premises*,[1] which are propositions that are affirmed by means of intuitive inference, which is to pass quickly from principles to [the knowledge] that is sought,[57] with both instantaneously occurring[2] to the mind. No [mental] movement is involved, unlike in reflective thought, which is a gradual process. An example is to state, "The light of the moon is derived from the light of the sun," on account of the differences in the shape of the moon's light depending on its proximity to or distance from the sun. The Sufis refer to this[3] as "divine clarification."
5. *massively reported premises*, which are propositions that are affirmed through the intermediate process of hearing them from such a great number of people that, by normative experience,[58] it would be impossible for them to have concurred on a falsehood. The sign that the prerequisite conditions for a massively reported premise[4] have been collectively met is that knowledge [of the reported fact] occurs; no particular number can be stipulated. Some examples are the statement "Our master Muḥammad ﷺ claimed prophethood, and miracles were manifested

٣- ومجرّبات وهي قضايا يحكم فيها بواسطة تكرار المشاهدة، كقولنا «شرب السقمونيا مُسهل الصفراء».

٤- وحدسيّات[١] وهي قضايا يحكم فيها بالحدس وهو سرعة الانتقال من المبادئ إلى المطالب وسنوحها[٢] للذهن دفعةً فلا حركة فيه بخلاف الفكر فإنه تدريجي، كقولنا «نور القمر مستفاد من نور الشمس» لاختلاف تشكّلاته النوريّة قربًا وبعدًا منها. ويعبّر عنه[٣] عند المتصوّفة بالظهورات الإلهيّة.

٥- ومتواترات وهي قضايا يحكم فيها بواسطة السمع من جمع كثير يستحيل عادةً تواطؤهم على الكذب، وحصول العلم آية اجتماع شرائطها[٤] ولا يشترط فيها عدد، كقولنا «سيّدنا محمد عليه الصلاة والسلام ادّعى النبوّة وأُظهرت[١٦] المعجزة

[1] [The letter *ḥāʾ* in *ḥadsiyyāt* is] correctly vowelized with *fatḥ*; a common mistake is to vowelize it with *kasr*.

[2] That is, their becoming apparent.

[3] That is, to intuitive inference.

[4] I.e., that the report is from a multitude of people, that they are such that their having concurred on a falsehood is impossible, and that the report is about a sensible thing. Al-Maḥallī, *al-Badr al-ṭāliʿ*, 2:39.

[١] بالفتح فصيح وبالكسر غلط مشهور.

[٢] أي ظهورهما.

[٣] أي عن الحدس.

[٤] وهي كون الخبر عن جمع وكونهم بحيث يمتنع تواطؤهم على الكذب وكونه عن محسوس (محلّي).

at his hands"[1] and the affirmation of distant cities and of past peoples in bygone ages.

6. *naturally evident premises*, which are propositions [implicitly] accompanied by their syllogisms, e.g., to state, "Four is even," on account of a middle term that is [naturally] present in the mind, namely, divisibility into equal numbers.

Experiential premises, intuitively inferred premises, and massively reported premises cannot be used to prove something to someone else unless the prerequisite conditions for these premises—namely, the [relevant] experience, intuitive inference, or mass reporting—[also] obtain for that person, whereby these premises could be used to prove something to him.

Now, demonstration is of two types. A demonstrative argument may be a *why-demonstration*, when one reasons from the cause to the effect,[2] e.g., to state, "This person has putrid humors,[3] and every person with putrid humors has a fever; therefore, this person has a fever." Or it may be a *that-demonstration*, when one reasons from the effect to the cause,[4] e.g., to state, "This person has a fever, and every person that has a fever has putrid humors; therefore, this person has putrid humors."

[Dialectical Argument]

The second is dialectical argument, which is a syllogism [that may be] composed of (1) *commonplace premises*, that is, propositions that all or some people

[1] That is, "And whoever is such is a prophet; therefore, our master and the delight of our eyes Muḥammad ﷺ is a prophet."

[2] That is, the middle term is the cause for the existence of the major term.[59]

[3] The humors are four: blood, phlegm, yellow bile, and black bile.

[4] That is, the middle term is the cause for one's knowledge that the major term holds true for the minor term.[60]

على يديه»،[١] وكالحكم بالبلدان النائية والأمم الماضية في الأزمنة الخالية.

٦- وفطريّات وهي قضايا قياساتها معها، كقولنا «الأربعة زوج» بسبب وسط حاضر في الذهن وهو الانقسام بمتساويين.

والمجرّبات والحدسيّات والمتواترات لا تكون حجّة على الغير إلا إذا وجدت فيه الأمور المقتضية لها من التجربة والحدس والتواتر فتكون حجّة عليه.

ثم البرهان قسمان: إما (١) لمّي إن استدلّ بالمؤثّر على الأثر،[٢] كقولنا «هذا متعفّن الأخلاط،[٣] وكل متعفّن الأخلاط محموم، فهذا محموم»؛ وإما (٢) إنّي إن استدلّ بالأثر على المؤثّر،[٤] كقولنا «هذا محموم، وكل محموم متعفّن الأخلاط، فهذا متعفّن الأخلاط».

[الجدل]

الثاني الجدل وهو قياس مؤلّف من (١) المشهورات وهي قضايا يعترف بها جميع الناس أو بعضهم لمصلحة

[١] أي «وكل من كذلك فهو نبي، فسيّدنا وقرّة أعيننا محمد صلى الله عليه وسلّم نبي».

[٢] أي الحدّ الأوسط علّة لوجود الأكبر.

[٣] وهي أربعة: الدم والبلغم والصفراء والسوداء.

[٤] أي الحدّ الأوسط علّة للعلم بثبوت الأكبر للأصغر.

would accept—this owing either to a common interest, e.g., the statements "Justice is good" and "Injustice is bad"; to a sympathetic inclination, e.g., the statements "Caring for the weak is praiseworthy" and "Being gracious to one's parents is good"; to an ingrained impulse, e.g., the statement "Exposing one's nakedness is blameworthy"; to particular customs, e.g., the Magians' belief that slaughtering animals is bad; or to being religious prescriptions and rules of conduct, e.g., religious [principles] like "Modesty is a part of faith."[61]

Commonplace premises are liable to be confused for self-evident premises, but the two are distinguishable by the fact that the intellect, if left to its natural disposition, would affirm self-evident premises but not commonplace premises. The latter may be true and they may be false, but self-evident premises are necessarily true. Every group of people has its own commonplaces in accordance with its customs, practices, and trades.

Dialectical argument may also be composed of (2) *conceded premises*, which are propositions conceded by an opponent. One may base an argument on such propositions to rebut the opponent. An example of [conceded premises] is the concession by jurists of the propositions of jurisprudential theory.[1]

The purpose of this type of argument[2] is to defeat the opponent or to convince someone who is incapable of apprehending the premises of a demonstrative argument.

[1] E.g., when the opponent says: Is the jewelry of women subject to zakat? And the jurists reply: It is obligatory to give zakat on the jewelry of women because we are informed of the [obligation to give] zakat on the jewelry of women in his statement ﷺ "Zakat is due on jewelry," and that of which we are informed by this hadith is obligatory; therefore, it is obligatory to give zakat on the jewelry of women.

[2] Namely, that of dialectical argument.

عامّة، كقولنا «العدل حسن» و«الظلم قبيح»؛ أو لرقّة، كقولنا «مراعاة الضعفاء محمودة» و«الإحسان إلى الآباء حسن»؛ أو لحميّة، كقولنا «كشف العورة مذموم»؛ أو لعادات، كقبح ذبح الحيوان عند[١٧] المجوس؛ أو لكونها شرائع وآدابًا، كالأمور الشرعية نحو «الحياء من الإيمان».

وقد تلتبس المشهورات بالأوّليّات ويفرّق بينهما بأن العقل لو خلّي وطبعَه حكَم بالأوّليّات دون المشهورات، وهي قد تكون صادقة وقد تكون كاذبة والأوّليّات صادقة البتة. ولكل قوم مشهورات بحسب عاداتهم وآدابهم وصناعاتهم.

أو (٢) من المسلّمات وهي قضايا تسلّم من الخصم فيبنى عليها الكلام لدفعه، كتسليم الفقهاء مسائل أصول الفقه.[١]

والغرض منه[٢] إلزام الخصم وإقناع من هو قاصر عن إدراك مقدّمات البرهان.

[١] كما إذا قال الخصم «هل كان في حلي النساء زكاة؟» فيقول الفقهاء «الزكاة في حلي النساء واجبة لأن الزكاة في حلي النساء مخبَر بها بقوله عليه الصلاة والسلام "في الحلي زكاة"، والمخبَر بها بهذا الحديث واجب، فالزكاة في حلي النساء واجبة».

[٢] أي من الجدل.

[Rhetorical Argument]

The third is rhetorical argument, which is a syllogism [that may be] composed of (1) *authoritative premises*, which are propositions taken from someone about whom one has a good opinion, either owing to a supernatural reason, i.e., a prophetic or saintly miracle, as with prophets[62] ﵏ and saints, or owing to the person's possession of surpassing intelligence or religiosity, as with scholars and ascetics.

Rhetorical argument may also be composed of (2) *suppositional premises*, which are propositions one deems to be true by way of preponderant judgment while allowing that, albeit unlikely, the contradictory may be true, e.g., to say, "Zayd goes about at night; therefore, he is a thief," or, "This wall is giving off dirt; therefore, it is collapsing."

The purpose of rhetorical argument is to make people desirous of what is good and averse to what is evil, as is done by those who give sermons and public admonition.

[Poetical Argument]

The fourth is poetical argument, which is a syllogism composed of *imaginative premises*, which are propositions that when presented to the soul have the effect of either comfort, straitness, ease, or fright. The following examples, in order, illustrate these effects: "Wine[1] is flowing ruby," "Honey[2] is vomit-inducing[3] bile," "Attaining lofty stations is a matter of but a few nights," and "Neglecting custom is a thing destructive."

The purpose of poetical argument is to affect the soul by enticing or frightening it.

[1] That is, "This is wine," and so on.

[2] That is, "This is honey," and so on.

[3] [*Muhawwi'a*] means *muqayyi'a* (vomit-inducing).

[الخطابة]

الثالث الخطابة وهو قياس مؤلّف من (١) المقبولات وهي قضايا تؤخذ ممن يعتقد فيه حسنًا إما لأمر سماوي من المعجزات والكرامات كالأنبياء عليهم السلام والأولياء وإما لاختصاصه بمزيد عقل ودين كأهل العلم والزهد.

أو من (٢) المظنونات وهي قضايا يحكم بها حكمًا راجحًا مع تجويز نقيضه تجويزًا مرجوحًا، كقولنا «زيد يطوف بالليل فهو سارق» و«هذا الحائط ينتثر منه التراب فهو ينهدم».

والغرض من الخطابة ترغيب الناس في الخير وتنفيرهم عن الشرّ كما يفعله الخطباء والوعّاظ.

[الشعر]

الرابع الشعر وهو قياس مؤلّف من المخيّلات وهي قضايا إذا أوردت على النفس أثّرت فيها بسطًا أو قبضًا أو تسهيلًا أو تهويلًا، أمثلة ذلك مرتّبًا نحو «الخمر[١] ياقوتة سيّالة» و«العسل[٢] مِرّة مُهوِّعة»[٣] و«كسب المعالي بكم ليالي» و«ترك العادات من المهلكات».

والغرض منه انفعال النفس بالترغيب والترهيب.

[١] أي هذا خمر إلخ.

[٢] أي هذا عسل إلخ.

[٣] أي مُقيِّئة.

Poetical statements that comprise imaginative propositions are minor premises for implicit universal major premises. For example, a poetical statement about the qualities of the beloved is a minor premise for an implicit universal major premise, which would be "Everyone that is such ought to be loved." In syllogistic form, this is "This person ought to be loved: he is generous, and everyone that is such ought to be loved; therefore, this person ought to be loved."

والأشعار المشتملة على المخيّلات صغريات لكبريات كلّية مطويّة، فشعر أوصاف المحبوب مثلًا صغرى لكبرى كلّية مطويّة وهي هنا هذه: «كل من هذا شأنه وجب أن يُحَبّ»؛ صورة قياسه هكذا: «هذا واجب أن يحبّ لأنه سخي، كل من هذا شأنه واجب أن يحبّ، فينتج هذا واجب أن يحبّ».

[Fallacious Argument]

The fifth is fallacious argument, which is of two types. The first is termed *sophistry*, i.e., fraudulent knowledge, and the second is termed *contentious disputation*, i.e., disputation neither for the truth nor to elicit concession.[63] The first is a syllogism composed of false premises that resemble the truth or resemble commonplace premises.[64] The second is a syllogism composed of false estimative premises posited by the estimative faculty[1] with respect to matters that are not sensible.[2] Estimation is derivative of sensation; when its judgment pertains to sensible things it is true, and when its judgment pertains to other things it is false.

[المغالطة]

الخامس قياس مغالطة وهو قسمان يقال لأوّلهما سفسطة أي علم مزخرف ولثانيهما مشاغبة أي منازعة لا للصواب ولا للإلزام. الأول هو قياس مؤلّف من مقدّمات كاذبة شبيهة بالحقّ أو بالمشهورات، والثاني هو قياس مؤلّف من مقدّمات وهميّة كاذبة يحكم بها الوهم[١] في أمور غير محسوسة.[٢] والوهم تابع للحسّ فإذا حكم على المحسوسات كان صادقًا وإن حكم على غيرها كان كاذبًا.

Fallacious argument of either type is invalid. The invalidity of a fallacious argument may, on the one hand, be due to (A) its *form*. [This applies in the following cases:]

1. *The conditions for productivity are unmet*, e.g., when in the first figure either the minor premise is negative or the major premise particular.

والمغالطة فاسدة بقسميها، إما (أ) من حيث الصورة:

١- بأن ينتفي شرط الإنتاج، ككون الصغرى في الشكل الأول سالبة أو الكبرى جزئيّة.

[1] Which is a faculty of the soul by which it apprehends non-sensible particulars, e.g., the friendship of Zayd and the enmity of ʿAmr.

[2] The reason we say "not sensible" is that the estimative faculty is *not* incorrect in its judgments about sensible things, e.g., when it judges that a beautiful woman is beautiful or that an ugly woman is ugly. Al-Rāzī, *Sharḥ*, 2:248.

[١] وهو قوّة للنفس بها تدرك المعاني الجزئيّة كصداقة زيد وعداوة عمرو مثلًا.

[٢] وإنما قلنا غير محسوسة لأن حكم الوهم في المحسوسات ليس بكاذب كما إذ حكم بحسن حسناء وقبح شوهاء (شرح الشمسية).

2. *A nature-proposition*[65] *is put in place of a universal proposition*, e.g., to say, "The human being is an animal, and 'animal' is a genus; therefore, the human being is a genus," and to say, "A noun is a word, and 'word' [divides into] 'noun', 'verb', and 'particle'; therefore, a noun [divides into] 'noun', 'verb', and 'particle'," the fallacy being that the major premise in both examples is not universal.

3. *The middle term does not repeat*, e.g., to say in reference to the image of a horse engraved on something like a wall, "This [image] is a horse, and every horse neighs; therefore, this image neighs," the fallacy being that "horse" is nonliteral in the minor premise and literal in the major premise, so the middle term does not repeat.

On the other hand, the invalidity of a fallacious argument may be due to (B) its meaning and its *matter*. [This applies in the following cases:]

1. *The minor premise comprises two propositions of different quality*, e.g., to say, "Humans alone write, and everything that writes is an animal; therefore, humans alone are animals." Since the word "alone" has the function of the statement "Things other than humans do not write," the minor premise is implicitly negative, and the conditions for productivity are vitiated. The fallacy in this is to treat two propositions of different quality as a single premise.

2. *The conclusion and a premise are the same*, e.g., to say, "Every human being (*insān*) is human (*bashar*), and every human (*bashar*) laughs; therefore, every human being (*insān*)

٢- أو بأن توضع القضيّة الطبيعيّة مقام الكلّية، كقولنا «الإنسان حيوان، والحيوان جنس، ينتج الإنسان جنس» وكقولنا «الاسم كلمة، والكلمة اسم وفعل وحرف، ينتج الاسم اسم وفعل وحرف»؛ والغلط أن الكبرى فيهما ليست كلّية.

٣- أو بأن لا يتكرّر الحدّ الأوسط، كقولنا لصورة الفرس المنقوشة على نحو الجدار «هذه فرس، وكل فرس صهّال، ينتج هذه الصورة صهّالة»؛ والغلط فيه أن الفرس مجاز في الصغرى وحقيقة في الكبرى فلم يتكرّر الحدّ الأوسط.

وإما (ب) من حيث المعنى والمادّة:

١- بأن تكون الصغرى مشتملة على قضيّتين مختلفتين بالكيف، كقولنا «الإنسان وحده كاتب، وكل كاتب حيوان، ينتج الإنسان وحده حيوان»؛ ولمّا كانت لفظة «وحده» في قوّة قولنا «غير الإنسان ليس بكاتب» كانت الصغرى سالبة ضمنًا فانتفى شرط الإنتاج؛ والغلط فيه وضع قضيّتين مختلفتين في الكيف موضع مقدّمة واحدة.

٢- أو بأن يكون المطلوب وبعض المقدّمات شيئًا واحدًا، كقولنا «كل إنسان بشر، وكل بشر

laughs." The fallacy in this is that it begs the question, because the conclusion is the major premise itself since *insān* is synonymous with *bashar*.

3. *The subject does not have extramental existence*, e.g., to say, "Everything that is both human and horse is human, and everything that is both human and horse is a horse; therefore (by the third figure) some human is a horse." The fallacy in this is that the subject of the premises does not exist since there is nothing of which it is true that it is both human and horse.

4. *Things that are mental are treated as things that have extramental existence*, e.g., to say, "A partner to the Creator exists in the mind, and everything that exists in the mind has extramental existence; therefore, a partner to the Creator extramentally exists"—exalted is Allah far beyond such a notion!

5. *Things that have extramental existence are treated as things that are mental*, e.g., to say, "Substances exist in the mind, and everything that exists in the mind is an accident that inheres in it; therefore, substances are accidents that inhere in the mind." The fallacy in the latter two arguments is that the judgment of existence in the mind pertains only to the mental and imaginal form of a thing, not to the thing itself in extramental existence.

The purpose of fallacious argument is to show that the opponent is wrong and to silence him, and this is religiously prohibited unless he is an obstinate disputant who does not seek the truth. The greatest benefit in knowing this kind of argument is that one can avoid it, as the poet says,

> I studied evil not for evil, but to ward it off;
>
> One who is not learned in evil into evil falls

ضاحك، ينتج كل إنسان ضاحك»؛ والغلط فيه المصادرة على المطلوب لأن النتيجة عين الكبرى لمرادفة «الإنسان» لـ«البشر».

٣- أو بأن لا يرى وجود الموضوع في الخارج، كقولنا «كل إنسان وفرس فهو إنسان، وكل إنسان وفرس فهو فرس، ينتج من الشكل الثالث بعض الإنسان فرس»؛ والغلط فيه أن موضوع المقدّمتين ليس بموجود إذ لا شيء يصدق عليه أنه إنسان وفرس.

٤- أو بأن يؤخذ الذهنيّات مكان الخارجيّات، كأن يقال «شريك الباري موجود في الذهن، وكل موجود فيه يتحقّق في الخارج، شريك الباري يتحقّق في الخارج» تعالى الله عن ذلك علوًّا كبيرًا.

٥- أو يؤخذ الخارجيّات مكان الذهنيّات، كأن يقال «الجوهر موجود في الذهن، وكل موجود فيه عرض قائم به، ينتج الجوهر عرض قائم به»؛ والغلط فيهما أن الحكم بالوجود في الذهن على صورة الشيء الذهنيّة وخياله لا على نفسه وذاته في الخارج.

والغرض من المغالطة تغليط الخصم وإسكاته وهو حرام إلا أن يكون معاندًا لا طالبًا للحقّ. وأعظم فائدة معرفتها الاحتراز عنها كما قال الشاعر:

عَرَفْتُ الشَّرَ لَا لِلشَّرِّ لَكِنْ لِتَوَقِّيهِ

فَمَنْ لَمْ يَعْرِفِ الشَّرَّ يَقَعْ فِيهِ

Of the five arts,[66] demonstration is the ultimate recourse. With respect to His saying ﷻ, “Call to the way of your Lord with wisdom and goodly exhortation and dispute with them in the most virtuous manner” (Q 16:125), it has been said that “wisdom” is an allusion to demonstrative argument, “goodly exhortation” to rhetorical argument, and “dispute with them” to dialectical argument, all three being worthy of recourse in calling to the way of truth.

والعمدة من الصناعات الخمس البرهان. قيل في قوله تعالى ﴿ٱدْعُ إِلَىٰ سَبِيلِ رَبِّكَ بِٱلْحِكْمَةِ وَٱلْمَوْعِظَةِ ٱلْحَسَنَةِ وَجَٰدِلْهُم بِٱلَّتِي هِيَ أَحْسَنُ﴾ [١٦/ ١٢٥] إن «الحكمة» إشارة إلى البرهان و«الموعظة الحسنة» إلى الخطابة و«جادلهم» إلى الجدل فيكون كل من هذه الثلاثة معتمدًا عليه في الدعوة إلى سبيل الحق.

By the assistance of Allah ﷻ, the treatise entitled *The Ancient Abundance: On the Science of Logic* is complete. May Allah ﷻ by His grace and generosity render it of benefit to us and all believers. Allah! “Take us not to task if we forget or err!” (Q 2:286). “Glory to your Lord, Lord of Might, transcending what they describe! Peace be upon the messengers. And praise to Allah, Lord of the worlds” (Q 37:180–82). By His permission ﷻ, the fourth treatise follows, entitled *The Gushing Wellspring: On the Science of Language Theory.*

تمّت بعون الله تعالى الرسالة المسمّاة بالفيض العتيق في علم المنطق جعلها الله تعالى بمنّه وكرمه نافعة لنا ولسائر المؤمنين. اللّهم لا تؤاخذنا إن نسينا أو أخطأنا. ﴿سُبْحَٰنَ رَبِّكَ رَبِّ ٱلْعِزَّةِ عَمَّا يَصِفُونَ ١٨٠ وَسَلَٰمٌ عَلَى ٱلْمُرْسَلِينَ ١٨١ وَٱلْحَمْدُ لِلَّهِ رَبِّ ٱلْعَٰلَمِينَ﴾ [٣٧/ ١٨٠-١٨٢]. وتليها بإذنه تعالى الرسالة الرابعة المسمّاة الورد الصدع في علم الوضع.

٢٧٣

NOTES TO TREATISE III

1 Or *simple apprehension.*

2 The combination of these three conceptions with the judgment itself of either affirmation or negation makes up the assent according to the position attributed to Imām al-Rāzī.

3 This refers to the well-known theologian Fakhr al-Dīn al-Rāzī (d. 606/1209).

4 Knowledge (*ʿilm*) here is to be understood as knowledge that is certain and conclusive, in contrast with presumption (*ẓann*), the kind of knowledge that consists in apprehending what is merely the most likely or most reasonable of the available possibilities.

5 Or the *significate.*

6 The Arabic word is *nāṭiq*, which should be read in English as the substantive "rational thing" rather than as the mere adjective "rational."

7 This is because whenever there is signification of a part of a whole, there must be signification of a whole, but not vice versa; likewise, whenever there is signification of something that follows from an assigned meaning there must be an assigned meaning, but not vice versa.

8 The point is that the definition stands as valid because lexical matter and morphological structure do not count as distinct parts.

9 Since there is only one sun extramentally (at least for the sake of the example), "sun" is given as an example of a universal whose *mental* instances are equivalent with respect to the concept: all suns that can be conceived in the mind are equally suns.

10 As in *raʾaytu rajulan* (I saw a man), where *rajulan* cannot comprehend all men. Because it signifies a single man, *rajulan* in such a sentence is not general.

11 Because it is restricted in number, *ʿashara* is not general.

12 This is also termed *technical* (*iṣṭilāḥī*) convention, that is, the special jargon of a particular group.

13 *Intension* (*mafhūm*) refers to the conceptual meaning that a term signifies, and it is often juxtaposed with *extension* (*mā-ṣadaq* or *miṣdāq*), which refers to the actual things to which the term and its intension apply. For example, the intension of the word "human" is the conceptual meaning 'rational animal', which it signifies, and its extension is all of the individual humans that are instances (*afrād*) of this concept. Thus, there are three things that must be diligently distinguished in the study of logic: (1) the word, or verbal expression (*lafẓ*); (2) the conceptual meaning, or intension (*mafhūm*); and (3) the individual referents, or extension (*mā-ṣadaq*).

14 In a restrictive expression, one part of the expression specifies or "restricts" another part, whether the "restricting" expression is an adjective, a *muḍāf ilayhi*, or an adverb of place or time. In a non-restrictive expression, like *fī al-dāri* (in the house), no such specification occurs. See notes 13 and 14 in al-Yazdī, *Sharḥ Tahdhīb al-manṭiq*, 115.

15 Literally, "A universal is that the mere conception *of whose intension* (*mafhūmihi*) does not preclude that it could be shared." Now, because the definition of *universal* in the Arabic text implies that universals *have* an intension, it would follow that universals are verbal expressions rather than the intension itself. (On

these terms, see note 13.) However, as the logicians point out, it is more accurate to say that universals are concepts; they are indeed the intension itself that is signified by the expression. Accordingly, we chose to adjust the phrasing of the text in translation, thereby also simplifying the definition.

16 A concept is considered "shared" when it applies (i.e., *extends*) to more than one individual instance.

17 The Arabic term *ḍāḥik*, here rendered "laughing thing," is not to be understood as "thing that actually laughs" but rather as that thing that has the capacity or faculty for laughter, or simply the *kind of thing* that laughs, i.e., a risible thing. The same principle applies to other examples below that are rendered with the English present participle.

18 A *sort* (*ṣinf*) is a subset of a species, delimited by accidental universals: 'Turk' is a subset of 'human', delimited by the accidental universal of being Turkish. (Being Turkish is accidental since it is external to the essence of 'human'.) In descending order from the general to the specific, the genus (*jins*) is above the species (*nawʿ*), which is above both the sort (*ṣinf*) and the individual (*shakhṣ*). Now, when a higher genus is predicated of something, it is predicated by the intermediary predication of the intervening essential universals, that is, the intervening genera and species. When there are no intervening essential universals, the predication is termed *primary predication* (*ḥaml awwalī*). For example, while 'animal' is predicated of 'Zayd' and 'Turk' by the intermediary predication of 'human', it is predicated of 'human' by way of primary predication.

19 According to this position, an expression ("A") signifies a meaning ('B') by concomitance (*iltizām*) if and only if that meaning ('B') is a strictly evident inseparable accident of the expression's intension ('A').

20 In this case, there are two universals, A and B, where A is more specific than B. From the perspective of A, the two universals overlap entirely, which means that every instance of A is an instance of B. From the perspective of B, however, this is not the case, because some instances of B are not instances of A. Thus, if A were 'human' and B were 'animal', it would be correct to say that B subsumes A.

21 That is, the two universals do overlap in some instances, but each also has instances that it does not share with the other.

22 In these examples, what is being defined, or the *definiendum* (*muʿarraf*), is 'human'.

23 A real definition (*taʿrīf ḥaqīqī*) defines a real quiddity (*māhiyya ḥaqīqiyya*) as it is in extramental reality. By contrast, a nominal definition (*taʿrīf ismī*) defines a quiddity as denoted by a given term, whether or not that quiddity is extramentally real. While a real definition gives knowledge of a quiddity as it really is (whether this means conceiving its essence or simply distinguishing it from other things through nonessential aspects), a nominal definition simply gives knowledge of the concept that a given term has been assigned, as conceived by the assigner. Hence, nonexistent quiddities (like unicorns) can only be defined nominally. Real quiddities, on the other hand, can be defined both through real definitions (like when we want to know what an oak tree really is) and through nominal definitions (like when we want to conceptualize the meaning of the term "oak tree"). Al-Taftāzānī, *al-Talwīḥ*, 1:18.

24 The great philosopher and polymath Ibn Sīnā (d. 428/1037) brought the period of the "early scholars" (*mutaqaddimūn*) of logic to its culmination.

25 *Qawl*, literally "saying" or "something that is said," technically denotes a composite (*murak-*

kab), whether in mental conception or verbal expression. Strictly speaking, propositions are mental conceptions, but the author treats them as verbal statements (in the same way he previously treated universals as verbal expressions; see note 15). The aim of this common practice in introductory logic texts is to simplify the subject matter for the student.

26 In other words, the proposition is distinguished from other composites (like phrases, questions, and commands) in that it conceptually involves an informing (*ḥikāya*) about reality; it says something about what is or is not the case. Only because propositions have this function does it make sense to call a proposition true (when it performs its function correctly) or false (when it fails to do so). This is what is meant by propositions' having the kind of "conceptual form" (*mafhūm*) that makes truth and falsity applicable. When one considers only the conceptual form of the composite without considering what is truly the case in reality (*al-wāqiʿ*), truth and falsity are both applicable to every proposition—even to propositions that are (in consideration of reality) known to be absolutely true or absolutely false. See Gelenbevī, *Sharḥ Gelenbevī*, 74–75; al-ʿAṭṭār, *Ḥāshiya ʿalā sharḥ al-Khabīṣī*, 225.

27 An extreme's being "potentially simple" (*mufrad bi-l-quwwa*) means that it is effectively or functionally simple: its role with regard to the judgment—i.e., its role of serving as the subject about which the judgment is made or the predicate by which the judgment is made—could potentially be fulfilled by a simple term. Al-Taftāzānī, *Sharḥ al-Risāla*, 408.

28 While logicians writing in Arabic acknowledge the logical role of the copula, the use of an independent copula is unnecessary in Arabic syntax because inflection serves the function that the copula would have had, like the *ḍamm* for the nominative case in the example *Zaydun ʿālimun*. English, for its part, does use a copula: the various forms of the infinitive "to be," as in "Zayd *is* a scholar" and "We *are* students."

29 According to this second interpretation of the coincidental—namely, that the proposition is true if and only if the consequent is true—this example proposition is true since the consequent is true: donkeys do in fact bray.

30 The interpretation of the coincidental that suffices with the truth of the consequent is inclusive of the interpretation that requires the truth of both the antecedent and the consequent, since when the stricter requirement is met, so too is the looser requirement.

31 These definitions apply only to affirmative disjunctions. The negative form of each disjunction, as the author will mention shortly, states that such a judgment does not hold, as in "It is not the case that every tree is either an oak or a pine."

32 A sub-proposition, or *juzʾ* (part), within a disjunction is termed a *disjunct*.

33 These are technical terms in number theory, treated and defined in classical arithmetic (*ʿilm al-ḥisāb*). A *perfect number* is an integer equal to the sum of its proper divisors, or its positive factors excluding itself. An *abundant number* is an integer less than this sum, and a *deficient number* is an integer greater than this sum. Thus six is a perfect number because $6=1+2+3$; twelve is an abundant number because $12<1+2+3+4+6$; and four is a deficient number because $4>1+2$.

34 These quantifiers all carry the same meaning. In English we would use "all" or "every."

35 In English, "whenever."

36 In English, "in all cases" or "always."

37 In English, "some" or "one."

38 In English, "in some cases" or "sometimes."

39 In English, "no" or "every…is not."

40 In English, "in no case" or "never."

41 In English, "some...is not," "one...is not," or "not all."

42 In English, "it is not that whenever" or "not in every case."

43 In English, "not in every case" or "not always."

44 As opposed to "some is not."

45 In English, "if."

46 In English, "or."

47 The matter (*mādda*) of the propositions is the content of their actual terms, in contradistinction to their form.

48 See note 25.

49 Strictly speaking, the part that is considered to be the syllogism is the two premises alone: "This is a human, and every human is an animal."

50 A "discrepancy" is present when a given figure with true premises of a given quantity and quality produces affirmative conclusions in some cases and negative conclusions in other cases. This sort of discrepancy in the conclusions indicates that they are not entailed by the syllogism *inherently*. Al-Taftāzānī, *Sharḥ al-Risāla*, 556; al-Yazdī, *Sharḥ Tahdhīb al-manṭiq*, 292.

51 This refers to the affirmation or negation and the universality or particularity of the minor and major premises considered together.

52 An "unfamiliar syllogism" is a formally valid syllogism with a form different than the ones recognized and categorized in the classical tradition of logic. El-Rouayheb, *Islamic Intellectual History*, 85–96.

53 For a commercial good to be *ribawī* in this sense means that it would be unlawful, as an act of *ribā*, to exchange it for a good of the same kind in unequal amounts.

54 This is a classification of the combinative syllogism in terms of the types of propositions it contains; it does not include replicative syllogisms.

55 An evenly even number (*zawj al-zawj*) can be halved more than once and still yield whole numbers; an oddly even number (*zawj al-fard*) can be halved only once.

56 Strictly speaking, this should be "I am experiencing fear" and "I am experiencing anger." Internal sensation itself cannot inform us about the internal states of others.

57 Recall the definition of reflective thought (*fikr*) in the introduction of this treatise, where the process of knowledge acquisition was described as a transition from "knowns" (*maʿlūmāt*) to "unknowns" (*majhūlāt*).

58 The term *normative experience* (*ʿāda*, literally "habit" or "custom") refers to the regular association of events as experienced in the created universe. Some occurrences that are, strictly speaking, rationally possible, involving no rational contradiction, are at the same time known to be impossible by normative experience. An example is a fire's being cold: while this is rationally possible in the strict sense, it is known to be impossible by our experience of the way the world is. Thus, a prophetic miracle (*muʿjiza*), e.g., the coolness of the fire for the prophet Ibrāhīm, is called a "disruption of normative experience" (*kharq al-ʿāda*).

59 This kind of reasoning is also termed *propter quid* reasoning.

60 This kind of reasoning is also termed *quia* reasoning.

61 It is possible for a premise to be commonplace in consideration of its common acceptance while also being demonstrable by demonstrative argument. This would apply, for example, to matters of religion that are indisputably sound. From the perspective that they are

universally accepted by the community of the faithful, they are commonplace premises; from the perspective that they are demonstrable through the logical proofs for religious truth, they are demonstrative premises.

62 See the previous note about the possibility of a premise's belonging to multiple categories. Also note that the stronger position is that premises supported by prophetic miracles do not belong to this category at all but rather to the category of demonstrative premises. Al-Khayrābādī, *al-Mirqāh*, 99.

63 For example, to avoid looking ignorant in front of an audience or to deliberately incite disagreement and sow discord in an audience when both you and your interlocuter know that your position is incorrect.

64 As the distinction is sometimes explained, sophistry (*safsaṭa*) utilizes false premises that are deceptively similar to the true and certain premises that a genuine philosopher would use, and contentious disputation (*mushāghaba*) utilizes false premises that are deceptively similar to the commonplace premises that a genuine disputant would use. See Fenārī, *al-Fawāʾid*, 130.

65 A nature-proposition (*qaḍiyya ṭabīʿiyya*) is a proposition whose subject is a natural universal, that is, a nature or essence, and is considered from this perspective rather than from the perspective of its instances.

66 The five arts (*al-ṣināʿāt al-khams*) are the five kinds of syllogistic arguments just discussed.

IV

THE GUSHING WELLSPRING

On the science of language theory

الورد الصدع في علم الوضع

In the Name of Allah,
All-Merciful, Most Compassionate

بسم الله الرحمن الرحيم

ALL PRAISE IS due to Allah, Lord of the worlds. May blessings and peace be upon the seal of the prophets, Muḥammad, and upon all of his family and Companions.

الحمـد لله رب العالمين والصلاة والـسلام على خاتم النبيين محمـد وعلى آله وصحبه أجمعين.

To Proceed This is a treatise on the science of language theory. I have presented it in a manner that renders it easy for the student to grasp. Yet success is from Allah ﷻ alone.

أمـا بعـد فهذه رسـالة في علـم الوضع جعلتهـا على وجه يسـهّل ضبطه على طالبـه. ومن الله تعـالى وحـده التوفيق.

INTRODUCTION

Lexically, *waḍʿ* (positing) means placing something in a delimited area. As a technical term, *waḍʿ* (assignment) means making one thing specific to another such that whenever the first thing is understood, the second thing is thereby understood by someone aware of the specification. The first thing, in the case of expressions and otherwise,[1] is termed the *assigned* and the second the *denotation*.

The science of language theory is a science in which one investigates the modes of conventional linguistic assignment in terms of being general or specific and individual or collective. Its subject matter is the assigned word[2] in terms of its assignation to a meaning. The aim of the science is that one know how to distinguish the literal significance of expressions from their nonliteral significance, how to distinguish assigned expressions from unassigned expressions, and how to distinguish terms whose assignment is lexical from those whose assignment is technical. The science has two parts.

المقدمة

الوضع لغةً جعل شيء في حيّز واصطلاحًا تعيين شيء لشيء متى فُهم الشيء الأول فُهم منه الشيء الثاني للعالِم بالتعيين. والشيء الأول لفظًا كان أو غيره يسمّى موضوعًا والثاني موضوعًا له.

وعلم الوضع هو علم يبحث فيه عن أحوال الوضع العرفى من حيث العموم والخصوص والشخصية والنوعية. وموضوعه الأسماء المعيّنة من حيث تعيينها للمعنى. وغايته معرفة حقائق الألفاظ عن مجازاتها وتمييز الموضوعات عن المهملات والموضوعات اللغويّة عن الاصطلاحيّة بعضها عن بعض. وهو قسمان.

[Chapter 1]

INDIVIDUAL ASSIGNMENT

The first of the two parts of the science of language theory concerns individual assignment. What is it? How many categories does it comprise?

Individual assignment is that in which the assigned expression is a single expression[1]—e.g., *Zayd, Usāma, huwa* (he), *hādhā* (this), *alladhī* (which), and *min* (from)—that, conceived in its specific individuality, is assigned either to a particular meaning, like the meaning 'Zayd', or to a universal meaning, like the meaning 'man'. It is of three categories.

1. Specific Assignment to the Specific

This category includes the assignment of *personal proper names*, e.g., *Zayd*, and *generic proper names*, e.g., *Usāma*. The assigner (1) considers the expression *Zayd* or the expression *Usāma*, for example, and (2) conceives a specific meaning, whether it be individuated in external reality[2] (e.g., the real person Zayd) or [individuated] in the mind[3] (e.g., [an individualized conception of] the predatory animal).3 Then (3) he states, "I assign this expression to this meaning."

[1] As in the assignment of personal proper names, generic nouns, personal pronouns, demonstrative pronouns, relative pronouns, and particles.

[2] As is the case with respect to personal proper names.

[3] As is the case with respect to generic proper names.

[الباب الأول]

الوضع الشخصي

الأول من قسمي الوضع الوضع الشخصي: ما هو؟
وكم قسمًا؟

هو ما كان اللفظ الموضوع لفظًا واحدًا[١] كـ«زيد» و«أسامة» و«هو» و«هذا» و«الذي» و«مِنْ» ملحوظًا بخصوصه موضوعًا لمعنًى جزئي كمعنى «زيد» أو لمعنًى كلي كمعنى «رجل». وأقسامه ثلاثة.

١. وضع خاص لموضوع له خاص

كوضع الأعلام الشخصية كـ«زيد» والجنسية كـ«أسامة»، بأن: (١) لاحظ الواضع لفظ «زيد» أو «أسامة» مثلًا (٢) وتصوّر معنًى معيّنًا بتعيين خارجي[٢] كذات زيد أو ذهني[٣] كالحيوان المفترس، (٣) ثم قال: وضعتُ هذا اللفظ لهذا المعنى.

[١] كما في وضع الأعلام وأسماء الأجناس والضمائر وأسماء الإشارة والموصولات والحروف.

[٢] كما في العلَم الشخصي.

[٣] كما في العلَم الجنسي.

According to some, the assignment of generic proper names belongs to the second category, i.e., general assignment to the general.[1]

قيل وضع علم الجنس من القسم الثاني أي من الموضوع بالوضع العامّ لموضوع له عامّ.[١]

2. General Assignment to the General

٢. وضع عام لموضوع له عام

This category includes the assignment of generic nouns, e.g., *asad* (lion) and *insān* (human); of infinitive nouns, e.g., *ḍarb* (hitting) and *ikrām* (honoring); of quasi-infinitive nouns, e.g., *salām* (peace) and *kalām* (speech); and of the lexical roots of verbs and derivative nouns. The assignment proceeds as follows. The assigner (1) conceives a universal concept generally, like the concept 'rational animal', then (2) states, "I assign the expression *insān* to this universal concept." You may extrapolate from this to [the assignment of] infinitive nouns and quasi-infinitive nouns like *salām* and *kalām*.

كوضع أسماء الأجناس كـ«أسد» و«إنسان» والمصادر كـ«ضَرْب» و«إكرام» وأسمائها كـ«سلام» و«كلام» وموادّ الأفعال والمشتقّات، بأن: (١) تصوّر الواضع مفهومًا كليًّا بعمومه كمفهوم الحيوان الناطق، (٢) ثم قال: وضعت لفظة «إنسان» لهذا المفهوم العامّ. وقِسْ عليه المصادر وأسماءها كـ«السلام» و«الكلام».

In this category, the denotation and the *assigner's meaning*[4] are thus the same thing considered from different perspectives. For, in this category, the meaning to which an expression is assigned is regarded as the assigner's meaning with respect to [his] conceiving [it], and it is regarded as the denotation with respect to the expression's being assigned to it.

فالموضوع له وآلة الوضع في هذا القسم متّحدان بالذات مختلفان بالاعتبار؛ فإنّ المعنى الموضوع له فيه من حيث التصوّر آلة الوضع ومن حيث وضع اللفظ له موضوع له.

[1] This [latter] view is founded on the assumption that generic proper names are assigned to an essence in terms of what the essence itself is, without consideration of its individuation in the mind; as such, a generic proper name is simply a generic noun, only termed a "proper name" to serve certain grammatical functions. [By contrast], the former view is founded on the assumption that a generic proper name is assigned to an essence insofar as that essence is individuated in the mind. In sum, this former takes into account, together with the essence, the qualification of individuation, while the latter does not—which leaves it under the category of the generic noun.

[١] وهذا مبنيّ على أن علَم الجنس موضوع للماهية من حيث هي هي أي مع قطع النظر عن كونه معيّنًا في الذهن. وحينئذ يكون اسم جنس؛ وإطلاق «العلَم» عليه لأحكام لفظية. والأول مبنيّ على أنه موضوع للماهيّة المعيّنة في الذهن من حيث تعيّنها فيه. والحاصل أن الأول اعتبر مع الماهيّة قيد التعيين، والثاني لم يعتبره فيكون داخلًا في اسم الجنس.

3. General Assignment to the Specific

This category includes the assignment of particles, personal pronouns, non-personal pronouns (i.e., demonstrative and relative pronouns), quasi-verbal nouns, and those place/time adverbs with auxiliary meaning:

1. For example, the assigner (1) conceives the expression *min* (from) in its specific individuality, and (2) conceives certain specific instances—that is, particular commencements-*from*[1]—through a universal concept, that is, the universal concept 'commencement'. Then (3) he states, "I assign the expression *min* to each one of these instances in its specific individuality." The assignment proceeds in this manner for the remaining particles.[2]
2. He[3] (1) conceives the expression *huwa* (he) in its specific individuality, and (2) conceives certain particulars through a universal concept, e.g., 'previously mentioned[4] masculine singular'.[5] Then (3) he states, "I assign the expression *huwa* to each one of these partic-

[1] E.g., the commencement of travel from Basra, the commencement of the recital of the Quran, the commencement of the obligation to perform the ritual prayer upon the attainment of maturity and intellect, and so forth.

[2] Thus we would say: The assigner (1) conceives the expression *'alā* (on), for example, in its specific individuality, and (2) [conceives] specific particulars—that is, particular situations-*on* (e.g., Zayd's being situated on the surface and 'Amr's being situated on the horse)—through a universal concept, namely, the universal concept 'being above'. Then (3) he states, "I assign the expression *'alā* to every one of these particulars in its specific individuality." You may extrapolate from this to the assignment of *fī* (in), the *lām*, and other particles.

[3] Namely, the assigner.

[4] Whether [mentioned] in words, in meaning, or in effect.

[5] This concept is universal and includes every real particular, e.g., Zayd and 'Amr, and every relative particular, e.g., 'human', 'animal', 'tree', and 'rock'.5

٣. وضع عام لموضوع له خاص

كوضع الحروف والمضمرات والمبهمات أي أسماء الإشارة والموصولات وأسماء الأفعال وبعض الظروف مما يتضمّن معنى الحرف. مثلًا:

١- تصوّر الواضع (١) لفظة «مِن» بخصوصها (٢) وحصصًا مخصوصة أي ابتداآت معيّنة[١] بمفهوم كلّي أي الابتداء المطلق، (٣) ثم قال: وضعتُ لفظة «مِن» لكل واحد من تلك الحصص بخصوصه. وهكذا وضع سائر الحروف.[٢]

٢- وتصوّر[٣] (١) لفظة «هو» بخصوصها (٢) وجزئيات بمفهوم كلّي مثل المفرد المذكّر المتقدّم[٤] ذكره،[٥] (٣)

[١] من ابتداء السير من البصرة ومن ابتداء القراءة من القرآن ومن ابتداء وجوب الصلاة من البلوغ والعقل إلى غير ذلك.

[٢] فنقول: تصوّر الواضع (١) لفظة «على» مثلًا بخصوصها (٢) وجزئيات مخصوصة أي استعلاءات معيّنة من استعلاء زيد على السطح واستعلاء عمرو على الفرس بمفهوم كلي وهو الاستعلاء المطلق، (٣) ثم قال: وضعتُ لفظة «على» لكل واحد من تلك الجزئيات بخصوصه. وقِسْ عليه وضع «في» واللام وغيرها من الحروف.

[٣] أي الواضع.

[٤] أي لفظًا أو معنًى أو حكمًا.

[٥] فهذا المفهوم كلي شامل لكل جزئي حقيقي كزيد وعمرو و إضافي كالإنسان والحيوان والشجر والحجر.

ulars in its specific individuality." You may extrapolate from this to [the assignment of] the remaining personal pronouns.

3. He (1) conceives the expression *dhālika* (that), for example, in its specific individuality, and (2) conceives certain particulars through a universal concept, like 'distant masculine singular that is physically pointed out'. Then (3) he states, "I assign the expression *dhālika* to each one of these particulars in its specific individuality." The process is the same for the remaining demonstrative pronouns.

4. He (1) conceives the expression *alladhī* (which), for example, in its specific individuality, and (2) conceives certain particulars through a universal concept, e.g., 'masculine singular that is rationally pointed out (by the specific reference borne within the relative clause)'. Then (3) he states, "I assign the expression *alladhī* to each one of these particulars in its specific individuality."

Thus, in the case of particles, personal pronouns, and non-personal pronouns, the assigner's meaning is a universal concept, and the denotation is certain particulars. But while the assigner's meaning in the case of particles is essential and intrinsic to the concept, in the case of personal and non-personal pronouns it is accidental and extrinsic to the concept.

This is in accordance with the view of the late-period scholars. According to the early-period scholars, the denotation in [the assignment of] these four and similar classes is the universal concept, though it is a condition that [expressions belonging to these four classes] be used solely in reference to particulars. It follows that this type of assignment belongs to the category of general assignment to the general. But the chosen position is the former, because the latter position entails that [expressions belonging to this category] are nonliteral expressions that lack literal significance, since they are

ثـم قال: وضعـتُ لفظة «هـو» لكل واحـد من تلك الجزئيـات بعينه. وقـسْ عليه سـائر الضمائر.

٣- وتصـوّر (١) لفظـة «ذلـك» مثـلًا بخصوصهـا (٢) وخصوصيــات بمفهــوم كلي مثــل المفــرد المذكــر المشــار إليــه البعيــد بالإشــارة الحســية، (٣) ثــم قــال: وضعــتُ لفظــة «ذلــك» لــكل واحــد مــن تلــك الخصوصيــات بعينــه. وعلى هــذا القيــاس ســائر أســماء الإشــارة.

٤- وتصـوّر (١) لفظـة «الذي» مثـلًا بخصوصهـا (٢) وجزئيـات بمفهـوم كلي مثـل المفـرد المذكـر المشـار إليـه بالإشـارة العقليـة أي بمعهوديّـة مضمـون الصلة له، (٣) ثـم قال: وضعتُ لفظـة «الذي» لكل واحـد مـن تلـك الجزئيـات بعينه.

فآلـة الوضـع في الحـروف والمضمـرات والمبهمـات المفهـوم الكلي، والموضـوع له الجزئيـات. إلا أن آلـة الوضـع في الحـروف ذاتيـة داخلـة في مفهومهـا وفي المضمـرات والمبهمـات عرضيـة خارجـة عـن مفهومهـا.

هــذا عنــد المتأخّريــن. وأمــا عنــد المتقــدّمين فالموضـوع له في هـذه الأربعـة ونحوهـا هـو المفهـوم الكلي بشرط اسـتعمالها في الجزئيـات؛ فهي إذن مـن الموضـوع بالوضـع العـامّ لموضـوع له عامّ. والمختـار هـو الأول إذ يلـزم على الثاني أن تكـون مجـازات لا حقائـق لها إذ لـم

never used for the universal concept. It also entails that particles are conceptually independent and that assignment is futile.[6]

These four classes—namely, personal pronouns, e.g., *huwa*; demonstrative pronouns, e.g., *hādhā*; relative pronouns, e.g., *alladhī*; and particles, e.g., *min*—lack meaning save through contextual indicants that are specific to each, since the act of assignment bears an equal relation to each denotation. That contextual indicant for the first class is previous mention, for the second class physical pointing, for the third class rational pointing, and for the fourth class the word that bears the connection, e.g., the word *sirtu* (I traveled) in *sirtu min al-Baṣrati ilā al-Kūfa* (I traveled from Basra to Kufa).

تستعمل في المفهوم الكلي، وأن تكون الحروف مستقلّة بالفهم، وأن يخلو الوضع عن الفائدة.

وهذه الأربعة أعني الضمير كـ«هو» والإشارة كـ«هذا» والموصول كـ«الذي» والحرف كـ«من» لا تفيد إلا بقرينة معيّنة لها لاستواء نسبة الوضع إلى المسمّيات. وتلك القرينة في الأول تقدّم الذكر، وفي الثاني الإشارة الحسية، وفي الثالث الإشارة العقلية، وفي الرابع المتعلّق كـ«سرت» في «سرت من البصرة إلى الكوفة».

[Chapter 2]

COLLECTIVE ASSIGNMENT

The second of the two parts of the science of language theory concerns collective assignment. What is the definition of collective assignment? What are its categories?

Collective assignment is that in which what is assigned consists of multiple expressions conceived through a universal concept, as in "Each expression that is such and such I assign to such and such," rather than a single expression conceived in its specific individuality as in the case of individual assignment. Like individual assignment, it is of three categories.

1. Specific Assignment to the Specific

The first of the categories of collective assignment is that of specific assignment to the specific. The assignment proceeds as follows. The assigner first considers a group of expressions through a universal concept, e.g., 'any word of the pattern *faʿ_la*'. Then he states, "Each instance to which that universal applies I hereby assign to signify the respective structure of the active perfect tense verb."[7] You may extrapolate to other cases.

If one counts the formal structures [of words with] different lexical matter as multiple [structures],[8] then the denotation is a universal concept individuated in the mind, and, accordingly, [the assigned expression] is categorized as a generic proper name. Otherwise, it is categorized as a personal proper name.

[الباب الثاني]

الوضع النوعي

الثاني من قسمي الوضع الوضع النوعي: ما تعريف الوضع النوعي؟ وما أقسامه؟

هو ما كان اللفظ الموضوع ألفاظًا متعدّدة متصوّرة بمفهوم كلي — مثل: كل ما كان كذا وضعتُه لكذا — لا لفظًا واحدًا مقصودًا[١] بخصوصه كما في الوضع الشخصي. وأقسامه كالشخصي ثلاثة.

[١. وضع خاص لموضوع له خاص]

الأول من أقسام الوضع النوعيّ وضع خاصّ لموضوع له خاصّ، بأن لاحظ الواضع أوّلًا طائفة من الألفاظ بمفهوم كلي مثل «كل ما كان على فَعَلَ»، ثم قال: وضعتُ ما صدق عليه ذلك الأمر الكلي لهيئة الماضي المعلوم المعيّنة. وقِسْ عليه غيره.

فإن اعتبر تعدّد الهيئة بتعدّد المادّة فالموضوع له كلي معيّن بتعيّن ذهني فهي حينئذ من قبيل الأعلام الجنسيّة؛ وإلا فهي من قبيل الأعلام الشخصيّة.

2. General Assignment to the General

The second of the categories of collective assignment is that of general assignment to the general.

This category includes the assignment of words[9] possessing any of the derivative forms, which are of eight types: the verb,[1] the active participle, the passive participle, the participial, the noun of instrument, the noun of place, the noun of time, and the comparative/superlative. The rationale [behind this division] is that the derivative form is either regarded insofar as the action inheres in it as a transient occurrence, and this is the active participle; or it is regarded insofar as the action befalls it, and this is the passive participle; or it is regarded insofar as the action [or quality] inheres in it as a lasting quality, and this is the participial; or it is regarded insofar as it is an instrument for the action's occurrence, and this is the noun of instrument; or a place in which the action occurs, and this is the noun of place; or a time at which the action occurs, and this is the noun of time; or it is regarded insofar as the action [or quality] inheres in it to a greater extent, and this is the comparative/superlative.

The assignment proceeds, for example, as follows. The assigner, after (1) considering the category of the assigned expression and (2) considering the category of the meaning to which it is assigned, (3) states, "Each word that possesses the formal structure of the active participle I hereby assign to signify that in which the source notion inheres."

[1] Know that with respect to verbs there are three assignations: (1) the assignation of their lexical roots to actions, by general individual assignment to the general; (2) the assignation of the syntactic structures that arise from their interactions with grammatical agents to the specific relations [between real actions and agents], by general collective assignment to the specific; and (3) the assignation of their morphological structures to times, by general collective assignment to the general. Eğīnī, *al-'Ujāla*, 54.

[٢. وضع عام لموضوع له عام]

الثاني من أقسام الوضع النوعي وضع عام لموضوع له عام:

كوضع صيغ عامّة المشتقّات؛ وهي ثمانية: الفعل،[١] واسم الفاعل، واسم المفعول، والصفة المشبّهة، واسم الآلة، واسم المكان، واسم الزمان، واسم التفضيل. وذلك لأن المشتقّ إما أن يعتبر قيام الحدث به من حيث الحدوث وهو اسم الفاعل، أو وقوع الحدث عليه وهو اسم المفعول، أو قيامه به من جهة الثبوت وهو الصفة المشبّهة، أو كونه آلة لحصوله وهو اسم الآلة، أو مكانًا وقع فيه وهو اسم المكان، أو زمانًا وقع فيه وهو اسم الزمان، أو يعتبر قيام الحدث به على وصف الزيادة وهو اسم التفضيل.

وذلك مثل أن يقول الواضع بعد ملاحظة (١) نوع اللفظ الموضوع (٢) ونوع المعنى الموضوع له: (٣) كل ما كان على صيغة الفاعل وضعتُه لمن قام به مأخذ الاشتقاق.

[١] اعلم أن للأفعال ثلاثة أوضاع: (١) وضع موادّها للأحداث بوضع شخصي بطريق وضع عامّ لموضوع له عامّ، وثانيها (٢) وضع هيئاتها التركيبية التي تحصل من مقارنتها للفواعل بإزاء النسب الجزئية بطريق وضع عامّ لموضوع له خاصّ من النوعي، وثالثها (٣) وضع هيئاتها الإفرادية للزمان بطريق وضع عامّ لموضوع له عامّ من النوعي أيضا (العجالة الرحميّة لمحمد رحمي الأكيني).

This category also includes the assignment of words possessing the form of the relational noun. The assigner states, for example, "Each word that possesses the form of the relational noun I hereby assign to signify a thing related to a specified notion."

Also included is the assignment of words possessing the form of the diminutive noun. The assigner states, for example, "Each word that possesses the morphological quality of diminution I hereby assign to signify an entity with a small amount of the [signified] quality."

It also includes the assignment of *composite structures*, whether (A) *sentential*, as in *Zaydun qāʾimun* (Zayd is standing), or (B) *non-sentential*, that is, either (1) *iḍāfī*, as in *ghulāmu Zaydin* (Zayd's servant boy); (2) restrictive, as in *al-ḥayawānu al-nāṭiqu* (the rational animal); (3) numeral, as in *khamsata ʿashara* (fifteen); (4) synthetic, as in *Baʿlabakk* (Baalbek); or (5) vocal, as in *Sībawayhi*. The assignment proceeds by the assigner's stating, "I hereby assign each declarative sentence to signify the informing about reality." You may extrapolate to other cases.

3. General Assignment to the Specific

The third of the categories of collective assignment is that of general assignment to the specific. This category includes (1) the assignment of all verbs, for they are collectively assigned by means of the consideration of a universal concept that includes every complete relation, in its specific individuality, [between a verb and grammatical agent or between an action and real agent]. The denotation is thus those particular relations considered by means of that universal concept.[10] Also included are (2) words in the singular or the plural prefixed with the universal *lām*; (3) phrases in a universal or a specific *iḍāfa*; (4) phrases with the negated indefinite; and (5) verbs of the perfect, imperfect, imperative, or prohibitive forms, if verbs are assigned to refer to

وكوضع صيغ اسم المنسوب مثل أن يقول الواضع: كل ما هو على صيغة اسم المنسوب وضعتُه لشيء منسوب إلى وصف معيّن.

ووضع صيغ اسم التصغير مثل أن يقول الواضع: كل ما هو على صفة تصغير وضعتُه لذات متّصف بصغر الصفة.

ووضع الهيئة التركيبيّة سواء كانت (أ) كلاميّة كـ«زيد قائم» أو (ب) غير كلاميّة وهي (١) الإضافيّة كـ«غلام زيد» أو (٢) التقييديّة كـ«الحيوان الناطق» أو (٣) العدديّة كـ«خمسة عشر» أو (٤) المزجيّة كـ«بعلبك» أو (٥) الصوتيّة كـ«سيبويه». وذلك مثل أن يقول الواضع: كل جملة خبريّة وضعتُها للإخبار عن الواقع؛ وقِسْ عليه غيره.

[٣. وضع عام لموضوع له خاص]

الثالث من أقسام الوضع النوعي وضع عامّ لموضوع له خاصّ، كوضع (١) عامّة الأفعال فإنها موضوعة بالنوع بملاحظة عنوان كلي شامل لخصوصية كل نسبة جزئية من النسب التامّة، فالموضوع له تلك النسب الجزئية الملحوظة بذلك العنوان الكلي. (٢) وكالمفرد والجمع المحلّى بلام الاستغراق، (٣) والإضافة الاستغراقية والعهدية، (٤) والنكرة المنفية. (٥) والماضي والمضارع والأمر والنهي إذا كان وضع الأفعال للحدث والزمان والنسبة إلى فاعل

an action, a time, and a specified agent. But if verbs are assigned to refer to an action, a time, and an unspecified agent, their assignment belongs to the category of general assignment to the general, as discussed above in the second category.[11]

معيّن؛ وأما إذا كان وضعها للحدث والزمان والنسبة الى فاعل ما فيكون وضعها من قبيل الوضع الكلي والموضوع له الكلي، كما مرّ في القسم الثاني.

A Fuller Exposition of Collective Assignment

إيضاح ما أجملناه في الوضع النوعي

Collective assignment, like individual assignment, is of three categories.

إن الوضع النوعي كالشخصي ثلاثة أقسام.

1. Specific Assignment to the Specific

[١. جزئى الوضع والموضوع له]

The first of the categories of collective assignment is that of specific assignment to the specific. This category comprises the assignment of words of the various forms and structures that are taken by the lexical root *f-ʿ-l*—whether the forms be verbal, e.g., *faʿala* / *yafʿalu* and *afʿala* / *yufʿilu*, or nonverbal, e.g., *fāʿilun* / *mafʿūlun*, and whether they be triliteral or non-triliteral—to the categories of specific words possessing these forms. The assignment proceeds, for example, as follows. The assigner, after (1 & 2) considering the specific assigned words and the specific denotations, both through their categories,[12] (3) states, "Each word of a form taken by the lexical root *f-ʿ-l* is hereby assigned to [the category of] that which is patterned on it." Thus, *faʿala*, for instance, is assigned to [the category of] *naṣara* (he helped) and similar words, *yafʿulu* (the letter *ʿayn* vowelized with *ḍamm*) is assigned to *yanṣuru* (he helps), *faʿlan* is assigned to *naṣran* (helping), and *fāʿilun* is assigned to *nāṣirun* (one that helps).[13]

الأول من أقسام الوضع النوعي جزئى الوضع والموضوع له، كوضع الهيئات والصيغ الطارئة على «ف-ع-ل» — فعلًا كانت الصيغ كـ«فَعَلَ/ يَفْعَلُ» و«أَفْعَلَ/ يُفْعِلُ» أو غيره كـ«فَاعِلٌ/ مَفْعُولٌ» ثلاثيًّا أو غيره — لأجناس الصيغ المشخّصة. مثل أن يقول الواضع بعد ملاحظة (١) أفراد الموضوع (٢) والموضوع له بنوعيها[١]: (٣) كل ما يطرأ على «ف-ع-ل» فهو موضوع لما يوزن به. فإذن «فَعَلَ» مثلًا موضوع لـ«نَصَرَ» ونحوه، و«يَفْعُلُ» بضمّ العين موضوع لـ«يَنْصُرُ»، و«فَعْلًا» موضوع لـ«نَصْرًا»، و«فَاعِلٌ» موضوع لـ«نَاصِرٌ».

2. General Assignment to the General

[٢. كلي الوضع والموضوع له]

The second of the categories of collective assignment is that of general assignment to the general.

الثاني من أقسام الوضع النوعي كلي الوضع والموضوع له.

This category includes the assignment of words possessing any of the derivative forms. The assigner, after (1) considering the category of the assigned expression and (2) considering the category of the meaning to which it is assigned, (3) states, for example, "Each word possessing the form of the active participle I hereby assign to signify that in which the source notion inheres." This assignment includes the assignment of *ḍāriban* (one that hits) to 'that in which hitting inheres', and *qātilan* (one that kills) to 'that in which killing inheres'. All the derivative forms are assigned in this way.

This category also includes the assignment of sentential compounds, e.g., *Zaydun qā'imun* (Zayd is standing). The assigner states, for example, "I hereby assign every declarative sentence to signify the informing about reality." You may extrapolate to other cases.

Also included is the assignment of words possessing the form of an adjective-like noun, like words possessing the form of the relational noun, e.g., *madanī* (one that is ascribed to the city). The assigner states, for example, "Each word possessing the form of the relational noun I hereby assign to signify something ascribed to some specified thing."

Also included is the assignment of words possessing the form of the diminutive noun, e.g., *Hudhayl*. The assigner states, for example, "Each word possessing the form of the diminutive I hereby assign to signify an entity with a small amount of the [signified] quality."

Also included are the assignations of the nouns of place, time, and instrument.

Also included are the assignations of *generic* or *mentally specific iḍāfa structures*. The assigner states, for example, "Each phrase possessing the composite structure of a [generic] *iḍāfa* I hereby assign to signify that the *muḍāf* is a generic category," and, "Each phrase possessing the composite structure of a mentally [specific] *iḍāfa* I hereby assign to signify that the *muḍāf* is a category insofar as it exists within an unspecified instance."

كوضع صيغ عامّة المشتقّات، مثل أن يقول الواضع بعد (١) ملاحظة نوع اللفظ الموضوع (٢) وملاحظة نوع المعنى الموضوع له: (٣) كل ما كان على صيغة الفاعل وضعتُه لمن قام به مأخذ الاشتقاق. ويدخل في ضمن هذا الوضع «ضاربًا» لمن قام به الضرب و«قاتلًا» لمن قام به القتل. وهكذا سائر المشتقّات.

وكوضع المركّبات التامّة كـ«زيد قائم»، مثل أن يقول الواضع: كل جملة خبرية وضعتُها للإخبار عن الواقع. وقِسْ عليه غيره.

وكوضع صيغ الأسماء المشبّهة بالصفات مثل صيغ اسم المنسوب كـ«المدني»، مثل أن يقول الواضع: كل ما هو على صيغة اسم المنسوب وضعتُه لشيء منسوب إلى شيء معيّن[٣].

ووضع صيغ اسم التصغير كـ«هذيل»، مثل أن يقول: كل ما هو على صيغة التصغير وضعتُه لذات متّصف بصغر الصفة.

وأسماء المكان والزمان والآلة.

والإضافة الجنسية والعهدية الذهنية، مثل: كل ما كان على هيئة التركيب الإضافي [الجنسي] وضعتُه لإفادة جنسية المضاف، وكل ما كان على هيئة التركيب الإضافي [العهدي] الذهني[٤] وضعتُه لإفادة جنسية المضاف من حيث وجوده في ضمن فرد غير معيّن[٥].

3. General Assignment to the Specific

The third of the categories of collective assignment is that of general assignment to the specific.

This category includes the assignment of singular nouns prefixed with the *universal lām*. The assigner states, for example, "Each singular noun prefixed with the universal *lām* I hereby assign to indicate that the judgment holds for every one of its individuals."

Also included is the assignment of plural nouns prefixed with the universal *lām*. The assigner states, for example, "Each plural noun prefixed with the universal *lām* I hereby assign to indicate that the judgment applies to every one of its individuals."

Also included is the assignment of phrases in *universal iḍāfa structures*. The assigner states, for example, "Each phrase possessing the composite structure of a universal *iḍāfa* I hereby assign to indicate the universal inclusion of the *muḍāf*."

Also included is the assignment of phrases in *specific iḍāfa structures*. The assigner states, for example, "Each phrase possessing the composite structure of a specific [*iḍāfa*] I hereby assign to indicate that the *muḍāf* is a category insofar as it is actualized in a specified individual," according to one view.

Also included is the assignment of negated indefinite nouns. The assigner states, for example, "Each indefinite noun that falls within the confines of negation I hereby assign to indicate that the judgment holds for every individual respectively."

Also included are the assignations of verbs of the perfect, imperfect, imperative, and prohibitive forms. The assignment proceeds, for example, as follows. The assigner, after (1) considering certain words possessing the perfect tense structure, and (2) considering the [real] relation of the inherently signified action to a specified agent in the past, (3) states, "Each word possessing the perfect tense structure I hereby assign to signify the relation of

[٣. كلي الوضع جزئي الموضوع له]

الثالث من أقسام الوضع النوعي كلي الوضع جزئي الموضوع له.

كوضع المفرد المُحلّى بلام الاستغراق، كأن يقول الواضع: كل مفرد مُحلًّى بلام الاستغراق وضعتُه لإفادة ثبوت الحكم لكل واحد منه.

كوضع الجمع المُحلّى بلام الاستغراق، كأن يقول الواضع: كل جمع مُحلًّى بلام الاستغراق وضعتُه لإفادة نسبة الحكم إلى كل واحد من أفراده.

كوضع الإضافة الاستغراقية، كأن يقول الواضع: كل ما كان على هيئة التركيب الإضافي الاستغراقي وضعتُه لإفادة استغراق المضاف.

كوضع الإضافة العهدية، كأن يقول الواضع: كل ما كان على هيئة التركيب [الإضافي] العهدي وضعتُه لإفادة جنسية المضاف من حيث تحققه في ضمن فرد معيّن، على رأي.

كوضع النكرة المنفية، كأن يقول الواضع: كل نكرة وقعت في حيّز النفي وضعتُها لإفادة ثبوت الحكم إلى كل واحد واحد.

كوضع الماضي والمضارع والأمر والنهي، مثل أن يقول الواضع بعد (١) ملاحظة ما كان على الهيئة الماضوية (٢) وملاحظة نسبة الحدث المدلول ضمنًا إلى فاعل معيّن في الزمان الماضي: (٣) كل ما كان على هيئته

the inherently signified action to a specified agent in the past." This assignment includes the assignment of *ḍaraba* (he hit) to the relation between the action of hitting and a specified agent in the past, *naṣara* (he helped) to the relation between the action of helping and a specified agent in the past, and so on. You may extrapolate from this to the respective processes of assignation for the imperfect, imperative, and prohibitive. If, however, the assignment of a verb pertains to an action, a time, and a relation to any agent whatever, then the assignment of verbs belongs to the category of general assignment to the general.

الماضوية وضعتُه لنسبة الحدث المدلول ضمنًا إلى فاعل معيّن في الزمان الماضي. ويدخل في ضمن هذا «ضَرَبَ» لنسبة حدث الضرب إلى فاعل معيّن في الزمان الماضي، و«نَصَرَ» لنسبة حدث النصرة إلى فاعل معيّن في الزمان الماضي، إلى غير ذلك. وقِسْ عليه صور أوضاع المضارع والأمر والنهي. وإذا كان وضع الأفعال للحدث والزمان والنسبة إلى فاعل ما فيكون وضعها من قبيل الوضع الكلي والموضوع له الكلي.

INSTRUCTIVE NOTES

تنبيهات

I. Assignment entails a significatory relationship, though the converse is not true because signification is possible through natural or rational means [as well].

الأول أن الوضع يستلزم الدلالة بدون العكس لجواز أن تكون بالطبع أو بالعقل.

II. Intention is not a condition for signification according to the majority view, in opposition to the view of Ibn Sīnā.

الثاني أن الإرادة ليست شرطًا للدلالة عند الجمهور خلافًا لابن سينا.

III. A *univocal expression* is a single expression assigned to a single meaning whose multiple instantiation is nonetheless validated by the intellect, e.g., *insān* (human). An *equivocal expression* is a single expression assigned to two or more meanings, whether particular, e.g., *Zayd*; universal, e.g., *ʿayn* (eye, spring, spy...); or different, e.g., *asad* used as a name (Asad) or not used as a name (lion). Thus, *equivocity* is multiplicity in meaning and unity in expression, and *synonymy* is its opposite, that is, multiplicity in expression and unity in meaning, e.g., *layth* (lion) and *asad.*

الثالث المشترك المعنوي لفظ واحد موضوع لمعنًى واحد لكن العقل يجوّز صدقه على كثيرين، كـ«الإنسان». والمشترك اللفظي لفظ واحد لمعنيين أو أكثر جزئيين كـ«زيد» أو كليين كـ«العين» أو مختلفين كـ«الأسد» علَما وغير علَم. فالاشتراك اللفظي تعدّد المعنى واتّحاد اللفظ؛ والترادف عكسه أي تعدّد اللفظ واتّحاد المعنى كـ«الليث» و«الأسد».

❋ ❋ ❋

By the assistance of Allah ﷻ, the treatise entitled *The Gushing Wellspring: On the Science of Language Theory* is complete. May Allah ﷻ by His grace and generosity render it of benefit to us and to all believers. Allah! “Take us not to task if we forget or err!” (Q 2:286). “Glory to your Lord, Lord of Might, transcending what they describe! Peace be upon the messengers. And praise to Allah, Lord of the worlds” (Q 37:180–82). By His permission ﷻ, the fifth treatise follows, entitled *The Radiant Bloom: On the Science of Metaphor*.

تمّت بعون الله تعالى الرسالة المسمّاة بالورد الصدع في علم الوضع جعلها الله تعالى بمنّه وكرمه نافعة لنا ولسائر المؤمنين. اللّهم لا تؤاخذنا إن نسينا أو أخطأنا. ﴿سُبۡحَٰنَ رَبِّكَ رَبِّ ٱلۡعِزَّةِ عَمَّا يَصِفُونَ ١٨٠ وَسَلَٰمٌ عَلَى ٱلۡمُرۡسَلِينَ ١٨١ وَٱلۡحَمۡدُ لِلَّهِ رَبِّ ٱلۡعَٰلَمِينَ﴾ [٣٧/ ١٨٠-١٨٢]. وتليها بإذنه تعالى الرسالة الخامسة المسمّاة النضارة في علم الاستعارة.

NOTES TO TREATISE IV

1 The assignment of word patterns and syntactical forms to their respective significations and functions is no less important than the coinage of words. This will be apparent in Chapter 2.

2 Though the Arabic word *ism* is used here, one should not understand that the subject matter of the science is restricted to the grammatical noun or even that it is restricted to the word. See the previous note.

3 That is, he mentally conceives of the category 'lion', and then he applies the proper name Usāma to that specific conception of the category 'lion' that he has formed in his mind in that moment. From that point on, the name Usāma applies to the specific conception of 'lion' that anyone might form mentally in any particular moment. One might compare this to the way that the name John Doe is applied to the hypothetical generic man and the name Fido to the hypothetical generic dog.

4 The *assigner's meaning* (*ālat al-waḍʿ*) is the concept in the assigner's mind by which he conceives the referents—including any that are yet to exist—to which he intends to assign a given expression. The category to which an assignment belongs is partly determined by the assigner's meaning: a general assignment is one in which the assigner's meaning is universal, while a specific assignment is one in which the assigner's meaning is particular. In the first of the three categories discussed in the text, the assigner's meaning is the particular concept of the specific (i.e., particular) denotation to which the expression is assigned; in the second category, it is the universal concept of the general (i.e., universal) denotation to which the expression is assigned; and in the third category, it is the universal concept that unites all the specific denotations to which the expression is assigned.

5 Although the concept 'previously mentioned masculine singular' is expressed in grammatical terms, it refers here to real things rather than to words.

6 The act of assignment becomes futile because the purpose of assignment is that speakers use the assigned expression for the denotation that it is assigned, but the condition proposed by those holding the latter position disallows this.

7 Thus, *faʿala*, *faʿula*, and *faʿila*, for example, are all assigned as names for the corresponding perfect tense structures: *faʿala* becomes a name for the class that includes *naṣara* (he helped), *faʿula* becomes a name for the class that includes *ḥasuna* (he was good), and *faʿila* becomes a name for the class that includes *ʿalima* (he knew). Thus, when one sees the word *ḥasiba* (he deemed), one can say, "This word belongs to the class *Faʿila*."

8 According to this way of counting, two words with a common pattern but different lexical roots are counted as having separate structures. For example, the structures of *ḍaraba* (he hit) and *naṣara* (he helped) are counted as two distinct instances of a generic category (i.e., the general *fa-ʿa-la* pattern). That category is assigned a proper name.

9 The Arabic term *ṣīgha* can be used to refer broadly to the combination of a word's lexical root and its formal structure, or it can be used to refer strictly to the structure itself, abstracted of combination with any particular lexical root. When the author says here that the *ṣīgha*

is assigned, this is understood to mean the expression that is the combination of lexical root and formal structure, namely, the word.

10 This is highly condensed; refer to the fuller explanation below. In the meantime, note that the syntactic relation between the verb and grammatical agent is assigned to the real relation between the action and real agent.

11 There is a dispute over whether verbs are assigned to signify general or specific relations between actions and agents. For example, does the verb *ḍaraba* as used in the specific context of the statement *ḍaraba Zaydun* (Zayd hit) refer to the general performance of hitting or to Zayd's hitting? The discussion that the author is referring to is his note above in the second category on the assignment of verbs, which presents the position that verbs refer to specific relations. Bear in mind that the other two elements of the assignment of verbs mentioned in that note—the assignment of roots to action-notions and the assignment of tenses to times—belong to the second category by unanimous agreement.

12 The assigned words are conceived through the general concept 'words of the root *f-ʿ-l* as arranged in such and such morphological structure', and the denotations are conceived through the general concept 'such and such morphological structure'. Thus, for instance, the word *faʿala* (a specific individual of the former general concept) becomes a generic proper name for the perfect tense verb structure (a specific individual of the latter generic concept). See al-Bakshahrī, *Taṣwīr al-waḍʿ*, 8. The student may be surprised to learn that the denotation is conceived through a general concept, given that this is a category of specific assignment. The generality here, however, is only due to the collective assignment. In the two remaining categories, the student may observe that this generality is compounded with another, which is due to the assignment's being not only collective but also general.

13 Each is assigned as a name for the category of words that share the pattern it represents. Thus, for example, *faʿala* is assigned as a name for the perfect tense verb category, which is the category that unites *naṣara*, *fataḥa*, *ḍaraba*, and so on. Note that the wording in the text is somewhat imprecise here because it suggests that the name is assigned to the individual words themselves.

V

THE RADIANT BLOOM

On the science of metaphor

النضارة في علم الاستعارة

In the Name of Allah,
All-Merciful, Most Compassionate

بسم الله الرحمن الرحيم

ALL PRAISE IS due to Allah, Lord of the worlds. May blessings and peace be upon the seal of the prophets Muḥammad and upon his family, his Companions, and those who follow them in excellence until the day of judgment.

الحمد لله رب العالمين والصلاة والسلام على خاتم النبيّين محمد وعلى آله وصحبه والتابعين لهم بإحسان إلى يوم الدين.

To Proceed This is a treatise on the science of metaphor.[1] I have entitled it *The Radiant Bloom: On the Science of Metaphor*.

أما بعد فهذه رسالة في علم الاستعارة سمّيتها النضارة في علم الاستعارة.

[مقدمة]

تعريفه وموضوعه وغايته

هو علم يعـرف به إيراد المـعنى الواحد بطـرق مختلفة[١] في وضوح الدلالة عليـه[٢] كإيراد جود زيـد بـ«كثير الرماد» و«جبـان الكلـب» و«مهـزول الفصيـل».[٣] وموضوعـه

[١] الغـرض مـن معرفـة هـذا الإيـراد أن يحترز المتكلّم عـن الخطأ في تأديـة الكلام بحيث لا يـورد من الكلام مـا يدلّ على مقصوده خفيةً عنـد اقتضاء المقـام دلالة واضحـة، أو دلالة واضحة عـن اقتضائه دلالـة خفيـة، أو دلالـة أوضـح عنـد اقتضائه دلالـة متوسّـطة، أو دلالـة متوسّـطة عنـد اقتضائـه دلالة أوضـح أو أخفى.

[٢] بـأن يكـون بعضهـا أوضـح مـن بعض سـواء كانـت تلـك الطرق مـن قبيـل الكنايـة أو المجـاز أو التشبيـه. مثـال الكنايـة ذُكـر في المتن و«كـثير الرمـاد» أوضحهـا. ومثـال الاسـتعارة في وصف زيد بالجـود «رأيـت بحـرًا في الدار» في الاسـتعارة الحقيقيـة و«طـمّ زيد بإنعامـه جميـع الأنـام» و«لجّة زيـد تتلاطـم بالأمـواج» كلاهمـا في الاسـتعارة المكنيـة وأوضحهـا الأول. ومثال التشبيـه «زيد كالبحر في السـخاء» و«زيـد كالبحـر» و«زيـد بحـر» والأول أوضحها.

[٣] هــذه التراكيـب تفيـد وصـف زيـد بالجـود مـن طريـق الكنايـة لأن هـزال الفصيـل إنمـا يكـون بإعطـاء لبن أمّـه للضيفـان، وجبن الكلـب لألفـه للواردين عليـه منهـم بكثرة فلا يعـادي

[INTRODUCTION]

Definition, subject matter, and aim

The science of metaphor is a science by which one knows how to convey one meaning in diverse ways[1] that vary in how plainly they signify that meaning,[2] e.g., to convey the generosity of Zayd through “has abundant ashes,” “has a meek dog,” or “has a lean young camel.”[3] The subject matter of

[1] The purpose of learning how to convey meanings in this way is that a speaker avoid errors in communication by not speaking in a way that (1) signifies his intent subtly when the situation calls for overt signification, (2) signifies his intent overtly when the situation calls for subtle signification, (3) signifies his intent especially overtly when the situation calls for moderately [plain] signification, or (4) signifies his intent moderately [plainly] when the situation calls for especially overt or especially subtle signification.

[2] Such that some ways are more plain than others, whether these ways belong to the category of implication, nonliteral language, or simile. The main text provides examples of implication, and the plainest of them is “has abundant ashes.” Examples of metaphor in describing Zayd as generous are “I saw an ocean in the house” for *actual metaphor* and “Zayd has flooded all creatures with his kindness” and “Zayd’s gulf crashes with waves” both for *implicit metaphor*; the first is the plainest. Examples of simile are “Zayd is like the sea in generosity,” “Zayd is like the sea,” and “Zayd is a sea”; the first is the plainest.

[3] These phrases convey the attribution of generosity to Zayd by implication: the leanness of a young camel can only imply that one serves its mother’s milk to one’s guests, the meekness of a dog is the result of its becoming accustomed to the frequent arrival of guests such

the science is the verbal expression with respect to simile, nonliteral language, implication, and allusion. The aim of the science is that one know how to convey one meaning in different ways.

اللفظ مـن حيث التشبيـه والمجـاز والكنايـة والتعريض. وغايتـه معرفة إيـراد المـعنى الواحد بطـرق مختلفة.

I have arranged [this treatise] into three chapters.

ورتّبتها على ثلاثة أبواب.

that the dog does not attack anyone, and an abundance of ashes is the result of frequently burning firewood to cook due to the abundance of guests (as explained in al-Dasūqī, *Kitāb ḥāshiyat al-Dasūqī*, 3:8).

أحـدًا؛ كـذا في الدسـوقي. وكثرة الرمـاد مـن كثرة إحـراق الحطـب للطبـخ مـن أجـل كثرة الضيفـان.

Chapter 1

SIMILE

Comprising the definition of simile and an explanation of its components

Simile is to use the *kāf* or the like[2] to indicate that one thing has a commonality with another thing, but not in the manner of metaphor.

[The Components of Simile]

Simile has four components: the two objects of comparison,[1] the ground, and the instrument.

1–2. The Objects of Comparison: the Tenor and the Vehicle The objects of comparison could be (a) both sensory, e.g., "Zayd is like a rose"; (b) both abstract, e.g., "Knowledge is like life";[2] or (c) different [in this respect], e.g., "Death is like a predator."[3]

---

[1] Namely, the *tenor of the simile* and the *vehicle for the simile*.

[2] The ground for comparison between knowledge and life is that both are aspects of conscious apprehension, though knowledge is a cause of apprehension while life is a prerequisite for it. What is meant by knowledge here is the trained faculty by which one has the capacity for particular instances of apprehension, not apprehension itself.

[3] This is an example of an abstract tenor and sensory vehicle. *Al-maniyya*, or death, is abstract since it is the absence of life within a thing that could have life. *Al-sabuʿ*, or a predator, is sensory. The ground for comparison between the two is the seizing or destroying of lives without any discrimination between those who are beneficent and those who are pernicious. An example of the reverse is to say, "Perfume is like noble character."

الباب الأول

التشبيه

فيه تعريف التشبيه وبيان أركانه

التشبيه[١] الدلالة على مشاركة أمر لآخر في معنًى بالكاف ونحوه بحيث لا تكون على سبيل الاستعارة.

[أركان التشبيه]

وأركانه أربعة: طرفاه[١] ووجهه وأداته.

١-٢. طرفاه أي المشبه والمشبه به وهما إما حسيّان نحو «زيد كالورد»، وإما عقليّان نحو «العلم كالحياة»،[٢] وإما مختلفان نحو «المنيّة السبع».[٣]

---

[١] وهما المشبّه والمشبّه به.

[٢] وجه الشبه بينهما كونهما جهتي إدراك، وإن كان العلم سببًا له والحياة شرطًا له. فالمراد بالعلم هنا الملكة التي يقتدر بها على الإدراكات الجزئيّة لا نفس الإدراك.

[٣] هذا المثال لما كان المشبّه عقليًا والمشبّه به حسّيًا. فإن المنيّة أي الموت عقليّ لأنه عدم الحياة عمّا من شأنه الحياة، والسبع أي المفترس من الحيوان حسّيّ. ووجه الشبه بينهما اغتيال النفوس أي إهلاكها من غير تفرقة بين نفّاع وضرّار. ومثال العكس أن يقال «العطر كخلق كريم».

Furthermore, the objects of comparison could be (a) both simple, as above; (b) both composite, e.g., Bashshār's saying,

> *ka'anna muthāra al-naqʿi fawqa ru'ūsinā*
> As though the rising dust above our heads
>
> *wa-asyāfanā laylun tahāwā kawākibuh*[1]
> With our swords were a night of plunging stars

or (c) different [in this respect], e.g., another [poet's] saying,

> *wa-ka'anna muḥmarra al-shaqīqi*
> It is as if the red poppy anemone
>
> *idhā taṣawwaba aw taṣaʿʿad*
> In an upward or downward bend
>
> *aʿlāmu yāqūtin nushirna*
> Were flags of ruby splayed
>
> *ʿalā rimāḥin min zabarjad*[2]
> Upon poles of peridot

[1] *Muthār* (made to rise) is a passive participle derived from *athāra al-ghubāra* (He made the dust rise), i.e., "stirred it up and moved it." *Naqʿ* is dust. The phrase *fawqa ru'ūsinā* (above our heads) means "gathered above our heads." The *wāw* in the phrase *wa-asyāfanā* means "with." The word *tahāwā* is originally *tatahāwā* (plunging) (one of the two *tā*'s was elided) and means "falling down one after the other." The ground for comparison is the configuration that consists of the falling of shining bodies—namely, swords and stars—that are protracted and proportional and are dispersed throughout something dark: the swords are in the darkness of dust, and stars are in the darkness of night.

[2] The phrase *muḥmarr al-shaqīq* (a reddened poppy anemone) is grammatically analogous to *jardu qaṭīfa* (a threadbare body covering). A *shaqīq* is a red flower with black at its center, and it grows on mountains. *Idhā* (when) is an adverb for [the implicit] *ushabbihu* (I liken), which is understood from *ka'anna* (as if). *Taṣawwaba* means "leaned downward"; *taṣaʿʿada* means "leaned upward." *Aʿlām* is the plural of *ʿalam*, or a flag. *Zabarjad* is a green gemstone. Now, the tenor of the simile here is a simple sensory thing, and the vehicle is an imaginary composite.

وأيضا طرفاه إما (١) مفردان كما مرّ، وإما (٢) مركّبان كما في قول بشّار:

> كَأَنَّ مُثَارَ النَّقْعِ فَوْقَ رُؤُوسِنَا
> وَأَسْيَافَنَا لَيْلٌ تَهَاوَى كَوَاكِبُهُ[١]

وإما (٣) مختلفان كما في قول الآخر:

> وكَأَنَّ مُحْمَرَّ الشَّقِيقِ
> إِذَا تَصَوَّبَ أَوْ تَصَعَّدْ
> أَعْلَامُ يَاقُوتٍ نُشِرْنَ
> عَلَى رِمَاحٍ مِنْ زَبَرْجَدْ[٢]

[١] «المثار» اسم مفعول من «أثار الغبارَ» أي «هيّجه وحرّكه». و«النقع» الغبار. وقوله «فوق رؤوسنا» أي «المنعقد فوق رؤوسنا». والواو في قوله «وأسيافنا» بمعنى «مع». وقوله «تهاوى» أصله «تتهاوى» — حذفت إحدى التائين — أي «يتساقط بعضها إثر بعض». ووجه الشبه هو الهيئة الحاصلة من سقوط أجرام مشرقة — وهي السيوف والنجوم — مستطيلة متناسبة المقدار متفرّقة في جوانب شيء مظلم؛ أما السيوف ففي ظلمة الغبار وأما الكواكب ففي ظلمة الليل.

[٢] قوله «محمرّ الشقيق» من باب «جرد قطيفة». و«الشقيق» ورد أحمر في وسطه سواد ينبت بالجبال. و«إذا» ظرف لـ«أشبه» المأخوذ من «كأنّ». و«تصوّب» أي «مال إلى أسفل»، و«تصعّد» أي «مال إلى علوّ». و«الأعلام» جمع «علَم» وهي الراية. و«الزبرجد» حجر أخضر من المعادن النفيسة. فالمشبّه هنا مفرد حسّيّ والمشبّه به مركّب خيالي.

3. The Ground for Comparison The ground for comparison is that in which the objects of comparison share *actually*, as above, or *imaginarily*, e.g., "The Sunna is like light in illumination," "Deviant innovation is like dusk in blackness," and [the poet's] saying,

> *wa-ka'anna al-nujūma bayna dujāhu*
> As though the stars amid its gloom
>
> *sunanun lāḥa baynahunna ibtidāʿu*[1]
> Were sunnas amid deviance gleaming

4. The Instrument The instrument of simile can be the *kāf*, *ka'anna*, *mithl*, or the like.

Sometimes the instrument is not mentioned, such that (a) the vehicle of the simile is the predicate of a tenor that is either implicit, e.g., *ṣummun bukmun ʿumyun* (Deaf, dumb, and blind) (Q 2:18),[2]

[1] The word *dujāhu* is the plural of *dujya* (gloom), which resembles *ẓulma* (darkness) in morphological pattern and in meaning. The pronoun refers to the night in the preceding phrase *rubba laylin...* (How many a night...). Another narration attests *dujāhā* with the pronoun referring to the stars. *Sunan* is the plural of *sunna*. *Lāḥa* means "appeared." *Ibtidāʿ* means "deviant innovation." Now, it should be clear that the phrase *sunanun lāḥa baynahunna ibtidāʿu* (sunnas amid which deviance gleams) is a case of inversion and means *sunanun lāḥat bayna al-ibtidāʿi* (sunnas gleaming amid deviance). It should also be clear that this is a simile between the sensory and the abstract, but, hyperbolically, the sunnas are treated as though they were sensory and as though they were the basis [for the comparison]. Alternatively, the [entire] simile could be construed inversely, the intended meaning being *wa-ka'anna al-sunana bayna al-ibtidāʿi nujūmun bayna dujāhu* (As if sunnas amid deviance were stars within its gloom). The ground for comparison is the configuration that consists of shining white objects dispersed throughout something dark and black. This configuration is absent in the vehicle for the simile, namely, the sunnas, except by means of imagination.

[2] I.e., "They are deaf, dumb, and blind." *Ṣumm* is the plural of *aṣamm* (deaf); *bukm* is the plural of *abkam* (dumb), that is, someone who is mute; and *ʿumy* is the plural of *aʿmā* (blind).

٣. وجهه ووجهه ما يشتركان فيه تحقيقًا كما مرّ أو تخييلًا نحو «السنّة كالنور في الإضاءة» و«البدعة كالظلمة في السواد» وكقوله:

> وَكَأَنَّ النّجُومَ بَيْنَ دُجَاهُ
>
> سُنَنٌ لَاحَ بَيْنَهُنَّ ابْتِدَاعُ[١]

٤. أداته وأداته الكاف و«كأنّ» و«مثل» ونحوها.

وقد لا تذكر الأداة بأن (١) يكون المشبّه به خبرًا لمشبّه مقدّر نحو ﴿صُمٌّ بُكْمٌ عُمْيٌ﴾ [٢/ ١٨][٢] أو مذكور؛

[١] قوله «دجاه» جمع «دُجية» وهي كـ«الظلمة» وزنًا ومعنًى. والضمير لليل في قوله قبلَه «ربّ ليل» إلخ. وروي «دجاها» والضمير للنجوم. و«السنن» جمع «سنّة». و«لاح» أي «ظهر». و«ابتداع» أي «بدعة». ثم لا يخفى أن قوله «سنن لاح بينهنّ ابتداع» من باب القلب أي «سنن لاحت بين الابتداع». ولا يخفى أن هذا أيضا من تشبيه المحسوس بالمعقول، فيقدّر أن السنن محسوسة ويجعل كأنها أصل على طريق المبالغة أو يجعل من عكس التشبيه والأصل «وكأنّ السنن بين الابتداع نجوم بين دجاه». ووجه الشبه وهو الهيئة الحاصلة من حصول أشياء مشرقة بيض في جوانب شيء مظلم أسود، فهي غير موجودة في المشبّه به الذي هو السنن إلا على طريق التخييل.

[٢] أي «هم صمّ بكم عمي». و«الصمّ» جمع «أصمّ»، و«البكم» جمع «أبكم» وهو الأخرس، و«العمي» جمع «أعمى».

or explicit; or such that (b) the vehicle of the simile has a status comparable to that of a predicate, as in

1. the predicate of the category of *kāna*, e.g., *kāna Zaydun asadan* (Zayd was a lion).
2. [the predicate] of the category of *inna*, e.g., *inna Zaydan asadun* (Zayd is indeed a lion).
3. the second object in the category of *ʿalimtu* (I knew), e.g., *ʿalimtu Zaydan asadan* (I knew Zayd to be a lion).
4. the third object in the category of *aʿlamtu* (I informed), e.g., *aʿlamtu Zaydan Bakran asadan* (I informed Zayd that Bakr is a lion).
5. a circumstance, e.g., *jāʾanī Zaydun asadan* (Zayd came to me as a lion).
6. an adjective, e.g., *jāʾanī Zaydun al-asadu* (Zayd, the lion, came to me).

أو (٢) يكون في حكم الخبر:

١- كخبر باب كَانَ نحو «كان زيد أسدًا».

٢- وباب إِنَّ نحو «إن زيدًا أسد».

٣- والمفعول الثاني لباب عَلِمْتُ نحو «علمتُ زيدًا أسدًا».

٤- والثالث لباب أَعْلَمْتُ نحو «أعلمتُ زيدًا بكرًا أسدًا».

٥- والحال نحو «جاءني زيد أسدًا».

٦- والصفة نحو «جاء زيد الأسد».

[The Purpose of Simile]

[When the Purpose Pertains to the Tenor] The purpose of simile most often pertains to the tenor. That purpose may be

1. to show that the tenor is possible, as in [the poet's] saying,

   fa-in tafuq al-anāma wa-anta minhum
   If you surpass all creatures though you be of them,

   fa-inna al-miska baʿḍu dami al-ghazāli[1]
   Musk is indeed a part of the blood of the gazelle

[الغرض من التشبيه]

[عود الغرض من التشبيه إلي المشبه] والغرض من التشبيه في الأغلب يعود إلى المشبّه. وهو إما:

١- بيان إمكانه، كما في قوله:

فَإِنْ تَفُقِ الأَنَامَ وَأَنْتَ مِنْهُمْ
فَإِنَّ المِسْكَ بَعْضُ دَمِ الغَزَالِ[١]

[1] The phrase *fa-in tafuq* derives from *fāqa / yafūqu*, meaning "to be above." *Anām* according to [the dictionary] *al-Miṣbāḥ* [*al-munīr*] refers to the jinn and humankind (according to some, it refers to any creature upon the face of the earth); the poet intended those creatures alive in his time. The phrase *wa-anta minhum* (while you are of them) is a circumstantial clause. The statement *fa-inna al-miska...* (Musk is indeed...) is not a result clause for the condition; rather, it is the reason for the result clause

[١] قوله «فإن تفق» من «فاق / يفوق» أي «علا». و«الأنام» قال في المصباح الجنّ والإنس، وقيل ما على وجه الأرض من جميع الخلق؛ وأراد الشاعر الأنام الموجودين في زمانه. وقوله «وأنت منهم» جملة حاليّة. وقوله «فإن المسك...» الخ ليس جوابًا للشرط وإنما هو علّة للجواب أُقيم مقامه، والأصل «فلا بُعد

that is, "Your case is like that of musk."

2. to explain its condition, e.g., "This garment is like that garment in blackness."
3. to explain the extent or degree [to which the ground applies to it], e.g., "This garment is like a crow in the intensity [of its color]."
4. to reinforce [its condition],3 e.g., "So-and-so is like one who writes on water or builds on air in that his effort is futile."
5. to beautify it,[1] e.g., a simile between a black face and the pupil of a gazelle.
6. to render it ugly, e.g., a simile between a pock-marked face and a dry piece of dung that was pecked by roosters.[2]

أي «حالك كحال المسك».

٢- أو بيـان حـاله، نحو «هـذا الثـوب مثـل ذاك الثوب في السواد».

٣- أو بيان مقداره، نحو «هذا الثوب كالغراب في شدّته».

٤- أو تقريـره، نحـو «فـلان كمـن يرقـم على المـاء أو يبـني على الهـواء في أنّ سـعيه لا طائـل تحتـه».

٥- أو تزيينه[١] كما في تشبيه وجه أسود بمقلة الظبي.

٦- أو تشـويهه كمـا في تشـبيه وجـه مجـدور بسـلحة جامـدة قـد نقرتهـا الديكـة.[٢]

---

and takes its place. The underlying meaning is "...then this is not at all strange, because musk is..." and so on. The simile in the verse is tacit and implied since [the poet] mentions an implicate of the simile—the ground, namely, the lofty status of the vehicle—and intends the implicant, which is the simile, i.e., "Your condition is like that of musk in surpassing all else of its kind." In other words, just as musk was originally blood and then became musk and, by its noble qualities which were not present in blood, entirely surpassed blood, likewise the person being praised was of humankind and then, by his qualities of perfection which were not present in others, surpassed them and rose above them in nobility and rank such that he became like an independent principle and a category in himself.

[1] Grammatically conjoined to "to show that the tenor is possible"; that is, to beautify the tenor of the simile in the eye of the listener.

[2] *Tashwīhuhu* (to render it ugly) means to make it repulsive. *Salḥa* (dung) (with an undotted *ḥā'*) is feces. *Diyaka* (roosters) (on the pattern of *qirada* [apes]) is the plural of *dīk* (rooster). As a play on words, they say, *dīk wadīk*, meaning "a fat rooster," where the *wāw* in the word *wadīk* is original to the word and not for conjunction; *wadīk* is derived from *wadak*, which is the grease of meat and fat.

في ذلـك لأن المسـك...» إلـخ. والتشبيـه في البيت ضـمنيّ ومكنيّ عنـه لأنه ذكـر فيـه لازم التشبيه وهو وجه الشـبه الذي هـو فوقان الأصـل وأراد الملـزوم وهـو التشبيـه أي «حالك كحال المسـك في التفـوّق على الجنس» أي كما أن المسـك كان في أصلـه دمًا ثم صار مـسكًا وفـاق سـائر الدمـاء لما فيه مـن الأوصـاف الشريفـة التي لا توجـد في الدم كذلـك الممـدوح كان من الإنسـان ثم فاقهـم وفاق عليهـم بالشرف والرتبـة لما فيه مـن أوصاف الكمـال التي لا توجد في غيره حتى صـار كأنـه أصل برأسـه وجنس بنفسـه.

[١] عطف على بيان إمكانه أي تزيين المشّبه في عين السامع.

[٢] تشـويهه أي تقبيحـه. و«السـلحة» بحاء مهملـة الغائـط. و«الديكـة» وزان «قـردة» جمـع «ديـك»؛ ويلغـز فيقـال «ديـك وديـك» أي «ديـك سـمين»، فالـواو في قـوله «وديـك» مـن أصل الكلمـة لا للعطـف، مـن «الـودك» وهـو دسـم اللحـم والشـحم.

The vehicle of the simile should be more familiar and well-known [than the tenor] in its possession of the ground.

When the Purpose of the Simile Pertains to the Vehicle Sometimes the purpose of the simile pertains to the vehicle. Such a purpose bears two possibilities.

The first is in giving the impression that the vehicle is more fully endowed [with the ground] than the tenor. This occurs in an *inverted simile*, as in [the poet's] saying,

> *wa-badā al-ṣabāḥu ka'anna ghurratahu*
> And morn appeared as though its blaze
>
> *wajhu al-khalīfati ḥīna yamtadiḥu*[1]
> Were the caliph's face when he is praised

and as in "Abū Ḥanīfa is like Abū Yūsuf."[4]

The second is in showing the interest that one has in it, e.g., when one who is hungry likens a face that resembles the full moon in roundness and brilliance to a round piece of bread. This is called *displaying what is desired.*

وينبغي أن يكون المشبّه به أعرف وأشهر بوجه الشبه.

عود الغرض من التشبيه إلى المشبه به وقد يعود[٢] الغرض من التشبيه إلى المشبّه به. وهذا الغرض قسمان.

أحدهما إيهام أنّه أتمّ من المشبّه؛ وذلك في التشبيه المقلوب، كقوله:

> وَبَدَا الصَّبَاحُ كَأَنَّ غُرَّتَهُ
>
> وَجْهُ الخَلِيفَةِ حِينَ يُمْتَدَحُ[١]

ونحو «أبو حنيفة كأبي يوسف».

وثانيها بيان الاهتمام به، كأن يشبّه الجائع وجهًا كائنًا كالبدر في الاستدارة والاستنارة بالرغيف. ويسمّى هذا إظهار المطلوب.

❋ ❋ ❋

[1] The phrase *wa-badā al-ṣabāḥu*, or "And morn appeared," refers either to the morning or to its light. A *ghurra* (blaze) is a white streak larger than a dirham on the face of a horse, and it is being used as a metaphor for the whiteness of the morning. The poet has rendered the blaze a tenor and the face of the caliph a vehicle despite the fact that the former is more fully endowed [with the ground] than the latter, intending to convey the impression that the face of the caliph is richer in clarity and brilliance than the morning, in hyperbolic praise.

[١] قوله «وبدا الصباح» أي «ظهر الصباح» بمعنى الصبح أو ضيائه. والغرّة بياض في جبهة الفرس فوق الدرهم استعير لبياض الصبح. فإن الشاعر جعل الغرّة مشبّهًا ووجه الخليفة مشبّهًا به مع أن الأول أتمّ من الثاني قصدًا إلى إيهام أن وجه الخليفة أتمّ من الصباح في الوضوح والضياء مبالغةً في المدح.

The highest level of simile is to omit the ground and the instrument, e.g., *Zaydun asadun* (Zayd is a lion) and *ṣummun bukmun ʿumyun* (Deaf, dumb, and blind) (Q 2:18).[1] The lowest level of simile is to explicitly provide all of its components. Any other way [of formulating a simile] is at an intermediate level.[2] Sometimes the vehicle is made *muḍāf* to the tenor for hyperbole, e.g., *lujaynu al-māʾi* (the silver of the water).

[1] Regardless whether the tenor of the simile is explicitly mentioned, as in the first example, or omitted, as in the second example.[5]

[2] To expound on this, the force of a simile may be due to (1) the apparent inclusion of all [qualities] as grounds. This occurs when the ground is omitted, for when the ground is omitted, this conveys the apparent impression that *every* quality of the tenor and the vehicle serves as a basis for comparing the tenor to the vehicle. This is because with the omission, one cannot give preponderance to any one quality over another [to serve as the sole basis] of the comparison. This reinforces the sameness [between the tenor and vehicle] and stands in contrast to the case when the ground is explicitly mentioned, because [in the latter case] the reason for the comparison is specified. Alternatively, [the force of a simile] may be due to (2) predicating the vehicle of the tenor. This occurs when the instrument is omitted since explicitly mentioning the instrument implies a distinction between that which is compared [i.e., the tenor] and that to which it is compared [i.e., the vehicle], while omitting the instrument gives the apparent impression that the one is applicable to the other and extends to it, thereby reinforcing the sameness between them. Now, [similes] that utilize both [of these force-giving omissions], i.e., omission of the ground and omission of the instrument, carry the most possible force and are at the highest level; as for those which lack both omissions, they carry no force and are at the lowest level. [Similes] that utilize [only] one omission are at an intermediate level.

وأعلى مراتب التشبيه حذف وجهه وأداته، نحو «زيد أسد» و﴿صُمٌّ بُكْمٌ عُمْيٌ﴾ [٢/ ١٨]؛[١] وأدناها ذكر جميع الأركان؛ وأوسطها غيرهما.[٢] وقد يضاف المشبّه به إلى المشبّه للمبالغة، نحو «لجين الماء».

[١] سواء ذكر المشبّه كالمثال الأول أو حذف كالمثال الثاني.

[٢] وبيان ذلك أن القوّة إما (١) بعموم وجه الشبه ظاهرًا، وذلك يحصل بحذفه لأنه إذا حُذف الوجه أفاد بحسب الظاهر أن جهة إلحاق المشبّه بالمشبّه به كل وصف إذ لا ترجيح لبعض الأوصاف على بعض في الإلحاق عند الحذف. وذلك يقوّي الاتحاد بخلاف ما إذا ذكر الوجه فإنه يتعيّن وجه الإلحاق؛ وإما (٢) بحمل المشبّه به على المشبّه، وذلك يحصل بحذف الأداة لأن ذكرها يدلّ على المباينة بين الملحق والملحق به وحذفها يُشعر بحسب الظاهر بجريان أحدهما على الآخر وصدقه عليه فيتقوّى الاتحاد بينهما. فما اشتمل على الوجهين أي حذف الوجه والأداة فهو في غاية القوّة فهو أعلى، وما خلا عنهما فلا قوّة فيه فهو أدنى، وما اشتمل على أحدهما فهو متوسّط.

Chapter 2

الباب الثاني

NONLITERAL LANGUAGE

المجاز

Because literal language serves as the basis for nonliteral language, we will deal with the former first and then turn to nonliteral language.

ولأنّ الحقيقة كالأصل للمجاز فأولًا نتعرض لها ثم للمجاز.

[Preliminary Classification]

[تمهيد]

Literal Language

الحقيقة

Our discussion here concerns the definition of literal language, its classification into *literal expressions* and *literal predication*, the definitions of both, and the classification of literal predication into four categories.

كلامنا هنا في تعريفها وانقسامها إلى اللغويّة والعقليّة وتعريفهما وانقسام العقليّة إلى أربعة أقسام.

A *ḥaqīqa* (instance of literal language) is an expression used for that to which it was assigned.[6] Literal language is classified into literal expressions and literal predication: *literal expressions* are expressions used for their assigned meanings according to the vocabulary referenced by the speech,[7] and *literal predication* is that a verb, a word with verbal import, or the like be predicated of an [agent] to which the

الحقيقة كلمة استعملت فيما وضعت له. وتنقسم إلى اللغويّة والعقليّة. أما اللغويّة فهي الكلمة المستعملة فيما وضعت له في اصطلاح به التخاطب. وأما الحقيقة العقليّة فهي نسبة الفعل أو معناه أو غيرهما إلى ما هو له

speaker apparently believes that it belongs.[1] Literal predication is classified into four types since the [predication] may

1. correspond to reality alone, e.g., a Muʿtazilī's telling someone unaware of his doctrine, "Allah has created all actions."[8]
2. correspond to [the speaker's] belief alone, e.g., an ignorant person's stating, "Spring made the vegetation sprout."
3. correspond to both, e.g., a believer's stating, "Allah made the vegetation sprout."
4. correspond to neither, e.g., to state, "Zayd came," when you know that he did not come.[2]

Nonliteral Language

Our discussion here concerns the definition of nonliteral language, its classification into nonliteral predication and tropes, [the classification of] nonliteral predication into four categories, [the classification of] tropes into metonymy and metaphor, the classification of each of these into

عند المتكلّم في الظاهر.[١] وهي تنقسم إلى أربعة أقسام، لأنه إما:

١- يطابق الواقع فقط، كقول المعتزلي لمن لا يعرف حاله «خلق الله الأفعال كلّها».

٢- أو يطابق الاعتقاد فقط، كقول الجاهل «أنبت الربيع البقل».

٣- أو يطابقهما جميعًا، كقول المؤمن «أنبت الله البقل».

٤- أو لا يطابقهما جميعًا، نحو قولك «جاء زيد» وأنت تعلم أنه لم يجئ.[٢]

المجاز

كلامنا هنا في تعريفه وانقسامه إلى العقلي واللغوي، والعقلي إلى أربعة أقسام، واللغوي إلى مرسل واستعارة،

---

[1] "According to the speaker's belief" and "apparent" are both connected to the phrase "to which it belongs." The qualification "apparent" includes [predications] that do not [actually] correspond to [the speaker's] belief, as in the first example. For when a Muʿtazilī says, "Allah has created all actions," he has predicated the creating of actions of [a subject] that is not what he believes to be the actual agent. The qualification "according to the speaker's belief" includes [predications] that correspond to [the speaker's] belief but not to reality, as in the second example.

[2] That is, when the addressee is unaware that Zayd did not come. For, if the addressee were aware as well, then the usage would not necessarily be literal, since it would be possible that the speaker made use of the fact that the person knows that Zayd did not come as a contextual indicant that the apparent meaning was not his intent. In this case, the predication would be of a [subject] to which it does not belong and would be an instance of nonliteral predication.

[١] «عند المتكلّم» و«في الظاهر» كلاهما متعلّق بقوله «له». ودخل بقوله «في الظاهر» ما لا يطابق الاعتقاد كالمثال الأول فإن المعتزلي إذا قال «خلق الله الأفعال كلّها» فقد نسب خلقًا إلى غير فاعله الحقيقي في اعتقاده، وبقوله «عند المتكلّم» ما يطابق الاعتقاد دون الواقع كالمثال الثاني.

[٢] أي ولا يعلم المخاطَب أنه لم يجئ، إذ لو علمه المخاطب أيضا لما تعيّن كونه حقيقة لجواز أن يكون المتكلّم قد جعل علم السامع بأنه لم يجئ قرينة على أنه لم يرد ظاهره فيكون الإسناد إلى غير ما هو له فيكون مجازًا عقليًا.

simple and composite, and [the classification of] simple metaphor into explicit and implicit.

Definition and Classification of Nonliteral Language A *majāz* (instance of nonliteral language) is an expression used for that to which it was *not* assigned, in consideration of a *semantic link* and [with] a *contextual indicant* that precludes that the assigned meaning could be intended.9 Nonliteral language is classified into nonliteral predication[1] and tropes.

[Nonliteral Predication] Nonliteral predication is that a verb, a word with verbal import, or the like be predicated of a [subject] with which it is associated rather than one to which it belongs by means of [its prompting] an interpretive process,[2] i.e., by contextual indication. This includes the following:

1. attributive relations like *ʿīshatun rāḍiyatun* (a content life) for an example in which the active voice is attributed to the object; *saylun mufʿamun* (an inundated flood) for the reverse;[3] *jadda jidduhu* (His exerting of

[1] [The word *ʿaqlī* in *majāz ʿaqlī*] is related to *ʿaql* (intellect) because nonliteral usage is the manipulation of something that is rational and apprehensible to the intellect, namely, predication. This can also be termed *predicative nonliterality* (*ḥukmī* is related to *ḥukm* [predication]), *nonliteral affirmation*, or *nonliteral predication* (*isnād majāzī*).

[2] [*Bi-taʾawwul* (by [prompting] an interpretive process)] grammatically modifies *nisba* (be predicated); this entails that the intellect seek that to which the [predication truly] belongs, i.e., the literal truth or that to which [the predication] belongs according to the intellect. Ultimately, this entails that [the speaker] has employed a contextual indicant that deflects the predication from that to which it belongs.

[3] This is an example of that which is in the passive voice yet predicated of the agent, because the flood is what inundates, or fills. The phrases "for the infinitive," "for the time," "for the place," and "for the means" mean "which is in the active voice yet predicated of the infinitive," "...of the time," "...of the place," or "...of the means," as in the examples provided in the text.

وانقسام كل منهما إلى مفرد ومركب، والاستعارة المفردة الى المصرّحة والمكنية.

تعريف المجاز وانقسامه: المجاز هو ما استعمل في غير ما وضع له لعلاقة وقرينة مانعة عن إرادة المعنى الموضوع له. وينقسم إلى عقليّ[١] ولغويّ.

[المجاز العقلي] المجاز العقلي هو نسبة الفعل أو معناه أو غيرهما إلى مُلابس له غير ما هو له بتأوّل[٢] أي بقرينة. فيشمل النسبة:

١- الإسنادية نحو «عيشة راضية» فيما بني للفاعل وأسند إلى المفعول به، و«سيل مفعم» في عكسه،[٣] و«جدَّ جدُّه» في المصدر، و«نهاره

[١] نسبة للعقل لأن التجوّز التصرّف في أمر معقول يدرَك بالعقل وهو الإسناد. ويسمّى مجازًا حكميًّا أي منسوبًا للحكم، ومجازًا في الإثبات، وإسنادًا مجازيًّا.

[٢] متعلّق بـ«نسبة» أي تطلب ما يؤول إليه من الحقيقة أو الموضع الذي يؤول إليه من العقل. وحاصله أن ينصب قرينة صارفة عن أن يكون الإسناد إلى ما هو له.

[٣] أي فيما بُني للمفعول وأُسند إلى الفاعل، لأن السيل هو الذي يفعم أي يملأ. وقوله في المصدر وفي الزمان وفي المكان وفي السبب أي فيما بني للفاعل وأسند إلى المصدر أو إلى الزمان أو إلى المكان أو إلى السبب كالأمثلة المذكورة في المتن.

صائم» في الزمـان، و«نهر جـارٍ» في المكان، و«بنى الأمير المدينة» في السـبب.

٢- والإضافية[١] نحو «مخالب المنيّة نشبت بفلان».

٣- والإيقاعيـة نحـو «نوّمـت الليـل» و«أجريـت النهـر».

وأقسامه أربعة، لأن طرفيه إما:

١- حقيقتان لغويّتان، نحو «أنبت الربيع البقل».[٢]

٢- أو مجازان، نحو «أحيا الأرض شباب الزمان».[٣]

٣- أو مختلفـان بـأن يكـون المسـند حقيقة والمسـند إليه مجـازًا، نحـو «أنبت البقـل شـباب الزمان».

٤- أو بالعكس،[٤] نحو «أحيا الأرض الربيع».

[١] عطف على «الإسنادية»، وكذا قوله «والإيقاعية».

[٢] فـإن الإنبات والربيـع حقيقتان لغويّتـان والنسـبة التي بينهما مجاز عقلي.

[٣] فـإن الإحيـاء مجـاز عـن الإنبـات، والشـباب مجـاز عـن الربيـع؛ والنسـبة التي بينهمـا مجـاز عـقلي.

[٤] أي يكون المسند مجازًا والمسند إليه حقيقة.

effort exerted effort) for an example with [the signified notion of] the infinitive noun; *nahāruhu ṣāʾimun* (His day is fasting) for the time; *nahrun jārin* (a flowing riverbed) for the place; and *banā al-amīru al-madīnata* (The governor built the city) for the cause.

2. *iḍāfa* relations[1] like *makhālibu al-maniyyati nashibat bi-fulānin* (The claws of death dug into so-and-so).
3. causative relations like *nawwamtu al-layla* (I put the night to sleep) and *ajraytu al-nahra* (I made the river flow).

Nonliteral predication is of four types because the two terms may be

1. both literal expressions, e.g., "Spring made the vegetation sprout."[2]
2. both tropes, e.g., "The youthfulness of the season enlivened the earth."[3]
3. different such that the predicate is a literal expression and the subject is a trope, e.g., "The youthfulness of the season made the vegetation sprout."
4. the reverse,[4] e.g., "Spring enlivened the earth."

[1] *Iḍāfiyya* is grammatically conjoined to *isnādiyya* (attributive). The same goes for *īqāʿiyya* (causative).

[2] "Made sprout" and "spring" are literal expressions, and the predication between them is a nonliteral predication.

[3] "Enlivened" is a trope for making something sprout, "youthfulness" is a trope for spring, and the predication between them is a nonliteral predication.

[4] That is, the predicate is a trope and the subject is a literal expression.

The Trope and Its Categories Tropes are expressions used for meanings other than those assigned to them according to the vocabulary[1] referenced by the speech, in consideration of a semantic link[2] and [with] a contextual indicant that precludes that the assigned meaning could be intended,[3] regardless whether that vocabulary be (1) the *lexical code*,[10] e.g., *asad* (lion / courageous man)[4] for the predatory animal and a courageous man; (2) *revelational usage*, e.g., *ṣalāh* (ritual prayer / supplication)[5] for the act of worship and supplication; (3) a *specific convention*, e.g., *fiʿl* (verb / action)[6] for the word and the occurrence; or (4) *general* [*convention*], e.g., *dābba* (riding animal / thing that walks or crawls upon the ground)[7] for the four-legged creature and a human being.

[1] [*Fī iṣṭilāḥin* (according to the vocabulary)] grammatically modifies *ghayri* (other than).

[2] [*Li-ʿalāqatin* (in consideration of a semantic link)] grammatically modifies *al-mustaʿmala* (used).

[3] [*Irādatihi* (intending it)], i.e., intending the assigned meaning.

[4] *Asad* is either lexically literal, in reference to the predatory animal, or lexically nonliteral, in reference to a courageous man.

[5] *Ṣalāh* is literal with regard to revelational usage in reference to the specific act of worship and nonliteral with regard to revelational usage in reference to supplication.

[6] *Fiʿl* is literal by a specific convention, namely, grammatical convention, in reference to [words] that signify [meanings in] themselves that are bound to one of the three times, and it is nonliteral by grammatical convention in reference to an occurrence.

[7] *Dābba* is literal by general convention in reference to the four-legged creature and nonliteral by general convention in reference to a human being.

المجاز اللغوي وأقسامه المجاز اللغوي هو الكلمة المستعملة في غير ما وضعت له في اصطلاح[١] به التخاطب لعلاقة[٢] مع قرينة مانعة عن إرادته[٣] سواء كان ذلك الاصطلاح لغةً كـ«الأسد»[٤] للسبع والرجل الشجاع، أو شرعًا كـ«الصلاة»[٥] للعبادة والدعاء، أو عرفًا خاصًّا كـ«الفعل»[٦] للفظ والحدث، أو عامًّا كـ«الدابّة»[٧] لذوات الأربع والإنسان.

[١] متعلّق بـ«غير».

[٢] متعلق بـ«المستعملة».

[٣] أي إرادة ما وضعت له.

[٤] فإنه حقيقة لغوية في السبع أو مجاز لغوي في الرجل الشجاع.

[٥] فإنها حقيقة شرعيّة في العبادة المخصوصة، مجاز شرعيّ في الدعاء.

[٦] فإنها حقيقة عرفيّة خاصّة أي نحويّة فيما دلّ على [معنًى في] نفسه مقترنًا بأحد الأزمنة الثلاثة، مجاز نحويّ في الحدث.

[٧] فإنها حقيقة عرفيّة عامّة في ذوات الأربع، مجاز عرفيّ عامّ في الإنسان.

Tropes are of two types: (1) *metonymy*,[1] when the semantic link is not resemblance, or else[2] (2) *metaphor*. Each of these is either (a) simple or (b) composite. Thus, there are four categories [of tropes].

وهـو قسـمان: (١) مرسـل[١] إن كانـت علاقتـه غير المشـابهة وإلا[٢] (٢) فاسـتعارة. وكل منهما إما (١) مفرد أو (٢) مركّـب. فالأقسـام أربعة.

❋ ❋ ❋

[I. Simple Metonymy]

[(١) المجاز المرسل المفرد]

The first category is simple metonymy, which is to refer to a thing by such as the name of

1. a cause of the thing, as in *yad* (hand)[3] for favors or for power and as in "We let [the cattle] graze on the rain," i.e., "the vegetation."[4]
2. an effect of the thing, as in "The sky rained vegetation," i.e., "rain."

الأول المجاز المرسل المفرد، وهو كتسمية الشيء باسم:

١- سـببه، كـ«اليـد»[٣] في النعمـة والقـدرة ونحـو «رعينـا الغيـث» أي «النبـات».[٤]

٢- أو مسبّبه، نحو «أمطرت السماء نباتًا» أي «مطرًا».

---

[1] Metonymy (*majāz mursal*) is termed *mursal* (released) because *irsāl* (releasing) lexically means "to free from restriction": while metaphor is restricted by the [implicit] claim that the tenor is of the same kind as the vehicle, metonymy is free from this restriction. According to some: The reason it is termed *mursal* is that it is free from the restriction to a specific kind of semantic link and may involve many different kinds of semantic links, in contrast to metaphor, which is restricted to a single kind of semantic link, namely, that of resemblance.

[2] When the semantic link is resemblance.

[3] As in *kathurat ayādī fulānin ʿindī* (The hands of so-and-so were abundant with me), i.e., "his favors," and *li-l-amīri yadun* (The commander has a hand), i.e., "power." For, the hand is a causal means for the granting of favors and the displaying of power.

[4] Rain causes vegetation.

[١] سمّي مـرسلًا لأن الإرسـال في اللغـة الإطلاق والمجـاز الاسـتعاري مقيّـد بادّعاء أن المشـبّه مـن جنس المشـبّه به والمرسـل مطلق عن هـذا القيـد. وقيـل إنمـا سمّي مرسلًا لإرسـاله عـن التقيّـد بعلاقة مخصوصـة بـل ردّد بين علاقـات كـثيرة مختلفـة بخلاف المجـاز الاسـتعاري فإنـه مقيّـد بعلاقـة واحـدة هي المشـابهة.

[٢] بأن كانت علاقته المشابهة.

[٣] مثـل «كثرت أيادي فلان عنـدي» أي «نعمـه» و«للأمير يد» أي «قـدرة»، فإنهـا سـبب لصـدور النعمـة ولظهـور القدرة.

[٤] فإن الغيث سبب للنبات.

3. the whole of the thing,[1] as in “They place their fingers in their ears” (Q 2:19), i.e., “their fingertips.”
4. a part of the thing,[2] as in *ʿayn* (eye) for someone on the lookout.
5. the location of the thing,[3] as in “So let him call his assembly-place” (Q 96:17), i.e., “the people of his assembly.”
6. something located within it,[4] as in “And as for those whose faces whiten, they will be in the mercy of Allah” (Q 3:107), i.e., “in paradise.”
7. something to which it applies,[5] as in “…in which of you is the afflicted one” (Q 68:6), i.e., “the affliction.”
8. something juxtaposed with it,[6] as in *rāwiya* (water-bearing animal) (meaning “camel”) for a *mazāda*, or a leather waterbag.

٣- أو كلّه،[١] نحو ﴿يَجْعَلُونَ أَصَٰبِعَهُمْ فِيٓ ءَاذَانِهِم﴾ [٢/ ١٩] أي «أناملهم».

٤- أو جزئه،[٢] كـ«العين» في الشخص الرقيب.

٥- أو محلّه،[٣] نحو ﴿فَلْيَدْعُ نَادِيَهُۥ﴾ [٩٦/ ١٧] أي «أهل ناديه».

٦- أو حالّه،[٤] نحو ﴿وَأَمَّا ٱلَّذِينَ ٱبْيَضَّتْ وُجُوهُهُمْ فَفِي رَحْمَةِ ٱللَّهِ﴾ [٣/ ١٠٧] أي «في الجنّة».

٧- أو متعلّقه،[٥] نحو ﴿بِأَييِّكُمُ ٱلْمَفْتُونُ﴾ [٦٨/ ٦] أي «الفتنة».

٨- أو مجاوره،[٦] كـ«الراوية» أي البعير في المزادة أي القربة.

[1] That is, to refer to a thing, like fingertips, by the name of its whole, like fingers.

[2] That is, to refer to a thing, like someone on the lookout, or a spy, by the name of a part of that thing, like an eye.

[3] That is, to refer to a thing, like the people of an assembly, by the name of its location, like an assembly-place, or a place of gathering.

[4] That is, to refer to a thing, like paradise, by the name of something that is located within it, or occurs in it, like mercy.

[5] That is, to refer to a thing, like affliction, by the name of an object to which it applies (*mutaʿallaqihi*, with *fatḥ* of the *lām*), like someone with an affliction.

[6] That is, to refer to a thing, like a *mazāda* (with *fatḥ*), which is a vessel of water from which one drinks while atop an animal, by the name of something juxtaposed with that thing, like a camel, for *rāwiya* is a word for a camel.

[١] أي تسمية الشيء كالأنامل باسم كلّه كالأصابع.

[٢] أي تسمية الشيء كالشخص الرقيب أي الجاسوس باسم جزئه كالعين.

[٣] أي تسمية الشيء كأهل النادي باسم محلّه كالنادي أي المجلس.

[٤] أي تسمية الشيء كالجنّة باسم حالّه أي الواقع فيه كالرحمة.

[٥] أي تسمية الشيء كالفتنة باسم متعلّقه بفتح اللام كالمفتون.

[٦] أي تسمية الشيء كالمزادة بفتح وهو ظرف الماء الذي يستقى به على الدابّة باسم ما يجاوره وهو البعير فإن «الراوية» اسم له.

9. the opposite of the thing,[1] as in *mafāza* (place of safety or escape) for a perilous desert.
10. an instrumental means of the thing,[2] as in “And make for me a faithful tongue among later generations” (Q 26:84), i.e., “good mention.”
11. a qualified sense of the thing,[3] as in *mishfar* (lip of a camel) for a lip.
12. an unqualified sense of the thing,[4] as in the reverse of this example.
13. or [a name] that refers to what the thing was,[5] and this is termed *past metonymy*, as in “Give orphans their property” (Q 4:2), i.e., “those who were orphans.”

[1] That is, to refer to a thing, like a perilous desert, by the name of its opposite, e.g., *mafāza*, a word for a place of *fawz* (escape), or deliverance.

[2] That is, to refer to a thing, like good mention, by the name of an instrumental means of that thing, like a tongue.

[3] That is, to refer to a thing, like a lip in the general sense, by the name of a qualified instance of that thing, e.g., *mishfar* (with *kasr* of the *mīm*), which is for the lip of a camel.

[4] That is, to refer to a thing, like the lip of a camel, by the name of its unqualified sense, like a lip in general.

[5] That is, to refer to a thing, like children who have come of age, by the name of a condition that the thing had in the past, e.g., “orphans” in the noble verse, i.e., “those who were orphans,” since there is no orphanhood after the age of maturity.

٩- أو مضادّه،[١] كـ«المفازة» في البرّيّة المهلكة.

١٠- أو آلته،[٢] نحو ﴿وَٱجْعَل لِّي لِسَانَ صِدْقٍ فِي ٱلْأٓخِرِينَ﴾ [٢٦/ ٨٤] أي «ذكرًا حسنًا».

١١- أو مقيّده،[٣] كـ«المشفر» في الشفة.

١٢- أو مطلقه،[٤] كعكس هذا المثال.

١٣- أو باعتبار ما كان[٥] ويسمّى مجازًا بالكون، نحو ﴿وَءَاتُوا۟ ٱلْيَتَٰمَىٰٓ أَمْوَٰلَهُمْ﴾ [٤/ ٢] أي «الذين كانوا يتامى».

[١] أي تسمية الشيء كالبرّيّة المهلكة باسم ضدّه كـ«المفازة» فإنه اسم لمكان الفوز أي النجاة.

[٢] أي تسمية الشيء كالذكر الحسن باسم آلته كاللسان.

[٣] أي تسمية الشيء كالشفة المطلقة باسم مقيّده كـ«المِشفر» بكسر الميم لشفة البعير.

[٤] أي تسمية المقيّد كالمشفر باسم مطلقه كالشفة المطلقة.

[٥] أي تسمية الشيء كالأولاد البالغين باسم الشيء الذي كان هو عليه في الزمان الماضي كـ«اليتامى» في الآية الكريمة أي «الذين كانوا يتامى» إذ لا يُتمَ بعد البلوغ.

14. or what the thing will be,[1] and this is termed *future metonymy*, as in "Surely you will die and surely they will die [lit., 'are dead']" (Q 39:30)[2] and "'Truly I saw myself in a dream pressing wine'" (Q 12:36), i.e., "grapes."

١٤- أو مـا يـؤول إليـه[١] ويسـمّى مجـازًا بـالأوْل، نحـو ﴿إِنَّـكَ مَيِّـتٌ وَإِنَّهُـم مَّيِّتُـونَ﴾ [٣٩/ ٣٠][٢] و﴿إِنِّيٓ أَرَىٰنِيٓ أَعۡصِرُ خَمۡـرٗا﴾ [١٢/ ٣٦] أي «عنبًـا».

These are examples of simple metonymy.

هذه أمثلة المجاز المرسل المفرد٣.

[II. Composite Metonymy]

[(٢) المجاز المرسل المركب]

The second category is that of composite metonymy, which is like the poet's saying,

> *hawāya maʿa al-rakbi al-yamānīna muṣʿidun*
> Away with the Yemeni riders journeys my love,

والثاني المجاز المرسل المركّب، وهو كقول الشاعر:

> هَـوَايَ مَـعَ الرَّكْـبِ اليَمَـانِينَ مُصْعِـدٌ

[1] That is, to refer to a thing, like a living person, by the name of what it will become, like a dead person.

[2] Some have said: *Mayyit* with vowelization [*bi-l-taḥrīk*, lit., "with being moved"] is for what moves and *mayt* without vowelization [*bi-l-sukūn*, lit., "with being motionless"] is for what is motionless. As the poet says,

> *ayā sāʾilī tafsīra maytin wa-mayyitin*
> O you who'd have me explain *mayt* and *mayyit*,
>
> *fa-dūnaka qad fassartu in kunta taʿqilu*
> Attend; I've explained, if you'll understand:
>
> *fa-mā kāna dhā rūḥin fa-dhālika mayyitun*
> We call *mayyit* that which has a living soul,
>
> *wa-mā al-maytu illā man ilā al-qabri yuḥmalu*
> And *mayt* is only what we carry to the grave

Nonetheless, the prevailing view is that they have the same meaning: both the lightened [*mayt*] and the doubled [*mayyit*] are literal in reference to someone who has actually died and nonliteral in reference to someone who will die.

[١] أي تسمية الشيء كالحيّ باسم ما يؤول إليه كالميّت.

[٢] قيل «الميت» بالتحريك للمتحرك وبالسكون للساكن كما قال:

> أَيَـا سَـائِلِي تَفْـسِيرَ مَيْـتٍ وَمَيِّـتٍ
>
> فَدُونَـكَ قَـدْ فَسَّرْتُ إِنْ كُنْـتَ تَعْقِـلُ
>
> فَمَـا كَـانَ ذَا رُوحٍ فَذَلِـكَ مَيِّـتٌ
>
> وَمَـا المَيْـتُ إِلَّا مَـنْ إِلَى الـقَبْرِ يُحْمَـلُ

وإلا ظهـر القـول بالاتّحاد فكلّ مِـن المخفّف والمشـدّد حقيقة فيمن مـات بالفعل مجاز فيمن سـيموت.

janībun wa-juthmānī bi-Makkata mūthaqu[1]
Led alongside, while my body to Makka
is tied

This composite structure is linguistically assigned [the function] of informing, but its aim [here] is the implicate, which is the expression of sorrow and regret.[11]

[III. Simple Metaphor]

The third category of the trope is simple metaphor.

[The Definition and Components of Simple Metaphor]

A simple metaphor is that whose semantic link is one of resemblance. The two objects of comparison are termed the *vehicle for the metaphor* and the *tenor of the metaphor*, the expression is termed a *metaphorical expression*,[2] that in which[3] the objects of comparison are conceived to share is termed a *commonality*, and that which precludes that the literal meaning could be intended is termed a *contextual indicant.*

[1] *Hawāya* (my love) means "my beloved." *Rakb* is the plural of *rākib* (rider). *Yamānīna* is the plural of *yamānin*, which means "Yemeni"; *yamānin* is originally *yamānī* but undergoes the same morphological modification as *qāḍin* (judge). *Muṣʿid* (journeys) (with *kasr* of the *ʿayn*) is the predicate of *hawāya* and is derived from *aṣʿada fī al-arḍi* ("he journeyed in the land"): it means "becoming distant and traveling the land." *Janīb* means "one who is made to follow alongside another," i.e., someone whose people lead and keep before them; this implies that the beloved is unable to free herself from the riders and will not come to him. *Juthmānī* means "my body." *Mūthaq* means "shackled."

[2] The vehicle is the literal meaning [of the expression], and the tenor is the [intended] nonliteral referent. The metaphorical expression is like clothing that was borrowed from someone and then used to clothe someone else.

[3] *Mā* (that) is grammatically conjoined to *ṭarafayhā* (its objects of comparison).

جَنِيــــبٌ وَجُثْمَـــانِي بِمَكَّـــةَ مُوثَـــقُ؛[١]

فـإن هـذا المركّب موضـوع للإخبـار؛ والغرض منـه لازمه الذي هو إظهـار التحـزّن والتحسّر.

[(٣) الاستعارة المفردة]

الثالث من المجاز اللغوي الاستعارة المفردة.

[تعريف الاستعارة المفردة وأركانها]

وهي مـا تكـون علاقته المشـابهة. يقال لطرفيها مسـتعار منه ومسـتعار له، وللفـظ مسـتعار،[٢] ولِما[٣] قُصد اشتراك الطـرفين فيه جامـع، ولِما يَمنع إرادة المـعنى الحقيقي قرينة.

[١] «هـواي» أي «مهـواي».° و«الركـب» اسـم جمـع لـ«راكـب». و«اليمـانين» جمـع «يمـان» بمـعنى «يـمنيّ»، وأصـل «يمـان» «يمـانيّ» أُعـلّ إعلال «قـاضٍ». و«مصعـد» بكسر الـعين خبر «هـواي» مـن «أصعـد في الأرض» مضى فيهـا أي «مبعـد ذاهب في الأرض». و«الجنيـب» المجنوب المستتبـع أي الذي يُتبعـه قومـه ويقدّمونـه أمامهم. وهـو كناية عـن أن المحبوبـة لا يمكـن انفلاتهـا عـن الركب ولن تـأتي إليـه. و«جثماني» أي «شـخصي». و«موثـق» أي «مقيّـد».

[٢] المستعار منه هو المعنى الحقيقي، والمستعار له هو المعنى المجازي، واللفظ المستعار بمنزلة اللباس الذي استعير من أحد فلبّس غيره.

[٣] عطف على «طرفيها».

[Types of Simple Metaphor]

[Explicit and Implicit Metaphor] It[1] is (1) an *explicit metaphor* if the vehicle is mentioned but the tenor is intended, e.g., "I saw a lion in the bathhouse," and (2) an *implicit metaphor*[12] if the tenor is mentioned but some specific characteristic of the vehicle is affirmed for the tenor as a contextual indicant, e.g., al-Hudhalī's saying,

> *wa-idhā al-maniyyatu anshabat aẓfārahā*
> And when death digs in its claws
>
> *alfayta kulla tamīmatin lā tanfaʿu*[2]
> You will find no amulet of any avail

This—namely, the contextual indicant of an implicit metaphor—is termed a *metaphorical characterization.* The rhetoricians hold that implicit metaphor and metaphorical characterization are inseparable.

Now, the tenor might be mentioned verbatim as above, or it might be mentioned in another way as in His saying ﷻ, "So Allah made it taste the garment of hunger and fear" (Q 16:112). Here, the detrimental condition that overcomes the human being in the state of hunger and fear is compared to a garment in that it envelops, and thus the word "garment" is used metaphorically in reference to that condition. [Moreover, the same condition is compared] to distasteful, bitter food in its repugnancy. This, then, is a case of explicit metaphor in consideration of the former and a case of implicit metaphor in consideration of the latter, with "making taste" being a metaphorical characterization.

[1] A metaphor.

[2] *Maniyya* means "death," and it is the grammatical agent of an omitted verb interpreted by *anshabat* (digs in), i.e., "fastens." *Alfayta* means "you will find." A *tamīma* is a bead (*kharaza*, with *fatḥ* of the *khāʾ* and *rāʾ*) that is used as an amulet, that is, hung on the necks of children to protect them from the evil eye or jinn, as they claim.

[أقسام الاستعارة المفردة]

[الاستعارة المصرّحة والمكنيّة] وهي[١] (١) استعارة مصرّحة إن ذكر المشبّه به وأريد المشبّه، نحو «رأيت أسدًا في الحمّام»؛ (٢) واستعارة مكنية إن ذكر المشبّه وأثبت له ما يختصّ بالمشبّه به قرينة، كقول الهذلي:

> وَإِذَا المَنِيَّةُ أَنْشَبَتْ أَظْفَارَهَا
>
> أَلْفَيْتَ كُلَّ تَمِيمَةٍ لَا تَنْفَعُ[٢]

وتسمّى هذه أي قرينة المكنيّة استعارة تخييلية ويحكمون بعدم انفكاك المكنيّة عنها.

ثم إن المشبّه قد يذكر بلفظه كما مرّ وقد يذكر بغير لفظه كقوله تعالى ﴿فَأَذَاقَهَا ٱللَّهُ لِبَاسَ ٱلْجُوعِ وَٱلْخَوْفِ﴾ [١٦/ ١١٢] فإنه شبّه ما غشي الإنسان عند الجوع والخوف من أثر الضرر من حيث الاشتمال باللباس فاستعير له اسمه ومن حيث الكراهة بالطعم المرّ البشيع فيكون استعارة مصرّحة نظرًا إلى الأول ومكنيّة نظرًا إلى الثاني وتكون الإذاقة تخييلًا.

[١] أي الاستعارة.

[٢] «المنيّة» الموت، وهو فاعل فعل محذوف يفسّره «أنشبت» أي «علّقت». و«ألفيت» أي «وجدت». و«التميمة» الخرزة بفتح الخاء والراء التي تُجعل معاذة أي تعلّق على عنق الصبيان صونًا لهم عن العين أو الجن على زعمهم.

[Classifying Explicit Metaphor in Terms of the Tenor] Al-Sakkākī[13] divides explicit metaphors into two types: first, (1) *actual metaphors*, which are those whose tenor either has actual sensible reality, as in "I saw a lion flinging," or has actual intelligible reality, as in "Guide us upon the straight path" (Q 1:6), i.e., "the true religion," and, second, (2) *fanciful metaphors*, which he defines as those whose tenor has no actual reality, whether sensible or intelligible, but is rather a merely fanciful image,[14] as with the word "claws" in one of the previous examples—for, when death is compared to a predator in that it snatches,[1] one's faculty of fancy[15] proceeds to generate[2] for 'death' the image and properties of a predator and gives it the imaginary likeness of claws. But [al-Sakkākī's division] is overly contrived.

[Classifying Explicit Metaphor in Terms of the Expression] There are two types of [explicit metaphor] in consideration of the metaphorical expression. A metaphor is (1) *primary* if the expression is a generic noun—that is, a noun that is universal either in reality or in effect—irrespective of its qualities and regardless whether it be a concrete noun, e.g., "lion" for a brave man, or an abstract noun, e.g., "killing"

[1] I.e., in that it kills.

[2] *Ikhtirā'* means "generating." The upshot of what al-Sakkākī proposes is that when death is compared to a predator, one's faculty of fancy imagines and supposes that it has claws like the claws of a predator and then compares its imagined, supposed claws to the real claws of a predator. Then, one uses the word "claws," which is assigned to real claws, for this imagined, supposed tenor. Thus, this is a fanciful explicit metaphor: it is an explicit metaphor because the vehicle is mentioned but the tenor intended, and it is a fanciful metaphor because the tenor is suppositional and imaginal, not real.

[تقسيم الاستعارة المصرّحة باعتبار المستعار له] وجعل السكّاكي الاستعارة المصرّحة قسمين: أحدهما تحقيقية، وهي ما يكون المستعار له فيه محقّقًا حسًّا نحو «رأيت أسدًا يرمي» أو عقلًا نحو ﴿ٱهْدِنَا ٱلصِّرَٰطَ ٱلْمُسْتَقِيمَ﴾ [١/ ٦] أي «الدين الحقّ»؛ وثانيهما تخييلية، وفسّرها بما لا تحقّق لمعناه حسًّا ولا عقلًا بل هو صورة وهمية محضة كلفظ الأظفار فيما مرّ فإنه لمّا شبّه المنيّة بالسبع في الاغتيال[١] أخذ الوهم في تصويرها بصورته واختراع[٢] لوازمه لها فاخترع لها مثل صورة الأظفار. وفيه تعسّف.[٦]

[تقسيم الاستعارة المصرّحة باعتبار اللفظ المستعار] [والاستعارة المصرّحة] باعتبار اللفظ المستعار[٧] قسمان: إما (١) أصليّة إن كان اسم جنس أي اسمًا كليًّا حقيقةً أو حكمًا من غير اعتبار وصف فيه سواء كان اسم عين كـ«أسد» للرجل الشجاع أو اسم معنًى كـ«قتل»

[١] أي في الإهلاك.

[٢] أي إيجاد. وحاصل ما ذكره السكّاكي هو أنه لمّا شبّه المنيّة بالسبع خيّل الوهم وفرض أن لها أظفارًا مثل أظفار السبع فشبّه أظفارها المخيّلة المفروضة بأظفار السبع الحقيقيّة واستعمل في المشبّه المخيّل المفروض لفظ «الأظفار» الموضوع للأظفار الحقيقيّة. فهي استعارة مصرّحة تخييليّة؛ أما كونها استعارة مصرّحة فلأنه ذكر المشبّه به وأريد المشبّه وأما كونها تخييليّة فلأن المشبّه فرضي خيالي لا حقيقي.

for a forceful hitting. A metaphor is (2) *secondary* if the expression is (a) a verb, (b) a derivative noun,[1] or (c) a particle.

With respect to [a verb or derivative noun], the metaphor applies first to the infinitive noun and then to the word: thus, in the statement *naṭaqat al-ḥālu... / al-ḥālu nāṭiqatun bi-kadhā* (The circumstance told... / the circumstance tells of such and such), [the circumstance's function of] indicating is likened to [the action of] speaking (*nuṭq*) in that it conveys meaning to the mind; the word *nuṭq* (speaking) becomes a metaphor, and then the verb [*naṭaqat*] or the derivative noun [*nāṭiqatun*] is derived from it. Thus, the metaphor is primary with respect to the infinitive noun and secondary with respect to the verb or derivative noun.

The contextual indicant[2] in both primary and secondary metaphor may be the mention of a particular (1) agent, as above; (2) object, as in "He slew miserliness" (i.e., eliminated it) and "He revived generosity" (i.e., made it abundant); or (3) genitive noun, as in *fa-bashshirhum bi-ʿadhābin alīmin* (Give them glad tidings of a painful punishment) (Q 3:21) (i.e., warn them); or it may be (4) the situation or circumstantial context, e.g., "I killed Zayd" (i.e., struck him forcefully).

With respect to a particle,[3] the metaphor applies first to the related notion of the particle's

[1] *Yushtaqqu minhu* means "[derived] from a verb" assuming that words are morphologically derived from verbs, as is the position of the Kufans, or it means "[derived] from the infinitive noun of the verb" (with omission of the *muḍāf*), as is the position of the Basrans.

[2] The contextual indicant of the metaphor.

[3] *Fī al-ḥarf* (with respect to a particle) is grammatically conjoined to *fī al-awwalayn* (with respect to the first two). That is, with respect to a particle, metaphors apply first to the related notion of the particle's meaning, which is a universal meaning like 'commencement in general', and then apply secondarily to the instances and particulars of that particle.

للضرب الشديد؛ وإما (٢) تبعيّة إن كان فعلًا أو ما يشتقّ منه[١] أو حرفًا.

فالاستعارة في الأوّلين تجري أوّلًا في المصدر ثم فيهما، ففي قولنا «نطقتْ الحال... والحال ناطقة بكذا» يشبّه الدلالة بالنطق في إيصال المعنى إلى الذهن فيستعار لها لفظ «النطق» ثم يشتقّ منه الفعل أو الصفة، فتكون الاستعارة في المصدر أصليّة وفي الفعل والصفة تبعيّة.

وقرينتها[٢] فيهما ذكر (١) الفاعل كما مرّ، أو (٢) المفعول نحو «قتل البخلَ» أي «أزاله» و«أحيا السماحَ» أي «كثّره»، أو (٣) المجرور نحو ﴿فَبَشِّرْهُم بِعَذَابٍ أَلِيمٍ﴾ [٣/ ٢١] أي «أنذرهم»، أو (٤) الحال أو المقام نحو «قتلت زيدًا» أي «ضربته ضربًا شديدًا».

وفي الحرف[٣] تجري أوّلًا في متعلّق معناه ثم في معناه تبعًا له. والمراد بمتعلّق معناه ما يعبّر به

[١] أي «من الفعل» بناءً على أن الاشتقاق منه كما هو مذهب الكوفيين، أو «من مصدره» على حذف مضاف كما هو مذهب البصريين.

[٢] أي قرينة الاستعارة.

[٣] عطف على قوله «في الأوّلين» أي والاستعارة في الحرف تجري أوّلًا في متعلّق معنى الحرف وهو المعنى الكلّي كالابتداء المطلق ثم في حصصه وجزئيّاته ثانيًا.

meaning and then, secondarily, to the particle's meaning. What is meant by the related notion of the particle's meaning is that general meaning by which one expresses the meaning of the particle,[1] as when one says that *min* (from) is for 'commencement', *ilā* (to) is for 'termination', and so on. Thus, in His saying ﷻ, *wa-la-uṣallibannakum fī judhūʿi al-nakhli* ("And I shall surely crucify you on [lit., 'in'] the trunks of palm trees") (Q 20:71), the general notion of 'being above' is likened to the general notion of 'being within' in that it involves the general notion of being settled somewhere. Thus, the name of the vehicle[2] first becomes a metaphor for the tenor, and then, secondarily, the particle assigned to the particulars of the vehicle is used for the particulars of the tenor.

Al-Sakkākī prefers to account for secondary metaphor in terms of implicit metaphor by considering the contextual indicant of a secondary metaphor to be an implicit metaphor and the secondary metaphor itself to be a contextual indicant of the implicit metaphor. Thus, in *naṭaqat al-ḥālu... / al-ḥālu nāṭiqatun bi-kadhā* (The circumstance told... / the circumstance tells of such and such), he considers "the circumstance" to be an implicit metaphor that refers to a speaking human being in view of [the common action of] indicating what is sought, and [he considers] the attribution of [the action of] speaking to "the circumstance" to be a contextual indicant of this. [Similarly], in His saying ﷻ, *wa-la-uṣallibannakum fī judhūʿi al-nakhli* ("And I shall surely crucify you on [lit., 'in'] the trunks of palm trees"), al-Sakkākī considers "the trunks" to be an implicit metaphor for things that contain other things, and [he considers] the use of the word *fī* (in) to be a contextual indicant—and so on in this manner.

[1] *Mā* refers to the general meanings. The pronoun in *bihi* refers to *mā*, and the pronoun in *ʿanhu* refers to *maʿnā al-ḥarf* (the meaning of the particle).

[2] Namely, the general notion of 'being within'; the tenor is the general notion of 'being above'.

عنه[١] من المعاني المطلقة، كقولنا «مِنْ للابتداء» و«إِلَى للانتهاء» إلى غير ذلك. ففي قوله تعالى ﴿وَلَأُصَلِّبَنَّكُمْ فِي جُذُوعِ ٱلنَّخْلِ﴾ [٢٠/٧١] يشبّه الاستعلاء المطلق بالظرفية المطلقة في مطلق الاستقرار. فيستعار لفظ المشبّه به[٢] للمشبّه أوّلًا ثم يستعمل الحرف الموضوع لجزئيّات المشبّه به في جزئيّات المشبّه ثانيًا.

واختار السكّاكي ردّ التبعية إلى الاستعارة بالكناية بجعل قرينتها مكنيًّا عنها وجعل نفسها قرينة لها. ففي «نطقت الحال... والحال ناطقة بكذا» يجعل «الحال» استعارة بالكناية عن إنسان متكلّم في الدلالة على المقصود ونسبة النطق إليها قرينة لها، وفي قوله تعالى ﴿وَلَأُصَلِّبَنَّكُمْ فِي جُذُوعِ ٱلنَّخْلِ﴾ يجعل «الجذوع» استعارة بالكناية عن الظروف واستعمال لفظة «في» قرينة، وعلى هذا القياس.

[١] «ما» عبارة عن المعاني المطلقة. وضمير «به» راجع إلى «ما». وضمير «عنه» راجع إلى معنى الحرف.

[٢] وهو الظرفيّة المطلقة والمشبّه الاستعلاء المطلق.

[Classifying Explicit Metaphor in Terms of the Objects of Comparison] There are two types of explicit metaphor in consideration of the objects of comparison. This is because the combination of both within a single thing may be either

1. possible, e.g., "to whom We give life" in "Is then he who was dead and to whom We give life…" (Q 6:122), i.e., "at loss and whom we guided": the giving of life is being used as a metaphor for granting guidance, and both acts together are attributable to Allah ﷻ.[1] This is termed a *concordant metaphor.*
2. or impossible, e.g., "dead" in the same verse;[2] death is being used as a metaphor for being at loss, and both states cannot occur together in the same thing.[3] This is termed *discordant metaphor,* and it includes metaphors of sarcastic or witty irony, which are used in reference to the contrary or contradictory meaning,[4] like the use of "generous"

[1] For, indeed, Allah ﷻ gives life and guides.

[2] Namely, "Is then he who was dead and to whom We give life…" (Q 6:122).

[3] Since someone who is dead cannot be described as being at loss.

[4] The difference between a contrary opposite and a contradictory opposite is that contraries are two existential things that cannot simultaneously exist [in a single thing] but can simultaneously be negated, e.g., blackness and whiteness, while contradictories are two things that can neither simultaneously exist nor simultaneously be negated, one of which is existential and the other privative, e.g., affirmation and negation. The difference between a metaphor of sarcastic irony and a metaphor of witty irony lies in the purpose: if the purpose that motivates one to use a word for the contrary of its meaning is to mock and deride the person one is speaking about, then the metaphor is one of sarcastic irony, but if the motivating purpose is to delight one's listeners and to dissipate their boredom by means of something witty and clever, then the metaphor is one of witty irony.

[تقسيم الاستعارة المصرّحة باعتبار الطرفين] الاستعارة المصرّحة باعتبار الطرفين قسمان لأن اجتماعهما في شيء إما:

١- ممكن، نحو «أحييناه» في ﴿أَوَمَن كَانَ مَيْتًا فَأَحْيَيْنَٰهُ﴾ [٦/ ١٢٢] أي «ضالًّا فهديناه»؛ استعير الإحياء للهداية وقد اجتمعا في الله سبحانه.[١] وتسمّى وفاقية.

٢- وإما ممتنع، نحو «ميتًا» فيما مرّ؛[٢] استعير الموت للضلالة ولا يجتمعان في شيء.[٣] وتسمّى عنادية. ومنها التهكّمية والتمليحية، وهما ما استعمل في ضدّه أو نقيضه،[٤] كإطلاق «الكريم»

[١] فإن الله سبحانه يحيي ويهدي.

[٢] وهو ﴿أَوَمَن كَانَ مَيْتًا فَأَحْيَيْنَٰهُ﴾.

[٣] إذ الميت لا يوصف بالضلالة.

[٤] والفرق بين الضدّ والنقيض هو أن الضدّين هما الأمران الوجوديّان٨ اللذان لا يجتمعان وقد يرتفعان٩ كالسواد والبياض، وأن١٠ النقيضين الأمران اللذان لا يجتمعان ولا يرتفعان وأحدهما وجودي والآخر عدمي كالثبوت والنفي. والفرق بين التهكّميّة والتمليحيّة بحسب الغرض لأنه إن كان الغرض الحامل على استعمال اللفظ في ضدّ معناه الهزؤ والسخريّة بالمقول فيه كانت الاستعارة تهكّميّة، وإن كان الغرض الحامل على ذلك بسط السامعين وإزالة السآمة عنهم بواسطة الإتيان بشيء مليح مستظرف كانت تمليحيّة.

for a miser or "lion" for a coward and like His saying ﷻ, "Give them glad tidings of a painful punishment" (Q 3:21): "glad tidings" is used as an ironic metaphor for warning.

[Classifying Explicit Metaphor in Terms of the Commonality] There are two types of explicit metaphor in consideration of the commonality as well. This is because the commonality may be either

1. conceptually internal to both the tenor and the vehicle, as in His saying ﷻ, "And We sundered them into communities on the earth" (Q 7:168): the dispersion of the group is likened to sundering (which is lexically assigned to signify the severing of the physical continuum between attached bodies), then "sundering" is used as a metaphor for dispersing, and then the verb[1] is derived from it. The commonality is the elimination of cohesion, which is conceptually internal to both sundering and dispersing.
2. or not conceptually internal to both the tenor and the vehicle, as in the usage of "lion" as a metaphor for a courageous man or "the sun" for a radiant face.

[Classifying Explicit Metaphor in Terms of the Objects of Comparison and the Commonality] In consideration of all three elements, explicit metaphors are of six types. This is because if the vehicle and tenor are both sensory, the commonality may be

[1] Namely, *qaṭṭaʿnā* (We sundered).

على البخيل و«الأسد» على الجبان وكقوله تعالى ﴿فَبَشِّرْهُم بِعَذَابٍ أَلِيمٍ﴾ [٣/ ٢١]؛ استعير البشارة للإنذار على سبيل التهكّم.

[تقسيم الاستعارة المصرّحة باعتبار الجامع] وباعتبار الجامع أيضا قسمان لأنه إما:

١- داخل في مفهوم المستعار له والمستعار منه، كما في قوله تعالى ﴿وَقَطَّعْنَٰهُمْ فِى ٱلْأَرْضِ أُمَمًا﴾ [٧/ ١٦٨]. فإنه شبّه تفريق الجماعة بالتقطيع الموضوع لإزالة الاتّصال بين الأجسام الملتزقة، واستعير «التقطيع» للتفريق ثم اشتقّ منه الفعل.[١] والجامع إزالة الاجتماع وهي داخلة في مفهومهما.

٢- وإما غير داخل في مفهومهما، كاستعارة «الأسد» للرجل الشجاع و«الشمس» للوجه المتهلّل.

[تقسيم الاستعارة المصرّحة باعتبار الثلاثة] وباعتبار الثلاثة ستّة أقسام، لأن المستعار منه والمستعار له إن كانا حسّيّين فالجامع إما:

[١] وهو «قطّعنا».

1. sensory, as in His saying ﷻ, "Then he brought forth for them a calf as a lifeless body with a lowing sound" (Q 20:88): the vehicle is a young cow, the tenor is the creature[1] that Allah ﷻ created from the jewelry of the Egyptians, and the commonality is the shape. Each of these is sensory.

2. abstract, as in His saying ﷻ, "And a sign for them is the night: We strip the day therefrom" (Q 36:37). The vehicle is the stripping of skin,[2] and the tenor is the withdrawing of light from the place of night;[3] both are sensory in view of their objects, which are skin and light. The commonality is one event's following another—in the former, the appearance of flesh follows the stripping of skin, and in the latter, the appearance of the dark of night follows the removal of the light of day—and this commonality is abstract. The objects involved in the process of following are not always sensory;[4] thus, the commonality is not considered sensory.

١- حسّي، نحو قوله تعالى ﴿فَأَخْرَجَ لَهُمْ عِجْلًا جَسَدًا لَّهُۥ خُوَارٌ﴾ [٢٠/ ٨٨]. فالمستعار منه ولد البقرة، والمستعار له الحيوان[١] الذي خلقه الله تعالى من حلي القبط، والجامع الشكل. والجميع حسّي.

٢- وإما عقلي، نحو قوله تعالى ﴿وَءَايَةٌ لَّهُمُ ٱلَّيْلُ نَسْلَخُ مِنْهُ ٱلنَّهَارَ﴾ [٣٦/ ٣٧]. فالمستعار منه كشط الجلد،[٢] والمستعار له كشف الضوء[٣] عن مكان الليل؛ وهما حسّيّان باعتبار متعلّقهما وهو الجلد١١ والضوء. والجامع ترتّب أمر على آخر وهو في الأول ترتّب ظهور اللحم على كشط الجلد وفي الثاني ترتّب ظهور ظلمة الليل على إزالة ضوء النهار، وهو عقلي. ومتعلّق الترتيب ليس محسوسًا دائمًا[٤] فلم يُجعل حسّيًا.

---

[1] Which had the form of a calf.

[2] That is, the removal of skin from a sheep or the like.

[3] That is, the removal of light. What is meant by "the place of night" is the atmospheric stratum between the sky and the earth, though some say that it is the surface of the earth. What is meant by this being "the place of night" is that it is the place of its shade, i.e., its darkness, which means that it is the place where the darkness of night appears.

[4] This is an answer to an implicit question that may be expressed as follows:

> When one considers the stripping (*kashṭ*) of skin, the withdrawing (*kashf*) of light, and the process of following (*tarattub*), respectively, none of them are sensory because each is an infinitive noun, and infinitive notions have no extramental existence. However, when one considers the objects of each, they are sensory: in the first, this is skin; in the second, it is light; and in the third, it is flesh and darkness. Why,

---

[١] وهو على صورة العجل.

[٢] أي إزالته عن الشاة ونحوها.

[٣] أي إزالته. والمراد بمكان الليل الهواء الذي بين السماء والأرض وقيل سطح الأرض. والمراد بكون ما ذكر مكانًا لليل أنه مكان لظلّه أي لظلمته أي إنه مكان تظهر فيه ظلمته.

[٤] جواب سؤال مقدّر تقديره:

> إنّ كلًّا من كشط الجلد وكشف الضوء والترتّب إذا نُظر إلى نفسه ليس بمحسوس لأنه مصدر والمعنى المصدري لا وجود له في الخارج، وإذا نُظر إلى متعلّقه كان محسوسًا وهو في الأوّل الجلد١٢ وفي الثاني الضوء وفي الثالث اللحم والظلمة؛ فلِمَ

3. mixed, as in your stating, *ra'aytu shamsan* (I saw a sun), when you mean a human who is like the sun in facial beauty and eminence.[1]

If (4) both are abstract or they differ such that (5) the vehicle is sensory and the tenor is abstract or (6) vice versa,[2] then the commonality can only be abstract.

The same division from another perspective:

1. The vehicle, tenor, and commonality are all abstract, as in His saying ﷻ, "'Who has raised us from our place of sleep?'" (Q 36:52): the vehicle is sleep, the tenor is death, and the commonality is that [the person] does not manifest voluntary action. All three are abstract.
2. The vehicle is sensory while the tenor and commonality are abstract, as in His saying ﷻ, "So break forth as you have been commanded" (Q 15:94): the vehicle is breaking a glass vessel, which is sensory, while the tenor is proclaiming [the prophetic message] and the commonality is producing an effect, both of which are abstract.

---

then, are the first two considered sensory while the third is not considered sensory?

The author answers by stating:

The objects involved in the process of following are not always sensory. Following applies not only when one sensory thing follows another sensory thing, as here, but also when one abstract thing follows another abstract thing, as in how knowledge of a conclusion follows knowledge of the premises. Thus, following is not considered sensory.

[1] *Ṭalʿa* means "face," which is called a *ṭalʿa* because it is what one looks at (*al-muṭṭalaʿu ʿalayhi*) when one sees and stands face-to-face [with a person]. *Nabāha* means "eminence."

[2] Such that the vehicle is abstract and the tenor is sensory.

٣- وإما مختلف، كقولك «رأيت شمسًا» وأنت تريد إنسانًا كالشمس في حسن الطلعة ونباهة الشأن.[١]

وإن (٤) كانا عقليَّين أو مختلفَين بأن (٥) كان المستعار منه حسّيًّا والمستعار له عقليًّا أو (٦) بالعكس[٢] فالجامع عقلي لا غير.

التقسيم بوجه آخر:

١- الجميع من المستعار منه وله والجامع عقلي، كقوله تعالى ﴿مَن بَعَثَنَا مِن مَّرْقَدِنَا﴾ [٣٦/ ٥٢] فالمستعار منه الرقاد والمستعار له الموت والجامع عدم ظهور الفعل الاختياري، والجميع عقلي.

٢- المستعار منه حسّي والمستعار [له] والجامع عقليّان، كقوله تعالى ﴿فَٱصْدَعْ بِمَا تُؤْمَرُ﴾ [١٥/ ٩٤] فالمستعار منه كسر الزجاجة وهو حسّي، والمستعار له التبليغ والجامع التأثير وهما عقليان.

جعل الأوّلان حسيّين ولمْ يجعل الثالث حسيًّا؟

فأجاب بقوله:

ومتعلّق[٣] الترتيب ليس محسوسًا دائمًا. فإنه صادق بترتّب محسوس على محسوس كما هنا وترتّب معقول على معقول كترتّب العلم بالنتيجة على العلم بالمقدّمات، فلم يجعل حسيًّا.

[١] «الطلعة» الوجه، وسمّي «طلعة» لأنه المطّلع عليه عند الشهود والمواجهة. و«النباهة» الرفعة.

[٢] بأن كان المستعار منه عقليًّا والمستعار له حسيًّا.

3. The tenor is sensory while the vehicle and commonality are abstract, as in His statement ﷻ "Truly when the waters transgressed, We carried you upon the ship" (Q 69:11): the tenor is the abundance of water, which is sensory, while the vehicle is arrogance and the commonality is excessive elevation, both of which are abstract.

[Classifying Explicit Metaphor in Terms of Suitable Accompaniment] In consideration of *suitable accompaniment*, there are three types of explicit metaphor. A metaphor is

1. *plain* when not accompanied by anything that suits either the vehicle or the tenor,[1] e.g., "I saw a lion throwing."
2. *inflated* when accompanied by what suits the vehicle, e.g., His saying ﷻ, "They have purchased error at the price of guidance. Their commerce has not brought them profit" (Q 2:16).[2]
3. *deflated* when accompanied by what suits the tenor, e.g., the [poet's] saying,

   ghamru al-ridāʾi idhā tabassama ḍāḥikan
   Possessed of a copious cloak; when he smiles in laughter,

[1] That is, excluding the contextual indicant, seeing as it would suit the tenor. If the contextual indicant were brought into consideration, there would never be a plain metaphor. Or such has been said. Yet there is truly no need for this [qualification] because the contextual indicant is part of the metaphor; without it, it would not be called a metaphor.

[2] Exchanging falsehood for truth and choosing the former over the latter is likened to making a purchase, the word *ishtirāʾ* (purchasing) is used as a metaphor, and then the verb, namely, *ishtaraw* (they have purchased) is derived from *ishtirāʾ*. The mention of profit is an inflation [of the metaphor]. [The term] *murashshaḥa* (inflated) is derived from *tarshīḥ* (inflation), which means "strengthening." This kind of metaphor is termed *inflated* due to the strength that it has because the vehicle is mentioned along with that which suits it.

٣- المستعار له حسّي والمستعار منه والجامع عقليّان، كقوله تعالى ﴿إِنَّا لَمَّا طَغَا ٱلْمَآءُ حَمَلْنَٰكُمْ فِى ٱلْجَارِيَةِ﴾ [٦٩/ ١١] فالمستعار له كثرة الماء وهو حسّي، والمستعار منه التكبّر والجامع الاستعلاء المفرط وهما عقليّان.

[تقسيم الاستعارة المصرّحة باعتبار الملائم] وباعتبار الملائم ثلاثة أقسام، لأنها:

١- إن لم تقترن بما يلائم شيئًا[١] من المستعار منه والمستعار له فمطلقة، نحو «رأيت أسدًا يرمي».

٢- وإن اقترنت بما يلائم المستعار منه فمرشّحة، نحو قوله تعالى ﴿ٱشْتَرَوُاْ ٱلضَّلَٰلَةَ بِٱلْهُدَىٰ فَمَا رَبِحَت تِّجَٰرَتُهُمْ﴾ [٢/ ١٦].[٢]

٣- وإن اقترنت بما يلائم المستعار له فمجرّدة، كقوله:

غَمْرُ الرِّدَاءِ إِذَا تَبَسَّمَ ضَاحِكًا

[١] أي بعد تمام القرينة إذ هي ممّا يلائم المستعار له فلو اعتبرت لم توجد مطلقة. كذا قيل، وفيه أنه لا حاجة إلى ذلك لأن القرينة من جملة الاستعارة فبدونها لا يقال لها استعارة.

[٢] شبّه استبدال الباطل بالحق واختياره عليه بالاشتراء فاستعير له اسمه ثم اشتقّ منه الفعل أي «اشتروا». وذكر الربح ترشيح. و«المرشّحة» من «الترشيح» وهو التقوية؛ سمّيت هذه الاستعارة «مرشّحة» لقوّتها حيث ذكر المشبّه به مع ملائمه.

ghaliqat li-ḍaḥkatihi riqābu al-māli[1]
The necks of his wealth are foreclosed by his laugh

i.e., "The person being praised gives copiously: when he smiles, the necks of his wealth pass securely into the possession of beggars." The poet uses "cloak" as a metaphor for 'giving' by virtue of the commonality of its serving as a protection from undesirable things, and then he deflates the metaphor by describing it as "copious," which suits giving.

Both[2] may be combined, e.g., the [poet's] saying,

ladā asadin shākī al-silāḥi muqadhdhafin
In the presence of a lion armed to the teeth and oft-flung

lahu libadun aẓfāruhu lam tuqallami[3]
Who has a mane and whose claws are not pared

[1] *Ghamr* (copious) (with *fatḥ* of the *ghayn*) is the predicate of an omitted subject, which can be expressed as *huwa ghamr* (He is [possessed of] a copious...), i.e., "of an abundance of giving." *Ḍāḥikan* means "beginning to laugh" or "taking to laughter." *Ghaliqat* (of the same [pattern] as *ʿalimat* [she knew]) means "were secured." *Ḍaḥka* (with *fatḥ* of the *ḍād*) refers to an instance of laughter. The meaning is that when the praised one smiles, the necks of his wealth are foreclosed and pass securely into the possession of beggars.[16]

[2] That is, the inflation and deflation of a single metaphor.

[3] *Ladā asadin* (in the presence of a lion) is the predicate of an omitted subject, which may be expressed as *ana ladā asadin* (I am in the presence of a lion), or it is the predicate of a *kāna* that is omitted along with its subject-noun, i.e., *ana kuntu ladā asadin* (I was in the presence of a lion). *Shākī al-silāḥi* (armed to the teeth) means "fully armed" and is deflationary because it suits the tenor, namely, the courageous man. *Muqadhdhaf* (oft-flung) can be interpreted to mean "one who was flung and thrown into battles and wars," which would make it suit the tenor and thus be deflationary; it could also be interpreted to mean "one into whom muscular flesh was flung and thrown," which would make it suit

غَلِقَتْ لِضَحْكَتِهِ رِقَابُ المَالِ[١]

أي الممدوح كثير العطاء إذا تبسّم تمكّنت رقاب أمواله في أيدي السائلين؛ استعار الرداء للعطاء بجامع الصون عمّا يكره ثم وصفه بالغمر الذي يناسب العطاء تجريدًا.

وقد يجتمعان،[٢] كقوله:

لَدَى أَسَدٍ شَاكِي السِّلَاحِ مُقَذَّفٍ
لَهُ لِبَدٌ أَظْفَارُهُ لَمْ تُقَلَّمِ[٣]

[١] «غمر» بفتح الغين خبر لمبتدأ محذوف تقديره «هو غمر...» إلخ أي «كثير العطاء». و«ضاحكًا» أي «شارعًا في الضحك آخذًا فيه». و«غلقت» كـ«علمت» أي «تمكّنت». و«الضحكة» بفتح الضاد المرّة من الضحك. أي إذا تبسّم الممدوح غلقت وتمكّنت رقاب أمواله في أيدي السائلين.

[٢] أي الترشيح والتجريد في استعارة واحدة.

[٣] «لدى أسد» خبر مبتدأ محذوف تقديره «أنا لدى أسد»، أو خبر لـ«كان» المحذوفة مع اسمها أي «أنا كنت لدى أسد». و«شاكي السلاح» أي «تامّه». وهذا تجريد لأنه ملائم المستعار له وهو الرجل الشجاع. و«مقذّف» يحتمل أن المراد «قُذف به ورمي به في الوقائع والحروب» فيكون ملائمًا للمستعار له فيكون تجريدًا، ويحتمل أن المراد «قُذف ورمي باللحم» فيكون ملائمًا لهما فلا يكون تجريدًا ولا ترشيحًا [بل هو في][١٤] معنى الإطلاق. و«لبد» كـ«عنب» جمع «لبدة» وهي ما تلبد وتضامّ من شعر الأسد على منكبه فيكون ملائمًا للمستعار منه فيكون ترشيحًا. و«أظفاره

i.e., "I am with a man who resembles a lion in courage."

Inflation is most emphatic, then leaving [the metaphor] plain, then deflation. Inflation is most emphatic because it entails an actualization of the hyperbole in the comparison.[1] Leaving [a metaphor] plain is more emphatic than deflation. The combination of inflation and deflation is at the same level [of emphasis] as leaving [a metaphor] plain.

Inflation and deflation are taken into account only after the metaphor is complete. Thus, the contextual indicant of an explicit metaphor is not counted as deflation, and the contextual indicant of an implicit metaphor is not counted as inflation.[2]

Inflation may involve the use of that which suits the vehicle as a metaphor for that which suits the tenor. [In such a case], it would also be possible for the inflation to retain its literal meaning, serving

---

both the tenor and the vehicle and thus be neither deflationary nor inflationary, [carrying rather] the meaning of rendering [the metaphor] plain. *Libad* (mane) (of the same [pattern] as *ʿinab* [grapes]) is the plural of *libda*, which refers to any part of a lion's fur that is matted and clings to its flank; it suits the vehicle and is thus inflationary. *Aẓfāruhu lam tuqallami* (whose claws/nails are not pared) can be interpreted to mean that [the creature being talked about] is not the kind that would pare its claws, which would make it inflationary; it can be interpreted to negate that its nails are pared in any emphatic sense, thereby affirming the basic action [of paring], which would make it deflationary; and it can be interpreted as an emphatic negation (instead of the negation of emphasis), meaning that its claws are emphatically not pared, which would again make it inflationary.

[1] That is, reinforcing the hyperbole, since metaphor involves hyperbolized simile. Inflating a metaphor by means of that which suits the vehicle brings actualization and strength to the metaphor. The metaphor provides the basis of the hyperbole by rendering the tenor an instance of the vehicle, and the reinforcement of this hyperbole occurs by means of the inflation.

[2] The contextual indicant of an implicit metaphor is like "the claws" in "The claws of death dug into to so-and-so."

أي أنا عند رجل كالأسد في الشجاعة.

الترشيح أبلغ ثم الإطلاق ثم التجريد: الترشيح أبلغ لاشتماله على تحقيق المبالغة في التشبيه؛[١] والإطلاق أبلغ من التجريد؛ وجمع الترشيح والتجريد في مرتبة الإطلاق.

واعتبار الترشيح والتجريد إنما يكون بعد تمام الاستعارة فلا تعدّ قرينة المصرّحة تجريدًا ولا قرينة المكنيّة ترشيحًا.[٢]

والترشيح يجوز أن يكون مستعارًا من ملائم المستعار منه لملائم المستعار له، ويحتمل أن يكون باقيًا على معناه الحقيقي لا يقصد به إلا

لم تقلّم» يحتمل أن يراد به أنه ليس من جنس من شأنه تقليم الأظفار فيكون ترشيحًا، ويحتمل أن يراد به أن أظفاره انتفت المبالغة في تقليمها فيكون أصله ثابتًا لها فيكون تجريدًا، ويحتمل أن يكون من المبالغة في النفي لا من نفي المبالغة والمعنى أن أظفاره انتفى تقليمها انتفاء مبالغًا فيه فيكون ترشيحًا أيضا.

[١] أي تقوية المبالغة لأن في الاستعارة مبالغة في التشبيه فترشيحها بما يلائم المستعار منه تحقيق وتقوية لها؛ فأصل المبالغة جاء من الاستعارة بجعل المشبّه فردًا من أفراد المشبّه به وتقويتها حصلت بالترشيح.

[٢] وقرينة المكنيّة كالأظفار في «أظفار المنيّة نشبت بفلان».

only to strengthen the metaphor. Both possibilities are present in His statement ﷻ "And hold fast to the rope of Allah, all together" (Q 3:103): "rope" is used as a metaphor for 'covenant', and that metaphor is inflated by the mention[1] of "holding fast"—which either retains its literal meaning or becomes a metaphor for upholding faith in the covenant.

تقوية الاستعارة. ويحتمل الوجهين قوله تعالى ﴿وَٱعْتَصِمُواْ بِحَبْلِ ٱللَّهِ جَمِيعًا﴾ [٣/ ١٠٣]؛ استعير الحبل للعهد وذكر[١] الاعتصام ترشيحًا إما باقيًا على معناه الحقيقي أو مستعارًا للوثوق بالعهد.

[IV. Composite Metaphor]

[(٤) الاستعارة المركبة]

The fourth category of the trope is composite metaphor. A composite metaphor is a composite expression used for a meaning likened to its original meaning, as when one tells a person who is being indecisive about some matter, "I see you putting a foot forward and then withdrawing it again."[2] If [the expression][3] is not in widespread use, it is termed an *analogy*, a *metaphorical analogy*, or an *analogical metaphor*; if widespread, it is termed a *proverb*. Proverbs are not to be altered from the [grammatical] form of their original context to fit the context of their usage:[4] one says to a man just as to a woman, *fī al-ṣayfi ḍayyaʿti al-labana* (You [f.] lost that milk in the summer), with *kasr* of the *tāʾ* because [the statement] was originally addressed to a woman.[17]

·الرابع من أقسام المجاز الاستعارة المركّبة، وهو اللفظ المركّب المستعمل فيما شبّه بمعناه الأصلي، كما يقال للمتردّد في أمر «إني أراك تقدّم رجلًا وتؤخّر أخرى».[٢] وهذه[٣] إن لم يشتهر استعمالها تسمّى تمثيلًا وتمثيلًا[١٥] على سبيل الاستعارة واستعارةً تمثيليّةً؛ وإن اشتهرت تسمّى مثلًا. والأمثال لا تغيَّر في مضربها عن حال موردها،[٤] فيقال للرجل كما يقال للمرأة أيضا «في الصيف ضيّعتِ اللبن» بكسر التاء لأنه كان في الأصل لامرأة.[١٦]

---

[1] [*Dhukira al-iʿtiṣāmu* ("holding fast" was mentioned)] is in the passive voice so that it corresponds to the preceding [verb]. *Iʿtiṣām* (holding fast) in the literal sense means to grasp the rope.

[2] The word *ukhrā* (another) is an adjective for an implicit *tāratan* (a time). This can be expressed as, "I see you putting a foot forward at one time and then withdrawing that foot at another time." The meaning is not "You put one foot forward and withdraw the other foot" as may initially occur to the mind.

[3] The composite metaphor.

[4] The "original context" of a proverb is that for which the statement was first used, and the "context of its usage" is that for which it is now used.

[١] بالبناء للمجهول ليناسب ما قبله. والمعنى الحقيقي للاعتصام التمسّك بالحبل.

[٢] قوله «أخرى» نعت لـ«تارة» مقدّرة، والتقدير «أراك تقدّم رجلًا تارة وتؤخّر تلك الرجل تارة أخرى»؛ وليس المعنى «تقدّم رجلًا وتؤخّر رجلًا أخرى» كما يتبادر إلى الذهن في الوهلة الأولى.

[٣] أي الاستعارة المركّبة.

[٤] مورد المثل ما استعمل فيه الكلام أوّلًا ومضربه ما استعمل فيه الكلام الآن.

❁ ❁ ❁

The Difference between Metaphor and Lying Metaphor is different from lying in that, unlike lying, it is based on interpretation, and [the speaker] makes use of a contextual indicant to indicate that he intends a metaphorical meaning. It is different from error in that, unlike error, it involves a commonality.

الفرق بين الاستعارة والكذب الاستعارة تفارق الكذب ببنائها على التأويل وبنصب قرينة على إرادة المعنى المجازي دونه؛ وتفارِق الغلط بوجود الجامع فيها دونه.

❁ ❁ ❁

Sometimes [the term] *majāz* is used in reference to a word whose inflection has changed by the omission of a word, as in His saying ﷻ, *wa-s'al al-qaryata* ("Ask the town") (Q 12:82), i.e., *ahla al-qaryati* (the people of the town), or by the addition of a word, as in His statement ﷻ *laysa ka-mithlihi shay'un* (There is nothing like Him) (Q 42:11), i.e., *laysa mithlahu shay'un.*[1]

وقد يطلق[١] «المجاز» على كلمة تغيّر إعرابها بحذف لفظ نحو قوله تعالى ﴿وَسْـَٔلِ ٱلْقَرْيَةَ﴾ [١٢/ ٨٢] أي «أهل القرية» أو بزيادة لفظ نحو قوله تعالى ﴿لَيْسَ كَمِثْلِهِۦ شَىْءٌ﴾ [٤٢/ ١١] أي «ليس مثله شيء».

---

[1] The word *majāz* is used for this meaning either (1) by way of equivocity, having been subject to two assignations—one assignation to 'an expression used for a meaning other than that to which it was assigned…' and one assignation to 'a word whose inflection has changed…'—such that the use of the term *majāz* in reference to this meaning is literal, or (2) by way of simile, where 'a word diverted from its original inflection' is likened to 'a word diverted from its original meaning' in virtue of the commonality of 'being diverted', and then the name of the vehicle (i.e., the term *majāz*) is used as a metaphor for the tenor such that the use of the word *majāz* for the tenor is an instance of nonliteral language through metaphor.

[١] أي يطلق عليها لفظ «المجاز» (١) على سبيل الاشتراك اللفظي بأن وضع لفظ «المجاز» مرّتين — مرّة للكلمة المستعملة في غير ما وضعت له إلخ وأخرى للكلمة التي تغيّر إعرابها إلخ — فيكون إطلاق لفظ «المجاز» عليها حقيقة، أو (٢) على سبيل التشبيه بأن شبّهت الكلمة المنتقلة عن إعرابها الأصلي بالكلمة المنتقلة عن معناها الأصلي بجامع الانتقال واستعير اسم المشبّه به وهو لفظ «المجاز» للمشبّه فيكون إطلاق لفظ «المجاز» عليها مجازًا بالاستعارة.

Chapter 3

IMPLICATION

Our discussion in this chapter concerns the definition of *implication* and its three-way classification, [namely, as pertaining to] an entity, an attribute, or an attribution.

An implicative expression is an expression by which one intends an implicate of the meaning while it remains possible that the meaning [itself] could have been intended along with the implicate,[1] e.g., "Zayd has long sword straps."[2] This is intended to refer to his tall stature, while it remains possible that reference to the length of his sword straps could simultaneously be intended as well. Thus, implication differs from nonliteral language in that if there is a contextual indicant that precludes that the literal meaning could be intended, [the expression] is nonliteral, but otherwise it is implicative.

Implications are of three types:

The first[3] is that by which the thing [described] is intended, e.g., to say, "one with upright stature and broad nails," to imply 'human being'.

---

[1] The pronoun in *irādatihi* (intending it) refers to *maʿnāhu* (its meaning) and the pronoun in *maʿahu* (along with it) refers to the *lāzim* (an implicate).

[2] *Nijād* (of the morphological pattern of *kitāb* [book]) refers to the straps used to carry a sword. What is intended by "having long sword straps" is "being of tall stature," while it remains possible for one to also mean by it that the straps used to carry the person's sword are long.

[3] The author says *al-ūlā* (the first [f.]) and not *al-awwal* (the first [m.])—while the latter would be expected since the word *qism* (type) is masculine—in consideration of the fact that the reference is to [the feminine noun] *al-kināya* (implication).

الباب الثالث

الكناية

كلامنا فيه في تعريف الكناية وانقسامها إلى ثلاثة: إلى ذات أو صفة أو نسبة

الكناية لفظ أريد به لازم معناه مع جواز إرادته معه،[١] نحو «زيد طويل النجاد»؛[٢] المراد منه طول القامة مع جواز إرادة طول النجاد معه. فهي تخالف المجاز في أنه إن قامت قرينة مانعة عن إرادة المعنى الحقيقي فمجاز وإلا فكناية.

وهي ثلاثة أقسام:

الأولى[٣] المطلوب بها الذات، كقولنا كناية عن الإنسان «مستوي القامة عريض الأظفار».

---

[١] ضمير «إرادته» راجع إلى «معناه»، وضمير «معه» راجع إلى «لازم».

[٢] «النجاد» بوزن «كتاب» حمائل السيف. والمراد من «طويل النجاد» «طويل القامة» مع جواز أن يراد منه أنه طويل حمائل السيف أيضا.

[٣] وإنما قال «الأولى» ولم يقل «الأول» — مع أنه الظاهر لأن لفظ «قسم» مذكّر — باعتبار كونها عبارة عن الكناية.

The second is that by which an attribute [of the thing described], like generosity or nobleness, is intended. If the transition does not involve an intermediate step [of inference], it is *direct*, e.g., to say, "having a wide nape," to imply 'dull fellow'; otherwise, it is *far-removed*, e.g., to say, "So-and-so has abundant ashes," to imply a hospitable host[1]—one transitions from 'having abundant ashes' to 'frequently burning firewood under cooking pots' to 'abundantly cooking food'[2] to 'having a great number of people eating'[3] to 'having frequent guests'[4] to the intended meaning, namely, 'being a hospitable host'.

The third is that by which an attribution is intended, that is, either (1) one thing's being affirmed of another, e.g., the [poet's] saying,

> *inna al-samāḥata wa-l-murūʾata wa-l-nadā*
> Truly, openhandedness, magnanimity, and largesse
>
> *fī qubbatin ḍuribat ʿalā Ibni al-Ḥashraji*[5]
> Are within a round tent pitched over Ibn al-Ḥashraj

[1] That is, 'being of abundant hospitability', which is to properly observe the rights of the guest.

[2] *Ṭabāʾikh* is the plural of *ṭabīkh*, or "that which is cooked."

[3] *Akala* (of the pattern of *fajara* [ones who are immoral]) is the plural of *ākil* (one who eats).

[4] *Ḍīfān* (with *kasr* of the *ḍād*) is the plural of *ḍayf* (guest).

[5] *Samāḥa* (openhandedness) is to gladly give of wealth what one is not required to give, whether one gives little or much. *Nadā* (largesse) is to give abundant wealth in order to merit matters of significance that are general, like the praise of every person. In common to both is generosity. *Murūʾa* (magnanimity) by convention means being vast in kindness with one's wealth and other things, as by pardoning offenses. It may be interpreted as the perfection of manliness, though this would lead to the problem that [this virtue] would be specific to men to the exclusion of women, which is at odds with the fact that women can indeed be magnanimous as well. This is so unless one says that the intended meaning of manliness is 'humanity' in a sense that includes the male and

والثانيـة المطلـوب بهـا الصفـة كالجـود والكـرم. فإن لـم يكـن الانتقال فيه بواسـطة قريبـةٌ كقـولنا كناية عن الأبلـه «عريـض القفـا» وإلا فبعيـدة كقـولنا كنايـة عن المضياف[١] «فلان كـثير الرماد» فإنه ينتقـل منه إلى كثرة إحـراق الحطـب تحت القـدور ومنهـا إلى كثرة الطبائخ[٢] ومنها إلى كثرة الأكلة[٣] ومنهـا إلى كثرة الضيفان[٤] ومنها إلى المقصـود وهـو المضياف.

والثالثـة المطلوب بها نسبة أي (١) إثبـات أمر لآخر، كقوله:

> إِنَّ السَّـمَاحَةَ وَالمَـرُوءَةَ وَالنَّـدَى
>
> فِي قُبَّـةٍ ضُرِبَـتْ عَلَى ابْـنِ الحَشْرَجِ[٥]

[١] أي «كثير المضيافية» التي هي القيام بحقّ الضيف.

[٢] جمع «طبيخ» أي «ما يُطبخ».

[٣] بوزن «الفَجَرَة» جمع «آكل».

[٤] بكسر الضاد جمع «ضيف».

[٥] «السـماحة» بـذل مـا لا يجـب بـذله مـن المال عـن طيـب نفـس سـواء كان المبـذول قلـيلًا أو كـثيرًا. و«النـدى» بـذل الأمـوال الكـثيرة لاكتسـاب الأمـور الجليلـة العامّـة” كثنـاء كل أحـد. ويجمعهـا الكـرم. و«المـروءة» في العـرف سـعة الإحسـان بالأمـوال وغيرهـا كالعفـو عـن الجنايـة، وتـفسّر بكمـال الرجوليّـة لكـن يـرد عليـه أنـه يقـتضي اختصاصهـا بالرجـل دون المـرأة مـع أنهـا تتّصـف بالمـروءة أيضـا إلا أن يقـال المـراد بالرجوليّـة الإنسـانيّة الشـامِلة للذكـر والأنثى،

which implies that these attributes are affirmed of him, or (2) one thing's being negated[1] of another, e.g., [someone's quoting the Prophet's] statement ﷺ "A Muslim is one from whose tongue and hand Muslims are safe"[18] in indirect reference to a [specific] person who is hurting Muslims to imply negating his Islam.[2]

This [last] type is also termed *allusion*: an expression used in its literal sense while being used to point to a different meaning. Such an expression may be nonliteral, e.g., to say, "You hurt me, so you will learn," intending someone else in the presence of the person whom you are addressing. If you intend both people together, it is an implicative expression. In either case—i.e., in the case of nonliteral language or implication—there must be a contextual indicant of the intended meaning.[3]

فإنه كناية عن إثبات هذه الصفات له؛ أو (٢) نفيه[١] عنه، كقوله ﷺ في عرض من يؤذي المسلمين كناية عن نفي الإسلام عنه:[٢] «المسلم من سلِم المسلمون من لسانه ويده».

ويقال لهذا القسم التعريض، وهو لفظ استُعمل في معناه الحقيقي وأشير به إلى معنًى آخر. وقد يكون مجازًا، كقولك «آذيتني فستعرف» وأنت تريد إنسانًا مع المخاطب دونه؛ وإن أردتهما جميعًا كان كناية. ولا بدّ فيهما أي في المجاز والكناية من قرينة تدلّ على المقصود[١٨].[٣]

the female. Magnanimity may also be interpreted as a desire to maintain one's guard against those attributes that disgrace a person and to maintain those attributes that raise a person above his peers; and this interpretation is similar to the previous one. Now, situating these three qualities within a round tent pitched over Ibn al-Ḥashraj implies that they are firmly established in him; for when something is affirmed within the physical place or location of the man, it is affirmed of the man himself.

[1] *Nafyuhu* (its negation) is grammatically conjoined to *ithbātu amrin* (one thing's affirmation).

[2] The way that the implication here works is that the import of the statement is that Islam is restricted to those people who do not cause hurt, and the restriction to such people can only be true if Islam is negated of the hurtful person. Thus, the implicant is expressed and through it the implicate is intended.

[3] When there is contextual indication that the threat is directed only at the person who is not being addressed (as, for example, when the person being addressed is a friend who caused no hurt), the expression is nonliteral. When there is contextual indication that the threat is directed at both (as when both are enemies of the speaker and have hurt him) the expression is implicative. Thus, there must be a contextual indicant to distinguish one case from the other. May Allah send blessings and peace upon our mas-

وتفسّر أيضا بالرغبة في المحافظة على دفع ما يعاب به الإنسان وعلى ما يرفع به على الأقران وهذا قريب مما قبله. ثم في جعل هذه الصفات الثلاث في قبّة مضروبة على ابن الحشرج كناية عن ثبوتها له لأنه إذا أُثبت الأمر في مكان الرجل وحيّزه فقد أُثبت له.

[١] عطف على قوله «إثبات أمر».

[٢] وجه الكناية هنا أن مدلول الجملة حصر الإسلام فيمن لا يؤذي ولا ينحصر فيه إلا بانتفائه عن المؤذي؛ فأطلق الملزوم وأريد اللازم.

[٣] فإذا وجدت قرينة دالّة على أن المهدّد غير المخاطب فقط كأن يكون المخاطب صديقًا له وغير مؤذ كان اللفظ مجازًا، وإذا وجدت قرينة دالّة على أنهما هدّدا كأن يكونا عدوّين للمتكلّم ومؤذيين له كان اللفظ كناية؛ فلا بدّ من قرينة تميّز أحدهما من

❋ ❋ ❋

The rhetoricians concur that nonliteral language is more emphatic than literal language and that implication is more emphatic than direct language, because in nonliteral language and implication one transitions from the implicant to the implicate, and this is like bringing forth a claim with evidence. For when you say, "I saw a lion in the bathhouse," it is as though you have said, "I saw a courageous man in the bathhouse because he resembles a lion," and when you say, "So-and-so has abundant ashes," it is as though you have said, "So-and-so is generous because he has abundant ashes."

أطبق البلغاء على أن المجاز أبلغ من الحقيقة وأن الكناية أبلغ من التصريح لأن الانتقال فيهما من الملزوم إلى اللازم فهو كدعوى الشيء ببيّنة. فإذا قلت «رأيت أسدًا في الحمّام» فكأنّك قلت «رأيت شجاعًا في الحمّام لأنه كالأسد»؛ وإذا قلت «فلان كثير الرماد» فكأنك قلت «فلان جواد لأنه كثير الرماد».

❋ ❋ ❋

By the assistance of Allah ﷻ, the treatise entitled *The Radiant Bloom: On the Science of Metaphor* is complete. May Allah ﷻ by His grace and generosity render it of benefit to us and all believers. Allah! "Take us not to task if we forget or err!" (Q 2:286). "Glory to your Lord, Lord of Might, transcending what they describe! Peace be upon the messengers. And praise to Allah, Lord of the worlds" (Q 37:180–82). By His permission ﷻ, the sixth treatise follows, entitled *The Quintessence: On the Science of Dialectics.*

تمّت بعون الله تعالى الرسالة المسمّاة بالنضارة في علم الاستعارة جعلها الله تعالى بمنّه وكرمه نافعة لنا ولسائر المؤمنين. اللّهم لا تؤاخذنا إن نسينا أو أخطأنا. ﴿سُبْحَٰنَ رَبِّكَ رَبِّ ٱلْعِزَّةِ عَمَّا يَصِفُونَ ۝١٨٠ وَسَلَٰمٌ عَلَى ٱلْمُرْسَلِينَ ۝١٨١ وَٱلْحَمْدُ لِلَّهِ رَبِّ ٱلْعَٰلَمِينَ﴾ [٣٧/ ١٨٠-١٨٢]. وتليها بإذنه تعالى الرسالة السادسة المسمّاة اللباب في علم المناظرة والآداب.

---

ter and prophet Muḥammad and upon all of his family and Companions, and may peace be upon the messengers. All praise is due to Allah, Lord of the worlds.

الآخر. وصلّى الله على سيّدنا ونبيّنا محمّد وعلى آله وصحبه وسلّم أجمعين وسلام على المرسلين والحمد لله رب العالمين.

NOTES TO TREATISE V

1 The author names this treatise after one topic (metaphor) which is prominent within the science of figurative language (*ʿilm al-bayān*). However, both the definition of the science given in the introduction of this treatise and the material covered for the most part overlap with Treatise VIII, which is on the science of figurative language.

2 That is, to use the particle *kāf,* which means "like" or "as," or any word with the same meaning, such as the noun *mithl.*

3 That is, to use the simile not simply as a means of describing the tenor (which would be explaining its condition, as listed above) but also of building up an image in the mind of the listener to confirm or strengthen that description.

4 Abū Yūsuf Yaʿqūb b. Ibrāhīm al-Anṣārī (d. 182/798) was one of the main students of the imam of the Ḥanafī school of jurisprudence, Abū Ḥanīfa al-Nuʿmān b. Thābit (d. 150/767).

5 In English, this is considered to be metaphor, but in Arabic rhetoric, it is considered a type of simile, namely *hyperbolic simile* (*tashbīh balīgh*).

6 As this definition stands, it applies only to literal expressions (*ḥaqīqa lughawiyya*); it does not apply to literal predication (*ḥaqīqa ʿaqliyya*). If one wanted to define *ḥaqīqa* in a broad sense that embraces both divisions, one could say that a *ḥaqīqa* is that which maintains its proper, default meaning, whether as an expression (*lafẓ*) in relation to its assigned meaning or as a predication (*isnād*) in relation to the speaker's apparent belief.

7 In other words, a *literal expression* (*ḥaqīqa lughawiyya*) is an expression that is used according to its literal meaning within the relevant speech conventions, i.e., the particular vocabulary that is relevant to the context.

8 The Muʿtazila were a theological group well known for maintaining that human beings are the creators of their own deeds, arguing that this is a prerequisite for moral responsibility. Thus, the example statement does not correspond to the Muʿtazilī's belief. In line with Sunni orthodoxy, the author uses the example as a statement that *does* correspond to reality, however: Allah the Exalted is the creator of all things, even human actions, though it remains true that humans *perform* those created actions in the sense of "acquisition" (*kasb*) and are therefore responsible for them.

9 As with the definition of *ḥaqīqa* above, this definition applies only to tropes (*majāz lughawī*); it does not apply to nonliteral predication (*majāz ʿaqlī*). If one wanted to define *majāz* in a broad sense that embraces both divisions, one could appeal to the lexical meaning of *majāz* as "passing," as in that which "passes" or deviates from its proper, default meaning in a specific way. See al-Dardīr, *Ḥāshiyat al-Ṣāwī*, 9.

10 That is, the vocabulary of the Arabic language in its original state, where every expression refers to the meanings it was originally assigned.

11 This is an example of a trope because it is being used for a semantic function other than its assigned one. It is metonymy rather than metaphor because the semantic link is the relationship of entailment rather than that of resemblance. Finally, it is composite rather than simple because the assigned expression here is the composite

grammatical structure of a declarative sentence rather than a simple word or phrase.

12 This is also termed a *metaphor with concealment*. The above translation is used for both.

13 The linguistic master Sirāj al-Dīn al-Sakkākī (d. 626/1229), author of *Miftāḥ al-ʿulūm*.

14 Unlike the first example, which refers to a real person (say, Zayd), and the second example, which refers to the real religion of Islam, fanciful metaphors refer to fictional, imaginary tenors made up by one's fancy. In the example that follows in the text, the tenor is not the actual, real phenomenon of death; it is a particular fictional image of death made up in the speaker's mind.

15 This faculty is technically termed the "estimation" or "estimative faculty" (*quwwa wahmiyya*).

16 The implication is that beggars would take of his wealth without his knowledge and bring it before him, which would cause him to smile, signifying approval and finalizing the transfer. The word *ghaliq* refers to a practice involving a creditor's foreclosure, or seizure, of some pledged property (such as "necks," i.e., slaves) when the debtor who made the pledge is unable to redeem it. See al-Dasūqī, *Kitāb ḥāshiyat al-Dasūqī*, 3:372.

17 The story goes that the woman had demanded a divorce from her wealthy but old husband one summer and then had remarried. When the new couple came upon a hard winter of drought and famine, she sent her former husband a request for some milk, which he declined, remarking that she had squandered the advantages of her previous marriage. Al-Taftāzānī, *Mukhtaṣar*, 2:149n5.

18 Al-Bukhārī, *al-Jāmiʿ al-ṣaḥīḥ*, 1:11 (no. 10).

VI

THE QUINTESSENCE

On the science of dialectics

اللباب في علم المناظرة والآداب

In the Name of Allah,
All-Merciful, Most Compassionate

ALL PRAISE IS due to Allah, Lord of the worlds. May blessings and peace be upon the seal of the prophets, Muḥammad, and upon his family, Companions, Helpers, and those who follow them in excellence until the day of judgment.

To Proceed This is a treatise on the science of dialectical disputation and protocol that draws selectively from *al-Waladiyya fī al-munāẓara wa-l-ādāb*[1] and other sources.

By convention, *munāẓara* (dialectical disputation) means the rebutting of one another—that is, the objector's rebutting the assertion of the proponent and the proponent's rebutting the assertion of the objector—to manifest the truth.[1] The science of dialectics is a science by which one knows what constitutes a sound or an unsound rebuttal.[2]

[1] This is meant to exclude [mere] disputation, which is the rebutting of one another so that the opponent is silenced. In other words, each of the disputants aims to defend his own assertion regardless whether it be right or wrong and to tear down the opponent's assertion regardless whether it be right or wrong.

[2] In the phrase *fann al-munāẓara* (the science of dialectics), *fann* means *ʿilm* (science), and the grammatical *iḍāfa* is of the same type as that in *yawm al-aḥad* (the

بسم الله الرحمن الرحيم

الحمد لله رب العالمين والصلاة والسلام على خاتم النبيين محمد وعلى آله وصحبه وأنصاره والتابعين لهم بإحسان إلى يوم الدين.

أما بعد فهذه رسالة في فنّ المناظرة والآداب منتخبة من الرسالة الولديّة في المناظرة والآداب وغيرها.

المناظرة في العرف هي المدافعة؛ أعني دفع السائل قول المعلّل ودفع المعلّل قول السائل ليظهر الحقّ.[١] وفنّ المناظرة فنّ يعرف به صحيح الدفع وفاسده.[٢]

[١] قوله «ليظهر الحقّ» احتراز عن الجدل فإنه المدافعة لإسكات الخصم، ومعناه أن كلًّا من المجادلين يقصد حفظ مقاله سواء كان حقًّا أو باطلًا ويريد هدم مقال الخصم سواء كان حقًّا أو باطلًا.

[٢] قوله «فنّ المناظرة» الفنّ بمعنى العلم، وإضافته من قبيل «يوم الأحد» فاسم الفنّ هو المناظرة. وبالجملة فإن «المناظرة» تطلق

INTRODUCTION

تقديم

Know that when you put forth declarative speech that is not self-evident, then if you are [merely] transmitting what you have stated and do not avow its truth, there is no expectation of you beyond that you show the soundness of your transmission by presenting a text that contains the transmitted statement, for example. As for when you are not transmitting but are rather making a claim, we will provide an exposition of [what is expected of you], by the will of Allah ﷻ, in three chapters and a conclusion. Chapter 1 concerns assent, that is, the claim; Chapter 2 concerns definition; and Chapter 3 concerns division. The conclusion concerns the end of a dialectical disputation.

Success and rectitude are from Allah ﷻ alone.

اعلم أنك إذا قلت كلامًا خبريًّا غير بديهي فإن كنت فيما قلت ناقلًا ولم تلتزم صحّة منقولك فلا يرد عليك شيء سوى تصحيح نقلك بإحضار كتاب منقول عنه مثلًا. وإن كنت غير ناقل بل كنت مدّعيًا فنذكر بيان هذا إن شاء الله تعالى في ثلاثة أبواب وخاتمة. الباب الأول في التصديق أي الدعوى؛ الباب الثاني في التعريف؛ الباب الثالث في التقسيم؛ الخاتمة فيما آلت إليه المناظرة.

ومن الله تعالى وحده التوفيق والسداد.

day of Sunday); thus, the name of the science is *dialectics*. In brief, [the term] *munāẓara* is conventionally used in two senses. One refers to the action of those engaged in dialectical disputation, and the other refers to the specific science that has here been defined.

في العرف على معنيين: أحدهما صفة المناظرين والآخر العلم المخصوص المعرّف ههنا.

Chapter 1

ASSENT, OR THE CLAIM

الباب الأول

التصديق أي الدعوى

Know that when one asserts a proposition, it is called the *claim*, the one who asserts it the *proponent* (*muʿallil*) because his role is to justify it (*al-taʿlīl ʿalayhi*), and the one who asks for a proof the *objector*. Now, if the claim is neither accompanied by a proof nor clearly evident, then the objector may challenge it, which means to request a proof for it. If it is clearly evident, then challenging it is invalid and considered obstinacy. If the claim is accompanied by a proof, then the objector has three dialectical functions: *challenge*, *counteraction*, and *confutation*.

اعلم أن التصديق إذا قاله أحد يقال له الدعوى والمدّعى، ولقائله المعلّل لأنّ من حقّه التعليل عليه، ولطالب الدليل السائل. فإن لم يكن مقرونًا بدليل ولم يكن بديهيًا جليًا فللسائل أن يمنعه ومعناه طلب الدليل عليه، وإن كان بديهيًا جليًا فلا يصحّ منعه ويسمّى منعه مكابرة، وإن كان مقرونًا بدليل فللسائل حينئذ ثلاث وظائف: المنع والمعارضة والنقض.

Challenge

The first dialectical function is to challenge. Challenging is of two types.

المنع

الوظيفة الأولى المنع، وهو قسمان.

[1. Challenging a Premise of a Proof]

The first type of challenge is to challenge a premise[2] of the proof, assuming that the proponent has not provided a proof for that premise and that it is not clearly self-evident. In such cases as these, it would be invalid to challenge the claim since to *challenge* is to request proof, and that request [in these cases] is already fulfilled. This is unless one in fact means to challenge a premise of the proof for the claim, though this is nonliteral.[3]

[١. منع مقدمة الدليل]

الأوّل منع مقدّمة الدليل إذا لم يستدلّ المعلّل عليها ولم تكن بديهيّة جليّة ولا يصحّ منع المدّعى حينئذ لأن المنع طلب الدليل والمطلوب حاصل، إلا أن يراد منع شيء من مقدّمات دليله وذا مجاز.

A challenge stands either without a corroboration or with one. A *corroboration* is an assertion made by the one issuing a challenge because he believes that it entails the contradictory of the challenged premise. One might provide a corroboration in the manner of asserting a possibility, e.g., by saying, "We do not concede that it is not human; why is it not possible that it be rational?" or one might provide it in the manner of a decisive assertion, e.g., by saying, "How so, when it is rational?"[4]

The Task of the Proponent When the Objector Challenges His Claim The task of the proponent when the objector challenges his unsupported claim or premise is to prove what the objector has challenged since this is what the challenger has requested. This proving is of two types. One type is to provide a proof that yields the challenged premise. The other type is to refute a corroboration that is coextensive with the challenge. For, by refutation of the corroboration, the contradictory of the challenged premise is [also] refuted, which results in the challenged premise itself being affirmed, since it is impossible to eliminate both of two contradictories.

Corroborations are of five rationally conceivable types: (1) coextensive, (2) narrower, (3) broader, (4) partially overlapping, and (5) distinct. Let us provide examples for each. When we assert, "This indistinct figure is not something that laughs because it is not human," then

1. if the objector says, "We do not concede that it is not human; why is it not possible that it be rational?" then this corroboration is *coextensive* with 'human'.
2. if he says, "Why is it not possible that it be Abyssinian?" then this is *narrower*.
3. if he says, "Why is it not possible that it be an animal?" then this is *broader*.

المنع إما مجرّد عن السند أو مقرون به. والسند ما ذكره المانع لزعمه أنه يستلزم نقيض الممنوع. فقد يذكر على سبيل التجويز كأن يقال «لا نسلّم أنه ليس بإنسان لِمَ لا يجوز أن يكون ناطقًا؟»، وقد يذكر على سبيل القطع كأن يقال «كيف وهو ناطق؟».

وظيفة المعلّل عند منع السائل مدّعاه وظيفة المعلّل عند منع السائل مدّعاه الغير المدلّل أو مقدّمة دليله إثبات ما منعه لأنّ هذا مطلوب المانع. وذلك الإثبات نوعان: أحدهما ذكر دليل ينتج الممنوع، والآخر إبطال السند المساوي للمنع لأنّ بإبطاله يبطل نقيضُ الممنوع فيثبت عينه لاستحالة ارتفاع النقيضين.

والسند بالاحتمال العقلي خمسة أقسام: (١) المساوي، (٢) الأخصّ مطلقًا، (٣) والأعمّ مطلقًا، (٤) والأعمّ من وجه، (٥) والمباين. ولنمثّل للكل، فإذا قلنا «هذا الشبح ليس بضاحك لأنه ليس إنسان»:

١- فإن قال السائل «لا نسلّم أنه ليس بإنسان لِمَ لا يجوز أن يكون ناطقًا؟» فهذا سند مساوٍ للإنسان.

٢- وإن قال «لِمَ لا يجوز أن يكون زنجيًّا؟» فهذا أخصّ مطلقًا.

٣- وإن قال «لِمَ لا يجوز أن يكون حيوانًا؟» فهذا أعمّ مطلقًا.

4. if he says, "Why is it not possible that it be white?" then this is *partially overlapping*.[1]
5. if he says, "Why is it not possible that it be a rock?" then this is *distinct*.

It is not valid to provide either distinct or partially overlapping corroborations, nor does it advantage the proponent to refute them if the objector were to provide them. As for coextensive or narrower corroborations, it is valid to provide them; however, refuting the narrower does not advantage the proponent—what rather does advantage him is to refute the coextensive. And as for broader corroborations, they cannot be provided, though it does advantage the proponent to refute them if the objector were to provide them.

Know that if what is challenged is a premise in the proof of the proponent, then he has another dialectical option by which to be rid of the challenge, namely, to provide another proof for the claim, though this means that he has been silenced from one perspective.

[1] 'White' is broader than 'human' from the more inclusive perspective [i.e., that of whiteness]. This is the same as the case if you were to assert, "This thing is not rational because it is not human, and whatever is not human is not rational," and someone were to challenge the minor premise by saying, "We do not concede that it is not human; why is it not possible that it be an animal?" This corroboration is broader than the contradictory of the challenged premise, namely 'human', and it partially overlaps with [the challenged premise] itself, namely 'not human'. For instance, while both 'animal' and 'not human' are true of horses, between the two, only 'animal' applies to humans, and only 'not human' applies to rocks. [Thus, 'not] animal' rules out being human but does not rule out *not* being human, since it is possible that it be a rock, for instance, which is not human.

٤- وإن قال «لمَ لا يجوز أن يكون أبيض؟» فهذا أعمّ من وجه.[١]

٥- وإن قال «لمَ لا يجوز أن يكون حجرًا؟» فهذا مباين.

والمباين والأعمّ من وجه لا يجوز الاستناد بهما ولا ينفع المعلّل إبطالهما لو استند بهما السائل. والمساوي والأخصّ مطلقًا يجوز الاستناد بهما لكن لا ينفع المعلّل إبطال الأخصّ بل ينفعه إبطال المساوي. وأما الأعمّ مطلقًا فلا يجوز الاستناد به لكن ينفع المعلّل إبطاله لو استند به السائل.

واعلم أن الممنوع لو كان مقدّمة دليل المعلّل فللمعلّل وظيفة أخرى للتخلّص عن المنع وهو إثبات المدّعى بدليل آخر؛ وذا إفحام من وجه.

[١] قوله «أعمّ من وجه» من عينه في الغالب، كما إذا قلت «هذا ليس بناطق لأنه ليس بإنسان وكل ما ليس بإنسان فهو ليس بناطق» فمنع أحد الصغرى بقوله «لا نسلّم أنه ليس بإنسان لمَ لا يجوز أن يكون حيوانًا؟» فهذا السند أعمّ مطلقًا من نقيض الممنوع وهو ‹الإنسان› وأعمّ من وجه من عينه وهو ‹ليس بإنسان› لتصادقهما في الفرس مثلًا وانفراد ‹الحيوان› عنه في الإنسان وانفراد ‹ما ليس بإنسان› عن ‹الحيوان› في الحجر. [ف‹ليس] حيوان› يوجب إبطال أنه إنسان ولا يوجب إبطال أنه ليس بإنسان لجواز أن يكون حجرًا مثلًا وهو ليس بإنسان.

When the proponent justifies his claim or a premise either by a proof or by refuting the corroboration, then the objector may challenge or refute one of the premises of that proof as long as it is not clearly evident. If he does so, then the preceding exposition applies.

وعند إثبات المعلّل مدّعاه أو مقدّمته بدليل أو إبطال السند للسائل أن يمنع شيئًا من مقدّمات الدليل أو يبطله ما لم تكن بديهيّة جليّة. فإذا منع يأتي فيه التفصيل السابق.

The Challenging of a Premise Could Be of No Detriment The objector's challenge of a premise in the proof of the proponent could be of no detriment to the proponent. This is so when the objector provides a corroboration that involves a concession of the proponent's claim. For example, if the believer asserts, "The universe originated in time because it undergoes change," justifying the minor premise by arguing that the universe is never devoid of motion and rest, and then the philosopher says, "We do not concede that it is never devoid of them; why is it not possible that it be devoid of them as it was at the moment of its origination?" then this corroboration involves a concession that the universe originated in time.

منع المقدمة قد لا يضرّ منع السائل مقدّمة دليل المعلّل قد لا يضرّ المعلّل. وذلك إذا ذكر المانع سندًا يشمل الاعتراف بدعوى المعلّل، كما قال المؤمن «العالم حادث لأنه متغيّر» وأثبت الصغرى بأنه لا يخلو عن الحركة والسكون فقال الفلسفي «لا نسلّم عدم خلوّه عنهما لمَ لا يجوز أن يخلو عنهما كما في آن حدوثه؟» فهذا السند فيه اعتراف بحدوث العالم.

Offering a Refutation for What Has Not Yet Been Supported with a Proof If the objector offers a refutation for a claim that has not yet been supported with a proof, or if he offers a refutation for a premise in the proof for the claim before the proponent provides a proof for that premise, this is termed *usurpation* because providing proof is the role of the proponent and the objector has usurped it.

إبطال شيء قبل الاستدلال عليه لو أبطل السائل بالدليل المدّعى الغير المدلّل أو مقدّمة دليل المدّعي قبل أن يستدلّ المعلّل على تلك المقدّمة يسمّى غصبًا لأن الاستدلال منصب المعلّل وقد غصبه السائل.

There is disagreement over whether such a refutation deserves consideration. Those who hold that it deserves consideration deem it necessary for the proponent to respond to it. The verifying scholars, however, hold that it does not deserve consideration. Now, those who hold that it deserves consideration maintain that the objector may say, "By what I have expressed in the semblance of refutation and proof, I intended to present a corroborated challenge"; in such a case it decidedly deserves a response. The author of *al-Tawḍīḥ* says that someone who deems a

واختلف في كونه مسموعًا. ومن قال إنه مسموع يوجب على المعلّل أن يجيب عنه. والمحقّقون قالوا إنه غير مسموع. ومن قال إنه مسموع يقول إن للسائل أن يقول «أردت بما ذكرته في صورة الإبطال والاستدلال المنع مع السند» فيستحقّ الجواب حينئذ البتة. قال في التوضيح: ينبغي لمن حكم بفساد مقدّمة معيّنة أن يورد اعتراضه

given premise to be false must present his objection in the manner of a challenge, not in the manner of a refutation, lest the opponent complain that it is a usurpation, whereupon it would need to be amended.[5]

By the convention of [the dialecticians], *usurpation* is the objector's providing a proof for the falsity of that which he could have validly challenged. Thus, *counteraction* is not usurpation because counteraction is to refute the claim with a proof after the proponent has supported it with a proof, and it would not be valid to challenge a claim after it has been supported. Likewise, *confutation* is not usurpation because confutation is to refute the proof, and it would not be valid to challenge a proof, since only that which it is possible to support with a proof can be validly challenged, [and it is not possible to support the proof itself with a second proof], because the proof is composed of two premises, whereas only one premise can be yielded by any proof.

2. Challenging the Consecution of a Proof

Know that the objector may challenge the consecution of the proponent's proof. *Consecution* means that the proof is formulated in a way that entails the claim. The challenging of a proof's consecution may be expressed as, "We do not concede that this proof entails this claim," and this might be summarily expressed: "We do not concede the consecution" or "We challenge the consecution."

The consecution is sound only when the proof yields either the claim itself, a coextensive proposition, or a narrower one. When it produces a broader proposition, there is no consecution, just as [there is no consecution] when the claim is a universal affirmative proposition but the proof produces a particular affirmative proposition.[6]

عليها على سبيل المنع لا على سبيل الإبطال لئلّا يقول الخصم إنه غصب فيحتاج إلى العناية.

وهو أي الغصب في عرفهم استدلال السائل على بطلان ما صحّ منعه. فالمعارضة ليست بغصب لأنه إبطال الدعوى بدليل بعد استدلال المعلّل عليه وليس منع الدعوى بعد الاستدلال عليه صحيحًا. وكذا النقض ليس بغصب لأنه إبطال الدليل ولا يصحّ منع الدليل لأن المنع إنما يصحّ على ما يمكن الاستدلال عليه [ولا يصحّ الاستدلال على الدليل] لأنه مركّب من مقدّمتين والدليل لا ينتج إلا مقدّمة واحدة.

القسم الثاني: منع تقريب الدليل ومعناه

اعلم أن السائل قد يمنع تقريب دليل المعلّل. ومعنى التقريب سوق الدليل على وجه يستلزم المدّعى. وتقرير منعه «أنّا لا نسلّم استلزام هذا الدليل المدّعى» وقد يُجمل ويقال «لا نسلم التقريب» أو «التقريب ممنوع».

والتقريب إنما يتمّ إذا أنتج الدليل عين المدّعى أو ما يساويه أو الأخصّ منه مطلقًا؛ وأما إذا أنتج الأعمّ فلا تقريب، كأن يكون المدّعى موجبة كلّيّة وينتج الدليل موجبة جزئيّة.

❋ ❋ ❋

Can Transmissions and Claims Be Challenged? According to some: Transmissions and claims can be "challenged" only in a nonliteral sense. This means that, for either of the two, the term *manʿ* (challenge) and its morphological derivatives are usable only nonliterally to express the request for proof. To clarify, *challenge* according to their usage means 'to request a proof for the premise of a proof'. Since neither transmissions nor claims are premises of a proof, then to say, "We challenge this transmission," or, "We challenge this claim," is to request proof in a general way by means of a nonliteral expression. But if you were to request a proof for a transmission or a claim by means of a different expression, the expression would *not* be nonliteral, e.g., to say, "We do not concede this transmission/claim," or, "We request that you explain this."

The above pertains to unsupported claims. As for when a claim is supported, then requesting proof at all, no matter the expression, is a case of nonliteral predication[7] with the intended meaning of requesting proof for one of the premises in the proponent's proof.

What It Does Not Avail the Proponent to Challenge Since the duty of the proponent when confronted with a challenge is to provide proof (as you have come to know in detail), (1) it does not avail him to challenge the challenge, i.e., to say, "We do not concede the validity of this challenge; why is it not possible that the challenged premise be clearly self-evident?" Likewise, (2) it does not avail him to challenge a corroboration that is expressed in a decisive manner. Nor (3) does it avail him to challenge the adequacy of a given corroboration for the role of corroboration, corroborating his [own] challenge by arguing that the corroboration is too broad;

هل يمنع النقل أو المدّعى قيل لا يمنع النقل أو المدّعى إلا مجازًا ومعناه لا يستعمل لفظ «المنع» وما يشتقّ منه في طلب الدليل عليهما إلا مجازًا. وبيان ذلك أن المنع في اصطلاحهم طلب الدليل على مقدّمة الدليل؛ ولمّا لم يكن النقل والمدّعى مقدّمة الدليل فقولك «هذا النقل ممنوع» و«هذا المدّعى ممنوع» مجاز عن طلب الدليل مطلقًا. وأما إذا استعملت لفظًا آخر في طلب الدليل عليهما فلا مجاز، كأن تقول «لا نسلّم هذا النقل أو... هذا المدّعى» أو «هو مطلوب البيان».

هذا في المدّعى الغير المدلّل؛ وأما إن كان مدلّلًا فطلب الدليل عليه بأي لفظ كان مجاز في النسبة والمراد طلب الدليل على شيء من مقدّمات دليله.

ما لا ينفع المعلّل منعه لمّا كان الواجب على المعلّل عند منع المانع هو الإثبات كما عرفت تفصيله (١) فلا ينفعه منع المنع. تقريره «لا نسلّم صحّة وجود هذا المنع لمَ لا يجوز أن يكون الممنوع بديهيًّا جليًّا؟». وكذا (٢) لا ينفعه منع السند الذي ذكر على سبيل القطع. وكذا (٣) لا ينفعه منع صلاحيّة السند للسنديّة مستندًا بعمومه، وكذا

nor (4) does it avail him to [go further and] prove its inadequacy for the role of corroboration on the basis that it is too broad. Likewise, (5) it does not avail him to prove that a given expression used by the challenger is incorrect in that it is inconsistent with the rules of the Arabic language.

For the proponent to be preoccupied with these objections means that he has moved to another discussion to which the objector must offer a rebuttal. If the proponent becomes preoccupied with this new discussion to the exclusion of proving what the objector challenged, then he has failed to justify his claim: he has been silenced with respect to that claim, and he has moved to another matter of discussion.

It does advantage the proponent to invalidate the challenge by arguing that the challenged premise is clearly self-evident. This is effectively a justification of the challenged premise. Likewise, it advantages him to refute the challenge by claiming that the challenged premise is something that the challenger concedes. But this would be a *disputative rebuttal* rather than a *verificatory rebuttal*; thus it is impermissible when the aim is to manifest the truth. If the proponent [nevertheless] offers such a refutation, the challenger may maintain that he revokes his concession of the proposition he had previously conceded, as long as it is not clearly self-evident.

(٤) إبطال صلاحيّته للسنديّة مستدلًّا بعمومه. وكذا (٥) لا ينفعه إبطال عبارة المانع بمخالفتها القانون العرفي.

فاشتغال المعلّل بهذه الاعتراضات انتقال منه إلى بحث آخر يجب على السائل دفعه. فإن كان اشتغاله بها بدون إثبات ما منعه السائل فقد عجز عن إثبات مدّعاه فأُفحم فيه وانتقل إلى بحث آخر.

نعم ينفع المعلّل إبطال المنع مستدلًّا عليه ببداهة الممنوع بداهة جليّة؛ وهذا بمنزلة إثبات الممنوع. وكذا ينفعه إبطال المنع بدعوى أن الممنوع مسلّم عند المانع؛ لكن هذا جواب إلزامي جدلي لا تحقيقي فلا يصحّ عند إرادة إظهار الحقّ. وللمانع أن يدّعي حينئذ الرجوع عن تسليم ما سلّمه ما لم يكن بديهيًّا جليًّا.

Counteraction

The second dialectical function is counteraction, which is for the objector either (1) to prove the contradictory of the proponent's supported claim, (2) to prove a [proposition] that is coextensive with the contradictory of the claim, or (3) to prove a [proposition] that is narrower. For example, the proponent might assert the non-humanness of something and argue for it, and then the objector might counteract this by proving its humanness, by proving its ability to laugh, or by proving that it is Abyssinian.

المعارضة

الوظيفة الثانية المعارضة. هي (١) إثبات السائل نقيض ما ادّعاه المعلّل واستدلّ عليه أو (٢) إثبات ما يساوي نقيضه أو (٣) إثبات الأخصّ منه، كأن ادّعى المعلّل لاإنسانيّة شيء واستدلّ عليها فعارضه السائل بإثبات إنسانيّته أو بإثبات ضاحكيّته أو بإثبات أنه زنجي.

When the objector intends counteraction, he may tell the proponent, "Even granting that your proof entails your claim, I have [a proof] that negates your claim."

To rebut a counteraction, the proponent must either (1) challenge one of the premises in the proof of the counteractor; (2) prove that his proof is invalid (this is *confutation*); or (3) justify the claim through another proof (this is counteraction of the counteraction of the objector). There is further discussion on whether this kind of counteraction rebuts the counteraction of the objector.

[Counteraction of the Claim and of a Premise] Counteraction is also of two types:

1. *counteraction of the claim*, that is, that the objector argue for a proposition opposed to the proponent's claim after the proponent has justified his claim.
2. *counteraction of a premise*, that is, that the objector argue for a proposition opposed to a premise in the proof of the proponent after the proponent has justified that premise.

[Counteraction by Reversal, by Like, and by Unlike] Both types of counteraction are [further] divisible into three types: counteraction by reversal, by like, and by unlike. [The rationale behind this division] is that the proof of the counteractor [varies in relation to the proof of the proponent]:

1. If it is identical to the proponent's proof in matter and form[1] as occurs among the *universally-applicable fallacies*, the counteraction is termed *reversal* and *counteraction by reversal*. The universally-applicable fallacies are those proofs by which it is possible to argue

[1] In this case the proponent has no option but to counteract the counteraction, because if he were to confute the proof of the counteractor or challenge one of its premises then his objection would turn against him. Know this.

فللسائل عند إرادة المعارضة أن يقول للمعلّل «دليلك وإن دلّ على ما ادّعيت لكن عندي ما ينفي ما ادّعيت».

ودفع المعلّل المعارضة إما (١) بمنع بعض مقدّمات دليل المعارض أو (٢) بإثبات فساد دليله وهو النقض أو (٣) بإثبات الدعوى بدليل آخر وهو المعارضة على معارضة السائل. وفي كون هذه المعارضة دافعة لمعارضة السائل بحث.

[المعارضة في المدّعى وفي المقدّمة] وهي أيضا قسمان:

١- الأوّل المعارضة في المدّعى، وهي أن يثبت السائل خلاف مدّعى المعلّل بعد إثبات المعلّل مدّعاه.

٢- الثاني المعارضة في المقدّمة وهي أن يثبت السائل خلاف مقدّمة دليل المعلّل بعد إثبات المعلّل تلك المقدّمة.

[المعارضة قلبًا وبالمثل وبالغير] وينقسم كل منهما إلى ثلاثة أقسام: إلى المعارضة (١) قلبًا (٢) وبالمثل (٣) وبالغير، لأن دليل المعارض:

١- إن كان عين دليل المعلّل مادّة وصورة[١] كما في المغالطات العامّة الورود تسمّى تلك المعارضة قلبًا ومعارضة على سبيل القلب. المغالطات العامّة الورود هي الأدلّة التي يمكن أن يستدلّ بها

[١] فليس للمعلّل حينئذ إلا المعارضة على المعارضة إذ لو نقض دليل المعارض أو منع بعض مقدماته ينقلب اعتراضه عليه. فاعرف.

٣٥٢

for anything, even two contradictories. For example, one says, "That whose existence and nonexistence each entail the conclusion either exists or does not, and in either case the conclusion must be affirmed."[1] Thus, if the philosopher were to adduce this as proof for the eternality of the universe, we would counteract his argument by adducing this as proof for the temporal origination of the universe.

2. If it is different from it in matter but identical in form, it is termed *counteraction by like*. For example, the philosopher might say, "The universe is eternal because it is the effect of an eternal being, and whatever is the effect of an eternal being is eternal": we would counteract this with the argument that the universe originated in time because it undergoes changes and everything that undergoes change originated in time.

3. If it is different from it in form, it is termed *counteraction by unlike*. This is so whether (a) it is different also in matter—e.g., if we were to counteract the argument in the preceding case with the argument that the universe originated in time because it is the effect of a volitional being, and nothing eternal is the effect of a volitional being—or whether (b) it is identical in matter—as in the case of a universally-applicable fallacy, which the objector then counteracts by employing the fallacy in a different form from the form chosen by the proponent, to prove the contradictory of the proponent's claim.

[1] The response to this is that we maintain that the subject does not exist but do not concede the truth of the conclusion, because we maintain that the subject is nonexistent both with respect to its essence and with respect to its attribute, namely its entailment of the conclusion.

على جميع الأشياء حتى النقيضين، مثل أن يقال «الشيء الذي يكون وجوده وعدمه مستلزمًا للمطلوب إما موجود أو معدوم وأيًّا ما كان يلزم ثبوت المطلوب».[١] فإذا استدلّ به الفلسفي على قدم العالم فنعارضه بالاستدلال به على حدوثه.

٢- وإن كان غيره مادّة وعينه صورة تسمّى معارضة بالمثل، كأن يقول الفلسفي «العالم قديم لأنه أثر القديم وكل ما هو أثر القديم فهو قديم» فنعارضه بأنه حادث لأنه متغيّر وكل متغيّر حادث.

٣- وإن كان غيره صورة تسمّى معارضة بالغير سواء كان (١) غيره مادّة أيضا، كما إذا عارضناه في الصورة المذكورة بأن العالم حادث لأنه أثر المختار ولا شيء من القديم بأثر المختار؛ أو كان (٢) عينه مادّة، كما في مغالطة عامّة الورود فيعارضه السائل بإيراد تلك المغالطة على نقيض مدّعى المعلّل بصورة أخرى غير ما اختاره المعلّل.

[١] ويجاب عنه بـ«أنّا نختار أنه معدوم ولا نسلّم ثبوت المطلوب لأنّا نختار أنه معدوم ذاته وصفته التي هي استلزام المطلوب».١

Confutation

The third dialectical function is confutation (*naqḍ*), which may be qualified as *collective confutation* (*naqḍ ijmālī*)[8] and means the objector's asserting the invalidity of the proponent's proof by arguing that it entails a different claim and that the proponent's claim does not follow from his proof and by arguing [furthermore] that every such proof is invalid because a valid proof is never such that the claim does not follow, since claims are implicates of their proofs, and the nullity of the implicate indicates the nullity of the implicant.

For example, in response to the philosopher who adduces for the eternality of the universe the argument that it is the effect of an eternal being, and every effect of an eternal being is eternal, which entails that the universe is eternal, we say that this [same argument] applies to daily events, which originate in time as is self-evident. This confutation is not to be responded to by challenging the major premise but rather by challenging the minor premise.

The confuter may adduce for the invalidity of the proponent's proof that it entails circularity or infinite regress, which are absurd, and whatever entails an absurdity is itself absurd. In this case as well, there is no room to challenge the major premise. One may rather challenge the entailment or challenge the [charge of] absurdity since some cases of circularity and infinite regress are not absurd.[1]

[1] There is another way of formulating this. That is, one asserts, "The proof entails circularity or infinite regress, and whatever entails this is absurd," whereupon the respondent breaks up the minor premise and says, "If you mean that it entails an absurd circularity or an absurd infinite regress, we do not concede the minor premise, but if you mean [circularity and infinite regress] in the unqualified sense, we do not concede the major premise."

النقض

الوظيفـة الثالثـة النقـض. قـد يقيّـد فيقـال له النقـض الإجمـالي[٢]. معنـاه أن يـدّعي السـائل بـطلان دليـل المعلّل مسـتدلًّا بأنـه جـارٍ في مـدّعى آخـر مـع تخلّـف ذلـك المـدّعى عنـه وكل دليـل هـذا شـأنه فباطـل لأن الدليـل الصحيـح لا يتخلّـف عنـه المـدّعى لأن المـدّعى لازم له وبـطلان اللازم يـدلّ على بـطلان الملـزوم.

كأن قلنـا للفلـسفي المسـتدلّ على قـدم العالـم بأنـه أثـر القديـم وكل أثـر القديـم قديـم ينتـج العالـم قديـم «إنـه جـارٍ في الحـوادث اليوميّـة مـع أنهـا حادثـة بالبداهـة». ولا يجـاب عـن هـذا النقـض بمنـع الـكبرى بـل بمنـع الصغـرى.

وقـد يسـتدلّ الناقـض على بـطلان دليـل المعلّـل بأنـه مسـتلزم للدور أو التسلسـل وهـو محـال[١] وكل مـا يسـتلزم المحـال فهـو محـال. ولا مجـال لمنـع الـكبرى هنـا أيضـا بـل قـد يمنـع الاسـتلزام وقـد يمنـع الاسـتحالة لأن بعـض الدور والتسلسـل غير محـال.

[١] وهنـا تقرير آخـر، وهو أن يقـال «إنه مسـتلزم للدور أو التسلسـل وكل ما يسـتلزمهما[٣] فهو محـال» فحينئذ يردّد المجيـب في الصغرى ويقـول «إن أردت أنـه مسـتلزم للدور المحال أو التسلسـل المحال فلا نسـلّم الصغـرى وإن أردت المطلـق فلا نسـلّم الكبرى».

One may respond to confutation by justifying the claim through another proof, though this means that one has been silenced from one perspective.

وقد يجاب عن النقض بإثبات المدّعى بدليل آخر وهذا إفحام من وجه.

❋ ❋ ❋

The Counteractor and the Confuter When They Provide No Proof Know that when the counteractor or confuter provides no proof, his charge of unsoundness is not given consideration.

المعارض والناقض إذا لم يذكرا دليلًا اعلم أن المعارض والناقض إذا لم يذكرا دليلًا فلا يُسمع دعويهما البطلان.

The proof for a confutation is termed *evidence*.

ويسمّى دليل النقض شاهدًا.

If you were to ask: May the objector not challenge the entirety of the proof in the sense of asking for a proof for the proof? I would respond: No, as that is to assign an unfulfillable task: a proof produces only a single premise, [not an entire other proof].

إن قلت: أليس للسائل منع مجموع الدليل بمعنى طلب الدليل عليه؟ قلت: لا، لأنه تكليف بما لا يطاق لأن الدليل لا ينتج إلا مقدّمة واحدة.

When the Confuter Omits Some Particulars of the Proponent's Proof Know that the confuter might omit some particulars of the proponent's proof when applying the proof to a different claim. This is termed *partial confutation*. In such a case, the proponent may challenge the applicability, corroborating his challenge by asserting that the omitted particulars are integral to the entailment. The objector could refute this corroboration by proving that the omitted particulars have no integral role in the entailment.

ترك الناقض بعض أوصاف دليل المعلّل اعلم أن الناقض قد يترك بعض أوصاف دليل المعلّل عند إجراء الدليل في مدّعى آخر فيسمّى ذلك نقضًا مكسورًا. فللمعلّل حينئذ منع الجريان مستندًا بأن للوصف المتروك مدخلًا في العلّيّة. وقد يبطل السائل هذا السند بإثبات أن لا مدخل لذلك الوصف في العلّيّة.

For example, al-Shāfiʿī says, "Selling an absent item is invalid because it is the sale of that whose qualities are unknown," and we confute this with the argument that this then would apply to the case of marrying an absent woman, for her qualities are unknown, yet such a marriage is valid.[9] We have thus omitted the qualification of selling.

مثاله قال الشافعي «لا يصحّ بيع الغائب لأنه مبيع مجهول الصفة» فنقضناه بأنه جارٍ في تزوّج امرأة غائبة لأنها مجهولة الصفة مع أنه صحيح، فقد حذفنا قيد المبيعة.

That by Which a Proof May Not Be Confuted Neither a proof nor anything else may be confuted for involving verbosity, redundancy, obscurity, or other factors that would compromise its good form. Thus, it is not correct for one disputant to tell the other, "What you have expressed is invalid because it was possible to convey the meaning you expressed in better form." The reason such confutation is invalid is that the presence of a superior alternative does not necessarily entail the invalidity of the inferior alternative. It *is* valid to merely remonstrate on the point of good form, and this remonstration is termed a *practical pointer*. This, however, is not the habit of the dialecticians.

There is an exception [in which obscurity is a valid reason for confutation], namely when the definition is more obscure than the definiendum, e.g., to define fire as "something that resembles the soul in its subtle nature."

Confutation of an Expression, and the Response to Such Confutation An expression might be confuted, meaning that it be declared incorrect on the grounds that it is inconsistent with the Arabic lexicon, morphology, or syntax. One responds to this by challenging the inconsistency, corroborating one's challenge by citing one of the schools of Arabic language according to which the expression in question is valid.

It is widely understood that the one confuting an expression takes the burden of proof. This means that the objection that an expression is inconsistent with the Arabic language cannot validly be formulated as a challenge, because the confuter, like the counteractor, is a proponent, and the one who used the expression is a challenger. Moreover, confuting an expression does not avail the confuter when the one who used the expression challenges the confuter's claim or a premise in his proof.

ما لا ينقض به الدليل لا ينقض الدليل ولا غيره بالاشتمال على التطويل أو الاستدراك أو الخفاء إلى غير ذلك مما يزيل حسنه. فلا يصحّ لأحد المناظرين أن يقول للآخر «إن ما ذكرته باطل لأن المعنى الذي أدّيته بما ذكرته من العبارة يصحّ أداؤه بأحسن منها». وإنما لا يصحّ ذلك النقض لأن وجود الطريق الراجح لا يوجب بطلان المرجوح. وإنما يصحّ الاعتراض به على حسن العبارة، ويسمّى هذا الاعتراض تعيين الطريق؛ وهو ليس من دأب المناظرين.

وهنا استثناء وهو أن يكون التعريف أخفى من المعرّف، كأن يقال في تعريف النار بأنه شيء يشبه النفس في اللطافة.

نقض العبارة والجواب عنه قد ينقض العبارة، ومعناه دعوى بطلانها مستدلًّا بمخالفتها قانون اللغة أو الصرف أو النحو. ويجاب عنه بمنع مخالفتها مستندًا بمذهب من مذاهب أهل العربيّة يصحّ عليه تلك العبارة.

وقد اشتهر أن ناقض العبارة مستدلّ، ومعناه أن الاعتراض على العبارة بمخالفتها القانون العرئى لا يصحّ على طريق المنع لأن الناقض كالمعارض معلّل وصاحب العبارة مانع. ثم إن نقض العبارة لا ينفع الناقض إذا منع صاحب العبارة مدّعاه أو مقدّمة دليله.

Instructive Notes

The first note is that there are four [types of] confutation:[1] (1) confutation of a proof; (2) confutation of an expression, and these two we have already discussed in this chapter; (3) confutation of a definition, which we will discuss by the will of Allah ﷻ in Chapter 2; and (4) confutation of a division, which we will discuss by the will of Allah ﷻ in Chapter 3. As for requesting a proof for a claim or premise, this is not termed *confutation* (*naqḍ*) in the unqualified sense; rather it is termed *analytic confutation* (*naqḍ tafṣīlī*). Thus there can be no objection to the confinement of confutation to four [types].

The second note is that when an incomplete composite expression like *rūmī* (Roman) qualifies a proposition, this is semantically an affirmation, and hence it is susceptible to challenge. An example: You say, "This is a Roman human," thereby effectively asserting, "This human is Roman." The objector may then challenge merely his being Roman. And if you offer a proof that he is Roman, then the objector may challenge a premise of that proof, counteract it, or confute it. The intelligent student will not find this difficult to grasp. Now, when an incomplete composite expression does not qualify a proposition—for example, if someone says, "servant boy," or, "fifteen"—then no objection to it may be made unless the expression in question is inconsistent with the rules of the Arabic language.

[1] If you were to say: Rather, there are six because *naqḍ* means destruction and nullification, bringing into its scope the refutation of an unsubstantiated claim and the refutation of an unsubstantiated premise. Then I would respond: The discussion concerns *naqḍ* (confutation) in the technical sense [rather than the lexical sense], and in the technical terminology of the dialecticians these two are termed *usurpation* (*ghaṣb*). One might also respond: The discussion concerns [the kinds of] confutation that deserve consideration by consensus, and these two do not deserve consideration according to the verifying scholars, as mentioned previously.

تنبيهان

الأوّل أن النقض أربعة:[١] (١) نقض الدليل، (٢) نقض العبارة، فقد ذكرناهما في هذا الباب، (٣) نقض التعريف، سنذكره إن شاء الله تعالى في الباب الثاني، (٤) نقض التقسيم، سنذكره في الباب الثالث. أما طلب الدليل على المدّعى أو المقدّمة فلا يسمّى نقضًا على الإطلاق بل يسمّى نقضًا تفصيليًّا؛ فلا اعتراض على حصر النقض في أربعة.

التنبيه الثاني أن المركّب الناقص كـ«رومي» إذا كان قيدًا للقضيّة فهذا تصديق معنى فيرد عليه المنع، كأن تقول «هذا إنسان رومي» فهو بمنزلة قولك «هذا الإنسان رومي» فللسائل أن يمنع روميّته فقط فإن أثبتّ روميّته بدليل فللسائل أن يمنع مقدّمة ذلك الدليل أو يعارضه أو ينقضه؛ والمتفطّن لا يخفى عليه ذلك. وإذا لم يكن قيدًا للقضيّة كأن قال أحد «غلام» أو «خمسة عشر» فلا يعترض عليه بشيء إلا إذا خالف ذلك اللفظ القانون العربي.

[١] إن قلت: بل هو ستّة لأن معنى النقض الهدم والإبطال فيدخل فيه إبطال الدعوى الغير المدلّل وإبطال المقدّمة الغير المدلّلة، قلت: الكلام في النقض المصطلح وهما مسمّيان غصبًا في اصطلاح المناظرين، أو يقال: الكلام في النقض المسموع بالاتّفاق وهما غير مسموعين عند المحقّقين كما سبق.

Disputative Rebuttals and Their Validity

When the proponent rebuts the objector's objection with a response founded on a [premise] that the objector accepts—proving a [proposition] that the objector had challenged by means of a proof that incorporates a premise the objector accepts, in spite of the proponent's knowledge that the [premise that the objector] accepts is false—this is a *disputative rebuttal* rather than a verificatory one. Its purpose is not to manifest the truth but rather merely to force the opponent to concede. The same is the case when he proves it by means of a fallacious argument knowing that it is fallacious. The proponent should not offer such a response unless the objector is obstinate, i.e., seeking to show up the proponent, not seeking to manifest the truth. (A *verificatory rebuttal* is a response that [the proponent] founds on a proof he knows to be true.) Yet if the objector is passively silent in such a case, concession obtains. If he challenges what he had previously accepted, that is his prerogative, as he may profess being hesitant after having been certain, so long as the [proposition] he had [previously] accepted is not clearly self-evident. On this account, it is said that a challenger commits to no doctrine.

الجواب الإلزامي وجوازه

إذا أجاب المعلّل عن اعتراض السائل بجواب مبنيّ على ما سلّمه السائل بأن يثبت ما منعه السائل بدليل مشتمل على مقدّمة مسلّمة عند السائل مع علم المعلّل بأن الذي سلّمه باطل فهذا جواب إلزامي جدلي لا تحقيقي وليس الغرض منه إظهار الحقّ بل إلزام الخصم فقط. وكذا إثباته بمغالطة مع علمه بأنه مغالطة. فلا ينبغي للمعلّل ذلك الجواب إلا إذا كان السائل معاندًا أي طالبًا لذلّة المعلّل لا طالبًا لإظهار الحقّ. والجواب التحقيقي هو الجواب الذي بناه على دليلٍ علم حقّيته. لكن السائل إذا سكت حينئذ يحصل الإلزام؛ فإن منع ما سلّمه من قبل فله ذلك إذ له أن يدّعي التردّد بعد الجزم ما لم يكن ما سلّمه بديهيًّا جليًّا. ولذا قيل إن المانع لا مذهب له.

Chapter 2

DEFINITION

الباب الثاني

في التعريف

Our discussion of definition concerns confuting a definition on account of its insufficient inclusiveness, its insufficient exclusiveness, its entailing the impossible, or its not being clearer than the definiendum. It also concerns challenging a definition when it incorporates an inherent claim. And it concerns responding to these forms [of objection] by means of clarification.

The objector may confute [the definition], which means that he refute it for being insufficiently inclusive or insufficiently exclusive or for entailing the impossible. The cause for the first case is that the definition be narrower than [the defined term], as in the definition of 'human' as 'Abyssinian'. The cause for the second case is that it be broader, as in its definition as 'animal'. The first and second [cases] might obtain simultaneously, that is, when the definition partially overlaps with [the definiendum], as in the definition [of 'human'] as 'white'.

Formulating the Confutation for Insufficient Inclusiveness or Exclusiveness

Confutation [of a definition] on account of its being insufficiently inclusive or exclusive is formulated as follows: "This definition is insufficiently inclusive of the instances of the definiendum and insufficiently exclusive of other instances. All definitions of which this is the case are invalid."

قولنا فيه في نقضه بعدم جمعه وعدم منعه وباستلزامه المحال وبعدم كونه أجلى من المعرّف، وفي منعه عند اشتماله على الدعوى الضمنية°، وفي الجواب عن هذه الصور بتحرير المراد.

للسائل أن ينقضه ومعناه أن يبطله بعدم جمعه أو بعدم منعه أو باستلزام المحال. وسبب الأوّل كون التعريف أخصّ مطلقًا كتعريف الإنسان بالزنجي، وسبب الثاني كونه أعمّ مطلقًا كتعريفه بالحيوان. وقد يجتمع الأوّل والثاني وذلك إذا كان التعريف أعمّ من وجه، كتعريفه بالأبيض.

تقرير الإبطال بعدم الجمع وعدم المنع

تقرير الإبطال بعدم الجمع وعدم المنع «إن هذا التعريف غير جامع لأفراد المعرّف وغير مانع عن أغياره وكل تعريف هذا شأنه ففاسد».

The one offering the definition may challenge the major premise, corroborating his challenge by arguing that that the definition is *lexical*—namely, the specification of an expression's meaning through another expression[1] that clearly signifies that meaning to the one who hears it. This is the procedure of the lexicologists. It is valid [even] by means of [verbal expressions] that are broader or narrower, as, in the former case, when they say that *saʿdān* is a plant,[2] and, in the latter case, when the dictionary says, "*lahā* / *lahwan* (he amused himself / amusement), meaning *laʿiba* (he played)" (play is a type of amusement). [Thus, he may maintain that the definition is lexical] and not *logical*—namely, that in which precision is sought through mention of the general first and the specific second, e.g., when you say, "A human is an animal that is rational."10

According to the late-period scholars, coextension is a condition for definition; thus, a definition is invalidated by insufficient inclusiveness or insufficient exclusiveness. The early-period scholars, however, permitted definition through the broader or the narrower. [They permitted definitions] of the former type in cases where the definition is meant to distinguish the definiendum from something due to its similarity—e.g., if 'triangle' and 'circle' were indistinguishable to the listener, and one intended merely to distinguish the two and thus said, "A triangle is a polygon." [And they permitted definitions] of the latter type in cases where the definition is meant to illustrate prominent instances.

[1] This is like the definition of *ghaḍanfar* as *asad* (lion), and this is definition by synonyms. *Asad* clearly signifies the predatory animal to the one who hears it, in contrast to *ghaḍanfar*, which is a rare term for the predatory animal.

[2] *Saʿdān* is not synonymous with "plant"; it is a particular species of plant but more obscure in signifying its meaning, namely, 'a particular species of plant'. Thus, specification was sought, so "plant" was offered, that is, "species of plant," given that the nunation in *nabtin* indicates diversification. Reflect on this.

فلصاحب التعريف أن يمنع الكبرى مستندًا بأن التعريف لفظي — وهو تعيين معنى اللفظ بلفظ آخر[١] واضح الدلالة على ذلك المعنى بالنسبة إلى السامع؛ وهو طريق أهل اللغة. ويجوز بالأعمّ والأخصّ، والأوّل كقولهم «سعدان نبت»[٢] والثاني كقول القاموس «لها لهوًا أي لعبَ». أقول: اللعب نوع من اللهو — لا حقيقي وهو ما يراد به التفصيل بذكر العامّ أوّلًا والخاصّ ثانيًا، كقولك «الإنسان حيوان ناطق».

ويشترط فيه المساواة على مذهب المتأخّرين فيبطل بعدم الجمع أو عدم المنع؛ والقدماء جوّزوا التعريف بالأعمّ والأخصّ أما الأول ففي موضع يراد بالتعريف تمييز المعرّف عن بعض الأشياء لاشتباهه كما إذا شبّه المثلّث بالدائرة عند السامع وأريد تميّزه عنها فقط فيقال «المثلّث شكل مضلّع» وأما الثاني ففي موضع يراد بالتعريف بيان الأفراد

[١] وذلك كتعريف «الغضنفر» بـ«الأسد» وهذا تعريف المرادف و«الأسد» واضح الدلالة على الحيوان المفترس بالنسبة إلى السامع بخلاف «الغضنفر» فإنه لغة نادرة في الحيوان المفترس.

[٢] فإن «سعدان» ليس بمرادف لـ«نبت» بل نوع مخصوص منه لكنه أخفى دلالة على معناه وهو النوع المخصوص من النبت فأريد التعيين فقيل «نبتٌ» أي «نوع من النبت» على أن التنوين في «نبتٌ» للتنويع. تأمّل.

The one offering the definition may therefore challenge the major premise, corroborating his challenge by arguing that the goal was to distinguish the definiendum from something or to illustrate its prominent instances.

المشـــــهورة، فلصاحـــب التعريـــف منـــع الـــكبرى مستنـــدًا بـــأن المـــراد تـــميّز المعـــرّف عـــن بعـــض الأشـــياء أو بيـــان أفـــراده المشـــهورة.

He may also challenge the minor premise—namely, the objector's assertion "This definition is insufficiently inclusive of the defined term's instances and insufficiently exclusive of other instances"—by means of *clarification*.[11]

وله منـع الصغـرى وهـو قـول السـائل «إن هـذا التعريـف غير جامـع لأفـراد المعـرّف وغير مانـع عـن أغيـاره» بتحريـر المـراد.

Know that the minor premise resolves into two propositions. When you say that a definition is insufficiently inclusive of such and such instance, it is as if you have said, "The definiendum extends to such and such, but the definition does not extend to it." And when you say that it is insufficiently exclusive of such and such matter, it is as if you have said the converse of this. Now, the one offering the definition may challenge both of these propositions, and the corroboration for this challenge will in most cases be to clarify what was intended by either the definiendum or the definition. Be aware of this; may Allah ﷻ facilitate [your study].

واعلـم أن الصغـرى تنحـلّ إلى قضـيّتين فـإذا قلـت إنــه غير جامـع لفـرد فلاني فكأنـك قلـت «إن المعـرّف صادق عليـه والتعريف غير صـادق»، وإذا قلـت إنه غير مانـع عـن مـادّة فلانيـة فكأنـك قلـت عكـس المذكـور. فلصاحـب التعريـف أن يمنـع كلًّا مـن تَينـك القضيّتين، وسـند ذلـك المنـع في الغالـب تحريـر المـراد بالمعـرّف أو التعريـف. فاعـرف سـهّل الله تعـالى عليـك.

Formulating the Refutation for the Definition's Entailment of Circularity or Infinite Regress

تقرير الإبطال باستلزام التعريف الدور أو التسلسل

Refutation [of a definition] on account of its entailing circularity or regress is formulated as follows: "This definition entails circularity or infinite regress, either of which is an absurdity, and every definition that entails an absurdity is invalid." There is no room to challenge the major premise here; what may be challenged is rather the entailment. The corroboration for this will in most cases be to clarify the intended meaning. Or one may challenge the [charge of] absurdity, with the corroboration being "This circularity is not absurd" or "This infinite regress is not absurd." The distinction between when they are absurd and when they are not absurd belongs to the science of rational theology.

وتقريـر الإبطـال باسـتلزام التعريـف الدور أو التسلسـل «إن هـذا التعريف مسـتلزم للدور أو التسلسـل وهو محال وكل تعريـف يسـتلزم المحـال فهو فاسـد». ولا مجـال لمنع الـكبرى هنا؛ بـل يمنع الاسـتلزام وسـنده في الغالب تحرير التعريـف أو يمنع الاسـتحالة مستندًا بأن هـذا الدور غير محـال أو أن هذا التسلسـل غير محـال، وبيـان محالهما عن عـدم محالهما في علـم الكلام.

[The Confutation of a Definition for Lack of Clarity]

Know that a definition is subject to confutation when it is not clearer than the definiendum, e.g., the definition of 'fire' as 'something that resembles the soul in its subtle nature', while 'soul' is more obscure than 'fire'.[1] One of the conditions for the soundness of a definition is that it be clearer than the definiendum. If one uses rare expressions, intends meanings signified by concomitance, uses equivocal terms, or [uses] nonliteral language without any clear contextual indicant specifying the intended meaning, this vitiates the good form of a definition but not its soundness, given that the definition is clearer than the definiendum.

The Confuter of a Definition and His Opponent

It is widely understood that the confuter of a definition takes the burden of proof and his opponent is a challenger. This means that to object to a definition is inevitably to claim that it is invalid, and one substantiates this claim, as you know, by [proving] that it is insufficiently inclusive, insufficiently exclusive, or entails circularity or infinite regress. And the response to this is to challenge the premises of that proof, as you know.

[1] That is, *nafs* (soul), with the *fā'* vowelless. What is meant by "fire" is the heat that diffuses through live coals, and it can also be used in reference to the coals, though the intended meaning here is the former. The soul is an immaterial substance connected to a material one, but because it holds it in common with the intellect that it is illumined with intelligible forms, it sometimes takes its name. The *nafs* (with the *fā'* vowelless) is the *rūḥ* (soul). According to most of the *kalām* theologians it is a corporeal substance of subtle nature that diffuses through and inheres in the body and is never replaced or dissolved. According to the philosophers it is an immaterial substance connected to the body such that it directs and governs it. Such has been said.

[نقض التعريف بالخفاء]

واعلم أنه قد ينقض التعريف بأنه ليس بأجلى من المعرَّف، كتعريف النار بأنه شيء يشبه النفس في اللطافة والنفس أخفى من النار.[١] ومن شرائط صحّة التعريف كونه أجلى من المعرَّف. وأما استعمال الألفاظ الغريبة وإرادة المدلول الالتزامي واستعمال اللفظ المشترك أو المجاز بدون القرينة الواضحة المعيّنة للمراد فهو يُذهب حسن التعريف لا صحّته إذا كان التعريف أجلى من المعرَّف.

ناقض التعريف وموجهه

اشتهر أن ناقض التعريف مستدلّ وموجّهه مانع. ومعناه أن الاعتراض على التعريف لا يكون إلا بطريق دعوى بطلانه والاستدلال على تلك٦ الدعوى بما عرفت من أنه غير جامع أو غير مانع أو مستلزم للدور أو التسلسل. والجواب عن ذلك بمنع مقدّمات ذلك الدليل؛ وقد عرفت.

[١] قوله «النفس» بسكون الفاء. والمراد من «النار» الحرّ الساري في الجمر وقد يطلق على الجمر والمراد هنا هو الأول. النفس جوهر غير مادّي متعلّق بالمادّي إلا أنها لمضاهاتها بالعقل في التجلّي بالصورة قد يسمّى باسمه. «النفس» بسكون الفاء الروح وهو عند أكثر المتكلّمين جسم لطيف سارٍ في البدن حالّ فيه لا يتبدّل ولا يتحلّل، وعند الحكماء جوهر مجرّد يتعلّق بالبدن تعلّق التدبير والتصرّف؛ كذا قيل.

This pertains, however, when the one offering the definition does not state whether the definition is an essential definition or a descriptive definition.[12] If he asserts that it is an essential definition, it is as if he has asserted that the general and specific elements are essential universals; thus the general element is named a *genus* and the specific element a *differentia*. And if he asserts that it is a descriptive definition, it is as if he has asserted that one or both of the elements are accidental. Thus one may object by challenging their essentialness or by challenging the accidentality of one or both. That which occasions the challenge here is the implicit claim; be aware of this. The only way one can respond to this is by proving the essentialness or accidentality, and this is difficult for the reason usually cited, namely, that to distinguish the essential from the accidental is difficult.[1]

Know that the construal of definitions as being composed of essential [universals] is only the convention of the logicians and those who concur with them. As for the convention of the linguists, a definition is that which is sufficiently inclusive and exclusive in defining a thing, regardless whether by means of essential or accidental [universals]. Thus, one who says, "It is defined as such and such," may ward off the above challenge by [responding] that [his definition] is intended according to the convention of the linguists.

لكن هذا إذا لم يدّع صاحب التعريف بأن هذا التعريف حدّ أو رسم؛ فإذا ادّعى أنه حدّ فكأنّه ادّعى أن العامّ والخاصّ من الذاتيّات فيسمّى العامّ جنسًا والخاصّ فصلًا وإذا ادّعى أنه رسم فكأنّه ادّعى أن أحدهما أو كليهما من العرضيّات فيجوز الاعتراض بمنع كونهما من الذاتيّات وبمنع[٧] كون أحدهما أو كليهما من العرضيّات؛ ومورد المنع هنا الدعوى الضمنيّة فاعرف. ودفع هذا إنما يمكن بإثبات الذاتيّة أو العرضيّة وهذا[٨] عسير لما قيل أن تمييز الذاتي عن العرضي عسير.[١]

واعلم أن كون الحدّ بمعنى التركّب عن الذاتيّات إنما هو عرف أهل الميزان ومن وافقهم وأما في عرف أهل العربيّة فهو التعريف الجامع المانع سواء كان بالذاتيّات أو بالعرضيّات؛ فلمن قال «يحدّ بكذا» أن يدفع المنع المذكور بأن المراد به عرف أهل العربيّة.

---

[1] That is, to distinguish the genus from a general accident and the differentia from a special accident is difficult—rather, practically impossible. The verifying scholar al-Sharīf [al-Jurjānī] says: "It is difficult to apprehend real things by what is essential to them and to distinguish what is essential to them from what is accidental to them, to the point that it is practically impossible. For the genus resembles a general accident, and the differentia resembles a special accident." Naḥīfī, [in the margin of al-Āmidī, *Sharḥ al-Waladiyya*, 142.][13]

[١] أي تمييز الجنس عن العرض العامّ والفصل عن الخاصّة عسير بل متعذّر. قال الشريف المحقّق: إن الحقائق الموجودة يتعسّر الاطّلاع على ذاتيّاتها والتمييز بينها وبين عرضيّاتها تعسّرًا تامًّا[٩] واصلًا إلى حدّ التعذّر فإن الجنس شبيه بالعرض العامّ والفصل بالخاصّة (نحيفي).

Chapter 3

DIVISION

الباب الثالث

في التقسيم

Our investigation in this chapter concerns the confutation of a division on account of (1) its being inexhaustive, (2) its entailing that what is actually a subdivision of something is a condivision of that thing or that what is actually a condivision of something is a subdivision of that thing, (3) its being too broad, (4) its being the division of a thing into itself and other things, or (5) its comprising overlapping subdivisions. Our investigation also concerns the response to these confutations by clarification and the meaning of clarification.

بحثنا فيه في نقضه (١) بعدم حصره (٢) وباستلزام قسم الشيء في الواقع قسيمًا له أو قسيم الشيء في الواقع قسمًا له (٣) وبأن التقسيم أعمّ (٤) وبأنه تقسيم الشيء إلى نفسه وإلى غيره (٥) وبأن فيه تصادق الأقسام، وفي الجواب عن هذه النواقض بتحرير المراد ومعنى تحرير المراد.

Preliminary Discussion

Division is of two types: either the division of a universal into its particulars or the division of a whole into its parts. The universal and the whole are termed the *dividendum* and the *source of the division*, and the particulars and the parts are termed *subdivisions*. Each subdivision in relation to the other subdivisions is termed a *condivision*. A subdivision that falls under the dividendum but is not mentioned in the division process is termed a *residual subdivision*.

It is a condition for a division's validity that it be *sufficiently inclusive* and *sufficiently exclusive*. The former [condition] is also termed *exhaustiveness* and means that the division does not omit mention of anything that falls within the dividendum; the latter means that nothing that does *not* fall within

تمهيد

التقسيم قسمان: إما تقسيم الكلّي إلى جزئيّاته وإما تقسيم الكل إلى أجزائه. والكلّي والكل يسمّى مَقسمًا ومورد القسمة، وتسمّى الجزئيّات والأجزاء أقسامًا، ويسمّى كل قسم بالنسبة إلى القسم الآخر قسيمًا، ويسمّى القسم الذي دخل في المقسم ولم يذكر في التقسيم واسطة بين الأقسام.

وشرط صحّة التقسيم الجمع والمنع؛ ويسمّى الأول الحصر ومعناه أن لا يترك في التقسيم ذكر بعض ما دخل في المقسم، ومعنى الثاني أن لا يذكر في

the dividendum is mentioned in the division. Another of the conditions for a division's validity is that its subdivisions be mutually distinct.

What It Means to Divide a Universal into Its Particulars

To divide a universal into its particulars means to attach qualifications to the divided universal. After it is qualified, the divided universal may be explicitly mentioned in its subdivisions, e.g., to say, "A human is either a white human or a black human"; it may lie within the meanings of the subdivisions, e.g., to say, "A word is either a noun, a verb, or a particle"; or it may be omitted while being intended, e.g., to say, "A human is either white or black."

Now, such a division is either *deductive* or *inductive*. The former is that in which the intellect does not allow another subdivision and the listing of subdivisions proceeds by alternation between affirmation and negation, e.g., to say, "Something knowable is either existent or not." The latter is that in which the intellect allows another subdivision, though the subdivisions listed are those which are known by induction, e.g., "A natural element is either earth, water, air, or fire."

It is proper for an inductive division not to comprise an alternation between negation and affirmation, but one may express it in the same form as a division that has become rationally exhaustive by means of alternation in this manner. In such a case, some of its subdivisions will inevitably be *extended*, which means that the intension of the subdivision will be broader in applicability than to those instances to which it applies[1] that have been found by induction. Being broader means that the intellect allows the concept to apply to other instances

[1] That is, those instances to which the intension of the subdivision applies. The phrase [*mimmā ṣadaqa ʿalayhi*] is an explanation of the relative pronoun [in *mā wujida*].

التقسيم ما لم يدخل في المقسم. ومن شرائطه أيضا تباين الأقسام.

معنى تقسيم الكلي إلى جزئياته

معناه ضمّ قيود إلى المقسم. فقد يذكر المقسم في الأقسام صريحًا كقولك «الإنسان إما إنسان أبيض وإما إنسان أسود»، وقد يدخل في مفهوم الأقسام كقولك «الكلمة إما اسم أو فعل أو حرف»، وقد يحذف وهو مراد كقولك «الإنسان إما أبيض أو أسود».

ثم إن هذا التقسيم إما عقلي وإما استقرائي. الأول ما لا يجوّز العقل فيه قسمًا آخر ويكون ذكر الأقسام فيه بالترديد بين الإثبات والنفي، كقولك «المعلوم إما موجود أو لا». والثاني ما يجوّز العقل فيه قسمًا آخر لكن ذكر فيه ما علم بالاستقراء، كقولك «العنصر إما أرض أو ماء أو هواء أو نار».

والتقسيم الاستقرائي حقّه أن لا يردّد فيه بين النفي والإثبات؛ لكن قد يذكر في صورة الحصر العقلي بالترديد كذلك فيكون بعض الأقسام مرسلًا البتة. ومعنى إرساله أن يكون مفهوم القسم أعمّ مما وجد بالاستقراء مما صدق عليه[١] ومعنى هذا العموم أن يجوّز العقل صدق ذلك المفهوم على غير ما وجد، كقولك

[١] أي صدق مفهوم القسم عليه، والظرف بيان الموصول.

than those found. For example, when you say, "An element is either earth or not, and the latter is either water or not, and that third is either air or not, which is fire," the final subdivision is extended; that is, it is not exhaustively confined to fire according to the intellect but rather according to induction.

«العنصر إما أرض أو لا، والثاني إما ماء أو لا، والثالث إما هواء أو لا، وهو النار» فالقسم الأخير مرسل أي لا ينحصر في النار بحسب العقل بل بحسب الاستقراء.

What It Means to Divide a Whole into Its Parts

To divide a whole into its parts is to explicate its essence by recounting its parts. Thus, it does not involve attaching qualifications to the divided whole. The conditions [for its validity] are that it be exhaustive, that its subdivisions be mutually distinct, and that each subdivision fall within the divided whole, as in the division of *maʿjūn* paste into honey and nigella seed.

معنى تقسيم الكل إلى أجزائه

هو تحصيل ماهية المقسم بذكر أجزائه؛ فليس فيه ضمّ قيود إلى المقسم. وشرطه الحصر وتباين الأقسام ودخول كل قسم في المقسم، كتقسيم المعجون إلى عسل وشونيز.

Confuting a Division

1. Being Inexhaustive If the division is deductive, the objector confutes it by finding another subdivision that the intellect allows. If it is inductive, he confutes it by finding another subdivision that actually exists.

The objector might mistakenly suppose an inductive division that alternates between negation and affirmation to be a deductive division and hence claim that it is invalid since the intellect allows another subdivision. For example, he might say of the division of natural elements in the manner previously mentioned:[1] "The final subdivision[2] is not exhaustively confined to fire, since it is rationally possible that this subdivision be subdivided into fire and other than fire." He is to be told in response: "The division is inductive, and the subdivision you have deemed possible does not actually exist. An inductive division is invalidated only by the actual existence of another subdivision."

نقض التقسيم

١. بعدم حصره فإن كان عقليًّا ينقضه السائل بوجود قسم آخر يجوّزه العقل، وإن كان استقرائيًّا ينقضه بوجود قسم آخر متحقّق في الواقع.

وقد يظنّ السائل التقسيم الاستقرائي المتردّد بين النفي والإثبات تقسيمًا عقليًّا فيقول إنه باطل لتجويز العقل قسمًا آخر، كأن يقول في تقسيم العنصر كما ذكرنا[١] أن «القسم الأخير[٢] لا ينحصر في النار إذ يجوز بحسب العقل أن ينقسم إلى النار وغيرها»، فيجاب عنه بأن «القسمة استقرائيّة والقسم الذي جوّزته غير متحقّق في الواقع والتقسيم الاستقرائي لا يبطل إلا بوجود قسم آخر في الواقع».

[1] The phrase "in the manner previously mentioned" modifies "the division of elements."

[2] The sentence [beginning with] "The final subdivision" is a direct quote.

[١] قوله «كما ذكرنا» متعلّق بـ«تقسيم» العنصر».

[٢] قوله «أن القسم الأخير» مقول القول.

Now, if the objector invalidates either kind of division on account of inexhaustiveness, the proponent of the division may respond by clarifying the dividendum, i.e., that he intends thereby a meaning that does not include the residual subdivision.

فإذا أبطلهما السائل بعدم الحصر فقد يجيب عنه القاسم بتحرير المقسم أعني أن يريد منه معنًى لا يشمل الواسطة.

[2. Entailing That Something's Subdivision Is Its Condivision] A division may be confuted for entailing that what is actually something's subdivision is its condivision. This occurs when some subdivisions subsume others, e.g., when you say, "A body is either an animal or a growing thing." For 'animal' is actually a subdivision of 'growing thing', yet in this division it is rendered its condivision. One responds by challenging the cited entailment, corroborating this by clarification—i.e., [for example], responding that one intended 'growing non-animal'.

A division may also be confuted for entailing that what is actually something's condivision is its subdivision. This occurs when some of the subdivisions are distinct from the dividendum, e.g., when you say, "A human is either a horse or an Abyssinian." For 'horse' is a condivision of 'human' since both are divisions of 'animal', yet in this division it is rendered a subdivision of it.

[٢. باستلزام القسم قسيمًا أو القسيم قسمًا] وقد ينقض التقسيم بأنه يلزم فيه أن يكون قسم الشيء في الواقع قسيمًا له[١٢] وذلك إذا كان بعض الأقسام[١٣] أعمّ من الآخر، كما إذا قلت «الجسم إما حيوان أو نامٍ» فإن الحيوان قسم من النامي في الواقع وجُعل في هذا التقسيم قسيمًا له. ويجاب عنه بمنع اللزوم المذكور مستندًا بالتحرير، أعني به أن يراد نامٍ غير الحيوان.

وقد ينقض بأنه يلزم فيه أن يكون قسيم الشيء في الواقع قسمًا له وذلك إذا كان بعض الأقسام مباينًا للمقسم، كما إذا قلت «الإنسان إما فرس أو زنجي» فالفرس قسيم للإنسان لأنهما قسمان من الحيوان وقد جُعل في هذا التقسيم قسمًا له.

[3. Being Too Broad] A division may be confuted because the division it comprises is too broad, e.g., to say, "A human is either white or black." One responds that the dividendum is assumed in the subdivisions.[14]

[٣. بأنه أعمّ] وقد ينقض بأن التقسيم فيه أعمّ، كما إذا قلت «الإنسان إما أبيض أو أسود». فيجاب عنه بأن المقسم معتبر في الأقسام.

[4. Being the Division of Something into Itself and Other Than Itself] A division may be confuted for being the division of something into itself and other things. This occurs when one of the subdivisions is coextensive with the dividendum, e.g., the division of 'human' into 'man' and 'Abyssinian'.

[٤. بأنه تقسيم الشيء إلي نفسه وإلى غيره] وقد ينقض بأنه تقسيم الشيء إلى نفسه وإلي غيره وذلك إذا كان بعض الأقسام مساويًا للمقسم، كتقسيم الإنسان إلى البشر والزنجي.

[5. Comprising Overlapping Divisions] A division may be confuted for comprising overlapping subdivisions, that is, subdivisions that extend to the same thing. This occurs when all or some of the subdivisions are in a relation of partial overlap, e.g., to say, "An animal is either a human or white," for both are true predicates of a white human.[1]

But only a *real division* is invalidated by overlap—namely, the division of the dividendum into things that are distinguished from each other in actual reality. Overlap is of no detriment to a *perspectival division*, which is the division of a universal into concepts that are mentally distinguished, even if they extend to the same thing in actual reality. An example is the division of 'universal' into its five subdivisions though they all extend to 'colored thing,' as Fenārī[15] has shown. Thus, it may be objected that a division is invalid because its subdivisions overlap, and one may respond: "The division is perspectival; it is sufficient that the subdivisions be distinguished conceptually, and their extending to the same thing is of no detriment." For, one thing as characterized by different concepts is considered multiple things and can hence fall into multiple subdivisions.

One may also escape these objections by clarification.

The Meaning of Clarification

Know that *clarification* means to intend by an expression a meaning that is not apparent, e.g., to intend a specific [meaning] by a general [expression] by means of the context of juxtaposition.[16] However, it is not valid to intend a nonliteral meaning without a relevant semantic link as discussed in the science of figurative language. Thus, for example, 'horse' cannot be intended by "book." As for a

[1] The author of *Sharḥ al-Maṭāliʿ* says, "What is sought in division is to distinguish the subdivisions." Al-Rāzī, *Lawāmiʿ al-asrār*, 1:194.

[٥. بتصادق الأقسام] قد ينقض التقسيم بأن فيه تصادق الأقسام أي صدقها على شيء واحد وذلك إذا كان بين الأقسام كلها أو بعضها عموم من وجه، كما إذا قلنا «الحيوان إما إنسان وإما أبيض» لأنهما يصدقان على الإنسان الأبيض.[١]

لكن التصادق إنما يبطل به التقسيم الحقيقي وهو جعل المقسم أشياء متمايزة في الواقع ولا يضرّ التقسيم الاعتباري وهو تقسيم الكلي إلى مفهومات متباينة متمايزة في العقل وإن كانت متصادقة في الواقع، كتقسيم الكلي إلى أقسامه الخمسة مع أنها متصادقة في الملوّن كما بيّنه الفناري. فقد يعترض على التقسيم بأنه باطل لتصادق الأقسام فيه فيجاب عنه بأنه تقسيم اعتباري يكفي فيه تمايز الأقسام بحسب المفهوم ولا يضرّه التصادق. فالشيء الواحد باعتبار اتّصافه بمفهومات متخالفة يعتبر أشياء متعدّدة فيدخل في الأقسام المتعدّدة.

ويخرج عنها بتحرير المراد.

معنى تحرير المراد

اعلم أن معنى تحرير المراد إرادة معنًى غير ظاهر من اللفظ، كإرادة الخاصّ من العامّ بقرينة المقابلة. لكن لا تصحّ إرادة المجاز بدون العلاقة المعتبرة المذكورة في

[١] قال في شرح المطالع: المقصود من التقسيم التمايز بين الأقسام.

contextual indicant that precludes that the literal meaning could be intended, this is not necessary when the one offering the clarification is a challenger,[1] since possibility suffices for the challenger. A contextual indicant is a condition only to decisively determine that the meaning is nonliteral, not to make it possible.

علم البيان، فلا يراد الفرس من «الكتاب» مثلًا. وأما القرينة المانعة عن إرادة الحقيقة فلا تجب إذا كان المحرِّر مانعًا[١] لأن المانع يكفيه الجواز والقرينة المانعة إنما تشترط للقطع بالمعنى المجازي لا لتجويزه.

[1] If, however, he is someone advancing a proof and he makes his clarification a premise in his proof, then nonliteral usage must be clarified by a contextual indicant that precludes that the literal meaning could be intended. This is the case if the one responding by way of clarification is someone responding on behalf of the proponent. But if the one responding is the proponent himself, then his stating, "What I intend is such," is one of the strongest kinds of contextual indicants.

[١] وأما إذا كان مستدلًّا وجعل تحريره مقدّمة من دليله فلا بدّ للمجاز من بيان قرينة مانعة عن إرادة الحقيقة؛ هذا إذا كان المجيب بالتحرير شخصًا غير المعلّل يريد الجواب عن طرف المعلّل. وأما إذا كان المجيب هو المعلّل فقوله بأن مرادي هذا من أقوى القرائن المانعة.

CONCLUSION

This conclusion concerns two matters: an explanation of the end of a dialectical disputation and an explanation of the outcome of challenge and confutation.

The End of a Dialectical Disputation

Know that the discussion between the proponent and the objector either resolves in the failure of the proponent to rebut the objections of the objector or in the failure of the objector to object to the responses of the proponent, since it is impossible for the discussion to continue indefinitely. The failure of the proponent is conventionally termed *silencing*, and the failure of the objector *forced concession*; thus one says, "The proponent was silenced," or, "The objector was forced to concede" (that is, *mufḥam* and *mulzam*, respectively, with *fatḥ* of the *ḥāʾ* and *zāy*). The grammatical *iḍāfa* of *ifḥām* (silencing) to *al-muʿallil* (the proponent) is the *iḍāfa* of an infinitive noun to its object, and the same applies to *ilzām al-sāʾil* (the forced concession of the objector).

Now, *questioning* might take the meaning of objecting, and the questioning of the dialecticians is such. But it may also take the meaning of inquiry—that is, inquiring about the meaning of an expression, about the reason for a [particular] phrasing, or about the details of something ambiguous. This is not within the scope of dialectics (though *al-Kashshāf* is replete with it),[17] but there is no fault in it when one is asking about something obscure.

الخاتمة

هي في أمرين: في بيان انتهاء المناظرة وبيان حاصل المنع والنقض.

بيان انتهاء المناظرة

اعلم أن البحث بين المعلّل والسائل إما أن ينتهي إلى عجز المعلّل عن دفع اعتراض السائل أو إلى عجز السائل عن الاعتراض على جواب المعلّل إذ لا يمكن جريان البحث إلى غير النهاية. وعجز المعلّل يسمّى في العرف إفحامًا وعجز السائل إلزامًا ويقال «المعلّل مُفحَم» و«السائل مُلزَم» بفتح الحاء والزاي؛ فإضافة «الإفحام» إلى «المعلّل» إضافة المصدر إلى مفعوله وكذا «إلزام السائل».

ثم إن «السؤال» قد يكون بمعنى الاعتراض وذا سؤال المناظرين؛ وقد يكون بمعنى الاستفسار أي الاستفسار عن معنى اللفظ أو عن وجه التركيب أو عن تفصيل المجمل وهذا ليس داخلًا في المناظرة، والكشّاف مشحون به، ولا بأس بذلك عند خفاء المسؤول عنه.

The Outcome of Challenge and Confutation

Know that the outcome when the premise of a proof is challenged and confuted is that the claim of the proponent is left without proof; the proponent's claim is not invalidated when confuted. This is because the proof is an implicant of the claim, and the invalidation of the implicant does not entail the invalidation of the implicate. After all, it is possible that there be another implicant since it is possible that the implicate be general. Thus, there may be another proof for the claim.[18]

Likewise, the outcome of counteraction is mutual nullification, meaning that the proof of the proponent is nullified and invalidated, and vice versa, for a sound proof does not prove the opposite of its conclusion. The proponent's claim, then, is left without proof. Again, the outcome of counteraction is not an invalidation of the proponent's claim.[19]

The strongest kind of objection is to invalidate a claim that has no proof, even though that is called *usurpation*. The mildest kind is to challenge since neither corroboration nor proof is necessary.

بيان حاصل المنع والنقض

اعلم أن حاصل منع مقدّمة الدليل ونقضه إبقاء دعوى المعلّل بلا دليل وليس حاصل نقضه إبطالًا لدعوى المعلّل إذ الدليل ملزوم للدعوى ولا يلزم من إبطال الملزوم إبطال اللازم إذ يجوز أن يكون له ملزوم آخر لجواز عموم اللازم فيجوز أن يكون للمدّعى دليل آخر.

كذا حاصل المعارضة المساقطة أعني أن يسقط ويبطل دليل المعلّل[١٤] وبالعكس إذ الدليل الصحيح لا يدلّ على خلاف مدلوله فيبقى مدّعى المعلّل بلا دليل فليس حاصل المعارضة أيضا إبطالًا لدعوى المعلّل.

فأقوى الاعتراضات إبطال المدّعى الغير المدلّل وإن سمّي ذلك غصبًا وأسلمها المنع إذ لا يجب سند ولا دليل.

❋ ❋ ❋

By the assistance of Allah ﷻ, the treatise entitled *The Quintessence: On the Science of Dialectics* is complete. May Allah ﷻ by His grace and generosity render it of benefit to us and all believers. Allah! "Take us not to task if we forget or err!" (Q 2:286). "Glory to your Lord, Lord of Might, transcending what they describe! Peace be upon the messengers. And praise to Allah, Lord of the worlds" (Q 37:180–82). By His permission ﷻ, the seventh treatise follows, entitled *The Lordly Profusion: On the Science of Rhetorical Semantics.*

تمّت بعون الله تعالى الرسالة المسمّاة باللباب في علم المناظرة والآداب جعلها الله تعالى بمنّه وكرمه نافعة لنا ولسائر المؤمنين. اللّهم لا تؤاخذنا إن نسينا أو أخطأنا. ﴿سُبْحَٰنَ رَبِّكَ رَبِّ ٱلْعِزَّةِ عَمَّا يَصِفُونَ ۝١٨٠ وَسَلَٰمٌ عَلَى ٱلْمُرْسَلِينَ ۝١٨١ وَٱلْحَمْدُ لِلَّهِ رَبِّ ٱلْعَٰلَمِينَ﴾ [٣٧/ ١٨٠-١٨٢]. وتليها بإذنه تعالى الرسالة السابعة المسمّاة الفيض الربّاني في علم المعاني.

NOTES TO TREATISE VI

1 A commonly studied primer on dialectics authored by Meḥmed Sāçaḳlīzāde (d. 1145/1732).

2 The term *premise* (*muqaddima*) is more inclusive in dialectics than it is in logic; here, it is anything that is a direct prerequisite for the soundness of a proof. This includes not only the propositions that constitute the proof but also the formal conditions for the validity of the proof, like the conditions of quantity and quality associated with each syllogistic figure (*shakl*). Al-Āmidī, *Sharḥ al-Āmidī*, 126–27; al-Anṣārī, *Fatḥ al-Wahhāb*, 316–17.

3 That is, it would be a nonliteral usage of the term *challenge* (*manʿ*) to say that one challenges the claim while intending that one challenges a premise.

4 In these examples, the claim being challenged is that some given thing is not a human. We might imagine in this case that the interlocutors have observed an indistinct figure emerge in the distance and are debating what it is. We might also imagine that this indistinct figure has displayed what could be construed as intelligent or rational activity (perhaps it seems to be making gestures or sending signals). The proponent has made the claim that the figure is not a human being, and the objector is challenging this claim.

5 Al-Maḥbūbī, *al-Tawḍīḥ*, 2:187–88.

6 For example, if the claim is 'Every bird has a beak', but the proponent's proof only yields 'Every bird has a facial feature' (which is broader than having a beak), the consecution is flawed just as it would be flawed for the proponent to try proving his claim with a proof that only yields 'Some bird has a beak'.

7 *Majāz fī al-nisba* here refers to *majāz ʿaqlī*, a category of nonliteral language juxtaposed with *majāz lughawī*. This is discussed in Treatise V, pp. 313–14, and Treatise VII, pp. 389–91.

8 The term *confutation* distinguishes the technical term *naqḍ* from the more general *ibṭāl*, which is usually translated as *refutation*. The English word "confutation" contains a sense of rendering futile or bringing to nothing, which is fitting since the Arabic word *naqḍ* literally means to undo or destroy. Note that it is difficult to translate the term *naqḍ* in way that shows any parallel between *naqḍ ijmālī* and *naqḍ tafṣīlī* (another term for the challenging of a proposition), since the connection between the technical meanings of the two terms is not very close.

9 The disputation outlined in this example is presented from the vantage of the Ḥanafī jurist.

10 In the Arabic phrase *ḥayawānun nāṭiqun* (rational animal), the word *ḥayawānun* (animal) precedes the adjective *nāṭiqun* (rational).

11 Clarification (*taḥrīr al-murād*) is defined at the end of Chapter 3, p. 368.

12 Refer to Treatise III, pp. 243–44.

13 Al-Sayyid al-Sharīf al-Jurjānī (d. 816/1413), theologian and polymath. See al-Jurjānī, *Ḥāshiyat al-Jurjānī*, 1:340.

14 That is, he clarifies that he did not intend to divide 'human' into white things *as such* and black things *as such*; rather, he intended to divide 'human' into white *humans* and black *humans*.

15 Muḥammad al-Fanārī (or Meḥmed Fenārī, also known as Mollā Fenārī) (d. 834/1431), author

of *al-Fawāʾid al-fanāriyya*, a frequently taught commentary on the logic primer *Īsāghūjī*.

16 For example, when "human" and "animal" are juxtaposed, it is understood from context that the general expression "animal" is being used to refer specifically to non-human animals.

17 The famous work of Quran exegesis by Maḥmūd b. ʿUmar al-Zamakhsharī (d. 538/1144) titled *al-Kashshāf ʿan ḥaqāʾiq ghawāmiḍ al-tanzīl wa-ʿuyūn al-aqāwīl fī wujūh al-taʾwīl* is well-known for its method of rigorous linguistic inquiry.

18 If proof A would entail claim C, but the proponent was unsuccessful in defending A, that does not entail the falsity of C. It is possible that C can be demonstrated through a different proof, B. In other words, it is possible that C is more "general" or "broader" than to depend on A.

19 Although the proponent has failed to make a successful case for his claim, meaning that he has left it unsubstantiated, this does not necessarily mean that his claim is false. What it does mean is that the objector has succeeded in showing that the proponent could not prove it.

VII

THE LORDLY PROFUSION

On the science of rhetorical semantics

الفيض الرباني في علم المعاني

In the Name of Allah,
All-Merciful, Most Compassionate

بسم الله الرحمن الرحيم

ALL PRAISE IS due to Allah for blessing us with belief, submission, spiritual excellence, and knowledge of what we knew not. May blessings and peace be upon the best of His creation, Muḥammad, and upon his family, Companions, and all who follow them in excellence as long as the stars remain in the universe.

الحمد لله على ما أنعم علينا من الإيمان والإسلام والإحسان وبيان ما لم نعلم، والصلاة والسلام على خير خلقه محمد وعلى آله وصحبه والتابعين لهم بإحسان ما دام النجم في العالم.

To Proceed Says the destitute servant, needful of his self-sufficient Lord, may Allah ﷻ by His manifest and subtle kindness grant him pardon, Muḥammad Emīn b. Dhulfiqār b. ʿAlī b. Aḥmad al-Mīrānī al-Kuluyānī and, later, al-Anqarawī: This is a treatise on the science of rhetorical semantics in which I have included the best parts of the *Talkhīṣ*, *Mukhtaṣar al-maʿānī*,[1] and assorted parts of other works to ease comprehension and memorization.

أما بعد فيقول العبد الفقير المفتقر إلى ربّه الغني سامحه الله تعالى بلطفه الجلي والخفي محمد الأمين بن ذي الفقار بن علي بن أحمد الميراني الكلياني ثم الأنقروي: هذه رسالة في علم المعاني أدرجت فيها زبدة ما في التلخيص ومختصر المعاني ونبذة من غيرهما تسهيلًا للضبط والحفظ.

The science of rhetorical semantics is a science through which one knows the modes of verbal expressions by which they correspond to what the situation demands. I have arranged the treatise into an introduction and eight chapters.

علم المعاني علم يعرف به أحوال اللفظ التي بها يطابق اللفظ مقتضى الحال. رتّبتها على مقدّمة وثمانية أبواب.

INTRODUCTION

المقدمة

This introduction serves to explain what *articulateness* and *eloquence* mean and to explain that the science of rhetoric resolves into the sciences of rhetorical semantics, figurative language, and embellishment.

وهي هنا لبيان معنى الفصاحة والبلاغة، وبيان أن مرجع علم البلاغة إلى علم المعاني وعلم البيان وعلم البديع.

Articulateness

Faṣāḥa (articulateness) is a word that refers to clarity and distinctness. It may be used to describe simple expressions, e.g., "an articulate word"; speech, e.g., "articulate speech"; or speakers, e.g., "an articulate speaker."

Articulateness in Simple Expressions For a simple expression to be articulate means that it is clear of dissonance between its letters, of obscurity, and of aberrancy.

1. An example of *dissonance* is [the word] *mustashzirātun* (upturned) in Imruʾ al-Qays's saying,

   ghadāʾiruhu mustashzirātun ilā al-ʿulā
   The braids of [her hair] are turned aloft

   that is, "Its braids are raised."
2. An example of *obscurity* is [the word] *musarrajan* (like a Surayjī sword / like a lamp) in al-ʿAjjāj's saying, *wa-marsinan musarrajan*, that is, "a nose like a Surayjī sword in its fineness and regularity" or "…like a lamp in its radiance and brilliance."
3. An example of *aberrancy* is [the word] *al-ajlali* (the most glorious), with dissolution of the assimilated [doubled *lām*] in [the poet's] statement *al-ḥamdu li-Llāhi al-ʿaliyyi al-ajlali* (All praise is due to Allah, the Exalted, the Most Glorious).

الفصاحة

الفصاحة هي كلمة تنبئ عن الظهور والإبانة. ويوصف بها المفرد مثل «كلمة فصيحة»، والكلام مثل «كلام فصيح»، والمتكلّم مثل «متكلّم فصيح».

الفصاحة في المفرد الفصاحة في المفرد هي خلوصه من تنافر الحروف والغرابة ومخالفة القياس.

١- فالتنافر نحو «مستشزرات» في قول امرئ القيس:

غَدَائِرُهُ مُسْتَشْزِرَاتٌ إِلَى العُلَى

أي «ذوائبه مرتفعات».

٢- والغرابة نحو «مسرّجًا» في قول العجّاج «وَمَرْسِنًا مُسَرَّجًا» أي أنفًا كالسيف السريجي في الدقّة والاستواء أو كالسراج في البرق واللمعان.

٣- ومخالفة القياس نحو «الأجلل» بفكّ الإدغام في قوله «الحَمْدُ لِلّٰهِ العَلِيِّ الأَجْلَلِ».

Articulateness in Speech For speech to be articulate means that it is clear of weak composition, of dissonance between its words, and of overcomplication and that its [individual] words are articulate.

1. *Weakness* means that the composition of the speech violates grammatical rules, e.g., placing a personal pronoun before mentioning [the referent] in words, in meaning, or in effect, as in *ḍaraba ghulāmuhu Zaydan* (His [i.e., Zayd's] boy hit Zayd).

2. *Dissonance* means that the words are heavy on the tongue [in combination], even if they are [individually] each articulate, e.g., al-Jinnī's saying in a eulogy of his,

   wa-laysa qurba qabri Ḥarbin qabru
   And no grave lies near to the grave of Ḥarb

   and another's saying,

   karīmun matā amdaḥhu amdaḥhu wa-l-warā
   A noble man: when I praise him I praise him and all humanity

   maʿī wa-idhā mā lumtuhu lumtuhu waḥdī
   Joins me, but when I censure him I censure him alone[1]

3. *Overcomplication* means that due to some deficiency, the speech does not clearly signify the intended meaning. The deficiency may lie (a) in the ordering,[2] e.g., al-Farazdaq's saying,

[1] The verse means the following: He is noble such that when I praise him, all people agree with me in praising him because he has treated them well as he has treated me well; I never praise him in any way without people declaring me truthful. Or it means that everyone has agreed with me that he possesses those qualities of virtue by which a person deserves praise, and when I censure him, nobody agrees with me in censuring him since he lacks the qualities that would render him deserving of censure.

الفصاحة في الكلام الفصاحة في الكلام خلوصه من ضعف التأليف وتنافر الكلمات والتعقيد مع فصاحة الكلمات.

١- فالضعف أن يكون تأليف الكلام على خلاف القانون النحوي، كالإضمار قبل الذكر لفظًا أو معنًى أوحكمًا نحو «ضرب غلامُه زيدًا».

٢- والتنافر أن تكون الكلمات ثقيلة على اللسان وإن كان كل منها فصيحة، كقول الجنّي في مرثيته:

وَلَيْسَ قُرْبَ قَبْرِ حَرْبٍ قَبْرُ

وكقول غيره:

كَرِيمٌ مَتَى أَمْدَحْهُ أَمْدَحْهُ والوَرَى

مَعِي وَإِذَا مَا لُمْتُهُ لُمْتُهُ وَحْدِي[١]

٣- والتعقيد أن لا يكون الكلام ظاهر الدلالة على المراد لخلل إما (١) في النظم، كقول الفرزدق:

[١] معنى البيت: هو كريم إذا مدحتُه وافقني الناس على مدحه فيمدحونه لإسداء إحسانه إليهم كإسدائه إليّ ولا أمدحه بشيء إلا صدّقني الناس فيه، أو أن الناس وافقوني على وجود ما يوجب المدح للإنسان من صفات الكمال فيه وإذا لمته فلا يوافقني أحد على لومه لعدم وجود المقتضي له فيه.

wa-mā mithluhu fī al-nāsi illā mumallakan
Among humanity there is not like him—
except one crowned as sovereign

abū ummihi ḥayyun abūhu yuqāribuh
The father of whose mother—anyone
alive—is his father—related to him[1]

that is, among humanity there is not a living relative like him (i.e., one who resembles him in his virtues) except someone crowned as sovereign (i.e., a man invested with royal sovereignty) the father of whose mother is the father of the one being praised. Or the deficiency may lie (b) in the connection[3] because one meant to imply far-removed implications that presuppose many intermediate steps, e.g., Ibn Aḥnaf's saying,

sa-aṭlubu buʿda al-dāri ʿankum li-taqrabū
I shall seek an abode distant from you to
bring you near,

[1] The verse means the following: Among humanity there is not a relative of his (i.e., the one being praised) alive who is like him (i.e., anyone who resembles him in virtues) except someone crowned as sovereign (i.e., Hishām), the father of whose mother (i.e., the father of the mother of Hishām) is his father (i.e., the father of the one being praised). The personal pronoun in *ummihi* (his mother) refers to the person crowned as sovereign and in *abūhu* (his father) to the one being praised. Now, between the subject *abū ummihi* (the father of his mother) and its predicate *abūhu* (his father), there intervenes the unrelated word *ḥayyun* (alive). Similarly, between *ḥayyun* (one who is alive) and its adjective *yuqāribuhu* (related to him), there intervenes the unrelated word *abūhu* (his father). Moreover, the grammatical exception is made to precede that from which it is excepted. Thus, the verse, as you can see, is overcomplicated to the utmost; the poet could just as well have said, *wa-mā mithluhu fī al-nāsi aḥadun yuqāribuhu illā mumallakun abū ummihi abūhu* (Among humanity there is not like him anyone related to him except one crowned as sovereign, the father of whose mother is his father).

وَمَا مِـثْـلُـهُ فِـي الـنَّاسِ إِلَّا مُـمَـلَّـكًا

أَبُـو أُمِّـهِ حَـيٌّ أَبُـوهُ يُـقَـارِبُـهْ[١]

أي «ليس مثله في الناس حيّ قاربه (أي أحد يشبهه في الفضائل) إلا مملّكًا (أي رجلًا أُعطى له الملك) أبو أمّه أبو الممدوح». وإما (٢) في الانتقال بسبب إيراد اللوازم البعيدة المفتقرة إلى الوسائط الكثيرة، كقول ابن أحنف:

سَأَطْلُبُ بُعْدَ الدَّارِ عَنْكُمْ لِتَقْرَبُوا

[١] والمعنى فيه: وما مثله (يعني الممدوح) في الناس حيّ يقاربه (أي أحد يشبهه في الفضائل) إلا مملّكًا (يعني هشامًا) أبو أمه (أي أبو أمّ هشام) أبوه (أي أبو الممدوح). فالضمير في «أمّه» للمملّك وفي «أبوه» للممدوح. ففصل بين «أبو أمه» وهو مبتدأ و«أبوه» وهو خبره بأجنبيّ وهو «حيّ»، وكذا فصل بين «حيّ» و«يقاربه» وهو نعته بأجنبيّ وهو «أبوه»، وقدّم المستثنى على المستثنى منه؛ فهو كما تراه في غاية التعقيد. وكان من حقّ الناظم أن يقول «وما مثله في الناس أحد يقاربه إلا مملّك أبو أمه أبوه».

wa-taskubu ʿaynāya al-dumūʿa li-tajmudā
And my eyes will pour tears that they might dry[1]

since dryness of the eye is a far-removed implication of happiness: [the step] between them is the eye's becoming free of tears.[4]

Articulateness in Speakers With respect to a speaker, articulateness is a proficiency in giving articulate expression to intended meanings.

Eloquence

Balāgha (eloquence) refers [lexically] to arrival and reaching the end. It may be used to describe speech and speakers but not words; one may say "eloquent speech" and "an eloquent speaker," but one may not say *kalima balīgha* (an eloquent word) since the Arabs were not heard to say this. Eloquence, then, is of two types: eloquence in speech and eloquence in a speaker.

[Eloquence in Speech] The first type, namely, eloquence in speech, means that the speech corresponds to what the situation demands. The *situation* refers to any state of affairs that calls for the speaker to take into account specific considerations in addition to [the substance of] the speech that will convey what he essentially intends to convey. These specific considerations are *what the situation demands*. For example, the denial of [the speaker's] claim by the addressee is a situation that demands emphasis of the claim: [in this case], that which the situation demands is emphasis.

وَتَسْكُبُ عَيْنَايَ الدُّمُوعَ لِتَجْمُدَا[١]

فجمود العين لازم بعيد للسرور وبينهما خلوّ العين من الدموع.

الفصاحة في المتكلّم الفصاحة في المتكلّم ملكة يقتدر بها على التعبير عن المقصود بلفظ فصيح.

البلاغة

البلاغة[٤] تنبئ عن الوصول والانتهاء. ويوصف بها الكلام والمتكلّم دون الكلمة، إذ يقال «كلام بليغ» «متكلّم بليغ» ولا يقال «كلمة بليغة» إذ لم يُسمع ذلك عن العرب. فالبلاغة قسمان: بلاغة في الكلام وبلاغة في المتكلّم.

[البلاغة في الكلام] القسم الأول أي البلاغة في الكلام مطابقته لمقتضى الحال مع فصاحته. والحال هو الأمر الداعي للمتكلّم إلى أن يعتبر مع الكلام الذي يؤدّي به أصل المراد خصوصيّة ما وهذه الخصوصيّة هي مقتضى الحال، مثلًا كون المخاطب منكرًا للحكم حال يقتضي تأكيد الحكم والتأكيد مقتضى الحال.

---

[1] The verse means the following: I will seek and intend to be distant from you, my beloved, so that you might become near, since it is the habit of destiny to bring about the opposite of what one intends: if one intends distance, destiny will bring about proximity. And I intend and seek sorrow, which is entailed by tears, so that, by the habitual course of destiny, I might become happy.

[١] معنى البيت: أطلب وأريد البعد عنكم أيها الأحبّة لتقربوا إذ من عادة الزمان الإتيان بضدّ المراد فإذا أريد البعد يأتي الزمان بالقرب، وأريد وأطلب الحزن الذي هو لازم البكاء ليحصل السرور بما هو من عادة الزمان.

Speech is enhanced in beauty and acceptance to the extent that it corresponds to the appropriate considerations, and it is depreciated to the extent that this correspondence is lacking.

ارتفاع شأن الكلام[٣] في الحسن والقبول بمطابقته للاعتبار المناسب وانحطاطه بعدمها فمقتضى الحال هو الاعتبار المناسب.

There are two extremes to eloquence. There is the higher extreme, which is the point of miraculous inimitability or anything that approaches it, and there is the lower extreme, which is the point at which if the speech degrades any further, then according to the rhetoricians it has become indistinguishable from animal sounds. Between these two extremes there are many levels.

للبلاغة طرفان: أعلى وهو حدّ الإعجاز وما يقرب منه، أسفل وهو ما إذا غيّر الكلام عنه إلى ما دونه التحق عند البلغاء بأصوات الحيوانات؛ وبينهما مراتب كثيرة.

There are other aspects beyond [its corresponding to the appropriate considerations] that give beauty to speech; these are *embellishments*.

وتتبعها وجوه أخرى تورث الكلام حسنًا وهي المحسّنات البديعيّة.

[Eloquence in Speakers] The second type, namely, eloquence in speakers, is a proficiency in composing eloquent speech.

[البلاغة في المتكلّم] القسم الثاني أي البلاغة في المتكلم ملكة يقتدر بها على تأليف كلام بليغ.

* * *

One learns from the definitions of articulateness and eloquence, then, that everything eloquent is articulate but that not everything articulate is eloquent, since it is possible for articulate speech not to correspond to what the situation demands and, similarly, it is possible for one to have a proficiency in giving articulate expression to intended meanings without their correspondence to what the situation demands, e.g., saying, *inna Zaydan qā'imun* (Zayd is indeed standing) when the addressee is neutral to the information.

فقد علم من تعريفَي الفصاحة والبلاغة أن كل بليغ فصيح وليس كل فصيح بليغًا لجواز أن يكون كلام فصيح غير مطابق لمقتضى الحال. وكذا يجوز أن يكون لأحد ملكة يقتدر بها على التعبير عن المقصود بلفظ فصيح من غير مطابقة لمقتضى الحال، نحو قولك «إن زيدًا قائم» حال كون المخاطب خالي الذهن.

The Principles of Eloquence

مرجع البلاغة

According to scholarly verification, the principles of eloquence reside in two—rather, three—things:

1. The first is that by which one avoids errors in conveying the intended meaning:[5] this is the science of rhetorical semantics.
2. The second is that by which one avoids overcomplication in meaning:[6] this is the science of figurative language.
3. The third is that by which one knows the ways to beautify [one's speech]: this is the science of embellishment.[1]

مرجع البلاغة عند التحقيق إلى شيئين بل إلى ثلاثة أشياء.

١- الأول ما يحترز به عن الخطأ في تأدية المعنى المراد، وهو علم المعاني.

٢- الثاني ما يحترز به عن التعقيد المعنوي، وهو علم البيان.

٣- الثالث ما يعرف به وجوه التحسين، وهو علم البديع.[١]

These then are the three sciences we will discuss in this treatise[7] by the will of Allah. All success is through Allah.

فهذه ثلاثة فنون نتكلّم عليها إن شاء الله في هذه الرسالة، وبالله التوفيق.

❁ ❁ ❁

The object of the science of rhetorical semantics is confined to eight main topics in the way that a whole is confined to its parts.

ينحصر المقصود من علم المعاني في ثمانية أبواب انحصار الكل في الأجزاء.

Here concludes the introduction. It is followed, with His permission ﷻ, by an exposition of the eight main topics, which are the following:

1. the modes of declarative predication.
2. the modes of the subject.

إلى هنا تمّت المقدّمة تليها بإذنه تعالى بيان الأبواب الثمانية، وهي:

١- أحوال الإسناد الخبري.

٢- أحوال المسند إليه.

---

[1] Rhetoric does not *depend* on the science of embellishment, but the latter makes speech beautiful and gives it a delightful quality and is thus included in the science of rhetoric.

[١] البلاغة لا تتوقّف على علم البديع إلا إنه يورث الكلام حسنًا وبهجة فلذا يذكر في علم البلاغة.

3. the modes of the predicate.	٣- أحوال المسند.
4. the modes of verbal objects.	٤- أحوال متعلقات الفعل.
5. restriction.	٥- القصر.
6. non-declarative speech.	٦- الإنشاء.
7. breaking and joining.	٧- الفصل والوصل.
8. brevity, prolixity, and proportionality.	٨- الإيجاز والإطناب والمساواة.

Chapter 1

MODES OF DECLARATIVE PREDICATION

الباب الأول

أحوال الإسناد الخبري

Declarative predication is to bring together a word or anything that has the function of a word with another word such that this indicates the judgment that the meaning of the one word is either affirmed or negated of the meaning of the other.

وهو أي الإسناد الخبري ضمّ كلمة أو ما يجري مجراها إلى أخرى بحيث يفيد الحكم بأن مفهوم إحداهما ثابت لمفهوم الأخرى أو منتفٍ عنه.

The Declarer's Purpose in a Declaration

In making a declaration, the purpose of a declarer (that is, one who declares or informs) is to give the addressee either (1) knowledge of the judgment or (2) knowledge of the fact that he knows the judgment. The first is termed the *information*, and the second its implication, that is, the *implication of the information*. Sometimes, one might treat a person who knows both [the judgment and the fact that one knows the judgment] as ignorant because that person has failed to observe the consequences of what he knows.

قصد المخبر بخبره

قصد المخبر أي من يكون بصدد الإخبار والإعلام بخبره إما إفادة المخاطب الحكم أو كونه عالمًا به؛ ويسمّى الأول فائدة الخبر والثاني لازمها أي لازم فائدة الخبر. وقد ينزّل العالم بهما منزلة الجاهل لعدم جريه على مقتضى علمه.

The Modes of a Judgment

When a declarer intends by his declaration to convey knowledge [of a judgment] to the addressee, he should express it with no more [emphasis] than is necessary, [considering the state of the addressee], so that he avoids useless speech.

Judgments are of three classes with respect to the state of the addressee:

أقسام الحكم

ينبغي للمخبر إذا قصد بخبره إفادة المخاطب أن يقتصر من التركيب على قدر الحاجة حذرًا من اللغو.؛

أقسام الحكم من حيث حال المخاطب ثلاثة:

1. If the mind of the addressee is neutral to the judgment and is not hesitant about it, then the judgment does not need emphasis.
2. If the addressee is hesitant regarding the judgment and solicits it, then it is advisable to reinforce the judgment with something that would give it emphasis in order that it eliminate his hesitation.
3. If the addressee is denying the judgment, then it becomes necessary to add emphasis commensurate to the denial, that is, it becomes necessary to amplify the emphasis in proportion to the denial in order to eliminate it.

    Thus Allah ﷻ says, relating the words of the messengers sent to the town after they had been accused of lying the first time, *innā ilaykum mursalūna* ("Verily, we have been sent to you!") (Q 36:14), adding emphasis with *inna* (verily) and by the fact that the sentence is nominal. He says the second time, *rabbunā yaʿlamu innā ilaykum la-mursalūna* ("Our Lord knows: verily we have indeed been sent to you!") (Q 36:16), adding emphasis with an oath, *inna*, the *lām*, and the fact that the sentence is nominal, because the people being addressed had amplified their denial in saying, "You are but human beings like us, and the All-Merciful has not sent down anything. You are but lying" (Q 36:15).

The first mode [of expressing a judgment] is termed *initiating*, the second *answering*, and the third *insisting*. Expressing one's speech in these ways is termed the *expected mode of expression*, i.e., in accordance with what the apparent situation demands, for it does not involve diverging from the apparent situation.

Formulating One's Speech in an Unexpected Manner

This is of three types.

١- فإن كان المخاطب خالي الذهن من الحكم والتردّد فيه استغنى عن مؤكّدات الحكم.

٢- وإن كان متردّدًا فيه طالبًا له حَسُن تقويته بمؤكّد ليزيل ذلك المؤكّد تردّده.

٣- وإن كان المخاطب منكرًا للحكم وجب توكيده بحسب الإنكار أي يجب زيادة التأكيد بحسب ازدياد الإنكار إزالة له.

كما قال الله تعالى حكاية عن الرسل إلى القرية إذ كُذّبوا في المرّة الأولى ﴿فَقَالُوٓاْ إِنَّآ إِلَيۡكُم مُّرۡسَلُونَ﴾ [٣٦/ ١٤] مؤكّدًا بـ«إنّ» وإسميّة الجملة، وفي المرّة الثانية ﴿رَبُّنَا يَعۡلَمُ إِنَّآ إِلَيۡكُمۡ لَمُرۡسَلُونَ﴾ [٣٦/ ١٦] مؤكّدًا بالقسم و«إنّ» واللام وإسميّة الجملة لمبالغة المخاطبين في الإنكار حيث قالوا ﴿مَآ أَنتُمۡ إِلَّا بَشَرٞ مِّثۡلُنَا وَمَآ أَنزَلَ ٱلرَّحۡمَٰنُ مِن شَيۡءٍ إِنۡ أَنتُمۡ إِلَّا تَكۡذِبُونَ﴾ [٣٦/ ١٥].

ويسمّى الضرب الأول ابتدائيًّا والثاني طلبيًّا والثالث إنكاريًّا. ويسمّى إخراج الكلام على هذه الوجوه إخراجًا على مقتضى الظاهر أي مقتضى ظاهر الحال حيث لم يكن فيه عدول عن ظاهر الحال.

إخراج الكلام على خلاف مقتضى ظاهر الحال

وهو ثلاثة أنواع.

Type 1: Treating Someone Who Has Not Asked a Question As Someone Who Has Speech is oftentimes formulated in an unexpected manner such that someone who has *not* asked a question is treated as someone who has. This occurs when the person who has not asked a question is presented with [a situation] that intimates some information, causing him to anticipate the information in the manner of an inquirer who has not made up his mind. An example [of such formulation] is His saying ﷻ to Nūḥ ﷺ, "And address Me not concerning those who did wrong; surely they shall be drowned" (Q 11:37), that is, "And entreat me not, O Nūḥ, on behalf of your people nor ask that I delay their punishment." These words imply that their punishment was deserved, so the case became a case of the addressee's being unsure whether they were sentenced to drown or not; thus, "Surely they shall be drowned" was stated with emphasis. His statement ﷻ "Surely they shall be drowned" was formulated differently from what the apparent situation demanded since the apparent situation would not have called for emphasis, yet He added emphasis on account of the anticipation and uncertainty just mentioned.

Type 2: Treating Someone Who Has Not Denied As Someone Who Has Someone who has *not* issued any denial might be treated as someone who has done so when he manifests some sign of denial, e.g.,

jā'a Shaqīqun ʿāriḍan rumḥahu
Shaqīq came forth, his spear unpoised—

inna banī ʿammika fīhim rimāḥ
"Indeed, your uncle's tribe has spears!"[1]

[1] The meaning is as follows: This man came forth with his spear displayed at width, pridefully handling his spear in a careless manner to demonstrate his courage, which betrays great self-conceit on his part and a belief that none of his uncle's tribe would rise to challenge him, as if all of them were unarmed and not one of them had a spear. Thus, he was told, "Steer clear and out of their way, lest their spears fall upon you all at once and the tips of their spears be heaped on you—indeed, your uncle's tribe has spears aplenty!"

النوع الأول: جعل غير السائل كالسائل وكثيرًا ما يخرج الكلام على خلافه فيجعل غير السائل كالسائل إذا قدّم إلى غير السائل ما يشير له بالخبر فيستشرف الخبر وينظر إليه استشراف الطالب المتردّد، نحو قوله تعالى لنوح عليه السلام ﴿وَلَا تُخَٰطِبْنِي فِي ٱلَّذِينَ ظَلَمُوٓاْ إِنَّهُم مُّغْرَقُونَ﴾ [١١/ ٣٧] أي «ولا تدعني يا نوح في شأن قومك واستبطاء العذاب عنهم» فهذا كلام يشعر بأنه قد حقّ عليهم العذاب فصار المقام مقام أن يتردّد المخاطب في أنهم هل صاروا محكومًا عليهم بالإغراق أم لا فقيل «إنهم مغرقون» مؤكّدًا. فقوله تعالى «إنهم مغرقون» أخرج على خلاف مقتضى الظاهر لأن مقتضاه أن لايؤكّد لكنه أكّد لما ذكر من الاستشراف والتردّد.

النوع الثاني: جعل غير المنكر كالمنكر ويجعل غير المنكر كالمنكر إذا لاح عليه شيء من أمارة الإنكار، نحو:

جَـــاءَ شَـقِـيـــقٌ عَـارِضًـــا رُمْـحَـــهُ
إِنَّ بَـنِـــي عَـمِّـــكَ فِـيـهِـــمْ رِمَـــاحْ[١]

[١] والمعنى: جاء هذا الرجل واضعًا رمحه عرضًا مفتخرًا بتصريف الرماح مدلًّا بشجاعته دالًّا ذلك على إعجاب شديد منه واعتقاد بأنه لا يقوم إليه أحد من بني أعمامه كأنهم كلّهم عزلٌ ليس مع أحد منه رمح فقيل له «تنكّب وخلّ لهم طريقهم لئلّا تتزاحم عليك رماحهم وتتراكم عليك أسنّتها؛ إن بني عمّك فيهم رماح كثيرة».

which bears emphasis with *inna*.

مؤكّدًا بـ«إنّ».

Type 3: Treating Someone Who Has Denied As Someone Who Has Not Someone who *has* issued a denial might be treated as someone who has not done so when he has proofs and evidence available that would make him desist from his denial if he were to contemplate them, e.g., to tell someone who denies Islam, "Islam is true," without adding emphasis because that denier [already] possesses proofs that indicate the truth of Islam. His statement ﷻ "There is no doubt in it" (Q 2:2) is in this vein, treating something that exists as if it did not on the basis that there exists another thing that should eliminate it, for He has treated the doubt of those who doubt as though it did not exist, in consideration of the fact that there exists what should dispel it.

النوع الثالث: جعل المنكر كغير المنكر ويجعل المنكر كغير المنكر إذا كان مع المنكر ما أي شيء من الدلائل والشواهد إن تأمّله ارتدع عن إنكاره، كقولك لمنكر الإسلام «الإسلام حقّ» من غير تأكيد لأن مع ذلك المنكر دلائل دالّة على حقيّة الإسلام. ونظير هذا المثال قوله تعالى ﴿لَا رَيْبَ فِيهِ﴾ [٢/ ٢] لتنزيل وجود شيء منزلة عدمه بناء على وجود ما يزيله فإنه نزّل ريب المرتابين منزلة عدمه تعويلًا على وجود ما يزيله.

❋ ❋ ❋

The same—that is, the same as what applies in the case of affirmation—applies in the case of negation. To a person who is neutral [to the judgment], one says, *mā Zaydun qā'iman* (Zayd is not standing); to a person soliciting the judgment, *mā Zaydun bi-qā'imin* (Zayd truly is not standing); and to a person denying [the judgment], *wa-Llāhi mā Zaydun bi-qā'imin* (By Allah, Zayd truly is not standing!). One may extrapolate to other cases.

وهكذا أي مثل اعتبارات الإثبات اعتبارات النفي، فتقول لخالي الذهن «ما زيد قائمًا» ولطالب الحكم «ما زيد بقائم» وللمنكر «والله ما زيد بقائم»؛ وعلى هذا القياس.

Predication As Such May Be Either Literal or Nonliteral

كون مطلق الإسناد إما حقيقة عقلية أو مجازا عقليا

Literal Predication Literal predication[8] is that a verb or a word with verbal import—e.g., the infinitive noun, the active participle, the passive participle, the participial, the comparative/superlative, or the adverb of place/time—be predicated of [an agent] to which the speaker apparently believes that it belongs, i.e., insofar as can be discerned from his out-

الحقيقة العقلية وهو إسناد الفعل أو معناه كالمصدر واسم الفاعل واسم المفعول والصفة المشبّهة وأفعل التفضيل والظرف إلى ما هو له عند المتكلّم في الظاهر أي فيما يفهم من ظاهر

ward state by the fact that he provides no contextual indication that he believes that [the verb or the word with verbal import] does not belong to [that agent].

Literal predication is of four types:

1. The first is that which corresponds to both reality and [the speaker's true] belief, e.g., a believer's stating, "Allah made the vegetation sprout."
2. The second is that which corresponds to [the speaker's] belief alone, e.g., an ignorant person's stating, "Spring made the vegetation sprout."
3. The third is that which corresponds to reality alone, e.g., a Muʿtazilī's telling someone unaware of his doctrine, which he is concealing from the person, "Allah has created all actions."
4. The fourth is that which corresponds to neither reality nor [the speaker's] belief, e.g., to state, "Zayd came," when you know that he did not come.

Nonliteral Predication Nonliteral predication is that a verb or a word with verbal import be predicated of [a subject] associated with it to which it does *not* belong—i.e., of [a subject] other than the agent in the active voice or of [a subject] other than the object in the passive voice—regardless whether that other [subject] be other [than the agent or object] in actual reality or according to what the speaker apparently believes, [and that this predication prompt] an interpretive process. That entails that the verb or the word with verbal import be predicated of [a subject] other than that to which it belongs by [prompting] an interpretive process in which one seeks that to which it [really] belongs. Ultimately, this entails that the speaker has employed a contextual indicant that deflects the predication from that to which it belongs.

Verbs and words with verbal import have numerous associations. They associate with the agent, the object, the infinitive [notion], the time, the place,

حاله بأن لا ينصب قرينة دالّة على أنه غير ما هو له في اعتقاده.

وأقسامها أربعة:

١- الأول ما يطابق الواقع والاعتقاد جميعًا، كقول المؤمن «أنبت الله البقل».

٢- الثاني ما يطابق الاعتقاد فقط، نحو قول الجاهل «أنبت الربيع البقل».

٣- الثالث ما يطابق الواقع فقط، كقول المعتزلي لمن لا يعرف حاله وهو يخفيها منه «خلق الله الأفعال كلها».

٤- الرابع ما لا يطابق الواقع ولا الاعتقاد، نحو قولك «جاء زيد» وأنت تعلم أنه لم يجئ.

المجاز العقلي وهو إسناد الفعل أو معناه إلى ملابس له غير ما هو له أي غير الفاعل في المبني للفاعل وغير المفعول به في المبنى للمفعول سواء كان ذلك الغير غيرًا في الواقع أو عند المتكلّم في الظاهر بتأوّل أي يكون إسناد الفعل أو معناه إلى غير ما هو له بتأوّل بأن تطلب ما يؤول إليه وحاصله أن ينصب المتكلّم قرينة صارفة عن أن يكون الإسناد إلى ما هو له.

للفعل ومعناه ملابسات شتّى: يلابس الفاعل والمفعول به والمصدر والزمان والمكان والسبب،

and the cause, but they do not associate with the action-accompaniment, the circumstance, or their like. Literal [predication] is their being predicated of the agent in the active voice and of the object in the passive voice; their being predicated of anything else by virtue of association is nonliteral [predication]. Examples:

1. *ʿīshatin rāḍiyatin* (a content life) (Q 101:7), an example of that which, though active, is predicated of the object (since the life is what one is content with).[9]
2. *saylun mufʿamun* (an inundated flood), an example of that which, though passive, is predicated of the agent (since the flood is what inundates, i.e., fills, a valley).[10]
3. *jadda jidduhu* (His exerting of effort exerted effort) for [the signified notion] of the infinitive noun.[11]
4. *nahāruhu ṣāʾimun* (His day is fasting) for the time (since the person is fasting in the day).[12]
5. *nahrun jārin* (a flowing riverbed) for the place (since the water is flowing in the riverbed).[13]
6. *banā al-amīru al-madīnata* (The governor built the city) for the cause.[14]

Nonliteral predication is of four types:

1. The predicate and its subject are both literal, e.g., "Spring made the vegetation sprout," for this is nonliteral only in the relation and not in the terms.
2. The predicate and its subject are both nonliteral,[15] e.g., "The youthfulness of the season enlivened the earth," that is, "Springtime activated the forces of growth within the earth."
3. The subject is nonliteral but not its predicate, e.g., "The youthfulness of the season made the vegetation sprout."

ولا يلابس المفعول معه والحال ونحوهما. فإسناده إلى الفاعل إذا كان مبنيًّا للفاعل أو المفعول إذا كان مبنيًّا له حقيقة وإسناده إلى غيرهما للملابسة مجاز. الأمثلة:

١- ﴿عِيشَةٍ رَّاضِيَةٍ﴾ [١٠١/ ٧] فيما بني للفاعل وأسند إلى المفعول به، إذ العيشة مرضيّة.

٢- «سيل مفعَم» فيما بني للمفعول وأسند إلى الفاعل، لأن السيل هو الذي يفعِم أي يملأ الوادي.

٣- «جدّ جدّه» في المصدر.

٤- «نهاره صائم» في الزمان، لأن الشخص صائم في النهار.

٥- «نهر جارٍ» في المكان، لأن الماء جارٍ في النهر.

٦- «بنى الأمير المدينة» في السبب.

أقسام المجاز العقلي أربعة:

١- كون المسند والمسند إليه حقيقة، نحو «أنبت الربيعُ البقل» فالمجاز في النسبة فقط دون الطرفين.

٢- كونهما مجازين، نحو «أحيا الأرض شبابُ الزمان» أي «هيّج الربيعُ القوى النامية فيها».

٣- كون المسند إليه مجازًا دون المسند، نحو «أنبت البقل شبابُ الزمان».

4. The predicate is nonliteral but not its subject, e.g., "Spring enlivened the earth," that is, it "activated" it.

Nonliteral Predication in the Quran There is much nonliteral predication in the Quran—as in His statement ﷻ "And when His signs are recited to them, they increase in faith" (Q 8:2), where bringing an increase is predicated of the signs because they are a cause—and His saying, "He would slay their sons" (Q 28:4), His saying, "...when he stripped them of their raiment" (Q 7:27), and His saying, "...a day that would make children gray-haired" (Q 73:17).

[Contextual Indicants for Nonliteral Predication] Nonliteral predication must be indicated by a contextual indicant. The contextual indicant may be (1) *expressed*, e.g., [the phrase] *afnāhu qīlu Allāhi* (The word of Allah spells its end), i.e., "Allah's command and will,"[1] in the words of Abū al-Najm:

> *mayyaza ʿanhu qunzuʿan ʿan qunzuʿi*
> Upon [my head] is tuft from tuft withdrawn
>
> *jadhbu al-layālī abṭiʾī aw asriʿī*
> By the nightly tug—"Slow!" or "Quickly now!"—
>
> *afnāhu qīlu Llāhi li-l-shamsi iṭluʿī*
> Allah's word to the sun "Rise!" spells its end

[1] The fact that the poet placed [the word] *qīl* (word, saying) into grammatical *iḍāfa* with [the word] *Allāh* in his sentence is a contextual indicant that the attribution of *mayyaza* (withdrew, separated) to *jadhbu al-layālī* (the tug of nights) is nonliteral in his statement *mayyaza ʿanhu qunzuʿan ʿan qunzuʿin jadhbu al-layālī* (The tug of nights drew apart tuft from tuft [of hair] upon [my head]) (that is, the elapsing of nights). This is because this *iḍāfa* indicates that the one making the statement believes that it is Allah who wills, originates, and brings back.

٤- كون المسند مجازًا دون المسند إليه، نحو «أحيا الأرض الربيعُ» أي «هيّجها».

المجاز العقلي في القرآن المجاز العقلي في القرآن كثير، كقوله تعالى ﴿وَإِذَا تُلِيَتْ عَلَيْهِمْ ءَايَٰتُهُۥ زَادَتْهُمْ إِيمَٰنًا﴾ [٨/ ٢] أسندت الزيادة إلى الآيات لكونها سببًا، وقوله ﴿يُذَبِّحُ أَبْنَآءَهُمْ﴾ [٢٨/ ٤]، وقوله ﴿يَنزِعُ عَنْهُمَا لِبَاسَهُمَا﴾ [٧/ ٢٧]، وقوله ﴿يَوْمًا يَجْعَلُ ٱلْوِلْدَٰنَ شِيبًا﴾ [٧٣/ ١٧].

[قرينة المجاز العقلي] ولا بدّ له أي للمجاز العقلي من قرينة دالّة عليه سواء كانت (١) لفظيّة كـ«أفناه قيل الله» أي «أمر الله وإرادته»[١] في قول أبي النجم:

> مَيَّزَ عَنْهُ قُنْزُعًا عَنْ قُنْزُعِ
> جَذْبُ اللَّيَالِي أَبْطِئِي أَوْ أَسْرِعِي
> أَفْنَاهُ قِيلُ اللهِ لِلشَّمْسِ اِطْلُعِي

[١] فإضافة «قيل» إلى «الله» في كلامه قرينة على أن إسناد «ميّز» إلى «جذب الليالي» في قوله «ميّز عنه قنزعًا عن قنزعْ جذبُ الليالي» أي «مضيها» مجاز لأن هذه الإضافة تدلّ على أن القائل يعتقد أن الله هو المريد المبدئ المعيد.

Or the contextual indicant may be (2) *unexpressed*, as when it is rationally impossible for the predicate to belong to the subject, e.g., the statement "Love of you brought me to you"; when it would be impossible by normative experience, e.g., "The commander vanquished the troop"; or [when there are other considerations] like the fact that a monotheist is the one speaking, as in

> *ashāba al-ṣaghīra wa-afnā al-kabīra*
> The youth's hair is grayed, the aged man killed
>
> *karru al-ghadāti wa-marru al-ʿashī*
> By the recurrence of morn and the passing of eve[1]

for that fact is an unexpressed contextual indicant of nonliteral [predication].

[The Dispute about Nonliteral Predication] Al-Sakkākī denies nonliteral predication and considers it to be *metaphor with concealment*, which according to him is when one mentions the tenor of a simile and intends thereby the vehicle by means of a contextual indicant. A number of objections were raised against this view, but they can be rebutted by the response that his position is not that the tenor is mentioned and the vehicle intended literally, but his position is rather that the vehicle is intended by way of allegation and hyperbole, since it is obvious that the intended meaning of "death" in the statement "The claws of death dug into so-and-so" is not literally 'a predatory animal'. Al-Sakkākī mentions this explicitly in his book *al-Miftāḥ*, but the author [of *Talkhīṣ al-Miftāḥ*] was not aware of this.

أو (٢) معنويّة كاستحالة قيام المسند بالمسند إليه عقلًا كقولك «محبّتك جاءت بي إليك» أو عادةً نحو «هزم الأميرُ الجند» وكصدور الكلام عن الموحّد في مثل:

> أَشَابَ الصَّغِيرَ وأَفْنَى الكَبِيرَ
>
> كَرُّ الغَدَاةِ ومَرُّ العَشِي[١]

فإنه قرينة معنويّة على المجاز.

[الاختلاف في المجاز العقلي] وأنكر المجاز العقلي السكّاكي وجعله استعارة بالكناية وهي عنده أن تذكر المشبّه وتريد به المشبّه به بواسطة قرينة. ورُدّ باعتراضات، ودُفع بأنه ليس مذهبه أن يذكر المشبّه ويراد المشبّه به حقيقةً بل مذهبه أن يراد المشبّه به ادّعاءً ومبالغةً، لظهور أن ليس المراد بـ«المنيّة» في قولنا «مخالب المنيّة نشبت بفلان» هو السبع حقيقةً. والسكّاكي صرّح بذلك في كتابه المفتاح والمصنّف لم يطّلع عليه.

---

[1] The meaning of the verse is that the recurrence of days and the passing of nights makes the young old, gives the child white hair, and brings the aged man death.

[١] معنى البيت أن كرور الأيّام ومرور الليالي يجعل الصغير كبيرًا والطفل شائبًا والشيخ فانيًا.

Chapter 2

MODES OF THE SUBJECT

[What is meant by *modes of the subject*] is the modes that the subject may adopt by which to correspond to what the situation demands. These are numerous and include the following:

[1. Omission]

[The following are possible reasons] for omission of the subject:

1. to avoid what is unnecessary given the apparent meaning.
2. to give the impression that [the speaker] is employing the stronger of the two indicators, which are the intellect and the verbal expression,[16] e.g., [the poet's] saying,

   qāla lī kayfa anta qultu ʿalīlu
   He asked me, "How are you?" I said, "Ill:[1]

   saharun dāʾimun wa-ḥuznun ṭawīlu
   "Endless sleeplessness and lengthy grief"
3. to test the attentiveness of the listener or the extent of his attentiveness, given the presence of a contextual indicant.
4. to give the impression that one is safeguarding the subject from one's tongue or the reverse.[17]
5. [to leave room to deny one's intent] should need arise for denial.

[1] I.e., "I am ill."

الباب الثاني

أحوال المسند إليه

أي الأحوال العارضة التي بها يطابق اللفظ مقتضى الحال. وهي كثيرة، منها ما يلي:

[١. الحذف]

أما حذفه:

١- فللاحتراز عن العبث بناء على الظاهر.

٢- أو تخييل العدول إلى أقوى الدليلين من العقل واللفظ، كقوله:

قَالَ لِي كَيْفَ أَنْتَ قُلْتُ عَلِيلُ[١]

سَهَرٌ دَائِمٌ وحُزْنٌ طَوِيلُ

٣- أو اختبار تنبّه السامع عند القرينة أو مقدار تنبّهه.

٤- أو إيهام صونه عن لسانك أو عكسه.

٥- أو تأتّي الإنكار لدى الحاجة.

[١] أي «أنا عليل».

6. because there is nothing else that could be the subject or to give the impression that nothing else could be the subject.[18]

...or other reasons of this sort.

[2. Mention]

[The following are possible reasons] for mention of the subject:

1. because mention is the default mode and [the particular situation presents] no reason to depart from it.
2. out of precaution because [in the particular situation] it would be weak to depend on contextual indication.
3. to imply the stupidity of the listener.
4. to add clarity and confirmation.
5. to display the magnification or debasement of the subject.[19]
6. to seek blessings by or take pleasure in mentioning the subject.
7. to prolong one's speech when one wants to keep the attention [of the listener], e.g., "He said, 'It is my staff. I lean upon it...'" (Q 20:18).

[3. Rendering Definite]

As for rendering the subject definite:[20]

[Rendering Definite As a Personal Pronoun] [Rendering the subject definite] as a personal pronoun is done because the [particular] context pertains to the first person, the second person, or the third person.[21] The default case in the second person is that [the pronoun] refers to a specific person, but this can be disregarded so that it includes everyone who could be addressed, e.g., "Could you but see when the guilty bend their heads low before

٦- أو تعينّه أو ادّعاء التعيّن.

...أو نحو ذلك.

[٢. الذكر]

وأما ذكره:

١- فلكونه الأصل ولا مقتضى للعدول عنه.

٢- أو للاحتياط لضعف التعويل[٧] على القرينة.

٣- أو التنبيه على غباوة السامع.

٤- أو زيادة الإيضاح والتقرير.

٥- أو إظهار تعظيمه أو إهانته.

٦- أو التبرّك بذكره أو استلذاذه.

٧- أو بسط الكلام حيث الإصغاء مطلوب، نحو ﴿قَالَ هِيَ عَصَايَ أَتَوَكَّؤُاْ عَلَيْهَا﴾ [٢٠/ ١٨].

[٣. التعريف]

وأما تعريفه:

[التعريف بالإضمار] فبالإضمار لأن المقام للتكلّم أو الخطاب أو الغيبة. وأصل الخطاب أن يكون لمعيّن وقد يترك إلى غيره ليعمّ كل مخاطب، نحو ﴿وَلَوْ تَرَىٰٓ إِذِ ٱلْمُجْرِمُونَ نَاكِسُواْ رُءُوسِهِمْ عِندَ

their Lord" (Q 32:12), that is, "their condition will be manifest to the fullest extent [for all to see]": [the pronoun] is not restricted to any specific addressee.

[Rendering Definite As a Proper Name] [The following are possible reasons for rendering the subject definite] as a proper name:

1. to bring the subject specifically to mind for the listener immediately through a name specific to it, e.g., "Say, 'He, Allah, is One'" (Q 112:1).
2. to magnify or debase.
3. to utilize *implication*.[22]
4. to give the impression that one takes pleasure in the name or is seeking blessings through it.

[Rendering Definite As a Relative Pronoun] [The following are possible reasons for rendering the subject definite] as a relative pronoun:

1. because the addressee does not know the circumstances pertaining to the subject except for the relative clause, e.g., the statement "The person who was with us yesterday is a knowledgeable man."
2. because one finds it would be improper to explicitly mention the name.
3. to add confirmation, e.g., "But she in whose house he was staying sought to lure him from himself" (Q 12:23).[23]
4. to intensify, e.g., "And they were overwhelmed by that which enshrouded them of the sea" (Q 20:78).
5. to alert the addressee of an error, e.g.,

   inna alladhīna tarawnahum ikhwānakum
   Truly those whom you see as brothers
   of yours

رَبِّهِمْ﴾ [٣٢/ ١٢] أي «تناهت حالهم في الظهور» فلا يختصّ به مخاطب.

[التعريف بالعلميّة] وبالعلمية:

١- لإحضاره بعينه في ذهن السامع ابتداء باسم مختصّ به، نحو ﴿قُلْ هُوَ ٱللَّهُ أَحَدٌ﴾ [١١٢/ ١].

٢- أو تعظيم أو إهانة.

٣- أو كناية.

٤- أو إيهام استلذاذه أو التبرّك به.

[التعريف بالموصوليّة] وبالموصولية:

١- لعدم علم المخاطب بالأحوال المختصّة به سوى الصلة، كقولك «الذي كان معنا أمس رجل عالم».

٢- أو استهجان التصريح بالاسم.

٣- أو زيادة التقرير، نحو ﴿وَرَٰوَدَتْهُ ٱلَّتِي هُوَ فِي بَيْتِهَا عَن نَّفْسِهِۦ﴾ [١٢/ ٢٣].

٤- أو التفخيم، نحو ﴿فَغَشِيَهُم مِّنَ ٱلْيَمِّ مَا غَشِيَهُمْ﴾ [٢٠/ ٧٨].

٥- أو تنبيه المخاطب على خطأ، نحو:

إِنَّ الَّذِينَ تَرَوْنَهُمْ إِخْوَانَكُمْ

yashfī ghalīla ṣudūrihim an tuṣraʿū
Would have the thirst of their chests
quenched should you be felled[1]

6. to point to the reason that the predicate applies, e.g., "Truly those who are too arrogant to worship Me shall enter hell debased" (Q 40:60). [This pointing], furthermore, might be used as a means to allude to the magnification of [the predicate], e.g.,

inna alladhī samaka al-samāʾa banā lanā
He who elevated the heavens indeed
built for us

baytan daʿāʾimuhu aʿazzu wa-aṭwalu
A house whose pillars are stronger
and taller still[2]

Or [the pointing might be used as a means to allude to the magnification] of something besides [the predicate], e.g., "Those who denied Shuʿayb were themselves the losers" (Q 7:92);[25] or it might be utilized to affirm the predicate.

[Rendering Definite As a Demonstrative Pronoun]
[The following are possible reasons for rendering the subject definite] as a demonstrative pronoun:

1. to distinguish it in the most complete way, e.g., [the poet's] saying,

hādhā Abū al-Ṣaqri fardan fī maḥāsinihi
This is Abū al-Ṣaqr, unique in his merits,

يَـشْفِي غَلِيـلَ صُدُورِهِـمْ أَن تُصْرَعُـوا[١]

٦- أو الإيمـاء إلى وجـه بنـاء الخـبر، نحـو ﴿إِنَّ ٱلَّذِيـنَ يَسْـتَكْبِرُونَ عَـنْ عِبَادَتِي سَـيَدْخُلُونَ جَهَنَّـمَ دَاخِرِيـنَ﴾[٨] [٤٠/ ٦٠]؛ ثـم إنـه ربّما جُعـل ذريعة إلى التعريـض بالتعظيـم لشـأنه، نحـو:

إِنَّ الَّذِي سَـــمَكَ السَّـــمَاءَ بَنَى لَـنَـــا

بَـيْـتًـــا دَعَـائِمُـــهُ أَعَـــزُّ وأَطْـــوَلُ[٢]

أو شـأن غيره، نحـو ﴿ٱلَّذِيـنَ كَذَّبُـواْ شُـعَيْبًا كَانُـواْ هُـمُ ٱلْخَـٰسِرِيـنَ﴾ [٧/ ٩٢]؛ وقـد يُجعـل ذريعـة إلى تحقيـق الخبر.

[التعريف بالإشارة] وبالإشارة:

١- لتمييزه أكمل تمييز، نحو قوله:

هَـذَا أَبُو الصَّقْـرِ فَـرْدًا فِي مَـحَـاسِـنِـهِ

[1] I.e., O my sons, the people you believe are your brothers and upon whom you therefore depend in times of difficulty are such that it would satisfy the rancor and fire of enmity in their hearts were you to be brought down and afflicted with calamities. Beware, then! Do not trust them or depend on them. This evokes the sayings "Prudence is to think the worst" and "To trust all is impotence."

[2] *Samaka al-shayʾa / samkan* (he elevated the thing / *elevating*) is said of one's raising something up.[24]

[١] والمعنى: يـا بَنِيّ إن القـوم الذيـن تظنّونهـم إخوانكـم وتعتمـدون عليهـم في الشـدائد بمـا ظننتـم يـشفي مـا في صدورهم مـن غليل العـداوة وحرقتهـا أن تُصرعـوا وتُصابـوا بالحـوادث فإيّاكـم واستئمانهـم والاعتمـاد عليهـم. وفيـه إشـعار بقولهم «الحزم سـوء الظـنّ» و«الثقـة بكل أحـد عجـز».

[٢] يقال «سمك الشيء سمكًا» إذا رفعه.

min nasli Shaybāna bayna al-ḍāli wa-l-salami
Of the progeny of Shaybān between the *ḍāl* and *salam* trees[1]

2. to allude to the stupidity of the listener, e.g., [the poet's] saying,

   ulāʾika ābāʾī fa-jiʾnī bi-mithlihim
   Those are my forefathers; bring me then their like

   idhā jamaʿatnā yā Jarīru al-majāmiʿu
   If there be commonalities, Jarīr, that truly unite us[2]

3. to show the state of the subject in terms of proximity, remoteness, and intermediate distance, e.g., the statements *hādhā... / dhālika... / dhāka Zaydun* (This... / That [in the distance]... / That [right over there] is Zayd).
4. to demean through proximity, e.g., "Is this the one who makes mention of your gods?" (Q 21:36).
5. to magnify through remoteness, e.g., "Alif. Lām. Mīm. That is the book" (Q 2:1–2), or to demean [through remoteness], as when one says, "That accursed fellow did such and such."
6. to indicate, when what is pointed to takes successive descriptions, that it deserves the following [description] because of [the preceding description], e.g., "Those are the ones who act upon guidance from their Lord, and those are the ones who shall prosper" (Q 2:5).

مِـن نَسْـلِ شَيْبَـانَ بَيْنَ الضَّالِ والسَّـلَمِ[١]

٢- والتعريض بغباوة السامع، كقوله:

أُولَـئِـكَ آبَائِـي فَـجِـئْـنِـي بِـمِثْلِـهِـمْ
إِذَا جَـمَعَـتْـنَـا يَـا جَرِيـرُ المَجَامِـعُ[٢]

٣- أو بيـان حـاله في القـرب أو البعـد أو التوسّـط، كقولـك «هـذا... أو ذلـك... أو ذاك زيـد».

٤- أو تحقـيره بالقـرب، نحـو ﴿أَهَـٰذَا ٱلَّذِى يَذْكُرُ ءَالِهَتَكُمْ﴾ [٢١/ ٣٦].

٥- أو تعظيمـه بالبعـد، نحـو ﴿الٓمٓ ۝١ ذَٰلِكَ ٱلْكِتَـٰبُ﴾ [٢/ ١-٢]؛ أو تحقـيره، كمـا يقـال «ذلـك اللعـين فعـل كـذا».

٦- أو للتنبيـه عنـد تعقيـب المشـار إليـه بأوصـاف على أنـه جديـر بمـا يـرد بعـده مـن أجلهـا، نحـو ﴿أُوْلَـٰٓئِكَ عَلَىٰ هُدًى مِّن رَّبِّهِمْ وَأُوْلَـٰٓئِكَ هُمُ ٱلْمُفْلِحُونَ﴾ [٢/ ٥].

---

[1] The meaning is that this person being pointed to is the one who possesses the name that is well-known whenever it is mentioned, a man unique in his merits and virtues, of the progeny of Shaybān and the sons of this tribe who live in the desert. The Arabs consider living in the desert to be something praiseworthy because dignity is lost in urban life.

[2] The meaning of the verse is to reveal the incapacity [of the addressee], since [the poet] has already concluded that the addressee does not have the like of his forefathers.

[١] والمـعنى: هـذا المشـار إليـه صاحـب الاسـم المشـهور إذا ذكـر رجلًا فـردًا في محاسـنه وفضائلـه مـن نسـل شيبـان وأولاد هـذه القبيلـة المقيـمين بالباديـة، والإقامـة بهـا ممـا تمـدح بـه العـرب لأن فقـد العـزّ في الحضر.

[٢] ومـعنى البيـت التعـجيز لأنـه قـد تحقّـق عنـده أن ليـس للمخاطـب مثـل آبائـه.

[Rendering Definite with the *Lām*] [The following are possible reasons for rendering the subject definite] with the *lām*:

1. to signify a specific referent, e.g., *wa-laysa al-dhakaru ka-l-unthā* (And the male is not like the female) (Q 3:36), that is, "The one that she asked for is not like the one granted to her."[26]
2. to signify the very essence, e.g., to state, *al-rajulu khayrun min al-marʾati* (Men are better than women).[27]
3. [The *lām*] can also signify a thing that is single in virtue [merely] of its having specificity in the mind, e.g., to state, *udkhul al-sūqa* (Enter the market) when not referring specifically [to any market]. In terms of its meaning, this is like an indefinite noun.
4. It can also impart universality, e.g., *inna al-insāna la-fī khusrin* (Truly [every] man is in loss) (Q 103:2).

This is of two types. The first is that which is literal, e.g., *ʿālimu al-ghaybi wa-l-shahādati* (the Knower of the unseen and the seen) (Q 32:6), i.e., "all that is unseen or seen." The second is that which is conventional, e.g., to state, *jamaʿa al-amīru al-ṣāghata* (The governor gathered all the goldsmiths), i.e., "the goldsmiths of his city or realm."

Universality is more inclusive when applied to a singular noun, as shown by the fact that [the statement] *lā rijāla fī al-dāri* (There are not men in the house) is correct when there are one or two men,[28] unlike [the statement] *lā rajula...* (There is no man [in the house]). There is no incompatibility between universality and the noun's being singular, because the [universal *lām*] particle is affixed to a [singular noun] only when it lacks the meaning of

[التعريف باللام] وباللام:

١- للإشارة إلى معهود، نحو ﴿وَلَيْسَ ٱلذَّكَرُ كَٱلْأُنثَىٰ﴾ [٣/ ٣٦] أي «ليس الذي طلبت كالتي وهبت لها».

٢- أو إلى نفس الحقيقة، كقولك «الرجل خير من المرأة».

٣- وقد يأتي لواحد باعتبار عهديّته في الذهن، كقولك «ادخل السوق» حيث لا عهد؛ وهذا في المعنى كالنكرة.

٤- وقد يفيد الاستغراق، نحو ﴿إِنَّ ٱلْإِنسَٰنَ لَفِى خُسْرٍ﴾ [١٠٣/ ٢].

وهو ضربان: الأول حقيقي، نحو ﴿عَٰلِمُ ٱلْغَيْبِ وَٱلشَّهَٰدَةِ﴾ [١٣/ ٩] أي كل غيب وشهادة؛ الثاني عرفي، كقولنا «جمع الأمير الصاغة» أي صاغة بلده أو مملكته.

واستغراق المفرد أشمل بدليل صحّة «لا رجال في الدار» إذا كان فيها رجل أو رجلان دون «لا رجل...». ولا تنافي بين الاستغراق وإفراد الاسم لأن الحرف إنما يدخل عليه مجرّدًا عن معنى الوحدة

individuality and also because [the affixion of the particle to a singular noun] means "each individual" rather than "the individuals collectively." It is for this reason that one cannot qualify [such a noun] with a plural adjective.

[Rendering Definite through *Iḍāfa*] [The following are possible reasons for rendering the subject definite] through *iḍāfa*:

1. because it is the shortest way [in the particular situation] to bring the subject to the mind of the listener, e.g.,

   hawāya ma'a al-rakbi al-yamānīna muṣ'idun
   Away with the Yemeni riders journeys
   my love[1]

2. because it comprises (a) magnification of the *muḍāf ilayhi*, the *muḍāf*, or something else, e.g., to state, *'abdī ḥaḍara* (My servant was present), *'abdu al-khalīfati rakiba* (The servant of the caliph rode), or, *'abdu al-sulṭāni 'indī* (The servant of the sultan is with me), or it comprises (b) a demeaning,[29] e.g., *waladu al-ḥajjāmi ḥāḍirun* (The son of the cupper is present).

[4. Rendering Indefinite]

[The following are possible reasons] for rendering the subject indefinite:

1. to signify singularity, e.g., "And from the outskirts of the city, a man came running" (Q 36:20).

[1] *Hawāya* (my love) means "my beloved." *Rakb* (riders) is a collective noun for *rākib* (rider). *Yamānīna* is the plural of *yamān* in the sense of *yamanī* (Yemeni); the original form of *yamān* is *yamānī*, which was modified in the same way as *qāḍin* (judge). *Muṣ'idun* (journeying), the *'ayn* vowelized with *kasr*, is the predicate of *hawāya* (my love) and is derived from *aṣ'ada fī al-arḍi* (he journeyed upon the earth), i.e., "proceeded forward" through it, with the meaning that it is moving distant and traveling upon the earth.

ولأنه بمعنى «كل فرد» لا «مجموع الأفراد»[٩]، ولهذا امتنع وصفه بنعت الجمع.

[التعريف بالإضافة] وبالإضافة:

١- لأنها أخصر طريق لإحضاره في ذهن السامع، نحو:

هَوَايَ مَعَ الرَّكْبِ اليَمَانِينَ مُصْعِدٌ[١]

٢- أو لتضمّنها (١) تعظيمًا لشأن المضاف إليه أو المضاف أو غيرها، كقولك «عبدي حضر» و«عبد الخليفة ركب» و«عبد السلطان عندي»؛ أو (٢) تحقيرًا، نحو «ولد الحجّام حاضر».

[٤. التنكير]

وأما تنكيره:

١- فللإفراد، نحو ﴿وَجَآءَ مِنْ أَقْصَا ٱلْمَدِينَةِ رَجُلٌ يَسْعَىٰ﴾ [٣٦/ ٢٠].

[١] «هواي» أي «مهواي».[١٠] و«الركب» اسم جمع لـ«راكب». و«اليمانين» جمع «يمان» بمعنى «يمني» وأصل «يمان» «يماني» أعلّ إعلال «قاضٍ». و«مصعد» بكسر العين خبر «هواي» من «أصعد في الأرض» «مضى فيها» أي «مبعد ذاهب في الأرض».

2. to signify a special kind, e.g., "Upon their eyes is a covering" (Q 2:7).
3. to magnify or demean, e.g., [the poet's] saying,

   lahu ḥājibun fī kulli amrin yashīnuhu
   He takes [great] guard against all that
   would bring him disgrace

   wa-laysa lahu ʿan ṭālibi al-ʿurfi ḥājibu[1]
   Yet not [the least] guard before one who
   would seek his kindness

4. to signify (a) abundance, e.g., to state, "He has camels indeed," or, "He has sheep indeed," or (b) paucity, e.g., "But contentment from Allah is greater" (Q 9:72).[30]

The indefinite has been used to both magnify and signify abundance, e.g., "If they deny you, messengers [before you] were denied" (Q 35:4), i.e., "messengers of a great number with mighty signs."

[Cases] of rendering something besides the subject indefinite to signify singularity or a special kind include, for example, "And Allah created every beast from water" (Q 24:45); those to magnify include, for example, "Then take notice of a war from Allah and His messenger" (Q 2:279); and those to demean include, for example, "We do naught but make conjecture" (Q 45:32).

[5. Describing with Adjectives]

[The following are possible reasons] for describing the subject with adjectives:

1. because the adjectives clarify it and disclose its meaning, e.g., the statement *al-jismu al-ṭawīlu al-ʿarīḍu al-ʿamīqu yaḥtāju ilā farāghin yushghiluhu* (A height-possessing, width-possessing, and depth-possessing body requires empty space to occupy), and similar in terms of disclosure is [the poet's] saying,

[1] *Ḥājib* means *māniʿ* (preventative), *shayn* means *ʿayb* (disgrace), and *ʿurf* and *maʿrūf* mean *iḥsān* (good treatment).

٢- أو النوعيــة، نحو ﴿وَعَلَىٰٓ أَبْصَـٰرِهِمْ غِشَـٰوَةٌ﴾ [٢/ ٧].

٣- أو التعظيم أو التحقيقر، كقوله:

لَـهُ حَـاجِـبٌ فِـي كُـلِّ أَمْـرٍ يَـشِـيـنُـهُ
وَلَـيْـسَ لَه عَنْ طَالِبِ العُـرْفِ حَاجِبُ[١]

٤- أو (١) التكثـير، كقولهـم «إنّ له لَإبـلًا» و«إنّ له لَغنمًـا»؛ أو (٢) التقليـل، نحـو ﴿وَرِضْـوَٰنٌ مِّـنَ ٱللَّهِ أَكْبَرُ﴾ [٩/ ٧٢].

وقد جاء للتعظيم والتكثير، نحو ﴿وَإِن يُكَذِّبُوكَ فَقَدْ كُذِّبَتْ رُسُلٌ﴾ [٣٥/ ٤] أي «ذوو عدد كثير وآيات عظام».

ومـن تنـكير غيره للإفـراد أو النوعيـة نحـو ﴿وَٱللَّهُ خَلَـقَ كُلَّ دَآبَّـةٍ مِّـن مَّـآءٍ﴾ [٢٤/ ٤٥] وللتعظيـم نحـو ﴿فَأْذَنُـواْ بِحَـرْبٍ مِّـنَ ٱللَّهِ وَرَسُـولِهِۦ﴾ [٢/ ٢٧٩] وللتحـقير نحـو ﴿إِن نَّظُـنُّ إِلَّا ظَنًّـا﴾ [٤٥/ ٣٢].

[٥. الوصف]

وأما وصفه:

١- فلكونـه مبيّنًـا له كاشـفًا عـن معنـاه، كقولـك «الجسـم الطويـل العريض العميق يحتـاج إلى فراغ يشـغله». ونحـوه في الكشـف قـوله:

[١] و«الحاجــب» المانــع. و«الــشين» العيــب. و«العــرف» و«المعروف» الإحسان.

al-almaʿiyyu alladhī yaẓunnu laka al-ẓanna
A brilliant man, who makes deductions about you

ka-an qad raʾā wa-qad samiʿa
As though he had seen and had heard[1]

الأَلْـــمَعِيُّ الَّذِي يَظُـــنُّ لَـــكَ الظَّـــنَّ
كَأَنْ قَـــدْ رَأَى وَقَـــدْ سَـــمِعَا[١]

2. because the adjective specifies, e.g., *Zaydun al-tājiru ʿindanā* (Zayd the trader is with us).
3. because the adjective praises or censures, e.g., *jāʾanī Zaydun al-ʿālimu / al-jāhilu* (Zayd the scholar / the ignorant fellow came to me), when what is described is already specified prior to the introduction of the adjective.
4. because the adjective imparts emphasis, e.g., *amsi al-dābiru kāna yawman ʿaẓīman* (The just-elapsed past day was a great day).

٢- أو مخصّصًا، نحو «زيد التاجر عندنا».

٣- أو مدحًا أو ذمًّا، نحو «جاءني زيد العالم أو... الجاهل» حيث يتعيّن الموصوف قبل ذكره.

٤- أو تأكيدًا، نحو «أمس الدابر كان يومًا عظيمًا».

[6. Emphatic Apposition]

[The following are possible reasons] for emphatic apposition to the subject:

1. for confirmation.
2. to ward off the supposition of nonliteral usage, error, or lack of total inclusion.

[٦. التوكيد]

وأما توكيده:

١- فللتقرير.

٢- أو دفع توهّم التجوّز أو السهو أو عدم الشمول.

[7. Clarifying Apposition and Substitute Apposition]

As for clarifying apposition to the subject, [this may be done] to explain what it is with a name specific to it, e.g., "Your friend Khālid arrived."

As for substitute apposition to the subject, [this may be done] to add confirmation, e.g., *jāʾanī akhūka Zaydun* (Your brother Zayd came to me), *jāʾa al-qawmu aktharuhum* (Most of the people came), and *suliba ʿAmrun thawbuhu* (The garment of ʿAmr was stolen).

[٧. البيان والإبدال]

وأما بيانه فلإيضاحه باسم مختصّ به، نحو «قدم صديقك خالد».

وأما الإبدال منه فلزيادة التقرير، نحو «جاءني أخوك زيد» و«جاء القوم أكثرهم» و«سلب عمرو ثوبه».

[1] *Almaʿī* and *yalmaʿī* mean "an intelligent one with burning acumen."[31]

[١] «الألمعي» و«اليلمعي» الذكي المتوقّد ذكاء.

[8. Conjunction]

[The following are possible reasons] for conjunction:

1. to detail the subject in an abridged way, e.g., *jā'a Zaydun wa-'Amrun* (Zayd and *'Amr* came).
2. to detail the predicate likewise,[32] e.g., *jā'anī Zaydun fa-'Amrun / thumma 'Amrun* (Zayd and then [immediately / later] *'Amr* came to me), or *jā'anī al-qawmu ḥattā Khālidun* (The people, even Khālid, came to me).
3. to redirect the listener to the truth, e.g., *jā'anī Zaydun lā 'Amrun* (Zayd, not 'Amr, came).
4. to divert the predication to something else, e.g., *jā'anī Zaydun bal 'Amrun* (Zayd—rather, 'Amr—came) and *mā jā'anī 'Amrun bal Zaydun* (Not 'Amr but rather Zayd came).
5. because of doubt or to evoke doubt, e.g., *jā'anī Zaydun aw 'Amrun* (Zayd or 'Amr came).

[9. Separation]

As for separating the subject,[33] [this may be done] to render the predicate specific to it, e.g., *Zaydun huwa al-qā'imu* (Zayd is the one standing).

[10. Foregrounding]

[The following are possible reasons] for foregrounding the subject:

1. because the mention of the subject is more important, that is, either (1) because [foregrounding the subject] is the default condition and [the particular situation presents] no reason to depart from it or (2) in order to give the predicate a greater effect on the mind of the listener, since the subject leaves [the listener] in suspense with respect to the predicate, as in [the poet's] saying,

   wa-alladhī ḥārat al-bariyyatu fīhi
   That about which mankind is perplexed

[٨. العطف]

وأما العطف:

١- فلتفصيل المسند إليه مع اختصار، نحو «جاء زيد وعمرو».

٢- أو المسند كذلك، نحو «جاءني زيد فعمرو أو ...ثم عمرو» أو «جاءني القوم حتى خالد».

٣- أو ردّ السامع إلى الصواب، نحو «جاءني زيد لا عمرو».

٤- أو صرف الحكم إلى آخر، نحو «جاءني زيد بل عمرو» و«ما جاءني عمرو بل زيد».

٥- أو الشكّ أو التشكيك، نحو «جاءني زيد أو عمرو».

[٩. الفصل]

وأما فصله فلتخصيصه بالمسند، نحو «زيد هو القائم».

[١٠. التقديم]

وأما تقديمه:

١- فلكون ذكره أهمّ إما (١) لأنه الأصل ولا مقتضي[١] للعدول عنه وإما (٢) ليتمكّن الخبر في ذهن السامع لأن في المبتدأ تشويقًا إليه، كقوله:

وَالَّذِي حَارَتْ البَرِيَّةُ فِيهِ

ḥayawānun mustaḥdathun min jamādi
Is an animal made from lifeless matter

2. to hasten joy or distress in order to engender optimism or pessimism, e.g., "Saʿd [lit., 'good fortune'] is in your house" and "Saffāḥ [lit., 'shedder of blood'] is in the house of your friend."
3. to give the impression that the subject remains in one's mind or that one takes delight in nothing else.

...or other reasons of this sort.

[The Position of ʿAbd al-Qāhir] ʿAbd al-Qāhir[34] states: The subject might be foregrounded in order to imply that the verbal predicate[35] applies to it alone if it follows the negative particle, e.g., *mā ana qultu hādhā* (Not I [was it who] said this), i.e., "I did not say it, but it was said by someone else." For this reason it is not valid [to say], *mā ana qultu wa-lā ghayrī* (Not I [was it who] said [this] nor anyone else), *mā ana ra'aytu aḥadan* (Not I [was it who] saw anyone), nor, *mā ana ḍarabtu illā Zaydan* (Not I [was it who] hit [anyone] except Zayd).

If the subject does not follow a negative particle, then it might be foregrounded for the sake of specification in response to someone who claims either (1) that the verbal predicate applies exclusively to something other than the subject or (2) that that other thing shares in the verbal predicate, e.g., *ana saʿaytu fī ḥājatika* (I [am the one who] strove to fulfill your need). One adds emphasis in the former case by [a phrase] like "not someone else," and one adds emphasis in the latter case by [a phrase] like "by myself."

The subject might also be foregrounded to reinforce the predication, e.g., *huwa yuʿṭī al-jazīla* (He gives a great much). The same applies when the verb is negated, e.g., *anta lā takdhibu* (You do not lie), which is more emphatic in its negation of lying than *lā takdhibu* (You do not lie) and also more emphatic

حَيَوَانٌ مُسْتَحْدَثٌ مِنْ جَمَادِ

٢- وإما لتعجيل المسرّة أو المساءة للتفاؤل أو التطيّر، نحو «سعد في دارك» و«السفّاح في دار صديقك».

٣- وإما لإيهام أنه لا يزول عن الخاطر أو أنه لا يستلذّ إلا به.

...وإما لنحو ذلك.

[قول عبد القاهر] قال عبد القاهر: وقد يقدّم ليفيد تخصيصه بالخبر الفعلي إن ولي حرف النفي، نحو «ما أنا قلت هذا» أي «لم أقله مع أنه مقول لغيري» ولهذا لم يصح «ما أنا قلت ولا غيري» ولا «ما أنا رأيت أحدًا» ولا «ما أنا ضربت إلا زيدًا».

وإن لم يل[١٢] حرف النفي فقد يأتي للتخصيص ردًّا على من زعم (١) انفراد غيره به أو (٢) مشاركته فيه، نحو «أنا سعيت في حاجتك». ويؤكّد على الأول بنحو «لا غيري» وعلى الثاني بنحو «وحدي».

وقد يأتي لتقوية الحكم، نحو «هو يعطي الجزيل». وكذا إذا كان الفعل منفيًّا، نحو «أنت لا تكذب» فإنه أشدّ لنفي الكذب من «لا تكذب»

than *lā takdhibu anta* (You yourself do not lie) since the latter serves to emphasize the subject of the predication rather than the predication.

If the verb is predicated of an indefinite [subject], then [foregrounding the subject] gives it the function of specifying a category or a single thing, e.g., *rajulun jāʾanī* (A man [is who] came to me), i.e., "not a woman or two men."

And ʿAbd al-Qāhir states: If *kull* falls within the confines of a negation by succeeding a negative particle, e.g.,

> *mā kullu mā yatamannā al-marʾu yudrikuhu*
> Not all that a man wishes for does he attain

or by being governed by a negated verb—e.g., *mā jāʾa al-qawmu kulluhum* (Not all of the people came), *mā jāʾa kullu al-qawmi* (Not all of the people came), *lam ākhudh kulla al-darāhimi* (I did not take all of the dirhams), and *kulla al-darāhimi lam ākhudh* (All of the coins I did not take)—then the negation applies specifically to the universality, and [the statement] imparts that the action or quality does apply to some instances [of the grammatical agent or object]. Otherwise, the negation applies to every instance, as when Dhū al-Yadayn asked, "Did you shorten the ritual prayer or did you forget?" and the Prophet ﷺ stated, *kullu dhālika lam yakun* (Neither of those occurred), and this is the case with [the poet's] saying,

> *qad aṣbaḥat Ummu al-Khiyāri taddaʿī*
> Umm al-Khiyār has begun to accuse
>
> *ʿalayya dhanban kulluhu lam aṣnaʿi*
> Me of wrongs: None have I wrought

[11. Postponement]

As for postponing the subject, this may be done because the [particular] situation demands that one foreground the predicate.

وكذا من «لا تكذب أنت» لأنه لتأكيد المحكوم عليه لا الحكم.

وإن بني الفعل على منكر أفاد تخصيص الجنس أو الواحد به، نحو «رجل جاءني» أي لا امرأة ولا رجلان.

وقال عبد القاهر: إن كانت «كلّ» داخلة في حيّز النفي بأن تلت أداته نحو:

> مَا كُلُّ مَا يَتَمَنَّى المَرْءُ يُدْرِكُهُ

أو كانت معمولة للفعل المنفي — نحو «ما جاء القوم كلهم» أو «ما جاء كل القوم» أو «لم آخذ كل الدراهم» أو «كل الدراهم لم آخذ» — توجّه النفي إلى الشمول خاصّة وأفاد ثبوت الفعل أو الوصف لبعض أو تعلّقه به. وإلا عمّ كل فرد، كقول النبي ﷺ لمّا قال له ذو اليدين «أقصّرتَ الصلاة أم نسيتَ» «كل ذلك لم يكن»، وعليه قوله:

> قَدْ أَصْبَحَتْ أُمُّ الخِيَارِ تَدَّعِي
>
> عَلَيَّ ذَنْبًا كُلُّهُ لَمْ أَصْنَعِ

[١١. التأخير]

وأما تأخيره فلاقتضاء المقام تقديم المسند.

These abovementioned modes of the subject are all according to what the apparent situation demands. But speech can be formulated otherwise.

Alternative Formulations to What the Apparent Situation Demands

[Substituting with a Personal Pronoun]   A personal pronoun might be put in the place of an explicit noun, e.g., saying, *ni'ma rajulan* [*Zaydun*], in the place of *ni'ma al-rajulu Zaydun* (What a good man Zayd is), according to one of two positions,[36] and saying *huwa* or *hiya* in the place of *al-sha'nu* (the case is...) or *al-qiṣṣatu* (the fact is...) so that what follows has a greater effect on the mind of the listener, since when the listener does not understand a meaning from the pronoun, he awaits it.

[Substituting with an Explicit Noun]   This might be reversed; that is, an explicit noun[37] might be put in the place of a personal pronoun.

If [the explicit noun] is a demonstrative pronoun, then [the following are possible reasons why it may substitute for a personal pronoun]:

1. to give [the subject] the utmost distinction on account of its special possession of a noteworthy attribute, e.g., [the poet's] saying,

    kam 'āqilin 'āqilin a'yat madhāhibuhu
    How many a brilliant thinker whose doctrines fail

    wa-jāhilin jāhilin talqāhu marzūqā
    And an utter ignoramus you will find provisioned!

هذا الذي ذكر من أحوال المسند إليه كلّه مقتضى الظاهر، وقد يخرج الكلام على خلافه.

:إخراج الكلام على خلاف مقتضى الظاهر[13]

[الإبدال بالمضمر]   فيوضع المضمر موضع المظهر، كقولهم «نِعم رجلًا...» مكان «نِعم الرجل زيد» في أحد القولين وقولهم «هو» أو «هي» مكان الشأن أو القصّة ليتمكّن ما يعقبه في ذهن السامع لأنه إذا لم يفهم منه معنًى انتظره.

[الإبدال بالمظهر]   وقد يعكس أي وقد يوضع المظهر موضع المضمر.

فإن كان اسم إشارة:

١- فلكمال العناية بتمييزه لاختصاصه بحكم بديع، كقوله:

كَــمْ عَاقِــلٍ عَاقِـلٍ أَعْيَــتْ مَذَاهِبُــهُ

وَجَاهِــلٍ جَاهِــلٍ تَلْــقَاهُ مَــرْزُوقَــا

hādhā alladhī taraka al-awhāma ḥāʾiratan
This is what has left all minds perplexed

wa-ṣayyara al-ʿālima al-niḥrīra zindīqā
And made the well-versed scholar
a heretic[1]

2. to mock the listener, as when he lacks sight.
3. to announce how absolutely dull or clever the listener is.
4. to give the impression that the subject is entirely obvious. An example of this, applied to other than the subject, is

taʿālalti kay ashjā wa-mā biki ʿillatun
You feign illness to distress me, yet
you are not ill;

هَــذَا الَّــذِي تَــرَكَ الأَوْهَـامَ حَائِـرَةً

وَصَيَّــرَ العَالِــمَ النِّحْرِيــرَ زِنْدِيقَــا[١]

٢- أو التهكّم بالسامع، كما إذا كان فاقدًا البصر.

٣- أو النداء على كمال بلادته أو فطانته.

٤- أو ادّعاء كمـال ظهـوره، وعليـه مـن غـير بـاب المسـند إليـه:

تَعَالَلْـتِ كَــيْ أَشْجَى وَمَـا بِــكِ عِلَّـةٌ

---

[1] These two verses belong to Ibn al-Rāwandī and [are on the poetic meter called] *al-basīṭ*. Before them is

subḥāna man waḍaʿa al-ashyāʾa mawḍiʿahā
Glory to Him who placed all things in their places

wa-farraqa al-ʿizza wa-l-idhlāla tafrīqā
And made clear separation between nobility
and debasement

The second *ʿāqil* [in *ʿāqilin āqilin* (a brilliant thinker)] is an adjective for the first *ʿāqil* (thinker, one who is intelligent) and means "consummately intelligent," as in the statement *marartu bi-rajulin rajulin* (I passed by a manly man), i.e., "consummately manly." The meaning of *aʿyat madhāhibuhu* (his doctrines failed him) is that they incapacitated him and made his means of living difficult. A *niḥrīr* (one who is well-versed) (with the *nūn* vowelized with *kasr*) is someone who is proficient, skilled, intelligent, experienced, astute, and insightful in all matters because he slits the throat of knowledge. A *zindīq* (heretic) (with the *zāy* vowelized with *kasr*) is a dualist, someone who affirms light and darkness, someone who does not believe in the hereafter or in lordship, or someone who maintains a concealed disbelief while displaying belief, or it is an Arabization of *zin dīn*, which means "the woman's religion."

[١] البيتان لابن الراوندي، من البسيط. وقبلهما:

سُــبْحَانَ مَــنْ وَضَــعَ الأَشْــيَاءَ مَوْضِعَهَــا

وَفَــرَّقَ العِــزَّ وَالإِذْلَالَ تَـفْـرِيـقَـــا

و«عاقـل» الثاني صفـة لـ«عاقـل» الأول بمـعنى «كامـل العقـل متنـاه فيـه» كمـا يقـال «مـررت برجـل رجـل» أي «كامـل في الرجوليّـة». ومـعنى «أعيـت مذاهبـه» «أعجزتـه وصعّبـت عليه طرق معايشـه». و«النحريـر» بكسر النون الحاذق الماهـر العاقل المجـرّب المتقـن الفطن البـصير بكل شيء لأنه ينحـر العلم نحرًا. و«الزنديـق» بكسر الزاي مـن الثانوية أو القائل بالنـور والظلمة أو مـن لا يؤمـن بالآخـرة وبالربوبيّة أو مـن يبطن الكفـر ويظهر الإيمـان أو هـو معـرب «زن ديـن» أي «ديـن المرأة».

turīdīna qatlī qad ẓafirti bi-dhāliki
You desire to kill me—that
you have achieved[1]

i.e., *qad ẓafirti bihi* (you have achieved it).

If [the explicit noun that has been put in place of a personal pronoun] is something else, i.e., other than a demonstrative pronoun, then [the following are possible reasons for the substitution]:

1. to reinforce the impression [of the subject on the mind], e.g., "Say, 'He, Allah, is One. Allah is the Indomitable Recourse for all needs'" (Q 112:1–2). An analogous example applied to other than the subject is "In truth We sent it down, and in truth it descended" (Q 17:105).
2. to strike fear into the heart of the listener, inculcate (i.e., reinforce) a sense of awe, or further motivate compliance in someone whom one is commanding, e.g., the caliph's saying, "The commander of the believers orders you to do such and such." An example applied to other than the subject is "And when you are resolved, trust in Allah" (Q 3:159), since He did not say "in Me."
3. to seek sympathy, e.g., [the poet's] saying,

   ilāhī ʿabduka al-ʿāṣī atāka
   O God, Your sinful slave has come to you

[Shift of Person] Al-Sakkākī states: This[38] is not restricted to the subject or to this extent.[39] Rather, the grammatical first person, second person, and third person can each be changed for one another. This change is termed *shift of person*, e.g., [the poet's] saying, addressing himself,

تُرِيدِينَ قَتْلِي قَدْ ظَفِرْتِ بِذَلِكِ[١]

أي «قد ظفرتِ به».

وإن كان غيره أي غير اسم الإشارة:

١- فلزيادة التمكّن، نحو ﴿قُلْ هُوَ ٱللَّهُ أَحَدٌ ۝١ ٱللَّهُ ٱلصَّمَدُ﴾ [١١٢/ ١-٢]، ونظيره من غيره ﴿وَبِٱلْحَقِّ أَنزَلْنَٰهُ وَبِٱلْحَقِّ نَزَلَ﴾ [١٧/ ١٠٥].

٢- أو إدخال الروع في ضمير السامع أو تربية المهابة أي تقويتها أو تقوية داعي المأمور للامتثال، كقول الخلفاء «أمير المؤمنين يأمرك بكذا»، وعليه من غيره ﴿فَإِذَا عَزَمْتَ فَتَوَكَّلْ عَلَى ٱللَّهِ﴾ [٣/ ١٥٩] أي حيث لم يقل «عليّ».

٣- أو الاستعطاف، كقوله:

إِلَهِي عَبْدُكَ العَاصِي أَتَاكَ

[الالتفات] قال السكّاكي: هذا غير مختصّ بالمسند إليه ولا بهذا القدر بل ينقل من كل من التكلّم والخطاب والغيبة مطلقًا إلى الآخر ويسمّى هذا النقل التفاتًا، كقوله خطابًا لنفسه:

[1] *Taʿālalti* (you feigned illness) means *tamāraḍti*, which means "you put on the appearance of illness though you were not ill." *Kay ashjā* (to distress me) means *kay aḥzana*, which means "[so that] I grieve."

[١] «تعاللت» أي «تمارضت» يعني «أظهرتِ المرض مع أنك غير مريضة». «كي أشجى» أي «كي أحزن» يعني «أكون حزينًا».

taṭāwala layluka bi-l-Athmudi
Long was your night at Athmud[1]

The predominant view is that shift of person is to express a meaning in one of the three grammatical persons after having expressed it in a different one, and this is more specific [than on al-Sakkākī's view].

1. An example of shift from the first person to the second person is "'Why should I not worship Him who originated me and to whom you will be returned?'" (Q 36:22).
2. [From the first person] to the third person: "Truly We have bestowed abundant good upon you. So pray to your Lord and sacrifice" (Q 108:1–2).
3. From the second person to the first person:

ṭaḥā bika qalbun fī al-ḥisāni ṭarūbu
A heart enraptured by the fair ones
has carried you away

(i.e., "The exhilaration of your heart has taken you, O soul, upon every path and [made you expend] every effort in pursuit of the fair women")

buʿayda al-shabābi ʿaṣra ḥāna mashību
After the lapse of youth and at the onset
of old age;

yukallifunī Laylā wa-qad shaṭṭa walyuhā
It burdens me with Laylā. Far has her
nearness gone,

تَطَاوَلَ لَيْلُكَ بِالأَثْمُدِ[١]

والمشهور أن الالتفات هو التعبير عن معنًى بطريق من الثلاثة بعد التعبير عنه بآخر منها؛ وهذا أخصّ.

١- مثال الالتفات من التكلّم إلى الخطاب ﴿وَمَا لِيَ لَآ أَعْبُدُ ٱلَّذِى فَطَرَنِى وَإِلَيْهِ تُرْجَعُونَ﴾ [٣٦/ ٢٢].

٢- وإلى الغيبة ﴿إِنَّآ أَعْطَيْنَٰكَ ٱلْكَوْثَرَ ۝١ فَصَلِّ لِرَبِّكَ وَٱنْحَرْ﴾ [١٠٨/ ١-٢].

٣- ومن الخطاب إلى التكلّم:

طَحَا بِكَ قَلْبٌ فِي الحِسَانِ طَرُوبُ

أي «ذهب بك أيّها النفس كل طريق فرحُ القلب ونشاط في طلب الامرآت الحسان»

بُعَيْدَ الشَّبَابِ عَصْرَ حَانَ مَشِيبُ

يُكَلِّفُنِي لَيْلَى وَقَدْ شَطَّ وَلْيُهَا

[1] The poet is Imruʾ al-Qays al-Kindī the Companion ﵁, and [the poem] is the first qasida of the *mutaqārib* era. The rest of the verse is

wa-nāma al-khaliyyu wa-lam tarqudi
The carefree one slept but you did not sleep

Athmud (with *fatḥ* of the *hamza* and *ḍamm* of the *mīm*, though *kasr* of both has been transmitted) is the name of a place. In Meḥmed Zihnī Efendī's *al-Qawl al-jayyid*, it is vowelized with *fatḥ* of the *hamza* and *mīm*.

[١] قائله امرؤ القيس الكندي الصحابي رضي الله عنه وهو أول قصيدة من المتقارب وتمامه:

وَنَامَ الخَلِيُّ وَلَمْ تَرْقُدِ

و«الأثمد» بفتح الهمزة وضمّ الميم وروي بكسرهما اسم موضع، وفي القول الجيّد لمحمد ذهني أفندي بفتح الهمزة والميم.

wa-ʿādat ʿawādin baynanā wa-khuṭūbu
And vicissitudes and circumstances set between us anew[1]

i.e., "It burdens you with Laylā and the situation is that her nearness has become far and obstacles and momentous matters have come between us." Thus this involves a shift from the second person to the first person.

4. [From the second person] to the third person: "Even when you are sailing in ships, till, when they travel on them by [good] winds…" (Q 10:22).
5. From the third person to the first person: "And Allah is He who sends the winds; then they cause clouds to rise. Then We drive them…" (Q 35:9).
6. [From the third person] to the second person: "…Master of the day of judgment. You we worship" (Q 1:4–5).

The principle behind shift of person is that when speech changes from one mode to another, this better refreshes the energy of the listener and rouses his attention. Shifts of person sometimes carry specific subtleties, as is the case in [Sūrat] al-Fātiḥa. For when the servant mentions with a mindful heart Him who is deserving of praise he finds an impulse within himself that moves him to turn to

[1] *Ṭaḥā bika* (has carried you away) means "has expanded and taken you upon every path." *Ṭarūbu* (enraptured) is derived from *ṭarab*, which is giddy delight; in other words, "it is enraptured in pursuit of the fair ones and energetic in wooing them." *Buʿayda al-shabābi* (after the lapse of youth) means "when youth has elapsed just on the point of availing [your heart]." *ʿAṣra ḥāna mashību* (at the onset of old age) means "the time at which old age had approached and advanced to attack." *Shaṭṭa* means *baʿuda* (has become far). *Waly* means *qurb* (nearness). *ʿAwādī* are obstacles, and *ʿawādī al-dahr* are the obstacles of destiny. *Khuṭūb* is the plural of *khaṭb*, namely, a momentous matter.

وَعَادَتْ عَــوَادٍ بَـيْـنَـنَــا وَخُطُــوبُ[١]

أي «يكلّفك ليلى والحال قد بعُد وليُها وصارت موانع بيننا وأمور عظيمة» ففيه التفات من الخطاب إلى التكلّم[١٤].

٤- وإلى الغيبة ﴿حَتَّىٰٓ إِذَا كُنتُمْ فِى ٱلْفُلْكِ وَجَرَيْنَ بِهِم بِرِيحٍ﴾ [١٠/ ٢٢].

٥- ومن الغيبة إلى التكلّم ﴿وَٱللَّهُ ٱلَّذِىٓ أَرْسَلَ ٱلرِّيَٰحَ فَتُثِيرُ سَحَابًا فَسُقْنَٰهُ﴾ [٣٥/ ٩].

٦- وإلى الخطاب ﴿مَٰلِكِ يَوْمِ ٱلدِّينِ ۝٤ إِيَّاكَ نَعْبُدُ﴾ [١/ ٤-٥].

ووجهه أن الكلام إذا نقل من أسلوب إلى أسلوب كان أحسن تطرية لنشاط السامع وأكثر إيقاظًا للإصغاء إليه. وقد تختصّ مواقعه بلطائف كما في الفاتحة فإن العبد إذا ذكر الحقيق بالحمد عن قلب حاضر يجد من نفسه محرّكًا للإقبال عليه وكلّما أجرى

[١] ومعنى «طحا بك» أي «اتّسع وذهب بك كل مذهب». و«طروب» مأخوذ من «الطرب» وهو استخفاف القلب في الفرح أي «له طرب في طلب الحسان ونشاط في مراودتهنّ». ومعنى «بعيد الشباب» «حين ولّى وكاد ينصره». ومعنى «عصر حان مشيب» أي «زمان قرب المشيب وإقباله على الهجوم». ومعنى «شطّ» «بعُد». و«الولى» القرب. و«العوادي» الصوارف، و«عوادي الدهر» عوائقه. و«الخطوب» جمع «خطب» وهو الأمر العظيم.

Him. And every time he proceeds to recount one among those great attributes, that impulse grows stronger, until reaching the culmination: that He is the master of the entire affair on the day of recompense. At this point that impulse—on account of its having attained the utmost strength—necessarily moves [the servant] to turn to Him and address Him, singling Him out for complete submission and for assistance in all matters of significance.

[Responding in a Way Different Than What the Interlocutor Expects] One way of diverging from what the [apparent situation] demands is to respond to an interlocutor in a way that he does not expect by interpreting his words differently than he intended in order to make the point that such is what he should more rightly have intended, e.g., al-Qabaʿtharā's saying to al-Ḥajjāj—the latter having told him as a threat, *la-aḥmilannaka ʿalā al-adhami* (I will have you conveyed in shackles)—*mithlu al-amīri yuḥmilu ʿalā al-adhami wa-l-ashhabi* (Someone like the emir has people conveyed upon both black horses and gray horses), i.e., "For someone like the emir in sovereignty and openhandedness, it is fitting that he give (*yuṣfid*), not that he shackle (*yaṣfid*)."

[Giving an Answer Different Than What the Questioner Seeks] [Another way of departing from the apparent situation] is to give someone who asks a question an answer different from what he seeks by treating his question as if it were a different question in order to make the point that such is more befitting of his circumstance or more important for him, e.g., His saying ﷻ, "They ask you about the new moons. Say, 'They are markers of time for mankind and for the hajj'" (Q 2:189), and His saying ﷻ, "They ask you what they should spend. Say, 'Let whatever of your wealth you spend be for parents, kinsfolk, orphans, the indigent, and the traveler'" (Q 2:215).

[Referring to the Future with Expressions That Signify the Past] Another [way of departing from the apparent situation] is to refer to the future by an ex-

عليه صفة من تلك الصفات العظام قوي ذلك المحرّك إلى أن يؤول الأمر إلى خاتمتها المفيدة أنه مالك الأمر كلّه في يوم الجزاء فحينئذ يوجب ذلك المحرّك لتناهيه في القوّة[١٥] الإقبال عليه والخطاب بتخصيصه بغاية الخضوع والاستعانة في المهمّات.

[تلقّي المخاطب بغير ما يترقّب] ومن خلاف المقتضى تلقّي المخاطب بغير ما يترقّب بحمل كلامه على خلاف مراده تنبيهًا على أنه هو الأولى بالقصد، كقول القبعثرى للحجّاج وقد قال له متوعّدًا «لأحملنّك على الأدهم» «مثل الأمير يحمل على الأدهم والأشهب» أي «من كان مثل الأمير في السلطان وبسطة اليد فجدير بأن يُصفد (أي يعطي) لا أن يَصفد (أي يقيّد)».

[تلقّي السائل بغير ما يتطلّب] أو تلقّي السائل بغير ما يتطلّب بتنزيل سؤاله منزلة غيره تنبيهًا على أنه الأولى بحاله أو المهمّ له، كقوله تعالى ﴿يَسْـَٔلُونَكَ عَنِ ٱلْأَهِلَّةِ قُلْ هِىَ مَوَٰقِيتُ لِلنَّاسِ وَٱلْحَجِّ﴾ [٢/ ١٨٩] وكقوله تعالى ﴿يَسْـَٔلُونَكَ مَاذَا يُنفِقُونَ قُلْ مَآ أَنفَقْتُم مِّنْ خَيْرٍ فَلِلْوَٰلِدَيْنِ وَٱلْأَقْرَبِينَ وَٱلْيَتَـٰمَىٰ وَٱلْمَسَـٰكِينِ وَٱبْنِ ٱلسَّبِيلِ﴾ [٢/ ٢١٥].

[التعبير عن المستقبل بلفظ الماضي] ومنه التعبير عن المستقبل بلفظ الماضي تنبيهًا على

pression that signifies the past in order to make the point that [the event] will really occur, e.g., *wa-nufikha fī al-ṣūri fa-ṣaʿiqa man fī al-samāwāti wa-man fī al-arḍi* (And the trumpet will be blown [lit., "was blown"], whereupon whosoever is in the heavens and on the earth will swoon [lit., "swooned"]) (Q 39:68). Similar to this is *wa-inna al-dīna la-wāqiʿun* (And truly the judgment will come to pass) (Q 51:6), and similar is *dhālika yawmun majmūʿun lahu al-nāsu* (That is a day on which mankind will be gathered together) (Q 11:103).

[Inversion] Another [way of departing from the apparent situation] is inversion, e.g., "I presented the camel to the trough." Al-Sakkākī accepts inversion unconditionally and others reject it unconditionally, but the truth is that it is to be accepted when it contains some subtle significance, e.g., [the poet's] saying,

> *wa-mahmahin mughbarratin arjāʾuhu*
> And many a wasteland of dusty boundaries
>
> *Kaʾanna lawna arḍihi samāʾuhu*
> As though the color of its ground were
> its sky[1]

i.e., "were the color of its sky." Otherwise, it is rejected, e.g., [the poet's] saying in describing a camel as fat,

> *kamā ṭayyanta bi-l-fadani al-sayāʿā*
> As you plastered the mud and straw
> with the castle

meaning, "as you plastered the castle with mud and straw." A *fadan* is a castle, and *sayāʿ* is mud mixed with chopped straw.

[1] A *mahmah* (wasteland) is a distant desert and a desolate region, and its plural is *mahāmih*. *Mughbarra* (dusty) means colored with dust. *Arjāʾ* (boundaries) means limits and side regions and is the plural of *rajan*, which is *maqṣūr* [meaning that its original *yāʾ* has been converted to an *alif*].40

تحقّق وقوعه، نحو ﴿وَنُفِخَ فِي ٱلصُّورِ فَصَعِقَ مَن فِي ٱلسَّمَٰوَٰتِ وَمَن فِي ٱلْأَرْضِ﴾ [٣٩/ ٦٨] ومثله ﴿وَإِنَّ ٱلدِّينَ لَوَٰقِعٌ﴾ [٥١/ ٦] ونحوه ﴿ذَٰلِكَ يَوْمٌ مَّجْمُوعٌ لَّهُ ٱلنَّاسُ﴾ [١١/ ١٠٣].

[القلب] ومنه القلب، نحو «عرضتُ الناقةَ على الحوض». وقبله السكّاكي مطلقًا وردّه غيره مطلقًا والحقّ أنه إن تضمّن اعتبارًا لطيفًا قُبل، كقوله:

> وَمَهْمَهٍ مُغْبَرَّةٍ أَرْجَاؤُهُ
> كَأَنَّ لَوْنَ أَرْضِهِ سَمَاؤُهُ[١]

أي «لون سمائه»؛ وإلا ردّ، كقوله في وصف الناقة بالسمن:

> كَمَا طَيَّنْتَ بِالفَدَنِ السَّيَاعَا

والمعنى «كما طيّنت الفدن بالسياع». «الفدن» القصر و«السياع» الطين المخلوط بالتبن.

[١] و«المهمه» المفازة البعيدة والبلد المقفر، والجمع «مهامه». و«المغبرة» المتلوّنة بالغبرة. و«الأرجاء» الأطراف والنواحي جمع «رجًا» مقصورًا.

Chapter 3

MODES OF THE PREDICATE

1. As for the omission and mention of the predicate, [this may be done] for the rhetorical effects discussed regarding the subject.

2. As for rendering the predicate a simple expression, [this may be done] because [the particular situation entails that] the predicate not be resumptive, e.g., *Zaydun qā'imun* (Zayd is standing). An example of a *resumptive predicate* is *Zaydun abūhu munṭaliqun* (Zayd his father [sic] is departing).

3. As for [rendering] the predicate a verb, [this may be done] to qualify it with one of the [three] times while signifying renewal.[41]

4. As for [rendering] the predicate a noun, [this may be done] to indicate that it is not bound to one of the [three] times.

5. As for qualifying a verb with an actional accusative or its like,[42] this is done to convey additional meaning.

6. As for qualifying a verb with a condition, this is done due to considerations that cannot be understood without understanding the specific differences between the conditional operators[43] as explained in the science of grammar. Here, however, we must examine [the conditional particles] *in*, *idhā*, and *law*.

In and *idhā* are used for future conditions, but the default signification of *in* is lack of certainty that the

الباب الثالث

أحوال المسند

١- أما حذفه وذكره فلما مرّ في المسند إليه من النكات.

٢- وأما إفراده فلكونه غير سببي، نحو «زيد قائم». والسببي نحو «زيد أبوه منطلق».

٣- وأما كونه فعلًا فللتقييد بأحد الأزمنة مع إفادة التجدّد.

٤- وأما كونه اسمًا فلإفادة عدم التقيّد بأحد الأزمنة.

٥- وأما تقييد الفعل بمفعول ونحوه فلزيادة الفائدة.

٦- وأما تقييده بالشرط فلاعتبارات لا تعرف إلا بمعرفة ما بين أدواته من تفصيل بُيّن في علم النحو؛ ولكن لا بدّ من النظر ههنا في «إن» و«إذا» و«لو».

فـ«إن» و«إذا» للشرط في الاستقبال؛ لكن أصل «إن» عدم الجزم بوقوع الشرط وأصل «إذا»

condition will be met, and the default signification of *idhā* is certainty that it will be met. And because both are used to connect one thing to another in the future, each clause in both cases is a future verbal sentence. This [rule] cannot be contravened in terms of the verbal expression except to make some rhetorical point, like treating an event that has not occurred as an event that has occurred, [which is done] (a) due to the collective strength of the factors that will cause its occurrence, (b) due to the effective similarity of the future event to an event that has occurred, (c) to evoke optimism, or (d) to display desire that the event occur.

Law is used for a condition in the past when one is certain that the condition has not been met, entailing nonoccurrence in the past with respect to both of its clauses. Thus, when it precedes an imperfect tense verb as in *wa-law tarā idh wuqifū ʿalā al-nāri* (If you could see when they are arraigned before the fire) (Q 6:27), this serves to conjure the image, as in His stating ﷻ, *fa-tuthīru saḥāban* (Then they cause clouds to rise) (Q 30:48), conjuring that wondrous image that bespeaks the dazzling divine power.

١٠الجزم بوقوعه. ولكونهما لتعليق أمر بغيره في الاستقبال كان كلٌّ من جملتَي[١٦] كلٍّ فعليّةً استقباليّةً. ولا يخالَف ذلك لفظًا إلا لنكتة كإبراز غير الحاصل في معرض الحاصل (١) لقوّة الأسباب المتآخذة في حصوله أو (٢) كون ما هو للوقوع كالواقع أو (٣) التفاؤل أو (٤) إظهار الرغبة في وقوعه.

و«لو» للشرط في الماضي مع القطع بانتفاء الشرط فيلزم عدم الثبوت والمضي في جملتيها. فدخولها على المضارع في نحو ﴿وَلَوْ تَرَىٰٓ إِذْ وُقِفُوا۟ عَلَى ٱلنَّارِ﴾ [٦/ ٢٧] لاستحضار الصورة كما في قوله تعالى ﴿فَتُثِيرُ سَحَابًا﴾ [٣٠/ ٤٨] استحضارًا لتلك الصورة البديعة الدالّة على القدرة الباهرة.

7. As for rendering the predicate indefinite, [this may be done] (a) because one intends neither exhaustiveness nor specific reference or (b) to intensify, e.g., *hudan li-l-muttaqīna* (a [great] guidance for the reverent) (Q 2:2).

٧- وأما تنكيره (١) فلإرادة عدم الحصر والعهد أو (٢) للتفخيم نحو ﴿هُدًى لِّلْمُتَّقِينَ﴾ [٢/ ٢].

8. As for specifying the predicate with *iḍāfa* or by describing it with an adjective, this is done to more fully complete the conveyed meaning.

٨- وأما تخصيصه بالإضافة أو الوصف فلتكون الفائدة أتمّ.

9. As for rendering the predicate definite, [this may be done] (a) to convey a judgment to the listener about [a subject] that he would recognize through one of the modes of definiteness by [using a predicate that he would likewise recognize through one of the modes of definiteness] , e.g., *Zaydun akhūka* (Zayd is your brother) and *ʿAmrun al-munṭaliqu* (ʿAmr is the one departing). Rendering definite can

٩- وأما تعريفه (١) فلإفادة السامع حكمًا على أمر معلوم له بإحدى طرق التعريف [بآخر مثله] نحو «زيد أخوك» و«عمرو المنطلق»،

also convey (b) that a generic category is confined to an individual thing either actually, e.g., *Zaydun al-amīru* (Zayd is the [only] emir), or hyperbolically, when that category is perfected in the thing, e.g., *ʿAmrun al-shujāʿu* (ʿAmr is the courageous one).

(٢) وقــد يفيــد التعريــف قصر الجنــس على شيء تحقيقًــا نحــو «زيــد الأمير»، أو (٣) مبالغــة لكمــاله فيــه نحــو «عمــرو الشــجاع».

10. As for [rendering] the predicate a clause, [this may be done] (a) to strengthen [the predication] or (b) because [the particular situation entails that] the predicate be resumptive as discussed above.

١٠- وأمــا كونــه جملــة (١) فللتقــوّي أو (٢) لكونــه سببيًّــا كمــا مــرّ.

11. As for foregrounding the predicate, this is done to single it out for the subject, e.g., *lā fīhā ghawlun* (Therein [i.e., in the drinks of paradise] no headiness lies) (Q 37:47), i.e., as opposed to the wines of this worldly life.

١١- وأمــا تقديمــه فلتخصيصــه بالمســند إليــه، نحــو ﴿لَا فِيهَــا غَــوْلٌ﴾ [٣٧/ ٤٧] أي بخلاف خمــور الدنيــا.

Chapter 4

MODES OF VERBAL OBJECTS

الباب الرابع

أحوال متعلقات الفعل

A verb alongside an object is like a verb alongside an agent in that the purpose of mentioning either of them alongside the verb is to convey that the action is connected with it: as for the agent, [that connection concerns] the agent's performance of the action, and as for the object, [that connection concerns] the object's receipt of the action.

الفعل مع المفعول كالفعل مع الفاعل في أن الغرض من ذكره معه إفادة تلبّس الفعل بكل منهما؛ أما بالفاعل فمن جهة وقوعه عنه وأما بالمفعول فمن جهة وقوعه عليه.

[Providing No Object]

When no object is provided for a transitive verb, then if the intended purpose is simply to affirm or negate of an agent [the performance of] the action (i.e., the occurrence),[44] without regard for the recipient of the action, then the verb is relegated to the status of an intransitive verb, and no implicit object is supplied, so that the [action] becomes general and is not arbitrarily specified. But if the intended purpose involves the action's connection to an unmentioned object, it is necessary to supply an implicit [object] as suits the context.

[عدم ذكر المفعول به]

فإذا لم يذكر المفعول به مع الفعل المتعدّي فالغرض إن كان إثبات الفعل أي الحدث لفاعله أو نفيه عنه مطلقًا من غير تعلّقه بمن وقع عليه نزّل منزلة اللازم ولم يقدّر له مفعول قصدًا للتعميم دفعًا للتحكّم، وإن قصد تعلّقه بمفعول غير مذكور وجب التقدير بحسب القرائن.

[Omitting the Object]

Now, [the following are possible reasons] for the omission of [an intended, implicit] object [merely] from the expressed speech:

[حذف المفعول به]

ثم إن حذف المفعول من اللفظ:

1. to [produce the effect of] clarification after ambiguity, as with the verb of will, e.g., "Had He willed,[1] He could surely have guided you[2] all" (Q 6:149), i.e., "Had Allah willed that you be guided, He could surely have guided you all."
2. to prevent the mistaken supposition that something is intended that is not intended, e.g.,

   wa-sawrati ayyāmin ḥazazna ilā al-ʿaẓmi
   And the brutality of days that cut
   to the bone

   i.e., "the brutality of days that cut flesh to the bone." Had flesh been mentioned, one might have imagined before the rest was mentioned that the cutting did not reach to the bone.
3. to maintain [a rhyme on] the final word [in successive segments of speech].
4. because one finds the object's mention would be improper.
5. for some other fine point.

[1] Ambiguity.

[2] This is clarification.

١- إمـا للبيـان بعـد الإبهام، كمـا في فعل المشـيئة نحو ﴿فَلَوْ شَآءَ[١] لَهَدَىٰكُمْ[٢] أَجْمَعِينَ﴾ [٦/ ١٤٩] أي «فلـو شـاء الله هدايتكـم لهداكـم أجمعين».

٢- وإما لدفع توهّم إرادة غير المراد، نحو:

وَسَوْرَةِ أَيَّامٍ حَزَزْنَ إِلَى العَظْمِ

أي «شـدّة أيّـام قطعن اللحـم إلى العظـم» فلو ذكر اللحـم لربّمـا توهّـم قبل ذكـر ما بعـده أن الحـزّ لم ينتـه إلى العظم.

٣- وإما لرعاية الفاصلة.

٤- وإما لاستهجان ذكره.

٥- وإما لنكتة أخرى.

[١] إبهام.

[٢] هذا بيان.

Chapter 5

RESTRICTION

Lexically, *qaṣr* (restriction) means "confining"; technically, it means "specifying one thing with another in a specific way." What is meant by the "way" is the methods of restriction that we will discuss below.

[The Types of Restriction]

Restriction is of two types: *real restriction*, in which the specification pertains to what is real and in actual fact, and *relative restriction*, in which the specification pertains to something else.

Real restriction may be (1) to restrict the thing described to the attribute, e.g., "Zayd is nothing but a writer." There are virtually no instances of this because it is practically impossible to comprehensively know the attributes of a thing and to affirm one but negate all others. Or it may be (2) to restrict an attribute to the thing described, e.g., "There is not in the house but Zayd," i.e., "There are no others in it." One might intend this hyperbolically, when one does not give full consideration except to the thing mentioned.

Relative restriction may be (1) to restrict the thing described to the attribute, e.g., "Zayd is nothing but standing" in the sense of "not sitting" but without the meaning that he has no attributes at all beyond standing. Or it may be (2) to restrict an attribute to

الباب الخامس

القصر

وهو لغة الحبس واصطلاحًا تخصيص شيء بشيء بطريق مخصوص، والمراد بالطريق ما يفيد القصر مما سيأتي ذكره.

[أقسام القصر]

وهو قسمان: (١) حقيقي بأن يكون التخصيص بحسب الحقيقة وفى نفس الأمر (٢) وإضافي بأن يكون التخصيص بالنسبة إلى شيء آخر.

القصر الحقيقي إما (١) قصر الموصوف على الصفة، نحو «ما زيد إلا كاتب»، وهو لا يكاد يوجد لتعذّر الإحاطة بصفات شيء وإثبات واحدة منها ونفي ما عداها؛ وإما (٢) قصر الصفة على الموصوف، نحو «ما في الدار إلا زيد» أي «ليس فيها غيره»، وقد يقصد به المبالغة لعدم الاعتداد بغير المذكور.

القصر الإضافي إما (١) قصر الموصوف على الصفة، نحو «ما زيد إلا قائم» أي «لا قاعد» لا أنه لا يتجاوز من القيام إلى صفة أخرى أصلًا؛ (٢) وإما قصر الصفة

the thing described, e.g., "No one is standing but Zayd" in the sense of "ʿAmr is not" but without the meaning that no one at all besides Zayd can be described as standing.

Restriction is of three types with respect to the belief of the addressee: restriction for exclusivity, restriction for inversion, and restriction for specification. These [three types are all possible in] His saying, "'You we worship'" (Q 1:5): this is *restriction for exclusivity* if the addressee believes that worship is due to Allah and to idols both; it is *restriction for inversion* if he believes that worship is due to idols but not Allah ﷻ; and it is *restriction for specification* if he believes that worship is due to either Allah or idols, that is, to whichever one chooses. In restriction for specification, the two descriptions need not be mutually exclusive. Consequently, restriction for specification is possible in any instance where restriction for exclusivity or inversion is possible, but not vice versa.

The Methods of Restriction

There are six methods of restriction. Two of these we have already mentioned in the chapters on the predicate and the subject: they are (1) the intervention of the *separative pronoun*, e.g., *Zaydun huwa al-ʿālimu* (Zayd is *the* scholar), and (2) rendering definite with the *lām*, e.g., *wa-laysa al-dhakaru ka-l-unthā* (And the male is not like the female) (Q 3:36) and the statement *al-dhahabu khayrun min al-fiḍḍati* (Gold is better than silver).

There remain four:

1. The first is conjunction with *lā*, *bal*, or *lākin*, e.g., the statements *Zaydun shāʿirun lā kātibun* (Zayd is a poet, not a writer), *mā Zaydun kātiban bal shāʿirun* (Zayd is not a writer but rather a poet), and *mā Zaydun qāʿidan lākin qāʾimun* (Zayd is not sitting but rather standing).

على الموصوف، نحو «ما قائم إلا زيد» أي «لا عمرو» لا أنه لا يوصف بالقيام غير زيد أصلًا.

وهو باعتبار اعتقاد المخاطب ثلاثة أقسام: قصر إفراد، قصر قلب، قصر تعيين. وهذه قوله تعالى ﴿إِيَّاكَ نَعْبُدُ﴾ [١/ ٥] هو قصر إفراد إن اعتقد المخاطب أن العبادة تكون لله وللأصنام جميعًا، وقصر قلب إن اعتقد أن العبادة تكون للأصنام لا لله تعالى، وقصر تعيين إن اعتقد أن العبادة إما لله وإما للأصنام يعني أيّهما شئت. وهو أي قصر التعيين أعمّ من أن يكون الوصفان فيه متنافيين أو لا فكل مثال يصلح للإفراد والقلب يصلح للتعيين من غير عكس.

طرق القصر

طرق القصر[١٨] ستّة: اثنتان منها قد ذكرناهما في باب المسند والمسند إليه وهما توسّط ضمير الفصل نحو «زيد هو العالم» والتعريف باللام نحو ﴿وَلَيْسَ ٱلذَّكَرُ كَٱلْأُنثَىٰ﴾ [٣/ ٣٦] ونحو قولك «الذهب خير من الفضّة».

وبقيت منها أربعة:

١- الأول العطف بـ«لا» و«بل» و«لكنْ»، كقولك «زيد شاعر لا كاتب»، «ما زيد كاتبًا بل شاعر»، «ما زيد قاعدًا لكن قائم».

2. The second is negation followed by exception, e.g., the statement "Zayd is nothing but a poet."
3. The third is *innamā*, e.g., <u>*innamā*</u> *Zaydun kātibun* (Zayd is but a writer).
4. The fourth is to foreground what would otherwise be postponed, e.g., the statement *tamīmiyyun ana* (A Tamīmī I am).

٢- الثـاني النـفي والاسـتثناء، كقولـك «مـا زيـد إلا شـاعر».

٣- الثالث «إنما»، كقولك «إنما زيد كاتب».

٤- الرابع تقديـم مـا حقّـه التأخـير، كقولـك «تميـمي أنـا».

Chapter 6

NON-DECLARATIVE SPEECH

الباب السادس

الإنشــــاء

Lexically, *inshāʾ* (non-declarative speech) means "to create"; technically, it refers to speech that cannot take on truth or falsity. Non-declarative speech [divides into] that which comprises a request and that which does not comprise a request. This science concerns the kind that comprises a request—like commands, prohibitions, and so forth. The kind that does not comprise a request includes the forms of praise, censure, speech acts, oaths, expressions of wonderment, expressions of hope, and so forth.

وهــو لغــة الإيجــاد واصطلاحًــا كلام لا يحتمــل صدقًــا ولا كذبًــا. وهــو طــلبي وغير طــلبي؛ والطــلبي هــو المقصــود في هــذا الفــنّ كالأمــر والنهي وغيرهمــا وغير الطــلبي كصيــغ المــدح والذمّ والعقــود والقســم والتعجّــب والرجــاء ونحوهــا.

There are various kinds of non-declarative speech.

والإنشاء أنواع.

[Command]

[الأمر]

The first type is command, which is to request the addressee's performance of an act. The chosen position regarding commands and prohibitions is that it is not a necessary condition that one see oneself as superior in rank—whether the one issuing [the command or prohibition] is actually superior or not—since [the request to perform an act] is what one immediately understands when one hears the form of a command or prohibition. There are four forms of command:

1. the second-person imperative, e.g., *iḍrib* (Hit).
2. the third-person imperative, e.g., *li-yaḍrib* (Let him hit).

الأول الأمــر وهــو طلــب حصــول الفعــل مــن المخاطــب. والمختــار عــدم اشتراط الاســتعلاء في الأمــر والنهي ســواء صــدر مــن العــالي في الواقــع أم لا لتبــادر الفهــم عنــد ســماع صيغتيهمــا إليــه. وصيغتــه أربعــة:

١- أمر الحاضر، كـ«اضرب».

٢- أمر الغائب، نحو «ليضرب».

3. an imperative quasi-verbal noun, e.g., *mah* (Stop!).
4. an infinitive noun substituting for an imperative verb.

The imperative form can diverge from its original meaning, which is obligating, to other meanings like supplicating, threatening, demonstrating incapable, declaring permissible, giving one's permission, posing a choice, and other things.

[Prohibition]

The second type is prohibition, which is to request that [the addressee] refrain from something. It has one form, namely, the imperfect tense verb preceded by *lā*. The prohibitive form can diverge from its original meaning to other meanings like supplicating, politely soliciting, instructing, wishing, threatening, and other things.

[Inquiry]

The third type is inquiry, which may be [expressed by the following]:

1. *hal* (Is it so that...?) for assentive knowledge, e.g., *hal qāma Zaydun* (Did Zayd stand?).
2. *mā* (what?) for the explanation of a noun.
3. *man* (who?) for an identification of rational beings, e.g., *man fī al-dāri* (Who is in the house?).
4. *ay* (which?) for distinction between two things that have something in common.
5. *kam* (how much/many?) for number.
6. *kayfa* (how?) for state.

٣- اسم الفعل الأمري، نحو «مه».

٤- المصدر النائب عن فعل الأمر.

وقد تخرج صيغة الأمر عن معناها الأصلي الذي هو الإيجاب والإلزام إلى معانٍ أخرى كالدعاء والتهديد والتعجيز والإباحة والإذن والتخيير وغير ذلك.

[النهي]

وهو طلب الكفّ عن شيء. وله صيغة واحدة وهي الفعل المضارع الداخل عليه «لا». وقد تخرج صيغة النهي عن معناها الأصلي إلى معانٍ أخرى كالدعاء والالتماس والإرشاد والتمنّي والتهديد وغيرها.

[الاستفهام]

الثالث الاستفهام وهو:

١- بـ«هل» للتصديق، نحو «هل قام زيد؟».

٢- بـ«ما» لشرح الاسم.

٣- بـ«من» للعارض المشخّص لذي العقول، نحو «من في الدار؟».

٤- بـ«أيّ» للتمييز بين المشتركين.

٥- بـ«كم» للعدد.

٦- بـ«كيف» للحال.

7. *ayna* (where?) for place.
8. *matā* (when?) for time.
9. *annā* with the meaning of *kayfa*.

Except *hal*, all of these mentioned above are [requests] for conceptual knowledge.

10. the *hamza* for conceptual or assentive knowledge.

[The following are possible reasons] for using interrogative words:

1. to express that one deems something slow, e.g., *kam daʿawtuka fa-lā tujību* (How many times has it been that I called you and you did not respond?).
2. to threaten, e.g., *a-lam uʾaddibu fulānan* (Did I not discipline so-and-so?).
3. to express wonderment, e.g., *mā liya lā arā al-hudhuda* ("How is it that I do not see the hoopoe?") (Q 27:20).
4. to elicit acknowledgment, e.g., *a-laysa Allāhu bi-kāfin ʿabdahu* (Does Allah not suffice His slave?) (Q 39:36).
5. to reject by way of rebuke, e.g., *a-taʾtūna al-dhukrāna* ("Do you approach males?") (Q 26:165).
6. to repudiate as false, e.g., *a-fa-aṣfākum rabbukum bi-l-banīna* (Did your Lord favor you with sons?) (Q 17:40).
7. to mock, e.g., *a-ṣalātuka taʾmuruka an natruka mā yaʿbudu ābāʾunā* ("Does your manner of praying require that we forsake what our fathers worshipped?") (Q 11:87).
8. to demean, e.g., *man hādhā* (Who is this?) though you know the person, to debase his status.

٧- بـ«أين» للمكان.

٨- بـ«متى» للزمان.

٩- بـ«أنّى» بمعنى «كيف».

وكل هذه المذكورات غير «هل» للتصوّر.

١٠- بالهمزة للتصوّر والتصديق.

وقد تستعمل أداة الاستفهام:

١- للاستبطاء، نحو «كم دعوتك فلا تجيب؟».

٢- وللوعيد، نحو «ألم أؤدّب فلانًا؟».

٣- وللتعجّب، نحو ﴿مَا لِيَ لَآ أَرَى ٱلْهُدْهُدَ﴾ [٢٧/ ٢٠].

٤- وللتقرير، نحو ﴿أَلَيْسَ ٱللَّهُ بِكَافٍ عَبْدَهُۥ﴾ [٣٩/ ٣٦].

٥- وللإنكار توبيخًا، نحو ﴿أَتَأْتُونَ ٱلذُّكْرَانَ﴾ [٢٦/ ١٦٥].

٦- أو تكذيبًا، نحو ﴿أَفَأَصْفَىٰكُمْ رَبُّكُم بِٱلْبَنِينَ﴾ [١٧/ ٤٠].

٧- وللتهكّم، نحو ﴿أَصَلَوٰتُكَ تَأْمُرُكَ أَن نَّتْرُكَ مَا يَعْبُدُ ءَابَآؤُنَآ﴾ [١١/ ٨٧].

٨- أو للتحقير، نحو «من هذا؟» استحقارًا لشأنه مع أنك تعرفه.

9. to evoke frightful awe, e.g., *man Ḥajjāj* (Who is Ḥajjāj?).
10. to evoke remorse or to reproach with a perfect tense verb, e.g., *hallā akramta Zaydan* (Why did you not honor Zayd?).
11. to exhort with an imperfect tense verb, e.g., *hallā taqūmu* (Why do you not stand?).

٩- أو للتهويل، نحو «من حجّاج؟».

١٠- وللتنديم أو التنديب في الماضي، نحو «هلّا أكرمتَ زيدًا؟».

١١- والتحضيض في المضارع، نحو «هلّا تقوم؟».

❋ ❋ ❋

Now, declarative speech may take the place of non-declarative speech

1. for the sake of optimism, [treating the predication] as if it has occurred and is now being conveyed as information, e.g., *waffaqaka Allāhu li-l-taqwā* (May Allah providentially lead you to God-consciousness).[45]
2. to display an eagerness that it occur, e.g., *wa-l-wālidātu yurḍiʿna awlādahunna* (And let mothers nurse their children...) (Q 2:233) and *wa-l-muṭallaqātu yatarabbaṣna* (Divorced women shall wait...) (Q 2:228).[46]

ثم الخبر قد يقع موقع الإنشاء:

١- تفاؤلًا حتى كأنه وقع فأُخبر عنه، نحو «وفّقك الله للتقوى».

٢- أو إظهارًا للحرص في وقوعه، نحو ﴿وَٱلْوَٰلِدَٰتُ يُرْضِعْنَ أَوْلَٰدَهُنَّ﴾ [٢/ ٢٣٣]، ﴿وَٱلْمُطَلَّقَٰتُ يَتَرَبَّصْنَ﴾ [٢/ ٢٢٨].

Chapter 7

BREAKING AND JOINING

الباب السابع

الفصل والوصل

Joining is to use conjunctions between sentences; breaking is to leave [sentences without conjunctions between them].

الوصل عطف بعض الجمل على بعض والفصل تركه.

Now, when a sentence follows another sentence, then either the first sentence possesses *positional inflection* or it does not.[47]

فإذا أتت جملة بعد جملة فالأُولى إما أن يكون لها محلّ من الإعراب أو لا.

[When the First Sentence Possesses Positional Inflection] If the first sentence possesses positional inflection, then if the second sentence is meant to share its inflection, it is conjoined to it like a word. The condition on which it is acceptable [to conjoin two sentences] with a *wāw* or the like is that there be some commonality between the [sentences], e.g., *Zaydun yaktubu wa-yushʿiru* (Zayd writes [prose] and he composes poetry) or …*yuʿṭī wa-yamnaʿu* ([Zayd] gives and he withholds), as opposed to cases like *Zaydun yaktubu wa-yuʿṭī* (Zayd writes and he gives) or … *yushʿiru wa-yamnaʿu* ([Zayd] composes poetry and he withholds); conjunction is invalid in the last two.

[إن كان للأولى محل من الإعراب] فإن كان للأولى محلّ من الإعراب فإن قصد تشريك الثانية لها في حكمه عطفت عليها كالمفرد. فشرط كونه مقبولًا بالواو ونحوه أن يكون بينهما جهة جامعة، نحو «زيد يكتب ويشعر أو ...يعطي ويمنع» بخلاف نحو «زيد يكتب ويعطي أو ...يشعر ويمنع» فلا يجوز فيهما العطف.

But if the second sentence is not meant to share the inflection of the first sentence, they are broken apart, e.g., *wa-idhā khalaw ilā shayāṭīnihim qālū innā maʿakum innamā naḥnu mustahziʾūna Allāhu yastahziʾu*

وإن لم يقصد تشريك الثانية للأولى فصلت عنها، نحو ﴿وَإِذَا خَلَوْاْ إِلَىٰ شَيَٰطِينِهِمْ قَالُوٓاْ إِنَّا مَعَكُمْ إِنَّمَا نَحْنُ مُسْتَهْزِءُونَ ١٤ ٱللَّهُ يَسْتَهْزِئُ

bihim (But when they are alone with their satans they say, "We are with you. We were only mocking." Allah mocks them...) (Q 2:14–15): in order to avoid implying that it is a direct quotation of the hypocrites, He did not conjoin *Allāhu yastahziʾu bihim* (Allah mocks them) to *innā maʿakum* (We are with you).

[When the First Sentence Lacks Positional Inflection] If the first sentence does not possess positional inflection, then if the second sentence is meant to be linked to it with the meaning of a conjunction other than the *wāw*, it is conjoined by means of that conjunction without the condition that [the sentences have] a common aspect, e.g., *dakhala Zaydun fa-kharaja ʿAmrun* (Zayd came in, then ʿAmr [immediately] went out) or ...*thumma kharaja ʿAmrun* ([Zayd came in], then ʿAmr [eventually] went out) when one intends immediate or delayed succession.

But if the second sentence is not meant to be linked to the first sentence with the meaning of a conjunction other than the *wāw*, then if the first sentence contains a semantic property (that is, a qualification) that is not meant to be given to the second sentence, it is necessary to break them up (i.e., not to conjoin them) so that the joining does not imply that they share that semantic property, e.g., *wa-idhā khalaw...* (But when they are alone...): in order to prevent *Allāhu yastahziʾu bihim* (Allah mocks them) from sharing the adverbial specification,[48] He did not conjoin it to *qālū* (they say).

However, if the first sentence does not have a semantic property (that is, a qualification that is extraneous to the meaning of the second sentence) or has a semantic property that is meant to be given to the second sentence as well, then look further:

بِهِمْ﴾ [٢/ ١٤-١٥] لم يعطف «الله يستهزئ بهم» على «إنا معكم» لئلّا يلزم أن يكون مقول قول المنافقين.

[إن لم يكن للأولى محل من الإعراب] وإن لم يكن للأولى محلّ من الإعراب فإن قصد ربطها بها على معنًى عاطف سوى الواو عطفت بذلك العاطف من غير اشتراط جهة جامعة، نحو «دخل زيد فخرج عمرو أو ...ثم خرج عمرو» إذا قصد التعقيب أو المهلة.

وإن لم يقصد ربط الثانية بالأولى على معنًى عاطف سوى الواو فإن كان للأولى حكم أي قيد لم يقصد إعطاؤه للثانية فالفصل أي ترك العطف واجب لئلّا يلزم من الوصل التشريك في ذلك الحكم، نحو «وإذا خلوا...» الآية لم يعطف «الله يستهزئ بهم» على «قالوا» لئلّا يشاركه في الاختصاص بالظرفيّة.

وإن لم يكن للأولى حكم أي قيد زائد على مفهوم الجملة الثانية أو يكون ولكن قصد إعطاؤه للثانية أيضا فانظر:

(A) If [one of the following is the case]:

1. There is *total disconnection* between the two sentences, and there is nothing that would misleadingly imply anything contrary to the intended meaning. This is the case when the sentences differ such that one is declarative and the other non-declarative, e.g., *māta fulānun raḥimahu Allāhu* (So-and-so died; may Allah have mercy on him)...
2. There is *total connection* between the two sentences by virtue of the second sentence's serving as (a) an emphatic appositive for the first, e.g., *dhālika al-kitābu lā rayba fīhi* (That is the book in which there is no doubt) (Q 2:2); (b) a substitute appositive for it, e.g., *amaddakum bi-mā taʿlamūna amaddakum bi-anʿāmin wa-banīna* (...who has succored you with what you know—who has succored you with cattle and children) (Q 26:132–133); or (c) a clarifying appositive for it, e.g., *fa-waswasa ilayhi al-Shayṭānu qāla yā Ādamu* (Then Satan whispered to him. He said, "O Adam...") (Q 20:120)...
3. There is *virtual disconnection* between the two sentences, e.g.,

   wa-taẓunnu Salmā annanī abghī bihā
   And Salmā supposes I would have another

   badalan urāhā fī al-ḍalāli tahīmu
   In her place. I find she wanders in delusion[1]

   since had *urāhā* (I find she...) been conjoined to *taẓunnu* (supposes), one might have mistakenly assumed that it were conjoined to *abghī* (I seek), and the meaning would have been vitiated...
4. There is *virtual connection* between the two sentences, e.g.,

[1] *Abghī* means *aṭlub* (I seek). The meaning of *urāhā fī al-ḍalāli tahīmu* (I find she wanders in delusion) is "My soul tells me that she is lost in delusion."

(أ) فإن:

١- كان بين الجملتين كمال الانقطاع بلا شيء يوهم خلاف المقصود وذلك بأن تختلفا خبرًا وإنشاءً، نحو «مات فلان رحمه الله»؛

٢- أو كان بينهما كمال الاتّصال بأن تكون الثانية مؤكّدة للأولى، نحو ﴿ذَٰلِكَ ٱلْكِتَٰبُ لَا رَيْبَ فِيهِ﴾ [٢/ ٢]؛ أو بدلًا منها، نحو ﴿أَمَدَّكُم بِمَا تَعْلَمُونَ ﴿١٣٢﴾ أَمَدَّكُم بِأَنْعَٰمٍ وَبَنِينَ﴾[١٩] [٢٦/ ١٣٢-١٣٣]؛ أو عطف بيان لها، نحو ﴿فَوَسْوَسَ إِلَيْهِ ٱلشَّيْطَٰنُ قَالَ يَٰٓـَٔادَمُ...﴾ الآية [٢٠/ ١٢٠]؛

٣- أو كان بينهما شبه كمال الانقطاع، نحو:

وَتَظُنُّ سَلْمَى أَنَّنِي أَبْغِي بِهَا
بَدَلًا أُرَاهَا فِي الضَّلَالِ تَهِيمُ[١]

إذ لو عطف «أراها» على «تظنّ» لتوهّم أنه معطوف على «أبغي» وفسد المعنى؛

٤- أو كان بينهما شبه كمال الاتّصال، نحو:

[١] «أبغي» بمعنى «أطلب». ومعنى «أراها في الضلال تهيم» «تُريني نفسي أنها تتحيّر في الضلال».

qāla lī kayfa anta qultu ʿalīlu
He asked me, "How are you?" I said, "Ill:

saharun dāʾimun wa-ḥuznun ṭawīlu
"Endless sleeplessness and lengthy grief"

قَالَ لِي كَيْفَ أَنْتَ قُلْتُ عَلِيلُ
سَهَرٌ دَائِمٌ وَحُزْنٌ طَوِيلُ

It is as if he were asked, "What is the cause of your illness?" and he responded, "Endless sleeplessness and lengthy grief"...

كأنه قيل «ما سبب علّتك؟» فقال «سهر دائم وحزن طويل»...

In these four cases, breaking is specifically required because joining entails some difference and some relatedness, and relatedness is not present in the case of total disconnection and virtual disconnection.[49]

فيتعيّن الفصل في هذه الصور الأربع لأن الوصل يقتضي مغايرة ومناسبة والمناسبة غير موجودة في كمال الانقطاع وشبهه.

(B) If, however, there is *not* total disconnection between the two sentences without misleading implication (as in *qāla lī kayfa anta qultu ʿalīlu saharun dāʾimun wa-ḥuznun ṭawīlu*), nor is there total connection, nor is there virtually [total disconnection or connection] (as in one's uttering the prayer, *lā wa-ayyadaka Allāhu* (No; may Allah assist you): if the *wāw* were omitted, [the addressee] would mistakenly understand it as a prayer against him),[50] then joining (that is, conjunction with the *wāw*) is specifically required since there is cause for joining (i.e., the presence of difference and relatedness) and there is no preventive consideration (i.e., the presence of either kind of totality together with the abovementioned kind of misleading implication or a similar one).

(ب) وإن لم يكن بينهما كمال الانقطاع بلا إيهام — نحو «قال لي كيف أنت قلت عليل سهر دائم وحزن طويل»[٢٠] — ولا كمال الاتصال ولا شبه أحدهما — نحو قول الداعي «لا وأيّدك الله» ولو حذف الواو لتوهّم أنه دعاء عليه — فالوصل أي العطف بالواو متعيّن لوجود الداعي وهو وجود المغايرة والمناسبة وعدم المانع وهو وجود أحد الكمالين مع الإيهام المذكور وشبهه.

Instructive Point One thing that aesthetically enhances the joining [of sentences] is that the two sentences agree in being verbal or nominal and in having perfect or imperfect tense verbs. In the case of agreement, it is preferable to conjoin [the sentences], but in the case of non-agreement, what is preferable is to break them up. For this reason, the accusative takes priority in a case like *ḍarabtu Zaydan wa-ʿAmran akramtuhu* (I hit Zayd, and ʿAmr I honored) in order to make it a case of the conjunction of one verbal sentence to another.

تنبيه من محسّنات الوصل تناسب الجملتين في الفعليّة والاسميّة والماضويّة والمضارعة، فالعطف على مناسبه أولى؛ وأما عند التخالف فالأولى الفصل. ولذا رجح النصب في نحو «ضربت زيدًا وعمرًا أكرمته» ليكون من عطف الفعليّة على مثلها.

Chapter 8

PROPORTIONALITY, BREVITY, AND PROLIXITY

Proportionality, *brevity*, and *prolixity* refer, respectively, to the conveying of a primarily intended meaning through a verbal expression that is (1) equal to it,[51] (2) briefer than it but sufficient, or (3) lengthier than it for some purpose.

Proportionality

An example of proportionality is "Yet evil plotting besets none but those who plot" (Q 35:43).

Brevity

Brevity is of two types.

The first is *brevity by parsimony*, which is that which does not involve omission, e.g., "There is life for you in requital" (Q 2:179).[52]

The second is *brevity by omission*. That which is omitted is either

1. a *muḍāf*, e.g., *wa-s'al al-qaryata* ("Ask the town") (Q 12:82), i.e., *ahla al-qaryati* (the people of the town).
2. the subject of an adjective, e.g., *ana ibnu jalā* (I am the son of...unmistakable), i.e., *ibnu rajulin jalā* (the son of an unmistakable man).

الباب الثامن

المساواة والإيجاز والإطناب

هي تأدية أصل المراد بلفظ (١) مساوٍ له أو (٢) ناقص عنه وافٍ أو (٣) زائد عليه لفائدة.

المساواة

نحو ﴿وَلَا يَحِيقُ ٱلْمَكْرُ ٱلسَّيِّئُ إِلَّا بِأَهْلِهِۦ﴾ [٣٥/ ٤٣].

الإيجاز

وهو ضربان:

الأول إيجاز القصر وهو ما ليس بحذف، نحو ﴿وَلَكُمْ فِي ٱلْقِصَاصِ حَيَوٰةٌ﴾ [٢/ ١٧٩].

والثاني إيجاز الحذف. والمحذوف إما:

١- مضاف، نحو ﴿وَسْـَٔلِ ٱلْقَرْيَةَ﴾ [١٢/ ٨٢] أي «أهل القرية».

٢- أو موصوف، نحو «أنا ابن جلا» أي «ابن رجل جلا».

3. an adjective, e.g., *ya'khudhu kulla safīnatin* (...seizing every ship...) (Q 18:79), i.e., *kulla safīnatin ṣaḥīḥatin* (every sound ship).
4. a condition.
5. a result clause. Furthermore, omission of a result clause is either
   (a) purely for the sake of brevity, e.g., "And when it is said to them, 'Be mindful of that which is before you and of that which is behind you, that haply you may receive mercy—'" (Q 36:45), that is to imply, "they turned away."
   (b) to indicate that [the omitted result] is not such that knowledge could comprehend it, e.g., "If you could see when they are arraigned before the fire—" (Q 6:27), that is to imply, "you would see a tremendous thing."
   (c) to send the listener down every possible course.[53]

That which is omitted might also be more than one sentence, e.g., "'I shall inform you of its interpretation, so send me forth.' 'Yūsuf...'" (Q 12:45–46), that is to imply, "'So send me forth to Yūsuf so that I might seek from him an interpretation of the dream.' So they sent him forth, whereupon he came to him and said, 'O Yūsuf....'"

Now, sometimes something might be put in place of what was omitted, e.g., "If they deny you, messengers before you were denied" (Q 35:4), that is to imply, "Be steadfast and grieve not." Other times there might be nothing put in its place, the context being regarded as sufficient.

It is reason that determines that omission has occurred, but there are a number of things that may determine the specific content [of the omission].

The first is the most probable intention, as in "Carrion is forbidden to you" (Q 5:3). Reason determines that there is an omission, since religious

٣- أو صفة، نحو ﴿يَأْخُذُ كُلَّ سَفِينَةٍ﴾ [١٨/ ٧٩] أي «كل سفينة صحيحة».

٤- أو شرط.

٥- أو جواب شرط. ثم إن حذف الجواب إما:

(أ) لمجرّد الاختصار، نحو ﴿وَإِذَا قِيلَ لَهُمُ ٱتَّقُوا۟ مَا بَيْنَ أَيْدِيكُمْ وَمَا خَلْفَكُمْ لَعَلَّكُمْ تُرْحَمُونَ﴾ [٣٦/ ٤٥] أي «أعرضوا».

(ب) وإما للدلالة على أنه ما لا يحاط به العلم، نحو ﴿وَلَوْ تَرَىٰٓ إِذْ وُقِفُوا۟ عَلَى ٱلنَّارِ﴾ [٦/ ٢٧] أي «لرأيت أمرًا عظيمًا».

(ج) أو ليُذهب السامع كل مذهب ممكن.

وقد يكون المحذوف أكثر من جملة، نحو ﴿أَنَا۠ أُنَبِّئُكُم بِتَأْوِيلِهِۦ فَأَرْسِلُونِ ۝٤٥ يُوسُفُ...﴾ [١٢/ ٤٥-٤٦] أي «فأرسلوني إلى يوسف لأستعبره الرؤيا فأرسلوه فأتاه فقال يا يوسف».

ثم قد يقام مقام المحذوف شيء، نحو ﴿وَإِن يُكَذِّبُوكَ فَقَدْ كُذِّبَتْ رُسُلٌ مِّن قَبْلِكَ﴾ [٣٥/ ٤] أي «فاصبر ولا تحزن». وقد لا يقام مقامه شيء ويكتفى بالقرينة.

والدليل على الحذف العقل؛ وعلى التعيين أمور:

الأول المقصود الأظهر، نحو ﴿حُرِّمَتْ عَلَيْكُمُ ٱلْمَيْتَةُ﴾ [٥/ ٣] دلّ العقل على أن هناك حذفًا إذ الأحكام

rulings pertain to acts, not to things, and the specification of eating is determined by its being what is most probably intended by the prohibition of carrion.

The second is normative experience, as in "'This is the one on whose account you blamed me'" (Q 12:32). Conceivably, the implicit phrase could be "on account of loving whom" or "on account of attempting to seduce whom," but normative experience indicates that it is specifically the latter since a person who has excessive love is not normally blamed, because that love is not by choice.

The third is contextual indication, as in "In the name of Allah." One mentally supplies [a word for the activity] before which Allah's name is invoked, as in "I recite" when reciting, "I depart" when traveling, and so on.

Prolixity

Prolixity occurs either

1. by elucidating something after expressing it indistinctly so that the meaning takes lingering hold in the soul, e.g., "He said, 'My Lord! Expand for me my breast!'" (Q 20:25).[54]
2. by mentioning something specific after something general to indicate its superiority, as if it did not belong to the category of the general thing, e.g., "Be mindful of your prayers and the middlemost prayer" (Q 2:238).
3. by repeating for the sake of a fine point like emphasizing the warning in *kallā sawfa taʿlamūna thumma kallā sawfa taʿlamūna* (Nay! Soon you will know. Indeed! Soon you will know) (Q 102:3–4). *Thumma* contains an indication that the second warning is more emphatic.

الشرعيّة تتعلّق بالأفعال لا بالأعيان ودلّ المقصود الأظهر من حرمة الميتة على تعيين الأكل.

الثاني العادة، نحو ﴿فَذَٰلِكُنَّ ٱلَّذِي لُمْتُنَّنِي فِيهِ﴾ [١٢/ ٣٢] يحتمل أن يكون التقدير «في حبّه» أو «في مراودته» ودلّت العادة على تعيين الثاني لأن الحبّ المفرط لا يلام صاحبه عليه عادةً إذ ليس اختياريًّا.

الثالث الاقتران، نحو «بسم الله» فيقدّر ما جُعلت التسمية مبدأ له كـ«أقرأ» في القراءة و«أرتحل» في السفر ونحو ذلك.

الإطناب

وهو إما:

١- بالإيضاح بعد الإبهام ليتمكّن المعنى في النفس فضل تمكّن، نحو ﴿قَالَ رَبِّ ٱشْرَحْ لِي صَدْرِي﴾ [٢٠/ ٢٥].

٢- وإما بذكر الخاصّ بعد العامّ للتنبيه على فضله حتى كأنه ليس من جنس العامّ، نحو ﴿حَٰفِظُواْ عَلَى ٱلصَّلَوَٰتِ وَٱلصَّلَوٰةِ ٱلْوُسْطَىٰ﴾ [٢/ ٢٣٨].

٣- وإما بالتكرير لنكتة كتأكيد الإنذار في ﴿كَلَّا سَوْفَ تَعْلَمُونَ ۝٣ ثُمَّ كَلَّا سَوْفَ تَعْلَمُونَ﴾ [١٠٢/ ٣-٤] وفي «ثم» دلالة على أن الإنذار الثاني أبلغ.

4. by *epiphrase*, which is to end one's speech by adding a fine point without which the meaning would have been complete, e.g., "He said, 'O my people! Follow the messengers! Follow those who ask not of you any reward and who are guided'" (Q 36:20–21). The fine point here is additional urging that they follow [the messengers].

5. by *epiphonema*, which is to put after one sentence another sentence that comprises its meaning for the sake of emphasis, e.g., "Thus did We punish them for having disbelieved. And do We punish any but the ungrateful?" (Q 34:17) and "Say, 'Truth has come and falsehood has vanished. Truly falsehood is ever vanishing'" (Q 17:81).

6. by *complementing* (also called *preempting*), which is that one provide, in speech that might lead to a misunderstanding of the intended meaning, that which would ward off that misunderstanding, e.g., "…humble toward the believers, stern toward the disbelievers" (Q 5:54).

7. by *enriching*, which is that one provide, in speech that would *not* lead to any misunderstanding of the intended meaning, something additional for a fine purpose like amplification, e.g., "And they give food despite cherishing it" (Q 76:8).

8. by *interjecting*, which is that one express, in the middle of a sentence or between two sentences that are connected in meaning, one or more sentences that have no positional inflection for some fine purpose other than warding off a misunderstanding, like the declaration of divine transcendence in His saying ﷻ, "And they assign to Allah daughters—transcendent is He!—while they have that which they desire" (Q 16:57).

٤- وإما بالإيغال وهو ختم الكلام بما يفيد نكتة يتمّ المعنى بدونها، نحو ﴿قَالَ يَٰقَوْمِ ٱتَّبِعُوا۟ ٱلْمُرْسَلِينَ ۝٢٠ ٱتَّبِعُوا۟ مَن لَّا يَسْـَٔلُكُمْ أَجْرًا وَهُم مُّهْتَدُونَ﴾ [٣٦/ ٢٠-٢١] النكتة هنا زيادة حثّ على الاتّباع.

٥- وإما بالتذييل وهو تعقيب جملة بجملة أخرى تشتمل على معناها للتأكيد، نحو ﴿ذَٰلِكَ جَزَيْنَٰهُم بِمَا كَفَرُوا۟ وَهَلْ نُجَٰزِىٓ إِلَّا ٱلْكَفُورَ﴾ [٣٤/ ١٧] ونحو ﴿وَقُلْ جَآءَ ٱلْحَقُّ وَزَهَقَ ٱلْبَٰطِلُ إِنَّ ٱلْبَٰطِلَ كَانَ زَهُوقًا﴾ [١٧/ ٨١].

٦- وإما بالتكميل ويسمّى الاحتراس أيضا وهو أن يؤتى في كلام يوهم خلاف المقصود بما يدفعه، نحو ﴿أَذِلَّةٍ عَلَى ٱلْمُؤْمِنِينَ أَعِزَّةٍ عَلَى ٱلْكَٰفِرِينَ﴾ [٥/ ٥٤].

٧- وإما بالتتميم وهو أن يؤتى في كلام لا يوهم خلاف المقصود بفضلة لنكتة كالمبالغة، نحو ﴿وَيُطْعِمُونَ ٱلطَّعَامَ عَلَىٰ حُبِّهِۦ﴾ [٧٦/ ٨].

٨- وإما بالاعتراض وهو أن يؤتى في أثناء كلام أو بين كلامين متّصلين معنًى بجملة أو أكثر لا محلّ لها من الإعراب لنكتة سوى دفع الإيهام، كالتنزيه في قوله تعالى ﴿وَيَجْعَلُونَ لِلَّهِ ٱلْبَنَٰتِ سُبْحَٰنَهُۥ وَلَهُم مَّا يَشْتَهُونَ﴾ [١٦/ ٥٧].

٩- وإما بغير ذلك، كقوله تعالى ﴿ٱلَّذِينَ يَحۡمِلُونَ ٱلۡعَرۡشَ وَمَنۡ حَوۡلَهُۥ يُسَبِّحُونَ بِحَمۡدِ رَبِّهِمۡ وَيُؤۡمِنُونَ بِهِۦ﴾ [٤٠/ ٧] وحَسُن ذكر «ويؤمنون به» إظهارًا لشرف الإيمان.

9. in some other way like His saying ﷻ, "Those who bear the throne and those who surround it hymn the praise of their Lord and believe in Him" (Q 40:7). The mention of "and believe in Him" is apt in that it manifests the dignity of belief.

❁ ❁ ❁

واعلم أنه قد يوصف الكلام بالإيجاز والإطناب باعتبار كثرة حروفه وقلّتها بالنسبة إلى كلام آخر مساوٍ له في أصل المعنى.

Know that a statement might be described as brief or prolix in consideration of whether it has more or fewer letters than another statement that equally expresses the [same] primarily intended meaning.[55]

❁ ❁ ❁

تمّت بعون الله تعالى الرسالة المسمّاة بالفيض الربّاني في علم المعاني جعلها الله تعالى بمنّه وكرمه نافعة لنا ولسائر المؤمنين. اللّهم لا تؤاخذنا إن نسينا أو أخطأنا. ﴿سُبۡحَٰنَ رَبِّكَ رَبِّ ٱلۡعِزَّةِ عَمَّا يَصِفُونَ ١٨٠ وَسَلَٰمٌ عَلَى ٱلۡمُرۡسَلِينَ ١٨١ وَٱلۡحَمۡدُ لِلَّهِ رَبِّ ٱلۡعَٰلَمِينَ﴾ [٣٧/ ١٨٠-١٨٢]. وتليها بإذنه تعالى الرسالة الثامنة المسمّاة التبيان في علم البيان.

By the assistance of Allah ﷻ, the treatise entitled *The Lordly Profusion: On the Science of Rhetorical Semantics* is complete. May Allah ﷻ by His grace and generosity render it of benefit to us and all believers. Allah! "Take us not to task if we forget or err!" (Q 2:286). "Glory to your Lord, Lord of Might, transcending what they describe! Peace be upon the messengers. And praise to Allah, Lord of the worlds" (Q 37:180–82). By His permission ﷻ, the eighth treatise follows, entitled *The Elucidation: On the Science of Figurative Language.*

NOTES TO TREATISE VII

1 *Talkhīṣ al-Miftāḥ*, authored by Muḥammad b. ʿAbd al-Raḥmān al-Qazwīnī (d. 739/1338), is an abridgement of the portion of Sirāj al-Dīn al-Sakkākī's (d. 626/1229) *Miftāḥ al-ʿulūm* that deals with rhetoric (*balāgha*). *Mukhtaṣar al-maʿānī* is Saʿd al-Dīn al-Taftāzānī's (d. 792/1390) commentary on *Talkhīṣ al-Miftāḥ*.

2 This kind of overcomplication is called "overcomplication in the expression" (*al-taʿqīd al-lafẓī*).

3 This kind of overcomplication is called "overcomplication in the meaning" (*al-taʿqīd al-maʿnawī*).

4 Moreover, an eye's becoming dry could imply that the person has ceased to care or has become hard of heart. See al-Taftāzānī, *Mukhtaṣar*, 1:48.

5 That is, errors that would arise from failing to account for what the situation demands.

6 This is necessary for eloquence because it is necessary for articulateness (*faṣāḥa*) and eloquence depends on articulateness. The other prerequisites for articulateness are satisfied by means of other sciences: knowledge of lexicology (*ʿilm al-lugha*) equips one to avoid obscurity in word choice; morphology, aberrancy in word patterns; grammar, weakness in syntax and the overcomplicated ordering of expressions. Natural good taste (*dhawq salīm*) guides the speaker to avoid dissonant words and phrases. See al-Taftāzānī, *Mukhtaṣar*, 1:68–70; al-Dasūqī, *Kitāb ḥāshiyat al-Dasūqī*, 1:264.

7 The discussion in fact spans three consecutive treatises.

8 As discussed in Treatise V, pp. 311–16, literal and nonliteral *predication* (*ḥaqīqa ʿaqliyya* and *majāz ʿaqlī*) are distinct from literal and nonliteral *expressions* (*ḥaqīqa lughawiyya* and *majāz lughawī*).

9 The complete sentence is *fa-ammā man thaqulat mawāzīnuhu fa-huwa fī ʿīshatin rāḍiyatin* (As for one whose scales are heavy, he shall enjoy a contenting [lit., "content"] life) (Q 101:6–7). Although *rāḍiya* (content) is an active participle, it is predicated of what is in reality the object of the contentment (namely, the life in paradise) instead of the agent who is content (namely, the believer who has been rewarded).

10 Although *mufʿam* (inundated) is a passive participle, it is predicated of what is in reality the agent of the inundation (namely, the flood) instead of the object of the inundation (like a valley).

11 Since *jadda* (exerted effort) is an active verb, it belongs to the agent (namely, the person in question who is exerting effort); instead, it is here predicated of the abstract notion of the action.

12 As an active participle, *ṣāʾimun* (fasting) belongs to the agent, namely, the person who is fasting.

13 As an active participle, *jārin* (flowing) belongs to the agent, namely, the actual water that makes up the river. In this example, *nahr* as the riverbed, or the channel in which the river water flows, is to be understood as distinct from the "river," or the water, itself.

14 As an active verb, *banā* (built) belongs to the agent, namely, the actual builders.

15 That is, both the subject and the predicate are *tropes* (*majāz lughawī*).

16 The stronger indicator is the intellect.

17 Just as the speaker may consider himself unworthy to mention the subject by name, he may consider the subject unworthy of his mentioning it by name.

18 When it is obvious that there is only one possible thing that the predicate could refer to, it would be redundant to mention the subject explicitly. Better yet, in some cases, the speaker may want to convey the impression that he considers the predicate to belong exclusively to one subject and that it would be redundant to mention the subject, even though he knows that, strictly, this is not true.

19 That is, by the speaker's using a name, title, or description that inherently magnifies or debases the subject, like "the honorable judge" or "the wretched convict."

20 That is, choosing to use a definite subject instead of an indefinite subject.

21 The text is especially terse here. The purpose of rendering the subject definite is to convey meaning to the addressee in the most complete way (*ifādat al-mukhāṭab atamm fā'ida*) by using expressions that are specific and unambiguous. Since the personal pronoun is the most specific form of the definite, the use of a personal pronoun for the subject in the context of the first person, the second person, or the third person (of a previously mentioned subject) has the advantage of accomplishing this purpose in the fullest possible sense. See al-Dasūqī, *Kitāb ḥāshiyat al-Dasūqī*, 1:488–89.

22 Implication (*kināya*), studied in the science of figurative language (*bayān*), is the use of an expression for a nonliteral implied meaning when the literal meaning of the expression is also applicable. Here, the use of implication would be to refer to someone by his personal name in order to imply its context-appropriate lexical meaning, as in *karīm* (generous one) for a person named Karīm who is being generous.

23 Since seduction is not expected in such a relationship, the relative clause confirms that this was indeed the situation: none other than the woman in authority over Yūsuf ﷺ and in whose house he was staying made the attempt.

24 The point of the example is that by using the relative clause to mention that it is none other than the Creator of the heavens who built the house, the poet magnifies its status. This also helps him make the point that other houses are comparatively insignificant. Al-Taftāzānī, *Mukhtaṣar*, 1:152–53.

25 The relative clause alludes to the magnified status of Shuʿayb ﷺ.

26 The wife of ʿImrān wanted a son (whom she vowed to devote to the worship of Allah) but instead gave birth to a daughter, Maryam.

27 The speaker of this sentence would be making the (obviously problematic) claim that the general essence of 'man' is superior to that of 'woman'.

28 Since the plural form in Arabic signifies at least three, the negation of the plural negates three or more but does not necessarily negate one or two.

29 That is, a demeaning of the *muḍāf*, *muḍāf ilayhi*, or something else. The example provided demeans the *muḍāf*.

30 That is, even the smallest portion of contentment from Allah is greater than all else. Al-Bannānī, *al-Tajrīd*, 2:131. Another reading is that the indefinite magnifies Allah's contentment by indicating that it is given only to few. Al-Dasūqī, *Kitāb ḥāshiyat al-Dasūqī*, 1:578.

31 Note that in this example *al-almaʿī*, which is the word described by the adjectival phrase, is not the subject since the example is not a complete sentence.

32 That is, an abridged way, which means that one does not spell out the entire sentence each time. The difference between detailing the subject and detailing the predicate is that

the purpose of detailing the subject is to mention every person or thing to which the predicate applies, while the purpose of detailing the predicate is to mention every application of the predicate—as, in the following example, both the coming of Zayd and the coming of ʿAmr. See al-Taftāzānī, *Mukhtaṣar*, 1:183–85.

33 In this context, separation is the use of the *separative pronoun* (*ḍamīr al-faṣl*) *huwa*. Note that there are other purposes for the use of the separative pronoun, the most important of which is to distinguish the grammatical structure of subject and predicate from that of noun and adjective: *Zaydun al-qāʾimu* could mean either "Zayd, the one who is standing..." or "Zayd is the one standing."

34 ʿAbd al-Qāhir b. ʿAbd al-Raḥmān al-Jurjānī (d. 471/1078 or 474/1081), renowned rhetorician and grammarian.

35 A verbal predicate (*khabar fiʿlī*) is a clause that begins with a verb whose grammatical agent is a pronoun, whether implicit or explicit, that refers to the subject. See the example.

36 This example only works according to the position that divides statements of praise into two sub-sentences, where the subject (*musnad ilayhi*) of the first sub-sentence is the grammatical agent (e.g., *al-rajulu*) for the verb of praise (e.g., *niʿma*) as in *niʿma al-rajulu* [How good a man!]), and the subject of the second sub-sentence is an implicit noun (e.g., *huwa*) whose predicate is the noun qualified by praise (e.g., *Zaydun*) as in *huwa Zaydun* (He is Zayd). When the subject of the first sub-sentence (*al-rajulu*) is replaced by an explanatory indefinite noun (*rajulan*), the subject becomes an implicit agent pronoun in the verb (*niʿma*). Thus the two sentences would be *niʿma rajulan* (How good he is as a man!) *huwa Zaydun* (He is Zayd). However, this example does not work according to the other position regarding statements of praise, which treats them as a single sentence in which the subject (*musnad ilayhi*) is the noun qualified by praise—which here is *Zaydun*—and the preceding part of the sentence is the predicate. Al-Taftāzānī, *Mukhtaṣar*, 1:224.

37 Here the "explicit noun" is to be understood as opposed to the personal pronoun and thus includes demonstrative pronouns, as the student will observe.

38 That is, using the third person instead of the first person as in the examples immediately above.

39 That is, in addition to the use of the third person instead of the first person, there are other configurations in which one person can be used instead of another, as the text will now explain.

40 The subtle significance that makes this verse acceptable is its hyperbolic description of the color of the sky: instead of comparing the sky to the ground with respect to its color, the poet compares the sky to the very color of the ground itself. In the following example, by contrast, the inversion does not achieve any worthwhile effect: it simply makes no sense for a castle to be plastered onto mud and straw. Al-Taftāzānī, *Mukhtaṣar*, 1:245–46.

41 "Renewal" refers to the action's coming into existence after being nonexistent. The point is that the temporality of the action signified by the verb entails that there is a reason for the action's occurring in the specific time in question. "Renewal" is the opposite of "permanence" (*thubūt*), which is the default signification of nouns. Al-Dasūqī, *Kitāb ḥāshiyat al-Dasūqī*, 2:38.

42 *Actional accusatives* (*mafāʿīl*) include the action-notion (*mafʿūl muṭlaq*), the object (*mafʿūl bihi*), the action-place/time (*mafʿūl fīhi*), the action-reason (*mafʿūl lahu*), and the action-accompaniment (*mafʿūl maʿahu*). "Its like" refers to the circumstance (*ḥāl*), the specification (*tamyīz*), and the exception (*istithnāʾ*). Refer to

the section on accusative nouns in Treatise II, Chapter 4 (pp. 150–54).

43 The term *operator* (*adāh*) is used to include nouns as well as particles.

44 This parenthetical explanation is meant to clarify that *fiʿl* here should be understood not as the grammatical verb but rather the action signified by that verb, that is, the real occurrence that the agent brings about.

45 The point is that the sentence has the form of the declarative sentence "Allah has providentially led you to God-consciousness."

46 These example sentences have the forms of the declarative sentences "And mothers nurse their children…" and "Divorced women wait…."

47 Clauses that have a syntactical role within a larger sentence can be said to have "positional inflection." See Treatise II, note 33.

48 The adverbial specification is the clause "But when they are alone…."

49 The attentive student will complete this by observing that in cases of total connection and virtual connection, difference is not present.

50 *Lā ayyadaka Allāhu* would be understood as a single sentence with the meaning "May Allah not assist you."

51 These relations are measured by reference to an expression's signification (*dalāla*) by correspondence (*muṭābaqa*). Refer to the introduction of Treatise III, p. 227.

52 This Quranic statement is regarded to be a model of concision. In one phrase, it conveys the idea that a person's prior knowledge that he would be killed in retribution for wrongful killing functions as a deterrence; thus, the legislation of retaliatory killing prevents wrongful killing and results ultimately in the protection of human life. It has been observed that the Quranic phrase *fī al-qiṣāṣi ḥayātun* successfully conveys this idea in fewer vocalized letters than the old Arab saying "Killing is best averted by killing" (*al-qatlu anfā li-l-qatli*). Al-Taftāzānī, *Mukhtaṣar*, 1:528–29.

53 That is, omitting the result clause might have the effect of making the outcome seem open to various possibilities, inducing the listener to consider them one by one.

54 "Expand for me" (*ishraḥ lī*) expresses the request for expansion indistinctly, and "my breast" (*ṣadrī*) provides elucidation. The general idea is that indistinctness induces anticipation in the listener for elucidation, which makes the latter more impactful. Al-Taftāzānī, *Mukhtaṣar*, 1:538–39.

55 That is, according to a different technical usage of these terms than the one presented above.

VIII

THE ELUCIDATION

On the science of figurative language

التبيان في علم البيان

In the Name of Allah,
All-Merciful, Most Compassionate

بسم الله الرحمن الرحيم

ALL PRAISE IS due to Allah, Lord of the worlds. May blessings and peace be upon our messenger, Muḥammad, and upon his all family and Companions.

To Proceed This is a treatise on the science of figurative language. I have entitled it *The Elucidation: On the Science of Figurative Language* and arranged it into an introduction and three chapters. The introduction concerns the definition, aim, and subject matter of the science of figurative language. Chapter 1 concerns simile, Chapter 2 concerns nonliteral language, and Chapter 3 concerns implication.

الحمد لله ربّ العالمين والصلاة والسلام على رسولنا محمد وعلى آله وصحبه أجمعين.

أما بعد فهذه رسالة في علم البيان سمّيتها التبيان في علم البيان. رتّبتها على مقدّمة وثلاثة أبواب: المقدّمة في تعريف علم البيان وغايته وموضوعه، الباب الأول في التشبيه، الباب الثاني في المجاز، الباب الثالث في الكناية.

INTRODUCTION

المقدمة

What is the science of figurative language? What is its aim? What is its subject matter?

ما علم البيان؟ وما غايته؟ وما موضوعه؟

The science of figurative language is a science by which one knows how to convey one meaning in various ways that differ in how plainly they signify that meaning, e.g., to convey the generosity of Zayd through "has abundant ashes," "has a meek dog," or "has a lean young camel." The aim of the science is that one know how to convey one meaning in different ways. The subject matter of the science is the verbal expression with respect to simile, nonliteral language, and implication.

علم البيان علم يعرف به إيراد المعنى الواحد بطرق مختلفة في وضوح الدلالة عليه، كإيراد جود زيد بـ«كثير الرماد» و«جبان الكلب» و«مهزول الفصيل»؛ وغايته معرفة إيراد المعنى الواحد بطرق مختلفة؛ وموضوعه اللفظ من حيث التشبيه والمجاز والكناية.

If a verbal expression is used to convey some implicate of the assigned meaning, then if some contextual indicant indicates that the assigned meaning is not intended, that verbal expression is a *trope*, e.g., "They put their fingers in their ears" (Q 2:19). Otherwise, it is an *implicative expression*, e.g., "Zayd's ashes are abundant." If a contextual indicant indicates that one thing shares [an attribute] with another thing but not in the manner of metaphor, then the verbal expression is a *simile*, e.g., "Zayd is a lion."

اللفظ المراد به لازم المعنى الموضوع له؛ إن دلّت قرينة على عدم إرادة المعنى الموضوع له فمجاز كـ«يجعلون أصابعهم في آذانهم» وإلا فكناية كـ«زيد كثير الرماد». وإن دلّت قرينة على مشاركة أمر لأمر لا على وجه الاستعارة فتشبيه كـ«زيد أسد».

Chapter 1

SIMILE

What is simile? How many components does it have? What is the highest level of simile?

[The Definition of Simile]

Lexically, *tashbīh* (simile) means to use the [particle] *kāf* or the like to indicate that one thing shares some commonality with another thing.[1] In the science of figurative language, *simile* means that which is neither in the manner of *actual metaphor*, e.g., "I saw a lion in the bathhouse"; nor in the manner of *implicit metaphor*, e.g., "Death dug in its claws"; nor in the manner of *extraction*, which is discussed in the science of embellishment, e.g., *laqītu bi-Zaydin asadan* (I encountered in Zayd a lion), i.e., *laqītu maʿa Zaydin asadan* (I encountered with Zayd a lion), for the *bāʾ* means *maʿa* (with).

The definition [of simile] thus includes statements like "Zayd is a lion," with an omission of the instrument of simile, and His saying ﷻ, "Deaf, dumb, and blind" (Q 2:18), with an omission of both the instrument and the tenor of the simile.

How Many Components Does Simile Have?

Simile has four components:

1. the *tenor* of the simile.
2. the *vehicle* for the simile.

الباب الأول

التشبيـه

ما التشبيه؟ كم ركنًا له؟ وما أعلى مراتب التشبيه؟

[تعريف التشبيه]

التشبيـه في اللغـة الدلالة على مشـاركة أمر لأمـر في معنًى بـالكاف ونحوه؛ والمـراد بالتشبيـه في علـم البيـان مـا لـم يكـن على وجـه الاسـتعارة التحقيقيّـة نحو «رأيت أسـدًا في الحمـام» ولا على وجـه الاسـتعارة المكنيّة نحو «أنشـبت المنيّة أظفارهـا» ولا على وجه التجريـد الذي يذكر في علم البديع مـن نحو «لقيـت بزيد أسـدًا» أي «لقيـت مع زيد أسـدًا» فالباء بمـعنى «مع».

فدخـل في التعريـف نحـو «زيـد أسـد» بحـذف أداة التشبيه وقـوله تعالى ﴿صُمٌّ بُكۡمٌ عُمۡيٌ﴾ [٢/ ١٨] بحذف الأداة والمشـبّه جميعًـا.

كم ركنا للتشبيه؟

للتشبيه أربعة أركان:

١- المشبّه.

٢- المشبّه به.

These two either are (a) both sensory, e.g., "Zayd's cheek is like a rose"; are (b) both abstract, e.g., "Knowledge is like life"; or (c) are different [in this respect], e.g., "Death is like a predator."

3. the *ground* for the simile, which either (a) is *not* external to the essences of the tenor and the vehicle, as when one garment is likened to another with respect to their species or genus, e.g., to say, "This shirt is like that one in that they are both linen garments / ...in that they are both garments made of cotton";[2] [or (b) is external to] the essences of the tenor and the vehicle and is an attribute of both (otherwise, it could not possibly be the ground). That attribute is either *real*, i.e., a state of being that is established and inherent in the thing, or it is *relational*, i.e., that which is *not* a state of being that is inherent in the thing but rather an attribute involving two things, e.g., [the attribute of] disclosure when one says, "The proof is like the sun," for disclosure is not a state of being that is inherent in the proof or the sun themselves. The ground can also be divided in another way, which we saw more fitting to omit.

4. the *instrument of simile*, which may be the *kāf*, *ka'anna*, *mithlu*, or words of the same meaning. By default, when the *kāf* or its like is used, the vehicle comes after it. But in some cases another word comes after [instead], e.g., "Set forth for them a parable of the life of this world: [It is] like water We send down from the sky" (Q 18:45), meaning that the condition of the life of this world is like the condition of vegetation, not that it is like water as might be supposed ostensibly.

The Highest Level of Simile

Simile is divided into various levels with respect to emphatic force in consideration of whether all or some of its components are mentioned.

وهما إما حسيّان كـ«خدّ زيد كالورد» أو عقليّان كـ«العلم كالحياة» أو مختلفان كـ«المنيّة كالسبع».

٣- وجهه وهو إما (١) غير خارج عن حقيقتهما، كما في تشبيه ثوب بآخر في نوعهما وجنسهما كأن يقال «هذا القميص مثل ذاك في كونهما كتانًا أو ثوبًا من القطن»؛ [أو (٢) خارج] عن حقيقة المشبّه والمشبّه به صفة لهما وإلا لا يصلح أن يكون وجه الشبه. وتلك الصفة إما حقيقيّة أي هيئة متمكّنة في الذات متقرّرة فيها وإما إضافيّة أي ما لا يكون هيئة مقرّرة في الذات بل يكون معنًى متعلّقًا بشيئين كإزالة الحجاب في قولنا «الحجّة كالشمس» فإنها ليست هيئة مقرّرة في ذات الحجّة والشمس. ولوجه الشبه تقسيم آخر رأينا تركه أحسن.

٤- أداته وهي الكاف، و«كأنّ»، و«مثل»، وما في معناها. والأصل في نحو الكاف أن يليه المشبّه به؛ وقد يليه غيره نحو ﴿وَٱضْرِبْ لَهُم مَّثَلَ ٱلْحَيَوٰةِ ٱلدُّنْيَا كَمَآءٍ أَنزَلْنَـٰهُ مِنَ ٱلسَّمَآءِ﴾ [١٨/ ٤٥] أي «حال الحياة الدنيا كحال النباتات» لا الماء كما يظنّ ظاهرًا.

أعلى مراتب التشبيه

ينقسم التشبيه في قوّة المبالغة باعتبار ذكر أركانه كلّها أو بعضها إلى مراتب.

فـالأعلى مـا حـذف منـه وجهـه وأداتـه فقـط، نحـو «زيـد أسـد» أو مـع حـذف المشـبه نحـو «أسـد» في مقـام الإخبـار عـن زيـد.

ويلي هـذه المرتبة ما حذف منه وجهـه أو حذف أداته فقط، نحو «زيد كالأسـد» أو «زيد أسـد في الشجاعة»، أو مع حذف المشـبّه، نحو «كالأسـد» أو «أسـد في الشجاعة» عنـد الإخبـار عـن زيـد. ولا قـوّة في غيرهـا، نحـو «زيـد كالأسـد في الشجاعة».

The highest level is that in which only the ground and the instrument are omitted, e.g., "Zayd is a lion," or [these are omitted] along with omission of the tenor, e.g., "A lion" in the context of speaking about Zayd.

After this level comes that in which either the ground alone or the instrument alone is omitted, e.g., "Zayd is like a lion" or "Zayd is a lion in courage," or [one of these is omitted] along with omission of the tenor, e.g., "Like a lion" or "A lion in courage" when speaking about Zayd. There is no force in any other kind of simile, as in "Zayd is like a lion in courage."

Chapter 2

TROPES

Tropes are of two types: simple and composite.

Simple Tropes

As for simple tropes, they are words used for a [meaning] other than that to which they were assigned according to the vocabulary referenced by the speech, with a contextual indicant that precludes that the assigned meaning could be intended. There must be some semantic link, thereby excluding error and implication.

Literal expressions and tropes are each classified into those which are *lexical, revelational, conventional in the specific sense,* or *conventional in the general sense,* e.g., *asad* (lion / courageous man) for the predatory animal and a courageous man, *ṣalāh* (ritual prayer / supplication) for the specific form of worship and supplication, *fiʿl* (verb / action) for the word and the occurrence, and *dābba* (riding animal / thing that walks or crawls upon the ground) for the four-legged creature and a human being.

[Simple] tropes, with respect to the semantic link, are of two types: *metonymy*, if the semantic link is not similarity, or else *metaphor*. Oftentimes, [the term] *metaphor* is used to refer to using the name of the vehicle for the tenor; in such a case, they are the *vehicle* and *tenor* of a metaphor and the word is a *metaphorical expression*.

الباب الثاني

المجاز

وهو قسمان: مفرد، مركّب.

[المجاز المفرد]

أمّا المجاز المفرد فهو الكلمة المستعملة في غير ما وضعت له في اصطلاح به التخاطب مع قرينة مانعة عن إرادة الموضوع له. ولا بدّ من العلاقة ليخرج الغلط والكناية.

وكلّ من الحقيقة والمجاز لغوي وشرعي وعرفيّ خاصّ أو عامّ، كـ«أسد» للسبع والرجل الشجاع و«صلاة» للعبادة المخصوصة والدعاء و«فعل» للّفظ والحدث و«دابّة» لذات الأربع والإنسان.

والمجاز باعتبار العلاقة قسمان: (١) مرسل إن كانت العلاقة غير المشابهة، وإلا (٢) فاستعارة. وكثيرًا ما تطلق «الاستعارة» على استعمال اسم المشبّه به في المشبّه فهما مستعار منه ومستعار له واللفظ مستعار.

Metonymy is like using *yad* (hand) for favors or for power or using *rāwiya* (water-bearing animal) for *mazāda* (leather waterbag). It also includes referring to a thing by the name of (1) a part of it, as in *ʿayn* (eye) for *rabīʾa* (scout), which means someone on the lookout; (2) the reverse, as in "fingers" for fingertips; or referring to a thing by the name of (3) a cause of the thing, as in "We let [the cattle] graze on the rain"; (4) an effect of the thing, as in "The sky rained vegetation"; (5) what it previously was, as in "Give orphans their property" (Q 4:2); (6) what it will be in the future, as in "'Truly I see myself pressing wine'" (Q 12:36); (7) its location, as in "So let him call his assembly-place" (Q 96:17); (8) something located within it, as in "As for those whose faces whiten, they will be in the mercy of Allah" (Q 3:107), i.e., "in paradise"; (9) or an instrumental means of the thing, e.g., "'And make for me a faithful tongue among later generations'" (Q 26:84), i.e., "good mention."[3]

Composite Tropes

As for composite tropes, they are composite expressions that are used for a meaning likened to their original meaning in the manner of analogy for hyperbolic emphasis, e.g., when someone hesitating about some matter is told, "I see you putting a foot forward and then withdrawing it again": the image of his hesitation about the matter is likened to the image of the hesitation of a person who rises to leave and at one moment wants to leave, so he puts a foot forward, then at another moment wants not to, so he withdraws it again. To refer to the former image, a phrase is used that signifies the latter image by correspondence.[4] This kind of composite trope is termed a *metaphorical analogy* and sometimes termed simply an *analogy*. When its use in this manner becomes widespread, it is termed a *proverb*. Because of this, proverbs are not to be altered from the [grammatical] form of their original context to fit the context of their usage.[5]

والمجاز المرسل كـ«اليد» في النعمة والقدرة و«الراوية» في المزادة. ومنه تسمية الشيء باسم (١) جزئه، كـ«العين» في الربيئة وهي الشخص الرقيب؛ (٢) وعكسه، كـ«الأصابع» في الأنامل؛ وتسميته باسم (٣) سببه، نحو «رعينا الغيث»؛ أو (٤) مسبّبه، نحو «أمطرت السماء نباتا»؛ أو (٥) ما كان عليه، نحو ﴿وَءَاتُواْ ٱلۡيَتَٰمَىٰٓ أَمۡوَٰلَهُمۡ﴾ [٤/ ٢]؛ أو (٦) ما يؤول إليه، نحو ﴿إِنِّيٓ أَرَىٰنِيٓ أَعۡصِرُ خَمۡرٗا﴾ [١٢/ ٣٦]؛ أو (٧) محلّه، نحو ﴿فَلۡيَدۡعُ نَادِيَهُۥ﴾ [٩٦/ ١٧]؛ أو (٨) حالّه، نحو ﴿وَأَمَّا ٱلَّذِينَ ٱبۡيَضَّتۡ وُجُوهُهُمۡ فَفِي رَحۡمَةِ ٱللَّهِ﴾ [٣/ ١٠٧] أي «في الجنّة»؛ أو (٩) آلته، نحو ﴿وَٱجۡعَل لِّي لِسَانَ صِدۡقٖ فِي ٱلۡأٓخِرِينَ﴾ [٢٦/ ٨٤] أي «ذكرًا حسنًا».

[المجاز المركب]

وأما المجاز المركّب فهو اللفظ المركّب المستعمل فيما شبّه بمعناه الأصلي تشبيه التمثيل للمبالغة، كما يقال للمتردّد في أمر «إنّي أراك تقدّم رجلًا وتؤخّر أخرى» شبّه صورة تردّده في ذلك الأمر بصورة تردّد من قام ليذهب فتارة يريد الذهاب فيقدّم رجلًا وتارة لا يريد فيؤخّر أخرى فاستعمل في الصورة الأولى الكلام الدالّ بالمطابقة على الصورة الثانية. وهذا المجاز المركّب يسمّى التمثيل على سبيل الاستعارة وقد يسمّى التمثيل مطلقًا؛ ومتى فشا استعماله كذلك سمّي مثلًا، ولهذا لا تغيّر الأمثال في مضربها عن موردها.

❁ ❁ ❁

[Metaphor]

A metaphor may be qualified as *actual* when that to which it refers actually exists to the senses or to the intellect, as in [the poet's] saying,

> *ladā asadin shākī al-silāḥi muqadhdhafin*
> In the presence of a lion armed to the teeth and oft-flung[1]

i.e., "a courageous man," and as in His saying ﷻ, "'Guide us upon the straight path'" (Q 1:6), i.e., "the true religion."[6]

Metaphor is different from untruth in that metaphor is based on interpretation and on the utilization of a contextual indicant that indicates that what is intended is different than the apparent meaning.

A metaphor cannot be a proper name, since proper names are incompatible with generic import, unless the name bears some kind of attributive meaning, e.g., *Ḥātim*.[7]

---

[1] *Ladā asadin* (in the presence of a lion) is the predicate of an omitted subject; the implicit [sentence] is *ana ladā asadin* (I am in the presence of a lion). Or it is the predicate of *kāna*, which is omitted along with its subject-noun, i.e., *ana kuntu ladā asadin* (I was in the presence of a lion). *Shākī al-silāḥi* (armed to the teeth) means "fully armed"; it is deflationary because it is appropriate for the tenor of the metaphor, which is the courageous man. It is possible for *muqadhdhafin* (oft-flung) to mean "he is flung and thrown into engagements and battles," rendering it appropriate for the tenor of the metaphor and thus deflationary. But it is possible for it to mean "flesh was flung at him and he was pelted with flesh [i.e., he is muscular]," rendering it appropriate for both and thus neither deflationary nor inflationary but rather a plain metaphor.

[الاستعارة]

والاستعارة قد تقيّد بالتحقيقيّة لتحقّق معناها حسًّا أو عقلًا، كقوله:

> لَدَى أَسَدٍ شَاكِي السِّلَاحِ مُقَذَّفٍ[١]

أي «رجل شجاع»، وقوله تعالى ﴿ٱهْدِنَا ٱلصِّرَٰطَ ٱلْمُسْتَقِيمَ﴾ [١/ ٦] أي «الدين الحقّ».

والاستعارة تفارق الكذب بالبناء على التأويل ونصب القرينة على إرادة خلاف الظاهر.

ولا تكون علَمًا لمنافاة العلَم الجنسيّة إلا إذا تضمّن نوع وصفيّة، كـ«حاتم».

---

[١] «لدى أسد» خبر مبتدأ محذوف تقديره أنا لدى أسد أو خبر لكان المحذوفة مع اسمها أي أنا كنت لدى أسد، و«شاكي السلاح» أي تامّه وهذا تجريد لأنه ملائم المستعار له وهو الرجل الشجاع، و«مقذّف» يحتمل أن المراد قذف به ورمي به في الوقائع والحروب فيكون ملائمًا للمستعار له فيكون تجريدًا ويحتمل أن المراد قذف ورمي باللحم فيكون ملائمًا لهما فلا يكون تجريدًا ولا ترشيحًا بل هو [في] معنى الإطلاق.

[Types of Metaphor]

There are many classifications of metaphor in accordance with different considerations. Metaphor divides into two types in consideration of the objects of comparison, and likewise in consideration of the commonality; in consideration of all three, it is of six types.

[In Consideration of the Objects of Comparison] In consideration of the objects of comparison, metaphor is of two types. This is because the combination of both within a single thing may be either

1. possible, e.g., "to whom We give life" in His saying ﷻ, "Is then he who was dead and to whom We give life…" (Q 6:122), i.e., "at loss and whom we guided." The combination of giving life, which is the vehicle, with guiding, which is the tenor, is possible within a single thing. This type of metaphor is termed *concordant* on account of the concordance between the objects of comparison.
2. or impossible, e.g., to metaphorically refer to something existent as nonexistent on account of its lack of benefit. This type of metaphor is termed *discordant* and includes that whose purpose is sarcastic or witty irony, which applies to metaphors that are used to mean the contrary or contradictory opposite for such [a purpose], e.g., "Give them glad tidings of a painful punishment" (Q 3:21).

[In Consideration of the Commonality] In consideration of the commonality, metaphor is again of two types. For the commonality may be (1) conceptually internal to both objects of comparison, e.g., "Whenever he hears a frightening sound he flies toward it," for the commonality between running and flying is the traversal of distance with speed, and this is internal to both. Or the commonality may be (2) *not* conceptually internal [to both objects of comparison], e.g., "I saw a lion in the bathhouse."

[أقسام الاستعارة]

الاستعارة بالاعتبارات أقسام. الاستعارة باعتبار الطرفين قسمان وكذا باعتبار الجامع وباعتبار الثلاثة ستّة أقسام.

[باعتبار الطرفين] فهي باعتبار الطرفين قسمان لأن اجتماعهما في شيء إما:

١- ممكن، نحو «أحييناه» في قوله تعالى ﴿أَوَمَن كَانَ مَيْتًا فَأَحْيَيْنَـٰهُ﴾[1] [٦/ ١٢٢] أي «ضالًّا فهديناه» فجمع الإحياء الذي هو المستعار منه للهداية التي هي المستعار له يمكن في شيء واحد، وتسمّى وفاقيّة لما بين الطرفين من الوفاق.

٢- وإما ممتنع، كاستعارة اسم المعدوم للموجود لعدم نفعه، وتسمّى عنادية، ومنها التهكّميّة والتمليحيّة وهما لما استعمل في ضدّه أو نقيضه لما مرّ، نحو ﴿فَبَشِّرْهُم بِعَذَابٍ أَلِيمٍ﴾ [٣/ ٢١].

[باعتبار الجامع] وباعتبار الجامع أيضا قسمان لأنه إما (١) داخل في مفهوم الطرفين، نحو «كلما سمع هيعة طار إليها» فإن الجامع بين العدو والطيران هو قطع المسافة بسرعة وهو داخل فيهما؛ وإما (٢) غير داخل، نحو «رأيت أسدًا في الحمّام».

Furthermore, a metaphor is either (1) *common*, namely, that which is commonplace because of the apparentness of the commonality in it, e.g., "I saw a lion flinging"; or (2) *special*, namely, that which is abstruse and which only a specific group will recognize, e.g.,

> *wa-idhā iḥtabā qarabūsuhu bi-ʿinānihi*
> And when his saddlebow sits upright
> enwrapped with his reins
>
> *ʿalaka al-shakīma ilā inṣirāfi al-zāʾiri*
> He champs the bit until the departure
> of the visitor[1]

i.e., "When the owner of the horse fastens the bridle, the horse stands still."

[In Consideration of All Three] In consideration of all three, metaphor is of six types because

(A) if both of the objects of comparison are sensory, then

1. the commonality may be sensory, e.g., "Then he brought forth for them a calf" (Q 20:88). The vehicle is a young cow, the tenor is the creature that Allah ﷻ created from the jewelry of the Egyptians, and the commonality between them is the shape. Each of these is sensory.

[1] *Qarabūs* (saddlebow) (with *fatḥ* of the *rāʾ*, which may only be left vowelless by poetic license) means the arch [at one end] of a saddle, and the two are *qarabūsān*. *ʿInān* (reins) (with *kasr* of the *ʿayn*) means the strap of a bridle by which one controls an animal. *Shakīm* and *shakīma* (bit) mean the piece of metal that lies across in the mouth of a horse and on which lies the port. By "the visitor" [the poet] means himself, as evidenced by the previous verse, namely,

> *ʿawwadtuhu fī-mā azūru ḥabāʾibī*
> I have accustomed him when visiting those I love
>
> *ihmālahu wa-ka-dhāka kulla makhāṭiri*
> To inattention; likewise to every peril

وأيضا إما (١) عاميّة وهي المبتذلة لظهور الجامع فيها، نحو «رأيت أسدًا يرمي»؛ أو (٢) خاصّيّة وهي الغريبة التي لا يطّلع عليها إلا الخاصّة، نحو:

> وَإِذَا احْتَبَى قَرَبُوسُهُ بِعِنَانِهِ
> عَلَكَ الشَّكِيمَ إِلَى انْصِرَافِ الزَّائِرِ[١]

أي «إذا شدّ صاحب الفرس مقدّم لجامه وقف».

[باعتبار الثلاثة] وباعتبار الثلاثة ستّة أقسام لأن:

(أ) الطرفين إن كانا حسّيّين:

١- فالجامع إما حسّي، نحو ﴿فَأَخْرَجَ لَهُمْ عِجْلًا جَسَدًا﴾ [٢٠/ ٨٨] فإن المستعار منه ولد البقرة والمستعار له الحيوان الذي خلقه الله تعالى من حليّ القبط والجامع لهما الشكل والجميع حسّي.

[١] و«القربوس» بفتح الراء ولا تسكن إلا في ضرورة الشعر وهو حنو السرج وهما قربوسان. و«العنان» بكسر العين سير اللجام الذي تمسك به الدابّة. و«الشكيم» و«الشكيمة» الحديدة المعترضة في فم الفرس فيها الفأس. وأراد بـ«الزائر» نفسه بدليل ما قبله وهو:

> عَوَّدْتُهُ فِيمَا أَزُورُ حَبَائِبِي
> إِهْمَالَهُ وَكَذَاكَ كُلَّ مَخَاطِرِ

2. the commonality may be abstract, e.g., "And a sign for them is the night: We strip the day therefrom" (Q 36:37). The vehicle is the stripping of skin from [an animal] like a sheep, and the tenor is the withdrawing of light from the place of night. Both are sensory. The commonality is the concept of one event's following another, which is abstract.

3. the commonality may be mixed, being made up of something sensory and something abstract, e.g., to say, "I saw a sun," intending a human who is like the sun in facial beauty and eminence. The former (namely, the face) is sensory, and the latter (namely, eminence) is abstract.

(B) if the objects of comparison are not both sensory, then

4. both may be abstract, e.g., "'Who has raised us from our place of sleep?'" (Q 36:52). The vehicle is sleep, the tenor is death, and the commonality is that the person does not manifest any voluntary action. Each of these is abstract.

5. the vehicle may be sensory and the tenor and commonality abstract, e.g., "So break forth as you have been commanded" (Q 15:94). The vehicle is breaking a glass vessel, which is sensory; the tenor is proclaiming [the prophetic message], and the commonality is producing an effect, which are both abstract.

6. the tenor may be sensory and the vehicle and commonality abstract, e.g., "Truly when the waters transgressed, We carried you upon the ship" (Q 69:11). The tenor is the abundance of water, which is sensory; the vehicle is arrogance, and the commonality is excessive elevation, which are both abstract.

٢- وإما [عقلي] أي الجامع عقلي، نحو ﴿وَءَايَةٌ لَّهُمُ ٱلَّيْلُ نَسْلَخُ مِنْهُ ٱلنَّهَارَ﴾ [٣٦/ ٣٧] فإن المستعار منه كشط الجلد عن نحو الشاة والمستعار له كشف الضوء عن مكان الليل وهما حسّيّان والجامع هو ما يعقل من ترتّب أمر على آخر وهو عقلي.

٣- وإما مختلف أي إما الجامع مختلف مركّب من حسّي وعقلي، كقولك «رأيت شمسًا» وأنت تريد إنسانًا كالشمس في حسن الطلعة ونباهة الشأن فالأول أي من الطلعة حسّي والثاني أي نباهة الشأن عقلي.

(ب) وإلا أي وإن لم يكن الطرفان حسّيّين:

٤- فإما الجميع عقلي، نحو ﴿مَن بَعَثَنَا مِن مَّرْقَدِنَا﴾ [٣٦/ ٥٢] فإن المستعار منه الرقاد والمستعار له الموت والجامع عدم ظهور الفعل والجميع عقلي.

٥- وإما المستعار منه حسّي والمستعار له والجامع عقليّان، نحو ﴿فَٱصْدَعْ بِمَا تُؤْمَرُ﴾ [١٥/ ٩٤] فإن المستعار منه كسر الزجاجة وهو حسّي والمستعار له التبليغ والجامع التأثير وهما عقليّان.

٦- وإما المستعار له حسّي والمستعار منه والجامع عقليّان، نحو ﴿إِنَّا لَمَّا طَغَا ٱلْمَآءُ حَمَلْنَـٰكُمْ فِى ٱلْجَارِيَةِ﴾ [٦٩/ ١١] فإن المستعار له كثرة الماء وهو حسّي والمستعار منه التكبّر والجامع الاستعلاء المفرط وهما عقليّان.

Primary and Secondary Metaphor

When the metaphorical expression is a generic noun, the metaphor is *primary*, e.g., “lion” and “killing”; otherwise, it is *secondary*, e.g., verbs, derivative nouns, and particles. The simile in the first two [i.e., verbs and derivative nouns] concerns the infinitive meaning—that is, the meaning that is the source notion—while in the third (i.e., the particle) it concerns the related notion of the particle’s meaning—that is, the general meanings by which one expresses the meanings of particles, such as the general notion of ‘being within’, by which one expresses the meaning of *fī*. For example, one says, *Zaydun fī niʿmatin* (Zayd is in a blessed state): the vehicle here is the literal, [physical] notion of ‘being within’.

Thus, in *naṭaqat al-ḥālu… / al-ḥālu nāṭiqatun bi-kadhā* (The circumstance told… / The circumstance tells of such and such), [the function of] indicating is implicitly likened to [the action of] speaking (*nuṭq*). And in the *lām* of causality—e.g., “Thus the house of Pharaoh picked him up so that he would become (*li-yakūna*) to them an enemy and a sorrow” (Q 28:8)—the consequentiality of enmity and sorrow in relation to the picking up [of Mūsā is implicitly likened to] the consequentiality of a thing’s purpose in relation to the thing. [To express this simile], the *lām*, which is assigned to the vehicle, has been used for the tenor.

The default contextual indicant of metaphor in the first two [i.e., verbs and derivative nouns] is the mention of a [particular] (1) agent, e.g., *naṭaqat al-ḥālu* (The circumstance told); (2) object, e.g.,

> *qatala al-bukhla wa-aḥyā al-samāḥa*
> He slew miserliness and revived generosity[1]

[1] The first hemistich of the verse is *jumiʿa al-ḥaqqu lanā fī imāmin* (The truth was consolidated for us in an imam). *Samāḥ* means *karam* (generosity).

الاستعارة الأصلية والتبعية

اللفظ المستعار إن كان اسم جنس فالاستعارة أصليّة كـ«أسد» و«قتل» وإلا فتبعيّة كالفعل وما اشتقّ منه والحرف. فالتشبيه في الأولين في المعنى المصدري أي في المعنى الذي هو المصدر وفي الثالث الذي هو الحرف في متعلّق معناه وهو ما يعبّر به عن معاني الحروف من المعاني المطلقة وذلك كمطلق الظرفيّة المعبّر به عن معنى «في» نحو قولك «زيد في نعمة» والمشبّه بها هنا الظرفيّة الحقيقيّة.

فيقدّر التشبيه في «نطقت الحال... والحال ناطقة بكذا» للدلالة بالنطق وفي لام التعليل نحو ﴿فَٱلْتَقَطَهُۥٓ ءَالُ فِرْعَوْنَ لِيَكُونَ لَهُمْ عَدُوًّا وَحَزَنًا﴾ [٢٨/ ٨] لترتّب العداوة والحزن على الالتقاط بترتّب علّته الغائيّة عليه ثم استعمل في المشبّه اللام الموضوعة للمشبّه به.

ومدار قرينتها في الأولين على ذكر (١) الفاعل نحو «نطقت الحال» أو (٢) المفعول نحو:

> قَتَلَ البُخْلَ وَأَحْيَا السَّمَاحَا[١]

[١] صدره «جُمِعَ الحَقُّ لَنَا فِي إِمَامٍ». ومعنى «السماح» الكرم.

or (3) genitive noun, e.g., *fa-bashshirhum bi-'adhābin alīmin* (Give them glad tidings of a painful punishment) (Q 3:21).

Plain, Deflated, and Inflated Metaphor

In consideration of whether accompanied by what suits the vehicle or suits the tenor, metaphor is of three types:

1. *plain*, i.e., that which is not accompanied by anything that suits either the tenor or the vehicle, e.g., "I saw a lion in the bathhouse."
2. *deflated*, i.e., that which is accompanied by something that suits the tenor, e.g., [the poet's] saying,

   ghamru al-ridā'i idhā tabassama ḍāḥikan
   Possessed of a copious cloak; when he smiles in laughter,

   ghaliqat li-ḍaḥkatihi riqābu al-māli
   The necks of his wealth are foreclosed by his laugh[1]

3. *inflated*, i.e., that which is accompanied by something that suits the vehicle, e.g., "It is they who have purchased error at the price of guidance. Their commerce has not brought them profit" (Q 2:16).

It is possible for the latter two to be combined, as in [the poet's] saying,

[1] *Ghamr* (copious) (with *fatḥ* of the *ghayn*) is the predicate of an omitted subject; the implicit sentence is *huwa ghamru...* (He is possessed of a copious...), i.e., one who gives much. *Ḍāḥikan* (laughing) means he has begun to laugh or has just taken to laughing. *Ghaliqat* (foreclosed) (vowelized like *'alimat* [she knew]) means "became legally possessed by [a creditor]." *Ḍaḥka* (laugh) (with *fatḥ* of the *ḍād*) is an instance of laughing. The meaning [of the verse] is that when the person being praised smiles, the necks of his wealth are foreclosed and enter legally into the hands of those who had asked.

أو (٣) المجرور نحو ﴿فَبَشِّرْهُم بِعَذَابٍ أَلِيمٍ﴾ [٣/ ٢١].

الاستعارة المطلقة والمجردة والمرشحة

وهي باعتبار الاقتران بما يلائم المستعار منه أو له ثلاثة أقسام:

١- مطلقة وهي ما لم تقترن بما يلائم المستعار له ولا بما يلائم المستعار منه، نحو «رأيت أسدًا في الحمّام».

٢- ومجرّدة وهي ما قرن بما يلائم المستعار له، كقوله:

غَمْرُ الرِّدَاءِ إِذَا تَبَسَّمَ ضَاحِكًا
غَلِقَتْ لِضَحْكَتِهِ رِقَابُ المَالِ[١]

٣- ومرشّحة وهي ما قرن بما يلائم المستعار منه، نحو ﴿أُوْلَٰٓئِكَ ٱلَّذِينَ ٱشْتَرَوُاْ ٱلضَّلَٰلَةَ بِٱلْهُدَىٰ فَمَا رَبِحَت تِّجَٰرَتُهُمْ﴾ [٢/ ١٦].

وقد يجتمعان، كقوله:

[١] «غمر» بفتح الغين خبر لمبتدأ محذوف تقديره «هو غمر...» إلخ أي «كثير العطاء». و«ضاحكًا» أي «شارعًا في الضحك آخذا فيه». و«غلقت» كـ«عَلِمَتْ» أي «تمكّنت». و«الضحكة» بفتح الضاد المرّة من الضحك. أي «إذا تبسّم الممدوح غلقت وتمكّنت رقاب أمواله في أيدي السائلين».

ladā asadin shākī al-silāḥi muqadhdhafin
In the presence of a lion armed to the teeth and oft-flung,

lahu libadun aẓfāruhu lam tuqallami
Who has a mane and whose claws are not pared[1]

Inflation is most emphatic because it entails actualizing the hyperbole and because it is based on disregarding the simile, such that one may speak about high esteem on the basis of what applies to high location, e.g., [the poet's] saying,

wa-yaṣʿadu ḥattā yaẓunna al-jahūlu
He ascends until the ignoramus supposes

bi-anna lahu ḥājatan fī al-samāʾi
That he has some business in the sky

لَدَى أَسَدٍ شَاكِي السِّلَاحِ مُقَذَّفٍ
لَهُ لِبَدٌ أَظْفَارُهُ لَمْ تُقَلَّمِ[١]

والترشيح أبلغ لاشتماله على تحقيق المبالغة ومبناه على تناسي التشبيه، حتى أنه يبنى على علوّ القدر ما يبنى على علوّ المكان، كقوله:

وَيَصْعَدُ حَتَّى يَظُنَّ الجَهُولُ
بِأَنَّ لَهُ حَاجَةً فِي السَّمَاءِ

[1] *Ladā asadin* (in the presence of a lion) is the predicate of an omitted subject; the implicit [sentence] is *ana ladā asadin* (I am in the presence of a lion). Or it is the predicate of *kāna*, which is omitted along with its subject-noun, i.e., *ana kuntu ladā asadin* (I was in the presence of a lion). *Shākī al-silāḥi* (armed to the teeth) means "fully armed"; it is deflationary because it is appropriate for the tenor of the metaphor, which is the courageous man. It is possible for *muqadhdhafin* (oft-flung) to mean "he is flung and thrown into engagements and battles," rendering it appropriate for the tenor of the metaphor and thus deflationary. But it is possible for it to mean "flesh was flung at him and he was pelted with flesh [i.e., he is muscular]," rendering it appropriate for both and thus neither deflationary nor inflationary but rather plain. *Libad* (mane) (vowelized like *ʿinab* [grapes]) is the plural of *libda*, which is any part of the fur of a lion that is matted and clings to its flank; it is appropriate for the vehicle and thus inflationary. "Whose claws are not pared" can mean that his claws are not of the kind that is subject to paring, rendering it inflationary; it can mean the negation of an emphatic paring of his nails, such that the unemphatic meaning is affirmed for them, rendering it deflationary; and it can be a case of emphasizing the negation instead of negating the emphasis, such that the meaning is that the paring of his claws is negated emphatically, rendering it, again, inflationary.

[١] «لدى أسد» خبر مبتدأ محذوف تقديره «أنا لدى أسد» أو خبر لـ«كان» المحذوفة مع اسمها أي «أنا كنت لدى أسد». و«شاكي السلاح» أي «تامّه» وهذا تجريد لأنه ملائم المستعار له وهو الرجل الشجاع. و«مقذّف» يحتمل أن المراد «قُذف به ورُمي به في الوقائع والحروب» فيكون ملائمًا للمستعار له فيكون تجريدًا، ويحتمل أن المراد «قُذف ورُمي باللحم» فيكون ملائمًا لهما فلا يكون تجريدًا ولا ترشيحًا بل هو [في] معنى الإطلاق. و«لبد» كـ«عنب» جمع «لبدة» وهي ما تلبد وتضامّ من شعر الأسد على منكبه فيكون ملائمًا للمستعار منه فيكون ترشيحًا. و«أظفاره لم تقلم» يحتمل أن يراد به أنه ليس من جنس من شأنه تقليم الأظفار فيكون ترشيحًا، ويحتمل أن يراد به أن أظفاره انتفت المبالغة في تقليمها فيكون أصله ثابتًا لها فيكون تجريدًا، ويحتمل أن يكون من المبالغة في النفي لا من نفي المبالغة والمعنى أن أظفاره انتفى تقليمها انتفاءً مبالغًا فيه فيكون ترشيحًا أيضا.

And since it is valid to speak on the basis of what applies to the newly introduced [vehicle for a simile] while still acknowledging the originally intended [tenor of the simile]—as in [the poet's] saying,

> *hiya al-shamsu maskanuhā fī al-samāʾi*
> She is the sun; her dwelling is in the sky,
>
> *fa-ʿazzi al-fuʾāda ʿazāʾan jamīlā*
> So condole with your heart in sweet patience:
>
> *fa-lan tastaṭīʿa ilayhā al-ṣuʿūda*
> Never can you ascend to it,
>
> *wa-lan tastaṭīʿa ilayka al-nuzūlā*
> And never can it descend to you[8]

—it is even more proper that it be valid to speak on the basis of the newly introduced [vehicle for a metaphor] in cases when one discards the originally intended [tenor of the metaphor].

Implicit Metaphor

One might internally conceal a simile, explicitly expressing none of its components except the tenor, indicating the simile by affirming for the tenor something specific to the vehicle.[9] Such a simile is termed a *metaphor with concealment* or an *implicit metaphor*.

Affirming that thing for the tenor is *metaphorical characterization*, as when al-Hudhalī says,

> *wa-idhā al-maniyyatu anshabat aẓfārahā*
> And when death digs in its claws,
>
> *alfayta kulla tamīmatin lā tanfaʿu*
> You will find no amulet of any avail[1]

[1] *Maniyya* means *mawt* (death), and it is the agent of an omitted verb that is interpreted by *anshabat* (dug in), which means *ʿallaqat* (attached). A *tamīma* (amulet) is a *kharaza* (strung bead) that is made into a protective charm and hung on the necks of children to ward off the evil eye and the jinn, they claim.

وإذا جاز البناء على الفرع مع الاعتراف بالأصل كما في قوله:

هِيَ الشَّمْسُ مَسْكَنُهَا فِي السَّمَاءِ
فَعَزِّ الفُؤَادَ عَزَاءً جَمِيلَا
فَلَنْ تَسْتَطِيعَ إِلَيْهَا الصُّعُودَ
وَلَنْ تَسْتَطِيعَ إِلَيْكَ النُّزُولَا

فمع جحد الأصل يكون البناء على الفرع أولى بالجواز.

الاستعارة بالكناية

قد يضمر التشبيه في النفس فلا يصرّح بشيء من أركانه سوى المشبّه ويدلّ عليه بأن يثبت للمشبّه أمر يختصّ بالمشبّه به فيسمّى التشبيه استعارة بالكناية أو مكنيًّا عنها.

وإثبات ذلك الأمر للمشبّه استعارة تخييليّة، كما في قول الهذلي:

وَإِذَا المَنِيَّةُ أَنْشَبَتْ أَظْفَارَهَا
أَلْفَيْتَ كُلَّ تَمِيمَةٍ لَا تَنْفَعُ[١]

[١] «المنيّة» الموت وهو فاعل فعل محذوف يفسّره «أنشبت» أي «علّقت». و«ألفيت» أي «وجدت». و«التميمة» الخرزة بفتح الخاء والراء التي تجعل معاذة أي تعلّق على عنق الصبيان صونًا لهم عن العين أو الجنّ على زعمهم.

He likens death to a predator in that it seizes lives by force and overwhelming power without discriminating between those who are beneficent and those who are pernicious; then he affirmed for death claws, without which such seizing would be incomplete. Another example of metaphorical characterization is another [poet's] saying,

> *wa-la-in naṭaqtu bi-shukri birrika mufṣihan*
> Indeed, were I to clearly articulate
> gratitude for your kindness—
>
> *fa-lisānu ḥālī bi-l-shikāyati anṭaqu*
> The tongue of my condition, bespeaking
> complaint, is more articulate

i.e., "more articulate in the absence of gratitude." He likens his condition to a speaking human being in that it can express an intended meaning; then he affirms for his condition a tongue, by which this is possible for a speaking human being.

What Gives Aptness to a Metaphor?

The aptness of actual metaphors and of analogies derives from their fulfilling the conditions for an apt simile without their even catching the scent of simile in terms of their expressed form. On this account, it is advisable that the commonality between the two objects of comparison be evident, lest the metaphor become a puzzle, e.g., if one were to say, "I saw a lion," meaning a human being with bad breath, or, "I saw a hundred camels not a single one of which was fit for use," meaning people. This shows that simile is broader than metaphor in terms of the situations in which one can use it.

In connection with this, when the similarity between the objects of comparison is so strong that they are as one, e.g., knowledge and light and doubt and darkness, simile becomes unsuitable: one must use metaphor. Implicit metaphor is like actual metaphor [in the conditions for its suitability], and the suitability of metaphorical characterization is determined by [the same conditions as] the suitability of implicit metaphor.

شبّه المنيّة بالسبع في اغتيال النفوس بالقهر والغلبة من غير تفرقة بين نفّاع وضرّار فأثبت لها الأظفار التي لا يكمل ذلك الاغتيال فيه بدونها، وكما في قول الآخر:

> وَلَئِنْ نَطَقْتُ بِشُكْرِ بِرِّكَ مُفْصِحًا
>
> فَلِسَانُ حَالِي بِالشِّكَايَةِ أَنْطَقُ

أي «بعدم الشكر أنطق» — شبّه الحال بإنسان متكلّم في الدلالة على المقصود فأثبت لها اللسان الذي به قوامها في الإنسان المتكلّم.

حسن الاستعارة بم؟

حسن كل من التحقيقيّة والتمثيل برعاية جهات حسن التشبيه[٢] وأن لا يشمّ رائحته لفظًا. ولذلك يوصى أن يكون ما به الشبه بين الطرفين جليًّا لئلّا تصير إلغازًا كما لو قيل «رأيت أسدًا» وأريد إنسانًا أبخر و«رأيت إبلًا مائةً لا تجد فيها راحلة» وأريد الناس. وبهذا ظهر أن التشبيه أعمّ من الاستعارة محلًّا.

ويتّصل به أنه إذا قوي الشبه بين الطرفين حتى اتّحدا كالعلم والنور والشبهة والظلمة لم يحسن التشبيه وتعيّنت الاستعارة. والمكنيّ عنها كالتحقيقيّة والتخييليّة حسنها بحسب حسن المكنيّ عنها.

❁ ❁ ❁

Terming As *Majāz* a Word the Status of Whose Inflection Has Changed

[The term] *majāz* is sometimes used to refer to a word the status of whose inflection has changed by the omission or addition of a word, e.g., His saying ﷻ, "And your Lord comes" (Q 89:22), "'Ask the town'" (Q 12:82), and *laysa ka-mithlihi shay'un* (There is nothing like Him) (Q 42:11), i.e., "the command of your Lord," "the people of the town," and *laysa mithlahu shay'un* (There is nothing like Him). None of these is *majāz* (nonliteral language) in the technical sense; [the term] *majāz* is only used for them in an extended kind of usage.

إطلاق المجاز على كلمة تغير حكم إعرابها

وقد يطلق «المجاز» على كلمة تغيّر حكم إعرابها بحذف لفظ أو زيادة لفظ، كقوله تعالى ﴿وَجَآءَ رَبُّكَ﴾ [٨٩/ ٢٢]، ﴿وَسْـَٔلِ ٱلْقَرْيَةَ﴾ [١٢/ ٨٢]، و﴿لَيْسَ كَمِثْلِهِۦ شَىْءٌ﴾ [٤٢/ ١١] أي «أمر ربّك» و«أهل القرية» و«ليس مثله شيء». كل من هذه ليس من المجاز المصطلح عليه وإنما أطلق «المجاز» عليه بنوع من التجوّز.

Chapter 3

IMPLICATION

What is implication? How many types of it are there? Are nonliteral language and implication more emphatic than literal and direct language?

[The Definition of the Implicative Expression]

An implicative expression is a verbal expression by which one intends an implicate of the meaning while it remains possible that the meaning [itself] could be intended along with the implicate. One can see that implication is different from nonliteral language with respect to intending the literal meaning of the expression along with its implicate. [Others] have made the distinction that while in implication one transitions from the implicate, in nonliteral language one transitions from the implicant. This distinction is refuted by [pointing out] that one cannot transition from the implicate unless it implies in itself, but if the implicate does imply in itself, then to transition [from it] is to transition from an *implicant.*

[The Types of Implication]

Implication is of three types: (1) that by which the very thing described is intended, (2) that by which an attribute is intended, and (3) that by which an attribution is intended.

1. The first type of implication is that by which the very thing described is intended, e.g., [the poet's] saying,

   wa-l-ṭāʿinīna majāmiʿa al-aḍghāni
   And those who thrust at the gathering places of rancor

الباب الثالث

الكنـايـة

ما الكناية؟ وكم قسمًا هي؟ هل المجاز والكناية أبلغ من الحقيقة والتصريح؟

[تعريف الكناية]

الكنايــة لفــظ أريــد بــه لازم معنــاه مــع جــواز إرادتــه معــه. فظهــر أنهــا تخالــف المجــاز مــن جهــة إرادة المــعنى الحقــيقي للفــظ مــع إرادة لازمــه؛ وفُــرّق بــأن الانتقــال فيهــا مــن اللازم وفيــه مــن الملــزوم ورُدّ بــأن اللازم مــا لــم يكــن ملزومًــا لــم ينتقــل منــه وحينئــذ يكــون الانتقــال مــن الملــزوم.

[أقسام الكناية]

الكنايــة ثلاثــة أقســام: (١) المطلــوب بهــا نفــس الموصــوف (٢) والمطلــوب بهــا الصفــة (٣) والمطلــوب بهــا النســبة.

١- الأولى مــن أقســام الكنايــة المطلــوب بهــا نفــس الموصــوف، كقــوله:

وَالطَّاعِــنِينَ مَجَامِــعَ الأَضْغَــانِ

i.e., "I praise those who strike by sword and thrust by spear at the gathering places of rancor." *Ḍighn* (rancor) means *ḥiqd* (hatred). "The gathering places of rancor" implies 'hearts'. Another example is to say, "a living being of upright stature and wide nails," to imply 'human being'. It is a condition in both of these that [the description] be specific to the thing being implied.

أي «أمدح الضاربين بالسيف والطاعنين بالرمح مجامع الأضغان». و«الضغن» الحقد، و«مجامع الأضغان» كناية عن القلوب. وكقولنا كناية عن الإنسان «حيّ مستوي القامة عريض الأظفار». وشرطهما الاختصاص بالمكني عنه.

2. The second type of implication is that by which an attribute is intended. If the transition does not occur through an intermediate step, the implication is either (a) *direct* and clear, e.g., when one implies 'having tall stature' by "having long sword straps"; or (b) *obscure*, e.g., when one implies 'dull fellow' by "one who has a wide nape." If the transition occurs through an intermediate step, the implication is (c) *far-removed*, e.g., "one who has abundant ashes" to imply 'hospitable host', since [the listener's mind] transitions from 'having abundant ashes' to 'frequently burning firewood under cooking pots' to 'abundantly cooking food' to 'having a great number of people eating' to 'having frequent guests' to the intended meaning.

٢- الثانية منها المطلوب بها صفة، (١) فإن لم يكن الانتقال بواسطة فقريبة واضحة كقولهم كناية عن طول القامة «طويل نجاده» أو «طويل النجاد»، أو خفيّة كقولهم كناية عن الأبله «عريض القفا»؛ (٢) وإن كان بواسطة فبعيدة كقولهم «كثير الرماد» كناية عن المضياف فإنه ينتقل من كثرة الرماد إلى كثرة إحراق الحطب تحت القدور ومنها إلى كثرة الطبائخ ومنها إلى كثرة الأكلة ومنها إلى كثرة الضيفان ومنها إلى المقصود.

3. The third type of implication is that by which an attribution is intended, e.g., [the poet's] saying,

> *inna al-samāḥata wa-l-murūʾata wa-l-nadā*
> Truly, openhandedness, magnanimity, and largesse
>
> *fī qubbatin ḍuribat ʿalā Ibni al-Ḥashraji*
> Are within a round tent pitched over Ibn al-Ḥashraj[1]

٣- الثالثة منها المطلوب بها نسبة، كقوله:

إِنَّ السَّمَاحَةَ وَالمُرُوءَةَ وَالنَّدَا
فِي قُبَّةٍ ضُرِبَتْ عَلَى ابْنِ الحَشْرَجِ[١]

[1] Openhandedness is to gladly give of wealth what one is not required to give, whether one gives little or much. Largesse is to give abundant wealth in order to merit matters of significance that are general, like the praise of every person. In common to both is generosity. Magna-

[١] «السماحة» بذل ما لا يجب بذله من المال عن طيب نفس سواء كان المبذول قليلًا أو كثيرًا، و«الندى» بذل الأموال الكثيرة لاكتساب الأمور الجليلة العامّة كثناء كل أحد؛ ويجمعها الكرم. و«المروءة» في العرف سعة الإحسان بالأموال وغيرها كالعفو عن الجناية؛ وتفسّر بكمال الرجولية لكن يرد عليه أنه يقتضي

since the poet meant to affirm that these qualities are specific to Ibn al-Ḥashraj. He did not use direct language, as by saying, "They are particular to him," or anything of the sort; he opted for implication by situating the qualities within a dome cast over him. A similar example is when they say, "Glory lies between his garments," or, "Generosity lies between his shawls."

فإنه أراد أن يثبت اختصاص ابن الحشرج بهذه الصفات فترك التصريح بأن يقول «إنه مختصّ بها» أو نحوه إلى الكناية بأن جعلها في قبّة مضروبة عليه، ونحوه قولهم «المجد بين ثوبيه» و«الكرم بين برديه».

In the latter two types, the thing described might remain unmentioned, e.g., to indirectly allude to a [specific] person who hurts Muslims by saying, "A Muslim is one from whose tongue and hand Muslims are safe,"[10] which implies the negation of the attribute of Islam from the hurtful person while he remains unmentioned in the sentence.

والموصوف في هذين القسمين قد يكون غير مذكور، كما يقال في عرض من يؤذي المسلمين «المسلم من سلم المسلمون من لسانه ويده» فإنه كناية عن نفي صفة الإسلام عن المؤذي وهو غير مذكور في الكلام.

❋ ❋ ❋

Al-Sakkākī states: Implication varies from allusion to hinting to intimation to pointing to direct indication. The appropriate [name for an implicative

قال السكّاكي: الكناية تتفاوت إلى تعريض وتلويح ورمز وإشارة وإيماء. والمناسب

nimity by convention means being vast in kindness with one's wealth and other things, as by pardoning offenses. It may be interpreted as the perfection of manliness, though this would lead to the problem that [this virtue] would be specific to men to the exclusion of women, which is at odds with the fact that women can indeed be described as magnanimous. This is so unless one says that the intended meaning of manliness is 'humanity' in a sense that includes the male and the female. Magnanimity may also be interpreted as a desire to maintain one's guard against those attributes that disgrace a person and to maintain those attributes that raise a person above his peers; and this interpretation is similar to the previous one. Now, placing these three qualities into a round tent pitched over Ibn al-Ḥashraj implies that they are firmly established; for when something is affirmed in the place and location of the man, it is affirmed of the man himself.

اختصاصها بالرجل دون المرأة مع أنها تتّصف بالمروءة، إلا أن يقال المراد بالرجوليّة الإنسانيّة الشاملة للذكر والأنثى؛ وتفسّر أيضا بالرغبة في المحافظة على دفع ما يعاب به الإنسان وعلى ما يرفع به على الأقران وهذا قريب ممّا قبله. ثم في جعل هذه الصفات الثلاث في قبّة مضروبة على ابن الحشرج كناية عن ثبوتها لأنه إذا أثبت الأمر في مكان الرجل وحيّزه فقد أثبت له.

expression] that indirectly alludes is *allusion.*[1] Otherwise, if there are many intermediate steps [of inference], it is *hinting*. If there are few intermediate steps but there is obscurity, it is *intimation*; without obscurity it is *direct indication* or *pointing*.

للعرضيّة «التعريض»[١] ولغيرها إن كثرت الوسائط «التلويح» وإن قلّت مع خفاء «الرمز» وبلا خفاء «الإيماء» و«الإشارة».

He states furthermore: Allusion may be nonliteral, e.g., to say, "You hurt me, so you will learn," intending someone else in the presence of the person you are addressing. If you intend both people, it is implication. In either case there must be a contextual indicant.

ثم قال: والتعريض قد يكون مجازًا كقولك «آذيتني فستعرف» وأنت تريد إنسانًا مع المخاطب دونه، وإن أردتهما جميعًا كان كناية. ولا بدّ فيهما من قرينة.

Are Nonliteral Language and Implication More Emphatic Than Literal and Direct Language?

The rhetoricians concur that nonliteral language and implication are more emphatic than literal language and direct language because in the former two one transitions from the implicant to the implicate and this is like bringing forth a claim with evidence. And [they concur] that metaphor is more emphatic than simile because metaphor is a kind of nonliteral language.

هل المجاز والكناية أبلغ من الحقيقة والتصريح؟

أطبق البلغاء على أن المجاز والكناية أبلغ من الحقيقة والتصريح لأن الانتقال فيهما من الملزوم إلى اللازم فهو كدعوى الشيء ببيّنة، وأن الاستعارة أبلغ من التشبيه لأنها نوع من المجاز.

❁ ❁ ❁

By the assistance of Allah ﷻ, the treatise entitled *The Elucidation: On the Science of Figurative Language* is complete. May Allah ﷻ by His grace and generosity render it of benefit to us and all believers. Allah! "Take us not to task if we forget or err!" (Q 2:286). "Glory to your Lord, Lord of Might, transcending what they describe! Peace be upon the messengers. And praise to Allah, Lord of the worlds" (Q 37:180–82). By His permission ﷻ, the ninth treatise follows, entitled *The Vernal Downpour: On the Science of Embellishment*.

تمّت بعون الله تعالى الرسالة المسمّاة بالتبيان في علم البيان جعلها الله تعالى بمنّه وكرمه نافعة لنا ولسائر المؤمنين. اللّهم لا تؤاخذنا إن نسينا أو أخطأنا. ﴿سُبْحَٰنَ رَبِّكَ رَبِّ ٱلْعِزَّةِ عَمَّا يَصِفُونَ ۝١٨٠ وَسَلَٰمٌ عَلَى ٱلْمُرْسَلِينَ ۝١٨١ وَٱلْحَمْدُ لِلَّهِ رَبِّ ٱلْعَٰلَمِينَ﴾ [٣٧/ ١٨٠-١٨٢]. وتليها بإذنه تعالى الرسالة التاسعة المسمّاة الغيث الربيع في علم البديع.

---

[1] That is, the appropriate [name] for an implication that indirectly alludes to someone who fits the description without his being explicitly mentioned is *allusion*.

[١] أي والمناسب للكناية إذا كانت تعريضًا مسوقًا لموصوف غير مذكور «التعريض».

NOTES TO TREATISE VIII

1 In its lexical sense, *tashbīh* need not even involve the particle *kāf* or an independent word. Even a statement like *qātala Zaydun ʿAmran* (Zayd fought with ʿAmr) is an instance of "simile" in the lexical sense because the form of the verb signifies that Zayd and ʿAmr share in the action of fighting, an attribute common to both of them. Al-Taftāzānī, *Mukhtaṣar*, 2:17.

2 The source text for this passage, al-Taftāzānī's *Mukhtaṣar al-maʿānī*, lists three possibilities for the ground in this category: the species, the genus, and the differentia. Thus, the original example reads *hādhā al-qamīṣu mithlu dhālika fī kawnihimā kattānan aw thawban aw min quṭnin* (This shirt is like that one in that they are both linen garments / ...in that they are both garments / ...in that they are both made of cotton), where linen garments are an example of a species, garments are an example of a genus, and being made of cotton is an example of a differentia. Al-Taftāzānī, *Mukhtaṣar*, 2:29.

3 Refer to Treatise V, pp. 316–18, for a more comprehensive list.

4 Refer to Treatise III, pp. 226–28, for discussion of the modes of signification.

5 See the section on composite metaphor in Treatise V, p. 332.

6 Courageous men exist to the senses, and the true religion exists to the intellect.

7 In Arab culture, the name Ḥātim is associated with a legendary person by that name who was known for being extraordinarily generous.

8 This is an example of simile (*tashbīh*), specifically *hyperbolic simile* (*tashbīh balīgh*). The point is that although hyperbolic simile acknowledges the original tenor of the simile (the beloved), it still speaks about that tenor on the basis of the vehicle (the sun). Since metaphor (*istiʿāra*) does not even acknowledge the original tenor to begin with, it makes even more sense that metaphor would speak about the tenor on the basis of the vehicle.

9 The definition of implicit metaphor as a concealed simile belongs to Muḥammad b. ʿAbd al-Raḥmān al-Qazwīnī (d. 739/1338). See al-Taftāzānī, *Mukhtaṣar*, 2:149–50.

10 That is, quoting a prophetic statement narrated in al-Bukhārī, *al-Jāmiʿ al-ṣaḥīḥ*, 1:11 (no. 10).

IX

THE VERNAL DOWNPOUR

On the science of embellishment

الغيث الربيع في علم البديع

In the Name of Allah,
All-Merciful, Most Compassionate

ALL PRAISE IS due to Allah, Lord of the worlds. May blessings and peace be upon our messenger, Muḥammad, and upon all of his family and Companions.

To Proceed This is a treatise on the science of embellishment. I have entitled it *The Vernal Downpour: On the Science of Embellishment*. By His leave ﷻ, we will discuss in this treatise the principal questions of the science of embellishment.

The science of embellishment is a science by which one knows the methods by which speech is beautified after it is ensured that the speech corresponds to what the situation demands, is free of overcomplication, and clearly signifies [the intended meaning].[1] The aim of the science is to know the methods, both semantic and verbal, of beautifying speech. Its subject matter is the investigation into the methods of beautifying speech.

These methods are numerous. The most important of them are the following.

I. Antithesis

Antithesis, which is also termed "correspondence" or "contrast," is the juxtaposition of contraries—that is, two opposing ideas—in a sentence. It may

بسم الله الرحمن الرحيم

الحمد لله ربّ العالمين والصلاة والسلام على رسولنا محمد وعلى آله وصحبه أجمعين.

أما بعد فهذه رسالة في علم البديع سمّيتها الغيث الربيع في علم البديع نذكر فيها بإذنه تعالى عيون مسائل علم البديع.

علم البديع هو علم يعرف به وجوه تحسين الكلام بعد رعاية المطابقة لمقتضى الحال وخلوّه عن التعقيد ووضوح الدلالة. وغايته معرفة وجوه تحسين الكلام معنويّة كانت الوجوه أو لفظيّة. وموضوعه البحث عن وجوه تحسين الكلام.

وهي كثيرة وأهمّها:

١. المطابقة

ويقال له الطباق والتضادّ أيضا وهي جمع بين المتضادّين أي معنيين متقابلين في الجملة. ويكون بلفظين من

occur with words that belong to the same part of speech, whether as (1) nouns, e.g., *wa-taḥsabuhum <u>ayqāẓan</u> wa-hum <u>ruqūdun</u>* (You would have thought them awake, though they were asleep) (Q 18:18), as (2) verbs, e.g., *yuḥyī wa-yumītu* (He gives life and causes death) (Q 2:258); or as (3) particles, e.g., *<u>lahā</u> mā kasabat wa-<u>ʿalayhā</u> mā iktasabat* (It shall have what it has earned and be subject to what it has perpetrated) (Q 2:286). [It may also occur with words] that belong to different parts of speech, e.g., *a-wa-man kāna <u>maytan</u> fa-<u>aḥyaynāhu</u> wa-jaʿalnā lahu nūran yamshī bihi* (Is then he who was dead and to whom we gave life, making for him a light by which to walk...) (Q 6:122).

II. Association

Association is also termed "harmony" or "conformity" and is the juxtaposition of an [idea] with a matching [idea] without contrast, e.g., "The <u>sun</u> and the <u>moon</u> are upon an exact reckoning" (Q 55:5).

III. Semblance

Semblance is to give one thing the name of another because it stands in its contextual vicinity either explicitly or implicitly. An example of the former is "'You know what is in my self and I know not what is in Your <u>Self</u>'" (Q 5:116). An example of the latter is "The <u>baptism</u> (*ṣibgha*) of Allah" (Q 2:138)—i.e., "the purification of Allah" since belief purifies souls—an emphatic infinitive that modifies "We believe in Allah": by semblance, belief in Allah is expressed as "the baptism of Allah."[2]

IV. Double Entendre

Double entendre[3] is the use of an expression that has two meanings, one immediate and one remote, intending the remote meaning. It is of two types: (1) *bare double entendre*, which is not combined with what would suit the immediate meaning, e.g.,

نوع واحد (١) اسمين نحو ﴿وَتَحۡسَبُهُمۡ أَيۡقَاظٗا وَهُمۡ رُقُودٞۚ﴾ [١٨/ ١٨]، أو (٢) فعلين نحو ﴿يُحۡيِۦ وَيُمِيتُ﴾ [٢/ ٢٥٨]، أو (٣) حرفين نحو ﴿لَهَا مَا كَسَبَتۡ وَعَلَيۡهَا مَا ٱكۡتَسَبَتۡۗ﴾ [٢/ ٢٨٦]؛ أو من نوعين نحو ﴿أَوَمَن كَانَ مَيۡتٗا فَأَحۡيَيۡنَٰهُ وَجَعَلۡنَا لَهُۥ نُورٗا يَمۡشِي بِهِۦ﴾ [٦/ ١٢٢].

٢. مراعاة النظير

يسمّى التناسب والتوفيق وهو جمع أمر وما يناسبه لا بالتضادّ، نحو ﴿ٱلشَّمۡسُ وَٱلۡقَمَرُ بِحُسۡبَانٖ﴾ [٥٥/ ٥].

٣. المشاكلة

وهي ذكر الشيء بلفظ غيره لوقوعه في صحبته تحقيقًا أو تقديرًا، فالأول نحو ﴿تَعۡلَمُ مَا فِي نَفۡسِي وَلَآ أَعۡلَمُ مَا فِي نَفۡسِكَۚ﴾ [٥/ ١١٦] والثاني نحو ﴿صِبۡغَةَ ٱللَّهِ﴾ [٢/ ١٣٨] وهو مصدر مؤكّد لـ﴿ءَامَنَّا بِٱللَّهِ﴾ أي «تطهير الله» لأن الإيمان يطهّر النفوس فعبّر عن الإيمان بالله بـ«صبغة الله» للمشاكلة.

٤. التورية

وهي أن يطلق لفظ له معنيان قريب وبعيد ويراد البعيد. وهي ضربان: (١) مجرّدة وهي التي لا تجامع

al-Raḥmānu ʿalā al-ʿarshi istawā (The All-Merciful reigns [lit., "mounted"] upon the throne) (Q 20:5), and (2) *amplified double entendre*, e.g., *wa-l-samāʾa banaynāhā bi-aydin* (And the sky have We built with might [lit., "hands"]) (Q 51:47).[4]

V. Reutilization

Reutilization is either (1) to intend by an expression that carries two meanings one of those meanings and to intend by a personal pronoun that refers to it the other, as in the [poet's] saying,

> *idhā nazala samāʾun bi-arḍi qawmin*
> When rain befalls the land of a people,
>
> *raʿaynāhu wa-in kānū ghiḍābā*
> We graze it, spiteful though they be

By *samāʾ* (sky) he means "rain," but by the pronoun referring to it in *raʿaynāhu* (we graze it) he means "the vegetation." Or it is (2) to intend by one of two personal pronouns one referent and by the other another, whether the referents be both literal, both nonliteral, or different [in this respect], as in the [poet's] saying,

> *fa-saqā al-ghaḍā wa-sākinīhi wa-in humu*
> So He watered the saxaul tree and its dwellers though they
>
> *shabbūhu bayna jawāniḥī wa-ḍulūʿī*
> Kindled it between the fore and hind of my ribs

By one of the two pronouns that refer to "the saxaul tree" (namely, the genitive pronoun in *sākinīhi* [its dwellers]) he means "the locale of the saxaul tree," and by the other (namely, the accusative pronoun in *shabbūhu* [they burned it]) he means "the fire lit from the saxaul tree." The meaning [of the verse] is "So Allah watered the locale in which the saxaul tree lives though those people ignited and kindled it in my heart, burning me with the fire of love, which is like the fire of the saxaul tree."

شيئًا مما يلائم القريب، نحو ﴿ٱلرَّحۡمَٰنُ عَلَى ٱلۡعَرۡشِ ٱسۡتَوَىٰ﴾ [٢٠/ ٥]؛ (٢) ومرشّحة، نحو ﴿وَٱلسَّمَآءَ بَنَيۡنَٰهَا بِأَيۡيْدٖ﴾ [٥١/ ٤٧].

٥. الاستخدام

وهو (١) أن يراد بلفظ له معنيان أحدهما وبضميره الآخر، كقوله:

> إِذَا نَزَلَ سَمَاءٌ بِأَرْضِ قَوْمٍ
>
> رَعَيْنَاهُ وَإِنْ كَانُوا غِضَابَا

أراد بـ«السماء» الغيث وبضميره في «رعيناه» النبت؛ أو (٢) يراد بأحد الضميرين أحدهما ثم بالآخر الآخر سواء كان المعنيان حقيقيّين أو مجازيّين أو مختلفين، كقوله:

> فَسَقَى الغَضَا وَالسَّاكِنِيهِ[١] وَإِنْ هُمُ
>
> شَبُّوهُ بَيْنَ جَوَانِحِي وَضُلُوعِي

أراد بأحد الضميرين الراجعين إلى «الغضا» أعني المجرور في «الساكنيه»[٢] المكان الذي فيه شجرة الغضا وبالآخر أعني المنصوب في «شبّوه» النار الحاصلة من شجرة الغضا، أي «فسقى الله المكان الذي فيه شجرة الغضا وإن هم أوقدوه وأحرقوه في قلبي وأحرقوني بنار الهوى التي تشبه نار الغضا».

VI. Respective Correlation

Respective correlation is to introduce multiple subjects either (1) individually or (2) collectively and then to discuss each of them without specifying [which subject one is referring to], trusting that the listener will make the respective connections.

The first, in which subjects are introduced individually, is of two subtypes, for the discussion either (a) follows the order in which the subjects were introduced, e.g., "Out of His mercy He made for you night and day, that you may rest therein and that you may seek of His bounty" (Q 28:73), or (b) it does not follow the same order, e.g., the [poet's] saying,

> *kayfa aslū wa-anti ḥiqfun wa-ghuṣnun*
> How could I forget [you], when you
> are a dune and a bough
>
> *wa-ghazālun laḥẓan wa-qaddan wa-ridfā* [1]
> And a gazelle in your glance, figure,
> and behind?

The glance refers to the gazelle, the figure refers to the bough, and the behind refers to the dune. [Another such example] is the statement "He is a sun, a lion, and an ocean in generosity, radiance, and courage."

The second, in which subjects are introduced collectively, is as in His saying ﷻ, "And they said, 'No one will enter paradise unless he be a Jew or a Christian'" (Q 2:111); that is, "The Jews said, 'No one will enter paradise unless he be a Jew,' and the Christians said, 'No one will enter paradise unless he be a Christian.'" The subjects were introduced collectively since this would not be confusing, for it is known that each group deems the other misguided.

---

[1] *Aslū* (forget) means "lose my love for you." A *ḥiqf* (dune) is a protracted and curved body of sand. *Laḥaẓahu / laḥẓan* (he glanced at him / to glance) means "he looked at him from one side out of the corner of his eye." *Qadd* means "figure" or "physique." The *ridf* is the backside or rump, and according to some, it is specific to the buttocks of a woman; regardless, its plural form is *ardāf*.

٦. اللف والنشر

وهو ذكر متعدّد على التفصيل أو الإجمال ثم يُؤتى ما لكل واحد من غير تعيين ثقةً بأن السامع يردّه إليه.

فالأول أي اللفّ تفصيلًا ضربان لأن النشر إما (١) على ترتيب اللفّ، نحو ﴿وَمِن رَّحْمَتِهِۦ جَعَلَ لَكُمُ ٱلَّيْلَ وَٱلنَّهَارَ لِتَسْكُنُواْ فِيهِ وَلِتَبْتَغُواْ مِن فَضْلِهِۦ﴾ [٢٨/ ٧٣]؛ وإما (٢) على غير ترتيبه، كقوله:

> كَيْفَ أَسْلُو وَأَنْتِ حِقْفٌ وَغُصْنٌ
>
> وَغَزَالٌ لَحْظًا وَقَدًّا وَرِدْفَا [١]

و«اللحظ» للغزال و«القدّ» للغصن و«الردف» للحقف، وقولك «هو شمس وأسد وبحر جودًا وبهاءً وشجاعةً».

والثاني أي اللفّ إجمالًا نحو قوله تعالى ﴿وَقَالُواْ لَن يَدْخُلَ ٱلْجَنَّةَ إِلَّا مَن كَانَ هُودًا أَوْ نَصَٰرَىٰ﴾ [٢/ ١١١] أي «قالت اليهود لن يدخل الجنّة إلا من كان هودًا وقالت النصارى لن يدخل الجنّة إلا من كان نصارى» فلفّ لعدم الإلباس للعلم بتضليل كل فريق صاحبه.

---

[١] «أسلو» أي «أخلص عن حبّك». «الحقف» ما استطال واعوجّ من الرمل. «لحظه لحظًا»: «نظر إليه بمؤخّر عينه من أحد جانبيه». «القدّ» القامة أو القوام. و«الردف» الكفل والعجز وخصّ بعضهم به عجيزة المرأة، والجمع من كل ذلك «أرداف».

VII. Combination

Combination is to include multiple subjects in a predication, as in His statement ﷻ "Wealth and children are the adornment of the life of this world" (Q 18:46).

VIII. Acceptable Hyperbole

Hyperbole is to affirm regarding some quality a degree of strength or weakness that is impossible or far-fetched. All hyperbole is either (1) *reasonable*, (2) *extravagant*, or (3) *excessive*. If the claim is possible rationally and by normative experience, it is reasonable, and if it is possible rationally but not by normative experience, it is extravagant. Both are acceptable. Otherwise, it is excessive, e.g., the [poet's] saying,

> *akhafta ahla al-shirki ḥattā innahu*[1]
> So greatly have you terrified the people of idolatry
>
> *la-takhāfuka al-nuṭafu allatī lam tukhlaqi*
> That you are dreaded even by uncreated sperm

IX. Paronomasia

Paronomasia is the phonetic resemblance between two expressions, e.g., *wa-yawma taqūmu al-sāʿatu yuqsimu al-mujrimūna mā labithū ghayra sāʿatin* (And on the day when the hour is come, the guilty will swear that they had tarried naught but an hour) (Q 30:55). Related to paronomasia are the following two devices:

1. The first is that the two expressions be derived from the same root,[5] e.g., *fa-aqim wajhaka li-l-dīni al-qayyimi* (And set your face to the upright religion) (Q 30:43).

٧. الجمع

وهو أن يجمع بين متعدّد في حكم، كقوله تعالى ﴿ٱلْمَالُ وَٱلْبَنُونَ زِينَةُ ٱلْحَيَوٰةِ ٱلدُّنْيَا﴾ [١٨/ ٤٦].

٨. المبالغة المقبولة

والمبالغة أن يدّعى لوصف بلوغه في الشدّة أو الضعف حدًّا مستحيلًا أو متبعّدًا. وينحصر في (١) التبليغ (٢) والإغراق (٣) والغلوّ لأن المدّعى إن كان ممكنًا عقلًا وعادةً فتبليغ وإن كان ممكنًا عقلًا لا عادةً فإغراق وهما مقبولان وإلا فغلوّ كقوله:

> أَخَفْتَ أَهْلَ الشِّرْكِ حَتَّى إِنَّهُ[١]
>
> لَتَخَافُكَ النُّطَفُ الَّتِي لَمْ تُخْلَقِ

٩. الجناس بين اللفظين

وهو تشابههما في اللفظ، نحو ﴿وَيَوْمَ تَقُومُ ٱلسَّاعَةُ يُقْسِمُ ٱلْمُجْرِمُونَ مَا لَبِثُواْ غَيْرَ سَاعَةٍ﴾ [٣٠/ ٥٥].
ويلحق بالجناس شيئان:

١- أحدهما أن يجمع اللفظين الاشتقاقُ، نحو ﴿فَأَقِمْ وَجْهَكَ لِلدِّينِ ٱلْقَيِّمِ﴾ [٣٠/ ٤٣].

---

[1] In [Meḥmed Zihnī Efendī's] *al-Qawl al-jayyid*, the *hamza* [in *innahu*] is vowelized with *fatḥ* [as *annahu*].

[١] وفي القول الجيّد بفتح الهمزة.

2. The second is that they bear a pseudo-etymological resemblance in a manner similar to derivation, e.g., *qāla innī li-ʿamalikum min al-qālīna* (He said, "Truly I am of those who detest what you do") (Q 26:168).

X. Echo

Echo is to place at the beginning of a segment of speech one of a pair of words that make up a repetition, a paronomasia, or either of the devices related to paronomasia and at its end the other, e.g., *wa-takhshā al-nāsa wa-Allāhu aḥaqqu an takhshāhu* (… as you feared the people, though Allah is more worthy of your fear) (Q 33:37); *sāʾilu al-laʾīmi yarjiʿu wa-damʿuhu sāʾilun* (One who asks of a miser returns with flowing tears); and

> *ammaltuhum thumma taʾammaltuhum*
> I placed hopes in them, but then
> I considered them,
>
> *fa-lāḥa lī an laysa fīhim falāḥ*
> And it dawned on me that in them
> there was no success

XI. Prose Rhyme

Prose rhyme is that a pair of final words in prose have the same terminal letter-sound, just as end rhymes have in poetry. It is of three types:

1. *peripheral rhyme*, if the final words are of different morphological patterns, e.g., *mā lakum lā tarjūna li-Llāhi waqāran wa-qad khalaqakum aṭwāran* ("What ails you that you hope not to find in Allah some dignity, when He has created you stage by stage?") (Q 71:13–14).
2. *inlaid rhyme*, if all or most of that within one of the paired segments resembles the corresponding portion within the other in its pattern

٢- وثانيهما أن يجمعهما المشابهة وهي ما يشبه الاشتقاق، نحو ﴿قَالَ إِنِّي لِعَمَلِكُم مِّنَ ٱلْقَالِينَ﴾ [٢٦/ ١٦٨].

١٠. رد العجز على الصدر

وهو أن يجعل أحد اللفظين المكرّرين أو المتجانسين أو الملحقين بهما في أول الفقرة والآخر في آخرها، نحو ﴿وَتَخْشَى ٱلنَّاسَ وَٱللَّهُ أَحَقُّ أَن تَخْشَىٰهُ﴾ [٣٣/ ٣٧] ونحو «سائل اللئيم يرجع ودمعه سائل» ونحو:

أَمَّلْتُهُمْ ثُمَّ تَأَمَّلْتُهُمْ
فَلَاحَ لِي أَنْ لَيْسَ فِيهِمْ فَلَاحْ

١١. السجع

وهو تواطؤ الفاصلتين من النثر على حرف واحد كالقافية في الشعر. وهو ثلاثة أضرب:

١- مطرّف إن اختلفا في الوزن، نحو ﴿مَّا لَكُمْ لَا تَرْجُونَ لِلَّهِ وَقَارًا ۝١٣ وَقَدْ خَلَقَكُمْ أَطْوَارًا﴾ [٧١/ ١٣-١٤].

٢- ترصيع إن كان ما في إحدى القرينتين أو أكثر مثل ما يقابله من الأخرى في الوزن

and ending, e.g., *fa-huwa yaṭbaʿu al-asjāʿa bi-jawāhiri lafẓihi wa-yaqraʿu al-asmāʿa bi-zawājiri waʿẓihi* (He studs every rhyme with the gems of his words and raps every ear with the rebukes of his admonition).[6]

3. *parallel rhyme*, if that within one of the paired segments does *not* resemble the corresponding portion within the other in its pattern,[7] e.g., *fīhā sururun marfūʿatun wa-akwābun mawḍūʿatun* (Therein are raised couches, and goblets set out) (Q 88:13–14).

والتقفية، نحو «فهو يطبع الأسجاع بجواهر لفظه ويقرع الأسماع بزواجر وعظه».

٣- موازٍ إن لم يكن في أحدهما مثل ما يقابله من الأخرى في الوزن، نحو ﴿فِيهَا سُرُرٌ مَّرْفُوعَةٌ ⑬ وَأَكْوَابٌ مَّوْضُوعَةٌ﴾ [٨٨/ ١٣-١٤].

XII. Equilibrium

Equilibrium is that a pair of final words have the same morphological pattern,[8] e.g., *wa-namāriqu maṣfūfatun wa-zarābiyyu mabthūthatun* (And cushions arrayed, and carpets spread) (Q 88:15–16).

١٢. الموازنة

وهي تساوي الفاصلتين في الوزن، نحو ﴿وَنَمَارِقُ مَصْفُوفَةٌ ⑮ وَزَرَابِيُّ مَبْثُوثَةٌ﴾ [٨٨/ ١٥-١٦].

XIII. Palindrome

An example of a palindrome[9] is the [poet's] saying,

mawaddatuhu tadūmu li-kulli hawlin
His love endures through all that would dismay—

wa-hal kullun mawaddatuhu tadūmu
Now, does the love of every man endure?

١٣. القلب

كقوله:

مَوَدَّتُهُ تَدُومُ لِكُلِّ هَوْلٍ
وَهَلْ كُلٌّ مَوَدَّتُهُ تَدُومُ[٣]

❋ ❋ ❋

In all of the devices of embellishment mentioned above, the principle of beauty is that the expressions remain subordinate to the meanings. Meanings should not be subordinated to expressions such that contrived and labored expressions be produced [first] and then meaning made to fit them however they be, as is done by one who is obsessed

أصل الحسن في جميع ما ذكر من المحسّنات أن تكون الألفاظ تابعة للمعاني لا أن تكون المعاني توابع للألفاظ بأن يؤتى بألفاظ متكلّفة مصنوعة فيتبعها المعنى كيف ما كانت كما فعله من له شغف بإيراد المحسّنات

with the production of verbal embellishments and does not care how obscure their signification may be or how flimsy their meaning, his words thus becoming like a scabbard of gold for a sword of wood. Rather, the proper way is to leave the meanings as they are and to seek out for those meanings themselves the words that best suit them. Only then are eloquence and prowess manifested, and the consummate master distinguished from the unskilled amateur.

اللفظيّة بلا مبالاة بخفاء الدلالة وركاكة المعنى فيصير الكلام كغمد من ذهب على سيف من خشب. بل الوجه أن تترك المعاني على سجيّتها فتطلب لأنفسها ألفاظًا تليق بها؛ وعند هذا تظهر البلاغة والبراعة ويتميّز الكامل من القاصر.

❁ ❁ ❁

By the assistance of Allah ﷻ, the treatise entitled *The Vernal Downpour: On the Science of Embellishment* is complete. May Allah ﷻ by His grace and generosity render it of benefit to us and all believers. Allah! "Take us not to task if we forget or err!" (Q 2:286). "Glory to your Lord, Lord of Might, transcending what they describe! Peace be upon the messengers. And praise to Allah, Lord of the worlds" (Q 37:180–82). By His permission ﷻ, the tenth treatise follows, entitled *Understanding Law: On Jurisprudential Theory*.

تمّت بعون الله تعالى الرسالة المسمّاة بالغيث الربيع في علم البديع جعلها الله تعالى بمنّه وكرمه نافعة لنا ولسائر المؤمنين. اللّهم لا تؤاخذنا إن نسينا أو أخطأنا. ﴿سُبْحَٰنَ رَبِّكَ رَبِّ ٱلْعِزَّةِ عَمَّا يَصِفُونَ ۝١٨٠ وَسَلَٰمٌ عَلَى ٱلْمُرْسَلِينَ ۝١٨١ وَٱلْحَمْدُ لِلَّهِ رَبِّ ٱلْعَٰلَمِينَ﴾ [٣٧/ ١٨٠-١٨٢]. وتليها بإذنه تعالى الرسالة العاشرة المسمّاة فهم الفقه في أصول الفقه.

NOTES TO TREATISE IX

1 Refer to the end of the introduction of Treatise VII, p. 383.

2 *Ṣibgha* in the sense of "baptism" is implicitly in the contextual vicinity of the verse because, along with the surrounding verses, it engages the Jews and Christians. Since true religious belief is that which consists in the purification of Allah, the belief pronounced in the statement "We believe in Allah" comprises the meaning of purification, allowing the phrase *ṣibghat Allāhi* in the sense of "the purification of Allah" to function grammatically as an emphatic infinitive (*maṣdar mu'akkid*). Al-Taftāzānī, *Mukhtaṣar*, 2:219–20.

3 Although the Arabic term *tawriya*, like the term *double entendre*, can be used to describe the allusion to unseemly or risqué meanings, it is not confined in this way as a technical term, as is clear from the Quranic examples in the text.

4 Building suits hands.

5 This device can be termed *polyptoton*.

6 The entirety of the second segment, beginning with *wa-yaqraʿu*, corresponds with the words of the first; the only element within the pair that does not have a match is the word *huwa* in the first segment.

7 The difference between parallel rhyme and peripheral rhyme is that the final words in a parallel rhyme are of the same pattern.

8 The two words must also have different terminal letter-sounds (*taqfiya*). In the provided example, *maṣfūfa* has a *fā'* and *mabthūtha* has a *thā'*; the *tā' marbūṭa* is not counted.

9 Palindromes are sentences or phrases that remain the same when the order of their letters is reversed.

X

UNDERSTANDING LAW

On jurisprudential theory

فهم الفقه في أصول الفقه

In the Name of Allah,
All-Merciful, Most Compassionate

بسم الله الرحمن الرحيم

ALL PRAISE IS due to Allah, Lord of the worlds. May blessings and peace be upon the best of His creation, Muḥammad, the seal of the prophets, and upon all of his family and Companions.

الحمد لله ربّ العالمين والصلاة والسلام على خير خلقه محمد خاتم النبيّين وعلى آله وأصحابه أجمعين.

To Proceed Says the destitute servant, needful of his self-sufficient Lord, Muḥammad Emīn b. Dhulfiqār b. ʿAlī b. Aḥmad al-Mīrānī al-Kuluyānī and, later, al-Anqarawī, may Allah ﷻ by His manifest and subtle kindness grant him and his parents forgiveness: This is a treatise on jurisprudential theory that I have authored by drawing selectively from (1) *Lubb al-uṣūl* and its commentary *Ghāyat al-wuṣūl,* both works of Shaykh al-Islām Abū Yaḥyā Zakariyyā al-Anṣārī[1] and from (2) *Jamʿ al-jawāmiʿ*

أما بعد فيقول العبد الفقير المفتقر إلى ربّه الغني محمد أمين بن ذو الفقار بن علي بن أحمد الميراني الكلياني ثم الأنقروي سامحه الله تعالى ووالديه بلطفه الجلي والخفي: إن هذه رسالة في أصول الفقه انتخبتها من (١) لبّ الأصول وشرحه غاية الوصول[١] تأليفي شيخ الإسلام أبي يحيى زكريّا الأنصاري[١] ومن (٢) جمع

[1] Zayn al-Dīn Abū Yaḥyā Zakariyyā b. Muḥammad b. Zakariyyā al-Anṣārī al-Miṣrī al-Shāfiʿī was born in the village of Sunayka, Egypt, in the year 824 AH and passed away in the year 925 or 926 AH. Zakariyyā al-Anṣārī was a judge, Quran exegete, jurist, Sufi, and master of hadith. He authored many works, including *Fatḥ al-Raḥmān* and *Fatḥ al-Jalīl* (notes on *Tafsīr al-Bayḍāwī*) in Quran exegesis; *Tuḥfat al-Bārī ʿalā Ṣaḥīḥ al-Bukhārī* in hadith; *Sharḥ Īsāghūjī* in logic; *Sharḥ Alfiyyat al-ʿIrāqī* in hadith terminology; *Sharḥ Shudhūr al-dhahab* in grammar; *Tuḥfat nujabāʾ al-ʿaṣr* in the science of *tajwīd*; *al-Daqāʾiq al-muḥakkama* in the Quran recita-

[١] زين الدين أبو يحيى زكريّا بن محمد بن زكريّا الأنصاري المصري الشافعي ولد في قرية سُنَيكة[١] بمصر عام ٨٢٤هـ وتوفّي عام ٩٢٥ أو ٩٢٦هـ. زكريّا الأنصاري قاضٍ مفسّر فقيه متصوّف ومن حفّاظ الحديث. له تصانيف كثيرة منها فتح الرحمن وفتح الجليل تعليق على تفسير البيضاوي في التفسير، وتحفة الباري على صحيح البخاري في الحديث، وشرح إيساغوجي في المنطق، وشرح ألفيّة العراقي في مصطلح الحديث، وشرح شذور الذهب في النحو، وتحفة نجباء

by Imām al-Subkī[1] and its commentary by Jalāl al-Dīn al-Maḥallī.[2]

I have entitled this treatise *Understanding Law: On Jurisprudential Theory.* It comprises sixteen preliminary discussions, i.e., discussions that serve as a prelude to the topics of primary concern, and seven chapters concerning the topics of primary concern. Five of these chapters concern the

tions; *Tanqīḥ Taḥrīr al-Lubāb*, *Asnā al-maṭālib fī sharḥ Rawḍat al-ṭālib*, *al-Ghurar al-bahiyya fī sharḥ al-Bahja al-wardiyya*, and *Manhaj al-ṭālib* in law; *Lubb al-uṣūl* (which he abridged from *Jamʿ al-jawāmiʿ*) and *Ghāyat al-wuṣūl* in jurisprudential theory; and other works. See al-Ziriklī, *al-Aʿlām*, 3:46; al-Ghazzī, *al-Kawākib al-sāʾira*, 1:198–208; and al-Shaʿrānī, *al-Ṭabaqāt al-kubrā*, 2:222–26.

[1] Abū al-Naṣr Tāj al-Dīn al-Subkī al-Miṣrī al-Adīb al-Shāfiʿī was born in the year 727 AH and passed away in the year 771 AH. He authored a number of invaluable books, including *Jamʿ al-jawāmiʿ*, *Manʿ al-mawāniʿ* (a commentary on *Jamʿ al-jawāmiʿ*), *al-Ibhāj* (a commentary on al-Bayḍāwī's *al-Minhāj*), *Rafʿ al-ḥājib fī mukhtaṣar Ibn Ḥājib*, and *al-Ashbāh wa-l-naẓāʾir* in jurisprudential theory; *al-Ṭabaqāt al-shāfiʿiyya* in the genre of biographical references; *al-Sayf al-mashhūr fī ʿaqīdat Ibn Manṣūr* in creed; *Muʿīd al-niʿam wa-mubīd al-niqam* in ethics; and other works. See al-Baghdādī, *Hadiyyat al-ʿārifīn*, 1:639, and al-Laknawī, *al-Fawāʾid al-bahiyya*, 196n1.

[2] Muḥammad b. Aḥmad b. Muḥammad b. Ibrāhīm b. Hishām al-Jalāl Abū ʿAbdallāh al-Maḥallī al-Shāfiʿī was born in the year 791 AH in Cairo and passed away in the year 864 AH. A few of his works are *Tafsīr al-Qurʾān* (known as *Tafsīr al-Jalālayn*) in Quran exegesis; *al-Badr al-ṭāliʿ bi-sharḥ Jamʿ al-jawāmiʿ* (the book referred to in this text) and *Sharḥ Waraqāt Imām al-Ḥaramayn* in jurisprudential theory; *Kanz al-rāghibīn sharḥ Minhāj al-ṭālibīn* in law; *Sharḥ Tashīl al-fawāʾid* and *Sharḥ al-Iʿrāb ʿan qawāʿid al-iʿrāb* in grammar; and other works. See al-Shawkānī, *al-Badr al-ṭāliʿ*, 2:115, and the introduction of the editor Ḥusām al-Dīn b. Mūsā in al-Maḥallī, *Sharḥ al-Waraqāt*, 27–36.

الجوامع للإمام السبكي[١] وشرحه لجلال الدين المحلّي.[٢]

سمّيتها فهم الفقه في أصول الفقه. فيه ستّ عشرة مقدّمة أي أمور متقدّمة على المقصود بالذات وسبعة كتب في المقصود بالذات خمسة منها في مباحث

العصر في التجويد، والدقائق المحكمة في القراءات، وتنقيح تحرير اللباب وأسنى المطالب في شرح روض الطالب والغرر البهيّة في شرح البهجة الورديّة ومنهج الطلّاب في الفقه، ولبّ الأصول اختصره من جمع الجوامع وغاية الوصول في أصول الفقه، وغير ذلك. انظر الأعلام للزركلي (٣/ ٤٦) والكواكب السائرة للغزّي (١/ ١٩٨-٢٠٨) والطبقات الكبرى للشعراني (٢/ ٢٢٢-٢٢٦).

[١] أبو النصر تاج الدين السبكي المصري الأديب الشافعي ولد سنة ٧٢٧هـ وتوفّي سنة ٧٧١هـ وصنّف كتبًا نفيسة منها جمع الجوامع ومنع الموانع شرح جمع الجوامع والإبهاج في شرح المنهاج للبيضاوي ورفع الحاجب في مختصر ابن حاجب والأشباه والنظائر في أصول الفقه، والطبقات الشافعيّة في الطبقات، والسيف المشهور في عقيدة ابن منصور في العقائد، ومعيد النعم ومبيد النقم في الأخلاق، وغير ذلك. انظر هديّة العارفين للبغدادي (١/ ٦٣٩) والفوائد البهيّة للّكنوي (١٩٦).

[٢] محمد بن أحمد بن محمد بن إبراهيم بن هاشم الجلال أبو عبد الله المحلّي الشافعي ولد سنة ٧٩١هـ بالقاهرة وتوفّي سنة ٨٦٤هـ. بعض مؤلّفاته تفسير القرآن المعروف بتفسير الجلالين في التفسير، والبدر الطالع بشرح جمع الجوامع الكتاب الذي أشير إليه في النصّ وشرح ورقات إمام الحرمين في أصول الفقه، وكنز الراغبين شرح منهاج الطالبين في الفقه، وشرح تسهيل الفوائد وشرح الإعراب عن قواعد الإعراب في النحو، وغير ذلك. انظر البدر الطالع للشوكاني (٢/ ١١٥) ومقدّمة شرح الورقات للمحقّق حسام الدين بن موسى (٢٧-٣٦).

indicants of jurisprudence, which are the Quran, the Sunna, consensus, analogy, and adopted indicants; the sixth concerns the weighing of indicants; and the seventh concerns legal reasoning and the related questions of imitation and of the etiquette of giving fatwas.

أدلّـة الفقـه التي هي الكتاب والسـنّة والإجمـاع والقياس والاسـتدلال والسـادس في التعـادل والتراجيح والسـابع في الاجتهـاد ومـا يتبعه مـن التقليـد وأدب الفتيا.

My hope is that Allah ﷻ accept this and bring through it benefit to me, to the reader, to the listener, and to every believer. Indeed, He is the best in whom to hope, the best from whom to seek aid.

والمأمـول مـن الله تعـالى القبـول والنفـع بهـا لي ولقارئهـا ومسـتمعها وسـائر المؤمـنين فإنـه خير مأمـول وخير مـعين للمسـتعينين.

SIXTEEN PRELIMINARY DISCUSSIONS

المقدمات الست عشرة

1. The Meaning of *Uṣūl al-Fiqh*

Uṣūl al-fiqh (principles of jurisprudence) refers to (1) the general (i.e., non-determinative) indicants of jurisprudence, e.g., "Any imperative verb used in a literal sense indicates obligation" and "Consensus is authoritative";[1] (2) the methods of deriving the specific indicants of jurisprudence from which law is in turn derived (that is, from the specific indicants); and (3) the condition of one who derives them, that is, the qualifications of one who derives specific instances of the general indicants of jurisprudence, namely, the mujtahid, for he (as opposed to an imitator) is the one who derives them by considering the factors that give preponderance in cases of conflict.[2]

It has also been said that *uṣūl al-fiqh* refers to knowledge of the indicants of jurisprudence and matters connected to them. The first definition is preferable because the indicants and the matters connected to them do not cease to be *uṣūl* (principles) when they are not known.

١. معنى أصول الفقه

أصـول الفقـه (١) أدلّـة الفقـه الإجماليّـة أي غير المعيّنة، كـ«مطلـق الأمـر للوجوب حقيقـة» و«الإجمـاع حجّة»؛ (٢) وطـرق اسـتفادة أدلّـة الفقـه التفصيليّة المسـتفاد هو (أي الفقـه) منهـا أي أدلّـة الفقـه التفصيليّـة؛ (٣) وحال مسـتفيدها أي صفـات مسـتفيد جزئيّـات أدلّـة الفقـه الإجماليّـة وهـو المجتهد لأنـه الذي يسـتفيدها بالمرجّحات عنـد تعارضهـا دون المقلّد.

وقيـل أصـول الفقـه معرفـة أدلّـة الفقه ومـا عطف عليهـا. ورجّـح الأول لأن الأدلّـة وما عطف عليهـا إذا لم تعـرف لـم تخرج عـن كونهـا أصولًا.

2. Jurisprudence

Jurisprudence is knowledge of practical religious rulings that is derived from specific indicants, e.g., the knowledge that the ritual prayer is obligatory, which is derived from His saying ﷻ, "Perform the ritual prayer" (Q 6:72).

٢. الفقه

وهـو علـم بحكـم شرعي عـملي مكتسـبٌ مـن دليـل تفصـيلي، كعلـم وجـوب الصلاة مكتسـب من قـوله تعالى ﴿أَقِيمُـواْ ٱلصَّلَـوٰةَ﴾ [٦/ ٧٢].

3. Rulings

A ruling is the addressed speech of Allah ﷻ, that is, His eternal internal speech—which was named "addressed speech" in preeternity, according to the soundest position—as pertains to the acts of morally responsible individuals, (1) decreeing (i.e., requesting) acts [or the refraining from acts][3] that are obligatory, recommended, prohibited, reprehensible, or suboptimal; (2) granting the choice between acting and not acting; or (3) determining causes, conditions, impediments, valid acts, or invalid acts. Thus, rulings can only be learned from Allah ﷻ.

٣. الحكم

وهو خطاب الله تعالى أي كلامه النفسي الأزلي المسمّى في الأزل خطابًا على الأصحّ المتعلّق بفعل المكلّف (١) قضاءً أي طلبًا للفعل وجوبًا أو ندبًا أو حرمةً أو كراهةً أو خلاف الأولى، أو (٢) تخييرًا أي بين الفعل والترك، (٣) والوارد بكون الشيء سببًا أو شرطًا أو مانعًا أو صحيحًا أو فاسدًا؛ فلا يدرك حكم إلا من الله تعالى.

4. The Positions regarding Situations That Lack Rulings

Were there to occur after the prophetic mission a situation [in which a given act] lacks a ruling, there are three positions regarding its status: (1) prohibition on account of the verse "They ask you what is lawful for them..." (Q 5:4), because the verse indicates that prohibition is the default status; (2) permission on account of the verse "He it is who created for you all that is on the earth" (Q 2:29); and (3) suspension of judgment on account of the conflict between these two indicants.

٤. الأقوال في صورة لا حكم فيها

لو وقع بعد البعثة صورة لا حكم فيها ففيها ثلاثة أقوال: (١) الحظر لآية ﴿يَسْـَٔلُونَكَ مَاذَآ أُحِلَّ لَهُمْ﴾ [٥/ ٤] فإنها تدلّ على سبق التحريم؛ (٢) والإباحة لآية ﴿خَلَقَ لَكُم مَّا فِي ٱلْأَرْضِ جَمِيعًا﴾ [٢/ ٢٩]؛ (٣) والوقف لتعارض الدليلين.

5. Types of Address

The addressed speech [of Allah] bears a hypothetical relation to the nonexistent.[4]

If it requests an act firmly, the address is one of *obligation*; if it does so mildly, it is one of *recommendation*. If it requests the refraining from an act firmly, it is one of *prohibition*; if it does so mildly but specifies the act, it is one of *reprehension*; and if it does not specify the act, it is one of [designating the act] *suboptimal*. If it gives the choice to act or not, the address is one of *permission*. If it designates something a cause, condition, impediment, or the like, it is one of regulative

٥. أقسام الخطاب

يتعلّق الخطاب بالمعدوم تعلّقًا معنويًا.

فإن اقتضى الفعل اقتضاءً جازمًا فالخطاب إيجاب أو غير جازم فندب أو الترك جازمًا فتحريم أو غير جازم بنهي مخصوص فكراهة أو بغير مخصوص فخلاف الأولى أو خيّر بين الفعل والترك فإباحة. وإن ورد بكون الشيء سببًا أو شرطًا أو مانعًا أو نحوها فوضع أي فهذا الخطاب

imposition; that is, such address is termed *regulative imposition* or *address of regulative imposition* because the [regulation] in question comes to be by Allah's imposition, i.e., His making it the case. Likewise, address that makes a request or gives a choice is termed *address of injunctive imposition* (*taklīf*) because it pertains to the acts of one who is morally responsible (*mukallaf*) inasmuch as he is morally responsible.

6. Causes, Conditions, and Impediments

A *cause* is that which occasions the ruling, e.g., adultery in relation to the statutory punishment.[5] A *condition* is that whose absence entails absence but whose presence entails neither presence nor absence, e.g., ablutions for prayer. An *impediment* is a feature that indicates the negation of a ruling, e.g., murder in that it negates inheritance and parenthood in that it negates [the obligation of] retaliatory punishment.[6]

7. Timely Fulfillment

According to the soundest position: *Timely fulfillment* is to perform an act of worship or a unit of prayer within its time, that is, the time legally appointed for it; *late fulfillment* is to perform such an act after its time to make amends for an [unperformed] action whose performance was required in the past; and *repetition* is to perform such an act again within its time for any reason at all. According to some: Repetition is specifically when the first performance was deficient, and this is the majority position. It has also been said that repetition may be for any genuine reason, whether a deficiency or to acquire some virtue that had been lacking in the first performance.

8. Types of Rulings That Are Relaxed

If a ruling is relaxed on account of an excuse despite the existence of the cause for the original ruling,[7] then it is a *dispensation*, which may be either (1) obligatory, e.g., eating carrion in the case of someone

يسمّى وضعًا ويسمّى خطاب وضع أيضا لأن متعلّقه بوضع الله أي بجعله كما يسمّى الخطاب المقتضي أو المخيّر خطاب تكليف لتعلّقه بفعل المكلّف من حيث إنه مكلّف.

٦. السبب والشرط والمانع

السبب ما يضاف الحكم إليه، كالزنا للحدّ[٢]. والشرط ما لزم من عدمه عدم ولا يلزم من وجوده وجود ولا عدم، كالوضوء للصلاة. والمانع وصف معرّف نقيض الحكم، كالقتل في منع الإرث والأبوّة في منع القصاص.

٧. الأداء

الأصحّ أن الأداء فعل العبادة أو ركعة في وقتها وهو الزمن المقدّر لها شرعًا، وأن القضاء فعلها بعد وقتها تداركًا لما سبق لفعله مقتضٍ، وأن الإعادة فعلها في وقتها ثانيًا مطلقًا. وقيل الإعادة مختصّة بخلل في الأول وعليه الأكثر، وقيل بالعذر الشامل للخلل أو لحصول فضيلة لم تكن في الأول.

٨. أنواع الحكم المتغير إلى سهولة

الحكم إن تغيّر إلى سهولة لعذر مع قيام السبب للحكم الأصلي فرخصة (١) واجبة كأكل الميتة للمضطر

in dire need; (2) recommended, e.g., shortening the prayer in the case that the conditions [for shortening] are met; (3) permissible, e.g., forward purchasing; or (4) suboptimal, e.g., breaking the fast in the case of a traveler whom fasting would not harm. Otherwise, the ruling is a *stringent ruling*.

9. Indicants

An indicant is that through which, if one uses sound reasoning, it is possible to arrive at a declarative conclusion, e.g., to say, "The universe originated in time, and everything that originated in time has a creator; therefore, the universe has a creator," and, "'Perform the ritual prayer' is a command, and every command used in a literal sense indicates obligation; therefore, 'Establish prayer' used in a literal sense indicates obligation."

10. Types of Apprehension

Apprehension without a judgment is *conception* and with it *assent*. Assent when held with conviction and when unsusceptible to change is *knowledge*. Otherwise, if it corresponds to reality, it is *correct belief*, and if it does not, it is *incorrect*. Assent that is not held with conviction is either *presumption*, *fancy*, or *doubt* because there is either preponderance in favor of it or against it or there is neither.[8]

11. The Good and the Bad and Permissibility

According to the soundest position: A *good* act is one that merits praise, and a *bad* act is one that merits blame. That which fits neither description occupies a middle status.

[According to the soundest position:] *Permissibility* is a legal ruling.[9]

أو (٢) مندوبة كقصر الصلاة بشرطه أو (٣) مباحة كالسلم (٤) وخلاف الأولى كفطر مسافر لا يضرّه الصوم، وإلا فعزيمة.

٩. الدليل

الدليل ما يمكن التوصّل بصحيح النظر فيه إلى مطلوب خبري، كأن تقول «العالم حادث وكل حادث له صانع فالعالم له صانع» و«أقيموا الصلاة أمر بها وكل أمر بشيء لوجوبه حقيقة فأقيموا الصلاة لوجوبها حقيقة».

١٠. أنواع الإدراك

الإدراك بلا حكم تصوّر ومعه تصديق. وجازمه إن لم يقبل تغيّرًا فعلم وإلا فاعتقاد صحيح إن طابق الواقع وإلا ففاسد؛ وغير الجازم ظنّ ووهم وشكّ لأنه إما راجح أو مرجوح أو مساوٍ.

١١. الحسن والقبيح والإباحة

الأصحّ أن الحسن ما يمدح عليه والقبيح ما يذمّ عليه فما لا ولا فواسطة.

والإباحة حكم شرعي.

[According to the soundest position:] When obligatoriness is abrogated, *acceptability* remains, which, according to the soundest position, means that there is no harm [in acting or refraining]. According to some, [what remains after the abrogation] is simply permissibility; according to some, what remains is simply recommendation.

وأن الوجـوب إذا نسـخ بقي الجـواز وهـو عـدم الحـرج في الأصـحّ وقيـل هـو الإباحـة فقـط وقيـل هـو النـدب فقـط.

12. Communal Obligation and Communal Sunna

A *communal obligation* is something important whose realization is firmly requested without inherent consideration for who it is that performs the act. According to the soundest position, communal obligations are lower [in priority] than individual obligations, are due upon all, and are fulfilled through the acts of a few. A *communal sunna* is the same as a communal obligation, substituting [the qualification] "firmly" with the opposite, meaning that it is requested mildly.

١٢. فرض الكفاية وسنتها

فـرض الكفايـة مهـمّ يقصـد جزمًـا حصـوله مـن غير نظـر بـالذات إلى فاعلـه. والأصـحّ أنـه دون فـرض الـعين وأنـه على الكل ويسـقط بفعـل البعـض. وسـنّة الكفايـة كفرضهـا بإبـدال «جزمًـا» بضـدّه أي يقصـد غير جـزم.

13. The Obligatoriness of Acts Required to Accomplish Obligations

An act within one's capacity without which an obligatory act of any kind could not be accomplished is [itself also] obligatory, according to the soundest position. Thus, if it is impossible to avoid a prohibited act except by avoiding some other act, then it is obligatory to avoid [that other act].

١٣. وجوب ما لا يتم الواجب إلا به

المقـدور الذي لا يتـمّ الواجـب المطلـق إلا بـه واجـب على الأصـحّ، فلـو تعـذّر تـرك محـرّم إلا بترك غيره وجـب الترك.

14. A General Command Does Not Extend to Reprehensible Acts

A general command does not extend to reprehensible acts according to the soundest position. Thus, prayer is not valid during times when it is reprehensible, e.g., from sunrise until the sun rises the length of a spear [from the horizon], and according to the soundest position this is the case even when the act is mildly reprehensible. If the reprehensible act has two aspects

١٤. عدم تناول الأمر المطلق المكروه

مطلـق الأمـر لا يتنـاول المكـروه في الأصـحّ، فلا تصـحّ الـصلاة في الأوقـات المكروهـة كعنـد طلـوع الشـمس حتى ترتفـع كرمـح، ولـو كراهـة تنزيـه في الأصـحّ. فـإن كان للمكـروه جهتـان لا لـزوم بينهمـا

that are separable, e.g., praying in places where it is reprehensible, then a general command certainly extends to the act if it is mildly reprehensible and [also], according to the soundest position, if it is prohibited. Thus, the soundest position is that it is valid to pray in a usurped [land] and that one is not rewarded for such a prayer, as a penalty in consideration of the aspect [of the act that pertains to] the usurpation.

كالـصلاة في الأمكنـة المكروهـة تنـاوله مطلـق الأمـر قطعًـا في نهي التنزيـه وعلى الأصـحّ في التحريـم، فالأصـحّ صحّـة الـصلاة في مغصـوب وأنـه لا يثـاب عليهـا عقوبـة له مـن جهـة الغصـب.

15. The Dispute about the Possibility of Imposing an Impossible Obligation

According to the soundest position: It is possible [for Allah] to obligate an [act] that is in any sense impossible. It does occur that [He] obligates [acts] that are impossible in the mere sense that Allah knows that the acts will not be performed. It is possible [for Allah to obligate an act] whose legal conditions did not occur, e.g., obligating the [acts of] derived law upon the disbeliever, and this does occur, and the disbeliever is punished for his failure to comply.

١٥. الخلاف في جواز التكليف بالمحال

الأصـحّ جـواز التكليـف بالمحـال مطلقًـا ووقوعـه بالمحـال لتعلّـق علـم الله بعـدم وقوعـه فقـط وجـوازه بمـا لـم يحصـل شرطـه الشرعي كتكليـف الكافـر بالفروع ووقوعـه فيعاقـب على تـرك امتثـاله.

16. Sequential and Alternative Rulings and Their Subclasses

A ruling may pertain to two or more acts in a tiered sequence. In such cases, to combine the acts may be prohibited, e.g., eating both a legally slaughtered animal and carrion; permitted, e.g., making both water ablutions and dry ablutions; or a sunna, e.g., the methods of expiating intercourse [in Ramadan]. Likewise, [a ruling may pertain to two or more acts] alternatively. In such cases, to combine the acts may be prohibited, e.g., marrying off a woman to both of two suitable candidates; permitted, e.g., covering with two garments the area of one's body that one is legally required to cover; or a sunna, e.g., the methods of expiating an oath.

١٦. الحكم على الترتيب وعلى البدل وأقسامه

الحكـم قـد يتعلّـق بأمريـن فـأكثر على الترتيـب فيحـرم الجمـع كأكل المـذكّى والميتـة أو يبـاح كالوضـوء والتيمّـم أو يسـنّ كخصـال كفّـارة الوقـاع؛ وعلى البـدل كذلـك فيحـرم الجمـع كتزويـج المـرأة مـن كفـئين أو يبـاح كـستر العـورة بثـوبين أو يسـنّ كخصـال كفّـارة اليـمين.

THE SEVEN CHAPTERS

الكتب السبعة

Chapter 1

THE QURAN

الكتاب الأول

القرآن

The first of the seven chapters concerns the Quran, which is termed "the Book" according to the convention of the religious scholars.

الكتاب الأول من الكتب السبعة القرآن ويقال له في عرف أهل الشرع الكتاب.

The Definition of Quran

In creedal theology, *Quran* is a name for the signified meaning of [revelation's] verbal expression. In jurisprudential theory, it is the [body of] verbal expressions revealed to Muḥammad ﷺ that proves inimitable in every one of its chapters and whose recitation is an act of worship.

According to the soundest position: The *basmala* is part of the Quran, and noncanonical readings are not. The seven canonical recitations are massively transmitted—including those aspects related to correctly rendering the pronunciation, like the prolongation of long vowels. The recitation of noncanonical readings [in prayer] is prohibited; the soundest position is that any reading besides the ten canonical readings is a noncanonical reading and has the status of a unit report.

تعريف القرآن

وهو في أصول الدين اسم لمدلول اللفظ، وفي أصول الفقه هو اللفظ المنزّل على محمد ﷺ المعجز بسورة منه المتعبّد بتلاوته.

ومنه البسملة لا الشاذّ في الأصحّ. والقراءات السبع متواترة ولو فيما هو من قبيل الأداء كالمدّ. وتحرم القراءة بالشاذّ والأصحّ أنه ما وراء القراءات العشر وأنه يجري مجرى الآحاد.

It is not possible that there be any expression in the Quran or Sunna that lacks meaning or any expression by which a meaning other than the apparent meaning is intended in the absence of an indicant that clarifies the intended meaning. Nor is there any indeterminate expression that one will be held responsible for putting into practice which is left without explanation.

[According to the soundest position:] Transmissional indicants can produce certainty when supplemented by external [conditions], as by mass transmission and sensory observation, e.g., the indicants for the obligatoriness of prayer.

Articulated Meanings and Their Division into Unequivocal and Apparent

An articulated meaning is a meaning that an expression signifies within its actual articulation, e.g., the prohibition of muttering *uff* (Ugh!) to one's parents in His saying ﷻ, "Say not to them, 'Uff!'" (Q 17:23). [This is] in contrast to an *implicature*, whose signification by means of an expression is nonverbal and not within its actual articulation, e.g., the prohibition of striking one's parents.

If an expression that signifies within its actual articulation signifies a given meaning and cannot possibly mean anything else, e.g., "Zayd" in a statement like "Zayd came," then it is *unequivocal*. [Another example is] *bayʿ* (buying and selling) in His statement ﷻ "Allah has permitted buying and selling" (Q 2:275).

If it signifies a meaning but can sustain a secondary meaning, e.g., "the lion" in a statement like "I saw the lion today," then it is *apparent*.[10] [Another example is] "the dead" in His statement ﷻ "He brings forth the living from the dead" (Q 30:19).

وأنه لا يجوز ورود ما لا معنى له في الكتاب والسنّة ولا ما لا يعنى[٣] به غير ظاهره إلا بدليل يبيّن المراد منه وأنه لا يبقى مجمل كلّف بالعمل به غير مبيّن.

وأن الأدلّة النقليّة قد تفيد اليقين بانضمام غيرها من تواتر ومشاهدة كما في أدلّة وجوب الصلاة.

المنطوق وتقسيمه إلى النص والظاهر[٤]

المنطوق معنًى دلّ عليه اللفظ في محلّ النطق كتحريم التأفّف للوالدين بقوله تعالى ﴿فَلَا تَقُل لَّهُمَآ أُفٍّ﴾ [١٧/ ٢٣] بخلاف المفهوم فإن دلالة اللفظ عليه في محلّ السكوت لا في محلّ النطق كتحريم الضرب لهما.

اللفظ الدالّ في محلّ النطق إن أفاد معنًى لا يحتمل غيره كـ«زيد» في نحو «جاء زيد» فنصّ وكـ«البيع» في قوله تعالى ﴿وَأَحَلَّ ٱللَّهُ ٱلْبَيْعَ﴾ [٢/ ٢٧٥].

وإن أفاد معنًى يحتمل بدله معنًى مرجوحًا كـ«الأسد» في نحو «رأيت اليوم الأسد» فظاهر وكـ«الميت» في قوله تعالى ﴿يُخْرِجُ ٱلْحَىَّ مِنَ ٱلْمَيِّتِ﴾ [٣٠/ ١٩].

[The Division of Signification]

The Division of Signification into Correspondence, Containment, and Concomitance An expression's signification of its complete meaning is *correspondence*, of a part of its meaning *containment*, and of a mentally concomitant meaning *concomitance*. The first two are verbal; the last is rational.

The Division of Concomitance into Textually Required, Indirectly Entailed, and Directly Entailed Now, a case of signification by concomitance in which the truth or validity of the articulated meaning presupposes an implicit [word or phrase] is *textually required signification* , e.g., the hadith, "Error and forgetfulness are removed from my *umma*,"[1] i.e., "liability therein," and His saying ﷻ, "'Ask the town'" (Q 12:82), i.e., "its inhabitants." Otherwise, if it signifies a meaning that is not integral to the intent, it is *indirectly entailed signification*, e.g., "Intimacy with your wives is permitted for you during the nights of fasting" (Q 2:187) signifying the validity of the fast of one who began the day in a state of major ritual impurity. If it signifies a meaning that is integral to the intent, it is *directly entailed signification*, e.g., the Prophet's saying ﷺ, "Free a slave,"[2] in the report of the Bedouin "I had intercourse with my wife during the day in Ramadan" signifying that intercourse is a cause for manumission.

Implicatures and Their Division into Congruous, Counter, and *A Fortiori*

An implicature is a meaning that an expression signifies *not* within its actual articulation. Implicatures can be divided into three types:

[1] Ibn Ḥibbān, *Ṣaḥīḥ Ibn Ḥibbān*, 16:202; al-Ḥākim, *al-Mustadrak*, 2:236.

[2] Al-Bukhārī, *al-Jāmiʿ al-ṣaḥīḥ*, 8:23 (no. 6087); al-Bayhaqī, *al-Sunan al-kubrā*, 4:374.

[تقسيم الدلالة]

تقسيم الدلالة إلى مطابقة وتضمن والتزام دلالة اللفظ على تمام معناه مطابقة وعلى جزئه تضمّن وعلى لازمه الذهني التزام؛ والأوليان لفظيّتان والأخيرة عقليّة.

تقسيم الالتزام إلى دلالة اقتضاء ودلالة إشارة ودلالة إيماء ثم دلالة الالتزام إن توقّف صدق المنطوق أو صحّته على تقدير فدلالة اقتضاء، كحديث «رفع عن أمّتي الخطأ والنسيان»[١] أي «المؤاخذة بهما» وكقوله تعالى ﴿وَسْـَٔلِ ٱلْقَرْيَةَ﴾ [١٢/ ٨٢] أي «أهلها». وإلا فإن دلّ على ما لا يقصد فدلالة إشارة، كدلالة ﴿أُحِلَّ لَكُمْ لَيْلَةَ ٱلصِّيَامِ ٱلرَّفَثُ إِلَىٰ نِسَآئِكُمْ﴾ [٢/ ١٨٧] على صحّة صوم من أصبح جنبًا. وإن دلّ على ما يقصد فدلالة إيماء، كدلالة قول النبي ﷺ «أعتق رقبة»[٢] في خبر الأعرابي «واقعت أهلي في نهار رمضان» على أن الوقاع علّة للإعتاق.

المفهوم وتقسيمه إلى موافقة ومخالفة وفحوى الخطاب

المفهوم معنًى دلّ عليه اللفظ لا في محلّ النطق. وينقسم إلى ثلاثة أقسام:

[١] ابن حبّان، صحيح ابن حبّان، ١٦/ ٢٠٢؛ الحاكم، المستدرك، ٢/ ٢٣٦.

[٢] البخاري، الأدب، ٦٨؛ البيهقي، السنن الكبرى، ٤/ ٣٧٤.

1. If the meaning agrees with the articulated meaning, it is termed a *congruous implicature*, e.g., the prohibition of setting an orphan's wealth on fire as signified by the verse "Truly those who consume the property of orphans unjustly..." (Q 4:10).[11]
2. If it disagrees with the articulated meaning, it is termed a *counter implicature*, e.g., "[Zakat is due on] grazing animals" signifying that zakat is not due on stall-fed animals.
3. If it applies with greater reason than the articulated meaning, it is termed an *a fortiori implicature*, e.g., the prohibition of striking one's parents as signified by His saying ﷻ, "Say not to them, 'Uff!'" (Q 17:23).

Particular, Universal, Simple, Composite, and Meaningless Expressions

The signified meaning of an expression is either a particular meaning or a universal meaning: if conceiving the meaning precludes that it could be shared [by multiple things] (e.g., the signified meaning of "Zayd"), it is *particular*. If it does not preclude that it could be shared [by multiple things] (e.g., the signified meaning of "human"), it is *universal*. Furthermore, an expression is either *simple*, in which case it is either meaningful (e.g., "man," "hit," and "Is...?") or meaningless (e.g., the letter-sounds *bah*, *lah*, and *sah*), or it is *composite* and either meaningful (e.g., "Zayd is standing") or meaningless (e.g., anything denoted by the term "nonsense").[12]

Unambiguous and Ambiguous Expressions

Unambiguous expressions are expressions whose meaning is clear, namely, unequivocal or apparent expressions. Ambiguous expressions are those that are not such,[13] according to the soundest position,[14] though Allah may clarify them for some among His select servants.[15]

١- فإن وافق المنطوق فيسمّى مفهوم موافقة، كتحريم إحراق مال اليتيم الدالّ عليه آية ﴿إِنَّ ٱلَّذِينَ يَأْكُلُونَ أَمْوَٰلَ ٱلْيَتَٰمَىٰ ظُلْمًا﴾ [٤/ ١٠].

٢- وإن خالفه فيسمّى مفهوم مخالفة، كدلالة «السائمة» على عدم وجوب الزكاة في المعلوفة.

٣- وإن كان أولى من المنطوق فيسمّى فحوى الخطاب، كتحريم ضرب الوالدين الدالّ عليه قوله تعالى ﴿فَلَا تَقُل لَّهُمَآ أُفٍّ﴾ [١٧/ ٢٣].

الجزئي والكلي والمفرد والمركب والمهمل

مدلول اللفظ إما معنًى جزئي أو كلّي لأنه إن منع تصوّره من الشركة فيه كمدلول «زيد» فجزئي، وإن لم يمنع منها كمدلول «الإنسان» فكلي. وإما لفظ مفرد فهو إما مستعمل كـ«رجل» و«ضرب» و«هل» أو مهمل كحروف «بَه» «لَه» «سَه»، أو مركّب مستعمل كـ«زيد قائم» أو مهمل كمدلول لفظ «الهذيان».

المحكم والمتشابه

المحكم من اللفظ المتّضح المعنى من نصّ أو ظاهر والمتشابه غيره في الأصحّ، وقد يوضّحه الله لبعض أصفيائه.

Particulars and Univocal and Modulative Universals

If there is a single expression and a single meaning, then if conceiving the expression's meaning precludes that it could be shared, the expression is a *particular*. Otherwise, the expression is a *univocal universal* if its meaning is equivalent within its instances, e.g., "human," or else a *modulative universal*, e.g., "whiteness," whose meaning is more intense in snow than it is in ivory.

Mutually Distinct, Synonymous, Equivocal, Literal, and Nonliteral Expressions

If multiple expressions have multiple meanings (e.g., "human" and "horse"), they are *mutually distinct*. If the multiplicity is only in the expressions (e.g., *insān* [human] and *bashar* [human]), they are *synonymous*. If the multiplicity is in the meanings and not their expressions, then if an expression applies literally to each meaning, it is *equivocal* (e.g., *qur*ʾ [phase of menstruation *or* phase of purity]), and if it does not, it is *literal* [with respect to one meaning] and *nonliteral* [with respect to the other], e.g., "lion" with respect to the predatory animal and a courageous man.

Proper Names Classified into Personal and Generic

A proper name is an expression that specifies its referent by means of linguistic assignment. If its specification is extramental, it is a *personal proper name*, e.g., *Zayd*; if it is not, its specification being mental, it is a *generic proper name*, e.g., *Usāma*.

Morphological Derivation

Morphological derivation is to ascribe one word to another[16] on account of an affinity in their meanings and root letters; e.g., *nāṭiq* (rational) is from *nuṭq* (rationality).

الجزئي والكلي المتواطئ والمشكك

اللفظ والمعنى إن اتّحدا فإن منع تصوّر معناه الشركة فجزئي كـ«زيد» وإلا فكلّي متواطئ إن استوى معناه في أفراده كـ«الإنسان» وإلا فمشكّك كـ«البياض» فإن معناه في الثلج أشدّ منه في العاج.

المباين والمترادف والمشترك والحقيقة والمجاز

إن تعدّد اللفظ والمعنى كـ«الإنسان» و«الفرس» فمباين، أو اللفظ فقط كـ«الإنسان» و«البشر» فمترادف، أو تعدّد المعنى دون اللفظ فإن كان اللفظ حقيقة فيهما فمشترك كـ«القرء» وإلا فحقيقة ومجاز كـ«الأسد» للحيوان المفترس والرجل الشجاع.

العلم وانقسامه إلى عين وجنس

العلَم لفظ عيّن مسمّاه بوضع فإن كان تعيينه خارجيًّا فعلم شخص كـ«زيد» وإلا بأن كان تعيينه ذهنيًّا فعلم جنس كـ«أسامة».

الاشتقاق

الاشتقاق ردّ لفظ إلى آخر لمناسبة بينهما في المعنى والحروف الأصليّة، كـ«الناطق» من «النطق».

The Possible and Actual Presence of Equivocal Expressions in Spoken Language

According to the soundest position: Equivocal expressions actually occur in spoken language, which is possible [rather than necessary], e.g., *qurʾ* with respect to 'phase of purity' and 'phase of menstruation'. It is lexically valid to use equivocal expressions for both of their meanings together, which is nonliteral usage because such expressions were not assigned to both meanings together but rather to each individually. Thus, the like of "And do good" (Q 22:77) may refer to obligatory or recommended acts, respectively, as the [imperative] form *ifʿal* is interpreted literally or nonliterally.

Literal Expressions and Their Classification

Literal expressions are expressions used for [the meaning] to which they were first assigned. Literal usage can be *lexical*, e.g., "lion" for the predatory animal; *conventional*, e.g., *dābba* for animals with hooves; and *revelational*, e.g., *ṣalāh* for the specific act of worship.

Nonliteral Expressions and the Reason to Resort to Them

Nonliteral expressions[17] are expressions used with reference to a second assignation on account of a semantic link between the meaning to which they were assigned first and that to which they were assigned second. Nonliteral expressions may be resorted to [for the following reasons]:

1. because the literal expression is difficult to pronounce, e.g., *khanfaqīq* for a calamity, in place of which one might resort to [a word] like *mawt* (death).
2. because the literal expression is repugnant, e.g., *khirʾa* (defecation), in place of which one might resort to *ghāʾiṭ*, which literally means a low area.

وقوع المشترك في الكلام جوازا

الأصحّ أن المشترك واقع في الكلام جوازًا كـ«القرء» للطهر والحيض، وأنه يصحّ لغةً إطلاقه على معنييه معًا مجازًا لأنه لم يوضع لهما معًا بل لكل واحد منهما منفردًا، فنحو ﴿وَٱفۡعَلُواْ ٱلۡخَيۡرَ﴾ [٢٢/ ٧٧] يعمّ الواجب والمندوب حملًا لصيغة «اِفْعَل» على الحقيقة والمجاز.

الحقيقة وانقسامها

الحقيقة لفظ مستعمل فيما وضع له أوّلًا. وهي لغويّة كـ«الأسد» للحيوان المفترس وعرفيّة كـ«الدابّة» لذات الحوافر وشرعيّة كـ«الصلاة» للعبادة المخصوصة.

المجاز وسبب العدول إليه

المجاز لفظ مستعمل بوضع ثانٍ لعلاقة بين ما وضع له أوّلًا وما وضع له ثانيًا. ويعدل إليه:

١- لثقل الحقيقة على اللسان، كـ«الخنفقيق» للداهية يعدل عنه إلى «الموت» مثلًا.

٢- أو بشاعتها، كـ«الخرأة» يعدل عنها إلى «الغائط» وحقيقته المكان المطمئنّ.

3. because one does not know the literal expression.
4. for the eloquence of the nonliteral expression, e.g., “Zayd is a lion,” which is more eloquent than “courageous.”
5. because the nonliteral expression is [more] well-known.
6. other reasons, like obscuring the intended meaning from people other than the person you are addressing.

Nonliteral and transferred usage are not the primary, default [modes of usage]. By default, one understands an expression according to its literal meaning.

Expressions are to be interpreted according to the terminological context of the speaker. In [the context of] revelation, they are [interpreted as] revelational; in [the context of] a convention, they are [interpreted as] conventional; and in [the context of] lexical usage, they are [interpreted as] lexical.

Implication and Allusion

If an expression is used in its literal sense in order to have [the listener] infer a concomitant meaning, it is an *implicative expression*, that is, a literal expression that is not used in a straightforward way, e.g., “Zayd has long sword straps.” If it is used for its meaning, in general,[18] in order to hint at other meanings, it is an *allusive expression*, e.g., “A Muslim is one from whose tongue and hand Muslims are safe.”[19]

[General Expressions]

[A general expression is an expression that comprehends all of its possible referents without restriction.][20]

٣- أو جهلها.

٤- أو لبلاغة المجاز، نحو «زيد أسد» فإنه أبلغ من «شجاع».

٥- أو شهرته.

٦- أو غير ذلك كإخفاء المراد عن غير المخاطبين.

وهو والنقل خلاف الأصل الراجح فالأصل حمل اللفظ على معناه الحقيقي.

اللفظ محمول على عرف المخاطِب ففي الشرع الشرعي وفي العرف العرفي وفي اللغة اللغوي.

الكناية والتعريض

اللفظ إن استعمل في معناه الحقيقي للانتقال إلى لازمه فكناية فهي حقيقة غير صريحة، نحو «زيد طويل النجاد». وإن استعمل في معناه مطلقًا للتلويح بغير معناه فتعريض، نحو «المسلم من سلم المسلمون من لسانه ويده»[٦].

[العام]

[العامّ لفظ يستغرق الصالح له بلا حصر.]

Specification and What Can Be Specified

Specification is to confine [the ruling of] a general expression to certain individual instances. According to the soundest position: Specification can be by means of the intellect. Quran can be specified by means of Quran; Sunna can be specified by means of Sunna; either can be specified by means of either; and either can be specified by means of analogy, the suggestion of the speech,[21] or the drift of the speech.[22] This amounts to eight types [of cases of specification].

The first is the specification of Quran by means of the intellect, e.g., His saying ﷻ, "Say, 'Allah is the Creator of all things'" (Q 13:16); the intellect necessarily apprehends that He ﷻ did not create Himself.

The second is the specification of Quran by means of Quran, which means the specification of a decisive text by means of [another] decisive text, e.g., the specification of His statement ﷻ "Divorced women shall wait by themselves for three courses" (Q 2:228) by means of His statement "But as for those who are pregnant, their term is until they deliver" (Q 65:4) and His saying, "O you who believe! If you marry believing women and then divorce them before you have touched them, there shall be no waiting period for you to reckon against them" (Q 33:49).

The third is the specification of Sunna by means of Sunna, e.g., the specification the report [found in] the two *Ṣaḥīḥ*s[23] "On that which the sky waters a tenth is due"[1] by means of the report [also found] in the two *Ṣaḥīḥ*s "There is no zakat due on what is less than five *awsuq*."[2]

The fourth is the specification of Quran by means of Sunna, e.g., the specification of the verse of inheritance for non-Muslim children by means of the

[1] Al-Bukhārī, *al-Jāmiʿ al-ṣaḥīḥ*, 2:126 (no. 1483); Muslim, *Ṣaḥīḥ*, 400 (no. 981).

[2] Al-Bukhārī, *al-Jāmiʿ al-ṣaḥīḥ*, 2:116 (no. 1447); Muslim, *Ṣaḥīḥ*, 399 (no. 979); 400 (no. 980).

التخصيص وما يتخصص به

التخصيص قصر العامّ على بعض أفراده. يجوز في الأصحّ التخصيص بالعقل وتخصيص الكتاب به والسنّة بها وكل بآخر وبالقياس وبدليل الخطاب وبالفحوى. فهذه ثمانية أقسام:

الأول تخصيص الكتاب بالعقل، نحو قوله تعالى ﴿قُلِ ٱللَّهُ خَٰلِقُ كُلِّ شَيۡءٖ﴾ [١٣/ ١٦] فإن العقل يدرك بالضرورة أنه تعالى ليس خالقًا لنفسه.

الثاني تخصيص الكتاب بالكتاب وهو من تخصيص قطعي المتن بقطعيه[٧]، كتخصيص قوله تعالى ﴿وَٱلۡمُطَلَّقَٰتُ يَتَرَبَّصۡنَ بِأَنفُسِهِنَّ ثَلَٰثَةَ قُرُوٓءٖ﴾ [٢/ ٢٢٨] بقوله تعالى ﴿وَأُوْلَٰتُ ٱلۡأَحۡمَالِ أَجَلُهُنَّ أَن يَضَعۡنَ حَمۡلَهُنَّ﴾ [٦٥/ ٤] وبقوله ﴿يَٰٓأَيُّهَا ٱلَّذِينَ ءَامَنُوٓاْ إِذَا نَكَحۡتُمُ ٱلۡمُؤۡمِنَٰتِ ثُمَّ طَلَّقۡتُمُوهُنَّ مِن قَبۡلِ أَن تَمَسُّوهُنَّ فَمَا لَكُمۡ عَلَيۡهِنَّ مِنۡ عِدَّةٖ تَعۡتَدُّونَهَا﴾ [٣٣/ ٤٩].

الثالث تخصيص السنّة بالسنّة، كتخصيص خبر الصحيحين «فيما سقته السماء العشر»[١] بخبرهما «ليس فيما دون خمسة أوسق صدقة».[٢]

الرابع تخصيص الكتاب بالسنّة، كتخصيص آية المواريث للولد الكافر بخبر الصحيحين «لا يرث المسلم

[١] البخاري، الزكاة، ٥٥؛ مسلم، الزكاة، ٧.

[٢] البخاري، الزكاة، ٣٢؛ مسلم، الزكاة، ١-٦.

report in the two *Ṣaḥīḥ*s "A Muslim does not inherit from a non-Muslim and a non-Muslim does not [inherit from] a Muslim."[1] This is specification by means of a unit report; [specification] by means of mass reports, then, is [valid] with all the more reason.

The fifth is the specification of Sunna by means of Quran, e.g., the specification of the report of Muslim "An unmarried person [who commits fornication] with an unmarried person [is to receive] one hundred lashes,"[2] which would include slave girls, by means of His statement "[Slave girls] shall be liable to half the punishment of free women" (Q 4:25).

The sixth is the specification of either Quran or Sunna by means of an analogy that relies on a specific text, even if it be a unit report, e.g., the specification of the verse "As for the adulterer and the adulteress..." (Q 24:2), which would include slave girls, by means of His statement ﷻ "They shall be liable to half the punishment of free women" (Q 4:25): male slaves are analogized to slave girls.

The seventh is the specification of either [Quran or Sunna] by means of the suggestion of the speech (i.e., by a counter implicature), e.g., the specification of the report of Ibn Mājah "Nothing renders water impure except what overpowers its smell, taste, or color"[3] by means of the implicature of his report "When the water [in a vessel] amounts to two *qulla*s, it does not carry impurity."[4]

The eighth is the specification of either [Quran or Sunna] by means of the drift [of the speech] (i.e., congruous implicature), e.g., the specification of the report of Abū Dāwūd and others "The delaying of repayment by a person who possesses the means renders it permissible to [impugn] his honor and

[1] Al-Bukhārī, *al-Jāmiʿ al-ṣaḥīḥ*, 8:156 (no. 6764); Muslim, *Ṣaḥīḥ*, 678 (no. 1614).

[2] Muslim, *Ṣaḥīḥ*, 720 (no. 1690).

[3] Ibn Mājah, *al-Sunan*, 1:327 (no. 521).

[4] Ibn Mājah, *al-Sunan*, 1:325 (no. 517).

الكافر ولا الكافر المسلم»[١] وهذا تخصيص بخبر الواحد فبالمتواترة أولى.

الخامس تخصيص السنّة بالكتاب، كتخصيص خبر مسلم «البكر بالبكر جلد مائة»[٢] الشامل للأَمَة بقوله ﴿فَعَلَيْهِنَّ نِصْفُ مَا عَلَى ٱلْمُحْصَنَٰتِ مِنَ ٱلْعَذَابِ﴾ [٤/ ٢٥].

السادس تخصيص كل من الكتاب والسنّة بالقياس المستند إلى نصّ خاصّ ولو خبر واحد، كتخصيص آية ﴿ٱلزَّانِيَةُ وَٱلزَّانِي﴾ [٢٤/ ٢] الشاملة للأَمَة بقوله تعالى ﴿فَعَلَيْهِنَّ نِصْفُ مَا عَلَى ٱلْمُحْصَنَٰتِ مِنَ ٱلْعَذَابِ﴾ [٤/ ٢٥] وقيس بالأمة العبد.

السابع تخصيص كل منهما بدليل الخطاب أي مفهوم المخالفة، كتخصيص خبر ابن ماجه «الماء لا ينجسه شيء إلا ما غلب على ريحه وطعمه ولونه»[٣] بمفهوم خبره «إذا بلغ الماء قلّتين لم يحمل الخبث».[٤]

الثامن تخصيص كل منهما بالفحوى أي بمفهوم الموافقة، كتخصيص خبر أبي داود وغيره «لَيُّ الواجد يُحل

[١] البخاري، الفرائض، ٢٥؛ مسلم، الفرائض، ١.

[٢] مسلم، الحدود، ١٢.

[٣] ابن ماجه، الطهارة وسننها، ٧٦.

[٤] ابن ماجه، الطهارة وسننها، ٧٥.

to punish him"[1] (i.e., to detain him) by means of the implicature of "Say not to them, 'Uff!'" (Q 17:33); thus, a child's detaining [his parents for delaying repayment] is impermissible.

Unqualified and Qualified Expressions, the Abrogation of Unqualified Expressions, and Their Modification by Certain Qualifications or the Opposite

According to the chosen position: *Unqualified expressions* are those which signify a quiddity without qualification. Unqualified and qualified expressions are analogous to general and specific expressions with respect to the discussion above: that by which general expressions are specified is that by which unqualified expressions are qualified, and that by which they are not is not. This is because unqualified expressions are general with respect to their meaning.

According to the soundest position: When an unqualified and a qualified expression share the same ruling and the same cause for the ruling and are both affirmative (e.g., that it be said regarding the expiation of *ẓihār* in one situation, "Free a slave,"[2] and in another situation, "Free a believing slave"), then if the qualified expression comes after the unqualified expression is put into practice, it abrogates it. If the qualified expression comes after the time of the address [that contained] the unqualified expression but not after it is put into practice, it qualifies it.

When one of the two is affirmative and the other is not (e.g., "Free a slave" and "Do not free a disbelieving slave"), then the unqualified expression

عرضه وعقوبته»[١] أي «حبسه» بمفهوم ﴿فَلَا تَقُل لَّهُمَآ أُفٍّ﴾ [١٧/ ٢٣] فيحرم حبسهما للولد.

المطلق والمقيد ونسخ المطلق وتقييده بصفة أو ضدها

المختار أن المطلق ما دلّ على الماهيّة بلا قيد وهما كالعامّ والخاصّ فيما مرّ فما يخصّ به العامّ يقيّد به المطلق وما لا فلا لأن المطلق عامّ بحسب المعنى.

وإنهما^٨ في الأصحّ إن اتّحد حكمهما وسبب الحكم وكانا مثبتين كأن يقال في كفّارة الظهار في محلّ «أعتق رقبة»[٢] وفي محلّ آخر «أعتق رقبة مؤمنة»^٩ فإن تأخّر المقيّد عن العمل بالمطلق نسخه وإن تأخّر عن وقت الخطاب بالمطلق دون العمل قيّده.

وإن كان أحدهما مثبتًا والآخر خلافه، نحو «أعتق رقبة» «لا تعتق رقبة كافرة» قيّد المطلق

[1] Al-Bukhārī, *al-Jāmiʿ al-ṣaḥīḥ*, 3:118; Abū Dāwūd, *al-Sunan*, 4:231 (no. 3623).

[2] Abū Dāwūd, *al-Sunan*, 3:82 (no. 2208); Ibn Mājah, *al-Sunan*, 3:213 (no. 2062).

[١] البخاري، الاستقراض وأداء الديون والحجر والتفليس، ١٢؛ أبو داود، الأقضية، ٢٩.

[٢] أبو داود، الطلاق، ٨١؛ ابن ماجه، الطلاق، ٢٥.

takes the opposite of the qualification. Otherwise, it takes the qualification, according to the soundest opinion, and the qualified expression is considered to be specified rather than qualified.

If (1) their rulings differ but the causes for the rulings are the same—e.g., His saying ﷻ, "And wipe your faces and your hands" (Q 4:43), with respect to dry ablutions and, "Wash your faces and your hands up to the elbows" (Q 5:6), with respect to water ablutions—or (2) the causes differ but the rulings are the same—e.g., His saying ﷻ, "Let them free a slave" (Q 85:3), with respect to the expiation for *ẓihār* and, "Let him set free a believing slave" (Q 4:92), with respect to the expiation for murder—then the unqualified expression takes the qualification of the qualified expression.

Apparent and Interpreted Expressions

An *apparent expression* is that which signifies a meaning presumptively, i.e., preponderantly. An *interpreted expression* is the interpretation of an apparent expression in accordance with one of its less evident possible meanings.[24] If it is interpreted on account of a proof, it is *sound*; if it is interpreted on account of what is [incorrectly] supposed to be a proof, it is *unsound*; and if it is interpreted without proof, it is *trifling* [with revelation].

Interpretation is of two types:

The first type is an initially plausible [interpretation] that preponderates over the apparent expression through the slightest proof, e.g., His saying ﷻ, "When you rise to perform the ritual prayer..." (Q 5:6), i.e., "intend to perform it."

The second type is an initially implausible [interpretation] that does not preponderate over the apparent expression through the slightest proof,[25] e.g., interpreting "retain" in his saying ﷺ to Ghaylān when the latter accepted Islam while married to ten wives,

بضدّ الصفة والا قيّد المطلق بالصفة في الأصحّ ويكون المقيّد مخصّصًا لا مقيّدًا.

وإن اختلف حكمهما مع اتّحاد سببهما كما في قوله تعالى في التيمّم ﴿فَٱمْسَحُواْ بِوُجُوهِكُمْ وَأَيْدِيكُم﴾ [٤/ ٤٣] وفي الوضوء ﴿فَٱغْسِلُواْ وُجُوهَكُمْ وَأَيْدِيَكُمْ إِلَى ٱلْمَرَافِقِ﴾ [٥/ ٦] أو اختلف سببهما مع اتّحاد حكمهما كما في قوله تعالى في كفّارة الظهار ﴿فَتَحْرِيرُ رَقَبَةٍ﴾ [٥٨/ ٣] وفي كفّارة القتل ﴿فَتَحْرِيرُ رَقَبَةٍ مُّؤْمِنَةٍ﴾ [٤/ ٩٢] قيّد المطلق بالمقيّد.

الظاهر والمؤول

الظاهر ما دلّ دلالة ظنّيّة أي راجحة. والمؤوّل حمل الظاهر على المحتمل المرجوح؛ فإن حمل لدليل فصحيح أو لما يظنّ دليلًا ففاسد أو لا لشيء فلعب.

والتأويل قسمان:

الأول قريب يترجّح على الظاهر بأدنى دليل، نحو قوله تعالى ﴿إِذَا قُمْتُمْ إِلَى ٱلصَّلَوٰةِ﴾ [٥/ ٦] أي «عزمتم على القيام إليها».

والثاني بعيد لا يترجّح على الظاهر بأدنى دليل، كتأويل «أمسك» من قوله ﷺ لغيلان لما أسلم

"Retain four and divorce the rest of them,"[1] as "Renew your marriage to four." The implausibility lies in the fact that no renewal of marriage has been transmitted regarding him or anyone else who accepted Islam.

على عشر نسوة «أمسك أربعًا وفارق سائرهنّ»[١] بـ«ابتدئ نكاح الأربع» ووجه بعده أنه لم ينقل تجديد نكاح منه ولا من غيره ممن أسلم.

The Indeterminate and the Explained

The *indeterminate* is [an expression or action] whose signification is unclear, e.g., *qur'*, since it can be used just as well for the phase of purity as for the phase of menstruation, being equivocally applicable to both—the Shāfiʿī jurist interprets *qur'* as the phase of purity, and the Ḥanafī jurist interprets it as the phase of menstruation, each based on his own [legal principles]. The *explained* is to bring something from a state of uncertainty to a state of clarity.26 According to the soundest position, this can occur through an action.

المجمل والمفسر

المجمل ما لم تتضح دلالته، كـ«القرء» لتردّده بين الطهر والحيض لاشتراكه بينهما وحمله الشافعي على الطهر والحنفي على الحيض لما قام عندهما. المفسّر هو إخراج الشيء من حيّز الإشكال إلى حيّز التجلّي، والأصحّ أنه يكون بالفعل.

Abrogation

[This topic] comprises a number of questions.

Abrogation is the annulment of a legal ruling by means of a legal indicant. The position according to which abrogation means revealing the termination of a legal ruling's time span resolves to the same [meaning]; thus, there is no dispute concerning the meaning.

According to the soundest position: It is possible that some of the Quran be abrogated with respect to its recitation and rulings or with respect to either but not the other. All three cases have occurred. The first case is the abrogation of the recitation and rulings [together]. Muslim narrates from ʿĀ'isha ﵂, "In revelation there used to be 'ten distinct acts of suckling,' then this was abrogated by 'five

النسخ

فيه مسائل.

هو رفع حكم شرعي بدليل شرعي. والقول بأنه بيان لانتهاء أمد حكم شرعي يرجع إلى ذلك؛ فلا خلاف في المعنى.

ويجوز في الأصحّ نسخ بعض القرآن تلاوةً وحكمًا أو أحدهما دون الآخر، والثلاثة واقعة. الأول نسخ التلاوة والحكم: روى مسلم عن عائشة رضي الله عنها «كان فيما أنزل عشر رضعات معلومات فنسخ بخمس

[1] Al-Bayhaqī, *al-Sunan al-kubrā*, 7:294–97.

[١] البيهقي، السنن الكبرى، ٧/ ٢٩٤-٢٩٧.

distinct acts.'"[1] The second case is that of [verses] whose recitation was abrogated but not the rulings. Al-Shāfiʿī and others narrate from ʿUmar ﷺ, "Were it not that people would say, "Umar added to the Book of Allah,' I would have written, 'As for the married man and the married woman, do certainly stone them if they commit adultery,' for we used to recite it"[2]—this is [a verse] whose recitation was abrogated but not the ruling, since he ﷺ ordered the stoning of the married [adulterer], as narrated by the two shaykhs [al-Bukhārī and Muslim]. The third case is that of [verses] whose rulings were abrogated but not the recitation. There are many cases of this; e.g., His saying ﷻ, "And those among you who are taken by death and leave behind wives, [let them] bequeath..." (Q 2:240), was abrogated by His saying, "...and [who] leave behind wives, let them wait by themselves..." (Q 2:234), since the latter was revealed after the former.

According to the soundest position: It is possible for Sunna to be abrogated by Quran, e.g., the abrogation of the prohibition of intimacy between the fasting man and his wife during the night, which had been established by the Sunna, by His statement ﷻ "You are permitted, on the nights of the fast, to be intimate with your wives" (Q 2:187).

According to the soundest position: It is possible for Quran to be abrogated by Sunna, whether by means of mass transmission or unit transmission. He ﷻ states, "And We have sent down the Reminder to you that you might clarify for mankind that which has been sent down to them" (Q 16:44).

Whenever Quran is abrogated by Sunna, there are [verses of] Quran that support the Sunna, and likewise whenever Sunna is abrogated by Quran, there are [sources of] Sunna that support the Quran,

[1] Muslim, *Ṣaḥīḥ*, 597–98 (no. 1452).

[2] Al-Bukhārī, *al-Jāmiʿ al-ṣaḥīḥ*, 9:69; Muslim, *Ṣaḥīḥ*, 720–21 (no. 1691); Ibn Mājah, *al-Sunan*, 3:588 (no. 2553); al-Shāfiʿī, *al-Umm*, 10:204.

معلومات».[١] الثاني منسوخ التلاوة دون الحكم: روى الشافعي وغيره عن عمر رضي الله عنه «لولا أن يقول الناس زاد عمر في كتاب الله لكتبت "الشيخ والشيخة إذا زنيا فارجموهما البتة" فإنا قرأناها»[٢] فهذا منسوخ التلاوة دون الحكم لأمره ﷺ برجم المحصن، رواه الشيخان. الثالث منسوخ الحكم دون التلاوة وهذا القسم كثير كقوله تعالى ﴿وَٱلَّذِينَ يُتَوَفَّوْنَ مِنكُمْ وَيَذَرُونَ أَزْوَٰجًا وَصِيَّةً﴾ [٢/ ٢٤٠] إلى آخره نسخ بقوله ﴿وَيَذَرُونَ أَزْوَٰجًا يَتَرَبَّصْنَ﴾ [٢/ ٢٣٤] إلى آخره لتأخّره في النزول عن الأول.

ويجوز في الأصحّ نسخ السنّة بالقرآن، كنسخ تحريم مباشرة الصائم أهله ليلًا الثابت بالسنّة بقوله تعالى ﴿أُحِلَّ لَكُمْ لَيْلَةَ ٱلصِّيَامِ ٱلرَّفَثُ إِلَىٰ نِسَآئِكُمْ﴾ [٢/ ١٨٧].

ويجوز في الأصحّ نسخ القرآن بالسنّة متواترةً أو آحادًا. قال تعالى ﴿وَأَنزَلْنَآ إِلَيْكَ ٱلذِّكْرَ لِتُبَيِّنَ لِلنَّاسِ مَا نُزِّلَ إِلَيْهِمْ﴾ [١٦/ ٤٤].

وحيث وقع نسخ القرآن بالسنّة فمعها قرآن عاضد لها وكذا حيث نسخِ السنّة بالقرآن فمعه سنّة عاضدة له

[١] مسلم، الرضاع، ٢٤-٢٥.

[٢] البخاري، الحدود، ٣٠؛ مسلم، الحدود، ١٥؛ ابن ماجه، الحدود، ٩؛ الشافعي، الأم، ١٠/ ٢٠٤.

showing their mutual agreement. An example of this is the abrogation of [the ruling of] facing Jerusalem in ritual prayer, which had been established through his actions ﷺ, by His saying ﷻ, "Turn your face toward the Sacred Mosque" (Q 2:149), which he put into practice ﷺ.

According to the soundest position: It is possible for an analogy that was made in the time of the Prophet ﷺ to be abrogated by (1) a textual statement or by (2) an analogy more apparent than the abrogated analogy. An example of the first is for him ﷺ to say, "Quantitative disparity in wheat is forbidden because it is food," then for rice to be analogized to wheat, and then for him later to say, "You may sell rice for rice with quantitative disparity." An example of the second is that after the abovementioned analogy there come a textual statement permitting the sale of corn for corn with quantitative disparity, and then an analogy be made to the sale of rice for rice with quantitative disparity.

According to the soundest position: It is possible for a congruous implicature to be abrogated, regardless whether it is the type that applies with greater or equal reason.

According to us, in contrast to certain of the Mu'tazila, it is possible for a more burdensome [ruling] to replace [another ruling], just as it is possible for an equally burdensome or less burdensome [ruling] and just as it is possible for there to be no replacement. [However,] according to the soundest position, this has not actually occurred.

An abrogating source can be identified by the fact that it succeeds [what it abrogates]. Whether a source succeeds [another] can be known through (1) consensus, (2) a statement by the Prophet ﷺ, (3) his saying something that opposes what he had said before, or (4) the narrator's saying, "This was later."

تبيّن توافقهما،[١١] كما في نسخ التوجّه في الصلاة إلى بيت المقدس الثابت بفعله ﷺ بقوله تعالى ﴿فَوَلِّ وَجْهَكَ شَطْرَ ٱلْمَسْجِدِ ٱلْحَرَامِ﴾ [٢/ ١٤٩] وقد فعله ﷺ.

ويجوز في الأصحّ نسخ القياس الموجود في زمن النبي ﷺ بنصّ أو قياس أجلى من القياس المنسوخ به. فالأول كأن[١٢] يقول ﷺ «المفاضلة في البُرّ حرام لأنه مطعوم» فيقاس به الأرز ثم يقول «بيعوا الأرز بالأرز متفاضلًا». والثاني كأن يأتي بعد القياس المذكور نصّ بجواز بيع الذرة بالذرة متفاضلًا فيقاس بيع الأرز بالأرز متفاضلًا.

ويجوز في الأصحّ نسخ الفحوى أي نسخ مفهوم الموافقة بقسميه الأولى والمساوي.

يجوز عندنا خلافًا لبعض المعتزلة ببدل أثقل كما يجوز بمساوٍ وبأخفّ وبلا بدل، ولم يقع في الأصحّ.

يتعيّن الناسخ بتأخّره ويعلم تأخّره بالإجماع وقول النبي وبذكره شيئًا على خلاف ما ذكره أوّلًا وبقول الراوي هذا متأخّر.

Chapter 2

THE SUNNA

الكتاب الثاني

في السـنـة

This chapter comprises a number of issues.

فيه مسائل.

The Definition of Sunna

The Sunna is the statements and actions of the Prophet ﷺ, and included among his actions is his *tacit approval* since it is the refraining from expressing disapproval, and to refrain is an action.

تعريف السنة

وهي أقـوال النـبي ﷺ وأفعاله، ومـن الأفعـال تقريره لأنه كـفّ عن الإنـكار والكـفّ فعل.[١٣]

That Prophets Are Infallible

The prophets ﷺ are safeguarded even from committing minor sins unintentionally, though according to the majority position, it is possible for them to commit minor sins unintentionally unless the sin indicates baseness, e.g., stealing a scrap of food or being stingy over a date. They would be informed were they to commit them.

كون الأنبياء معصومين

الأنبيـاء عليهـم الـصلاة والـسلام معصومـون حتى عـن الصـغيرة سـهوًا؛ والأكثر على جـواز صـدور الصـغيرة عنهـم سـهوًا إلا الصـغيرة الدالّة على الخسّـة كسرقـة لقمة والتطفيـف بتمـرة، وينبّهـون عليهـا لـو صـدرت.

That the Prophet's Actions Are Never Reprehensible

His actions ﷺ are never reprehensible—in a sense that includes what is suboptimal—because he is infallible. Any act he does which would be reprehensible with respect to us is not reprehensible with respect to him, because he intended by the act to demonstrate its permissibility.

كون فعل النبي غير مكروه

فعلـه ﷺ غير مكـروه بالمعنى الشـامل لخلاف الأولى للعصمـة. ومـا يفعله مما هـو مكـروه في حقّنـا غير مكروه في حقّـه لأنـه قصـد بـه بيان الجـواز.

The Rulings of the Prophet's Actions with Respect to Us

Those of his actions that (1) were natural [human acts], e.g., his standing and sitting; that (2) alternated [between being natural human acts and acts of revealed legislation], e.g., his performance of the hajj pilgrimage while riding and his sitting to rest; that (3) were [acts of] clarification, e.g., his severing a thief's hand up to the wrist; or that (4) were specific to him, e.g., marrying more than four wives, are all clear cases. [The acts] in the first case are permissible for us, the second recommended, and the third obligatory, and our religious practice does not extend to [the acts] in the fourth case.

With respect to any of his other actions, if the [legal] status of the act is known to be one of obligation, recommendation, or permission, then according to the soundest position, his *umma* is the same as him with respect to it. The [legal] status of his actions is known through the indication of textual statements, e.g., his saying, "This is obligatory."

Certainty about the Falsity of a Report Immediately or by Proof

A report is known to be false with certainty either (1) immediately, e.g., contradictory opposites, or (2) by proof, e.g., the assertion of a philosopher that the universe is eternal.

Every Report That Suggests a Falsity Is Fabricated or Missing Crucial Elements

Every report that suggests a falsity and is not amenable to interpretation either is (1) *fabricated*, e.g., the narrated report that He ﷻ created Himself, which is false since it indicates something false—i.e., His originating in time, when a conclusive proof shows that He ﷻ transcends origination—or is (2) missing, by [the omission of] the narrator, elements that would dispel from the report

حكم أفعال النبي في حقنا

وما كان من أفعاله (١) جبلِّيًّا كقيامه وقعوده أو (٢) متردّدًا كحجّه راكبًا وجلسته للاستراحة أو (٣) بيانًا كقطعه يد السارق من الكوع أو (٤) مخصَّصًا به كزيادة في النكاح على أربع نسوة فواضح فيباح لنا في الأول ويندب في الثاني ويجب في الثالث ولسنا في الرابع متعبّدين به.

وفي سوى ما ذكر في فعله إن عُلمت صفته من وجوب أو ندب أو إباحة فأمّته مثله في ذلك في الأصحّ؛ وتُعلم صفة فعله بنصّ عليها، كقوله «هذا واجب» مثلًا.

القطع بكذب الخبر ضرورة أو استدلالا

الخبر إما مقطوع بكذبه ضرورةً كالنقيضين أو استدلالًا كقول الفلسفي «العالم قديم».

كل خبر أوهم باطلا إما موضوع أو نقص منه شيء يضر

كل خبر أوهم باطلًا ولم يقبل تأويلًا فهو إما (١) موضوع، كما روي أنه تعالى خلق نفسه فهو كذب لإيهامه باطلًا وهو حدوثه وقد دلّ الدليل القطعي على أنه تعالى منزّه عن الحدوث؛ وإما (٢) نُقص منه من جهة الراوي ما يزيل الوهم الحاصل بالنقصان

the false suggestion resulting from the omission, e.g., the report narrated in the two *Ṣaḥīḥ*s from Ibn ʿUmar ﷺ, who said, "The Prophet ﷺ led us in the *ʿishā'* prayer at the end of his life, and when he completed the *salām*, he stood and said, 'Do you see this night of yours? A hundred years from it, no one who is today on the face of the earth will remain.'"[1] Ibn ʿUmar then said, "The people were frightened by the Messenger of Allah's statement ﷺ,"[2] meaning that they misunderstood what he meant since they did not hear the word "today."

منه، كما في خبر الصحيحين عن ابن عمر قال «صلّى بنا النبي ﷺ صلاة العشاء في آخر حياته فلمّا سلّم قام فقال "أرأيتكم ليلتكم هذه على رأس مائة سنة منها لا يبقى ممن هو اليوم على ظهر الأرض أحد"»[١] قال ابن عمر «فوهل الناس في مقالة رسول الله صلّى الله عليه وسلّم»[٢] أي غلطوا في فهم المراد منها حيث لم يسمعوا لفظة «اليوم».

Causes for the Fabrication of Reports

[Causes for the fabrication of reports include the following]:

1. a narrator's forgetting his narration such that he mentions something else, deeming it the narration.
2. intentional falsification, e.g., the fabrication by heretics of reports that offend the intellect in order to drive intelligent people away from the pure revealed law.
3. an error by the narrator, such as a slip of his tongue [causing him to utter] something other than his narration, replacing it with what he assumes conveys its meaning or narrating what he deems to be a hadith.
4. other causes, like the fabrication of reports by certain people to motivate others towards religious obedience and frighten them away from sin, and so on.

سبب وضع الخبر

[سبب وضعه]:

١- نسيان من الراوي لمرويّه فيذكر غيره ظانًّا أنه مرويّه.

٢- أو افتراء، كوضع الزنادقة أخبارًا تخالف العقول تنفيرًا للعقلاء عن الشريعة المطهّرة.

٣- أو غلط من الراوي بأن يسبق لسانه إلى غير مرويّه فيضع مكانه ما يظنّ أنه يؤدّي معناه أو يروي ما يظنّه حديثًا.

٤- أو غيرها كما في وضع بعضهم أخبارًا في الترغيب في الطاعة والترهيب عن المعصية أو غير ذلك.

---

[1] Al-Bukhārī, *al-Jāmiʿ al-ṣaḥīḥ*, 1:34 (no. 116); 1:117 (no. 564); 1:123 (no. 601); Muslim, *Ṣaḥīḥ*, 1057 (no. 2537); 1058 (no. 2538, no. 2539).

[2] Muslim, *Ṣaḥīḥ*, 1057 (no. 2537).

[١] البخاري، العلم، ٤١؛ مواقيت الصلاة، ٢٠؛ مسلم، فضائل الصحابة، ٢١٧-٢٢٠.

[٢] مسلم، فضائل الصحابة، ٢١٧.

Reports with Respect to Truth and Falsity

الخبر بحسب الصدق والكذب

There are two types of reports with respect to truth and falsity: those whose falsity is certain and those whose truth is certain.[27]

الخبر بحسب الصدق والكذب قسمان: إما مقطوع بكذبه وإما مقطوع بصدقه.

As for those whose falsity is certain, [they may be]

1. reports that were scrutinized (that is, looked into) in the books of hadith and were not traced to the right sources, i.e., reliable narrators.
2. reports that were transmitted by unit chains in cases where there would have been strong reasons to expect their mass transmission, either on account of their standing out as peculiar, e.g., a preacher falling from the pulpit during the sermon, or on account of their pertaining to religious foundations, e.g., a report on which the Shia rely regarding the imamate of ʿAlī (may Allah honor his countenance), namely, "You are the caliph after me": the fact that this report is not massively transmitted proves that it is not sound.

أما المقطوع بكذبه:

١- فخبر نُقّب أي فُتّش عنه في كتب الحديث ولم يوجد عند أهله من الرواة الثقات.

٢- خبر نُقل آحادًا فيما تتوفّر الدواعي على نقله تواترًا إما لغرابته كسقوط الخطيب عن المنبر وقت الخطبة أو لتعلّقه بأصل ديني كخبر يستند إليه الشيعة على إمامة عليّ كرّم الله وجهه وهو «أنت الخليفة من بعدي» فعدم تواتره دليل على عدم صحّته.

As for reports whose truth is certain, [they may be]

1. reports from a truthful source, that is, the statements of Allah ﷻ, for He transcends telling falsehoods, and the massively transmitted statements of His messenger ﷺ, for he is infallible.
2. reports that are *massively transmitted* in their wording or meaning, i.e., reports from such a number of people that it would be impossible by the standard of normative experience that they had concurred (that is, agreed) on a falsehood in reporting a sensory [event] (rather than an intellectually apprehended one, since one can be mistaken in such things, e.g., the assertion of the philosophers that the universe is eternal).

   If people of such [a number] agree on the wording and the meaning, it is a *verbatim*

وأما المقطوع بصدقه:

١- كخبر الصادق أي خبر الله تعالى لتنزّهه عن الكذب وخبر رسوله المتواتر عنه ﷺ لعصمته عنه.

٢- والمتواتر لفظًا أو معنًى وهو خبر جمع يمتنع عادة تواطؤهم أي توافقهم على الكذب خبرًا عن محسوس لا عن معقول — لجواز الغلط فيه كخبر الفلاسفة بقدم العالم.

فإن اتّفق الجمع المذكور في اللفظ والمعنى فهو لفظي وإن اختلفوا فيهما مع وجود

mass report; if they disagree on both but there remains a common meaning [that they do agree on], it is a *substantive mass report*, e.g., if someone were to report that Ḥātim gave a dinar, another that he gave a horse, another that he gave a camel, and so forth, then they would have agreed on a common meaning: the giving.

معنًى كلّي فهو معنوي كما لو أخبر واحد عن حاتم بأنه أعطى دينارًا وآخر بأنه أعطى فرسًا وآخر بأنه أعطى بعيرًا وهكذا فقد اتّفقوا على معنًى كلّي وهو الإعطاء.

According to the soundest position: The knowledge [acquired] through mass reports is immediate and does not require that one reflect after hearing the report. Someone who reports [about a sensory event] in the presence of [witnesses] of such a number as would be sufficient for mass transmission and who do not deny [his report], there being no reason for them to withhold their denial—whether fear, ambition, or ignorance of the reported [event]—is truthful. This is because the silence [of the witnesses] is understood, by normative experience, as confirmation of his report; the report, then, would be true.

والأصحّ أن العلم فيه ضروري من غير احتياج إلى نظر عقب السماع. وإن المخبِر[١٤] بحضرة عدد التواتر ولم يكذّبوه ولا حامل على سكوتهم عن تكذيبهم من نحو خوف أو طمع في شيء أو عدم علم بخبره صادق فيما أخبر به لأن سكوتهم تصديق له عادة فيكون الخبر صادقًا.

As for reports whose truth is presumed, these are *unit reports*, i.e., [reports] that do not reach the point of mass transmission, whether they are narrated by one person or more, and whether or not they impart (conclusive) knowledge when considered alongside independent indicants.

وأما مظنون الصدق فهو خبر الواحد وهو ما لم ينته إلى التواتر سواء أكان رواته واحدًا أم أكثر أفاد العلم بالقرائن المنفصلات أو لا.

One type of unit report is the *widely known report*, i.e., that which is widespread among people and has a basis, and this type of report is sometimes termed *well-known*. The minimum number of narrators for such reports is two; this is the position of the jurists. According to some, the number must be greater than three; this is the position of the jurisprudential theorists. According to others, it must be three; this is the position of the hadith scholars.

ومنه المستفيض وهو الشائع بين الناس عن أصل وقد يسمّى مشهورًا. وأقلّ عدد راويه اثنان؛ وهو قول الفقهاء. وقيل ما زاد على ثلاثة؛ وهو قول الأصوليّين. وقيل ثلاثة؛ وهو قول المحدّثين.

The Omission of Part of a Report

According to the soundest position: Omitting part of a report is permissible unless the rest depends on [the omitted part], in which case it is unanimously agreed that omission is impermissible because it is detrimental to the intended meaning. For example, [an omission is detrimental] when [the omitted part contains] the purpose or an exception. This differs from a case in which the rest [of the report] does not depend on [the omitted part]: such an omission is permissible because [the omitted part] is like an independent report, as in his statement ﷺ in the report "It is that whose water is pure and whose unslaughtered animals are permissible,"[1] in which the phrase "whose unslaughtered animals are permissible" does not depend on the part before it.

Those Whose Reporting Is Accepted and Those Whose Reporting Is Not

According to the soundest position: The conveying [of a report] by a discerning child who retained [the report], matured, and then conveyed what he had retained is accepted. [Likewise, the conveying of a report by] a disbeliever who retained [the report], accepted Islam, and then conveyed it and that of an immoral person who repented and then conveyed is accepted. [The reporting of] a deviant innovator is accepted if he (1) recognizes the prohibition of lying, (2) does not openly call others to his deviancy, and (3) is not to be pronounced a disbeliever thereby. This is because he can be trusted not to lie and has an interpretive argument for his deviancy, and stands in contrast to one who does not recognize the prohibition of lying, calls people to his deviancy, or is to be pronounced a disbeliever thereby, e.g., one who denies the origination of the universe, the resurrection, or Allah's knowledge of nonexistent things or of particulars; [reports] belonging to any of these three categories are not accepted.

[1] Ibn Ḥibbān, *Ṣaḥīḥ Ibn Ḥibbān*, 4:49; al-Ḥākim, *al-Mustadrak*, 1:223–27.

حذف بعض الخبر

الأصحّ أن حذف بعض الخبر جائز إلا أن يتعلّق به الباقي فلا يجوز حذفه حينئذ اتّفاقًا لإخلاله بالمعنى المقصود كأن يكون غاية أو مستثنى بخلاف ما لا يتعلّق به الباقي فيجوز حذفه لأنه كخبر مستقلّ. مثاله قوله ﷺ في الخبر «هو الطهور ماؤه الحلّ ميتته»[١] إذ قوله «الحلّ ميتته» لا تعلّق له بما قبله.

من يقبل أداؤه ومن لا

والأصحّ أنه يقبل أداء صبي مميز تحمّلَ فبلغَ فأدّى ما تحمّله؛ أو تحمّل كافر فأسلم فأدّى أو فاسق فتاب فأدّى قُبل؛ وأنه يقبل مبتدع (١) يحرّم الكذب (٢) وليس بداعية (٣) ولا يكفر ببدعته لأمنه الكذب مع تأويله في الابتداع بخلاف من لا يحرّم الكذب أو يدعو الناس إلى بدعته أو يكفر ببدعته كمنكر حدوث العالم والبعث وعلم الله بالمعدوم وبالجزئيّات فلا يقبل واحد من هذه الثلاثة.

[١] ابن حبّان، صحيح ابن حبّان، ٤/ ٤٩؛ الحاكم، المستدرك، ١/ ٢٢٣-٢٢٧.

The Condition for a Narrator

The condition for a narrator is that he be upright (*ʿadāla*). Lexically, *ʿadāla* is to occupy the mean, and in the religious [sciences] it is used in a sense that includes *dignity*, i.e., a habit (that is, a fixed disposition in the soul) that bars one from committing major sins, base minor sins like stealing a scrap of food, or permissible but contemptible actions like urinating in a path. Performing any of these kinds of acts vitiates uprightness.

According to the chosen position: Major sins are those singled out with threats like His anger or with being cursed.

Mursal Hadiths and Their Authority

According to the common [definition] among the jurisprudential theorists, jurists, and some hadith scholars, [*mursal* hadiths] are hadiths attributed to the Prophet ﷺ by anyone other than a Companion—whether a Follower or someone later—omitting the intermediate narrator between the narrator and the Prophet. According to the majority of the hadith scholars, [*mursal* hadiths] are hadiths attributed to the Prophet by a Follower.

According to the soundest position: *Mursal* hadiths are not accepted (which means that they cannot be used as authoritative proofs), because it cannot be known whether the omitted narrator was upright, even if he was a Companion—he might have been subject to a disqualifying event.[28] This applies unless the narrator of the *mursal* hadith is one of the eminent Followers and [his narration] is bolstered by (1) the fact that he narrates only from upright narrators—in such a case the report takes the status of an uninterrupted hadith because it is the same to omit an upright narrator as to cite him—or bolstered by (2) the statements or actions of a Companion, (3) the position of the scholarly majority, (4) an uninterrupt-

شرط الراوي

شرط الراوي العدالة وهي لغةً التوسّط وشرعًا بالمعنى الشامل للمروءة ملكة أي هيئة راسخة في النفس تمنع اقتراف الكبائر والصغائر الخسّة كسرقة لقمة والرذائل الجائزة كبول بطريق فباقتراف فرد منه تنتفي العدالة.

والمختار أن الكبيرة ما تُوُعِّد عليه بنحو غضبه ولعن بخصوصه غالبًا.

الحديث المرسل وحجيته

المشهور عند الأصوليّين والفقهاء وبعض المحدّثين هو مرفوع غير صحابي تابعيًّا كان أو من بعده إلى النبي ﷺ مسقطًا الواسطة بينه وبين النبي. وعند أكثر المحدّثين هو مرفوع تابعي إلى النبي.

والأصحّ أنه لا يقبل أي لا يحتجّ به للجهل بعدالة الساقط وإن كان صحابيًّا لاحتمال أن يكون ممن طرأ له قادح؛ إلا إن كان مرسله من كبار التابعين وعضّده (١) كونُ مرسله لا يروي إلا عن عدل وهو حينئذ مسند حكمًا لأن إسقاط العدل كذكره أو عضّده (٢) قول صحابي أو فعله أو (٣) قول الأكثر من العلماء أو (٤)

ed hadith or [another narrator's] *mursal* hadith, (5) the fact of being well known, (6) an analogy, (7) the practice of the people of the era, or the like.

When considered together, a *mursal* hadith and its bolstering proof are an authoritative proof as long as the bolstering proof is not used as an authoritative proof [on its own]; otherwise, they are two [distinct] indicants since the bolstering proof is in that case an indicant on its own and the *mursal* hadith, when bolstered by it, becomes another indicant. If the *mursal* hadith lacks a bolstering proof and there is no other indicant regarding the matter, then the soundest position is that it is obligatory to refrain out of caution.[29]

The Transmission of Hadiths by Meaning

According to the soundest position: It is permissible for one who knows the meanings of the expressions to transmit a hadith by [merely conveying its] meaning.[30] As for one who does not know this, it is absolutely impermissible for him to change the wording.

Considering the Statement of a Companion As Authoritative Proof

According to the soundest position: It is considered an authoritative proof when a Companion states, (1) “The Prophet said…”; (2) “From him…”; (3) “I heard him…,” “He commanded…,” “He prohibited…,” “We were commanded,” similar [verbs] in the passive voice like “We were prohibited [from]…,” or “It is of the Sunna that such and such”; (4) “During his lifetime, all of us people would do…” or “During his lifetime, the people used to do…”; (5) “We used to do…”; (6) “The people used to do…”; or (7) “They would not sever [a thief's hand] for a trivial theft,”[31] for this [habit] was apparent in all the people, which amounts to consensus. The conjunction of the above forms of expression with a *fā'* indicates that each form is lower in rank than the one before it.[32]

مسند أو مرسل (٥) أو انتشار أو (٦) قياس أو (٧) عمل أهل العصر أو نحوها.

والمجموع من المرسل وعاضده حجّة إن لم يحتجّ بالعاضد وإلا فدليلان إذ العاضد حينئذ دليل برأسه والمرسل لما اعتضد به صار دليلًا آخر. فإن تجرَّد هذا المرسل عن عاضد ولا دليل في الباب سواه فالأصحّ أنه يجب الانكفاف احتياطًا.

نقل الحديث بالمعنى

الأصحّ جواز نقل الحديث بالمعنى لعارف بمعاني الألفاظ. أما غير العارف فلا يجوز له تغيير اللفظ قطعًا.

الاحتجاج بقول الصحابي

الأصحّ أنه يحتجّ بقول الصحابي (١) «قال النبي» (٢) فـ«عنه» (٣) فـ«سمعته» أو «أمر» و«نهى» أو «أمرنا» أو نحوه مما بني للمفعول كـ«نُهينا» و«من السنّة كذا» (٤) فـ«كنّا معاشر الناس نفعل في عهده» أو «كان الناس يفعلون [في عهده]» (٥) فـ«كنّا نفعل» (٦) فـ«كان الناس يفعلون» (٧) فـ«كانوا لا يقطعون في الشيء التافه» لظهور ذلك في جميع الناس الذي هو إجماع. وعطف الصور بالفاء إشارة إلى أن كل صورة دون ما قبلها رتبةً.

The Levels of Reception

The sources of transmission to someone other than a Companion are of eleven types, [listed in descending order of strength]:

1. the shaykh dictating aloud to [the student][33] from memory or a text.
2. narration without dictation.
3. the student reciting to the teacher.
4. the student hearing another's recitation to the teacher. This and preceding level are termed *presentation*.
5. the student being given [the teacher's text] or copying [from the teacher's text] with authorization [regarding the transmission], e.g., the teacher handing to the student the original text [of narrations that the student had heard] or a text copied from the original or writing some hadith for [a student] in his presence or elsewhere and telling him, "I authorize you to narrate it from me."
6. the teacher giving authorization—without handing or writing [any text]—to a specific [student] regarding a specific [text], e.g., "I authorize you to narrate *al-Bukhārī*."
7. [authorizing] a specific [student] regarding a general [body of narrations], e.g., "I authorize you to narrate all that you have heard from me."
8. [authorizing] a general [body of students] regarding a specific [text], e.g., "I authorize those who have met me to narrate *Muslim*."
9. [authorizing] a general [body of students] regarding a general [body of narrations], e.g., "I authorize those who are contemporaneous with me to narrate all of my narrations."

مراتب التحمل

مستند غير الصحابي في الرواية إحدى عشرة:

١- قراءة الشيخ عليه إملاء من حفظه أو من كتابه.

٢- فتحديثًا بلا إملاء.

٣- قراءته على الشيخ.

٤- فسماعه بقراءة غيره على الشيخ ويسمّى هذا والذي قبله بالعرض.

٥- فمناولة أو مكاتبة مع إجازة كأن يدفع له الشيخ أصل سماعه أو فرعًا مقابلًا به أو يكتب شيئًا من حديث لحاضر عنده أو غائب عنه ويقول له «أجزت لك روايته عنّي».

٦- فإجازة[١٥] بلا مناولة شيء ولا مكاتبة لخاصّ في خاصّ كـ«أجزتك رواية البخاري».

٧- فخاصّ في عامّ كـ«أجزت لك رواية جميع مسموعاتي».

٨- فعامّ في خاصّ كـ«أجزت لمن أدركني رواية مسلم».

٩- فعامّ في عامّ كـ«أجزت لمن عاصرني رواية جميع مرويّاتي».

10. [authorizing] such and such a person and those of his lineage who succeed him.

11. handing [a student a text] or writing down [hadith for him] without authorizing him if [the teacher] says in doing so, "I heard this."

١٠- فلفلان ومن يوجد من نسله تبعًا له.

١١- فمناولـة أو مكاتبـة بـلا إجـازة إن قال معهـا «هذا من سـماعي».

Chapter 3

CONSENSUS

This chapter comprises several investigations.

I. According to the soundest position: Consensus is possible. According to some: Consensus is impossible by normative experience, as is reaching a consensus on a single food to eat. The response is that in such a case there is no factor that would bring about a unanimous opinion.

II. According to the soundest position: Consensus, granting its possibility, is legally authoritative even if transmitted through unit reports. He says ﷻ, "But whosoever opposes the Messenger after guidance has been made clear to him and follows a way other than that of the believers..." (Q 4:115), warning therein against following a way other than that of the believers. It is obligatory, then, to follow their way, namely, their speech and actions, which renders [consensus] authoritative.

III. According to the soundest position: Consensus, granting its authority, is *conclusive* if those [whose assessment is] given consideration agree that consensus has occurred, but not if they differ [on whether consensus has occurred], as in the case of tacit consensus, which is *presumptive*.

IV. To contravene conclusive consensus—or even presumptive consensus among those who recognize it—is prohibited on account of the warning against it

الكتاب الثالث

في الإجماع

فيه مباحث.

١- الأصحّ إمكان الإجماع. وقيل لا يمكن عادة كالاجتماع على أكل طعام واحد؛ وردّ بأنه لا جامع لهم عليه.

٢- والأصحّ أن الإجماع بعد إمكانه حجّة شرعيّة وإن نقل آحادًا. قال تعالى ﴿وَمَن يُشَاقِقِ ٱلرَّسُولَ مِن بَعْدِ مَا تَبَيَّنَ لَهُ ٱلْهُدَىٰ وَيَتَّبِعْ غَيْرَ سَبِيلِ ٱلْمُؤْمِنِينَ﴾ ...الآية [٤/ ١١٥] توعّد فيها على اتّباع غير سبيل المؤمنين فيجب اتّباع سبيلهم وهو قولهم وفعلهم فيكون حجّة.

٣- والأصحّ أن الإجماع بعد حجّيّته قطعي إن اتّفق المعتبَرون على أنه إجماع لا إن اختلفوا كالسكوتي فإنه ظنّي.

٤- وخرق الإجماع القطعي وكذا الظنّي عند من اعتبره حرام للتوعّد عليه كما مرّ في الآية السابقة. فعلم من

حرمة خرقه تحريم إحداث قول ثالث في مسألة اختلف أهل عصر فيها على قولين وإحداث تفصيل بين مسألتين لم يفصّل بينهما أهل عصر إن خرقاه أي إن خرق الثالث والتفصيل الإجماع بأن خالفا ما اتّفق عليه أهل عصر بخلاف ما إذا لم يخرقاه.

as in the verse cited above. Moreover, on the basis of the prohibition of contravening consensus, one infers that it would be prohibited to introduce a third opinion on a question regarding which the scholars of the time are divided into two positions or to introduce a distinction between two questions that the scholars of the time do not distinguish[34] if in doing either of these things one were to contravene consensus, that is, if the third position or the distinction were to contravene consensus by breaking from those points on which the scholars of the time did agree. By contrast, it would not [be prohibited to do either of these things] in a way that does not contravene consensus.

٥- وعلم أنه يجوز إظهار دليل لحكم أو تأويل لدليل ليوافق غيره أو علّة لحكم غير ما ذكروه من الدليل والتأويل والعلّة لجواز تعدّد المذكورات إن لم يخرق ما ذكر ما ذكروه.

V. One also infers [from the prohibition of contravening consensus] that it would be permissible to posit (1) an indicant for a ruling, (2) the interpretation of an indicant to support a different ruling, or (3) a cause for a ruling, [this posited indicant, interpretation, or cause] being other than the indicants, interpretations, or causes that have already been agreed upon—since a multiplicity of these things is possible—so long as it does not contravene what has already been agreed upon.[35]

٦- وعلم أن الإجماع لا يضادّ إجماعًا أي لا يجوز انعقاده على ما يضادّ ما انعقد عليه إجماع قبله لاستلزامه تعارض قاطعين؛ وهو الأصحّ في الكل. ولا يعارَض الإجماع بناء على أنه دليل قطعي إذ لا تعارض بين قاطعين لاستحالته، إذ التعارض بين شيئين يقتضي خطأ أحدهما.

VI. One also infers that a consensus cannot oppose a consensus. That is, it would be invalid to form a consensus that opposes an already existing consensus since this would entail contradiction between conclusive [indicants]. This is the soundest position regarding all [of these questions].[36] As a conclusive indicant, consensus cannot be contradicted [by another indicant] because there can be no contradiction between conclusive indicants;[37] such would be impossible since a contradiction between two things entails that one of them is incorrect.

٧- جاحدُ مجمعٍ عليه معلوم من الدين ضرورة كافر إن كان فيه نصّ وكذا إن لم يكن فيه نصّ على الأصحّ.

VII. One who rejects a point of consensus that is necessarily known to be part and parcel of the religion is a disbeliever if there exists an unequivocal text regarding the matter and, according to the soundest position, even if there exists no unequivocal text regarding the matter.

Chapter 4

ANALOGY

الكتاب الرابع

في القياس

Lexically, *qiyās* (analogy) means determination and equalization. Technically, it means referring one conceivable thing to another, i.e., extending the latter's ruling to the former because the former equally possesses the cause of the latter's ruling. This occurs when the one who is doing the referring—that is, the mujtahid, whether a mujtahid in the absolute sense or in the restricted sense—judges that the cause of the latter's ruling is entirely present in the former.

وهو لغةً التقدير والمساواة، واصطلاحًا حمل معلوم على معلوم أي إلحاقه به في حكمه لمساواته له في علّة حكمه بأن توجد بتمامها في المحمول عند الحامل وهو المجتهد مطلقًا أو مقيّدًا.

Analogy is authoritative in worldly matters, e.g., [in determining what is] nourishing food. [It is also authoritative] otherwise, as in legal matters, according to the soundest position, as evidenced by (1) the fact that it was consistently and prevalently practiced by many Companions without any objection from the others—which would normally be considered to amount to acceptance in comparable everyday situations—and due to (2) His saying ﷻ, "So take heed" (Q 59:2). To take heed means to analogize one thing to another.

وهو حجّة في الأمور الدنيويّة كالأغذية وكذا في غيرها كالشرعيّة في الأصحّ لعمل كثير من الصحابة به متكرّرًا شائعًا مع سكوت الباقين الذي هو في مثل ذلك من الأمور العامّة وفاق عادةً، ولقوله تعالى ﴿فَٱعْتَبِرُواْ﴾ [٥٩/ ٢] والاعتبار قياس الشيء بالشيء.

Analogy is valid, then, with respect to these matters. But it is invalid with respect to experiential and natural matters, that is, matters that refer to normative experience or bodily nature, e.g., the minimum or maximum duration of menstruation, postnatal bleeding, or pregnancy, because these cannot be ascertained through analogy, according to the soundest position, since the reason for them cannot be apprehended. In these cases, one refers instead to the opinions of experts.

فيجوز القياس في ذلك إلا في العاديّة والخلقيّة أي التي ترجع إلى العادة والخلقة كأقلّ الحيض أو النفاس أو الحمل وأكثره فيمتنع ثبوتها بالقياس في الأصحّ لأنها لا يدرك المعنى فيها بل يرجع فيها إلى قول من يوثق به.

Nor is analogy valid with respect to [all] legal rulings: it is impossible for [the entire body of legal rulings] to be ascertained through analogy, according to the soundest position, because there are some legal rulings whose reasons cannot be apprehended, e.g., the obligation of a clan's payment of the blood money. According to some: Analogy is valid [with respect to every legal ruling] in the sense that any ruling could be ascertained through analogy by apprehension of its reason, and the obligation of a clan's payment of the blood money has an apprehensible reason, namely, to assist the perpetrator in fulfilling a task he is incapable to fulfilling in the same way that a debtor is assisted in rectifying his dealings with [his creditor] through the zakat money that he receives.

Nor is analogy valid that is based on abrogated rulings; according to the soundest position, analogy is impossible in such cases since, by virtue of abrogation, the common element no longer merits consideration. According to some: Analogy remains valid because analogy reveals the ruling of the derivative case, and the abrogation of [the ruling of] the original case does not abrogate [the ruling of] the derivative case.[38]

According to the soundest position: A textual statement of the cause for a ruling (including [rulings about] refraining from action) is not a command to utilize analogy, regardless whether the ruling relates to a positive act, e.g., "Honor Zayd because of his knowledge," or to the refraining from an act, e.g., "Wine is prohibited because it intoxicates." According to some: [Such a statement] is in either case a command to utilize analogy because there is no other point in mentioning the legal cause. We respond: We do not concede the exclusivity; it is possible that the point be to explain the apprehensible reason for the ruling in order to render it more impactful on the soul.

وإلا في [كل] الأحكام فيمتنع ثبوتها بالقياس في الأصحّ لأن منها ما لا يدرك معناه، كوجوب الدية على العاقلة. وقيل يجوز بمعنى أن[١٦] كلاً من الأحكام صالح لأن يثبت بالقياس بأن يدرك معناه ووجوب الدية على العاقلة له معنًى يدرك وهو إعانة الجاني فيما هو معذور فيه كما يعان الغارم لإصلاح ذات البين بما يصرف إليه من الزكاة.

وإلا في القياس على منسوخ فيمتنع فيه في الأصحّ لانتفاء اعتبار الجامع بالنسخ. وقيل يجوز فيه لأن القياس مظهِر لحكم الفرع ونسخ الأصل ليس نسخًا للفرع.

وليس النصّ على العلّة لحكم ولو في جانب الكفّ أمرًا بالقياس في الأصحّ لا في جانب الفعل غير الكفّ كـ«أكرم زيدًا لعلمه» ولا في جانب الكفّ نحو «الخمر حرام لإسكارها». وقيل إنه أمر به في الجانبين إذ لا فائدة لذكر العلّة إلا ذلك. قلنا لا نسلّم الحصر لجواز كون الفائدة بيان مدرك الحكم ليكون أوقع في النفس.

The Components of Analogy

Analogy has four components: an original case, a ruling, a derivative case, and a cause, which is a feature that the original case and the derivative case have in common. The ruling of the original case extends to the derivative case by means of the commonality.

1. The Original Case

The first component is the original case. The original case is termed the *source of the analogy* and the derivative case the *object of the analogy*. According to the soundest position: The original case, or the source of the analogy, is the locus of the ruling, and it is that to which the comparison is made. According to the soundest position: It is not a necessary condition that there be an indicant pertaining to the original case that validates the use of its category or the specific case in an analogy.

2. The Ruling of the Original Case

The second component is the ruling of the original case. Its conditions are [as follows]:

1. The ruling of the original case must be established by some means (including consensus) other than analogy because were it to be established by means of analogy, then (a) in the scenario that the legal cause is the same, a second analogy would be superfluous since it would have sufficed to analogize the derivative case of the second analogy to the original case of the first analogy, and (b) in the scenario that the legal cause is different, the second analogy would be unsound since the original case and the derivative case would lack a common cause for the ruling.

   An example in which [the legal cause] is the same is when apples are analogized to wheat in being *ribawī*[39] by virtue of the commonali-

أركانه

أركان القياس أربعة: أصل، حكم، فرع، علة وهي معنًى مشترك بين الأصل والفرع. وحكم الأصل يتعدّى بواسطة المشترك إلى الفرع.

١. الأصل

الركن الأول الأصل. يسمّى الأصل مقيسًا عليه والفرع مقيسًا. والأصحّ أنه أي الأصل المقيس عليه محلّ الحكم والمشبّه به. والأصحّ أنه لا يشترط في الأصل دليل على جواز القياس عليه بنوعه أو شخصه.

٢. حكم الأصل

الركن الثاني حكم الأصل. شرطه:

١- ثبوته بغير قياس ولو إجماعًا، إذ لو ثبت بقياس كان القياس الثاني (١) عند اتّحاد العلّة لغوًا للاستغناء عنه بقياس الفرع فيه على الأصل في الأول (٢) وعند اختلافها غير منعقد لعدم اشتراك الأصل والفرع فيه في علّة الحكم.

فالاتّحاد كقياس التفّاح على البرّ في الربويّة بجامع الطعم ثم قياس السفرجل على التفّاح

ty of being food, and then quinces are analogized to apples in the same manner: the [second analogy] is superfluous because it would have sufficed to analogize quinces to wheat.

An example in which [the legal cause] is different is when *ratq* (a blockage of the site of intercourse) is analogized to castration in annulling marriage by virtue of the commonality of vitiating the enjoyment of sexual intercourse, and then leprosy is analogized to *ratq* in the same manner: the [second analogy] is unsound because leprosy does not vitiate the enjoyment of sexual intercourse.

2. The ruling of the original case must be of the same kind as the ruling of the derivative case: it must be legal if one seeks to ascertain a legal ruling, rational if one seeks to ascertain a rational ruling, and lexical if one seeks to ascertain a lexical ruling.

3. The ruling of the original case should not deviate from the paradigm of analogy. The locus of a ruling that deviates from the paradigm of analogy, i.e., diverges from its normal way, cannot be subjected to analogy because in such a case the [ruling] cannot transfer. An example is the solitary testimonial authority of Khuzayma b. Thābit; one cannot analogize other [narrators] to him even when they are superior to him in rank, like [Abū Bakr] al-Ṣiddīq ﷺ.

4. The indicant for the ruling of the original case must not include the ruling of the derivative case, since this would leave no need for analogy.

5. [In the context of a jurisprudential disputation,] according to all, the disputing parties need to agree upon the ruling of the original case. [According to the soundest position, the agreement of the disputing parties is sufficient] since the inquiry does not concern anyone else. According to some: [The ruling must be agreed upon] by the entire *umma* such that there could never be

فيما ذكر؛ وهو لغو للاستغناء عنه بقياس السفرجل على البرّ.

والاختلاف كقياس الرتق وهو انسداد محلّ الوطء على جبّ الذكر في فسخ النكاح بجامع فوات التمتّع ثم قياس الجذام على الرتق فيما ذكر؛ وهو غير منعقد لأن فوات التمتّع غير موجود فيه.

٢- وكونه من جنس حكم الفرع، فيشترط كونه شرعيًّا إن كان المطلوب إثباته حكمًا شرعيًّا وكونه عقليًّا إن كان المطلوب إثباته حكمًا عقليًّا وكونه لغويًّا إن كان المطلوب إثباته حكمًا لغويًّا.

٣- وأن لا يعدل حكم الأصل عن سنن القياس، فما عدل عن سننه أي خرج عن طريقه لا يقاس على محلّه لتعذّر التعدية حينئذ، كشهادة خزيمة بن ثابت وحده فلا يقاس به غيره وإن فاقه رتبةً كالصدّيق رضي الله عنه.

٤- وأن لا يكون دليل حكم الأصل شاملًا لحكم الفرع للاستغناء به حينئذ عن القياس.

٥- وكون حكم الأصل متّفقًا عليه جزمًا بين الخصمين لأن البحث لا يعدوهما. وقيل بين كل

occasion to challenge it in the first place.

3. The Derivative Case

The third component is the derivative case. According to the soundest position: The derivative case is the locus[40] that is compared to the original case.

According to the chosen position: [In the context of jurisprudential disputation,] it is acceptable to counteract [a disputant's analogy] regarding a derivative case with [an analogy] that entails a contradictory or contrary ruling. The form of [this objection] with regard to the derivative case is that the objector tells the proponent, "Granting that the feature[41] you have cited entails the application of the ruling to the derivative case, I can cite a different feature that entails the contradictory or contrary ruling."

An example of [citing a feature that entails] the contradictory [ruling] is [that the proponent state,] "Wiping [one's head] is an integral component of ablutions; therefore, performing it thrice is a sunna just like [washing] the face," to which the objector responds, "It is not a sunna to wipe the head thrice just as [it is not a sunna] to wipe a leather sock [thrice]."[42]

An example of [citing a feature that entails] the contrary [ruling] is [that the proponent state,] "The *witr* prayer is a duty that the Prophet ﷺ consistently maintained; therefore, it is obligatory just like declaring the testimony of faith," to which the objector responds, "[The *witr* prayer is] fixed to the time period of one of the five prayers; therefore, it is a sunna just like the dawn sunna prayer."[43]

The preferred way to rebut such a counteraction—in addition to rebutting the arguments that were used to object to the proponent first of all—is to rebut it by arguing that the feature favored by the proponent preponderates over the feature favored by the objector according to the relevant standards that determine preponderance (which we will discuss in their place), because action ought to be in accordance with the preponderant [feature].

الأمّة حتى لا يتأتّى المنع أصلًا.

٣. الفرع

الركن الثالث الفرع وهو المحلّ المشبّه بالأصل في الأصحّ.

والمختار قبول المعارضة في الفرع بمقتضي[١٧] نقيض الحكم أو ضدّه. وصورتها في الفرع أن يقول المعترض للمستدلّ «ما ذكرتَه من الوصف وإن اقتضى ثبوت الحكم في الفرع فعندي وصف آخر يقتضي نقيضه أو ضدّه».

فالنقيض نحو «المسح ركن في الوضوء فيسنّ تثليثه كالوجه» فيقول المعارض «مسح الرأس في الوضوء لا يسنّ تثليثه كمسح الخفّ».

والضدّ نحو «الوتر واجب واظب عليه النبي صلّى الله عليه وسلّم فيجب كالتشهّد» فيقول المعارض «...مؤقّت بوقت صلاة من الخمس فيسنّ كسنّة الفجر».

والمختار في دفع المعارضة المذكورة زيادة على دفعها بكل ما يعترض به على المستدلّ ابتداءً دفعُها بالترجيح لوصف المستدلّ على وصف المعارض بمرجّح مما يأتي في محلّه لتعيّن[١٨] العمل بالراجح.

The derivative case must meet the following conditions:

1. The cause in the original case must be entirely present in the derivative case (e.g., [the feature of] being intoxicating in the analogy of date wine to grape wine and [the feature of] being hurtful in the analogy of striking to grumbling "Uff!") such that the legal ruling transfers to the derivative case.

   If the cause is (1) conclusive such that one knows conclusively that it is the cause in the original case and that it is present in the derivative case, like [the feature of] being hurtful in the example above, then the analogy with respect to that cause is a *conclusive analogy*. As a result, it is as if the derivative case is included by the indicant for the original case: if the indicant is presumptive, the ruling of the derivative case is the same.

   If the cause is (2) presumptive, then the analogy with respect to that cause is a *presumptive* or *"lower-grade" analogy*, like the analogy of apples to wheat through the commonality of being food, for this is the legal cause in the original case according to us, though we grant that it is possible that the cause is, as held by some, [the feature of] being [storable] provision or being subject to weighable measure—and the only [feature] among these that is present in apples is that of being food—thus, the ruling's application to apples is lower in grade than its application to wheat.

2. The derivative case must not be counteracted; there must be no conclusive [evidence] standing against it, that is, against the derivative case with respect to the ruling; and also, according to the soundest position, [there must be no] unit report [standing against it] since unit reports have priority over analogy.

وشرط الفرع:

١- وجود تمام العلّة التي في الأصل فيه، كالإسكار في قياس النبيذ بالخمر والإيذاء في قياس الضرب بالتأفيف فيتعدّى الحكم إلى الفرع.

(أ) فإن كانت العلّة قطعيّة بأن قطع بكونها علّة في الأصل ووجودِها في الفرع كالإسكار والإيذاء فيما مرّ فقطعيٌّ قياسُها حتى كأن الفرع فيه شمله دليل الأصل فإن كان دليله ظنيًّا فحكم الفرع كذلك.

(ب) أو كانت ظنّيّة فقياسها ظنّي وأدوَن كقياس التفّاح بالبرّ بجامع الطعم فإنه العلّة عندنا في الأصل مع احتمال ما قيل إنها القوت أو الكيل وليس في التفّاح إلا الطعم فثبوت الحكم فيه أدون من ثبوته في البرّ.

٢- وأن لا يعارَض ولا يقوم القاطعُ على خلافه أي خلاف الفرع في الحكم وكذا خبرُ الواحد في الأصحّ لأنه مقدّم على القياس.

3. The ruling of the derivative case and the ruling of the original case must be the same conceptually.[44]
4. The ruling of the derivative case must not precede the ruling of the original case when there is no indicant for the ruling of the derivative case besides the analogy, e.g., analogizing water ablutions to dry ablutions in the obligatoriness of the intention.[45]

4. The Legal Cause

The fourth component is the legal cause. It is a prerequisite condition for extending the ruling of an original case through a cause that [the cause in the original case] comprise some rationale, or benefit, that motivates, or drives, morally responsible agents to comply and serves to vouch for basing the ruling on that cause. An example of this is the protection of human lives: a person who knows that a retaliatory punishment is imposed on murderers refrains from committing murder.

Is It Valid for the Cause to Be the Rationale or to Be Privative? It is invalid for the cause to be the rationale [itself] if it cannot be precisely delimited,[46] e.g., hardship in travel, for this cannot be precisely delimited. But if it can be precisely delimited, it is valid, as argued by al-Āmidī,[47] Ibn al-Ḥājib,[48] and others, due to the absence of the problematic concern.

According to the source text:[49] It is invalid for the cause of a positive ruling to be privative, because a cause (in the sense of a sign) must be clearer than that of which it is the cause, and that which is privative is more obscure than that which is positive. It is valid for the cause of a positive ruling to be of its like, e.g., for the cause of the prohibition of wine to be that it is intoxicating, and it is valid for the cause of a privative ruling to be of its like, e.g., for the cause of the invalidity of financial prerogative to be the lack of intellect.

٣- وأن يتّحد حكمه بحكم الأصل في المعنى.

٤- وأن لا يتقدّم حكم الفرع على حكم الأصل حيث لا دليل له غير القياس، كقياس الوضوء بالتيمّم في وجوب النيّة.

٤. العلة

الركن الرابع العلة. وشرط للإلحاق بحكم الأصل بالعلّة أن تشتمل على حكمة أي مصلحة تبعث أي تحمل المكلّف على الامتثال وتصلح شاهدًا لإناطة الحكم بالعلّة، كحفظ النفوس فإن مَن علم أن مَن قَتل اقتُصّ منه انكفّ عن القتل.

هل يجوز كون العلة الحكمة أو كونها عدميًّا؟

لا يجوز كون العلّة الحكمة إن لم تنضبط، كالمشقّة في السفر لعدم انضباطها؛ فإن انضبطت جاز كما رجّحه الآمدي وابن الحاجب وغيرهما لانتفاء المحذور.

ولا يجوز في الأصل كون العلّة عدميّة في الحكم الثبوتي لأن العلّة بمعنى العلامة يجب أن تكون[١٩] أجلى من المعلَّل والعدمي أخفى من الثبوتي. ويجوز تعليل الثبوتي بمثله كتعليل حرمة الخمر بالإسكار والعدمي بمثله كتعليل عدم صحّة التصرّف بعدم العقل.

The Persistence of a Ruling When It Is Certain That the Rationale Is Absent According to the soundest position: A ruling persists [in those particular cases] where it is certain that the rationale is absent, since [the cause remains] a presumptive locus [for that ruling in general], as in the permissibility of shortening the prayer during travel for a person who boards a ship that has traveled the prerequisite distance for the shortening of prayers in a moment that is free of hardship.

Among the Conditions for Extending [a Ruling] Is the Absence of Two Things In order for [a ruling] to be extended through a cause, the following conditions must be met:

1. The legal cause must not contradict a textual statement or consensus, since these have priority over analogy.

   An example of contradicting a textual statement is that a Ḥanafī say, "A woman can possess [wealth] by nature; therefore, by analogy to her [prerogative] to sell her commodities, she may validly marry without the permission of her guardian," for this contradicts the report of Abū Dāwūd and others "Whenever a woman marries herself off without the permission of her guardian, her marriage is null."[1]

   An example of contradicting consensus is to analogize the prayer of travelers to the fast of travelers in being non-obligatory by means of the commonality of difficult travel, for this contradicts the consensus that timely fulfillment of the prayer is obligatory on travelers.

2. The legal cause that has been ascertained must not comprise any addition to textual statements or consensus that would negate their effects.

[1] Ibn Ḥibbān, *Ṣaḥīḥ Ibn Ḥibbān*, 9:384; al-Ḥākim, *al-Mustadrak*, 2:199–200; Abū Dāwūd, *al-Sunan*, 3:20 (no. 2076).

ثبوت الحكم فيما يقطع بانتفاء الحكمة

يثبت الحكم فيما يقطع بانتفائها فيه للمظنّة في الأصحّ، كجواز القصر بالسفر لمن ركب سفينة قطعت به مسافة القصر في لحظة بلا مشقّة.

من شرط الإلحاق انتفاء شيئين شرط للإلحاق بالعلّة:

١- أن لا تخالف نصًّا أو إجماعًا لتقدّمهما على القياس.

فمخالفة النصّ كقول الحنفي «المرأة مالكة بطبعها فيصحّ نكاحها بغير إذن وليّها قياسًا على بيع سلعتها» فإنه مخالف لخبر أبي داود وغيره «أيّما امرأة نكحت نفسها بغير إذن وليّها فنكاحها باطل».[١]

ومخالفة الإجماع كقياس صلاة المسافر على صومه في عدم الوجوب بجامع السفر الشاقّ فإنه مخالف للإجماع على وجوب أدائها عليه.

٢- وأن لا تتضمّن العلّة المستنبطة زيادةً على النصّ والإجماع منافيةً مقتضاه.

[١] ابن حبّان، صحيح ابن حبّان، ٩/ ٣٨٤؛ الحاكم، المستدرك، ٢/ ١٩٩-٢٠٠؛ أبو داود، النكاح، ٢٠.

The Means for Determining a Legal Cause

These are methods that indicate whether something is a cause, and they are numerous.

[1. Consensus]

The first is consensus, e.g., the consensus that the legal cause in the report of the two *Ṣaḥīḥ*s "No one should settle a dispute between two individuals while he is angry"[1] is the way that anger confounds thought; thus, other states that confound thought are analogized to anger, like excessive hunger and excessive satiety.

[2. Textual Statements]

The second of the means for determining a legal cause is a textual statement, whether unequivocal or apparent. Unequivocal textual statements are [expressed through] the like of "due to such and such cause"; next [in rank], "due to such and such reason"; and next [in rank], "due to such and such," e.g., His saying ﷻ, "Due to this, We prescribed for the children of Israel..." (Q 5:32). Apparent textual statements are [expressed through] the like of the *lām*, whether explicit, e.g., *Kitābun anzalnāhu ilayka li-tukhrija al-nāsa min al-ẓulumāti ilā al-nūri* (A book that We have sent down to you that you might bring forth mankind out of darkness into light) (Q 14:1), or implicit, e.g., *Wa-lā tuṭiʿ kulla ḥallāfin mahīnin...* (So obey not any vile oath-monger) up until He says ﷻ, *...an kāna dhā mālin wa-banīna* (... simply because he possesses wealth and children) (Q 68:10–14), i.e., *li-an* (because).

[1] Al-Bukhārī, *al-Jāmiʿ al-ṣaḥīḥ*, 9:65 (no. 7158); Muslim, *Ṣaḥīḥ*, 733 (no. 1717).

مسالك العلة

أي الطرق الدالّة على علّيّة الشيء. وهي كثيرة.

[١. الإجماع]

·الأول الإجماع، كالإجماع على أن العلّة في خبر الصحيحين «لا يحكم أحد بين اثنين وهو غضبان»[١] تشويش الغضب للفكر فيقاس بالغضب غيره مما يشوّش٢ الفكر نحو جوع وشبع مفرطين.

[٢. النص]

الثاني من مسالك العلّة النصّ صريحًا كان أو ظاهرًا. والصريح كـ«لعلّة كذا» فـ«لسبب كذا» فـ«من أجل كذا»، كقوله تعالى ﴿مِنْ أَجْلِ ذَٰلِكَ كَتَبْنَا عَلَىٰ بَنِيٓ إِسْرَٰٓءِيلَ﴾ ...الآية [٥/ ٣٢]. والنصّ الظاهر كاللام ظاهرة كانت نحو ﴿كِتَٰبٌ أَنزَلْنَٰهُ إِلَيْكَ لِتُخْرِجَ ٱلنَّاسَ مِنَ ٱلظُّلُمَٰتِ إِلَى ٱلنُّورِ﴾ [١٤/ ١] أو مقدّرة نحو ﴿وَلَا تُطِعْ كُلَّ حَلَّافٍ مَّهِينٍ﴾ إلى قوله ﴿أَن كَانَ ذَا مَالٍ وَبَنِينَ﴾ [٦٨/ ١٠-١٤] أي «لأن».

[١] البخاري، الأحكام، ١٣؛ مسلم، الأقضية، ١٦.

[3. Direct Entailment]

The third of the means for determining a legal cause is direct entailment, as in the report of the bedouin "I had intercourse with my wife during daytime in Ramadan," to which the Prophet ﷺ responded, "Free a slave":[1] his command to free a slave in response to the mention of intercourse indicates that [the act] is the cause for [the ruling].

[4. The Process of Elimination]

The fourth of the means for determining a legal cause is the process of elimination, namely, to enumerate all the qualities of the original case, which is the source of the analogy, and to rule out those among them that are not fit to be the cause, e.g., enumerating all the qualities of wheat when analogizing corn to it as food and then ruling out all the qualities besides that of being food, which determines that [the feature of] being food is the cause.

[5. Suitability]

The fifth of the means for determining a legal cause is suitability. Deducing the suitable cause is termed *extraction of the basis*, for it consists in revealing that on which the ruling depends, i.e., that to which the ruling is attached; *manāṭ* (basis) is from *nawṭ* (to make s.th. dependent on s.th.), and it refers to the legal cause. To extract the basis is to specify the cause by revealing the mutual suitability between the ruling and the specified cause, given that they are mutually concomitant, e.g., [the feature of] being intoxicating.[50] *Munāsib* (suitable legal consideration)—which is morphologically derived from the preceding term *munāsaba* (suitability)—refers to a feature that (1) is apparent, (2) can be precisely delimited, and (3) leads logically, by the application of the ruling, to an

[1] Al-Bukhārī, *al-Jāmiʿ al-ṣaḥīḥ*, 8:23 (no. 6087); al-Bayhaqī, *al-Sunan al-Kubrā*, 4:374.

[٣. الإيماء]

الثالث من مسالك العلّة الإيماء، كما في خبر الأعرابي «واقعت أهلي في نهار رمضان» فقال النبي ﷺ «أعتق رقبة»[١] فأمرُه بالإعتاق عند ذكر الوقاع يدلّ على أنه علّة له.

[٤. التقسيم]

الرابع من مسالك العلّة التقسيم وهو حصر أوصاف الأصل المقيس عليه وإبطال ما لا يصلح منها للعلّيّة، كأن يحصر أوصاف البرّ في قياس الذرة عليه في الطعم ويبطل ما عدا الطعم فيتعيّن الطعم للعلّيّة.

[٥. المناسبة]

الخامس من مسالك العلّة المناسبة. ويسمّى استخراج العلّة المناسبة تخريج المناط لأنه إبداء ما ينوط به الحكم أي ما تعلّق به الحكم فـ«المناط» من «النوط» وهو العلّة. وتخريج المناط تعيين العلّة بإبداء المناسبة بين العلّة المعيّنة والحكم مع الاقتران بينهما كالإسكار. و«المناسب» المأخوذ من «المناسبة» المتقدّمة وصف (١) ظاهر (٢) منضبط (٣) يحصل عقلًا من ترتّب الحكم

[١] البخاري، الأدب، ٦٨؛ البيهقي، السنن الكبرى، ٤/ ٣٧٤.

attainment of benefit or a repelling of harm that[1] could be specifically intended by the Lawgiver.

Suitable legal considerations are of several types. With regard to the legislation of rulings for their sake, they are of three types: considerations of fundamental necessity, considerations of practical necessity, and considerations of practical benefit.

1. Considerations of Fundamental Necessity Considerations of fundamental necessity are of several types: (1) the preservation of the religion, for the sake of which the slaying of disbelievers [in war] is legislated; next, (2) the preservation of life, for the sake of which retribution is legislated; next, (3) the preservation of intellect, for the sake of which the statutory punishment for intoxication is legislated; next, (4) the preservation of lineage, for the sake of which the statutory punishment for adultery is legislated; next, (5) the preservation of wealth, for the sake of which the statutory punishments for theft and banditry are legislated; and, next, (6) the preservation of honor, for the sake of which the punishments for slander and cursing are legislated. That by which a fundamental necessity is fully achieved has the same [rank] and thus adopts the same status, e.g., the statutory punishment for consuming small amounts of an intoxicating substance, since small amounts lead to large amounts.

2. Considerations of Practical Necessity Considerations of practical necessity are things that are needed but not to the point of fundamental necessity, e.g., commercial transactions and commercial agreements.[51] A practical necessity might be fundamentally necessary in some situations, e.g., an agreement regarding the raising of a child. That by which a practical necessity is fully achieved has the same [rank and adopts the same status], e.g., the option to void a transaction for safety from fraud.

[1] [In the Arabic phrasing of the sentence,] *mā* is the grammatical agent of [the preceding] *yaḥṣulu*.

عليه ما[١] يصلح كونه مقصودًا للشارع من حصول مصلحة أو دفع مفسدة.

للمناسب أقسام. المناسب من حيث شرع الحكم له ثلاثة أقسام: ضروري فحاجي فتحسيني.

١. المناسب الضروري وهو أنواع: (١) حفظ الدين المشروع له قتل الكفّار، (٢) فحفظ النفس المشروع له القود، (٣) فحفظ العقل المشروع له حدّ السكر، (٤) فحفظ النسب المشروع له حدّ الزنا، (٥) فحفظ المال المشروع له حدّ السرقة وحدّ قطع الطريق، (٦) فحفظ العِرض المشروع له عقوبة القذف والسبّ. ومثل الضروري مكمّله فيكون في مرتبته، كالحدّ بتناول[٢٢] قليل المسكر إذ قليله يدعو إلى كثيره.

٢. المناسب الحاجي وهو ما يحتاج إليه ولا يصل إلى حد الضرورة، كالبيع فالإجارة. وقد يكون الحاجي ضرورة في بعض الصور، كالإجارة لتربية الطفل. ومثل الحاجي مكمّله، كخيار البيع ليسلم عن الغبن.

[١] فاعل «يحصل».

3. Considerations of Practical Benefit Considerations of practical benefit are things that are deemed good by custom without being necessary. They are of two types:

1. those that stand in conflict with legal maxims, e.g., contracts of *kitāba*,[52] which bypass the maxim that it is invalid for an individual to sell part of his wealth for another part of his wealth; after all, any [wealth] earned by a contracting slave would be the property of the master were the slave to judge himself incapable [of procuring the full sum].
2. those that do not stand in conflict with any legal maxim, e.g., the disqualification of slaves from giving testimony; although this is not necessary, it is deemed good by custom because slaves fall short of the noble rank that entails [such] rights, unlike [their qualification] to narrate.[53]

[6. Isolation of the Basis]

The sixth of the means for determining the legal cause is isolation of the basis. This is when an apparent textual statement indicates that the causal basis for a ruling lies in a given feature, and then the case-specific aspects of that feature are disregarded by the exercise of ijtihad, and the ruling is based on a more general [feature]. An example of this is the way that Abū Ḥanīfa and Mālik disregarded—with respect to the report of the bedouin who had intercourse with his wife during daytime in Ramadan—the case-specific fact of the intercourse and based the expiation on the breaking of the fast as such.

Disqualifying Factors

A disqualifying factor is that which disqualifies an indicant, whether the indicant be a legal cause or otherwise.[54] According to the soundest position: One such

٣. المناسب التحسيني وهو ما استحسن عادة من غير احتياج إليه. وهو قسمان:

١- معارض للقواعد الشرعيّة، كالكتابة وهي خارمة لقاعدة امتناع بيع الشخص بعض ماله ببعض آخر إذ ما يحصّله المكاتَب في قوّة ملك السيّد له بتعجيزه نفسه.

٢- غير المعارض لشيء من القواعد، كسلب أهليّة الشهادة عن العبد فإنه غير محتاج إليه لكنه مستحسن عادة لنقص الرقيق عن هذا المنصب الشريف الملزم للحقوق بخلاف الرواية.

[٦. تنقيح المناط]

والسادس من مسالك العلّة تنقيح المناط بأن يدلّ نصّ ظاهر على التعليل لحكم بوصف فيحذَف خصوصُه عن الاعتبار بالاجتهاد ويناط الحكم بالأعمّ، كما حذف أبو حنيفة ومالك من خبر الأعرابي الذي واقع زوجته في نهار رمضان خصوص الوقاع عن الاعتبار وأناطا الكفّارة بمطلق[٢٣] الإفطار.

القوادح

وهي ما يقدح في الدليل علّة كان الدليل أو غيرها. منها تخلّف الحكم عن العلّة

factor is that a ruling fail to accompany a deduced cause neither due to a preventative factor nor due to the non-satisfaction of a condition—[simply speaking,] that the [presumed] cause be present in some cases without the ruling—for, had the [presumed] cause truly been the cause of the ruling, the ruling would have been present in such cases. [Disqualification] does not apply to causes that are indicated by unequivocal texts, since they cannot be contradicted, nor does it apply when the absence of a ruling is due to a preventative factor or to the non-satisfaction of a condition; despite the absence [of the ruling], the cause could [nonetheless] be paired with it in both cases. This is the chosen position of Ibn al-Ḥājib and other verifying scholars. According to some: [The absence of the ruling] always entails disqualification; this is the position preferred in the source text.[55] According to some: It never entails disqualification; this is the position of the majority of the Ḥanafīs, who term such a case *specification of the cause*.

المستنبطـــة بلا مانـــع أو فقـــد شرط في الأصـــحّ بـــأن وجـــدت في بعـــض صـــور بـــدون الحكـــم لأنهـــا لـــو كانـــت علّـــة للحكـــم لثبـــت حينئـــذ؛ بخلاف المنصوصـــة إذ لا نقـــض معهـــا وبخلاف مـــا إذا كان التخلّـــف لمانـــع أو فقـــد شرط لأن العلّـــة عنـــد التخلّـــف تجامـــع كلًّا منهمـــا. وهـــذا مـــا اختـــاره ابـــن حاجـــب وغيره مـــن المحقّـــقين. وقيـــل يقـــدح مطلقًـــا؛ ورجّحـــه الأصـــل. وقيـــل لا يقـــدح مطلقًـــا وقـــال بـــه أكثر الحنفيّـــة وســـمّوه تخصيـــص العلّـــة.

Conclusion

خاتمة

That analogy is part of the religion and that it is of two types

كون القياس من الدين وأنه قسمان

According to the soundest position: Analogy is a part of religion since it is commanded by His saying ﷻ, "So take heed, O you who are possessed of sight" (Q 59:2), and it is one of the principal sources of jurisprudence (*uṣūl al-fiqh*), as one learns from the definition of the latter. [Rulings derived by analogy] are the religious legislation of Allah. [However, with respect to such rulings,] one may not say, "Allah said…," nor may he say, "His prophet ﷺ said…," since they are deduced rather than textually stated. Analogy is communally obligatory on mujtahids, and it becomes individually obligatory on any mujtahid who [is placed in a situation in which] he needs to use it.[56]

١٠ الأصحّ أن القيـاس من الدين لأنـه مأمور به لقـوله تعالى ﴿فَٱعْتَبِرُواْ يَـٰٓأُوْلِي ٱلْأَبْصَـٰرِ﴾ [٥٩/ ٢] وأنـه مـن أصول[٢٤] الفقـه كمـا عُـرِف من حـدّه وأنـه ديـن الله وشرعـه. ولا يقـال فيـه «قـاله الله» ولا «...نبيُّـه» لأنـه مسـتنبط لا منصـوص. وهـو أي القياس فـرض كفايـة على المجتهدين ويتعـيّن على مجتهـد احتـاج إليه.

Legal analogies are of two types:

وهو قسمان:

1. those which are *evident*, i.e., those where it is either conclusively known that there are no discrepancies [between the original case and the derivative case] (that is, the discrepancies are judged to be insignificant) or nearly conclusively so, e.g., the analogy of blind [animals] to lame [animals] in that they cannot be used for ritual sacrifice, [this original ruling] being established through the report "Four [types of animals] cannot be used for sacrifices: lame animals with clear impairments...."[1]
2. those which are not evident, e.g., the analogy of committing murder with a blunt object to committing murder with a sharp object in that retribution is obligatory.

١- الأول جلي وهو ما قطع فيه بنفي الفارق أي بإلغائه أو قرب منه، كقياس العمياء على العوراء في المنع من التضحية الثابت بخبر «أربع لا تجوز في الأضاحي العوراء البيّن عورها...» الحديث.[١]

٢- والثاني بخلاف الجلي، كقياس القتل بمثقل على القتل بمحدّد في وجوب القود.

[1] Ibn Ḥibbān, *Ṣaḥīḥ Ibn Ḥibbān*, 13:240–46; al-Ḥākim, *al-Mustadrak*, 1:642, 4:349.

[١] ابن حبّان، صحيح ابن حبّان، ١٣/ ٢٤٠-٢٤٦؛ الحاكم، المستدرك، ١/ ٦٤٢؛ ٤/ ٣٤٩.

Chapter 5

ADOPTED INDICANTS

An adopted indicant is any indicant that is neither a textual statement of the Quran or Sunna, nor consensus, nor legal analogy.[57] This indisputably includes combinative and replicative syllogisms, which are the two types of the logical syllogism, namely, a composite of propositions that, when accepted, inherently entails another [proposition], i.e., the conclusion.

There are a number of questions concerning this topic.

That Exhaustive Induction Is an Indicant

An inductive argument that proceeds from the particular to the universal by accounting for the particulars of a given universal to affirm for it their ruling is a conclusive indicant if the induction is exhaustive, according to the majority position, and is a presumptive indicant if the induction is inexhaustive. The jurists term this "subsuming the individual case into the predominant case."

That Presumption of Continuity Is a Proof

According to the soundest position: Presumption of the continuity of (1) the default state of negation,[58] (2) the generality [of general expressions], (3) textual statements, or (4) [rulings] which revelation has indicated exist on account of the presence of their

الكتاب الخامس

في الاستدلال

وهو دليل ليس بنصّ من كتاب أو سنّة ولا إجماع ولا قياس شرعي؛ فدخل فيه قطعًا القياس الاقتراني والقياس الاستثنائي وهما نوعا القياس المنطقي وهو قول مؤلّف من قضايا متى سلّمت لزم عنها لذاتها قول آخر وهو النتيجة.

في هذا مسائل.

كون الاستقراء التام دليلا

الاستقراء بالجزئي على الكلّي بأن يُتتبّع جزئيّات كلّي ليُثبت حكمها له إن كان تامًّا فهو دليل قطعي عند الأكثر أو كان ناقصًا فظنّي؛ ويسمّى هذا عند الفقهاء إلحاق الفرد بالأغلب.

كون الاستصحاب حجة

الأصحّ أن (١) استصحاب العدم الأصلي (٢) واستصحاب العموم أو (٣) النصّ (٤) واستصحاب ما دلّ الشرع على ثبوته لوجود سببه كثبوت الملك

causes (e.g., the obtainment of ownership through the act of buying) is a proof unconditionally and is thus the basis for action until there arises an altering factor. The original condition takes priority over what is apparent unless opposed by a preponderant apparent condition that has a cause and is presumed to be more likely, in which case the apparent condition takes priority. An example of this is urine that fell into a large quantity of water which was then found in an altered condition,[59] evincing the possibility that the alteration was due to the urine as well as the possibility that it was due to a different and benign cause, like having been stagnant for a long time.

بـالشراء حجّـة مطلقًـا فيعمـل بـه إلى ورود المـغيّر فيقـدّم الأصـل على الظاهـر إلا إن عارضـه ظاهـر غالـب ذو سـبب ظُـنّ أنـه أقـوى فيقـدّم عليـه كبـول وقـع في مـاء كـثير فوجـد متـغيرًا واحتمـل تـغيّره بـه وبـغيره ممـا لا يضرّه كطـول المكـث.

Does One Who Negates Something Bear the Burden of Proof?

According to the chosen position: One who negates something bears the burden of proof if the negation is not immediately knowable; otherwise, he does not.

هل يطالب النافي بدليل؟

المختـار أن النافي يطالَـب بدليـل إن لـم يُعلَـم النفي ضرورة وإلا فلا.

[Adopting the Most Lenient or Most Difficult Ruling]

[According to the chosen position:] It is not obligatory to adopt the most lenient [ruling] or the most difficult [ruling] on a matter; rather, either alternative is permissible because the default condition is the absence of obligation.

[الأخذ بالأخف وبالأثقل]

وأنـه لا يجـب الأخـذ بالأخـفّ ولا بالأثقـل في شيء بـل يجـوز كل منهمـا لأن الأصـل عـدم الوجـوب.

That the Prophet Was Held to Revealed Law Before His Prophethood

According to the chosen position: He ﷺ was held to a revealed law before his prophethood. The chosen position is to desist from identifying that law and that after his prophethood, it was impermissible for him to practice a revealed law that had preceded him because he had a revealed law specific to him.

كون النبي متعبدا بالشرع قبل البعثة

المختـار أنـه ﷺ كان متعبّـدًا قبـل البعثـة بشرع. والمختـار الوقـف عـن تعيينـه وبعدهـا المنع مـن تعبّـده بشرع مـن قبلـه لأن له شرعًا يخصّـه.

[The Default Ruling with Respect to Benefits or Harms]

According to the chosen position: The default [ruling] with respect to benefits is permissibility and with respect to harms prohibition.

Is Juristic Preference a Legal Indicant?

According to the chosen position: Juristic preference is not a legal indicant unless it is interpreted as abandoning one analogy in favor of a stronger analogy. Given this meaning, there is no dispute since the stronger of two analogies indisputably takes priority over the other.

That the Position of a Companion Is Not a Proof and That He Is Not to Be Imitated

The position of a Companion, by agreement, is not a proof with respect to another Companion, and, according to the soundest position, it is not a proof with respect to others, like Followers, either. The soundest position is that of the verifying scholars: Companions are not to be imitated [in matters of religious law]; others are not to imitate them because their legal positions cannot be ascertained since they were not formally recorded, unlike the legal positions of certain others, namely, the four imams.[60] As for the fact that al-Shāfiʿī agreed with Zayd ﷺ regarding inheritance laws, this was founded on proof and not an imitation of Zayd; his ijtihad coincided with that of Zayd.

That Spiritual Inspiration Is Not a Proof

According to the soundest position: *Ilhām* (spiritual inspiration)—namely, that something be cast into the heart that gives assurance in the chest, which Allah ﷻ specially gifts to some of His elect—is not a proof when [experienced] by someone fallible, since the thoughts of such a person are not absolutely reliable: one cannot trust that they are safe from the schemes of Satan.

[الأصل في المنافع والمضار]

والمختار أن الأصل في المنافع الحلّ وفي المضارّ التحريم.

هل الاستحسان دليل؟

المختار أن الاستحسان ليس دليلًا إلا إذا فُسِّر بعدول عن قياس إلى قياس أقوى منه؛ ولا خلاف فيه بهذا المعنى إذ أقوى القياسين مقدّم على الآخر قطعًا.

كون قول صحابي غير حجة وأنه لا يقلد

قول الصحابي غير حجّة على صحابي وفاقًا وعلى غيره كتابعي في الأصحّ. والأصحّ ما عليه المحقّقون أن الصحابي لا يقلَّد وليس لغيره أن يقلّده لأنه لا يوثق بمذهبه إذ لم يدوَّن بخلاف مذهب غيره من الأئمّة الأربعة. وأما موافقة الشافعي زيدًا في الفرائض فلدليل لا تقليدًا لزيد بأن وافق اجتهاده اجتهاده.

كون الإلهام غير حجة

·الأصحّ أن الإلهام وهو[٢٥] إلقاء شيء في القلب يطمئنّ له الصدر يخصّ به الله تعالى بعض أصفيائه غير حجّة من غير معصوم لعدم الثقة بخواطره لأنه لا تؤمن دسيسة الشيطان فيها.

Jurisprudence Is Built on Four Things

Jurisprudence is built on four things, though the majority of [its questions] only resolve to these by contrived effort:[61]

1. The first is that certainty is not vitiated by doubt. One issue to which this applies is the [ruling] that a person who was certain of his ritual purity and then encounters doubt regarding whether he annulled his purity should proceed on the assumption of purity.
2. The second is that harm is necessarily removed. One issue to which this applies is the obligation to return usurped objects and to take liability for damage.
3. The third is that hardship brings facilitation. One issue to which this applies is the permissibility of shortening and combining [prayers] and breaking fast during travel, given that the conditions are met.
4. The fourth is that normative experience is authoritative; that is, revealed law is enacted in accordance with it. One issue to which this applies is [the determination of] the minimum and maximum periods of menstruation.

Some have added to these four that things are according to their purposes. One issue to which this applies is the obligation of the intention for ritual purification.

مبنى الفقه على الأربعة

مـبنى الفقـه على أربعـة أمـور وإن لـم يرجـع أكثره إليهـا إلا بتكلّـف:

١- الأول أن اليقـين لا يرفـع بالشـك، ومـن مسـائله مَـن تيقّـن الطهـر وشـكّ في الحـدث يأخـذ بالطهـر.

٢- الثـاني أن الـضرر يـزال وجوبًـا، ومـن مسـائله وجـوب ردّ المغصـوب وضمانـه بالتلـف.

٣- الثالـث أن المشـقّة تجلـب التيسـير، ومـن مسـائله جـواز القـصر والجمـع والفطـر في السـفر بشرطـه.

٤- الرابـع أن العـادة محكَّمـة أي معمـول بهـا شرعًا، ومـن مسـائله أقـلّ الحيـض وأكـثره.

وزاد بعضهـم على الأربعـة أن الأمـور بمقاصدهـا، ومـن مسـائله وجـوب النيّـة في الطهـر.

Chapter 6

THE WEIGHING OF INDICANTS

This comprises a number of questions.

The Impossibility of a Contradiction between Conclusive Indicants

It is impossible for two conclusive indicants to contradict each other, whether they be two rational indicants, two transmissional indicants, or one rational indicant and one transmissional indicant. [This impossibility] does not apply to [a contradiction between] one conclusive and one presumptive indicant, nor does it apply, according to the soundest position, to [a contradiction] in reality [between] two presumptive indicants. If two presumptive indicants contradict each other, the chosen position is that both fall out of consideration, as with a conflict between two points of court evidence.

Distinguishing between Two Positions of a Mujtahid

If two positions have been transmitted from a mujtahid, then if one succeeded the other, his position is the later position. Otherwise, it is the one whose preference he indicated by any remark, e.g., by saying, “this is more fitting.” If he made no such remark, his position is uncertain. The soundest position is that the preponderance [of one transmitted position of a mujtahid over another] be determined by

الكتاب السادس

في التعادل والتراجيح

وفيه مسائل.

امتناع التعارض بين القاطعين

يمتنع تعادل قاطعين عقليّين أو نقليّين أو عقلي ونقلي لا تعادل قطعي وظنّي وكذا أمارتان في الواقع في الأصحّ فإن تعادلتا فالمختار التساقط كما في تعارض البيّنتين.

التفصيل بين قوى المجتهد

وإن نقل عن مجتهد قولان فإن تعاقبا فالمتأخّر قوله وإلا فما ذكر فيه شيئًا مشعرًا بترجيحه كقوله «هذا أشبه» وإن لم يذكر ذلك فهو متردّد. والأصحّ الترجيح بالنظر فإن وقف عن الترجيح

means of reflective reasoning; if one is to withhold from giving preponderance, one should withhold judgment. According to the soundest position: If a mujtahid is not known to have asserted a position regarding a question but is known to have done so regarding an analogous one, the latter becomes his derived position regarding the [former] question; that is, those jurists of his school who are qualified to derive rulings derive the position by subsuming it under the analogous question. According to the soundest position: The derived position should not be ascribed without qualification to the mujtahid; it should be ascribed to him with the qualification that it is a derived position so that it is not confused for a position that he explicitly asserted.

وقف عن الحكم. وإن لم يعرف للمجتهد قول في مسألة لكن في نظيرها فهو قوله المخرج فيها في الأصحّ أي أخرجه الأصحاب إلحاقًا لها بنظيرها والأصحّ لا ينسب إليه مطلقًا بل ينسب إليه مقيّدًا بأنه مخرَج حتى لا يلبّس بالمنصوص.

The Meaning of Giving Preponderance; Acting in Accordance with the Preponderant Indicant

معنى الترجيح والعمل بالراجح

Giving preponderance is to judge one of two indicants stronger. According to the soundest position: It is obligatory to act in accordance with the preponderant [indicant].

الترجيح تقوية أحد الدليلين. والعمل بالراجح واجب في الأصحّ.

Giving preponderance does not apply with respect to conclusive [indicants]. A later [textual indicant] abrogates [an earlier one] even if transmitted through unit reports.

ولا ترجيح في القطعيّات. والمتأخّر ناسخ وإن نقل المتأخّر بالآحاد.

The Preferability of Acting in Accordance with Two Contradictory Indicants

أولوية العمل بالمتعارضين

According to the soundest position: Acting in accordance with two contradictory [indicants] is preferable to disregarding either one. An example is the report "Any hide that has been tanned is pure"[1] considered together with the report "Do not make use of the hides or sinews of carrion,"[2] which [as

والأصحّ أن العمل بالمتعارضين أولى من إلغاء أحدهما، مثاله خبر «أيّما إهاب دُبغ فقد طهر»[١] مع خبر «لا تنتفعوا من الميتة بإهاب ولا عصب»[٢]

[1] Ibn Mājah, *al-Sunan*, 4:602 (no. 3609).

[2] Abū Dāwūd, *al-Sunan*, 4:431 (no. 4124); al-Tirmidhī, *al-Jāmiʿ al-kabīr*, 3:343 (no. 1729).

[١] ابن ماجه، اللباس، ٢٥.

[٢] أبو داود، اللباس، ٤١؛ الترمذي، اللباس، ٧.

such] would include both hides that are tanned and those that are untanned: we interpret the latter as referring to untanned hides in order to reconcile the two indicants.

Considerations by Which Preponderance Is Given

[An indicant] may be given preponderance by virtue of an abundance of indicants and narrators, according to the soundest position, or by virtue of a short chain of transmission.

[Giving Preponderance by Consideration of the Narrator] [An indicant may also be given preponderance by virtue of] the narrator's jurisprudential knowledge; his lexical or grammatical knowledge; his scrupulousness, accuracy, sagacity, or awareness; his being free of creedal deviancy or being known to be trustworthy; the vindication of his credibility through firsthand experience; his being of known lineage (or, according to some, of well-known lineage); the explicit vindication of his credibility; his having memorized what he is narrating; his mentioning the occasioning reason [for the narrated incident]; his reliance on memory instead of on writing; the manifestness of his method of [taking] narrations; his having heard [the narrated report] without an intervening barrier; his being male and free,[62] according to the soundest position; his being of the senior Companions; his relatively late acceptance of Islam, according to the soundest position; his receiving [the narrated report] after [the age of] moral accountability; his not being a disingenuous narrator; his not possessing two names; his direct presence [at the narrated incident]; his being the one whom the incident concerns; his use of the original wording in narrating; his original narrator's not having denied [narrating the report]; or his hadith's being in [either of] the two *Ṣaḥīḥ*s.

الشامل للإهاب المدبوغ وغيره فحملناه على غير المدبوغ جمعًا بين الدليلين.

ما به الترجيح

يرجّح بكثرة الأدلّة والرواة في الأصحّ وبعلوّ الإسناد.

[الترجيح بحسب الراوي] وفقه الراوي، ولغته ونحوه، وورعه وضبطه وفطنته ويقظته، وعدم بدعته، وشهرة عدالته، وكونه مزكًّى بالاختبار، ومعروف النسب (قيل ومشهوره)، وصريح التزكية، وحفظ المروي، وذكر السبب، والتعويل على الحفظ دون الكتابة، وظهور طريق روايته[٢٦]، وسماعه بلا حجاب، وكونه ذكرًا وحرًّا في الأصحّ، ومن أكابر الصحابة، ومتأخّر الإسلام في الأصحّ، ومتحمّلًا بعد التكليف، وغير مدلّس، وغير ذي اسمين، ومباشرًا، وصاحب الواقعة، وراويًا باللفظ، ولم ينكره الأصل، وكون حديثه في الصحيحين.

[Giving Preponderance by Consideration of the Narrated Report] [Preponderance is given to] statements, then actions, then tacit approvals. Preponderance is given to articulate [narrations] (and, according to one position, those that are more articulate); hadiths with additional content, according to the soundest position; those that are transmitted in the dialect of Quraysh; those that are Madinan;[63] those that indicate the lofty status of the Prophet ﷺ;[64] those that include the cause as well as the ruling; those in which the cause is mentioned before the ruling, according to the soundest position; and those that contain threats or emphasis.

[Preponderance is given to] general expressions that are unqualified over general expressions with reasons due to the possibility that they (that is, the general expressions) be restricted to those reasons, except when the reasons apply (that is, except for general expressions in reference to the cases in which those reasons do apply), in which case the general expressions with reasons take priority over general expressions that are unqualified. [Preponderance is also given to] conditional general expressions (e.g., the conditional *man* [whoever] and *mā* [whatever]) over negative indefinite nouns, according to the soundest position, since the former, unlike the latter, indicate legal causality; to the latter over all of the remaining forms that signify generality; to definite plural nouns over the non-conditional *man* (who) and *mā* (what); and to each of these over definite generic nouns. [Preponderance is also given to expressions] that are not specified and to those which are least specified.

[Preponderance is given to] textually required signification, then directly entailed signification, then indirectly entailed signification; both of the latter are given preponderance over both types of implicature; and congruous implicature is given preponderance over counter implicature.

·**[الترجيح بحسب المروي]** والقول فالفعل فالتقرير. ويرجّح الفصيح (وكذا زائد الفصاحة في قول)، والحديث[٢٧] المشتمل على زيادة في الأصحّ، والوارد بلغة قريش، والمدني، والمشعر بعلوّ شأن النبي ﷺ، وما فيه الحكم مع العلّة، وما قدّم فيه ذكرها عليه في الأصحّ، وما فيه تهديد أو تأكيد.

والعامّ مطلقًا على العامّ ذي السبب لاحتمال قصره أي العامّ على السبب إلا في السبب أي إلا عامًّا كائنًا في صورة السبب فإذًا يقدّم هو على العامّ المطلق؛ والعامّ الشرطي كـ«من» و«ما» الشرطيّين على النكرة المنفيّة في الأصحّ لإفادته التعليل دونها؛ وهي على الباقي من صيغ العموم؛ والجمع المعرّف على «من» و«ما» غير شرطيّتين؛ وكلّها على الجنس المعرّف. وما لم يخصّ، والأقلّ تخصيصًا.

والاقتضاء فالإيماء فالإشارة؛ ويرجّحان على المفهومين؛ وكذا الموافقة على المخالفة.

[Giving Preponderance by Consideration of the Meaning of the Report] [Preponderance is given to reports] that indicate a change from the original condition and, according to the soundest position, to those that are affirmative. [Preponderance is given to] declaration, then prohibition, then obligation, then reprehension, then recommendation, and then permission, according the source text (regarding some of these).[65] [Preponderance is given to reports] whose meaning is comprehensible; to those which negate punishments; and, according to the soundest position, to those which are regulative over those which are injunctive.

[Giving Preponderance by External Considerations] [Preponderance is given to] indicants that accord with other indicants or with *mursal* hadiths, [the legal positions of] Companions, [the practice of] the inhabitants of Madina, or the [scholarly] majority, according to the soundest position. Regarding inheritance law, preponderance is given to [indicants] that accord with [the position of] Zayd, then Muʿādh, and then ʿAlī, and regarding rulings besides inheritance law, to Muʿādh and then ʿAlī.

[Giving Preponderance among Consensuses] [Preponderance is given to] consensus over textual indicants; to the consensus of preceding generations; to an all-inclusive consensus over a [strictly scholarly] consensus with which the commoners disagree; to the consensus of an era that has elapsed over one that is otherwise; and to consensus that was not preceded by disagreement, according to the soundest position.

[الترجيح بحسب مدلول الخبر] والناقل عن الأصل، والمثبت في الأصحّ، والخبر فالحظر فالإيجاب فالكراهة فالندب فالإباحة في الأصل في بعضها، المعقول معناه، وكذا نافي العقوبة، والوضعي على التكليفي في الأصحّ.

[الترجيح بالأمور الخارجيّة] والدليل الموافق دليلًا آخر، وكذا مرسلًا أو صحابيًّا أو أهل المدينة أو الأكثر في الأصحّ. ويرجّح موافق زيد في الفرائض فمعاذ فعلي، ومعاذ في أحكام غير الفرائض فعلي.

[ترجيح الإجماعات] والإجماع على النصّ، وإجماع السابقين، وإجماع الكل على ما خالف فيه العوامّ، والمنقرض عصره على غيره، وكذا ما لم يسبق بخلاف في الأصحّ.

[The Equality of Massively Transmitted Textual Indicants] According to the soundest position: Two massively transmitted [textual indicants] of the Quran or Sunna are equal.

[Giving Preponderance among Legal Analogies] Preponderance is given to one analogy over another analogy by virtue of the strength of the indicant for the ruling of the original case and the analogy's consistency with the due patterns of analogy, i.e., that the derivative case belong to the same category as the original case.

[Preponderance is given to a legal cause] that is present in two original cases over one that is present in a single original case and to an essential cause over a legally dictated cause.[66] [Preponderance is given by virtue of] a cause's possessing less qualifications, according to the soundest position; its entailing precaution with respect to an obligatory act; its universal presence in [all instances of] the original case; and there being agreement on the cause's causality in the original case. [Preponderance is given to] a cause that agrees with a number of principles over a cause that agrees with one; to a cause that agrees with another cause; and to causes ascertained by means of conclusive consensus, then conclusive textual indicants, then nonconclusive consensus, then nonconclusive textual indicants, according to the soundest position, and then direct entailment.

[Preponderance is given to] *analogy by causal force*[67] over *analogy by indication*;[68] to [causal] features that are real, then customary, then legally dictated; [to features that are] existential, then privative, without dispute; [to features that are] simple, then composite, according to the soundest position; [to legal causes] that motivate over those that [merely] indicate [the ruling]; [to causes] that extend to other cases; and [to causes that have] a greater number of derivative cases, according to the soundest position.

[تساوي المتواترين] والأصحّ تساوي المتواترَين من كتاب وسنّة.

[ترجيح الأقيسة] ويرجّح القياس على قياس آخر بقوّة دليل حكم الأصل؛ وكونه على سنن القياس أي فرعه من جنس أصله.

وكذا ذات أصلين على ذات أصل؛ وعلّة ذاتيّة على حكميّة؛ وكونها أقلّ أوصافًا في الأصحّ؛ والمقتضية احتياطًا في فرض؛ وعامّة الأصل؛ والمتّفق على تعليل أصلها؛ والموافقة لأصول على الموافقة لواحد؛ وكذا الموافقة لعلّة أخرى؛ وما تثبت علّته بإجماع فنصّ قطعيّين فظنيّين في الأصحّ فإيماء.

وقياس المعنى على الدلالة؛ والوصف الحقيقي فالعرفي فالشرعي؛ الوجودي فالعدمي قطعًا؛ البسيط فالمركّب في الأصحّ؛ والباعثة على الأمارة؛ وكذا المتعدّية، والأكثر فروعًا في الأصحّ.

[Giving Preponderance regarding Legal Definitions] [Preponderance is given to legal definitions][69] that are more familiar over those that are more obscure; to those that are essential over those that are accidental; to those that are explicit;[70] to those that are broader,[71] according to the soundest position; to those that conform to revealed and lexical usage; and to those that are derived in a better way.

[ترجيــح الحــدود] والأعــرف على الأخفى، والذاتي على العــرضي، والصريــح، وكــذا الأعــمّ في الأصــحّ، وموافــق نقــل الســمع واللغــة، ومــا طريــق اكتســابه أرجــح.

❋ ❋ ❋

The factors that give preponderance cannot be exhaustively enumerated. The criterion [for preponderance] is prevailing presumption.

والمرجّحات لا تنحصر؛ ومثارها غلبة الظنّ.

Chapter 7

IJTIHAD

And the related questions of imitation
and of fatwas

الكتاب السابع

في الاجتهاد

وما معه من التقليد والفتاوى

Ijtihad and the Mujtahid

Ijtihad is a jurisprudent's expenditure of his utmost effort to attain presumptive knowledge of a ruling. A mujtahid is a jurisprudent,[72] that is, someone who is mature; sane; inherently intelligent, i.e., naturally possessed of deep understanding; possessed of an intermediate level of knowledge of Arabic, jurisprudential theory, and what bears a connection with legal rulings—i.e., the Quran and Sunna, to which legal rulings are connected in virtue of being indicated thereby—even if he has not memorized a text on any of these [sciences].

For legitimate ijtihad,[73] such a person must be well aware of the points of consensus; of the abrogating and the abrogated; of the occasions of revelation; of what is massively transmitted and what is transmitted through unit reports; of authentic reports and reports of other ranks; and of the statuses of narrators.[74] With regard to being well aware of the statuses of narrators, it suffices in our age to defer to the imams of that discipline. Consideration is not given to [one's knowledge of] rational theology or the derived rulings of law or to one's being male or free. Nor is consideration given to one's moral integrity, according to the soundest position. [Preferably, a mujtahid] should search for indicants that would conflict with [his conclusion].

الاجتهاد والمجتهد

الاجتهاد استفراغ الفقيه الوسع لتحصيل الظنّ بالحكم. والمجتهد الفقيه وهو البالغ العاقل فقيه النفس أي شديد الفهم بالطبع ذو الدرجة الوسطى عربيّةً وأصولًا للفقه ومتعلَّقًا للأحكام أي ما تتعلّق هي به لدلالته عليها من كتاب وسنّة وإن لم يحفظ متنًا لها.

ويُعتبر للاجتهاد كونه خبيرًا بمواقع الإجماع والناسخ والمنسوخ وأسباب النزول والمتواتر والآحاد والصحيح وغيره وحال الرواة، ويكفي في الخبرة بحال الرواة في زمننا الرجوع لأئمة ذلك. ولا يعتبر علم الكلام وتفاريع الفقه والذكورة والحريّة وكذا لا يعتبر العدالة في الأصحّ؛ وليبحث عن المعارض.

The rank beneath that of the mujtahid[75] is that of the *mujtahid within a school*, that is, one who is able to deduce legal positions in accordance with the statements of his imam. The rank beneath this is that of the *mujtahid of fatwas*, that is, one who has comprehensive knowledge [of his imam's school] and is able to determine the preponderance of one transmitted position over another.

According to the soundest position: It is possible for [a mujtahid's ability to perform] ijtihad to be limited to particular areas of law; it is possible and did in fact occur that the Prophet ﷺ engaged in ijtihad; his ijtihad was never wrong; and ijtihad [by others] was permissible and did in fact occur during his lifetime.

ودونه مجتهد المذهب وهو المتمكّن من تخريج الوجوه على نصوص إمامه. ودونه مجتهد الفتيا وهو المتبحّر المتمكّن من ترجيح قول على آخر.

والأصحّ جواز تجزّي الاجتهاد في بعض الأبواب، وجواز الاجتهاد للنبي ﷺ ووقوعه، وأن اجتهاده لا يخطئ، وأن الاجتهاد جائز في عصره فإنه واقع.

Correct and Incorrect Judgments

There is [exactly] one correct judgment in matters that can be known rationally, and someone who makes an incorrect judgment [in such matters] is sinful—in fact, if he rejects Islam, he is a disbeliever. Undisputedly, there is [also exactly] one correct judgment in those matters known conclusively by revelation, whether the indicant be a textual statement or consensus. According to the soundest position: There is [also exactly] one correct judgment in those matters known by revelation in the absence of any conclusive indicants (though according to some, every mujtahid is correct in these matters); Allah has a specific ruling prior to the ijtihad; a presumptive indicant of that ruling is available; the mujtahid is held responsible for arriving at that ruling; a [mujtahid] who makes an incorrect judgment is not sinful but rather is rewarded; and one who performs ijtihad with negligence is sinful.

المصيب والمخطئ

المصيب في العقليّات واحد والمخطئ آثم بل كافر إن نفى الإسلام. والمصيب في نقليّات فيها قاطع من نصّ أو إجماع واحد قطعًا. والأصحّ أنه أي المصيب في النقليّات ولا قاطع فيها واحد (وقيل كل مجتهد فيها مصيب) وأن لله فيها حكمًا معيّنًا قبل الاجتهاد وأن عليه أمارة وأنه مكلّف بإصابته وأن المخطئ لا يأثم بل يؤجر ومتى قصّر مجتهد أثم.

That Rulings Based on Ijtihad Cannot Be Nullified

A ruling based on ijtihad cannot be nullified. If a ruling violates a textual statement, consensus, or an evident analogy, or if one gives a ruling that conflicts with his own ijtihad or with a statement of his imam and the ruling is not based on his imitating the position of another [imam], then that ruling is null.[76] According to the soundest position: If one were to marry without the permission of [the woman's] guardian after which one's ijtihad or the ijtihad of the [mujtahid] whom one imitates were to change, then the woman would become impermissible.[77] One whose ijtihad changes must inform those who had sought his judgment so that they desist [from acting in accordance with the first judgment]. Their actions are not invalidated[78] and [the mujtahid] is not liable for damage unless his judgment changes on account of a conclusive indicant; but if it does, that is, if his judgment changes on account of a conclusive indicant, then their actions are invalidated and [the mujtahid] is liable for damage due to his negligence.

That It Is Possible That He ﷻ Tell a Prophet or Tell a Scholar through a Prophet, "Rule As You Will"

According to the chosen position: It is possible that a prophet or scholar be told, "Rule as you will; it will be correct." [Such a statement] would be a revealed indicant. This is termed *consignment*. [According to the chosen position:] This has not actually occurred. [According to the chosen position:] It is possible that a command be conditioned on the choice of the person being commanded.

عدم نقض الحكم في الاجتهاديات

لا ينقض الحكم في الاجتهاديّات. فإن خالف نصًّا أو إجماعًا أو قياسًا جليًّا أو حَكم بخلاف اجتهاده أو بخلاف نصّ إمامه ولم يقلّد غيرَه نُقِض. ولو نكح بغير ولي ثم تغيّر اجتهاده أو اجتهاد مقلَّده فالأصحّ تحريمها. ومن تغيّر في اجتهاده أعلم المستفتي ليكفّ؛ ولا ينقض معموله. ولا يضمن المتلَف إن تغيّر لا لقاطع وإلا أي وإن تغيّر لقاطع فينقض معموله ويضمن المتلَف لتقصيره.

جواز قوله تعالى لنبي أو عالم على لسانه «احكم بما شئت»

المختار أنه يجوز أن يقال لنبي أو عالم «احكم بما تشاء فهو حقّ» ويكون مدركًا شرعيًّا ويسمّى التفويض؛ وأنه لم يقع؛ وأنه يجوز تعليق الأمر باختيار المأمور.

Imitation and Its Obligatoriness on Those Who Are Not Mujtahids

Imitation is to adopt the position of another without knowing the indicant for it.[79] According to the soundest position: With respect to non-creedal matters, imitation is obligatory on those who are not mujtahids. Imitation is prohibited for one who possesses presumptive knowledge of a ruling by means of his own [actual] ijtihad and, according to the soundest position, it is prohibited for [one with the qualifications of] a mujtahid.

That It Is Obligatory to Repeat One's Reasoning or Seek a Fatwa When an Incident Recurs

According to the soundest position: If an incident recurs for a mujtahid who does not remember the indicant, he must repeat his reasoning. If an incident recurs for a commoner who had sought a fatwa from a scholar, he must seek a fatwa again, even if the scholar were imitating a deceased [mujtahid].[80]

That It Is Permissible to Imitate One Who Is Outranked

According to the chosen position: It is permissible to imitate [a mujtahid] who is outranked—it is not obligatory to search for the best; the more knowledgeable [mujtahid] ranks above the more scrupulous; [it is permissible] to imitate a deceased [mujtahid]; and [it is permissible] to seek a fatwa from a person whom one either knows or presumes to be qualified, even if he be a judge. If one does not know, the chosen position is that one may regard as sufficient the abundance of the person's knowledge and appearance of his integrity. A commoner may ask a [mufti] for his source for the sake of his own instruction, and the mufti should explain it if it is not obscure.

التقليد ووجوبه على غير المجتهد

التقليد أخذ قول الغير من غير معرفة دليله. ويلزم غير المجتهد في غير العقائد في الأصحّ ويحرم على ظانّ الحكم باجتهاده وكذا على المجتهد في الأصحّ.

وجوب إعادة النظر أو الاستفتاء عند تكرر الواقعة

الأصحّ أنه لو تكرّرت واقعة لمجتهد لم يذكر الدليل وجب تجديد النظر أو لعامّي استفتى عالمًا وجب إعادة الاستفتاء ولو كان مقلِّدَ ميت.

جواز تقليد المفضول

المختار جواز تقليد المفضول فلا يجب البحث عن الأرجح؛ وأن الراجح علمًا فوق الراجح ورعًا؛ وتقليد الميت؛ واستفتاء من عرفت أهليّته أو ظنّت ولو قاضيًا فإن جهلت فالمختار الاكتفاء باستفاضة علمه وبظهور عدالته. وللعامّي سؤاله عن مأخذه استرشادًا؛ ثم عليه أي المفتي بيانه إن لم يخْفَ.

That It Is Permissible for an Imitator to Give a Fatwa

According to the soundest position: It is permissible for an imitator who is capable of determining preponderance[81] to give fatwas in accordance with the school of his imam.

جواز إفتاء المقلد

الأصحّ أنــه يجـوز لمــقلّد قــادر على الترجيــح الإفتــاء بمذهـــب إمامـــه.

❋ ❋ ❋

[According to the soundest position:] It is possible for an age to lack mujtahids, and this will occur.

وأنه يجوز خلوّ الزمان عن مجتهد وأنه يقع.

[According to the soundest position:] If a mujtahid gives a fatwa to a commoner regarding an incident, the commoner may withdraw from the mujtahid's fatwa if he has not [yet] put it into practice and if there is another [available] mufti.

وأنـــه لـــو أفتى مجتهـــد عاميًّـــا في حادثـــة فلـــه الرجـــوع عنـــه فيهـــا إن لـــم يعمـــل بقـــوله فيهـــا وثمّـــة مفـــتٍ آخـــر.

[According to the soundest position:] An imitator must adhere to a particular school that he believes to be either superior or equivalent [to the others], though it is preferable that he strive to arrive at belief in the superiority of a particular school. According to some: His adherence need not be on these conditions, i.e., he need not adhere to one that is entailed by evidence; this is the position of al-Nawawī.[82] [According to the soundest position:] An imitator may depart from [the school]. [According to the soundest position:] It impermissible to insistently seek after convenient rulings.

وأنـــه يلـــزم المـــقلّد التزام مذهـــب مـــعيّن يعتقـــده أرجـــح أو مســـاويًا والأولى الـــسعي في اعتقـــاده أرجـــح (وقيـــل لا يلزمـــه التزامـــه هـــذا أي عـــدم التزامـــه مـــا يقتضيـــه الدليـــل، قـــاله النـــووي)؛ وأن له الخـــروج عنـــه؛ وأنـــه يمتنـــع تتبّـــع الرخـــص.

❋ ❋ ❋

By the assistance of Allah ﷻ, the treatise entitled *Understanding Law: On Jurisprudential Theory* is complete. May Allah ﷻ by His grace and generosity render it of benefit to us and all believers. Allah! “Take us not to task if we forget or err!” (Q 2:286). “Glory to your Lord, Lord of Might, transcending what they describe! Peace be upon the messengers. And praise to Allah, Lord of the worlds” (Q 37:180–82). By His permission ﷻ, the eleventh treatise follows, entitled *The Sturdy Rope: On Creedal Theology*.

تمّت بعون الله تعالى الرسالة المسمّاة بفهم الفقه في أصول الفقه جعلها الله تعالى بمنّه وكرمه نافعة لنا ولسائر المؤمنين. اللّهم لا تؤاخذنا إن نسينا أو أخطأنا. ﴿سُبْحَـٰنَ رَبِّكَ رَبِّ ٱلْعِزَّةِ عَمَّا يَصِفُونَ ۝١٨٠ وَسَلَـٰمٌ عَلَى ٱلْمُرْسَلِينَ ۝١٨١ وَٱلْحَمْدُ لِلَّهِ رَبِّ ٱلْعَـٰلَمِينَ﴾ [٣٧/ ١٨٠-١٨٢]. وتليها بإذنه تعالى الرسالة الحادية عشرة المسمّاة الحبل المتين في أصول الدين.

NOTES TO TREATISE X

1 To clarify, an example of a general indicant is 'the imperative verb' insofar as it indicates obligation when used literally, and an example of a specific indicant is the Quranic command *aqīmū al-ṣalāta* (Perform the ritual prayer), which uses the imperative verb form literally in *aqīmū* (perform). The legal ruling derived from the specific indicant is that the ritual prayer is obligatory. General indicants can be thought of as the middle terms in syllogisms where the minor terms are specific indicants (*adilla tafṣīliyya*). For example, consider the syllogism "'Perform the ritual prayer' is an imperative, and the imperative indicates obligation." Here, the middle term 'the imperative' is the general indicant. But the general indicant is non-determinative (*ghayr muʿayyina*), which means that it does not determine the ruling on its own. If we had no information besides the theoretical principle that the imperative indicates obligation, we could not tell that the ritual prayer is obligatory. To determine that it is so, we need to consider the specific indicant, namely, the Quranic command "Perform the ritual prayer."

2 Together, these three components of the definition account for the seven chapters of the treatise: the first five chapters treat the general indicants (*adilla ijmāliyya*) of jurisprudence, the sixth treats the methods by which specific indicants are derived from general indicants, and the seventh treats the mujtahid and matters pertaining to his exercise of ijtihad.

3 Refraining (*kaff*) from doing something is considered an act. Al-Anṣārī, *Ghāyat al-wuṣūl*, 117.

4 The relation of the divine speech to the nonexistent agent is such that *if* the latter were to exist as a morally responsible being, he would be subject to the address. That is to say that the nonexistent agent is not *actually* subject to the address while nonexistent. Al-Anṣārī, *Ghāyat al-wuṣūl*, 127.

5 The cause is the act of adultery, and the ruling is the obligation of the punishment. Note that in the context of analogy (*qiyās*), the *sabab* is termed the *ʿilla*.

6 That murder impedes inheritance means that when an inheritor murders a person from whom he would normally inherit, the fact of the murder prevents the application of the ruling despite the presence of the cause for the ruling (that is, death). That parenthood impedes the obligation of retaliatory punishment means that when a father or mother murders his or her child, the fact that the murderer is the parent prevents the application of the ruling that retaliatory punishment is obligatory despite the presence of the cause of the ruling (that is, murder).

7 Strictly speaking, what changes is not the ruling itself; it is the ruling's particular application (*taʿalluq*).

8 According to another position, only knowledge (*ʿilm*) and presumption (*ẓann*) are assents. Fancy (*wahm*) and doubt (*shakk*) are not considered types of assent because they are not cases in which the intellect actually makes an affirmation or negation. See al-Anṣārī, *Ghāyat al-wuṣūl*, 163.

9 Declaring an act permissible means giving agents the choice to perform the act or not. This status is granted by revelation; it is not a

default rational ruling. Al-Anṣārī, *Ghāyat al-wuṣūl*, 173–74.

10 The secondary, "outweighed" (*marjūḥ*) meaning of "lion" is the metaphorical meaning of a courageous man. Al-Anṣārī, *Ghāyat al-wuṣūl*, 227.

11 The remainder of the verse is "...only consume fire in their bellies, and they will burn in a blazing flame."

12 An example of a meaningless composite expression is *dayzun murikmun*, which is nonsense. Al-Bannānī, *Ḥāshiyat al-Bannānī*, 1:264.

13 Note that indeterminate (*mujmal*) expressions, which will be defined below, are not considered ambiguous if they are explained. Al-Bannānī, *Ḥāshiyat al-Bannānī*, 1:268.

14 According to this position, Verse 3:7 in Sūrat Āl ʿImrān is read with a stop after "except Allah" (*illā Allāh*), which means that even those who are "firmly grounded in knowledge" (*al-rāsikhūna fī al-ʿilm*) lack clarity on the meaning of the ambiguous (*mutashābih*) verses of the Quran. Al-Anṣārī, *Ghāyat al-wuṣūl*, 253–54.

15 These are technical meanings of the terms *muḥkam* and *mutashābih*. The former can also be used to mean "perfected," as in Sūrat Hūd (Q 11:1), and the latter can also be used to mean "having parts that are similar to each other," as in Sūrat al-Zumar (Q 39:23). By reference to these non-technical usages of the terms, one would say that the Quran is entirely *muḥkam* and entirely *mutashābih*.

16 *Ishtiqāq* (morphological derivation) is sometimes defined as the etymological study of derivations and other times as the act of derivation itself. This definition is given from the former perspective.

17 Also termed *tropes*.

18 Regardless whether that meaning is its literal meaning or not.

19 This prophetic statement would be quoted to indirectly make the point that some specific person being alluded to is not a true Muslim. Al-Bukhārī, *al-Jāmiʿ al-ṣaḥīḥ*, 1:11 (no. 10). Refer to the discussions of allusion in Treatise V, pp. 335–36, and Treatise VIII, pp. 457–58.

20 The text's lack of a section on the general expression (*ʿāmm*) is a surprising omission considering the concept's importance in jurisprudential theory. We have provided the definition of the term as present in *Lubb al-uṣūl*. Al-Anṣārī, *Ghāyat al-wuṣūl*, 385–86. See also al-Maḥallī, *al-Badr al-ṭāliʿ*, 1:335. For what is excluded by this definition, refer to the author's brief mention of the *ʿāmm* in the section on simple expressions in the introduction of Treatise III, p. 230.

21 This refers to counter implicature (*mafhūm al-mukhālafa*).

22 This refers to congruous implicature (*mafhūm al-muwāfaqa*).

23 That is, the two well-known *ṣaḥīḥ* hadith collections of al-Bukhārī and Muslim.

24 The source text gives this as the definition of *taʾwīl* (interpretation), as a result of which a given expression would be considered an interpreted expression. Al-Anṣārī, *Ghāyat al-wuṣūl*, 461.

25 That is, a stronger proof than required for the first type is necessary to validate the interpretation.

26 This would strictly be a definition of *tafsīr* (explanation). Compare al-Anṣārī, *Ghāyat al-wuṣūl*, 474.

27 This obviously should not be read as a strictly exhaustive division, since it does not include the category of reports whose truth is presumptive, which is discussed directly below.

28 According to the soundest position, all of the Companions are recognized as upright; however, even those who hold this position acknowledge that since the Companions are not

infallible, it is possible for them to sin, and the implications of sins like theft or adultery remain significant for them. Al-Anṣārī, *Ghāyat al-wuṣūl*, 574.

29 That is, if the *mursal* hadith in such a case prohibits an act, it would be obligatory to refrain from that act. Al-Anṣārī, *Ghāyat al-wuṣūl*, 578.

30 He must know the meanings of the expressions used in the hadith and the expressions used in their place. He must also have a general facility with language such that he can discern what kind of construction is appropriate to a given context. Al-Bannānī, *Ḥāshiyat al-Bannānī*, 2:171.

31 A statement attributed to ʿĀʾisha ☙.

32 The *fāʾ* is represented in the translation by a semicolon and a number.

33 The student would be expected to write down what his teacher is dictating.

34 For example, when there is scholarly disagreement on whether aunts inherit or not, with both parties acknowledging that the legal cause of the ruling is that aunts belong to the category of 'relatives connected through females' (*dhawū al-arḥām*), it would be a contravention of consensus to introduce a distinction between paternal aunts and maternal aunts and to say that only one or the other inherits. The problem with this newly drawn distinction would be that it effectively disregards the earlier consensus on the legal cause. Al-Anṣārī, *Ghāyat al-wuṣūl*, 599.

35 That is, if a particular indicant, interpretation, or cause has already been ruled out by consensus, then its affirmation would be impermissible because it would contravene consensus.

36 That is, all of the cases of invalid consensus considered above are invalid because they would involve an opposition between conclusive indicants.

37 In the case when consensus is opposed by a presumptive indicant, there is no contradiction because the presumptive indicant is automatically disregarded in the face of the opposing conclusive indicant. Al-Anṣārī, *Ghāyat al-wuṣūl*, 602.

38 According to this position, since analogy merely reveals an existing ruling rather than actually establishing a new ruling, the mere fact that the original case, which was the means for discovering the ruling of the derivative case, has been abrogated does not abrogate the ruling of the derivative case.

39 This means that it is unlawful, as an act of *ribā*, to exchange wheat for wheat in unequal amounts.

40 The derivative case is the locus (*maḥall*) of a ruling (that is, the thing about which there is a ruling) in the same way that the original case is the locus of a ruling.

41 The feature (*waṣf*) is the proposed cause (*ʿilla*).

42 "It is not a sunna to wipe the head thrice" is contradictory to "It is a sunna to wipe the head thrice."

43 "The *witr* prayer is a sunna" is contrary to "The *witr* prayer is obligatory."

44 Al-Anṣārī prefers the simple phrase *fī al-maʿnā* to saying, as al-Subkī does in *Jamʿ al-jawāmiʿ*, that the two rulings must belong to the same species or genus. See al-Anṣārī, *Ḥāshiyat Shaykh al-Islām*, 3:271.

45 Since dry ablutions were legislated after water ablutions, dry ablutions cannot serve as the original case in this example.

46 The legal cause cannot be identified with an elusive rationale that varies from case to case, from person to person, or by considerations of circumstance that make it difficult to be precisely clear about what the constant factor is that provides the basis for the ruling. Al-Āmidī, *al-Iḥkām*, 3:255.

47 Sayf al-Dīn ʿAlī al-Āmidī (d. 631/1233), *kalām* theologian and author of *al-Iḥkām fī uṣūl al-aḥkām*, an important work of jurisprudential theory.

48 Jamāl al-Dīn ʿUthmān b. ʿUmar, known as Ibn al-Ḥājib (d. 646/1249), prominent grammarian and Mālikī jurist who authored *Mukhtaṣar al-Muntahā fī al-uṣūl*, an abridgement a larger work of his on jurisprudential theory.

49 That is, according to Zakariyyā al-Anṣārī's *Lubb al-uṣūl*.

50 On account of the fact that intoxication impairs the intellect, there is mutual suitability between a drink's being intoxicating and the ruling that the drink is prohibited. Thus, because the ruling of prohibition was found to always apply to intoxicating drinks (that is, the ruling and the quality are concomitant), the jurists determined that the quality of being intoxicating must be the legal cause of the prohibition.

51 The *fāʾ* indicates a sequential ranking, as was the case with the preceding list.

52 In a contract of *kitāba*, the slave and the master agree that the slave is to be released to earn a certain sum which he is then to pay in order to purchase his freedom.

53 Related to this is the idea that, on account of the undignified personal conditions often entailed by slavery, freemen would generally be expected to hold themselves to a higher standard of conduct than slaves. In a related inquiry in Chapter 6 (p. 530), the text states that, all else being equal, the soundest position (though disputed, as al-Anṣārī mentions) is to give precedence to the narrations of freemen over those of slaves. See al-Anṣārī, *Ghāyat al-wuṣūl*, 779; al-Anṣārī, *Ḥāshiyat Shaykh al-Islām*, 4:68.

54 This is the definition of Zakariyyā al-Anṣarī. Jalāl al-Dīn al-Maḥallī gives the slightly different definition "That which disqualifies an indicant with respect to either the legal cause or another element" (*mā yaqdaḥu fī al-dalīli min ḥaythu al-ʿillati aw ghayrihā*). Commenting on al-Maḥallī's definition, Ḥasan al-ʿAṭṭār explains,

> What is meant by "an indicant" (*dalīl*) is an analogy (*qiyās*) and what is meant by "another element" (*ghayrihā*) is the components of analogy, e.g., the derivative case and the original case. Shaykh al-Islām [Zakariyyā al-Anṣārī] says that it is clearer to say, "Whether the indicant be a legal cause or otherwise." However, one issue with [al-Anṣārī's preferred phrase] is that the indicant, which is an analogy, cannot [itself] be a legal cause.

Al-ʿAṭṭār, *Ḥāshiyat al-ʿAṭṭār ʿalā sharḥ al-Jalāl*, 2:340.

55 The text in question is Tāj al-Dīn al-Subkī's *Jamʿ al-jawāmiʿ*, which is the source for Zakariyyā al-Anṣārī's *Lubb al-uṣūl*. The statement "This is the position preferred in the source text" is from al-Anṣārī's commentary on *Lubb al-uṣūl*.

56 That is, analogy becomes individually obligatory on a mujtahid who cannot find another qualified mujtahid and is faced with a case that requires the use of analogy. Al-Anṣārī, *Ghāyat al-wuṣūl*, 743.

57 Although the Arabic word *istidlāl* can be understood to mean "inference" or "reasoning," it is helpful to interpret the *istifʿāl* pattern here to carry the sense of "adopting" (*ittikhādh*): *istidlāl* is to adopt something as a *dalīl*, to affirm or defend its status as an indicant. Technically defined, *istidlāl* refers to the indicants themselves that are thus adopted, which is why we translate the term as "adopted indicants." Unlike the Quran, Sunna, consensus, and analogy, adopted indicants are indicants whose legitimacy is a matter of ijtihad. Thus, various adopted indicants are disputed on an individual level, though it is a point of consensus that

there are indeed legitimate adopted indicants. See al-Shirbīnī, *Taqrīr al-Shirbīnī*, 2:342.

58 This refers to the presumption that things negated by the intellect and not affirmed by revealed law remain null, e.g., an obligation to fast in the month of Rajab. Al-Anṣārī, *Ghāyat al-wuṣūl*, 753.

59 The original condition in this example is that the water is pure, and the preponderant apparent condition that has a cause is that the water is impure.

60 The four imams of jurisprudence, Abū Ḥanīfa al-Nuʿmān b. Thābit (d. 150/767), Mālik b. Anas (d. 179/796), Muḥammad b. Idrīs al-Shāfiʿī (d. 204/820), and Aḥmad b. Ḥanbal (d. 241/855).

61 Not indicants in the strict sense, the following legal maxims (*qawāʿid fiqhiyya*) are general rules that are consistently reflected in the revealed law and thus can be said to underlie the entire structure of jurisprudence. In truth, these maxims are so general and the scope of the sacred law so expansive that in the case of many legal rulings it would be difficult to attribute the ruling to any of these maxims as such.

62 Both qualifications are disputed. The rationale for the first qualification is that males generally (*fī al-jumla*) have more technical precision (*aḍbaṭ*), though some disagreed, arguing that many females are more technically precise than many males. Regardless, the commentators of *Jamʿ al-jawāmiʿ* point out that in the case when the report concerns matters pertaining to women, this qualification conflicts with the general rule mentioned below that preponderance is to be given to the narrations of the one whom the content of a report directly concerns. Al-Bannānī, *Ḥāshiyat al-Bannānī*, 2:364; al-ʿAṭṭār, *Ḥāshiyat al-ʿAṭṭār ʿalā sharḥ al-Jalāl*, 2:407–8. With respect to the second qualification, see note 53.

63 That is, hadiths from the period after the hijra to Madina.

64 The rationale behind this qualification is that the elevation of the status of the Prophet ﷺ manifested more and more clearly throughout the unfolding stages of his prophetic mission; thus, a report that indicates a higher status is likely to belong to a later stage in his blessed life. Al-Anṣārī, *Ḥāshiyat Shaykh al-Islām*, 4:77.

65 That is, some of these comparative rankings—in particular, the ranking of prohibition, obligation, and recommendation above permission—represent the position of *Lubb al-uṣūl* but are disputed. See al-Anṣārī, *Ghāyat al-wuṣūl*, 788.

66 That is, all else being equal, an analogy based on a cause that is essential to the original case (like intoxication with respect to drinking wine) takes precedence over an analogy based on a cause that is the legal ruling of the original case (like prohibition). Al-Anṣārī, *Ghāyat al-wuṣūl*, 793.

67 Analogy by causal force (*qiyās al-maʿnā*) refers to an analogy made by reference to a commonality between two cases that is determined to be the legal cause on account of its mutual suitability with the ruling.

68 Analogy by indication (*qiyās al-dalāla*) refers to an analogy made by reference to a commonality between two cases that is either concomitant (*lāzim*) to the legal cause, an effect (*athar*) of the legal cause, or the ruling (*ḥukm*) occasioned by the legal cause. A commonality of this kind entails the presence of a legal cause but does not identify it specifically.

69 The following considerations apply to cases in which competing presumptive definitions of the same thing can be derived from the revealed texts. See al-Bannānī, *Ḥāshiyat al-Bannānī*, 2:377.

70 That is, those that do not employ nonliteral or equivocal terms. Al-Anṣārī, *Ghāyat al-wuṣūl*, 798.

71 That is, broader than the competing definition. Al-Bannānī, *Ḥāshiyat al-Bannānī*, 2:377–78.

72 Here and in the definition of ijtihad above, the term "jurisprudent" (*faqīh*) is not meant in the sense of an actual jurist who has mastered the sacred law; it is meant in the sense of someone predisposed for jurisprudence, meaning that he has the aptitude and prerequisite base of knowledge for jurisprudence. This is a technical usage of the term *faqīh* specific to jurisprudential theory. See al-ʿAṭṭār, *Ḥāshiyat al-ʿAṭṭār ʿalā sharḥ al-Jalāl*, 2:421.

73 There is a distinction between ijtihad in the sense of the necessary qualifications of the mujtahid in general (*ṣifat al-ijtihād*), as discussed just above, and ijtihad in the sense of the mujtahid's actual exercise of ijtihad on a particular issue (*īqāʿ al-ijtihād*), as here. It is not sufficient that the person doing ijtihad simply be a "qualified scholar": he must also thoroughly research and know the indicants pertaining to the subject. See al-Bannānī, *Ḥāshiyat al-Bannānī*, 2:383–84.

74 The mujtahid is only required to be well aware of these things insofar as they are connected with the subject of his ijtihad. Al-Anṣārī, *Ghāyat al-wuṣūl*, 805.

75 A mujtahid of the highest rank, as defined above, is considered an absolute mujtahid (*mujtahid muṭlaq*).

76 Strictly speaking, there would have been no *ruling* as such in the first place; there would simply have been an invalid position advanced by the mujtahid. Al-Anṣārī, *Ghāyat al-wuṣūl*, 814.

77 The purpose of this example is to illustrate the legal consequences of a change in a mujtahid's conclusion based on ijtihad. In this case, a given mujtahid arrives at the conclusion, through an initial performance of ijtihad, that marriage without the formal permission of the woman's guardian stands as valid. This same mujtahid or an imitator (*muqallid*) deferring to his ijtihad marries a woman without her guardian's formal permission, after which the mujtahid's ijtihad leads him to change his position; reconsidering the evidence, he concludes that marriage without the guardian's formal permission is actually invalid. Consequently, the mujtahid or the imitator is now committed to the position that the marriage is invalid and should proceed accordingly.

78 That is, actions that an imitator had performed in the past are not retroactively rendered invalid, given that the first ijtihad was legitimate. However, after the imitator is informed of the new ijtihad, he should proceed to act accordingly, as illustrated above.

79 That is, without being sufficiently aware of the relevant indicants and satisfying the qualifications of the mujtahid such that one could perform ijtihad on the matter for oneself. See al-Anṣārī, *Ghāyat al-wuṣūl*, 817.

80 This because the commoner cannot be sure that the scholar will not discover that his first fatwa was invalid. But this uncertainty is not always the case: the commoner need not ask again if he knows that the answer was based on a textual statement or consensus or if the scholar he had asked the first time has died. Al-Anṣārī, *Ghāyat al-wuṣūl*, 820–21.

81 Namely, a mujtahid of fatwas.

82 The famous Shāfiʿī jurist and master of hadith Muḥyī al-Dīn Yaḥyā b. Sharaf al-Nawawī (d. 676/1277).

XI

THE STURDY ROPE

On the science of creedal theology

الحبل المتين في علم أصول الدين

In the Name of Allah,
All-Merciful, Most Compassionate

بسم الله الرحمن الرحيم

ALL PRAISE IS due to Allah, Lord of the worlds. May blessings and peace be upon our messenger, Muḥammad, and upon all of his family and Companions.

الحمد لله ربّ العالمين والصلاة والسلام على رسولنا محمد وعلى آله وصحبه أجمعين.

To Proceed This is a treatise on the science of creedal theology. I have entitled it *The Sturdy Rope: On the Science of Creedal Theology*. I have based the treatise on those of the principles of creedal theology which it is necessary [to know].

أما بعد فهذه رسالة في علم أصول الدين سمّيتها الحبل المتين في علم أصول الدين بنيتها على ما تمسّ إليه الحاجة من عيون مسائل أصول الدين.

[The Principles of Creedal Theology]

[عيون مسائل أصول الدين]

The Prohibition yet Validity of Mere Imitation

امتناع التقليد وصحته

I. The chosen position is that mere imitation [of the positions of others] is prohibited in matters of creed—e.g., in that the universe is originated, in that the Creator exists, in those things that are necessary and those that are impossible with respect to Him, and so forth—because what is sought is certainty. He ﷻ said to His prophet, "Know, then, that there is no god but Allah" (Q 47:19), and He said to

١- المختار أنه يمتنع التقليد في أصول الدين كحدوث العالم ووجود الباري وما يجب له ويمتنع وغير ذلك لأن المطلوب هو اليقين. قال تعالى لنبيّه ﴿فَٱعۡلَمۡ أَنَّهُۥ لَآ إِلَٰهَ إِلَّا ٱللَّهُ﴾ [٤٧/١٩]

humanity, "Follow him, that haply you may be guided" (Q 7:158). Other [creedal] matters are in analogy to divine oneness.[1] Imitation is valid, however, when held with conviction.[2]

Thus, let one have firm conviction that the universe is originated, that it has an Originator, that He is Allah who is not subject to division, who does not resemble anything, and whom nothing resembles in any way.

The Essence of Allah ﷻ Is Different from All Essences

II. Allah ﷻ is eternal without beginning, and His essence is different from all essences. The verifying scholars hold that none know it at present, and the chosen position is that it is impossible [to know it] in the hereafter.

III. Allah ﷻ is not a corporeal object,[1] nor is He a substance,[2] nor is He a property.[3] He existed eternally by Himself without place or time, and then He originated this universe without any need; had He willed, He would not have originated it. Nothing came into being in the essence of Allah by His originating the universe. "He does whatsoever He wills" (Q 85:16), and "Nothing is at all like Him" (Q 42:11).

All of destiny, the good and the bad, is from Him. His knowledge extends to every knowable thing, His power to every subjectable thing.[4] Everything that He knows will exist He has willed to be; everything that He knows will not He has not.

His eternality is without end. He remains with His names and the attributes of His essence, these including both those attributes indicated by His acts, namely, power, knowledge, life, and will, and

[1] A corporeal object is something that has three dimensions: height, width, and depth.

[2] A substance is something that subsists in itself.[3]

[3] A property is something that subsists in another thing.

وقال للناس ﴿وَٱتَّبِعُوهُ لَعَلَّكُمْ تَهْتَدُونَ﴾ [٧/ ١٥٨]، ويقاس بالوحدانيّة غيرها.

ولكن يصحّ إذا كان بجزم؛ فليجزم عقده بأن العالم حادث وله محدِث وهو الله الواحد الذي لا ينقسم ولا يشبه شيئًا ولا يشبهه شيء بوجه من الوجوه.

حقيقته تعالى مخالفة للحقائق

٢- الله تعالى قديم وحقيقته مخالفة لسائر الحقائق. قال المحقّقون ليست معلومة الآن؛ والمختار أنها ليست ممكنة في الآخرة.

٣- وأنه تعالى ليس بجسم[١] ولا جوهر[٢] ولا عرض[٣] لم يزل وحده ولا مكان ولا زمان ثم أحدث هذا العالم بلا احتياج؛ ولو شاء ما أحدثه؛ لم يحدث به في ذاته حادث. فعّال لما يريد؛ ليس كمثله شيء.

القدر خيره وشرّه منه؛ علمه شامل لكل معلوم وقدرته لكل مقدور؛ ما علم أنه يوجد أراده وما لا فلا.

بقاؤه غير متناه لم يزل بأسمائه وصفات ذاته وهي ما دلّ عليها فعله من قدرة وعلم وحياة وإرادة

[١] الجسم ما له أبعاد ثلاثة الطول والعرض والعمق.

[٢] الجوهر ما يقوم بنفسه.

[٣] العرض ما يقوم بالغير.

those indicated by His transcending of imperfection, namely, hearing, sight, speech, and endless eternality.

أو دلّ عليها تنزيهه عن النقص من سمع وبصر وكلام وبقاء.

What We Believe about the Divine Attributes

اعتقادنا في الصفات

IV. We believe in the apparent meaning of every authentic affirmation of a divine attribute in the Quran and Sunna, and we affirm the transcendence of Allah upon hearing anything that poses a problematic difficulty.[5] Now, our imams differ on whether we should find a suitable interpretation or whether, while maintaining His transcendence, we should consign the meaning to Allah; they agree, however, that our lacking knowledge of the precise meaning does not vitiate [a simple kind of knowledge].

٤- ما صحّ في الكتاب والسنّة من الصفات نعتقد ظاهر معناه وننزّه الله عند سماع مشكله. ثم اختلف أئمّتنا أنؤوّل أم نفوّض منزّهين له مع اتّفاقهم على أن جهلنا بتفصيله لا يَقدح.

V. The pre-expressional speech [of Allah] is uncreated. It is literally true that it is written in our copies of the Quran, memorized in our hearts, and recited on our tongues.

٥- الكلام النفسي غير مخلوق مكتوب في مصاحفنا محفوظ في صدورنا مقروء بألسنتنا على الحقيقة.

VI. Allah ﷻ rewards obedience and punishes disobedience—save when He pardons and forgives a sin short of associating partners with Him. It is within His prerogative to reward the sinner and punish the obedient or to inflict pain on beasts or children. It is impossible that He be unjust.[6]

٦- الله سبحانه وتعالى يثيب على الطاعة ويعاقب على المعصية إلا أن يعفو ويغفر غير الشرك. وله إثابة العاصي وتعذيب المطيع وإيلام الدوابّ والأطفال؛ ويستحيل وصفه بالظلم.

VII. Believers will see Him in the hereafter, and the chosen position is that seeing Him in this life is possible. In *al-Maktūbāt*,[7] Imam al-Rabbānī states that Allah is not seen in this life. Allah knows best.

٧- يراه المؤمنون في الآخرة والمختار جواز رؤيته في الدنيا. قلت قال الإمام الربّاني في المكتوبات: لا يُرى في الدنيا. والله أعلم.

The Blissful and the Damned

السعيد والشقي

VIII. The *blissful* is one who Allah has eternally decreed will die a believer, regardless whether he had previously disbelieved and then Allah ﷻ had pardoned. The *damned* is one who is the opposite, regardless whether he had previously believed and then that belief had come to nothing. These two [eternally decreed conditions] do not interchange.

٨- السعيد من كتب الله في الأزل موته مؤمنًا وإن تقدّم منه كفر وقد غفر الله تعالى والشقي عكسه وإن تقدّم منه إيمان وقد حبط. ثم لا يتبدّلان.

IX. The chosen position is that [for Allah] to be pleased with or love something is different than [for Him] to decree or will it.

٩- المختار أن الرضى والمحبّة غير المشيئة والإرادة.

X. *Provision* is whatever occasions benefit, even if it be prohibited.

١٠- الرزق ما ينتفع به ولو حرامًا.

XI. It is in Allah's hand to guide or send astray, i.e., to create guidance or straying.

١١- بيده الهداية والإضلال أي خلق الاهتداء والضلال.

XII. The chosen position is that *grace* is to create the ability to obey, and so too is *providence*; *forsaking* is the opposite. *Khatm* (sealing), *ṭab*ʿ (sealing), *akinna* (coverings), and *aqfāl* (locks) are to create straying in the heart.[8]

١٢- المختار أن اللطف خلق قدرة الطاعة والتوفيق كذلك والخذلان ضدّه. والختم والطبع والأكنّة والإقفال خلق الضلالة في القلب.

XIII. According to the soundest position, quiddities are made to be [by Allah].[9]

١٣- والماهيّات مجعولة في الأصحّ.

XIV. He ﷻ sent His messengers with miracles and specially chose Muḥammad ﷺ as the seal of the prophets, who was sent to all creatures and granted superiority over them. After him [in superiority] are the prophets and then the distinguished angels.

١٤- أرسل تعالى رسله بالمعجزات وخصّ محمدًا ﷺ بأنه خاتم النبيّين المبعوث إلى الخلق كافّة المفضّل عليهم ثم الأنبياء ثم خواصّ الملائكة.

XV. A *prophetic miracle* is a disruption of normative experience that is accompanied by a challenge and is not countered [by its like].[10]

١٥- والمعجزة أمر خارق للعادة مقرون بالتحدّي مع عدم المعارضة.

Belief, Submission, and Spiritual Excellence

الإيمان والإسلام والإحسان

XVI. *Belief* is the assent of the heart, and consideration is given to one's verbalization of the two testimonies if one is capable. *Submission* is the verbalization of the two testimonies, and consideration is given to one's belief.[11] *Spiritual excellence* is to worship Allah as though you see Him, for if you do not see Him, He yet sees you.

١٦- الإيمان تصديق القلب ويعتبر فيه تلفّظ القادر بالشهادتين. والإسلام التلفّظ بالشهادتين يعتبر فيه الإيمان. والإحسان أن تعبد الله كأنّك تراه فإن لم تكن تراه فإنه يراك.

XVII. *Sinfulness* does not vitiate belief. One who dies a sinful believer is subject to the divine will: he may be punished and then admitted into paradise, or he may be pardoned.

١٧- والفسق لا يزيل الإيمان والميّت مؤمنًا فاسقًا تحت المشيئة يعاقب ثم يدخل الجنّة أو يسامح.

XVIII. The first and foremost intercessor is our prophet Muḥammad ﷺ.

١٨- وأوّل شافع وأولاه نبيّنا محمد ﷺ.

XIX. No person dies but at his appointed time.

١٩- ولا يموت أحد إلا بأجله.

The Enduring of the Soul after Death

بقاء الروح بعد الموت

XX. The *soul* endures after the body dies. The soundest position is that, like the tailbone, the soul will never perish. Our prophet ﷺ did not discuss its essential reality, so we withhold from doing so.

٢٠- الروح باقية بعد موت البدن والأصحّ أنه لا يفنى أبدًا كعجب الذنب؛ وحقيقتها لم يتكلّم عليها نبيّنا ﷺ فنمسك عنها.

XXI. *Saintly miracles* are a reality and are not restricted to being unlike [the birth of] a child without a father, in opposition to the view of al-Qushayrī.[12]

٢١- كرامات الأولياء حقّ ولا تختصّ بغير نحو ولد بلا والد خلافًا للقشيري.

XXII. According to the chosen position, we do not declare any of the people of the qibla to be a disbeliever.

٢٢- لا نكفّر أحدًا من أهل القبلة على المختار.

XXIII. We hold that punishment in the grave, questioning by the two angels, bodily resurrection—which is [either] to bring [a thing] into existence after its nonexistence or to bring [a thing] together after its dispersion, and the correct position is to withhold judgment—the Gathering, the Bridge, and the Scale are real. We hold that paradise and hell have already been created.

٢٣- نرى أن عذاب القبر وسؤال الملكين والمعاد الجسماني – وهو إيجاد بعد فناء أو جمع بعد تفرّق والحقّ التوقّف – والحشر والصراط والميزان حقّ. والجنّة والنار مخلوقتان الآن.

The Obligation to Appoint a Leader

وجوب نصب الإمام

XXIV. It is obligatory for the people to appoint a leader, even if he is not the best [of them]. It is impermissible to rebel against him.

٢٤- يجب على الناس نصب إمام ولو مفضولًا؛ ولا يجوز الخروج عليه.

XXV. Nothing is obligatory on Allah.

٢٥- لا يجب على الله شيء.

XXVI. We hold that the best of people after the prophets ﷺ is Abū Bakr, then ʿUmar, then ʿUthmān, and then ʿAlī ؓ. We hold that ʿĀʾisha ؓ is innocent.

٢٦- نرى أن خير البشر بعد الأنبياء صلّى الله عليهم وسلّم أبو بكر فعمر فعثمان فعلي رضي الله عنهم؛ وبراءة عائشة.

XXVII. We abstain from [pronouncing opinions] on the events that transpired between the Companions; we hold that they will be rewarded [for their good intentions].

٢٧- نمسك عما جرى بين الصحابة ونراهم مأجورين.

XXVIII. The imams of the juristic schools and all the other imams of the Muslims, like the two Sufyāns,[13] are rightly guided by their Lord.

٢٨- أئمّة المذاهب وسائر أئمّة المسلمين كالسفيانَين[١] على هدًى من ربّهم.

XXIX. Al-Ashʿarī[14] is an imam for the Sunnis.

٢٩- أن الأشعري إمام في السنّة.

XXX. The spiritual path of al-Junayd[15] is a well creditable path.

٣٠- طريق الجنيد طريق مقوَّم.

From *al-Fiqh al-Akbar* and Its Commentaries

عن الفقه الأكبر وشروحه

I wanted to include here some theological questions taken from *al-Fiqh al-akbar* by the grandest imam Abū Ḥanīfa ؓ which are needed, elucidating some obscure points in accordance with the work's commentaries. Success and rectitude are through Allah ﷻ alone.

أحببت أن أذكر هنا بعض ما يحتاج إليه من مسائل علم التوحيد عن الفقه الأكبر[٢] للإمام الأعظم أبي حنيفة رضي الله تعالى عنه مفسّرًا بعض ما كان مغلقًا وفق ما في شروحه. وبالله تعالى وحده التوفيق والسداد.

I. Affirming divine oneness (*tawḥīd*) means affirming that the divine entity transcends anything that might be conceived in our comprehension or imagined in our supposition.

١- حقيقة التوحيد هو تنزيه الذات الإلهيّة عن كل ما يتصوّر في الأفهام ويتخيّل في الأوهام.

II. The basis of belief is one's assenting [verbally and mentally] to the six articles mentioned in the hadith of Jibrīl (may blessings and peace be upon our prophet and upon him).

٢- أصل الإيمان الإقرار والتصديق بالأشياء الستّة المذكورة في حديث جبريل على نبيّنا وعليه الصلاة والسلام.

III. Everything is by decree, which means that the knowledge of Allah ﷻ relates eternally to all possible things in a comprehensive manner; that the divine will relates to the things that Allah ﷻ knows; and that His power relates to the things that His will specifies. Thus there is no determinism.

٣- كل شيء بقدر وهو عبارة عن تعلّق علم الله تعالى أزلًا بالممكنات على وجه الإحاطة، وعن تعلّق الإرادة بما علم الله تعالى، وعن تعلّق قدرته تعالى بما خصّصت الإرادة فلا جبر أصلًا.

IV. Allah ﷻ eternally was and eternally will remain possessed of His names, attributes of essence and attributes of action. The difference between attributes of essence and attributes of action is this: any attribute alongside which the opposite can be attributed to Allah ﷻ is an *attribute of action*, e.g., giving life and taking life, and if an attribute's opposite cannot be attributed to Him, then it is an *attribute of essence*, e.g., life and knowledge.

٤- لم يزل الله تعالى ولا يزال بأسمائه وصفاته الذاتيّة والفعليّة[٣] والفرق بين الصفات الذاتيّة والفعليّة أن كل صفة يوصف الله تعالى بها وبضدّها فهي من الصفات الفعليّة كالإحياء والإماتة وإن كان لا يوصف بضدّها فهي الصفات الذاتيّة كالحياة والعلم.

V. When He ﷻ brings a thing about, He does so by His acting (*fa'l*, with *fatḥ* of the *fā'*), which is an eternal attribute of His; He does not do so by some originated acting, for originated things are the effects of His acting. In the same way, anything upon which He acts is a receptacle in which the effects of His acting occur and is thus considered by consensus to be a created thing.

٥- أنه تعالى إذا فعل شيئًا يفعله بفَعله (بفتح الفاء) الذي هو صفة أزليّة له لا بفَعل حادث لأن الحادث هو أثر فعله وكذا المفعول فإنه محلّ لوقوع أثر الفعل وهو مخلوق بالاتّفاق.

VI. The speech of Allah ﷻ is uncreated, while the speech of created beings is created. That is, the verbal uttering of the speech of Allah ﷻ by one other than Allah ﷻ is created. Ultimately, we consider who it is that originally arranged the speech: the arrangement of the speech of Allah originates from Him ﷻ, not from another.[16] See now, would you not say after quoting a hadith, "This that I have quoted—these are not my words but the words of the Messenger of Allah ﷺ," since the arrangement of the statement originates from the Messenger of Allah ﷺ?

٦- كلام الله تعالى غير مخلوق وكلام غيره من المخلوقين مخلوق أي تلفّظ غير الله تعالى بكلام الله تعالى مخلوق لأن العبرة بمبدأ نظم الكلام ومبدأ نظمه منه تعالى لا من غيره ألا ترى أنك إذا قرأت حديثًا قلت «هذا الذي قرأته ليس قوئى بل قول رسول الله صلّى الله عليه وسلّم» لأن مبدأ نظم ذلك القول من رسول الله ﷺ.

VII. Allah ﷻ had spoken to Mūsā before he was created. After he was created, He addressed him with the import of His eternal speech, in the same way that the inscription of words in the Preserved Tablet indicates [the import of His eternal speech]. He addressed him in accordance with those recorded words. Thus, the recorded words that Mūsā ﷷ heard from the tree were originated and created things, but they were also indications of the speech of His that is a real, eternal attribute.

٧- كان الله تعالى كلّم موسى قبل أن يُخلق؛ كلّمه بعد خلقه بمضمون كلامه القديم الأزلي كما يدلّ عليه نقش الكلمات في اللوح المحفوظ فكلّمه على وفق تلك الكلمات المسطورة فالكلمات المسطورة التي سمعها موسى عليه السلام من الشجرة حادثة مخلوقة إلا أنها أدلّة كلامه الذي هو صفته الأزليّة الحقيقيّة.

VIII. Allah ﷻ speaks not as we speak: we speak by means of organs and letters, while Allah ﷻ speaks without organs or letters. All letters are created, but the speech of Allah ﷻ is uncreated; it subsists in His essence and is not subject to separation or transferal to hearts or ears.

٨- الله تعالى يتكلّم لا كما نتكلّم؛ نحن نتكلّم بالآلات والحروف والله تعالى يتكلّم بلا آلات ولا حروف؛ والحروف مخلوقة وكلام الله تعالى غير مخلوق قائم بذاته لا يقبل الانفصال والانتقال إلى القلوب والآذان.

IX. When Allah ﷻ makes mention in the Quran of a countenance, a hand, and a self, these are attributes that He possesses "without how," i.e., without [our] knowing the modality, for the modality is unknown.

٩- ما ذكره الله تعالى في القرآن من ذكر الوجه واليد والنفس فهو له صفات بلا كيف أي بلا معرفة الكيفيّة فإن الكيفيّة مجهولة.

X. Nothing exists in this world or in the hereafter save by His knowledge, His will, His decree, His foreordainment, and its being written in the Preserved Tablet. It is written in the manner of description rather than in the manner of decree. That is, everything is written in the Preserved Tablet with its qualities—one's obedience or disobedience, one's character, and other qualities—but nothing is written by way of the mere decree that it occur without any description or reason. There is not, for example, written in it, "Let Zayd be a believer and 'Amr a disbeliever."

١٠- لا يكون في الدنيا ولا في الآخرة شيء إلا بعلمه ومشيئته وقضائه وقدره وكَتبه في اللوح المحفوظ؛ وكتبه بالوصف لا بالحكم أي كتب في اللوح المحفوظ كل شيء بأوصافه من الطاعة والمعصية والأخلاق وغيرها ولم يكتب فيه شيء بمجرّد الحكم بوقوعه بلا وصف ولا سبب، مثلًا لم يكتب فيه «ليكن زيد مؤمنًا وعمرو كافرًا».

XI. Allah ﷻ extracted the progeny of Ādam ﵇ from his loins in the form of little specks, and then He granted them intelligence and addressed them, commanding them to believe and forbidding them to disbelieve, upon which they acknowledged His lordship. This having been an act of belief on their part, they are born into that instinct.

١١- أخـرج الله تعـالى ذريّـة آدم عليـه السلام مـن صلبه على صـور الذرّ فجعـل لهـم عـقلًا فخاطبهـم وأمرهـم بالإيمـان ونهاهـم عـن الكفـر فأقـرّوا له بالربوبيّة فكان ذلـك منهـم إيمانـًا فهـم يـولدون على تلـك الفطـرة.

XII. Allah ﷻ created the human being to try him, for this life is the abode of trial.

١٢- خلق الله تعالى الإنسان ابتلاءً لأن الدنيا دار الابتلاء.

XIII. It is obligatory on us to believe in the unseen realm.

١٣- وعلينا الإيمان بالغيب.

XIV. Allah ﷻ created people free of disbelief and belief, i.e., the acquired kind, while the instinctive kind of belief was present [in them]. Then He addressed them, commanding and forbidding, after which anyone who disbelieves does so by his own act, i.e., voluntarily, by denial and rejection of the truth out of obstinacy and arrogance, and by Allah's ﷻ forsaking him, and anyone who believes does so by his own act, by his own affirmation and assent, and by Allah's ﷻ providentially guiding him.

١٤- خلـق الله تعـالى الخلق سـليمًا مـن الكفـر والإيمان أي الكسبـيّين؛ وكان الإيمان الفطري موجـودًا ثم خاطبهم وأمرهـم ونهاهـم فكفـر مـن كفـر بفعلـه أي باختياره وإنكاره وجحوده الحـقّ عنـادًا واسـتكبارًا وبخـذلان الله تعـالى إيّـاه وآمـن مـن آمـن بفعلـه وإقـراره وتصديقه وبتوفيـق الله تعـالى إيّاه.

XV. Allah ﷻ does not create people believers with an acquired [kind of] belief or disbelievers with an acquired [kind of] disbelief. Belief, disbelief, obedience, and disobedience are acts of the servant.

١٥- إن الله سـبحانه وتعـالى لا يخلـق المخلـوق مؤمنـًا بالإيمـان الكسـبي ولا كافـرًا بالكفر الكسـبي. والإيمان والكفـر والطاعـة والعصيـان مـن أفعـال العبـاد.

XVI. Every act of disobedience occurs by His knowledge, decree, foreordainment, and will, but not with His love, nor with His pleasure, nor by His command.

١٦- المعـاصي كلّهـا بعلمـه وقضائـه وتقديـره ومشيئته لا بمحبّتـه ولا برضـاه ولا بأمـره.

XVII. When ostentation enters into any act, it vitiates the reward of that act. Self-conceit does the same.

١٧- الريـاء إذا وقـع في عمـل مـن الأعمـال يبطـل أجـره وكـذا العجـب.

XVIII. Allah ﷻ fulfills the needs of His enemies to lead them on; His punishment befalls them in the hereafter. They become deluded by this and increase in disobedience and disbelief.

١٨- إن الله تعالى يقضي حاجات أعدائه استدراجًا لهم وعقوبته لهم في العقبى فيغترّون به ويزدادون عصيانًا وكفرًا.

XIX. With respect to the content of their belief, all believers are equal in their belief and monotheism. But they are on unequal levels with respect to denying that [Allah has] any partner in [His] essence, attributes, or acts.

١٩- والمؤمنون مستوون في الإيمان والتوحيد من حيث المؤمَن به ومتفاضلون من حيث نفي الشريك عن الذات والصفات والأفعال.

XX. *Islām* means surrender and submission to the commands of Allah ﷻ. There is a lexical difference between *īmān* (belief) and *islām* (submission): lexically, *islām* means submission while *īmān* means assent. Belief cannot exist, however, without submission, nor can submission exist without belief. They are like exterior and interior, i.e., mutually concomitant: neither can be separated from the other, just as neither the exterior can be separated from the interior nor the interior from the exterior.

٢٠- الإسلام هو التسليم والانقياد لأوامر الله تعالى فمن حيث اللغة فرق بين الإيمان والإسلام إذ الإسلام لغة التسليم والإيمان التصديق ولكن لا يكون إيمان بلا إسلام ولا يوجد إسلام بلا إيمان. وهما كالظهر والبطن أي هما متلازمان° لا ينفكّ أحدهما عن الآخر كما لا ينفكّ الظهر عن البطن والبطن عن الظهر.

XXI. *Dīn* (religion) is a noun that refers to belief, to submission, and to all religious precepts. That is, the word *dīn* might be used where one intends "belief," it might be used where one intends "submission," and it might be used where one intends the revealed religion of our prophet ﷺ, which comprises belief, submission, and spiritual excellence.

٢١- الدين اسم واقع على الإيمان والإسلام والشرائع كلّها أي إن لفظ «الدين» قد يطلق ويراد به الإيمان وقد يراد به الإسلام وقد يراد به شريعة نبيّنا الجامعة للإيمان والإسلام والإحسان.

XXII. The settling of accounts between adversaries through good deeds on the day of resurrection is a reality. If one lacks any good deeds, one takes of the evil deeds of the other and bears the burden of those deeds.

٢٢- القصاص فيما بين الخصوم بالحسنات يوم القيامة حقّ؛ وإن لم يكن له حسنات أخذ من سيّئات صاحبه فحمل عليه.

XXIII. The returning of the soul to the body, the interrogation by Munkar and Nakīr, and the constriction and punishment of the grave are realities that will befall all disbelievers and some Muslims.[17]

٢٣- إعادة الروح إلى الجسد وسؤال منكر ونكير وضغطة القبر وعذابه حقّ للكفّار كلّهم ولبعض المسلمين.

XXIV. When a person encounters a difficulty with any intricate point of theology, he must for the time being believe that which is true with Allah ﷻ until he finds a scholar and asks him. He is not permitted to postpone his inquiry nor is he allowed an excuse, and if he dismisses the matter he disbelieves, that is, assuming that the matter be one of the fundamentals of the religion. But if he says, "I believe in Allah ﷻ, and I affirm whatever is true with Allah ﷻ," then belief is established in a general manner.

٢٤- إذا أشكل على الإنسان شيء من دقائق علم التوحيد ينبغي له أن يعتقد في الحال ما هو الصواب عند الله تعالى إلى أن يجد عالمًا فيسأله؛ ولا يسعه تأخير الطلب ولا يعذر؛ ويكفر إن وقف فيه أي إذا كان من ضروريّات الدين. وإذا قال «آمنت بالله تعالى واعتقدت ما هو الحقّ عند الله تعالى» يثبت إيمان الإجمال.

Matters of Which Ignorance Is Harmless and Knowledge Beneficial

مما لا يضر جهله وتنفع معرفته

I. The soundest position is that a thing's existence is identical to the thing. Thus, the nonexistent is not a thing, nor is it an entity, nor does it subsist. The same holds [even] according to the weaker view.[18]

١- الأصحّ أن وجود الشيء عينه فالمعدوم ليس بشيء ولا ذات ولا ثابت؛ وأنه كذلك على المرجوح.

II. [The soundest position is] that the name is the named.

٢- وأن الاسم هو المسمّى.

III. The names of Allah are taken strictly from revelation.

٣- أن أسماء الله توقيفيّة.

IV. A person is allowed to say, "I am a believer if Allah wills," so long as he does not doubt his present status.

٤- وأن للمرء أن يقول «أنا مؤمن إن شاء الله» لا شكًّا في الحال.

V. The enjoyment of a disbeliever exists to lead him on.

٥- وأن تمتّع الكافر استدراج.

VI. The thing signified by [the word] "I" is the specified body.[19]

٦- وأن المشار إليه بـ«أنا» الهيكل المخصوص.

VII. The *atom*, i.e., the indivisible particle, exists.

VIII. There is no such thing as a *quasi-ontic mode*; that is, there is no intermediate status between the existent and the nonexistent. Relations are perspectival things. A property cannot subsist in another property, persist for two instants, or inhere in two things.

IX. Two [opposites] of the same kind cannot coincide, as in two contrary opposites, unlike two things that are [merely] different. Two contradictory opposites can be neither simultaneously present nor simultaneously absent.

X. Neither alternative in a contingent thing [intrinsically] takes precedence over the other.[20]

XI. A contingent thing that remains in existence [remains] in need of something that gives it existence.

XII. *Space* is a hypothetical dimension in which the dimensions of a corporeal object extend, and it is a void. A *void* is possible according to our view; it refers to two corporeal objects' not being in physical contact and not having anything in between them that is in physical contact with both. *Time* is the association of an imagined renewing thing with a known renewing thing.[21]

XIII. The interpenetration of substances is impossible, as is a substance's lacking any properties. Corporeal objects are not composed of properties. Their dimensions are finite.

XIV. The effect is posterior to the cause in rank, and the soundest position is that it is simultaneous with it in time.

XV. *Pleasure* is to feel gratified when apprehending [a thing], such that apprehending [the thing] entails pleasure. Its opposite is *pain*.

٧- أن الجوهر الفرد وهو الجزء الذي لا يتجزّأ ثابت.

٨- وأنه لا حال أي لا واسطة بين الموجود والمعدوم؛ وأن النسب والإضافات أمور اعتباريّة؛ وأن العرض لا يقوم بعرض ولا يبقى زمانين ولا يحلّ محلّين.

٩- وأن المثلين لا يجتمعان كالضدّين بخلاف الخلافين؛ والنقيضان لا يجتمعان ولا يرتفعان.

١٠- وأن أحد طرفَي الممكن ليس أولى من الآخر.

١١- وأن الممكن الباقي محتاج إلى مؤثّر.

١٢- وأن المكان بُعد مفروض ينفذ فيه بُعد الجسم وهو الخلاء؛ والخلاء جائز عندنا والمراد به كون الجسمين لا يتماسّان ولا بينهما ما يماسّهما. وأن الزمان مقارنة متجدّد موهوم لمتجدّد معلوم.

١٣- ويمتنع تداخل الجواهر وخلوّ الجوهر عن كل الأعراض. والجسم غير مركّب منها؛ وأبعاده متناهية.

١٤- والمعلول يعقب علّته رتبة والأصحّ أنه يقارنها زمانًا.

١٥- وأن اللذة ارتياح عند إدراك فالإدراك ملزومها ويقابلها الألم.

XVI. Anything that the intellect conceives is either necessary, impossible, or possible.

١٦- وما تصوّره العقل إما واجب أو ممتنع أو ممكن.

* * *

By the assistance of Allah ﷻ, the treatise entitled *The Sturdy Rope: On Creedal Theology* is complete. May Allah ﷻ by His grace and generosity render it of benefit to us and all believers. Allah! "Take us not to task if we forget or err!" (Q 2:286). "Glory to your Lord, Lord of Might, transcending what they describe! Peace be upon the messengers. And praise to Allah, Lord of the worlds" (Q 37:180–82). By His permission ﷻ, the twelfth treatise follows, entitled *The Plenitude of the Gracious One: On the Science of Spiritual Principles.*

تمّت بعون الله تعالى الرسالة المسمّاة بالحبل المتين في أصول الدين جعلها الله تعالى بمنّه وكرمه نافعة لنا ولسائر المؤمنين. اللّهم لا تؤاخذنا إن نسينا أو أخطأنا. ﴿سُبْحَٰنَ رَبِّكَ رَبِّ ٱلْعِزَّةِ عَمَّا يَصِفُونَ ۝١٨٠ وَسَلَٰمٌ عَلَى ٱلْمُرْسَلِينَ ۝١٨١ وَٱلْحَمْدُ لِلَّهِ رَبِّ ٱلْعَٰلَمِينَ﴾ [٣٧/ ١٨٠-١٨٢]. وتليها بإذنه تعالى الرسالة الثانية عشرة المسمّاة فيض[٦] الرؤوف في علم مبادي التصوّف.

NOTES TO TREATISE XI

1 The Prophet ﷺ is commanded to know that Allah is one, and we are commanded to follow him. By analogy, we are commanded to know the rest of our creed.

2 That is, even though belief based on mere imitation of the doctrines of others is prohibited and sinful, it still counts as belief.

3 Although it is true that Allah subsists in Himself, which means that He exists without depending on any other entity in which to inhere, *substance* (*jawhar*) is a technical term that applies as a category of created things and is hence inappropriate to use in reference to Allah the Exalted.

4 That is, to everything that is intrinsically contingent (*mumkin*). That a thing be contingent means that neither existence nor nonexistence is necessitated by its very essence. This excludes Allah the Exalted Himself, whose existence is not contingent upon anything, and it excludes intrinsically impossible things, like square circles, which by definition cannot exist.

5 That is, anything whose apparent sense might carry implications that are incompatible with divine transcendence.

6 His being unjust is rationally impossible since He has created and owns everything in the cosmos, and there is no higher principle above Him. Any conceivable act, regardless how it might seem to His creatures, would by definition be just if He did it. But, by His mercy, He is not merely just; He is also compassionate and generous to an extent humanity cannot even nearly fathom.

7 A collection of over 500 letters written by the Sufi master Aḥmad Sirhindī, also known as Imām-i Rabbānī (d. 1034/1624 or 1625).

8 These are all Quranic terms.

9 That is, Allah brings quiddities into being by creating them, or giving them existence. Thus, when Allah creates humans, He makes the quiddity 'human' be. This is based on the understanding of *jaʿl* as 'giving existence'. Others who define *jaʿl* in a different sense, namely, as the determination of quiddities in themselves essentially, maintain that quiddities are *not* made to be what they are (*ghayr majʿūla*). The debate is a semantic one. See al-Anṣārī, *Ghāyat al-wuṣūl*, 847–48.

10 The challenge can be simply the prophet's claim to prophethood, which is a challenge to the people to produce miracles of their own if they would deny that Allah created the miracle to confirm the prophet's claim. One further qualification can be added to the definition: the miracle must not undermine the claimant. This would rule out the kind of miracle known as an *ihāna*, or "humiliation," by which Allah discredits false prophets.

11 That is, submission is a condition (*sharṭ*) for belief, and belief is a condition for submission.

12 The Sufi imam and exegete Abū al-Qāsim ʿAbd al-Karīm al-Qushayrī (d. 465/1072 or 1073).

13 That is, Sufyān al-Thawrī (d. 161/778) and Sufyān b. ʿUyayna (d. 198/813 or 814).

14 Abū al-Ḥasan al-Ashʿarī (d. 324/935 or 936), founder of the Ashʿarī school of theology.

15 The Sufi imam Abū al-Qāsim al-Junayd b. Muḥammad (d. 297/910).

16 Thus, when someone utters the Quran, we say both that his uttering is created and also that what he is uttering is literally the uncreated speech of Allah. The fact that Allah is the original speaker, or arranger, of that speech makes it literally His speech; the person is merely performing a verbal utterance of it.

17 That is, the constriction and punishment of the grave will befall all disbelievers and some Muslims.

18 That is, even according to the view that a thing's existence is not identical to the thing, the nonexistent is not a thing, nor is it an entity, nor does it subsist.

19 The body is understood here to include the soul (*mushtamil ʿalā al-nafs*). The opposing view is that which holds that "I" refers exclusively to the soul and not to the body. Al-Anṣārī, *Ghāyat al-wuṣūl*, 871.

20 The alternatives are existence and nonexistence.

21 That is, time is a hypothetical abstraction by which we make associations between things, referring to events and conventional intervals that are well-known for the purpose of marking and measuring events and durations that are imagined, that is, less distinctly known. Thus, when someone imagines Zayd's arriving but does not know exactly when it occurred or will occur, he might ask when Zayd arrived or will arrive, and we might respond by referring to an event he would remember ("The day that ʿAmr came over for dinner") or to a conventional interval he would recognize ("In three hours"). Note that a renewing thing (*mutajaddid*) is an originated thing (*ḥādith*), especially insofar as it undergoes change.

XII

THE PLENITUDE OF THE GRACIOUS ONE

On the science of spiritual principles

فيض الرؤوف في علم مبادي التصوف

In the Name of Allah,
All-Merciful, Most Compassionate

بسم الله الرحمن الرحيم

ALL PRAISE IS due to Allah, Lord of the worlds. May blessings and peace be upon our prophet, Muḥammad, and upon all of his family, Companions, and Followers.

الحمد لله ربّ العالمين والصلاة والسلام على نبيّنا محمد وعلى آله وصحبه وأتباعهم أجمعين.

To Proceed This is a treatise on the principles of the science of spiritual devotion. I have entitled it *The Plenitude of the Gracious One: On the Science of Spiritual Principles* and restricted it to the definition and principles of spiritual devotion.

أما بعد فهذه رسالة في مبادي علم التصوّف سمّيتها فيض الرؤوف في علم مبادي[1] التصوّف قصرتها على تعريف التصوّف ومباديه.

❋ ❋ ❋

What is spiritual devotion? How many divisions do its principles comprise?

ما التصوّف؟ وكم قسمًا مباديه؟

Spiritual devotion is the pure devotion of one's heart to Allah ﷻ and disdain of everything besides Him, i.e., in relation to His magnificence ﷻ. This ultimately relates to what one does with one's heart and bodily parts.

التصوّف هو تجريد القلب لله تعالى واحتقار ما سواه أي بالنسبة إلى عظمته تعالى. وحاصله يرجع إلى عمل القلب والجوارح.

There are many principles of spiritual devotion. The most important of them are [the following] three.

مباديه كثيرة أهمّها ثلاثة.

[Important Spiritual Principles]

Principle 1: To Know Allah ﷻ To know Allah, as stated by al-Ghazālī, is the first of all obligations according to the soundest position, because without it no [moral ruling of] obligation or even recommendation holds valid. One who knows his Lord can understand how his sins put him at distance from his Lord and his pious acts bring him nearer to Him. Thus, he fears His punishment and hopes for His reward; he gives heed to [his Lord's] commands and prohibitions; he conforms and he refrains; and his Master therefore loves him, becoming his hearing, his sight, and his hand, and taking him as a close friend, such that if he were to ask Him He would give him and if he were to seek His protection He would protect him, as is in the hadith of al-Bukhārī ؓ.[1] Out of His love, Allah takes care of him in all of his states just as the parents of a child out of their love take care of all of their child's states, such that the child never eats but from the hand of one of them and never walks but by the foot of one of them, and so on.

Principle 2: That One Seeking the Afterlife Have High Aspirations One who has high aspirations raises himself upward from paltry things to lofty matters, while one who has low aspirations gives no care: he waxes ignorant and renounces religion. Proceed, then, to either piety or corruption, bliss or wretchedness, felicity or the blaze.

Principle 3: To Assess One's Thoughts Whenever a thought occurs to you, assess it by the standard of revealed law.

If it is commanded, hasten to act on it, for it comes from the All-Merciful. If you fear the act will occur in a prohibited manner, e.g., with self-conceit or ostentation, without your intending it, then there is nothing wrong in proceeding. If such a thing does occur, whether unintentionally or intentionally,

[1] Al-Bukhārī, *al-Jāmiʿ al-ṣaḥīḥ*, 8:105 (no. 6502).

[من أهم مبادي التصوف]

أولها: معرفة الله تعالى هي كما قال الغزالي أوّل الواجبات على الأصحّ إذ لا يصحّ بدونها واجب بل ولا مندوب. ومن عرف ربّه تصوّر تبعيده عنه بذنبه وتقريبه له بطاعته فخاف عذابه ورجا ثوابه فأصغى إلى الأمر والنهي فامتثل واجتنب فأحبّه مولاه فكان سمعه وبصره ويده واتّخذه وليًّا إن سأله أعطاه وإن استعاذ به أعاذه كما في حديث البخاري رحمه الله تعالى[١] لحبّه يتولّاه في جميع أحواله كما أن أبوي الطفل لحبّهما له يتولّيان جميع أحواله فلا يأكل إلا بيد أحدهما ولا يمشي إلا برجله إلى غير ذلك.

وثانيها: كون طالب الآخرة علي الهمة عليّ الهمّة يرفع نفسه عن سفساف الأمور إلى معاليها ودنيء الهمّة لا يبالي فيجهل ويمرق من الدين. فدونك صلاحًا أو فسادًا وسعادةً أو شقاوةً ونعيمًا أو جحيمًا.

ثالثها: وزن الخاطر إذا خطر لك شيء فزنه بالشرع.

فإن كان مأمورًا به فبادر إلى فعله فإنه من الرحمن. فإن خفت وقوعه على صفة منهيّة كعجب أو رياء بلا قصد لها فلا بأس عليك فإن وقع بلا قصد أو بقصد

[١] البخاري، الرقاق، ٣٨.

seek pardon immediately. The fact that our seeking pardon will require [another] seeking of pardon should not cause us to neglect it.

If it is prohibited, beware, for it comes from Satan. If you incline [to the thought], seek pardon. You are excused for [entertaining the thought] in internal dialogue and considering it, so long as you do not speak or act accordingly. If your evil-inciting[1] soul will not obey you, fight it. Now, if you act on the thought because your evil-inciting soul overwhelms you, you are obligated to desist immediately. If you fail to desist because of enjoyment or laziness, remember that which severs all pleasures[1] and that it comes suddenly. If [you fail to desist] because of despair, then fear the hatred of your Lord, remember the vastness of His mercy, and bring before His mercy repentance, which is remorse. Repentance is actualized when one desists, resolves not to revert, and makes amends for anything he can. The soundest position is that repentance from a sin is valid even if that repentance [later] becomes null or if one persists in committing major sins, and that it is necessary to repent from minor sins.

If you are unsure whether the thought be something commanded or something prohibited, then refrain.

Additional Principles [Have] little of food, little of sleep, and little of mingling with people.

[1] *Evil-inciting* excludes (1) the *self-blaming soul*, namely, that which blames itself even when it strives for excellence; (2) the *well-content soul*, namely, that which is secure in standing upright in obedience; and (3) the *comfort-seeking soul*, namely, that which inclines toward the permissible, like recreation, listening to beautiful voices, and delicious food. All four [names] refer to one and the same soul: it sometimes assumes the character of the well-content soul, other times of the evil-inciting soul, other times of the self-blaming soul, and other times of the comfort-seeking soul. The soul's effective status is that of its predominant character, just as with the four elements of the human [body]—black bile, yellow bile, [blood], and phlegm.

فاستغفر منه فورًا. واحتياج استغفارنا إلى استغفار لا يوجب تركه.

وإن كان منهيًّا فإيّاك فإنه من الشيطان. فإن ملت فاستغفر؛ وحديث النفس والهمّ ما لم تتكلّم أو تعمل به مغفوران. وإن لم تطعك الأمّارة[١] فجاهدها، فإن فعلت الخاطر المذكور لغلبة الأمّارة عليك فاقلع على الفور وجوبًا، فإن لم تقلع لاستلذاذ أو كسل فاذكر هاذم اللذّات وفجأته أو لقنوط فخف مقت ربّك واذكر سعة رحمته. واعرض عليها التوبة وهي الندم؛ وتتحقّق بالإقلاع وعزم أن لا يعود وتدارك ما يمكن تداركه؛ والأصحّ صحّتها عن ذنب ولو نقضت أو كانت مع الإصرار على كبير، ووجوبها عن صغير.

وإن شككت في الخاطر أمأمور هو أم منهي فأمسك.

ومن مباديه أيضا قلّة الطعام، قلّة المنام، قلّة الاختلاط بالأنام.

[١] وخرج بالأمّارة (١) اللوّامة وهي التي تلوم نفسها وإن اجتهد في الإحسان، (٢) والمطمئنّة وهي الآمنة باستقامتها بالطاعة، (٣) والروحانيّة وهي التي تميل إلى المباح كالتنزه وسماع الصوت الحسن والمأكل الطيّب. والأربعة ترجع إلى نفس واحدة لكنها تتشكّل تارة مطمئنّة وتارة أمّارة وتارة لوّامة وتارة روحانيّة؛ والحكم فيها للغالب كالعناصر الأربعة في الإنسان: السوداء والصفراء [والدم]٢ والبلغم.

Additionally, rein in the soul with the reins of God-consciousness; bar it from dubious matters, an excess in permissible matters, and whimsical inclination; and rouse it with fear and a raging hellfire and with hope for the pleasure of Allah ﷻ and the groves of the everlasting abode.

Furthermore, make continual invocation, and show gratitude with sincerity by employing the seven bodily organs with which He endowed you—which are the eyes, the hearing, the hands, the feet, the stomach, the heart, [and the genitals]—for the purposes for which they were created. Attend to all of this as though you see Him ﷻ, for although you do not see Him, He sees you.

Instructive Points

Everything, including one's thoughts and one's acting upon them or refraining, occurs by the power and will of Allah. He creates the acquisition of the servant, having allotted to him a kind of power that serves to acquire but not to create. For Allah creates and does not acquire, while the reverse is true of the servant. The soundest position is that the servant's power is simultaneous with the action and does not supply the capacity for two opposite [actions], and that incapacity is a real quality that is opposed to power by way of contrariety.

Whether it be preferable to trust [in Allah][2] or to pursue worldly provision varies by person. To seek detachment from all that preoccupies one from Allah ﷻ when Allah has given one occasion to [seek] the means of provision is [in fact] a subtle desire. To take means of provision that preoccupy one from Allah when one has occasion to detach is to sink below a high rank. The best thing for a person for whom Allah has allotted the circumstances to [take] the means of provision is to take them instead of detaching, and the best

ثم إلجام النفس بلجام التقوى ونهيها عن الشبهات وفضول المباحات والهوى؛ وتهييجها بالخوف ونارٍ تلظّى ورَجا رِضى الله تعالى وجنّة المأوى.

ثم دوام الذكر والشكر مع الإخلاص بصرف ما أنعم عليك من الأعضاء السبعة التي هي العين والسمع واليد والرجل والبطن والقلب [والفرج][٣] إلى ما خلقت لها ملاحظًا في جميع ذلك كأنك تراه تعالى فإن لم تره فإنه يراك.

التنبيهات

كلُّ واقعٍ — ومن جملته الخاطر فعله وتركه — بقدرة الله وإرادته فهو خالق كسب العبد قدّر له قدرة تصلح للكسب لا للإيجاد؛ فالله خالق لا مكتسب والعبد بعكسه. والأصحّ أن قدرته مع الفعل فهي لا تصلح للضدّين وأن العجز صفة وجوديّة تقابِل القدرة تقابُل الضدّين.

وأن التفضيل بين التوكّل والاكتساب يختلف باختلاف الناس فإرادة التجريد عما يشغل عن الله تعالى مع داعية الأسباب من الله في مريد التجريد شهوة خفيّة، وسلوك الأسباب الشاغلة عن الله مع داعية التجريد في سالك انحطاط عن الرتبة العليّة. فالأصلح لمن قدّر الله فيه داعية

٥٧٠

thing for a person for whom Allah has allotted the circumstances to detach is to seek detachment instead of provision.

Satan may tempt one to cast off Allah's proximity ﷻ in the guise of [taking] the means of provision, and he may tempt one to laziness in the guise of trust [in Allah], this all being a plot on his part. For example, he may say to a seeker of detachment for whom it is better to seek detachment than not, "For how long will you neglect the means of provision? Do you not know that neglecting these means makes hearts covet what other have? Pursue these means, then, so that you may be safe from this." And he may say to a seeker of provision for whom it is better to seek provision than not, "If you were to leave this off, to seek detachment, and to put your trust in Allah, your heart would become pure and you would be given sufficient [provision] from Allah. Leave this off, then, so that you may attain this." Leaving off the pursuit of provision, which was not what was best for him, would then lead him to depend on other people and to be anxious about his provision. The successful person seeks both detachment and the means of provision and knows that nothing occurs save what Allah ﷻ wills.

الأسباب سلوكها دون التجريد ولمن قدّر الله فيه التجريد سلوكه دون الأسباب.

وقد يأتي الشيطان باطّراح[٤] جانب الله تعالى في صورة الأسباب أو بالكسل في صورة التوكّل كيدًا منه، كأن يقول لسالك التجريد الذي سلوكه له أصلح من تركه له «إلى متى تترك الأسباب؟ ألم تعلم أن تركها يطمع القلوب لما في أيدي الناس؟ فاسلكها لتسلم من ذلك»، ويقول لسالك الأسباب الذي سلوكه لها أصلح من تركه لها «ولو تركتها وسلكت التجريد فتوكّلت على الله لصفى قلبك وأتاك ما يكفيك من عند الله فاتركها ليحصل لك ذلك» فيؤدّي تركها الذي هو غير أصلح له إلى الطلب من الخلق والاهتمام بالرزق. والموفَّق يبحث عنهما ويعلم أنه لا يكون إلا ما يريد الله تعالى.

❁ ❁ ❁

Says this destitute and impoverished servant, Muḥammad Emīn, may Allah, Lord of the worlds, pardon him: Every perfection and felicity is contained in a single matter, namely, to be constant in following the Prophet ﷺ in the most complete manner in one's speech, action, and states, i.e., character. This includes everything one may do in following him ﷺ that Allah ﷻ loves, and it excludes everything He does not love—every deviance and laxity that is at odds with the Sunna and with firm purpose. Success is from Allah ﷻ alone.

يقول هذا العبد الفقير المسكين محمد أمين سامحه الله ربّ العالمين: إن كل كمال وسعادة منحصر في شيء واحد وهو التزام كمال الاتبّاع للنبي ﷺ قولًا وفعلًا وحالًا أي أخلاقًا؛ فدخل فيه ما يحبّ الله تعالى من الاتبّاع له ﷺ وخرج ما لا يحبّ من البدعة والرخصة المخالفتين للسنّة والعزيمة. ومن الله تعالى وحده التوفيق.

❋ ❋ ❋

The treatise entitled *The Plenitude of the Gracious One: On the Science of Spiritual Principles* is complete. “Our Lord, take us not to task if we forget or err!” (Q 2:286). Join us through this among “those whom [Allah] has blessed, the prophets, the truthful ones, the witnesses, and the righteous. What beautiful companions they are!” (Q 4:69). “Glory to your Lord, Lord of Might, transcending what they describe! Peace be upon the messengers. And praise to Allah, Lord of the worlds” (Q 37:180–82). May Allah ﷻ bless our prophet Muḥammad and give him peace and so all of his family, Companions, and those who follow them in excellence forever and ever.

تمّت الرسالة المسمّاة فيض° الرؤوف في علم مبادي التصوّف. ربّنا لا تؤاخذنا إن نسينا أو أخطأنا واجعلنا بها مع الذين أنعم عليهم من النبيّين والصدّيقين والشهداء والصالحين وحسن أولئك رفيقًا. ﴿سُبْحَٰنَ رَبِّكَ رَبِّ ٱلْعِزَّةِ عَمَّا يَصِفُونَ ﴿١٨٠﴾ وَسَلَٰمٌ عَلَى ٱلْمُرْسَلِينَ ﴿١٨١﴾ وَٱلْحَمْدُ لِلَّهِ رَبِّ ٱلْعَٰلَمِينَ﴾ [٣٧/ ١٨٠-١٨٢]. وصلّى الله تعالى على نبيّنا محمد وسلّم وعلى آله وصحبه والتابعين لهم بإحسان أبد الآبدين.

NOTES TO TREATISE XII

1 Abū Hurayra ؓ narrates that the Prophet ﷺ said, "Remember often that which severs all pleasures," that is, death. Al-Tirmidhī, *al-Jāmiʿ al-kabīr*, 4:141 (no. 2307).

2 That is, to trust Allah in the sense that one abandons the active pursuit of worldly provision and lives an ascetic life. In the sense of one's spiritual state, however, every believer must trust in Allah.

NOTES TO THE ARABIC TEXT

Introduction

١ في الأصل: علم مبادئ علم التصوف.

٢ في الأصل: مشعرًا.

٣ في الأصل: والفلاحة كالحياكة.

٤ في الأصل: عنبة.

٥ في الأصل: يجب.

٦ في الأصل: السميا.

٧ في الأصل: يقلبها.

I. Morphology

١ في الأصل: فعلي.

٢ حذفنا: أي قال لا حول ولا قوة إلا بالله.

٣ في الأصل: للازم.

٤ في الأصل: للازم.

٥ في الأصل: للازم.

٦ في الأصل: الصيغة.

٧ حذفنا: نحو: مجرور به.

٨ في الأصل: أحمر.

٩ في الأصل: هُزَيْلِيٌّ هُزَيْلِيَّانِ هُزَيْلِيُّونَ هُزَيْلِيَّةٌ هُزَيْلِيَّتَانِ هُزَيْلِيَّاتٌ.

١٠ في الأصل: بَصْرِيٌّ بَصْرِيَّانِ بَصْرِيُّونَ بَصْرِيَّةٌ بَصْرِيَّتَانِ بَصْرِيَّاتٌ.

١١ في الأصل: دسَّي.

١٢ في الأصل: تَظَنّي.

١٣ في الأصل: يستمدّ ويتمادّ.

١٤ حذفنا قبله: ومادّ أصله الثاني مادد على وزن فاعل كقاتل.

١٥ في الأصل: انفيل.

١٦ في الأصل: وبالقلب.

١٧ في الأصل: إلا.

١٨ في الأصل: مفول.

١٩ حذفنا قبله: إعلال باب ضرب أجوف ماضياً إعلاله ماضياً بالقلب أي.

٢٠ في الأصل: فالقلب.

٢١ حذفنا بعده: إعلاله.

٢٢ حذفنا من الحاشية: وتكسر الفاء فيهما نظرًا لحركة عين الفعل.

٢٣ في الأصل: كمعلوم.

٢٤ حذفنا بعده: إعلاله ماضياً.

٢٥ في الأصل: مُفِعْلٌ.

٢٦ في الأصل: يستدعى.

٢٧ حذفنا: راضٍ، سارٍ.

٢٨ في الأصل: على أصله مرميون.

٢٩ في الأصل: موئّى.

٣٠ في الأصل: موئى.

٣١ في الأصل: انقوى.

٣٢ في الأصل: بالحذف.

٣٣ في الأصل: انقوى.

٣٤ في الأصل: القوى.

٣٥ في الأصل: ينقوي.

٣٦ في الأصل: يرضي.

٣٧ في الأصل: ارض.

٣٨ في الأصل: التق.

٣٩ في الأصل: لا ترض.

٤٠ في الأصل: راضٍ.

٤١ في الأصل: أأمل.

٤٢ في الأصل: أأمل.

٤٣ في الأصل: لا تؤمل.

٤٤ في الأصل: مدّ.

٤٥ حذفنا: لا تمادّ.

٤٦ حذفنا: إن كان من الثلاثي المجرد.

٤٧ حذفنا: إعلالها.

٤٨ في الأصل: يكنّ.

٤٩ حذفنا: نحو أحسن وأحمر.

٥٠ في الأصل: انفال.

٥١ في الأصل: انفلن.

٥٢ في الأصل: تقبل.

٥٣ حذفنا: كاختير.

٥٤ حذفنا: إن كان من الثلاثي المجرد.

٥٥ حذفنا: فبالحذف صارت: لا تغز، لا تغزوا، لا تغزوا، لا تغزي.

٥٦ في الأصل: نحو: رامي. حذف الضمة لثقلها على حرف العلة وحذف الياء لالتقاء الساكنين نحو: رام، أصله رامي على وزن فاعل كضارب. وبالحذفين صار: رام على وزن فاع.

٥٧ في الأصل: لام اللام.

٥٨ في الأصل: مضار.

٥٩ في الأصل: تفتعل.

٦٠ في الأصل: روى.

٦١ في الأصل: يرضى، أصله يرضيُ.

٦٢ في الأصل: يرضى.

٦٣ في الأصل: التق.

٦٤ في الأصل: رقٍّ.

٦٥ في الأصل: واسم.

٦٦ في الأصل: كمرموي.

٦٧ في الأصل: أأمن.

٦٨ في الأصل: إتخذ.

٦٩ في الأصل: نحو: ايتعد، أصله اوتعد، فبالإعلال صار: اتّعد.

٧٠ في الأصل: أأمل، أأدب.

٧١ في الأصل: ايذر.

٧٢ في الأصل: الذال.

٧٣ في الأصل: تأذر.

٧٤ في الأصل: آذر.

٧٥ في الأصل: أاذر.

٧٦ في الأصل: آذر.

٧٧ في الأصل: مأذور.

٧٨ في الأصل: مأذر.

٧٩ في الأصل: يكنّ.

٨٠ حذفنا: نحو: مكرم يكرم.

II. Grammar

١ في الأصل: يُجرّ.

٢ حذفنا: وهو كل اسم نسب إليه شيء بواسطة حرف الجر لفظاً نحو: مررت بزيد، أو تقديراً نحو: غلام زيد أي غلام لزيد.

٣ حذفنا: وهي.

٤ في الأصل: تام.

٥ في الأصل: نحوه.

٦ حذفنا: ونحو: نضربُ ولن نضربَ ولم نضربْ.

٧ حذفنا: ونحو: نغزو، ولن نغزوَ، ولم يغزُ.

٨ في الأصل: جره.

٩ في الأصل: تمت.

١٠ حذفنا: بالتاء.

١١ في الأصل: احضر.

١٢ حذفنا: والجمع المصحح كالمسلمون والمسلمات.

١٣ في الأصل: مشدد.

١٤ في الأصل: جاءني هندان وزيدون ورأيت هندَين وزيدين ومررت بهندَين وزيدِين. وأما من يجعل الإعراب على النون كما في سكران وعلّيون فهو يقول جاءني هنداني وزيدوئى.

١٥ في الأصل: الفُضْل.

١٦ في الأصل: ضربتْ.

١٧ في الأصل: وللبيتين.

١٨ في الأصل: يختلْ.

١٩ في الأصل: جائنئ.

٢٠ في الأصل: الفوق.

٢١ في الأصل: وهي للتشبيه كأن زيداً أسد.

٢٢ حذفنا: النافية.

٢٣ حذفنا: لا النافية.

٢٤ حذفنا: وهما.

٢٥ في الأصل: لأكرمتك.

٢٦ في الأصل: أحد.

III. Logic

١ حذفنا من المتن: فإنه جزء.

٢ في الأصل: الغير النامي.

٣ في الأصل: -إن نحوياً زيد-.

٤ في الأصل: المنادي.

٥ في الأصل: أنه.

٦ في أصل المتن: **وبالعكس**. ولإزالة التكرار حذفنا من الحاشية عليه: **أي كل مقسم للسافل مقسم للعالي ولا عكس كلياً**.

٧ في الأصل: لأن.

٨ في الأصل: الجسم.

٩ في الأصل: طبيعة الطبائع.

١٠ بعد أن حذفنا من آخر الجملة السابقة: أو في الجملة كالأبيض والإنسان.

١١ كما في الشمسيّة، والأصل: لا يفصل أحدهما عن.

١٢ حذفنا من الحاشية: هذا التقسيم باعتبار الرابطة.

١٣ في الأصل: لا شجراً.

١٤ في الأصل: العالم حادث.

١٥ في الأصل: أو.

١٦ في الأصل: أظهر.

١٧ في الأصل: عن.

IV. Language Theory

١ في الأصل: مقصوراً.

٢ في الأصل: بنوعيه.

٣ في الأصل: غير معين.

٤ حذفنا: الجنسي.

٥ حذفنا: بالعهدي.

V. Metaphor

١ حذفنا من الحاشية: لم يأت بالضمير بأن يقال هو لئلا يعود إلى التشبيه الاصطلاحي المبني عليه الاستعارة الذي هو أخص من مطلق التشبيه مع أنه المراد وما يقال إن المعرفة إذا أعيدت كانت عين الأول فقاعدة أغلبية لا كلية فلا يرد أن الظاهر كالضمير في العود إلى المذكور.

٢ حذفنا من الحاشية: أي الغرض من التشبيه.

٣ في الأصل: المفرد المجاز المرسل.

٤ في أصل المتن: موثوق.

٥ في الأصل: مهوئى.

٦ حذفنا بعده: **الاستعارة المصرحة باعتبار المستعار له وهي باعتبار المستعار له قسمان: تحقيقية، وتخييلية** لعدم الاتّفاق مع مضمون الفقرة. وكذا حذفنا من الحاشية: [**وهي] أي الاستعارة المصرحة**.

٧ في الأصل: **وباعتبار اللفظ المستعار أيضا** والتغيير من أجل ما سبق من الحذف أعلاه. وحذفنا من الحاشية: [**وهي] عطف على قوله باعتبار المستعار منه**.

٨ في الأصل: والوجوديان.

٩ في الأصل: يرتفع.

١٠ في الأصل: وإن.

١١ في أصل المتن: **اللحم**. وحذفنا من الحاشية: **لعلّ الصواب «الجلد»**.

١٢ في الأصل: **اللحم**. وحذفنا بعده: (**لعلّ الصواب «الجلد»**).

١٣ في الأصل: ومتعقل.

١٤ في الأصل: أو هو.

١٥ في الأصل: وتمثيلياً.

١٦ حذفنا من الحاشية: وقوله «بكسر التاء» لأنه كان في الأصل لامرأة.

١٧ في الأصل: العام.

١٨ حذفنا من الحاشية: ضميرها راجع إلى المجاز والكناية.

VI. Dialectics

١ في الأصل: استلزام عدم المطلوب.

٢ في الأصل: الإجمال.

٣ في الأصل: يستلزم.

٤ في الأصل: على الدليل على ما.

٥ في الأصل: الضمني.

٦ في الأصل: ذلك.

٧ في الأصل: ويمنع.

٨ حذفنا من الحاشية: قوله «وهذا» في التقسيم الحقيقي وأمثلته لا تحصى، ومنها تقسيم الحيوان إلى الإنسان والفرس والبغل والحمار والبقر إلى غيرها، ومن أمثلتها قولك «زيد إما قائم أو قاعد أو مضطجع» لأن حاصله تقسيم وصف زيد إلى القيام والقعود والاضطجاع ولا يتصادق هذه الأوصاف على شيء واحد.

٩ في الأصل: عسير تام.

١٠ في الأصل: وشوينز.

١١ في الأصل: بقسيم.

١٢ حذفنا قبل الجملة: قد ينقض التقسيم باستلزامه قسم الشيء قسيماً له.

١٣ في الأصل: القسم.

١٤ في الأصل: لمعلل.

VII. Rhetorical Semantics

١ في الأصل: أمه.

٢ حذفنا: هي ما.

٣ حذفنا: ارتفاع شأن الكلام.

٤ أتت هذه الجملة في الأصل قبل العنوان.

٥ في الأصل: قزعاً عن قزع.

٦ في الأصل: يُنْزَعُ.

٧ في الأصل: لضعف تعويل.

٨ حذفنا قبل «إن الذين»: لكم.

٩ في الأصل: الإفراد.

١٠ في الأصل: مهوئ.

١١ في الأصل: مقتضى.

١٢ في الأصل: يك.

١٣ في الأصل: الحال.

١٤ في الأصل: التكلم إلى الخطاب.

١٥ في الأصل: قوة.

١٦ في الأصل: الجملتين.

١٧ في الأصل: خززن.

١٨ في الأصل هنا وقبله: طرق التخصيص.

١٩ حذفنا: الآية.

٢٠ حذفنا: كأنه قيل: ما سبب علتك؟ فقال: سهر دائم وحزن طويل.

VIII. Figurative Language

١ في الأصل: وجعلنا.

٢ في الأصل: الشبيه.

IX. Embellishment

١ في الأصل: وَساكِنِيهِ.

٢ في الأصل: ساكنيه.

٣ (مَوَدَّتُهُ) في الأصل: مَوَدَّةٍ.

X. Jurisprudential Theory

١ في الأصل: الأصول.

٢ في الأصل: كالحد للزنا.

٣ في الأصل: يعني.

٤ حذفنا: وتقسيم الدلالة.

٥ في الأصل: وتنقسم.

٦ حذفنا من الحاشية: البخاري، الإيمان، ٤.

٧ في الأصل: بقطعية.

٨ في الأصح: إنهما.

٩ حذفنا من الحاشية: عبد الرزّاق، مصنّف، ٩/ ١٧٩.

١٠ في الأصل: [٥/ ٦].

١١ حذفنا: لما مرّ.

١٢ في الأصل: كان.

١٣ حذفنا: كما تقرّر في محلّه.

١٤ في الأصل: الخبر.

١٥ في الأصل: فأجازه.

١٦ في الأصل: حتى إن.

١٧ في الأصل: بمقتضى.

١٨ في الأصل: ليتعيّن.

١٩ في الأصل: يكون.

٢٠ في الأصل: ومخالف.

٢١ في الأصل: يوشوش.

٢٢ في الأصل: يتناول.

٢٣ في الأصل: لمطلق.

٢٤ في الأصل: أصل.

٢٥ حذفنا: لغة.

٢٦ في الأصل: رواية.

٢٧ في الأصل: الحديث.

XI. Creedal Theology

١ في الأصل: كالسفيانيين.

٢ هنا وقبله في الأصل: فقه الأكبر.

٣ في الأصل: والعملية.

٤ في الأصل: الكسبين.

٥ في الأصل: مثلاً زمان.

٦ في الأصل: الفيض.

XII. Spiritual Principles

١ في الأصل: مبادي علم.

٢ في الأصل: والخلط.

٣ زدناه وحذفنا: **والبصر** بعد ذكر العين والسمع.

٤ في الأصل: بإطراح.

٥ في الأصل: الفيض.

GLOSSARY

THIS ENGLISH–ARABIC GLOSSARY lists the English technical terms contained in the treatises of this volume along with (1) the corresponding Arabic term in transliteration, (2) a literal translation of the Arabic when it diverges from the English technical term, (3) page references to locations in the text where the term is introduced, defined, or used in a notable way, along with abbreviations for the subjects of the treatises containing these references, (4) definitions or notes about the term's relation to other terms or about the term's translation when deemed helpful. The definitions provided in the glossary are, in the main, the definitions provided by the author, though in many instances they have been reworded for clarity. In cases where the author introduces a technical term in the text but does not provide a definition, one is often supplied in this glossary; these are mainly drawn from the source texts that the author would have consulted or from standard technical glossaries like the *al-Taʿrīfāt* of al-Jurjānī (d. 816/1413) or the *Kashshāf iṣṭilāḥāt al-funūn* of al-Tahānawī (d. later than 1158/1745). Parenthetical page references are added to notable locations in other treatises where the term is similarly defined or introduced. Readers in search of a particular term that they know in Arabic will find the corresponding English term in the Arabic–English glossary key.

A

***a fortiori* implicature** [*faḥwā al-khiṭāb* – "the import of the addressed speech"] JRT 487 Implicature (*mafhūm*) that applies with greater reason than the articulated meaning. Note that the term *faḥwā* is sometimes used in the text in reference to congruous implicature (*mafhūm al-muwāfaqa*).

aberrancy [*mukhālafat al-qiyās* – "contravention of the standard"] SEM 378 The use of a word with a non-standard morphological pattern. A defect that vitiates the articulateness (*faṣāha*) of a simple expression.

abrogation [*al-naskh*] JRT 495 The removal of a legal ruling by means of a legal indicant.

abstract governor [*al-ʿāmil al-maʿnawī* – "the meaning-based maker or effector"] GRA 124 Governor that is not verbally expressed; opposed to the expressed governor (*ʿāmil lafẓī*).

acceptability [*al-jawāz*] JRT 482 The legal status of an act that there is no harm in either performing or not performing.

acceptable hyperbole [*al-mubālagha al-maqbūla*] EMB 467 Hyperbole (*mubālagha*), or the affirmation of a quality to an impossible or far-fetched degree, in a way that is not excessive (*ghulū*).

accidental universal [*al-kullī al-ʿaraḍī*] LOG 238 A universal that is external to the essence of its particulars.

accidentally indeclinable noun [*al-mabnī al-ʿāriḍī*] GRA 156 Noun that is indeclinable in virtue of its resemblance to those categories of expressions that are indeclinable by default.

accusative/subjunctive [*al-manṣūb* – "erected; set up"] GRA 150, 173 Noun in the accusative case or verb in the subjunctive mood.

acquired [*al-kasbī*] LOG 226 Another term for reflective (*naẓarī*) knowledge.

action-accompaniment [*al-mafʿūl maʿahu* – "the done-with"] GRA 151 Actional accusative (*mafʿūl*) that follows the *wāw* that means *maʿa* (with), expressing something accompanying a verbal action.

actional accusative [*al-mafʿūl* – "the done"] GRA 150 Noun belonging to the principal category of accusative nouns.

action-notion [*al-mafʿūl al-muṭlaq* – "the absolute done"] GRA 150 Actional accusative (*mafʿūl*) emphasizing a verbal action or expressing its kind or number.

action-place/time [*al-mafʿūl fīhi* – "the done-in"] GRA 151 Actional accusative (*mafʿūl*) expressing the time or place of a verbal action.

action-reason [*al-mafʿūl lahu* – "the done-for"] GRA 152 Actional accusative (*mafʿūl*) expressing the reason for a verbal action.

active participle [*ism al-fāʿil* – "the noun of the doer"] MOR 40, 43 Derivative noun form; two examples are *nāṣirun* and *mukrimun*. GRA 126 Noun with verbal import that signifies the doer of an action, or a temporary occurrence. LTY 289, 292 Formal structure assigned to signify that in which the source notion inheres.

active voice [*al-mabnī li-l-fāʿil* – "the built for the doer"] [*al-maʿlūm* – "the known"] GRA 178 Form of the verb that signifies that the grammatical agent is the doer of the action. Opposed to the passive voice (*al-mabnī li-l-majhūl*). (MOR 46–47)

actual metaphor [*al-istiʿāra al-taḥqīqiyya; al-istiʿāra al-ḥaqīqiyya*] MET 322 Explicit metaphor whose tenor has actual sensible reality or actual intelligible reality, according to al-Sakkākī. Opposed to a fanciful metaphor (*istiʿāra takhyīliyya*) as al-Sakkākī defines the latter, namely, a metaphor whose tenor is purely invented in the imagination or fancy. FIG 446 Metaphor referring to a tenor that actually exists to the senses or to the intellect. When juxtaposed in the text with the implicit metaphor (*istiʿāra makniyya*), "actual metaphor" refers primarily to the explicit metaphor (*istiʿāra muṣarraḥa*), of which it is technically a subdivision.

actually separating accident [*al-ʿaraḍ al-mufāriq bi-l-fiʿl*] LOG 239 Separable accident that actually separates, whether quickly or gradually. Opposed to the possibly separable accident (*ʿaraḍ mufāriq bi-l-imkān*).

addition [*al-ziyāda*] MOR Phonetic change undergone by some words in modification (*iʿlāl*) by the addition of a vowel or letter.

adjectival derivatives [*al-amthila al-waṣfiyya*] MOR 47 Category of uniform derivatives (*amthila muṭṭarida*) featuring the grammatical affixes of number and gender for adjectival nouns.

adjective [*al-ṣifa*] GRA 136, 147 Appositive (*tābiʿ*) that indicates a meaning in the principal noun (*matbūʿ*). (SEM 400)

adopted indicants [*al-istidlāl* – "adopting as an indicant; taking as a proof"] JRT 524 General indicants (*adilla ijmāliyya*) aside from textual statements of the Quran or Sunna, consensus, and analogy.

adverb of place [*ẓarf makān* – "container of place"] GRA 151 Subclass of the action-place/time accusative (*mafʿūl fīhi*); expresses the place of the action.

adverb of time [*ẓarf zamān* – "container of time"] GRA 151 Subclass of the action-place/time accusative (*mafʿūl fīhi*); expresses the time of the action.

affirming divine oneness [*al-tawḥīd* – "making one"] CRD 554 Affirming that the divine entity transcends anything that might be conceived or imagined.

agent [*al-fāʿil* – "the doer"] GRA 133, 149 Noun of which a verb or its like is predicated. The basis of the category of nominative nouns.

allusion [*al-taʿrīḍ*] MET 336 An expression used in its literal sense while being used to point to another meaning. FIG 458–59 Type of implication that makes indirect reference to someone that fits the description without his having been explicitly mentioned. JRT 490 Expression used for a meaning, whether literal or nonliteral, to hint at other meanings.

ambiguous expression [*al-lafẓ al-mutashābih*] JRT 487 Expression whose meaning is not clear. Opposed to the unambiguous (*muḥkam*) expression.

analogical metaphor [*al-istiʿāra al-tamthīliyya*] MET 332 Another term for a metaphorical analogy (*tamthīl ʿalā sabīl al-istiʿāra*), which can also be simply called an "analogy" (*tamthīl*).

analogy (1) [*al-qiyās*] JRT 510 To refer one conceivable thing to another, conferring on the former a ruling of the latter on the basis of evaluating that the former equally and entirely possesses the cause of the latter's ruling.

analogy (2) [*al-tamthīl*] MET 332 Composite metaphor (*istiʿāra murakkaba*) that is not in widespread use. FIG 445 Composite trope (*majāz murakkab*) used for a meaning that is likened to its original meaning for exaggerative emphasis. When a particular expression of this kind comes into widespread use, it is called a proverb.

analogy by causal force [*qiyās al-maʿnā* – "analogy pertaining to the idea or import"] JRT 533 Analogy made by reference to a common element that is determined to be the legal cause on account of its mutual suitability with the ruling. Opposed to analogy by indication (*qiyās al-dalāla*).

analogy by indication [*qiyās al-dalāla*] JRT 533 Analogy made by reference to a common element that is either concomitant to the legal cause, an effect of the legal cause, or the ruling occasioned by the legal cause. Opposed to analogy by causal force (*qiyās al-maʿnā*).

analytic confutation [*al-naqḍ al-tafṣīlī* – "confutation pertaining to distinct parts"] DIA 357 Another term for challenge (*manʿ*). Targets a specific premise, as opposed to collective confutation (*naqḍ ijmālī*), which targets the proof as a whole.

answering mode [*al-ṭalabī* – "relating to inquiry"] SEM 386 The normal way of expressing a judgment to a person who is hesitant about it and has solicited it, namely, with some degree of emphasis.

antecedent [*al-muqaddam* – "the placed-before"] LOG 248 First part of a hypothetical proposition.

anti-exceptive [*waṣliyya* – "connective"] MOR 51 A clause of the form *wa-in faʿala* or *wa-law faʿala* (even if he does/did/had done).

anti-exclusive disjunctive proposition [*al-munfaṣila al-māniʿat al-khulū* – "the disjunctive proposition that precludes emptiness"] LOG 250 Disjunctive proposition whose affirmative judgment is that the two disjuncts are not both false.

anti-inclusive disjunctive proposition [*al-munfaṣila al-māniʿat al-jamʿ* – "the disjunctive proposition that precludes joining"] LOG 250 Disjunctive proposition whose affirmative judgment is that the two disjuncts are not both true.

antithesis [*al-muṭābaqa* – "correspondence"] EMB 463 Juxtaposition of two contrary or opposing ideas in a sentence. Two other names for this device are *ṭibāq* (correspondence) and *taḍādd* (contrast).

apparent expression [*al-ẓāhir*] JRT 485 Expression that signifies a meaning with preponderance.

appositives [*tawābiʿ al-muʿrab* – "followers of the inflected"] GRA 147 Nouns that follow a declinable noun and adopt its declension in the same manner.

articulated meaning [*al-manṭūq*] JRT 485 Meaning that an expression signifies within its actual articulation.

articulateness [*al-faṣāḥa*] SEM 378 Clarity and distinctness, including the purity and correctness of language, as used to describe simple expressions, speech, or speakers.

assent [*al-taṣdīq*] LOG 225 Combination of three conceptions—a subject or antecedent, a predicate or consequent, and a relation between them—and a judgment (*ḥukm*), according to Fakhr al-Dīn al-Rāzī and the logicians who follow him. According to the philosophers (and the verifying logicians after al-Rāzī and his followers), assent is simply the judgment (*ḥukm*). JRT 481 Apprehension with a judgment. Note that Zakariyyā al-Ansārī, author of the source text, defines assent as the judgment itself, in line with the verifying scholars (*muḥaqqiqūn*). *Ghāyat al-wuṣūl*, 161.

assigned expression [*al-mawḍūʿ* – "that which is placed or imposed"] LTY 282 Expression or structure that is made specific to a meaning by an act of assignment (*waḍʿ*) such that when someone aware of the assignment understands the expression, he understands the meaning thereby signified.

assigned signification [*al-dalāla al-waḍʿiyya*] LOG 227 Signification established by someone's effective act, that is, his act of assigning the signifier to the meaning.

assigner's meaning [*ālat al-waḍʿ* – "the tool or medium of the assignment"] LTY 284 The concept in the assigner's mind through which he conceives at once the denotation (*mawḍūʿ lahu*), or the referents of the expression or structure that he is assigning.

assignment [*al-waḍʿ* – "placing; imposition"] LTY 282 Making one thing specific to another such that when someone aware of the specification understands the former, he thereby understands the latter.

assignment to the general [*al-waḍʿ li-mawḍūʿ lahu ʿāmm; kullī al-mawḍūʿ lahu*] LTY Assignment of an expression or structure to a general, or universal (*kullī*), denotation, or signified meaning.

assignment to the specific [*al-waḍʿ li-mawḍūʿ lahu khāṣṣ; juzʾī al-mawḍūʿ lahu*] LTY Assignment of an expression or structure to a specific, or particular (*juzʾī*), individual denotation, or signified meaning.

assimilation [*al-idghām*] MOR Phonetic change undergone by some words in modification (*iʿlāl*) by the merging or blending of the sounds of two letters.

association [*murāʿāt al-naẓīr* – "giving consideration to what is comparable"] EMB 464 Juxtaposition of two suitable ideas without contrast. Two other names for this device are *tanāsub* (harmony) and *tawfīq* (conformity).

atom [*al-jawhar al-fard* – "the singular substance"] CRD 560 Indivisible physical particle.

attached pronoun [*al-ḍamīr al-muttaṣil*] GRA 157 Personal pronoun that cannot stand as a separate word. Opposed to the detached pronoun (*ḍamīr munfaṣil*).

attributes of action [*ṣifāt al-afʿāl* – "attributes of the acts"] CRD 555 Divine attributes alongside which the opposite can also be attributed to Allah the Exalted since they pertain to His creative action.

attributes of essence [*ṣifāt al-dhāt*] CRD 555 Divine attributes alongside which the opposite cannot also be attributed to Allah the Exalted since they pertain to the perfection of His essence.

attributive *iḍāfa* [*al-iḍāfa al-maʿnawiyya* – "significant or meaningful *iḍāfa*"] GRA 155, 213n9 *Iḍāfa* where the *muḍāf* is not a participle with verbal governance over the *muḍāf ilayhi*. With regard to the meaning it signifies, an attributive *iḍāfa* is equivalent to either the *lām* (e.g., signifying possession), *min* (composition), or *fī* (place or time).

authoritative premises [*al-maqbūlāt* – "those which are accepted"] LOG 269 Propositions taken from someone for whom you have high esteem either because he is endorsed by supernatural signs or because of his intelligence or religiosity. Used as premises in rhetorical argument.

auxiliary verbs [*al-afʿāl al-nāqiṣa* – "the incomplete verbs"] GRA 125, 179–81 Verbs that cannot make a complete sentence together with their grammatical agent without an accusative predicate. Opposed to complete verbs (*afʿāl tāmma*).

B

bad act [*al-qabīḥ* – "the repugnant"] JRT 481 Act that merits blame.

beginning *lām* [*lām al-ibtidāʾ*] GRA 209 Emphatic *lām* as in *la-Zaydun qāʾimun.*

belief [*al-īmān*] CRD 552 Internally assenting to the six articles mentioned in the hadith of Jibrīl.

blissful [*saʿīd*] CRD 551 One who Allah the Exalted has eternally decreed will die a believer.

breaking [*al-faṣl* – "disjunction"] SEM 424 To leave two consecutive sentences without a conjunction between them; opposed to joining (*waṣl*).

brevity [*al-ījāz*] SEM 428 Conveying a primarily intended meaning through a verbal expression that, while sufficient, is briefer than that expression which would have signified the meaning by correspondence (*muṭābaqa*), for an appropriate rhetorical end.

brevity by omission [*ījāz al-ḥadhf*] SEM 428 Brevity that is achieved by omitting a part of the expression.

brevity by parsimony [*ījāz al-qaṣr*] SEM 428 Brevity that is achieved without omitting any part of the expression.

broadly evident inseparable accident [*al-ʿaraḍ al-lāzim al-bayyin bi-l-maʿnā al-aʿamm* – "the inseparable accident that is evident in the broad sense"] LOG 239 Inseparable accident regarding which one becomes certain upon conceiving the relation between the accident and the implicant (*malzūm*) that the accident is inseparable from the implicant.

broken plural noun [*al-majmūʿ al-mukassar*] GRA 161 Any plural noun form that breaks apart the structure of the singular, as in *rijālun.*

C

categorical proposition [*al-qaḍiyya al-ḥamliyya* – "the predicative proposition"] LOG 247 Proposition whose two extremes are simple either actually or potentially. Opposed to the hypothetical proposition (*qaḍiyya sharṭiyya*).

certain premises [*al-yaqīniyyāt* – "those of certainty"] LOG 265 Propositions that afford certainty, whether immediate (*ḍarūrī*) or reflective (*naẓarī*), and can be used as premises in demonstrative argument.

challenge [*al-manʿ* – "preventing"] DIA 345, 349 To request proof for an unproven premise or the consecution (*taqrīb*) of a proof.

circumstance [*al-ḥāl* – "the state"] GRA 135, 152 Accusative noun that explains the state of the agent or object.

claim [*al-daʿwā; al-muddaʿā*] DIA 345 Proposition that is asserted by the proponent and must be proven or justified in a disputation.

clarification [*taḥrīr al-murād* – "rendering accurate the intended meaning"] DIA 368 Explaining the unapparent but valid meaning that one intended by a given expression.

clarifying apposition [*ʿaṭf al-bayān; al-bayān*] GRA 137, 148 The use of a clarifying appositive, that is, an appositive (*tābiʿ*) that clarifies a previous noun by a more recognizable name. (SEM 401)
coextension [*al-tasāwī* – "equality"] LOG 231, 241 Relation between universals that have the same extension (*miṣdāq*), meaning that they apply to all the same individual instances. (DIA 346)
coincidentally conditional proposition [*al-muttaṣila al-ittifāqiyya* – "the coincidental connected"] LOG 249 Conditional proposition that affirms a conditional connection ('If X then Y') between the antecedent and consequent without a causal or conceptual connection.
coincidentally disjunctive proposition [*al-munfaṣila al-ittifāqiyya* – "the coincidental disconnected"] LOG 250 Disjunctive proposition that affirms a disjunction ('Either X or Y') between the antecedent and consequent that is not due to their respective essences.
collective assignment [*al-waḍʿ al-nawʿī* – "assignment pertaining to the kind"] LTY 288 Assignment at once of multiple expressions conceived through a general concept, namely, their common structure.
collective confutation [*al-naqḍ al-ijmālī* – "summary demolition"] DIA 354 Another term for confutation (*naqḍ*), as distinguished from piecemeal confutation (*naqḍ tafṣīlī*), which is another term for challenging (*manʿ*).
combination (1) [*al-jamʿ*] EMB 467 Inclusion of multiple subjects in a predication.
combination (2) [*al-qarīna*] LOG 257 The coupling of the minor with the major premise, with given quality and quantity, in a combinative syllogism. Also termed a mood (*ḍarb*).
combinative syllogism [*al-qiyās al-iqtirānī*] LOG 256 Syllogism that does not explicitly incorporate the conclusion or its contradictory within either of its premises.
comfort-seeking soul [*al-nafs al-rawḥāniyya*] SPR 569n1 Aspect of the human soul that inclines toward permissible pleasures.
command [*al-amr*] LOG 232–33 Non-declarative speech that is linguistically assigned the function of signifying the asking while in a superordinate position that someone bring about something. SEM 420 Non-declarative speech that requests the occurrence of an action from the addressee. (GRA 177)
common metaphor [*al-istiʿāra al-ʿāmmiyya*] FIG 448 Metaphor that is commonplace because the commonality (*jāmiʿ*) that it involves is apparent.
commonality [*al-jāmiʿ*] MET 320 That in which the objects of comparison are conceived to share in a metaphor. (FIG 447)
commonplace premises [*al-mashhūrāt* – "those which are widespread"] LOG 267–68 Propositions that all or some people would accept on account of a common interest, sympathetic inclination, ingrained impulse, particular customs, or religious precepts. Used as premises in dialectical argument.
communal obligation [*farḍ al-kifāya* – "obligation of sufficiency"] JRT 482 Something important whose realization is firmly requested without inherent consideration for who it is that performs the act.
communal sunna [*sunnat al-kifāya* – "sunna of sufficiency"] JRT 482 Something important whose realization is mildly requested without inherent consideration for who it is that performs the act.
comparative/superlative noun [*ism al-tafḍīl*] MOR 42, 45 {"the noun of deeming greater or superior"] Derivative noun form; an example is *anṣaru*. Sometimes formed by the mediation of a word, as in *aktharu ikrāman*. GRA 126, 169 Signifies the possession of a quality to a greater degree than some or all other things. LTY 289 Derivative form assigned to signify that in which the source notion inheres to a greater extent than in something else or to the greatest extent.

complementing [*al-takmīl* – "completing"] SEM 431 To add to speech that might lead to a misunderstanding of the intended meaning a phrase or qualification that wards off that possible misunderstanding. Also termed "preempting" (*iḥtirās*).

complete composite expression [*al-lafẓ al-murakkab al-tāmm*] LOG 232 Composite expression after whose utterance it would be valid to stop speaking. (LTY 290)

complete descriptive definition [*al-rasm al-tāmm* – "the complete description"] LOG 244 Definition composed of the direct genus and an inseparable special accident of the definiendum.

complete essential definition [*al-ḥadd al-tāmm* – "the complete definition"] LOG 243 Definition composed of the direct genus and direct differentia of the definiendum.

complete verbs [*al-afʿāl al-tāmma*] GRA 125 Verbs that can make a complete sentence together with their grammatical agent. Opposed to auxiliary verbs (*afʿāl nāqiṣa*).

composite expression [*al-lafẓ al-murakkab*] LOG 232 Expression whose parts signify parts of the expression's meaning. Opposed to the simple expression (*lafẓ mufrad*). (LTY 290) (JRT 487)

composite metaphor [*al-istiʿāra al-murakkaba*] MET 332 Composite expression used nonliterally for a meaning likened to its original meaning.

composite metonymy [*al-majāz al-mursal al-murakkab*] MET 319 Composite expression used nonliterally for a meaning or function other than its linguistically assigned meaning or function with a semantic link other than resemblance.

composite structure [*al-hayʾa al-tarkībiyya*] LTY 290 Syntactic, as opposed to simple, or morphological (*ifrādiyya*), expressional structure.

compound nouns [*al-murakkabāt*] GRA 160 Indeclinable nouns composed of two words between which there is no predicative relation.

conceded premises [*al-musallamāt*] LOG 268 Propositions conceded by an opponent. Used as premises in dialectical argument.

conception [*al-taṣawwur*] LOG 225 Knowledge, or apprehension (*idrāk*), that is unaccompanied by a judgment (*ḥukm*). Also termed *taṣawwur sādhaj* (pure conception) or "simple apprehension." JRT 481 Apprehension without a judgment.

conceptual correlation [*al-taḍāyuf* – "mutual relation; correlation"] LOG 249 Relation between two things such that the conception of either is contingent on the conception of the other.

conceptualized universal [*al-kullī al-ʿaqlī* – "the intellective universal"] LOG 240 Combination of a natural universal (*kullī ṭabīʿī*) and the logical concept of the universal (*kullī manṭiqī*); a universal quiddity considered as a universal.

conclusion [*al-natīja; al-maṭlūb* – "that which is produced; that which is sought"] LOG 257 Proposition that a syllogism intrinsically entails when its premises are accepted.

conclusive cause [*al-ʿilla al-qaṭʿiyya*] JRT 515 Something that is known to be the legal cause in a given original case conclusively, or with certainty. Opposed to a presumptive cause (*ʿilla ẓanniyya*).

conclusive consensus [*al-ijmāʿ al-qaṭʿī*] JRT 508 Consensus whose realization is agreed on by the relevant authorities. Opposed to presumptive consensus (*ijmāʿ ẓannī*).

conclusive indicant [*al-dalīl al-qaṭʿī*] JRT Indicant that imparts certainty, as opposed to a presumptive indicant (*dalīl ẓannī*).

concomitance [*al-iltizām*] LOG 228 An expression's signification of meanings that are mentally concomitant with its assigned meaning inasmuch as they are concomitant. JRT 486 An expression's signification of a meaning mentally concomitant with its meaning.

concordant metaphor [*al-istiʿāra al-wifāqiyya*] MET 325 Metaphor in which the combination of the objects of comparison is possible. (FIG 447)

condition [*al-sharṭ*] JRT 480 That whose absence entails a given thing's absence but whose presence entails neither its presence nor its absence.

condition clause [*jumlat al-sharṭ*] GRA 206 Verbal clause followed by the result clause (*jumlat al-jawāb*).

condition verb [*al-sharṭ* – "the condition"] GRA 132 Jussive verb followed by the jussive result verb.

conditional [*al-sharṭiyya*] MOR 50 A clause of the form *in faʿala* (if he does/did).

conditional particles [*ḥurūf al-sharṭ*] GRA 205 The particles *in*, *law*, and *ammā*.

conditional proposition [*qaḍiyya sharṭiyya muttaṣila* – "connected conditional proposition"] LOG 248–49 Hypothetical proposition that affirms that one sub-proposition or judgmental relation, whether affirmative or negative, follows from the truth of another, as in the form 'If A is B, then C is D'. Note that this describes the affirmative conditional proposition; negative conditional propositions negate such a relationship between two sub-propositions.

condivision [*al-qasīm* – "copart; counterpart"] DIA 364 A subdivision in relation to its counterpart subdivisions in a given division.

confutation [*al-naqḍ* – "undoing; destroying"] DIA 354 The objector's asserting the invalidity of the proponent's proof by arguing that the claim does not follow from the proof.

congruous implicature [*mafhūm al-muwāfaqa* – "understood meaning of agreement"] JRT 487 Implicature (*mafhūm*) that agrees with the articulated meaning.

conjointly weak root [*al-lafīf al-maqrūn* – "the conjointly gathered"] MOR 85 Root whose second and third radicals are weak letters.

conjunct [*al-maʿṭūf*] GRA 136, 148 Appositive conjoined by a conjunction (*ḥarf ʿaṭf*) to a primarily governed expression. A conjunct noun fully shares with the principal noun in a predication.

conjunction [*al-ʿaṭf* – "conjunction"] [*al-ʿaṭf bi-l-ḥurūf* – "conjunction by means of particles"] GRA 136, 148 Putting an expression that is directly preceded by a conjunction (*ḥarf ʿaṭf*) after a primarily governed expression, thereby making the second expression a secondarily governed conjunct (*maʿṭūf*). (SEM 402)

conjunctions [*ḥurūf al-ʿaṭf* – "the particles of conjunction"] GRA 192 The particles *wāw*, *fāʾ*, *thumma*, *ḥattā*, *aw*, *immā*, *am*, *lā*, *bal*, and *lākin*.

connected exception [*al-mustathnā al-muttaṣil*] GRA 152 Exception (*mustathnā*) that is excluded from a group. Opposed to the disconnected exception (*mustathnā munqaṭiʿ*).

connective *hamza* [*hamzat al-waṣl*] MOR *Hamza* added at the beginning of a word to facilitate pronunciation.

consecution [*al-taqrīb* – "bringing near"] DIA 349 The formulation of a given proof in a way that entails the claim.

consensus [*al-ijmāʿ*] JRT 508 One of the four primary indicants of jurisprudence; the agreement of the independent scholars of the *umma* after the passing of the Prophet (peace and blessings be upon him) at some time concerning some matter.

consequent [*al-tālī* – "the following"] LOG 248 Second part of a hypothetical proposition.

consideration of fundamental necessity [*al-munāsib al-ḍarūrī* – "that which is suitable and relates to necessity"] JRT 520 Type of suitable legal consideration (*munāsib*) that consists in the preservation of the religion, life, intellect, lineage, wealth, or honor.

consideration of practical benefit [*al-munāsib al-taḥsīnī* – "that which is suitable and relates to betterment or amelioration"] JRT 521 Type of suitable legal consideration (*munāsib*) that consists in the securing of benefits that are not necessary but are deemed good by custom.

consideration of practical necessity [*al-munāsib al-ḥājī* – "that which is suitable and relates to need"] JRT 520 Type of suitable legal consideration (*munāsib*) that consists in the securing of things that are needed but not to the point of fundamental necessity.

constitutive differentia [*al-faṣl al-muqawwim*] LOG 237 Differentia insofar as it constitutes the essence of a thing, distinguishing it from other things. Opposed to the divisive differentia (*faṣl muqassim*).

containment [*al-taḍammun*] LOG 227 An expression's signification of meanings that are contained within its assigned meaning inasmuch as they are contained. JRT 486 An expression's signification of a part of its meaning.

contentious disputation [*al-mushāghaba*] LOG 270 As defined in the text: a syllogism composed of false estimative premises posited by the estimative faculty with respect to matters that are not sensible. Alternatively: a syllogism composed of false premises that are deceptively similar to the commonplace premises that a genuine disputant would use. Used as premises in fallacious argument neither for the sake of truth nor to elicit concession.

contextual indicant [*al-qarīna* – "evidence; context"] MET 313, 320 In general, something that indicates or determines a meaning by context rather than assignment. With respect to figurative language, something in a given context that indicates that the assigned, normal, or proper meaning could not have been intended. (SEM 391) (FIG 444, 446)

contradiction (1) [*al-tanāquḍ*] LOG 253 Relation of difference between two propositions in affirmation and negation in a way that inherently mandates that one be true and one false.

contradiction (2) [*al-taʿādul* – "equivalence; mutual counterbalancing"] JRT 528 That two indicants each negate the other.

conversion (1) [*al-ʿaks al-mustawī* – "straight inversion"] LOG 254 Mutual transposition of the extremes of a proposition in a way that preserves its truth and quality.

conversion (2) [*al-qalb* – "transformation"] MOR Phonetic change undergone by some words in modification (*iʿlāl*) by the replacement of one vowel or letter with another.

copula [*al-rābiṭa*] LOG 248 The part of a proposition that signifies the relation (*nisba*).

corporeal object [*al-jism* – "body"] CRD 550 Substance (*jawhar*) with three spatial dimensions; physical body.

correct belief [*al-iʿtiqād al-ṣaḥīḥ*] JRT 481 Assent that is susceptible to change but held with conviction and corresponds to reality.

correspondence [*al-muṭābaqa*] LOG 227 An expression's signification of its complete assigned meaning inasmuch as it is complete. JRT 486 An expression's signification of its complete meaning.

corroboration [*al-sanad* – "support"] DIA 346 Assertion made by one issuing a challenge (*manʿ*) on the grounds that the assertion allegedly entails the contradictory of the challenged premise.

counter implicature [*mafhūm al-mukhālafa* – "understood meaning of disagreement"] JRT 487 Implicature (*mafhūm*) that disagrees with the articulated meaning.

counteraction [*al-muʿāraḍa* – "opposing; contending"] DIA 349, 351 The objector's proving a proposition that is the contradictory of the proponent's supported claim, coextensive with the contradictory, or narrower (i.e., more specific) than the contradictory.

counteraction by like [*al-muʿāraḍa bi-l-mithl*] DIA 353 Counteraction (*muʿāraḍa*) through a proof that is different in matter from the proponent's proof but identical to it in form.

counteraction by reversal [*al-muʿāraḍa bi-l-qalb*] DIA 352 Counteraction (*muʿāraḍa*) through a proof that is identical in both matter and form to the proponent's proof. Also called simply "reversal" (*qalb*).
counteraction by unlike [*al-muʿāraḍa bi-l-ghayr*] DIA 353 Counteraction (*muʿāraḍa*) through a proof that is different in form from the proponent's proof, whether or not it is identical to it in matter.
counterfactual hypothetical [*al-imtināʿiyya* – "that which relates to impossibility"] MOR 51 A clause of the form *law faʿala* (if he had done). Expresses a counterfactual condition.
counterpart nunation [*tanwīn al-muqābala*] GRA 211 Nunation of the sound feminine plural that is a counterpart to the *nūn* of the sound masculine plural.

D

damned [*shaqī* – "wretched"] CRD 551 One who Allah the Exalted has eternally decreed will die a disbeliever.
declarative [*khabarī* – "informative"] LOG 232 Related to or serving to constitute a statement or proposition, that is, an "information-bearing" or "truth apt" composite expression, or an expression that can be true or false. (LTY 292) (SEM 385)
declarative expression [*khabar* – "information; report"] LOG 232 Complete expression that bears truth or falsity; a statement or proposition (*qaḍiyya*).
declarative predication [*al-isnād al-khabarī*] SEM 385 To bring together a word or anything that has the function of a word with another, thereby indicating the affirmation or negation of the meaning of one with respect to the meaning of the other.
declinable noun [*al-ism al-muʿrab*] GRA 145 Noun whose inflection varies by means of governors.
deductive division [*al-taqsīm al-ʿaqlī* – "rational division"] DIA 365 Division that proceeds by alternating between affirmation and negation such that the intellect does not allow another subdivision.
defective root [*al-nāqiṣ* – "the deficient"] [*muʿtall al-lām* – "that which has a weak *lām*"] MOR 79 Root whose third radical is a weak letter.
definite *lām* [*lām al-taʿrīf*] GRA 208 Vowelless *lām* that makes a noun grammatically definite.
definite noun [*al-maʿrifa*] GRA 162 Noun that indicates a thing with specificity. Opposed to the indefinite noun (*nakira*).
definition [*al-taʿrīf*] LOG 243 That whose conception causes one to acquire conception of a thing in its essence or in some nonessential aspect that distinguishes it from all else. Also termed a *muʿarrif* (definiens) or a *qawl shāriḥ* (explanatory composite phrase or concept).
deflated metaphor [*al-istiʿāra al-mujarrada* – "divested metaphor"] MET 329 Metaphor that is accompanied by what suits the tenor. (FIG 451)
demonstration [*al-burhān*] LOG 227 Indicant (*dalīl*) that imparts knowledge (*ʿilm*) that is certain. Also called a "demonstrative proof" (*dalīl burhānī*).
demonstrative argument [*al-burhān*] LOG 265 Syllogism consisting of two certain premises (*yaqīniyyāt*). Of the five arts (*al-ṣināʿāt al-khams*), the one whose purpose is to yield certainty.
demonstrative pronoun [*ism al-ishāra*] GRA 158 Indeclinable noun whose lexically assigned function is to signify a thing that is physically pointed to.
demonstrative proof [*dalīl burhānī*] LOG 227 Indicant (*dalīl*) that imparts knowledge (*ʿilm*) that is certain. Also called a "demonstration" (*burhān*).
denotation [*al-mawḍūʿ lahu* – "that to or for

which the assignment is made"] LTY 282 In the relation of assignment (*waḍʿ*), the thing to which another is assigned such that it is understood whenever the assigned thing is understood by someone aware of the assignation.

derivative case [*al-farʿ* – "the branch"] JRT 514 One of the four components of analogy (*qiyās*); the case to which the ruling of the original case is extended.

derivatives [*al-amthila* – "the patterns"] MOR 39 Words derived from the infinitive noun (*maṣdar*), sharing its lexical root, or matter (*mādda*), but bearing different forms that signify various relations affecting the meaning of the abstract notion signified by the infinitive noun.

destiny [*al-qadar*] CRD 550 Every eternally decreed thing or event, including the good and evil acts of humans.

detached pronoun [*al-ḍamīr al-munfaṣil*] GRA 158 Personal pronoun that stands as a separate word. Opposed to the attached pronoun (*ḍamīr muttaṣil*).

dialectical argument [*al-jadal* – "disputation"] LOG 267–68 Syllogism consisting of commonplace or conceded premises. Of the five arts (*al-ṣināʿāt al-khams*), the one whose purpose is to defeat the opponent or to convince someone who is incapable of apprehending the premises of a demonstrative argument.

dialectical disputation [*al-munāẓara* – "exchanging opinions"] DIA 343 Process of mutual rebuttal between an objector and proponent to manifest the truth. Distinguished from mere disputation (*jadal*), whose purpose is not necessarily to manifest the truth.

dialectics [*ʿilm al-munāẓara*] DIA 343 Science by which one knows what constitutes a sound or unsound rebuttal in a disputation for the purpose of manifesting the truth.

differentia [*al-faṣl* – "separation; division"] LOG 236 Essential universal that is predicated of a thing in response to the question "What kind of thing is it essentially?" One of the five universals.

diminutive noun [*ism al-taṣghīr*] MOR 42, 44 Derivative noun form; two examples are *nuṣayrun* and *ukayrimun*. GRA 165 Signifies smallness. LTY 290, 292 Form assigned to signify an entity possessed of a small amount of a quality.

direct differentia [*al-faṣl al-qarīb* – "proximate differentia"] LOG 236 Differentia that distinguishes the thing from things with the same direct genus. Opposed to the remote differentia (*faṣl baʿīd*).

direct genus [*al-jins al-qarīb* – "proximate genus"] LOG 235 Genus that is correctly given in response to the question "What are they?" asked about every quiddity under a given genus. Opposed to the remote genus (*jins baʿīd*).

direct implication [*al-kināya al-qarība* – "proximate implication"] MET 335 Implication (*kināya*) by which an attribute is implied and understood without intermediate steps of inference. (FIG 457)

direct indication [*al-īmāʾ*] FIG 459 Implication (*kināya*) that, like pointing (*ishāra*), involves few intermediate steps of inference on the part of the listener and does not contain obscurity.

directly entailed signification [*dalālat al-īmāʾ* – "signification of indication"] JRT 486 Signification by concomitance of a meaning that is integral to the intent.

disambiguated noun [*al-ism al-mubham al-tāmm* – "the complete ambiguous noun"] GRA 127 Ambiguous noun whose meaning is completed by means of nunation, the *nūn* of the dual, the *nūn* of the quasi-plural, or *iḍāfa*. Governs the specifying noun (*tamyīz*), making it accusative.

disconnected exception [*al-mustathnā al-munqaṭiʿ*] GRA 153 Exception (*mustathnā*) that is not excluded from a group. Opposed to the connected exception (*mustathnā muttaṣil*).

discordant metaphor [*al-istiʿāra al-ʿinādiyya*] MET 325 Metaphor in which the combination of the objects of comparison is impossible. (FIG 447)

disjointly weak root [*al-lafīf al-mafrūq* – "the disjointly gathered"] MOR 84 Root whose first and third radicals are weak letters.

disjunct [*al-juzʾ* – "the part"] LOG Sub-proposition in a disjunctive proposition.

disjunctive proposition [*al-qaḍiyya al-sharṭiyya al-munfaṣila* – "disconnected conditional proposition"] LOG 249–51 Hypothetical proposition that affirms that one sub-proposition or judgmental relation, whether affirmative or negative, is in some kind of disjunction, or incongruity, with another, as in the form 'Either A is B or C is D'. Note that this describes the affirmative disjunctive proposition; negative disjunctive propositions negate such a relationship between two sub-propositions.

dispensation [*al-rukhṣa*] JRT 480 Ruling whose application is relaxed on account of an excuse despite the existence of its cause.

displaying what is desired [*iẓhār al-maṭlūb*] MET 309 Using a simile as a means to display one's interest in the vehicle.

disputative rebuttal [*al-jawāb al-ilzāmī* – "response of forcing concession"] DIA 358 Rebuttal founded on a premise that the opponent accepts even though the disputant offering it believes it to be false. Opposed to a verificatory rebuttal (*jawāb taḥqīqī*).

disqualifying factor [*al-qādiḥ*] JRT 521 Something pertaining to any of the components of an analogy that disqualifies it.

dissonance [*tanāfur al-ḥurūf* – "the disharmony of the letters"] [*tanāfur al-kalimāt* – "the disharmony of the words"] SEM 378–79 Defect that vitiates the articulateness (*faṣāḥa*) of words or speech when it is difficult to pronounce the constituent letters or words in combination.

dividendum [*al-maqsim* – "place or locus of division"] DIA 364 A universal or whole as divided into particulars or parts. This term is borrowed from Latin, in analogy with "definiendum," for its utility.

divisive differentia [*al-faṣl al-muqassim*] LOG 237 Differentia insofar as it divides all the genera of a thing, distinguishing all else from the thing. Opposed to the constitutive differentia (*faṣl muqawwim*).

double entendre [*al-tawriya* – "concealment; dissimulation"] EMB 464 To use an expression with two meanings, one immediate and one remote, and intend the remote meaning.

doubled root [*al-muḍāʿaf*] MOR 52 In triliteral classes, a root whose second and third radicals are the same. In quadriliteral classes, a root whose first and third radicals are the same and whose second and fourth radicals are the same.

doubly privative proposition [*al-qaḍiyya al-maʿdūlat al-ṭarafayn* – "proposition whose extremes are diverted"] LOG 248 Proposition in which a negative particle is part of the subject and a negative particle is part of the predicate.

doubt [*al-shakk*] JRT 481 Apprehension of a judgmental relation without any preponderance in favor of either its truth or its falsity.

dual noun [*al-muthannā*] GRA 160 Noun ending in *-āni* or *-ayni* to signify duality.

E

echo [*radd al-ʿajuz ʿalā al-ṣadr* – "bringing the rear back to the front"] EMB 468 To place at the beginning of a segment of speech one and at its end the other of a pair of words that make up a repetition, a paronomasia, or a device appended to paronomasia.

effort [*al-takalluf*] MOR 31n1 The signification of undertaking to gradually bring about an outcome, as sometimes carried by the pattern *tafaʿʿala*, for example.

eight unities [*al-waḥadāt al-thamānī*] LOG 253 The aspects in which two propositions must concur as a condition for their being contradictories of each other: subject, predicate, time, place, relation, potentiality and actuality, part and whole, and condition. This is not an exhaustive list; other relevant unities can be thought of, like cause, instrument, and so forth. As a totality, all of these unities can be collapsed into one unity, namely, that of the judgmental relation (*nisba ḥukmiyya*).

elision [*al-ḥadhf*] MOR Phonetic change undergone by some words in modification (*iʿlāl*) by the omission of a vowel or letter.

eloquence [*al-balāgha* – "arriving at or attaining an end"] SEM 381 When used to describe speech, the correspondence of that speech to what the situation calls for, that is, the rhetorical effectiveness of the speech. When used to describe a speaker, a proficiency in composing such speech. The term *balāgha* is also used to denote the science (*ʿilm al-balāgha*, or "rhetoric") that studies the principles of eloquence and thus includes rhetorical semantics (*ʿilm al-maʿānī*), figurative language (*ʿilm al-bayān*), and embellishment (*ʿilm al-badīʿ*).

embellishment [*ʿilm al-badīʿ* – "the science of what is original and wonderful"] EMB 463 Within the larger science of rhetoric (*balāgha*), the discipline that studies the ways to beautify language. (SEM 383)

embellishments [*al-muḥassināt al-badīʿiyya* – "embellishments relating to the original and wonderful"] SEM 382 Linguistic devices by which speech is beautified. Studied in the discipline, or science, of embellishment (*ʿilm al-badīʿ*). (EMB 469)

emphasis [*al-taʾkīd; al-tawkīd*] GRA 137, 147 Appositive (*tābiʿ*) that gives confirmation to the principal noun (*matbūʿ*) with respect to the predication or with respect to its inclusiveness. (SEM 401)

emphatic apposition [*al-taʾkīd; al-tawkīd*] GRA 137, 147 Rendering an expression an emphasis (*taʾkīd*). (SEM 401)

emphatic *nūn* [*al-nūn al-muʾakkida*] GRA 209 Particle suffixed to a future verb that contains the meaning of a request or oath, emphasizing it. The *nūn* can be heavy, as in *iḍribanna*, or light, as in *iḍriban*.

enriching [*al-tatmīm* – "completing"] SEM 431 To make an addition to one's speech for a fine purpose like amplification when the speech would not have been susceptible to misunderstanding anyway.

entreaty [*al-suʾāl*] LOG 233 Non-declarative speech that deferentially expresses a request that someone bring about or abstain from something. Also called "supplication" (*duʿāʾ*).

epiphonema [*al-tadhyīl* – "appending"] SEM 431 To emphasize a point made in one sentence by following it up with another that comprises the same meaning.

epiphrase [*al-īghāl* – "traveling far; pushing onward"] SEM 431 To end one's speech by adding a fine point without which the meaning would still have been complete.

equilibrium [*al-muwāzana*] EMB 469 That a pair of final words have the same pattern.

equivocal expression [*al-mushtarak al-lafẓī* – "that whose utterance is shared"] LOG 230 Simple expression that possesses multiple meanings to which it was distinctly assigned. LTY 295 Single expression assigned to two or more meanings, whether each meaning is particular, each universal, or some particular and some universal. JRT 488 Expression that applies literally to multiple meanings.

essential universal [*al-kullī al-dhātī*] LOG 234–35 Universal that is not external to the essence of its particulars. Opposed to the accidental universal (*kullī ʿaraḍī*).

essentially inseparable accident [*lāzim al-māhiyya* – "that which is inseparable from the quiddity"] LOG 238 Accident that is inseparable from a given thing both in extramental existence and in the mind.

eternality [*al-qidam*] CRD 550 Existence without

beginning.

evidence [*al-shāhid*] DIA 355 Proof for a confutation.

evident analogy [*al-qiyās al-jalī*] JRT 523 Legal analogy in which it is definitively or nearly definitively known that there is no discrepancy between the original case and the derivative case.

evil-inciting soul [*al-nafs al-ammāra bi-l-sū'*] SPR 569 Aspect of the human soul that incites it to do what is evil.

exception [*al-mustathnā* – "that which is excepted"] GRA 135, 152 Accusative noun that follows *illā* or one of its sisters.

exceptive particles [*ḥurūf al-istithnā'*] GRA 199 The particles *illā*, *khalā*, *ʿadā*, and *ḥāshā*; according to the majority view, however, *khalā* and *ʿadā* are verbs.

excessive hyperbole [*al-ghulū* – "exceeding the limits"] EMB 467 Hyperbole that is rationally impossible and hence not considered acceptable hyperbole (*mubālagha maqbūla*).

exhaustiveness [*al-ḥaṣr*] DIA 364 Another term for a division's being sufficiently inclusive.

existential proposition [*al-qaḍiyya al-wujūdiyya*] LOG 248 Another term for a non-privative (*muḥaṣṣala*) proposition.

expected mode of expression [*al-ikhrāj ʿalā muqtaḍā al-ẓāhir* – "expressing according to the dictates of what is apparent"] SEM 386 Expressing a judgment (*ḥukm*) in a way that aligns with the apparent situation, that is, with the degree of emphasis appropriate for initiating, answering, or insisting.

experiential premises [*al-mujarrabāt*] LOG 266 Class of certain propositions (*yaqīniyyāt*) that are judged to be true by means of repeated observation; used as premises in demonstrative argument.

explained [*al-mufassar*] JRT 495 Expression or action brought from a state of uncertainty to a state of clarity. Opposed to the indeterminate (*mujmal*).

explicit inflection [*al-iʿrāb al-lafẓī* – "verbally expressed inflection"] GRA 143 Inflection that appears in the expression.

explicit metaphor [*al-istiʿāra al-muṣarraḥa*] MET 321 Metaphor in which the vehicle is mentioned but the tenor intended. Opposed to the implicit metaphor (*istiʿāra makniyya*).

expressed contextual indicant [*al-qarīna al-lafẓiyya*] SEM 391 Verbally expressed contextual indicant of nonliteral predication.

expressed governor [*al-ʿāmil al-lafẓī* – "the utterance-based maker or effector"] GRA 125 Governor that is verbally expressed; opposed to the abstract governor (*ʿāmil maʿnawī*).

expression with verbal import [*maʿnā al-fiʿl* – "the meaning of the verb"] GRA 127 Expression from which the meaning of a verb is understood.

expressive of ability [*al-qudratiyya*] MOR 51 The modal verb construction *yaqdiru an yafʿala* (he can do).

expressive of exhortation [*al-taḥḍīḍiyya*] MOR 51 The verbal construction *hallā yafʿalu* (why does he not do?).

expressive of hope [*al-rajā'iyya*] MOR 51 The verbal construction *laʿallahu faʿala* (perhaps he will do).

expressive of obligation or necessity [*al-wujūbiyya*] MOR 51 The modal verb construction *lā budda an yafʿala* (he must do).

expressive of persistence [*al-dā'imiyya*] MOR 50 The modal verb construction *mā zāla yafʿalu* (he continues doing; he still does).

expressive of reproach [*al-tandībiyya*] MOR 51 The verbal construction *hallā faʿala* (why did he not do?).

expressive of the place [*al-maḥalliyya*] MOR 50 A clause of the form *ḥaythu faʿala* (where he did). Often used to mean "in view of the fact that he did."

expressive of the point of termination [*al-intihā'iyya*] MOR 51 A clause of the form *ḥattā faʿala* (until he did; to the point that he did).

expressive of the time [*al-tawqītiyya*] MOR 50 A clause of the form *ḥīna faʿala* (when he did).

expressive of the time of commencement [*al-ibtidāʾiyya*] MOR 51 A clause of the form *mundhu faʿala* (since he did).

expressive of what is proper or appropriate [*al-liyāqatiyya*] MOR 51 The modal verb construction *yanbaghī an yafʿala* (he should do).

expressive of wish [*al-tamanniyya*] MOR 51 The verbal construction *laytahu faʿala* (would that he had done).

extended subdivision [*al-qism al-mursal* – "unbound part"] DIA 365 Subdivision whose intension (i.e., conceptual meaning) is applicable not only to the instances of the subdivision that have actually been identified by induction but also to any hypothetical instance that does not have another distinct place in the division. In plainer words, the subdivision that includes "everything else" that is not expressly included by the other subdivisions.

extension [*al-mā-ṣadaq* – "the it-is-true-of-it] [*al-miṣdāq* – the truth-criterion"] LOG The things to which a concept or term applies.

extraction [*al-tajrīd*] FIG 441 To hyperbolically extract, or derive, from something that possesses a certain attribute another thing with the same attribute, thereby emphasizing the extent to which the original possesses the attribute. For example, the sentence "I saw in Zayd a lion" emphasizes Zayd's courage by "extracting" from him an animal known for courage. This device is studied in the science of embellishment (*badīʿ*).

extraction of the basis [*takhrīj al-manāṭ*] JRT 519 Determining a legal cause by revealing the mutual suitability (*munāsaba*) between a given ruling and a concomitant factor that might serve as its basis (*manāṭ*), or cause.

extramentally inseparable accident [*al-lāzim al-wujūdī* – "the existential inseparable"] LOG 238 Accident that is inseparable from a given thing in extramental existence.

extravagant hyperbole [*al-ighrāq* – "taking something to its full extent"] EMB 467 Hyperbole that is possible rationally but not by normative experience (*ʿāda*); considered to be an acceptable kind of hyperbole (*mubālagha maqbūla*).

F

fabricated report [*al-mawḍūʿ* – "that which is placed or posited"] JRT 499–500 Report that is not true of the Prophet ﷺ.

fallacious argument [*al-mughālaṭa*] LOG 270 Syllogism consisting of premises of sophistry (*safsaṭa*) or contentious disputation (*mushāghaba*); unsound either due to its form or due to its matter. Of the five arts (*al-ṣināʿāt al-khams*), the one whose purpose is to make an opponent appear to be wrong.

fanciful metaphor [*al-istiʿāra al-takhyīliyya* – "imaginative borrowing"] MET 322 Explicit metaphor (*istiʿāra muṣarraḥa*) whose tenor has no actual sensible or intelligible reality but is rather a merely fanciful, or imagined, image. Part of al-Sakkākī's classification of metaphors; opposed to the actual metaphor (*istiʿāra taḥqīqiyya*).

fancy [*al-wahm*] JRT 481 Apprehension of a judgmental relation whose falsity is preponderant, that is, whose truth is less probable. The term *wahm* can also refer to the faculty that is sometimes termed the "estimation" or "estimative faculty." (LOG 270) (MET 322)

far-removed implication [*al-kināya al-baʿīda* – "remote implication"] MET 335 Implication (*kināya*) by which an attribute is implied and understood through intermediate steps of inference. (FIG 380)

feminine noun [*al-ism al-muʾannath*] GRA 163 Noun possessing the *tāʾ* of femininity or one of the *alif*s of femininity.

figurative language [*ʿilm al-bayān* – "the science of clear expression"] FIG 440 Within the larger science of rhetoric (*balāgha*), the discipline that studies how to express meanings in language with different degrees of plainness, from the overt to the subtle. SEM 383 Within the larger science of rhetoric, the discipline that studies how to avoid overcomplication in meaning (*taʿqīd maʿnawī*).

figure [*al-shakl*] LOG 257 The form of the composition of the minor and major premises, that is, the configuration that results from the respective positions of the minor and major terms in a syllogism.

forced concession [*al-ilzām*] DIA 370 The failure of the objector to sustain objections to the responses of the proponent in a disputation.

foregrounding [*al-taqdīm* – "making precede"] SEM 402 Putting an element before others: in the case of foregrounding the subject, putting the subject first; in the case of foregrounding the predicate, putting the predicate first.

forsaking [*al-khidhlān*] CRD 552 Allah's creating in someone the ability to disobey Him ﷻ.

fully declinable noun [*al-munṣarif* – "the variable"] GRA 145 Declinable noun that takes genitive inflections and nunation; triptote, as opposed to the partially declinable (*ghayr munṣarif*) noun.

G

general accident [*al-ʿaraḍ al-ʿāmm*] LOG 238 Accidental universal that is predicable of, or applies to, multiple essences. One of the five universals.

general assignment [*al-waḍʿ al-ʿāmm* – "general assignment"] [*al-waḍʿ al-kullī* – "universal assignment"] LTY Assignment of an expression or structure to denotations or meanings considered by means of a general, or universal (*kullī*), concept. That is, in general assignment, the assigner's meaning (*ālat al-waḍʿ*) is a universal concept, regardless whether the expression is assigned to a universal meaning or to particulars that fall under that universal concept. Opposed to specific assignment (*waḍʿ khāṣṣ*).

general convention [*al-ʿurf al-ʿāmm*] LOG 230 The customary usage of the users of the language in general—without restriction to a specific group, art, or discipline—insofar as it influences the transfer of the original lexical meanings of expressions to new meanings. General convention is sometimes referred to simply as "convention" (*ʿurf*). (MET 315) (FIG 444) (JRT 489)

general expression [*al-lafẓ al-ʿāmm*] LOG 230 Simple expression that comprehends everything to which it is applicable without restriction. Although the author introduces this classification in the treatise on logic, it typically appears in texts of jurisprudential theory. (JRT 490)

general indicants of jurisprudence [*adillat al-fiqh al-ijmāliyya*] JRT 478 Indicants that are not determinative (*ghayr muʿayyina*), meaning that they are high-level principles that do not specifically determine the actual rulings of law, as opposed to the specific indicants of jurisprudence (*adillat al-fiqh al-tafṣīliyya*).

generic *iḍāfa* structure [*al-iḍāfa al-jinsiyya*] LTY 292 *Iḍāfa* structure by which the generic kind is signified.

generic *lām* [*lām al-jins*] GRA 208 Definite *lām* by which the noun signifies the generic kind.

generic noun [*ism al-jins*] GRA 145 Noun that signifies something and all that is like it in essence.

generic proper name [*al-ʿalam al-jinsī*] JRT 488 Proper name that applies to a category insofar as it is conceived specifically in the mind. (LTY 283)

genitive [*al-majrūr* – "the dragged"] GRA 135, 154 Noun in the genitive case.

genus [*al-jins*] LOG 235 Essential universal that can be predicated of multiple things that have different essences in response to a question asking what they are. One of the five universals.

genus of genera [*jins al-ajnās*] LOG 235 Another term for a highest genus (*jins ʿālī*).

giving preponderance [*al-tarjīḥ*] JRT 529 To judge one of two presumptive indicants stronger than the other.

good act [*al-ḥasan*] JRT 481 Act that merits praise.

governance [*ʿamal* – "activity; work"] GRA 124 The effect or influence of a governor on a governed expression, reflected in the latter's inflection. The term *ʿamal* is sometimes used as a synonym for inflection (*iʿrāb*).

governed expression [*al-maʿmūl* – "the made"] GRA 133 Expression on which a governor has an effect, whether the effect be explicit, implicit, or positional.

governor [*al-ʿāmil* – "the maker or effector"] GRA 124 That which mandates a specific kind of inflection at the end of a word.

grace [*al-luṭf* – "gentleness; kindness"] CRD 552 Allah's creating in someone the ability to obey Him.

grammar [*ʿilm al-naḥw*] GRA 123 Science of principles (*uṣūl*) concerning word endings in terms of inflection (*iʿrāb*) and the absence of inflection, or indeclinability (*bināʾ*). Gelibolī, *Tuḥfat al-ikhwān*, 62–63. This science could also be named "syntax" to distinguish it from morphology (*ʿilm al-ṣarf*), since the term "grammar" is sometimes used as a general and inclusive term that includes both morphology and syntax.

ground for comparison [*wajh al-tashbīh; wajh al-shabah* – "the aspect of comparison; the aspect of similarity"] MET 306 The point of similarity shared by the objects compared in a simile; one of the four components of simile. Abbreviated as "ground." (FIG 442)

H

***hāʾ* of pause** [*hāʾ al-sakt*] GRA 210 *Hāʾ* added to words ending in a non-inflectional short vowel when one pauses after pronouncing the word.

hamzated root [*al-mahmūz*] MOR 88 Root containing the letter *hamza*.

highest genus [*al-jins al-ʿālī*] LOG 235 Genus without a superior, or higher, genus above it in the hierarchical ordering of all genera. Also called a "genus of genera" (*jins al-ajnās*).

highest species [*al-nawʿ al-ʿālī*] LOG 236 Species without a superior, or higher, species above it in the hierarchical ordering of all species.

hinting [*al-talwīḥ*] FIG 459 Implication (*kināya*) that involves many intermediate steps of inference on the part of the listener.

hollow root [*al-ajwaf*] MOR 62 Root whose second radical is a weak letter.

hypothetical proposition [*al-qaḍiyya al-sharṭiyya* – "the conditional proposition"] LOG 248 Proposition whose extremes are not simple, meaning that they could stand as propositions on their own. Opposed to the categorical proposition (*qaḍiyya ḥamliyya*).

I

iḍāfa [*al-iḍāfa* – "subjoining; annexing"] GRA 135, 155 Construction in which the first noun, the *muḍāf*, puts the second noun, the *muḍāf ilayhi*, into the genitive case. Divided into attributive *iḍāfa* and nonattributive *iḍāfa*.

ijtihad [*al-ijtihād* – "diligent exertion"] JRT 535 A

qualified jurist's expenditure of his utmost effort to attain presumptive knowledge of a legal ruling.

imaginative premises [*al-mukhayyilāt* – "those which elicit images"] LOG 269 Propositions that have either an appealing effect or a repelling effect, enticing the soul or turning it away. Used as premises in poetical argument.

imitation [*al-taqlīd* – "adorning; investing with authority"] JRT 538 To adopt the position of another without complete knowledge of its evidence or proof. (CRD 549)

imitator [*al-muqallid*] JRT 538–39 Someone who is not an independent jurist and must therefore defer to the legal positions of others.

immediate [*al-ḍarūrī* – "the necessary"] LOG 225 Category of knowledge, including both conception and assent, that is obtained without the process of reflective reasoning or thought.

impediment [*al-māniʿ*] JRT 480 Feature of a given case that prevents a given ruling from applying.

imperative [*al-amr*] MOR 40–41, 44 {"the command"} Derivative verb form (as in *unṣur*) or construction (as in *li-yanṣur*). GRA 177 Verb form or construction that indicates a command, or the request to do something.

imperative *lām* [*lām al-amr* – "the *lām* of command"] GRA 131, 177, 209 The particle *lām* with *kasr*; a prefix that makes an imperfect tense verb jussive. One of the ways of constructing an imperative verb (*amr*).

imperative proper [*al-amr bi-l-ṣīgha*] MOR 44, 66, 69 {"the command by form"} The distinctive imperative verb form used for the second person, as opposed to the third-person imperative formed by prefixing the imperative *lām*. (GRA 177)

imperfect tense verb [*al-fiʿl al-muḍāriʿ*] MOR 40, 43 {"the resembling verb"} Derivative verb form; two examples are *yanṣuru* and *yukrimu*. GRA 172 Signifies action in the present or future. Named *muḍāriʿ* (resembling) because it resembles the active participle (*ism al-fāʿil*).

implicant [*al-malzūm* – "the clung-to or attached-to"] LOG Something that implies or entails another thing, which is called an implicate (*lāzim*): whenever the implicant is true or exists, the implicate is true or exists.

implicate [*al-lāzim* – "that which clings, attaches, or is inseparable"] LOG Something that is implied by, entailed by, or concomitant to another thing, which is called the implicant (*malzūm*): whenever the implicant is true or exists, the implicate is true or exists. An implicate can also be called an "implication," but we avoid this where it might lead to confusion with *luzūm*, or the *relationship* of implication. *Lāzim* could also be translated as "concomitant" or "that which is entailed" (or "entailment," though, like "implication," this could cause confusion in some contexts).

implication [*al-kināya*] MET 334 Use of an expression to indicate an implicate (*lāzim*) of its proper, or assigned, meaning in a case where the proper meaning itself is valid. The term *kināya* can also refer to the implicative expression itself. JRT 490 Expression used in its literal sense in order to have the listener infer an implicate, i.e., a concomitant meaning. (FIG 456)

implication of the information [*lāzim fāʾidat al-khabar* – "that which is inseparable from the benefit of the report"] SEM 385 An addressee's knowledge of the fact that the speaker knows the judgment conveyed in a declarative sentence insofar as the addressee's knowledge of this fact is the aim of the speaker.

implicature [*al-mafhūm* – "that which is understood"] JRT 485–86 A meaning that an expression signifies without actually articulating. Opposed to an articulated meaning (*manṭūq*).

implicit inflection [*al-iʿrāb al-taqdīrī*] GRA 143 Inflection that is implicit in the ending of a word but lacks verbal expression.

implicit metaphor [*al-istiʿāra al-makniyya*] MET

321 Metaphor where the tenor (rather than the vehicle) is explicitly mentioned, but it is characterized as if it were the vehicle. (FIG 453)

incapacity [*al-ʿajz*] SPR 570 Attribute that is the contrary opposite (*ḍidd*) of power (*qudra*).

incomplete composite expression [*al-lafẓ al-murakkab al-nāqiṣ*] LOG 232 Composite expression after whose utterance it would be invalid to stop speaking since the expression does not convey a complete thought on its own. (LTY 290)

incomplete descriptive definition [*al-rasm al-nāqiṣ* – "the deficient description"] LOG 244 Definition with accidental elements that is not composed specifically of the direct genus and an inseparable special accident.

incomplete essential definition [*al-ḥadd al-nāqiṣ* – "the deficient definition"] LOG 243 Definition composed of a remote genus and the direct differentia.

incorrect belief [*al-iʿtiqād al-fāsid*] JRT 481 Assent that is held with conviction, is susceptible to change, and does not correspond to reality.

indeclinable noun [*al-ism al-mabnī* – "the built noun"] GRA 156 Noun whose ending does not vary by means of governors.

indefinite noun [*al-nakira*] GRA 163 Noun that indicates a thing without specificity. Opposed to the definite noun (*maʿrifa*). (LOG 230)

indefinite nunation [*tanwīn al-tankīr*] GRA 211 Nunation that indicates that the noun is indefinite as in *ṣahin*.

indeterminate [*al-mujmal*] JRT 495 Expression or action whose legal signification is unclear; may be clarified by explanation (*tafsīr*).

indicant [*al-dalīl*] JRT 481 Something that can lead one to draw a declarative, or propositional, conclusion if one reflects about it correctly. (LOG 227)

indirectly entailed signification [*dalālat al-ishāra*] JRT 486 Subdivision of signification by concomitance in which the signified meaning is neither textually required nor integral to the intent of the speaker.

individual assignment [*al-waḍʿ al-shakhṣī*] LTY 283 Category of assignment in which what is assigned is a single expression, or a word. Opposed to collective assignment (*waḍʿ nawʿī*).

inductive division [*al-taqsīm al-istiqrāʾī*] DIA 365 Division where the intellect allows the possibility of other subdivisions, the ones listed in the division being simply those identified by induction.

inevident inseparable accident [*al-ʿaraḍ al-lāzim ghayr al-bayyin*] LOG 239 Inseparable accident whose inseparability can only be known with certainty by means of proof.

infinitive noun [*al-maṣdar* – "the source"] GRA 126, 168 Noun from which verbs and nouns related to verbs are derived; signifies the action abstracted from any particular time or agent; can take on the governance of its corresponding verbs. (MOR 39)

infinitive noun of kind [*maṣdar bināʾ al-nawʿ*] MOR 41, 44 {"the source of the form of the kind"] Derivative noun form; an example is *niṣratan*. Signifies an action with respect to a specific kind of that action, abstracted from any particular time or agent. In non-triliteral classes, this meaning can only be obtained through the mediation of additional words, like the adjective in *ikrāmatan ʿāẓīmatan*.

infinitive particles [*al-ḥurūf al-maṣdariyya*] GRA 202 Particles that precede verbal clauses, giving the entire clause the meaning and syntactic role of a simple infinitive noun.

inflated metaphor [*al-istiʿāra al-murashshaḥa* – "the nurtured or strengthened metaphor"] MET 329 Explicit metaphor that is built up and taken further by means of descriptions or qualifications that suit the vehicle. (FIG 451)

inflection [*al-iʿrāb* – "making clear"] GRA 138 Variations in the ending of an inflectable expression that are determined by governors.

information [*fāʾidat al-khabar* – "the benefit of the report or declaration"] SEM 385 Knowledge of the judgment conveyed in a declarative sentence insofar as the aim of the speaker is to impart that knowledge to the addressee.

inherently conditional proposition [*al-muttaṣila al-luzūmiyya* – "the necessary connected"] LOG 249 Conditional proposition that affirms a causal or conceptual connection between the antecedent and consequent.

inherently disjunctive proposition [*al-munfaṣila al-ʿinādiyya*] LOG 250 Disjunctive proposition in which the disagreement of the disjuncts is due to their respective essences.

initiating mode [*al-ibtidāʾī*] SEM 386 The normal way of expressing a judgment to a person who neither has already made the judgment nor is hesitant about it.

injunctive imposition [*al-taklīf* – "burdening"] JRT 480 The speech of the Lawgiver addressed to morally responsible agents insofar as it comprises the request to act or refrain or the giving of choice.

inlaid rhyme [*sajʿ al-tarṣīʿ*] EMB 468 Prose rhyme in which all or most of the corresponding words in the paired segments have the same morphological pattern.

inquiry [*al-istifhām*] SEM 421 Non-declarative speech that requests knowledge or information.

inseparable accident [*al-ʿaraḍ al-lāzim*] LOG 238 Accidental universal whose separation from a thing is impossible, whether extramentally, mentally, or both extramentally and mentally. May be a special or general accident. Opposed to the separable accident (*ʿaraḍ mufāriq*).

insisting mode [*al-inkārī* – "relating to denial"] SEM 386 The normal way of expressing a judgment to a person who denies it, namely, with the necessary degree of emphasis commensurate to the denial.

instantial infinitive noun [*maṣdar bināʾ al-marra* – "the source of the form of the instance"] MOR 41, 44 Derivative noun form; two examples are *naṣratan* and *ikrāmatan*. Signifies one instance of an action abstracted from any particular time or agent.

instrument of simile [*adāt al-tashbīh*] MET 306 The *kāf*, *kaʾanna*, *mithlu*, or any other word that means "like." A component of simile. (FIG 442)

intension [*al-mafhūm* – "that which is understood"] LOG The conceptual meaning that a term signifies as opposed to the extension (*miṣdāq*) of that term or concept. For example, the intension of "human" as commonly given is 'rational animal'.

interjecting [*al-iʿtirāḍ*] SEM 431 The insertion of one or more sentences with no positional inflection or syntactical role into speech, deliberately disrupting its continuity.

intermediate genus [*al-jins al-mutawassiṭ*] LOG 235 Genus that ranks anywhere between a highest genus and a lowest genus in the hierarchical ordering of genera.

intermediate species [*al-nawʿ al-mutawassiṭ*] LOG 236 Species that ranks anywhere between a lowest species and a highest species in the hierarchical ordering of species.

interpreted expression [*al-muʾawwal*] JRT 494 An apparent expression (*ẓāhir*) interpreted in accordance with one of its less evident possible meanings.

interrogative [*istifhāmiyya*] MOR 51 The verbal construction *a-faʿala* / *hal faʿala* (did he do?).

interrogative particles [*ḥarfā al-istifhām*] GRA 204 The particles *hamza* and *hal*, which stand at the beginning of a sentence to signify the request for knowledge or information.

intimation [*al-ramz*] FIG 459 Implication (*kināya*) that involves few intermediate steps of inference on the part of the listener but contains obscurity.

intransitive verb [*al-fiʿl al-ghayr al-mutaʿaddī; al-fiʿl al-lāzim*] GRA 177 Verb that is restricted to the agent, which means that it does not take an object. Opposed to the transitive verb (*fiʿl mutaʿaddī*). (MOR 28)

intransitivity [*al-luzūm*] MOR 28n3 Property

of a verb or noun with verbal import by which it takes no object. The opposite of transitivity (*taʿaddī*).

intuitively inferred premises [*al-ḥadsiyyāt*] LOG 266 Class of certain propositions (*yaqīniyyāt*) that are judged to be true by intuitive inference, or the passing instantaneously from premises to conclusions. Used as premises in demonstrative argument.

inversion [*al-qalb*] SEM 411 The switching of two parts of a sentence or speech with each other.

inverted simile [*al-tashbīh al-maqlūb*] MET 309 Simile whose vehicle, in reality, possesses the ground to a lesser extent or degree than the tenor. Such a simile is hyperbolic because it gives the impression that the vehicle is more fully endowed with the ground.

irregular roots [*al-muʿtall* – "the weak"] [*ghayr al-sālim* – "the unsound"] MOR 52 General category of all roots that include weak letters, doubled letters, or the letter *hamza* and as such are subject to irregularity in one or more of their derivative forms as a result of modification (*iʿlāl*), usually for phonetic considerations.

isolation of the basis [*tanqīḥ al-manāṭ* – "trimming the place of suspension"] JRT 521 Exercise of ijtihad by which specific aspects of a case with a textually indicated cause for its ruling are determined not to be part of that cause. That is, the mujtahid "trims away" those case-specific qualifications that would make the legal cause too specific if they were retained and reduces the cause to those isolated features that are pertinent to the ruling.

J

joining [*al-waṣl*] SEM 424 The use of conjunctions between sentences or clauses. Opposed to breaking (*faṣl*).

judgment [*al-ḥukm*] LOG 225 Affirmation or negation.

judgmental relation [*al-nisba al-ḥukmiyya*] LOG 253 The relation that is affirmed or negated in a proposition. This relation must be identical in contradictory propositions.

jurisprudence [*al-fiqh*] JRT 478 Knowledge of practical religious rulings that is derived from specific indicants (*adilla tafṣīliyya*).

jurisprudential theory [*ʿilm uṣūl al-fiqh* – "the science of the principles of jurisprudence"] JRT 478 Science that studies the principles of jurisprudence, after which it is named.

juristic preference [*al-istiḥsān*] JRT 526 The departure from an analogy-based ruling.

jussive [*al-majzūm* – "the truncated"] GRA 136, 174–76 Verb in the jussive mood.

jussive operators [*al-kalimāt al-jāzima* – "the jussive-making words"] GRA 131 Words that put the imperfect tense verb into the jussive mood.

jussive particles [*al-ḥurūf al-jāzima*] GRA 131 Particles that put a single verb into the jussive mood; subset of the jussive operators.

K

knowledge [*al-ʿilm*] LOG 225 The obtaining of a thing's representation, or form (*ṣūra*), in the mind, whether by way of conception or assent. If the "thing" is a real state of affairs represented as true or as "being the case," the knowledge is assentive; otherwise, it is conceptual. JRT 481 Assent held with conviction and unsusceptible to change and thus also corresponding to reality. Note that this definition is narrower than the one in provided in logic; here, the term "knowledge" is applied only to a subset of "knowledge" in the broader sense defined there. This is a difference in the usage of the term in the two contexts, not a substantive inconsistency.

L

***lām* of oath** [*lām al-qasam*] GRA 208 The particle *lām* that connects the main clause to a clause containing an oath under certain conditions when the main clause is not a request.

***lām* particles** [*al-lāmāt*] GRA 208 Category of the various distinct uses of the particle *lām*.

***lām* that anticipates an oath** [*al-lām al-muwaṭṭiʾa li-l-qasam* – "the *lām* that smooths the ground for the oath"] GRA 208 The particle *lām* that precedes the conditional clause in an oath to signal that the forthcoming main clause is connected to the oath.

language theory [*ʿilm al-waḍʿ* – "the science of imposition; the science of assignment"] LTY 282 Science concerned with the assignment (*waḍʿ*) of words and linguistic structures to their meanings and functions. Although word coinage might be its most prominent aspect, this science studies the semantics of language as a whole, from the lexical roots and internal forms of words to the syntactical structures of phrases and sentences.

late fulfillment [*al-qaḍāʾ* – "to fulfill; to conclude; to settle"] JRT 480 Performance of a required act of worship or unit of prayer after its legally appointed time to make amends for not fulfilling the requirement during its time.

legal cause [*al-ʿilla*] JRT 516 Component of analogy (*qiyās*) that is the basis and occasion of the ruling.

lexical code [*al-lugha* – "the language"] MET 315 The vocabulary of the Arabic language in its original state, where every expression refers to the meanings to which it was originally assigned. The lexical code provides the basis for later transfers in the meanings of words through convention or revelation, which produce new sets of vocabulary. (FIG 444) (JRT 489)

lexical definition [*al-taʿrīf al-lafẓī* – "verbal definition"] LOG 246 Elucidating a word or expression by means of a clearer or better-known word or expression. The kind of definition that is appropriate when the focus is on the words themselves and what they mean; sometimes opposed to logical definition (*taʿrīf ḥaqīqī*), which is concerned primarily with concepts. (DIA 360)

literal expression [*al-ḥaqīqa al-lughawiyya; al-ḥaqīqa* – "the lexically literal"] MET 311 Expression used for its proper assigned meaning in the relevant vocabulary set. Which vocabulary set is relevant— whether the lexical code (*lugha*), the vocabulary of revelation (*sharʿ*), or a vocabulary developed by general social convention (*ʿurf ʿāmm*) or the specialized convention or technical jargon of a specific group (*ʿurf khāṣṣ*)—is determined by the context of the speech. (LOG 230) (FIG 444) (JRT 488)

literal language [*al-ḥaqīqa* – "the literal"] MET 311 Language that maintains its proper, default meaning; divided into literal expressions (*ḥaqīqa lughawiyya*) and literal predication (*ḥaqīqa ʿaqliyya*).

literal predication [*al-ḥaqīqa al-ʿaqliyya* – "the rationally literal"] MET 311–12 A speaker's predicating an action (or quality) of an agent when he apparently does believe that the action (or quality) belongs to that agent. Opposed to nonliteral predication (*majāz ʿaqlī*). (SEM 388)

logic [*ʿilm al-manṭiq*] LOG 224 Science concerned with the procedures for correct thinking, where "thinking" means reflective thought (*fikr*), or the process of using one's knowledge to obtain new knowledge.

logical concept of the universal [*al-kullī al-manṭiqī* – "the logical universal"] LOG 240 The very concept 'universal' as defined in logic.

logical definition [*al-taʿrīf al-ḥaqīqī* – "real definition"] DIA 360 Definition that aims to precisely identify a given concept by combining a general term, like its genus, with a specific term, like a differentia or special accident. Opposed to lexical definition (*taʿrīf lafẓī*).

lowest genus [*al-jins al-sāfil*] LOG 235 Genus without an inferior, or lower, genus below it in the hierarchical ordering of all genera.

lowest species [*al-nawʿ al-sāfil*] LOG 236 Species without an inferior, or lower, species below it in the hierarchical ordering of all species. Also called the "species of species" (*nawʿ al-anwāʿ*).

M

major premise [*al-kubrā*] LOG 257 Proposition containing the major term in a syllogism.

major term [*al-ḥadd al-akbar*] LOG 257 The term in a syllogism that is the predicate of the syllogism's conclusion.

masculine noun [*al-ism al-mudhakkar*] GRA 163 Noun without the *tāʾ* of femininity or an *alif* of femininity.

mass report [*al-khabar al-mutawātir* – "the continuously recurring report"] JRT 501 Report about a sense-perceptible event that is massively transmitted (*mutawātir*), meaning that it is transmitted by such a great number of people that the possibility of all their reports collectively being false, whether by deliberate collusion or pervasive error, is conclusively ruled out by normative experience (*ʿāda*). Divided into the verbatim mass report (*mutawātir lafẓī*) and the substantive mass report (*mutawātir maʿnawī*).

massively reported premises [*al-mutawātirāt* – "those that are sequential or continuous"] LOG 266 Class of certain propositions (*yaqīniyyāt*) reported by such a massive number of people that the possibility of all the reports collectively being false is conclusively ruled out by normative experience (*ʿāda*). Used as premises in demonstrative argument.

mentally inseparable accident [*al-lāzim al-dhihnī*] LOG 238 Accident that is inseparable from a thing as conceived in the mind.

mentally specific *iḍāfa* structure [*al-iḍāfa al-ʿahdiyya al-dhihniyya*] LTY 292 *Iḍāfa* structure that is used to signify that the *muḍāf* is a category insofar as it exists within an unspecified instance, like saying that you are looking for *maḥall al-wuḍūʾ* ("the" *wuḍūʾ* station) without intending any *wuḍūʾ* station in particular: the specificity is only a hypothetical specificity in your mind, but really you are concerned with the category, and any specific instance will do.

mention [*al-dhikr*] SEM 394 Explicitly including a given element in a sentence; the default mode of the subject and the predicate as opposed to omission (*ḥadhf*), which is rhetorically superior in certain situations.

metaphor [*al-istiʿāra* – "borrowing"] MET 316, 320 Trope (*majāz lughawī*) based on a comparison. Unlike metonymy (*majāz mursal*), the semantic link (*ʿalāqa*) between the chosen expression and the intended referent in metaphor is always one of resemblance. In simple terms, a metaphor is the nonliteral use of a term based on some point of resemblance between its meaning and the intended meaning when context makes the intended meaning clear. (FIG 444, 446)

metaphor with concealment [*al-istiʿāra bi-l-kināya*] SEM 392 Mentioning the tenor of a simile and using a contextual indicant to indicate hyperbolically that one intends the vehicle. This is based on al-Sakkākī's definition. FIG 453 Simile that one internally conceives while explicitly mentioning only the tenor and characterizing it as if it were the vehicle. This is based on al-Qazwīnī's definition; he equates it with implicit metaphor (*istiʿāra makniyya*).

metaphorical analogy [*al-tamthīl ʿalā sabīl al-istiʿāra* – "analogy in the way of metaphor"] MET 332 Another name for a composite metaphor, or analogy (*tamthīl*). (FIG 445)

metaphorical characterization [*al-istiʿāra al-*

takhyīliyya – "imaginative borrowing"] MET 321 Affirming characteristics for the tenor, which is explicitly mentioned, that are specific to the vehicle, which is not explicitly mentioned, thereby providing contextual indication of an implicit metaphor (*istiʿāra makniyya*). FIG 453 Affirming for the tenor, which is explicitly mentioned, something specific to the vehicle, which is not explicitly mentioned.

metaphorical expression [*al-lafẓ al-mustaʿār* – "the borrowed expression"] MET 320 The expression used in a metaphor to refer to the tenor; literally signifies the vehicle. (FIG 444)

metonymy [*al-majāz al-mursal* – "the unrestricted trope"] MET 316 Trope (*majāz lughawī*) based on any kind of semantic link (*ʿalāqa*) other than resemblance; opposed to metaphor (*istiʿāra*). In simple terms, metonymy is the nonliteral use of a term based on some association or relation (like a part–whole or cause–effect relation) between its meaning and the intended meaning when context makes the intended meaning clear. (FIG 444–45)

middle term [*al-ḥadd al-awsaṭ*] LOG 257 The term repeated in the minor and major premises of a syllogism.

mimated infinitive [*al-maṣdar al-mīmī*] MOR 41, 43 Derivative noun with the same signification as the infinitive noun; has a form that begins with a *mīm* and is shared by the nouns of time and place.

minor premise [*al-ṣughrā*] LOG 257 Proposition containing the minor term in a syllogism.

minor term [*al-ḥadd al-aṣghar*] LOG 257 The term in a syllogism that is the subject of the syllogism's conclusion.

modality [*al-kayfiyya*] CRD 556 The qualitative reality or precise nature of a thing as it really is. It is beyond our capacity to know the modality of what is affirmed in the revealed descriptions of Allah the Exalted, including those descriptions that are seemingly anthropomorphic.

modification [*al-iʿlāl*] MOR {"making weak; deeming weak"] Phonetic changes that a word undergoes because of the irregularity of its root. Such changes may include assimilation (*idghām*), elision (*ḥadhf*), transfer (*naql*), conversion (*qalb*), or addition (*ziyāda*).

modulative universal [*al-kullī al-mushakkik* – "the doubt-causing universal"] LOG 229–30 Simple expression applicable to multiple things with varying degrees of priority and intensity. (JRT 488)

mood [*al-ḍarb* – "kind"] LOG 257 The status of the premises in a syllogism, considered together, with regard to affirmation and negation and universality and particularity.

morphological classes [*abwāb al-ṣarf* – "the gates of morphology"] MOR 27 Families of vowel patterns and augment letters built around a base of three or four radicals, often affecting the root meaning and determining properties like transitivity, intransitivity, quasi-passivity, and reciprocity. The morphological class of a word also determines its set of derivative forms.

morphological derivation [*al-ishtiqāq*] JRT 488 The ascription of one word to another, or identification of an etymological relationship between the two, on account of an affinity in their meanings and root letters. The term *ishtiqāq* is sometimes used to refer to the act of deriving a word from another.

morphology [*ʿilm al-ṣarf* – "the science of deflecting or shifting"] MOR 25 The science of those principles by which one knows the states of word forms in terms of derivation and modification.

muḍāf ilayhi [*al-muḍāf ilayhi* – "that to which there is annexation"] GRA 135, 154 Genitive noun governed by a *muḍāf* noun. The second term in an *iḍāfa* structure.

***muḍāf* noun** [*al-ism al-muḍāf* – "the annexed noun"] GRA 127, 155 First term in an *iḍāfa*. Also termed simply the "*muḍāf*."

mujtahid [*al-mujtahid*] JRT 535 Someone with

the natural qualifications and prerequisite base of knowledge that makes him "predisposed for jurisprudence" (*faqīh*) who furthermore meets a number of scholarly conditions pertaining to a given subject of inquiry such that he is able to actually perform ijtihad on the matter. There are various ranks of mujtahids.

mujtahid of fatwas [*mujtahid al-futyā*] JRT 536 Mujtahid who is able to weigh the available opinions within his school. The rank beneath the rank of the "mujtahid within a school" (*mujtahid al-madhhab*).

mujtahid within a school [*mujtahid al-madhhab*] JRT 536 Mujtahid who is able to extract legal proofs from the statements of the imam of his school of jurisprudence. The rank beneath the rank of the unconditional mujtahid (*mujtahid muṭlaq*).

***mursal* hadith** [*al-ḥadīth al-mursal* – "the loose or released hadith"] JRT 504 Hadith attributed to the Prophet ﷺ by someone other than a Companion—or, according to most hadith scholars, by a Follower specifically—with an omission of the immediate narrator from the chain of transmission.

mutual distinction [*al-tabāyun* – "difference"] LOG 231, 241 Mutual relation between universals whose extension (*miṣdāq*) has no common instances at all. (DIA 347) (JRT 488)

mutual suitability [*al-munāsaba*] JRT 519 Relation between a legal cause and a concomitant ruling in which the cause serves as a suitable consideration (*munāsib*) on which to base the ruling. Revealing a mutual suitability by "extraction of the basis" (*takhrīj al-manāṭ*) of a ruling is one means for determining a cause.

N

name simpliciter [*al-ism* – "name"] GRA 145 Proper name (*ʿalam*) that is neither a surname (*kunya*) nor a title (*laqab*).

natural signification [*al-dalāla al-ṭabīʿiyya*] LOG 227 Signification that is established and understood by the operation of human nature. Opposed to assigned signification (*dalāla waḍʿiyya*) and rational signification (*dalāla ʿaqliyya*).

natural universal [*al-kullī al-ṭabīʿī*] LOG 240 A nature or essence that can be characterized as a universal.

naturally evident premises [*al-fiṭriyyāt* – "those relating to the natural disposition"] LOG 267 Class of certain propositions (*yaqīniyyāt*) that are implicitly accompanied by their syllogisms: the middle term always comes to the mind when the proposition is conceived. Used as premises in demonstrative argument.

negative of coincidental conditionality/disjunction [*al-sāliba al-ittifāqiyya* – "the coincidental negative"] LOG 251 Hypothetical proposition, whether conditional or disjunctive, that negates coincidental conditionality or disjunction between the antecedent and consequent.

negative of inherent conditionality [*al-sāliba al-luzūmiyya* – "the necessary negative"] LOG 251 Conditional proposition that negates the presence of any causal or conceptual connection between the antecedent and consequent.

negative of inherent disjunction [*al-sāliba al-ʿinādiyya*] LOG 251 Proposition that negates essential or inherent disagreement between two disjuncts.

negative particles [*ḥurūf al-nafy*] GRA 195 Category of particles that can signify negation: *mā*, *lā*, *in*, *lam*, *lammā*, and *lan*.

nominal definition [*al-taʿrīf al-ismī*] LOG 245 Definition of a quiddity as denoted by a given term, irrespective of whether the quiddity is extramentally real. Opposed to real definition (*taʿrīf ḥaqīqī*).

nominal derivatives [*al-amthila al-ismiyya*] MOR 49 Category of uniform derivatives (*amthila muṭṭarida*) featuring the grammatical affixes of number for non-adjectival nouns.

nominative/indicative [*al-marfūʿ* – "the raised"] GRA 133, 148, 172 Noun in the nominative case or verb in the indicative mood.

nonattributive *iḍāfa* [*al-iḍāfa al-lafẓiyya* – "verbal *iḍāfa*"] GRA 155 *Iḍāfa* where the *muḍāf* is a participle with verbal governance over the *muḍāf ilayhi*. This kind of *iḍāfa* utilizes the grammatical form of an *iḍāfa* merely to simplify the phrase.

non-declarative speech [*al-inshāʾ* – "bringing about"] LOG 232 The kind of complete expression that cannot be true or false. (SEM 420)

nonliteral expression [*majāz lughawī* – "lexical nonliteral expression"] LOG 231 Simple expression lexically assigned to a meaning and then used for another without the first meaning's having been discarded. Another term for "trope." JRT 488 Expression used for a second assigned meaning on account of a semantic link between the first and the second assigned meaning.

nonliteral language [*al-majāz* – "passing across; moving beyond; place or locus of passing or crossing"] MET 313 Category that includes the trope, or nonliteral expression (*majāz lughawī*), and also nonliteral predication (*majāz ʿaqlī*). Deviation from the proper or default meaning; opposed to literal language (*ḥaqīqa*).

nonliteral predication [*al-majāz al-ʿaqlī* – "rational nonliteral usage"] MET 313 That a verb or the like be predicated of an agent with which it is associated rather than an agent to which it really belongs, with the use of a contextual indicant to prompt an interpretive process in the listener. One of the two categories of nonliteral language (*majāz*), the other being the trope, or nonliteral expression (*majāz lughawī*). Can also be termed "predicative nonliterality" (*majāz ḥukmī*) or "nonliteral affirmation" (*majāz fī al-ithbāt*), or, guiding our preferred translation, *isnād majāzī* (nonliteral predication). (SEM 389)

non-personal pronouns [*al-mubhamāt* – "those which are ambiguous"] GRA 162 Category of pronouns that includes demonstrative pronouns and relative pronouns but excludes personal pronouns. (LTY 285)

non-privative proposition [*al-muḥaṣṣala* – "the obtained"] LOG 248 Categorical proposition that is not subject-privative, predicate-privative, or doubly privative.

non-restrictive composite expression [*al-lafẓ al-murakkab ghayr al-taqyīdī*] LOG 233 Composite expression without parts that specify or restrict other parts of the expression. Opposed to the restrictive composite expression (*lafẓ murakkab taqyīdī*).

non-sentential composite structure [*al-hayʾa al-tarkībiyya ghayr al-kalāmiyya*] LTY 290 The composite structure of an incomplete composite expression (*murakkab ghayr tāmm*). The structure of a phrase rather than a sentence.

nonverbal signification [*al-dalāla ghayr al-lafẓiyya*] LOG 227 Signification in which the signifier is not a verbal expression.

notification [*al-tanbīh*] LOG 233 Non-declarative speech that does not have the function of asking, that is, does not signify any kind of request.

noun [*al-ism*] GRA 144 Word that signifies a meaning in itself that is not bound to the past, present, or future. One of the three principal categories of words, along with the verb (*fiʿl*) and the particle (*ḥarf*). LOG 229 Independent word whose morphological structure does not signify the past, present, or future.

noun of instrument [*ism al-āla*] MOR 41 Derivative noun form; an example is *minṣarun*. Signifies the instrument by which an action occurs. Does not occur in intransitive or non-triliteral classes. (LTY 289)

noun of place [*ism al-makān*] MOR 41, 43 Derivative noun form; two examples are *manṣarun* and *mukramun*. Signifies the place where an action occurs. (LTY 289)

noun of time [*ism al-zamān*] MOR 41, 43 Derivative noun form; two examples are *manṣarun* and *mukramun*. Signifies the time when an action occurs. (LTY 289)

nouns of sound [*al-aṣwāt* – "sounds"] GRA 160 Category of nouns that are expressions whose purpose is to mimic sounds.

nouns related to verbs [*al-asmāʾ al-muttaṣila bi-l-afʿāl*] GRA 168 Category of nouns that always carry verbal import. This includes infinitive nouns, active and passive participles, participials, and comparative/superlative nouns.

numeral noun [*ism al-ʿadad*] GRA 166 Noun that signifies a discrete quantity. (LOG 230)

nunation [*al-tanwīn*] GRA 211 Vowelless and unwritten *nūn* pronounced after a word's final short vowel but not to emphasize it (because that would be the emphatic *nūn*).

nunation of compensation [*tanwīn al-ʿiwaḍ*] GRA 211 Nunation of a *muḍāf* that "compensates" for an omitted *muḍāf ilayhi*, as in *yawmaʾidhin*.

nunation of establishment [*tanwīn al-tamakkun*] GRA 211 Nunation that indicates that a fully declinable noun is well established in its nominal nature.

nunation of nasalization [*tanwīn al-tarannum* – "nunation of quavering or trilling"] GRA 211 Nunation that in some dialects replaces a long vowel in an unbound metrical rhyme (*qāfiya muṭlaqa*), one that ends in a long vowel rather than a vowelless consonant. So called because the nunation that replaces a long vowel can be modulated with a melodious nasalized quavering and prolongation.

nunation of prolongation [*al-tanwīn al-ghālī* – "exceeding nunation"] GRA 212 Nunation that is added to a fettered metrical rhyme (*qāfiya muqayyada*), one that ends in a vowelless consonant. So called, according to one view, because the addition of nunation makes the verse exceed the poetic meter (*wazn*). Al-Mīlānī, *Sharḥ al-Mughnī*, 438.

O

object [*al-mafʿūl bihi* – "the done-to"] GRA 134, 150 Actional accusative (*mafʿūl*) that expresses the object or recipient to which an action is done or occurs.

object of the analogy [*al-maqīs* – "that which is analogized to something"] JRT 512 The derivative case (*farʿ*) in an analogy.

objector [*al-sāʾil* – "questioner"] DIA 345 Disputant whose role is to scrutinize the proponent's claims and raise objections to his proofs; counterpart of the proponent (*muʿallil*) in a disputation.

objects of comparison [*ṭarafā al-tashbīh* – "the extremes of the comparison or simile"] MET 304 The two things compared in a simile or a metaphor, that is, the tenor (*mushabbah* or *mustaʿār lahu*) and the vehicle (*mushabbah bihi* or *mustaʿār minhu*).

obligation [*al-ījāb*] JRT 479 The divine address insofar as it firmly requests an act.

obscurity [*al-gharāba* – "strangeness"] SEM 378 The use of an unfamiliar word whose meaning is unclear. A defect that vitiates the articulateness (*faṣāha*) of a simple expression.

observational premises [*al-mushāhadāt* – "those that are observed"] LOG 265 Class of certain propositions (*yaqīniyyāt*) that are affirmed by mere sensation. This includes internal sensation as well as sensation by the five external senses. Used as premises in demonstrative argument. Also termed "sensate premises" (*maḥsūsāt*).

omission [*al-ḥadhf*] SEM 393 Leaving out a given element in a sentence; rhetorically effective in certain situations. Opposed to mention (*dhikr*).

original case [*al-aṣl* – "the root; the original"] JRT 512 One of the four components of analogy (*qiyās*); the case with the original ruling that is the source of the analogy to the derivative case.

overcomplication [*al-taʿqīd*] SEM 379 The failure of the speech to clearly signify the intended meaning either because the ordering of its parts has been unduly tangled or because the listener is expected to make an unlikely connection to properly grasp the meaning. A defect that vitiates the articulateness (*faṣāḥa*) of speech.

P

palindrome [*al-qalb* – "inversion"] EMB 469 Embellishing device in which a sentence or phrase is used that would remain the same if the order of its letters were reversed.

parallel rhyme [*al-sajʿ al-muwāzī*] EMB 469 Prose rhyme in which the paired segments do not correspond in terms of their patterns except for their respective final words.

partial confutation [*al-naqḍ al-maksūr* – "fragmented confutation"] DIA 355 Kind of confutation in which the objector omits some particular aspects of the proponent's proof and then shows that the proof produces a conclusion that is at odds with the proponent's claim, discrediting the latter's proof by exposing a deviation or discontinuity (*takhalluf*) between it and the conclusion it was supposed to prove. Partial confutation is valid only when the omitted aspects are not essential to the proof's entailment of the proponent's claim.

partial overlap [*al-ʿumūm wa-l-khuṣūṣ min wajh* – "generality and specificity from a perspective"] LOG 241 Relation between two universals whose extension (*miṣdāq*) overlaps in some instances but diverges in others, each of the two universals having instances that the other does not. (DIA 347)

partially declinable noun [*ghayr al-munṣarif* – "the invariable"] GRA 146 Declinable noun that cannot take the standard genitive inflection or nunation; diptote, as opposed to the fully declinable (*munṣarif*) noun.

participial [*al-ṣifa al-mushabbaha* – "the likened adjective or attribute"] MOR 42 Derivative noun with several different forms; two examples are *aṭshānu* and *wajīhun*. GRA 126, 169 Noun with verbal import that signifies the possessor of the quality or attribute of its associated verb. Derives its name from its resemblance to the active participle. Aside from their forms, the difference between participials and active participles is that participials are always associated with intransitive verbs that signify qualities. (LTY 289)

particle [*al-ḥarf*] GRA 184 Word that signifies a meaning in another word rather than in itself, i.e., lacks independent meaning. Note that many particles are prefixed or suffixed to other words; although they do not have the full appearance of words in such cases, they are still words in the sense that they are grammatically distinct, at least in some sense, from the words that they are affixed to. [*al-adāh* – "the tool"] LOG 229 Simple expression that is not independent.

particle of proximity [*ḥarf al-taqrīb* – "the particle of deeming close"] GRA 203 The particle *qad* insofar as it expresses the recency of a past event when used before a perfect tense verb.

particle of rebuke [*ḥarf al-radʿ*] GRA 208 The particle *kallā* insofar as it expresses decisive disapproval. Also called the "particle of reprimand" (*ḥarf al-zajr*).

particles expressing the reason [*ḥarfā al-taʿlīl*] GRA 207 The particles *kay* and the *lām* insofar as they express the reason for an action.

particles of address [*ḥarfā al-khiṭāb*] GRA 200 The particles of the *kāf* and the *tāʾ* insofar as they point to the addressee when suffixed to certain pronouns. The particles of address lack a syntactical role.

particles of affirmation [*ḥurūf al-taṣdīq wa-l-ījāb* – "particles of deeming true and affirming"] GRA 198 Category of particles that indicate assent or the affirmation or confirmation of something: *naʿam*, *balā*, *ajal*, *jayri*, *inna*, and *ay*.

particles of alerting [*ḥurūf al-tanbīh*] GRA 196–97 Category of three particles with the function of getting the attention of the addressee: *hā*, *amā*, and *alā*.

particles of connection [*ḥurūf al-ṣila*] GRA 200 Category of particles that can be removed from a sentence without impairing its meaning but nevertheless have a place in articulate speech, serving subtle purposes like emphasis. Also called "additional particles" (*ḥurūf al-ziyāda*). These particles are *in*, *an*, *mā*, *lā*, *min*, the *bāʾ*, and the *lām*, all of which have their own distinct meanings apart from their usage as particles of connection.

particles of explanation [*ḥarfā al-tafsīr*] GRA 201 The particles *ay* and *an* insofar as they indicate that what follows is an explanation of the foregoing.

particles of futurity [*ḥurūf al-istiqbāl*] GRA 203 Category of particles that indicate that an action will or will not occur in the future: the *sīn*, *sawfa*, *lā*, and *lan*.

particles of reproach and exhortation [*ḥurūf al-taḥḍīḍ*] GRA 203 Category of particles that stand before a verb to express a reproach for the failure to perform an action in the past or an exhortation to perform an action in the future: *lawlā*, *lawmā*, *hallā*, and *alā*.

particular [*al-juzʾī*] LOG 231 That whose mere conception precludes that multiple instances of it could exist. Opposed to the universal (*kullī*). The term *particular* can also be considered a category that includes the real particular (*juzʾī ḥaqīqī*), as defined here, and the relative particular (*juzʾī iḍāfī*). (JRT 488)

passive participle [*ism al-mafʿūl*] MOR 40, 43 {"the noun of the done-to"] Derivative noun form; two examples are *manṣūrun* and *mukramun*. GRA 126, 168 Noun with verbal import that signifies the object to whom or which an action occurs. (LTY 289)

passive voice [*al-bināʾ li-l-majhūl* – "being built for the unknown"] GRA 178 The form of a derived noun or verb insofar as it indicates that the grammatical agent (*fāʿil*) is the object of the signified action. A verb in the passive voice is said to be "built for the unknown" (*mabnī li-l-majhūl*) because the real agent of the action is not indicated by the grammatical agent. Such a verb is also described as "built for the object" (*mabnī li-l-mafʿūl*). (MOR 46–47)

past conditional [*al-sharṭiyya al-ḥikāʾiyya*] MOR 50 A clause of the form *in kāna faʿala* (if he did; if he had done).

past perfect [*al-ḥikāʾiyya*] MOR 50 The compound tense *kāna faʿala* (he had done).

past perfect interrogative [*al-istifhāmiyya al-ḥikāʾiyya*] MOR 51 The verbal construction *a-kāna faʿala* / *hal kāna faʿala* (had he done?).

perfect tense verb [*al-fiʿl al-māḍī*] MOR 40, 43 {"the past verb"] Derivative verb form; two examples are *naṣara* and *akrama*. GRA 172 Verb that signifies action or occurrence in the past. (LTY 293–94)

peripheral rhyme [*al-sajʿ al-muṭarraf*] EMB 468 Prose rhyme in which the final words have different morphological patterns.

permission [*al-ibāḥa*] JRT 479 The divine address insofar as it gives the agent the choice of whether or not to perform a given act.

personal pronoun [*al-muḍmar* – "the internally concealed"] GRA 157 Indeclinable noun that signifies either the speaker, the addressee, or a third-person entity that has already been explicitly, implicitly, or effectively mentioned. (LTY 285–86)

personal proper name [*al-ʿalam al-shakhṣī* – "name pertaining to the individual"] LTY 288 Proper name that refers to a person or thing that is extramentally individual or specific. Opposed to the generic proper name (*ʿalam jinsī*). (JRT 488)

perspectival division [*al-taqsīm al-iʿtibārī*] DIA 368 Division (*taqsīm*) of a universal into mentally distinct concepts, regardless of whether or not they are actually distinct from each other with respect to their individual instances in extramental reality. Opposed to real division (*taqsīm ḥaqīqī*).

persuasive proof [*al-dalīl al-iqnāʿī*] LOG 227 Indicant that imparts presumption (*ẓann*) rather than certain and conclusive knowledge. Also called a "suggestive indicant" (*amāra*).

plain metaphor [*al-istiʿāra al-muṭlaqa*] MET 329 Metaphor that is neither inflated (*murashshaḥa*) nor deflated (*mujarrada*); that is, it stands unaccompanied by any additional phrases or qualifications that would particularly suit either the tenor or the vehicle. (FIG 451)

plural noun [*al-majmūʿ* – "the gathered"] GRA 161 Noun that signifies three or more referents by means of its form. Opposed to the singular (*mufrad*) and the dual (*muthannā*).

plural of abundance [*jamʿ al-kathra*] GRA 161–62 Plural form used to signify an abundance—as in more than ten—of something. Opposed to the plural of paucity (*jamʿ al-qilla*).

plural of paucity [*jamʿ al-qilla*] GRA 161 Plural form used to signify a fewness or paucity—as in ten or less—of something. Opposed to the plual of abundance (*jamʿ al-kathra*).

poetical argument [*al-shiʿr*] LOG 269 Syllogism consisting of imaginative premises (*mukhayyilāt*). Of the five arts (*al-ṣināʿāt al-khams*), the one whose purpose is to bias someone in favor of or against something.

pointing [*al-ishāra*] FIG 459 Implication (*kināya*) that, like direct indication (*īmāʾ*), involves few intermediate steps of inference on the part of the listener and does not contain obscurity.

positional inflection [*al-iʿrāb al-maḥallī*] GRA 143 The kind of inflection that an inherently uninflectable expression (like a pronoun or an entire clause) or an expression that is "preoccupied" with another inflection has in virtue of its syntactic role as part of a sentence; that is, the inflection that the expression would possess if it were an inflectable expression or were not preoccupied. Opposed to both explicit inflection (*iʿrāb lafẓī*) and implicit inflection (*iʿrāb taqdīrī*).

possible [*al-mumkin*] CRD 561 Neither necessary nor impossible, when used in its strict sense. Sometimes used in the broad one-sided sense of non-impossibility.

possibly separable accident [*al-ʿaraḍ al-mufāriq bi-l-imkān*] LOG 239 Separable accident that does not actually separate from a thing. Opposed to the actually separating accident (*ʿaraḍ mufāriq bi-l-fiʿl*).

postponement [*al-taʾkhīr*] SEM 404 Putting an element after others: in the case of postponing the subject, putting the subject last; in the case of postponing the predicate, putting the predicate last.

practical pointer [*taʿyīn al-ṭarīq* – "distinguishing the way"] DIA 356 A disputant's remonstration with his opponent that something could have been expressed in better form.

predicate [*al-khabar*] GRA 134, 149 Nominative expression that indicates what is said of the subject (*mubtadaʾ*) in a nominative clause (*jumla ismiyya*). [*al-maḥmūl*] LOG 248 The second extreme (*ṭaraf*) in a categorical proposition; the term or concept that is linked to the subject in a relation of affirmation or negation. [*al-musnad* – "what is made to lean on something"] SEM Anything that is affirmed or negated of something else in speech, including a grammatical predicate (*khabar*) in relation to its subject (*mubtadaʾ*), a verb in relation to its agent (*fāʿil*), and an adjective (*ṣifa*) in relation to the noun that it modifies.

predicate-privative proposition [*maʿdūlat al-maḥmūl* – "that whose predicate is diverted"] LOG 248 Categorical proposition with a negative particle as part of its predicate.

pre-expressional speech [*al-kalām al-nafsī* – "inward speech"] CRD 551 Speech that is considered insofar as the speaker has not actually expressed it to another. In reference to the eternal and uncreated attribute of divine speech, the term is used to distinguish it from the created, temporal utterance and recitation of that speech.

prepositional *lām* [*lām al-jarr* – "the *lām* of the genitive"] GRA 209 The particle *lām* that makes a subsequently attached noun genitive; typically indicates possession, specification, or the reason for something.

prepositions [*ḥurūf al-jarr* – "the particles of the genitive"] GRA 128, 185 Category of particles that are prefixed to nouns, adding relational meanings to them and making them genitive.

presentation [*al-ʿarḍ*] JRT 506 Form of hadith transmission in which a student recites to a teacher.

presumption [*al-ẓann*] LOG 226–27 The kind of knowledge that is tentative or probable rather than certain. Opposed to certainty (*yaqīn*), which is sometimes simply called "knowledge" (*ʿilm*). JRT 481 Assent (*taṣdīq*) that is preponderant but not held with conviction (*jazm*).

presumption of continuity [*al-istiṣḥāb* – "association; accompaniment"] JRT 524 The juristic principle that an existing indicant or legal qualification remains in effect so long as nothing occurs that would change it.

presumptive analogy [*al-qiyās al-ẓannī*] JRT 515 Analogy whose legal cause is presumed, but not conclusively known, to be the cause in the original case. Also called a "lower-grade" analogy (*qiyās al-adwan*).

presumptive consensus [*al-ijmāʿ al-ẓannī*] JRT 508 Consensus that is not universally acknowledged by mujtahids and thus only makes for a presumptive proof.

presumptive indicant [*al-dalīl al-ẓannī*] JRT Indicant whose indication is only presumptive, that is, most likely, as opposed to definitive or certain (*qaṭʿī*).

primarily governed expression [*al-maʿmūl bi-l-aṣāla*] GRA 133 Expression on which a governor has a direct effect; opposed to the secondarily governed expression (*maʿmūl bi-l-tabaʿ*).

primary metaphor [*al-istiʿāra al-aṣliyya*] MET 322 Metaphor that applies to the expression directly instead of applying to the expression by means of another expression, with generic import, from which the expression is derived. This is the case when the expression is a generic noun. Opposed to secondary metaphor (*istiʿāra tabaʿiyya*). (FIG 450)

principal noun [*al-matbūʿ* – "the followed"] GRA 136 Noun to which a secondarily governed noun conforms grammatically.

principles of jurisprudence [*uṣūl al-fiqh*] JRT 478 A term that refers to the subject matter of the science of jurisprudential theory, namely, the general indicants of jurisprudence, the methods of deriving specific indicants from them, and the prerequisite qualifications of the juristic expert, or mujtahid, who does so.

principles of spiritual devotion [*mabādī al-taṣawwuf*] SPR 567 Principles pertaining to the practice of the heart and the body in pure devotion to Allah the Exalted.

process of elimination [*al-taqsīm* – "division"] JRT 519 Means for determining a legal case; the enumeration of all the qualities of the original case to rule out those unfit to be the cause.

prohibition (1) [*al-nahy*] LOG 232–33 Mode of non-declarative speech; to ask someone, while in a superordinate position, to bring about an abstinence from something. SEM 421 Mode of non-declarative speech; to request that the addressee refrain from something.

prohibition (2) [*al-taḥrīm*] JRT 479 The divine address insofar as it firmly requests the

refraining from an act.
prohibitive [*al-nahy* – "prohibition"] GRA 177 Verbal construction that signifies prohibition by use of the particle *lā*.
prolixity [*al-iṭnāb*] SEM 428, 430 Conveying a primarily intended meaning through a verbal expression that is lengthier than that expression which would have signified the meaning by correspondence (*muṭābaqa*), for an appropriate rhetorical end. Also termed "periphrasis."
proper name [*al-ʿalam*] GRA 145 Noun assigned to a thing individually. JRT 488 Expression that specifies its referent by means of linguistic assignment.
property [*al-ʿaraḍ*] CRD 550 In the classification of contingent things, something that subsists in another thing; opposed to a substance (*jawhar*).
prophetic miracle [*al-muʿjiza* – "thing that incapacitates or proves someone incapable"] CRD 552 A disruption of normative experience that is accompanied by a challenge, is not countered by its like, and does not undermine the claimant.
proponent [*al-muʿallil* – "the one justifying with reasons"] DIA 345 Disputant who asserts a claim in a dialectical disputation and bears the burden of justifying it.
proportionality [*al-musāwāh* – "equality"] SEM 428 Conveying a primarily intended meaning through an expression that signifies it by correspondence (*muṭābaqa*), rather than an expression that signifies more or less than it.
proposition [*al-qaḍiyya*] LOG 232, 247 The kind of composite (*qawl*) that can be true or false. Propositions are primarily conceptual entities, but for the sake of simplicity they are often identified with the verbal statement that conveys the concept.
prose rhyme [*al-sajʿ*] EMB 468 Device of embellishment in prose in which corresponding final words end in the same letter-sound.
proverb [*al-mathal*] MET 332 Metaphorical analogy that becomes widespread such that when used, it is not altered from the grammatical form specific to its original context to fit the context of its usage. (FIG 445)
providence [*al-tawfīq*] CRD 552 Allah's creating in a servant the ability to obey.
provision [*al-rizq*] CRD 552 Whatever occasions benefit for one.
pure conception [*al-taṣawwur al-sādhaj*] LOG 225 Conception (*taṣawwur*) without a judgment (*ḥukm*). Also called "simple apprehension." Opposed to assent (*taṣdīq*).

Q

qualified expression [*al-muqayyad*] JRT 493–94 Expression that signifies a quiddity with qualification; opposed to the unqualified expression (*muṭlaq*).
quantifier [*al-sūr* – "the wall"] LOG 251 The part of a proposition that indicates whether it is particular or universal.
quasi-ontic mode [*al-ḥāl* – "the state or condition"] CRD 560 Intermediate ontological status between the existent and the nonexistent, affirmed most notably by certain Muʿtazilī theologians.
quasi-verbal nouns [*asmāʾ al-afʿāl* – "the nouns of verbs"] GRA 159 Category of nouns with the meaning of either an imperative verb or a perfect tense verb.
question [*al-istifhām*] LOG 232 Non-declarative speech that is assigned the function of asking someone to tell something.
questioning [*al-suʾāl*] DIA 370 In the context of a dialectical disputation, the posing of objections. In other contexts, inquiry into the meanings of expressions, the reason why something was phrased in a particular way, detail about something ambiguous, or the like.

R

rational signification [*al-dalāla al-ʿaqliyya*] LOG 227 Relation of signification that was established neither by someone's determining act nor as a consequence of human nature; opposed to assigned signification (*dalāla waḍʿiyya*) and natural signification (*dalāla ṭabīʿiyya*).

real definition [*al-taʿrīf al-ḥaqīqī*] LOG 245 Definition of a real quiddity as it is in extramental reality. Opposed to nominal definition (*taʿrīf ismī*).

real division [*al-taqsīm al-ḥaqīqī*] DIA 368 Division of a dividendum into things that are distinguished from each other in actual reality. Opposed to perspectival division (*taqsīm iʿtibārī*).

real femininity [*al-taʾnīth al-ḥaqīqī*] GRA 163 The kind of femininity that has a counterpart in a male sentient being; opposed to verbal femininity (*taʾnīth lafẓī*).

real particular [*al-juzʾī al-ḥaqīqī*] LOG 229, 231 Concept whose mere conception precludes that it could be shared; opposed to the real universal (*kullī ḥaqīqī*). On the level of verbal expressions, a simple expression with individual reference by assignment.

real restriction [*al-qaṣr al-ḥaqīqī*] SEM 417 Use of the device of restriction when the specification pertains to what is real and factual; opposed to relative restriction (*qaṣr iḍāfī*).

real species [*al-nawʿ al-ḥaqīqī*] LOG 236 What is said of multiple things with identical essences in response to "What is it?"

real universal [*al-kullī al-ḥaqīqī*] LOG 231–32 Concept whose mere conception does not preclude that it could be shared and under which other things can fall in the supposition of the mind, irrespective of whether they fall under it in extramental existence or not; opposed to the real particular (*juzʾī ḥaqīqī*).

reasonable hyperbole [*al-tablīgh*] {"delivering or conveying"] EMB 467 Hyperbole that is possible rationally and by normative experience (*ʿāda*); considered to be an acceptable kind of hyperbole (*mubālagha maqbūla*).

received expressed governor [*al-ʿāmil al-lafẓī al-samāʿī*] GRA 127 Category of governors concerning whose governance one cannot give a universal rule but must instead resort to what is received from the early users of the language. Opposed to the regular expressed governor (*ʿāmil lafẓī qiyāsī*).

recommendation [*al-nadb*] JRT 479 The divine address insofar as it mildly requests an act.

reflective [*al-naẓarī*] LOG 226 Said of conceptions or assents whose obtaining in the mind depends on reflective reasoning (*naẓar*), or thought (*fikr*); opposed to the immediate (*ḍarūrī*).

reflective thought [*al-fikr*] LOG 224, 226 The mental process of arranging things one knows so that one arrives at something one does not know.

regular expressed governor [*al-ʿāmil al-lafẓī al-qiyāsī*] GRA 125 Category of governors concerning whose governance one can give a universal rule. Opposed to the received expressed governor (*ʿāmil lafẓī samāʿī*).

regulative imposition [*al-waḍʿ* – "putting in place"] JRT 479–80 Allah's addressed speech insofar as it designates something a legal cause, condition, impediment or the like. Juxtaposed with the address of injunctive imposition (*taklīf*).

relational noun [*al-ism al-mansūb*] MOR 42, 44 Derivative noun form; two examples are *naṣriyyun* and *ikramiyyun*. GRA 165 Noun to the end of which a doubled *yāʾ* is added to signify an ascription or relation to the thing that is signified by the word without the *yāʾ*.

relative particular [*al-juzʾī al-iḍāfī*] LOG 231 Concept that is subsumed under another inasmuch as it is more specific than that other concept.

relative pronoun [*al-ism al-mawṣūl* – "the connected noun"] GRA 159 Indeclinable noun that signifies an object that is mentally indicated by means of a relative clause. (LTY 286)

relative restriction [*al-qaṣr al-iḍāfī*] SEM 417 Use of the device of restriction when the specification does not pertain to what is real or factual; opposed to real restriction (*qaṣr ḥaqīqī*).

relative species [*al-nawʿ al-iḍāfī*] LOG 236 Universal of which together with other universals a genus is predicated in response to "What is it?" by way of primary predication.

relative universal [*al-kullī al-iḍāfī*] LOG 231–32 Concept under which other things are subsumed in actual reality.

religion [*al-dīn*] CRD 558 The whole system of creed and worship that Allah has revealed to His servants through His messengers, leading people of sound intellect, by a praiseworthy exercise of their choice, to righteousness in their worldly lives and felicity in the hereafter.

remote differentia [*al-faṣl al-baʿīd*] LOG 237 Differentia that distinguishes a thing from that with which it shares a remote genus.

remote genus [*al-jins al-baʿīd*] LOG 235 Genus that cannot be correctly given in response to a question about a quiddity and all with which it shares the genus but can correctly be given in response to a question about the quiddity and some other quiddities with which it shares the genus.

replicative syllogism [*al-qiyās al-istithnāʾī* – "the exceptive syllogism; the doubled syllogism; the repetitive syllogism"] LOG 262 Syllogism that explicitly incorporates the conclusion or its contradictory within either of its premises. On the etymology of the term *istithnāʾ* in logic, see Gyekye, "The Term." "Replicative" has been chosen to translate *istithnāʾī* because aside from capturing the idea of doubling and repetition, it gives a sense of the role of what Gyekye calls the "additional assumption" introduced by the second premise in replying to and resolving the implicit uncertainty in the hypothetical first premise of the syllogism.

reprehension [*al-karāha*] JRT 479 The divine address insofar as it mildly requests the refraining from an act and specifies the act.

request [*al-iltimās*] LOG 233 Non-declarative speech that is linguistically assigned the function of signifying the asking while in a coordinate position that someone bring about something or the abstinence from something.

resemblant root [*al-mithāl* – "something similar"] MOR 57 Root whose first radical is a weak letter.

residual subdivision [*al-wāsiṭa bayna al-aqsām* – "that which intervenes among the parts"] DIA 364 Subdivision that falls under the dividendum (*maqsim*) but is not mentioned in the division process.

respective correlation [*al-laff wa-l-nashr* – "rolling and unrolling; folding and unfolding"] EMB 466 To introduce multiple subjects either individually or collectively and then discuss each of them without specification, trusting that the listener will make the respective connections. The interested student may compare correlative verse and epanodos, two related figures of speech.

restriction [*al-qaṣr*] SEM 417 The specification of one thing with another in a specific way, whether the specification of something to a specific attribute or the specification of an attribute to a specific thing.

restriction for exclusivity [*qaṣr al-ifrād* – "the restriction of singling out"] SEM 418 Use of the device of restriction (*qaṣr*) when the addressee believes in the non-exclusivity of what is stated.

restriction for inversion [*qaṣr al-qalb* – "the restriction of inversion"] SEM 418 Use of the device of restriction (*qaṣr*) when the addressee believes the inverse of what is stated.

restriction for specification [*qaṣr al-taʿyīn*] SEM 418 Use of the device of restriction (*qaṣr*) when the addressee believes in the non-specificity of what is stated.

restrictive composite expression [*al-lafẓ al-murakkab al-taqyīdī*] LOG 233 Composite expression in which one part restricts, or specifies, another part, whether the restricting part is an adjective, a *muḍāf ilayhi*, or an adverb of place or time.

result clause [*jumlat al-jawāb* – "the clause of the response"] GRA 206 In a conditional sentence, the clause that follows the condition clause (*jumlat al-sharṭ*).

result verb [*al-jazāʾ* – "the consequence"] GRA 132 In a conditional sentence, the verb that follows the condition verb (*sharṭ*).

resumptive predicate [*al-musnad al-sababī* – "the predicate of suspension"] SEM 412 Predicate (*musnad*) containing a pronoun that refers to the subject (*musnad ilayhi*).

reutilization [*al-istikhdām* – "utilization"] EMB 465 The use of personal pronouns to refer to the same expression while respectively intending different meanings borne by that expression.

revelational usage [*al-sharʿ* – "the way; the religion"] MET 315 The set of vocabulary established by the way certain words and terms are used in revelation. (LOG 230) (FIG 444) (JRT 489)

rhetorical argument [*al-khiṭāba* – "rhetoric; oratory"] LOG 269 Syllogism consisting of authoritative premises (*maqbūlāt*) or suppositional premises (*maẓnūnāt*). Of the five arts (*al-ṣināʿāt al-khams*), the one whose purpose is to make people desirous of what is good and averse to what is evil.

rhetorical semantics [*ʿilm al-maʿānī* – "the science of meanings and intended effects"] SEM 377, 383 Within the larger science of rhetoric (*balāgha*), the discipline that studies how speech may be made to correspond to what the situation demands, that is, to fit the rhetorical situation, thereby avoiding errors in conveying the intended meaning.

ruling [*al-ḥukm*] JRT 479 The addressed speech of Allah the Exalted as pertains to the acts of morally responsible individuals, whether by way of decreeing, granting the choice to act or not, or determining legal causes, conditions, impediments, valid acts, or invalid acts.

ruling of the original case [*ḥukm al-aṣl*] JRT 512 The ruling of a given original case in an analogy; one of the four components of analogy.

S

saintly miracle [*al-karāma* – "mark of honor or favor"] CRD 553 A miracle, that is, a disruption of normative experience (*kharq al-ʿāda*), gifted to a saint or righteous believer.

science of metaphor [*ʿilm al-istiʿāra*] MET 302 A science defined in the same way as the science of figurative language (*ʿilm al-bayān*). In this *Compendium*, the treatise on metaphor predictably delves into further detail on metaphor (*istiʿāra*) and its types; metaphor is one of the most important concepts in the science of figurative language.

secondarily governed expression [*al-maʿmūl bi-l-tabaʿ*] GRA 133, 136 Expression on which a governor has an effect through an intermediary and which thus conforms grammatically to the principal expression (*matbūʿ*). Opposed to the primarily governed expression (*maʿmūl bi-l-aṣāla*).

secondary metaphor [*al-istiʿāra al-tabaʿiyya*] MET 323 Metaphor that applies to the expression by means of another expression, with generic import, from which the expression is derived. This is the case when the expression is a verb, derivative noun, or particle. Opposed to primary metaphor (*istiʿāra aṣliyya*) (FIG 450)

self-blaming soul [*al-nafs al-lawwāma*] SPR 569n1 Aspect of the human soul that blames itself even when it strives for excellence.

self-evident premises [*al-awwaliyyāt* – "those which are primary"] LOG 265 Class of certain propositions (*yaqīniyyāt*) that are affirmed by mere conception of the terms and the relation between them. Used as premises in demonstrative argument.

semantic link [*al-ʿalāqa* – "the link or connection"] MET 313 The relationship in meaning between a trope (*majāz lughawī*) and the literal expression that it replaces, whether a relationship of resemblance, as is the case in metaphor (*istiʿāra*), or another kind of relationship, as is the case in metonymy (*majāz mursal*). (FIG 444)

semblance [*al-mushākala* – "resemblance"] EMB 464 Device of embellishment in which one thing is given the name of another because it explicitly or implicitly stands in its contextual vicinity.

sensate premises [*al-maḥsūsāt* – "those which are sensed"] LOG 265 Another term for observational premises (*mushāhadāt*).

sentential composite structure [*al-hay'a al-tarkībiyya al-kalāmiyya*] LTY 290 Composite structures that express a complete thought in a sentence; opposed to a non-sentential structure (*hay'a tarkībiyya ghayr kalāmiyya*).

separable accident [*al-ʿaraḍ al-mufāriq*] LOG 239 Accidental universal whose separation from the things of which it is an accident is possible. May be a special or general accident. Opposed to the inseparable accident (*ʿaraḍ lāzim*).

separation [*al-faṣl*] SEM 402 The use of the separative pronoun (*ḍamīr al-faṣl*).

shift of person [*al-iltifāt* – "turning around or toward"] SEM 407 Shifting one's discourse from one grammatical person (the first person, second person, or third person) to another grammatical person while still referring to the same subject.

significate [*al-madlūl*] LOG 227n5 That which is signified in the relation of signification (*dalāla*).

signification [*al-dalāla*] LOG 226 Relation between two things such that knowledge or presumption of the one entails knowledge or presumption of the other.

signifier [*al-dāll*] LOG 227 That which signifies in the relation of signification (*dalāla*).

silencing [*al-ifḥām*] DIA 370 The failure of the proponent to justify his claim by rebutting the objections of his opponent in a dialectical disputation.

simile [*al-tashbīh* – "likening; comparison"] MET 304 The use of the *kāf* or a word with the same meaning to indicate that one thing has a commonality with another without making a metaphor. (FIG 441)

simple expression [*al-lafẓ al-mufrad* – "the single or singular expression"] LOG 228 Expression whose parts are not intended to signify parts of the expression's meaning; opposed to the composite expression (*lafẓ murakkab*). (JRT 487)

simple metaphor [*al-istiʿāra al-mufrada* – "the single or singular metaphor"] MET 320 Standard metaphor (*istiʿāra*) that is not composite, that is, not an analogy.

simple metonymy [*al-majāz al-mursal al-mufrad* – "the single or singular unrestricted trope"] MET 316 Standard use of metonymy (*majāz mursal*) that is opposed to composite metonymy (*majāz mursal murakkab*).

simple triliteral [*al-thulāthī al-mujarrad* – "that which is bare and consists of three"] MOR 26–27 Category of those six variously vowelized morphological classes that consist of three radicals without augment letters.

situation [*al-ḥāl* – "the state or circumstance"] SEM 381 State of affairs that a speaker must take into consideration in addition to the primary substance of what he wants to say in order to communicate effectively. May also be termed the "rhetorical situation."

sophistry [*al-safsaṭa*] LOG 270 Kind of fallacious argument in which the premises are false but resemble premises that are true and certain.

sound [*al-sālim*] MOR 25–26 Root without weak letters, doubled letters, or a *hamza.*
sound interpretation [*al-taʾwīl al-ṣaḥīḥ*] JRT 494 The interpretation of an apparent expression in accordance with one of its less evident possible meanings on account of a proof.
sound plural noun [*al-majmūʿ al-muṣaḥḥaḥ*] GRA 161 Plural noun that is not a broken plural and thus has a regular plural pattern.
source of the analogy [*al-maqīs ʿalayhi* – "that in relation with which analogy is made"] JRT 512 The original case (*aṣl*) in an analogy.
source of the division [*mawrid al-qisma*] DIA 364 Another term for the dividendum (*maqsim*).
space [*al-makān*] CRD 560 Hypothetical dimension in which corporeal objects extend.
special accident [*al-khāṣṣa*] LOG 238 Accidental universal that is predicable of, or applies to, only a single essence. One of the five universals. Also called a "proprium."
special metaphor [*al-istiʿāra al-khāṣṣiyya*] FIG 448 Metaphor whose commonality (*jāmiʿ*) is abstruse such that the metaphor would be recognized only by a specific group; opposed to a common metaphor (*istiʿāra ʿāmmiyya*).
species [*al-nawʿ*] LOG 236 Essential universal that can be predicated of multiple things with identical essences in response to a question asking what they are. One of the five universals.
species of species [*nawʿ al-anwāʿ*] LOG 236 Another term for a lowest species (*nawʿ sāfil*).
specific assignment [*al-waḍʿ al-khāṣṣ* – "specific assignment"] [*juzʾī al-waḍʿ* – "having particular assignment"] LTY Assignment of an expression or structure to denotations or meanings considered by means of a specific, or particular (*juzʾī*), concept. In specific assignment, both the assigner's meaning (*ālat al-waḍʿ*) and the denotation (*mawḍūʿ lahu*) are particular. Opposed to general assignment (*waḍʿ ʿāmm*).
specific convention [*al-ʿurf al-khāṣṣ*] LOG 230 The set of vocabulary established by the way certain words and terms are used by a specific group. Also termed technical (*iṣṭilāḥī*) convention. (MET 315) (FIG 444)
specific *iḍāfa* structure [*al-iḍāfa al-ʿahdiyya* – "the *iḍāfa* of what is previously known"] LTY 290 *Iḍāfa* structure that is assigned to signify something specific.
specific indicants of jurisprudence [*adillat al-fiqh al-tafṣīliyya*] JRT 478 The indicants by which particular rulings are determined; subsumed by the general indicants of jurisprudence (*adillat al-fiqh al-ijmāliyya*).
specific *lām* [*lām al-ʿahd* – "the *lām* of what is previously known"] GRA 208 Definite *lām* by which the noun signifies a specific referent.
specification (1) [*al-takhṣīṣ*] JRT 491 Confining the ruling of a general expression to certain individual instances.
specification (2) [*al-tamyīz*] GRA 135, 152 Accusative noun that removes ambiguity from a word or from the predication in a sentence.
spiritual devotion [*al-taṣawwuf*] SPR 567 The pure devotion of one's heart to Allah the Exalted and comparative disdain of everything besides Him.
spiritual excellence [*al-iḥsān* – "excellence"] CRD 558 One of the three primary aspects of religion, together with belief (*īmān*) and submission (*islām*): in the prophetic definition, to worship Allah as though one sees Him.
spiritual inspiration [*al-ilhām*] JRT 526 The direct depositing of knowledge and certainty about some matter into the consciousness of a saint or righteous believer.
strict disjunctive proposition [*al-munfaṣila al-ḥaqīqiyya* – "the proper disjunctive proposition"] LOG 249 Disjunctive proposition whose affirmative judgment is that the two disjuncts are neither both true nor both false.
strictly evident inseparable accident [*al-ʿaraḍ al-lāzim al-bayyin bi-l-maʿnā al-akhaṣṣ* – "the

inseparable accident that is evident in the narrow sense"] LOG 238 Inseparable accident that one always conceives upon conceiving the implicant (*malzūm*).

stringent ruling [*al-ʿazīma*] JRT 481 The opposite of a dispensation (*rukhṣa*).

subdivision [*al-qism* – "part"] DIA 364 In the division of a universal, one of its particulars; in the division of a whole, one of its parts. Can also be termed a "division."

subject [*al-mubtadaʾ* – "the beginning"] GRA 134, 149 Nominative expression that introduces something so that something can be said about it by means of the predicate (*khabar*) in a nominative clause (*jumla ismiyya*). [*al-mawḍūʿ* – "that which is placed or posited"] LOG 248 The first extreme (*ṭaraf*) in a categorical proposition; the term or concept that is linked to the predicate (*maḥmūl*) in a relation of affirmation or negation. [*al-musnad ilayhi* – "that on which something is made to lean"] SEM Anything of which something is affirmed or negated in speech, including a grammatical subject (*mubtadaʾ*) in relation to its predicate (*khabar*), an agent (*fāʿil*) in relation to its verb, and a noun in relation to its adjective (*ṣifa*).

subject-privative proposition [*maʿdūlat al-mawḍūʿ* – "that whose subject is diverted"] LOG 248 Categorical proposition with a negative particle as part of its subject.

subjunctive particles of the imperfect tense verb [*al-ḥurūf al-nāṣiba li-l-fiʿl al-muḍāriʿ* – "those particles that make the imperfect tense verb subjunctive"] GRA 131 Class of received (*samāʿī*) governors; category of particles that precede an imperfect tense verb and make it subjunctive.

submission [*al-islām*] CRD 552 The component of the religion (*dīn*) that pertains to practice; begins with the verbalization of the testimony of faith and includes obedience to all the commands and prohibitions of Allah the Exalted.

suboptimal [*khilāf al-awlā* – "the state of being at variance with what is most preferable"] JRT 479 Legal status, or ruling, determined by the divine address insofar as it mildly requests the refraining from an act without specifying the act.

substance [*al-jawhar*] CRD 550 In the categorization of contingent things, something that subsists in itself; opposed to a property (*ʿaraḍ*).

substantive mass report [*al-mutawātir al-maʿnawī* – "that which is massively transmitted in terms of the meaning"] JRT 502 A common meaning that emerges from a number of reports that, aside from variances in expression, collectively satisfy the conditions for mass transmission. Opposed to a verbatim mass report (*mutawātir lafẓī*).

substitute agent [*nāʾib al-fāʿil*] GRA 133 Nominative noun governed by a passive verb. In place of the agent, signifies the object of the action signified by the verb.

substitute apposition [*al-badal* – "substitution"] GRA 137, 147 The use of a substitute, that is, an appositive (*tābiʿ*) to which what is predicated of the principal noun is meant to apply instead. (SEM 401)

subsumption [*al-ʿumūm wa-l-khuṣūṣ al-muṭlaq* – "absolute generality and specificity"] LOG 241 Relation between two universals that overlap in their extension from one perspective, such that every instance of one of them is also an instance of the other but not vice versa.

sufficient exclusiveness [*al-manʿ* – "preventing"] DIA 364–65 That a division (*taqsīm*) not omit anything that falls within the dividendum (*maqsim*).

sufficient inclusiveness [*al-jamʿ* – "gathering"] DIA 364 That a division (*taqsīm*) not include anything that does not fall within the dividendum (*maqsim*).

suggestive indicant [*al-amāra*] LOG 227 An indicant (*dalīl*) that imparts presumption. Also called a "persuasive proof" (*dalīl iqnāʿī*).

suitable accompaniment [*al-mulāʾim* – "that which is suitable"] MET 329 Description, phrase, or expression that suits either the vehicle or the tenor in a metaphor, thereby inflating or deflating the metaphor, respectively. (FIG 451)

suitable legal consideration [*al-munāsib* – "that which is suitable"] JRT 519 A feature that is fit to serve as the cause in an analogy because it is apparent, can be precisely delimited, and leads logically, by application of the ruling, to a benefit or avoidance of harm that could be specifically intended by the Lawgiver.

suppositional premises [*al-maẓnūnāt* – "those which are supposed or presumed"] LOG 269 Propositions one deems to be true by way of preponderant judgment, or presumption, while allowing that the contradictory, albeit unlikely, may be true. Used as premises in rhetorical argument.

surname [*al-kunya*] GRA 145 Proper name (*ʿalam*) that begins with a familial relation like *ab* or *umm*.

suspension [*al-taʿlīq*] GRA 179 The necessary nullification of the verbally expressed governance of verbs of mental consideration (*afʿāl al-qulūb*) when they occur before the *lām* of beginning, a question, or a negation.

syllogism [*al-qiyās*] LOG 256 Composite of propositions that, when accepted, inherently entails a proposition as a conclusion.

synonymy [*al-tarāduf*] LOG 231 Relation between different expressions with the same intension and extension. (LTY 295) (JRT 488)

synthetic composite [*al-murakkab al-mazjī* – "the mixed composite"] LTY 290 Composite word made by the fusing together of two words.

synthetic infinitive noun [*al-maṣdar al-ṣanʿī*] MOR 41, 44 Derivative noun form made by the addition of the relational *yāʾ* and the transmutative *tāʾ*; two examples are *naṣriyyatun* and *ikrāmiyyatun*. Signifies the abstract notion or idea of doing, having, or being something (depending on the base word), abstracted from any particular time or agent.

T

tacit approval [*al-taqrīr* – "confirmation"] JRT 498 The refraining from expressing disapproval, specifically as pertains to the Prophet ﷺ and the consideration of his Sunna as a legal indicant.

tacit consensus [*al-ijmāʿ al-sukūtī* – "the consensus of silence"] JRT 508 Presumptive consensus that occurs when the community of a given generation of mujtahids collectively refrains from expressing disapproval about a ruling advanced by a mujtahid.

temporally extensive [*al-tawqītiyya al-imtidādiyya*] MOR 50 The modal verb construction *mā dāma yafʿalu* (as long as he does).

tenor of the metaphor [*al-mustaʿār lahu* – "that for which something is borrowed"] MET 320 The real subject of a metaphor (*istiʿāra*), represented by the vehicle (*mustaʿār*), with which it shares an aspect of resemblance. Abbreviated as "tenor." (FIG 444)

tenor of the simile [*al-mushabbah* – "that which is likened to something"] MET 304 Of the two objects of comparison in a simile (*tashbīh*), the one that is said to be like the other. Abbreviated as "tenor." (FIG 441)

textually required entailment [*dalālat al-iqtiḍāʾ* – "signification of requirement"] JRT 486 Signification by concomitance of a meaning that is presupposed for the truth or validity of the articulated meaning.

that-demonstration [*al-burhān al-innī*] LOG 267 Demonstrative argument that reasons from the effect to the cause: the middle term is the cause of one's knowledge that the major term holds true for the minor term. This kind of reasoning can also be termed "*quia* reasoning." The term *innī* is derived from *inna* (that).

the *mā* and *lā* that resemble *laysa* [*mā wa-lā al-mushabbahatāni bi-laysa*] GRA 130 The particles *mā* and *lā* insofar as they constitute a class of received governors that make the subject nominative and the predicate accusative. When used in this way, these particles bear the meaning of the particle *laysa*.

three-part proposition [*al-qaḍiyya al-thulāthiyya*] LOG 248 Categorical proposition in which the copula is mentioned; opposed to the two-part proposition (*qaḍiyya thunāʾiyya*).

time [*al-zamān*] CRD 560 The association of an imagined renewing thing with a known renewing thing.

timely fulfillment [*al-adāʾ* – "performance; fulfillment"] JRT 480 Performance of an act of worship or a unit of prayer within its legally appointed time.

title [*al-laqab*] GRA 145 Proper name (*ʿalam*) with the function of indicating something that is praiseworthy or blameworthy about a person.

total connection [*kamāl al-ittiṣāl*] SEM 426 Relation between two consecutive sentences in which the second is an emphatic appositive, a substitute appositive, or a clarifying appositive for the first, entailing that the sentences must be broken up by forgoing the use of a conjunction.

total disconnection [*kamāl al-inqiṭāʿ*] SEM 426 Relation between two consecutive sentences in which one is declarative and the other is non-declarative, entailing that the sentences must be broken up by forgoing the use of a conjunction.

transfer [*al-naql*] MOR Phonetic change undergone by some words in modification (*iʿlāl*) by the movement of a vowel from one letter to another.

transferred by a specific convention [*al-manqūl al-ʿurfī al-khāṣṣ*] LOG 230 Said of a simple expression used for a meaning that is not its assigned lexical meaning but rather a new meaning established by a special convention (*ʿurf khāṣṣ*), assuming that it is no longer used for the originally assigned meaning without contextual indicants.

transferred by general convention [*al-manqūl al-ʿurfī al-ʿāmm*] LOG 230 Said of a simple expression used for a meaning that is not its assigned lexical meaning but rather a new meaning established by general convention (*ʿurf ʿāmm*), assuming that it is no longer used for the originally assigned meaning without contextual indicants.

transferred by revelation [*al-manqūl al-sharʿī*] LOG 230 Said of a simple expression used for a meaning that is not its assigned lexical meaning but rather a new meaning established by revelation (*sharʿ*), assuming that it is no longer used for the originally assigned meaning without contextual indicants.

transitive verb [*al-fiʿl al-mutaʿaddī*] GRA 177 Verb that takes a direct object (*mafʿūl bihi*). Opposed to the intransitive verb (*fiʿl lāzim*). (MOR 28n2)

transitivity [*al-taʿaddī*] MOR 28n2 Property of a verb or noun with verbal import by which it takes an object. The opposite of intransitivity (*luzūm*). (GRA 177)

transmission by meaning [*al-naql bi-l-maʿnā*] JRT 505 Transmission of a hadith by merely conveying the meaning, that is, with a change in the wording.

trifling [*al-laʿib*] JRT 494 Interpretation of an apparent expression in accordance with one of its less evident possible meanings without proof.

trope [*al-majāz al-lughawī* – "lexical nonliteral expression"] MET 315 Expression used for a meaning other than that assigned to it according to the vocabulary referenced by the speech in consideration of a semantic link in the presence of a contextual indicant that precludes that the assigned meaning could be intended. One of the two categories of nonliteral language (*majāz*), the other being nonliteral predication (*majāz ʿaqlī*). Can also be termed a "nonliteral expression." (FIG 440, 444–45)

two-part proposition [*al-qaḍiyya al-thunāʾiyya*] LOG 248 Categorical proposition in which the copula is not mentioned; opposed to the three-part proposition (*qaḍiyya thulāthiyya*).

U

unambiguous expression [*al-lafẓ al-muḥkam* – "fixed or secured expression"] JRT 487 Unequivocal or apparent expression whose meaning is clear. Opposed to the obscure (*mutashābih*) expression.

unequivocal expression [*al-naṣṣ*] JRT 485 Expression that cannot possibly mean anything besides its articulated meaning; opposed to the apparent (*ẓāhir*) expression. Note that the Arabic term *naṣṣ* is often used in reference to textual indicants as such, irrespective of whether they are unequivocal or apparent.

unexpressed contextual indicant [*al-qarīna al-maʿnawiyya*] SEM 392 Contextual indicant of nonliteral predication that is not verbally expressed, as when reason or experience dictates that the predication is impossible.

uniform derivatives [*al-amthila al-muṭṭarida*] MOR 45 Category of derivatives (*amthila*) sharing a common lexical root and form but featuring different grammatical affixes.

unit report [*khabar al-wāḥid* – "the report of one"] JRT 502 Report that does not reach the point of mass transmission (*tawātur*).

universal [*al-kullī*] LOG 231, 234 That whose mere conception does not preclude that it could be shared by multiple instances; opposite of the particular (*juzʾī*). (JRT 487)

universal *iḍāfa* structure [*al-iḍāfa al-istighrāqiyya*] LTY 293 *Iḍāfa* structure assigned to signify the total and universal inclusion of the *muḍāf*.

universal *lām* [*lām al-istighrāq*] LTY 293 Noun prefix whose assigned function is to signify that the judgment applies to every one of the noun's individuals. Type of definite *lām*.

univocal universal [*al-kullī al-mutawāṭiʾ* – "the agreeing universal"] LOG 229–30 Universal expression whose mental or extramental instances are equivalent with respect to it. (JRT 488) [*al-mushtarak al-maʿnawī* – "that whose meaning is shared"] LTY 295 Single expression assigned to signify a single meaning whose multiple instantiation is nonetheless validated by the intellect. Note that the term *mushtarak maʿnawī* might be used synonymously with *mutawāṭiʾ* or it might be used as a higher category that also includes the modulative (*mushakkik*) expression.

unknown [*al-majhūl*] LOG 226 In the process of reflective thought (*fikr*), the knowledge that is to be attained by means of what is already known.

unqualified expression [*al-muṭlaq*] JRT 493 Expression that signifies a quiddity without qualification; opposed to the qualified expression (*muqayyad*).

unquantified proposition [*al-qaḍiyya al-muhmala* – "the proposition that was left to be or neglected"] LOG 252 Proposition that omits quantification; in the case of categorical propositions, this means the absence of a quantifier, and in hypothetical propositions, this means the use of such generic particles as *law*, *in*, *idh*, *immā*, or *aw*.

unsound [*ghayr al-sālim*] MOR 26, 52 Another term for the irregular root (*muʿtall*).

unsound interpretation [*al-taʾwīl al-fāsid*] JRT 494 The mistaken interpretation of an apparent expression in accordance with one of its less evident possible meanings on account of what is presumed to be proof.

usurpation [*al-ghaṣb*] DIA 348–49, 371 Breach of disputational protocol in which the objector (*sāʾil*) undertakes to prove a claim, to refute an unsupported claim, or to otherwise assume the role of a proponent (*muʿallil*).

V

vague pronouns [*al-kināyāt*] GRA 160 Expressions that refer to specific referents but without specifying their number or kind, as in *kam*, *kadhā*, and *kaʾayyin*.

variform derivatives [*al-amthila al-mukhtalifa*] MOR 39 Category of derivatives (*amthila*) sharing a common lexical root but featuring different forms and grammatical affixes.

vehicle for the metaphor [*al-mustaʿār minhu* – "that from which something is borrowed"] MET 320 The expression used nonliterally to represent the tenor, or real subject of a metaphor (*istiʿāra*), with which it shares an aspect of resemblance. Abbreviated as "vehicle." (FIG 444)

vehicle for the simile [*al-mushabbah bihi* – "that to which something is likened"] MET 304 Of the two objects of comparison in a simile (*tashbīh*), the one that the other is said to resemble. Abbreviated as "vehicle." (FIG 441)

verb [*al-fiʿl*] GRA 171 Word that signifies a meaning in itself that is bound to the past, present, or future. One of the three principal categories of words, along with the noun (*ism*) and the particle (*ḥarf*). [*al-kalima* – "word"] LOG 229 Independent word whose morphological structure signifies the past, present, or future.

verb of wonderment [*fiʿl al-taʿajjub*] MOR 42, 45 Derivative verb form formed by means of the particle *mā* or the letter *bāʾ* as in *mā anṣarahu* or *akrim bihi*. GRA 183 Verb in a composite form that is assigned to indicate wonderment.

verbal derivatives [*al-amthila al-fiʿliyya*] MOR 45 Category of uniform derivatives (*amthila muṭṭarida*) featuring the grammatical affixes of person, number, and gender for verbs.

verbal expression [*al-lafẓ* – "throwing; ejecting or emitting; uttering"] LOG 228 Anything that may be articulated by the human being. Abbreviated as "expression" when not liable to be confused for physical gestures or other nonverbal modes of expression.

verbal femininity [*al-taʾnīth al-lafẓī*] GRA 163 The kind of femininity that does not have a counterpart in a male sentient being, meaning that it is a merely grammatical femininity. Opposed to real femininity (*taʾnīth ḥaqīqī*).

verbal signification [*al-dalāla al-lafẓiyya*] LOG 227 Relation of signification (*dalāla*) in which the signifier is a verbal expression.

verbatim mass report [*al-mutawātir al-lafẓī* – "that which is massively transmitted in terms of the wording"] JRT 501–2 Report that satisfies the conditions for mass transmission with respect to both its meaning and its particular wording. Opposed to a substantive mass report (*mutawātir maʿnawī*).

verb-like particles [*al-ḥurūf al-mushabbaha bi-l-fiʿl*] GRA 129, 189 Class of received governors; category of particles that make the subject accusative and the predicate nominative. Termed "verb-like particles" on account of the comparison with auxiliary verbs (*afʿāl nāqiṣa*) in that they take a subject-noun and predicate. There are six: *inna*, *anna*, *kaʾanna*, *lākinna*, *layta*, and *laʿalla*.

verbs of mental consideration [*afʿāl al-qulūb* – "verbs of the hearts"] GRA 178 Category of seven verbs that signify a mental act and take two accusative objects: *ẓanantu*, *ḥasibtu*, *khiltu*, *ʿalimtu*, *zaʿamtu*, *raʾaytu*, and *wajadtu*.

verbs of praise or blame [*fiʿlā al-madḥ wa-l-dhamm*] GRA 182 The two verbs *niʿma* and *biʾsa*, which are assigned to express praise or blame; used with two nominative nouns, the agent and the noun qualified with praise or blame.

verbs of proximity [*afʿāl al-muqāraba*] GRA

181 Category of verbs assigned to signify that the predicate is near to being the case with respect to either the hopes of the speaker or actual reality or that the action just began.

verificatory rebuttal [*al-jawāb al-taḥqīqī* – “response meant to establish the truth”] DIA 358 Rebuttal founded on a proof known to be true by the disputant who offers it. Opposed to a disputative rebuttal (*jawāb ilzāmī*).

virtual connection [*shibh kamāl al-ittiṣāl*] SEM 426–27 Relation between two consecutive sentences that, though not a relation of total connection (*kamāl al-ittiṣāl*), is close enough that the sentences must be broken up by forgoing the use of a conjunction.

virtual disconnection [*shibh kamāl al-inqiṭāʿ*] SEM 426 Relation between two consecutive sentences that, though not a relation of total disconnection (*kamāl al-infiṣāl*), entails that the sentences must be broken up by forgoing the use of a conjunction to ensure that the sentences are not read in continuity.

vocal composite [*al-murakkab al-ṣawtī*] LTY 290 Class of the synthetic composite (*murakkab mazjī*) with the *-wayhi* ending of certain Persian names, like Sībawayhi.

vocative object [*al-munādā* – “he who is called”] GRA 151 Accusative noun signifying the person whose response is sought through the use of a particle that stands for the verb *adʿū* (I call) either explicitly or implicitly.

vocative particles [*ḥurūf al-nidāʾ* – “the particles of calling”] GRA 197 Category of particles by which someone is called: *yā*, *ayā*, *hayā*, *ay*, and the *hamza*.

void [*al-khalāʾ*] CRD 560 Two corporeal objects’ not being in physical contact and not having anything in between them that is in physical contact with both.

vowelless *tāʾ* of femininity [*tāʾ al-taʾnīth al-sākina*] GRA 209 The *tāʾ* that attaches to the end of a perfect tense verb to indicate that the subject is feminine.

W

weak letter [*ḥarf al-ʿilla*] MOR The letter *wāw*, *yāʾ*, or *alif*.

weakness [*ḍuʿf al-taʾlīf* – “weakness of composition”] SEM 379 The composition of speech in a way that violates syntactical or grammatical rules. A defect that vitiates the articulateness (*faṣāḥa*) of speech.

well-content soul [*al-nafs al-muṭmaʾinna*] SPR 569n1 Aspect of the human soul that is secure in standing upright in obedience.

well-known report [*al-khabar al-mashhūr*] JRT 502 Another term for the widely known report (*khabar mustafīḍ*).

what the situation demands [*muqtaḍā al-ḥāl*] SEM 381 The specific considerations, as determined by the rhetorical situation, that an effective and eloquent speaker must take into account in addition to the primary substance of his speech.

why-demonstration [*al-burhān al-limmī*] LOG 267 Demonstrative argument that reasons from the cause to the effect: the middle term is the cause of the major term. This kind of reasoning can also be termed “*propter quid* reasoning.” The term *limmī* is derived from *lima* (why?).

widely known report [*al-khabar al-mustafīḍ*] JRT 502 Type of unit report (*khabar al-wāḥid*) that is widespread and has a basis; the minimum number of narrators for such a report is two according to the *fuqahāʾ*, greater than three according to the *uṣūliyyūn*, and three according to the *muḥaddithūn*.

word [*al-kalima*] MOR 25 In morphology, a noun or verb. In grammar, a noun, verb, or particle.

word-formation [*al-taṣrīf* – “deflecting; shifting”] MOR 25 Formation of a derivative word by transforming an original infinitive noun to signify various meanings in relation to its root meaning.

ARABIC–ENGLISH GLOSSARY KEY

abwāb al-ṣarf – morphological classes
adāt al-tashbīh – instrument of simile
adillat al-fiqh al-ijmāliyya – general indicants of jurisprudence
adillat al-fiqh al-tafṣīliyya – specific indicants of jurisprudence
afʿāl al-muqāraba – verbs of proximity
afʿāl al-qulūb – verbs of mental consideration
al-adāʾ – timely fulfillment
al-adāh – particle
al-afʿāl al-nāqiṣa – auxiliary verbs
al-afʿāl al-tāmma – complete verbs
al-ajwaf – hollow root
al-ʿajz – incapacity
al-ʿaks al-mustawī – conversion (1)
al-ʿalam al-jinsī – generic proper name
al-ʿalam al-shakhṣī – personal proper name
al-ʿalam – proper name
al-ʿalāqa – semantic link
al-amāra – suggestive indicant
al-ʿāmil al-lafẓī al-qiyāsī – regular expressed governor
al-ʿāmil al-lafẓī al-samāʿī – received expressed governor
al-ʿāmil al-lafẓī – expressed governor
al-ʿāmil al-maʿnawī – abstract governor
al-ʿāmil – governor
al-amr bi-l-ṣīgha – imperative proper
al-amr (1) – command
al-amr (2) – imperative
al-amthila al-fiʿliyya – verbal derivatives
al-amthila al-ismiyya – nominal derivatives
al-amthila al-mukhtalifa – variform derivatives
al-amthila al-muṭṭarida – uniform derivatives
al-amthila al-waṣfiyya – adjectival derivatives
al-amthila – derivatives
al-ʿaraḍ al-ʿāmm – general accident
al-ʿaraḍ al-lāzim al-bayyin bi-l-maʿnā al-aʿamm – broadly evident inseparable accident
al-ʿaraḍ al-lāzim al-bayyin bi-l-maʿnā al-akhaṣṣ – strictly evident inseparable accident
al-ʿaraḍ al-lāzim ghayr al-bayyin – inevident inseparable accident
al-ʿaraḍ al-lāzim – inseparable accident
al-ʿaraḍ al-mufāriq bi-l-fiʿl – actually separating accident
al-ʿaraḍ al-mufāriq bi-l-imkān – possibly separable accident
al-ʿaraḍ al-mufāriq – separable accident
al-ʿaraḍ – property
al-ʿarḍ – presentation
al-aṣl – original case
al-asmāʾ al-muttaṣila bi-l-afʿāl – nouns related to verbs
al-aṣwāt – nouns of sound
ālat al-waḍʿ – assigner's meaning
al-ʿaṭf bi-l-ḥurūf – conjunction
al-ʿaṭf – conjunction
al-awwaliyyāt – self-evident premises
al-ʿazīma – stringent ruling
al-badal – substitute apposition
al-balāgha – eloquence
al-bayān – clarifying apposition
al-bināʾ li-l-majhūl – passive voice

al-burhān al-innī – that-demonstration
al-burhān al-limmī – why-demonstration
al-burhān (1) – demonstration
al-burhān (2) – demonstrative argument
al-dāʾimiyya – expressive of persistence
al-dalāla al-ʿaqliyya – rational signification
al-dalāla al-lafẓiyya – verbal signification
al-dalāla al-ṭabīʿiyya – natural signification
al-dalāla al-waḍʿiyya – assigned signification
al-dalāla ghayr al-lafẓiyya – nonverbal signification
al-dalāla – signification
al-dalīl al-iqnāʿī – persuasive proof
al-dalīl al-qaṭʿī – conclusive indicant
al-dalīl al-ẓannī – presumptive indicant
al-dalīl – indicant
al-dāll – signifier
al-ḍamīr al-munfaṣil – detached pronoun
al-ḍamīr al-muttaṣil – attached pronoun
al-ḍarb – mood
al-ḍarūrī – immediate
al-daʿwā – claim
al-dhikr – mention
al-dīn – religion
al-fāʿil – agent
al-farʿ – derivative case
al-faṣāḥa – articulateness
al-faṣl al-baʿīd – remote differentia
al-faṣl al-muqassim – divisive differentia
al-faṣl al-muqawwim – constitutive differentia
al-faṣl al-qarīb – direct differentia
al-faṣl (1) – differentia
al-faṣl (2) – breaking
al-faṣl (3) – separation
al-fikr – reflective thought
al-fiʿl al-ghayr al-mutaʿaddī – intransitive verb
al-fiʿl al-lāzim – intransitive verb
al-fiʿl al-māḍī – perfect tense verb
al-fiʿl al-muḍāriʿ – imperfect tense verb
al-fiʿl al-mutaʿaddī – transitive verb
al-fiʿl – verb
al-fiqh – jurisprudence
al-fiṭriyyāt – naturally evident premises
al-gharāba – obscurity
al-ghaṣb – usurpation
al-ghulū – excessive hyperbole
al-ḥadd al-akbar – major term
al-ḥadd al-aṣghar – minor term
al-ḥadd al-awsaṭ – middle term
al-ḥadd al-nāqiṣ – incomplete essential definition
al-ḥadd al-tāmm – complete essential definition
al-ḥadhf (1) – elision
al-ḥadhf (2) – omission
al-ḥadīth al-mursal – *mursal* hadith
al-ḥadsiyyāt – intuitively inferred premises
al-ḥāl (1) – circumstance
al-ḥāl (2) – situation
al-ḥāl (3) – quasi-ontic mode
al-ḥaqīqa al-ʿaqliyya – literal predication
al-ḥaqīqa al-lughawiyya – literal expression
al-ḥaqīqa (1) – literal expression
al-ḥaqīqa (2) – literal language
al-ḥarf – particle
al-ḥasan – good act
al-ḥaṣr – exhaustiveness
al-hayʾa al-tarkībiyya al-kalāmiyya – sentential composite structure
al-hayʾa al-tarkībiyya ghayr al-kalāmiyya – non-sentential composite structure
al-hayʾa al-tarkībiyya – composite structure
al-ḥikāʾiyya – past perfect

al-ḥukm – judgment
al-ḥukm – ruling
al-ḥurūf al-jāzima – jussive particles
al-ḥurūf al-maṣdariyya – infinitive particles
al-ḥurūf al-mushabbaha bi-l-fiʿl – verb-like particles
al-ḥurūf al-nāṣiba li-l-fiʿl al-muḍāriʿ – subjunctive particles of the imperfect tense verb
al-ibāḥa – permission
al-ibtidāʾī – initiating mode
al-ibtidāʾiyya – expressive of the time of commencement
al-iḍāfa al-ʿahdiyya al-dhihniyya – mentally specific *iḍāfa* structure
al-iḍāfa al-ʿahdiyya – specific *iḍāfa* structure
al-iḍāfa al-istighrāqiyya – universal *iḍāfa* structure
al-iḍāfa al-jinsiyya – generic *iḍāfa* structure
al-iḍāfa al-lafẓiyya – nonattributive *iḍāfa*
al-iḍāfa al-maʿnawiyya – attributive *iḍāfa*
al-iḍāfa – *iḍāfa*
al-idghām – assimilation
al-ifḥām – silencing
al-īghāl – epiphrase
al-ighrāq – extravagant hyperbole
al-iḥsān – spiritual excellence
al-ījāb – obligation
al-ījāz – brevity
al-ijmāʿ al-qaṭʿī – conclusive consensus
al-ijmāʿ al-sukūtī – tacit consensus
al-ijmāʿ al-ẓannī – presumptive consensus
al-ijmāʿ – consensus
al-ijtihād – ijtihad
al-ikhrāj ʿalā muqtaḍā al-ẓāhir – expected mode of expression
al-iʿlāl – modification
al-ilhām – spiritual inspiration
al-ʿilla al-qaṭʿiyya – conclusive cause
al-ʿilla – legal cause
al-ʿilm – knowledge
al-iltifāt – shift of person
al-iltimās – request
al-iltizām – concomitance
al-ilzām – forced concession
al-īmāʾ – direct indication
al-īmān – belief
al-imtināʿiyya – counterfactual hypothetical
al-inkārī – insisting mode
al-inshāʾ – non-declarative speech
al-intihāʾiyya – expressive of the point of termination
al-iʿrāb al-lafẓī – explicit inflection
al-iʿrāb al-maḥallī – positional inflection
al-iʿrāb al-taqdīrī – implicit inflection
al-iʿrāb – inflection
al-ishāra – pointing
al-ishtiqāq – morphological derivation
al-islām – submission
al-ism al-mabnī – indeclinable noun
al-ism al-mansūb – relational noun
al-ism al-mawṣūl – relative pronoun
al-ism al-muʾannath – feminine noun
al-ism al-mubham al-tāmm – disambiguated noun
al-ism al-muḍāf – *muḍāf* noun
al-ism al-mudhakkar – masculine noun
al-ism al-muʿrab – declinable noun
al-ism (1) – noun
al-ism (2) – name simpliciter
al-isnād al-khabarī – declarative predication
al-istiʿāra al-ʿāmmiyya – common metaphor
al-istiʿāra al-aṣliyya – primary metaphor
al-istiʿāra al-ḥaqīqiyya – actual metaphor
al-istiʿāra al-ʿinādiyya – discordant metaphor

al-istiʿāra al-khāṣṣiyya – special metaphor
al-istiʿāra al-makniyya – implicit metaphor
al-istiʿāra al-mufrada – simple metaphor
al-istiʿāra al-mujarrada – deflated metaphor
al-istiʿāra al-murakkaba – composite metaphor
al-istiʿāra al-murashshaḥa – inflated metaphor
al-istiʿāra al-muṣarraḥa – explicit metaphor
al-istiʿāra al-muṭlaqa – plain metaphor
al-istiʿāra al-tabaʿiyya – secondary metaphor
al-istiʿāra al-taḥqīqiyya – actual metaphor
al-istiʿāra al-takhyīliyya (1) – fanciful metaphor
al-istiʿāra al-takhyīliyya (2) – metaphorical characterization
al-istiʿāra al-tamthīliyya – analogical metaphor
al-istiʿāra al-wifāqiyya – concordant metaphor
al-istiʿāra bi-l-kināya – metaphor with concealment
al-istiʿāra – metaphor
al-istidlāl – adopted indicants
al-istifhām – inquiry; question
al-istifhāmiyya al-ḥikāʾiyya – past perfect interrogative
al-istiḥsān – juristic preference
al-istikhdām – reutilization
al-istiṣḥāb – presumption of continuity
al-iʿtiqād al-fāsid – incorrect belief
al-iʿtiqād al-ṣaḥīḥ – correct belief
al-iʿtirāḍ – interjecting
al-iṭnāb – prolixity
al-jadal – dialectical argument
al-jamʿ (1) – combination (1)
al-jamʿ (2) – sufficient inclusiveness
al-jāmiʿ – commonality
al-jawāb al-ilzāmī – disputative rebuttal
al-jawāb al-taḥqīqī – verificatory rebuttal
al-jawāz – acceptability
al-jawhar al-fard – atom
al-jawhar – substance
al-jazāʾ – result verb
al-jins al-ʿālī – highest genus
al-jins al-baʿīd – remote genus
al-jins al-mutawassiṭ – intermediate genus
al-jins al-qarīb – direct genus
al-jins al-sāfil – lowest genus
al-jins – genus
al-jism – corporeal object
al-juzʾ – disjunct
al-juzʾī al-ḥaqīqī – real particular
al-juzʾī al-iḍāfī – relative particular
al-juzʾī – particular
al-kalām al-nafsī – pre-expressional speech
al-kalima (1) – word
al-kalima (2) – verb
al-kalimāt al-jāzima – jussive operators
al-karāha – reprehension
al-karāma – saintly miracle
al-kasbī – acquired
al-kayfiyya – modality
al-khabar al-mashhūr – well-known report
al-khabar al-mustafīḍ – widely known report
al-khabar al-mutawātir – mass report
al-khabar – predicate
al-khalāʾ – void
al-khāṣṣa – special accident
al-khidhlān – forsaking
al-khiṭāba – rhetorical argument
al-kināya al-baʿīda – far-removed implication
al-kināya al-qarība – direct implication
al-kināya – implication
al-kināyāt – vague pronouns
al-kubrā – major premise

al-kullī al-ʿaqlī – conceptualized universal
al-kullī al-ʿaraḍī – accidental universal
al-kullī al-dhātī – essential universal
al-kullī al-ḥaqīqī – real universal
al-kullī al-iḍāfī – relative universal
al-kullī al-manṭiqī – logical concept of the universal
al-kullī al-mushakkik – modulative universal
al-kullī al-mutawāṭiʾ – univocal universal
al-kullī al-ṭabīʿī – natural universal
al-kullī – universal
al-kunya – surname
al-laff wa-l-nashr – respective correlation
al-lafīf al-mafrūq – disjointly weak root
al-lafīf al-maqrūn – conjointly weak root
al-lafẓ al-ʿāmm – general expression
al-lafẓ al-mufrad – simple expression
al-lafẓ al-muḥkam – unambiguous expression
al-lafẓ al-murakkab al-nāqiṣ – incomplete composite expression
al-lafẓ al-murakkab al-tāmm – complete composite expression
al-lafẓ al-murakkab al-taqyīdī – restrictive composite expression
al-lafẓ al-murakkab ghayr al-taqyīdī – non-restrictive composite expression
al-lafẓ al-murakkab – composite expression
al-lafẓ al-mustaʿār – metaphorical expression
al-lafẓ al-mutashābih – ambiguous expression
al-lafẓ – verbal expression
al-laʿib – trifling
al-lām al-muwaṭṭiʾa li-l-qasam – *lām* that anticipates an oath
al-lāmāt – *lām* particles
al-laqab – title
al-lāzim al-dhihnī – mentally inseparable accident
al-lāzim al-wujūdī – extramentally inseparable accident
al-lāzim – implicate
al-liyāqatiyya – expressive of what is proper or appropriate
al-lugha – lexical code
al-luṭf – grace
al-luzūm – intransitivity
al-mabnī al-ʿāriḍī – accidentally indeclinable noun
al-mabnī li-l-fāʿil – active voice
al-madlūl – significate
al-mafhūm (1) – intension
al-mafhūm (2) – implicature
al-mafʿūl al-muṭlaq – action-notion
al-mafʿūl bihi – object
al-mafʿūl fīhi – action-place/time
al-mafʿūl lahu – action-reason
al-mafʿūl maʿahu – action-accompaniment
al-mafʿūl – actional accusative
al-maḥalliyya – expressive of the place
al-maḥmūl – predicate
al-mahmūz – hamzated root
al-maḥsūsāt – sensate premises
al-majāz al-ʿaqlī – nonliteral predication
al-majāz al-lughawī – trope
al-majāz al-mursal al-mufrad – simple metonymy
al-majāz al-mursal al-murakkab – composite metonymy
al-majāz al-mursal – metonymy
al-majāz – nonliteral language
al-majhūl – unknown
al-majmūʿ al-mukassar – broken plural noun
al-majmūʿ al-muṣaḥḥaḥ – sound plural noun
al-majmūʿ – plural noun
al-majrūr – genitive
al-majzūm – jussive

al-makān – space
al-maʿlūm – active voice
al-malzūm – implicant
al-maʿmūl bi-l-aṣāla – primarily governed expression
al-maʿmūl bi-l-tabaʿ – secondarily governed expression
al-maʿmūl – governed expression
al-manʿ (1) – challenge
al-manʿ (2) – sufficient exclusiveness
al-māniʿ – impediment
al-manqūl al-sharʿī – transferred by revelation
al-manqūl al-ʿurfī al-ʿāmm – transferred by general convention
al-manqūl al-ʿurfī al-khāṣṣ – transferred by a specific convention
al-manṣūb – accusative/subjunctive
al-manṭūq – articulated meaning
al-maqbūlāt – authoritative premises
al-maqīs ʿalayhi – source of the analogy
al-maqīs – object of the analogy
al-maqsim – dividendum
al-marfūʿ – nominative/indicative
al-maʿrifa – definite noun
al-mā-ṣadaq – extension
al-maṣdar al-mīmī – mimated infinitive
al-maṣdar al-ṣanʿī – synthetic infinitive noun
al-maṣdar – infinitive noun
al-mashhūrāt – commonplace premises
al-matbūʿ – principal noun
al-mathal – proverb
al-maṭlūb – conclusion
al-maʿṭūf – conjunct
al-mawḍūʿ lahu – denotation
al-mawḍūʿ (1) – assigned expression
al-mawḍūʿ (2) – subject
al-mawḍūʿ (3) – fabricated report
al-maẓnūnāt – suppositional premises
al-miṣdāq – extension
al-mithāl – resemblant root
al-muʿallil – proponent
al-muʿāraḍa bi-l-ghayr – counteraction by unlike
al-muʿāraḍa bi-l-mithl – counteraction by like
al-muʿāraḍa bi-l-qalb – counteraction by reversal
al-muʿāraḍa – counteraction
al-muʾawwal – interpreted expression
al-mubālagha al-maqbūla – acceptable hyperbole
al-mubhamāt – non-personal pronouns
al-mubtadaʾ – subject
al-muḍāʿaf – doubled root
al-muḍāf ilayhi – *muḍāf ilayhi*
al-muddaʿā – claim
al-muḍmar – personal pronoun
al-mufassar – explained
al-mughālaṭa – fallacious argument
al-muḥaṣṣala – non-privative proposition
al-muḥassināt al-badīʿiyya – embellishments
al-mujarrabāt – experiential premises
al-muʿjiza – prophetic miracle
al-mujmal – indeterminate
al-mujtahid – mujtahid
al-mukhayyilāt – imaginative premises
al-mulāʾim – suitable accompaniment
al-mumkin – possible
al-munādā – vocative object
al-munāsaba – mutual suitability
al-munāsib al-ḍarūrī – consideration of fundamental necessity
al-munāsib al-ḥājī – consideration of practical necessity
al-munāsib al-taḥsīnī – consideration of practical benefit

al-munāsib – suitable legal consideration
al-munāẓara – dialectical disputation
al-munfaṣila al-ḥaqīqiyya – strict disjunctive proposition
al-munfaṣila al-ʿinādiyya – inherently disjunctive proposition
al-munfaṣila al-ittifāqiyya – coincidentally disjunctive proposition
al-munfaṣila al-māniʿat al-jamʿ – anti-inclusive disjunctive proposition
al-munfaṣila al-māniʿat al-khulū – anti-exclusive disjunctive proposition
al-munṣarif – fully declinable noun
al-muqaddam – antecedent
al-muqallid – imitator
al-muqayyad – qualified expression
al-murakkab al-mazjī – synthetic composite
al-murakkab al-ṣawtī – vocal composite
al-murakkabāt – compound nouns
al-musallamāt – conceded premises
al-musāwāh – proportionality
al-mushabbah bihi – vehicle for the simile
al-mushabbah – tenor of the simile
al-mushāghaba – contentious disputation
al-mushāhadāt – observational premises
al-mushākala – semblance
al-mushtarak al-lafẓī – equivocal expression
al-mushtarak al-maʿnawī – univocal universal
al-musnad al-sababī – resumptive predicate
al-musnad ilayhi – subject
al-musnad – predicate
al-mustaʿār lahu – tenor of the metaphor
al-mustaʿār minhu – vehicle for the metaphor
al-mustathnā al-munqaṭiʿ – disconnected exception
al-mustathnā al-muttaṣil – connected exception
al-mustathnā – exception
al-muṭābaqa (1) – correspondence
al-muṭābaqa (2) – antithesis
al-muʿtall – irregular roots
al-mutawātir al-lafẓī – verbatim mass report
al-mutawātir al-maʿnawī – substantive mass report
al-mutawātirāt – massively reported premises
al-muthannā – dual noun
al-muṭlaq – unqualified expression
al-muttaṣila al-ittifāqiyya – coincidentally conditional proposition
al-muttaṣila al-luzūmiyya – inherently conditional proposition
al-muwāzana – equilibrium
al-nadb – recommendation
al-nafs al-ammāra bi-l-sūʾ – evil-inciting soul
al-nafs al-lawwāma – self-blaming soul
al-nafs al-muṭmaʾinna – well-content soul
al-nafs al-rawḥāniyya – comfort-seeking soul
al-nahy (1) – prohibition (1)
al-nahy (2) – prohibitive
al-nakira – indefinite noun
al-naqḍ al-ijmālī – collective confutation
al-naqḍ al-maksūr – partial confutation
al-naqḍ al-tafṣīlī – analytic confutation
al-naqḍ – confutation
al-nāqiṣ – defective root
al-naql bi-l-maʿnā – transmission by meaning
al-naql – transfer
al-naskh – abrogation
al-naṣṣ – unequivocal expression
al-natīja – conclusion
al-nawʿ al-ʿālī – highest species
al-nawʿ al-ḥaqīqī – real species
al-nawʿ al-iḍāfī – relative species
al-nawʿ al-mutawassiṭ – intermediate species

al-nawʿ al-sāfil – lowest species
al-nawʿ – species
al-naẓarī – reflective
al-nisba al-ḥukmiyya – judgmental relation
al-nūn al-muʾakkida – emphatic *nūn*
al-qabīḥ – bad act
al-qaḍāʾ – late fulfillment
al-qadar – destiny
al-qādiḥ – disqualifying factor
al-qaḍiyya al-ḥamliyya – categorical proposition
al-qaḍiyya al-maʿdūlat al-ṭarafayn – doubly privative proposition
al-qaḍiyya al-muhmala – unquantified proposition
al-qaḍiyya al-sharṭiyya al-munfaṣila – disjunctive proposition
al-qaḍiyya al-sharṭiyya – hypothetical proposition
al-qaḍiyya al-thulāthiyya – three-part proposition
al-qaḍiyya al-thunāʾiyya – two-part proposition
al-qaḍiyya al-wujūdiyya – existential proposition
al-qaḍiyya – proposition
al-qalb (1) – conversion (2)
al-qalb (2) – inversion
al-qalb (3) – palindrome
al-qarīna al-lafẓiyya – expressed contextual indicant
al-qarīna al-maʿnawiyya – unexpressed contextual indicant
al-qarīna (1) – contextual indicant
al-qarīna (2) – combination (2)
al-qasīm – condivision
al-qaṣr al-ḥaqīqī – real restriction
al-qaṣr al-iḍāfī – relative restriction
al-qaṣr – restriction
al-qidam – eternality
al-qism al-mursal – extended subdivision
al-qism – subdivision
al-qiyās al-iqtirānī – combinative syllogism
al-qiyās al-istithnāʾī – replicative syllogism
al-qiyās al-jalī – evident analogy
al-qiyās al-ẓannī – presumptive analogy
al-qiyās (1) – syllogism
al-qiyās (2) – analogy (1)
al-qudratiyya – expressive of ability
al-rābiṭa – copula
al-rajāʾiyya – expressive of hope
al-ramz – intimation
al-rasm al-nāqiṣ – incomplete descriptive definition
al-rasm al-tāmm – complete descriptive definition
al-rizq – provision
al-rukhṣa – dispensation
al-safsaṭa – sophistry
al-sāʾil – objector
al-sajʿ al-muṭarraf – peripheral rhyme
al-sajʿ al-muwāzī – parallel rhyme
al-sajʿ – prose rhyme
al-sāliba al-ʿinādiyya – negative of inherent disjunction
al-sāliba al-ittifāqiyya – negative of coincidental conditionality/disjunction
al-sāliba al-luzūmiyya – negative of inherent conditionality
al-sālim – sound
al-sanad – corroboration
al-shāhid – evidence
al-shakk – doubt
al-shakl – figure
al-sharʿ – revelational usage
al-sharṭ (1) – condition
al-sharṭ (2) – condition verb
al-sharṭiyya al-ḥikāʾiyya – past conditional
al-sharṭiyya – conditional

al-shiʿr – poetical argument
al-ṣifa al-mushabbaha – participial
al-ṣifa – adjective
al-suʾāl (1) – entreaty
al-suʾāl (2) – questioning
al-ṣughrā – minor premise
al-sūr – quantifier
al-taʿaddī – transitivity
al-taʿādul – contradiction (2)
al-tabāyun – mutual distinction
al-tablīgh – reasonable hyperbole
al-taḍammun – containment
al-taḍāyuf – conceptual correlation
al-tadhyīl – epiphonema
al-taḥḍīḍiyya – expressive of exhortation
al-taḥrīm – prohibition (2)
al-tajrīd – extraction
al-takalluf – effort
al-taʾkhīr – postponement
al-takhṣīṣ – specification (1)
al-taʾkīd (1) – emphasis
al-taʾkīd (2) – emphatic apposition
al-taklīf – injunctive imposition
al-takmīl – complementing
al-ṭalabī – answering mode
al-tālī – consequent
al-taʿlīq – suspension
al-talwīḥ – hinting
al-tamanniyya – expressive of wish
al-tamthīl ʿalā sabīl al-istiʿāra – metaphorical analogy
al-tamthīl – analogy (2)
al-tamyīz – specification (2)
al-tanāquḍ – contradiction (1)
al-tanbīh – notification
al-tandībiyya – expressive of reproach
al-taʾnīth al-ḥaqīqī – real femininity
al-taʾnīth al-lafẓī – verbal femininity
al-tanwīn al-ghālī – nunation of prolongation
al-tanwīn – nunation
al-taqdīm – foregrounding
al-taʿqīd – overcomplication
al-taqlīd – imitation
al-taqrīb – consecution
al-taqrīr – tacit approval
al-taqsīm al-ʿaqlī – deductive division
al-taqsīm al-ḥaqīqī – real division
al-taqsīm al-istiqrāʾī – inductive division
al-taqsīm al-iʿtibārī – perspectival division
al-taqsīm – process of elimination
al-tarāduf – synonymy
al-taʿrīḍ – allusion
al-taʿrīf al-ḥaqīqī (1) – logical definition
al-taʿrīf al-ḥaqīqī (2) – real definition
al-taʿrīf al-ismī – nominal definition
al-taʿrīf al-lafẓī – lexical definition
al-taʿrīf – definition
al-tarjīḥ – giving preponderance
al-tasāwī – coextension
al-taṣawwuf – spiritual devotion
al-taṣawwur al-sādhaj – pure conception
al-taṣawwur – conception
al-taṣdīq – assent
al-tashbīh al-maqlūb – inverted simile
al-tashbīh – simile
al-taṣrīf – word-formation
al-tatmīm – enriching
al-tawfīq – providence
al-tawḥīd – affirming divine oneness
al-taʾwīl al-fāsid – unsound interpretation

al-taʾwīl al-ṣaḥīḥ – sound interpretation
al-tawqītiyya al-imtidādiyya – temporally extensive
al-tawqītiyya – expressive of the time
al-tawriya – double entendre
al-thulāthī al-mujarrad – simple triliteral
al-ʿumūm wa-l-khuṣūṣ al-muṭlaq – subsumption
al-ʿumūm wa-l-khuṣūṣ min wajh – partial overlap
al-ʿurf al-ʿāmm – general convention
al-ʿurf al-khāṣṣ – specific convention
al-waḍʿ al-ʿāmm – general assignment
al-waḍʿ al-khāṣṣ – specific assignment
al-waḍʿ al-kullī – general assignment
al-waḍʿ al-nawʿī – collective assignment
al-waḍʿ al-shakhṣī – individual assignment
al-waḍʿ li-mawḍūʿ lahu ʿāmm – assignment to the general
al-waḍʿ li-mawḍūʿ lahu khāṣṣ – assignment to the specific
al-waḍʿ (1) – assignment
al-waḍʿ (2) – regulative imposition
al-waḥadāt al-thamānī – eight unities
al-wahm – fancy
al-wāsiṭa bayna al-aqsām – residual subdivision
al-waṣl – joining
al-wujūbiyya – expressive of obligation or necessity
al-yaqīniyyāt – certain premises
al-ẓāhir – apparent expression
al-zamān – time
al-ẓann – presumption
al-ziyāda – addition
ʿamal – governance
asmāʾ al-afʿāl – quasi-verbal nouns
ʿaṭf al-bayān – clarifying apposition
dalālat al-īmāʾ – directly entailed signification
dalālat al-iqtiḍāʾ – textually required entailment
dalālat al-ishāra – indirectly entailed signification
dalīl burhānī – demonstrative proof
ḍuʿf al-taʾlīf – weakness
faḥwā al-khiṭāb – *a fortiori* implicature
fāʾidat al-khabar – information
farḍ al-kifāya – communal obligation
fiʿl al-taʿajjub – verb of wonderment
fiʿlā al-madḥ wa-l-dhamm – verbs of praise or blame
ghayr al-munṣarif – partially declinable noun
ghayr al-sālim – irregular roots; unsound
hāʾ al-sakt – *hāʾ* of pause
hamzat al-waṣl – connective *hamza*
ḥarf al-ʿilla – weak letter
ḥarf al-radʿ – particle of rebuke
ḥarf al-taqrīb – particle of proximity
ḥarfā al-istifhām – interrogative particles
ḥarfā al-khiṭāb – particles of address
ḥarfā al-tafsīr – particles of explanation
ḥarfā al-taʿlīl – particles expressing the reason
ḥukm al-aṣl – ruling of the original case
ḥurūf al-ʿaṭf – conjunctions
ḥurūf al-istiqbāl – particles of futurity
ḥurūf al-istithnāʾ – exceptive particles
ḥurūf al-jarr – prepositions
ḥurūf al-nafy – negative particles
ḥurūf al-nidāʾ – vocative particles
ḥurūf al-sharṭ – conditional particles
ḥurūf al-ṣila – particles of connection
ḥurūf al-taḥḍīḍ – particles of reproach and exhortation
ḥurūf al-tanbīh – particles of alerting
ḥurūf al-taṣdīq wa-l-ījāb – particles of affirmation
ījāz al-ḥadhf – brevity by omission
ījāz al-qaṣr – brevity by parsimony

ʿilm al-badīʿ – embellishment
ʿilm al-bayān – figurative language
ʿilm al-istiʿāra – science of metaphor
ʿilm al-maʿānī – rhetorical semantics
ʿilm al-manṭiq – logic
ʿilm al-munāẓara – dialectics
ʿilm al-naḥw – grammar
ʿilm al-ṣarf – morphology
ʿilm al-waḍʿ – language theory
ʿilm uṣūl al-fiqh – jurisprudential theory
ism al-ʿadad – numeral noun
ism al-āla – noun of instrument
ism al-fāʿil – active participle
ism al-ishāra – demonstrative pronoun
ism al-jins – generic noun
ism al-mafʿūl – passive participle
ism al-makān – noun of place
ism al-tafḍīl – comparative/superlative noun
ism al-taṣghīr – diminutive noun
ism al-zamān – noun of time
istifhāmiyya – interrogative
iẓhār al-maṭlūb – displaying what is desired
jamʿ al-kathra – plural of abundance
jamʿ al-qilla – plural of paucity
jins al-ajnās – genus of genera
jumlat al-jawāb – result clause
jumlat al-sharṭ – condition clause
juzʾī al-mawḍūʿ lahu – assignment to the specific
juzʾī al-waḍʿ – specific assignment
kamāl al-inqiṭāʿ – total disconnection
kamāl al-ittiṣāl – total connection
khabar al-wāḥid – unit report
khabar – declarative expression
khabarī – declarative
khilāf al-awlā – suboptimal
kullī al-mawḍūʿ lahu – assignment to the general
lām al-ʿahd – specific *lām*
lām al-amr – imperative *lām*
lām al-ibtidāʾ – beginning *lām*
lām al-istighrāq – universal *lām*
lām al-jarr – prepositional *lām*
lām al-jins – generic *lām*
lām al-qasam – *lām* of oath
lām al-taʿrīf – definite *lām*
lāzim al-māhiyya – essentially inseparable accident
lāzim fāʾidat al-khabar – implication of the information
mā wa-lā al-mushabbahatāni bi-laysa – the *mā* and *lā* that resemble *laysa*
mabādī al-taṣawwuf – principles of spiritual devotion
maʿdūlat al-maḥmūl – predicate-privative proposition
maʿdūlat al-mawḍūʿ – subject-privative proposition
mafhūm al-mukhālafa – counter implicature
mafhūm al-muwāfaqa – congruous implicature
majāz lughawī – nonliteral expression
maʿnā al-fiʿl – expression with verbal import
maṣdar bināʾ al-marra – instantial infinitive noun
maṣdar bināʾ al-nawʿ – infinitive noun of kind
mawrid al-qisma – source of the division
mujtahid al-futyā – mujtahid of fatwas
mujtahid al-madhhab – mujtahid within a school
mukhālafat al-qiyās – aberrancy
muqtaḍā al-ḥāl – what the situation demands
murāʿāt al-naẓīr – association
muʿtall al-lām – defective root
nāʾib al-fāʿil – substitute agent
nawʿ al-anwāʿ – species of species
qaḍiyya sharṭiyya muttaṣila – conditional proposition

qaṣr al-ifrād – restriction for exclusivity
qaṣr al-qalb – restriction for inversion
qaṣr al-taʿyīn – restriction for specification
qiyās al-dalāla – analogy by indication
qiyās al-maʿnā – analogy by causal force
radd al-ʿajuz ʿalā al-ṣadr – echo
saʿīd – blissful
sajʿ al-tarṣīʿ – inlaid rhyme
shaqī – damned
shibh kamāl al-inqiṭāʿ – virtual disconnection
shibh kamāl al-ittiṣāl – virtual connection
ṣifāt al-afʿāl – attributes of action
ṣifāt al-dhāt – attributes of essence
sunnat al-kifāya – communal sunna
tāʾ al-taʾnīth al-sākina – vowelless *tāʾ* of femininity
taḥrīr al-murād – clarification
takhrīj al-manāṭ – extraction of the basis
tanāfur al-ḥurūf – dissonance
tanāfur al-kalimāt – dissonance
tanqīḥ al-manāṭ – isolation of the basis
tanwīn al-ʿiwaḍ – nunation of compensation
tanwīn al-muqābala – counterpart nunation
tanwīn al-tamakkun – nunation of establishment
tanwīn al-tankīr – indefinite nunation
tanwīn al-tarannum – nunation of nasalization
ṭarafā al-tashbīh – objects of comparison
tawābiʿ al-muʿrab – appositives
taʿyīn al-ṭarīq – practical pointer
uṣūl al-fiqh – principles of jurisprudence
wajh al-shabah – ground for comparison
wajh al-tashbīh – ground for comparison
waṣliyya – anti-exceptive
ẓarf makān – adverb of place
ẓarf zamān – adverb of time

BIBLIOGRAPHY

Abū Dāwūd. *Kitāb al-sunan*. [See al-Sijistānī, Abū Dāwūd.]

al-Āmidī, ʿAbd al-Wahhāb. *Sharḥ al-Āmidī ʿalā al-Risāla al-waladiyya*. Edited by ʿAbd al-Ḥamīd al-ʿĪsāwī. Amman: Dār al-Nūr, 2014.

———. *Sharḥ al-Waladiyya*. Istanbul: Dār al-Ṭibāʿa al-ʿĀmira, 1845.

al-Āmidī, ʿAlī b. Muḥammad. *al-Iḥkām fī uṣūl al-aḥkām*. Edited by ʿAbd al-Razzāq ʿAfīfī. 4 vols. Riyadh: Dār al-Ṣumayʿī li-l-Nashr wa-l-Tawzīʿ, 2003.

al-Anṣārī, Zakariyyā. *Fatḥ al-Wahhāb bi-sharḥ al-Ādāb*. Edited by ʿArafah ʿAbd al-Raḥmān al-Nādī. Kuwait: Dār al-Ḍiyāʾ, 2014.

———. *Ghāyat al-wuṣūl ilā sharḥ Lubb al-uṣūl*. Edited by Muṣṭafā b. Ḥāmid b. Sumayṭ. Beirut: Dār al-Ḍiyāʾ, 2017.

———. *Ḥāshiyat Shaykh al-Islām Zakariyyā al-Anṣārī ʿalā sharḥ al-Imām al-Maḥallī ʿalā Jamʿ al-jawāmiʿ*. Edited by ʿAbd al-Ḥafīẓ Hilāl al-Jazāʾirī. 4 vols. Riyadh: Maktabat al-Rushd, 2007.

al-Astarābādī, Raḍī al-Dīn. *Sharḥ Shāfiyat Ibn Ḥājib*. Edited by Muḥammad Nūr al-Ḥasan, Muḥammad al-Zaqrāf, and Muḥammad Muḥyī al-Dīn ʿAbd al-Ḥamīd. 4 vols. Beirut: Dār al-Kutub al-ʿIlmiyya, 1982.

al-ʿAṭṭār, Ḥasan. *Ḥāshiya ʿalā sharḥ al-Khabīṣī*. In *al-Tadhhīb sharḥ ʿUbaydallāh b. Faḍlallāh al-Khabīṣī ʿalā Tahdhīb al-manṭiq wa-l-kalām*. Cairo: Maṭbaʿat Muṣtafā al-Bābī al-Ḥalabī, 1936.

———. *Ḥāshiyat al-ʿAṭṭār ʿalā sharḥ al-Jalāl al-Maḥallī ʿalā Jamʿ al-jawāmiʿ*. 2 vols. Beirut: Dār al-Kutub al-ʿIlmiyya, n.d.

al-Baghdādī, Ismāʿīl Pāshā. *Hadiyyat al-ʿārifīn: Asmāʾ al-muʾallifīn wa-āthār al-muṣannifīn*. Istanbul: Wakālat al-Maʿārif, 1951.

al-Bakshahrī, Aḥmad Shākir. *Taṣwīr al-waḍʿ ʿalā matn Numūdhaj al-waḍʿ*. Istanbul: Dār al-Ṭibāʿa al-ʿĀmira, 1305/1887 or 1888.

al-Bannānī, ʿAbd al-Raḥmān b. Jādallāh. *Ḥāshiyat al-Bannānī ʿalā sharḥ al-Maḥallī ʿalā matn Jamʿ al-jawāmiʿ*. 2 vols. Beirut: Dār al-Fikr, 1982.

al-Bannānī, Muṣṭafā b. Muḥammad. *al-Tajrīd*. In *Taqrīr al-Shams al-Anbābī ʿalā sharḥ Saʿd al-Dīn al-Taftāzānī li-Talkhīṣ al-Miftāḥ wa-ḥāshiyatihi al-shahīra bi-l-Tajrīd fī ʿilm al-maʿānī wa-l-bayān wa-l-badīʿ*. 4 vols. Cairo: Maṭbaʿat al-Saʿāda, 1330–1331/1912–1913.

al-Bayhaqī, Abū Bakr Aḥmad. *al-Sunan al-kubrā*. Edited by Muḥammad ʿAbd al-Qādir ʿAṭā. 11 vols. Beirut: Dār al-Kutub al-ʿIlmiyya, 2003.

Birgevī, Meḥmed. *Iẓhār al-asrār fī al-naḥw*. Edited by Anwar al-Dāghistānī. Beirut: Dār al-Minhāj, 2011.

———. *Risāla fī amthilat al-taṣrīf*. In *Majmūʿat al-ṣarf wa-shurūḥuhā wa-ḥawāshīhā*, edited by Ṣuhayb Mullā Muḥammad Nūrī ʿAlī, 629–52. Damascus: Dār Nūr al-Ṣabāḥ, 2016.

al-Buḥayrī, Muḥammad b. Saʿīd. *al-Inbāʾ bi-sharḥ matn al-Bināʾ fī ʿilm al-taṣrīf*. 1st ed. Cairo: al-Dār al-ʿĀlamiyya li-l-Nashr wa-l-Tajlīd, n.d.

al-Bukhārī, Muḥammad b. Ismāʿīl. *al-Jāmiʿ al-ṣaḥīḥ*. Edited by Muḥammad Zuhayr b. Nāṣir al-Nāṣir. 9 vols. Beirut: Dār Ṭawq al-Najāh, 2001.

al-Dardīr, Aḥmad. *Ḥāshiyat al-Ṣāwī ʿalā Sharḥ al-Dardīr li-risālatihi Tuḥfat al-ikhwān fī ʿilm al-bayān*. Cairo: Maṭbaʿat Muṣṭafā al-Bābī al-Ḥalabī, 1935.

al-Dasūqī, Muḥammad. *Kitāb ḥāshiyat al-Dasūqī ʿalā mukhtaṣar al-Saʿd*. Edited by ʿAbd al-Ḥamīd Hindāwī. Sidon: al-Maktaba al-ʿAṣriyya, 2007.

Eğīnī, Meḥmed Raḥmī. *al-ʿUjāla al-raḥmiyya*. Istanbul: Ṣafā wa-Anwar, 1894.

El-Rouayheb, Khaled. *Islamic Intellectual History in the Seventeenth Century: Scholarly Currents in the Ottoman Empire and the Maghreb*. Cambridge: Cambridge University Press, 2015.

Er, Muhammad Emin. *The Soul of Islam: Essential Doctrines and Beliefs*. Translated by Joseph Walsh. Atlanta: Shifa, 2008.

al-Fākihī, ʿAbdallāh. *Sharḥ Kitāb al-ḥudūd fī al-naḥw*. Edited by al-Mutawallī Ramaḍān Aḥmad al-Damīrī. Cairo: Dār al-Taḍāmun l-l-Ṭibāʿa, 1988.

Fenārī, Meḥmed. *al-Fawāʾid al-fanāriyya*. 2nd ed. Istanbul: Haşemi, 2015.

Gelenbevī, Ismāʿīl. *Sharḥ Gelenbevī fī ʿilm al-manṭiq ʿalā matn Īsāghūjī*. Edited by Jādallāh Bassām Ṣāliḥ. Amman: Dār al-Nūr, 2016.

Gelibolī, Muṣṭafā b. Ibrāhīm. *Tuḥfat al-ikhwān sharḥ al-ʿAwāmil*. 2nd ed. Istanbul: Dār al-Sirāj, 2022.

al-Ghazzī, Muḥammad. *al-Kawākib al-sāʾira bi-aʿyān al-miʾat al-ʿāshira*. Beirut: Dār al-Kutub al-ʿIlmiyya, 1997.

Gyekye, Kwame. "The Term *Istithnāʾ* in Arabic Logic." *Journal of the American Oriental Society* 92, no. 1 (1972): 88–92. https://www.jstor.org/stable/599652.

al-Ḥākim, Abū ʿAbdallāh. *al-Mustadrak ʿalā al-Ṣaḥīḥayn*. 5 vols. Cairo: Dār al-Ḥaramayn, 1997.

al-Ḥamawī, Aḥmad. *Ghamr ʿuyūn al-baṣāʾir sharḥ kitāb al-Ashbāh wa-l-naẓāʾir*. Beirut: Dār al-Kutub al-ʿIlmiyya, 1985.

Ibn ʿĀbidīn, Muḥammad Amīn. *Ḥāshiyat Radd al-muḥtār ʿalā al-Durr al-mukhtār sharḥ Tanwīr al-abṣār*. Cairo: Maṭbaʿat Muṣṭafā al-Bābī al-Ḥalabī wa-Awlādihi, 1966.

———. *Ḥāshiyat Ibn ʿĀbidīn Radd al-muḥtār ʿalā al-Durr al-mukhtār*. Edited by Ḥusām al-Dīn Farfūr. Damascus: Dār al-Thaqāfa wa-l-Turāth, 2000.

Ibn Aḥmad, Muḥammad b. Muḥammad. *Fatḥ al-asrār*. In *Shurūḥ al-Iẓhār*. 2 vols. Istanbul: Dār al-Maʿrūf li-l-Nashr wa-l-Tawzīʿ, 2019.

Ibn Aḥmad, Walī. *al-Maṭlūb fī sharḥ al-Maqṣūd*. In *Shurūḥ al-Maqṣūd*, edited by Jihād al-ʿUmarī. Istanbul: Şifa, 2021.

Ibn ʿAqīl, ʿAbdallāh. *Sharḥ Ibn ʿAqīl ʿalā Alfiyyat Ibn Mālik*. 4 vols. Damascus: Muʾassasat al-Risāla, 2019.

Ibn al-Ḥājib. *al-Kāfiya fī ʿilm al-naḥw*. Karachi: al-Bushrā, 2021.

———. *al-Shāfiya fī ʿilm al-taṣrīf*. Edited by Ḥasan Aḥmad al-ʿUthmān. Makkah: al-Maktaba al-Makkiyya, 1995.

Ibn Ḥibbān, Muḥammad and ʿAlāʾ al-Dīn b. Balbān [cited Ibn Ḥibbān]. *Ṣaḥīḥ Ibn Ḥibbān bi-tartīb Ibn Balbān*. Edited by Shuʿayb al-Arnaʾūṭ. 18 vols. Beirut: Muʾassasat al-Risāla, 1988.

Ibn Mājah al-Qazwīnī, Muḥammad. *al-Sunan*. Edited by Shuʿayb al-Arnāʾūṭ. 5 vols. Beirut: Dār al-Risāla al-ʿĀlamiyya, 2009.

Ibn Masʿūd, Aḥmad b. ʿAlī. *Marāḥ al-arwāḥ fī al-ṣarf*. In *Majmūʿat al-ṣarf wa-shurūḥuhā wa-ḥawāshīhā*, edited by Ṣuhayb Mullā Muḥammad Nūrī ʿAlī, 495–591. Damascus: Dār Nūr al-Ṣabāḥ, 2016.

al-Jāmī, Nūr al-Dīn ʿAbd al-Raḥmān. *al-Fawāʾid al-ḍiyāʾiyya al-mashhūr bi-Mullā Jāmī*. Edited by Ilyās Qablān. Istanbul: Şifa, 2015.

al-Jurjānī, al-Sayyid al-Sharīf. *Ḥāshiyat al-Jurjānī*. In *Shurūḥ al-Shamsiyya*. 2 vols. Cairo: al-Maktaba al-Azhariyya li-l-Turāth, 2020.

al-Khayrābādī, Faḍl-i Imām. *al-Mirqāh*. Karachi: al-Bushrā, 2019.

al-Laknawī, Muḥammad ʿAbd al-Ḥayy. *al-Fawāʾid al-bahiyya fī tarājim al-ḥanafiyya*. Edited by Muḥammad Badr al-Dīn Naʿsānī. Cairo: Maṭbaʿat al-Saʿāda, 1324/1906 or 1907.

al-Maḥallī, Jalāl al-Dīn Muḥammad. *al-Badr al-ṭāliʿ fī ḥall Jamʿ al-jawāmiʿ*. Edited by Murtaḍā ʿAlī al-Dāghistānī. 2 vols. Damascus: Muʾassasat al-Risāla, 2005.

———. *Sharḥ al-Waraqāt fī uṣūl al-fiqh*. Edited by Ḥusām al-Dīn b. Mūsā ʿAfāna. Jerusalem: Jāmiʿat al-Quds, 1999.

al-Maḥbūbī, ʿUbaydallāh. *al-Tawḍīḥ sharḥ al-Tanqīḥ*. [See al-Taftāzānī, *Sharḥ al-Talwīḥ*.]

al-Mīlānī, Muḥammad b. ʿAbd al-Raḥīm. *Sharḥ al-Mughnī fī al-naḥw*. Istanbul: Haşemi, 2019.

Muslim. *Ṣaḥīḥ Muslim*. [See al-Naysābūrī, Muslim b. al-Ḥajjāj.]

al-Naysābūrī, Muslim b. al-Ḥajjāj [cited Muslim]. *Ṣaḥīḥ Muslim*. Edited by Yāsir Ḥasan, ʿIzz al-Dīn Ḍalī, and ʿImād al-Ṭayyār. Damascus: Muʾassasat al-Risāla, 2016.

al-Shāfiʿī, Muḥammad b. Idrīs. *al-Umm*. Edited by Rifʿat Fawzī ʿAbd al-Muṭṭalib. Mansoura: Dār al-Wafāʾ, 2008.

al-Shaʿrānī, ʿAbd al-Wahhāb. *al-Ṭabaqāt al-kubrā*. Cairo: Maktabat al-Thaqāfa al-Dīniyya, 2005.

al-Shawkānī, Muḥammad. *al-Badr al-ṭāliʿ bi-maḥāsin man baʿd al-qarn al-sābiʿ*. Beirut: Dār al-Maʿrifa, n.d.

al-Shirbīnī, ʿAbd al-Raḥmān. *Taqrīr al-Shirbīnī*. In *Ḥāshiyat al-Bannānī ʿalā sharḥ al-Maḥallī ʿalā matn Jamʿ al-jawāmiʿ*. 2 vols. Beirut: Dār al-Fikr, 1982.

al-Sijistānī, Abū Dāwūd [cited Abū Dāwūd]. *Kitāb al-sunan*. Edited by Muḥammad ʿAwwāma. 5 vols. Jeddah: Dār al-Qibla li-l-Thaqāfa al-ʿIlmiyya, 1998.

al-Siyālkūtī, ʿAbd al-Ḥakīm. *Ḥāshiyat ʿAbd al-Ḥakīm al-Siyālkūtī ʿalā awākhir al-Jāmī*. In *al-Majmūʿa al-nūriyya al-mushtamila ʿalā sittati kutubin fī al-naḥw*, edited by Muḥammad Nūrī Nāṣ and Fuʾād Nāṣir. 2 vols. Midyat: Dār Nūr al-Ṣabāḥ, 2010.

Surūrī, Muṣṭafā b. Shaʿbān. *Sharḥ al-Amthila al-mukhtalifa*. In *Majmūʿat al-ṣarf wa-shurūḥuhā wa-ḥawāshīhā*, edited by Ṣuhayb Mullā Muḥammad Nūrī ʿAlī, 605–26. Damascus: Dār Nūr al-Ṣabāḥ, 2016.

al-Taftāzānī, Masʿūd b. ʿUmar. *Mukhtaṣar al-maʿānī*. Karachi: al-Bushrā, 2019.

———. *Sharḥ al-Risāla al-shamsiyya fī taḥrīr al-qawāʿid al-manṭiqiyya*. Edited by Masʿūd Aḥmad Saʿīdī. Beirut: Dār al-Ḍiyāʾ, 2022.

———. *Sharḥ al-Talwīḥ ʿalā al-Tawḍīḥ li-matn al-Tanqīḥ fī uṣūl al-fiqh*. Edited by Zakariyyā ʿUmayrāt. 2 vols. 1957. Reprint, Beirut: Dār al-Kutub al-ʿIlmiyya, n.d.

———. *Sharḥ Taṣrīf al-ʿIzzī*. In *Shurūḥ al-ʿIzzī*, edited by Anṣār Aṣlān and Muḥammad Yāsīn Eren. Istanbul: Dār al-Shifā, 2023.

al-Rāzī, Quṭb al-Dīn. *Lawāmiʿ al-asrār fī sharḥ Maṭāliʿ al-anwār*. Edited by Abū al-Qāsim al-Raḥmānī. 3 vols. Tehran: Muʾassasa-yi Pazhūhishī-yi Ḥikmat va Falsafa-yi Īrān, 2014.

———. *Sharḥ al-Rāzī li-l-Risāla al-shamsiyya fī al-manṭiq*. In *Shurūḥ al-Shamsiyya*. 2 vols. Reprint, Cairo: al-Maktaba al-Azhariyya li-l-Turāth, 2020.

al-Tirmidhī, Abū ʿĪsā. *al-Jāmiʿ al-kabīr*. Edited by Bashshār ʿAwwād Maʿrūf. 6 vols. Beirut: Dār al-Gharb al-Islāmī, 1996.

al-Yazdī, ʿAbdallāh. *Sharḥ Tahdhīb al-manṭiq*. Edited by ʿAbd al-Ḥamīd al-Turkmānī. Amman: Dār al-Nūr, 2018.

Wright, W. *Arabic Grammar*. 3rd ed. Mineola: Dover, 2005.

al-Ziriklī, Khayr al-Dīn. *al-Aʿlām: Qāmus tarājim li-ashhar al-rijāl wa-l-nisāʾ min al-ʿarab wa-l-mustaʿribīn wa-l-mustashriqīn*. Beirut: Dār al-ʿIlm li-l-Malāyīn, 2002.